Speaking of Sexuality

Interdisciplinary Readings

Speaking of Sexuality

Interdisciplinary Readings

THIRD EDITION

Nelwyn B. Moore
Texas State University-San Marcos

J. Kenneth Davidson, Sr.
University of Wisconsin-Eau Claire

Terri D. Fisher
The Ohio State University at Mansfield

New York   Oxford
OXFORD UNIVERSITY PRESS
2010

Oxford University Press, Inc., publishes works that further
Oxford University's objective of excellence
in research, scholarship, and education.

Oxford   New York
Auckland   Cape Town   Dar es Salaam   Hong Kong   Karachi
Kuala Lumpur   Madrid   Melbourne   Mexico City   Nairobi
New Delhi   Shanghai   Taipei   Toronto

With offices in
Argentina   Austria   Brazil   Chile   Czech Republic   France   Greece
Guatemala   Hungary   Italy   Japan   Poland   Portugal   Singapore
South Korea   Switzerland   Thailand   Turkey   Ukraine   Vietnam

Published by Oxford University Press, Inc.
198 Madison Avenue, New York, New York 10016
http://www.oup.com

Library of Congress Cataloging-in-Publishing Data
Speaking of sexuality / Nelwyn B. Moore, J. Kenneth Davidson, Terri D. Fisher. — 3rd ed.
    p.   cm.
  Includes bibliographical references.
  ISBN 978-0-19-538949-4 (alk. paper)
  1. Sex.   2. Sex (Psychology)   3. Hygiene, Sexual.   4. Interpersonal relations.
  I. Moore, Nelwyn B.   II. Davidson, J. Kenneth.   III. Fisher, Terri D.
  HQ21.S6244 2010
  306.7—dc22
                                                                2009002632

Printed in the United States of America
on acid-free paper

We dedicate this book to the countless thousands of
students who have touched our lives in more
years than we care to count . . .

and to our professional colleagues
with whom we share both a common
passion for teaching, and a common illusion . . .
the belief that we know more about the subject
of sexuality than do the students!

—Nelwyn B. Moore
J. Kenneth Davidson, Sr.
Terri D. Fisher

CONTENTS

sexually explicit videos of Black and White men that were used as a research stimulus.

psychosocial factors on sexual expression in later life.

A comprehensive literature review revealing that sexual dysfunction and depression in women often co-occur, and the role of cultural factors in shaping the response to sexual dysfunction that results from antidepressant medications and from depression itself.

*Chapter 40
THE RELATIONSHIP BETWEEN CHILDHOOD SEXUAL ABUSE AND ADULT MENTAL HEALTH AMONG UNDERGRADUATES

M. Scott Young, Kelli-Lee Harford, Bill Kinder, and Jodi K. Savell

This study examined whether gender moderated the relationship between childhood sexual abuse and adult mental health.

*Chapter 41
CONCEPTUALIZING THE "WANTEDNESS" OF WOMEN'S CONSENSUAL AND NONCONSENSUAL SEXUAL EXPERIENCES: IMPLICATIONS FOR HOW WOMEN LABEL THEIR EXPERIENCES WITH RAPE

Zöe D. Peterson and Charlene L. Muehlenhard

These researchers had three objectives: developing a multidimensional model for conceptualizing the wantedness of a sexual act; using the model to compare women's experiences with rape and consensual sex; and assessing whether wantedness is related to rape acknowledgement.

Chapter 42
TACTICS OF SEXUAL COERCION: WHEN MEN AND WOMEN WON'T TAKE NO FOR AN ANSWER

Cindy J. Struckman-Johnson, David L. Struckman-Johnson, and Peter B. Anderson

Contrary to popular opinion, while less often than men, women do sometimes use tactics to initiate sexual contact with unwilling sex partners, an interesting fact revealed by subjects in this fascinating piece of qualitative research.

*Chapter 43
HETEROSEXUAL FRONTERAS: IMMIGRANT MEXICANOS, SEXUAL VULNERABILITIES, AND SURVIVAL

Gloria González-López

The investigator examined how migration may destabilize the boundaries of heterosexuality among male immigrants, leading to same-sex encounters with employers and other immigrant men and, at times, other forms of sexual harassment.

Chapter 44
EFFECTS OF CYBERSEX ADDICTION ON THE FAMILY: RESULTS OF A SURVEY

Jennifer P. Schneider

Using qualitative analysis of poignant survey response data, this thought-provoking investigation reveals the major impact that cybersex can have on marital and family relationships.

Chapter 45
NAKED CAPITALISTS

Frank Rich

An engaging writer reveals the interworkings, major players, and financial assets found in the pornographic film industry in this wide-ranging account of an American growth industry.

*Chapter 46
TEMPORARILY YOURS: DESIRE, DEMAND, AND THE COMMERCE OF SEX

Elizabeth Bernstein

Using in-depth interviews, this compelling exploration of the changing landscape of sex work provides a brief sketch of the academic and political discourse surrounding commercialized sex and offers a glimpse of recent attempts by state agencies to reshape demand in the sexual marketplace.

With compelling wisdom and compassion, Levine writes about the need to focus on a sense of community in developing strategies to combat AIDS, using Minnesota's Twin Cities as a model.

Content analysis was used to study how major newspapers representative of the Northeast, Midwest, Southeast, and West regions framed stories about *True Love Waits*, a nationwide virginity pledge campaign, and ADD Health, a longitudinal study that evaluated the effects of virginity pledges.

The author argues that successful sex education programs must be transparent regarding the philosophies of sexuality and of education that undergird research and practice, and that educational efforts must be tailored specifically to the social-relational contexts that research finds to be related to solutions.

*Denotes a chapter new to this edition.

A visitor to the United States in 2009 would probably conclude that it is a completely open society with regard to sexuality. Every one of us is surrounded by sexual materials and information. On network television, sexual behavior and relationships are portrayed in prime-time programs, soap operas, and news magazines; on cable television, explicit sexual interactions are increasingly frequent. "News stories" about sexual topics fill our daily papers, news magazines, and TV news. Feature films display and provide scripts for a wide range of sexual behaviors and lifestyles. Advertisers use images of sexually attractive women and men to sell us everything from cosmetics and clothing, to beer and wine, automobiles and vacations. And then there is explicit pornography, available on cable television, in magazines, at your local video rental outlet, and on the Internet, where it is the largest single category of sites.

Unfortunately, young men and women who attempt to fashion their sexual expression and lifestyle using these media depictions are not likely to find sexual fulfillment or lasting relationships. The portrayals we see on television and in films are unrealistic; they feature young, attractive people who typically are not in long-term relationships, and these people do not worry about pregnancy or sexually transmitted infections (STIs). The portrayals in pornography are not realistic either; they feature people who are very attractive, have large breasts or penises (or both), and who engage in a wide variety of sexual acts with abandon. Either type of portrayal is difficult for most people in the United States to identify with. In contrast, the plots of soap operas and news stories often focus on the dangers associated with sexuality, such as rape, unwanted pregnancy, and STIs.

Fortunately, we have much better sources of information available to us. Scientific research on human sexuality dates back at least to the 1890s and the pioneering work of Sigmund Freud. Over the years, many biological, behavioral, and social scientists have contributed to our contemporary understanding of sexuality. Since the 1970s, textbooks written by knowledgeable scientist/educators and anthologies of professional readings have become increasingly accessible to students and the general public. The Moore, Davidson, and Fisher collection of articles and chapters is designed to introduce sexuality research and writings by biological scientists, psychologists, social psychologists, sociologists, and historians. The Editors have carefully selected these readings to reflect the diversity of materials published in this field. They have also edited the original readings to make them more concise and informative.

This is the Third Edition of this volume. Based on feedback from students and faculty, the Editors have replaced half of the chapters included in the Second Edition with new ones. One of us (JD) has used the book as an assigned reader for several semesters. He used it because he wanted students to have access to original articles, to see and appreciate the complexity of a research project or a theoretical argument. Many of these students spontaneously commented on how interesting or important they found the material in these articles to be. The students also appreciated the introductory paragraphs written by the Editors; these paragraphs provide both a context for and summarize the themes of each chapter.

The selections will introduce you to important influences on your sexual thoughts, emotions, and behavior. Biological development and aging, gender and race/ethnicity, parents, friends, lovers, sexuality education, religion, and culture all affect sexuality throughout the person's life. Such complex influences can lead to emotionally and sexually satisfying relationships and behavior. They can also lead to frustrating and painful outcomes, such as loneliness, problems in sexual functioning, STIs, and sexual victimization. Reading the articles in this book, you can learn about the influences on your sexuality, and gain a sense of agency and control, enabling you to avoid undesirable outcomes and increasing your chances of creating positive ones.

As you read, consider whether and how the content of an article relates to you and your relationships. For example, if the article discusses communication in relationships, consider whether you can improve communication with your partner(s) based on what you read. If you find a particular article especially interesting or thought-provoking and want more information, consult the sources listed in the references, or the relevant sections in your textbook.

Between us, we have been teaching human sexuality for 65 years. Many of our students have told us that it was the single most important course that they took, because they gained a greater understanding of their sexuality and of our society. We hope that these readings contribute to your own achievement of this understanding.

John D. DeLamater
Professor of Sociology
University of Wisconsin—Madison

Janet Shibley Hyde
Professor of Psychology and Women's Studies
University of Wisconsin—Madison

This Third Edition of *Speaking of Sexuality* is, like most things, better for having been tested and tinkered with. I am particularly happy with the choices in this edition because I, like many other professors who teach sexuality classes, keep or change our books, based, at least in large part, on student evaluations. With a first edition there is no chance to know student reaction, so one hopes that the breadth of topics and a generally high standard of writing will support lectures and keep students' interest, but there is no track record to depend on. Fortunately, the First and Second editions proved to be popular with my classes and I had no hesitation on re-adoption. Still, while most of the book got it right in the previous editions, I am glad that the Third edition has more articles on minorities and a larger section on sexual health. I think more students will be able to see themselves in many of these articles or learn about how ethnicity or race can change the nature of a sexual experience or pose an additional vulnerability or series of reactions. Of course, there is never enough room in one book to do justice to all the topics or permutations of experience a professor would want to include, but there is plenty here to start wide-ranging discussions and open windows into lives unexperienced by ourselves but important to understand.

Limits are even more frustrating when we add the problem of interdisciplinary approaches to sexuality. Of course, different academic disciplines would have made different choices. The vision of what are central observations and issues might be substantially altered if this book were, for example, on the medical aspects of sexuality. Still, I think this volume has taken into account what many disciplines consider cutting-edge issues in an attempt to give you, the reader, the widest possible view of the most important ways sexuality touches our lives. More interdisciplinary than others, but still using a socio-psychological lens, these authors focus on sexuality by using comparative and interdisciplinary materials. One of the unique aspects of *Speaking of Sexuality* is that sociology as one of the frames of references will illuminate how human interaction and social groups affect our sexuality—and you will have the benefit of historical, medical, legal, psychological and therapeutic materials to help you understand each issue. As a major bonus, most of the articles were also chosen for their readability so that the book won't seem like medicine: good for you, but hard going down.

What do I like about the book? Why do I use it in my class (an intimate lecture hall of over 700 students...)? First, I think the topics covered are extremely germane to the lives of college and graduate students. Second, I like the fact that the book includes both qualitative support for my lectures (articles that give us personal interviews with people about their sexual feelings or behavior) and quantitative material (so that the scientific data that predicts and describes trends and behaviors can be evaluated). Third, I like the organization—the earlier chapters help build a basis for understanding the later ones.

The first section of the book gives students a "framework," a way of seeing how culture, history, and even a sex researcher's own discipline or background influences which questions on sexuality are asked and how sexual practices or changing sexual values become seen as "crises" or critical problems. The authors delineate gender, race, class, age, sexual orientation and marital status as mediating variables that have to be taken into account in order to understand how sexuality affects individuals and society. Once we understand the need to pay attention to these social factors, we can analyze the changing sexual issues that occur throughout the life cycle. In the simplest sense, we know that children have a different level of physiological and emotional development from teenagers, and teenagers are equally different from adults. Other factors, such as the fact that younger children are more constrained by parental values, beliefs and fears, and are treated differently from adults by legal systems and other institutions have to be taken into account. The feelings, beliefs and behaviors of children and adolescents are consequential for adulthood—and so quite a bit of space in this book is devoted to the sexual behavior of preadolescents, adolescents and young adults.

Adolescence however is a tricky concept. It seems to have lengthened into what might have been called early adulthood in other periods of history. That caveat not withstanding, we need to look at those pivotal moments of first intercourse, the meaning of virginity (and "experience"), committed versus uncommitted sexual experiences and how young people do or do not learn how to talk about what they want sexually. The truth is, as many of you know, that talking about sex is often a lot harder to do than having sex (and as we can see from some articles in the book, it seems to be extremely hard for parents to talk about it as well—when it comes to educating their children!). This dearth of communication from parent to child is also depressing for teenagers and young adults who need information. When people are learning about themselves at the same time they are falling in love (or lust), clear expression of needs, wants (and "don't wants") are extremely difficult. Yet while communication is at the center of an ability to conduct a satisfying and safe sexual relationship, most people negotiate sexual desire awkwardly and sometimes downright disastrously. This may sound familiar: many, perhaps most, college students are still inexperienced when it comes to expressing their sexual thoughts and desires to a partner, which is why putting in articles on sexuality and communication seems like critical content to me.

This doesn't mean, of course, that communication and honesty cease to be a challenge after adolescence. The section in this book on young adulthood indicates how important these issues continue to be in the maintenance of longerterm relationships. In fact, as Part Four shows us, creating and keeping desire in relationships cannot be taken for granted, nor since issues vary from one race, gender, class, or age group to another, can one answer be assumed to be relevant for all populations.

Finally, the last third of the book pays attention to sexual health, sexual problems and policy issues. While the first part of the book is on how sexuality works in "ordinary" situations (if any situations are ever ordinary!), the last sections make us face up to aspects of sexual health that can prove painful, or even fatal, if healthy practices are not observed. The specter of HIV, AIDS and even nonlethal sexually transmitted infections (STIs) has had a disastrous impact on some minority communities and several articles in this book look at how STIs or even the possibility of contracting one changes lives.

Other challenges also exist because of differential exposure to stigmatization or victimization. No book on sexuality can ignore the fact that the right to sexual consent is often abused and that we as citizens need to know who is at risk and how to protect ourselves and our children. As social scientists, however, we know that consent to engage in sexual activity is often ambiguous and that gender norms may make it more likely for one person to feel violated while the other feels betrayed and mystified. Good research in this area has created articles that every person needs to read in order to understand how interpretation of what happened can be so different between two people.

Cultural battles over sexuality are going on now, and perhaps they will always be going on. Sexuality education itself, the very process you are voluntarily entering into, is quite controversial and a battleground in many school districts. Sexual social policy is fought over in the schools, courts, legislatures, and religious institutions. This conflict and litigation over values is perhaps most vividly played out in the current debate over how homosexuality shall be regarded and treated in Western culture. While gay men and lesbians are far more open and integrated into general society than ever before in the United States, this is not true in some areas of the country and in many parts of the world. Homophobia (loathing for and aversion to homosexuals) exists and debates rage about whether homosexuality should be accepted because it is a biological inheritance involving no choice or option for an individual, or whether it is a "lifestyle." Others question whether or not homosexuality is able to be stifled by denying homosexuals their civil rights. Polls indicate split opinions about acceptance of homosexual civil rights, although, in general, values on sexual orientation in the United States and Europe have become more liberal. However, one issue is quite incendiary, and that is the issue of whether or not same-sex couples have the right to marry.

Some people, even those who accept other civil rights for homosexuals, do not feel comfortable about including legal marriage as a right. Legislatures throughout the country heatedly debate gay marriage, coming to different conclusions about whether or not same-sex marriages are allowed under their state constitutions. Sometimes, rights are given—and then taken back. California had approved same-sex marriage, and many same-sex couples had married legally, but Proposition 8, a bill to cancel gay marriage in California, passed by referendum. Now the issue is making its way through the courts and as of this writing, it has been accepted for review by the Supreme Court of California. It is not clear what the outcome will be, and in the meantime, legal experts debate about whether already married same-sex couples will retain legal standing. Some states wish to avoid the battle by endorsing "civil unions" or "domestic partnerships" instead of same-sex marriage. Naturally, hot debates have ensued whether or not civil union is an acceptable "middle ground" by which same-sex couple rights can be preserved but marriage as an institution remains heterosexual.

Certainly other hot issues will emerge as well. For example, see the article on how morality and medicine are now intertwined and how that has become a debate and a cause for some people's activism and protest. These battles over sexual morality and practice occur because we all hold deeply held beliefs about sexuality and we are all affected by what laws and social policies are made. This book is so constructed as to give you solid research on which to test your beliefs, add information to your decision making on personal issues, and be able to be an informed citizen as you vote on issues that will affect your sexual life, your personal happiness, and, perhaps, the health, welfare, and safety of your friends and fellow citizens. Enjoy the readings, examine your assumptions, and profit from the thoughtful and provocative moments that this book will encourage.

Pepper Schwartz
Professor of Sociology
University of Washington

OVERVIEW

> No aspect of human life seethes with so many unexorcised demons as does sex. No human activity is so hexed by superstition, so haunted by residual tribal lore, and so harassed by socially induced fear.
>
> —*Harvey Cox*

The captivating words by noted theologian Harvey Cox alluding to the unstateable state of the subject of this anthology, sexuality, are less than rhetorical. They portend that all is not well in the real world of sexuality. We agree. But neither is all lost. This latter belief is the basis of the paradigm for this work.

By choosing to reframe many of today's considered-to-be sexuality issues, we hope to dispel a number of sexual myths that have been formed from society's free-floating sexual anxieties. To accomplish this feat, we called upon academicians—women and men of letters in the fields of health care, anthropology, theology, sexology, sociology, marriage and family therapy, psychology, social work, psychiatry, and family studies. Most have spoken with empirical authority, based on their own research. Some few by virtue of the respect gained over a lifetime of work in the field of sexology were selected for their accumulated acumen. For balance, a number of challenging selections were included from authors whose writings appear in popular sources such as *Commentary* and *The New York Times Magazine*, as well as award-winning books.

English educator Robert Grimm once said that if you want to know what individuals are really like at their very core, look at the way they use their sexuality. If, for you, this book has a voice, you may well hear it ask, "How are we, as a part of humankind, collectively using our sexuality?" We invite you to accompany us into the pages of this book in order that we may all more authoritatively answer this question.

ABOUT THE ANTHOLOGY

Speaking of Sexuality (SOS) is the alternative for instructors of human sexuality courses who prefer a student-friendly, yet more rigorous, less sensationalized, book of readings than any currently on the market. No other sexuality reader has both comprehensive Part Openers, with absorbing discussions of each chapter topic, and insightful Chapter Lead-Ins that encourage students to think critically about the subject as they read.

Combining the best of "the old with the new," this edition has retained the same distinctive features that made the First and Second Editions of *SOS* the leading sexuality reader in its class. Presenting an array of personal and societal sexuality issues at a scholarly level that other works have failed to achieve, it also uniquely addresses the subject of human sexuality from a personal perspective of strength, one that is sex positive but realistic. The framework for this anthology, as in the first two editions, is lifetime sexual health, an organizing principle based on two assumptions: Sexuality is an inseparable part of an individual's persona and sexuality spans the life cycle from birth to death. The core belief that a healthy sexual script is a realistic goal for every person is the book's bottom-line rationale.

To enable the reader to encounter leading sexuality authorities, past and present, seminal works in sexuality research and theory are included here. The balance achieved by also offering articles that reveal popular treatment of today's timely topics enables students to become more discriminating consumers of sexuality materials in the mass media, competencies that we believe to be essential in a sex-saturated society.

Respect for the integrity of the professor and the student has guided this professional endeavor. Because we believe that professors bring their own personality to the process of facilitating learning and that students are both interested in and capable of learning, the narrative in this anthology is purposefully classic in format, challenging in content, and devoid of jargon.

Instructors using the first two editions of SOS (2001, 2005) cited the following unique benefits to students and professors:

- High readability and style;
- Blending of contemporary and classic works in research and theory;
- Multi-disciplinary approach to studying sexuality;
- Breadth of editorial team's professional experience;
- Balance of the physical, psychological, and sociological aspects of sexuality;
- Timely and interesting coverage of topics students most want to know about;
- Eclectic mix of articles from scholarly and popular sources;
- Extensive, absorbing discussion of each topic in Part Openers;
- Strong introductory Lead-Ins for each chapter that promote critical thinking;
- Coverage of the historical and political contexts of sexuality;
- Theme of health promotion and the life cycle as organizing principles;
- Rationale for critiquing the various forms of sexuality-related media; and

- Easy application to a variety of teaching methods.

We have listened to our respected colleagues who reviewed the Second Edition of SOS, many of whom had "hands on" experience using it in their own courses. As a result, twenty-eight new selections have been added, expanding the topical areas so that each Part has one or more new chapters. In addition, two new Parts, "Relationships and Sexuality" and "Sexual Health," have added considerably to the breadth of the book.

This Third Edition of *Speaking of Sexuality* features timely and thought-provoking topics, many of which are not found in other sexuality readers: asexuality; bisexuality; Asian parents and sexual communication; Viagra and the medicalization of male sexuality; close relationships of lesbians and gays; queer theory; bogus pipeline experiment of self-reported sexuality; female depression and sexual dysfunction; American Indian youth and HIV/AIDS protectors; newspapers and virginity pledges; gender and sexual desire; cybersex addition; the economics of pornography; "wantedness" of women's sexual experiences; communication with new sex partners; and Mexican male immigrants and sexual boundaries.

In weaving together the Third Edition of *Speaking of Sexuality*, the following unique selections from recent highly-acclaimed scholarly books were added:

- In her new award-winning book, *Temporarily Yours: Intimacy, Authenticity, and the Commerce of Sex*, Elizabeth Bernstein examines the social features that undergird the changing face of commercialized sex and the academic and political discourse surrounding it.
- From Mark Regnerus' startling new book, *Forbidden Fruit: Sex and Religion in the Lives of American Teenagers*, evidence is presented of a rationale for an emerging religious and social class patterning of sexual substitution activities by teenagers, i.e., oral and anal sex.

- Using a sociological lens in her widely acclaimed book, *Hooking Up*, Kathleen Bogle explores the phenomenon, evoking words like "booty calls" and "friends with benefits" to illuminate facts and myths concerning casual sex on college campuses.

- Anthropologist Helen Fisher examines the chemistry of sexual desire in lust, romantic love, and attachment from an evolutionary biological perspective in her book, *Web of Love*.

- *Virginity Lost* by Laura Carpenter, a provocative book based on in-depth interviews, is a valuable contribution to understanding ways young people navigate the transition from virginity, and how meanings differ by gender and sexual orientation.

- In *Damaged Goods*, Adina Nack investigates the emergence of a gendered morality associated with the medical treatment of STIs, resulting in shame, especially for female patients.

- Evolutionary psychology is used as a framework to explore the role of sexual strategies as adaptive solutions to human mating problems by David Buss in his book, *The Evolution of Desire*.

With every product, there is a parallel process story. In this case, negotiating the sometimes slippery slope between a sociologist/researcher, a family scientist/family therapist, and a psychologist was not always an easy task. However, we feel the results are considerably stronger because of our team efforts. Together, we have interwoven complex phenomena from fields known for their diversity of theories, concepts, and issues. The final product is an anthology with professional integrity and pragmatic pedagogical purposes. If we provoke critical thinking about today's timely topics surrounding sexuality, and motivate students to continue their efforts to learn about sexuality after their course has ended, we will have achieved our combined purposes in this edition of *SOS*.

INSTRUCTOR'S MANUAL/TESTING PROGRAM

A full-scale *Instructor's Manual* is available to provide assistance when integrating the anthology material into sexuality courses and when evaluating student achievement. The components for each entry include general summarizing statements, key points, and general conclusions. These features are available to adopters in *PowerPoint* presentations. Additionally, there are multiple choice, true/false, and essay questions for student evaluation. Finally, the following pedagogical tools are provided: a Topical Matrix, based on current sexuality texts; an Article Review Form, a one-page document that can be reproduced as needed; and Web site addresses, which focus on sexuality and sexual health issues and topics.

Nelwyn B. Moore
J. Kenneth Davidson, Sr.
Terri D. Fisher

Elisa S. Abes is an Assistant Professor of Educational Leadership at Miami University. She has studied the relationship between lesbian college students' perceptions of their sexual-orientation identity and other dimensions of identity, such as race, social class, religion, and gender as well as the theoretical and practical implications of introducing queer theory to student development theory.

Antonia Abbey, who is a Professor of Psychology at Wayne State University, studies sexual risk taking and sexual assault.

Paul R. Abramson, Professor of Psychology at the University of California, Los Angeles (UCLA), has research interests in the epidemiology of HIV and sex and the law. His books include *A House Divided: Suspicions of Mother-Daughter Incest* (2000) and *With Pleasure: Thoughts on the Nature of Human Sexuality* (1995).

Joseph Adelson is Professor Emeritus of Psychology at the University of Michigan.

Michele G. Alexander was Assistant Professor of Psychology at the University of Maine when she met an untimely death in 2003. She was a social psychologist with an interest in ethnic and racial stereotypes and how they are activated, as well as sex-role stereotypes and how they contribute to sex differences in various aspects of behavior.

Veanne N. Anderson, Associate Professor of Psychology and Women's Studies at Indiana State University, has research interests in the areas of gender and sexuality, attitudes toward transgendered individuals, and feminism and sexuality.

Peter B. Anderson is currently a Professor of Human Services at Walden University. Prior to Hurricane Katrina, he was Professor of Human Performance and Health Promotion at the University of New Orleans. His research interests include sexual violence, the impact of alcohol consumption on sexual risk behavior, gender, and the intersection of race, gender, and class. He is coauthor of *Does Anyone Still Remember When Sex Was Fun?: Positive Sexuality in the Age of AIDS* (Third Edition, 1996) and coeditor of *Sexually Aggressive Women: Current Perspectives and Controversies* (1998).

Natalie Angier, author and science writer for *The New York Times*, received a Pulitzer prize in 1991 for a 10-article series on scientific topics that included the biology of scorpions, disputes over the Human Genome Project, and the ubiquity of philandering in the animal kingdom. She has written hundreds of popular science articles on various aspects of sexuality. Her books include *The Canon: A Whirligig Tour of the Beautiful Basics of Science* (2007), *Woman: An Intimate Geography* (1999), *The Beauty of the Beastly: New Views on the Nature of Life* (1995), and *Natural Obsessions: Striving to Unlock the Deepest Secrets of the Cancer Cell* (1988).

J. Michael Bailey, Professor of Psychology at Northwestern University, focuses his research on sexual orientation in the areas of gender nonconformity, sexual arousal, and genetics. He is the author of *The Man Who Would Be Queen* (2003).

Elizabeth Bernstein is Assistant Professor of Women's Studies and Sociology at Barnard College, Columbia University. She is the author of *Temporarily Yours: Intimacy, Authenticity, and the Commerce of Sex* (2007) and coeditor of *Regulating Sex: The Politics of Intimacy and Identity* (2005).

Kathleen A. Bogle, Assistant Professor of Sociology and Criminal Justice at LaSalle University, is the author of *Hooking Up: Sex, Dating, and Relationships on Campus* (2008).

Philip O. Buck is Manager of Health Economics and Outcomes Research at Teva Neuroscience, Inc.

David M. Buss, Professor of Psychology at the University of Texas at Austin, studies various aspects of human mating strategies. He has written numerous books including *Evolutionary Psychology: The New Science of the Mind* (2008), *The Handbook of Evolutionary Psychology* (2005), *The Evolution of Desire: Strategies of Human Mating* (2003), and *The Dangerous Passion: Why Jealousy Is as Necessary as Love and Sex* (2000).

Bethany Butzer has a Ph.D. in Psychology from the University of Western Ontario. Her research interests include links between adult attachment and aspects of sexuality as well as the association between adult attachment orientations, sexual satisfaction, and relationship satisfaction.

William M. Byne holds an appointment as Associate Professor of Psychiatry in the Mount Sinai School of Medicine. He has conducted research on sexual differentiation of the brain in laboratory mammals and humans, and has written on the difficulties encountered in extrapolating data across species and the importance of considering both biological and psychosocial contributions to human phenomena.

Lorne Campbell, Associate Professor of Psychology at the University of Western Ontario, investigates predictors of sexual satisfaction, focusing on how sexual satisfaction is linked with global perceptions of relationship quality.

Laura M. Carpenter, an Assistant Professor of Sociology at Vanderbilt University, is author of *Virginity Lost: An Intimate Portrait of First Sexual Experiences* (2005). Her areas of scholarly interest include gender, sexual behavior, sexuality over the life course, virginity and virginity loss, and the politics of sexuality and sexual health.

F. Scott Christopher, Professor in the School of Social and Family Dynamics at Arizona State University, maintains research interests in the intersection of sexuality and close relationships. Much of his current research has focused on sexual aggression. He is the author of *To Dance the Dance: A Symbolic Interactional Exploration of Premarital Sexuality* (2001).

J. Kenneth Davidson, Sr. is Professor Emeritus of Sociology and Past Coordinator of Family Studies at the University of Wisconsin-Eau Claire. His research interests include sexual attitudes and behavior of college students; the Grafenberg spot and female ejaculation; sexual fantasies; female and male masturbation; sexuality education; and the orgasmic response in women. He is coauthor of *Marriage and Family: Change and Continuity* (1996) and *Marriage and Family* (1992) and coeditor of *Speaking of Sexuality* (2001, 2005); and *Cultural Diversity and Families* (1992).

Robert Davis, Professor of Sociology at North Carolina Agricultural and Technological State University, is interested in the sexual attitudes and behavior of college students.

John D. DeLamater is Professor of Sociology at the University of Wisconsin-Madison, with primary research interests in sexuality and the life cycle. He is coauthor of *Understanding Human Sexuality* (2008), *Understanding Human Sexuality: Canadian Edition* (2007), and *Premarital Sexuality: Attitudes, Relationships, Behavior* (1979) and former editor of *The Journal of Sex Research*.

Lisa M. Diamond, Associate Professor of Psychology and Gender Studies at the University of Utah, is a researcher on adult attachment, adolescent and young adult intimate relationships, and the development of sexual orientation and identity. She is the author of *Sexual Fluidity: Understanding Women's Love and Desire* (2008).

Roseanne D. Dobkin, Assistant Professor of Psychiatry at University of Medicine and Dentistry of New Jersey-Robert Wood Johnson Medical School, has research interests in the areas of menopause, depression and sexuality, and sexual dysfunction with antidepressants.

John R. Earle is Professor Emeritus of Sociology at Wake Forest University, with an interest in the sexual attitudes and behavior of college students.

Pamela I. Erickson, Professor of Psychology at the University of Connecticut, has research interests in adolescent sexual and reproductive behavior and the social context of sexual behavior among emergent adults. She is author of *Latina Adolescent Childbearing in East Los Angeles* (1998).

Adam W. Fingerhut, an Assistant Professor of Psychology at Loyola Marymount University, has research interests in gay and lesbian identity, sexual orientation and mental health, prejudice and stereotyping, and straight allies.

Helen E. Fisher is Research Professor and member of the Center for Human Evolutionary Studies in the Department of Anthropology, Rutgers University. She has conducted extensive research on the evolution and future of human sex, love and marriage, and gender differences in the brain and behavior. She is the author of five books: *Why Him? Why Her?* (2009), *Why We Love: The Nature and Chemistry of Romantic Love* (2004), *The First Sex: The Natural Talents of Women and How They Are Changing the World* (1999; 2000), *Anatomy of Love: The Natural History of Monogamy, Adultery and Divorce* (1992; 1994), and *The Sex Contract: The Evolution of Human Behavior* (1982; 1983).

Terri D. Fisher, Associate Professor of Psychology at The Ohio State University at Mansfield, has current research interests in gender and personality differences in various aspects of sexuality, and the impact of the research context on those differences. She has also published numerous studies on parent-child communication about sexuality. She is coeditor of *Current Directions in Sexuality and Relationships* (2010) and the *Handbook of Sexuality-Related Measures* (2010).

Robert T. Francoeur, Professor Emeritus of Biology and Psychology at Fairleigh Dickinson University, has written extensively about cross-cultural sexual attitudes, values, and behavior. He has coauthored, edited, and coedited over thirty books, including *Scent of Eros: Mysteries of Odor in Human Sexuality* (2002), *Sex, Love, and Marriage in the Twenty-First Century* (1999), *Sexuality in America* (1990), *The International Encyclopedia of Sexuality* (1997), and *Becoming a Sexual Person* (1984).

William N. Friedrich was a psychologist in the Department of Psychiatry and Psychology at the Mayo Clinic in Rochester, Minnesota until he died in 2005.

John H. Gagnon is Distinguished Professor of Sociology Emeritus at the State University of New York at Stony Brook and a past president of the International Academy of Sex Research. His many books, which reflect his research interests in sexual conduct, include *Sexuality in the Arab World* (2006), *Sexual Conduct: The Social*

Sources of Human Sexuality (2005), *An Interpretation of Desire: Essays in the Study of Sexuality* (2004), *In Changing Times: Gay Men and Lesbians Encounter HIV/AIDS* (1997), *Conceiving Sexuality: Approaches to Sex Research in a Postmodern World* (1995), *The Social Organization of Sexuality* (1994), and *Sex in America* (1994).

Susan Golombok, Director, Centre for Family Research at the University of Cambridge, is interested in children's gender development. She is the author of *Parenting: What Really Counts?* (2000) and coauthor of *Growing Up in a Lesbian Family: Effects on Child Development* (1997).

Gloria González-López, Associate Professor of Sociology at the University of Texas at Austin, conducts sexuality research with populations of Mexican origin. She is currently conducting sociological research on the sexual, romantic, and life experiences of adult women and men living in urban Mexico with histories of incestuous relationships. Her book, *Erotic Journeys: Mexican Immigrants and Their Sex Lives*, was published in 2005.

Cynthia A. Graham is a Research Tutor at Oxford Doctoral Course in Clinical Psychology and a Research Fellow at The Kinsey Institute for Research in Sex, Gender, and Reproduction. Her research interests include women's sexuality, sexual dysfunction, condom errors and problems, and contraception. She is the editor of *The Journal of Sex Research*.

Kelli-Lee Harford is a Pediatric Psychologist at the University of Wisconsin Hospital and Clinics, Department of Rehabilitation. Her primary research interest is resilience in survivors of child sexual abuse.

Katrenia Y. Reed Hughes has a Psy.D. in Clinical Psychology from Indiana State University, and is currently with Butler Business Accelerator. Her research interests include choice of sexual partners across the lifespan and the effects of age on racial preference of sexual partners.

David Kasch is a doctoral student in the Department of Higher Education and Organizational Change at the University of California, Los Angeles, where he studies the influence of sociocultural power dynamics on sexual identity definition and development for college students.

Janna L. Kim is Assistant Professor of Child and Adolescent Studies, California State University, Fullerton. Her research interests include sexual socialization; adolescent sexual health; intersections of culture, gender, and sexuality; mass media influences on sexuality development; and mixed method and qualitative approaches to studying sexuality.

Young J. Kim (deceased) was a Professor of Biostatistics at Johns Hopkins University, Bloomberg School of Public Health.

Edward O. Laumann is George Herbert Mead Distinguished Service Professor, Department of Sociology at the University of Chicago, where his major research interests include sexual dysfunction, sexually transmitted infections, sexual networks, *AIDS* prevention, and population studies of sexual behavior. He has authored or coauthored numerous books, including *Sexual Behavior and Attitudes in China: 1999–2000* (2005), *The Sexual Organization of the City* (2004), *Sex, Love, and Health in America: Private Choices and Public Policy* (2001), *The Social Organization of Sexuality* (1994), and *Sex in America: A Definitive Survey* (1994).

Sandra R. Leiblum is Professor of Psychiatry (Retired) at University of Medicine and Dentistry of New Jersey-Robert Wood Johnson Medical School and Director of Psychological Services at the New Jersey Center for Sexual Wellness. She is interested in male and female sexuality; persistent genital arousal disorder; menopause; sexual compulsivity, infertility and

sex; and the Internet and sexual compulsivity. Her numerous books include *Principles and Practice of Sex Therapy* (4th edition, 2007), *Getting the Sex You Want: A Woman's Guide to Becoming Proud, Passionate and Pleased in Bed* (2003), *Infertility: Psychological Issues and Counseling Strategies* (1996), *Case Studies in Sex Therapy* (1995), *Erectile Disorders: Assessment and Treatment* (1992), and *Sexual Desire Disorders* (1988).

Judith Levine, a writer who explores the influence of history, culture, and politics on intimate life, including sexuality, has authored *Not Buying It: My Year Without Shopping* (2006); *Do You Remember Me? A Father, a Daughter, and a Search for the Self* (2004), *Harmful to Minors: The Perils of Protecting Children from Sex* (2002), which won the Los Angeles Book Prize, and *My Enemy, My Love: Women, Masculinity, and the Dilemmas of Desire* (1992).

Jenna Mahay is a postdoctoral fellow at the Population Research Center at the University of Chicago, working on the Chicago Health and Social Life Survey Project.

Humberto Marin is Assistant Professor of Psychiatry at University of Medicine and Dentistry of New Jersey-Robert Wood Johnson Medical School and is interested in sexual dysfunction caused by antidepressants.

Barbara L. Marshall, Professor of Sociology at Trent University, is interested in gender and sexuality, aging and sexuality, and the biomedicalization of sexuality. She is author of *Configuring Gender: Explorations in Theory and Politics* (2000) and *Engendering Modernity: Feminism, Social Theory and Social Change* (1994) and coeditor of *The Routledge Encyclopedia of Social Theory* (2006) and *Engendering the Social: Feminist Encounters with Sociological Theory* (2004).

Flavio F. Marsiglia is a Foundation Professor of Cultural Diversity and Health in the School of Social Work at Arizona State University and Director of the Southwest Interdisciplinary Research Center (SIRC). With research interests in health and health disparities, he is the author of *Diversity, Oppression and Change* (2009).

Felicia E. Mebane is Clinical Assistant Professor of Health Policy and Management and Assistant Dean for Student Affairs in the School of Public Health at the University of North Carolina, Chapel Hill. Her interests include the impact of news media on health policy, politics, and health policy communication. She is the author of *Medicare Politics: Exploring the Roles of Media Coverage, Political Information, and Political Participation* (2000).

Matthew Menza, Professor of Psychiatry at University of Medicine and Dentistry of New Jersey-Robert Wood Johnson Medical School, conducts research on sexual dysfunction caused by antidepressants. He is coeditor of *Psychiatric Issues in Parkinson's Disease: A Practical Guide* (2006).

Robert T. Michael is Eliakim Hastings Moore Distinguished Service Professor Emeritus, Harris School of Public Policy Studies, University of Chicago. His research interests include the economic analysis of sexual behavior and social policy related to sexual behavior. He has coauthored *Social Awakening: Adolescent Behavior as Adulthood Approaches* (2001), *Sex, Love, and Health in America: Private Choices and Public Policies* (2001), *The Social Organization of Sexuality* (1994), and *Sex in America: A Definitive Survey* (1994).

Stuart Michaels is the Assistant Director of the Center for Gender Studies at the University of Chicago. He is interested in gender and sexuality, the social construction and the science of sexuality, and international comparative research on homosexuality. Michaels is coauthor of *The Social Organization of Sexuality* (1994) and *Sex in America: A Definitive Survey* (1994).

Nelwyn B. Moore is Professor Emerita of Family and Child Studies at Texas State University-San Marcos and a certified marriage and family therapist. Her research interests include sexual attitudes and behavior of college students, teen pregnancy, adoption attitudes and practices, and cross-cultural sexuality education. She is coauthor of *Marriage and Family: Change and Continuity* (1996) and *Marriage and Family* (1992) and coeditor of *Speaking of Sexuality* (2001, 2005) and *Cultural Diversity and Families* (1992).

Sara M. Moorman has an M.S. in Sociology from the University of Wisconsin-Madison with a research interest in married couples in later life.

Charlene Muehlenhard is Professor of Psychology and Women, Gender, and Sexuality Studies at the University of Kansas, and a former President of the Society for the Scientific Study of Sexuality. Her research interests are on sexual consent and coercion, gender similarities and differences in sexuality, and meanings attributed to sexuality.

Adina Nack, Associate Professor of Sociology at California Lutheran University, has research interests in sexually transmitted diseases, reproductive health, deviance and stigma, and HIV/AIDS. She is the author of *Damaged Goods? Women Living with Incurable Sexually Transmitted Diseases* (2008).

Constance A. Nathanson is Professor of Clinical Sociomedical Sciences and Population and Family Health at Columbia University Mailman School of Public Health. Her interests include gender, sexual behavior, and the political, historical, and social movement dimensions of gender and sexuality. Her published books are *Disease Prevention as Social Change: The State, Society,* *and Public Health in the United States, France, Great Britain, and Canada* (2007) and *Dangerous Passage: The Social Control of Sexuality in Women's Adolescence* (1991).

Tanya Nieri is an Assistant Professor of Sociology at University of California, Riverside, with interests in the sociology of health and illness, acculturation and ethnic identity, prevention interventions, and health promotion.

Paul Okami is an Adjunct Professor of Psychology at Widener University, with an interest in the evolutionary psychology of sex differences.

Richard Olmstead is an Associate Researcher in the Department of Psychiatry and Biobehavioral Sciences at the University of Los Angeles-California (UCLA).

Terrance D. Olson is a Professor in the School of Family Life at Brigham Young University. He focuses his interests in ethical foundations of quality of life; philosophy of moral agency; philosophy of social science and applied problem solving; adoption; and individual ethical and legal responsibilities.

Michele R. Parkhill is a Research Scientist at the Alcohol and Drug Abuse Institute at the University of Washington who studies sexual risk taking and sexual assault.

Laura Pendleton (Okami) is a registered nurse at Penn-Presbyterian Hospital in Philadelphia.

Letitia Anne Peplau is a Professor of Psychology at the University of California, Los Angeles, where she does research on sexuality in close relationships, gender differences in sexuality, and sexual orientation and identity. She is coauthor of *Social Psychology* (2006) and *Psychology* (1993) and coeditor of *Women's Sexualities: Perspectives on Sexual Orientation* *and Gender* (special issue of *Journal of Social Issues*, 2000) and *Gender, Culture and Ethnicity* (1999).

Zöe D. Peterson, Assistant Professor of Psychology and Women and Gender Studies at University of Missouri – St. Louis, has research interests in the areas of sexual coercion, perpetration and victimization, unwanted sex, and ambivalence about sex.

Richard C. Pillard, Professor of Psychiatry at Boston University School of Medicine, has primary research interests in sexual orientation, especially the genetics of sexual orientation.

Nicole Prause, an Assistant Professor at Idaho State University, has research interests in digital signal processing, women's sexual health, alcohol effects on sexual response, models of sexual arousal, and models of sexual risk taking.

Mark D. Regnerus, Associate Professor of Sociology at the University of Texas at Austin, is interested in sexual decision making and relationship dynamics and is the author of *Forbidden Fruit: Sex and Religion in the Lives of American Teenagers* (2007).

Frank Rich, an Op-Ed columnist for *The New York Times*, received the George Polk Award for commentary in 2005. His books include *The Greatest Story Ever Sold: The Decline and Fall of Truth From 9/11 to Katrina* (2006), *Ghost Light: A Memoir* (2000), and *Hot Seat: Theatre Criticism for The New York Times, 1980–1993* (1998).

Barbara K. Rimer is Alumni Distinguished Professor of Health Behavior and Health Education and Dean of the School of Public Health, University of North Carolina, Chapel Hill. Dr. Rimer has conducted research in a number of areas, including informed decision making, long-term maintenance of behavior changes,

and dissemination of evidence-based interventions. She is coeditor of *Health Behavior and Health Education: Theory, Research, and Practice* (Fourth Edition, 2008) and *Prostate Cancer Trends, 1973–1995: Seer Program, National Cancer Institute* (1994).

Raymond C. Rosen is Chief Scientist at New England Research Institutes. He has coauthored or coedited numerous books, including *Case Studies in Sex Therapy* (Second Edition, 2004), *Principles and Practice of Sex Therapy* (Third Edition, 2000), *Sexual Happiness for Men: A Practical Approach* (1992), *Erectile Disorders: Assessment and Treatment* (1992), and *Patterns of Sexual Arousal: Psychophysiological Processes and Clinical Applications* (1988). He also served as editor of the *Annual Review of Sex Research* from 1995 to 1999.

Virginia E. Rutter, an Assistant Professor of Sociology at Framingham State College, concentrates her research interests in the area of gender and sexuality as well as contraceptive decision making. She is coauthor of *The Gender of Sexuality* (1998) and *The Love Test: Romance and Relationship Self-Quizzes Developed by Psychologists and Sociologists* (1998).

Christopher Saenz is a research scientist at Wayne State University who studies sexual assault and pornography.

Jodi Savell is in the College of Education at the University of South Florida. Her research interests include sexual abuse, human sexuality, and stress and trauma as they relate to memory, neurobiology, and emotional functioning.

David M. Schnarch, a licensed clinical psychologist and certified sex therapist, is Director of the Marriage and Family Health Center in Evergreen, Colorado, where he focuses on the treatment of sexual desire and intimacy problems. He is the author of *Resurrecting Sex: Resolving*

Sexual Problems and Rejuvenating Your Relationship (2002), *Passionate Marriage: Sex, Love, & Intimacy in Emotionally Committed Relationships* (1997), and *Constructing the Sexual Crucible: An Integration of Sexual and Marital Therapy* (1991).

Jennifer P. Schneider, affiliated with Arizona Community Physicians, has coauthored numerous books on sex addiction, cybersex addiction, and effects of sex addiction on the family, including *Untangling the Web: Breaking Free from Sex, Porn, and Fantasy Addiction in the Internet Age* (2006), *Disclosing Secrets: When, to Whom, and How Much to Reveal Addiction Secrets* (2002), *Cybersex Exposed: Simple Fantasy or Obsession?* (2001), and *The Wounded Healer: Addiction-Sensitive Approach to the Sexually Exploitative Professional* (1999).

Pepper Schwartz, is Elsa and Clarence Schrag Fellow and Professor of Sociology at the University of Washington. She is primarily interested in studying sexuality in intimate relationships, both heterosexual and homosexual. She is the author of sixteen books, including *Prime: Adventures and Advice About Sex, Love and the Sensual Years* (2007), *Ten Talks Parents Must Have with Children about Sex and Character* (2002), and *Everything You Know About Love and Sex is Wrong* (2002). Her book *American Couples: Money, Work and Sex*, with Philip Blumstein (1983) still sets the standard for comparative work on heterosexual, gay, and lesbian couples.

Susan Sprecher, Professor of Sociology (with a joint appointment in Psychology) at Illinois State University, has primary research interests in the area of sexuality in the context of close relationships and other topics related to close relationships. She is coauthor of *Sexuality* (1993) and coeditor of *Handbook of Sexuality in Close Relationships* (2004), *Sexuality in Close Relationships* (1991), and *Human Sexuality: The Societal and Interpersonal Context* (1989).

Arlene Rubin Stiffman, George Warren Brown School of Social Work, Washington University in St. Louis, is a Social Work Senior Scholar and Barbara A. Bailey Professor Emeritus. She is the editor of *The Field Research Survival Guide* (2009).

Cindy Struckman-Johnson, a Professor of Psychology at the University of South Dakota, has research interests in the sexual coercion of men and women on campus and in prisons, condom use, masculinity and homophobia. She is coeditor *of Aggressive Women: Current Perspectives and Controversies* (1998).

Dave Struckman-Johnson is a Professor of Computer Science at the University of South Dakota. He has scholarly interests in sexual coercion of men and women on campus and in prisons, as well as condom use.

Fiona Tasker, Senior Lecturer in Psychology at Birkbeck College University of London, has research interests in LGBT parenting. She is coauthor of *Growing Up in a Lesbian Family: Effects on Child Development* (1997) and coeditor of *Gay and Lesbian Parenting: New Directions* (2007).

Jay Teachman is Professor of Sociology at Western Washington University. He is interested in the relationship between early sexual experiences and marital success and is coauthor of *The Sexual Bond: Rethinking the Family and Close Relationships* (1989).

L. Monique Ward is an Associate Professor of Psychology at the University of Michigan with research interests in sexual socialization, gender socialization, media effects on emergent sexuality, and the intersections of body image and sexuality.

Eileen A. Yam is a Research and Evaluation Specialist on Population and Social Transitions at the International Center for Research on Women (ICRW). Her research interests include international family planning, abortion, sexually transmitted infections, and maternal health.

M. Scott Young is Coordinator of Statistical Research in the Department of Mental Health Law and Policy at the University of South Florida. His research interests include long-term effects of childhood sexual abuse on adult functioning, particularly as it relates to adult substance use; sexual behavior and psychopathology; and evaluation of alternative case-processing approaches.

Nelwyn B. Moore, Professor Emerita of Family and Consumer Sciences at Texas State University-San Marcos received her Ph.D. in Child Development and Family Relations from the University of Texas, Austin where she also completed a post-doctoral program in Family Therapy. She taught courses in family studies and child development for thirty-seven years. Moore is a Certified Marriage and Family Therapist (American Association of Marriage and Family Therapists); a Diplomate, American Psychotherapy Association; a Licensed Marriage and Family Therapist; a Licensed Professional Counselor; and a Certified Family Life Educator, with professional training in the area of human sexuality. Moore is a past recipient of the Ernest G. Osborne Excellence in Teaching Award from the National Council on Family Relations and is recognized for her contributions to sexuality education as well as her publications in professional journals on sexual attitudes and behavior of college women and men, adoption, teen pregnancy, family life education, and family and interpersonal relations. She is coauthor of *Marriage and Family: Change and Continuity* (1996) and *Marriage and Family* (1992) and coeditor of *Speaking of Sexuality* (2001, 2005) and *Cultural Diversity and Families* (1992).

In this edition of *Speaking of Sexuality*, Moore shared literary responsibilities including article selection and the writing of the Part Openers and Chapter Lead-Ins.

J. Kenneth Davidson, Sr., Professor Emeritus of Sociology and Past Coordinator of Family Studies at the University of Wisconsin-Eau Claire, received his Ph.D. in Family Sociology from the University of Florida. Nationally recognized as an authority in the field of human sexuality, he taught a course in the sociology of human sexuality for twenty-nine years. His teaching materials appear in the *Sociology of Sexuality and Sexual Orientation: Syllabi and Teaching Materials* (1997, 2002) published by the American Sociological Association. A Fellow in the National Council on Family Relations, he is a past recipient of their Ernest G. Osborne Excellence in Teaching Award. Davidson is also one of the most widely published researchers in the field of human sexuality, with numerous papers in professional journals concerning sexual attitudes and behavior of college women and men, the female sexual response and sexual satisfaction, the Gräfenberg Spot and female ejaculation, pretending orgasm among women, sexual fantasies, and adoption. He is coauthor of *Marriage and Family: Change and Continuity* (1996) and *Marriage and Family* (1992) and coeditor of *Speaking of Sexuality* (2001, 2005) and *Cultural Diversity and Families* (1992). The **Davidson-Moore Archives** at the Kinsey Institute for Research in Sex, Gender and Reproduction at Indiana University reflect the past 25 years of collaborative research and publications between Davidson and Moore.

In this edition of *Speaking of Sexuality*, Davidson assumed management and production responsibilities including literature searches, article selection, copyediting, and proofreading.

Terri D. Fisher, Associate Professor of Psychology and Program Coordinator at The Ohio State University at Mansfield, has a Ph.D. in experimental/developmental psychology from the University of Georgia. She has been a sexuality researcher for almost 30 years, and teaches courses in human sexual behavior and adolescent sexuality, among others. Fisher served as the President of the Midcontinent Region of the Society for the Scientific Study of Sexuality in 2000 and has been a Consulting Editor for *The Journal of Sex Research* since 1994. She is coauthor of an article selected to receive the Hugo G. Beigel Award for the best research published in *The Journal of Sex Research* in 1983. Fisher has published numerous studies on gender and personality differences in sexuality, parent-child communication about sexuality, contextual effects on the reporting of sexual behavior, and the role of sexual satisfaction within relationships. She is coeditor of *Current Directions in Sexuality and Relationships* (2010) and *Handbook of Sexuality-Related Measures* (2010).

In this edition of *Speaking of Sexuality*, Fisher shared both production and literary responsibilities including literature searches, article selection, and the writing of the Part Openers and Chapter Lead-Ins.

ACKNOWLEDGMENTS

First among persons acknowledged for contributions to this book must be those thousands who shall remain nameless: students who over many years of teaching have taught us far more valuable lessons about life and humanity than we ourselves have taught. And, the many family and sexuality professionals along the way who have served as mentors may be unaware of their influence in our lives, but it is present just the same. Some, but not all, are names instantly recognizable, such as Azalete Little (NBM), James Leslie McCary (NBM), Gerald R. Leslie (JKD), Felix M. Berardo (JKD), Robert H. Pollock (TDF), and Elizabeth Rice Allgeier (TDF). Some are no longer with us, some are retired, while still others remain in our current networks of professional colleagues. Many of those who have touched our lives significantly and kept us true to our purpose are today's promising young scholars.

Our faith in the review process has been strengthened by the significant contributions made by our colleagues who served as reviewers for this work. We express sincere appreciation to these consummate professionals, without whose numerous comments and recommendations this anthology would not be as pragmatic, student friendly, or interesting. They are Kelly A. Dorgan, East Tennessee State University; Yasmina Katsulis, Arizona State University; Karen McKinney, University of Louisville; Anna Muraco, Loyola Marymount University; Adina Nack, California Lutheran University; Philip Osteen, University of Maryland-Baltimore; and Elizabeth Rink, Montana State.

We are indebted to Sherith H. Pankratz, Senior Editor, Oxford University Press, without whose able assistance and encouragement the Third Edition of this sexuality anthology would never have come to fruition. In addition, we want to acknowledge the helpful suggestions and cordial assistance provided by Whitney Laemmli, Assistant Editor; Amy Krivohlavek, Marketing Manager; and Marianne Paul, Production Editor.

The support of capable assistants has enabled the completion of this complex endeavor. Paul J. Loeber provided proofreading and editorial assistance. Stuart Hall contributed clerical assistance along with Shaye McAlexander and Marna Utz of The Ohio State University at Mansfield.

Finally, this Third Edition would not have been possible without the loving support of our families: husband Jerry, son Jay and daughter Amy Moore Meeks and her children Madeleine and Max (NBM); sons John and Stephen, John's sons John III and William (JKD); husband Paul Loeber, sons Stuart and Spencer Hall, and parents, Norris and Naomi Fisher (TDF).

And, the paw prints that have warmed these words belong to G.B. (NBM), who has walked across these pages of our lives time and time again. Her cohorts, Emma (TDF) and Katrina (TDF), also provided hours of feline companionship, while serving as living paperweights on the writing desk.

Nelwyn B. Moore
J. Kenneth Davidson, Sr.
Terri D. Fisher

Historical, Theoretical, and Research Perspectives on Sexuality

As the most ambitious of the offerings in this anthology, Part I almost assumes a life of its own. Most of the selections were purposely chosen because they reflect seminal works in the field of sexuality research. Names like Kinsey, Masters and Johnson, Lauman, Gagnon, and Buss are instantly recognizable as standard-bearers in the field of sexuality research, yesterday and today. Although most students may not be primarily interested in the theory and history of sexuality research, they will be fascinated with the insights furnished by the authors.

The selections in Part I introduce readers to highly detailed portraits of American sexuality—who does what, with whom, how, and how many times—a feat certainly more easily accomplished with the click of a mouse to browse the Internet. But the difference between Internet browsing and mining the minds of the last century's giants in the field of sexuality research is immeasurable. Applying their scientific orientation to the study of sexual behavior and attitudes, each of the authors helps students reframe the issues to fit into broader social contexts. The picture that emerges for avid readers is a sum that is truly greater than the individual parts.

Considered to be one of the world's leading authorities on the history of sex and the nature of gender, Vern L. Bullough was uniquely qualified to document the work of sexologists of the twentieth century. Bullough, who died in 2006, authored, co-authored, edited, or co-edited over 50 books and hundreds of articles (Davis, 2007). Known primarily as a historian, in mid-career he obtained a degree in nursing before becoming Professor and Dean of Natural and Social Sciences at the State University of New York at Buffalo. Bullough's pioneering work on topics such as prostitution, homosexuality, gender, and pornography helped to legitimize the study of these marginalized subjects as well as that of sexuality itself (Davis, 2007).

In the first two chapters, Vern Bullough not only recorded interesting facts, but also revealed the colorful personalities of three key players—Kinsey and Masters and Johnson. This prolific writer's unbiased treatment of the life and work of these giants in the field of sexuality research documented their singular, rare contributions, while also acknowledging their shortcomings as researchers.

Born on the cusp of the nineteenth century in 1894, Alfred Kinsey entered the field of sexuality research at a time when two circumstances occurred simultaneously: a growing awareness of the importance of sexuality, and an increasing volume of studies about human sexuality. His study of human males, published in 1948, and his study of females, published in 1952, were hailed as benchmarks for changes in American society. Perhaps best known for his distinctive interviewing techniques, Kinsey's most valuable contribution is said to be his success in treating the study of sexuality as a scientific discipline.

Although Kinsey pioneered the use of case histories to study human sexuality, Masters and Johnson were the first to use clinical techniques of observing, measuring, and recording actual sexual behaviors in a laboratory setting. Technological advances made after the Kinsey data were collected, such as the development of an artificial coital device with a miniature camera and intrauterine electrodes, enabled the latter research team to achieve its goal of replacing many "phallic fallacies" with facts. Vern Bullough carefully detailed the unprecedented clinical research conducted by the Masters and Johnson team.

The Laumann et al. selection and the Adelson selection stand alone, but students will miss an interesting exercise in analysis and synthesis if they fail to read both. Hailed by *Time* (Elmer-Dewitt, 1994) as probably the "First truly scientific study of sexuality in America," the Laumann team's study, published as *The Social Organization of Sexuality* (1994), exploded many sexuality myths. Whether the findings were received as reassuring or alarming depended upon one's personal agenda. The first chapter is included here as a significant piece of work in that it clarifies the rationale and theoretical base of the study.

Joseph Adelson's treatment of the Laumann et al. data in "Sex Among the Americans" is at once compelling and practical. Students will enjoy the fast read with its astonishing facts, guaranteed to shatter at least some myths about Americans and sexuality. Adelson's critique points to the authors' avoidance of a value construct and their questionable choice of social networks and the sexual marketplace as theoretical structures. He is troubled by the authors' lack of consideration of the "inner world," the motives and character that influence sexual behavior and attitudes. He does conclude, however, that the data have great value. This offering, more than most, will motivate students to move closer to their own position statements about sexuality in America.

One criticism of past research in sexuality is that it was often relatively atheoretical. In the 1980s, a new theoretical viewpoint began to emerge in psychology: evolutionary psychology. This perspective applied the biological concepts of natural selection, adaptation, and survival of the fittest to the area of human behavior. While initially quite controversial, evolutionary psychology has made serious inroads such that it is now a common theoretical perspective used by many psychologists and sexuality researchers. David Buss is arguably the most well-known evolutionary psychologist. He has certainly worked hard to publicize and disseminate an evolutionary understanding of mating research. As the final selection in this Part, an excerpt from Buss's book, *The Evolution of Desire*, lays out the basic premises of this perspective.

This controversial book that claims to be the first to present a unified theory of human mating behavior is based on the most massive study ever undertaken, encompassing more than 10,000 people of all ages from 37 cultures around the world. For students, the good news from evolutionary psychology is that human beings are designed to fall in love. The bad news is that they are not designed to stay there. Both finding and keeping a mate are important adaptive problems in which students will be vitally interested.

REFERENCES

Davis, C. M. 2007. Vern L. Bullough. *The Journal of Sex Research* 44: 1–2.

Elmer-Dewitt, P. 1994. Now for the truth about Americans and sex. *Time*, 17 October, 62–66, 68, 70.

CHAPTER I

Alfred Kinsey

Vern L. Bullough

"... The most influential American sex researcher of the twentieth century." Readers do not have to be experts in the area of sex research to recognize that this quote refers to Alfred Kinsey. A biologist turned sexologist, Kinsey is portrayed in the literature as both a colorful character and a consummate researcher. Kinsey's advocates and adversaries alike agree that his controversial life's work sparked a revolution in sexuality research. But there has long been disagreement about the nature of his influence. Was the greatest significance of Kinsey's work that it was a marker of changes occurring at that time as claimed by one historian? Or, as suggested by others, was his work seminal because it was instrumental in bringing about the changes? Noted therapist David Mace, who defined the sexual revolution of the 1960s as a grassroots uprising against organized religion's teachings about sexuality, alluded to the latter position when he identified Kinsey along with Sigmund Freud and Albert Ellis as the three most influential forces in the sexual revolution. Mace believed their contributions to the knowledge about human sexuality was unparalleled.

Regardless of how one views the influence of Kinsey's work, facts cannot be ignored. The radical changes in public attitudes that followed his first published report on male sexuality in 1948 foreshadowed a new discipline of sexology, a new profession of sex therapy, and new materials and methodology for sexuality education. Nevertheless, Kinsey today is still a controversial figure, attracting both detractors who would defame him and advocates who would vindicate him.

Kinsey has been criticized by many professionals in the field, including a former Director of the Kinsey Institute. Critics point to problems such as the following:

- His difficulties with sampling and survey research, illustrated by the fact that he confused, in some cases, the concepts of random sampling and representativeness.
- His infamous seventeen-hour interview with a pedophile that admittedly was the basis for much of his data about the onset of childhood sexual activity.
- His use of data collected from an Indiana State Prison for the bulk of his male study.

Kinsey, however, has been recognized, even by his detractors for the following singular contributions made to sexuality research:

- His Seven-point scale, which placed persons along a continuum of sexual activity from exclusively heterosexual to exclusively homosexual and is still in use today.
- His objectifying the existence of homosexuality and his conclusion that one

From Science in the Bedroom: A History of Sex Research (pp. 168–185; 334–337) by V. L. Bullough. 1994. New York: Basic Books. Copyright © 1994 by Basic Books, a member of Perseus Books Group. Reprinted by Permission.

or a few homosexual experiences do not classify a person as homosexual.

- *His reported data on the percentage of the population that is exclusively homosexual are amazingly consistent with national probability samples today.*
- *His early data reporting multiple orgasms among women, which are still cited today.*
- *His landmark federal court case (1957) decided after his death, which resulted in scientists and scholars being treated as a "community"; therefore, they can possess obscene materials for scientific purposes. Today, the Kinsey Institute at Indiana University has the largest collection of pornography in the world.*

After reading Vern Bullough's treatment of the life of Alfred Kinsey, on which side of the Kinsey controversy do you find yourself? What factors most influenced your position either as an advocate or an adversary?

It was in a setting of a growing awareness of the importance of sexuality and an ever-increasing volume of studies on human sexuality that Alfred Kinsey began to do his research. Kinsey was born in 1894 in Hoboken, New Jersey; he was at the height of his career in 1938 when he shifted from the study of gall wasps to the study of human sexuality. He probably also was going through what might be called a midlife crisis, hunting for new fields to conquer. In the summer of that year, Indiana University began to teach a course in marriage, one of the many colleges and universities to venture into this new area. Because no professor on the faculty was considered qualified to teach it singlehand-edly, teachers (all men) were gathered together from the departments of law, economics, sociology, philosophy, medicine, and biology to do so. Kinsey ended up as coordinator of the course.

To add to his own knowledge, he soon began taking histories of the students, many of whom came to him for counseling. He sought information on age at first premarital intercourse,

the frequency of sexual activity, the number of partners, and similar data. Gradually, he amplified his search for information by including questions about prostitutes, the age of the partner with whom the subject had his or her first intercourse, the percentage of partners who were married, and so forth. Kinsey, a compulsive data gatherer, began an extensive reading program into all aspects of sexual behavior. This led him to build up a personal library, since serious studies on sex were difficult to find in most public or university libraries. To extend his collection of data beyond the classroom, Kinsey took a field trip to Chicago in June 1939 to conduct interviews. About this time, he also began working with inmates at the Indiana State Penal Farm and their families, compiling their sexual histories. All of this he did in consultation with the university officials, who had ruled that the histories were to be kept completely confidential. His students apparently trusted him, and many of them who had taken the class continued to write Kinsey about their sexual problems long after they had graduated.

Kinsey's expanding research into human sexuality was not without controversy, and one of his most persistent critics was Thurman Rice, a bacteriology professor at the university who had written extensively on sex, primarily from the point of view of eugenics. Rice had long given the sex lecture that was part of a required course in hygiene at the university and for which males were separated from females. Rice was typical of an earlier generation of sex experts, in that he considered moral education a part of sex education. He believed masturbation was harmful, condemned premarital intercourse, and was fearful that Kinsey's course on marriage was a perversion of academic standards. He charged Kinsey with, among other things, asking some of the women students about the length of their clitorises, and then demanded the names of students in the class so he could verify such classroom voyeurism. Rice totally opposed Kinsey's questioning in general, because he believed that sexual behavior could not be analyzed by scientific methods as it was a moral subject, not a scientific one. Some parents also objected to the specific sexual data given in the course, and university president Herman Wells, a personal friend of Kinsey, offered him the alternative of either continuing to teach the course or to conduct his sex research.[1] In any case, Kinsey would continue to teach in the biology department. He elected to do the research and dropped his participation in the marriage course.

Kinsey was not only interested but well prepared. As a bench scientist, he felt the researcher had to be directly involved in the project. He was somewhat disdainful of the work of most of his predecessors in sex research. He was appalled at how Freud and the early analysts, still under the influence of Krafft-Ebing, had looked on masturbation as a sickness. He was also concerned that Freud relied on subjective impressions and did not test them. Similarly, he disagreed with Stekel and, ultimately, with the whole psychoanalytic approach. He had no use for Kraft-Ebing's unscientific cataloging of sexual behavior. Kinsey believed that American psychologists and American followers of Freud were not objective scientists and were too highly influenced by traditional moral codes. Though he had good words to say about Ellis, his esteem dwindled when he learned that the British researcher was so timid about his work that he could not talk to his subjects face to face and depended entirely on letters written to him. Kinsey was also offended by Hirschfeld's open proclamation of his own homosexuality, which led him to regard Hirschfeld as a special pleader and not an objective scientist. Similarly, he was disdainful of Malinowski because in his mind Malinowski was not only afraid of sex but had been taken in by the Islanders. He and Mead disagreed publicly, because Mead accused him of talking only about sex per se and not about such things as maternal behavior. Kinsey thought they were different things and said he wanted to study sex, not love. Obviously, Kinsey was a strong-minded individual—some might call him arrogant; he was critical of most of his predecessors, although

he was always careful to cite them in his work if they had broken new ground. Moreover, in spite of his criticism, he recognized that some, particularly Freud and Ellis, had made important contributions for their time. They just fell short of what Kinsey felt was necessary, namely the study of human sexual activity in as detached and scientific a way as possible. He had the commitment and the temperament to do so, since he thought he had to be rigorously neutral and nonjudgmental and let his data speak for him.[2]

In short, after years of skirting around the subject of human sexuality, the CRPS (Committee for Research in the Problems of Sex) jumped in with full support for Kinsey. The result was a revolution in sex research. Aiding this revolution was what for a time was believed to be the elimination of the threat of venereal diseases, or as the Centers for Disease Control began to call them, sexually transmitted diseases.[3]

The first big step in this direction was the discovery of sulfa drugs in 1935, and this was followed by the development of a commercial process for making penicillin during World War II. Sulfa proved effective against gonorrhea, while penicillin was effective against both gonorrhea and syphilis. Other new antibiotics soon appeared in the postwar period, and for a time at least, the fear of sexually transmitted diseases was no longer an issue and, more important, no longer an inhibitor, in sexual relations. In sum, Americans, who had been among the most sexually inhibited, proved to be a receptive audience for the new findings about human sexuality.

The two decades following the appearance of the first Kinsey report in 1948 saw a radical change in public attitudes about sexuality spurred both by the development of the oral contraceptive and by new studies in human sexuality, including additional ones by Kinsey and his team and by William Masters and Virginia Johnson. The results of these studies included the establishment of a new discipline, sexology; the emergence of a new helping profession, sex therapist; and a reorientation of the way sex was taught. Individually and collectively, there was also a changing attitude, more positive if you will, toward sexuality.

KINSEY'S RESEARCH

Kinsey is a good marker of these changes because, unlike almost all previous American sex researchers, Kinsey emphasized the sex part of sex research and held that sex was as legitimate a subject to study as any other. He recognized the many facets of sexual behavior from biology to history and gathered together one of the great resource libraries of the world devoted entirely to sex. He openly challenged the traditional medical dominance of sexual topics and, in the process, opened up the field to many other disciplines. Though some of his statistics can be challenged, it was the combination of all his contributions that make him the most influential American sex researcher of the twentieth century.

His two major works, the male study in 1948 and the female study in 1952, serve as effective indicators of the change taking place in American society.[4] Though Kinsey is known for his diligent interviewing and summation of data, his work is most significant because of his attempt to treat the study of sex as a scientific discipline, compiling and examining the data and drawing conclusions from them without moralizing.

THE KINSEY INTERVIEW

The key to Kinsey's studies was the interview, since Kinsey was convinced that it was only through this means that accurate data could be compiled. His interview technique included a number of checks for consistency, and if inconsistencies appeared, either from attempts to deceive or from faulty memory, the interviewer probed deeper until the apparent disagreement could be explained or eliminated. Kinsey strongly believed he could detect

fraudulent answers, and certainly his ingenious coding system was designed to detect the most obvious ones.

Exaggeration proved almost impossible in the system in which questions were asked rapidly and in detail, because few subjects could give consistent answers. Though he recognized that some subjects might not remember accurately, he felt errors resulting from false memories would be offset by errors other subjects made in an opposite direction. A deliberate cover-up was a more serious problem, but he felt his numerous cross-checks made it difficult. If histories were taken of a husband and wife, the two were cross-checked to see how they conformed; some retakes were conducted after a minimum interval of two years and an average interval of four years to see if people would give the same basic answers.

Kinsey was also concerned with potential bias by the interviewer, and he sought to overcome this by limiting the number of interviewers to four: himself, Wardell Pomeroy, Clyde Martin, and eventually Paul Gebhard. These men engaged in discussion sessions after a series of interviews to see if they agreed on the coding of certain kinds of responses. Collaboratively, the four interviewed some eighteen thousand individuals; eight thousand each by Kinsey and Pomeroy and two thousand by Martin and Gebhard.[5] Kinsey actually hoped to get one hundred thousand sexual histories, but his death ended this long-term plan.

The interview covered a basic minimum of about 350 items, and these items remained almost unchanged throughout all the interviews. A maximum history covered 521 items, and whenever there was any indication of sexual activity beyond what the basic questions covered, the interviewer could go as far as he thought necessary to get the material. All the questions had been memorized by the interviewers, and there was no referral to any question sheet. Questions were asked directly and without apology, and the interviewer waited for a response from the subject. Initial questions were simply informational ones about the informant's age, birthplace, educational experience, marital status, and children. These were followed by questions on religion, personal health, hobbies, special interests, and so on. It was not until 20 minutes into the interview that sex questions appeared, and these started with sex education, proceeded to ages when a person first became aware of where babies came from, and then on to menstruation and growth of pubic hair and various anatomical changes. From here, the questions went on to early sex experiences, including age at first masturbation. Techniques of masturbation were investigated for both men and women. There were questions on erotic fantasies during masturbation and about erotic responses, and next was a series of questions about actual sex practices. The answers to the basic 350 questions could be coded on one page; Pomeroy estimated that the code sheet provided information equivalent to twenty-five typewritten pages.[6]

Before any specific questions about homosexuality were asked, twelve preliminary inquiries were scattered throughout the early questions, the answers to which would give the interviewer hints about the subject's sexual preference in partners. If the interviewer thought the subject was not being honest, he told the person so and generally refused to finish the interview. In some cases, the interview continued, but at the end the interviewer then told the subject that he wanted to go through some questions again, so that the subject could answer accurately questions that he or she had not been honest about the first time. In general, the interview ran from 1.5 hours to 2 hours. Children were also interviewed, but a different approach was used and at least one parent was always present.

Some individuals were interviewed for much longer periods of time. For example, those individuals who had extensive homosexual experiences were asked more questions than those who did not; subjects who had engaged in prostitution were also asked more questions. The longest interview was of a pedophile. It took some 17 hours and involved both Pomeroy and Kinsey. This man was sought out because he was known to have kept accurate written records of his sexual activity, a not uncommon occurrence among pedophiles. The man had sexual relations with six hundred preadolescent males and two hundred preadolescent females, as well as intercourse with countless adults of both sexes and with animals of many species. He had developed elaborate techniques of masturbation and reported that his grandmother had introduced him to heterosexual intercourse and that his first homosexual experience was with his father.

His notes on his sexual relations with preadolescents furnished much of the information on childhood activity that Kinsey reported, since it included the length of time it took the child to be aroused, the child's response, and other such data. Kinsey's use of these data has been much criticized,[7] in part because Kinsey did not report his subject to the authorities. During the interview, the man was boastful about his ability to masturbate to ejaculation in 10 seconds from a flaccid start, and when Kinsey and Pomeroy openly expressed their disbelief at such a statement, the man effectively demonstrated his ability to them then and there. Pomeroy added that this was the only sexual demonstration that took place during the eighteen thousand interview sessions.[8] There were, however, laboratory observations from which data were derived, but these were separate from the interview and did not necessarily include the same individuals.

KINSEY AND STATISTICS

One of the major criticisms of Kinsey was the way in which he drew his sample. Two difficulties were at the heart of the criticism: (1) it was not random, and (2) it depended on volunteers. His critics urged him to undertake at least a small interviewing project on randomly selected individuals to test the validity of his findings,[9] but he refused. His reason for the refusal is that he believed some of those chosen randomly would not consent to answering the questions, and thus he argued it would no longer be a random sample. Though sampling techniques when Kinsey began in the 1930s were not as advanced as they later became, the issue of Kinsey's sampling concerned the Committee for Research in the Problems of Sex very early in their support. They had concluded, however, that the cluster method he advocated was as good as could be expected.[10] After the first Kinsey volume was published, Kinsey took greater care to explain his sampling method in his second book, and also eliminated some of the more controversial data gathered from interviews with prisoners.[11]

Kinsey's sample is clearly overrepresented in some areas; for example, there are too many midwesterners, particularly from Indiana, and in the male study there is a disproportionate number of prison inmates and perhaps also of homosexuals.[12] Critics also charged that those who volunteered for the project were among the less inhibited members of society, and this gave an erroneous picture of the American public. There probably is some truth in this charge, but Kinsey tried to guard against it through what he called 100 percent sampling. When he turned to organized groups to obtain subjects, all members had to agree to be interviewed about their sexual histories, whether the group was a college fraternity, a woman's club, or the residents of a particular building. About a quarter of his sample was picked this way, and since he found few significant differences between the reports of those who belonged to groups and those he contacted in other ways, he felt he was able to establish the resentativeness of his sample. Though this was an ingenious resolution to the problem, his sample was, by any definition, not a cross-sample of the total population.[13]

One of the problems with any statistical summary of sex life is what is reported and how it is reported. Kinsey, for example, put sexual activity on a 7-point continuum that ranged from 0 to 6; exclusively heterosexual behavior was on one

end (0) and exclusively homosexual or lesbian behavior was on the other (6). The effect of this was to emphasize the variety of sexual activity and to demonstrate that homosexuality and lesbianism were more or less a natural aspect of human behavior. This was a partial solution to an impossible question: What is homosexuality, or for that matter what is heterosexuality? Kinsey avoided these questions by defining sex in terms of outlet, any activity that resulted in orgasm. This was something that could be measured with his 7-point bipolar scale.

At the time Kinsey began his research, 5-, 6-, and 7-point scales seem to have been the most popular, and he probably adopted such a scale for this reason. Although the Kinsey scale can be improved on and although it does not measure all the things that many researchers would now want to measure, it did two things of great importance. It offered comfort to both homosexuals and heterosexuals. Kinsey, in effect, demonstrated that homosexual activity was widespread in the American population: 37 percent of his American male sample had at least one homosexual experience to orgasm sometime between adolescence and old age.[14] This statistic gave assurance to many worried heterosexuals who had experimented briefly with same-sex activities that they were not homosexuals and could relax in their normality.

Homosexuals, on the other hand, found that they were more numerous than the general public (and perhaps they themselves) realized and that many heterosexuals had experimented with homosexuality. It also led many writers on homosexuality to claim a higher percentage of homosexuals in society than probably existed. Reports of the proportion of gays in the population ranged from one person in twenty to one person in ten to even higher ratios, depending on which Kinsey statistic was used.[15] However, only 4 percent of Kinsey's subjects could be labeled as exclusively homosexual; this percentage is close to what has been found in more recent studies Kinsey noted that the proportion of women engaging in same-sex activity was less than half that of the men.

KINSEY'S DEFINITIONS AND HOMOSEXUALITY

Kinsey's insistence on a behavioral definition of homosexuality has led to speculation about his own potential homosexuality,[16] a question that seems to arise about almost every investigator of homosexuality. There is no evidence for this, but Kinsey did not condemn homosexuality, which might have been the basis for the charge. He also rejected the popular stereotype of the homosexual as effeminate, temperamental, and artistic; instead, he held there were wide variations among homosexuals. To gauge this he turned to measuring sexual activity. He did, however, believe that homosexual relations were characterized by promiscuity and instability, a statement somewhat contrary to his own data, as homosexual contacts accounted for only 6 to 7 percent of all male orgasms.[17]

Undoubtedly, Kinsey's findings and the publicity about homosexuality were valuable in assuring many a parent and many a client that one experience does not a homosexual make. On the other hand, his conclusion that a significant percentage of his sample was exclusively homosexual or almost exclusively homosexual allowed American society to come to terms with the facts of life and to recognize the widespread existence of this phenomenon. These are extremely important contributions, and the modern gay movement would probably not have come into being without them, at least at the time it did. Kinsey, in effect, accepted the bisexual potential of humans as a reality and this in itself was a major challenge to existing concepts in the psychoanalytic community, which tended to argue that bisexuals were really homosexuals trying to adjust to societal norms.[18] Kinsey's emphasis on outlet and his bipolar scale not only challenged traditional attitudes about sex but undermined them.

OTHER FINDINGS

Kinsey was also important in emphasizing that there are class distinctions in sexual practices, that highly educated individuals have a different history of sexual activity than do the less educated, and the affluent have patterns that are different from the poor. This finding basically challenged the validity of most of the studies that had gone before his, which for the most part were based on college-educated or upper-middle-class samples. He also found that the younger generation in his male study was less likely to visit prostitutes than the older, suggesting not only that there was a generational change, but that age cohorts also must be taken into account. Kinsey was not the first to recognize generational change; it had been much commented on by others, including Terman, even though the phenomenon had not been measured effectively by his predecessors.

Kinsey challenged all sorts of myths about sexuality. One such challenge had to do with female frigidity, or what is now called anorgasmia. A total of 49 percent of the females he studied had experienced orgasm within the first month of marriage, 67 percent by the first six months, and 75 percent by the end of the first year. More remarkable was the fact that nearly 25 percent of the women in the sample recalled experiencing orgasm by the age of fifteen, and more than 50 percent by the age of twenty and 64 percent before marriage. The orgasms occurred through masturbation (40 percent), through heterosexual petting without penetration (24 percent), and through premarital coitus (10 percent). For 3 percent it was through a homosexual experience.[19]

Women varied enormously in the frequency of their orgasmic responses, with some reporting only one or two orgasms during their entire lives, while some 40–50 percent responded being orgasmic almost every time they had coitus. Still, 10 percent of his sample who had been married at least fifteen years had never had an orgasm. He also reported cases in which women failed to reach orgasm until after twenty years of marital intercourse. He also documented (as had others) the female ability to achieve multiple orgasm. Some 14 percent of the females in his sample responded that they had multiple orgasms. Several managed to have a dozen or more orgasms while their husbands ejaculated only once.[20] He concluded from his data that the human female, like the human male, is an "orgasm experiencing animal."[21]

Sometimes Kinsey seemed deliberately to flaunt the differences between widely held beliefs about traditional conduct and reality. He showed that fewer than half of the orgasms achieved by American males were derived from intercourse with their wives, which meant, he said, that more than half were derived from sources that were "socially disapproved and in large part illegal and punishable under the criminal codes."[22] He seemed to imply that premarital abstinence was unnatural and argued that nearly all cultures other than those in the Judeo-Christian tradition made allowance for sexual intercourse before marriage.[23] Similarly, he found that nearly 50 percent of the women in his sample had coitus before they were married, although in a "considerable portion" it had been confined to their fiancé and had taken place within one or two years preceding marriage.[24] He also argued that his data did not justify the general opinion then existing that premarital coitus was of necessity "more hurried and consequently less satisfactory than coitus usually is in marriage."[25] Kinsey, in effect, ended up defending premarital intercourse just as he had masturbation and petting, arguing that premarital experience contributed to sexual success in marriage.[26]

The two reports hit different emotional responses in the American public. For the male study it was the incidence of homosexuality that received much of the headlines, while for the female study it was the generalized premarital and even extramarital activity of the women. Some 26 percent of the women had engaged in extramarital coitus,[27] and about 50 percent of

the married male population had.[28] Still, it was the case of the women "adulteress" that roused public opinion.

Kinsey reported that 50 percent of the males who remained single until age thirty-five had overt homosexual experiences, and some 13 percent of his sample had more homosexual than heterosexual experiences between the ages of sixteen and fifty-five, and Kinsey noted that between 4 and 5 percent of the male population were exclusively homosexual.[29] This figure corresponds to some of Hirschfeld's figures and, as indicated, tends to be supported by more recent data. Women in his sample reported considerably fewer homosexual contacts than the men. Some 28 percent had reported homosexual arousal by age forty-five, but only 13 percent had actually reached orgasm.[30] The homosexual pattern, however, differed between men and women by social class. Among men it was the lower socioeconomic class that had more homosexual experiences, whereas among women, it was the upper class, better-educated group that had more homosexual activity.[31] He did not really explain this difference, which might well have been due to the ability of the upper-class women to have more choices in their partners and the economic capability to be independent of a man.

Kinsey openly and willingly challenged many basic societal beliefs. Though there is considerable evidence of Kinsey's commitment to marriage, and he demanded that his interviewers be happily married,[32] his data seemed to many to undermine the belief in marriage and traditional family. Kinsey had questioned the assumption that extramarital intercourse always undermined the stability of marriage and held that the full story was more complex than the most highly publicized cases led one to assume. He seemed to feel that the most appropriate extramarital affair, from the standpoint of preserving a marriage, was an alliance in which neither party became overly involved emotionally. He was, however, more cautious in the female book and conceded that extramarital affairs probably contributed to divorces in more ways and to "a greater extent than the subjects themselves realized."[33] Inevitably, his ideas came under attack, because he seemed to be assaulting traditional religious teachings.[34]

Interestingly, Kinsey ignored what might be called sexual adventure, paying almost no attention to swinging, group sex, and alternate lifestyles as well as such phenomena as sadism, masochism, transvestism, voyeurism, and exhibitionism. He justified this neglect by arguing that such practices were statistically insignificant. But the real answer is probably that Kinsey was not interested in them. He was also not particularly interested in pregnancy[35] or sexually transmitted diseases. What he did, however, was to demystify discussions of sex as much as it was possible to do so. Sex, to him, became just another aspect of human behavior, albeit an important part. He made Americans and the world at large aware of just how big a part human sexuality played in the life cycle of the individual and how widespread many kinds of heterosexual and homosexual activity were.

CRITICISM

Though the general public accepted the importance of the study,[36] many people attacked it, including Harold W. Dodds, president of Princeton University, and the Reverend Henry P. Van Dusen, president of Union Theological Seminary as well as a member of the Rockefeller Foundation.[37] While a significant proportion of the more serious criticisms was based on the sampling method and the statistical reliability of the data, the vast majority of criticism was based on what can only be called moralism and prudery. Kinsey was surprised and upset by the criticism, but since he basically had challenged much of psychoanalytic thinking, disagreed with and criticized the findings of many of his predecessors in the social sciences, and stated that much of Western moral teaching ignored reality, it is difficult to understand why he did not expect severe criticism. Moreover, as Lionel

Trilling reported, in spite of Kinsey's scientific stance, his book was "full of assumptions and conclusions; it makes very positive statements on highly debatable matters, and it editorializes very freely."[38] This made criticism easier than it might have been if he had not, either consciously or unconsciously, engaged in editorializing.

Though in terms of serious criticism, he had as many defenders as he did hostile critics, most of his defenders also had some criticism not only of his results but of his plans.[39] Despite the criticisms of the first report, the CRPS continued to fund Kinsey.

Because the response to the first volume had made it a best-seller, the press had eagerly anticipated the publication of the second volume on the female. By the time the book was ready to appear, the advance interest was so great that Kinsey and co-workers were literally besieged by the press, which was engaging in what has since come to be called a frenzy. The center of the assault on the female volume was essentially by the moralists, particularly by the clergy, who seemed to feel that Kinsey had undermined the virginal status of American womanhood. Some who had supported the first study, such as Karl Menninger, joined in the denunciation of the second. In part, some of the criticism was a turf war. For example, Menninger said, "Kinsey's compulsion to force human sexual behavior into a zoological frame of reference leads him to repudiate or neglect human psychology, and to see normality as that which is natural in the sense that it is what is practiced by animals."[40]

For public relations purposes, it was announced that Kinsey's support was not renewed because he had failed to request support, but there is ample evidence in the Rockefeller Archives that he did. Some of the slack in funding for Kinsey was taken up by Indiana University through the effort of its president, Wells. The scope of the project, however, was severely curtailed. Kinsey continued to try to gain funding from the Rockefeller Foundation. He continued to pursue his research and tried desperately to raise more funds, up until his death on

August 25, 1956. In spite of the trauma of his last years and the serious and legitimate criticism of his studies, he was probably the major figure in transforming American public attitudes about sex, helping Americans to come to terms with the existence of real sexual behaviors that had been previously ignored.[41]

KINSEY AND CENSORSHIP

Kinsey also broke new legal ground in disseminating information about sex. This was because he was nothing if not thorough, and typical of his research was his attempt to survey exhaustively the literature about human sexuality. This, among other things, involved collecting materials from all over the world. Inevitably, he ran into difficulty with postal and customs officials. Alden H. Baker, Collector of Customs at Indianapolis, called some of the incoming materials, "Damned dirty stuff," and held in 1950 it was inadmissible. Kinsey believed that the law specifically granted exceptions to scientists and medical individuals in matters dealing with possible obscenity, and he argued it was under this category that the materials should be admitted. Washington, D.C. customs officials said there was nothing in the materials that was of intrinsic value or that made it valuable to scientists. Rather than destroy the material outright, as they held was their right, they agreed to wait for final court adjudication.[42] The case, *U.S. v. 31 Photographs*, was finally decided after Kinsey's death in the Federal Court of New York.[43] Judge Edmund L. Palmieri, ruling in Kinsey's favor, stated that there was no warrant for either custom officials or the court to sit in review of the decisions of scholars as to the bypaths of learning on which they would tread. The legal question was narrowly defined, whether among those persons who sought to see the material, there was a reasonable probability that it would appeal to prurient interest.[44] In this case, Palmieri decided it would not. The important aspect of the case was that the court, in determining community standards for defining whether a material was obscene, recognized those scientists and scholars interested in studying human sexuality as a community when it could be shown that this was the audience for which the material was intended. Customs decided not to appeal the ruling, and this has allowed various institutions and professionals to collect materials essential for sex research.

Kinsey was determined to make the study of sex a science and had projected a number of projects and book-length reports. Though some of these studies on which data had been collected were brought to fruition by his successors in Indiana and other new projects were initiated, Kinsey's death led to a greater dispersion of sex research across the United States than might have been the case had he lived.

A good example is the study of the biological factors involved in sexual behavior, for which Kinsey had been gathering data. At his death, his collection included, among other things, more than four thousand sets of measurements of penises made by subjects who gave their case histories, and another twelve thousand measurements made by a person who turned his records over to Kinsey. In the Kinsey files, the longest authenticated measurement of a penis was 10.5 inches in erection, although there were unofficial reports of longer ones. The average length was nearly 6.5 inches.

Kinsey had also attempted to measure clitorises, but this was more complicated because the amount of fleshy material and the position of the material in the prepuce. Still, clitorises that measured as long as 3 inches were reported (primarily in black women), and Kinsey noted that peep shows had exhibited women with 4-inch clitorises. Kinsey also turned to gynecologists to determine the extent to which women were aware of tactile and heavier stimulation in every part of the genitalia. He thought that clitoral stimulation was the key to female orgasm.[45] Kinsey, ever the entrepreneur, had grand plans to do much more in this area and had requested funds for a physiologist, a neurologist and a specialist in the sexual behavior of lower animals, but nothing had come of these requests. Instead, William Masters and Virginia Johnson were the pioneers in this area.

NOTES

1. Wardell B. Pomeroy, *Dr. Kinsey and the Institute for Sex Research* (New York: Harper & Row, 1972). Judith Reisman has charged that Kinsey was not simply chosen for the university's new marriage course but that he had maneuvered for many years to gain approval for the course and to be able to direct it. See Judith A. Reisman and Edward W. Eichel, *Kinsey, Sex and Fraud: The Indoctrination of a People* (Lafayette, LA: Lochinvar-Huntington House, 1990).
2. George W. Corner, *The Seven Ages of a Medical Scientist* (Philadelphia: University of Pennsylvania Press, 1981), 314.
3. Ibid., 268.
4. Alfred Kinsey, Wardell Pomeroy, and Clyde Martin, *Sexual Behavior in the Human Male* (Philadelphia: Saunders, 1948); and Alfred Kinsey, Wardell Pomeroy, Clyde Martin, and Paul Gebhard, *Sexual Behavior in the Human Female* (Philadelphia: Saunders, 1953).
5. Wardell B. Pomeroy, *Dr. Kinsey and the Institute for Sex Research* (New York: Harper & Row, 1972).
6. Ibid., 121; and Wardell Pomeroy, personal communication.
7. See Judith A. Reisman and Edward W. Eichel, in *Kinsey, Sex, and Fraud*, ed. J. Gordon Muir and John H. Court (Lafayette, LA.: Lochinvar-Huntington House, 1990). This is a badly written and poorly edited book, in which Kinsey is described as unscientific for relying on either the memory of older subjects or data gathered from a pedophile. See the reply from Gebhard, "Dr. Paul Gebhard's Letter to Dr. Judith Reisman Regarding Kinsey Research Subjects and Data" (March 11, 1981) [Appendix B], in *Kinsey, Sex, and Fraud*, 223.
8. Ibid., 122–3.
9. William G. Cochran, Frederick Mosteller, and John W. Tukey, *Statistical Problems of the Kinsey Report* (Washington, D.C.: American Statistical Association, 1954), 23.
10. See "Report" Foundation 1, Ser. 200, Box 41, Rockefeller Foundation Archives, Pocantico Hills, North Tarrytown, New York.
11. George W. Corner, *The Seven Ages of a Medical Scientist: An Autobiography* (Philadelphia: University of Pennsylvania Press, 1981), 315–6.
12. Pomeroy, *Dr. Kinsey*, 464.
13. See Kinsey et al., *Sexual Behavior in the Human Female*, 28–31.
14. Kinsey et al., *Sexual Behavior in the Human Male*, 161, 610–50.
15. See Vern L. Bullough, "The Kinsey Scale in Historical Perspective," in *Homosexuality/Heterosexuality: Concepts of Sexual Orientation*, ed. David P. McWhirter, Stephanie A. Sanders, and June Machover Reinisch (New York: Oxford University Press, 1990), 3–14.
16. See Pomeroy, *Dr. Kinsey*, 46; and Paul Robinson "Dr. Kinsey and the Institute for Sex Research," *Atlantic* 229 (May 1972): 99–102.
17. Kinsey et al., *Sexual Behavior in the Human Male*, 610, 633–6. This is the explanation advanced by Paul Robinson, *The Modernization of Sex* (New York: Harper & Row, 1976), 70–71.
18. See Kenneth Lewes, *The Psychoanalytic Theory of Male Homosexuality* (New York: Simon & Schuster, 1988).
19. Kinsey et al., *Sexual Behavior in the Human Female*, 375–408.
20. Ibid., 377, 383.
21. Edward M. Brecher, *The Sex Researchers* (Boston: Little, Brown, 1969), 124.
22. Ibid., 568.
23. Ibid., 547, 549, 559; and Kinsey et al., *Sexual Behavior in the Human Female*, 284.
24. Ibid., 186.
25. Ibid., 311.
26. Ibid., 328.
27. Ibid., 416.
28. Kinsey et al., *Sexual Behavior in the Human Male*, 585.
29. Ibid., 650–1.
30. Kinsey et al., *Sexual Behavior in the Human Female*, 450–1.
31. Ibid., 460.
32. Pomeroy, *Dr. Kinsey*, 101.
33. Kinsey et al., *Sexual Behavior in the Human Female*, 435–6.
34. See Reinhold Niebuhr, "Kinsey and the Moral Problems of Man's Sexual Life," in *An Analysis of the Kinsey Reports*, ed. Donald Porter Geddes (New York: New American Library, 1954), 62–70.
35. Actually, he had collected data on pregnancy, birth, and abortion, which appeared in Paul H. Gebhard,

Wardell B. Pomeroy, Clyde E. Martin, and Cornelia V. Christenson, *Pregnancy, Birth, and Abortion* (New York: Harper, 1958).

36. A Gallup poll following the book's publication found that 58 percent of the men and 55 percent of the women thought Kinsey's research was a good thing; only 10 and 14 percent, respectively, thought it a bad thing. See Pomeroy, *Dr. Kinsey*, 283–4.

37. Dodds went so far as to meet with officials of the Rockefeller Foundation to express his unhappiness and that of Van Dusen. See Memo of June 28, 1948, Foundation Ser. 200, Box 40, Rockefeller Foundation Archives.

38. Lionel Trilling, *The Liberal Imagination* (1950; reprint, New York: Viking, 1957), 218.

39. Pomeroy, *Dr. Kinsey*, 298–9.

40. Quoted in Ibid., 367.

41. Corner, *Seven Ages of a Medical Scientist*, 316–7.

42. *The New York Times*, "U.S. Customs Refuses to Pass Obscene European Photos," November 18, 1950, n18, 9:5, and in *Indianapolis Star-News*, December 8, 1950. See Foundation Records [National Research Council] Ser. 200, Box 41, 463, Rockefeller Foundation Archives.

43. *United States v. 31 Photographs*, 156 F. Supp. 350 (S.D.N.Y., 1957).

44. Morris L. Ernst and Alan U. Schwartz, *Censorship: The Search for the Obscene* (New York: Macmillan, 1964), 125.

45. Pomeroy, *Dr. Kinsey*, 317–9.

CHAPTER 2

Masters and Johnson

Vern L. Bullough

Building on a baseline of Alfred Kinsey's sociological data about patterns of sexual behavior, Masters and Johnson emphasized the application of clinical scientific methods in studying the physiology of sexual response in women and men. Through such methods, they clearly delineated varied physiological responses to sexual stimulation in women and, to a lesser degree, in men. For example, they clinically documented multiple orgasms in women and discovered the source of vaginal lubrication during sexual arousal to be the walls of the vagina, rather than the Glands of Bartholin as previously believed. Even though they clinically verified Kinsey's findings concerning the similarity of the anatomy and physiology of the sexual response in females and males, they rejected his claim that the differences were centered in the brain's capacity to respond to psychological stimuli. Masters and Johnson are perhaps best recognized for their arbitrary four-stage division of the sexual response cycle still in use today: the excitement, plateau, orgasmic, and resolution stages.

The Masters and Johnson team was the first to challenge the assumption that psychiatry and psychoanalysis should be the sole providers of the treatment for sexual dysfunction. By moving the focus to the medical model, they expanded treatment options to include obstetrics and gynecology, urology, and later, sex therapy. Today, medical and behavioral professionals across many disciplines can more competently address the problems of sexual dysfunction because of the remarkable work of this research team.

A careful reading of Vern Bullough's Kinsey and Masters and Johnson chapters will enable you to establish an imaginary time line of sexuality advances in the mid-twentieth century. It would be interesting to consider who in your family tree was your present age in 1954, when the Masters and Johnson laboratory program for the investigation of the human sexual response began. Based on your knowledge of this ancestor, do you think she or he would have volunteered to be an experimental subject using miniature cameras and electronic devices? Would you do so today? These questions may border on the ridiculous, but they highlight the significance of an era that fostered not only the principal players in this chapter, but also other contemporary characters in sexuality advances, such as Alan Guttmacher and Mary Calderone.

From *Science in the Bedroom: A History of Sex Research* (pp. 196–205; 339–340) by V. L. Bullough. 1994. New York: Basic Books. Copyright © 1994 by Basic Books, a member of Perseus Books Group. Reprinted by permission.

William Masters and Virginia Johnson from the first were much more practice oriented than Kinsey. Masters was a physician who was concerned with helping his patients overcome their problems. Together, Masters and Johnson thought of themselves as therapists, which meant they accepted the world as they saw it existing and wanted to help their clients adjust to it. Kinsey, on the other hand, was a scientist, describing the world as it existed but also emphasizing the contradictions between actuality and accepted standards. Masters and Johnson conducted their research for a reason that was entirely different from Kinsey's.

When the laboratory program for the investigation in human sexual functioning was designed in 1954, the greatest handicap to successful treatment of sexual inadequacy was a lack of reliable physiological information in the area of human sexual response. It was presumed that definitive laboratory effort would develop material of clinical consequence that could be used by professionals in the field to improve methodology of therapeutic approach to sexual inadequacy.[1]

Just as Kinsey had challenged, sometimes with considerable hostility, the psychiatric monopoly on sexual treatment and research, Masters and Johnson offered whole new areas for the gynecologist, urologist, and other medical specialists to extend their services. Ultimately, Masters and Johnson also helped establish a whole new profession, the sex therapist, which was no longer restricted to the psychiatrist but included nurses, psychologists, social workers, and counselors. It should be added, however, that the initial promise of nonevasive therapeutic techniques for problems of sexual inadequacy was oversold by some therapists and that, as the years passed, the balance between medical intervention and nonintrusive therapy changed. The basic teaching techniques pioneered by Masters and Johnson and their contemporaries, however, still remain important.

Masters was a native of Cleveland and was born to a well-to-do family in 1915. He attended Lawrenceville Prep School and went on to Hamilton College, where he received his bachelor's degree in 1938. He then entered the University of Rochester School of Medicine and Dentistry, where he worked in Corner's laboratory. Interestingly, Corner had three of the leaders in what he called "the practical application of scientific thought to problems of human sex behavior" as students: Guttmacher, who became internationally prominent in the family planning movement; Mary Steichen Calderone, co-founder of the Sex Information and Educational Council of the United States (SIECUS); and Masters.[2]

Masters, who had always been more interested in medical research than in the practice of medicine, decided he would like to do sex research when he completed his degree, and went to Corner for advice. Corner essentially gave him three general principles to follow in pursuing sex research: (1) he should establish a scientific reputation in some other scientific field first, (2) he should secure the sponsorship of a major medical school or university, and (3) he should be at least forty years of age.[3]

Masters followed the advice almost to the letter, although he did start his research into sexuality at the age of thirty eight. After graduation from medical school, he accepted a position at Washington University in St. Louis. Willard Allen, another of Corner's students and an active researcher in endocrinology, helped Masters get the appointment as an intern in obstetrics and gynecology. Masters moved up the ladder through resident to assistant professor and associate professor. He married and had two children. Masters also published a number of papers covering a variety of obstetrical and gynecological topics, although the majority dealt with hormone-replacement therapy for aging and aged women, a treatment that he strongly advocated[4] and that is widely used today.

THE BEGINNINGS

Gradually, Masters turned to studying the sexual act itself. The pioneer in this respect had been the French physician Félix Roubaud, who had published his account of the female response cycle in 1855.[5] Kinsey had called Roubaud's description unsurpassed,[6] even though the Frenchman had been mistaken on two points, namely the claim that there was direct frictional contact between the penis and the clitoris, and that the semen was sucked up through the cervix.

Just as Masters was actively beginning to plan his own program, G. Klumbies and H. Kleinsorge, two physicians at the University Clinic in Jena, Germany reported on a patient who was capable of fantasizing to orgasm, a fact that made it possible to distinguish the direct effects of orgasm from the muscular exertion that ordinarily preceded it or accompanied it. With the aid of an electrocardiograph and a blood pressure recorder, Klumbies and Kleinsorge recorded physiological changes, including pulse rate, systolic and diastolic blood pressure, rhythm of heart chamber contractions, respiratory volume, and muscle irritability. The woman identified some of her orgasms as more intense than others, and Klumbies and Kleinsorge noted that the intensity of the orgasm as subjectively reported showed a close relation to the acuteness of the blood pressure peak.[7] Another investigator, Abraham Mosovich, recorded electroencephalograms (brain wave patterns) during sexual arousal and orgasm.[8]

The best and most complete observations made before Masters and Johnson's studies were Kinsey's. He reported that he had access to a considerable body "of observed data on the involvement of the entire body in the spasms following orgasm."[9] Actually, most of the observations had been made on volunteers by Kinsey or his staff, independent of the interview portion of his research.

When Masters began his studies in 1954, he interviewed at length and in depth 118 female and 37 male prostitutes. Of these 8 of the women and 3 of the men then participated as experimental subjects in a preliminary series of laboratory studies. Suggestions of this select group of techniques for support and control of the human male and female in situations of direct sexual response proved invaluable. They described many methods for elevating or controlling sexual tensions and demonstrated innumerable variations in stimulative technique. Ultimately many of these techniques have been found to have direct application in therapy of male and female sexual inadequacy and have been integrated into the clinical programs.[10]

Ultimately, however, the experimental results derived from the prostitute population were not included in the final published results, because Masters and Johnson wanted a baseline of what they regarded as "anatomic normalcy." To get this, they turned to patient populations and volunteers for data. It was during this phase that Virginia Johnson joined Masters's team, because Masters strongly believed that a woman should be involved in his research. Born Virginia Eshelman in Missouri in 1925, she had studied music at Drury College and later attended the University of Missouri. In 1950, Johnson married and had a son and daughter before separating from her husband in the late 1950s. Masters was seeking a woman to assist in research interviewing and had specified that he wanted a woman who had experience and interest in working with people. The Bureau sent Johnson, and she was hired. The two later married, but were divorced in 1992.

Johnson's work was particularly important in the first two books but played a lesser part in latter studies. The fact that Masters and Johnson were a male-female team separates them from Kinsey. Though Kinsey had added a woman to his team shortly before he died, he seems to have not felt it necessary to do so before. Masters, in general, gave more emphasis to the female than to the male not only in his team but in his studies. In the discussion of physiology, for example, the female is mentioned first. Masters seems to have emphasized that the female is not just an inferior imitation of the male, an attitude widely prevalent even at the time of his research.

SEXUAL RESPONSE CYCLE

Masters and Johnson held that the sexual response cycle involved much more than a penis and vagina, and they sought to measure heart rate, respiratory functions, muscle tension, breast response, and any other physiological measurement they could think of. A key element in the ability of Masters and Johnson to break new ground was technological. Advances in the miniaturization of cameras and electronic devices meant that they could be used inside of a plastic phallus. This allowed Masters and Johnson to record what took place inside the vagina during orgasm, and they could observe the phenomena in some detail. This new technology permitted them to give definitive answers to some of the questions about which there had been arguments or on which there had only been subjective data. It allowed Masters and Johnson to determine that there was a moistening of the vaginal lining with lubricating fluid within 10 to 30 seconds of the onset of erotic stimulation and to note that this fluid came from the coalescence of a "sweating" of the vagina's walls. They emphasized that neither the Bartholin's glands nor the cervix, previously believed to be the source of the lubrication, contributed to the fluid. Rather the sweating resulted from the increased blood supply and the engorgement of vaginal tissues.[11]

Masters and Johnson also noted a lengthening and distension of the vaginal walls, while the cervix and the uterus are pulled slowly back and up into the false pelvis (the part of the pelvis above the hip joint). The vagina's walls also undergo a distinct coloration change, from purplish red to a darker purple, as a result of vasocongestion, and the wrinkled or corrugated aspects of the vaginal wall (technically called the rugal pattern) are flattened. Gradually, the outer third of the vagina becomes grossly distended with venous blood, and the vasocongestion is so marked that the central lumen (interior) of the outer third of the vaginal barrel wall is reduced by a least a third. All this takes place during what Masters and Johnson called the plateau phase, or second phase of the sexual response cycle.

This is followed by the orgasmic phase, during which much of physiologic activity is confined to what Masters and Johnson called the orgasm platform in the upper third of the vagina. Here there are strong contractions at 0.8 second intervals, which recur within a normal range of three to five and up to ten to fifteen times per individual orgasm. The uterus elevates and contracts rhythmically with each contraction, beginning at the upper end of the uterus and moving like a wave through the midzone and down to the lower or cervical end. These uterine contractions had been long associated with the idea that the cervix sucks up sperm. Masters and Johnson, however, theorized that contractions in such a direction would, if anything, expel sperm. They then proceeded to demonstrate the uterine contractions could not possibly lead to a sucking up of the sperm into the uterus. They prepared a tight-fitting cervical cup that they filled with a semen-like liquid in a radiopaque base. Masters and Johnson then made radiograms during the orgasmic experience and found no such sucking action.[12]

To describe what took place during intercourse, Masters and Johnson developed a four-phase description: (1) excitement, (2) plateau, (3) orgasm, and (4) resolution. They found that men responded in terms of basic physiological changes along the same lines as women; in both sexes, there was an increase in heart rate, blood pressure, and muscle tension, and in the majority of both men and women a "sex flush" (a rosy measlelike rash over the chest, neck, face, shoulders, arms, and thighs) is observable. At orgasm the heart and respiratory rates are at a maximum and the sex flush at its peak, although the male has what are called ejaculatory contractions during the orgasm. The orgasm phase is followed by the resolution phase in which there is a return to conditions as they were before the sexual excitement phase began. Women were found to have a wider variety of orgasmic responses and many could have multiple orgasms.

Masters and Johnson criticized what they called the "phallic fallacy" of comparing the clitoris with the penis. They emphasized that even though the clitoris might be the anatomical analogue of the penis, it reacts to sexual stimulation in a manner quite different from the penis. It does not become erect during arousal but instead withdraws beneath its protective foreskin, and in fact, its length is reduced by at least half as orgasm approaches. When it is retracted, however, it responds to generalized pressure on the labial hood.[13]

Patient concerns were always present in Masters and Johnson's minds. For example, they reported that the average flaccid measurement of a penis was 7.5 centimeters (about 3 inches) and during erection the penis more than doubled in length. However, they recognized that not all men had the same size penis.[14] To allay the qualms of their readers, they emphasized that the vagina was a "potential rather than an actual space," and was "infinitely distensible."[15] Interestingly, however, there is no evidence that they ever asked any of their female subjects whether penis size made a difference, or if they did, the answer was not recorded.

SAMPLE

All told, 694 individuals, including 276 married couples, participated in the Masters and Johnson laboratory program. Of these, 142 were unmarried but 44 had been previously married. The men ranged in age from twenty-one to eighty-nine and the women, from eighteen to seventy-eight. Volunteers for the laboratory research program were involved in masturbation by hand, fingers, or a mechanical vibrator; in sexual intercourse with the woman on her back, with the male on his back; and in artificial coition with a transparent probe. Also studied were the anatomy and physiology of the aging male and aging female, although the data were not as complete as for the younger ages. Masters and Johnson emphasized, however, that if

opportunity for regularity of coitus exists, the elderly woman will retain a far higher capacity for sexual performance than her female counterpart who does not have similar coital opportunity. They reported that even though the postmenopausal woman has lost some of her hormone output, the psyche is as important, if not more important, in determining the sex drive.[16] Similarly, while in the aging male the entire ejaculatory process undergoes a reduction in physiological efficiency, the sexual response remains. Masters and Johnson concluded,

There is every reason to believe that maintained regularity of sexual expression coupled with adequate physical well-being and healthy mental orientation to the aging process will combine to provide a sexually stimulative climate within a marriage. This climate will, in turn, improve sexual tension and provide a capacity for sexual performance that frequently may extend to and beyond the 80-year level.[17]

SEXUAL DYSFUNCTION

A natural follow-up to the physiological studies of the human sexual response was treatment for dysfunctional clients. For this purpose, Masters and Johnson developed a sex therapy team (a woman and a man) and a methodology through which they said they were treating the "marriage," since the basic foundation of their treatment was that both the husband and wife in a sexually dysfunctional marriage be treated.[18] Such a statement emphasizes Masters and Johnson's marital orientation, something that probably contributed to their widespread acceptance on the American scene. Although a significant proportion of their clients were unmarried, most came to therapy accompanied by a partner.

Because Masters and Johnson always emphasized the therapeutic nature of their research, their aim in effect had always been the development of treatment modalities. In their treatment, they concentrated on specific symptoms rather than generalized disorders. In a way, they adopted some of the concepts of the behavioral psychologists who had begun treating sexual problems in the 1950s,[19] but in the process, they popularized sex therapy and systematized it on a physiological base.

One result was the development of a new specialty in the helping professions, that of sex therapist. Before their entrance on the scene, the predominant treatment of sexual dysfunction, at least in the United States, was through psychoanalysis. What Masters and Johnson essentially did was challenge perhaps the final bastion of the control that psychiatry, and particularly psychoanalysis, had over the sex field. Kinsey had basically undermined many of the assumptions that psychiatry had made about sexual behavior and furnished a new kind of database. With Masters and Johnson, even the treatment option, which psychiatry had dominated, was now redirected to other specialists, many of whom were not physicians. The result was to increase the number of individuals who were not only professionally but economically interested in sex. Kinsey, in effect, had reestablished the concept of sexology. Although sexological research was a somewhat limited field, the rise of sex therapy gave sexology enough other professionals to justify separate sexological societies and journals.

Masters and Johnson were also important because they, although in a much gentler form than Kinsey, emphasized the importance of sex education. For example, in their discussion of the anorgasmic female, they stated that women in general were victims of the double standard, because they more than men had been taught to repress their sexual feelings. Masters and Johnson concluded that repression, in the form of historical and psychological experience, was the most important factor in the development of frigidity.[20] Ignorance and superstition about sex were and remain the major problems in an inadequate sexual response, and when the sexual partners manage to have their prejudices, misconceptions, and misunderstandings of natural sexual functioning exposed, then and only then

can "a firm basis for mutual security in sexual expression" be established.[21] In short, for marriage to reach its full potential, and Masters and Johnson were always concerned with marriage, knowledge of sex was essential. This message was seized on not only by a new generation of sex educators to bring about reforms in sex education but by the public in general, who seemed to grow ever more interested in how to have a better marriage, which they believed was highly dependent on sexual performance.

The largest component of the expanding group of sex professionals in the 1960s was the sex therapist, the number of which grew rapidly. Masters and Johnson had established a two-week basic program that involved a male and female sex therapist and a client couple; this program served as the initial model. Masters and Johnson reported that the two-week session eliminated sexual difficulties for 80 percent of their clients. Not content with these immediate results, they followed up these studies five years later and stated that of those they were able to recontact, only 7 percent reported recurrence of the dysfunctions for which they originally had sought treatment.[22] The result of such claims was a demand by the public for help with sexual problems and an awareness by the various kinds of professionals that they could expand their client base if they could gain some expertise in sex.

Many would-be sex therapists went to St. Louis to take special training sessions with Masters and Johnson. Professionals who entered sex therapy from a slightly different background also offered special seminars. On the West Coast, for example, William Hartman and Marilyn Fithian, who had included sexual therapy as part of their marriage and family counseling, had begun to carry out their own set of experiments on the sexual response in their Long Beach, California, center. As the demand for sex therapists grew, Hartman and Fithian conducted training seminars not only in Long Beach but all over the country, introducing would-be professionals to new trends in sex therapy.

Another important early sex therapist was Helen Singer Kaplan, who tried to combine some of the insights and techniques of psychoanalysis with behavioral methods. She questioned Masters and Johnson's use of two therapists and felt that one therapist of either sex would be sufficient,[23] a finding made by others.[24] Kaplan agreed that many sexual difficulties stemmed from superficial causes, but she believed that when unconscious conflict was at the heart of the problem and involved deep-seated emotional problems the therapist should use more analytic approaches. As a result, her approach is designated as psychosexual therapy to distinguish it from sex therapy, and her entry into the field emphasizes how psychoanalysts themselves gradually adjusted to the new sex therapy techniques.

In the afterglow of success, the sex therapy originally presented by Masters and Johnson did not seem to hold true for a growing number of therapists as the field rapidly expanded. This was perhaps because of not only the existence of deep-seated emotional problems in some clients, as Kaplan had pointed out, but the presence of basic physiological problems such as diabetes. The result was an attack on the success claims of Masters and Johnson, as an increasing number of studies reported much higher failure rates.[25]

The difference in success rates, however, is probably the result of both the changing nature of clients and the differing methods of client selection. Many of the original problems presented by the early clients of Masters and Johnson resulted from a lack of knowledge of basic sexual activity, something that was comparatively easy to overcome. The very success of the books by Masters and Johnson made such clients increasingly less likely to seek the help of a therapist, since they could read about the sources of human sexual inadequacy and adjust their own practices. On the other hand, the physical exam required by Masters and Johnson for their patients undoubtedly eliminated many of those with physiological difficulties that other,

less knowledgeable therapists attempted to treat and failed to help. The major result of the criticism of Masters and Johnson was to emphasize that sex therapy at its best involved a team, not only of therapists but of medical professionals, particularly the urologist and gynecologist.

NOTES

1. William H. Masters and Virginia E. Johnson, *Human Sexual Inadequacy* (Boston: Little, Brown, 1970), 1. The therapeutic intent is not emphasized in their first study, William H. Masters and Virginia E. Johnson, *Human Sexual Response* (Boston: Little, Brown, 1966).
2. George W. Corner, *The Seven Ages of a Medical Scientist* (Philadelphia: University of Pennsylvania Press, 1981), 212.
3. Corner, *The Seven Ages of a Medical Scientist*, 213.
4. Among his articles are W. H. Masters, "Long Range Sex Steroid Replacement: Target Organ Regeneration," *Journal of Gerontology* 8 (1953): 33–39; W. H. Masters, "Endocrine Therapy in the Aging Individual," *Obstetrics and Gynecology* 8 (1956): 61–67; and W. H. Masters, "Sex Steroid Influence on the Aging Process," *American Journal of Obstetrics and Gynecology* 74 (1957): 733–46.
5. Félix Roubaud, *Trait de l'Impuissance et de la Sterilité chez l'Homme et chez la Femme* (1855; reprint, Paris: Baillière, 1876).
6. Alfred E. Kinsey, Wardell B. Pomeroy, and Clyde Martin, *Sexual Behavior in the Human Female* (Philadelphia: Saunders, 1953).
7. G. Klumbies and H. Kleinsorge, "Das Herz in Orgasmus," *Medizinische Klinik* 45 (1950): 952–8; and G. Klumbies and H. Kleinsorge, "Circulatory Dangers and Prophylaxis During Orgasm," *International Journal of Sexology* 4 (1950): 61–66.
8. Kinsey et al., *Sexual Behavior in the Human Female*, 630, fig. 140.
9. Ibid., 631, n. 46.
10. Masters and Johnson, *Human Sexual Response*, 10.
11. Ibid., 300.
12. Ibid., 124.
13. Ibid., 57–61.
14. Ibid., 192.
15. Ibid., 194–5.
16. Ibid., 242.
17. Ibid., 270.

18. Masters and Johnson, *Human Sexual Inadequacy*, 3.

19. Joseph Wolpe, *Psychotherapy by Reciprocal Inhibition* (Stanford, Calif.: Stanford University Press, 1958).

20. Ibid., 214–8, 222–6.

21. Ibid., 62.

22. Masters and Johnson, *Human Sexual Inadequacy*, 366, tab. 11 B.

23. Helen Singer Kaplan, *The New Sex Therapy* (New York: Brunner/Mazel, 1974).

24. Joseph LoPiccolo, J. R. Heiman, D. R. Hogan, and C. W. Roberts, "Effectiveness of Single Therapists Versus Cotherapy Teams in Sex Therapy," *Journal of Counsulting and Clinical Psychology* 53 (1985): 287–94.

25. S. Schumacher and C. W. Lloyd, "Physiology and Psychological Factors in Impotence," *Journal of Sex Research* 17 (1981): 40–53; and B. Zilbergeld and M. Evans, "The Inadequacy of Masters and Johnson," *Psychology Today* 14 (1980): 29–43.

CHAPTER 3

The Social Organization of Sexuality
Theoretical Background

Edward O. Laumann
John H. Gagnon
Robert T. Michael
Stuart Michaels

Following the work of Kinsey and of Masters and Johnson, little sexuality research was conducted in the United States from the mid-1950s to the mid-1960s. And even in the period of permissiveness that evolved during the sexual revolution, most of the survey research was based on samples from college students. By the early 1970s, it was evident that significant changes were occurring in sexual behavior and attitudes: rising percentages of young people were having premarital sexual intercourse, and the gay/lesbian movement and the feminist movement were in full swing.

Sex became a household word as the mass media contributed to the widespread belief that everyone, youth and adult, was actively involved in premarital sex and postmarital sexual affairs. Publications such as Playboy *and* Redbook *disseminated information from reader surveys of sexual behavior via "tear out and mail in" questionnaires. Shere Hite (1976) reported, in her*

From *The Social Organization of Sexuality: Sexual Practices in the United States* (pp. 3–34) by E. O. Laumann, J. H. Gagnon, R. T. Michael, & S. Michaels. 1994. Chicago: University of Chicago Press. Copyright © 1994 by Edward O. Laumann, Robert T. Michaels, CSG Enterprises, Inc., and Stuart Michaels. Reprinted by permission.

controversial bestseller, The Hite Report, *that 70 percent of married persons were having extramarital affairs within the first five years of marriage. Her claim was based on a survey of 100,000 women, which had a return rate of 3 percent. Her somewhat politicized sample included members of the National Organization for Women (NOW), the American Association of University Women (AAUW), and abortion rights groups. Scholars, lamenting that bad data are worse than no data, concluded that the ability of mass media to produce their own facts is a fact of life that even researchers must learn to live with. By the 1980s, it became apparent that not only were people looking at bad data, they also were looking backward at old data for answers.*

It was into such a world in the late 1980s that Laumann, Gagnon, Michael, and Michaels, a research team from the University of Chicago and the State University of New York at Stony Brook, launched their National Health and Social Life Survey, the goal of which was to develop a social scientific theory of sexual conduct. The $1.7 million study was financed in 1992 by eight private foundations after conservative senators had killed federal funding of the research project in 1991.

Although studies in the previous decades had chronicled changes in sexual behavior, the researchers of earlier periods had neglected the construction of theories to explain human sexual behavior. Because sexual behavior is social, the theorists proposed that it must be studied within relationships to explain it as a social phenomenon. Psychological studies invariably center on an individualistic approach to the study of sexuality, but sociological studies focus on the social, the external, the relational, and the public dimensions. Thus, social logic was suggested to be a missing variable in the study of sexuality and, therefore, chosen as a theoretical framework for the National Health and Social Life Survey.

The nation's most comprehensive, representative survey of sexual behavior in the general population to date, the Laumann et al. study utilized face-to-face, 90-minute interviews with subjects from a randomly selected sample of 3,432 American women and men between the ages of 18 and 59. The results of the survey led to a better understanding of how sexual behavior is organized in American society and its broad-ranging public policy implications. Two books were published with the findings: The Social Organization of Sexuality: Sexual Practices in the United States, *which included extensive statistical analyses for academic readers, and* Sex in America: A Definitive Survey, *intended for general readership.*

As chapter 1 from their scholarly book shows, the theoretical background for this study is carefully constructed from three theories: scripting theory to explain sexual conduct; choice theory to explain sexual decision making; and network theory to explain the sexual dyad. Together, they form at least a middle-range theoretical basis for construction of a social-scientific approach to sexuality. With a careful review of the following selection, readers may gain insight into the Laumann et al. study. More significantly they can broaden their awareness of theory construction and its importance in survey research.

———————

Human sexual behavior is a diverse phenomenon. It occurs in different physical locations and social contexts, consists of a wide range of specific activities, and is perceived differently by different people. An individual engages in sexual activity on the basis of a complex set of motivations and organizes that activity on the basis of numerous external factors and influences. Thus, it is unlikely that the tools and concepts from any single scientific discipline will suffice to answer all or even most of the questions one might ask about sexual behavior. This [narrative] introduces the several approaches that we have found especially helpful in formulating what we hope will prove to be a more comprehensive social scientific understanding of sexuality.

A SOCIAL SCIENTIFIC APPROACH TO SEXUALITY

Much of the previous scientific research on sexuality has been conducted by biologists and psychologists and has thus focused on sexual behavior purely as an "individual level" phenomenon. Thus, such research has defined sexual activity to be the physical actions that a person performs (or the thoughts and feelings that a person experiences), and has sought to explain individual variation in these actions in terms of processes endogenous to the individual. A good example of this approach is the study of sexual "drives" or "instincts." In drive theories, people are assumed to experience a buildup of "sexual tension" or "sexual need" during periods of deprivation or during particularly erotic environmental stimulation. When sexual activity is experienced, the drive is satiated and the need reduced. Such cycles of increased drive and its resultant satiation are often used to explain hunger and thirst and, by analogy, sexual conduct. Differences in drives across individuals are generally assumed to result from underlying biological or psychological differences in those individuals.

The major shortcoming of such studiously individualistic approaches is that they are able (at most) to explain only a very small part of the story. This is because, unlike the sexual behavior of certain animal species (e.g., salmon, who are genetically programmed to swim upstream at the appropriate time to spawn), human sexual behavior is only partly determined by factors originating within the individual. In addition, a person's socialization into a particular culture, his or her interaction with sex partners, and the constraints imposed on him or her become extremely important in determining his or her other sexual activities. This observation is perhaps obvious, yet research on social processes represents a disproportionately small amount of the extant scientific literature on human sexuality.

This does not mean that there have been no social scientific studies of sexual behavior. One prominent researcher, Ira Reiss (1990), recently enumerated more than a dozen national surveys of sexual attitudes and practices since Kinsey and his associates' work appeared in the late 1940s. Previous national studies of sexual behavior have targeted specific subpopulations or have focused on a relatively narrow range of sexual conduct. For example, Zelnik and Kantner (1972; 1980) conducted three national studies of pregnancy-related behavior among adolescents. Subsequently, Sonenstein, Pleck, and Ku (1991) conducted a more comprehensive study of sexual practices among adolescent males, and the CDC (1992) reported on a limited number of sexual behaviors among a national sample of high school students.

With regard to adults, the first nationally representative data were collected by Reiss in 1963. Later, Klassen, Williams, and Levitt (1989) conducted a study of adults age twenty-one and older (the data were collected in 1970) that focused primarily on sexual attitudes. In addition, the National Survey of Family Growth (Mosher and McNally 1991) asked its fifteen- to forty-four-year-old female respondents a limited number of questions about sexual behavior, and Tanfer's study of twenty- to twenty-nine-year-old women (Tanfer 1992) focused on a much broader range of sexual behaviors, relationships, and attitudes. These studies were followed in 1991 by a well-publicized study conducted by the Batelle Institute of twenty- to thirty-nine-year-old men that collected data on a wide range of sexual conduct (Billy et al. 1993). Finally, the National AIDS Behavioral Surveys (Peterson et al. 1993) collected behavioral data relevant to the transmission of AIDS from respondents in twenty-three "high-risk" U.S. cities. While these studies provide information on several important issues, few have attended seriously to the fact that sexual activity occurs in the context of a relationship (Blumstein and Schwartz 1983) or the epidemiological consequences of the structure of sexual networks.

We thus have in hand a number of important indications of where to look for the effects that social factors have on sexual behavior. One example is the persistent finding that a person's social class ("working" vs. "middle") is correlated with certain aspects of sexual behavior (Weinberg and Williams 1980), although there is some evidence that the strength of this association is diminishing with time (DeLamater 1981). Another persistent finding comes from the relatively large literature on adolescent sexuality (Brookman 1990).

Sociologists have found that adolescents involved in religious activities tend to delay first intercourse longer than those who are not (DeLamater and MacCorquodale 1979). These and other essentially descriptive findings are certainly interesting, yet, without a systematic theoretical framework within which to interpret them, they cannot help us understand how and why specific social processes or circumstances affect sexual behavior.

Biological and psychological studies of sexual behavior focus solely on the individual as the relevant "unit of analysis." That is, the objective of such research is to answer questions about why an individual exhibits certain sexual behaviors. But this line of inquiry can reveal only part of the story. Most sexual behavior is not performed by an individual alone and in the absence of others. Instead, sexual behavior is social in the sense that it involves two people (or more). Sex involves negotiation and interplay, the expectation and experience of compromise. There is competition; there is cooperation. The relationships between the partners and between their mutual actions make the sexual partnership or dyad an essential analytic unit in the study of sexuality. This focus on the social, the external, the relational, and the public dimensions is what distinguishes our inquiry from the psychological and biological orientations that have characterized much sex research in the past.

Although little progress has been made in the social sciences toward developing systematic theories about the social processes involved in sexual behavior, social psychology, sociology, and economics have each developed persuasive theories explaining other spheres of social behavior. Therefore, it seems sensible to draw on such theories in attempting to formulate a social scientific theory of sexual conduct. We have begun with three theoretical traditions—scripting theory, choice theory, and social network theory—each addressing certain aspects of sexual behavior.

SCRIPTING THEORY: EXPLAINING SEXUAL CONTENT

Previous researchers have generally adopted the perspective that there is an inevitable negative conflict between the biological nature of human beings and the cultures in which they are reared. With regard to sexual behavior, this implies that social factors function solely to inhibit or constrain people's intrinsic sexual desires and urges. For example, it is assumed that biologically mature adolescents will naturally have intercourse (that they both want to and have the opportunity to do so) and that those who do not are simply better at "controlling their urges." We reject this perspective, not because it allows for the influence of biological effects on sexual

behavior, but because it takes a narrow view of the role of social processes as merely constraining sexual conduct. We argue that sociocultural processes play a fundamental role in determining what we perceive to be "sexual" and how we construct and interpret our sexual fantasies and thoughts. Thus, although biological factors may indeed affect sexual behavior, they play at most a small role in determining what those specific behaviors will be and how they will be interpreted.

Scripting theories of sexual conduct address exactly these types of questions. The starting point for these theories can be expressed in terms of several assumptions about the ways in which specific sexual patterns are acquired and expressed. First, they assume that patterns of sexual conduct in a culture are locally derived (i.e., that what is sexual and what sex means differ in different cultures). Second, they assume either that human beings possess no biological instincts about how to act sexually or that the effects of such instincts are minor in comparison with the effects of an individual's socially determined scripts for conduct. People may vary biologically in activity level and temperament, but there are no direct links between this variation and what they will do sexually as adults. Third, they assume that, through a process of acculturation lasting from birth to death, individuals acquire patterns of sexual conduct that are appropriate to their culture (including those patterns that are thought to deviate from the norms of the culture). Fourth, they assume that people may not enact the scripts provided by their culture exactly but instead may make minor adaptations to suit their own needs. In complex and contradictory cultures, such individual adaptations will be very diverse.

On the basis of these four principles, sexual scripts specify with whom people have sex, when and where they should have sex, what they should do sexually, and why they should do sexual things. These scripts embody what the intersubjective culture treats as sexuality (cultural scenarios) and what the individual believes to be the domain of sexuality. Individuals improvise on the basis of the cultural scenarios and in the process change the sexual culture of the society. In this way, individual sexual actors as well as those who create representations of sexual life (e.g., the mass media, religious leaders, educators, and researchers) are constantly reproducing and transforming sexual life in a society. For example, introducing condoms into sexual activity as part of an AIDS education and prevention program requires changing scripts for sexual conduct on the part of individuals. If large numbers of individuals adopt this new script, they will change the effects that sexual activity has on health by reducing unwanted pregnancies, abortions, and the spread of sexually transmitted diseases.

The scripting perspective distinguishes between cultural scenarios (the instructions for sexual and other conduct that are embedded in the cultural narratives that are provided as guides or instructions for all conduct), interpersonal scripts (the structured patterns of interaction in which individuals as actors engage in everyday interpersonal conduct), and intrapsychic scripts (the plans and fantasies by which individuals guide and reflect on their past, current, or future conduct) (Gagnon and Simon 1987; Gagnon 1991).

Several studies provide evidence for the importance of sexual scripts in shaping both perception and behavior (Geer and Brussard 1990; Castillo and Geer 1993). For example, in one study, male subjects listened to one of two different narratives, during which time their level of sexual arousal was monitored. Both narratives began with identical stories describing a young woman getting into her car and driving to a building, where she goes into a room, closes the door, and removes her clothes. At this point, a man enters the room; he is identified in the first narrative as the woman's gynecologist, in the second as her boyfriend. Predictably, subjects hearing the first narrative experienced significantly less arousal than those who heard the second, despite the similarity of the two narratives. Since

the physician was not part of the subjects' sexual scripts, they had to reevaluate their perceptions of the situation.

With regard to the effects of scripts on actual behavior, research among adolescents has repeatedly demonstrated the existence of a general pattern of activities that young people follow as they acquire sexual experience (DeLamater and MacCorquodale 1979). The pattern begins with kissing, proceeding first to necking and then to the male fondling the female's breast (first over the clothing, then underneath) Next occurs fondling of each other's genitals, first by the male, then by the female. This is followed by genital-genital contact and then by vaginal intercourse. Only after intercourse do adolescents go on to try oral sex, again first by the male, then by the female. What this means is that those who have had vaginal intercourse are also likely to have engaged in kissing, necking, fondling, and apposition. Similarly, those who have not yet engaged in "heavy petting" are unlikely to move directly to intercourse. Of course, not all adolescents complete the entire program or, to use the especially apt euphemism, "go all the way." Moreover, any single interaction is subject to practical considerations (such as being restricted to the backseat of a car) that may result in temporary deviations from the script.

CHOICE THEORY: SEXUAL DECISION MAKING

While scripting theories are useful in explaining the range of activities (or scripts) available to an individual, they tell us little about how the individual chooses among these various possibilities. For example, an individual may have different scripts for how to act toward different partners (e.g., a new partner, a "one-night stand," and a spouse) and in different situations; however, the content of these scripts alone tells us little about why that individual may choose to pursue certain types of relationships to the exclusion of others. In order to address this important issue, we turn to an economic approach to decision making. Essentially, economic choice theory is concerned with how people utilize the resources available to them in the pursuit of one or more specific goals. Since one's resources are generally limited, choices arise regarding how these resources should be apportioned among various activities leading to one or another goal. Were there no scarcity of the necessary resources, there would be no constraint on the achievement of one's goals and no need for choices to be made. However, the necessary resources (i.e., time, money, emotional and physical energy, personal reputation) required to engage in sexual behavior are limited, and choices must therefore be made.

It is important to recognize that an economic approach presumes the existence of a goal or a set of goals. Thus, in order to utilize this approach, we must first identify what those goals (or at least some of them) are. For example, the goals of sexual behavior may include sexual pleasure itself, the emotional satisfaction that results from being intimately involved with someone toward whom one feels affection, having children, and acquiring a "good reputation" among one's friends. So we have listed four goals that may motivate a person to use his or her limited money, time, and energy to achieve one or another of these goals.

People differ in the importance that they accord these various goals and in their capacities to achieve them. Choice theory focuses on how these goals and capacities influence behavior. Invariably, the efforts of one person to achieve his or her goals affect the efforts of others. That is what makes this a social science—people's efforts do not take place in isolation. When it comes to selecting a sex partner, for example, if one person succeeds in attracting a partner, that person is "taken" or "spoken for," and is no longer available to anyone else. This social dimension of sexual behavior is less obvious but no less real when it comes to most other activities, from using contraception to selecting a "sexy" outfit to wear to a party.

In order to make our discussion more concrete, suppose that we are interested in explaining why people have the number of sex partners that they do. Our research shows that 71 percent of adults (aged eighteen to fifty-nine) report having only one sex partner during the previous year and that 53 percent report having only one sex partner over the previous five years. These data suggest that most people change sex partners relatively infrequently, choosing instead to remain in long-term, sexually exclusive relationships. As we stated above, we will assume that most people desire some amount of sexual stimulation and that this, together with other goals, leads them to pursue sexual relationships with one or more partners. Yet securing partners is not without cost; one must expend time, money, emotional energy, and social resources in order to meet people and negotiate a sexual relationship. Solely on the basis of this consideration, it would seem to be more cost effective to fulfill one's sexual needs by remaining in a long-term relationship than by constantly searching for new partners. One might "look around" and perhaps even fantasize about potential partners, but the costs involved in actually pursuing them relative to simply maintaining one's current relationship may be too high. Only those whose objectives explicitly include having sex with many partners (perhaps because of the excitement and uncertainty) will frequently choose to incur such costs.

In this example, an individual spends resources and engages in activities for the purpose of achieving sexual pleasure, in much the same way as an industrial firm manufactures a product in order to make a profit; both may be described as productive activities. And, like most productive activities, both can involve the creation of unintended by-products, desirable and undesirable. In the case of having sex with a partner, an unwanted pregnancy, a sexually transmitted infection or disease, a happier, more pleasant personality, and a greater ability to concentrate are examples of possible by-products.

These decisions are often made in the face of uncertainty: about detection, about the nature of the new partnership, and about the risk of disease, pregnancy, and harm. The more information one has about the outcome of a choice, the wiser will be the choice, of course, but then there is the decision about how much information to acquire before making the choice.

Like so many choices we make, choices regarding sexual behavior are often made under uncertainty. It is the case that people have different attitudes toward risk; some enjoy taking risks, while others prefer to avoid risk. One reason that couples discuss their views and their prior sexual histories is to share information about the probabilities of good and bad eventualities from having sex together. Similarly, people use contraception to avoid pregnancy and disease, travel to distant places to carry on affairs in order to avoid detection, and generally treat their decisions about sexual behavior with some degree of strategy and purpose that characterizes their choices in other domains.

While formal models of behavior often assume that risks are perceived accurately, research in psychology has shown that people do a rather poor job of estimating not only the absolute sizes but even the relative sizes of the risks that they encounter. For example, in a study of possible determinants of self-perceived risk for AIDS, Prohaska et al. (1990) found that respondents in those demographic subgroups with the highest prevalence of HIV infection (singles, males, Blacks, and Hispanics) were not more likely to perceive themselves as at risk than other respondents. The study did, however, show higher perceptions of risk among respondents with multiple partners during the past five years as well as among those who knew little or nothing about the previous sexual behavior of their partners. Finally, respondents who reported that they would be ashamed if they contracted AIDS were less likely to perceive themselves as being at risk. Although it is difficult to interpret this last finding, it suggests the possibility that people's emotional and moral reactions to the disease—factors that may have nothing to do with objective risk—may affect their subjective risk assessment.

In addition to risk management, another conceptual tool from economics that can be useful in understanding sexual behavior is that of human capital. Individuals invest in education and skills in order to achieve their objectives. This is obvious in the case of people preparing to enter or reenter the job market. However, there are also types of human capital that facilitate the pursuit of sexual objectives. One example is the skills necessary to attract potential sex partners. These might include a healthy and attractive appearance, good conversational skills, and the like. Clearly, such human capital is most valuable to those who are actively searching for a partner, so these people should be expected to invest more highly in these skills than others who are involved in long-term monogamous relationships. Since skills tend to deteriorate with disuse, people who have been out of the market for a period of time are likely to find their skills rusty on returning. Moreover, new expectations and protocols in dating may require learning the new "rules of the game."

Another type of human capital used to secure sexual activity is the skills necessary for maintaining an existing relationship. These might include the ability to satisfy one's partner physically as well as the ability to accommodate his or her personality and interests, to get along with his or her family and friends, and so forth. Such skills have been the focus of studies that seek to understand why married couples choose to remain married or to divorce. In a marriage (or in any long-term sexual relationship), each partner acquires specific skills that are beneficial in the couple's interactions. Yet these skills are valuable only as long as the couple remains together. This loss of value associated with dissolution provides incentive for couples to remain together.

Thus far, our discussion about choice theory has been oriented around an individual decision maker. However, the decisions of one person (or institution) often impinge on others through the marketplace in which people acquire the resources to achieve their goals. The key factor in determining an item's value in the market is desirability relative to scarcity. Value is determined by the competitive forces of demand (reflecting desirability) and supply (reflecting availability), while it is measured by the commodity's unit price relative to other goods.

Perhaps the most obvious example of a market in the context of sexual behavior is the market for sex partners. In most cases, this market does not involve a product being exchanged for money but consists instead of a barter exchange in which each person both seeks (i.e., demands) a sex partner and offers (i.e., supplies) himself or herself as a partner in exchange. Each prospective partner offers his or her own physical attributes, personality, skills, etc., in exchange for those of a partner of interest to him or her. This exchange is made explicit in advertisements that appear in the personals column of the newspaper, such as "SWM gd looking, seeks F undr 30 for fun/companionship."

Anyone who has participated in the market for sex partners knows that those possessing more of the traits most valued in a particular culture have more opportunities for exchange than those possessing fewer. The majority of these opportunities are likely to involve similarly or less attractive potential partners, from among whom each individual is expected to choose the "best deal" that he or she can get. If there is a disparity between the numbers of males and females on the market, those who are least desirable are likely to be left without a partner altogether. An example of this is the often talked about "marriage squeeze" in which middle-aged and older women lose out to younger women in the competition for an insufficient number of eligible men.

An important aspect of selecting a sex partner is that it involves little prior knowledge of the other's sexual competence. Like many other "products" acquired in the marketplace, one does not know all about the partner's sexual interests, capabilities, and limitations before a match is made. That, of course, is true of the car you buy or the job you accept. Consequently, one relies on reputation, on what you can tell from looking and talking, on the reliability of the broker or grocer. Buyers invest in information about the product, while sellers invest in presentation and persuasion.

In a day when one shunned sexual contact before marriage, the information that partners had about their sexual compatibility was probably far less at the time of the wedding than is the case in a day when most couples have sex with each other before they form marriage bonds. You would think that this more "intensive searching" would lead to more compatible matches and thus lower divorce rates, but that surely has not been the case in the United States over the past three decades.

In the marketplace for sex partners, there is a time of considerable searching and exploring and a time after a selection is made and a partnership formed when the searching stops or is at least greatly diminished. Interest in a new sex partner can be renewed when divorce or separation occurs, and it is during these times of more extensive searching that additional sex partners are more likely to be acquired. Over the lifetime of an individual we should expect to see certain periods of relatively extensive exploration of the sex partner marketplace and other times with little involvement in that marketplace.

When we think about the market for sex partners, despite the strangeness of the concept to some, there are many parallels to other, more familiar marketplaces. We noted above that individuals surely differ in their goals or objectives as they choose a sex partner—recreational sex, an intense companionship, a partner for raising children, for example. Not surprisingly, then, those active in the market will surely place different values on different attributes in prospective partners—some men might value companionship more than physical attractiveness, while others might value earning power or a strong sense of family loyalty in a prospective sex and marriage partner more than any other attribute.

Another aspect of markets is that they have physical dimensions. Geographic distance adds costs to matching just as much as acquiring information does. Most people search in local markets, and the partitioning of the market into the sex partners in the local community—even in the local social networks in which a person is active—reflects the costliness of searching more widely. That, like the fact that information about options is costly, is a reality in most markets.

As individuals, most of us are accustomed to thinking of sexuality in highly personal terms, consisting of our own thoughts and what we do with our partners. For this reason, our choices about which sexual activities to pursue are based on our personal assessments of the benefits and costs involved. However, the private choices that we make about sexual behaviors and attitudes can also have consequences at a collective or societal level. There can be both benefits and costs to society as a whole that are not immediately visible to the individual. Such benefits or costs are called externalities.

In the United States, an externality resulting from fertility, many would argue, is the burden on the welfare system of children whose parents are either unable or unwilling to support them financially. While many couples determine how many children they can afford to support and plan their fertility accordingly, other couples bear children they did not plan or plan children they subsequently cannot afford. Child welfare programs in effect lower the cost of raising a child to the natural or custodial parents and impose these costs on the taxpayer.

Another externality associated with sexual behavior is the possible transmission of diseases such as gonorrhea, chlamydia, and HIV. Such diseases not only threaten an individual's health but also contribute to collective costs such as the provision of subsidized medical care and research and the increased risk of being exposed to the infection as it becomes more widespread.

The choices that individuals make about sexual behavior that exposes them to the risk of unwanted pregnancy or disease are made in the context of the costs of avoiding these outcomes. Since there are negative externalities associated with these outcomes, it seems a sensible strategy to subsidize the costs of avoiding them. That is one rationale for government support of programs that distribute contraceptives and information about how to avoid pregnancy and sexually transmitted disease or infection.

Note how a brief discussion of externalities can quickly become a discussion of government policy or an advocacy of collective action. Choice theory promotes discussion of this nature since it facilitates an articulation of the relation between private choices and public repercussions between individual and collective action.

NETWORK THEORY: THE SEXUAL DYAD

So far, we have said little about how the sexual partnership (or dyad) is theoretically significant. Both scripting and choice theories focus on what individuals do, explaining it on the basis of the experiences, circumstances, and decisions of those individuals. However, sexual activity is fundamentally social in that it involves two or more persons either explicitly or implicitly (as in the case of sexual fantasy and masturbation). This simple fact has three important implications. First, since sexual partnerships are a special case of social relationships we may expect these partnerships to conform to certain regularities that have been observed regarding social relationships more generally. This provides a theoretical framework within which to study the dynamics of sexual parnerships—who becomes partners with whom, how these partnerships are maintained, and why some of them eventually dissolve. Second, since sexual activity is negotiated within the context of a social relationship, the features of the relationship itself become important in determining what activities will occur. This may seem obvious at first; however, such thinking represents a subtle major departure from previous research on sexuality (Sprecher and McKinney 1993). Finally, sexual dyads do not exist in a vacuum but are instead embedded within larger networks of social relationships. Thus, individual dyads are affected by the social networks surrounding them, and this in turn influences the sexual activity of their members. We now turn to a more detailed discussion of each of these implications.

One of the most persistent empirical regularities that has been observed among social relationships is the tendency toward equal status contact, meaning that people tend to initiate and maintain relationships with others who have the same or similar social characteristics as they themselves do. This general pattern of same-status contact has been observed in studies of friendship (Laumann 1966, 1973; Hallinan and Williams 1989), professional relationships (Heinz and Laumann 1982), and relationships among discussion partners (Marsden 1988). Specifically, these studies have shown that such relationships are more likely to exist among persons of the same gender, age, race, education, and religion. Several factors account for these findings, including the fact that our society is geographically and socially segregated in ways that greatly reduce an individual's opportunities to interact with people unlike himself or herself. In addition, some authors have suggested that people prefer to interact with similar others in order to reinforce their own self-identity, to validate their own behaviors and attitudes and, most obviously, because they are more likely to share common interests with such people. Finally, a person's family, friends, and other associates maintain control over the kinds of people with whom that person forms relationships, often decreasing the likelihood that he or she will interact with dissimilar others.

For similar reasons, we also expect sexual relationships to occur more frequently between people with the same or similar characteristics.

Research on similarity among married couples seems to confirm this general hypothesis, identifying large amounts of both educational (Mare 1991) and religious (Kalmijn 1991) homogamy (in other words, marriage partners share similar characteristics). More recently, the same has also been found among cohabiting couples (Schoen and Weinick 1993).

Just as the nature of asymmetries has changed over time, we also expect them to differ across different types of sexual relationships. More specifically, we expect the patterns of racial, age, educational, and religious similarity that have been observed in marital relationships to be different in noncohabitational sexual partnerships. An individual interested in pursuing an extramarital relationship, for example, might intentionally locate a socially dissimilar person in order to minimize the possibility of being discovered by his or her spouse, family, and friends.

In sum, sexual relationships differ markedly from other types of relationships with respect to the types of exchanges that occur within them, and these differences lead to different predictions about the occurrence of sexual relationships between persons with different social characteristics. Moreover, we expect the pattern of sex partner choice to differ across the different types of sexual relationships.

The social composition of sexual relationships also affects the type of behavior that occurs within them. These effects are distinct from those that are due to the individual characteristics of the partners; hence, they can be examined only by studying the dyad as whole. For example, we show that oral sex is a largely reciprocated activity, which implies that it is more likely to occur in those relationships where both parties are willing to perform the act.

In addition, other characteristics of respondents' sexual partnerships are likely to affect whether they engage in oral sex. Thus, while more educated people are more likely to have oral sex, it may also be the case that there is something about the types of sexual relationships that these more highly educated respondents have that increases the likelihood that oral sex will occur within them.

There are several elements of sexual relationships that might plausibly affect which sexual behaviors occur within them. We have already identified one of these as being related to the characteristics of the partners involved. This is the nature of the exchange between the two partners. Relationships that, in addition to sexual interaction, involve the exchange of items, such as economic resources, companionship, and other types of support, may place certain constraints on the types of sexual services that one partner can (or is willing to) extract from the other. For example, if a woman perceives that she is getting more from her partner than she is giving, she may feel obligated to correct this imbalance by performing sexual activities that her partner enjoys. Similarly, if a man perceives himself to be dependent on his partner, he might be willing to forgo his own sexual interests in order to please his partner (Emerson 1981). Conversely, people who perceive themselves as giving more than they receive or as being less dependent on their relationships than their partners might be more likely to ask their partners to perform certain activities or refuse to comply with their partner's wishes.

The exchanges that occur within a relationship are not the only features of that relationship that can affect sexual behavior. Another important feature is the way in which the relationship is socially defined and perceived by the participants. Some common examples of socially defined sexual relationships are "high school sweethearts," "lovers," "boyfriend and girlfriend," "husband and wife," and "one-night stand." Clearly, these may be interpreted differently by different people, and it is also possible that culturally distinct subgroups use a different set of definitions. Consequently, we learn and make decisions about what is and is not appropriate sexual behavior within the context of a specific type of relationship, rather than solely in terms of the individual performing the behavior. Thus, some men force their wives to have

sex with them because they believe that, within marriage, a husband is owed sex by his wife whenever and however he wants it, even though the same man might consider the exact same behavior directed toward a stranger or even a girlfriend to be rape.

Both scripting and choice theories combine with a network approach to generate more comprehensive explanations of sexual conduct. Although the network approach emphasizes the properties of relationships rather than persons, it cannot by itself be used to explain what goes on within a specific relationship. This requires an understanding of what motivates the individuals in that relationship, such as that provided by scripting and choice theory. Understandings about what is appropriate within the context of a specific relationship are nothing other than scripts—scripts that are specific not only to the persons involved but also to the relationship between those two people. Similarly, exchanges between partners result from the strategically motivated interests of both partners, implying that, if a relationship costs a partner more than it benefits him or her, he or she will withdraw from the exchange. Nevertheless, regardless of people's cultural understandings and their motivations, sexual activity can occur only when two people come together in a relationship. The fundamental contribution of the network approach is in showing how the social networks in which people are embedded affect whether two people will get together to form a sexual relationship and, if they do, which cultural understandings and economic motivations they will bring to that relationship.

Sexual scripts are learned through interaction with others, and this interaction is clearly shaped by the networks in which we are embedded. Most research on this subject has focused on the sexual behavior of adolescents and has generally found that sexually active adolescents tend to have friends who are also sexually active (Billy, Rodgers, and Udry 1984), although it is unclear which causes which. Similarly, the legitimacy of oral sex in youthful sexual relationships is dependent on gendered support networks that supply different legitimations for these forms of conduct to both male and female adolescents (Gagnon and Simon 1987). Another less common but still convincing illustration of the role of networks is provided by reports among young boys of "circle jerks," an activity in which a group will masturbate to orgasm, often in some competitive fashion (to see who will ejaculate the soonest, who has the largest penis, or how far the semen travels on ejaculation).

We also expect social networks to be important in determining the sexual behavior of adults. To understand these influences, we must specify the interests that third parties have in the occurrence (or nonoccurrence) of certain activities within specific types of partnerships. By third parties we mean people connected to either or both members of a focal sexual dyad by one or more types of social relationship. Thus, parents have interests in the sexual experiences of their children, such as wanting them to refrain from sexual activity until they are "ready," wanting them not to date people whom they consider to be "poor" influences, etc. Similarly, children of divorced parents also have interests in the sexual relationships of their parents since these can claim part of the parent's attention and lead to remarriage. Third-party interests are not limited to relatives; friends too can be interested in each other's happiness in a relationship and be wary of the threat that that relationship might pose for the stability of the friendship.

Probably the best organized of all groups that have an interest in sexuality are stakeholders in reproductive activity. They range from individual parents to large-scale organizations such as Planned Parenthood that supply services, participate in political lobbying, and seek private and government resources and support for their programs. Control of reproduction involves the control of sexual activity, necessarily a complicated relationship. Morally conservative stakeholders attempt to control both sexuality and reproduction through moral instruction,

policing the content of school curriculum and of the media, limiting information about contraception and the availability of contraceptive devices, limiting the access of the potentially sexually active to services for the prevention of sexually transmitted infection and disease (including HIV), and so forth. In contrast, liberal stakeholders seek to provide most of these services while remaining (somewhat) indifferent to the sexual expressions of consenting adults over the age of sixteen.

Other highly organized and politically active stakeholders are those who seek either to facilitate or to limit the acceptance of same-gender sexual relationships and the legal provision of the same rights and privileges for these couples as are enjoyed by heterosexual couples (e.g., allowing them to raise children, to show affection in public, etc.). Friends, relatives, and even parents often admonish or outright reject gay individuals because they do not know how to behave or are uncomfortable around them and, more important, because they are forced to justify or deny the individual's behavior in front of their own friends and associates. In fact, intolerance of homosexuality is so ubiquitous in this country that many homosexuals are forced either to conceal their sexual preference or to move to one of the few social environments where being gay is accepted.

An example of a less organized but still powerful third-party interest is that in maintaining exclusivity in established sexual partnerships, especially marriages. Part of this interest stems from the belief that extramarital sex is morally wrong, a belief that is almost universally accepted (roughly 90 percent of adults believe that extramarital sex is either "always wrong" or "almost always wrong"). In keeping with this attitude, our data suggest that the annual incidence of extramarital sexual activity is modest. Although we do not deny the fact that one's own moral and religious beliefs strongly influence the decision to limit oneself to a single partner at a time, we do argue that these beliefs are legitimated and reinforced through interaction with others who share such beliefs and who have concrete interests in the couple's sexual exclusivity. For example, in their attempts to support one spouse, the relatives and friends of that person are likely to regard any extramarital activity on the part of the other spouse as unjustifiable.

To acknowledge the potential for extramarital activity, even if only by discussing it with a friend, risks both personal temptation and the possibility of being labeled by others as a potential "cheater." This fact increases people's reluctance to address the topic in conversation, thus decreasing the possibility of locating potential partners or social approval for the behavior.

Opportunities to pursue extramarital sexual activity are also limited by the very large proportion of individuals in the society who are already in relationships. Especially after age thirty, the number of uncoupled individuals is small. This is exacerbated by the fact that marriage accustoms a couple to the conversations and activities of the other married couples to whom they usually restrict their associations. Presumably, some fraction of these married individuals might be willing to engage in extramarital sex; however, this number is almost certainly quite small and, more important, very difficult to identify for the reasons discussed above.

Sexual activity is not unique in being motivated and constrained by the interests of third parties. However, unlike other spheres of activity, sexual activity almost always occurs in private and is usually talked about in highly routine and nonrevealing ways. This fact makes the surveillance of the sexual dyad by outsiders remarkably difficult—third parties are privy only to the testimony of the individuals themselves about what happened. This has both positive and negative social consequences— sexual encounters may be conducted entirely by trial and error and independently of regulation, leading to sexual experimentation, or they may be occasions on which the participants deliberately or ignorantly exploit or violate each other.

INTERRELATIONS AMONG THE THEORIES

As we have indicated, each of these three theories is intended to answer different types of questions about sexual activity. However, since these questions are interrelated, so are the theories used to explain them. In most cases, these interrelations take the form of consistent or complementary predictions by the different theories. For example, we have already shown how both scripting and choice theories may be used to explain what occurs within specific relationships identified by the network approach. Occasionally, however, there are inconsistencies in what the theoretical approaches would predict and no clear way of reconciling these differences on the basis of theoretical arguments alone.

The sharpest inconsistency among the three approaches is between scripting and choice theories. As we have already noted, a fundamental assumption in choice theory is that individuals act strategically or rationally in the pursuit of goals. In contrast, scripting theory suggests that individuals model their actions on the basis of a predetermined (although somewhat flexible) set of cultural scenarios. Given the small number of scenarios relative to the number of different circumstances that people encounter, it is likely that certain people will be unable to locate a scenario that represents what would be considered "rational behavior" in their particular case. In such instances, the predictions of the two theories would conflict. Yet there is a more fundamental difference between scripting and choice theories than the existence of discrepant predictions. The two theories assume very different mechanisms underlying people's behavior. Choice theory assumes that individuals are constantly evaluating their situations and making choices, whereas scripting theory assumes that individuals are constrained by a script that they learned from those around them.

At this point, the reader might be wondering how these general theoretical approaches can be used to inform and interpret analyses of the actual data collected in this study. After all, using a survey instrument limits the researcher to asking only those questions that are easy to understand and to answer. Thus, for example, we were unable to measure sex scripts directly since doing so would require a complicated series of questions about numerous specific activities and the order in which they occurred. More important, the fact that ours was a national survey prohibited us from tailoring certain questions to particular locations or subpopulations. This meant that much fine-grained cultural (and, to some extent, regional) variation in these scripts was beyond our grasp. Similarly, our ability to measure people's networks was also quite limited; we could not ask them about specific places or events where they socialized, nor could we ask them about their relationships with specific persons other than their sex partners. For example, it would be very useful to know something about the larger network structures in which respondents are embedded since these structures certainly affect the structure of their sexual networks. Since such structures are unique to particular locations, however, they are beyond the scope of this type of study. Finally, the methods used to study rational decision making also require an intensive set of questions (such as those designed to determine an individual's preference ordering) targeted to a specific situation. These limitations are important ones, forcing us to relegate focused examinations of specific issues to future projects. However, a national study such as this one is a necessary precursor to more specialized work.

REFERENCES

Billy, John O. G., Joseph Lee Rodgers, and J. Richard Udry. 1984. Adolescent sexual behavior and friendship choice. *Social Forces*, 62:653–78.

Billy, John O. G., Koray Tanfer, William R. Grady, and Daniel H. Klepenger. 1993. The sexual behavior of men in the United States. *Family Planning Perspectives* 25, no. 2:52–60.

Blumstein, Philip, and Pepper Schwartz. 1983. *American Couples*. New York: Morrow.

Brookman, Richard R. 1990. Adolescent sexual behavior. In *Sexually Transmitted Diseases*, eds. King K. Holmes et al. New York: McGraw-Hill.

Castillo, C. O., and J. H. Geer. 1993. Ambiguous stimuli: Sex in the eye of the beholder. *Archives of Sexual Behavior* 22:131–43.

Centers for Disease Control (CDC). 1992. *STD/HIV Prevention 1991 Annual Report*. Atlanta.

DeLamater, John. 1981. The social control of sexuality. *Annual Review of Sociology* 7:263–90.

DeLamater, John, and Patricia MacCorquodale. 1979. *Premarital Sexuality: Attitudes, Relationships, Behavior*. Madison: University of Wisconsin.

Emerson, Richard M. 1981. Social exchange theory. In *Social Psychology: Sociological Perspective*, eds. M. Rosenberg and R. H. Turner. New York: Basic Books.

Gagnon, John H. 1991. The implicit and explicit use of scripts in sex research. In *The Annual Review of Sex Research*, ed. John Bancroft, Clive Davis, and Deborah Weinstein. Mt. Vernon, Iowa: Society for the Scientific Study of Sex.

Gagnon, John H., and William Simon. 1987. The scripting of oral-genital sexual conduct. *Archives of Sexual Behavior* 16, no. 1:1–25.

Geer, J. H., and D. B. Brussard. 1990. Scaling sex behavior and arousal: Consistency and sex differences. *Journal of Personality and Social Psychology* 58: 644–71.

Hallinan, Maureen T., and Richard A. Williams. 1989. Interracial freindship choices in secondary schools. *American Sociological Review* 54:67–78.

Heinz, John P., and Edward O. Laumann. 1982. *Chicago Lawyers: The Social Structure of the Bar*. Chicago: Russell Sage Foundation and American Bar Foundation.

Hite, S. 1976. *The Hite report: A nationwide study of female sexuality*. New York: Macmillan.

Kalick, S. Michael, and Thomas E. Hamilton III. 1986. The matching hypothesis reexamined. *Journal of Personality and Social Psychology* 51, no. 4: 673–82.

Kalmijn, Matthijs. 1991. Shifting boundaries: Trends in religious and educational homogany. *American Sociological Review* 57:706–800.

Klassen, A. D., C. J. Williams, and E. E. Levitt. 1989. In *Sex and Morality in the U.S.*, ed. H. J. O'Gorman. Middletown, Conn.: Wesleyan University Press.

Laumann, Edward O. 1966. *Prestige and Association in an Urban Community*. New York: Bobbs-Merrill.

———. 1973. *Bonds of Pluralism: The Form and Substance of Urban Social Networks*. New York: Wiley.

Mare, Robert D. 1991. Five decades of educational assortative mating. *American Sociological Review* 56: 15–32.

Marsden, Peter V. 1988. Homogeneity in confiding relations. *Social Networks* 10:57–76.

Mosher, William D., and James W. McNally. 1991. Contraceptive use at first premarital intercourse: United States, 1965–1988. *Family Planning Perspectives* 23, no. 3:108–16.

Peterson, John L., Joseph A. Catania, M. Margaret Dolcini, and Bonnie Faigeles. 1993. Multiple sexual partners among blacks in high risk cities. *Family Planning Perspectives* 25:263–67.

Prohaska, Thomas R., Gay Albrecht, Judith A. Levy, Noreen Sugrue, and Joung-Hwa Kim. 1990. Determinants of self-perceived risk for AIDS. *Journal of Health and Social Behavior* 31:384–94.

Reiss, Ira L. 1990. *An End to Shame: Shaping Our Next Sexual Revolution*. New York: Prometheus Books.

Schoen, Robert, and Robin M. Weinick. 1993. Partner choice in marriages and cohabitations. *Journal of Marriage and Family* 55:408–14.

Sonenstein, F. L., J. H. Pleck, and L. C. Ku. 1991. Levels of sexual activity among adolescent males in the United States. *Family Planning Perspectives* 23, no. 4:162–67.

Sprecher, Susan, and Kathleen McKinney. 1993. *Sexuality*. London: Sage Publications.

Tanfer, Koray. 1992. Coital frequency among single women: Normative constraints and situational opportunities. *Journal of Sex Research* 29:221–50.

Weinberg, Martin S., and Colin J. Williams. 1980. Sexual embourgeoisment? Social class and sexual activity: 1938–1970. *American Sociological Review* 45, no. 1:33–48.

Zelnick, Melvin, and John F. Kantner. 1972. Sexuality, contraception, and pregnancy among young unwed females in the U.S. In *Demographic and Social Aspects of Population Growth*, eds. Charles F. Westoff and R. Parke. Washington, D.C.: U.S. Government Printing Office.

———. 1980. Sexual activity, contraceptive use and pregnancy among metropolitan-area teenagers: 1971–1979. *Family Planning Perspectives* 12:230–37.

CHAPTER 4

Sex Among the Americans

Joseph Adelson

Juxtaposing the sexually inhibited and the sexually liberated, Joseph Adelson mines the fields of facts generated by the research of Laumann et al. with a 1990s survey that shocked Americans. The cover of Time *(October 17, 1994) announced the news: "Sex in America: Surprising News From the Most Important Survey Since the Kinsey Report!" As the news hit the airwaves and the press, Americans were surprised to learn that the hotbed of sex in the '90s was the marriage bed.*

Although media "sexperts," such as Cosmopolitan editor Helen Gurley Brown; Hugh Hefner, founder of Playboy; *and Bob Guccione, publisher of* Penthouse, *were uttering words like "outrageous," "stupid," "ridiculous," and "come on now," Europeans seemed less surprised by the findings. They were, in fact, parallel with studies in England and France that also had found low rates of homosexuality and high rates of marital fidelity.*

Critics abounded! They decried the absence of women among the study's directors, asking if this could have skewed the questions. Doubts were also raised about whether personal interviews could elicit truly candid answers to intimate questions, for example, about masturbation, or whether the sample was too small to generalize about some groups, like homosexuals. Adelson himself is less than ebullient about some of the interpretations,

given the findings by the researchers and the choice of the theories used as a framework for the study. He does, however, praise its technical competence and its findings, which "carry us beyond, and largely discredit, the data of earlier studies." Among those who praised the survey, Ira Reiss, sexuality scholar from the University of Minnesota, declared that of the major sex surveys to date, the Laumann et al. study was probably the best thought out and had the broadest coverage.

As readers today take a retrospective look at the findings that Adelson presents from the Laumann et al. survey, they can add their own cacophony of beliefs and disbeliefs. After all, their ideas will be no less reflective of their own experiential findings than were those of Brown, Hefner, and Guccione.

I teach a seminar for first-year undergraduates on the troubles of adolescence. During a discussion of teenage illegitimacy not too long ago, I mentioned in passing a surprising datum I had just come across: the average American woman, during her lifetime, has two sex partners. The reaction in my classroom was electric—amazement, disbelief. That can't be! It's more than that! They must be lying!

These are youngsters, mind, who can absorb the most horrendous social statistics—that the killing of adolescents has increased fourfold in the last decade, that two-thirds of all black children are born out of wedlock—without batting an eye. They may or may not find such data troubling (it is often hard to tell), but they do not find them shocking. What shocked them was the *not*-shocking—news of modesty, decorum, restraint.

After class, a young man came up to me who wanted to know the data for homosexuality in the source I had referred to. Well, I replied, if self-definition is the criterion, the figures are a bit under 3 percent for males, and between 1 and 2 percent for females. He was furious. I know that literature in detail, he told me. We're studying it in philosophy (!) class; those numbers are not only false but probably falsified, and I'm sure they're being circulated to discourage the gay community, which in fact is growing by leaps and bounds.

Later in the week, thinking these inflamed responses might reflect the passions of youth, I asked several friends and colleagues—each and every one of them (it goes without saying) wise and worldly-wise—to estimate the number of partners American women have over a lifetime. Their guesses ranged from a low of six to a high of twenty. When apprised of the figure I had come across, they, too, reacted with disbelief, in some cases mixed with heavy sarcasm about the pretensions of survey research and what one of them termed "social so-called science."

Where, then, did I get the numbers I had so innocently broadcast? From a recent sociological study, *Sex in America: A Definitive Survey*,[1] published in both a popular and scholarly edition, the latter under the appropriately academic title, *The Social Organization of Sexuality*.[2] This, the publishers tell us, is the "only comprehensive and methodologically sound survey of America's sexual practices and beliefs."

They were drawn to it, they tell us, by dissatisfaction with prior studies of American sexual behavior. At their best, earlier surveys like the famous one done by Alfred Kinsey and his associates in 1948 were well-intentioned but flawed, the most common problem being a reliance on catch-as-catch-can methods of recruiting interviewees. These studies also lacked any means for checking the truthfulness of the responses

given, and the worst of them, like the egregious *Hite Report* on female sexuality of 1976, solicited responses from selected and sometimes highly politicized groups. In the case of the *Hite Report* that meant that the data were drawn from members of the National Organization for Women, abortion-rights advocates, and the like; even so. *Hite* managed but a 3-percent response rate, making it certain that the respondents bore little likeness to American women in general.

The authors of *Sex in America* set out to do things right by sampling accurately our adult population (aged 18–60); preparing a carefully pre-tested questionnaire, training their interviewers rigorously; and introducing several methods of checking the veracity of the responses obtained. One may have some serious reservations, as I do, about what went into the questionnaire as well as what was left out and about the interpretations offered; but the sampling itself is state-of-the-art, and the authors are right to be pleased with themselves. Carrying out a national survey of this scope is extremely expensive ($450 per interview) and requires great technical expertise and a high level of patience and compulsiveness.

As a culture—and my students beautifully represent that culture—we have come to believe that the degree of individual sexual pleasure can be placed on a linear chart extending from "inhibited" at one end to "liberated" at the other. The sexually free are unattached and unencumbered. They have been everywhere and done everything, and are ready for more—more positions, more variations, more partners, more often. At the other extreme are those who have sex only within marriage and then only infrequently, who employ the missionary position, perform the act rapidly, and achieve shallow orgasms or none at all.

Though we might not say so openly, many of us also tend to believe that blacks are more active sexually than whites, and that those belonging to conservative religious denominations are bound to be more inhibited than those without any religious affiliation. And we may also believe that, sooner or later, sex with the same person becomes too familiar and boring, leading us to seek adventure elsewhere. After all, a cardinal rule in matters sexual is that we are drawn to those unlike us, to what is alien or taboo: opposites attract.

What the research gathered in *Sex in America* tells us is that none of the above is true. In fact, American sexuality is marked by moderation and fidelity. Husbands and wives are faithful to each other, and so are those living together though unmarried. Even the unattached rarely wander, and are certainly not promiscuous. As I had accurately reported to my students, one-half of all Americans of both sexes have three or fewer partners in a lifetime; as one might expect, men are more active sexually, but not by a wide margin. (And lest one protest that all this is the baleful legacy of American Puritanism, parallel studies throughout the Western world, in countries Catholic as well as Protestant, yield essentially the same findings.)

American sexual practices are, similarly, conventional. Vaginal intercourse is by far the most appealing mode, almost universally judged exciting and pleasurable. It is followed, at a distance, by the mild voyeurism of "watching partners undress," and then by oral sex. All other sexual practices—group sex, anal sex in its several variations, sadomasochism, the use of sexual toys and devices, homosexuality, sex with strangers, watching strangers have sex— all these are deemed unappealing, in most cases very unappealing, and by all segments of the population, men and women, young and old.

Sex in America (as I told my young student of philosophy) comes up with a dramatically lower figure for homosexual identity and practice. Until quite recently, the standard number was 10 percent, and when cited it was often preceded by the phrase "at least," suggesting that the true figure was higher and was being suppressed either by caution or by shame. Many psychologists and psychiatrists had their doubts about this, believing the true figure to be 5 to 6 percent for men, and half that for women; but for the most part these doubts went unvoiced. We now learn that even the reduced number was too high. Fewer than 3 percent of men identify themselves as homosexual; more inclusive criteria give us no more than 5 percent. Lesbianism is about half as common. European studies provide similar data.

Among the most interesting findings in *Sex in America* are what one might call the absent findings: in particular, the absence of expected variations associated with race, ethnicity, education, religion, and the like. Both the popular and the scholarly editions of this study are glutted with charts and tables illustrating these modest or nonexistent differences. How frequently do men achieve orgasm with their "primary partners"? About three-quarters of men say "always," no matter what their age, marital status, education, or race. "How many times do you have sex each month?" Again, little variation: almost always six to seven times a month, for men and women, well-educated or not, of all religious affiliations; the only blip is that those over fifty report a slightly lower rate (four or five times monthly).

To whom do we become attached? Here we come to a central emphasis of this study: we become dear to those who are near, that is, those who are like us and whom we come to know in the daily routines and venues of our lives. Sexual behavior, the authors tell us time and again, is shaped by the social networks we occupy. We choose (and are chosen by) those within our network, those like us in almost all respects—race, religion, education, class. We rarely venture out of these boundaries, and should we try to, those within them signal their disapproval.

If you enjoy wallowing in numbers, the tables in *Sex in America* provide what seem to be small surprises now and again. For example: more conservative Protestant women report always having orgasms than do women of any other religion. Really? Yes, really; but also not really— they do outpace others in the "always" category, but that aside, there are no other important differences by religion. Nor do the occasional variations by race and education add up to a consistent pattern. Blacks, for example, are high on a few measures, but average or low on others.

Still, that figure about conservative Protestant women and their orgasms does point to what is the real bombshell in this study. Not only does it turn out that, in the war between the prudes and the libertines, Americans in general have continued to hold fast on the side of the prudes. It also turns out—horror!—that the prudes are having much more fun.

This study, in fact, is a paean to sexual bonding, to marriage or its near-equivalents. Intimate, exclusive relationships between spouses or committed partners provide, by far, the greatest degree of sexual gratification. More: in a finding that turns the standard scenario of pornography on its head, these books reveal that those without committed partners are far less likely to engage in casual sex during a given period than to do without sex altogether. Twenty-three percent of unattached men report having had no sex, as opposed to less than 1 percent of those married or living with someone; among women, the figures are 32 percent compared to 2 percent. At the other extreme, attached men and women are twice as likely as unattached to have sex two or more times a week. In the pleasure sweepstakes, monogamy counts.

And we are not done. Perhaps the most astonishing single datum reported in these books has to do with those conducting extramarital affairs: they report that they are more gratified sexually by their spouses than by their lovers. To add insult to injury, they also have sex less often than those faithfully married. Among the unmarried, those who have at least two sexual partners are less pleased with their sex lives, emotionally and physically, than those married or living together. For women in particular, a close attachment is essentially a necessity for a gratifying sex life.

Let me sum up, in the authors' own words, the key findings of this research. Whether you count by "adult lifetime or in the past year," nearly all Americans have "a very modest number of partners." This number "varies little with education, race, or religion." Rather, it is determined by marital status or by whether a couple is living together. Once married, people tend to have one and only one partner, and those who are married and living together are almost as likely to be faithful. Sexual practices, moreover, are highly conventional. Only vaginal intercourse is universally attractive, while almost all the *outre* variations are disliked. Finally, when it comes to sexual pleasure, liberation carries a palpable cost, fidelity its own very great reward.

Which leads to a question: if all this is essentially correct, why are my students and my friends and all the rest of us so mistaken? Why do we think of ourselves as a society which has happily (or, for those scandalized by it, sinfully) thrown off most of the constraints of the past, a society in which more and more of us are sexually adventurous both before and during marriage, and are willing and even eager to try out exotic sexual combinations and practices?

Well, for one thing we believe what "empirical science" has taught us to believe. The Kinsey data, initially so shocking, were rather quickly absorbed into the conventional wisdom. The 10-percent "datum" for homosexuality, for example, had its origins in the Kinsey findings. That statistic and others like it were not superseded by more accurate ones, in large part because subsequent studies made the same sorts of sampling error. Kinseyesque findings were thus presumably confirmed and became accepted even by those distressed by what they implied morally. In this connection, it is ironically pertinent that the research in *Sex in America* failed to win federal support because of the opposition of conservative legislators who expected that it would show a high level of deviant behavior.

This in itself tells us that sexual information is not ideologically neutral. Sexuality is important terrain in the cultural wars that divide us, and what we believe to be true about it is conditioned by a larger set of assumptions and expectations about human nature and the social order. In particular, when we read about sex, or see it portrayed in films or on television, we do not see its mundane, quotidian side; we see persons taking dangerous risks to achieve pleasure, or struggling to realize their true selves by means of erotic liberation.

Robert Lichter of the Media Research Center reports that seven out of eight sexual encounters in television dramas involve extramarital relations. No surprise there—the illicit is all but a *sine qua non* of the dramatic. Yet this same partiality is found throughout the public culture. As I write, my local newspaper—small-city, staid, sober in most respects—has helpfully brought us a report of a bright new development in erotic practice called playful sadomasochism, wherein the gestures and rituals of the real thing are mimicked without serious pain being inflicted. My favorite national newspaper, the *Wall Street Journal*, recently ran a front-page story on another bright new trend, this one among women: serial bisexuality, or going back and forth between male and female partners. These accounts have in common the tone and feel of fashion reporting, complete with the tacit assurance to the shy that, however odd it may appear at the moment, this is indeed the coming style.

Missing in all these savvy, wide-eyed reports is any sense of the everyday torments freelance sexuality imposes on ordinary and (as we glean from *Sex in America*) even not-so-ordinary people. Will he (she) like it? Will she (he) have an orgasm? Is my body attractive? Do I smell badly? Can I keep going long enough? Will he (she) *really* like it? Am I better than he (she) has had before? Am I being too rough? Not rough enough? Too responsive? Not responsive enough? And on, and on. Not everyone is quite so anxious, but as any psychotherapist can testify, a great many are.

Nor does one need therapeutic testimony to confirm the part played in sexual life by self-doubt, shame, and narcissistic injury. Simply visit any good bookstore to find a substantial array of titles offering advice, instruction, encouragement, and spiritual uplift designed to calm your fears, assuage your guilt, overcome your embarrassment, and protect you against

humiliation, thus making the sexual act enjoyable, or in some cases simply possible. Media sex, with its incessant stress on triumph and variety, is blind to this side of sexual feeling; one might say it represents a manic defense against it, if not a denial of its existence.

And this leads us to yet another answer to the question of why we were all so mistaken. Those who construct the public image of sexuality in our country—journalists, dramatists, pundits, professors, etc.—occupy quite a special sociological niche within the population at large, and their constructions to a greater or lesser degree tend to mirror their own attitudes and practices. Significantly, only a quarter of the overall survey sample in *Sex in America*—those whom the authors term "recreationals"—see sex in terms of pleasure alone, removed from obligation, devotion, or moral concern, and these same "recreationals" are four to five times more likely to have committed adultery, and two to three times more likely to have engaged in deviant sex. We learn from the sociological charts provided by the authors that—surprise—these same "recreationals" tend to be without religious affiliation. In which academic and professional precincts they live, and what they do for a living, it is not hard to guess.

As opposed to the "recreationals," a substantial majority of those surveyed in *Sex in America* report that they are guided in their sexual practices by their religious beliefs, or link sex to marriage or a loving attachment. Here we begin to see most clearly how differences in moral outlook play out in behavior. And here, too, we edge close to the realm of values. This is a realm which our authors, for their part, sedulously strive to avoid.

They, after all, are sociologists (with the exception of Gina Kolata, a science journalist), and they bring to their enterprise a fierce belief in the heuristic powers of their discipline. Thus, they inform us quite solemnly that they have employed the "advanced and sophisticated methods of social-science research," the same ones that have worked so well in the study of such topics as "labor-force participation . . . or migration behavior." In analyzing their findings, they rely almost entirely on two quintessentially social-scientific concepts: social networks and the (sexual) marketplace.

They seem unable, however, to grasp how little these concepts explain. In a long discussion of racial barriers, for instance, the authors succeed in demonstrating that only rarely do American blacks and whites become sexual or marital partners. They cite this finding to support their emphasis on the general explanatory power of social networks as cementers of sexual bonds. But whatever the figures may be for whites and blacks, marriages between whites and Asian-Americans have now become commonplace. If race is so important, how did that happen, and why?

Nor do we hear anything from the authors about the Jews, whose rates of intermarriage are now high enough to threaten the group's survival. When I was a boy, one did not marry outside the faith because doing so would mortify one's family. Needless to say, that pattern changed, and rather quickly. Why? Is religion a less powerful barrier than race? Is family less powerful than class or peer group?

In illustrating the efficacy of social networks, the authors provide a fairly long discussion of how the sexes were kept apart on campuses during the 1950s and early 1960s, when colleges acted *in loco parentis* as guardians of sexual boundaries. Then, in the late 60s, they tell us, due to the pressures of the youth movement, these rules disappeared "virtually overnight," and the era of sexual liberation was unloosed. But no matter what was, or was not, happening in the dormitories between one moment and the next, the same tired notion of a social network is brought in to explain it. How can this be? A social network that stops on a dime, completely reverses direction, and still performs the same function, has no value as an explanatory concept. It is simply a piece of jargon.

Consider, finally, the concept of the sexual marketplace, which the authors invoke to explain how people choose mates. Each person in a pair—so the reasoning goes—trades his or her assets to make the most advantageous match available. Among the examples given are those of Ross Perot and Henry Kissinger, both of whom, the second time around, found women younger and more attractive than themselves, trading money and power for youth and beauty. The authors believe that all such calculations are unconscious; "certainly most people are not consciously aware" of them.

To the contrary, most of us are very much aware of them, and some of us can think of nothing else. My Aunt Sadie's truisms on marriage were largely devoted to such observations: "He didn't marry her for her looks, but her father has a nice business." Come to think of it, so are the truisms of Aunt Jane Austen, Uncle Anthony Trollope, and most of the other greats and not-so-greats who have written about what goes into the formation of domestic arrangements.

The concepts of "network" and "marketplace," in other words, allow us to fashion explanations after the fact—*post hoc ergo propter hoc*. They are a capacious umbrella under which we can place everything we already know—but little else. Why are a given network's boundaries sometimes permeable and sometimes not? How does a group's history influence its members? Which networks evolve in expectable directions, and which do not, and why? These questions are never asked by our authors because they cannot be answered with the equipment they have assembled.

Even more troubling is the avoidance of any consideration of the inner world—the world of motives and character—which influences sexual and mental behavior. Some of the findings simply cry out for the insights of sociobiology, a discipline mentioned briefly only to be firmly dismissed. And when it comes to the psychological sources of behavior, the authors are singularly myopic.

A small but revealing example can be found in the index; for the category "shame," the entry reads, "see guilt." But guilt and shame are very different emotions, different not only subjectively but also in origin and effect. Another small example: general happiness, the authors discover, is correlated with a good sex life—but which comes first? Amazingly, they confess to not having a clue.

The most revealing instance of such myopia concerns the treatment of forced sex. The authors find that about one-fifth of women report having been coerced sexually at some time. The coerced are not, as one might assume, strangers or casual pickups; most of them are husbands or loved ones. And it is usually not clear just what the coercion consists of, though it seems not to be physical assault or rape. Now, these same women also report having many problems in sexual response—pains, difficulty in lubricating, lack of pleasure. It would appear they are inhibited about sex, and would prefer to avoid it. But then we also learn that they have many more sexual partners, and engage in more deviant activities. Finally, sex aside, they are unhappy in general.

What does it all mean? The authors dance around, unable to venture a coherent explanation. It is a case of political correctness—a fear of blaming the victim—joined to a *deformation professionelle*, the limitations produced by vocational bias: in this case, an aversion to psychological inferences. They cannot, in short, bring themselves to state the obvious: these are troubled women whose troubles are almost certainly rooted in personality. Here, as elsewhere throughout their study, the authors have built a conceptual cage and locked themselves in.

But I do not want to end on a wholly critical note. Many of the reviews of this study have been negative, at times scathingly so, the burden of complaint being close to that voiced by my first-year undergraduates—that you cannot trust what people tell you in an interview on sex; that the researchers are self-deceived to think otherwise; that we need some objective, independent measures of the truth, otherwise we are at the mercy of those who lie, or fudge, or misremember, or leave things out.

Most psychological research, Freud's included, depends on self-reporting to some degree. It can rarely do independent checks on veracity, and hence it cannot fully guarantee the probity of its findings. This is an old problem—and those who do survey research are, most of them, especially aware of it. They do what can be done, practically speaking, and present their data honestly and modestly. What other choices do we have? Do we declare some topics off-limits to research? If so, we will soon enough substitute our own experience, writ large, or our own imaginings, or our stern beliefs about what ought to be.

That is just what we have done to sexuality—as this study, despite its flaws, allows us to see. Its strength rests on its technical competence and its findings, which carry us beyond, and largely discredit the data of earlier studies. That is a lot. The rest, which has to do with human happiness and how this won and lost, lies in the domain of subtler doctors of the soul than sociologists.

But is it not wonderful enough to learn, through graphs, charts, tables, and survey data, that many of the secrets of such human happiness, no matter how obscure they may be to undergraduates and their professors, have not altogether been lost to most men and women?

Notes

1. Robert T. Michael, John H. Gagnon, Edward O. Laumann, and Gina Kolata. Little, Brown, 300 pp.
2. Edward O. Laumann, John H Gagnon, Robert T. Michael, and Stuart Michaels. University of Chicago Press, 718 pp.

CHAPTER 5

Origins of Mating Behavior

David M. Buss

In 1989, psychologists Elaine Hatfield and Russell Clark (1989) published the results of a daring study in which college student researchers approached an attractive member of the other sex on campus and posed one of three questions: "Would you go out with me tonight?" "Would you come over to my apartment tonight?" or "Would you go to bed with me tonight?" While 75 percent of the young men agreed to have sex with this attractive stranger, none of the women acquiesced. This dramatic sex difference is often used to illustrate some of the basic tenets of evolutionary psychology, the idea that because women and men face different challenges in reproduction, over time they have evolved differential sexual strategies. These strategies include different degrees of willingness to engage in casual sex as well as different criteria for characteristics sought in a mate.

What do you look for in a potential partner? Do you know why these characteristics appeal to you? David Buss, the author of this chapter, would tell you that your mate preferences, at least in part, are tied to a long line of human evolutionary history. According to evolutionary psychologists, women seek the protection, resources, and genes of successful men, but men seek success to attract

women, especially younger ones who are likely to be fertile. Of course, both men and women seek different traits in a short-term partner (a "one-night stand" or a hookup partner) than they do in a long-term partner. There are those with whom we wish to mate, and those with whom we wish to share a life.

After reading this chapter, you will likely want to discuss these ideas with other students in your class. If evolutionary psychology makes sense to you, you might wish to design a study to test a sexual strategies hypothesis. On the other hand, if you have a negative reaction to these ideas, you may wish to engage in the intellectual exercise of designing a study to test an alternative theory that might be a more efficient explanation of some of the phenomena discussed in this reading.

From *The Evolution of Desire: Strategies of Human Mating* (pp. 1–18) by D. M. Buss. 2003. New York: Basic Books. Copyright © 1994 by David M. Buss. Revised edition © 2003 by David M. Buss. Reprinted by permission of Basic Books, a member of Perseus Books Group.

Human mating behavior delights and amuses us and galvanizes our gossip, but it is also deeply disturbing. Few domains of human activity generate as much discussion, as many laws, or such elaborate rituals in all cultures. Yet the elements of human mating seem to defy understanding. Women and men sometimes find themselves choosing mates who abuse them psychologically and physically. Conflicts erupt within couples, producing downward spirals of blame and despair. Despite their best intentions and vows of lifelong love, half of all married couples end up divorcing.

Pain, betrayal, and loss contrast sharply with the usual romantic notions of love. We grow up believing in true love, in finding our "one and only." We assume that once we do, we will marry in bliss and live happily ever after. But reality rarely coincides with our beliefs. Even a cursory look at the divorce rate, the 30 to 50 percent incidence of extramarital affairs, and the jealous rages that rack so many relationships shatters these illusions.

Discord and dissolution in mating relationships are typically seen as signs of failure. They are thought to signal personal inadequacy, immaturity, neurosis, failure of will, or simply poor judgment in the choice of a mate. This view is radically wrong. Conflict in mating is the norm and not the exception. It ranges from a man's anger at a woman who declines his advances to a wife's frustration with a husband who fails to help in the home. Such a pervasive pattern defies easy explanation. Something deeper, more telling about human nature is involved—something we do not fully understand.

The problem is complicated by the centrality of love in human life. Feelings of love mesmerize us when we experience them and occupy our fantasies when we do not. Contrary to common belief, love is not a recent invention of the Western leisure classes. People in all cultures experience love and have coined specific words for it. Its pervasiveness convinces us that love, with its key components of commitment, tenderness, and passion, is an inevitable part of the human experience, within the grasp of everyone.

Our failure to understand the real and paradoxical nature of human mating is costly, both scientifically and socially. Scientifically, the dearth of knowledge leaves unanswered some of life's most puzzling questions, such as why people sacrifice years of their lives to the quest for love and the struggle for relationship. Socially, our ignorance leaves us frustrated and helpless when we are bruised by mating behavior gone awry in the workplace, on the dating scene, and in our home.

We need to reconcile the profound love that humans seek with the conflict that permeates our most cherished relationships. We need to square our dreams with reality. To understand these baffling contradictions, we must gaze back into our evolutionary past—a past that has grooved and scored our minds as much as our bodies, our strategies for mating as much as our strategies for survival.

EVOLUTIONARY ROOTS

More than a century ago, Charles Darwin offered a revolutionary explanation for the mysteries of mating.[1] He had become intrigued by the puzzling way that animals had developed characteristics that would appear to hinder their survival. The elaborate plumage, large antlers, and other conspicuous features displayed by many species seemed costly in the currency of survival. He wondered how the brilliant plumage of peacocks could evolve, and become more common, when it poses such an obvious threat to survival, acting as an open lure to predators. Darwin's answer was that the peacock's displays evolved because they led to an individual's reproductive success, providing an advantage in the competition for a desirable mate and continuing that peacock's genetic line. The evolution of characteristics because of their reproductive benefits, rather than survival benefits, is known as sexual selection.

Sexual selection, according to Darwin, takes two forms. In one form, members of the same sex compete with each other, and the outcome of their contest gives the winner greater sexual access to members of the sex. Two stags locking horns in combat is the prototypical image of this intrasexual competition. The characteristics that lead to success in contests of this kind, such as greater strength, intelligence, or attractiveness to allies, evolve because the victors are able to mate more often and pass on more genes. In the other type of sexual selection, members of one sex choose a mate based on their preferences for particular qualities in that mate. These characteristics evolve in the other sex because animals possessing them are chosen more often as mates, and their genes thrive. Animals lacking the desired characteristics are excluded from mating and their genes perish. Since peahens prefer peacocks with plumage that flashes and glitters, dull-feathered males get left in the evolutionary dust. Peacocks today possess brilliant plumage because over evolutionary history peahens have preferred to mate with dazzling and colorful males.

Darwin's theory of sexual selection begins to explain mating behavior by identifying two key processes by which evolutionary change can occur: preferences for a mate and competition for a mate. But the theory was vigorously resisted by male scientists for over a century, in part because the active choosing of mates seemed to grant too much power to females, who were thought to remain passive in the mating process. The theory of sexual selection was also resisted by mainstream social scientists because its portrayal of human nature seemed to depend on instinctive behavior, and thus to minimize the uniqueness and flexibility of humans. Culture and consciousness were presumed to free us from evolutionary forces. The breakthrough in applying sexual selection to humans came in the late 1970s and 1980s, in the form of theoretical advances initiated by my colleagues and me in the fields of psychology and anthropology. We tried to identify underlying psychological mechanisms that were the products of evolution—mechanisms that help to explain both the extraordinary flexibility of human behavior and the active mating strategies pursued by women and men. This new discipline is called evolutionary psychology.

When I began work in the field, however, little was known about actual human mating behavior. There was a frustrating lack of scientific evidence on mating in the broad array of human populations, and practically no documented support for grand evolutionary theorizing. No one knew whether some mating desires are universal, whether certain sex differences are characteristic of all people in all cultures, or whether culture exerts a powerful enough influence to override the evolved preferences that might exist. So I departed from the traditional path of mainstream psychology to explore which characteristics of human mating behavior would follow from evolutionary principles. In the beginning, I simply wanted to verify a few of the most obvious evolutionary predictions about sex differences in mating preferences; for example, whether men desire youth and physical attractiveness in a mate and whether women desire status and economic security. Toward that end, I interviewed and administered questionnaires to 186 married adults and 100 unmarried college students within the United States.

The next step was to verify whether the psychological phenomena uncovered by this study were characteristic of our species. If mating desires and other features of human psychology are products of our evolutionary history, they should be found universally, not just in the United States. So I initiated an international study to explore how mates are selected in other cultures, starting with a few European countries, including Germany and the Netherlands. I soon realized, however, that since European cultures share many features, they do not provide the most rigorous test for the principles of evolutionary psychology. Over a period of five years, I expanded the study to include fifty collaborators from thirty-seven cultures located on six continents and five islands, from Australia to Zambia. We sampled large cities, such as Rio de Janeiro and Sao Paulo in Brazil, Shanghai in China, Bangalore and Ahmadabad in India, Jerusalem and Tel Aviv in Israel, and Tehran in Iran. We also sampled rural peoples, including Indians in the state of Gujarat and Zulus in South Africa. All major racial groups, religious groups, and ethnic groups were represented. In all, we surveyed 10,047 persons worldwide.

To explore as many mating domains as possible, I launched over fifty new studies, involving thousands of individuals. Included in these studies were men and women searching for a mate in singles bars and on college campuses, dating couples at various stages of commitment, newlywed couples in the first five years of marriage, and couples who ended up divorced.

The findings from all of these studies caused controversy and confusion among my colleagues, because in many respects they contradicted conventional thinking. They forced a radical shift from the standard view of men's and women's sexual psychology. One of my aims is to formulate from these diverse findings a unified theory of human mating, based not on romantic notions or outdated scientific theories but on current scientific evidence. Much of what I discovered about human mating is not nice. But a scientist cannot wish away unpleasant findings. Ultimately, the disturbing side of human mating must be confronted if its harsh consequences are ever to be ameliorated.

SEXUAL STRATEGIES

Strategies are methods for accomplishing goals, the means for solving problems. It may seem odd to view human mating, romance, sex, and love as inherently strategic. But we never choose mates at random. We do not attract mates indiscriminately. We do not derogate our competitors out of boredom. Our mating is strategic, and our strategies are designed to solve particular problems for successful mating. Understanding how people solve those problems requires an analysis of sexual strategies. Strategies are essential for survival on the mating battlefield.

Adaptations are evolved solutions to the problems posed by survival and reproduction. Over millions of years of evolution, natural selection has produced in us hunger mechanisms to solve the problem of providing nutrients to the organism; taste buds that are sensitive to fat and sugar to solve the problem of what to put into our mouths (nuts and berries, but not dirt or gravel); sweat glands and shivering mechanisms to solve the problems of extreme

hot and cold; emotions such as fear and rage that motivate flight and fight to combat predators or aggressive competitors; and a complex immune system to combat diseases and parasites. These adaptations are human solutions to the problems of existence posed by the hostile forces of nature—they are our survival strategies. Those who failed to develop appropriate characteristics failed to survive.

Correspondingly, sexual strategies are adaptive solutions to mating problems. Those in our evolutionary past who failed to mate successfully failed to become our ancestors. All of us descend from a long and unbroken line of ancestors who competed successfully for desirable mates, attracted mates who were reproductively valuable, retained mates long enough to reproduce, fended off interested rivals, and solved the problems that could have impeded reproductive success. We carry in us the sexual legacy of those success stories.

Each sexual strategy is tailored to a specific adaptive problem, such as identifying a desirable mate or besting competitors in attracting a mate. Underlying each sexual strategy are psychological mechanisms, such as preferences for a particular mate, feelings of love, desire for sex, or jealousy. Each psychological mechanism is sensitive to information or cues from the external world, such as physical features, signs of sexual interest, or hints of potential infidelity. Our psychological mechanisms are also sensitive to information about ourselves, such as our ability to attract a mate who has a certain degree of desirability. The goal is to peel back the layers of adaptive problems that men and women have faced in the course of mating and uncover the complex sexual strategies they have evolved for solving them.

Although the term *sexual strategies* is a useful metaphor for thinking about solutions to mating problems, it is misleading in the sense of connoting conscious intent. Sexual strategies do not require conscious planning or awareness. Our sweat glands are "strategies" for accomplishing the goal of thermal regulation, but they require neither conscious planning nor awareness of the goal. Indeed, just as a piano player's sudden awareness of her hands may impede performance, most human sexual strategies are best carried out without the awareness of the actor.

SELECTING A MATE

Nowhere do people have an equal desire for all members of the opposite sex. Everywhere some potential mates are preferred, others shunned. Our sexual desires have come into being in the same way as have other kinds of desires. Consider the survival problem of what food to eat. Humans are faced with a bewildering array of potential objects to ingest—berries, fruit, nuts, meat, dirt, gravel, poisonous plants, twigs, and feces. If we had no taste preferences and ingested objects from our environment at random, some people, by chance alone, would consume ripe fruit, fresh nuts, and other objects that provide caloric and nutritive sustenance. Others, also by chance alone, would eat rancid meat, rotten fruit, and toxins. Earlier humans who preferred nutritious objects survived.

Our actual food preferences bear out this evolutionary process. We show great fondness for substances rich in fat, sugar, protein, and salt and an aversion to substances that are bitter, sour, and toxic. These food preferences solve a basic problem of survival. We carry them with us today precisely because they solved critical adaptive problems for our ancestors.

Our desires in a mate serve analogous adaptive purposes, but their functions do not center simply on survival. Imagine living as our ancestors did long ago—struggling to keep warm by the fire; hunting meat for our kin; gathering nuts, berries, and herbs; and avoiding dangerous animals and hostile humans. If we were to select a mate who failed to deliver the resources promised, who had affairs, who was lazy, who lacked hunting skills, or who heaped physical abuse on us, our survival would be tenuous, our reproduction at risk. In contrast, a mate who

provided abundant resources, who protected us and our children, and who devoted time, energy, and effort to our family would be a great asset. As a result of the powerful survival and reproductive advantages that were reaped by those of our ancestors who chose a mate wisely, clear desires in a mate evolved. As descendants of those people, we carry their desires with us today.

Many other species have evolved mate preferences. The African village weaverbird provides a vivid illustration.[2] When the male weaverbird spots a female in the vicinity, he displays his recently built nest by suspending himself upside down from the bottom and vigorously flapping his wings. If the male passes this test, the female approaches the nest, enters it, and examines the nest materials, poking and pulling them for as long as ten minutes. As she makes her inspection, the male sings to her from nearby. At any point in this sequence she may decide that the nest does not meet her standards and depart to inspect another male's nest. A male whose nest is rejected by several females will often break it down and start over. By exerting a preference for males who can build a superior nest, the female weaverbird solves the problems of protecting and provisioning her future chicks. Her preferences have evolved because they bestowed a reproductive advantage over other weaverbirds who had no preferences and who mated with any males who happened along.

Women, like weaverbirds, prefer men with desirable "nests." Consider one of the problems that women in evolutionary history had to face: selecting a man who would be willing to commit to a long-term relationship. A woman in our evolutionary past who chose to mate with a man who was flighty, impulsive, philandering, or unable to sustain relationships found herself raising her children alone, without benefit of the resources, aid, and protection that another man might have offered. A woman who preferred to mate with a reliable man who was willing to commit to her was more likely to have children who survived and thrived. Over thousands of generations, a preference for men who showed signs of being willing and able to commit to them evolved in women, just as preferences for mates with adequate nests evolved in weaver-birds. This preference solved key reproductive problems, just as food preferences solved key survival problems.

People do not always desire the commitment required of long-term mating. Men and women sometimes deliberately seek a short-term fling, a temporary liaison, or a brief affair. And when they do, their preferences shift, sometimes dramatically. One of the crucial decisions for humans in selecting a mate is whether they are seeking a short-term mate or a long-term partner. The sexual strategies pursued hinge on this decision.

ATTRACTING A MATE

People who possess desirable characteristics are in great demand. Appreciating their traits is not enough for successful mating, just as spying a ripe berry bush down a steep ravine is not enough for successful eating. The next step in mating is to compete successfully for a desirable mate.

Among the elephant seals on the coast of California, males during the mating season use their sharp tusks to best rival males in head-to-head combat.[3] Often their contests and bellowing continue day and night. The losers lie scarred and injured on the beach, exhausted victims of this brutal competition. But the winner's job is not yet over. He must roam the perimeter of his harem, which contains a dozen or more females. This dominant male must hold his place in life's reproductive cycle by herding stray females back into the harem and repelling other males who attempt to sneak copulation.

Over many generations, male elephant seals who are stronger, larger, and more cunning have succeeded in getting a mate. The larger, more aggressive males control the sexual access to females and so pass on to their sons the genes conferring these qualities.

Female elephant seals prefer to mate with the victors and thus pass on the genes conferring this preference to their daughters. But by choosing the larger, stronger winners, they also determine the genes for size and fighting abilities that will live on in their sons. The smaller, weaker, and more timid males fail to mate entirely. Because only 5 percent of the males monopolize 85 percent of the females, selection pressures remain intense even today.

Male elephant seals must fight not just to best other males but also to be chosen by females. A female emits loud bellowing sounds when a smaller male tries to mate with her. The alerted dominant male comes bounding toward them, rears his head in threat, and exposes a massive chest. This gesture is usually enough to send the smaller male scurrying for cover. Female preferences are one key to establishing competition among the males. If females did not mind mating with smaller, weaker males, then they would not alert the dominant male, and there would be less intense selection pressure for size and strength. Female preferences, in short, determine many of the ground rules of the male contests.

People are not like elephant seals in most of these mating behaviors. For example, whereas only 5 percent of the male elephant seals do 85 percent of the mating, more than 90 percent of men are able at some point in their lives to find a mate.[4] Male elephant seals strive to monopolize harems of females, and the winners remain victorious for only a season or two, whereas many humans form enduring unions that last for years and decades. But men and male elephant seals share a key characteristic: both must compete to attract females. Males who fail to attract females risk being shut out of mating.

Throughout the animal world, males typically compete more fiercely than females for mates, and in many species males are certainly more ostentatious and strident in their competition. But competition among females is also intense in many species. Among patas monkeys and gelada baboons, females harass copulating pairs in order to interfere with the mating success of rival females. Among wild rhesus monkeys, females use aggression to interrupt sexual contact between other females and males, occasionally winning the male consort for herself. And among savanna baboons, female competition over mates serves not merely to secure sexual access but also to develop long-term social relationships that provide physical protection.[5]

Competition among women, though typically less florid and violent than competition among men, pervades human mating systems. The writer H. L. Mencken noted: "When women kiss, it always reminds one of prize fighters shaking hands." Members of each sex compete with each other for access to members of the opposite sex. The tactics they use to compete are often dictated by the preferences of the opposite sex. Those who do not have what the other sex wants risk remaining on the sidelines in the dance of mating.

KEEPING A MATE

Keeping a mate is another important adaptive problem; mates may continue to be desirable to rivals, who may poach, thereby undoing all the effort devoted to attracting, courting, and committing to the mate. Furthermore, one mate may defect because of the failure of the other to fulfill his or her needs and wants or upon the arrival of someone fresher, more compelling, or more beautiful. Mates, once gained, must be retained.

The problem of holding on to a mate is confronted by everyone who seeks a long-term relationship. In our evolutionary past, men who were indifferent to the sexual infidelities of their mates risked compromising their paternity. They risked investing time, energy, and effort in children who were not their own. Ancestral women, in contrast, did not risk the loss of parenthood if their mates had affairs, because maternity has always been 100 percent certain. But a woman with a philandering husband risked

losing his resources, his commitment, and his investment in her children. One psychological strategy that evolved to combat infidelity was jealousy. Ancestral people who became enraged at signs of their mate's potential defection and who acted to prevent it had a selective advantage over those who were not jealous. People who failed to prevent infidelity in a mate had less reproductive success.[6]

The emotion of jealousy motivates various kinds of action in overt response to a threat to the relationship. Sexual jealousy, for example, may produce either of two radically different actions, vigilance or violence. In one case, a jealous man might follow his wife when she goes out, call her unexpectedly to see whether she is where she said she would be, keep an eye on her at a party, or read her mail. These actions represent vigilance. In the other case, a man might threaten a rival whom he spotted with his wife, beat the rival with his fists, get his friends to beat up the rival, or throw a brick through the rival's window. These actions represent violence. Both courses of action, vigilance and violence, are different manifestations of the same psychological strategy of jealousy. They represent alternative ways of solving the problem of the defection of a mate.

Jealousy is not a rigid, invariant instinct that drives robotlike, mechanical action. It is highly sensitive to context and environment. Many other behavioral options are available to serve the strategy of jealousy, giving humans a flexibility in tailoring their responses to the subtle nuances of a situation.

REPLACING A MATE

Not all mates can be retained, nor should they be. Sometimes there are compelling reasons to get rid of a mate, such as when a mate stops providing support, withdraws sex, or starts inflicting physical abuse. Those who remain with a mate through economic hardship, sexual infidelity, and cruelty may win our admiration for their loyalty. But staying with a bad mate does not help a person successfully pass on genes. We are the descendants of those who knew when to cut their losses.

Getting rid of a mate has precedent in the animal world. Ring doves, for example, are generally monogamous from one breeding season to the next, but they break up under certain circumstances. The doves experience a divorce rate of about 25 percent every season; the major reason for breaking their bond is infertility.[7] When a ring dove fails to produce chicks with one partner during a breeding season, he or she leaves the mate and searches for another. Losing an infertile mate serves the goal of reproduction for ring doves better than remaining in a barren union.

Just as we have evolved sexual strategies to select, attract, and keep a good mate, we have also evolved strategies for jettisoning a bad mate. Divorce is a human universal that occurs in all known cultures. Our separation strategies involve a variety of psychological mechanisms. We have ways to assess whether the costs inflicted by a mate outweigh the benefits provided. We scrutinize other potential partners and evaluate whether they might offer more than our current mate. We gauge the likelihood of successfully attracting other desirable partners. We calculate the potential damage that might be caused to ourselves, our children, and our kin by the dissolution of the relationship. And we combine all this information into a decision to stay or leave.

Once a mate decides to leave, another set of psychological strategies is activated. Because such decisions have complex consequences for two sets of extended kin who often have keen interests in the union, breaking up is neither simple nor effortless. These complex social relationships must be negotiated, the breakup justified. The range of tactical options within the human repertoire is enormous, from simply packing one's bags and walking away to provoking a rift by revealing an infidelity.

Breaking up is a solution to the problem of a bad mate, but it opens up the new problem of replacing that mate. Like most mammals,

humans typically do not mate with a single person for an entire lifetime. Humans often reenter the mating market and repeat the cycle of selection, attraction, and retention. But starting over after a breakup poses its own unique set of problems. People reenter the mating market at a different age and with different assets and liabilities. Increased resources and status may help one to attract a mate who was previously out of range. Alternatively, older age and children from a previous mateship may detract from one's ability to attract a new mate.

Men and women undergo predictably different changes as they divorce and reenter the mating market. If there are children, the woman often takes primary responsibility for child rearing. Because children from previous unions are usually seen as costs rather than benefits when it comes to mating, a woman's ability to attract a desirable mate often suffers relative to a man's. Consequently, fewer divorced women than men remarry, and this difference between the sexes gets larger with increasing age.

CONFLICT BETWEEN THE SEXES

The sexual strategies that members of one sex pursue to select, attract, keep, or replace a mate often have the unfortunate consequence of creating a conflict with members of the other sex. Among the scorpionfly, a female refuses to copulate with a courting male unless he brings her a substantial nuptial gift, which is typically a dead insect to be consumed.[8] While the female eats the nuptial gift, the male copulates with her. During copulation, the male maintains a loose grasp on the nuptial gift, as if to prevent the female from absconding with it before copulation is complete. It takes the male twenty minutes of continuous copulation to deposit all his sperm into the female. Male scorpionflies have evolved the ability to select a nuptial gift that takes the female approximately twenty minutes to consume. If the gift is smaller and is consumed before copulation is completed, the female casts off the male before he has deposited all his sperm. If the gift is larger and takes the female more than twenty minutes to consume, the male completes copulation, and the two then fight over the leftovers. Conflict between male and female scorpionflies thus occurs over whether he gets to complete copulation when the gift is too small and over who gets to use the residual food resources when the gift is larger than needed.

Men and women also clash over resources and sexual access. In the evolutionary psychology of human mating, the sexual strategy adopted by one sex can trip up and conflict with the strategy adopted by the other sex in a phenomenon called strategic interference. Consider the differences in men's and women's proclivities to seek brief or lasting sexual relations. Men and women typically differ in how long and how well they need to know someone before they consent to sexual intercourse. Although there are many exceptions and individual differences, men generally have lower thresholds for seeking sex. For example, men often express the desire and willingness to have sex with an attractive stranger, whereas women almost invariably refuse anonymous encounters and prefer some degree of commitment.

There is a fundamental conflict between these different sexual strategies; men cannot fulfill their short-term wishes without simultaneously interfering with women's long-term goals. An insistence on immediate sex interferes with the requirement for a prolonged courtship. The interference is reciprocal, since prolonged courting also obstructs the goal of ready sex. Whenever the strategy adopted by one sex interferes with the strategy adopted by the other sex, conflict ensues.

Conflicts do not end with the wedding vows. Married women complain that their husbands are condescending, emotionally constricted, and unreliable. Married men complain that their wives are moody, overly dependent, and sexually withholding. Both sexes complain about infidelities, ranging from mild flirtations to serious affairs. All of these conflicts become understandable in the context of our evolved mating strategies.

Although conflict between the sexes is pervasive, it is not inevitable. There are conditions that minimize conflict and produce harmony between the sexes. Knowledge of our evolved sexual strategies gives us tremendous power to better our own lives by choosing actions and contexts that activate some strategies and deactivate others. Indeed, understanding sexual strategies, including the cues that trigger them, is one step toward the reduction of conflict between men and women.

CULTURE AND CONTEXT

Although ancestral selection pressures are responsible for creating the mating strategies we use today, our current conditions differ from the historical conditions under which those strategies evolved. Ancestral people got their vegetables from gathering and their meat from hunting, whereas modern people get their food from supermarkets and restaurants. Similarly, modern urban people today deploy their mating strategies in singles bars, at parties, through computer networks, and by means of dating services rather than on the savanna, in protected caves, or around primitive campfires. Whereas modern conditions of mating differ from ancestral conditions, the same sexual strategies operate with unbridled force. Our evolved psychology of mating remains. It is the only mating psychology we have; it just gets played out in a modern environment.

To illustrate, look at the foods consumed in massive quantities at fast food chains. We have not evolved any genes for McDonald's, but the foods we eat there reveal the ancestral strategies for survival we carry with us today. We consume in vast quantities fat, sugar, protein, and salt in the form of burgers, shakes, french fries, and pizzas. Fast food chains are popular precisely because they serve these elements in concentrated quantities. They reveal the food preferences that evolved in a past environment of scarcity. Today, however, we overconsume these elements because of their evolutionarily unprecedented abundance, and the old survival strategies now hurt our health. We are stuck with the taste preferences that evolved under different conditions, because evolution works on a time scale too slow to keep up with the radical changes of the past several hundred years. Although we cannot go back in time and observe directly what those ancestral conditions were, our current taste preferences, like our fear of snakes and our fondness for children, provide a window for viewing what those conditions must have been. We carry with us equipment that was designed for an ancient world.

Our evolved mating strategies, just like our survival strategies, may be currently maladaptive in the currencies of survival and reproduction. The advent of AIDS, for example, renders casual sex far more dangerous to survival than it ever was under ancestral conditions. Only by understanding our evolved sexual strategies, where they came from and what conditions they were designed to deal with, can we hope to change our current course.

One impressive advantage humans have over many other species is that our repertoire of mating strategies is large and highly sensitive to context. Consider the problem of being in an unhappy marriage and contemplating a decision to get divorced. This decision will depend upon many complex factors, such as the amount of conflict within the marriage, whether one's mate is philandering, the pressure applied by relatives on both sides of the family, the presence of children, the ages and needs of the children, and the prospects for attracting another mate. Humans have evolved psychological mechanisms that consider and weigh the costs and benefits of these crucial features of context.

Not only individual but also cultural circumstances vary in ways that are critical for evoking particular sexual strategies from the entire human repertoire. Some cultures have mating systems that are polygynous, allowing men to take multiple wives. Other cultures are polyandrous, allowing women to take multiple husbands. Still others are monogamous, restricting both sexes to one marriage partner at a time. And others are promiscuous, with a high rate of mate switching. Our evolved strategies of mating are highly sensitive to these legal and cultural patterns. In polygynous mating systems, for example, parents place tremendous pressure on their sons to compete for women in an apparent attempt to avoid the mateless state that plagues some men when others monopolize multiple women.[9] In monogamous mating cultures, in contrast, parents put less pressure on their sons' strivings.

Another important contextual factor is the ratio of the sexes, or the number of available men relative to available women. When there is a surplus of women, such as among the Ache Indians of Paraguay, men become more reluctant to commit to one woman, preferring instead to pursue many casual relationships. When there is a surplus of men, such as in contemporary cities of China and among the Hiwi tribe of Venezuela, monogamous marriage is the rule and divorce rates plummet.[10] As men's sexual strategies shift, so must women's, and vice versa. The two sets coexist in a complex reciprocal relation, based in part on the sex ratio.

From one perspective, context is everything. Contexts that recurred over evolutionary time created the strategies we carry with us now. Current contexts and cultural conditions determine which strategies get activated and which lie dormant.

BARRIERS TO UNDERSTANDING HUMAN SEXUALITY

Evolutionary theory has appalled and upset people since Darwin first proposed it in 1859 to explain the creation and organization of life. Lady Ashley, his contemporary, remarked upon hearing about his theory of our descent from nonhuman primates: "Let's hope that it's not true; and if it is true, let's hope that it does not become widely known." Strenuous resistance continues to this day. These barriers to understanding must be removed if we are to gain real insight into our sexuality.

One barrier is perceptual. Our cognitive and perceptual mechanisms have been designed by natural selection to perceive and think about events that occur in a relatively limited time-span—over seconds, minutes, hours, days, sometimes months, and occasionally years. Ancestral humans spent most of their time solving immediate problems, such as finding food, maintaining a shelter, keeping warm, selecting and competing for partners, protecting children, forming alliances, striving for status, and defending against marauders, so there was pressure to think in the short term. Evolution, in contrast, occurs gradually over thousands of generations in tiny increments that we cannot observe directly. To understand events that occur on time scales this large requires a leap of the imagination, much like the cognitive feats of physicists who theorize about black holes and eleven-dimensional universes they cannot see.

Another barrier to understanding the evolutionary psychology of human mating is ideological. From Spencer's theory of social Darwinism onward, biological theories have sometimes been used for political ends—to justify oppression, to argue for racial or sexual superiority. The history of misusing biological explanations of human behavior, however, does not justify jettisoning the most powerful theory of organic life we have. To understand human mating requires that we face our evolutionary heritage boldly and understand ourselves as products of that heritage.

Another basis of resistance to evolutionary psychology is the naturalistic fallacy, which maintains that whatever exists should exist. The naturalistic fallacy confuses a scientific description of human behavior with a moral prescription for that behavior. In nature, however, there are diseases, plagues, parasites, infant mortality, and a host of other natural events which we try to eliminate or reduce. The fact that they do exist in nature does not imply that they should exist.

Similarly, male sexual jealousy, which evolved as a psychological strategy to protect men's certainty of their paternity, is known to cause damage to women worldwide in the form of wife battering and homicide. As a society, we may eventually develop methods for reducing male sexual jealousy and its dangerous manifestations. Because there is an evolutionary origin for male sexual jealousy does not mean that we must condone or perpetuate it. Judgments of what should exist rest with people's value systems, not with science or with what currently exists.

The naturalistic fallacy has its reverse, the antinaturalistic fallacy. Some people have exalted visions of what it means to be human. According to one of these views, "natural" humans are at one with nature, peacefully coexisting with plants, animals, and each other. War, aggression, and competition are seen as corruptions of this essentially peaceful human nature by current conditions, such as patriarchy or capitalism. Despite the evidence, people cling to these illusions. The antinaturalistic fallacy occurs when we see ourselves through the lens of utopian visions of what we want people to be.

Opposition also arises to the presumed implications of evolutionary psychology for change. If a mating strategy is rooted in evolutionary biology, it is thought to be immutable, intractable, and unchangeable; we are therefore doomed to follow the dictates of our biological mandate, like blind, unthinking robots. This belief mistakenly divides human behavior into two separate categories, one biologically determined and the other environmentally determined. In fact, human action is inexorably a product of both. Every strand of DNA unfolds within a particular environmental and cultural context. Within each person's life, social and physical environments provide input to the evolved psychological mechanisms, and every behavior is without exception a joint product of those mechanisms and their environmental influences. Evolutionary psychology represents a true interactionist view which identifies the historical, developmental, cultural, and situational features that formed human psychology and guide that psychology today.

All behavior patterns can in principle be altered by environmental intervention. The fact that we can currently alter some patterns and not others is a problem only of knowledge and technology. Advances in knowledge bring about new possibilities for change, if change is desired. Humans are extraordinarily sensitive to changes in their environment, because natural selection did not create in humans invariant instincts that manifest themselves in behavior regardless of context. Identifying the roots of mating behavior in evolutionary biology does not doom us to an unalterable fate.

Another form of resistance to evolutionary psychology comes from the feminist movement. Many feminists worry that evolutionary explanations imply an inequality between the sexes, support restrictions on the roles that men and women can adopt, encourage stereotypes about the sexes, perpetuate the exclusion of women from power and resources, and foster pessimism about the possibilities for changing the status quo. For these reasons, feminists sometimes reject evolutionary accounts.

Yet evolutionary psychology does not carry these feared implications for human mating. In evolutionary terms, men and women are identical in many or most domains, differing only in the limited areas in which they have faced recurrently different adaptive problems over human evolutionary history. For example, they diverge primarily in their preference for a particular sexual strategy, not in their innate ability to exercise the full range of human sexual strategies.

Evolutionary psychology strives to illuminate men's and women's evolved mating behavior, not to prescribe what the sexes could be or should

be. Nor does it offer prescriptions for appropriate sex roles. It has no political agenda. Indeed, if I have any political stance on issues related to the theory, it is the hope for equality among all persons regardless of sex, regardless of race, and regardless of preferred sexual strategy; a tolerance for the diversity of human sexual behavior; and a belief that evolutionary theory should not be erroneously interpreted as implying genetic or biological determinism or impermeability to environmental influences.

A final source of resistance to evolutionary psychology comes from the idealistic views of romance, sexual harmony, and lifelong love to which we all cling. I cleave tightly to these views myself, believing that love has a central place in human sexual psychology. Mating relationships provide some of life's deepest satisfactions, and without them life would seem empty. After all, some people do manage to live happily ever after. But we have ignored the truth about human mating for too long. Conflict, competition, and manipulation also pervade human mating, and we must lift our collective heads from the sand to see them if we are to understand life's most engrossing relationships.

INTRODUCTION REFERENCE

Clark, R. D., III, and E. Hatfield. 1989. Gender differences in receptivity to sexual offers. *Journal of Psychology and Human Sexuality* 2: 39–5.

REFERENCES

1. Darwin, C. (1871). *The descent of man and selection in relation to sex.* London: Murray.
2. Collias, N. E., & Collias, E. C. (1970). The behavior of the West African village weaverbird. *Ibis, 112,* 457–480.
3. Le Boeuf, B. J. (1974). Male-male competition and reproductive success in elephant seals. *American Zoology, 14,* 163–176.
4. Vandenberg, S. (1972). Assortative mating, or who marries whom? *Behavior Genetics, 2,* 127–158.
5. Smuts, B. B. (1987). Sexual competition and mate choice. In B. B. Smuts, D. L. Cheney, R. M. Seyfarth, R. W. Wrangham, & T. T. Struhsaker (Eds.), *Primate*

societies (385–399). Chicago: University of Chicago Press.

6. Buss, D. M., Larsen, R. J., Westen, D., & Semmelroth, J. (1992). Sex differences in jealousy: Evolution, physiology, and psychology. *Psychological Science, 3,* 251–255.

7. Erickson, C. J., & Zenone, P. G. (1976). Courtship differences in male ring doves: Avoidance of cuckoldry? *Science, 192,* 1353–1354.

8. Thornhill, R. (1980). Mate choice in *Hylobittacus apicalis* (Insecta: Mecoptera) and its relation to some models of female choice. *Evolution, 34,* 519–538.

9. Low, B. S. (1989). Cross-cultural patterns in the training of children: An evolutionary perspective. *Journal of Comparative Psychology, 103,* 313–319.

10. Guttentag, M., & Secord, P. (1983). *Too many women?* Beverly Hills, CA: Sage.

PART II

Sexuality and the Life Cycle: Childhood and Adolescence

All the world's a stage and all the men and women merely players; They have their exits and their entrances; And one man in his time plays many parts, His acts being seven ages.

— *William Shakespeare*

William Shakespeare is one among many poets, prophets, and priests who have long proclaimed that the essence of life lies in its progression; that as individuals struggle to balance the inevitable intricacies of change and continuity, life is expressed. It was not until the latter part of the twentieth century that the multidisciplinary field of life-span development emerged from the disciplines of child development and developmental psychology. The study of the journey in human sexuality over the life span is the touchstone personally and professionally for those who seek a holistic understanding of sexuality.

Especially for the young, a life-cycle perspective of sexuality can lend continuity in a day characterized by disconnects. When using a life-span focus to understand the development of their psychosexual scripts, students may ask different questions that have somewhat surprising answers. For example, they may wonder, is it

possible to predict with whom I will have my longest sexual affair? Without referring to a crystal ball, scientists can answer this question. They can state the following fact with great accuracy: Your longest sexual affair will be with yourself. And, it will last a lifetime.

John DeLamater, a professor of sociology, and William Friedrich, a psychologist, teamed together to succinctly trace the tempestuous journey of human sexual development in the lead article of Part II. To do this in a coherent way, they divided the sexual life cycle into childhood (birth–7 years); preadolescence (8–12 years); adolescence (13–19 years); adulthood; and the period of aging, when adulthood fades into the latter part of life. This last stage occurs anywhere from age 40–60 when the periods of menopause for females and andropause for males signal that a fully evident aging process has begun. Because of their professional backgrounds, DeLamater and Friedrich were uniquely qualified to summarize the empirical research about the biological, sociological, and behavioral factors that impact human sexual development throughout life. Information in this chapter provides a needed overview for students of sexuality who are interested in relationships, sexuality, and the life cycle—all issues that are raised in the readings that follow in Parts II, III, IV and VI.

Robert Francoeur begins with the headwaters of life, the childhood and adolescent years that are significant in the development of psychosexual scripts. As such, they offer watershed opportunities for promoting healthy attitudes and behaviors about sexuality, a central core that touches every aspect of a person's being. But, conversely, when the headwaters are troubled, it is difficult to calm the downstream flow. For this reason, family life cycle and developmental theorists focus on the importance of the formative years in their efforts to understand human behavior. Defining childhood operationally as any time between infancy and the point at which the individual becomes a sexually mature adult, Francoeur broadens his topic beyond the years that are typically considered to be the childhood years.

His thesis that normative religious doctrines—the attitudes, values, and doctrines endorsed by a culture, society, and parents—are central factors in the psychosexual development throughout one's formative years is hardly debatable. However, what he so richly portrays about this topic will leave readers with an informed awareness of the lack of childhood sexual ethics in most religious traditions.

A neglected research arena is highlighted with an important study by Paul Okami, Richard Olmstead, Paul Abramson, and Laura Pendleton about the long-term effects of early childhood exposure to parental nudity and to the "primal scene." The authors tap into 18 years of longitudinal data from the UCLA Family Lifestyles Project to clarify what some clinicians and child development experts have postulated to be potentially harmful experiences in childhood. A major contribution of this important study is the review of the research literature that reveals a lack of empirical support for such claims. Particularly those students who bring an awareness of family systems theory to the Okami et al. reading may be puzzled by the authors' assertion

that their specific findings were not predicted by any theory with which they were familiar. Nevertheless, readers who understand developmental theory and psychosexual development throughout the formative years, emphasized in the beginning selections, may be better able to formulate questions for future research because of this study. Further, the results of this research may quiet alarmists whose references to phrases like "the emotional incest syndrome," "maternal seductress," and "sexualized attention" feed the paperback tradition of empirically unsubstantiated theories that abound in the popular genre. Then again, perhaps, it will not.

An exciting addition to Part II is from a well-researched book by sociologist Mark Regnerus with the alluring title, *Forbidden Fruit: Sex & Religion in the Lives of American Teenagers*. A variety of research methods were used to collect the data, including the National Survey of Youth and Religion (NSYR), of which the author was co-investigator. The NSYR was a national random-digit-dial telephone survey of a sample of all U.S. household telephone numbers, resulting in 3,370 adolescent and parent interviews. Personal interviews were also conducted with 267 teenagers who had completed the telephone survey. The second source of extensive data for the book was from the National Longitudinal Study of Adolescent Health, arguably the most comprehensive survey of adolescents and young adults ever accomplished.

The chapter chosen for inclusion here, "Imitation Sex and the New Middle-Class Morality," reveals a religious and social class patterning of sexual activity preference and a middle-class morality. Regnerus believes the new patterns of behavior are not about religion or abstinence, but rather about risk reduction, safeguarding one's future, and sexual substitution. The technical virginity debate surrounding oral and anal sex is explored in this chapter along with the influence of pornography, an industry believed to have outgrossed the box office receipts of all Hollywood films combined since the 1990s (Thio, 2001). This well-researched scholarly work details an intriguing subject that will stimulate student thinking, if not controversy.

The reporting of case studies in Pamela Erickson's chapter about Latino adolescent mothers differs significantly from research that has been characterized as "endless statistics in endless articles about endless teenage pregnancies." This selection should be of substantial interest to readers specifically because it is a different approach to gathering data: case studies of life-history interviews with 40 young Latino adolescent mothers and their partners. Such qualitative data in the literature are relatively rare because interviews are much more time consuming than are other methods of data collection, such as survey data, and also because qualitative data are more difficult to analyze.

Reviewers and editors often claim that "lack of rigor" in qualitative data produces results "too soft" to merit their inclusion in professional journals, an argument that rephrased means there are no "endless statistics" with which to formulate results and conclusions. Although all professionals in the research arena have a responsibility to maintain the highest standards of excellence for self and others in the discipline, students must learn that differences in research methods are not to be mistaken for deficiencies. Instead, embracing the diversity in methods of research so aptly demonstrated by Erickson in this chapter affirms the mutual quest for excellence, an important lesson for future researchers as well as those who are research consumers.

REFERENCE

Thio, A. 2001. *Deviant behavior*, 6th ed. Boston: Allyn and Bacon.

CHAPTER 6

Human Sexual Development

John D. DeLamater
William N. Friedrich

Have you checked your sexual health today? The issue of sexual health just might be the unspoken agenda of this selection by DeLamater and Friedrich, an important work that described the stages in the human sexual development process. In the absence of an instant sexual-health meter, we are left to our own devices in assessing how we are doing on this front. In actuality, a thorough check-up would follow a somewhat circuitous route that along the way must consider our sexual gender, sexual identity, sexual attitudes, and sexual behavior. Not only are all of these factors shaping forces, but more important, our subjective feelings about them may be the most significant markers of our sexual health.

By university age, most peoples' gender and sexual identities are fully formed and, thus, can be more objectively observed than can their sexual attitudes and behavior be assessed. As you read the developmental tasks that are to be achieved in childhood, preadolescence, adolescence, adulthood, and later life, ask yourself How am I doing thus far? In reading about the childhood years, for example, several questions may occur to you. At what childhood age did I become aware that cultural norms prohibited freedom of sexual play?

Who was important to me in the formation of my gender identity, or in my sense of femaleness or maleness? At what age did I begin to be socialized to the gender-role norms of society, learning how females and males are expected to behave? Are there specific sexual experiences from my childhood that are guilt-inducing? And if so, how have they influenced my adult life? Certainly, a thorough reading of this article will contribute to your understanding of human sexual development. But, on a more personal note, it could also lead to insight that would illuminate one of the most important journeys you will ever take with yourself: enhanced sexual health.

Empirical research by scholars from several disciplines provides the basis for an outline of the process of sexual development. The process of achieving sexual maturity begins at conception and ends at death. It is influenced by biological maturation/aging, by progression through the socially-defined stages of childhood, adolescence, adulthood, and later life, and by the person's relationships with others, including family members, intimate partners, and friends. These forces shape the person's gender and sexual identities, sexual attitudes, and sexual behavior. Adults display their sexuality in a variety of lifestyles, with heterosexual marriage being the most common. This diversity contributes to the vitality of society. Although changes in

From "Human Sexual Development" by J. DeLamater and W. N. Friedrich. 2002. *The Journal of Sex Research 39*: 10–14. Reprinted by permission of the publisher (Taylor & Francis, http://www.informaworld.com).

sexual functioning in later life are common, sexual interest and desire may continue until death.

Human beings are sexual beings throughout their entire lives. At certain points in life, sexuality may manifest itself in different ways. Each life stage brings with it pressures for change and sexual development milestones to be achieved if sexual health is to be attained or maintained. The stages of sexual development are a human developmental process involving biological and behavioral components.

Childhood (Birth to 7 Years)

The capacity for a sexual response is present from birth. Male infants, for example, get erections, and vaginal lubrication has been found in female infants in the 24 hours after birth (Masters, Johnson, & Kolodny, 1982). Infants have been observed fondling their genitals. The rhythmic manipulation associated with adult masturbation appears at ages 2 1/2 to 3 (Martinson, 1994). This is a natural form of sexual expression (Friedrich, Fisher, Broughton, Houston, & Shafran, 1998). Children engage in a variety of sexual play experiences while very young; this play becomes increasingly covert as the child ages (ages 6 to 9) and becomes aware of cultural norms (Reynolds, Herbenick, & Bancroft, in press). Infants and young children have many other sensual experiences, including sucking on their fingers and toes, and being rocked and cuddled. These experiences may establish preferences for certain kinds of stimulation that persist throughout life.

The quality of relationships with parents is also very important to the child's capacity for sexual and emotional relationships later in life. Typically, an attachment or bond forms between the infant and parent(s) (Bowlby, 1965). It is facilitated by positive physical contact. If this attachment is stable, secure, and satisfying, positive emotional attachments in adulthood are more likely (Goldberg, Muir, Kerr, 1995).

Early childhood is also the period during which each child forms a gender identity, a sense of maleness or femaleness. This identity is typically formed by age 3. The child is simultaneously being socialized according to the gender-role norms of the society, learning how males and females are expected to behave (Bussey & Bandura, 1999).

Between the ages of 3 and 7, there is a marked increase in sexual interest and activity. Children form a concept of marriage or long-term relationships; they practice adult roles as they "play house." They also learn that there are genital differences between males and females (Goldman & Goldman, 1982), and show interest in the genitals of other children and adults as part of their natural curiosity about the world. Children may engage in heterosexual play, including "playing doctor." There is little impact of childhood sex play on sexual adjustment at ages 17 and 18 (Okami, Olmstead, & Abramson, 1997). In response to such play, some parent teach children not to touch the bodies of others, and restrict conversation about sex. As a result, children turn to their peers for information about sex (Martinson, 1994).

Preadolescence (8 to 12 Years)

In this period, children have a social organization that is homosocial; that is, the social division of males and females into separate groups (Thorne, 1993). One result of this is that sexual exploration and learning at this stage is likely to involve persons of the same gender.

During this period, more children gain experience with masturbation. About 40 percent of the women and 38 percent of the men in a sample of college students recall masturbating before puberty (Bancroft, Herbenick, & Reynolds, in press). Adolescents report that their first experience of sexual attraction occurred at age 10 to 12 (Bancroft et al., in press; Rosario et al., 1996), with first experience of sexual fantasies occurring several months to 1 year later.

Group dating and heterosexual parties emerge at the end of this period. These experiences begin the process of developing the capacity to sustain intimate relationships.

ADOLESCENCE (13 TO 19 YEARS)

Biological Development

The biological changes associated with puberty, the time during which there is sudden enlargement and maturation of the gonads, other genitalia, and secondary sex characteristics (Tanner, 1967), lead to a surge of sexual interest. These changes begin as early as 10 years of age to as late as 14 years of age, and include rises in levels of sex hormones, which may produce sexual attraction and fantasies. Bodily changes include physical growth, growth in genitals and girls' breasts, and development of facial and pubic hair. These changes signal to the youth and to others that she or he is becoming sexually mature.

Whereas biological changes, especially increases in testosterone levels, create the possibility of adult sexual interactions, social factors interact with them, either facilitating or inhibiting sexual expression (Udry, 1988). Permissive attitudes regarding sexual behavior and father absence for girls are associated with increased masturbation and heterosexual intercourse, whereas church attendance and long-range educational and career plans are associated with lower levels of sexual activity. Many males begin masturbating between ages 13 and 15, whereas the onset among females is more gradual (Bancroft et al., in press).

Sexual Behavior

Toward the middle and end of adolescence, more young people engage in heterosexual intercourse: In 1999, 48 percent of females and 52 percent of males in grades 9 to 12 reported engaging in intercourse (CDC, 2000). Women today are engaging in intercourse for the first time at younger ages, compared with young women 30 years ago (Trussell & Vaughn, 1991). Patterns of premarital intercourse vary by ethnic group. African Americans have sex for the first time, on average, at 15.5 years; Cuban Americans and Puerto Ricans at 16.6 years, and Mexican Americans and Whites at 17 years; in each group, men begin having intercourse at younger ages than women (Day, 1992). These variations reflect differences between these groups in family structure (intact family), church attendance, and socioeconomic opportunities (parents' education, neighborhood employment rates).

These rates of premarital heterosexual intercourse are connected to two long-term trends. First, the age of menarche has been falling steadily since the beginning of the twentieth century. The average age today is 12.5 years for Blacks and 12.7 years for Whites (Hofferth, 1990). Second, the age of first marriage has been rising—in 1960, first marriages occurred at age 20.8 for women and 22.8 for men; in 1998, it was 25 for women and 26.7 for men (U.S. Bureau of the Census, 1999). The effect is a substantial lengthening of the time between biological readiness and marriage; the gap is typically 12 to 14 years today. Thus, many more young people are having sex before they get married than in 1960. Since many do not consistently use birth control, there was a corresponding rise in the rate of pregnancy among single adolescents from the 1970s to 1991; however, from 1991 to 1997 the rate of teen pregnancy declined 18 percent. This decline reflects increased attention in society to the importance of pregnancy prevention, increased access for teens to birth control, and increased economic opportunities for teenagers (Ventura, Mosher, Curtin, Abma, & Henshaw, 1998).

Between 5 percent and 10 percent of adolescent males report having sexual experiences with someone of the same gender, compared with 6 percent of adolescent females (Bancroft et al., in press; Turner et al., 1998). These adolescents usually report that their first experience was with another adolescent. In some cases the person has only one or a few such experiences, partly out of curiosity, and the behavior is discontinued.

Developmental Tasks

Several psychosocial developmental tasks face adolescents. One is resolving the conflict between identity and role confusion, developing a stable sense of who one is in the midst of conflicting social influences (Erikson, 1968). Gender identity is a very important aspect of identity; in later adolescence, the young person may emerge with a stable, self-confident sense of manhood or womanhood, or alternatively, may feel in conflict about gender roles. A sexual identity also emerges—a sense that one is heterosexual, homosexual, or bisexual, and a sense of one's attractiveness to others.

Another task of adolescence is learning how to manage physical and emotional intimacy in relationships with others (Collins & Sroufe, 1999). Youth ages 10 to 15 most frequently name the mass media, including movies, TV, magazines, and music, as their source of information about sex and intimacy. Smaller percentages name parents, peers, sexuality education programs, and professionals as sources (Kaiser Family Foundation, 1997).

ADULTHOOD

The process of achieving sexual maturity continues in adulthood. One task in this life stage is learning to communicate effectively with partners in intimate relationships; this is difficult for many persons, in part because there are few role models in our society showing us how to engage in direct, honest communication in such relationships. A second task is developing the ability to make informed decisions about reproduction and prevention of sexually transmitted infections, including HIV infection.

Sexual Lifestyle Options

Adults have several options with regard to sexual lifestyle. Some plan to remain single. They may remain celibate, participate in one long-term monogamous relationship, participate in sexual relationships with several persons, or engage in serial monogamy—a series of two or more relationships involving fidelity to the partner for the duration of each relationship. Among single persons, 26 percent of the men and 22 percent of the women report having sexual intercourse two or more times per week; 22 percent of the men and 30 percent of the women report not having sex in the preceding year (Laumann, Gagnon, Michael, & Michaels, 1994). Black men and women are more likely to remain single than their White counterparts; in 1999, 41 percent of Black men and 38 percent of Black women were never married, compared with 20 percent of White men and 16 percent of White women (U.S. Bureau of the Census, 2000). In part this reflects choice, but it also reflects the economic position of Blacks in American society. It is difficult for many Black men to find a job that provides the wages and benefits needed to support a family. Among Hispanics, 33 percent of men and 25 percent of women are never married (U.S. Bureau of the Census, 2000).

Living together is an option chosen by increasing numbers of couples. It is an important step in development not only because it represents commitment but because it is a public declaration of a sexual relationship. For some couples, cohabitation is an alternative to marriage. In 1999, 7 percent of all women were cohabiting (U.S. Bureau of the Census, 1999). These relationships tend to be shortlived; one third last less than 1 year, and only 1 out of 10 lasts 5 years (Bumpass et al., 1991).

Marriage is the most common sexual lifestyle in the United States. In 1999, 73 percent of men and 80 percent of women had been married at least once; by age 45, 95 percent of all women have married at least once (U.S. Bureau of the Census, 1999). Marriage is the social context in which sexual expression is thought to be most legitimate. The average couple engages in sexual intercourse 2 or 3 times per week (Laumann et al., 1994). At the same time, there is great variability in frequency. For example, 7 percent of couples report that they have not had coitus in the preceding year (Smith, 1994). Sexual frequency in marriage reflects the joint influence of biological and social factors. There is a decline in the frequency of intercourse with age (Smith, 1994). Biological factors include physical changes that affect sexual frequency, and chronic illnesses. Social factors include habituation to sex with the partner, and unhappiness with the relationship (Call, Sprecher, & Schwartz, 1995).

Couples report engaging in a variety of sexual activities in addition to vaginal intercourse, including oral-genital sexuality (70 percent of married men and 74 percent of married women), anal intercourse (27 percent and 21 percent), and hand-genital stimulation. Many adults continue to masturbate even though they are in a long-term relationship; 17 percent of married men and 5 percent of married women masturbate at least once a week (Laumann et al., 1994).

Sexual satisfaction with one's sexual relationship is an important component of sexual health. While many factors may contribute to satisfaction, three that differentiate people who are happy from those who are not are (a) accepting one's own sexuality, (b) listening to one's partner and being aware of the partner's likes and dislikes, and (c) talking openly and honestly (Maurer, 1994). In other words, successfully completing the developmental tasks of adolescence and young adulthood are keys to sexual health.

Most couples will experience fundamental changes in their sexual experience at least once over the course of the relationship. The change may result from developing greater understanding of oneself or partner, changes in communication patterns, accidents or illnesses that interfere with one's sexual responsiveness, or major stressors associated with family or career. Some couples will need professional support to enable them to successfully cope with these forces. Some relationships will not survive.

Extramarital sexual activity is reported by 25 percent of married men and 15 percent of married women (Laumann et al., 1994). Many of these persons will only engage in this activity once while they are married. The incidence varies by ethnicity; 27 percent of Blacks report extramarital sexual activity, compared with 14 percent of Whites (Smith, 1994). Hispanics have the same incidence as Whites (Laumann et al., 1994). Several reasons have been suggested for extramarital relationships, including dissatisfaction with marital sexuality, dissatisfaction with or conflicts in the marriage, and placing greater emphasis on personal growth and pleasure than on fidelity (Lawson, 1988).

Persons who lose their partner through divorce or death have the option of postmarital sexual relationships. Most divorced women, but fewer widows, develop an active sex life; 28 percent of divorced women and 81 percent of the widowed reported being sexually abstinent in the preceding year (Smith, 1994). By gender, 46 percent of divorced and widowed men and 58 percent of divorced and widowed women reported engaging in sexual intercourse a few times or not at all in the preceding year (Laumann et al., 1994). There is a higher probability of being sexually active postmaritally for those who are under 35 and those who have no children in the home (Stack & Gundlach, 1992).

Divorced persons, especially women, face complex problems of adjustment. These problems may include reduced income, lower perceived standard of living, the demands of single parenthood, and reduced availability of social support (Amato, 2001). These problems may increase the motivation to quickly reestablish a relationship with a partner.

Some adults engage in sexual activities that involve risks to their physical health, such as STIs and HIV infection. Examples of such activities include engaging in vaginal or anal intercourse without using condoms, engaging in sexual activity with casual partners, and engaging in sex with multiple partners. Since 1985 there has been substantial publicity about these risks. Have adults changed their sexual behavior to reduce their risk? Between 1981 and 1991, men who have sex with men reported reducing the number of partners, having fewer anonymous encounters, and engaging less often in anal intercourse or using condoms consistently (Ehrhardt, Yingling, & Warne, 1991). Among heterosexuals, the number of single adults who report having multiple partners has declined (Smith, 1991), and condom use by men and women at risk has increased (Catania, Canchola, Binson, Dolcini, & Paul, 2001).

SEXUALITY AND AGING

Biological Changes

Biology, a major influence in childhood and adolescence, again becomes a significant influence on sexual health at midlife.

In women, menopause—the cessation of menstruation—is associated with a decline in the production of estrogen; this occurs, on the average, over a 2-year period beginning around age 50 (it can begin at any age from 40 to 60). The decline in estrogen is associated with several changes in the sexual organs. The walls of the vagina become thin and inelastic. Further, the vagina shrinks in both width and length. These changes may make penile insertion more difficult, and intercourse uncomfortable. By 5 years after menopause, the amount of vaginal lubrication often decreases noticeably. Intercourse may become more difficult and painful. There are a number of ways to deal with these changes successfully, including estrogen-replacement therapy, supplemental testosterone, and use of a sterile lubricant.

As they age, men experience andropause (Lamberts, van den Beld, & van der Lely, 1997) or ADAM—androgen decline in the aging male (Morales, Heaton, & Carson, 2000), a gradual decline in the production of testosterone; this may begin as early as age 40. Erections occur more slowly. The refractory period, the period following orgasm during which the person cannot be sexually aroused, lengthens. These changes may be experienced as problems; on the other hand, they may be experienced as allowing the man greater control over orgasm.

These biological changes in women and men do not preclude satisfying sexual activity. Among older people who are healthy and active and have regular opportunities for sexual expression, sexual activity in all forms including masturbation and same-gender behavior-continues past 74 years of age (AARP, 1999).

Social Influences

An important influence on sexuality is the attitudes of others, especially those attitudes that define specific behaviors as acceptable or unacceptable. This is especially evident with regard to older persons. American society has a negative attitude toward sexual expression among the elderly. It seems inappropriate for two 75-year-old people to engage in intercourse, and especially inappropriate for persons of that age to masturbate. These negative attitudes are particularly obvious in nursing homes and care facilities where rules prohibit or staff members frown upon sexual activity among the residents. These attitudes affect the way the elderly are treated, and the elderly may hold such attitudes themselves. These attitudes may be a more important reason why many elderly people are not sexually active than the biological changes they experience.

SUMMARY

Human sexual development is a process that begins at conception and ends at death. The principal forces are biological maturation/aging; progression through the socially defined stages of childhood, adolescence, adulthood, and later life; and one's social relationships during each of these stages. These forces interact to influence the person's sexual identity, sexual attitudes, and sexual behavior. While similarities can be identified in the lives and sexual expression of many people, there is wide variation in sexual attitudes, behaviors, and lifestyles.

This diversity contributes to the vitality of society.

REFERENCES

Amato, P. (2001). The consequences of divorce for children and adults. In R. Milardo (Ed.), *Understanding families into the new millennium: A decade in review* (pp. 433–465). Minneapolis, MN: National Council on Family Relations.

American Association of Retired Persons. (1999). *AARP/Modern Maturity sexuality study.* Atlanta, GA: NFO Research, Inc.

Bancroft, J., Herbenick, D., & Reynolds, M. (In press). *Masturbation as a marker of sexual development In J. Bancroft (Ed.), Sexual development.* Bloomington, IN: Indiana University Press.

Bowlby, J. (1965). Maternal care and mental health. In J. Bowlby (Ed.), *Child care and the growth of love.* London: Penguin.

Bumpass, L. L., Sweet, J. A., & Cherlin, A. (1991). The role of cohabitation in declining rates of marriage. *Journal of Marriage and the Family, 53,* 913–927.

Bussey, K., & Bandura, A. (1999). Social cognitive theory of gender development and differentiation. *Psychological Review, 106,* 676–713.

Call, V., Sprecher, S., & Schwartz, P. (1995). The incidence and frequency of marital sex in a national sample. *Journal of Marriage and the Family, 57,* 639–652.

Catania, J. A., Canchola, J., Binson, D., Dolcini, M. M., & Paul, J. P. (2001). National trends in condom use among at-risk heterosexuals in the United States. *Journal of Acquired Immune Deficiency Syndromes, 27,* 176–182.

Centers for Disease Control and Prevention. (2000). Youth risk behavior surveillance-United States, 1999. *Morbidity and Mortality Weekly Report, 49,* SS–5.

Collins, W. A., & Sroufe, L. A. (1999). Capacity for intimate relationships: A developmental construction. In W. Furman, B. B. Brown, & C. Feiring (Eds.), *The development of romantic relationships in adolescence* (pp. 125–147). Cambridge, UK: Cambridge University Press.

Day, R. (1992). The transition to first intercourse among racially and culturally diverse youth. *Journal of Marriage and the Family, 54,* 749–762.

Ehrhardt, A. A., Yingling, S., & Warne, P. A. (1991). Sexual behavior in the era of AIDS: What has changed in the United States? *Annual Review of Sex Research, 2,* 25–48.

Erikson, E. H. (1968). *Identity: Youth and crisis.* New York: Norton.

Friedrich, W. N., Fisher, J., Broughton, D., Houston, M., & Shafran, C. R. (1998). Normative sexual behavior in children: A contemporary sample. *Pediatrics, 101,* e9.

Goldberg, S., Muir, R., & Kerr, J. (1995). *Attachment theory: Social, developmental, and clinical perspectives.* Hillsdale, NJ: Analytic Press.

Goldman, R. J., & Goldman, J. D. G. (1982). *Children's sexual thinking.* London: Routledge and Kegan Paul.

Hofferth, S. L. (1990). Trends in adolescent sexual activity, contraception, and pregnancy in the United States. In J. Bancroft & J. Reinisch (Eds.), *Adolescence and puberty* (pp. 217–233). New York: Oxford University Press.

Kaiser Family Foundation. (1997). *Talking with kids about tough issues.* Menlo Park, CA: Author.

Lamberts, S. W. J., van den Beld, A., & van der Lely, A. J. (1997). The endocrinology of aging. *Science, 278,* 419–424.

Laumann, E. O., Gagnon, J. H., Michael, R. T., & Michaels, S. (1994). *The social organization of sexuality: Sexual practices in the United States.* Chicago: The University of Chicago Press.

Lawson, A. (1988). *Adultery: An analysis of love and betrayal.* New York: Basic Books.

Martinson, F. M. (1994). *The sexual life of children.* Westport CT: Bergin and Garvey.

Masters, W. H., Johnson, V. E., & Kolodny, R. C. (1982). *Human sexuality.* Boston: Little, Brown

Maurer, H. (1994). *Sex: Real people talk about what they really do.* New York: Penguin Books.

Morales, A., Heaton, J. P. W., & Carson, C. C. (2000). Andropause: A misnomer for a true clinical entity. *Journal of Urology, 163,* 705–712.

Okami, P., Olmstead, R., & Abramson, P. (1997). Sexual experiences in early childhood: 18-year longitudinal data from the UCLA Family Lifestyles Project. *The Journal of Sex Research, 34,* 339–347.

Reynolds, M., Herbenick, D., & Bancroft, J. (in press). The nature of childhood sexual experience: Two studies 50 years apart. In J. Bancroft (Ed.), *Sexual development.* Bloomington, IN: Indiana University Press.

Rosario, M., Meyer-Bahlburg, H., Hunter, J., Exner, T., Swadz, M., & Keller, A. (1996). The psychosexual development of urban lesbian, gay and bisexual youths. *The Journal of Sex Research, 33,* 113–126.

Smith, T. W. (1991). Adult sexual behavior in 1989: Number of partners, frequency of intercourse, and risk of AIDS. *Family Planning Perspectives, 23*(3), 102–107.

Smith, T. W. (1994). The demography of sexual behavior. Menlo Park, CA: Kaiser Family Foundation.

Stack, S., & Gundlach, J. H. (1992). Divorce and sex. *Archives of Sexual Behavior, 21*, 359–368.

Tanner, J. M. (1967). Puberty. In A. McLaren (Ed.), *Advances in reproductive physiology* (Vol. II). New York: Academic Press.

Thorne, B. (1993). *Gender play: Girls and boys in school.* New Brunswick, NJ: Rutgers University Press.

Trussell, J., & Vaughn, B. (1991). *Selected results concerning sexual behavior and contraceptive use from the 1988 National Survey of Family Growth and the 1988 National Survey of Adolescent Males.* (Working Paper 91–12). Princeton, NJ: Office of Population Research.

Turner, C. F., Ku, L., Rogers, S. M., Lindberg, L. D., Pleck, J. H., & Sonenstein, F. L. (1998). Adolescent sexual behavior, drug use, and violence: Increased reporting with computer survey technology. *Science, 280,* 867–8.

Udry, J. R. (1988). Biological predispositions and social control in adolescent sexual behavior. *American Sociological Review, 53,* 709–722.

U.S. Bureau of the Census. (1999). *Statistical abstract of the United States, 1999.* Washington, DC: Author.

U.S. Bureau of the Census. (2000). *Statistical abstract of the United States, 2000.* Washington, DC: Author.

Ventura, S. J., Mosher, W. D., Curtin, S. A, Abma, J. C., & Henshaw, S. (2001). Trends in pregnancy rates for the United States, 1976–97. *National Vital Statistics Reports, 49*(4).

CHAPTER 7

Current Religious Doctrines of Sexual and Erotic Development in Childhood

Robert T. Francoeur

Students who wish to be informed about either religion and sexuality or childhood and sexuality will find Robert Francoeur's combination of the two concepts intriguing. The author, a university teacher of human sexuality with degrees in embryology, theology, and biology, is uniquely qualified to explore the relationship between religious doctrines and childhood sexuality. From his thorough literary review, he synthesizes current knowledge concerning the influence of religious doctrines as they relate to the sexual development of children. In so doing, he cuts a wide path through the doctrines of the major religious traditions in Western societies as they intersect with sexuality and childhood. Those whose interest extends to the Latino cultures of Latin America, the Islamic culture of the Middle East, or the Hindu, Buddhist, and Confucian Taoist cultures of the Far East are referred to the full text of his chapter.

Major points of interest are the various religious views toward sexual behaviors, such as masturbation, premarital sexual intimacy, and homosexuality. But perhaps of more importance to readers, the information may prompt an assessment of their own experiential data, gleaned from

"childhood sexuality lessons" via parents and religious leaders. Although a sample of one is admittedly less than scientific, each person is acutely aware of the significance of her/his own experiences in sexual scripting. Extrapolating from the broader context of adult beliefs and values as a model, Francoeur weaves plausible explanations of this scripting. For example, he postulates that parental efforts to prohibit, prevent, or punish natural sexual behavior in childhood and adolescence may vandalize the formation of normophilic lovemaps and promote the formation of paraphilic lovemaps. The review of Money's concept of the crucial periods of psychosexual development, through which the child passes in the preparation of her/his individual lovemap aids such an introspective journey.

Students may especially resonate to the carefully crafted thesis that as sexually mature single persons today, they are a new human subspecies. It is true that young adults today can claim that they had no ancestors to model appropriate sexual behaviors because the day in which they live is so uniquely characterized by socially prolonged adolescence and later marriages.

Though theoretical in nature, much of this information will be perceived as pragmatic, with tables particularly contributing to this end. The range of sexual moralities in different religious traditions, as related to their basic worldviews, are revealed in Table 7.1. In Table 7.2, the

From "Current Religious Doctrines of Sexual and Erotic Development in Childhood" by R. T. Francoeur. 1990. In *Handbook of Sexology: Vol. 7*, M. E. Perry, ed., 81–112. New York: Elsevier Science. Copyright © 1990, Elsevier Science. Reprinted by permission.

dichotomous "Hot and Cool Sex" paradigm, influenced by Western sexual values and behaviors, may strike a familiar chord with the parents of today's college students. The Francoeurs', earlier work (1974) furnishes a down-to-earth touch to an at times weighty offering. This treasury which traces independently developed paradigms from a variety of religious philosophies is a must-read for serious students of sexuality.

OBJECTIVE, DEFINITIONS, AND PREMISES

The purpose of this work is to summarize the relatively little information available on religious doctrines as they relate to and affect the sexual and erotic development of children in various contemporary cultures. The cultures surveyed are the Judaic, Christian (both Protestant and Catholic) and humanist traditions in Western societies.

Within this purview, certain premises need to be spelled out.

The child. The status of child is operationally and dynamically defined as including those phases of psychosexual development which occur between infancy and that point, somewhere after puberty, when the individual is socially recognized as a sexually mature adult.

Normative religious doctrines. This work assumes that the religious attitudes, values and doctrines endorsed by a culture, society and parents are a central factor in the psychosexual development of the child. Religious values and doctrines, both directly and indirectly, provide major affective and cognitive sources for establishing standards of acceptable and accepted behavior. Even when an individual, parent or society does not adhere to what would be termed a religious value system, as in the humanist tradition, the normative doctrines endorsed are usually articulated against the backdrop of a prevailing religious tradition.

Moreover, there is good evidence, both historical and contemporary, that in times of political and economic upheaval, societies commonly enlist religious doctrines, even to the point of creating new interpretations and rules, as a means of shoring up the status quo (1).

The dearth and derivative character of childhood sexual ethics. Religious traditions have seldom dealt with the sexual and erotic development of children as something of value in its own right. Childhood sexuality is seldom mentioned, let alone discussed in any detail, in religious studies and secular histories of sexuality.

Moreover, whatever is said about childhood sexuality in religious doctrines is, invariably, subordinate to and derived from the broader context of adult beliefs and values which focus on the pivotal adult sexual relationship, marriage. As the concept of marriage has changed in Europe and North America so have the doctrines about childhood sexuality derived from this adult model. When marriage was based on dynastic or political concerns, adolescent sexual relations were judged in terms of paternal property rights, the legitimacy of offspring and the avoidance of sexual behaviors that would complicate social organization. Premarital and extramarital erotic experiences may have been allowed, or even expected in this context. As the procreative function of marital sex decreased and dynastic/political concerns yielded increasingly to a norm of exclusive emotional and romantic bonding within marriage, so did the acceptability of extramartial erotic fulfillment wane (2–4).

The role of adult religious beliefs in sexual scripting. While Money has detailed the crucial periods or "gates" of psychosexual development through which the child passes after birth, a brief recapitulation here will situate our exploration of the role of parental religious beliefs in the psychosexual development of the child.

When parents first observe the sexual anatomy of their newborn infant and respond by assigning it a gender, as boy or girl, that gender of assignment triggers a sexually dimorphic scripting of the infant for masculine or feminine roles which, in part, reflects the religious beliefs and values of the parents and their adult society.

Infants quickly and spontaneously discover the sensuousness of their genitals. They explore their own bodies. They respond to the rhythmic pressure, squeezing, rubbing and touching that bring pleasurable sensations. In the process, many males and fewer females learn to masturbate. Young males also experience episodic nocturnal penile tumescence (NPT) on average three times per night, for a total duration of two to three hours. Later, during puberty, NPT will be enriched and associated with erotic dreams. Casual genital fondling and masturbatory activities are natural and common between ages three and five. Equally natural and common, when not inhibited or represented by adults, is the tendency of young children to engage in flirtatious rehearsal play with a parent or other older children of the opposite sex.

About age five, as the child's social context enlarges with the beginning of formal schooling, flirtatious play expands to incoporate boyfriend-girlfriend playmate romance. This is also the age when pelvic rocking or thrusting movements against the body of a partner while lying side by side gives way to the rehearsal play of coitus (5). In our repressed society, positioning rehearsal for coitus is frequently reduced to playing doctor and nurse.

In late childhood, prenatally encoded neural pathway tendencies are elaborated on by an unknown and variable combination of childhood and adolescent sexual fantasies, experiences and scriptings to determine the child's sexual orientation (status) and uniquely personal lovemap. At around age eight, pairbonding in a love affair may occur in a type of prepubertal mating rehearsal. Finally, with puberty, secondary sex characteristics make obvious the physical maturation of the child and its new sexual potential.

Parents are frequently oblivious of the many natural and spontaneous experiences of childhood psychosexual development. When,

however, these spontaneous explorations are observed, the parents become mentors and scriptors for what they consider sexually appropriate for children. Given the strong antisexual biases of Western societies, these natural explorations, sexual responses and masturbatory activity are frequently short-circuited because the parental religious beliefs judge these activities sinful and forbidden.

Parental efforts to prohibit, prevent or punish this natural behavior may well vandalize the formation of normophilic lovemaps and promote the formation of paraphilic lovemaps in early childhood and preadolescence, when nurturance or the lack of it elaborates on and reinforces neural templates laid down in the brain before birth (6).

A new human subspecies. In non-technological societies, the physical maturation of puberty is commonly marked with a rite of passage to adulthood which confers and celebrates all the sexual rights and responsibilities that status carries in a particular society. In the technological West, this concurrence has been radically disassociated by socioeconomic changes. In the days of Romeo and Juliet, marriages were arranged by the parents before their children entered sexual maturity, which came in the late teens. In this context, the prolonged period of adolescence we know today did not exist. Thus, adolescent sexual relations, premarital sex, were of minor concern to religious thinkers.

As the Industrial Revolution progressed, the length of adolescence was extended and children no longer married in their early teens. From the late nineteenth century on, the growing emphasis on public education reinforced the social prolongation of adolescence and later marriages. In the midtwentieth century, the advent of effective and convenient contraceptives culminated in the emergence of a new human subspecies, the sexually mature single person. Unfortunately, religious rites of passage which traditionally acknowledged adult status and responsibilities at puberty, Jewish bar (bat) mitzvah and Christian confirmation, remained devoid of any recognition of this new separation of sexual maturation and marriage.

The period of adolescence is a Western phenomenon. In it, the young person is sexuoerotically capable but socially prohibited from entering the marital state where he/she could legitimately express sexual drives and needs. This new subspecies, the sexually mature single and legally dependent adolescent, has created new questions of sexual morality with which religious groups are only just beginning to deal (7–8). The advent of sexuoerotic drives and interests at puberty and the postponement of adult status leaves the adolescent in a state of limbo. The adolescent's growing need for self-actualizing independence, erotic and romantic fantasies, erotic drives and early erotic experiences with self and others is immediate and real.

The tensions of this transition are evident in Piaget's model of moral development as the child moves from a heteronomous stage based on total acceptance of a morality imposed by others to an autonomous stage in which sexual and other norms are internalized in a morality of cooperation. Kohlberg has proposed a similar, more detailed model with a transition from a conventional morality based on conformity to societal and parental norms to the social contract and universal ethical principles of a postconventional morality (9–11). An application of these models to religious institutions appears at the end of the next section.

THE VALUE SPECTRUM WITHIN RELIGIOUS DENOMINATIONAL DOCTRINES

Although religious value systems are quite varied, their doctrines and norms focus primarily on the adult and adult relationships in marriage, the family and the world outside. Children are addressed mainly in terms of initiation rituals such as baptism and their education for adult responsibilities. Because of this, any discussion of religious doctrines related to childhood sexuality must begin with an analysis of adult religious doctrines.

Recent efforts to analyze doctrinal systems have revealed two distinct world philosophies (weltanschauungs) tenuously coexisting for centuries within the Judaic, Christian, Islamic and Hindu traditions. This author is not aware of evidence of a similar coexistent dualism of world views in the other religious traditions examined here, but the conclusion of Mayr is that no greater revolution has occurred in the history of human thought than the radical shift from a fixed cosmology rooted in unchanging archetypes to a dynamic, evolving cosmogenic world view based on populations and individuals (12). While the process or evolutionary world view may be gaining dominance in Western cultures and religious traditions, the Moral Majority and religious New Right in the United States, and the growing vitality of orthodox Judaism provide ample evidence that the fixed world view still has a clear influence in moderating human behavior (13–15).

Ideologically, the fixed and process world views are at the two ends of a continuum or spectrum that includes a wide range of approaches to moral and sexual issues. While individuals often take a fixed position on one issue and a process position on a second issue, these general categories are instructive when examining the impact of religious doctrines on childhood sexuality because individuals generally tend to adopt one or the other approach and maintain a fairly consistent set of intertwined religious values and attitudes.

Religious doctrines, and their adherents, can be divided by the weltanschauung which underlies their religious beliefs and doctrines. Either the world is a completely finished universe in which human nature was created by some supreme being, perfect, complete and unchanging in essence from the beginning, or the world is a universe characterized by continual change with human nature constantly evolving as it struggles to reach its fuller potential or what it is called upon to become by the deity. Either one believes that the first human beings were created by God as unchanging archetypes, thus determining standards of human behavior for all time, or one believes that human nature, behavior and moral standards have been evolving since the beginning of the human race. In the former view, a supreme being created human nature; in the latter view, the deity is creating human nature with human collaboration.

Deriving from these two views of the world and human nature, one finds two distinct views of the world and human nature, one finds two distinct views of the origins of evil and sexuality. If one believes that human nature, the purposes of sexuality and the nature of sexual relations were established in the beginning, then one also finds it congenial to believe that evil results from some original sin, a primeval fall of the first humans from a state of perfection and grace. If, on the other hand, one believes in an evolving human nature, then physical and moral evils are viewed as the inevitable, natural growth pains that come as humans struggle toward the fullness of their creation (16).

Divergent world views and sexual value systems in the Roman Catholic, Protestant, Judaic, Islamic, and Humanist religious traditions are illustrated in Table 7.1.

This general dichotomy of world views comes through with a powerful consistency in an analysis of traditional and contemporary Western sexual values, as Table 7.2 shows (17).

The convergence of independently developed value paradigms from a variety of different disciplines confirms the importance and necessity of ascertaining the weltanschauung that supports any religious doctrinal system and its sexual values. Once these premises are understood, the type of influence a particular religious doctrinal system is likely to have on children can be projected with some degree of accuracy. Since so little is available in terms of specific doctrines or moral precepts for childhood sexual development, this insight, however limited, is valuable as a starting point from which one can appreciate better the divergence of sexual values, for both adults and children.

In an adaptation of the moral development models of Piaget, Kohlberg and Gilligan to American religious institutions, Stayton

TABLE 7.1 A Spectrum of Ethical Systems with Typical Adherents in Different Traditions

Tradition Source	A Spectrum	
	Fixed Philosophy of Nature	Process Philosophy of Nature
Roman Catholic natural law tradition	Act-oriented natural law/divine order ethics expressed in formal Vatican pronouncements.	Person-oriented, evolving ethics expressed by many contemporary theologians.
Protestant Nominalism	Fundamentalism based on a literal interpretation of the Bible, as endorsed by the Moral Majority and the religious New Right: Seventh Day Adventists, Jehovah's Witnesses, Church of the Latter Day Saints.	An ethic based on the convenant between Jesus and humankind; examples in the 1970 United Presbyterian document on Sexuality and the Human Community.
Humanism	Stoicism and epicurean asceticism.	Situation ethics, e.g., the 1976 American Humanist Association: A New Bill of Sexual Rights and Responsibilities.
Judaism	Orthodox and Hassidic concern for strict observation of the Torah and Talmudic prescriptions.	Liberal and reformed application of moral principles to today's situations.

TABLE 7.2   A Dichotomous Paradigm Based on Western Sexual Values and Behavior

Hot Sex	Cool Sex
Definitions	
Reduction of genital sex.	Sexuality coextensive with personality.
Genitally focused feelings.	Diffused sensuality/sexuality.
Time and place arrangements.	Spontaneous.
Value System	
Patriarchal.	Egalitarian.
Male dominance by aggression.	Equal partnership as friends.
Double moral standard.	Single moral standard.
Behavioral Structures	
Closed possessiveness.	Open inclusiveness.
Casual, impersonal.	Involved, intimate.
Physical sex segregated from life, emotions and responsibility.	Sex integrated in whole framework of life.
Concerns	
Orgasm obsessed.	Engaging, pleasuring communications.
Extramarital relations as escape.	Comarital relations a growth of primary bond.
Fear of emotions and senses.	Embracing of emotions and senses.

(Ref. 8, p. 134) sees three institutional types. Corresponding to stage one in moral development are System A religious institutions, which focus on acts of masturbation, homosexuality, abortion or premarital sex. The act is either right or wrong. Absolute obedience to the authority is expected. At the other end of the spectrum are System C religious institutions, for whom acts are neither evil nor good in themselves and the focus is on the nature of relationships and individual responsibilities, as in stages five or six of the moral development models. System B religious institutions are more complex because they can reflect any of stages two to four, and individuals often fluctuate between stages depending on the extent of their personal involvement in a particular issue of sexuality. As Stayton notes,

> The dilemma for many adolescents is that they may be further along in their moral development than the religious institutions to which they belong. The Judaeo-Christian traditions have almost exclusively interpreted

sexual morality from a System A or absolutist position, although most religious groups have modified their positions slightly in the direction of increased sexual liberality, and a few rabbis, priests, and ministers have become considerably more modern in their views. (Ref. 8, p. 134)

JUDAIC DOCTRINES OF CHILDHOOD SEXUALITY

Judaism exhibits a clear doctrinal range within the fixed/process philosophies spectrum (Table 7.1). On the fixed world view end, Orthodox Judaism and its most conservative sect, Hassidic Judaism, claim to be most faithful to traditional religious principles, beliefs and rituals. On the liberal side of the spectrum, Reformed and humanistic Judaism are the most open and adaptable to insights from modern developmental psychology and sexology. Conservative Judaism represents the middle of the spectrum.

In general, the Jewish tradition has escaped the antisexualism of the neoplatonic dualism of body/soul that has been so influential in Christian thought. The Judaic tradition affirms sexuality as a blessing, a gift from God which grounds and stabilizes the family. Centuries of persecution and enforced emigration, coupled with a strong biblical tradition, have made the patriarchal family central in the Jewish experience. It is assumed that every Jewish man and woman will marry and have children. The first commandment of the Torah is "You shall be fruitful and multiply." Hence, there is no place for asceticism, sexual or otherwise. Celibacy is condemned and there is little tolerance or understanding of the single life (18).

Male-female dualism is, however, deeply rooted in the Jewish patriarchal family. Particularly in the orthodox sects, women are peripheral Jews. They are excluded from circumcision, the primary sign of Yahweh's covenant with his chosen people, from study of the Torah, and from ritual service as rabbis. Jewish women are honored as devoted wives and play a powerful role as mothers of the family. In orthodoxy, the sexes are segregated in ritual and much of daily life. There is a fear of female sexuality and the power of women to lure men into lascivious thoughts or untoward behavior that distract them from study of the Torah. "Family purity" is a significant concern for both men and women. At their wedding, Hassidic and orthodox women are given manuals providing meticulous directions about menstruation and its consequences. A woman is ritually unclean during menstruation and forbidden to have sexual intercourse or physical contact of any kind with her husband or any male until the evening of the seventh day after the last sign of vaginal discharge, when she immerses herself in a mikveh, or ritual bath (19–20). Most conservative and reformed Jews no longer adhere to the laws of niddah or menstruation and ritual purity.

As might be expected, Orthodox Judaism has made little if any accommodation to the new discoveries in sexology and child development because all that can be said about these issues has been set down in an unchanging tradition centuries ago. Orthodox Judaism adheres to a strict historical and legalistic interpretation of the Torah which views the pleasures of sexual relations as a mutual right and blessing exchanged between husband and wife. Since marriage and procreation are the most important responsibilities, contraception, masturbation, premarital sexual relations, adultery and homosexuality are all rigorously condemned. Single people are expected to avoid masturbation and premartial sex. In this respect, orthodox Judaism has much in common with the sexual restriction of formal Catholic doctrine and fundamentalist Protestantism. Reformed Jews, and to a lesser extent Conservative Jews, are more flexible, maintaining a loyalty to tradition while emphasizing themes that allow adherents to adapt to new scientific developments and social exigencies.

CHRISTIAN DOCTRINES OF CHILDHOOD SEXUALITY

A Historical Overview

Underlying the whole of Christian doctrine is the struggle to overcome the consequences of original sin. In attempting to differentiate themselves from the Jews, the early Christians unfortunately lost the positive Judaic view of sexuality. In its place, under the influence of Paul, Jerome, the Desert Fathers, and especially Augustine in the third century, Christianity adopted a pagan dualism from Hellenic and neoplatonic philosophy that has permeated Christian thinking about sexuality until the present. Linked with Judaic patriarchal dualism, this pagan body-versus-soul dualism created a strongly antisexual ethic. Men were portrayed as rational, spiritual and good, provided they avoided the contaminating touch of women. Women, for their part, were passionate, earthly, and "the outpost of hell, the gateway of the devil." They could, however, achieve salvation, preferably in virginity, but also through childbearing. A strong ascetic tradition exalted martyrdom, virginity and celibacy.

Early and medieval Christianity was dominated by a sexual morality based on a selective interpretation of the natural order and purpose of things. Marriage and sexual intercourse could be tolerated but only if they were used exclusively for continuation of the human race. Sex for pleasure was not allowed. The result, in medieval Christianity, was a complete catalog of sexual practices based on natural acts which were procreative (marital intercourse, fornication and rape) and those which were unnatural (masturbation, contraceptive intercourse and sodomy). Sex was licit only between husband and wife, and natural only when it was not enjoyed and nothing was done to interfere with its procreative purpose. For centuries, Christianity has struggled with a radical inability to cope theologically and ethically with the issues of self-love, pleasure and play. Spiritual love, agape, was the ideal and physical love, eros, a sinful indulgence in passion (21–22).

Recently, the analysis of Christian sexual ethics has moved beyond this obvious antisexual posture. Gardella (2) argues convincingly that the contemporary American ethic of sexual pleasure resulted in large part from the struggle of Protestants and Catholics to overcome original sin, gain freedom from guilt and find innocent ecstasy. Without the interplay of Catholic and Protestant sexual moralists in the past two centuries, the contemporary American ethic of sexual pleasure and ecstasy would not be what it is. This more positive interpretation, however, does not alter the fact that with rare exception Christian ethics has been quite uncomfortable with sexual pleasure and sexuality, especially outside the martial and heterosexual realms.

From the early Victorian era to the present, Christian morality in America has maintained two contradictory images of the child and its psychosexual development. In one view, the child, though conceived in original sin, enjoyed a period of sublime innocence which the sexual awakening of puberty shattered. Freud's belief in a period of preadolescent sexual latency reinforced this view.

In the second view, the doctrine of original sin emphasized the innate inclinations to evil and depravity in every child. Since original sin was frequently associated with sex, the parents' role was to watch over each child constantly and eradicate any sign of depraved activity, especially any hint of the vile practice of "self-pollution." Despite their seeming difference, the outcome of both religious views was the prohibition and punishment of any and all expressions of the psychosexual rehearsal behaviors natural to childhood. The Victorian hysteria over masturbation, which lasted well into this century, has been well documented (23).

Contemporary Doctrines

In Catholicism, formal statements from the Vatican continue adhering to the natural law interpretation of sexuality, focusing on acts, and concluding that any sexual activity outside heterosexual marital procreative sex is a gravely sinful, intrinsically evil and disordered act. This view has been balanced in the past decade by the vast majority of contemporary Catholic moralists who have shifted to a person-oriented, process-based moral thinking. On the subject of masturbation, this person-oriented view ranges from statements that "not every deliberately willed act of masturbation necessarily constitutes the grave matter required for mortal sin" to Catholic moralists who maintain that "it must be said once and for all that the masturbation of the child and of the adolescent is a normal act which has no unfavorable consequences, either physical or moral, as long as one does not make the mistake of placing these acts on a moral plane, with which they have nothing to do" (24).

Despite the disagreements of different sects within mainstream Protestant Christianity, sexuality is affirmed as a good gift of the Creator which has been marred and distorted by human sin and alienation. Unlike Catholicism,

Protestantism early on abandoned procreation as the primary purpose of marriage and sexual expression. It has also been more open to new empirical knowledge about sex and more willing to move from categories of acts to an interpersonal focus on the meanings of sexual expression (Ref. 25, pp. 364–392). The United Presbyterian Workstudy document of 1970, for instance, clearly states that morally good and evil sexual actions "are not susceptible of being catalogued" (26). This person-oriented approach is evident in a variety of denominational statements compiled by Genne (27). Typical is the following statement from the United Presbyterian Church:

> Since masturbation is often one of the earliest pleasurable sexual experiences which is identifiably genital, we consider it essential that the church, through its teachings and through the attitudes it encourages in Christian homes, contribute to a healthy understanding of this experience which will be free of guilt and shame. The ethical significance of masturbation depends entirely on the context in which it takes place. Therefore, we can see no objection to it when it occurs as a normal developmental experience or as a deliberately chosen alternative to inappropriate heterosexual activity. (Ref. 26, pp. 14–15)

On issues of adolescent sexual relations, premarital sexual intercourse and homosexuality, the mainstream Protestant churches have been more cautious in breaking with the traditional heterosexual marital ethics, asking questions rather than taking definitive positions:

> In a society where the sexes are moving more and more toward equal status and away from double standards, is it the responsibility of the Church to examine her traditional standards of sexuality for single adults and ask what values would be best to help single men and women to be themselves as whole human beings? (28)

> Sexual union as a communicative act has increasingly become associated with the showing of affection both within and without the institution of marriage and herein lies the problem. If we as a church have and do condone sexual union as a communicative act, can we and should we condone it only within the institution of marriage? (29)

> Sexual intercourse outside marriage is a growing reality in our time. To state categorically that it is wrong is to come at it legalistically rather than contextually. (30)

The ordination of acknowledged gay men and lesbian women to the ministry by the Episcopal Church and United Church of Christ (Congregational) and debates over this possibility in other Protestant denominations are indicative of a similar shift in sexual values which will inevitably affect childhood sexuality. John Boswell has noted that homosexually oriented children suffer a unique problem because of their "lack of social category" (1). Both secular and religious cultures ignore gay children as non-existent. Gay children fall off the map of human society. It is to be hoped that, as the mainstream Protestant Churches and process-oriented Catholic moralists adjust more to the realities of modern life, this destructive situation will change for the better.

In 1968, an interfaith statement developed by the National Council of Churches, the Synagogue Council of America and the U.S. Catholic Conference called for tolerance and acceptance of differences in school sexuality programs, informed and dignified discussion on all sides of moral questions, and promotion of our potential as human beings (8).

It is obvious from any cursory reading of religious doctrines based on the fixed world view that the conservative judgements of Orthodox Jews, Eastern Orthodox Christians, the Vatican, Jehovah's Witnesses (31–32), the Seventh Day Adventists, the Church of the Latter Day Saints (Mormons) and fundamentalist Moral Majority Protestant groups will remain unalterably opposed to any acceptance of masturbation, homosexual relations and heterosexual expressions of any kind for the unmarried, adolescents, or especially children. As mentioned earlier, Stayton suggests that most institutions within the Judaeo-Christian tradition, particularly recent pronouncements from the Vatican, reflect a moral development which has been arrested at stage one (Ref. 8, p. 134).

A 1987 report prepared by The Task Force on Changing Patterns of Sexuality and Family Life for Study by the Episcopal Diocese of Newark, New Jersey, is the most advanced and liberal document to be issued by any mainstream Christian church. In essence, this document would provide for gay unions "the same recognition and affirmation which nurtures and sustains heterosexual couples in their relationships, including, where appropriate, liturgies which recognize and bless such relationships." While this report calls for "maintaining the sacredness of the marital relationship in the sacrament of Holy Matrimony," it also calls for recognition and acceptance of young adults who choose to engage in premarital sexual relations or nonmarital cohabitation. Moral criteria urged by the report include: "life-enhancing for both partners and exploitative of neither . . . grounded in sexual fidelity and not involving promiscuity . . . founded on love and valued for the strengthening, joy, support and benefit of the couple and those to whom they are related." Recognition of premarital sex should create a most positive and responsible atmosphere for teenagers (33).

The Society of Friends (Quakers) and the Unitarian/Universalist Church have moved beyond stage-one morality, and have openly acknowledged and dealt positively with issues of sexuality in childhood and adolescence (34). In 1971, a nationwide controversy erupted with the release of a very explicit student-centered experiential program sponsored by the Unitarian/Universalist Church, in which sexually explicit filmstrips, student manuals and parent guides, "About Your Sexuality," dealt with a range of topics no church document had previously dared touch (35). For some, it may have been

acceptable for a program for adolescents to deal with male and female sexual anatomy and physiology, dating, partner choice, conception and childbirth, but the inclusion of explicit filmstrips and texts dealing with sexual intercourse, same sex behaviours, masturbation, contraception and sexual diseases was unheard of. In some states, criminal prosecutions were threatened against the main author, Derek Calderwood, and local Unitarian/Universalist Churches which used this program. Fifteen years later, the third updating of "About Your Sexuality" is still too controversial for use in many Christian churches although its preeminent position is widely recognized.

HUMANIST DOCTRINES

Drawing on input from 35 leading sexologists, Lester Kirkendall drafted "A New Bill of Sexual Rights and Responsibilities" for the American Humanist Association. Among the nine main points proposed in this statement was one related specifically to children:

> Individuals are able to respond positively and affirmatively to sexuality throughout life; this must be acknowledged and accepted. Childhood sexuality is expressed through genital awareness and exploration. This involves self-touching, caressing parts of the body, including the sexual organs. These are learned experiences that help the individual understand his or her body and incorporate sexuality as an integral part of his or her personality. Masturbation is a viable mode of satisfaction for many individuals, young and old, and should be fully accepted. Just as repressive attitudes have prevented us from recognizing the value of childhood sexual response, so have they prevented us from seeing the value of sexuality in the middle and later years . . . (36)

In Christianity and especially in Roman Catholicism, the patriarchal, marital, reproductive symbols of sexuality have dominated, often reinforced by a competitive or dichotomous dualism of body versus soul, a concept of an "original sin" linked in the common mind with sexual sin, and a redemption achieved by subordination and denial of the body with its passions and emotions. In Western sexual archetypes, the male is active and dominant, the female passive. The rational male is clearly superior to the emotional and passionate female. The world view of the early Persian philosopher Zoroaster split the world into a realm of light, goodness and spirit on one side and a world of darkness, evil and body on the other side. This dichotomy flourished in the West, especially in Roman Catholicism (37).

While the doctrines and symbols of the great religions of the world undoubtedly play a substantial normative role in guiding the sexual lives of adults, only scant indirect and inferential conclusions can be made about their impact on childhood sexual development. In the more dualistic Christian tradition, more can be concluded because of the pervading religious concerns expressed about controlling and regulating sexual expression for those who are not married and ready to have a family. Much more research is needed to answer the question of to what extent dysfunctional and paraphilic lovemaps can be traced to which religious doctrines.

INTRODUCTION REFERENCE

Francoeur, A. K., and R. T. Francoeur. 1974. *Hot and cool sex: Cultures in conflict*. New York: Harcourt Brace Jovanovich.

NOTES

1. Boswell J. (1980) *Christianity, Social Tolerance and Homosexuality*. University of Chicago Press, Chicago.
2. Gardella P. (1985) *Innocent Ecstasy: How Christianity Gave America an Ethic of Sexual Pleasure*. Oxford University Press, New York.
3. Bullough V.L. (1976) *Sexual Variance in Society and History*. Wiley, New York.
4. Brinton C. (1959) *A History of Western Morals*. Harcourt Brace and Co., New York.
5. Money J., Cawte J.E., Bianchi G.N., Nurcombe B. (1970) Sex training and traditions in Arnhem Land. *Br. J. Med. Psychol*, 43, 383.
6. Money J. (1986) *Lovemaps: Clinical Concepts of Sexual/Erotic Health and Pathology, Paraphilia, and Gender Transposition in Childhood, Adolescence, and Maturity*, pp. xvi and 18. Irvington Press, New York.
7. Francoeur R.T. (1972) *Eve's New Rib: 20 Faces of Sex, Marriage and Family*, pp. 43–64. Harcourt Brace Jovanovich, New York.
8. Stayton W.R. (1985) Religion and adolescent sexuality. *Semin. Adolescent Med.*, 1, 131–137.
9. Piaget J. (1965) *The Moral Judgment of the Child*. Free Press, New York.
10. Hersh R.D., Paolitto D., Reimer J. (1979) *Promoting Moral Growth: From Piaget to Kohlberg*. Longmans, New York.
11. Gilligan C., Kohlberg L. (1974) Moral reasoning and value formation. In Calderone M.S. (Ed), *Sexuality and Human Values*. Association Press, New York.
12. Mayr E. (1963) *Animal Species and Evolution*, p. 5. Harvard University Press, Cambridge, MA.
13. Francoeur R.T. (1965) *Perspectives in Evolution*. Helicon Press, Baltimore.
14. Francoeur R.T. (1970) *Evolving World Converging Man*. Holt Rinehart Winston, New York.
15. Francoeur R.T. (1984) Moral concepts in the year 2020: The individual, the family, and society. In Kirkendall L.A., Gravatt A.E. (Eds), *Marriage and the Family in the Year 2020*. Prometheus Press, Buffalo, NY.
16. Francoeur R.T. (1982) *Becoming a Sexual Person*, Ch. 14. John Wiley, New York.
17. Francoeur A.K., Francoeur R.T. (1974) *Hot and Cool Sex: Cultures in Conflict*. Harcourt Brace Jovanovich, New York.
18. Nelson J.B. (1983) *Between Two Gardens: Reflections on Sexuality and Religious Experience*, pp. 56–59. Pilgrim Press, New York.
19. Schneid H. (1973) *Marriage* (Popular Judaica Library). Keter Books, Jerusalem.
20. Blasz E. (1967) *Code of Jewish Family Purity: A Condensation of the Nidah Laws Committee for the Preservation of Jewish Family Purity*. Brooklyn, NY.
21. Bullough V.L., Brundage J. (1982) *Sexual Practices and the Medieval Church*, pp. 1–12. Prometheus Press, Buffalo, NY.
22. Bullough V.L., Bullough B. (1977) *Sin, Sickness, and Sanity*, Ch. 2. New American Library Meridian, New York.

23. Phipps W.E. (1977) Masturbation: Vice or virtue? *J. Relig. Health*, 16(3), 183.

24. Kosnik A., Carroll W., Cunningham A., Modras R., Schulte J. (1977) *Human Sexuality: New Directions in American Catholic Thought.* A Study Commissioned by The Catholic Theological Society of America, pp. 219–229. Paulist Press, New York.

25. Herz F.M., Rosen E.J. (1982) Jewish families. In McGoldrick M., Pearce J.K., Giordano J. (Eds), *Ethnicity and Family Therapy*, pp. 364–392. Guilford Press, New York.

26. United Presbyterian Church of the U.S. (1977) *Sexuality and the Human Community*, p. 11. U.P.C.U.S.A., Philadelphia.

27. Genne W.H. (Ed) (1970) *A Synoptic of Recent Denominational Statements on Sexuality.* National Council of Churches, New York.

28. *Christianity and Human Sexuality* (No date) p. 50. The Executive Council of the Episcopal Church.

29. A Staff Report of the Work of the Task Force on Sex Ethics (1969) p. 10. The United Church of Christ, Division of Christian Education, Philadelphia.

30. *Sex, Marriage, and Family: A Contemporary Christian Perspective* (1970) p. 67. Board of Social Ministry of the Lutheran Church in America, New York.

31. Watch Tower Bible and Tract Society of New York (1978) *Making Your Family Life Happy.* Watch Tower Bible and Tract Society of New York, Inc., New York.

32. Watch Tower Bible and Tract Society of New York (1976) *Your Youth: Getting the Best Out of It.* Watch Tower Bible and Tract Society of New York, Inc., New York.

33. Thayer N.S.T. (1987) (March) Report of the Task Force on Changing Patterns of Sexuality and Family Life. Episcopal Diocese, Newark, NJ.

34. Friends (1966) *Towards a Quaker View of Sex.* Friends Home Service Committee, London.

35. Calderwood D. (1971) *About Your Sexuality.* Beacon Press, Boston.

36. Kirkendall L.A. (1976) A new bill of sexual rights and responsibilities. *The Humanist*, 36(1), 4–6.

37. Cousins E.H. (1987) Male-female aspects of the Trinity in Christian Mysticism. In Gupta B. (Ed), *Sexual Archetypes, East and West*, pp. 45–49. Paragon House, New York.

CHAPTER 8

Early Childhood Exposure to Parental Nudity and Scenes of Parental Sexuality

Paul Okami
Richard Olmstead
Paul R. Abramson
Laura Pendleton

Is exposure of a child to parental nudity or scenes of parental sexual activity a subtle form of sexual abuse as suggested by some researchers and clinicians? According to Okami et al., empirical data on the longterm outcomes of such scenarios are scant, although seemingly authoritative statements alluding to this fact frequently appear in the popular literature. Thus, the authors' investigation of this subject is a welcome addition to the research literature.

Sigmund Freud coined the term "primal scene" to refer to visual or auditory exposure of children to parental sexual intercourse. Psychoanalysts have long related such exposure to mental health problems of children. The researchers conducting this study reasoned that any such harm from exposure to these events would result from interactions with specific ecological variables, such as age or sex of the child. They framed their study with a number of important outcome measures chosen to reflect long-term adjustment in areas of concern to clinicians.

Readers should be aware of some methodological limitations of the Okami et al. study: the sample was not from "average" U.S. families; the sample was limited in size; a non-random sample was used; and there were some problems of measurement. Nevertheless, this study is an important effort among the few other empirical studies that do exist, and readers will be better positioned to discriminate between myth and fact about this controversial topic.

From "Early Childhood Exposure to Parental Nudity and Scences of Parental Sexuality ('Primal Scenes'): An 18-Year Longitudinal Study of Outcome" by P. Okami, R. Olmstead, P. R. Abramson, and L. Pendleton. 1998. *Archives of Sexual Behavior* 27: 361–384. Copyright © 1998, Kluwer Academic/Plenum Publishers. With kind permission from Springer Science + Business Media.

INTRODUCTION

Increasing numbers of academic researchers and clinicians have suggested that behaviors such as exposure of a child to parental nudity or scenes of parental sexuality ("primal scenes") constitute subtle forms of sexual abuse that previously have gone unrecognized (Haynes-Seman and Krugman, 1989; Kritsberg, 1993; Krug, 1989). Such subtle sexual abuse—referred to as syndromes like "maternal seductiveness," "emotional incest syndrome," "emotional sexual abuse," "covert sexual abuse," and "sexualized attention"—may also include less easily defined behaviors such as parent "flirtatiousness," or inappropriate and excessive displays of physical affection (Sroufe and Fleeson, 1986).

As Okami (1995) suggested, however, such concern is not new. That is, although these "syndromes" have recently entered the discourse on sexual abuse, some of the behaviors that constitute them have long held positions in the pantheon of improper parenting practices. For example, Esman (1973) observed that just one of these practices—exposure of the child to primal scenes—has been indicted in 75 years of psychoanalytic, psychiatric, and psychological literature as the primary etiologic agent in virtually every form of child and adult pathology. However, Esman concluded that, "One is moved to wonder whether we are here confronted with one of those situations in which a theory, by explaining everything, succeeds in explaining nothing" (pp. 64–65). In the present article we report results of the first longitudinal investigation of long-term correlates of exposure to parental nudity and primal scenes.

Exposure to Parental Nudity

Only three empirical articles have addressed the issue of childhood exposure to parent and other adult nudity: Lewis and Janda (1988); Oleinick et al. (1966); and Story (1979). In several other cases, descriptive, self-report studies of social nudist or other groups practicing casual nudity have been conducted without comparison groups (Berger, 1977; Hartman et al., 1991; Smith and Sparks, 1986). In general, the tone of all of this work is antialarmist, representing childhood exposure to nudity as benign.

Apart from these tentative attempts to collect data, writings on this topic consist of theory-driven clinical opinion and commentaries by child rearing specialists. Clinical writings typically reflect the notion that exposure to nudity

may be traumatic as a result of (i) premature and excessive stimulation in a manner controlled by the adult, leaving the child feeling powerless; (ii) the child's unfavorable comparison between his or her own anatomy and the adult's; or (iii) the intensification of Oedipal desires and consequent anxiety (DeCecco and Shively, 1977; Justice and Justice, 1979).

Given the vehemence with which clinicians and child-rearing specialists often condemn childhood exposure to parental nudity, it is paradoxical that their dire predictions are not supported by the (scant) empirical work that does exist. Findings are at worst neutral, or ambiguous as to interpretation, and there is even the implication of possible positive benefits in these studies (particularly for boys) in domains such as self-reported comfort with physical affection (Lewis and Janda, 1988) and positive "body self-concept" (Story, 1979). Although these investigations are methodologically limited, their results are consistent with the view of a smaller group of child-rearing specialists and other commentators who have stressed the potential benefits to children of exposure to nudity in the home, in areas such as later sexual functioning, and capacity for affection and intimacy (Goodson, 1991; Martinson, 1977). Although some of these writers make reference to the cross-cultural ubiquity of childhood exposure to parental nudity—although objecting to alarmist positions taken by Western commentators who fail to provide supportive data—the cross-cultural record is not generally explicit on the question of actual exposure of children to parental nudity. It does, however, present a strong case for the universality of parent-child cosleeping or room sharing (Caudill and Plath, 1966; Lozoff et al., 1984; Morelli et al., 1992). It may tentatively be inferred that under such conditions large numbers of the world's population of children are exposed to parental nudity. Finally, a third group of writers stress the importance of the context in which childhood exposure to nudity takes place, insisting that outcomes are mediated by such contextual variations as gender of child, age of child, family climate, cultural beliefs, and so on (Okami, 1995; Okami et al., 1997).

Exposure to Scenes of Parental Sexuality (Primal Scenes)

Freud and his followers chose the term "primal scenes" to refer to visual or auditory exposure of children to parental intercourse, and subsequent fantasy elaborations on the event (Dahl, 1982). Despite the identification of such exposure by psychoanalysts and others as uniquely dangerous to the mental health of children, there are, once again, scant empirical data bearing on effects of primal scene exposure. We could locate only one prevalence study (Rosenfeld et al., 1980) and two studies of initial response and subsequent adult functioning (Hoyt, 1979, 1979). Of course, numbers of case studies exist, including a very rich psychoanalytic literature describing putative consequences of exposure to primal scenes. These writers have explained the traumatagenic issues by referring to "a) the erotically charged character of the exposure, resulting in undischarged libidinal energy and concomitant anxiety; b) the sadomasochistic content of fantasy misinterpretation of the event; and c) the exacerbation of oedipal desires and resultant castration anxiety or other fears of retaliation" (Okami, 1995, p. 56).

Again, however, the few attempts to validate these notions empirically do not support predictions of harm. For example, Rosenfeld et al. (1980) concluded that the extent of psychological damage has been exaggerated. These investigators arrived at their conclusion by two routes: First, exposure to primal scenes appeared to be rather prevalent, with the most conservative estimates as high as 41 percent. Rosenfeld et al. suggested that given this frequency of occurrence, factors other than the primal scene qua primal scene must be responsible for trauma when it occurs. Second, parents reported largely neutral and noncomprehending responses from their small children (ages 4–6). On the other hand, some children appeared to respond with amusement, giggling, and clear comprehension. Thus, the rather sinister portrait emerging from psychoanalytic literature was largely absent from these parent reports.

Hoyt (1978) queried college students about their childhood exposure to scenes of parental sexuality. He found that although these students reported that their exposure had resulted in largely negative emotional responses at the time, the exposed group did not differ from the nonexposed group on self-report ratings of "current happiness" or frequency of and satisfaction with current sexual relations. Moreover, these subjects recalled exposure primarily at prepubescent and pubertal ages. Given that the mean ages for first exposure reported by parents in the Rosenfeld et al. (1980) studies were between 4 and 6, it is conceivable that subjects in Hoyt's investigations were not reporting their first actual exposure to scenes of parental sexuality. Therefore, findings of exposure at peripubertal ages are of limited value in assessing outcome of exposure to primal scenes generally, because with a few exceptions, primal scenes have been defined in the literature as events of early childhood. That is, responses such as "castration anxiety" and "Oedipal desires" are said to be of most critical importance in the lives of very young children.

THE PRESENT STUDY

Despite the lack of empirical support, psychoanalytic and family systems theorists continue to stress the potential for harm in exposure to parental nudity and primal scenes. Therefore, longitudinal outcome data are important in beginning to resolve this question. In the present exploratory study, 204 families were enlisted during the mid-1970s as part of a multidisciplinary investigation of emergent family lifestyles, UCLA Family Lifestyles Project. Children were followed from birth to the current wave of data collection at ages 17–18. Because there was no indication in the literature that either of the target behaviors is harmful, we hypothesized no deleterious effects of early childhood exposure either to nudity or primal scenes.

Theories based in evolutionary biology, cognitive science, and ethology predict sex differences in psychological mechanisms mediating sexual behavior in humans (Abramson and Pinkerton, 1995; Buss, 1994, 1995). Although most evolutionary theorizing about human sex differences in sexuality has focused on reproductively mature individuals, sex differences in sexuality-related psychological response also have been found among children and early adolescents (Gold and Gold, 1991; Knoth et al., 1988). In their study of adolescents ages 12–18 who were asked to recall their earliest sexual arousal and sexual feelings, Knoth et al., (1988) reported outcomes markedly congruent with evolutionary theory. Specifically, these investigators found that girls, as compared with boys, reported later onset of arousal, less frequency of arousal, less intense arousal, less distracting arousal, and were less likely to have experienced first arousal in response to visual cues. In the study by Gold and Gold (1991), men, relative to women, reported that their boyhood fantasies were more explicit and focused on the sexual acts themselves, more likely to have resulted from visual cues, more likely to have resulted in positive rather than negative affect, and that they were first experienced at an earlier age. Thus, sex differences in sexuality-related psychological responses appear to be present at least from preadolescence.

Method

Outcome measures were chosen to reflect long-term adjustment in a number of areas of concern to clinicians. These areas included: (i) self-acceptance; (ii) relations with parents, peers, and other adults; (iii) drug use; (iv) antisocial and criminal behavior; (v) suicidal ideation; (vi) social "problems" associated with sexual behavior (getting pregnant or having gotten someone pregnant, and getting an STD); and (vii) quality of sexual relationships, attitudes, and beliefs.

The UCLA Family Lifestyles Project (FLS) is a longitudinal investigation founded in 1973 to examine emergent family life-styles of that era. Fifty "conventional" and 154 "nonconventional" families, matched for ethnicity and socioeconomic status (SES) according to Hollingshead's four-factor model (Hollingshead, 1975), were enrolled prior to the birth of the target child. All parents were of European American descent and were living in the State of California when recruited.

Conventional families were defined as those in a "married couple relationship" and were referred by a randomly selected sample of obstetricians from the San Francisco, San Diego, and Los Angeles areas. Nonconventional families were recruited through physician referral, birthing office records, alternative media announcements, and referral by already enrolled participants. Nonconventional family forms included intentional single mothers, couples living in communes or other group-living situations, and "social contract" (cohabiting) couples. During the most recent wave of data collection, target children were between the ages of 17 and 18 years.

For boys, exposure to primal scenes predicted reduced likelihood of having gotten an STD, or having gotten someone pregnant. The reverse was the case for girls, who were significantly more likely to have gotten an STD or to have become pregnant. This finding was independent of the extent of sexual behavior engaged in.

To determine extent of exposure to nudity and primal scenes, parents were asked two questions in a face-to-face interview at child's age 3: "Does mother (father) go nude in front of child?" and "Does mother (father) bathe or shower with the child?" The questions were followed by scales anchored by 1 (never) and 4 (regularly) or 1 (never) and 5 (daily). At child's age 6, parents were asked whether they (i) discouraged family nudity, (ii) felt OK about nudity within the family but not with others, or (iii) encouraged nudity within the family and with others.

Exposure to primal scenes was measured by two items. At child's age 3, parents were asked whether their child had ever seen them "have sex." They were offered a 4-point response format anchored by 1 (never) and 4 (regularly). At child's age 6, parents were again asked if their child had observed them having intercourse, and again offered a 4-point scale anchored by 1 (no) and 4 (regularly). Because of shifts in the identity of mothers' male partners for some of the families over the first 6 years, and the greater frequency of fathers working outside of the home and being unavailable for interview, missing data for fathers approach unacceptable levels. Therefore, only mothers' data were used for these analyses.

Results

The principal components analyses yielded five drug-use factors and four antisocial behavior factors. The drug-use factors are hence referred to as Hard Drugs (i) Sedatives, minor tranquilizers; (ii) Marijuana, hashish, psychedelic mushrooms, LSD, "Ecstasy"; (iii) PCP, major tranquilizers, other psychedelics, inhalants; (iv) Amyl nitrate, amphetamines, other narcotics; and (v) Heroin, barbiturates, cocaine, inhalants. The antisocial behavior variables are labeled antisocial behavior: theft, vandalism, felonies and fighting.

Frequencies for exposure to the main variables are as follows: For exposure to primal scenes, 32 percent of the children were exposed (boys, $n = 34$, girls, $n = 39$), whereas 68 percent of the children were not exposed. For exposure to parental nudity, 25 percent of children were not exposed to any parental nudity, 44 percent of children were exposed with moderate frequency, and 31 percent of children (boys, $n = 34$, girls, $n = 27$) were exposed frequently.

A number of trends were found that were significant. Exposure to parental nudity predicted lower likelihood of sexual activity in adolescence, but more positive sexual experiences among that group of participants who were

sexually active. Exposure to parental nudity also predicted reduced instances of petty theft and shoplifting, but this was mediated by a sex of participant interaction indicating that this effect was attenuated or absent for women. Similarly, exposure to parental nudity was associated with reduced use of drugs such as marijuana, LSD, Ecstasy, and psychedelic mushrooms, but again, this effect was experienced primarily by men. Indeed, exposed women were very slightly more likely to have used these drugs.

At the level of trend, exposure to primal scenes was associated with higher levels of self-acceptance and improved relations with adults other than parents. There was also a trend for women exposed to primal scenes to have been less likely to use drugs such as PCP, major tranquilizers, inhalants, and psychedelics other than LSD or mushrooms.

Although a number of nonsignificant trends emerged, the only significant finding was that family sexual liberalism was associated with sexual liberalism at adolescence.

DISCUSSION

This study, using a longitudinal design, is the first to examine long-term correlates of early childhood exposure to parental nudity and primal scenes. Consistent with the cross-sectional retrospective literature (and with our expectations), no harmful main effects of these experiences were found at ages 17–18. Indeed, trends in the data did not reach significance. Exposure to parental nudity was associated with positive, rather than negative, sexual experiences in adolescence, but with reduced sexual experience overall. Boys exposed to parental nudity were less likely to have engaged in theft in adolescence or to have used various psychedelic drugs and marijuana.

In the case of primal scenes, exposure was associated with improved relations with adults outside of the family and with higher levels of self-acceptance. Girls exposed to primal scenes were also less likely to have used drugs such as PCP, inhalants, or various psychedelics in adolescence. The one note of caution: males' exposure to primal scenes was associated with reduced risk of social "problems" associated with sexuality, while the opposite was the case for females. Women in our study who had been exposed to primal scenes reported increased instances of STD transmission and pregnancy. All findings were independent of the effects of SES, sex of participant, family stability, pathology, "pronaturalism," and beliefs and attitudes toward sexuality.

Taken as a whole then, effects are few, but generally beneficial in nature. Thus, results of this study add weight to the views of those who have opposed alarmist characterizations of childhood exposure both to nudity and incidental scenes of parental sexuality. Moreover, although the association of higher instance of sexually transmitted diseases and adolescent pregnancy among young women exposed to primal scenes might appear at first glance to represent harm unequivocally, more careful examination renders these findings somewhat ambiguous. In the case of increased instance of pregnancy among these women, for example, it should be noted that over half of those who reported having become pregnant (and almost half of the men who reported impregnating someone) rated their experience "good" rather than "bad." Although it is true that problems—sometimes serious problems—may attend such pregnancies in U.S. society, some data also suggest that these problems have been exaggerated (Stevens-Simon and White, 1991), and may often result more from low SES than from adolescent pregnancy itself (Trussell, 1988). Current treatment of adolescent pregnancy as intrinsically pathological may in part have generalized from an overall tendency to view adolescent sexual behaviors as problematic.

Even findings of increased instances of STD transmission among the women in our study need to be considered carefully. Symons (February 1995, personal communication) pointed out that increased instances of STDs and pregnancy among women exposed to primal scenes might be more parsimoniously understood as decreased use of condoms among the women. Regardless of problematic outcome, decreased use of condoms may be motivated by heightened desire (and capacity) for intimacy or higher levels of trust in partners—as well as by simple lack of sexual responsibility or self-destructive tendencies. In this respect it should be recalled that there was a (nonsignificant) trend toward higher levels of self-acceptance and improved relations with adults among these women.

Several outcome measures in the direction of beneficial correlates for boys were neutral or problematic correlates for girls. One interpretation would be that human males and females process sexuality-related events differently as the result of sexually dysmorphic psychological mechanisms that have evolved through natural and sexual selection (Buss, 1994). Moore (1995) has suggested the possibility that these mechanisms might begin to emerge reliably in childhood.

Other explanations of the gender interactions are also possible. For example, boys and girls are socialized differently throughout the world where sexuality is concerned, with girls being socialized more restrictively (Mead, 1967). Although these socialization procedures may also represent expressions of sexually dysmorphic psychological adaptation by natural and sexual selection, it could be argued that they instead represent temporally specific but worldwide sociocultural or socioeconomic forces related to patriarchal control of female sexuality. A third explanation of our results is more prosaic. These interactions by sex may be entirely artifactual statistical noise.

Additionally, while findings of beneficial outcomes are interesting, specific findings are not predicted by any theory that we know. In our view, then, the importance of the present investigation, apart from the suggestion of interactions by sex, lies not so much in positive findings as in the negative findings for harm—findings that converge on all of the available empirical data. Admittedly, any one set of negative results is not particularly informative. However, given virtually no evidence in this or any other empirical study that the behaviors examined in the current study are unambiguously harmful, the interesting question becomes: Why is it so widely believed in the United States and certain European nations that these practices are uniformly detrimental to the mental health of children? Such notions, certainly where exposure to parental nudity is concerned, are perhaps better conceptualized as myths. Whereas any of these behaviors of course may be experienced in an abusive context—and may also occasion harm under certain circumstances for certain individuals—their appearance per se does not appear to constitute cause for alarm.

Methodological limitations need to be addressed in interpreting results of this study. Most obviously, although the sample contains an interesting assortment of families that permitted the predictor variables to be studied in a number of contexts, these families undoubtedly differ in a number of potentially important ways from the "average" U.S. family. In addition to volunteer bias, the sample is made up entirely of European Americans residing in California at the time of enrollment, and "nonconventional" means exactly what it says—three-fourths of the sample were nonrepresentative of typical American life-style by definition. However, while not representative, the current sample was dedicated and attrition virtually nonexistent. This adds considerably to the meaningfulness of the analysis. Moreover, because the nonconventional families (whose members constituted approximately 75 percent of the total sample) were more likely to adhere to countercultural values supportive of free sexual expression, nudity within the family, and so forth, it is precisely in a data set such as this that one ought to expect to see elevated problems if these practices are in fact deleterious of themselves.

In any event, lack of reliability in the instruments used here would tend to reduce the probability of the type of findings that emerged. Lack of reliability should have produced null findings—not positive findings in a direction directly opposite that proposed by received wisdom. It is therefore difficult to imagine a methodological problem that could have erroneously painted such a consistent portrait of no harm.

Findings of the current study do not resolve the moral (or legal) issue of whether the behaviors we have examined represent "subtle sexual abuse." However, they do address the empirical question of whether these occurrences are harmful, at least within certain domains. Although evidence gathered for the present study is far from conclusive, at this point it is difficult to see the utility of referring to these events a priori as harmful, and even more difficult to see the utility of characterizing them globally as "abusive."

REFERENCES

Abramson, P. R., and Pinkerton, S. (1995). *Sexual Nature, Sexual Culture*, University of Chicago Press, Chicago.

Berger, B. (1977). Child-rearing research in communes: The extension of adult sexual behavior to young children. In Oremland, E. K., and Oremland, J. D. (eds.), *The Sexual and Gender Development of Young Children: The Role of the Educator*, Ballinger, Cambridge, MA, pp. 159–164.

Buss, D. M. (1994). *The Evolution of Desire*, Basic Books, New York.

Buss, D. M. (1995). Evolutionary psychology: A new paradigm for psychological science. *Psychol. Inq.* 6: 1–30.

Caudhill, W., and Plath, D. W. (1966). Who sleeps by whom? Parent-child involvement in urban Japanese families. *Psychiatry* 29: 344–366.

Dahl, G. (1982). Notes on critical examinations of the primal scene concept. *J. Am. Psychiat. Assoc.* 30: 657–677.

DeCecco, J. P., and Shively, M. G. (1977). Children's development: Social sex-role and the hetero-homosexual orientation. In Oremland, E. K., and Oremland, J. D. (eds.), *The Sexual and Gender Development of Young Children: The Role of the Educator*, Ballinger, Cambridge, MA, pp. 89–90.

Esman, A. H. (1973). The primal scene: A review and a reconsideration. *Psychanal. Quart.* 28: 49–81.

Gold, S. R., and Gold, R. G. (1991). Gender differences in first sexual fantasies. *J. Sex Educ. Ther.* 17: 207–216.

Goodson, A. (1991). *Therapy, Nudity, and Joy*, Elysium Growth Press, Los Angeles.

Hartman, W. E., Fithian, M., and Johnson, D. (1991). *Nudist Society*, 2nd ed., Elysium Growth Press, Los Angeles.

Haynes-Seman, C., and Krugman, R. D. (1989). Sexualized attention: Normal interaction or precursor to sexual abuse? *Am. J Orthopsychiat.* 59: 238–245.

Hollingshead, A. (1975). *Four Factor Index of Social Position*, Yale University, New Haven, CT.

Hoyt, M. F. (1978). Primal scene experiences as recalled and reported by college students. *Psychiatry* 41: 57–71.

Hoyt, M. F. (1979). Primal-scene experiences: Quantitative assessment of an interview study. *Arch. Sex. Behav.* 8: 225–245.

Justice, B., and Justice, R. (1979). *The Broken Taboo*, Human Sciences, New York.

Knoth, R., Boyd, K., and Singer, B. (1988). Empirical tests of sexual selection theory: Predictions of sex differences in onset, intensity, and time course of sexual arousal. *J. Sex Res.* 24: 73–79.

Kritsberg, W. (1993). *The Invisible Wound: A New Approach to Healing Childhood Sexual Trauma*, Bantam, New York.

Krug, R. S. (1989). Adult male report of childhood sexual abuse by mothers: Case descriptions, motivations and long-term consequences. *Child Abuse Neg.* 13: 111–119.

Lewis, R. J., and Janda, L. H. (1988). The relationship between adult sexual adjustment and childhood experiences regarding exposure to nudity, sleeping in the parental bed, and parental attitudes toward sexuality. *Arch. Sex. Behav.* 17: 349–362.

Lozoff, B., Wolf, A. W., and Davis, N. S. (1984). Co-sleeping in urban families with young children in the United States. *Pediatrics* 74: 171–182.

Martinson, F. M. (1977). Eroticism in childhood: A sociological perspective. In Oremland, E. K., and Oremland, J. D. (eds.), *The Sexual and Gender Development of Young Children: The Role of the Educator*, Ballinger, Cambridge, MA, pp. 73–82.

Mead, M. (1967). *Male and Female: A Study of the Sexes in a Changing World*, William Morrow, New York.

Moore, M. M. (1995). Courtship signaling and adolescents: "Girls just want to have fun"? *J. Sex Res.* 32: 319–328.

Morelli, G. A., Rogoff, B., Oppenheim, D., and Goldsmith, D. (1992). Culture variations in infant's sleeping arrangements: Questions of independence. *Dev. Psychol.* 28: 604–613.

Okami, P. (1995). Childhood exposure to parental nudity, parent-child co-sleeping, and "primal scenes": A review of clinical opinion and empirical evidence. *J. Sex Res.* 32: 51–64.

Okami, P., Olmstead, R., and Abramson, P. R. (1997). Sexual experiences in early childhood: 18-year data from the UCLA Family Life-styles Project. *J. Sex Res.* 34: 339–347.

Oleinick, M. S., Bahn, A. K., Eisenberg, L., and Lilienfield, A. M. (1966). Early socialization experiences. *Arch. Gen. Psychiat.* 15: 1966.

Rosenfeld, A. A., Smith, C. R., Wenegrat, M. A., Brewster, M. A., and Haavik, D. K. (1980). The primal scene: A study of prevalence. *Anti. J. Psychial.* 137: 1426–1428.

Smith, D. C., and Sparks, W. (1986). *The Naked Child: Growing Up Without Shame*, Elysium Growth Press, Los Angeles.

Sroufe, A. L., and Fleeson, J. (1986). Attachment and the construction of relationships. In Hartup, W. W., and Rubin, Z. (eds.), *Relationships and Development*, Erlbaum, Hillsdale, NJ, pp. 51–71.

Stevens-Simon, C., and White, M. (1991). Adolescent pregnancy. *Pediat. Ann.* 20: 322–331.

Story, M. D. (1979). Factors associated with more positive body self-concepts in preschool children. *J. Soc. Psychol.* 108: 49–56.

Trussell, J. (1988). Teenage pregnancy in the United States. *Fam. Plann. Perspect.* 20: 262–273.

CHAPTER 9

Forbidden Fruit
Imitation Sex and the New Middle-Class Morality

Mark D. Regnerus

"Red Sex, Blue Sex: Why Do So Many Evangelical Teen-agers Become Pregnant?" The title of this article in The New Yorker *magazine by Margaret Talbot (2008) will probably evoke an immediate, but distinctly different response from Red and Blue state readers. Americans remain almost as ambivalent about teenage sexuality as they do about their political ideology. If it is assumed that such ambivalence is rooted in religion, what is the role of religion in the formation of sexual values and actions of teenagers, and how is that pathway constructed? In* Forbidden Fruit: Sex & Religion in the Lives of American Teenagers, *Mark Regnerus explores this challenging question and a number of other queries in his book. For example, what difference, if any, does religion make in adolescent sexual lives? Are abstinence pledges effective? What does it mean to be emotionally ready for sex? Who feels guilty about their sexual activity and why?*

The chapter selected for inclusion in Part II, "Imitation Sex and the New Middle-Class Morality" addresses the topics of oral and anal sex as well as the influence of the pornography industry

that negatively impacts the lives of adolescents (Thio 2001). The burgeoning phenomenon of internet pornography that not only delivers but often introduces teenagers to sexual information and graphic sexual images is revealed. Questions that other researchers, educators, health professionals, and policymakers are asking that pertain to oral and anal sex among teenagers are posed, with the acknowledgment that very little factual information has been collected about these behaviors since the 1980s (Coles and Stokes 1985). The chapter raises issues without answers in some instances. For example, to what extent does adolescent sexual activity consist of non-coital behavior (i.e., mutual masturbation, oral sex, and anal intercourse)? And, are these behaviors more common than they were in the past, or are they just much more talked about? Given the scarcity of data on the frequency of oral and anal sex, can the evidence of the rise in STIs among teenagers be attributed to those practices?

The final questions pertain to "what is abstinence" and "what is sex?" In 1998, when President Bill Clinton claimed that he had not perjured himself because "I did not have sexual relations with that woman," he had, in fact, had something else—oral sex. At that time, 20 percent of adults also believed that oral sex did not constitute sexual relations (Remez 2000) as did 60 percent of a large random sample of college students at a Midwestern university (Sanders and Reinisch 1999).

Regnerus believes that religion can and does matter but that there is a disconnect between religious beliefs and sexual behavior. Outcomes of the abstinence-pledge movement where some 2.5 million teens pledged to remain celibate until marriage support such a belief. More than one-half of those who pledged celibacy ended up having sexual intercourse before marriage and usually not with their future spouse (Talbot 2008). In addition, those who pledged were less inclined to use condoms when they did have sex for the first time (Brückner and Bearman 2005).

In this offering, both the unanswered questions and the unquestioned answers may challenge some long-held concepts of religion, morality, and sexuality, sparking a lively class debate. But, hopefully, the issues raised in this work will force a continuing dialogue that helps to differentiate between health-promoting and health-threatening behaviors for adolescents.

As most teenagers figure out, there's more than one form of sexual activity. Since virginity is clearly valued—and, to a lesser extent, practiced—among more devoutly religious youth, one might wonder whether the same value applies to abstinence from other forms of sexual activity. The NSYR [National Survey of Youth and Religion] asked questions about oral sex and the use of pornography. What emerges when I evaluate these two is evidence of a religious and social class patterning of sexual activity preference and a nascent middle-class sexual morality that is neither about religion nor about abstinence, but about risk reduction, safeguarding one's future, and sexual substitution.

ORAL SEX

Much is made in the news media and in films, high school locker rooms, and parental conversations about the perceived rise in prevalence of oral sex. Media outlets have taken note of the "friends with benefits" phenomenon, which refers to casual oral sex (and occasionally intercourse) between friends who are not romantically involved with each other. Curiously, none of our interviewees volunteered the phrase "friends with benefits." Some no doubt experienced what the term captures, but the phenomenon is certainly less common than concerned parents may have been led to believe. Most adolescent sexual activity occurs within exclusive relationships, albeit comparatively short-term ones, not mere associations.

While oral sex can be given or received by either gender, when most adolescents talk about oral sex in the interviews, they are typically referring to the action that adolescent girls perform upon adolescent boys. Jeannette, an 18-year-old Catholic girl from New York state (who attends mass sporadically), intends to avoid sexual contact altogether until marriage, and she hasn't given much thought to distinguishing between oral and vaginal sex: "I don't even know what I think about oral sex. I don't know why anyone would want to do that." Among adolescent girls who have not had sex and are not dating anyone, this is the most common answer. Dating or being in a relationship with someone of the opposite sex, however, tends to color girls' perspectives on the topic.

There has also been a lot of talk about oral sex as a means by which youth maintain a technical virginity, as "third base," as "starter sex," and as a way to avoid pregnancy risks and some types of STDs (Remez 2000). Third base or not, oral sex is a more common introduction to sexual activity than is intercourse. Indeed, oral sex is about 50 percent more common than vaginal intercourse up until age 15. Somewhere between ages 15 and 17, intercourse catches up and surpasses oral sex in popularity. Whether its practitioners are trying to maintain a technical virginity is another matter, one to which I return shortly.

Teenagers of different religious affiliations range in oral sexual experience from a low of about 9 percent to a high of 30 percent. The difference in preference for *type* of sexual activity (in the NSYR) by religious affiliation is striking when contrasted to intercourse numbers. Whereas black Protestant youths are the most likely to have had sexual intercourse, they display one of the lowest rates of oral sex. On the flip side, Jewish and mainline Protestant youths display a much clearer preference for oral sex rather than intercourse. Youths who claim to be spiritual but not religious report slightly higher prevalences of both types of sex. Of the seven religious traditions listed, evangelicals are the fourth lowest in terms of oral sex—right in the middle of the pack, just like with intercourse.

Are these apparent religious influences more than just ephemeral? Yes. Black Protestants are statistically less likely than evangelicals to report having had oral sex. So are Catholic and Mormon youth. Prior to controls, youths who consider themselves spiritual but not religious are more likely than those who do not to report having experienced oral sex. And while personal religiosity curbs the likelihood of reporting oral sex, this association disappears after I account for strong influences from dating, attitudes about abstinence, and parents' sexual values. This should not surprise; youth for whom religion is an important part of their lives tend to hold less permissive attitudes about sex (and to have less permissive parents), and these attitudes reduce their likelihood of having had oral sex.

The 2002 NSFG [National Survey of Family Growth] helpfully distinguishes between giving and receiving oral sex, although its religious affiliation categories unfortunately do not allow me to distinguish Mormon and Jewish youth. Overall, 40 percent of adolescent boys aged 15–17 have received oral sex, and 28 percent have given it. Among 15- to 17-year-old girls, 38 percent have received and 30 percent have given oral sex. Such disjointed numbers suggest some level of misperception about what actually constitutes giving and receiving oral sex, since both males and females were more apt to report receiving oral sex than giving it.

Several numbers stand out. The nonreligious, the never-attenders, and the religion-isn't-important crowd distinguish themselves in all categories and in both genders. They are more than twice as likely as more religious youth to give or receive oral sex. Mainline Protestant girls exhibit comparably high rates of both giving and receiving oral sex, second only to nonreligious girls. Evangelical youths in the NSFG are the least likely to say they have *received* oral sex, which distinguishes them from their average rate in the NSYR, but they report middle-of-the-road numbers on *giving* oral sex.

Black Protestant adolescents display the most evidently disjointed answers—both girls and boys are more than twice as likely to report receiving oral sex as giving it. Why *both* genders state this is unclear, though it may have to do with distinctive interpretations of the survey questions themselves. Catholic boys are also twice as likely to have received it as to have given it. Religiosity again clearly distinguishes answers here: it is both very influential and linear in its association with oral sex. Between 13 and 27 percent of the most religious youth say yes to any one of the questions, far below the 40–60 percent among the least religious teenagers.

This remains true even when controlling for family structure, demographics, and parents' education. Both church attendance *and* the importance of religion are independently associated with a lower likelihood of either giving or receiving oral sex (in the NSFG). When controlling for these two forms of religiosity, no clear distinctions remain among the various religious affiliations.

The Technical Virginity Debate: Is Oral Sex Really Sex?

Do teenagers think oral sex is really sex, or something distinct and less serious than intercourse? We asked our interviewees this question, especially since we were interested in gauging whether oral sex is a popular means by which teenagers maintain their virginity technically, while still participating in nonvaginal forms of paired sexual activity. There is no clear consensus, however. For some, "sex" runs the gamut of all coupled sexual activity, especially when it results in the exchange of bodily fluids. For others, there are shades of gray. Religion often distinguishes opinions on the question. Evangelical Protestant and other religiously conservative teens tend to consider oral and vaginal sex in the same light, at least in theory. Jennifer, a 17-year-old evangelical from Georgia, takes a simple approach to the definition: "I think oral sex is sex, too. You know, I mean, it's all the same to me. If it has the word sex in it, then it's sex." This definition was repeated with regularity. Others we interviewed note that the two may be different yet equally wrong. For some religiously conservative adolescents, our even asking them about the definition of what constitutes sex is confusing. When we asked Kelli, a 16-year-old conservative Lutheran from Minnesota, to comment on or distinguish between the morality or acceptability of vaginal versus oral sex, she responds, "Can you explain that?" In general, most of the adolescent virgins we interviewed feel that they are just not ready for intercourse or oral sex yet.

Thus, I find it difficult to believe that very many religiously conservative adolescents would be using oral sex as a primary means for maintaining technical virginity. There is not a lot of technical virginity language articulated by adolescents, least of all by religious conservatives, in contrast to others' impressions (e.g., Clark 2004; DiMarco 2006).

Is there survey evidence for the technical virginity strategy? One study concluded that virgins in serious relationships are just as likely to have had oral sex as nonvirgins (Werner-Wilson 1998). Brückner and Bearman (2005) reported that about 13 percent of consistent abstinence pledgers reported having had oral sex but not intercourse, compared with just 2 percent of nonpledgers and 5 percent of inconsistent pledgers. This is the popular definition of technical virginity, which characterizes about

16 percent of all American teenagers. As you can see, it is not adolescents from any religious tradition, but the nonreligious, who are most likely to fit this profile. Over 22 percent of nonreligious teenagers have had oral or anal sex, but not intercourse. They are followed in prevalence by Catholics, the mix of those from other religions, evangelicals, mainliners, and—at bottom—black Protestants, who are far more likely to have already experienced vaginal intercourse.

Among NSYR 16-year-olds, about 19 percent of mainline Protestants and 23 percent of Jews opt for an oral-sex-only approach, compared with only 8 percent of evangelicals, 7 percent of Catholics, and a mere 3 percent of black Protestants. When I turn the tables and evaluate youth who have *only had vaginal intercourse*, this characterizes about 30 percent of 16- to 17-year-old black Protestant teenagers, but *zero* percent of 16-year-old mainline Protestant and Jewish youths, and only 3 out of 93 17-year-olds. Let me state this plainly: out of 113 Jewish adolescents in the NSYR, *not one* reported having had vaginal intercourse but not oral sex. Only 4 out of 341 mainline Protestant youths reported the same. There is certainly something to this pattern.

The interviews hint at this pattern as well. Naomi, an 18-year-old Jewish girl from Massachusetts, says about oral sex, "I don't think it's as serious, because you don't have to be as careful depending on who you're with. . . . But I think it's still intimate. I don't think you could just do that [have oral sex] for everybody." Rob, a 17-year-old mainline Protestant from New Jersey, doesn't have reservations about teenagers who want to have sex, provided they're in a relationship and are "serious about each other." However, when asked about his friends' sexual behavior, he says: "A lot is oral sex, or just like, you know, like fooling around and stuff. And I doubt, I don't think a lot of people are really getting into it, just like actual sex, for a while." A virgin himself, he sees sex as dangerous—what with the ever-present threat of pregnancy and STDs—but largely lacking a moral component.

Is Oral Sex in the Script?

There are good reasons to think that religiously conservative youth might uniquely avoid oral sex in a way that they might not avoid vaginal intercourse. After all, the Bible seldom explicitly addresses alternative sexual practices, but when it does, it tends to be disparaging. In other words, many religious youths may prefer to avoid oral sex because it is considered deviant, gross, or simply without precedent—in other words, it's not in their sexual script. Two of the most theologically conservative traditions—black Protestants and Mormons—each display *higher* percentages of vaginal intercourse than oral sex, and black Protestants are the least likely to be technical virgins. A mere 1.5 percent of African-American youth in the NSYR have *only* had oral sex. The same perspective characterizes the most devoutly religious youths, regardless of particular denomination: they are much more likely at age 17 to have experienced vaginal intercourse than to have experienced oral sex.

The interviews bear these claims out. Jamaal, an 18-year-old African American, disdains oral sex and wonders why anyone—male or female—would put their mouth on organs that also function to excrete waste products (to paraphrase his words). He prefers "just the regular" method of sex. Another African-American adolescent who has had oral sex complains, "I don't think it's really that rewarding. It's just really kind of boring, when you look at it." Janeena, an African American, thinks—in contrast to how many white youth tend to see it—that "regular" sex is acceptable "first," before marriage, and only then might other forms of sex become legitimate. Lisa, a 16-year-old white Mormon from Nevada, concurs:

> There's a big difference [between the two types of sex], but it's kind of opposite of what most people would believe. I feel that like oral sex is much more beyond than sex. So, beyond, you mean . . .] Like, more intimate even. Or like, like it would take a lot, like a long relationship or a really good relationship or something.

These are not the words of adolescents looking for alternative sexual pleasures yet keen on remaining virgins. Rather, oral sex is not in their sexual script, and for many it never will be.

Perhaps this preference among religious conservatives reflects their higher fertility rates and even a pronatalist and profamily orientation rather than an anti-sex approach. After all, evangelical Protestants were the most likely (29 percent) to report being married. This is nearly *twice* as high as mainline Protestants (15 percent) and almost *five times* as likely as Jews (6 percent). By contrast, Randall, a 14-year-old religiously unaffiliated youth from Montana, offered his primary reason for preferring oral sex: you can't get someone pregnant that way. Premarital pregnancy may still be scandalous among religious conservatives, but early family formation is not; it's still in their script. Family formation is no longer a central goal of many other young Americans. It's optional, and considered best delayed. Thus, technical virginity makes far more sense to less religious adolescents than to the most devout.

PRACTICING ORAL SEX OR JUST DABBLING?

Is oral sex a short-term, transitional replacement for more satisfying but riskier vaginal intercourse, or does it become a habit in its own right? While we did not ask pointed questions in our interviews about the frequency of oral sex, we did ask this on the NSYR survey. Youth who attend religious services more than once a week are the least likely to have had oral sex just once. Still, these religious adolescents are hardly exhibiting patterns of frequent oral sexual behavior. Only 12 percent of them report having oral sex "many times," which is about half the rate reported by youth of more modest attendance levels. The highest frequency of oral sex is among teenagers who attend sporadically (25 percent) and those who say religion is unimportant (30 percent).

Personal religious salience remains a steady predictor of the frequency of oral sex, even in more advanced statistical models. Youth for whom religion is important either avoid oral sex altogether or limit the number of times they experience it. This robust association holds up while controlling for powerful age, gender (male), and race (white) effects, among other influences. Even when accounting for several phenomena that predict more frequent oral sex (popularity, rebelliousness, currently dating, level of autonomy from parents, having "bad" friends, etc.), teenagers who think that religion is an important part of their daily lives are less likely to have frequent oral sex. Sources of moral authority eventually crowd out most of the *direct* religious influences, suggesting that adolescent religiosity is indirectly effective via its association with avoiding self-centered morality (making decisions based on what makes them happy or what gets them ahead), which in turn displays strong positive (and direct) effects on the frequency of oral sex.

Nevertheless, the NSYR and NSFG cannot yet answer the question of whether oral sex is a transitional experience for adolescents moving toward vaginal intercourse. But the evidence noted about youth who practice one or the other type of sex, but not both, hints at this conclusion: there's no one clear pattern. Some use oral sex as a transitional action, others combine it with intercourse, while the majority avoids them altogether until later in adolescence or adulthood.

ANAL SEX

Reports of anal sex were very unusual among adolescents in the Add Health study, so much so that I originally gave little thought to addressing the issue. After the 2002 NSFG data were released, however, I could no longer avoid it. The NSFG—several years newer than the Add Health—reported that 8.1 percent and 5.6 percent of 15- to 17-year-old males and females, respectively, say they have experienced

heterosexual anal sex. These numbers well exceeded Add Health's, possibly indicating its increasing popularity. Again, the least religious stand out: nearly one in five nonreligious teenage boys have had anal sex, followed at a distance by black Protestants (12 percent), Catholics (8 percent), Evangelicals (4 percent), and mainline Protestants (3 percent). Among girls, the nonreligious are also tops—at 14 percent—followed by mainline Protestants (10 percent), black Protestants (6 percent), evangelicals (4 percent), and Catholics (3 percent). Religiosity follows the same linear pattern we have seen. While about 15–17 percent of teens who never attend church report having anal sex, less than 2 percent of the most active religious youth say this. As with intercourse, the distinction between these most religious of all youth and teenagers who attend church weekly (still considered to be regular attendance) is notable: their prevalence rates of anal sex are twice as high as among those who attend church services more than once a week. The religious distinctions are strong: even after controlling for family structure, demographics, and parents' education, church attendance significantly curbs reports of anal sex.

PORNOGRAPHY

Sexual practices like anal sex no doubt receive a boost from their online visibility. The pornography industry is huge, thrives in the United States, and certainly affects adolescents (Stack, Wasserman, and Kern 2004). Assisted by technology, people are increasingly able to remove sexual expression from the context of interpersonal relationships. Pornography is no longer the exclusive domain of "adult" shops and the cordoned-off section of select bookstores. Pornography is, as we all know by now, widely available over the Internet and often delivered to us unsolicited in e-mail. For millions of young Americans, Internet pornography is their introduction to sexual information *and* expression. E-mail subject lines invite us to take a look at "sex-starved bitches" or "gorgeous gangbangers." Online, Americans are now never more than a click or two away from it. The popularity of online pictorial diaries at places like MySpace.com enable even amateurs (and teenagers) to participate in the porn industry. Unlike in the past, those who wish to avoid pornography have to go out of their way to do so. In a study released in 2003, one in four adolescents report unwanted exposure to sexually explicit pictures on the Internet in the past year (Mitchell, Finkelhor, and Wolak 2003). By now, that number is certainly much higher. Surprisingly, the level of parental supervision is not associated with such exposure. And filtering software is only modestly protective. Of that original 25 percent, one-quarter report being very or extremely upset by what they saw. One wonders if the same would be true today, considering the numbness that tends to accompany heightened exposure.

Since the 1990s, the pornography industry is thought to have outgrossed the box office receipts of all of Hollywood's films put together (Thio 2001). Many "normal" corporations and their stockholders directly or indirectly profit from the porn industry's success, since numerous multinational corporations often either own "entertainment" subsidiaries or profit from pornographic rentals. It is thought that roughly 40 percent of American hotels (more than 1.5 million rooms) offer pay-per-view pornography, accounting for several hundred million dollars in revenue per year, and up to 80 percent of total in-room entertainment charges (CNN, August 22, 2006). Despite such popularity, reliable data on and analyses of pornography use are exceptionally rare. Academics are in no hurry to collect such data (Slade 2001). And if studies of adult pornography use are unusual, research on adolescent usage is even more unique.

Perhaps because of this lack of data, speculation abounds about the prevalence of pornography among (mostly male) adolescents and adults. We *do* know that the personality predictors for "old style," offline pornography use are not very relevant to the study of online pornography use (Fisher and Barak 2000). Online porn is much more accessible, and the selection effects for it are different. Pamela Paul (2005) interviewed more than 100 people and noted that pornography tends to distract men from their real sexual partners and as a result harms their social relationships. The debate over these and other harmful effects of pornography continues, but the debate is hardly an informed one, since so few solid social scientists have waded into it.

Data on religion's influence on pornography use are limited as well. Darren Sherkat and Christopher Ellison (1997) note a strong connection between strength of religiosity and condemnation of pornography. Religious organizations, sometimes in unusual alliances with feminist organizations, have been and remain the most common sources of antiporn crusades. A descriptive study of Internet sex chat room participation finds that half of all users report no religious affiliation and that religion holds no influence in their lives (Wysocki 2001). More recently, a rare glimpse into the social science of adult pornography use revealed that the strongest predictors of Internet pornography use are weak ties to religion and the absence of a happy marriage (Stack, Wasserman, and Kern 2004). Religion, the authors conclude, functions as a social-control mechanism that may prevent adult men from doing what might otherwise come naturally to them (looking at pornography).

In the telephone survey component of the NSYR, adolescent respondents were queried in this way about Internet pornography use: "[i]n the last year, how often, if at all, have you used the Internet to view X-rated, pornographic Web sites?" Respondents could reply with: about once a day, a few times a week, about once a week, a few times a month, about once a month, less than once a month, or never. Pornography use is largely a gender-specific practice. The consumers of pornography among America's adolescents are almost exclusively male. Fully

97 percent of surveyed girls in the NSYR state that they never use the Internet for pornography, compared with 70 percent of all adolescent boys (60 percent of 16- and 17-year-old boys). I suspect there also is considerable social desirability bias at work in this question, prompting youths to underreport their involvement in pornography. From our in-person interviews, a majority of adolescent boys do not think there is a problem with viewing pornography, and they admit to doing this very thing ("infrequently," of course). Comparing the interview admissions with the survey data, then, suggests that the latter are undercounting.

Pornography use varies according to religiosity: whereas 18 percent of adolescent boys who never attend services report monthly use, only about 8 percent who attend more than once a week report comparably. Religion's importance in daily life sorts these youth even more extensively: 26 percent who say religion is not important at all report regular porn use, compared to only 5 percent who say religion is extremely important. Religious affiliation is also associated with this outcome: Jewish and nonreligious youths report the highest rates of pornography use—about 30 and 22 percent, respectively. Evangelicals, Mormons, and youths who identify with another (non-Christian) religion display the lowest stated rates of pornography use here, though these numbers may be artificially low due to stronger than average social desirability bias. The moral source variables (how youth decide between right and wrong) likewise show clear distinctions in their associations with Internet pornography.

The odds of Internet pornography use by spiritual-but-not-religious youth are elevated, even when controlling for their primary religious affiliation. With the addition of controls, the only two affiliations that remain distinctly different from evangelicals are Catholics and Jews, both of whom display significantly higher frequency. Thus, evangelical Protestants are among the least likely to report pornography use. They are statistically comparable to black

Protestants, mainliners, Mormons, and non-religious youth. Interestingly, religious attendance, the key indicator of public religiosity, exhibits little bearing on pornography usage, while religion's importance for daily life matters considerably.

Gendered and Religious Perspectives on Pornography

Very few adolescent girls with whom we spoke approve of pornography. Religion does not appear to augment their displeasure, either. Cassie, a 15-year-old evangelical from Georgia, is transparent in her repulsion, and her sentiment captures the opinion of the majority of the adolescent girls: "I feel betrayed by it really. Because a lot of it is watched by guys really, and I feel like I'm being stripped bare even if it's not my body. And it bothers me."

Samantha, a 15-year-old mainline Protestant from Virginia, speaks disparagingly of pornography, not so much for its immorality but rather because it indicates some pathetic ineptness on the part of users: "I think [pornography] is the dumbest thing.... Oh gosh. Seriously, though, you're a low life if, like, you can't go out and do your own thing. You have to watch someone else. I think that's disgusting. I think it's retarded. Uh, I think it's so low."

Other adolescent girls tolerate pornography, thinking it might be a safe outlet for adolescent boys' unstable libidos. Patti, a 14-year-old mainline Protestant girl from Pennsylvania, has mixed emotions about the subject:

I think that a lot of it is really, um, demeaning and degrading towards women. And it objectifies women; and I don't like to see that. I, it's not that I have a problem with the female or male body, because I think the body is a beautiful thing. And I think that art and pornography kind of get, sort of, done into one, because I mean there's a lot of really beautiful pieces of art that are of the naked body. [*Right.*] And obviously that's not pornography. [*Right.*] But I think that there's a fine line between art and pornography. And I think that pornography is disgusting and that there's no reason for it, so. But I think that people just have to realize there's a fine line between pornography and art form.

Patti's ambivalence concerns the portrait of the human female form, sans evident sexuality. However, most contemporary pornography is less concerned with conveying the *beauty* of a woman's body and more with its *sexuality*, either alone or with a partner(s) in a sexual act. That, Patti would agree, is objectionable.

Then, there is the other half of all adolescents—boys. I asked Jeff, a 17-year-old Catholic from Illinois, how he felt about pornography. He hemmed and hawed:

> Um, I think it's, I don't know. I don't think it's, oh man. Well you see, it depends on what you use it for, because I think it's good sometimes for teens because they're not having sex. They're taking all of that energy out on whatever, instead of going out and whatever, you know? But. I guess it's a way of, oh, I don't know, it's a way for teens to get out whatever they have to get out without making a baby or getting an STD.

Luke, a 16-year-old Catholic from New York, relays a common story about pornography use:

> Uh, it's, I don't know how to say it. I mean I'm not going to say I've never watched porn. I mean, what can you do? It's part of life. If you're going to look at it and you're going to watch it, that's your decision, I guess. [OK. So you mentioned you've seen it. Do you watch it at all on a regular basis?] Not on a regular basis. Every now and then of course, but . . . [How do you think viewing pornography affects us, do you think it changes us at all?] I guess it does some people. It really doesn't affect me.

I note above that what little research does exist on this topic suggests that evangelical Protestant adults tend to hold antipornography attitudes (Sherkat and Ellison 1997). From the NSYR survey and interviews, evangelical youth also tend to think uniquely about pornography, feeling distinctly hostile toward it, at least in concept. However, it is not at all clear that their usage patterns differ from other adolescents. We asked Tim, a 14-year-old evangelical from Georgia, about pornography: "It's wrong. [*Have you ever viewed pornographic Web sites or movies?*] Say that again? [*Have you ever viewed pornographic Web sites or movies?*] Can we skip this question?" Dale, a 15-year-old evangelical from Illinois, also takes his time when asked about pornography: "It's, I don't know. Skip it. [*OK. Ah, have you ever viewed any pornographic Web sites or movies or anything?*] Kind of inadvertently, like, but not really."

Despite their elevated proclivity for either avoiding the question or distorting the answer, evangelical adolescent boys are much more likely to identify the false "reality" of pornographic portrayals, less likely to take the matter lightly, and more likely to recognize its tempting allure. One 15-year-old notes that "you never know the person [in the picture], you're never going to meet them, and even if you did, would you have a chance with them? I don't view it as, as reasonable." Another calls it "not that satisfying. . . . there's a lot of fakeness to it. . . . it portrays a false sort of lifestyle." David, the evangelical from Texas, not only told me that he struggled for a time with a pornography "addiction" that "desensitized" him, but also that he feels "sorry for the people who watch that. And I feel sorry for the people who make it and star in them. It's sad." He quit looking at it when "it made me start feeling sick inside and empty."

Together, these accounts denote several conclusions about the majority of teenage boys and pornography:

- They look at it.
- They don't like to think that they look at it very often (although they may).
- Many believe it to be helpful (when combined with masturbation) for relieving pent-up sexual tension.

- Some feel guilty about it. Most feel embarrassed to admit it.
- They don't talk about it with their friends.
- Most believe that it doesn't affect them.

How to Make Love Like a Porn Star?

Not a few adolescent boys, however, express a perspective that most girls would certainly loathe—that of pornography as education about proper sexual technique. That is, some clearly think that what they see online or in videos is not only real sex (which it might be) but normal sex. Emilio, a 14-year-old Catholic from Arizona, thinks pornography is completely natural, " 'cause everybody does it. I mean, I'm not saying just 'cause everybody does it I do it, but I do it to learn. To learn or to, just to watch it. Most of the time to learn. [To learn what?] Like if I get in that situation, I'll know what to do." One of the more salient criticisms of pornography concerns this very thing—that it provides a false picture of what sexually intimate relations are like.

Although there is clearly variation, much contemporary pornography portrays women in submissive positions and men as sexual aggressors. In an enlightening look at the pornography industry and its delusional subtexts, Gail Dines and Robert Jensen (2004: 374) identify the main themes of heterosexual pornography: "(1) All women always want sex from men; (2) women like all the sexual acts that men perform or demand; and (3) any woman who does not at first realize this can be persuaded with a little force." Male-on-female violence—real, implied, or symbolic—pervades pornographic video. As a result, some adolescent boys approach girls "expecting them to be into anything and everything" (Hari 2005: 33).

Laura Carpenter (2002: 357) relays a similar experience from one of her interviewees who, in the process of losing his virginity, "tried to do what [he] saw the people do in the porno movies." His efforts did not lead to a mutually satisfying experience, to say the least. While it

is unclear how common Emilio's distorted perspective on pornography is, it is certainly disconcerting. An equally difficult question to answer is just how much adolescent girls have actually internalized the unrealistic (and emotionally harmful) norms of pornography. Do adolescent girls respond to the perceived "demand" for unusual sexual activities that their boyfriends are learning about online? Do they themselves log on to learn, or is any link between pornography and new sexual trends indirect, via its influence on popular teen magazines and their advice columns? While definitively answering these questions is not yet possible, the increase I note in the prevalence of anal sex among adolescents, however, hints at one answer.

MIDDLE-CLASS (SEXUAL) MORALITY

A key claim I want to make, and one which I believe the data support, is that a distinctly middle-class sexual morality is visible in the American religious scene, especially (but not exclusively) among mainline Protestant and Jewish youth—traditionally among the wealthiest of religious Americans. This sexual ethic trades the "higher" pleasures of vaginal intercourse for a set of low-risk substitutes: coupled oral sex, mutual masturbation, and solitary pornography use (and masturbation). By "low risk," I mean that the chance of pregnancy is nil, and the threat of transmitting STDs is diminished. Those who hold to this middle-class morality are more apt to think of sexual intercourse as "dangerous"—that is, conducive to pregnancy and diminished life chances.

White, strategically oriented youth with educated parents are among the least likely adolescents to object to contraception in theory and the most likely to say that having sex would upset their mother and that pregnancy would embarrass them. What are mainline Protestant and Jewish teenagers like? On average, they are white, not overly religious, very strategic, and from educated homes. Black Protestant, evangelical, Mormon, and some Catholic adolescents are more likely to say that premarital sex is wrong, but they also are quicker to engage in—and to tolerate the potential responsibilities that come with—sexual intercourse. While I don't have enough historical data to suggest that a widespread *change* has occurred in adolescents' sexual scripts, there is sufficient evidence that the behavior of white, middle-class, strategic mainline Protestant and Jewish teenagers reveals a script that is certainly distinct.

Adolescents espousing this new script are generally not interested in remaining technical virgins, though they may nevertheless exhibit that status for a time. They are sexually tolerant. They are interested in remaining free from the burden of teenage pregnancy and the sorrows and embarrassments of STDs. They perceive a bright future for themselves, one with college, advanced degrees, a career, and a family. Simply put, too much seems at stake. Sexual intercourse is not worth the risks. The pleasures of sex could be a foolish transaction, leading to pregnancy, which would in turn require hard thinking about abortion (to which they are generally not opposed, but don't take lightly, either). Thus, vaginal intercourse is replaced *for a time* by alternatives like oral sex and pornography.

Ironically, it is at its root a profamily sexual ethic, since such youths tend to come from what many scholars would label "good homes," and they want this for themselves in the future. Their eventual spouse simply need not be their first and only sexual partner. More important is emerging from pre-premarital sexual relationships free of children and disease. Sandra, a 13-year-old mainline Protestant girl from Washington, articulates the familial aspect of this sexual script. When asked under what conditions it would be OK to have sex, she responds: "(a) you're married. [Or] (b) you are having protected sex. . . . You know, just really safe, you know. I think marriage is a big, big deal." To Elisa, an articulate 14-year-old mainline

Protestant girl from northern Virginia, unprotected sex is even a moral mistake: "unprotected sex should wait until, not only marriage, but until you're really ready to have a child."

Elisa captures this middle-class morality script concisely: "I don't think that it's imperative that you wait until marriage, but I think it's a good, it's a wise decision." This ethic is not about religion. It's about being shrewd. Solidly middle- or upper-middle-class adolescents have considerable socioeconomic and educational expectations, courtesy of their parents and their communities' lifestyles. They are happy with their direction, generally not rebellious, tend to get along well with their parents, and have few moral qualms about expressing their nascent sexuality. In fact, nowhere in my NSYR analyses does the "parents, teachers, or respected adults" source of moral authority distinguish itself *except for contraceptive use*. Some parents are pushing sexual safety rather than abstinence, and their adolescent children are listening and obeying. Parental expectations are what shape their sexual values and scripts. If religion can help them live up to these values and avoid sexual pain, all the better. But it is not really expected to, since religion is a side item on their menu and not the main course (Smith and Denton 2005).

CONCLUSIONS

Oral sex, considered to be the primary substitute for vaginal intercourse (perhaps besides masturbation), is a more common *first* sexual activity until about age 16, at which point its preferred status begins to give way to intercourse. It is also more popular among nonreligious, mainline Protestant, and Jewish teenagers than it is among other religious groups.

Although some observers suggest that there is an emerging penchant among evangelicals and abstinence pledgers for technical virginity—the practice of oral or anal sex without vaginal intercourse—there is not much evidence of it when talking with them. Strictly by the numbers, it characterizes about 16 percent of youth. Technical virginity, however, is clearly less about religious rules and more about a strategic approach to steering clear of pregnancy and STDs. Indeed, most technical virgins have no moral objections to intercourse. They simply think it's a risk not worth taking.

Internet pornography is fast becoming a central source of adolescents' information about the sexual practices of others. It's a poor source, no doubt, fraught with unreal accounts of hypersexuality, group sex, fetishes, and women who live only to sexually satisfy men. It does not reflect sexual reality. Just how many American adolescents believe it does is, of course, impossible to gauge. Some interviewees suggested this to us, however. While religious patterns for pornography use are clear, the topic is subject to an elevated level of social desirability bias. Hems, haws, sighs, and long pauses accompanied lots of adolescent boys' answers to our questions about pornography, regardless of religiosity or religious affiliation. I suspect its use is more underreported than other sex-related practices. Its long-term influence on patterned sexual attitudes and behavior remains unknown.

The key story of the chapter, though, is about an evident sexual ethic among strategic, education-minded, moderately religious youth. I call it an emerging middle-class sexual morality, but in truth it is more characteristic of the upper middle class than those—like evangelical Protestants—who are newer to the middle class. It is future-oriented, self-focused (but not anti-family), risk aversive, parent-driven (and subtly class-oriented), yet largely sexually tolerant. It is most apparent among less religious and more affluent mainline Protestant and Jewish adolescents, though others subscribe to it as well. Oral sex is substituted for vaginal intercourse, and in so doing adolescents retain their technical virginity. But this is seldom *intentional*, in contrast to recent research claims to the contrary. Such youth see no need to abstain from intercourse until marriage. They're just

abstaining for the present to safeguard their future schooling plans, career trajectories, and life chances.

INTRODUCTION REFERENCES

Brückner, H., and P. Bearman. 2005. After the promise: The STD consequences of adolescent virginity pledges. *Journal of Adolescent Health 36*: 271–278.

Coles, R., and G. Stokes. 1985. *Sex and the American teenager.* New York: Harper & Row.

Remez, L. 2000. Oral sex among adolescents: Is it sex or is it abstinence? *Family Planning Perspectives 32*: 298–304.

Sanders, S. A., and J. M. Reinisch. 1999. Would you say you "had sex" if . . .? *Journal of the American Medical Association 281*: 275–77.

Talbot, M. 2008. Red sex, blue sex: Why do so many evangelical teen-agers become pregnant? *The New Yorker.* Http://www.newyorker.com/reporting/2008/11/03/081103fa_fact_talbot?yrail (accessed November 3).

Thio, A. 2001. *Deviant behavior* (6th ed.). Boston: Allyn and Bacon.

REFERENCES

Brückner, Hannah, and Peter S. Bearman. 2005. "After the Promise: The STD Consequences of Adolescent Virginity Pledges." *Journal of Adolescent Health 36*: 271–278.

Carpenter, Laura M. 2002. "Gender and the Meaning and Experience of Virginity Loss in the Contemporary United States." *Gender & Society 16*: 345–365.

Clark, Chap. 2004. *Hurt: Inside the World of Today's Teenagers.* Grand Rapids, MI: Baker Academic Press.

DiMarco, Hayley, 2006. *Technical Virgin: How Far Is Too Far?* Grand Rapids, MI: Revell.

Dines, Gail and Robert Jensen. 2004. "Pornography and Media: Toward a More Critical Analysis." pp. 369–380 in *Sexualities: Identities, Behaviors, and Society,* edited by Michael S. Kimmel and Rebecca F. Plante. New York: Oxford University Press.

Fisher, William, and Azy Barak. 2000. "Online Sex Shops: Phenomenological and Ideological Perspectives on Internet Sexuality." *Cyber Psychology & Behavior 3*: 575–589.

Hari, Johann. 2005. "It's Everywhere: Just Don't Talk about It." *New Statesman*, March 7, 32–33.

Mitchell, Kimberly J., David Finkelhor, and Janis Wolak. 2003. "The Exposure of Youth to Unwanted Sexual Material on the Internet: A National Survey of Risk, Impact, and Prevention." *Youth & Society* 34: 330–358.

Paul, Pamela, 2005. *Pornified: How Pornography Is Transforming Our Lives, Our Relationships, and Our Families*. New York: Times Books.

Remez, Lisa. 2000. "Oral Sex among Adolescents: Is It Sex or is It Abstinence?" *Family Planning Perspectives* 32: 298–304.

Sherkat, Darren E., and Christopher G. Ellison. 1997. "The Cognitive Structure of a Moral Crusade: Conservative Protestant Opposition to Pornography." *Social Forces* 75; 957–980.

Slade, Joseph W. 2001. *Pornography and Sexual Representation: A Reference Guide* (Vol. 1). Westport, CT: Greenwood.

Stack, Steven, Ira Wasserman, and Roger Kern. 2004. "Adult Social Bonds and Use of Internet Pornography." *Social Science Quarterly* 85: 75–88.

Thio, Alex. 2001. *Deviant Behavior*, 6th ed. Boston: Allyn and Bacon.

Werner-Wilson, Ronald Jay. 1998. "Are Virgins at Risk for Contracting HIV/AIDS?" *Journal of HIV/AIDS Prevention & Education for Adolescents & Children* 2: 63–71.

Wysocki, Diane K. 2001. "Let Your Fingers Do the Talking: Sex on an Adult Chat Line." pp. 258–263 in *Readings in Deviant Behavior*, edited by Alex Thio and Thomas Calhoun. Boston: Allyn and Bacon.

CHAPTER 10

Negotiation of First Sexual Intercourse Among Latina Adolescent Mothers

Pamela I. Erickson

Pamela Erickson assumes a laborious task as she investigates cultural and social factors affecting the initiation of sexual intercourse among Latina adolescent mothers using the case study method. The data were drawn from life-history interviews with the young mothers and their sexual partners from 1994 to 1997.

The author's careful review of the research literature revealed a number of stereotyped gender behaviors influenced by Latino cultural norms. These patterns included the fact that, in some cases, the female adolescent wants a baby; she has a high incidence of older men or adolescents as sex partners; and her role models are peers, relatives, and/or a mother who experienced teenage pregnancy. However, Erickson suggests that changes in socio-economic realities, such as the emergence of an educated Latino middle class and exposure to more egalitarian gender norms in the United States, have resulted in greater variations in actual gender behavior among Latina adolescents and less stereotypical behavior.

As the case studies in Erickson's research unfold, patterns emerge: scripting of relationships; male pressure and female resistance; the absence of

verbal consent; ignorance about sexuality; and male control along with female passivity. Readers are challenged to determine the role of cultural and societal factors in scenarios so deftly drawn by the data. How do these findings differ from those concerning other populations? Do these findings account for the fact that in 1995 the Latina adolescent birth rate surpassed that of African Americans for the first time? Is Erickson correct that Latino adolescent behavior is becoming less stereotypical? There is no lack of interesting questions for interested readers.

In the United States today, adolescent pregnancy and childbearing are perceived as serious health, social, and economic problems [1]. Despite a substantial research literature and numerous intervention programs, teenage childbearing rates have remained high for two decades [2]. The most recent statistics on adolescent birth rates indicate that those of Latina adolescent have now surpassed those of African Americans for the first time, and among Latina teens, birth rates are highest for those of Mexican descent [3]. This article explores the social and cultural context of romantic relationships in which Latina teen pregnancy occurs, using narratives from young mothers and their partners to illustrate experiences surrounding initiation of sexual intercourse and pregnancy.

From "Negotiation of First Sexual Intercourse among Latina Adolescent Mothers" by P. I. Erickson. 1998–1999. *International Quarterly of Community Health Education 18*: 121–137. Copyright © 1998, Baywood Publishing Company, Inc. Reprinted by permission.

The literature on teenage motherhood clearly demonstrates that adolescent childbearing is largely a socioeconomic class phenomenon intertwined with issues of race and ethnicity [2, 4]. Although it is commonly believed that teenage childbearing is disadvantageous for both mother and child [5], recent research suggests that adolescent childbearing may be an adaptive response to severe, generational, socioeconomic constraints experienced most acutely by adolescents of color [6–7].

Although political economy is an important factor in race and ethnic differences in adolescent childbearing, cultural expectations may also influence reproductive behavior [8]. In fact, Latina adolescents have distinct sexual behavior patterns. Compared to African-American and White (Non-Hispanic) adolescents, Latina adolescents have the lowest proportion of sexually active females, and they exhibit low use of family planning clinics, low use of contraceptive methods before becoming pregnant, and low use of abortion [9–11]. Latina adolescents may also be more likely to plan their pregnancies. Two surveys of primarily Mexican origin teen mothers in Los Angeles found that the proportion of young mothers who had planned to have a baby had increased from 34 percent in the 1986–87 survey to 58 percent in the 1992–94 survey [4]. In contrast, national data indicate that only 18 percent of pregnancies to adolescents of all races are planned [5]. In addition, greater acculturation has been associated with higher levels of sexual risk taking behavior and higher birth rates among Latina adolescents [9, 13–14].

Religious values are thought to buttress traditional gender role patterns through opposition to contraception and abortion [15]. In fact, however, Latinos are more similar to other Americans regarding both contraceptive use and attitudes about abortion [11, 15–16]. The use of abortion by Latinas actually exceeds that of Whites, although it may be used less often by Latina adolescents [11, 17].

Research and prevention efforts dealing with teenage pregnancy and childbearing have tended to assume three things: (1) that teenage motherhood is socially, economically, and often medically disadvantageous and should be prevented [1, 6]; (2) that all pregnancies should be consciously planned and young women should prevent unintended pregnancy through abstinence or contraception [5]; and (3) that young women have a choice about whether or not to engage in sex and they make decisions about sex and birth control after weighing the opportunity costs [18]. Yet, such a "rational decision-making" model of sex and reproduction seems to be a construct imposed by researchers, health practitioners, and other professionals dealing with adolescent pregnancy and childbearing issues. It is at odds with the emotional, highly intimate context in which sex is initiated by adolescents [19]. In the real world, sexual initiation is affected by a wide range of factors including emotions, sexual desire, coercion, and social, cultural, and moral norms [18–19].

In order to understand high rates of Latina adolescent childbearing it is important to understand how the social and cultural aspects of young Latinas' lives may put them at risk for early pregnancy. Latino culture places high value on family and motherhood, and childbearing occurs at younger ages than is normative in the broader American culture [20–21]. Latino cultural norms also tend to value premarital virginity and non-aggressive, modest, sexually ignorant, and sexually passive young women [21–23]. American cultural norms make young women the sexual gate-keepers in heterosexual relationships [19] and place high value on consciously chosen, responsible, planned motherhood [1, 5]. This non-traditional, essentially middle class, American gender role pattern may be one for which many Latina teens are not prepared.

THE CURRENT STUDY

Forty Latina teen mothers under age eighteen at the time they gave birth were recruited from a public hospital providing care to a low income, Latino population. The partners of the young mothers were also invited to participate subject to her permission. Fourteen male partners agreed to participate.[1]

Life histories of participants were collected during one to five informal interviews of one and two hours in length. Participants were simply asked to tell the story of their lives. Topics probed included neighborhood, school, and family, sex and romantic relationships, pregnancy and delivery, being a parent, school and work, migration history, acculturation, health care, and future life plans and goals.

Narratives are presented for five cases which illustrate the range of experiences surrounding sexual debut for young mothers. The interviews suggest that for these young mothers, it was not really sex that was being negotiated, but the couple's entire relationship.[2] "Rational" decision making regarding sex, contraception, and STD prevention could only become the norm for these young couples after they had been having intercourse for some time.

EVA AND RUDY[3]

At age sixteen, Eva moved out of her mother's house because they fought and she thought her mother drank too much, had too many boyfriends, and made her take care of her younger siblings all the time. Eva moved into a small apartment with her sister and another couple, but the situation was strained:

Eva: That's why I ended up living with Rudy.

Interviewer: When you were living with your sister, and you and Rudy were just *novios* (boyfriend/girlfriend)—you weren't really involved sexually yet. Did it happen after you moved in with Rudy?

Eva: After we moved to his house. He would like ask me, you know, if we could be together like. "No, no, no—I don't want it." Like, I didn't

wanna go that far, you know: I was, like, scared. So he—well, he respected me. But we had tried for (having intercourse) sometimes, but it was like—oh! I wouldn't even know what to do. So, just forget it, you know. I was scared, so, I was like, no.

After six months of resistance, Eva gave in to Rudy's urging for sex and got pregnant in the first month.

Eva: The first time (we had sex), I was living with him, he just came outside, but I still got pregnant. (Sex) scared me at first because I was never introduced to my body or even a male's body. I didn't even know how my body worked, you know? To me, in my head it (premarital sex) was wrong.

Interviewer: Were you willing to *entregar* (give yourself up, surrender) yourself to him?

Eva: Yeah, because, see like, I really did love him a lot and I really did care for him, but it was just the fact that I was gonna lose my virginity. I mean, for a Hispanic girl, you know, that's like, God, that's a big thing! That's like something precious. And, you know, like, you just have to wait 'til you're married and stuff, you know? I did love him a lot, but I just didn't want to go that far. I didn't even know why. I just didn't want to do it . . . may be because of what I had been taught. But I did. I didn't like being at home, and maybe it was a better way to stay away from home. So, being with him was better, and eventually I just gave up to it. But I was just looking for comfort, because I wasn't getting it at home.

Interviewer: Was it ever talked about, planned?

Eva: He would always ask me and I would say "No, no, no, no, no."

Eva and Rudy never talked about sex or contraception, but they had talked about a baby.

Eva: He had told me before that he wanted a baby, but I told him "I don't. I don't want a baby."

Eva was surprised that she got pregnant because they had only had sex that one time. By the time she realized she was pregnant she was about twelve to thirteen weeks and would not consider an abortion. After her daughter was born, Eva went back to high school and she is now in college. She and Rudy have a rocky relationship. They don't live together now, but he is very involved as a father and takes Sara frequently.

Rudy was born in Los Angeles and dropped out of school in ninth grade about the time his parents separated. He began working construction and met Eva when he was sixteen.

> *Rudy*: . . . I used to mess around with a lot of girls. But not in, you know . . . to put it this way, I was a virgin. I let her think that I—I was a big time player with the girls. And, uh, she was my first one.
>
> *Interviewer*: So, how did you decide to have sex?
>
> *Rudy*: Well, to me it wasn't really hard, but you know, for Eva it was.' cause . . . you know guys always they always leave them, you know. But the girl, like Eva, she was scared.
>
> *Interviewer*: Was she scared about getting pregnant? Did you guys ever talk about that?
>
> *Rudy*: She never did talk to me about that.
>
> *Interviewer*: And were you trying to get her pregnant?
>
> *Rudy*: Yeah, in a way, I was like . . . how does it feel to have a kid?
>
> *Interviewer*: Were you in love with Eva?
>
> *Rudy*: Well, see, I never loved someone, like really loved 'em (sic). You know? I don't know why. I'm just like that. I do like Eva and everything, but like, I miss her, but I don't like, love her, you know. Not yet. I don't know, we share a lot of things together, you know, but, I don't know how to love someone.

JULIA AND JUAN

Juan met Julia in Mexico. He was born and raised in Los Angeles but was visiting his grandparents in Mexico. Julia's family lived in the same neighborhood and they were family friends of his grandparents. She was twelve years old when they first met, but told him she was fifteen. He was sixteen. For two years, he visited whenever he could. He was in love. He wrote her poems and called her on the phone.

> *Juan*: I wasn't doing good (in school) 'cause all the time I was thinking about Julia—all the time . . . from one period to the next. I just couldn't stop. I couldn't help it. I tried not to think of her but I just couldn't stop.
>
> *Interviewer*: You were really in love with her.
>
> *Juan*: Yeah, but not—it was more, uh, spiritual, you know than just wanting to kiss her. No, it was true love. So I didn't want to have sex with her. I got tempted sometimes—when we were kissing so passionately—but I respected her. She was the first girl I respected.

Juan eventually found out that Julia had lied about her age and he agonized over how young she was. He wanted to wait until she was older before going out, to ask permission from her parents to date her, and then to have a long courtship. But when Julia was fourteen and Juan eighteen, her parents sent her to relatives in Los Angeles. She and Juan arranged to meet, and he took her to live with him at his mother's house.

> *Juan*: I decided to steal her with her permission. She was having troubles with her brothers and with her parents. And everybody was trying to talk me out of it because I was too young, but I was really in love with her and didn't want her to go through any more pain. So, when she was here, I stole her. That's when I got on the bad side of her parents. And they really got upset with me and I understood, 'cause that made me feel like less of a man. So, I decided to go ahead and live with her. I didn't want to 'cause I wanted to get

married first instead of taking her, because I knew that once she was there, where was she was gonna sleep? So, I just thought I might as well sleep with her, but I swear I wasn't thinking about the physical—the sexual part didn't hit me until a day before (she moved in).

Interviewer: So, did you and Julia talk about it (having sex)?

Juan: No, we just felt so free that it just happened. When you're in love, it's like a sense of freedom—like you could do anything. You feel real positive about things. I couldn't believe it that she was there with me. I mean one time she's in Mexico and the next she's in my room. She was so beautiful. And I was thinking, well, if I'm gonna marry her it might be OK. So, then, it just happened and it was like—we didn't—it wasn't even planned.

Julia was also in love with Juan.

Julia: He respected me a lot, and that day that I came (to live in his house)—I felt that I had to be with him.

Interviewer: Then, you didn't feel like he was pressuring you?

Julia: No, I knew what I was doing. He excites me, makes me happy. This is a love that is beautiful.

Interviewer: You intended to be his wife and have his children?

Julia: Yes.

Julia got pregnant about six months after they began having intercourse. They weren't using birth control because Julia had had an ovarian cyst in Mexico and she thought the doctor had told her she would never be able to have children. Juan and Julia wanted children someday, and they were hoping that Julia had been misdiagnosed, but they had not pursued medical follow-up in the United States. Thus, when she became pregnant, they were both surprised, but also very happy. They thought it was a little early

and that they were a little young, but they were happy. Juan and Julia now have two children and they were married shortly after Julia's eighteenth birthday.

SYLVIA

Sylvia, twenty years old at the time she was interviewed, was born in a small town in El Salvador. She came to the United States with her partner, Luís, when she was seventeen years old and three months pregnant with their daughter. Sylvia met and fell in love with Luís in El Salvador when she was fifteen. He was thirty. He had already moved to the United States, but had come back to visit relatives. Two years later when he returned to her village, she was still in love with him.

Luís began coming to her house and walking her to work. One day her stepfather caught them kissing, and her family tried to put an end to the relationship because he was so much older than she was. They threatened to call the police and have him put in jail, but Sylvia and Luís kept seeing each other secretly for about three months, and one day:

Sylvia: That's where it all started. He was going to take me to work, and from there we left. And the condemned man took me to a motel. And when I got there and he went in and I got to the door and I see the bed. Ay, I wanted to go but he grabbed me and wouldn't let me go. Well, maybe I wanted to, because then, we went together. I didn't know anything about condoms—nothing. And, I didn't protect myself. When I got pregnant he said: why didn't you take care of yourself (use contraception)?

In a later interview Sylvia continues with this theme:

Sylvia: Nobody educated me, nobody taught me (about sex). I think that's why I got pregnant so young. I'm not going to hide anything so that she (her daughter) can know. She has to know everything so she can choose what she wants to

Negotiation of First Sexual Intercourse Among Latina Adolescent Mothers 109

do. I never knew anything and because of that, I think, things happen.

Luís was surprised to find out that Sylvia was pregnant, and for awhile it was not clear what they would do. They finally decided that she would accompany him to the United States, but they have not married and Sylvia feels that their relationship is changing, or, perhaps that she thinks about things differently now.

> *Sylvia*: When I gave in and got pregnant I was head over heels in love with him. Now I don't know. It could be due to the problems we had when we got here. He drank a lot. Maybe I lost a little of all that I felt for him. Now I love him and all, but not like we were before.

Luís would like another child, but Sylvia does not—not yet anyway. Until things get better financially and emotionally she is using the oral contraceptive pill, despite Luís not wanting her to contracept.

ERIKA

Erika is a U.S.-born Latina who grew up in the housing projects. She was thirteen when she met Junior, who was twenty at the time. She had her first baby at fourteen.

> *Erika*: I met him on Halloween. I was just a Play-boy Bunny (her Halloween costume), so I didn't look my age. I was wearing heels and makeup—all of that. In the beginning I didn't really care for him, to tell you the truth. He kept coming and coming, so I guess that is what made me like him because he kept on coming.

Erika and Junior dated for about seven months before they had sex for the first time. Erika did not plan to have sex with Junior, but she was clear that he did not force her into it. She said that she didn't want to do it, but at the same time she wanted to do it. They never talked about having sex or about using birth control. She got pregnant within the first month.

> *Interviewer*: Were you trying to get pregnant, Erika?

> *Erika*: In a way I was, but in a way I was like no, no. It was in between.

> *Interviewer*: So, why did you want to get pregnant?

> *Erika*: The truth, the truth because I didn't want to be older.

> *Interviewer*: You didn't want to be a mother at an old age?

> *Erika*: Uhuh. My friend, she got a baby too, she got pregnant at thirteen. I had her (first baby) at fourteen. But her sister got pregnant at fifteen, had her (child) at sixteen. Everybody I know had a man, you know? Everybody I know has kids. I only know two people that don't have kids from everyone I know.

Erika and Junior are still together and they now have two children.

CORI

Cori came to the United States from Mexico with her mother after her parents' divorce when she was a small child. When Cori was ten, her mother sent her to live with her father in Mexico because she had a new partner and was beginning another family. When Cori turned thirteen she began having problems with her stepmother and came back to East L.A., where she lived with her mother and step-father until she was sixteen. They lived in a rough neighborhood with a lot of gang problems, but now Cori lives in an upscale beach community with her new partner. Cori thinks that the old neighborhood is part of the problem.

> *Cori*: My old friends there, a lot of them want to get out. They don't want to live in the neighborhood and they try to get out and it's too hard. They end up like me getting pregnant, but then they just get on welfare and they just say: "Oh well, I get on welfare I won't have to work."

They get all those girls pregnant and they just leave, and they don't think of their kids . . . when they need to give them money, to the girl, to take care of the kid, they are not there.

Cori met Carlos, her baby's father, through friends when she was fifteen. He was already eighteen and out of school, and she would ditch school to be with him. They went out for about a year before they had sex for the first time.

Cori: I mean it (sex) just happened. (laughs) We didn't talk about sex. He did once and got—I slapped him really hard. (laughter) He told me because we were six months together and all his friends were having sex and he wanted a girl-friend and a girlfriend was somebody he could sleep with and be with, and you know. I didn't let him, and he tried grabbing my butt, and I punched him so hard, (laughs) and he didn't like that, and he got mad for a while but then we went back together again, and it happened after a year. Then, we kind of broke off for a while and went back together.

Interviewer: So then, you guys went back together . . .

Cori: . . . for like six more months and then we did (had sex).

Interviewer: And how did that happen? Were you ready for it? Did you want to?

Cori: I don't know. I didn't really want to. It just happened, because I left my house. My mom threw me out. I didn't have anywhere to go, and so I stayed (at his house). I felt like I was trapped, and I am not going to say that he forced me but I was trapped . . . . I don't know, we did it for the wrong reasons. I felt like I was so desperate, I had nothing else to live for. (I thought) "I don't care about anything else, you know? Forget it, it's just you (him, Carlos) now." It would get to a point that I really didn't care. Then I let him. I let him but I didn't feel like it. I don't know, afterwards I felt like oh! What did I do? I just, we did it twice, then after that I didn't want to. I thought I was too young for that. (Then) I went to my friend's,

I didn't feel comfortable staying there (with Carlos), because he wanted me to sleep with him again, and I just didn't want to, so I left. And then I went to my other friend's house and I was just there with her. She has a baby and she is on welfare. She has been on welfare forever, since I know her. So then I said "I don't want to see myself like that—I don't," and I thought about it and I go "God! I could be pregnant." You know, it could happen. And I never, never let him touch me again. We did it twice or whatever, and he gave me something and got me pregnant. . . . I found out after, when I found out I was pregnant five months later, I had chlamydia. I was so mad. Afterwards, I found out that he was sleeping with my best friend. All my friends were sleeping with him. He was really cute.

DISCUSSION

These case studies reveal the complexity of negotiating sexual behavior within a romantic relationship. Having sex was an act that, in the words of so many of these young people, "just happened." It was not negotiated verbally. The couple did not discuss or plan it. Rather, sexual involvement was negotiated physically through a gradual escalation in the level of intimate sexual contact allowed by the young woman during the times they were together. Verbal negotiation that occurred in the context of sexual passion consisted of little else but "please" and "no, not yet." One young man, Cori's boyfriend, who tried to discuss sexual involvement outside the context of hugging and kissing, was slapped for his efforts. That slap was a signal that conscious discussion about sexual involvement was not appropriate or appreciated.

In all cases the young man was the initiator of sexual involvement, and the young woman was the resistor and controller of passion. This is a familiar sexual "script" in contemporary American culture [19]. Most of the young women were able to resist having intercourse for a considerable length of time (several months to a year) before giving in to their partner's urging and, in many cases their own desire as well. This period of waiting was called respect. The respect the young men had for their girlfriends (pressuring for sex, but not too hard, and allowing her to make the decision about the timing of their first sexual intercourse) is interpreted by the young women as an indication of their partner's emotional involvement in the relationship. It is a sign of the young man's good intentions, a test period during which he proves that he cares for her, is not just after sex, and will stay with her in a committed relationship.

In some cases, as with Julia and Juan, sexual intercourse became a spontaneous symbol of commitment and love within the context of the development of their relationship. As the relationship evolved and they became emotionally closer, they naturally wanted to express this closeness physically. As they fell in love, sex became a natural part of the union of their two selves into one, the much sought after goal of passionate, romantic love [24]. For Cori and Eva, allowing intercourse to occur seemed to be a bid for greater commitment in the relationship, a strategy that ultimately failed for both of them. Erika and Sylvia both had much older partners, and intercourse took them by surprise, but was not unwelcome. Perhaps the powerful feelings inherent in passionate love in combination with cultural expectations about the importance of female virginity and naivete about sex preclude these young women from planning for sex, the circumstances under which it should occur (the timing of the event), and the prevention of pregnancy and STDs (use of contraception and condoms).

One of the more unfortunate precipitators of sexual debut for three of the cases presented here was conflict within the young women's home. Eva and Cori both felt pressure to leave their mothers' homes and said they had nowhere else to go. Julia, too, was having difficulties at home, and was sent to her aunt in the United States. All three of these young women eventually chose to live with their boyfriends. Julia clearly loved Juan

and was ready to become his "wife." Eva and Cori both recognized that they were seeking a safe haven and comfort from their partners. Neither was ready to initiate intercourse. Eva thought it was morally wrong, and Cori thought she was too young. Both were also unsure of the depth of their own feelings for their partners—and their partner's feelings for them. Eva eventually came to love Rudy, but she was not in love with him when she moved in with him. She liked Rudy and was sexually attracted to him, but she needed a place to stay. Cori said she was not in love with Carlos. She gave in to sex because she needed a place to stay, because she thought he was cute, and because he was comforting.

An alternative reading of Cori's and Eva's stories, however, suggests that they only used the excuse of having nowhere else to go to justify the initiation of a sexual relationship with their boyfriends. Cori, it turns out, did have somewhere else to go, and Eva had a close school friend to whose family she probably could have turned had she wanted to do so. Instead, both arranged a scenario in which they could be blameless for engaging in sexual relations they felt were taboo.

Another striking chord in these narratives is the extent to which the young women were ignorant about the biology and physiology of human reproduction. Eva and Sylvia, in particular, thought this was a major reason for their unintended pregnancies—fear and ignorance of the mechanics of sex and contraception. For all except Julia, pregnancy was the consequence most feared by these young women. Although Erika wanted to get pregnant, she was somewhat ambivalent and considered abortion at the urging of her mother and Junior's mother, but all her friends had a man and kids, and she wanted to be like them. Junior was amenable to being a father and is still with her. Eva, Sylvia, and Cori had unintended pregnancies that changed their lives. Rudy wanted to see what being a father was like. He tried using withdrawal, but the method did not work well for him and Eva. Luís seemed to think pregnancy prevention was Sylvia's responsibility, but took on responsibility for her and their daughter. Carlos seemed to fit the pattern described by Cori in which young men take no responsibility for their sexual behavior at all. Cori contracted chlamydia and became pregnant. She was the only young mother who expressed any anger at her boyfriend's irresponsible behavior and at her own "stupidity." Interestingly, none of the young women talked about fear of STDs as a deterrent to having sex.

The role of older men dating teenage women and fathering children is just beginning to be addressed in the literature on adolescent pregnancy [25]. In the cases presented here, only Eva and Rudy were within two years in age. For the other four cases, age differences were three, four, six, and fifteen years. Certainly there can be knowledge and power differentials in such relationships, especially when the girl is a young teen (e.g., 12 to 15 years old) and the partner is an adult man. Sylvia's and Erika's families expressed concern about their dating much older men, and Juan also recognized it was problematic. In a later interview he said that he often felt more like Julia's father or her teacher than her husband and worried that perhaps he had stolen her girlhood. Despite their own and their families' concerns, they all persisted in their relationships.

Although none of these young women said they were forced into having sex, all, save Julia, did feel pressured by their partners. Cori came closest to describing a forced situation. She said she felt trapped, but it was a trap partly of her own making. The contradictions in some of these narratives both wanting and not wanting sex at the same time suggest the conflict in these young women's minds. For others, like Erika and Sylvia, sex was not unwelcome, but the timing was unexpected. Julia was the only one who seemed to embrace her sexual relationship with Juan, and her narrative stands in stark contrast to the other four, which depict conflicting desires, lack of preparation for sex, and uncertainty about their own or their partner's feelings.

Adult, middle-class health professionals working with adolescents tend to assume that anyone in a romantic relationship can be reasonably sure he or she might have sex and should be prepared to prevent unintended pregnancy and STDs. All of these respondents, however, indicated that their first intercourse experience together was neither expected nor planned. Moreover, almost all respondents, when asked how couples decide to have sex or use birth control, responded like Eva: "How do they decide? (long pause) They don't decide. They don't think about it." When adolescents say that they were not expecting or planning to have sex, even though they were involved in a romantic relationship that could reasonably be expected to include sexual involvement, we must take them at their word. As these cases indicate, both parties might have been thinking about sex, wanting to have sex, wondering when they would have sex, or trying to delay sex, but they were not consciously planning to have sex.

The implications of these findings for the prevention of pregnancy and STDs among young Latinas are not optimistic. The cultural scripting of gender roles in romantic relationships makes it almost certain that sex will be unplanned and unprotected. The young man pressures for sex, but allows his girlfriend to control the timing of the evolution of sexual intimacy within the relationship in order to prove his love and commitment. The young woman resists sex until she is sure of her partner's emotional commitment to her or wants to put it to the test, but she must remain unprepared for sex to be perceived as virtuous. Although this period of respect lasted six months to a year for these couples, abstinence eventually gave way to intercourse. These months were full of sexual uncertainty and emotional risk during which each person tested the other, and frank discussions about having sex, using birth control, or preventing STDs were culturally inappropriate and too emotionally risky for both parties. If either member of the couple violated these rules, he or she ran the risk of losing the partner.

Ironically, the initiation of sexual intercourse seemed to move the couple into another phase of their relationship in which they either broke up or developed mutual trust and affection that allowed for a more "rational" approach to sexual behavior and concern with its consequences. By this time, however, the young women were all pregnant and other decisions had to be made.

Cultural and social norms and values about appropriate sexual behavior, appropriate sexual partners, the importance of virginity, and contraception shape our experience of love and restrict what can be talked about at different stages of involvement in a romantic relationship. A script for romantic love that portrays spontaneous, unplanned, and unprotected sex after a protracted period of resistance by the female allows young women to retain their purity and relinquish their virginity at the same time. This script when enacted in the contemporary world of incurable STDs and the social and economic burdens of teenage motherhood places young women at enormous risk. Young couples will not behave as "rational decision-makers" in their sexual behavior until their society and community expect them to. Currently, as a society, we expect young people in love to behave "irrationally," to value spontaneous, unplanned (and therefore unprotected) sexual initiation. How, then, can we be surprised when they say, despite months of thinking about having sex, that they did not plan or expect to have sex. But, love can also accommodate prevention. Love, after all, is a valuing of the partner above the self. Surely, protection of the partner's health is part of love. We must teach our youth new scripts for falling in love, scripts that include this message.

NOTES

1. About half of the young women had no partner at the time of recruitment or did not want us to contact him. Many men who were contacted declined due to time constraints of employment.
2. All of the participants were in consensual relationships, and 90 percent had had only one sexual partner in their lifetime. However, about one-third revealed a history of sexual abuse in the past.
3. Names and details that would identify respondents have been changed to protect confidentiality.

REFERENCES

1. R. A. Hatcher, J. Trussell, F. Stewart et al., *Contraceptive Technology*, Irvington Publishers, Inc., New York, 1994.
2. K. Luker, *Dubious Conceptions: The Politics of Teenage Pregnancy, and Childbearing*, Harvard University Press, Cambridge, MA, 1996.
3. T. J. Mathews, S. J. Ventura, S. C. Curtin, and J. A. Martin, Births of Hispanic Origin, 1989–95, *Monthly Vital Statistics Report*, 46: (6 Supplement), pp. 1–28, 1998.
4. P. I. Erickson, *Latina Adolescent Childbearing in East Los Angeles*, University of Texas Press, Austin, 1998.
5. S. S. Brown and L. Eisenberg, *The Best Intentions: Unintended Pregnancy and the Well-Being of Children and Families*, National Academy Press, Washington, D.C., 1995.
6. L. S. Zabin and S. C. Hayward, *Adolescent Sexual Behavior and Childbearing*, Sage Publications, Newbury Park, California, 1993.
7. L. M. Burton, Teenage Childbearing as an Alternative Life Course Strategy in Multigenerational Black Families, *Human Nature*, 1: 2, pp. 123–143, 1990.
8. J. B. Lancaster and B. A. Hamburg, *School-Age Pregnancy and Parenthood: Biosocial Dimensions*, Aldine, DeGruyter, New York, 1986.
9. C. S. Aneshensel, E. Fielder, and R. M. Becerra, Fertility and Fertility-Related Behavior among Mexican-American and Non-Hispanic White Female Adolescents, *Journal of Health and Social Behavior*, 30, pp. 56–76, March 1989.
10. R. M. Becerra and D. de Anda, Pregnancy and Motherhood among Mexican American Adolescents, *Health and Social Work*, 9: 2, pp. 106–123, 1984.
11. P. I. Erickson and C. P. Kaplan, Latinas and Abortion, in *The New Civil War: The Psychology, Culture and Politics of Abortion* (Chapter 6), L. J. Beckman and S. M. Harvey (eds.), American Psychological Association, Washington, D.C., pp. 133–155, 1998.
12. T. Reynoso, M. E. Felice, and P. Shragg, Does American Acculturation Affect Outcome of

Mexican-American Teenage Pregnancy? *Journal of Adolescent Health*, 14: 4, pp. 257–261, 1993.

13. P. I. Erickson, Cultural Factors Affecting the Negotiation of First Sexual Intercourse among Latina Adolescent Parents, *International Quarterly of Community Health Education*, 18: 1, pp. 119–135, 1998–1999.

14. R. H. DuRant, R. Pendergast, and C. Seymore, Sexual Behavior among Hispanic Female Adolescents in the United States, *Pediatrics*, 85: 6, pp. 1051–1058, 1990.

15. H. Amaro, Women in the Mexican American Community: Religion, Culture, and Reproductive Attitudes and Experiences, *Journal of Community Psychology*, 16: 1, pp. 6–20, 1988.

16. H. Aviaro, Latina Attitudes towards Abortion, *Nuestro*, 5: 6, pp. 43–44, 1981.

17. L. M. Koonin, J. C. Smith, and M. Ramick, Abortion Surveillance—United States, 1991, *Morbidity and Mortality Weekly Report*, 44: SS-2, pp. 23–53, 1995.

18. J. Abma, A. Driscoll, and K. Moore, Young Women's Degree of Control over First Intercourse: An Exploratory Analysis, *Family Planning Perspectives*, 30: 1, pp. 12–18, 1998.

19. S. Thompson, *Going All the Way: Teenage Girls' Tales of Sex, Romance, and Pregnancy*, Hill and Wang, New York, 1995.

20. F. D. Bean and M. Tienda, *The Hispanic Population of the United States*, Russell Sage Foundation, New York, 1987.

21. B. R. Flores, *Chiquita's Cocoon: A "Cinderella Complex" for the Latina Woman*, Pepper Vine Press, Inc., Granite Bay, California, 1990.

22. N. Williams, *The Mexican-American Family: Tradition and Change*, General Hall, Inc., New York, 1990.

23. E. G. Pavich, A Chicana Perspective on Mexican Culture and Sexuality, *Journal of Social Work and Human Sexuality*, 4: 3, pp. 47–65, 1986.

24. E. S. Person, *Dreams of Love and Fateful Encounters: The Power of Romantic Passion*, Penguin Books, New York, 1988.

25. D. J. Landry and J. D. Forrest, How Old Are U.S. Fathers? *Family Planning Perspectives*, 27: 4, pp. 159–161, 1995.

Sexuality and the Life Cycle: Young Adulthood

The expanding definition of sexuality to encompass the entire life span is, perhaps, the most significant changing focus in human sexuality today. Sexuality researchers and clinicians who formerly worked to differentiate normative from nonnormative events first for children and, eventually, adolescents, are now addressing developmental and transformational issues about sexuality in young adulthood and beyond. The chapters in Part III contribute to that process.

Young adulthood poses specific challenges, one of which is intensifying personal individuation. According to Swiss psychiatrist Jung (1875–1961), individuation is a process of differentiation of self from others in the continuing development of the personality (Hinsie and Campbell 1970). Because our sexual self is an inseparable part of our persona, sex plays a considerable role in this real life drama. If, as claimed, emotions are the critical motivational forces promoting life-course individuation, it is prudent to explore the role of emotion in human sexual behavior. But, perhaps first, we must clarify the question, What is an emotion? Such queries have been the subject of debates by notables, ranging from Socrates to William

James, and now, to present-day philosophers. In the search for answers, emotion has been perceived by some as being inferior to reason and dismissed as merely an unintelligent feeling, while conversely, emotion has been couched by others as true wisdom, the master of reason (Solomon 1993). But even in the midst of such oppositional positions, most have agreed with two premises: virtually all emotion gets expressed in behavior and emotion has a cognitive dimension. Of the many contextual factors included in the negotiation of sexual activity, both emotion and cognition are critical to decision making.

In the beginning chapter of Part III, Davidson, Moore, Earle, and Davis report research about sexual decision making from a large-scale study that surveyed the sexual attitudes and behavior of never-married college students at four distinctly different universities. Focusing on the social institutions of education, religion, and family, the researchers pose the question, How do region, race, and religion matter in the sexual attitudes and behavior of college students today?

In seeking answers, several constructs were explored, beginning with DeLamater's (1987)

claim that institutions, such as universities, affect sexual attitudes and behavior by creating and maintaining different orientations toward sexuality. The research team then framed the broader social factors of race and regional differences by using constructs from *The Social Organization of Sexuality* (Laumann et al. 1994); the concept of sexual scripts (Simon and Gagnon 1987); and the theory of sex markets (Ellingson et al. 2004). Eventually, the authors proposed an additional framework by suggesting that "sense-of-place" as a concept laden with emotion may also serve as an influential variable in sexual choices. Davidson et al. argue that more than merely an institution, a regional location, or a sexual marketplace, a university has a heritage that evokes a nostalgic, legendary "sense-of-place." They contend that such an emotional concept can indeed be a variable in the mix of institutions, locations, sex markets, and sexual scripts that influence the sexual attitudes and behavior of college students.

Somewhat surprising answers revealed in this research provide valuable information for today's sexually active young adults who are in the process of achieving their own developmental task of individuation. This ambitious foray, mixing the mundane and the theoretical, is a challenge for students. But it is well worth the time for those who wish to better understand the interface of region, race, and religion with sexual attitudes and behavior, as well as how the process of individuation and sexual decisions are interrelated.

The chapter entitled, "Men, Women and the Sexual Double Standard," concerns a subject that is far from a new concept. The idea of a sexual double standard does, however, deserve a different scrutiny in a so-called "hooking-up culture." In a new bestseller entitled, *Hooking Up: Sex, Dating and Relationships on Campus*, Kathleen Bogle has written a book labeled by *Publishers Weekly* as "an evenhanded, sympathetic book on a topic that has received far too much sensational and shoddy coverage." Exploring many misconceptions about casual sex on college campuses, the book paints realistic portraits of young women and men who are the twenty-first century navigators in the newest sexual revolution. Noted sociologist Pepper Schwartz recommended, "this book should be required reading for college students *and* their parents" (Book Cover).

Bogle begins her exposé of the hooking-up phenomenon by reviewing how young people in the past century formed relationships. Details about the "Calling Era," the "Dating Era," and the "Hooking-Up Era" each illuminate a series of changes in the culture that created possibilities for new sexual scripts to emerge. And, with these scripts, apparently, the "rules of the road" for relationships have changed considerably. According to a Washington-based research group, today there are more high school seniors who say that they never date than those who say they frequently date (Dating 2008). Some may assume therefore, less dating equals less sex in relationships. The fallacy of this assumption is exposed by the paradigm shift in relationship formation whereby "dating is dated and hooking up is here to stay." In fact, more than one-half of sexually-active teens have had sexual intercourse with persons they are not dating (Manning, Giordano, and Longmore 2006). Op-Ed Columnist Charles Blow (2008) of the *New York Times* points out that under the old model, one dated a few times and if they really liked the person, they might consider having sex. Under the new model, after hooking up a few times, if you really like the person, you might consider going on a date.

Paula England, Stanford University sociologist, and her colleagues, who have studied the hooking up phenomenon by surveying students from 10 American universities, estimates that the shift in the relationship paradigm has been occurring for about two decades (England, Shafer, and Fogarty 2007). Bogle herself addresses both the pros and cons of this emerging relationship model. On the positive side, by emphasizing group friendship over the one-pair model of dating, those least likely to be dating are spared the stigma of not having a date.

The negative side of the ledger reflects issues of gender inequity, the subject of the Bogle chapter chosen for inclusion in Part III.

"Well-written and engaging," "a provocative book," and "a joy to read"—these and other similar accolades from respected sexology professionals attest to the acclaim garnered by Laura Carpenter's *Virginity Lost*, the first book to take an in-depth look at the meaning that women and men ascribe to their first experience with sexual intercourse. This well-researched book, grounded in sociocultural context, contains compelling personal stories from 61 young Americans of diverse race/ethnicity, class, gender and sexual orientation. By teasing out the complexities of this life-changing experience, the author offers students a rare window into one of life's most intimate and significant moments.

An interesting aspect of the book is the inclusion of a methodological appendix that includes a section entitled, "Interviewing Style: A Feminist Perspective." In these pages, Carpenter shares that one of her goals was to make the interviews as conversational as possible in order to enhance rapport, making it easier for persons to share such intimate details of their lives. An advocate of the belief of many ethnographers and feminist scholars that inequality characterizes a scholar's relationship with informants, she purposefully sought to correct this imbalance by concluding every interview with an invitation for participants to question her. Reportedly, of those who did ask questions, most were curious about what was "normal" or about her own virginity-loss experience.

In the words of Pepper Schwartz, author of *Everything You Know About Love and Sex is Wrong* (2001), "Laura Carpenter assumes nothing, and therefore, learns a great deal." Such a recommendation is not to be taken lightly. And, it is such an interesting, fast read that students will forget it is an assignment.

In a chapter that will require little professor prompting to be read, "Communicating With New Sex Partners: College Women and Questions That Make A Difference," Nelwyn Moore and Kenneth Davidson explore variables related to both rational decision making and its counterpart, emotion. They investigate the failure of college women to ask new partners about their sexual histories prior to sexual intercourse, differentiating between health-promoting and health-defeating sexual behavior. In spite of the constant media barrage and the efforts of sexuality educators, many young women report that they are not influenced by the information proclaiming the risk of contracting a sexually transmitted infection or initiating an unintentional pregnancy (Kusselling, Wenger, and Shapiro, 1995). In one study, 62 percent of college women indicated that awareness concerning AIDS had not affected their level of participation in sexual intercourse, and 72 percent had not changed their level of involvement in oral-genital sex (Weinberg, Lottes, and Aveline, 1998).

Providing valuable factual information for sexually-active young adults concerning health-promoting sexual communication skills may be of special significance for young persons today, many of whom will remain in uncommitted relationships for as much as a decade longer than their predecessors a generation ago. And, sexual communication skills when with a new sex partner may be particularly valuable if the relationship paradigm continues to shift from dating to hooking up, an emerging model for casual sexual encounters without expectations for future emotional commitment. England, Schafer, and Fogarty (2007) found that while one-fourth of all hook ups did not go further than "making out," 36–39 percent involved sexual intercourse. By demonstrating stark differences in communication style, leading to either health-promoting or health-defeating outcomes, this offering will likely spark a lively class discussion related to the questions that make a difference.

Reporting the differences and similarities in Black and White women's subjective sexual arousal to different erotica, Hughes and Anderson begin with a catchy, descriptive title, "What Turns Women On?: Black and White Women's Sexual Arousal." The subjects in this research, heterosexual Black and White college women, reported their subjective sexual arousal to erotic videos portraying Black or White actors. The fact that Black women were more aroused by the video with the Black actors while White women found both videos arousing is only one of the findings that will elicit varying opinions from class members.

The review of the literature that reveals how interracial dating and sexual/marital relationships are moderated by race and gender is, on its own, reason enough for students to read the chapter. Although the primary purpose of this study was to investigate differences and similarities in Black and White women's subjective sexual arousal to different erotica, the authors also examined other factors that may moderate or contribute to women's sexual arousal. Additionally, they considered the variables of sensation seeking and the attractiveness of the actors in the films, both of which should prove to be of great interest to students. With the Black/White racial differences revealed by this research, students are moved one step closer to understanding our racially and ethnically diverse world in which we live today.

REFERENCES

Blow, C. M. 2008, December 13. The demise of dating. *The New York Times*. http://www.nytimes.com/2008/12/13/opinion/13blow.html?scp=1&sq=charles%20blow%20hooking%20up&st=cse.

Dating. 2008, December 17. *Child Trends DataBank*. http:// www.childtrendsdatabank.org/indicators/73 Dating.cfm.

DeLamater, J. D. 1987. A sociological approach. In *Theories of sexuality* (pp. 237–56), eds. J. J. Geer and W. T. O'Donohue. New York: Plenum.

Ellingson, S., M. Van Haitsma, E. O. Laumann, and N. Tebbe. 2004. Religion and the politics of sexuality. In *The sexual organization of the city* (pp. 309–48), eds. E. O. Laumann, S. Ellingson, J. Hahay, A. Paik, and Y. Youm. Chicago: University of Chicago Press.

England, P., E. F. Schafer, and A. C. K. Fogarty. 2007. Hooking up and forming romantic relationships on today's college campuses. In *The gendered society reader*, 3rd ed., eds. M. D. Kimmel and A. Aronson 531–46. New York: Oxford University Press.

Hinsie, L. E., and R. J. Campbell. 1970. Individuation. *Psychiatric dictionary*. 4th ed. New York: Oxford University Press.

Kusselling, F. S., N. S. Wenger, and M. F. Shapiro. 1995. Inconsistent contraceptive use among female college students: Implications for interventions. *Journal of American College Health* 43: 191–95.

Laumann, E. O., J. H. Gagnon, R. T. Michael, and S. Michaels. 1994. *The social organization of sexuality: Sexual practices in the United States.* Chicago: University of Chicago Press.

Manning, W. D., P. C. Giordano, and M. A. Longmore. 2006. Hooking up: The relationship contexts of "nonrelationship" sex. *Journal of Adolescent Research* 21: 459–83.

Simon, W., and J. H. Gagnon. 1987. Sexual scripts: Permanence and change. *Archives of Sexual Behavior* 15: 97–120.

Solomon, R. C. 1993. The philosophy of emotions. In *Handbook of emotions*, eds. M. Lewis and J. M. Haviland, 3–15. New York: Guilford.

Weinberg, M. S., I. L. Lottes, and D. Aveline. 1998. AIDS risk reduction strategies among United States and Swedish heterosexual university students. *Archives of Sexual Behavior* 27: 385–401.

CHAPTER II

Sexual Attitudes and Behavior at Four Universities

Do Region, Race, and/or Religion Matter?

J. Kenneth Davidson, Sr.
Nelwyn B. Moore
John R. Earle
Robert Davis

The Associated Press reported in 2008 that the University of Florida Gators, known for wild celebrations following national championships in football and basketball, could raise a glass to another national title. The Princeton Review survey of 120,000 university students confirmed that the Gators now hold the title of "Best Party School in the Country" with last year's winner, West Virginia, slipping into fourth place, just ahead of the University of Mississippi, number two and Penn State, number three (Party School List, 2008). The annual list of 20 top party schools that reflect Eastern, Western, Northern and Southern escapades in the halls of ivy suggests that more than merely formal education may occur with matriculation at one's university of choice. Such speculations were the driving force for questions entertained in this chapter. The researchers asked, what, if anything,

do sex markets, sexual scripts, and sense-of-place have to do with a college student's sexual attitudes and behavior? How do region, race, and religion influence levels of premarital sexual involvement and risk-taking sexual practices? These questions and others are explored in the current chapter reporting a large-scale survey that compares the sexual attitudes and behavior at four distinctly different universities: a Southern historic Black public university, a Southern private university with a religious heritage, a Southwestern public university, and a Midwestern public university.

A vigorous class discussion is guaranteed as you as a reader relate to the changes occurring on other university campuses. You will be better able to contrast the numerous significant differences that were found between the universities and compare your own sense of the sexual environment that exists on your campus. As a class activity, you may even conduct a straw poll to predict the chances of your university ever claiming the dubious distinction of inclusion in the top twenty party school list. Sharing this bit of class trivia with the editor of your campus newspaper could raise

From "Sexual Attitudes and Behavior at Four Universities: Do Region, Race, and/or Religion Matter?" by J. K. Davidson, Sr., N. B. Moore, J. R. Earle, and R. Davis. 2008. *Adolescence* 43(170): 189–220. Copyright © 2008, Libra Publishers, Inc. Reprinted by permission.

the level of awareness concerning the influence of the somewhat obvious but obtuse concept, "sense-of-place."

Research now reveals that individuals engage in their most extensive identity exploration during emerging adulthood rather than early adolescence as previously believed (Arnett, 2000). This developmental stage of individuation is well in process for college-age students as they arrive on university campuses that no longer provide personnel acting *in loco parentis*. Instead, while surrounded by peer pressure that encourages premarital sexual activity, they encounter innumerable opportunities to develop a new sense of self. Decades of increases in rates of premarital sexual intercourse (PSI) and risk-taking sexual practices evidence these facts (Cooper, 2002). Although the National Youth Risk behavior Survey found no significant change in percentages of PSI between 1999–2003 by sex or race/ethnicity (Feijoo, 2004), this leveling trend is difficult to verify among college students because of variances in sample characteristics reflected in the research. Nevertheless, as sexual attitudes became more liberal, female and male views about sexuality converged, narrowing the gap in levels of PSI between women and men. But, Davidson (1993) found that motives for engaging in sexual intercourse remained divergent, with more women than men insisting that sexual intercourse occur within an affectionate relationship, findings corroborated a decade later by Hill (2002).

The gap between the levels of sexual activity by race/ethnicity also appears to be disappearing (Upchurch, Levy-Storms, Sucoff, & Aneshensel, 1998). Although PSI varies according to race/ethnicity, with the highest level of activity being among Blacks followed by whites, Hispanic-Americans, and Asian-Americans, the rate of increase among the general population has been greatest for white women (Langer, Warheit, & McDonald, 2001). Weinberg and Williams (1988) argued that the more liberal Black sexual patterns are associated with a distinct subculture that is more detached from family controls and less subject to moralistic dictates.

DeLamater (1987) claims that institutions affect sexual attitudes and behavior, not by dictating specific levels of permissiveness but by creating and maintaining different orientations toward sexuality. The institutions of education, religion, and family are believed to control sexual behavior through stigmatization, socialization, and surveillance, processes that unfold as individuals internalize the norms of sexuality and become self-regulating (Ellingson, Van Haitsma, Laumann, & Tebbe, 2004). But, consistently high rates of PSI and liberalization of attitudes toward sexuality suggest that the surveillance powers of religion and family have declined. However, Meier's (2003) findings that religiosity is still an important predictor of sexual behavior were confirmed by Davidson, Moore, and Ullstrup (2004) who found that students who were more devout and/or more involved in institutionalized religion were less likely to be sexually permissive. And, Laumann, Gagnon, Michael, and Michaels (1994) found that Black women were almost twice as likely as white women to indicate that religion shaped their sexual behavior. As the child's first reference group, the family is also an important predictor of sexual attitudes and behavior, with more positive sexual attitudes and safer sexual behaviors occurring among college women whose parents were the first source of information about sexual intercourse (Moore & Davidson, 1999).

Suggesting the significance of broader social factors, regional differences in sexual attitudes and behaviors were noted in the Laumann et al. (1994) study of the social organization of sexuality in the general population. Using the typology of normative orientations: *traditional*, *relational*, and *recreational*, they differentiated various sexuality orientations. Regional respondents who held a traditional orientation, West South Central (WSC), viewed the primary purpose of sexual intercourse as procreation; the relational respondents, East North Central (ENC), as a natural part of a loving relationship; and the recreational respondents, South Atlantic (SA), as pleasure.

Racial, gender, and religious differences in sexual orientations were noted in the Laumann et al. (1994) study, with 42% of white men found in the relational cluster compared to only 25% of Black men, more of whom (42%) were classified as recreational. Among women, the greatest percentage (48% of white and 46% of Black) were found in the relational cluster, with more white (21%) than Black (9%) women in the recreational cluster. Women and men indicating "no religion" were more likely to be in the recreational cluster; Mainline Protestants and Catholics in the relational cluster; and conservative Protestants in the traditional cluster.

THEORETICAL FRAMEWORKS

Although sexual scripts are based on sex drives, when enacted they reflect the sum of learning about being a sexual person. Simon and Gagnon (1987) theorized that sexual scripts determining sexual attitudes and behaviors operate at three levels: cultural (societal norms for broad sexual conduct); interpersonal (translating sexual desires into strategies); and psychic (sexual dialogues with self, eliciting and sustaining arousal). Additionally, Ellingson, Laumann, Paik, and Mahay (2004) articulated a theory of sex markets in their study of partner selection and relationship formation, characterizing sex markets as spatially and culturally bounded areas in which searches for sex partners and a variety of sexual transactions occur. If as proposed, an interrelated set of social forces organize sex markets and influence the outcomes, it is reasonable to conclude that when college students with individualized sexual scripts enter the university, "marketplace" interactions may alter their sexual attitudes and behaviors. But also, more than merely

a geographic location or a sexual marketplace, a university has a heritage that evokes a nostalgic, legendary "sense of place." Given such a "sense-of-place," do cultural forces, i.e., societal norms for broad social conduct, theorized by Simon and Gagnon (1987) influence sexual scripts that determine sexual attitudes and behavior? And, if so, how significant is that unique "sense of place" in altering the sexual attitudes and behavior of college students today? To investigate such queries, sex researchers need to be asking related questions. For example, how do variables such as age, family background, race/ethnicity, and religion factor into the "sexual marketplace" at various universities? And, are people or institutions more influential in determining behavioral outcomes? Accordingly, this study sought to ascertain any differences in sexual attitudes, levels of PSI, and risk-taking sexual practices of college students at four distinctly different universities. These universities are a historic Black public university (SA Region); a religiously affiliated Southern private university (SA Region); a Southwestern public university (WSC Region); and a Midwestern public university (ENC Region). The influence of region, race, and religion were considered.

REVIEW OF LITERATURE

Premarital Sexual Attitudes

Comparisons of studies at various times across different cohorts of college students reveal a gradual shift toward more permissive sexual attitudes and behavior, and a new set of sexual norms (Earle et al., in press). Religious affiliation and frequency of church attendance were significant variables in these changing attitudes. Although Conservative Protestants who attend church most often support traditional beliefs about PSI, traditional beliefs have declined among Catholics and Mainline Protestants at all levels of church attendance (Petersen & Donnenwerth, 1997). By 2004, no significant differences between Catholics and Protestants were found in their degree of religiosity and sexual attitudes (Lefkowitz, Gillen, Shearer, & Boone, 2004). Religious attitudes are known to increase levels of sexual guilt (Davidson et al., 2004).

Sexual Behavior

Premarital sexual intercourse. The percentage of never-married college women in general who have engaged in PSI ranges from 69% (Ratcliff-Crain, Donald, & Dalton, 1999) to 80% (Pinkerton, Bogart, Cecil, & Abramson, 2002). Among Black college women, the percentage who indicated having had PSI ranged from 71% (Braithwaite & Thomas, 2001) to 76% (Johnson et al., 1994). Among never-married college men, the percentage who have reported PSI ranges from 86% (Pinkerton et al., 2002) to 90% (Siegel, Klein, & Roghmann, 1999), while the percentages for Black college men varied from 83% (Johnson et al., 1994) to 85% (Ford & Goode, 1994).

Age at first intercourse. Among college students, the age at first intercourse continued to decline in the 1980s and early 1990s, so by the mid-1990s, 60% of women and 70% of men indicated having experienced sexual intercourse by age 17 (Feigenbaum, Weinstein, & Rosen, 1995). Today, the reported mean age for first intercourse for college women ranges from 16.7 years (Flannery, Ellington, & Votaw, 2003) to 17.5 years (Pinkerton et al., 2002) and for college men, 16.0 years (Nangle & Glover, 2001) to 17.6 years (Pluhar, Frongillo, Stycos, & Dempster-McClain, 1998). Race may be more important than gender in accounting for differences in the percentages of PSI before age 18 (Lehr, DiIorio, Dudley, & Lipana, 2000).

Number of sex partners. The gender gap in number of lifetime sex partners may also be converging. Among college women, the reported mean number of sex partners ranges from 3.7 partners (Davidson et al., 2004) to 5.2 partners (Weinberg, Lottes, & Gordon, 1997). For men, the mean number of sex partners varies from 3.5 partners (Ratcliff-Crain et al., 1999) to 6.6 partners (Pinkerton et al., 2002). Page, Hammerstein, and Scanlon (2002) found 29% of women and 30% of men indicated having had four or more lifetime sex partners. Persons who have PSI at earlier ages and those with lower levels of religiosity have higher numbers of sex partners (Christopher & Sprecher, 2001).

Sexual Risk-Taking

Casual sexual intercourse. Among women, 26% reported engaging in casual sex outside a monogamous relationship in contrast to 58% of men. Further, 51% of women reported engaging in a "one-night stand" compared to 65% of men (Seal & Agostinelli, 1996). The likelihood of having casual PSI increases with the number of sex partners, with sexual pleasure the strongest predictor of casual sex for both women and men (Feigenbaum et al., 1995). That 42% of college women and 55% of college men "never" or "rarely" asked a new sex partner about their sexual history reflects the risks of casual PSI (Hawkins, Gray, & Hawkins, 1995).

Alcohol consumption and sexual behavior. In the 1990s, the percentage of college students who were under the influence of alcohol at the time of first sexual intercourse ranged from 31% (Moore & Davidson, 1997) to 33% (Sprecher, Barbee, & Schwartz, 1995) for women and 24% (Sawyer & Smith, 1996) to 34% (Sprecher et al., 1995) for men. In fact, 17% of women and 22% of men reported being actually "drunk" at the time of their first intercourse experience (Sprecher et al., 1995).

Sexual risk-taking outcomes. The percentages of white college women who have been diagnosed with an STI ranges from 11% (Davidson & Moore, 1999) to 22% (Gilbert & Alexander, 1998) while the percentages for white college men varies from 8% (Nangle & Glover, 2001) to 17% (Dodge, Sandford, Yarber, & de Wit, 2004). In contrast, the percentage of Black college women who have been diagnosed with a STI ranged from 17% (Johnson et al., 1994) to 38% (Lewis,

Melton, Succop, & Rosenthal, 2000), while 45% of Black college men reported having had a STI (Johnson et al., 1994). Among white college women, 12% have reported having an unintended pregnancy (Davidson & Moore, 1999), while among white college men, 14% (Dodge et al., 2004) to 19% (Nangle & Glover, 2001) have impregnated a partner. By comparison, 41% of Black college women indicated having had an unintended pregnancy (Lewis et al., 2000).

METHOD

Procedure

An anonymous questionnaire was administered during regular university classes to volunteer respondents enrolled in select lower- and upper-division courses, including general education courses from social sciences and family studies, at four residential universities: a Southern private university (SPRU); a Midwesetern university (MWU); a Southwestern university (SWU); and a Southern historic Black university (SHBU). The questionnaire consisted of open-form and closed-form questions in the following areas: sexual history, contraceptive practices, sexually transmitted infection history, sexual attitudes, sexual guilt, and sexual satisfaction.

Sample

Given the nature of the research questions, the respondents were limited to never-married women and men. The subsamples were 1,618 never-married women (SPRU = 337, MWU = 626, SWU = 400, and SHBU = 255) and 884 never-married men (SPRU = 212, MWU = 296, SWU = 182; and SHBU = 194).

RESULTS

Personal and Family Background Characteristics

Dating. SWU women and SHBU men were more likely to be engaging in casual dating; and SHBU

women to be dating exclusively. MWU women were more likely to be pre-engaged, while MWU men were more likely to be engaged; and SPRU women and men were less likely to be dating.

Religion. As for religious denomination, SPRU women and men as well as SWU women and men were more likely to be Mainline Protestant, while SHBU women and men were more likely to be Baptist, and MWU women and men were more likely to be Catholic. Mothers of SHBU women and men attended religious services the most times per year, while mothers and fathers of MWU women and men attended the least number of times. Further, fathers of SPRU women and SHBU men attended services the most times per year. Among the respondents, SHBU women and men were more likely to consider themselves religious in comparison to others, while SWU women and men were least likely to do so.

Family composition. While growing up, SPRU women and men were the most likely to have mothers and fathers who were married to each other, while SHBU women and men were more likely to have mothers who were divorced/separated or never-married. Of the mothers of SHBU women and men, 15.9% and 14.1%, respectively had never been married.

Sexuality perspectives. To better understand how these women and men had developed their perspectives about sexuality, information was sought about participation in sex education in middle school; first information about sexual intercourse; and when growing up, frequency/ mother and father displayed affection. For women, the percentages who had had sex education were: SPRU = 82.8%, MWU = 84.6%, SWU = 73.6%, SHBU = 72.9%. Among men, the percentages were: SPRU = 84.4%, MWU = 76.6%, SWU = 70.1%, SBU = 73.5%. SPRU women were more likely and MWU women least likely to have received their first information about sexual intercourse from their parents. SWU women and men were more likely to have obtained their first information about sexual intercourse from peers, and MWU women, and men from teachers. SPRU women received information about sexual intercourse at the youngest age, and SHBU women at the oldest age, with no significant age differences found for men. SHBU women and men were more likely to have discussed sexually related topics with their mothers, and SPRU women and men were least likely to have done so. Displays of affection between parents occurred most frequently for SPRU women and men, and least frequently for SHBU women and men.

Sexual Standards

SPRU women and SHBU men were more likely and MWU women and men least likely to have their sexual decisions based on their own values. SHBU women and men were more likely to approve of PSI with a casual acquaintance and an occasional dating partner, and SPRU women and men least likely. With a regular dating partner, MWU women and SWU men were most likely and SPRU women and men least likely to approve of PSI. Both SWU women and men were more likely to approve of PSI if they were in a serious relationship and SPRU women and men were least likely. Finally, MWU and SWU women were more likely to approve of PSI if engaged, while SPRU women and SHBU men were least likely.

Sexual History

SHBU women and men were more likely to have had sexual intercourse, and more lifetime sex partners than other respondents. Further, SHBU men reported sexual intercourse more frequently than other men. But, SWU women had sexual intercourse more often and were more likely to have ever experienced orgasm. The SPRU women and men were least likely to have experienced sexual intercourse and to have had the fewest lifetime sex partners, and SPRU women were least likely to have had an orgasm. MWU women and SPRU men had had sexual intercourse least often.

First Sexual Intercourse

Circumstances. SHBU women and men had the youngest mean age at first sexual intercourse, while SPRU women and MWU men had the oldest mean age. SWU women and men were more likely to have given implied consent for their first intercourse experience and SPRU women and men were more likely to have given verbal consent. Further, SWU women and MWU men were more likely, and SHBU women and men least likely, to have been under the influence of alcohol during their first intercourse.

Contraceptive use. MWU women, or their sex partner, were more likely to have used a contraceptive at first sexual intercourse and SHBU women the least likely. SPRU men were most likely to have been contracepted and SHBU men least likely.

Personal reactions. Concerning guilt feelings about their first sexual intercourse, SWU women and SPRU men reported the greatest level of guilt and MWU women and SHBU men the least. No significant differences were found for physiological satisfaction for women or psychological sexual satisfaction for men. However, SPRU women were more likely and MWU women least likely to indicate psychological satisfaction, while SHBU men were more likely and MWU men least likely to indicate physiological satisfaction.

Sexual Risk Taking

Alcohol consumption. SWU women and men reported drinking more times per year and SHBU women and men the fewest times. SHBU women and men were most likely and SPRU women and men least likely to have engaged in sexual intercourse with someone they had just met.

Communication with new sex partners. SPRU women were most likely and SHBU women least likely to ask a new sex partner to reveal total number of past sex partners, while SPRU women and MWU men were most likely to reveal actual number of previous partners. There were no significant differences among women or men in asking if their sex partner had a STI or among men in asking their new sex partner about number of sex partners.

Current contraceptive usage. At their most recent PSI, SPRU women and men were more likely to have used a contraceptive. MWU women were more likely to have provided a condom for their sex partner during the past year.

Risk-taking outcomes. SHBU women were much more likely and SPRU women least likely to have been diagnosed with a STI, but for men, no significant differences appeared. In addition, SHBU women and men were much more likely to have experienced an unintended pregnancy, while SPRU women and SWU men were least likely.

DISCUSSION

Normative Sexual Orientation

SWU group. The SWU respondents from the West South Central (WSC) Region were more relational in sexual orientation, unlike the Laumann et al. (1994) WSC general population subjects who had a traditional orientation. More SWU women and men had cohabited; were more likely to be Mainline Protestants; considered themselves less religious; and had less traditional attitudes and behavior. However, gender differences in sexual attitudes revealed a traditional double standard, with women approving PSI in a serious relationship and men, with a regular dating partner.

The fact that more of these SWU women and men obtained their information about sexual intercourse from peers and that fewer men had sex education may have influenced the less emotionally healthy "implied consent" they gave for first sexual intercourse. Drinking more times per year placed both women and men in the less traditional and more risky categories. That more SWU women underreported the number of lifetime sex partners; were under the influence of alcohol at first intercourse; and felt guilty about

their first intercourse were plausibly factors that converged in their lower levels of psychological sexual satisfaction.

MWU group. MWU respondents from the East North Central (ENC) Region, where the majority of Laumann et al. (1994) subjects had a relational orientation, revealed a mixed but more relational sexual orientation, with more women pre-engaged and more men engaged. More likely to be Catholic they were less likely to make sexual decisions based on their own values, a finding that begs the question, on whose values did they depend? For the Laumann et al. (1994) relational respondents, religious values overwhelmingly shaped their sexual behavior. If these respondents did not use a logic-based personal morality (family and church), did they rely on a social logic related to reference groups (peers) to make sexual decisions? A likely scenario, but one refuted by the fact that the MWU Group exhibited the safest sexual behavior of all students, a factor inversely related to peer influence.

That women were more likely to use a contraceptive at first intercourse was plausibly related to having had sex education in school and teachers as their first source of information about sexual intercourse since teachers provide more contraceptive information than do parents (Davidson & Moore, 1999). Sex education may also explain why both MWU women and men took fewer risks during subsequent PSI, with more women providing condoms and more men revealing and asking about the number of previous partners. But, why did MWU women, who were most likely to be pre-engaged, have sexual intercourse less often and indicate less psychological sexual satisfaction at first sexual intercourse? This conundrum suggests that a preeminent role may have been played by the precepts of their Catholic religion in inducing guilt, a factor correlated with lack of sexual satisfaction (Moore & Davidson, 1997).

SPRU group. While Laumann et al. (1994) found the SA Region sexual orientation in the general population to be relational, these data indicate that the SPRU respondents were traditional. While relational individuals believe that there are certain situations in which PSI is not wrong (Laumann et al., 1994), fewer of the traditional SPRU women and men approved of PSI at any level: casual, occasional, regular, or serious dating.

Not surprisingly, these SPRU respondents with the most conservative sexual attitudes also had the most traditional family backgrounds. Women and men were more likely to be reared by mothers and fathers who were married to each other and who more often displayed affection toward each other. Women received their first information about sexual intercourse from parents and at the earliest age. More men had had sex education, but their first information about sexual intercourse came from peers, confirming Olson's (2005) theory that schools frequently offer sexuality education after the fact of need.

The convergence of positive family background factors and religious influences on the SPRU religiously affiliated campus possibly set the stage for the more traditional sexual attitudes and healthier sexual behaviors of SPRU students, fewer of whom had had PSI, and more of whom reported the fewest lifetime sex partners. The healthier response of verbal consent that women and men gave for first sexual intercourse was, for women, plausibly related to their older age at first intercourse and that their own values determined their sexual decisions. Sex education may have influenced the men who had experienced sexual intercourse less frequently and used contraception at first intercourse.

SHBU group. Laumann et al. (1994) found the normative sexual orientation of the general population respondents in the SA Region in which the SHBU respondents lived to be relational, while these data placed both SHBU women and men in the recreational category. For women, this fact may have been mitigated by education since more of them were juniors and seniors, and according to Laumann et al. (1994), the odds of being in the recreational cluster increases with each increment of education.

This research confirms decades of studies indicating that Blacks have more permissive attitudes toward PSI than whites (Mahay, Laumann, & Michaels, 2001). More SHBU women approved of PSI with casual, occasional, and regular dating partners and when engaged, and more men approved at every dating stage except engagement, an unexplained anomaly. That SHBU men based their sexual decisions on their own values supports the arguments of Weinberg and Williams (1988) that the black subculture is more detached from family controls and less subject to moralistic dictates of their conservative religion.

Confirming the recreational sexual orientation of SHBU women, and men, more had experienced PSI; experienced it at earlier ages; reported the highest number of lifetime sex partners; and fewer women had been contracepted at first intercourse. Their earlier and more frequent PSI corroborates the findings of Lehr et al. (2000) who found race to be an important factor in having PSI before age 18. That fewer of these women, more of whom had had a STI and an unintended pregnancy, had received sex education is suggestive of society's denial of reality and responsibility. Other risk-taking behaviors of SHBU respondents helped explain their higher percentages of STIs and unintended pregnancies: fewer women and men told or asked about number of previous sex partners at their most recent sexual intercourse and, more than others, they had had sexual intercourse with a person just met.

That SHBU respondents were less likely to be under the influence of alcohol at first intercourse than others was behavior possibly undergirded by their Black culture and/or their Fundamentalist religious values. Pragmatically, their earlier ages at PSI that made alcohol more difficult to obtain also may be explanatory. Supporting Staples' (1972) assertion that Blacks are less puritanical about sexuality than whites, more mothers of SHBU women and men had discussed sexually related topics with them than other respondents' mothers. That for men, the discussion occurred at the oldest age and for women at the youngest age seemingly acknowledges a reality: the lives of women are more disrupted by an unintended pregnancy than those of men.

This study supports Mahay et al. (2001) who found that race was a more defining factor of sexual orientation than religion. The recreational sexual orientation of SHBU students contradicted several religiosity findings. Their mothers attended religious services most frequently; respondents considered themselves more religious than others; and more were members of conservative denominations assumed to oppose recreational sexual activity. Work by Simon and Gagnon (1987) concerning sexual scripts may inform these apparent contradictions. Cultural scripts for sexual behavior evidenced in this research are more similar for Blacks and whites than are the interpersonal or interpsychic scripts that are more family related. That the SHBU families' milieus provided a wider variety of models of learning about sexuality partially supports the Weinberg and Williams (1988) argument that racial differences in sexual behavior are due to a distinct subculture created by Blacks as a result of specific historical and social circumstances. However, Willie's (1991) argument against the singular use of a historical perspective must be considered. He contends that differentiation in lifestyles among Black families can be understood by only examining the macro-environmental settings within which they live, factors beyond the scope of this study.

The recreational orientation of the more religious Black respondents in this study demonstrates the disjunctures between official religious teachings and behaviors, a fact labeled as commonplace among Blacks by Ellingson, Van Haitsma et al. (2004). Black family formation was the single most differentiating factor among groups, lending credence to DeLamater's (1987) thesis that social institutions such as religion and family create different sexual orientations. For the SHBU respondents, family, and perhaps the broader social circumstances as set forth by Willie (1991) and Weinberg and Williams (1988), appears to supersede religion as a determinant. For example, that mothers of SHBU women and men were more likely to have been divorced or separated and that 16% of the mothers of women and 14% of mothers of men were never married differs significantly from the two-parent or divorced/single parent family model found in the other groups. With more never-married mothers, there was less opportunity to observe displays of affection between parents, a variable correlated with safer sexual behaviors (Moore & Davidson, 1999). And, the macho Black male image of masculinity portrayed in media is harder to dispel without models to copy (Staples & Johnson, 1993). The degree to which diverse family forms are correlated with alterations in norms and values is yet unanswered, but a question worthy of further research.

In spite of these high-risk factors and their consequences, more SHBU men reported physiological and psychological sexual satisfaction and less guilt at first intercourse, and more women reported physiological sexual satisfaction. Such findings support those of Weinberg and Williams (1988) that Blacks were more sexually liberal; more accepting of sexual activity; more open about it; and pursued it more often. But, why did more SHBU women who subscribed to the myth that women should "always" have an orgasm during sexual intercourse feel guilty about PSI and both women and men feel guilty about heavy petting, findings that do not fit their patterns of sexual orientation? Possibly an anomaly, but more likely, the relationship of guilt and religiosity surfaces here. For the women who were more sexually active than others but more religious, cognitive dissonance plausibly induced guilt.

CONCLUSIONS

While comprehensiveness was a strength of this study, because of length limitations, this feature made it difficult to adequately explore all variables. Other limitations included the over-sampling of freshmen and sophomores on the SPRU campus, somewhat skewing their sample. To structure regional data, this study used the regional categories and the typology of normative sexual orientations referring to role behavior used by Laumann et al. (1994). Since it is unknown how many of their respondents from the general population were college students, specific comparisons with that study remain untenable.

This study supports the conclusions of Ellingson, Van Haitsma et al. (2004) that the surveillance powers of the institutions of both religion and family have declined. But, findings herein suggest that certain family background factors such as intact families and mothers and fathers who display affection toward each other supersede religion in affecting the sexual attitudes and behavior of college students. Less clear is why and how. While the Laumann et al. (1994) respondents who indicated "no religion" were more recreational and the Conservative and Fundamentalist Protestants were more traditional in their sexual orientation, the religiously conservative SHBU respondents (Baptists and Fundamentalists) in this study were more likely to be categorized as recreational. Thus, when religion and race intersected, race was more defining of sexual attitudes and behavior than religion, reiterating the Ellingson, Van Haitsma et al. (2004) thesis that although religious institutions try to shape sexual attitudes and behavior, their power does not translate into effective regulation.

Several regional questions were raised in this study. Why in the SA Region in which a relational sexual orientation was found among the general population (Laumann et al., 1994) did this study reveal different (SPRU—traditional and SHBU—recreational) and highly disparate sexual orientations at two universities less than 30 miles apart? These findings suggest that sex markets as defined by Ellingson, Laumann et al. (2004) may be too narrow a concept to offer adequate explanations of sexual behaviors. Instead, Simon and Gagnon's (1987) cultural level of sexual scripts appeared to be influential, inferring behavioral relevance when these students shared a university's legendary "sense of place," delineated by attributes related to religion and race. That of the four universities, SPRU, with the most traditional respondents, was the only religiously affiliated university and SHBU, with the most recreational respondents, was the only university with all Black respondents lends credence to these possibilities.

Another regional question concerned the WSC Region in which Laumann et al. (1994) found a traditional sexual orientation among the general population but this research found a relational orientation (SWU). The importance of the university as "place" is again suspected by the distinguishing features of SWU, a cosmopolitan campus located in a small town between two large cities with major universities and a variety of entertainment venues for young adults. Location plus a large sorority and fraternity presence on campus contributed to the SWU "party-school image" in the 1980s. Although a vastly different university today with the third highest admission standards in the state, a memorable legendary "sense of place" may still linger, influencing the sexual behavior of its students.

But, differences in regional variations reflected in university and general population samples are not straightforward. University students (SWU and SHBU) in this study displayed more liberal sexual attitudes and behavior than found in the general population in their regions and SPRU students more traditional ones (Laumann et al., 1994). That students at a religiously affiliated university (SPRU) were considerably more sexually conservative is not surprising but the reasons why are still unanswered in this study. Are these more religiously traditional students more conservative in sexual attitudes and behaviors because they came to a religiously affiliated campus or because they came from homes reflective of more traditional religious values? Probably both, but values of these respondents were more rooted in the family. But, why those from a historic Black university population (SHBU) were considerably more recreational in their sexual attitudes and behaviors than Laumann et al. (1994) found in the general population is puzzling. These results suggest that Black university students may experience more split loyalties between their families' cultural milieus and the world of academia than do white students. But, the question of specific effects of family background factors on college students when behavior patterns and belief systems in their home environments differ from new attitudes and beliefs on university campuses has been understudied. Finally, these findings raise another research query calling for clarification. Is the university milieu more influential in promoting certain sexual attitudes and behavior among college students whose personalities are not yet fully individuated than formerly acknowledged?

The research question, do region, race, and/or religion matter in the sexual attitudes and behavior of college students must be answered affirmatively. And, overall, although religion and other factors such as campus milieus in various regions are believed to be strong mediating variables, in this study, family background factors and race appeared to be most influential in differentiating the sexual attitudes and behavior of college students. Because each population was from a unique place, it is logical to assume that broad social factors by which sexual attitudes are adopted and maintained were also defining forces in their sexual behaviors. Future research needs to address the relative interface of region with institutionalized forces represented by family, race, and religion.

INTRODUCTION REFERENCE

Party school list from *Princeton Review* released: University of Florida on top. 2008. *The Huntington Post*, 28 July, 1.

REFERENCES

Arnett, J. J. (2000). Emerging adulthood: A theory of development from late teens through the twenties. *American Psychologist*, 55, 469–480.

Braithwaite, K., & Thomas, V. G. (2001). HIV/AIDS knowledge, attitudes, and risk-behaviors among African-American and Caribbean college women. *International Journal of the Advancement of Counseling*, 23, 115–129.

Christopher, F. S., & Sprecher, S. (2001). Sexuality in marriage, dating, and other relationships: A decade in review. In R. M. Milardo (Ed.), *Understanding families into the new millennium: A decade in review* (pp. 218–236). Minneapolis: National Council on Family Relations.

Cooper, M. L. (2002). Alcohol and risky sexual behavior among college students and youth: Evaluating the evidence. *Journal of Studies on Alcohol*, Suppl. 14, 101–107.

Davidson, J. K., Sr. (1993). Premarital sexual intercourse and axiomatic theory construction. *Sociological Inquiry, 63*, 84–100.

Davidson, J. K., Sr., & Moore, N. B. (1999). Age at first contraceptive information and risk taking among college women. *American Journal of Health Behavior*, 23, 293–302.

Davidson, J. K, Sr., Moore, N. B., & Ullstrup, K. M. (2004). Religiosity and sexual responsibility: Relationships of choice. *American Journal of Health Behavior, 28*, 335–346.

DeLamater, J. D. (1987). A sociological approach. In J. H. Geer & W. T. O'Donohue (Eds.), *Theories of sexuality* (pp. 237–256). New York: Plenum.

Dodge, B., Sandfort, T. G. M., Yarber, W. L., & de Wit, J. (2004). Sexual health among male college students in the United States and the Netherlands. *American Journal of Health Behavior, 29*, 172–182.

Earle, J. R., Perricone, P. J., Davidson, J. K., Sr., Moore, N. B., Harris, C. T., & Cotten, S. R. (In press). Premarital sexual attitudes and behavior at a religously-affiliated university: Two decades of change. *Sexuality & Culture*.

Ellingson, S., Laumann, E. O., Paik, A., & Mahay, J. (2004). The theory of sex markets. In E. O. Laumann, S. Ellingson, J. Mahay, A. Paik, & Y. Youm (Eds.), *The sexual organization of the city* (pp. 3–38). Chicago: University of Chicago Press.

Ellingson, S., Van Haitsma, M., Laumann, E. O., & Tebbe, N. (2004). Religion and the politics of sexuality. In E. O. Laumann, S. Ellingson, J. Mahay, A. Paik, & Y. Youm (Eds.), *The sexual organization of the city* (pp. 309–348). Chicago: University of Chicago Press.

Feigenbaum, R., Weinstein, E., & Rosen, E. (1995). College students' sexual attitudes and behaviors: Implications for sexuality education. *Journal of American College Health, 44,* 112–118.

Feijoo, A. N. (2004). Trends in sexual risk behaviors among high school students—United States, 1991 to 1997 and 1999 to 2003. Washington, D C: Advocates for Youth.

Flannery, D., Ellingson, L., & Votaw, K. S. (2003). Anal intercourse and sexual risk factors among college women, 1993–2000. *American Journal of Health Behavior, 27,* 228–234.

Ford, D. S., & Goode, C. R. (1994). African American college students' health behaviors and perceptions of related health issues. *Journal of American College Health, 42,* 206–210.

Gilbert, L., & Alexander, L. (1998). A profile of sexual health behaviors among college women. *Psychological Reports, 82,* 107–116.

Hawkins, M. J., Gray, C., & Hawkins, W. E. (1995). Gender difference of reported safer sex behavior within a random sample of college students. *Psychological Reports, 77,* 963–968.

Hill, C. A. (2002). Gender, relationship stages, and sexual behavior: The importance of partner emotional investment within specific situations. *Journal of Sex Research, 39,* 228–240.

Johnson, E. H., Jackson, L. A., Hinkle, Y., Gilbert, D., Hoopwood, T., Lollis, C. M., Willis, C., & Gant, L. (1994). What is the significance of the Black-White differences in risky sexual behavior. *Journal of the National Medical Association, 86,* 745–759.

Langer, L. M., Warheit, G. J., & McDonald, L. P. (2001). Correlates and predictors of risky sexual practices among a multi-racial/ethnic sample of university students. *Social Behavior & Personality, 29,* 133–144.

Laumann, E. O., Gagnon, J. H., Michael, R. T., & Michaels, S. (1994). *The social organization of sexuality: Sexual practices in the United States.* Chicago: University of Chicago Press.

Lefkowitz, E. S., Gillen, M. M., Shearer, C. L., & Boone, T. L. (2004). Religiosity, sexual behaviors, and sexual attitudes during emerging adulthood. *Journal of Sex Research, 41,* 150–159.

Lehr, S. T., DiIorio, C., Dudley, W. N., & Lipana, J. A. (2000). The relationship between parent-adolescent communication and safer sex behaviors in college students. *Journal of Family Nursing, 6,* 180–196.

Lewis, L. M., Melton, R. S., Succop, P. A., & Rosenthal, S. L. (2000). Factors influencing condom use and STD acquisition among African-American college women. *Journal of American College Health, 49,* 19–23.

Mahay, J., Laumann, E. O., & Michaels, S. (2001). Race, gender and class in sexual scripts. In E. O. Laumann & R. T. Michael (Eds.), *Sex, love and health in America: Private choices and public policies* (pp. 197–238). Chicago: University of Chicago Press.

Meier, A. M. (2003). Adolescents' transition to first intercourse, religiosity, and attitudes toward *sex. Social Forces, 81,* 1031–1052.

Moore, N. B., & Davidson, J. K., Sr. (1997). Guilt about first intercourse: An antecedent of sexual dissatisfaction among college women. *Journal of Sex & Marital Therapy, 26,* 85–106.

Moore, N. B., & Davidson, J. K., Sr. (1999). Parents as first sexuality information sources: Do they make a difference in daughters' sexual attitudes and behavior. *Journal of Sex Education and Therapy, 24,* 155–163.

Nangle, D. W., & Glover, R. L. (2001). Social behavior and condom use among males: A multidimensional assessment. *Journal of Sex Education and Therapy, 26,* 90–99.

Olson, T. D. (2005). Sexuality education: Philosophies and practices in search of a meaningful difference. In J. K. Davidson, Sr., & N. B. Moore (Eds.), *Speaking of sexuality,* (2nd ed.) (pp. 375–386). Los Angeles: Roxbury.

Page, R. M., Hammermeister, J. J., & Scanlon, A. (2002). Everybody's not doing it: Misperceptions of college students' sexual activity. *American Journal of Health Behavior, 24,* 387–394.

Petersen, L. R., & Donnenwerth, G. V. (1997). Secularization and the influence of religion on beliefs about premarital sex. *Social Forces, 75,* 1071–1089.

Pinkerton, S. D., Bogart, L. M., Cecil, H., & Abramson, P. R. (2002). Factors associated with masturbation in a collegiate sample. *Journal of Psychology & Human Sexuality, 14*(2/3), 103–121.

Pluhar, E., Frongillo, E. A., Jr., Stycos, J. M., & Dempster-McClain, D. (1998). Understanding the relationship between religion and the sexual attitudes and behaviors of college students. *Journal of Sex Education and Therapy, 23,* 288–296.

Ratliff-Crain, J., Donald, K. M., & Dalton, J. (1999). Knowledge, beliefs, peer norms, and past behaviors as correlates of risky sexual behaviors among college students. *Psychology & Health, 14,* 625–641.

Sawyer, R. G., & Smith, N. G. (1996). A survey of situational factors at first intercourse among college students. *American Journal of Health Behavior, 20,* 208–217.

Seal, D. W., & Agostinelli, G. (1996). College students' perceptions of the prevalence of risky sexual behavior. *AIDs Care, 8,* 453–466.

Siegel, D. M., Klein, D. I., & Roghmann, K. J. (1991). Sexual behavior, contraception, and risk among college students. *Journal of Adolescent Health, 25,* 336–343.

Simon, W., & Gagnon, J. H. (1987). Sexual scripts: Permanence and change. *Archives of Sexual Behavior, 15,* 97–120.

Sprecher, S., Barbee, A., & Schwartz, P. (1995). "Was it good for you, too?": Gender differences in first sexual intercourse experiences. *Journal of Sex Research, 32,* 3–15.

Staples, R. (1972). The sexuality of black women. *Sexual Behavior, 2,* 4–15.

Staples, R., & Johnson, L. B. (1993). *Black families at the crossroads.* San Francisco: Jossey-Bass.

Upchurch, D. M., Levy-Storms, L., Sucoff, C. A., & Aneshensel, C. S. (1998). Gender and ethnic differences in timing of first sexual intercourse. *Family Planning Perspectives, 30,* 121–127.

Weinberg, M., & Williams, C. (1988). Black sexuality: A test of two theories. *Journal of Sex Research, 25,* 197–218.

Weinberg, M. S., Lottes, I. L., & Gordon, L. E. (1997). Social class background, sexual attitudes, and sexual behavior in a heterosexual undergraduate sample. *Archives of Sexual Behavior, 26,* 625–642.

Willie, C. V. (1991). *A new look at Black families* (4th ed.). Dix Hills, NY: General Hall.

CHAPTER 12

Hooking Up

Men, Women, and the Sexual Double Standard

Kathleen A. Bogle

Over forty years ago, in his classic work Love and Will, *psychotherapist Rollo May (1969) decried the* Playboy *mentality that existed in our society, declaring that such a mind-set took the fig leaf from the genitals and placed it on the face. May predicted that much bed-hopping but little intimacy would result from such behavior. Although one-night stands and uncommitted sexual behaviors are obviously not of recent vintage, earlier research viewed them very differently. In the past, sexual behaviors in a committed relationship were somewhat less problematic, but unloving, uncommitted sexual relations needed an explanation. According to a new book about casual sex on college campuses, what was once viewed as questionable sexual behavior has now become a normative process known as "hooking up."*

Now in a best-seller entitled, Hooking Up: Sex, Dating and Relationships on Campus, *Kathleen A. Bogle uses a sociological lens to illuminate this phenomenon in a book that has been labeled "a page turner." In an interesting first chapter of the book, the author sets the stage by reviewing the three distinct scripts that have guided young women's and men's intimate lives over the past*

century. Showing how each era emerged during a period of social transition, Bogle describes the "Calling Era," the "Dating Era" and the "Hooking-Up Era."

In her 16 in-depth interviews that included undergraduate college students (ages 18–23) and alumni (ages 23–30), Bogle encountered an assortment of descriptive phrases ranging from "hooking up" to "friends with benefits" to "booty call." But even Bogle herself admittedly has difficulty in defining the ubiquitous term, "hooking up." The first team of psychologists to reveal that 28 percent of undergraduate students at a large Northeastern university had engaged in a "hookup" defined it as "a sexual encounter, usually lasting only one night, between two people who are strangers or brief acquaintances. Some physical interaction is typical but may or may not include sexual intercourse" (Paul, McManus, and Hayes, 2008, p. 79). Bogle concludes by noting that sexual activity on campus today is less rampant and promiscuous than many, including college students themselves, presume. This is a great "read" for college students who want to understand what hooking up really means to their classmates, but it is especially relevant for parents who, as so aptly stated in the Philadelphia Inquirer, *are trying to figure out why their darn kids are "running around the bases backwards."*

Certain Hollywood actresses of the 1950s and 1960s, such as Sandra Dee and Doris Day, epitomized the proverbial idea of a "good girl." These women had a squeaky clean, virginlike image that was promulgated both on and off screen. All actresses of this time period did not fit this mold, but there was something about maintaining this image that helped propel these women to stardom. An erotic image, on the other hand, also helped skyrocket the careers of actresses like Elizabeth Taylor and Marilyn Monroe. Interestingly, both Taylor and Monroe became the infamous "other women" in the marriages of "respectable" wives like Debbie Reynolds and first lady Jacqueline Kennedy. Thus, iconic women could be characterized either as a virginal "good girl" (i.e., the marrying kind), or a sexy "bad girl" whom a man should not bring home to Mother.

The women's movement of the late 1960s and 1970s aimed to free women of this kind of labeling by encouraging all women to embrace their sexuality. This era has been called the sexual revolution because it became increasingly socially acceptable for women to have sex prior to marriage. Although cultural expectations for women's sexual behavior changed after the sexual revolution, the good-girl image has remained relevant. The lasting popularity of women with an innocent persona begs the question: How much have attitudes on women's sexuality actually changed? The hookup culture on modern college campuses affords young people more freedom than ever before, yet there continues to be a double standard for the sexual lives of men and women.[1]

When men and women first enter college they seem to be on the same page. Freshman year is a time when all students can test limits. Both men and women enter college with ideas about what college life is supposed to be like, and they are eager to be a part of the social scene. Most students indicated that, as freshmen, they did not want to be "tied down" to a relationship because this would interfere with experiencing all that college life has to offer. Many students had had

exclusive relationships in high school and they reported looking forward to having a little freedom to see "who else is out there." During this time of sexual experimentation, many students, both male and female, spoke of enjoying partying and hooking up. Since they were still getting to know their fellow classmates on campus, many indicated that "random" hookups were common. After freshman year, things change. Men's and women's goals in the hookup culture diverge; men enjoy the status quo, while women begin to want something more. For many men, the hookup script worked, so they did not communicate that they wanted a different way of doing things. Men preferred a "no strings attached" approach to a hookup encounter, so they could hook up with different women whenever they had the opportunity. For men who had good social skills, the opportunities were many. Men who wanted more than "just a hookup" pursued relationships and they did not seem to have much difficulty finding them. However, many men indicated that they did not want relationships during college. Other men said they might be interested in a relationship if the "right girl" came along, but they were not planning to "go out of their way" to find her. Women, on the other hand, became increasingly relationship-oriented after freshman year. While many women were still willing to hook up, they wanted hookup encounters to turn into some semblance of a relationship.

GOALS AT ODDS

Since men and women want different things from the hookup culture, the intimate side of college life becomes somewhat of a battle of the sexes. Given that many women want relationships and many men do not, boyfriends are hard to come by. Lisa, a sophomore, discussed what college women want.

> *KB:* What about girls? What are they looking for, are they looking for sex, are they looking for relationships, what are they looking for?

Lisa: I think, like I said, when I first came in as a freshman, I wasn't looking for a real relationship at all, I just wanted to go out and have fun and do whatever I wanted to do. And I think a lot of my girlfriends were like that last year too. As time goes on, it gets kind of old [the whole hookup scene] and you're like: "All right, I'm sick of just kissing random people; it's not really that fun; it doesn't mean anything." And I think people, *at least girls*, as they progress through college they start to really want, I know a lot of them really want to find someone that they really like and have a real relationship.

KB: Do you think that is something they will be able to find or is that something that's hard for them to find?

Lisa: I don't know, I mean it is kind of hard to find in college. Like, the guy that I'm seeing now is someone from home.

Many of the women were not as fortunate as Lisa in terms of finding a boyfriend. It seemed it was easier for her to maintain a long-distance relationship than to find a boyfriend on campus among thousands of single men.

The college men were aware that some women wanted hookup encounters to evolve into relationships. So, they developed strategies for communicating their lack of interest in pursuing anything further. Specifically, men spoke about avoiding girls after a hookup, "not calling girls back," or "thinking of good excuses" to get out of spending time with them. Kevin, a senior, explained how he would get his point across without actually having to say so.

Kevin: If the next day [after a hookup] she's like: "I want to come over and hang out" and you didn't want to hook up with her again you'd be like: "Oh, I got practice tonight." Or I was the head of intramurals too . . . I'd be like: "I've got intramurals, I've got to run tonight over at the gym," that would be an easy way to get out of it. The other way is to just not talk to them.

KB: And why would you not want to talk to them again?

Kevin: If all I wanted was a hookup.

KB: But you didn't like the person?

Kevin: It's not that I didn't like them; I did not want to lead them on. I didn't want them to think that there might be something more [when] there's not.

For some men, hinting that they did not want a relationship did not work, so they had to verbalize it. This was the case with Brian, a sophomore.

KB: Of all the girls you've met at [Faith University], whom have you liked the most?

Brian: I don't know, I really don't know. I thought I liked . . . a chick last semester and then she just went crazy on me. Like she wanted the relationship, she wanted everything and I was just kind of like: "Oh I can't handle this right now." So I kind of backed out. . . . But, I mean, hooking up . . . can sometimes make things awkward.

KB: The girl last semester that you said went a little bit crazy, what happened? What did she do?

Brian: She started asking me out and I was like: "Uhhh, I'm not, I'm not [interested]."

KB: To be your boyfriend or asking you out on dates?

Brian: Yeah, to be her boyfriend. She's like: "Are you my boyfriend?" and I was like: "No." And she was like: "All right, well we're not hooking up unless you are my boyfriend." I was like: "All right." And that was the end of that.

Through experience, women learned that they could not expect a hookup encounter to turn into a relationship. Many of the women found that men's desire to avoid relationships often forced hookup partners to remain just that. Two women explained their disappointment in this way:

KB: And, it seems like [casual hookups] were a problem for you . . . because you seem like you wouldn't be interested in that in the future?

Susan: Yeah, it was a problem. [The guy I was hooking up with] . . . he would sleep in my bed and everything and we wouldn't do anything [sexual], like he wouldn't even kiss me . . . . But then, we hung out more and we started kissing and everything and then he never talked about . . . having it be a relationship. But I wanted . . . in my mind [I was thinking] like: "I want to be his girlfriend. I want to be his girlfriend." . . . I was like looking for a boyfriend, looking for that connection, looking for that dependency that I had [in a previous high school relationship]. And I found it [with] him, but he wasn't [interested in a relationship] . . . I didn't want to bring it up and just [say] like: "So where do we stand?" because I know guys don't like that question. So, it eventually led to sex and we only had sex once and then he continued to still want to talk and hang out with me but he never really brought up the "where do we stand" thing. That kind of pushed me away because I just didn't want to just be casually having sex with him and it not meaning something to him. So that stopped there. [Freshman]

KB: If people are [hooking up], is it usually with the same person repeatedly or is it more of random kind of one time thing?

Diane: [For] some people it's random. [For] some people I know it's from a week to week basis, [they] hook up or get with somebody they don't know. Not that they don't know them, but they're not like in a relationship with them. Some people will consistently hook up with the same person but then something will happen and . . . they'll stop but then they'll . . . find like another person and like consistently be with them [for hooking up].

KB: What typically happens to have one thing stop and another thing start? What kind of stops things?

Diane: Usually the girl gets . . . girls are crazy you know [if they found out the guy they were hooking up with] was [also] talking to somebody else. She'll be like: "Wait, are you talking to them?" . . . girls are like very predictable . . . if they're hooking up with someone for a while, they're going to want a relationship. They're going to want like some type of like title, not title but like . . .

KB: Commitment or something?

Diane: Right. Exactly, commitment. And usually guys don't want it.

KB: Why don't they want it?

Diane: Because they don't. They're in college, they don't want a girlfriend. They basically just want to get ass.

KB: So girls are looking more for relationships? Guys are looking more for a sexual relationship?

Diane: Yeah. [Sophomore]

Perhaps the concept of "hidden power" can help explain why Susan did not even want to ask her hookup partner if he would consider being in an exclusive relationship with her. Social scientist Aafke Komter, who studied the power dynamic between married couples, found that many hidden power struggles go on beneath the surface of purported equal relationships. In some cases, wives would not even bring up issues that were bothering them in the relationship for fear of "rocking the boat" and consequently jeopardizing the relationship. In Komter's analysis, the fact that women were afraid to even raise an issue that a man might "not like" shows that men have greater power in relationships. Similarly, in my study, although women were more likely to initiate "the talk" about the status of a relationship, in some cases they did not bring up the issue at all in anticipation of a negative reaction.[2]

WHY WOMEN SEEK RELATIONSHIPS

Students were not always cognizant of why women sought relationships more than men. Some cited psychological reasons, such as women are "more emotional" or women "need that kind of connection." Some women talked about wanting a relationship due to their affection for a particular man. However, there are likely reasons beyond psychology and personal biography. One possible reason why some women seek relationships during college is that they are interested in marrying a few years after graduation. Men, on the other hand, seemed willing to wait longer to get married. Many men suggested they would not get married until their late twenties (at the earliest) or possibly even well into their thirties. Thus, men's and women's timetables for getting married are at odds. This puts their timetables for finding potential marriage partners at odds, too, which in turn puts their timetables for having serious relationships at odds. For this reason, several women indicated that they would like to have a relationship with marriage potential.

> *KB*: Do you or [your] friends . . . think about marriage at all?
>
> *Gloria*: Yeah. We always talk about that. It's so weird, we are going to have to . . . not soon, I would like to be with who I'm going to marry for a good three years before [we get married] . . . someone I'm going to marry I'd want to be with for a long time.
>
> *KB*: So you [possibly] would want to meet someone in college . . . that you might end up with [permanently]?
>
> *Gloria*: Yeah. I would say junior year I would like to have a boyfriend and hopefully potential marriage [partner], but I don't know. [Freshman]

However, a couple of women in their junior and senior years mentioned no longer being naive regarding finding a future spouse during their college years.

> *KB*: Have you ever thought: "I wonder if this is someone I could marry?" Have you ever thought about it that way?
>
> *Marie*: I think about it all the time. Like anyone I have ever been serious with I'm always like: "I wonder if we could ever get married." . . . [But] I'm not that naive anymore. I know relationships come and go and you never know what is going to happen. I mean it would be nice, like my ex-boyfriend from over the summer, I really liked him a lot and I really wanted the kind of relationship my roommates have, even if it was a year or two, just something, like some stability, like you know, a possible marriage [partner], someone that you were close to and I definitely could see him as that. [Senior]

Another possible reason that women are more desirous of relationships than men is that women need relationships in order to protect their reputation. Over 30 years since the sexual revolution, there is still a double standard for male versus female sexual behavior on the college campus. In the hookup culture, men are free to choose whether to have a very active sex life or to "settle down" and maintain an exclusive relationship. Women, on the other hand, have considerably less freedom.

> *KB*: How do people get a bad reputation, assuming there's such a thing as getting a bad reputation?
>
> *Max*: Well it's kind of bad because if you're a girl and you hook up with a lot of guys, then that's looked down upon.
>
> *KB*: Okay. Looked down upon by everybody or looked down upon by guys?
>
> *Max*: By both genders, yeah. But, if you're a guy and you hook up with a lot of people, like from your peers, like your guy peers, they're going to be like: "Oh you're the man!" [Sophomore]

The sexual double standard leads to an environment where women need relationships in order to protect their reputations. For women who are active participants, the hookup system is fraught with pitfalls that can lead to being labeled a "slut." Rule number one for women is: Do not act like men in the sexual arena.

> *Larry*: The perception is that if a girl sleeps with a lot of guys she's a slut. If the guy sleeps with a lot of girls he's a stud . . . I mean, I see it every day. I mean, like I said, I bartend [and] I do go out to bars when I go out.
>
> *KB*: So when you say it's a perception [is it] a true perception?
>
> *Larry*: A complete true perception. It happens every day and you can ask anyone on campus randomly, and they would say that would be the perception. A girl sleeps with a lot of guys she's a slut. A guy sleeps with a lot of girls he's a stud. [Senior]

Prior to the sexual revolution era, women were expected to have sex, particularly intercourse, only with their husbands.[3] Since then, sex prior to marriage has become the norm for both men and women.[4] On the campuses I studied, most students assumed sex would be part of a committed, exclusive relationship; yet, students were also aware that sex (including intercourse) was often part of the hookup script. Students evaluated their peers, particularly their female peers, based on the context in which sex occurs. In the hookup culture, men and women are permitted to (and do) engage in sexual encounters that are, by definition, outside of the context of a committed relationship. However, there are prejudices against women who are seen as being too active in the hookup scene.

THE RULES FOR HOOKING UP

There are very few restrictions on sexual behavior for college men. Both male and female interviewees said college men were free to hook up as often as they had the opportunity to do so. For men, there is no stigma for engaging in "heavy" sexual activity. In fact, men are congratulated by their male peers for sexual conquests. Stigmatization occurs only for men who cannot "get any" (i.e., they are virgins or have difficulty getting women to hook up with them). However, such men were believed to be few and far between. The idea that men are free to engage in hooking up, including sexual intercourse, with a variety of women without risking their reputation was a point raised by many.

> *KB*: Are guys ever considered to be too loose sexually, or a pig?
>
> *Emily*: Oh, *I don't think so*. If you hear a guy who had sex with all these people, you're like "Hmm," but I think it's still much more for girls. [Sophomore]
>
> *Gloria*: Guys . . . don't get reps for hooking up with girls or having sex with girls. [Freshman]

According to Ed, a senior, men were aware that they were free to do as they please when it comes to hooking up.

> *KB*: So, is there any kind of standards among the people you know of what's acceptable and what's not acceptable to do as far as hooking up and sexual behavior?
>
> *Ed*: All the guys I know have no "don'ts."

Some students mentioned that a man who was very active in the hookup culture would be known as a "player." Although this term was considered derogatory by some students, others indicated that the term "player" also had somewhat of a positive connotation. An alternate description of a promiscuous man is "man-whore" or "male-slut." However, most students indicated that these terms are used as more of a joke than as a derogatory label per se.

For college men, there are virtually no rules, but for college women it is a very different story. In fact, there is a host of norms for the hookup script that, if violated, lead women to get bad reputations. Many of the men I interviewed mentioned that women would get a bad reputation if they hooked up too often with too many different partners.

> *KB:* For people that aren't in relationships, do you think that guys or girls have more partners as far as hooking up or sex?
>
> *Robert:* I think guys have more partners overall because they can do it more discreetly. A girl does it and a guy knows about it, the girl has a nickname or has this connotation about her. All the guys know who "puts out" [sexually] and who doesn't. Guys know that and want to steer away from girls that do it all the time. Whereas guys try to go for the trophy ones that hook up with people seldomly or with a select few.
>
> *KB:* So a trophy girl is someone who doesn't hook up as much?
>
> *Robert:* Correct.
>
> *KB:* So that would be someone sought after because it is more of a challenge?
>
> *Robert:* Yeah. As opposed to someone who sleeps with a lot of people. That is gross, everyone has been there, done that.
>
> *KB:* If girls are treated negatively if they hook up with or sleep with a lot of people, why do you think they do that?
>
> *Robert:* I think it goes back to the need factor. They want to be needed or loved and it's a quick fix or immediate gratification for them, the desire to be wanted or needed or [to] feel pretty. [Sophomore]

Despite men insisting that women should not hook up "too often" or with "too many partners," they were unable to offer a convincing operational definition of these terms. In other words, men had a sense that it was not acceptable for women to "get around," but they did not seem to know what "getting around" would really entail. When I pressed them to explain

what "too often" or "too many partners" meant, they always resorted to giving a somewhat preposterous definition. Larry, a senior, seems to have trouble identifying what qualifies as "a lot of guys."

> *KB:* You [said] "If a girl sleeps with a lot of guys she's a slut." How many would be a lot, in your opinion?
>
> *Larry:* In a short amount of time, it would be like twelve guys. If she was just randomly doing that and had like no . . . but just did it and was like: "Okay next." You know, something like that.
>
> *KB:* Okay.
>
> *Larry:* And would do it like that, sleep with five guys in a week. One every night, that would be like a slut.

The problem with Larry's explanation is that the behavior he defines as that of a "slut" does not generally happen. Rarely do college women sleep with "five guys in a week" or "twelve guys" in a short period of time. Even among the most sexually active college women, such behavior would be considered exceptional. None of the quantitative data on the sexual behavior of American women indicates that young women engage in this level of sexual activity with multiple partners.[5] Yet, many of the men I interviewed gave answers similar to Larry's about what women do in order to get labeled "sluts."

Although there are many norms governing the hookup script, there is simultaneously a sense of confusion, which is, in part, generated by the ambiguous nature of the term "hooking up." The rules for sexual behavior within the hookup script do not seem altogether clear and, to complicate matters, college students often have distorted perceptions of what others are doing sexually. Therefore, it is not surprising that students had difficulty articulating what constituted a rule violation when they were not entirely clear on what the rules were in the first place.

Another potential pitfall for women is hooking up with two different guys who know each other well. This is particularly problematic if the two different men are friends or fraternity brothers. The time span between the hookups is also a critical consideration. The men indicated that if a woman hooked up with two different men who knew each other without a reasonable amount of time between the hookup encounters, she would be labeled a "slut." Again, it was difficult to pinpoint what men considered a "reasonable amount of time." However, men seemed to object particularly to encounters that happened in the same month or even in the same semester (which generally equates to a three and a half month span of time).

> *Kevin*: If she has a reputation then we know who she is. And she would know who we were if we were a group of guys that were all friends. If she blew three or four guys, of course she would get a reputation.
>
> *KB*: What if it was just [a] hookup [which did not involve oral sex]?
>
> *Kevin*: Still, that's her writing her own fate.
>
> *KB*: So it's a no-no to hook up with several people in the same clique?
>
> *Kevin*: You are only making yourself trouble.... If one girl would hook up with me and then my friend and so on, of course she'd get a reputation.
>
> *KB*: Even if it was just kissing?
>
> *Kevin*: Bad idea. How do you expect these people not to talk [when] they're friends? "Did you hook up with Susan?" "Yeah, I hooked up with [her]." "Yeah, me too." She would have to realize that these guys are close buddies and of course they are going to know. I'd almost say that would be her fault. [Senior]

At State University, where fraternities were a more prominent feature of campus life, men indicated that the cardinal sin for women was hooking up with two or more men within the same fraternity. The same issues regarding hooking up with men who are friends applied here. However, the fraternity dimension seemed to add insult to injury.

> *Kyle*: If they have multiple partners in the same fraternity, I know other girls in other houses, even girls at our [fraternity] house who have hooked up with six or seven different guys. And you are like: "Maybe she'll hook up with everybody and we'll put her picture on the wall or something." Everyone knows her business and I think it is detrimental to her . . . reputation.
>
> *KB*: So, hooking up with people that are friends or in the same fraternity is not a good idea?
>
> *Kyle*: No. Because I think everyone talks about them. [Senior]

In addition to the problems for women regarding how often they hook up or with whom, there were also a number of other behaviors that could potentially lead to being negatively labeled. Several men mentioned how some women at their college dress, particularly how they dress for parties, bars, and other social gatherings where hooking up takes place. When women dress too seductively, they were often labeled "easy" or "stupid." In some cases, men indicated that girls who dressed in a seductive manner were purposely sought after by men looking for an easy, one-night hookup. Jack, a sophomore, said "If I want it to be something for one night, then I'm looking for someone that's showing a little midriff."

Another pitfall for college women was constantly hanging around a particular fraternity house. A couple of male fraternity members I interviewed mentioned that there were some girls who were always at their fraternity house. These girls became friends with some of the brothers in the fraternity and they started hanging out at the house even when no party or other social gathering was happening. These women were seen as the lowest of the low. In fact, one fraternity member said that these women were referred to by the fraternity brothers as "houserats." "House-rats" were stigmatized not only for what they did sexually within the hookup script, but also for their behavior outside the sexual arena.

Women's conduct in the hookup scene can also lead them to be negatively labeled. The men I spoke to said that women need to "watch themselves" in terms of flirting, drinking, and "letting go" at parties or bars where hooking up might take place.

KB: Are there people that have bad reputations?

Trent: Yeah.

KB: [How does someone get] a bad reputation?

Trent: Just doing stupid stuff. If you hear stories about them, you're going to think less of them.

KB: What would be a story that would earn someone a bad reputation?

Trent: This one girl was at this thing called "Mrs. Faith University" . . . for one of the frats. . . . It was this contest down at this one motor lodge place and they had to chug beer and do this drinking contest and the "dream girl" would be the one who won the most. But, this one girl comes out with this real short skirt and no underwear on and just starts flashing people and she was a mess and ever since then people just look at her and are like: "That's disgusting, what are you doing?" She's branded with that for the rest of her time here.

KB: At the time, were you there?

Trent: No, I wasn't there.

KB: So, the story kind of got around?

Trent: Yeah . . . people were just telling me about it and everyone looks at her and is just like . . . and I found out the next day, so you know the whole campus knew within the week.

KB: So, in that case it's not a bad reputation from something she did . . . with somebody else or sexually, but it was just how she was acting?

Trent: Yeah, in that case it was how she was acting. But, then you always hear stories about girls who will sleep around and you'll get a bad reputation that way [too]. [Senior]

Kyle: I think [freshman women] are a lot different than other women you encounter on this campus.

KB: Why are they different?

Kyle: Because they don't have a clue. They don't know what they are doing . . . . They can't get beer. They maybe feel out of place . . . . I just find that a lot of them hadn't drank a lot in high school and they go to a party and get sloshed, and then, it's funny to look at them sometimes.

KB: So you could almost spot at a party who is a freshman?

Kyle: Yeah. Definitely. And also they'll get . . . real sluttily dressed, I find. They wear those black sex pants and there will just be fifty of them rolling up to your house and you are just like: "Oh man, I don't want to drive anyone to the hospital tonight."

KB: Because they are going to drink so much?

Kyle: Or they just don't know how to handle themselves.

KB: What do you mean handle themselves, besides the drinking?

Kyle: That is what I mean. They drink too much and get themselves in trouble. Throw up all over the place, take their clothes off, or something stupid that they normally wouldn't do and I don't think they would do if they were a senior and had been exposed to the college culture and drinking.

KB: Do freshman males do that also or is it specifically girls?

Kyle: I think males do it too. It's just displayed differently. Guys would get drunk too, but maybe a guy would do something he wouldn't normally do like get in a fight or something, not like take his clothes off [the ways girls do].

KB: Would you say then that females change more over the four years [in college] than males do?

Kyle: Yeah. Definitely. Females change a lot more. They come to college and figure it's a big school and no one is going to find out what they do and then [they learn this is not the case]. [Senior]

Kyle refers to several of the ways women can get negatively labeled: how much they drink, what they wear, how wildly they behave, and so on. However, Kyle also noted that men did not have these same concerns. Men may need to learn their limits with drinking and to avoid starting fights, but men were not being judged in the same way as women. Moreover, women's behavior is specifically being scrutinized and sexualized. As Kyle points out, drinking may lead to guys getting in fights, but it is girls who "take their clothes off."

Just because these unwritten rules for women within the hookup scene exist does not mean all women follow them. The guidelines are sometimes vague and they may not be known to all women on campus. As Kyle and many other men I spoke with indicated, some women had to "learn the hard way" over time what is acceptable within the hookup script. This is particularly true for freshman women who may be naive about the rules at the outset of their college careers. Other college women may know the rules and flout them intentionally. However, most of the women I interviewed said they were aware of these rules and they "watched" their behavior accordingly.

BREAKING THE RULES

For women who break the rules there are consequences. One consequence is that students will label women who are seen as promiscuous. Being labeled a "slut" goes well beyond hurt feelings. Some students indicated that some women on campus were severely stigmatized. In my interview with Emily, a sophomore, she reveals how a label can overtake a woman's identity.

KB: Are there people who have bad reputations for how they act with guys?

Emily: Yeah, I think so, like . . . supposedly there's a girl named "Blow Job Jen" and supposedly she gives a lot of blow jobs, I don't know, but when I see her I think about that so I guess there are [people with bad reputations].

In addition to women being labeled by others, women also evaluate their own behavior by the standards set by their peers. As Adrienne, a senior, put it:

Guys talk about girls like this, like it's a number. It's like: "What did you do with this girl? Oh, she was hot." But I think for girls, if they like the guy or whatever [they hope it's not just a one-and-done hookup]. Or maybe it's because then [girls] don't feel like as much as a slut too if they can talk to the guy the next day. If they never talk to the guy again, then it's like: "Oh yeah, I hooked up with him one night and I haven't talked to him since." I think that [makes them feel like]: "Am I a slut for doing that?"

Another consequence for breaking the rules is being ostracized. Several women spoke about close female friends who were severely stigmatized for their behavior within the hookup scene. For instance, Gloria, a freshman, had a friend who "could not be seen" at a certain fraternity house because she had sex with a few different fraternity brothers during the course of a semester.

Gloria: I have a few [female] friends that have a rep, like a bad rep. First semester we couldn't go to certain frats because they were like with too many guys.

KB: What do you mean you couldn't go?

Gloria: Like she wasn't wanted there. She would have sex with this guy and then this guy [at some later point] and they'd be three frat brothers. They obviously don't want this girl at their parties.

KB: I don't understand why that is obvious . . . why would they not want her there?

Gloria: I don't know. Maybe she would feel . . . stupid going there. Say she had sex with this guy, she would get there and they would not acknowledge her. They would not talk to her, not even look at her . . . they would be . . . laughing at her [rather] than like [saying]: "What's up?"

It seems likely that a woman labeled this way (and treated accordingly) is affected both emotionally and, in turn, behaviorally. Sociologists argue that labeling can affect behavior by altering one's sense of identity and thereby ultimately creating a self-fulfilling prophecy, whereby people live up to the labels imposed on them.[6] If this is true, a young woman who is labeled the "campus slut" is likely to continue a pattern of behavior that will lead to further confirmation of the label. However, in some cases, life on campus might become too difficult. For instance, Violet, a junior, had a female friend who ultimately transferred to a different college in order to escape the negative label imposed on her.

KB: Do you know people that have a bad reputation on campus?

Violet: I know . . . one friend who was at another campus. She had to leave [school because] she had a bad rep.

KB: When you say "she had to leave" is it something she felt she had to [do] because she had a bad reputation? What made her leave?

Violet: Because she slept with a lot of people on campus . . . people look at her as though she was a slut. And I think it made her feel like people were looking down on her so she had to leave to make herself feel better.

Another consequence for women was that men indicated that they would not be willing to be in a relationship with a woman who has a reputation for being highly sexually active. Interestingly, even men who were highly sexually active themselves said that they would refuse to be involved with a woman who behaved in the same way. For instance, Tony, a senior, indicated that he had sexual intercourse with over forty women, but he would not want to be in a relationship with a woman who also had a high number of past sexual partners.

KB: When you say that you know people who might hook up with twenty different people in a semester, are you talking about guys or do you know girls who do that also?

Tony: Well, the one girl I was telling you about before, that's one of the girls that does it. She's like a guy, she loves sex.

KB: So, she hooks up with a lot of different people?

Tony: Oh yeah.

KB: Would you be willing to be in a relationship with a girl who was like that?

Tony: *No way*, no way.

KB: But, you were involved with her before?

Tony: Yeah, I was involved with her freshman year, when I first got to know her . . . . What was the question, you said: "Would I be involved with someone like that [a girl who had hooked up with a lot of guys] after I knew she was [with a lot of different guys]?" For that reason alone, I mean I don't want to date somebody that's been with a hundred guys.

This does not mean that the men I spoke with would not hook up with a woman who had a bad reputation on campus. Rather, men will not consider *relationships* with women who are known as "sluts." Thus, women who are not worthy of "respect" will likely have difficulty forming relationships with men on campus.

BOYFRIENDS, BENEFITS, AND BOOTY CALLS

As a result of the sexual double standard, participating in the hookup culture can be risky for women. Most college women were aware of the rules imposed on them and the consequences of breaking those rules. Although they may not have been cognizant of it, being in an ongoing relationship of some kind was a way for women to manage their reputations on campus. In the context of a relationship, college women are free to engage in sexual activity without the risk of being labeled or shunned. The students I spoke with often referred to women initiating "the talk" with men (i.e., a conversation to try to turn a hookup partner into a boyfriend). This was one way for women to try to gain control in the hookup scene, which is so fraught with pitfalls for them. Adrienne, a senior, had this to say about "the talk":

> *KB*: So were you [and your current boyfriend] considered exclusive at some particular point? When did things transition to that?
>
> *Adrienne*: I'd say . . . we don't really have an anniversary. We don't really subscribe to that, either. But like, um, I made it mid-June. That's when I have my own personal [anniversary] just to keep track. So, about mid-June going into junior year.
>
> *KB*: So what changed in June?
>
> *Adrienne*: Um, basically I'd come up [to visit him during the summer and] we had like a really fun time and I really liked him and he acted like he liked me. But he's always like, he kind of did this like pull away thing . . . . But, I was like: "Look I'm really, I'm really starting to like you and I really just don't want to get hurt. Like you tell me yes or you tell me no." He's like: "Oh, of course, you know, I really like you." And then we kind of made it I guess official. So then I started, I kept coming up on the weekends [to visit him over the summer break] . . . . So we hung out.

In the case of Adrienne, "the talk" worked; however, many women were not as successful with this strategy, as is evident in the following exchange with Patrick, a junior.

> *KB*: If you could have anything you wanted going on in terms of the opposite sex, what would be your ideal situation?
>
> *Patrick*: I think I would want a girlfriend, I think I would want to be in a relationship, but I'm like really sociable. So, when I was almost in a relationship, the girl [I was hooking up with] was upset because I would always be talking to other girls. So basically I would want somebody who would realize that I would want to be with one person but I would still like, like talking and hanging out and being close friends with other girls.
>
> *KB*: Okay, so tell me about that girl that had a problem with it. How did you meet her and how did things evolve?
>
> *Patrick*: We met first semester sophomore year and like we hooked up a couple times. Like we really never talked about a relationship until she brought it up the one time. And I'm like: "Well . . . yeah we could . . . like I'm not saying like I don't want to start dating and seeing you exclusively but it would be nice to like . . . maybe just see what it's like." And then when I would see her at parties [and] I would be talking to other girls and she would be all upset. I'm like: "Well, you know if that's going to get you upset, something small, just me talking to other girls, I mean I don't think we would be able to work this out." [But hooking up with her has] gone on. Like I still talk to her now and we still . . . hook up. But, I think she realizes that if we started seeing each other exclusively that I would still be talking to other girls and like being sociable to them.
>
> *KB*: She gets jealous?
>
> *Patrick*: I guess.
>
> *KB*: But it's been two years now that you guys have been hooking up off and on?

Patrick: Yeah.

KB: But you have freedom to hook up with someone else if you want to?

Patrick: Yeah.

KB: And she does?

Patrick: Yeah.

KB: And do you both take advantage of that freedom?

Patrick: Yes.

KB: Typically if people hook up with people repeatedly, would they talk on the phone in between or do they usually just run into them when they're out?

Patrick: I would say [they] run into them when they're out. That's when they're just hooking up. When it becomes more serious I would say they talk to each other on the phone.

KB: Okay, so what about you [and the girl you have been hooking up with for the past two years]? What do you do mostly?

Patrick: I haven't talked to her on the phone at all. I talk to her like on IM [instant message] every once and a while. But I don't like call her up and say: "Hey what's going on?"

KB: Okay, so you just see her in the course of things?

Patrick: Hmmm-hm [yes].

Like Adrienne and the woman Patrick refers to, many women indicated that they either want boyfriends or at least "something" beyond hooking up. Women who were able to find boyfriends could avoid hooking up altogether by being in an exclusive relationship (where hooking up with someone else would be considered cheating). However, for most women, boyfriends are not easy to come by during college. Generally, college men resist committing to an exclusive relationship in favor of remaining free to hook up with other partners.

For women who were unable to find men who were willing to be exclusively committed to them, there were other avenues they could pursue that would help protect them from the negative labels they might get from too much hooking up. A "friends with benefits" arrangement was one way to avoid acquiring "too many" new hookup partners. A friend with benefits refers to a man or woman who has someone of the opposite sex with whom he or she has sex on some level; however, they are not in an exclusive romantic relationship with that person. Friends with benefits are defined from the outset as "just friends"; the twist is that they are friends who are attracted enough to each other to want to engage in some version of a sexual relationship. Friends with benefits is not a step toward a romantic relationship and this is agreed upon in advance. Gloria, a freshman, talked about her friend with benefits.

Gloria: I have a friend who is like my best friend and we hook up every time we are out and pretty much drunk . . . we'll hang out during the day, he is my best friend, and we won't kiss or anything [during the day]. But when we're drunk, we hook up. But I guess you see that person out a lot and you hook up with [him] . . . [we] just kiss.

KB: You talked about this person you hooked up with repeatedly. Does he call you, do you call him?

Gloria: The guy that I hook up with repeatedly, we talk every day, five times a day. He lives far away from me so we don't really hang out that much.

KB: You don't think of him as your boyfriend?

Gloria: No, not at all, because he wants the same thing, just [to be] single. [We] can hook up with [other people], that way we don't get mad at each other.

KB: So you don't care that he hooks up with someone else at all?

Gloria: No. I don't care. I wouldn't be like mad but I would be like: "Oh, how is she?" You know what I mean, kind of jealous, but not like mad at all.

KB: And same for you . . . he doesn't care if you hook up with someone else?

Gloria: Yeah. I mean he'll say: "Oh, who'd you bring home tonight?" [just] kidding around. He gets . . . jealous, but not mad.

As Gloria indicated, friends with benefits represent more than "just a hookup." Someone who is just a hookup partner is not necessarily someone with whom you spend time beyond the night you hook up. Also, someone who is just a hookup partner is not necessarily someone you know that well or care about in any significant way. Thus, a friend with benefits relationship may represent a middle-of-the-road option for those who do not feel comfortable repeatedly hooking up with what some students referred to as "randoms" (i.e., people they did not know well). The advantage of friends with benefits for women is that, unlike a casual hookup partner, at least the man is supposed to care about them as a friend (just not as a girlfriend).

In addition to the positives for women, men may also find friends with benefits to be an attractive option. Many men indicated that finding hookup partners involves a certain degree of "work" or "skill." Having a friend with benefits provided a "steady hookup" option for those nights where finding a new hookup partner was not worth the effort. At the same time, friends with benefits does not imply an exclusive relationship; therefore, individuals are free to pursue other people whenever they choose. This level of freedom may make friends with benefits a very attractive option to many college students, particularly men.

Although both parties may agree that a friends with benefits relationship is not exclusive, the arrangement does not always play out so easily. Despite the positive spin that Gloria puts on it, many students talked about the potential

problems inherent in these relationships. Men were concerned that the woman would end up wanting more, while women were at risk for developing romantic feelings.

KB: Did you ever have an issue where someone wanted a relationship with you and you didn't want it?

Joseph: Yeah I had . . . one.

KB: Okay and how did that happen?

Joseph: We had something set up kind of where we were really close friends, we always had been, and one night we went a little further [sexually] than we probably should have. And [at first] we said that probably we shouldn't do that again. And then we were like: "Oh well, we can probably keep doing that but we can't let it go any further. We can't get attached."

KB: Kind of a friends with benefits thing?

Joseph: Yeah. That's how we agreed on, like if one person was going home with somebody that night, we can't be mad or anything like that. There wasn't a relationship. It was strictly, if for some reason we needed [each other], the other person was there. [But] she got attached and that's when things kind of went [wrong]. And I don't even talk to her anymore.

KB: So she wanted it to be a relationship?

Joseph: Yeah.

KB: Did you ever have an incident, a fight or something that blew up? Was she mad that you left with someone else or whatever?

Joseph: Yeah, that's kind of what started the whole thing because she got mad and I didn't understand why because I thought we had that agreement. I thought we had an agreement, so I didn't understand why and then that's what kind of finished off that. Then she wouldn't talk to me the next day. [Senior]

Ed: More girls than guys are looking for relationships, but not necessarily a permanent relationship, just something that's more than just a couple hookups or casual sex.

KB: And does that create issues that girls are looking for relationships more than guys are? Do you see that creating problems?

Ed: Yeah, because the next time you see them it's . . . very uncomfortable [and] awkward.

KB: So, you've had that issue where you thought girls were looking for a relationship [when you were not]?

Ed: Right.

KB: And how can you tell that they're looking for a relationship, do they tell you?

Ed: Yeah. Or they'll just, like I had one where [the girl] assumed that it was a relationship because we hooked up once. [She] just assumed that meant that suddenly you're girlfriend and boyfriend and she just took it way too fast.

KB: And how did you let her know that wasn't the case [that you weren't really her boyfriend]?

Ed: I just told her.

KB: How did she take it?

Ed: Then she was like: "Well, *can we still do that friends with benefits thing*?" And I was like: "No, I don't want to do that." What I was afraid of is if she was at the same party and she saw me talking to another girl and then she came up and made a big scene about it. [Senior]

Many students suggested that women may be more likely to get "emotionally involved" with a friends with benefits arrangement. Even Gloria, who suggested she was happy with her friends with benefits situation, admitted that her male friend is also "her territory." In other words, Gloria's female friends were not permitted to hook up with her particular male friend. Thus, for women, there is an emotional or territorial dimension that factors into friends with benefits arrangements.

KB: Are people that have a "friends with benefits" thing going, are they allowed to hook up with other people?

Violet: Yes.

KB: And does that ever create problems or issues? If you have . . . a female friend that has a friend with benefits [arrangement] and then she sees him hooking up with someone else, does that bother her?

Violet: I think it bothers girls more than boys. Because a male friend of mine has a girl [and] they were just friends [but] they would sleep together. And then he met somebody and she got very upset about it. I think girls get more emotionally involved with it, even though they are [supposed to be just] friends. [Junior] Another pseudo-relationship a number of students talked about was "booty calls."

A booty call is a late-night phone call placed, often via cell phone, to an earlier hookup partner, inviting him or her over for another hookup encounter.

Kevin: My friend would always have . . . he would fool around with a girl, but then he always had this one [other girl] . . . what did we call her?

KB: Plan B?

Kevin: No, it's his late-night call, no matter what. If he was going after some other girl all night, he could pick up the phone and call this girl and she would come over to his room.

KB: And sleep with him?

Kevin: [Yes] and sleep with him.

KB: Okay. You don't remember what the term was that you called her?

Kevin: I want to say "late night . . ." [wait it's] "booty call." That's your booty call! You pick up the phone and go: "Why don't you come over?" and not even say sex or anything, just: "Why don't you come over." She knows exactly what she's coming over there to do. [Senior]

KB: What does [booty call] mean?

Lisa: Like someone, well usually it occurs late at night when you're, like everyone is usually drunk or whatever and someone calls you and [says] like: "Do you want to come over?" And you both know what's going to happen. Like it's usually a friend or something like that and they basically just want to hook up and that's why they called you. Or computer IM's [Instant Messenger], they happen now too.

Students suggested that booty call partners often have an ongoing relationship, albeit not a romantic one.

KB: What about "booty call"? Does anyone use that term?

Brian: Definitely, definitely. I mean it's just, you use it jokingly. Like my one friend this past weekend was like: "Oops, booty call" and then left [the place we were hanging out]. Like, but I mean he's been hooking up with her for a while. [Sophomore]

A very interesting gender dynamic occurs with regard to booty calls. In this type of relationship, men often placed the call or sent the text message; women accepted their invitation. On the face of it, it would seem that such an invitation would not be particularly attractive to women. Booty calls were a man's last-ditch effort to find someone to hook up with for the evening. The man was often drunk when he placed the call and the woman generally would have to walk or drive over to his place late at night by herself. This does not seem like a very appealing combination. Yet, the students said women often took men up on their invitation. Why? One explanation is that women were on the same page as men. That is, the woman came home from a party or bar without finding someone else to hook up with that night. Thus, she was happy to have the opportunity to have a sexual encounter. Given how women are negatively labeled for having too many hookup partners, a repeat encounter with a previous hookup partner has its advantages. Consistent with this

explanation, some students described this type of relationship as all about the sex.

KB: What does [booty call] mean?

Kim: Um, that implies sex.

KB: What kind of scenario would that be? How does sex happen in that scenario?

Kim: I mean I think it's pretty much synonymous with friends with benefits. I mean, you know the person, you may be friends with them, but, you don't have a significant relationship and you just want your sexual needs to be fulfilled.

KB: And why do you think people end up in those kinds of situations?

Kim: Because they like sex. [Sophomore]

Another reason why women might agree to a booty call is that maintaining any kind of ongoing relationship is better than randomly hooking up. Additionally, since women are often looking for committed relationships, any attempts by a previous hookup partner to pursue further contact may seem like a step in the right direction toward evolving into "something more."

KB: Do people in your circle of friends [use the term booty call]? . . . Is that something people say?

Marie: Yeah. I'm not going to say that I've never done that or been used like that, but sometimes you don't realize that you're doing it. Like, the guy I was with for seven months . . . he started to get weird and I like . . . wasn't realizing that basically the only time he was calling me to come over (his place) was like one [o'clock] in the morning. But, I had liked him so much that I was like: "That's just how we are." But, that's basically what it was [a booty call relationship] . . . he was just using me when he felt like having me come over . . . . [Senior]

Although, as Marie noted, "guys love" having someone available as their booty call, women who were hoping the relationship would develop romantically were usually disappointed.

WHY NOT OPT OUT?

For those on the outside looking in, it may appear that men and women are on an equal playing field in the hookup culture on campus. Upon closer inspection, however, it becomes clear that college men are in a position of power. First, men are able to sustain the hookup system on campus despite the fact that it is not working for the majority of women. Most of the students indicated that college men favor casual sexual encounters or casual relationships, whereas women prefer more committed relationships. Therefore, while the hookup system works for men, it does not provide a good way for women to get what they want. Men's power in the hook up culture is also demonstrated by the fact that men control the intensity of relationships. They are able to keep most women as "just a hookup partner" and they decide if and when the relationship will turn into something more serious.

In addition to women's struggle to get the type of relationships they want, they also have difficulty navigating the hookup system. On one hand, the norms for hooking up (or at least the perceived norms) call for women to be sexually active. On the other hand, if women behave "too sexually" or are otherwise out of line with the unwritten rules for hooking up, they can be negatively labeled and treated accordingly. It may be that women seek relationships to avoid this dilemma. Entering into an exclusive relationship, in particular, is a way for women to manage the double bind that they face. Since full-fledged boyfriends are hard to come by, women often agree to other options, such as friends with benefits and booty calls. However, more often than not, these arrangements do not work to women's advantage.

Given the inherent problems for women, why don't they refuse to partake in hooking up? The answer seems to be that there is no clear alternative. If a student opts out as an individual, then she is no longer part of the mainstream on campus. Students who buck the system have few other options for engaging in sexual encounters and forming relationships. Theoretically, college women could ban together and refuse to participate in hooking up. However, this never occurred to any of the women I interviewed. Most college women did not necessarily object to hooking up per se; rather, they objected to how often it ends up leading to "nothing." They seemed to accept hooking up as a given and alter their expectations accordingly.

When I asked college women what their ideal scenario would be for meeting someone and getting together, it gave them pause. It was as if an alternative to hooking up had never crossed their mind. However, most revealed that they would want something different than the typical hookup scenario. Some women said that they would prefer to meet a man and "get to know him" without the first encounter involving sexual activity. Others suggested it was better to be "friends first" with a man and get to know him that way. Some women seemed to want to turn back the clock and go on dates. College women who yearned for something different than hooking up may not have long to wait to get their wish. As the twenty-something college graduates I interviewed told me, life after college begins a new phase for sex and relationships.

INTRODUCTION REFERENCES

May, R. 1969. *Love and will.* New York: Norton.

Paul, E. L., B. McManus, and A. Hayes. 2000. Hookups: Characteristics and correlates of college students' spontaneous and anonymous sexual experiences. *Journal of Sex Research* 37: 76–88.

REFERENCES

1. Reiss, Ira. 1997. *Solving America's Sexual Crises.* Amherst, NY: Prometheus Books.

2. Komter, Aafke. 1989. Hidden Power in Marriage. *Gender and Society* 3: 187–216.

3. Willis, Ellen. 1992. *No More Nice Girls: Countercultural Essays.* Hanover, NH: Wesleyan University Press.

4. Teachman, Jay. 2003. Premarital Sex, Premarital Cohabitation, and the Risk of Subsequent Marital Dissolution among Women. *Journal of Marriage and Family* 65: 444–455.

5. Glenn, Norval, and Elizabeth Marquardt. 2001. *Hooking Up, Hanging Out and Hoping for Mr. Right: College Women on Dating and Mating Today*. An Institute for American Values Report to the Independent Women's Forum.

6. Lemert, Edwin M. 1967. *Human Deviance, Social Problems, and Social Control*. Englewood Cliffs, NJ: Prentice Hall.

CHAPTER 13

Virginity Lost

A Natural Step

Laura M. Carpenter

"A lot of kids are putting off sex, and not because they can't get a date. They've decided to wait, and they're proud of their chastity, not embarrassed by it. Suddenly, virgin geek is giving way to virgin chic" (Ingrassia 1994). This 1994 Newsweek *quote, used to introduce the topic of virginity on college campuses, could aptly be titled "The Morals Revolution on Campuses." Oddly enough, that title belonged instead to a 1964* Newsweek *story about virginity ("The Morals Revolution," 1964). The article claimed that men no longer expected to marry virgins, but that because sexual intercourse with anyone except "Mr. Right" was suspect, the question of the day for young women was, How many "Mr. Rights" make a wrong? Thirty years apart, these accounts by the popular media were merely reporting news of the day—one, a sexual revolution and the other, its counterpart, a sexual retro-revolution. Could it possibly be true that the more things change, the more they stay the same? Now more than a decade later, after reading the Carpenter selection, "A Natural Step" from the provocative new book,* Virginity Lost, *readers may be better able to discern the meaning of this conundrum.*

Hailed as groundbreaking research, Virginity Lost *paints an intimate portrait of first sexual experience. By revealing essential information about this watershed moment of life, Laura Carpenter offers a glimpse into one of life's most intimate and significant sexual encounters. Using descriptors such as "a gift," "a stigma," and a "natural step," Carpenter vividly describes the transition from virginity with frank, fascinating first-person accounts of the never-to-be forgotten passage. Whether female, male, heterosexual, homosexual, younger or older, readers of this offering for whom this passage is no longer a mystery, will be able to compare and contrast their own journey in sexuality. Others will be enlightened and intrigued by the various meanings assigned to this significant life experience.*

Margaret Mead's best-selling volumes on South Pacific youth, published between 1928 and 1935, and Bronislaw Malinowski's sensationally titled 1929 monograph, *The Sexual Lives of Savages*, introduced educated Americans to the concept of puberty rites—ritualized celebrations of an individual's passage from childhood to adolescence or adulthood.[1] Anthropologists noted that these transitions typically entailed a shift from relative asexuality to potential or actual sexual activity, often marked by virginity loss (customarily defined as first vaginal sex).

From *Virginity Lost: An Intimate Portrait of First Sexual Experiences* (pp. 141–177) by L. M. Carpenter. 2005. New York: New York University Press. Copyright © 2005 by New York University. Reprinted by permission.

Virginity loss accordingly came to be understood as a *rite of passage* through which boys were transformed into men and girls into women.[2] In some non-Western societies, virginity loss was closely associated with marriage, as it is in Judeo-Christian tradition; in other societies, the two passages could be separable, a fact that, at the time, many Americans and Europeans found disturbingly "uncivilized."

Once Americans viewed virginity loss as a rite of passage in other cultures, it took but a small leap to train that interpretive lens on themselves. As college enrollments swelled following the Second World War, more and more young Americans had the opportunity to take anthropology courses in which they learned that virginity loss could be interpreted as a rite of passage. By the late 1950s, as the baby-boom generation began to enter adolescence, reassuring anxious parents with anthropological insights had become something of a cottage industry, with Margaret Mead at its helm.

The [young] women and men I interviewed described virginity loss as a central step in the transition from youth to adulthood—precisely the kind of event anthropologists refer to as a rite of passage. More specifically, they likened virginity loss to a step in two interrelated processes: becoming an adult, and acquiring knowledge about sexuality. Recalling discussions among her high school friends, Jessica Tanaka, a 27-year-old bisexual Japanese American from a working-class background, invoked both themes:

> I guess we sort of romanticized the whole, like, losing your virginity, like, becoming a woman, like, being grown-up kind of thing.... Like, we really couldn't figure out what it would be like, we'd have to go and find out on our own.... It was just sort of one of those things that eventually would happen, and then we would know. And ... we would be really disappointed or really not disappointed [laughs].

Heather Folger, a 28-year-old heterosexual middle-class White woman, compared virginity loss to other life transitions. "[It's a] pretty big milestone in people's lives.... Maybe not on a par with marriage or birth or death, but it's definitely one of the things that you'll always remember." People who liken virginity loss to a learning process or to a transition between life stages are effectively saying the same thing: that virginity loss represents a rite of passage, a process of transition from sexual youth to adulthood. I use the expressions *rite of passage* and *process* interchangeably, and call the metaphor's devotees "processers" for short.

Anthropologist Victor Turner compared the person undergoing a rite of passage to a "blank slate, on which is inscribed the knowledge and wisdom of the group, in those respects that pertain to the new status." Because of their relative ignorance about sexual intercourse (or whatever act they see as resulting in virginity loss), virgins are potentially at the mercy of their chosen sexual partners, especially experienced ones. Yet, since virginity loss is an informal passage, unregulated by formal institutions, virgins do have some control over it. Virgins and their sexual partners, like all informal initiates and their "helpers," both possess some power and must negotiate with one another as the passage proceeds.

Consistent with the gender-neutral application of the concept in anthropology and popular culture, the women I interviewed were only slightly more likely than men to describe virginity loss as a step in the process of growing up. Yet, although the rite of passage metaphor appears to offer an alternative to the traditionally feminine and masculine gift and stigma metaphors, it is not gender neutral. Because people tend to think in terms of becoming not just generic adults, but specifically adult *women* and *men*, when they draw on the process metaphor to guide their virginity-loss experiences they are constructing *gendered* adult identities. (In a similar manner, the metaphor helps people fashion specific sexual identities.) Whether the process perspective tends to disempower male or female virgins disproportionately, as do its stigma and gift counterparts, is a central question.

"I WAS A VIRGIN AT ONE POINT AND I ... NEVER REALLY THOUGHT ABOUT IT"

Meghan O'Brien hadn't attached much importance to virginity while she was growing up. To her, it was a simple designation for a certain stage in life:

> I guess I never really thought of virginity as, like, a qualitative thing. It was just . . . you have not had sex, you are a virgin. It wasn't like a feeling or anything like that to me. So if someone asked me how I felt about it, I think I would just say, you know, I was a virgin at one point and I . . . never really thought about it. That was just the way it just was.

The third daughter in a large Irish-American family, Meghan had grown up on the outskirts of Boston. She had attended an exclusive private high school and now, at 22, was within months of receiving her bachelor's degree from a prestigious liberal arts college. Meghan's reserved manner and appearance testified to her upbringing: she wore discreetly expensive sportswear and kept her straight brown hair brushed neatly back from her well-scrubbed face. By the time I interviewed Meghan, she no longer attended mass every Sunday, as she had when living at home, but she considered Catholic worship an indispensable part of her life.

Sex was rarely discussed in Meghan's family, but when she was about ten, her parents sat her down for "The Talk." This amounted to a review of basic reproductive biology and the decree, "You're Irish Catholic and you shouldn't have sex before marriage." Meghan took the latter with a grain of salt. Having once found a packet of condoms in her parents' bedside table, she figured that while they probably felt compelled to impart Catholic doctrine, they didn't expect their daughters to follow it to the letter. The sex education Meghan received at school was altogether different in breadth and tone. In formal health classes, sex was discussed with value-neutral candor—all consensual acts were "okay"—and when talk in the hallways and cafeteria turned to sex, as it often did, no one praised or condemned virginity or the lack thereof. Other students' sexual status was a topic of perennial interest, but Meghan recalled little if any peer pressure around sex. Typical of people who favored the process metaphor, she remembered feeling secure in the knowledge that virginity loss was an inevitable part of growing up. She didn't need to ask *whether* she would lose her virginity, though she did wonder about *when* and *with whom*—*choices* she saw as hers for the making. Virginity loss is, of course, not *literally* inevitable; but no one I interviewed saw lifelong celibacy as a desirable option—nor do any but a vanishingly small number of Americans.

Meghan's matter-of-fact approach didn't mean that she saw decisions about sex as inconsequential. But she looked forward to virginity loss for reasons quite different from those cited by gifters and the stigmatized. Instead of valuing virginity for its power to bind a special romantic relationship or longing desperately for its absence, Meghan desired the positive changes that accompanied virginity loss—changes like being one step closer to adulthood and gaining practical knowledge about sex's role in a caring relationship. She spoke of virginity loss not as significant in itself, but as "just like a steppingstone."

Perceiving sex as a natural part of a long-term romance, Meghan expected that she'd lose her virginity with one of her first steady boyfriends. She adamantly declared that this wasn't because she disapproved of casual sex—she didn't—but because she thought she'd be more comfortable learning about sex in an ongoing relationship. For one thing, losing her virginity with a boyfriend would give her the opportunity to learn about sex in stages. She explained:

> I just think that . . . when you're young, you're not . . . so comfortable with your own body, and you don't exactly know what you want, what you need. And I think it's more safe to just kind of

step into things, you know, slowly, than to just . . . to have sex very quickly.

Tellingly, no one who preferred the process metaphor considered remaining a virgin until marriage.

Sometimes Meghan imagined that virginity loss would be like "these mad sex scenes in movies," but more often she anticipated it being as physically awkward as other new experiences, like the first time she went skiing. Expecting some clumsiness was typical of women and men who shared her interpretation—as was the hope that one's own virginity-loss encounter might prove an exception to the rule. This stands in striking contrast with the perfect romantic scenes envisaged by most gifters and with stigmatized men's fear of awkwardness as a telltale sign of their sexual naiveté.

Meghan wasn't very experienced sexually when she started dating Rich in her freshman year in high school. "I did a lot of kissing when I was young," she recalled with a shy grin. "But, you know, innocent kissing." Rich, she said, "was the first person I did anything else with." Meghan and Rich were the same age, took many classes together, and were equally devoted to sports (tennis and track). The longer they dated, the more deeply they fell in love, and the more sexually intimate their relationship became. Meghan described their early encounters as a series of practice sessions. She said:

> I can remember lots of times like, being naked with each other. But we really wouldn't do anything, we would just kind of, like, lay around with each other. But that was enough . . . for us at that point. And I guess sometimes we would come close, I mean, the areas would touch or something. But I don't know if we were really ever trying. We weren't, we knew, both of us knew we did not want to be having sex at that point. . . . It was just, I think we were just kind of, like, getting to know each other's bodies.

By the time they were juniors, Rich and Meghan had fondled each other to orgasm many times and she'd given him fellatio once or twice. In effect, they learned about sex through a step-by-step process that they saw as (potentially) leading up to the big step of virginity loss. Incremental approaches to physical intimacy were universal among women and men in the rite-of-passage group. Unlike gifters, for whom incremental sexual activity represented a way of testing a partner's capacity for reciprocity, Meghan and her kindred spirits spoke of their expanding sexual repertoires as a kind of education. However, unlike Meghan, the majority went through this learning process with at least one partner before the person with whom they lost their virginity.

Although Meghan didn't think about it consciously, the fact that she was heterosexual provided the framework in which she made choices about sex and sexual partners. Nine of the ten heterosexual male and female processers lost their virginity with steady romantic partners, after engaging in increasingly intimate sexual activities with them, as did both bisexual women and two lesbians who hadn't come out at the time. In contrast, the two openly lesbian women and one openly gay man in the process group had virtually no experience with same-sex partners prior to losing their virginity; all three lost their virginity with friends. What poet and scholar Adrienne Rich has called *compulsory heterosexuality* contributes to these different trajectories.[3] Whereas high school youth are virtually expected to engage in heterosexual romance, relatively few adolescents openly identify as gay. (This was especially true in the early to mid-1990s, when the participants in question lost their virginity.) Given their predominance, greater visibility, and relative freedom from social sanctions, heterosexual teens may simply have more opportunities to develop romantic relationships than their gay and lesbian counterparts.[4]

Meghan's choices were further shaped by her understanding of virginity. Processers cared considerably more about who their partners were than did the stigmatized, and they were far more likely to lose their virginity with someone they were dating. But they did not speak of waiting for the "right" or "perfect" partner, as did gifters, nor did they insist on being in love, although about half of them, like Meghan, were. Rather, they described romantic relationships as the context best suited for satisfying in stages their curiosity about sex.

Meghan and Rich had both been virgins when they started dating, a fact they discussed with increasing frequency the longer they remained a couple. In framing virginity and nonvirginity as normal stages in an inevitable process, rather than as causes for shame or pride, she exemplifies the process frame. All but two processers told their partners that they were virgins. Half of the partners were virgins themselves. Under the circumstances, Meghan felt their mutual virginity had been an advantage:

> I think if one of us had been more experienced than the other, it would have been kind of like a, more of a pressure about, well, "You know what you're doing and I don't," kind of thing. So, neither of us knew what we were doing and, you know, we figured it out just fine . . . . I think that it was better like that.

In the fall of their senior year, when both of them were 18, Meghan and Rich were poised to take what she called the "natural" next step in their sexual relationship. When Rich's parents announced they were going away for a weekend, he and Meghan hastened to prepare. While Rich bought condoms, Meghan got her parents' permission to spend the night at a girlfriend's. But things didn't go according to plan.

> This was the weekend we were going to have sex, like, it was so dramatic! . . . And all of a sudden both of us were just really scared or nervous or something. . . . And he had a big track meet the next day or something. And, you know, we're up real late because neither of us wanted to just, like, initiate, you know what I mean? And . . . I was so nervous that it probably wouldn't have worked anyway, because I mean, I just wasn't enjoying

myself. He probably wasn't enjoying himself . . . . I think it was because we had planned it that it didn't work. So we were like, "Forget it," you know. "We'll do this another time."

Just a few weeks later, they found themselves together under less contrived circumstances:

> We didn't know we were going to be staying in the same place, we didn't know we were going to be in the same bed, and we ended up together. And it just kind of happened. You know, we were just kind of kissing, fooling around, and then one thing led to another and it was like, neither of us knew it was going to hap—[trails off]. Well, we probably did in the back of our minds somewhere, but it wasn't like this rigid or set plan, like it had been before. And it just happened naturally, so that was nice. Unprotected, though.

Not using a condom, even though they had planned to, was the one thing Meghan regretted about the encounter. "I didn't even think about protection at that point," she said, "because we didn't realize it was going to happen. And then it did . . . . It was very short because of, because we didn't have protection." Seeing virginity loss as a step in a process, ironically, contributed to their lapse. Meghan was one of four people in this group who, despite discussing safer sex with their partners and planning to use condoms, wound up losing their virginity when "one thing led to another" in a place and time where a condom wasn't available. (In contrast, when the stigmatized declined to practice safer sex, it was because they feared exposing their virginity.) Since Meghan and Rich both expected that they would continue having sex, she soon went on the Pill, alleviating their worries about unprotected encounters in the future.

Meghan found virginity loss emotionally "very enjoyable" but physically unremarkable, especially compared with the times she'd reached climax in other ways. Both the brevity of the act and their mutual inexperience with vaginal sex were, she felt, to blame. "Neither of us orgasmed," she explained. "I'd say it was just more that we were trying it out." Physically mediocre or even uncomfortable virginity-loss encounters were quite common among women who lost their virginity with men, due to the discomfort women often experience the first time inserting a penis into the vagina.

Like most who favored the passage metaphor, Meghan felt that her vision of virginity loss as a natural, if critical, step in learning about sex was confirmed by what happened when she lost her virginity, as well as by the experimentation that had gone before:

> Like, "That was it?" You know, like, "That's done? That was what we were waiting for, for so long?" 'Cause it's, I think it's a pretty natural thing, and once you do it, it's, I don't know. You, like, from what you see, you know, these mad sex scenes in movies, that was kind of like, "Oh, well, it wasn't quite like that." But that was also because it was our first time and everything.

Subsequent encounters bolstered Meghan's impression of taking part in an ongoing transformation. At first, "we didn't have sex a lot. And then . . . by the end of senior year and starting college, it was like, you know, we had sex more often . . . . I think it was just kind of like a natural progression." Happily, she found vaginal sex more physically pleasurable over time. This was a common trajectory: two-thirds of the processers continued to explore sex with their virginity-loss partners after virginity loss, for about 8 months on average. (Comparable figures for the stigmatized and gifters are 6 months and 2 years, respectively.) Looking back, Meghan described losing her virginity as a learning experience par excellence. "[It] just made me more aware of my sexuality," she said. "I mean, once . . . we had kind of decided that was where our relationship was going, we were more sexually experimenting." In short, virginity loss brought the enlightening changes she'd hoped for.

A few months after she lost her virginity, Meghan's father chanced across "this whole letter [from a friend] . . . about me having sex." She recalled:

He didn't say anything for about two days, to anyone . . . . Then finally he says . . ., "I need to have [a] talk with you." And he cried, he was so upset. He was so upset he just. I think . . . he was worried. I was in high school. I was, you know, I think he thought that this was just going to lead to trouble. That maybe I'd get pregnant or something bad would happen . . . . It was horrible, he was just so angry. And then I got upset and . . . He was like, "I really hope you stop this." And he never asked me again, hut I think he honestly thought that we had stopped after that."

Such intensely negative reactions were unusual among the parents of this group—a number of them had, in fact, helped their children obtain birth control or condoms—and was probably due in part to the O'Briens' devout Catholicism.

Meghan's frankness with her friends and partners throughout her sexual career was also typical. Overall, processers were much less concerned with others' impressions of their sexual status, before *and* after virginity loss, than gifters or the stigmatized. Seeing virginity and non-virginity as inevitable stages, rather than as causes for shame or pride, they felt neither compelled to conceal their virginity or boast of its absence, nor tempted to brag about it or hide its loss. No one in this group tried to pass as non-virgin; nor were they ashamed of having recently been virgins.

Deciding to have sex with a subsequent boyfriend, Rob, struck Meghan as another learning process. She explained:

> I think the first time I had sex with somebody else was . . . a really big deal to me because I had that same sense of, like, nervousness . . . . It wasn't about the act, it was more just being with this other person and, you know, it's going to be different . . . . It was funny, it was the same type of thing, like, "Well, I don't want to have sex until, you know, we're clear-cut and know what's going on."

Meghan's reaction to first sex with Rob highlights the significance of first times. Many rites of passage center on events that are first of their kind; as anthropologist Arnold van Gennep noted, the idea that "only the first time counts . . . is truly universal and . . . is everywhere expressed to some extent through special rites."[5] While virginity loss may represent the ultimate sexual first time, each sexual relationship offers the possibility of its own first time.

Meghan's beliefs and experiences were shaped by her gender and sexual identity. In American culture, it is acceptable for women and men to approach virginity loss as a rite of passage; overall, the women I interviewed were somewhat more likely to have done so. For women, the process metaphor offers an alternative to the traditional understanding of virginity as a gift, but one which carries less risk of being branded as promiscuous or unfeminine than treating virginity as a stigma. When women in this group lost their virginity, they constructed an identity as sexually "liberated," but not truly unorthodox, adult women. For those who lost their virginity with men, as Meghan did, the act offered a way of establishing a heterosexual identity, although only the women who subsequently came out as lesbians explicitly described it as such. The heterosexual women in my study were, in fact, less apt to see their own virginity loss as a step in a process than were the lesbians and bisexual women, a difference stemming from the fact that lesbian and bisexual women experienced the process of coming out as intertwined with virginity loss.

Meghan's beliefs and experiences may also have been influenced in subtle ways by her racial/ethnic background. Comparatively few women of color took this gender-atypical stance; being White probably made it easier for Meghan to do so. (Stigmatized women were also disproportionately White.) Previous studies have suggested that African American women and Latinas may feel pressured not to reject traditional ideals for feminine virginity, because doing so reinforces popular stereotypes of women of color as promiscuous.[6] Young Asian American women, for their part, may feel caught between the sexual stereotypes of the submissive "lotus blossom" and the sexually predatory "dragon lady"; treating virginity loss as a rite of passage may offer a welcome alternative to both images (whereas the gift and stigma metaphors, respectively, would help confirm them).

How gender and sexual identity shape, and are shaped by, virginity loss as seen through the rite-of-passage lens becomes even clearer when we explore the story of a gay man who shared Meghan's perspective.

"I THINK AWKWARD'S A GOOD WORD TO DESCRIBE IT"

Tom Hansen hadn't started thinking of virginity loss as a rite of passage until he was in his early twenties. He'd lost his virginity at 23, just a year before our interview. Closely intertwined with both changes in Tom's life was his gradual recognition that he was gay, which had prompted him in turn to question certain aspects of the evangelical Christian tradition in which he'd been raised. The box office manager of a repertory theater, Tom came from Scandinavian German heritage; he had fly-away blond hair, a round face, and a contagious smile.

As a youth, Tom had agreed wholeheartedly with his parents' understanding of virginity, which was endorsed by their independent Christian church.

> When I was younger, I guess I followed my parents. . . . They never told me it was wrong to lose my virginity—like if I were, I'd go to hell or anything. You know, that's not the way they worked. . . . But then I sort of respected them and respected their wishes. . . . So I considered that it would probably be better to wait until I got married. . . . In high school, I guess even through college, I was proud of it, the fact that I hadn't lost my virginity.

In effect, he had interpreted virginity as a gift. Such sentiments weren't particularly popular among his high school classmates, boys or girls; but Tom knew he wasn't entirely alone in feeling—or behaving—as he did. He recalled a conversation with one of his closest friends:

> At our graduation party we sat down with the yearbook and looked through all the pictures of our graduating class. And we decided who was sleeping with whom. You know, "Remember this guy, when he was with this girl?" and, you know, whatever. And out of the 419, we found that amongst us knew twelve to be confirmed virgins. I was one of the twelve, in high school. And so were, like, three or four of my friends. Not a lot of them, a lot of my friends were not virgins. But like three or four other kids that I knew and had grown up with . . . I knew that they were.

That knowledge had strengthened his convictions—he'd never wanted to hide his virginity from people who saw things differently—as did his parents' own example:

> It wasn't that they ever said, "No, and don't, because of this." But it was, you know, almost an expectation. "Oh, you wouldn't do that because you'll want to wait until you're married, because it's better that way." And I always assumed that they had, too.

What worked for them, he reasoned, would work for him.

But a series of events, beginning in college, spurred Tom to rethink his views on virginity. Chief among them was his growing recognition that he was sexually and romantically attracted to men. He'd felt the first inklings in high school and had attempted—unsuccessfully—to "protect" himself by choosing to attend a conservative Christian college. Since "one doesn't get married if one is gay," he said, "I . . . quickly realiz[ed] that it was not going to be a possibility for me to wait until I was married." Tom's beliefs were further shaken by what he saw around him at school. Some of his evangelical peers flouted their nonvirginity, while others interpreted the biblical ban on premarital sex in extremely broad terms, seeing oral sex with multiple partners as compatible with maintaining their virginity.

One day, a friend from Tom's dorm confided that, just before he left for school, his mother had instructed him: "Before you marry a girl, sleep with her. 'Cause if you don't like it, don't marry her. Then she's not the one . . . . You have to make sure you're compatible." Tom wasn't sure he agreed, but his friend's remark gave him another possibility to ponder.

If all that were not enough, when Tom was a senior in college, his father—on the brink of a divorce—vindictively announced that he and Tom's mother hadn't practiced what they'd preached. Tom said:

> I was clueless, completely clueless that . . . my parents had slept together before they were married . . . . My mom was 16, and he was 18. You know, they were still in high school! And I just thought, "Oh my God, what am *I* waiting for?" I was 22 years old, 23 years old, I'm like, "What a fool I am!" I think I was more open to it after that.

Gradually, Tom's conviction that virginity should be a special gift exchanged between spouses gave way to a new perspective, centered on learning and personal change:

> I didn't hold it against people if they had [lost their virginity], but I was sort of a little frightened, because I hadn't . . . . Because I felt like I was in a different, like, class of knowledge. That was sort of scary because they were so much further ahead than I was. So I was—I guess intimidated is a good word—by it. But I think my view was [not] that I had to wait, I just chose to. Just because I thought it was a good idea. Not religiously . . . I wasn't afraid of, you know, doing something wrong religiously. I wasn't ready and I didn't really find anyone that I wanted to sleep with.

He made a point of distinguishing himself from people who saw virginity as a stigma: "I don't think it's something that you want to do just, you know . . . to prove to yourself that you can do it, or prove to your friends that you've done it." In short, while he was still a virgin, Tom reinterpreted virginity loss, coming to see it as a step in a process. His recognition that he was gay, accompanied by his church's disapproval of homosexuality, his exposure to dissenting opinions and hypocrisy at school, and his parents' failings as role models all motivated this shift in beliefs.

Ever practical, Tom resolved "that I would have to lose my virginity.... I'm not going to go until I'm, like, 50 years old and decide, 'Oh, I'm going to have sex,' and then no one wants you," he said. Furthermore, before he met someone who might become a life partner, "I wanted to know what I was doing; I wanted to have a little bit of experience at least." Tom worried that a nonvirgin partner might try to take advantage of his novice status: "Of course there's the fear of the other person, who's had a ton of sexual experience, and you're like, 'I'm a blithering idiot, I don't know what I'm doing.'" Such caution, despite the desire to make the transition, is typical of irrevocable transitions.[2]

In high school, Tom had dated a number of women, but—fortunately, he said—he "wasn't in that group where you had to be sleeping together to be considered to be dating." He'd had lots of women friends in college, some of whom he had kissed, but never a girlfriend. Those friendships had, he believed, helped him pass as straight. Six months after college graduation, at which point he "had kissed maybe 20 girls probably total in my life," Tom's friend Amy tried to seduce him. Despite knowing that he was gay, he felt he should give sex with women one last chance: "I thought, all right, this is a shot.... So I tried. And nothing happened. The equipment did not function.... [We were] like, buck naked, fooling around and—nothing." With Tom unable to sustain an erection, they forwent vaginal intercourse.

Then, a week later, Amy confessed that she was now sure that she was a lesbian. She told Tom, "I just never felt it was right, but you were the closest thing I could think of as right. And it was better, but it wasn't what I wanted." When Amy asked if he thought *he* might be gay, Tom answered, "Yes." Their mutual relief was palpable. "The next week, she went out

and found a girlfriend.... And," he added ruefully, "I waited until September [i.e., several months], because I was foolish." In approaching sexual encounters with girls as a way of "testing" his sexual identity, Tom resembled many of the gay and bisexual boys anthropologist Gilbert Herdt and psychologist Andrew Boxer observed in their ethnography of a Chicago center for lesbigay youth.[7] Also consistent with Herdt and Boxer's findings, the younger generation of gay men and lesbians in my study (born 1973–1980) came out at younger ages on average and were more likely to lose their virginity with same-sex partners than their slightly older counterparts (regardless of how they interpreted virginity).

Tom had come out to a few friends before Amy, but after talking with her, he accelerated the process. He hoped that doing so would pave the way to virginity loss with another man. Once his closest friends knew about his sexual identity, Torn felt he could safely come out to Kent, "the only other gay [man] I had ever met and been friends with." The specter of sexual contact hovered in his mind when he told Kent that he, too, was gay:

> Because he was the one I was attracted to. And as my first opportunity, after all these years of being completely, you know, away from everybody else and safe.... And I was old enough and responsible enough, I figured I would, you know, take a chance. So that was the first time I ever said anything [to Kent], and then. Losing my virginity was much later. I said [that I was gay], and nothing happened between us until a good while later.

Tom was not alone in choosing a same-sex friend as a first sexual partner; the two lesbians in this group who had come out while they were virgins did likewise. In contrast, all but one of the heterosexual and bisexual processers lost their virginity with girlfriends or boyfriends. This is not to suggest that gay men and lesbians are less selective than their heterosexual counterparts; plenty of heterosexuals in the gift and stigma groups lost their virginity with friends or casual partners, after all. Rather, given the lack of openly gay people, especially at younger ages, some may opt to expand their sexual opportunities by including platonic friends among their prospective partners.[4] The ability to meet same-sex romantic partners also depends on where people live and the social circles in which they move. As a gay man living in a suburb well outside of Pittsburgh, with mostly conservative Christian acquaintances, Tom found meeting potential partners difficult.

After coming out to Kent, Tom tried several times to orchestrate a situation in which they would be alone. But "every time I made plans, it didn't work." Finally, more than a year after graduating from college, Tom invited Kent to join him and some college friends on a road trip to a concert in Cleveland. When they arrived,

> there were enough tickets for everybody but two people. So I of course volunteered not to go.... We went to see a movie, had dinner, whatever, and just went back to the house [of their former-classmate host] ... And she had a hot tub outside. So ... I had just gotten into the hot tub, and he's like, "Can I kiss you?" And I said, "Sure." And that was it. He whipped off his clothes so quickly [laughs]! I was like, "Oh my God" [laughs]. I had no. I mean, I had zero experience at that point.... I mean, I never had any sexual experience whatsoever with another guy.

Nor had Kent, as Tom knew. When Tom had come out to his friend, they'd talked about being virgins—with men as well as women—and agreed that virginity loss between men meant giving or receiving anal sex.

Tom's sexual identity and interpretation of virginity intertwined to influence his early sexual career. Suppressing his attraction to men, passing as straight, and trying to convince himself that he was had given Tom plenty of reasons and opportunities to experiment sexually with women, albeit not sufficient motivation to lose his virginity with one. In fact, the gay men and lesbians who told me they saw virginity loss as a

process—and who were openly gay as virgins—typically had as much experience with other-sex partners as their heterosexual counterparts, even though they'd had little if any intimate contact with same-sex partners prior to virginity loss.

After exchanging fellatio and attempting anal penetration—"which doesn't work in the hot tub, ever," Tom quipped, not to mention that "we were both new at this whole thing"—they made their way to the guest bedroom they'd been assigned.

> That pretty much ended the whole virginity thing. But I had conveniently packed condoms and lubricant and anything else that I could possibly think of that I'd need.... I always plan ... So I just. Yeah, I knew what I wanted, but I didn't know what was going to happen. So I just, I bought them maybe a month beforehand.... I just bought them hoping that I'd use them some day.

Tom's concern with safer sex was typical of people who saw virginity as a rite of passage. Two-thirds of them practiced safer sex during virginity loss, a rate comparable to that of gifters. Viewing virginity loss as a step in a process had encouraged these women and men to lose their virginity in ongoing romantic relationships or friendships, in which they were comfortable talking about condoms and/or contraception. Furthermore, perceiving sexual inexperience as a natural stage in life, rather than as a stigma, they felt no need to try to conceal their virginity by rejecting protective measures. (Lesbians who lost their virginity with other women were an exception, as I discuss below.)

> Virginity loss was everything Tom had hoped for—and yet at the same time it wasn't. I expected more out of it.... I didn't regret it. At the same time I didn't think it was something super incredible. I mean, I was nervous I was very nervous.... First of all, I was fooling around in somebody else's hot tub not knowing when they would be home.... I think, given a little bit more

freedom at the time . . . I would have been happier. . . . I mean . . . since then I've kissed . . . a couple other [men] who are much better kissers. . . . And at the same time, thinking, "Wow!" I mean, we were just fumbling around like idiots. But I knew I was old enough and, you know, I was ready.

In all, he said, "I think awkward's a good word to describe it." Though this awkwardness came as something of a surprise, Tom easily accepted it—not least because he thought it might have been inevitable given the physiology of receptive anal sex. Having a clumsy first time also confirmed his impression that virginity loss was a step in a longer process. As he put it, "I don't think my viewpoint has changed any, except for 'practice makes perfect'—maybe there's that adage added to it." Men and women who favored the process metaphor were far better prepared for "imperfect" or physically unremarkable encounters, and reacted to them with much greater aplomb, than people who saw virginity as a gift or stigma. They believed they still had a lot to learn about sex, and they had more reasonable expectations about physical sexual pleasure; few expected first sex to be intensely enjoyable. In contrast, gifters felt deeply let down by less-than-perfect partners and encounters, while the stigmatized typically worried that clumsiness betrayed their inexperience and/or that they'd missed out on the immense physical joy they'd expected.

Tom also found sex with Kent enlightening because it confirmed, in a very tangible way, his perception of himself as gay.

For the first time I just felt right. . . . It was the first time that I actually kissed somebody and actually didn't think it was, you know, boring. It was like, "Wow!" This is what I'm supposed to be doing . . . this is actually going through with things I feel, rather than what I'm supposed to do. So I didn't feel obligated or, you know, that this was the right thing to do or this was what my parents would have me do.

Tom didn't feel transformed overnight. Rather, losing his virginity had been the final step in a decade-long process changing him from an inexperienced boy unsure of his sexual identity into an openly and actively gay man. In most respects, however, processers' expectations and experiences of virginity loss differed very little by sexual identity.

Although Tom was happy not to be a virgin, he remained circumspect about revealing his new status. One disincentive was the fact that he and Kent moved in the same social circle, and it seemed inappropriate for two of the group to be sexually involved. Moreover, he feared that his more conservative (or less intimate) friends would be offended to learn he was gay. Like Meghan and others who shared their view of virginity, Tom wanted to be frank with his friends, and even his parents, but felt it prudent to tailor his disclosures according to social context.

Status passages often occur simultaneously, and almost all of the gay and bisexual male and female processers spoke of virginity loss as inextricably intertwined with the process of coming out. This sense of undergoing two linked processes at once was, I believe, the chief reason that the lesbigay individuals I interviewed subscribed to the process metaphor in greater proportions than did their heterosexual counterparts. Tom's story shows how concurrent rites of passage may complicate one another. On the one hand, he felt that if he had been able to come out earlier, it would have been easier to lose his virginity:

I would've dated girls, I would have dated guys, and started a lot earlier. . . . I probably wouldn't have had sex at the young age, still. I think that's something I was really way into being ready for. But if I had been more aware of what I was doing and dating and, like, hanging out with guys and, you know, fooling around, just getting more experience. Then I would have progressed faster.

On the other hand, being raised to see sex and virginity loss as a part of marriage—and thus reserved for heterosexuals—had made it more difficult for him to come out.

Not long after Tom and Kent lost their virginity together, Tom was lured away from Pittsburgh by a job offer from a theater in Philadelphia. He and Kent still visited one another 5 months later and, following Tom's new "practice makes perfect" adage, were continuing to explore sex together. This was unusual for someone who lost his virginity with a friend. Neither Tom nor Kent expected their relationship to blossom into anything more. "I'm not the type that will just have sex with anyone," Tom said, adding that he looked forward to discovering what it would be like to have sex with a man he loved.

"I Felt Different Afterwards, but I Didn't Feel Like I Had Crossed Over Some Great Line"

Feminist theorists often remark that lesbians' lives take distinctive shape from the ways their gender and sexual identities affect one another, or what theorists would term their intersection, such that their experiences cannot be simply equated with those of gay men or heterosexual women.[8] Abby Rosen's virginity-loss story is a case in point. When I interviewed her, Abby was 33 and had just embarked on a new career as a science librarian. She described her family as culturally Jewish but not particularly religious. A tall, athletic redhead, Abby had played soccer throughout high school and college and now coached a local girls' club team in her spare time. For the past 10 years, she identified herself as a lesbian. When I arrived at their house, she introduced her live-in partner as her wife. Neither woman had yet had children, although they hoped to in the future.

By her own account, Abby had never felt proud or ashamed of her virginity (or, later, her lack thereof). In the junior high and high schools she'd attended, virginity loss "was a big deal." But whereas many of her friends had perceived virginity loss as possessing "a significance

beyond a physical act," Abby herself "just never had that much significance attached to one particular event." Instead, she had seen virginity loss "in terms of growing up, getting more experiences in life in general." Thinking that it would be unrealistic to expect "stars shooting in the skies and violins playing and everything else," Abby had instead hoped that losing her virginity would be a learning experience. In fact, she said, "I would hate to think of someone hanging, like, this is going to be it for the rest of my life, on this one event, because almost no one I know is still with the same person that they had sex with."

Why had Abby come to interpret virginity loss so differently from her peers? She thought being Jewish among mostly Christian classmates had something to do with it; plus she had been a careful student of human behavior. She recalled her youthful reasoning:

> I knew that some kids in their religious classes were . . . told, "Don't have sex." So I knew that message was out there, I knew that certain people thought it was only . . . for marriage and not for beforehand. But . . . I was smart enough to figure out that perhaps the message wasn't an entirely accurate one . . . . I just knew it was out there and I knew it wasn't true.

On a less conscious level, Abby may have gravitated toward the process metaphor because she was going through the transition of coming out—first as bisexual and later as a lesbian—at the same time as she was becoming sexually active. As with gay men, the lesbians and bisexual women I interviewed were substantially more likely to have seen their own virginity loss as a step in a process than were their heterosexual counterparts.

Looking back, Abby believed that her nascent sexual identity had influenced the sexual decisions she made as a teenager, even though she hadn't been aware of it at the time. Before she recognized that she was sexually attracted to women, Abby hadn't really been interested in having sex or losing her virginity—both of which she had been taught to equate with vaginal intercourse. During high school, she had engaged in heavy petting, cunnilingus, and fellatio with several young men, but never seriously contemplated doing anything more. She explained:

> I don't think it was ever a conscious thing.
> I just . . . never did anything that I was
> uncomfortable with . . . and I never did any more
> than I wanted to. So I guess if I had wanted to,
> I would have, but I hadn't. And I was in the . . .
> very long process of figuring out my own
> sexuality, so that might have been part of it.

Other scholars have likewise found that lesbian and bisexual girls tend to see sexual experimentation with boys as a matter of course, rather than as a way of "testing" their sexual identity.[4]

By the time she came out as bisexual, as a 20-year-old college sophomore, Abby knew she wanted to have sex with a woman. Once she did, she reasoned (having revised her definition of sex since high school), she would no longer be a virgin. Abby looked forward to having romantic relationships, but her desire to satisfy her curiosity about sex was stronger than her inclination to lose her virginity with a girlfriend. She would be happy, she thought, if her first lesbian encounter was "trusting and caring and responsible." Among the women Abby trusted and liked "a whole lot" was Tara, a soccer teammate with whom she had been friends for several months. They had shared their sexual histories as friends, so Tara knew that Abby was a virgin and Abby knew that Tara was not. "[Tara] was actually straight, but had slept with both men and women before." Despite finding Tara attractive, Abby hadn't expected their relationship to take a sexual turn. They had never touched one another sexually before the spontaneous encounter in which they gave each other oral sex. "It was the kind of thing where one night it just happened," she recalled. "No great planning ahead of time."

Abby found sex with Tara physically and emotionally pleasurable. She was one of the few women in this group who described her virginity-loss encounter as very enjoyable physically; this may well be because she lost her virginity through cunnilingus, rather than penetrative vaginal sex, which many women find uncomfortable or even painful at first.

Abby also felt that the experience had enlightened and transformed her in small but meaningful ways. Having already given and received oral sex, albeit with men, she hadn't expected to learn anything new about sex per se from virginity loss. As she put it, "It wasn't like, 'Now I know what's it's like,' because I had actually done all those things before." Abby stood out in this interpretive group for expecting virginity loss *not* to be physically awkward, probably because she was one of the few not making the leap from oral to vaginal or anal sex. Having sex with a woman did, however, reinforce Abby's understanding that she wasn't heterosexual; and she felt subtly changed by virginity loss, in a way that confirmed her sense that it was part of a process.

> I felt different afterwards, but I didn't feel like I
> had crossed over some great line, that I was, you
> know, forever changed or any of those things. [It
> was] more coming to terms with my sexuality and
> finally doing something that I had wanted to do,
> than any physical change in myself or any, you
> know, "I am a woman now," kind of thing. . . . So
> I, I felt different because I had done something I
> had never done before. And I had, you know,
> been coming out to myself, coming out to friends,
> coming out wherever. This was sort of, I felt,
> another step in that process.

Her curiosity sated and her sexual interest in women confirmed, Abby knew that most of her future romantic and sexual partners would be women. She had sensed from the outset that Tara was ambivalent about sex with women, and therefore correctly assumed that while they would continue to be friends, their sexual encounter would remain an isolated incident. "[She] wasn't the person I was going to spend the rest of my life [with]," Abby explained. "I had no thought that [she] would be. So [virginity loss] wasn't any of that other stuff . . . that I guess some folks attach to it." When Abby had sex again, it was with her first girlfriend, Kris, whom she met several months after her night with Tara. Making love with Kris felt like just as much of a sexual turning point as losing her virginity had, Abby told me, because it had been her first sexual experience with someone she loved. Coming out had felt even more significant, for it involved "dealing with my own sexuality, and, you know, going through all that in my head was a lot more changing than . . . any specific act. Because that really had to do more with who I was." In short, Abby saw virginity loss, coming out, and having sex with a beloved partner as interrelated steps in the process of growing up and learning about sexuality.

Abby was, on the whole, pleased with the way she lost her virginity and said that she wouldn't change anything "at all." Unlike Tom and Meghan, who were glad to have lost their virginity with fellow virgins—people who knew as little about sex as they did—Abby hadn't given her partner's status much thought. Although knowledge is a source of power in a rite of passage, Tara hadn't abused her greater familiarity with sex; Abby had felt that she was in control of their encounter and that Tara had treated her as an equal. Was the encounter equitable because Abby and Tara were both women? We have, after all, seen that gender differences in power exacerbate the disadvantages faced by virgins who favor the gift and stigma metaphors (if they lose their virginity with an other-sex partner).

"EMOTIONAL PLEASURE, SURE. BUT PHYSICAL PLEASURE, THE FIRST TIME, NO"

Jennifer Gonzales felt she'd learned a lot from the process of losing her virginity, even though her own experience had been physically very painful. Now 25, she had spent her youth shuttling between her mother's house in northern Virginia, where she attended school, and her paternal grandparents' home in San Juan, Puerto Rico. Her parents, who shared little besides their Puerto Rican heritage and distaste for Roman Catholicism, had divorced when Jennifer was 8. Jennifer had been married for 2 years when I met her, and she was looking forward to starting a family—as soon as she could convince her husband, who wasn't Latino, that their future children should carry *her* last name as a public emblem of their ethnicity.

Twirling a strand of wavy dark hair around her finger, Jennifer explained that she saw virginity loss as one of many experiences through which people learned about sex. "There's not, like, one epiphanic moment," she declared. "It's part of a process, even." Yet, she had expected that the first time she had vaginal sex—the moment she lost her virginity—would be a uniquely memorable episode in that long and gradual journey. "I think you always remember the first time you have sex," she said.

Virginity loss was a central theme in many of the movies Jennifer saw as a teenager and in the novels she'd read. But the source of information about sex that Jennifer valued most, especially as a young girl, was her mother. Jennifer's mom brought home "all the books" about puberty and was open and comfortable talking about sex, which she said could and should be a source of great pleasure. Yet she also encouraged Jennifer to wait to have sex until she was at least 18. Jennifer suspects her mother's views were motivated not by any vestigial disapproval of premarital sex, her mother having repudiated the teachings of the Roman Catholic Church, but by concern for Jennifer's emotional maturity and, later, reluctance to acknowledge that her "little girl" was growing up.

Jennifer found the sex education she received in public school far less helpful, not least because, as she remembered it, the teachers were forbidden to mention birth control, much less illuminate specific aspects of sexual practice. She remembered in particular an incident from fifth or sixth grade, when she and her girlfriends had eagerly brought permission slips from home, only to discover that the "big sex ed talk" wasn't about sex at all, but about tampons and personal hygiene. By the time her ninth-grade biology teacher covered sexual reproduction, Jennifer was already well informed about "the basics," though she said she did learn some interesting, if trivial, facts.

From conversations with her mother and the films and fiction she devoured, Jennifer got the impression that all sex felt wonderful, even if the first time hurt a little or brought some blood. But she'd also heard, especially from more-experienced peers, that virginity loss could be boring, bumbling, or truly painful. As she put it:

> You always see in the movies, this beautiful scene . . . . I mean, I knew that it could be painful, I knew it could really . . . . So I didn't have as many expectations. But you know, I saw all the movies and, you know, the first time you want to be one of total pleasure.

She prepared herself for the worst, even while hoping that her own experience would be an exception.

Knowing that the first time could be disappointing as well as joyful kept Jennifer and her friends from feeling any particular urgency to lose their virginity, even as they looked forward to doing so. Nor did they feel much pressure from classmates who, as a rule, neither celebrated nor disparaged virginity. She recalled:

> My peers didn't really care one way or another . . . . If I had gone to college as a virgin, I think I would have felt pressure. I know my friends who were virgins felt pressure constantly . . . . If I were friends with a group of people who, everybody had sex but me, maybe then I would've felt pressure in high school. But that wasn't the case.

All in all, Jennifer approached virginity loss as inevitable but firmly in her command.

She didn't deliberately set out to abide by her mother's wishes; but as it turned out, Jennifer had scant opportunities to become sexually active during high school. She wasn't looking for the "perfect" partner, but none of the boys she dated piqued her interest in pursuing a relationship or in doing anything "more interesting" than kissing. Casual trysts were out of the question, because she wanted to work her way up to sex with a single partner. So Jennifer was still a virgin when she turned 18.

Many of the people I interviewed saw the transitions from virginity to nonvirginity and from high school to college (or work) as closely linked. For the stigmatized, these links were a source of anxiety and urgency, whereas processers like Jennifer tended to view them as a matter of fact. As Matt Bergquist, a 24-year-old White heterosexual engineer, put it, virginity loss was "just like one of the many changes when I was a senior and graduating high school. I don't think that it seemed that much more of a change than moving or going off to college."

Jennifer's romantic prospects took a turn for the better in December of her senior year, when she started spending time with Andy. Also 18, Andy was funny, smart, and kind—and Jennifer felt sexually attracted to him in a way she never had before. Within a month, they started to fall in love. They also began acting on their mutual attraction, starting with petting above the waist, then below, then experimenting with oral sex. Cunnilingus was simple enough—Andy had given it to his previous girlfriend, and Jennifer enjoyed receiving it—but Jennifer's first attempt to reciprocate was nothing short of comic. When she was younger, Jennifer had learned that fellatio was sometimes called a blow job, "but not that it didn't involve blowing." So during one intimate encounter, Jennifer took Andy's penis in her mouth and blew. He was confused at first, then laughed, then explained how fellatio usually worked in a way that, miraculously, kept her from feeling utterly embarrassed. Whereas people who saw virginity as a stigma felt deeply ashamed by beginners' mistakes, Jennifer quickly regained her composure and lost none of her interest in sex.

Andy knew that Jennifer was a virgin—she'd told him that well before the fellatio incident—and he'd only had sex with one girl before. Without belaboring the details, he let Jennifer know that he and his previous girlfriend, who had also been a virgin, had figured out what they liked to do through a process of trial and error (getting pleasure from vaginal sex had been particularly tricky for his girlfriend), and he imagined that he and Jennifer would do the same. Jennifer firmly believed that Andy's previous experience had prepared him to take the incremental approach to sex that she preferred. "We worked up to it," she quipped. "We'd get into it and we'd even get naked, but we wouldn't [have sex]." Rather than worry that Andy's greater experience would give him power over her, Jennifer was glad that he could help guide her. She said, "He was so patient, so understanding. It wasn't . . . that big of a deal that we couldn't wait another month." Likewise, most processers who were dating nonvirgin partners expressed gratitude for their partners' greater knowledge.

As the weeks passed and their emotional and physical intimacy intensified, Jennifer grew increasingly certain that she would lose her virginity with Andy. With her mother's grudging approval, she made an appointment with a gynecologist to get a prescription for the Pill. "I was on the Pill for two or three months before. But I could just . . . see it coming, so I wanted to be prepared. And I figured, well, you know, it regulates my period anyway." Altogether, two-thirds of people who viewed virginity loss as a rite of passage practiced some form of safer sex or birth control at virginity loss, a rate similar to that among women and men who saw virginity as a gift.

Andy and Jennifer had been dating about 5 months when they took the step from oral to vaginal sex.

> I don't think we actually made a conscious decision. Up to the point where we did it, we'd been messing around in his dad's house one day. You know, doing the regular thing and you say, "Okay," you know?

Jennifer liked the way sex with Andy made her feel emotionally; but unfortunately, that was the *only* part she liked. "Emotional pleasure, sure," she said. "But, physical pleasure, the first time, no. Physical pleasure the second time, no. The third, fourth—it took a while for me." Andy climaxed very quickly their first time together, and vaginal sex was much more painful than Jennifer had ever imagined it could be—so much so, in fact, that she had no desire to try it again. But the emotional pleasure she did feel, combined with Andy's empathy and reassurance, convinced her that it would be worth seeing if the physical side of sex might improve over time. In effect, Jennifer decided to interpret the physical pain of that first encounter as part of the process of learning about sex, rather than as a final verdict on vaginal intercourse. Later she made a point of warning her still-virgin friends that sex got a lot better with patient practice, hoping that they could benefit from her experience.

The physical pain Jennifer experienced is not unrelated to the fact that she lost her virginity through receptive vaginal intercourse. Women often feel some pain or discomfort the first time they have vaginal sex—though seldom as intense as Jennifer's.[9] More common are physically mediocre "first times" like Meghan's. Because gender and sexual identity determine which sexual practices individuals engage in, they effectively, if indirectly, help determine how physically enjoyable virginity loss is, on average, for members of different social groups.

At the end of summer, faced with the prospect of attending colleges hundreds of miles apart, Jennifer and Andy decided to break up. Ironically, Jennifer said, "[Sex] got better right around the time I left." Around that time she experienced her first orgasm, which seemed to mark the next big step in her ongoing education about sex.

All things considered, Jennifer was happy with the way she lost her virginity. Its physical shortcomings notwithstanding, the experience brought her emotional pleasure and more important, paved the way for her greater understanding and enjoyment of sex later on. In anthropologist Victor Turner's terms, virginity loss proved to be the passage of *status elevation* that she expected it to be.[10] She had no regrets. Indeed, none of the processers I interviewed regretted losing their virginity when, how, or with whom they did.

In approaching virginity loss as a rite of passage, Jennifer, like Meghan, adopted a stance that, while generally thought to be appropriate for women, is also somewhat unorthodox. Her heterosexuality shaped her expectations and experiences (and vice versa) in similar ways as well. But if Jennifer's interpretation of virginity was nontraditional for a woman, it was all the more so considering her Puerto Rican heritage. Latin American cultures, diverse as they are, typically revere unmarried women's virginity while allowing young men considerable latitude; U.S. Latinos and Latinas therefore tend to place a higher value on female virginity than do non-Hispanic Whites and African Americans.[11] Jennifer's beliefs about virginity clearly diverged from this traditional model. Yet, her personal conduct—losing her virginity relatively late and in a committed love relationship—was fairly typical of Latinas residing in the continental United States.[12]

Jennifer's family history provides a clue to her "mixed" stance. Her parents had abandoned the Catholic Church, along with its teachings about premarital sex, and become highly acculturated to Anglo America when Jennifer was just a child. Yet, Jennifer observed, they never wholly shook off the moral teachings of their conventional Puerto Rican families. Indeed, her grandparents did their best to indoctrinate her in traditional beliefs about women's sexuality during her many summers on the island. By refusing to see her virginity as a precious gift to be given in marriage, but waiting to lose it until she was 18 and in love, Jennifer managed to conform to her family's (admittedly ambivalent) teachings.

Jennifer's virginity-loss experience differed from those of Meghan, Tom, and Abby in two key respects. It was physically unpleasant—rather than unremarkable or enjoyable—and her partner was a nonvirgin of the other gender. Since knowledge represents a source of power in status passages, we might predict that a sexually experienced partner would try to take advantage of a virgin, especially if that partner enjoyed additional clout on the basis of his gender. But Jennifer felt that she'd been in charge of how and when she lost her virginity. In fact, none of the women who saw their loss of virginity as a step in a process had felt sexually disempowered, regardless of their partner's gender or level of experience; nor did they feel that their gender had worked to their special benefit. The contrast with women who interpreted virginity as a gift or as a stigma is dramatic. Jennifer's story therefore raises additional questions about people who favored the rite of passage metaphor: What kinds of power dynamics did *men* in this group face if they lost their virginity with women? And how did virgins whose experiences were unpleasant physically *and* emotionally react to the "lesson" that sex could be so disappointing?

"It Seemed Like It Should Be Really Easy to Do and It Wasn't Working"

Although Jennifer experienced an unusual degree of physical discomfort at virginity loss, she was not alone in trying to reconcile the unpleasant aspects of her experience with the conviction that virginity loss represents a desirable transition. Jason Cantor faced an even more formidable task, for he was one of six people in this group whose virginity-loss encounters fell short emotionally as well as physically.

Tall and rangy, Jason had lively brown eyes, dark wiry hair, and a subtle wit. Though only 24, he ran his own Web site design company. He had been active in the youth group at his parents' reform temple while growing up, and being Jewish had remained a central part of his identity. While he felt in no hurry to marry or have children, he looked forward to raising a family in the tradition he'd found so meaningful.

When Jason was a teenager, he had been eager to lose his virginity not because it embarrassed him, but because he had wanted to learn about sex. "I thought it [sex] would be pleasant, and I guess I thought there would be a very intense feeling of closeness and things like that." Virginity loss in particular had seemed to represent "sort of the year zero in between the part of life before sexual activity and then, the one after ... the moment between having never had sex and having had it." Jason had imagined that moment as an instant of supreme enlightenment. He expected the knowledge he'd gain through virginity loss to transform him profoundly.

Jason's curiosity about sex wasn't so intense that he felt compelled to seek out opportunities to lose his virginity. Rather, he figured, a chance would arise soon enough in the natural course of things. He and his friends had seen lots of movies in which peer pressure to have sex figured prominently but his own high school career was marked by an absence of such pressures, as well as by a liberal, value-neutral sex education curriculum. By the time he turned 17, Jason had experienced kissing and "petting, fondling, [and having] manual sex, oral sex, things like that," with a dozen girls he dated casually or "knew generally at parties." Although Jason enjoyed these casual liaisons immensely, he wanted to be in "a positive, pretty solid emotional relationship" when he lost his virginity. This wasn't because he felt that virginity loss would be meaningless if it weren't an expression of love and commitment, as gifters did, but rather because he thought that virginity loss was an experience "you're not going to forget."

Jason was a senior in high school when he fell in love for the first time. Fifteen-year-old Melissa's parents had just joined his family's synagogue, and they hit it off right away. After a few dates to movies and concerts, Melissa and Jason decided to see each other exclusively. In the weeks that followed, they engaged in "sex play at varying levels," from kissing to oral sex—the typical pattern for heterosexuals in this interpretive group. They discussed their mutual virginity; but neither gave it much thought beyond taking it for granted that, if they dated long enough, they would probably have vaginal sex. Eventually, the question was *when* they would lose their virginity together. Jason recounted:

> There were plenty of opportunities before it happened. I think it was more just timing.... At the time when it happened, I think it seemed like something that we both wanted to do. Whereas previous to that, I remember at least one, I remember specifically one instance before that, where I had brought up, you know, "Do you want to have sex now?" and she had said, "No, not now." And we let that lie. So it, it was sort of a timing thing.

They'd been a couple for almost 5 months when mutual interest and opportunity coincided. When a mandatory school play rehearsal prevented Jason from joining his family on a weekend trip, he invited Melissa to stay with him overnight. He made sure to change his sheets and have plenty of condoms on hand, just in case. But even careful planning didn't prepare them for the debacle that ensued. Jason recalled:

> We spent a good twenty minutes just trying to, to penetrate and eventually.... It just wasn't happening. So we stopped trying and went out and got some food or whatever, and I think we tried again later that day and it worked. And that was just—by the time it actually worked, it turned into sort of a frustration thing. You know, 'cause it was something, it seemed like it should be really easy to do and it wasn't working. And I know, I know that she felt ... pain when it actually worked.... And I was frustrated, so it was not very pleasant at all.

Despite the circumstances, Jason had an orgasm; Melissa did not.

Rather than renounce sex after such a fiasco, Jason and Melissa decided to give it another try.

Like Jennifer and Andy, they took encouragement from the strength of their relationship and from their enjoyment of earlier sexual encounters. Happily, their persistence was rewarded. "After the first time," Jason said, "when we went back and did it more, it was actually good, it was actually very pleasant. So I'd kind of had this idea that sex is something pleasant, and it panned out that way." In this way, they made their mutual transition to nonvirginity "stick." And, even though Jason's virginity-loss experience was more unpleasant than Jennifer's, and his frustration magnified by his preconception of first vaginal sex as "easy," he too came to value it for bringing him a step closer to a complete and fulfilling sexual life.

Jason and Melissa continued to date and to have sex for almost 2 years. He let his friends surmise that he wasn't a virgin anymore, but didn't broadcast his new status, since he wanted to maintain some semblance of privacy. The pair broke up after a frustrating year of dating long distance—while Melissa was a high school senior, Jason attended college 300 miles from home. When he was 21, Jason became involved in "another very serious relationship that went on for about a year." That romance reinforced his understanding of sex as a process in which virginity loss represented just one step:

> I think it was the first time where I really thought
> I was having sex that was pointedly good. And
> that my partner was contributing something
> unique and specific to the activity, you
> know . . . that she had skills and knowledge of
> how to do different things, to get different kinds
> of pleasure. And I remember . . . with this person
> that sex seemed a little more expansive then, there
> was more to it.

Jason's gender inevitably, if subtly, influenced his beliefs and experiences. For men, interpreting virginity loss as a step in a process served as a somewhat unorthodox compromise—acceptably masculine, according to popular opinion, but less extreme than the tradition equating men's virginity with stigma. Yet, Jason

did not experience virginity loss as gender neutral; he saw this rite of passage as transforming him from a boy into a man (at least in a sexual sense). Being male did not, however, appear to affect Jason's sense of sexual agency; he felt neither as though he'd been out of control nor that he'd been at Melissa's mercy. Similarly, the other male processers also felt that they'd remained in control.

BECOMING WOMEN AND MEN

Women and men who viewed virginity loss as a step in a process were, by and large, exposed to the same ideas about virginity as people who preferred other interpretations. But while they were aware that virginity could be seen as a stigma or as a gift, these approaches did not appeal to them. Different patterns of sexual socialization provide a partial explanation for the groups' different interpretive inclinations. Although individuals from working- and middle-class families were equally likely to have ever viewed virginity loss as a rite of passage, middle-class youth were overrepresented among those who drew on that metaphor at the time of their own virginity loss—that is, fairly early in life. Since the metaphor derives from anthropological studies that are a staple of college curricula but are seldom taught in secondary school, it may be that college-educated parents are better situated to share this perspective with their children. In general, the parents of men and women in the process group tended to hold fairly permissive attitudes about adolescent sexuality, typically taking it for granted that their offspring would have sex before marriage (though most parents frowned on virginity loss in early adolescence or with casual partners). With the exception of Tom, no one in the process group grew up in a conservative Protestant and/or devoutly religious family. Few recalled being exposed to, much less influenced by, religious teachings about virginity loss. Processers were also disproportionately likely to have participated in value-neutral comprehensive sex education pro-grams, such as those described by Meghan and Jason. Possibly for this reason, they described their peers as nonjudgmental more often than did members of the stigma and gift groups—even when those peers disagreed with their beliefs—and reported experiencing little if any peer pressure around sexual activity.

Beyond their sexual socialization, processers were acutely aware of the possibility of con-structing their identities through virginity loss—trading one social status for another being pre-cisely what their interpretation of that event entails. They invariably spoke of virginity loss as a signal event in their transformation from relatively naive adolescents to sexually know-ing adults. Many moreover described this trans-formation in gendered terms, as a process of becoming women or men. Because the rite of passage metaphor is seen as an appropriate, but not especially traditional, option for men and women in American culture, it provided the people in my study with a vehicle for challenging the sexual double standard by rejecting rather than reversing it (as when a man views virgin-ity as a gift). In this sense, viewing virginity loss as a step in a process helps young peo-ple to establish a truly unorthodox adult mas-culine or feminine self through virginity loss. More than half of processers had done "every-thing but" lose their virginity with at least one casual partner. By contrast, sex play with casual partners was exceedingly rare among gifters and seen as a kind of consolation prize by the stigmatized.

The passage metaphor also helps people to fashion sexual identities. Tom, Abby, and the other gay, lesbian, and bisexual women and men in this group experienced virginity loss as inter-twined with the process of coming out. Losing virginity with a same-sex partner enables indi-viduals to "prove" their lesbigay sexual identity to themselves and others. In fact, the two les-bians who lost their virginity with men before they came out noted that those experiences contributed to their growing sense that they weren't heterosexual. Heterosexual women and men likewise demonstrated their sexual identi-ties through virginity loss, although they were typically less conscious of doing so.

What youth learn about virginity and sex-uality from their parents, peers, schools, reli-gious institutions, and mass media—lessons that are patterned by gender, sexuality, race/ethnicity, social class, and religion—shapes their prefer-ences; as do the specific social contexts through which they move. But traditional links between social identity and interpretations of virgin-ity loss are weaker today than in the past, as the unconventional preferences of many of my study participants reveal. Broad social changes, especially those brought about by the feminist, gay rights, and civil rights movements, have opened new avenues, new ways of being men and women, gay and heterosexual, racially or ethni-cally identified, and so forth. Young women and men are, consequently, able to choose specific approaches to virginity loss based on the ver-sions of social identity that those approaches will help them achieve.

INTRODUCTION REFERENCES

Ingrassia, M. C. 1994. Virginity cool. *Newsweek*, 17 October, 59–62, 64, 69.

The morals revolution on campuses 1964. *Newsweek*, 6 April, 52.

REFERENCES

1. Malinowski, Bronislaw. 1929. *The sexual life of sav-ages*. New York: H. Liveright; Mead, Margaret, 1939. *From the South Seas: Studies of adolescence and sex in primitive societies*. New York: William Morrow.

2. Glaser, Barney G., and Anselm L. Strauss. 1971. *Status passage*. Chicago: Aldine-Atherton.

3. Rich, Adrienne. 1980. Compulsory heterosexuality and lesbian existence. In *Powers of desire: The poli-tics of sexuality*, edited by A. Snitow, C. Stansell, and S. Thompson, 177–205. New York: Monthly Review Press.

4. Savin-Williams, Ritch C. 2003. Dating and roman-tic relationships among gay, lesbian, and bisexual

youths. In *The gendered society reader*, edited by M. S. Kimmel and A. Aronson, 382–395. New York: Oxford University Press.

5. Van Gennep, Arnold. 1908. *The rites of passage.* Reprint, Chicago: University of Chicago Press, 1960.

6. Wyatt, Gail Elizabeth. 1997. *Stolen women: Reclaiming our sexuality, taking back our lives.* New York: Wiley.

7. Herdt, Gilbert, and Andrew Boxer. 1993. *Children of Horizons: How gay and lesbian teens are leading a new way out of the closet.* 2nd ed. Boston: Beacon Press.

8. Stein, Arlene, and Ken Plummer. 1994. I can't even think straight: Queer theory and the missing sexual revolution in sociology. *Sociological Theory* 12:178–187.

9. Sprecher, Susan, Anita Barbee, and Pepper Schwartz. 1995. "Was it good for you, too?": Gender differences in first sexual intercourse experiences. *JSR* 32: 3–15.

10. Turner, Victor. 1969. *The ritual process.* Ithaca, NY: Cornell University Press.

11. Raffaelli, Marcela, and Lenna L. Ontai. 2001. "She's 16 years old and there's boys calling over to the house": An exploratory study of sexual socialization in Latino families. *Culture, Health and Sexuality* 3:295–310.

12. Upchurch, Dawn M., Lene Levy-Storms, Clea A. Sucoff, and Carol S. Aneshensel. 1998. Gender and ethnic differences in the timing of first sexual intercourse. *FPP* 30:121–127.

CHAPTER 14

Communicating with New Sex Partners

College Women and Questions
That Make a Difference

Nelwyn B. Moore

J. Kenneth Davidson, Sr.

When queried about their sexual script, most college students would probably reply, "What sexual script?" Yet, by adulthood, all persons have one. That there is a complex network of interacting variables within the individual that affects sexual behavior may seem to be a self-evident fact. But, when sexual decisions are close at hand, most individuals seldom consider the influence of family history, their personality makeup, or the culture in which they grew up, all variables that do indeed influence sexual behavior. Of course, the interaction effects of such factors must also be considered for persons who would wish to scientifically analyze their sexual lives, if any such persons exist! And, the fact that this process is dynamic, continuing to evolve throughout life in relationships with others, must also be factored in the equation for accurate appraisal.

Moore and Davidson focus on just one aspect of sexual scripting among young adults as they ask the question: Why do women fail to ask new sex partners about their sexual histories? This question

should particularly resonate with women because lack of communication about sexual histories poses substantially greater risks for them than for men. This fact is based on widespread evidence that most college men have more lifetime sex partners than college women.

Although this study highlights primarily physiological factors, such as an unintended pregnancy or STIs in relation to lack of communication, can you suggest psychological risks that might also occur? If you are a sexually active-college female, you will find yourself in one of the three groups that differentiated the respondents. If so, what can you add from your own personal experience that might change the focus of future research on this topic? A heightened awareness of your own sexual script can enhance your role as director in the drama of your own developmental trajectory in life.

From "Communicating with New Sex Partners: Questions That Make a Difference" by N. B. Moore, and J. K. Davidson, Sr. 2000. *Journal of Sex & Marital Therapy 26:* 215–230. Reprinted by permission of the publisher (Taylor & Francis Ltd, http://www.tandf.co.uk/journals).

In today's society, numerous contextual factors surround the discussion and negotiation of sexual activity. Such sexual discourse often involves the representation of self and other in a creative game in which discussion of sexual pasts is avoided. This circumstance especially may be true for first sexual encounters. Added to this dilemma is the lack of an acceptable cultural language with which to negotiate disclosure of sexual histories (Pliskin, 1997). The fact that college women face gender-specific conflicts between the historically traditional and the more recent revolutionary understanding of their sexuality also is at issue. Society on the one hand condemns women who engage in casual sexual intercourse. At the same time, however, it advocates female sexual liberation (Dunn, 1998). And the very characteristics often associated with traditional gender roles, such as submissiveness, passivity, and nurturance, seemingly impair the woman's ability to effectively engage in rational decision making about involvement in sexual activity (Zellman & Goodchild 1983). Consequently, research suggests that women often are lacking in the training and socialization necessary to be effective communicators in sexual relationships (Murnen, Perot, & Bryne, 1989).

Despite the constant media barrage and the efforts of sexuality educators, many college women in the 1990s report being uninfluenced by information proclaiming the risks of contracting a sexually transmitted disease or initiating an unintentional pregnancy (Kusselling, Wenger, & Shapiro, 1995). Contrary to popular opinion, increased levels of awareness have not necessarily led to college women implementing behavioral changes in their sexual lives (Rubinson & De Rubertis, 1991). In one study, almost two thirds (62 percent) of college women indicated that awareness or concerns about AIDS had not affected their level of participation in sexual intercourse, and almost three fourths (72 percent) had not changed their level of involvement in oral-genital sex (Weinberg, Lottes, & Aveline, 1998). Even college women who claimed to have become more selective in their choice of sex partners were just as sexually active as those who had indicated no behavioral changes (Carroll, 1991). In fact, 19 percent of college women actually expressed the likelihood that they would eventually contract a sexually transmitted disease (STD) (Davidson & Moore, 1994).

REVIEW OF THE LITERATURE

First Sexual Intercourse

The age at first sexual intercourse for college women continued to decline during the 1990s, dropping to 16.5 years (Sprecher, Barbee, & Schwartz, 1995). Regardless of age, a person's first sexual intercourse experience often is viewed as a rite of passage to adulthood, potentially leading to affirmation of self-identity (Moore & Davidson, 1997). However, for many women, the first coital experience is disappointing both physically and emotionally (Darling, Davidson, & Passarello, 1992), perhaps in part, because only 50 percent of college women reported expecting first sexual intercourse to occur at that particular time (Sawyer & Smith, 1996). Additionally, the fact that college women are more likely to give implied consent rather than verbal consent for their first intercourse experience raises related questions (Moore & Davidson, 1997).

College women are more likely to experience feelings of anxiety, nervousness, embarrassment and guilt during their first sexual intercourse rather than excitement and pleasure (Guggino & Ponzetti, 1997). And only 38 percent of college women reported never feeling guilty about their first intercourse (Moore & Davidson, 1997). When asked to choose one word to describe their first sexual experience, only 24 percent of women chose a positive term, whereas 52 percent chose a negative term (Sawyer & Smith, 1996). Furthermore, the percentage of college women who indicated that they had experienced orgasm during first intercourse is only 7 percent (Sprecher, Barber, & Schwartz, 1995) to 8 percent (Sawyer & Smith, 1996).

In terms of safer sexual practices at first intercourse, the percentage of college women who were under the influence of alcohol ranges from 27 percent (Sprecher et al., 1995) to 31 percent (Moore & Davidson, 1997). In fact, 17 percent of the women reported being "drunk" (Sprecher et al., 1995). As for contraceptive usage during first intercourse, the ranges are from 55 percent (Moore & Davidson, 1997) to 74 percent

(Sawyer & Smith, 1996), with the condom being the most frequently employed contraceptive method (Sprecher et al., 1995).

Sexual Risk-Taking

In general, incidence of risk-taking sexual behavior is elevated by several factors: decreased age at first sexual intercourse (Mauldon & Luker, 1996), low sexual self-esteem (Seal, Minichiello, & Omodei, 1997); 2 or more sex partners within the past year (Seidman, Mosher, & Aral, 1994); and consumption of alcoholic beverages prior to sexual intercourse (Leigh, Schafer, & Temple, 1995). Alcoholic beverages continue to play a substantial role in the sexual lives of college women. In one survey, 75 percent of college women indicated that they had gotten drunk within the past year. Of these respondents, 10 percent indicated that while drunk they had sexual intercourse with a stranger (Carroll & Carroll, 1995). College women who consumed greater quantities of alcohol and on a more frequent basis ranked high on sexual insecurity, and they perceived that consumption of alcohol could enhance the sexual experience (Mooney, 1995). In fact, 17 percent of college women reported deliberately drinking "more than normal" to make it easier to have sexual intercourse with someone (Anderson & Mathieu, 1996). Binge drinking, in particular, is a crucial factor in the equation. Among college women, 66 percent of binge drinkers, in contrast with only 33 percent of nonbinge drinkers, had had sexual intercourse while under the influence of alcohol since coming to college (Piombo & Piles, 1996). Although alcohol may enhance their sexual experiences, many college women also indicated that alcohol at some time had led to a negative effect on their sexual experience (Paulson, Eppler, Satterwaite, Wuensch, & Bass, 1998).

Although the overall percentage of college women who use a contraceptive is increasing (Sprecher et al., 1995), a related phenomenon is puzzling. Women who delay initiating sexual intercourse for the longest period of time are least likely to use contraception at first sexual intercourse. This finding is especially troubling, because it suggests that strategies that encourage postponement of the initiation of sexual intercourse may inadvertently discourage safer sex practices (Cooksey, Rindfuss, & Guilkey, 1996).

Even though two-thirds (66 percent) of college women today report "always" using contraception (Raj & Pollack, 1995), the percentage who "usually/always" have their sex partner use a condom ranges from 26 percent (Prince & Bernard, 1998) to 32 percent (Weinberg et al., 1998). This inconsistent condom use is in spite of the fact that the primary motivation for using a condom among unmarried women is disease prevention and not contraception (Anderson & Mathieu, 1996). Lower condom use occurs among college women with high perceptions of relative invulnerability (Thompson, Anderson, Freedman, & Swan, 1996), absence of negative emotions (i.e., worry and regret over nonusage) (Richard, de Vries, & Van der Plight, 1998), low perceptions of present risk (Basen-Engquist, 1992), and endorsement of the "relational ideal" (i.e., love and commitment as prerequisite for sexual intercourse) (Hynie, Lyndon, Côté, & Wiener, 1998). Thus, it should not be surprising that college women frequently perceived using a condom or the pill as an either/or choice, rather than perceiving both as necessary for maximum protection against STDs and unwanted pregnancy (Beckman, Harvey, & Tiersky, 1996). The perception of present risk is greatly diminished with the consumption of alcohol, especially among those who are binge drinkers. Of female college binge drinkers, 49 percent reported having unprotected/unsafe sexual intercourse since coming to college in comparison to only 25 percent of nonbinge drinkers (Piombo & Piles, 1996).

Finally, the prevalence of risk-taking sexual practices is related to perceived risk and self-efficacy rather than knowledge. High self-efficacy is associated with both the intention to discuss STD prevention (Hale & Trumbetta, 1996) and reported discussion of past sex partners with a current sex partner (Basen-Engquist, 1992). Yet the percentage of college women who indicated having asked their last sex partner about his sexual history before engaging in sexual intercourse ranges from 26 percent (Hawkins, Gray, & Hawkins, 1995) to 55 percent (Hale, Char, Nagy, & Stockton, 1993). The reasons that college women most frequently give for not discussing past sexual histories of their prospective sex partners relate to the vulnerability of their self-image (i.e., embarrassment and fear of rejection as a person and/or as a sex partner) (Cline, Johnson, & Freeman, 1992). Discussion of sexual history is of crucial importance, because the number of lifetime sex partners for college men ranges from 7.0 partners (Weinberg et al., 1998) to 8.0 partners (Reinisch, Hill, Sanders, & Ziemba-Davis, 1995). Since widespread evidence exists that most college men have more lifetime sex partners than college women, the lack of communication about sexual histories poses substantially greater risks for women than for men (Reinisch et al., 1995).

Sexual Satisfaction

In general, sexually active college women tend to report low levels of sexual satisfaction, especially those with inconsistent contraceptive usage and consumption of alcohol prior to sexual intercourse (Raj & Pollack, 1995). The importance of relationship factors as determinants of women's sexual functioning, including orgasmic consistency, are strongly supported (Rosen, Taylor, Leiblum, & Bachmann, 1993). But behavioral factors such as age at first intercourse, number of lifetime sex partners, and frequency of sexual intercourse are unrelated to experiencing orgasm during sexual intercourse (Raboch & Raboch, 1992).

Among college women, 78 percent rated coital orgasm as an important component of their sexual experience (Loos, Bridges, & Critelli, 1997). And the absence of orgasm at first sexual intercourse for college women also leads to a lower rating for subjective pleasure regarding the first sexual experience (Sprecher et al., 1995). Furthermore, 60 percent of college women reported feeling guilty if no orgasm was experienced during sexual intercourse. These women were also more likely to report being asked by their sex partner if they had experienced orgasm and less likely to indicate psychological sexual satisfaction (Davidson & Moore, 1994).

Why then do women fail to ask new sex partners about their sexual histories? Is this failure to act just one of a cluster of risk-taking behaviors? Are there family and personal background variables that differentiate women who do not ask from those who do? To answer these questions, this study investigated the correlation, if any, between the failure of college women to ask new sex partners about their sexual history prior to engaging in sexual intercourse and participation in other risk-taking sexual practices, as well as cognitive decision making and family and personal background variables.

METHODOLOGY

An anonymous questionnaire was administered to volunteer respondents in the schools of arts and sciences, business, and nursing at a midwestern, residential state university. This investigation was part of a larger research project designed to assess whether or not any significant changes in the sexual attitudes and behaviors of college students have occurred during the 1990s. Given the nature of the research question, the focus of this investigation was 438 women (77.7 percent) who reported having experienced sexual intercourse. Those women who gave no response to the question/variable "frequency/ask new sex partner/total number of previous sex partners prior to having sexual intercourse" ($N = 28$) were declared as missing values, providing a final sample of 410 sexually active women.

RESULTS

Overview

The initial data analyses revealed that of these college women, 32.7 percent ($N = 134$)

reported "rarely", 19.5 percent ($N = 80$) reported "sometimes", and 47.8 percent ($N = 196$) reported "almost always" asking their new sex partner about his total number of previous sex partners. For ease of reporting the remaining data analyses, three respondent categories were subsequently established: AA group = almost always ask about previous sex partners; S group = sometimes ask about previous sex partners; and R group = rarely ask about previous sex partners. With regard to revealing their total number of sex partners, 44.0 percent of R group and 31.3 percent of S group women, in contrast to only 9.3 percent of AA group, reported "never" having discussed this matter with their new sex partner.

Of these women, 88.8 percent of R group, 92.5 percent of S group, and 88.7 percent of AA group women had received oral-genital stimulation. Further, 83.6 percent of R group, 90.0 percent of S group, and 87.2 percent of AA group had given oralgenital stimulation. S group women (65.0 percent) were more likely to have engaged in masturbation than either R group (45.5 percent) or AA group (45.9 percent) women. And 50.7 percent of R group, 53.8 percent of S group, and 60.7 percent of AA group women reported having experienced an orgasm while petting with an opposite-sex partner. However, S group (82.5 percent) and AA group women (72.4 percent) were more likely than R group (61.2 percent) women to indicate having ever experienced an orgasm during sexual intercourse.

Family and Personal Background

AA group women were more likely to have discussed sexually related topics with their mother figures than either R group or S group women. AA group women also were more likely than R group and S group women to believe that love should be a prerequisite for sexual intercourse and to desire to marry someone who had had sexual intercourse only with them. However, there were no significant differences between the groups for the following family

background variables: feelings toward mother while growing up; mother figure uncommunicative; feelings toward father figure while growing up; father figure uncommunicative; and discussion of sexually related topics with father figure. There were no significant differences in religious denominations between groups; most women were either Mainline Protestant (46.7 percent) or Roman Catholic (43.0 percent). However, AA group women attended religious services more frequently than either R group or S group women.

First Sexual Intercourse

AA group women reported being in a committed love relationship with their sex partner at the time of their first sexual intercourse experience more often than either R group or S group women. AA group women also were older than R group and S group women at their first intercourse. However, there were no significant differences between groups for the age of first sex partner. Although not significant, the data suggest that, though voluntarily consenting, R group and S group women were more likely to have given implied rather than verbal consent for their first intercourse experience. Furthermore, R group and S group women, in comparison to AA group women, more frequently had been under the influence of alcohol or some other mind-altering substance at their first intercourse. Thus, as might be expected, AA group women more often employed a contraceptive at their initial sexual encounter than either R group or S group women.

There were no significant differences between groups with regard to first sexual intercourse either being physiologically or psychologically satisfying. Nor did any significant differences exist between groups with regard to feelings of guilt after having engaged in sexual intercourse.

Risk-Related Sexual Behaviors

The advent of AIDS resulted in the R group and S group women becoming less sexually active when compared to AA group women. AA group women were more likely than either R group or S group women to respond that AIDS had had "no effect" on their sexual activity. However, AA group women reported fewer sex partners in the past year and fewer lifetime sex partners than either R group or S group women.

There were no significant differences between groups for the following risk-related sexual behavior variables: experienced anal intercourse, ever diagnosed with STD, used condom during oral-genital sex, and used contraceptive during most recent sexual intercourse. But significant differences did exist with regard to other sexual risk-taking. AA group women were more likely to have planned their most recent sexual intercourse and to have discussed contraception prior to their most recent sexual intercourse than R group or S group women. In contrast, R group and S group women were more likely to have sexual intercourse without contraceptive use than AA group women. Furthermore, AA group women, when compared to R group and S group women, more often asked a new sex partner about his STD history. In addition, AA group women were less likely to believe that they would eventually contract an STD than the other women. Finally, a greater percentage of S group women than R group and AA group reported having ever been pregnant.

Role of Cognitive Decision Making

In exploring the role of cognitive factors in the decision-making process in the lives of AA group women, two variables were significant. These women were more likely than R group and S group women to set goals for themselves and to make sexual decisions based on their own thoughts rather than being influenced by others. However, no differences were found for the variable frequency/"feel optimistic about life."

Sexual Adjustment and Sexual Satisfaction

For all of these women, sexual guilt was not a distinguishing variable. There were no significant differences between groups for the following sexual guilt-related Likert-scale variables: feel guilty about masturbation, feel guilty about petting, feel guilty about current sexual intercourse, and feel guilty if no orgasm experienced during sexual intercourse. Furthermore there were no significant differences between groups with regard to level of comfort with sexuality and frequency of orgasm experienced during sexual intercourse. However, the sex partners of R group and S group women were more likely to ask them if they had experienced an orgasm during sexual intercourse when compared to the sex partners of AA group women. Furthermore, no significant differences between groups were found for the variable physiological sexual satisfaction in their sexual lives. However, AA group women, in contrast to R group and S group women, were more likely to report psychological sexual satisfaction in their sexual lives.

DISCUSSION

Given the nonrandomness of this sample, questions can be raised regarding the generalizability of the data, specifically the appropriateness of making inferences about college women in general. However, because these college women constituted 15 percent of the female students in each of the freshman, sophomore, junior, and senior classes and were from classes in various disciplines, this sample is thought to be a representative, albeit nonrandomly selected, group of American college women. Consequently, the investigators believe that this study can contribute to a better understanding of the communication practices of college women with their new sex partners.

Ideally, an anticipated first-time sex partner should share her or his previous sexual history, including number of lifetime sex partners, sexually transmitted disease history, and length of time since last partnered sexual activity. Although the content of such sexual discussions by these women was not determined in this investigation, the researchers propose that this is an important question for future research. Such a focus could help discern how young women actually make decisions pertaining to sexual intercourse, furnishing valuable information for professionals.

As the data unfold about young women who almost always ask new sex partners about their total number of sex partners, a clear portrait emerges of an apparently self-confident young woman whose sexual self-esteem is intact. This is consistent with the findings of Basen-Engquist (1992) that high self-efficacy is associated with intent to discuss past sex partners with a current sex partner. A gestalt of family and personal background factors offers a clue to the basis of healthy sexual communications in the young adult years. Perhaps the prototype for communicating freely with a new sex partner about sexual histories, hers and his, evolved from early discussions about sexuality that AA group women had with their mothers. Also, the frequent church attendance and valuing sexual intercourse within the context of love (i.e., no sexual intercourse without love, marrying a man who has had sexual intercourse only with them) are more likely rooted in family values than peer values.

Although self-efficacy was not directly measured in this study, one could reasonably extrapolate a high degree of such abilities in AA group women from the constellation of health-promoting sexual decisions involving their first sexual intercourse. For example, first intercourse frequently occurred in a committed love relationship and at a later age than for their peers, R group and S group women. They were more likely to have used a contraceptive and were less likely to have been under the influence of alcohol.

The role of alcohol in risk-taking sexual behavior implied by this research supports the findings of others that risk-taking is elevated by consumption of alcohol (Leigh et al., 1995). Given the findings of Mooney (1995), one would at least have to ask the question whether or not

R and S group women who consumed greater quantities of alcohol and on a more frequent basis would rank high on sexual insecurity. Perhaps the risk takers in this study altered their perception of present risk with the consumption of alcohol as suggested by the Piombo and Piles (1996) study.

It is not surprising that in subsequent sexual intercourse experiences, AA group women exhibited healthier sexual behaviors than either R group or S group women, whose sexual behavior was characterized by risk-taking. Out of 11 statistically significant variables representing risk-related sexual behaviors, all but two variables were clearly health-promoting choices for AA group women. These women had fewer sexual intercourse partners in the past year and in their lifetime. Furthermore, they were less likely to have had sexual intercourse with a casual acquaintance or a person they had just met. Perhaps explicitly because of the foregoing health-promoting choices, they were least likely to believe that they would contract an STD in the future or to report that AIDS had had an effect on their current sexual activity. It is puzzling, however, that these low-risk women and the high-risk R group women were almost equally likely to have had a premarital pregnancy. Conceivably, this finding may be a function of the small n for this variable in general and for R group women in particular.

In assessing differences in the sexual behavior of these three groups of women, the key factor may lie in the cognitive dimension. AA group women were significantly more likely to base decisions on their own thoughts and goals that they had set for themselves. These cognitive variables may well be the chief ingredients in differentiating health-promoting and health-defeating sexual behavior among college women. Therefore, it is not surprising that AA group women were more likely than R and S group women to report psychological sexual satisfaction.

CONCLUSIONS

These findings do have at least two major implications for sex and family therapists. First, they lend further support to the crucial role that parent figures can play in the sexuality education of their children. Second, they demonstrate that the factors influencing young people to make healthy sexual decisions are far from simplistic. The health-promoting and health-defeating behaviors each appear to be constellations that, although observable, are by nature elusive in origin. If it is true that family/personal background factors and cognitive variables are singularly significant, practicing family professionals (such as sex educators, sex therapists, family therapists, and researchers) would be well-advised to focus less on the issue of imparting information about sexuality and more on strategies that support the development of high self-esteem and high self-efficacy in the developing person. Instruction and practice in decision-making skills and setting short-range and long-range goals for self may be essential precursors to enacting sexual health-promoting behaviors. This perspective suggests that perhaps family professionals need to emphasize subjective as well as objective methods in their work. Furthermore, it suggests that researchers need to probe deeper than their quantitative data for qualitative answers.

REFERENCES

Anderson, P. B., & Mathieu, D. A. (1996). College students' high-risk sexual behavior following alcohol consumption. *Journal of Sex & Marital Therapy, 22*, 259–264.

Basen-Engquist, K. (1992). Psychological predictors of "safer sex" behaviors in young adults. *AIDS Education and Prevention, 4*, 120–134.

Beckman, L. J., Harvey, S. M., & Tiersky, L. A. (1996). Attitudes about condom use among college students. *Journal of American College Health, 44*, 243–250.

Carroll, J. L., & Carroll, L. M. (1995). Alcohol use and risky sex among college students. *Psychological Reports, 76*, 723–726.

Carroll, L. M. (1991). Gender, knowledge about AIDS, reported behavioral change, and the sexuality of college students. *Journal of American College Health, 40*, 5–12.

Cline, R. J. W., Johnson, S. J., & Freeman, K. E. (1992). Talk among sexual partners about AIDS: Interpersonal communication for risk reduction or risk enhancement. *Health Communication, 4*, 39–56.

Cooksey, E. C., Rindfuss, R. B., & Guilkey, D. K. (1996). The initiation of adolescent sexual and contraceptive behavior during changing times. *Journal of Health and Social Behavior, 37*, 59–74.

Darling, C. A., Davidson, J. K., Sr., & Passarello, C. C. (1992). The mystique of first intercourse among college youth: The role of partners, contraceptive practices, and psychological reactions. *Journal of Youth and Adolescence, 21*, 97–117.

Davidson, J. K., Sr., & Moore, N. B. (1994). Guilt and lack of orgasm during sexual intercourse: Myth versus reality among college women. *Journal of Sex Education and Therapy, 20*, 153–174.

Dunn, J. L. (1998). Defining women: Notes toward an understanding of structure and agency in the negotiation of sex. *Journal of Contemporary Ethnology, 26*, 479–510.

Guggino, J. M., & Ponzetti, J. J., Jr. (1997). Gender differences in affective reactions to first coitus. *Journal of Adolescence, 20*, 189–200.

Hale, P. J., & Trumbetta, S. L. (1996). Women's self-efficacy and sexually transmitted disease preventative behaviors. *Research in Nursing and Health, 19*, 101–10.

Hale, R. W., Char, D. R., Nagy, K., & Stockert, N. (1993). Seventeen-year review of sexual and contraceptive behavior on a college campus. *American Journal of Obstretrics and Gynecology, 168*, 1833–1837.

Hawkins, M. J., Gray, C., & Hawkins, W. E. (1995). Gender differences of reported safer sex behaviors within a random sample of college students. *Psychological Reports, 77*, 963–968.

Hynie, M., Lydon, J. E., Côté, S., & Wiener, S. (1998). Relational sexual scripts and women's condom use: The importance of internalized norms. *Journal of Sex Research, 35*, 370–380.

Kusselling, F. S., Wenger, N. S., & Shapiro, M. F. (1995). Inconsistent contraceptive use among female college students: Implications for intervention. *Journal of American College Health, 43*, 191–195.

Leigh, B. C., Schafer, J., & Temple, M. T. (1995). Alcohol use and contraception at first sexual experiences. *Journal of Behavioral Medicine, 18*, 81–95.

Loos, V. E., Bridges, C. F., & Critelli, J. W. (1997). Weiner's attribution theory and female orgasmic consistency. *Journal of Sex Research, 23,* 348–361.

Mauldon, J., & Luker, K. (1996). The effects of contraceptive education on method use at first intercourse. *Family Planning Perspectives, 28,* 19–24, 41.

Mooney, D. K. (1995). The relationship between sexual insecurity, the alcohol expectation for enhanced sexual experience, and consumption patterns. *Addictive Behavior, 20,* 243–250.

Moore, N. B., & Davidson, J. K., Sr. (1997). Guilt about first intercourse: An antecedent of sexual dissatisfaction among college women. *Journal of Sex & Marital Therapy, 23,* 29–45.

Murnen, S. K., Perot, A., & Byrne, D. (1989). Coping with unwanted sexual activity: Normative responses, situational determinants, and individual differences. *Journal of Sexual Research, 26,* 85–106.

Paulson, R. L., Eppler, M. A., Satterwaite, T. N., Wuensch, K. L., & Bass, L. A. (1998). Alcohol consumption, strength of religious beliefs, and risky sexual behavior in college students. *Journal of American College Health, 46,* 227–232.

Piombo, M., & Piles, M. (1996). The relationship between college females' drinking and their sexual behaviors. *Women's Health Issues, 6,* 221–228.

Pliskin, K. L. (1997). Verbal communication and sexual communication. *Medical Anthropology Quarterly, 11,* 89–109.

Prince, A., & Bernard, A. L. (1998). Alcohol use and safer sex behaviors of students at a commuter university. *Journal of Alcohol and Drug Education, 43,* 1–19.

Raboch, J., & Raboch, J. (1992). Infrequent orgasms in women. *Journal of Sex & Marital Therapy, 18,* 114–120.

Raj, A., & Pollack, R. H. (1995). Factors predicting high-risk sexual behavior in heterosexual college females. *Journal of Sex & Marital Therapy, 21,* 213–224.

Reinisch, J. M., Hill, C. A., Sanders, S. A., & Ziemba-Davis, M. (1995). High-risk sexual behavior at a midwestern university: A confirmatory survey. *Family Planning Perspectives, 27,* 79–82.

Richard, R., de Vries, N. K., & Van der Plight, J. (1998). Anticipated regret and precautionary behavior. *Journal of Applied Social Psychology, 28,* 1411–1428.

Rosen, R. C., Taylor, J. F., Leiblum, S. R., & Bachmann, G. A. (1993). Prevalence of sexual dysfunction in women: Results of a survey study of 329 women in a gynecological clinic. *Journal of Sex & Marital Therapy, 19,* 171–188.

Rubinson, L., & De Rubertis, L. (1991). Trends in sexual attitudes and behavior of a college population over a 15-year period. *Journal of Sex & Marital Therapy, 17,* 32–41.

Sawyer, R. G., & Smith, N. G. (1996). A survey of situational factors at first intercourse among college students. *American Journal of Health and Behavior, 20,* 208–217.

Seal, A., Minichiello, V., & Omodei, M. (1997). Young women's sexual risk-taking behavior: Re-visiting the influence of sexual self-efficacy and sexual self-esteem. *International Journal of Sexually Transmitted Diseases and AIDS, 8,* 159–165.

Seidman, S. N., Mosher, W. D., & Aral, S. O. (1994). Predictors of high-risk behavior in unmarried American women: Adolescent environment as a risk factor, *Journal of Adolescent Health, 15,* 126–132.

Sprecher, S., Barbee, A., & Schwartz, P. (1995). "Was it good for you, too?": Gender differences in first sexual intercourse experiences. *Journal of Sex Research, 32,* 3–15.

Thompson, S. C., Anderson, K., Freedom, D., & Swan, J. (1996). Illusions of safety in a risky world: A study of college students' condom use. *Journal of Applied Social Psychology, 26,* 189–210.

Weinberg, M. S., Lottes, I. L., & Aveline, D. (1998). AIDS risk reduction strategies among United States and Swedish heterosexual university students. *Archives of Sexual Behavior, 27,* 385–401.

Zellman, G. L., & Goodchilds, J. K. (1983). Becoming sexual in adolescence. In E. R. Allgeier & N. B. McCormick (Eds.), *Changing boundaries. Gender roles and sexual behavior* (pp. 49–63). Palo Alto, CA: Mayfield.

CHAPTER 15

What Turns Women On?

Black and White Women's Sexual Arousal

Katrenia Y. Reed Hughes
Veanne N. Anderson

When Hughes and Anderson ask the question, "What Turns Women On?," they attempt to cross the generally male-dominated research divide. Not only does their research answer the question posed, it takes another step in the direction of understanding female sexuality by demonstrating differences between Black and White women's sexual arousal. Although humans generally need tactile stimulation to become fully sexually aroused, numerous studies have found that exposure to sexually-explicit erotic stimuli, such as pornographic films, can elicit sexual arousal (Exton et al. 2006).

Of the many factors believed to be involved in sexual arousal, gender differences have been found to be the most significant. In discussing the findings from a recent study of gender effects in sexual arousal, Youn (2006) admonished researchers to remember that both social and biological factors contribute to the process of gender formation, and, thus, both of these variables must be considered when interpreting gender differences. While gender differences in

sexual arousal are well-established, little is known about sexual arousal among women from different races. Research has, however, identified racial stereotypes as a factor in sexual arousal. In a study that examined White subjects' perceptions of Black and White characters in sexually explicit movies, Black men were stereotypically judged to be more sexually potent than White men (Davis and Cross 1979). Such stereotypes about Black male sexual prowess have been referred to frequently in historical and literary works, but little scientific data exists to support such assertions. Earlier, several Black writers indicated that a common denominator of racial prejudice among Whites was the attribution of higher sexual potency to Blacks, a claim that also remains unsubstantiated in the psychological and medical literature (Davis and Cross 1979).

As you read the Hughes and Anderson research, ask yourself the following questions: What role, if any, has stereotypical thinking played in interpreting the results? Also, have any stereotypical gender assumptions been made? If so, what is the relative role of both social and biological factors? And, why do you think that significantly more White female subjects declined participation in the phase of the study which involved viewing of the sexually explicit films? Finally, do you believe the Black/White differences can be better explained

From "What Turns Women On?: Black and White Women's Sexual Arousal" by K. Y. R. Hughes, and V. N. Anderson. 2007. *International Journal of Sexual Health 19*: 17–31. Reprinted by permission of the publisher (Taylor & Francis, http://www.informaworld.com).

by biological or sociological factors? Sharing your ideas with your classmates or your professor can expand your thinking about the balance of objective and subjective factors in research.

The enhanced eroticism of people of different races or from different cultures is a perception that has historical roots (Nagel, 2003) and that still exists today (Middleton, 2002). Clichés such as "jungle fever," "the forbidden fruit" and "opposites attract" have all been used to try to put into words the phenomenon that occurs when individuals who are considered to be unusual matches by the larger society, end up as sexual partners.

People who are considered different or exotic may be perceived as being more erotic; however, this perception does not necessarily lead to sexual relationships with exotic others. For example, surveys of convenience samples of university students indicate that at least half are willing to become romantically involved with or to date someone of another race (Fiebert, Karamol, & Kasdan, 2000; Knox, Zusman, Buffington, & Hemphill, 2000); however, most people in the United States actually date and have other types of intimate relationships with people of their own race. Based on the National Health and Social Life Survey (NHSLS) of a random sample of 18 to 59 year old American adults, Laumann, Gagnon, Michael, and Michaels (1994) found that the majority of people reported sexual relationships only with a person of the same race. Similarly, marriages between Blacks and Whites accounted for only .68% of the total marriages in 2002, up from .33% in 1980 (U.S. Bureau of the Census, 2004).

Interracial dating and sexual/marital relationships are also moderated by race and gender. Surveys of convenience samples of university students indicate that Black men are more likely than White men to report having dated (Fiebert et al., 2000) or having had sex with a woman of another race (Belcastro, 1985). No differences were found between Black and White women in

either study. In the NHSLS study, Black-White nonmarital or noncohabitational sexual relationships were more common among heterosexual Black men (7.6%) and White women (6.4%) than among heterosexual White men (.6%) and Black women (1%) (Laumann et al., 1994). Also, of the Black-White marriages in 2002, 70.6% were between a Black man and a White woman (U.S. Bureau of the Census, 2004).

It is probably not surprising that sexual and other intimate relationships are more likely to be intraracial, not interracial, given that people tend to be attracted to and fall in love with others who share similar values, social class, and family histories (Rubin, 1973). However, the fact that Black women are less likely than White women to be involved in interracial sexual or marital relationships (U.S. Bureau of the Census, 2004) deservers further explanation. Baumeister and Tice (2001) suggested that Black women may "hold prejudices against others and favor their own group, or possibly all other groups are prejudiced against them" (p. 257). These prejudices may, in turn, lead to fewer interracial sexual relationships among Black women.

Another factor that may contribute to the lower rate of interracial relationships among Black women is that Black women are not as sexually aroused by White men as White women are by Black men. This relative lack of sexual arousal may lead to less desire or motivation in Black women to pursue sexual relationships with White men. Although there is a fairly extensive literature on sex differences in what people find sexually arousing (e.g., Chivers, Rieger, Latty, & Bailey, 2004; Glascock, 2005; Mosher & McIan, 1994; Pearson & Pollack, 1997), studies investigating what different groups of women, i.e., Black women and White women, find sexually arousing are still lacking (Wiederman, Maynard & Fretz, 1996).

The primary purpose of this study was to explore the differences and similarities in Black and White women's subjective sexual arousal to different erotica. Several studies have demonstrated that women tend to prefer erotic films that are more woman-centered; that is, films where the woman is more active and the sexuality is more focused on the woman's pleasure (Mosher & McIan, 1994; Pearson & Pollack, 1997). In our study, women viewed woman-centered erotic films that featured heterosexual couples that were either Black or White. Ideally, we also wanted to include films that featured interracial couples, i.e., a Black man with a White woman and a White man with a Black woman. At the time we were looking we had difficulty finding interracial films that were woman-centered. Other researchers have noted the tendency for interracial erotica to exaggerate racial and gender stereotypes. For example, in interracial films, men, especially Black men, tend to be portrayed as "sex machines" and somewhat lacking in affection (Cowan & Campbell, 1994). Women, especially Black women, were portrayed as submissive to domination. Also, the men in the interracial videos tended to be more physically and verbally aggressive to their female partners than men in the same-race videos.

The second purpose of the study was to examine factors that may moderate or contribute to women's sexual arousal. First, willingness to date or have sex with someone of another race may enhance arousal to erotica featuring other-race actors. Increased willingness may cause the viewer to attribute more positive characteristics to the exotic actors, thus enhancing arousal. A second factor that may be related to subjective arousal in women is sex guilt, or guilt about one's sexual value system (Abramson & Mosher, 1975). Women who have high levels of sex guilt tend to report less sexual arousal to erotica than women who have low levels of sex guilt (Pearson & Pollack, 1997). Also, Black women may have higher levels of sex guilt than White women (Wyatt & Dunn, 1991). It is predicted that higher levels of sex guilt will be associated with a lower likelihood of reporting sexual arousal, especially in Black women.

A third factor that was investigated was sensation seeking, or the desire to seek novel or exciting adventures (Zuckerman, Kolin, Price, & Zoob, 1964). Higher levels of sensation seeking in women are associated with greater sexual desire, more sexual arousability, a more positive attitude toward sex, a higher frequency of sexual activities, and more sexual partners (Apt & Hurlbert, 1992; Gaither & Sellbom, 2003). Also, Williams (1982) found that high sensation seekers tend to exhibit more attraction to others who are dissimilar to them. Few studies have investigated racial or ethnic differences in sensation seeking, although Kurtz and Zuckerman (1978) found no significant differences between Black and White college students on the Sensation Seeking Scale. We predicted no significant differences between Black and White women in levels of sensation seeking. It was also expected that higher levels of sensation seeking, and hence more desire of novel experiences, would be predictive of more subjective arousal to both same-race and other-race erotica; however, sensation seeking would be a stronger predictor of erotica featuring other-race actors than erotica featuring same-race actors.

The final factor investigated was the attractiveness of the actors in the film. Janssen et al. (2003) found that the attractiveness of the male actor significantly predicted subjective arousal of heterosexual women to erotic films. We predicted that attractiveness of the male actor would be a significant predictor of arousal to the Black and White erotica for both Black and White women. However, given that most people tend to be attracted to those who are similar to them (Rubin, 1973), attractiveness of the male actor may be a stronger predictor for reported arousal when women are watching the video with actors similar to them in race.

The study was conducted in two parts. During Part One, Black and White women completed measures of sex guilt, sensation seeking, and demographic and intimate relationship information, including willingness to date and have sex with someone of the same or different race. Women returned for Part Two and rated their subjective sexual arousal to erotic videos, as well as other aspects of the videos (i.e., actor attractiveness).

METHOD

Participants

Part One. Participants were 46 African Descent/ Black (referred to as Black) and 75 European Descent/White (referred to as White) women who were students at a Midwestern university. Black women were over-sampled to insure an adequate sample size. At the time the data were collected, Black students accounted for about 10% (50.5% women and 49.5% men) and White students accounted for about 81.5% (53.4% women and 46.6% men) of the student population at the university. All women indicated they were heterosexual and at least 18 years old. Overall, the average age was 20.2; however, Black women were significantly younger than White women. First-year students accounted for the majority of the sample and most of the women were dating or single/not cohabiting.

Part Two. Thirty-six (78.3%) of the Black women and 37 (49.3%) of the White women who participated in Part One of the study returned to participate in Part Two of the study. Overall, the average age was 20.6 years. Similar to the participants in Part One, Black women were significantly younger than White women; first-year students accounted for the majority of the sample; and most of the women were single/not cohabiting or dating.

Measures and Stimuli

Part One. Participants completed the Revised Mosher Sex Guilt Inventory (Mosher, 1987), the Sensation Seeking Scale (Zuckerman et al., 1964), and a demographics questionnaire.

The Revised Mosher Sex Guilt Inventory is a 50-item, forced choice, pencil and paper, self-report measure of the level of guilt experienced with a person's sexual values system. Higher scores indicate more guilt related to their sexual values system.

The Sensation Seeking Scale is a 40-item, forced choice, pencil and paper, self-report measure of a person's need for novel sensations and experiences, with higher scores indicating more desire to seek out novel experiences and sensations.

The demographics questionnaire asked for information on race, age, educational level, relationship status, sexual orientation, and dating and sexual experiences with people of other races. Responses to four of the dating and sexual experiences items were included in subsequent analyses. Two items with a yes/no format asked if the participant had ever dated or engaged in sexual activity with someone of a different race. The other two items addressed how willing the participant would be to date a person of a different race and how willing the participant would be to have sex with a person of a different race (Likert-type scale with 1 being "not at all" and 7 being "extremely"). The remaining questions asked about dating and sexual experiences with older people and were used as filler items.

Three video excerpts with audio ranging from five to seven minutes in length were shown. Two of the videos were erotic and portrayed one man and one woman engaging in explicit, heterosexually oriented behavior including kissing, genital fondling, and vaginal intercourse. One of the erotic videos featured Black actors (Black video) and the other featured White actors (White video). The third, or neutral, video portrayed a nature scene that did not include any human activity. This neutral video was included to alleviate potential carryover effects from the first erotic video to the second erotic video.

The measure of subjective sexual arousal was constructed from components of the Ratings of Sexual Arousal (Mosher, Barton-Henry, & Green, 1988) and consisted of seven Likert-type items on a scale of 1 (no arousal at all) to 7 (extremely arousing). The items asked participants how sexually arousing they found the video segment and setting (two separate questions), how romantic they found the video segment and setting (two separate questions), and how enjoyable, exciting, and stimulating they found the video segment. Responses to each of the seven items were summed; total scores could range from 7 to 49 with higher scores indicating more subjective sexual arousal.

Participants also completed a measure to assess how similar the two erotic videos were in terms of general similarity, attractiveness of the male and female actors, the romantic quality, foreplay, and the portrayal of sexual behaviors (1 = "not at all similar" and 7 = "extremely similar"). Two additional questions asked how attractive the participants found the male actor and the female actor in each of the two erotic videos (1 = "not at all attractive" and 7 = "extremely attractive").

Procedures

Part One. The participants were tested in groups of 30 to 40 people. The women were informed that they would be eligible to participate in Part Two of the study and they were given information about the questionnaires and the sexually explicit nature of the videos that would be used in the second part.

The women then completed the Revised Mosher Sex Guilt Inventory, Sensation Seeking Scale, and the demographics questionnaire. Completed questionnaires were returned to the researcher in envelopes to protect privacy. The participants were then debriefed and reminded that they would be contacted regarding their participation in Part Two. They were also offered course extra credit, a small monetary reward, or a small gift for their participation.

Part Two. Testing for Part Two took place approximately two to three weeks after Part One. Each participant was tested individually. Participants were shown the first erotic video followed by the neutral video, and then the second erotic video. The erotic videos were presented in a counterbalanced order such that half of the participants received the video with the Black actors first, and half received the video with the White actors first. The neutral video was always

presented second. Participants were randomly assigned to each order with the stipulation that half of the Black and half of the White women viewed one order and the remaining women viewed the other order.

At the end of each video excerpt, the participant was asked to stop the videotape and complete the measure of subjective sexual arousal. The two questions asking about the attractiveness of the male and female actors were also completed at this time only for the erotic videos. Once she had completed the subjective measure for a given video, the woman was instructed to restart the tape to view the next video segment. This process was repeated until all three videos had been presented and all questionnaires had been completed and sealed in separate envelopes. After viewing the three video excerpts, the participant was requested to complete the comparability measures for the two erotic video segments. Participants were then debriefed and offered extra credit in a course, a small monetary reward, or a small gift for their participation.

RESULTS

Part One

Sex guilt and sensation seeking. Sex Guilt scores did not differ significantly between Black and White women. However, Black women had significantly lower scores than White women on the Sensation Seeking Scale. Higher sex guilt scores were associated with lower sensation seeking scores for both Black women and White women.

Dating and sexual experiences. There were no significant differences between the proportions of Black women (45.7%) and White women (33.3%) who indicated having dated someone of another race. Black and White women did not differ in their willingness to date, or have sex with someone of another race. Only 49 women responded to the question about having had sex with someone of a different race. Among these women, White women (80.8%) were more likely than Black women (43.5%) to report having had sex with someone of a different race.

Sex guilt scores did not correlate significantly with the dating and sexual experiences items for Black and White women. Sensation seeking scores were not significantly correlated with any of the dating and sexual experiences items for White women; however, there were significant correlations for the Black women. Black women with higher sensation seeking scores were more likely to be willing to date and to have sex with a person of another race.

Part Two

Compared to White women (50.7%), a significantly higher proportion of Black women (76.1%) agreed to return and participate in Part Two. As with Part One, there were no significant differences between the proportions of Black women (41.7%) and White women (24.3%) who indicated having dated someone of another race. Only 26 of the women who participated in Part Two had responded to the question about having had sex with someone of a different race. As with the sample in Part One, there was a tendency for more White women to report having had sex with someone of a different race than Black women (77.8% vs. 47.1%, respectively); however, unlike the results in Part One, this difference was not statistically significant.

Tests indicated that Black women were more likely than White women to find that the male and female actors differed in attractiveness in the two erotic videos. Further analyses of the two items assessing how attractive women found the male and female actors in each of the two erotic videos indicated that Black women rated the Black actors as more attractive than the White. There were no significant differences in the attractiveness ratings of the White women. There were no significant differences in the ratings of the general similarity, romantic quality, foreplay, and sexual behaviors of the two erotic videos.

The tests of within-subject contrasts revealed that subjective sexual arousal scores were higher for the erotic videos when compared to the neutral video.

Regardless of the video order, Black women reported significantly more arousal to the Black video than the White video. In contrast, White women reported similar arousal to the Black and White videos regardless of the video order. Nevertheless, when the Black video was shown first, Black and White women had similar levels of arousal to the Black video, but Black women's arousal to the White video was significantly less than White women's arousal. The reverse was true when the White video was shown first. Black and White women did not differ significantly in arousal to the White video, but Black women reported more arousal to the Black video than did White women.

There were no significant interaction effects for the type of video and the video order or for the interaction of the sensation seeking scores and the type of video.

In order to identify which variables would significantly predict sexual arousal scores, analyses were conducted separately for Black and White women for each of the two erotic videos. Predictor variables were the sex guilt scores, sensation seeking scores, attractiveness ratings for the male actor, and the ratings on the item assessing the willingness to have sex with someone of another race (White women's arousal to the Black video; Black women's arousal to the White video) or same race (White women's arousal to the White video; Black women's arousal to the Black video).

White women who found the Black male actor more attractive and who were less willing to have sex with someone of another race were more likely to report higher sexual arousal scores to the Black video. Lower sex guilt scores and higher attractiveness ratings for the White male actor significantly predicted White women's sexual arousal to the White video. None of the predictors were associated significantly with Black women's sexual arousal scores to the White video; however, Black women reported more arousal to the Black video when the Black male actor was rated as being more attractive.

A second analysis was conducted only on the sexual arousal scores for White women to the Black video and Black women to the White video. The predictors were the same as the preceding analyses except that instead of ratings of the willingness to have sex with a person of another race, ratings of the willingness to date a person of another race were included as a predictor variable. Results were similar to the preceding results. White women who found the Black male actor more attractive and were less willing to date someone of another race were more likely to report higher sexual arousal scores to the Black video. None of the predictors were associated significantly with Black women's sexual arousal scores to the White video.

DISCUSSION

Similar to the results of other studies (Todd & McKinney, 1992), Black and White women did not differ significantly in their reported willingness to date or have sex with someone of another race. Other studies report contradictory findings (Fiebert et al., 2000; Knox et al., 2000) that may be due to differences in samples (age, educational level, region of country, etc.). It would be worthwhile to examine the effects of the racial composition of a community on the willingness and opportunities available to have intimate interracial relationships. For example, the percentage of racial minorities at schools may affect students' willingness to establish interracial friendships and dating relationships (Korgen, Mahon, & Wang, 2003) and actual experiences with interracial dating (Yancey, 2002).

Although Black women were just as likely as White women to have dated someone of another race, White women were more likely than Black women to report having had sex with someone of another race. This latter finding may be biased

by the fact that not all women responded to the question about sex with someone of another race, but it agrees with other findings indicating stronger same-race preferences among Black women than White women for sexual (Laumann et al., 1994) and marital partners (U.S. Bureau of the Census, 2004).

Black and White women showed different patterns of subjective sexual arousal to the erotic videos. Black women reported more subjective arousal to the Black video than the White video, whereas White women did not show significant differences in their subjective sexual arousal to the two erotic videos. Historically Black women have experienced sexual exploitation by White men (Nagel, 2003) and have endured racist sexual stereotypes (Stephens & Phillips, 2003). These experiences may have produced negative attitudes or even prejudice (Baumeister & Tice, 2001) towards White men in general and a stronger allegiance to Black men. In turn, the negativity towards White men and the stronger allegiance to Black men may directly cause Black women to be less sexually aroused by videos depicting White actors. The effect may be more indirect as well; even though sexual arousal may be present, Black women may be reluctant to report such arousal to erotica that feature White actors. On the other hand, White women may have less prejudicial views of intimate relationships with Black men which may make them less reluctant to report their sexual arousal to erotica featuring people of another race. Future research should assess the strength of commitment to one's race, i.e., racial identity, and how that affects sexual arousal to videos portraying people of other races or ethnicities.

Significant predictors of sexual arousal also differed between Black and White women. Willingness to have sex with (or to date) someone of another race was a significant predictor of sexual arousal only for White women; however, the result was contrary to what was predicted. White women with higher levels of sexual arousal to the Black video were less willing to have sex with someone of another race. Although counterintuitive, this finding may be due in part to misattribution of the source of arousal (White, Fishbein, & Rutstein, 1981). White women who reported being less willing to have sex with someone of another race may experience discomfort or other negative emotions when viewing an erotic film with Black actors. These negative emotions may cause arousal which, given the circumstances of watching an erotic film, lead the women to attribute the arousal as being sexual. Additional research is needed to address the roles of negative emotions in arousal and how that arousal is labeled when viewing erotica. For example, Adams, Wright, and Lohr (1996) found that more homophobic men showed more physical sexual arousal, but reported less subjective sexual arousal, to gay male erotica than did less homophobic men. It would be worthwhile to include a measure of racial bias to determine if White women who hold more racist attitudes would report more or less subjective arousal to the Black video. Perhaps under other circumstances, positive associations with exotic stimuli may enhance sexual arousal.

Unlike Wyatt and Dunn (1991) we did not find significant differences between White and Black women's scores on the sex guilt scale. Different samples and the year of the study may account for this difference. Also, White women who reported more sexual arousal to the White video had lower levels of sex guilt (see also Pearson & Pollack, 1997). However, sex guilt was not predictive of White women's sexual arousal to the Black video or Black women's sexual arousal to either erotic video. It is possible that sex guilt may have specific effects depending on the type of erotica and the characteristics of the viewers (i.e., race or ethnicity). Also, the ready access to and proliferation of sexually explicit images in movies, on the Internet, and in advertising may result in some desensitization to such material, rendering sex guilt less likely to be predictive of sexual arousal (Gerrard, 1982).

Contrary to our prediction, White women had significantly higher levels of sensation seeking than Black women. Higher levels of sensation seeking were significantly correlated with Black women's willingness to date and have sex with a person of another race. Sensation seeking was also significantly and negatively correlated with levels of sex guilt in both groups of women. However, sensation seeking was not a significant predictor of sexual arousal for either group of women. One possible explanation for these findings is that sensation seeking tends to be fairly high in women who volunteer for sexuality research, hence reducing the variability in levels of sensation seeking (Wiederman, 1999). Also, we used a more general measure of sensation seeking which has been found to be less predictive of sexual measures than a scale that explicitly measures sexual sensation seeking (Gaither & Sellbom, 2003).

Higher ratings of physical attractiveness of the male actor were predictive of higher levels of sexual arousal for Black women to the Black video and for White women to both erotic videos. Physical attractiveness is an important element in sexual attraction (Langlois, Kalakanis, Rubenstein, Larson, Hallam, & Smoot, 2000) and has been found to predict sexual arousal of heterosexual women in other studies (Janssen et al., 2003). The fact that Black women's arousal to the White video was not predicted by the actor's attractiveness may be partly explained by the finding that Black women found the White male actor to be significantly less attractive than the Black male actor. White women did not rate the White and Black male actors differently on physical attractiveness. Black women may adhere more to the notion that people with similar characteristics to themselves are more attractive (Rubin, 1973). Once again, these beliefs may arise because of historical experiences of Black women with White men as alluded to earlier, or in-group biases concerning what is or is not socially acceptable sexual behavior, e.g., attraction to White men is bad.

The results of our study indicate that women are not a homogeneous group when it comes to sexual behavior. More research is needed on diverse groups of women to improve and advance theories of sexual arousal. For example, future studies should include woman-centered videos featuring an interracial couple, specifically Black women with White men and White women with Black men. It is possible that women may respond differently to interracial erotica, as compared to intraracial erotica, and that their sexual arousal depends on whether it is the male or female actor who is of the same or different race. Also, women and men may differ in the strength of the association between genital arousal and subjective sexual arousal (Chivers et al., 2004; however, see Rellini, McCall, Randall, & Meston, 2005 for a critique), but less is known about ethnic or racial differences and similarities in the correlations between these two types of sexual arousal. For example, do Black and White women differ in the correlation between subjective and genital sexual arousal and do different types of stimuli such as erotica featuring same-race or other-race actors affect that correlation? Including physiological measures other than genital, such as heart rate or skin sensitivity, would also be useful given that some women may perceive nongenital sources of arousal to be more salient than genital sources (Graham, Sanders, Milhausen, & McBride, 2004).

There are well known inherent biases in the types of college students who volunteer for sexuality research (Wiederman, 1999). Although some participant biases may be hard to control for, other biases may be alleviated. For example, sexuality research on women of different ethnicities is still lacking. We included heterosexual White and Black women in our sample, but other groups need to be studied, i.e., Latinas, Native Americans, women of Asian descent, multiracial women, and women of different sexual orientations.

In addition to volunteer biases, there may be effects of researcher characteristics on the responses of participants. For example, the ethnicity or race of the researcher(s) is rarely mentioned in studies of sexual behavior. We found that a higher percentage of Black women than White women returned to participate in the second part of our study and speculated that this may be due to the fact that the researcher was a Black woman. This Black researcher's effects on other aspects of the participants' behavior or study are unknown, but research is needed to clarify these effects. For example, participants may differ in their self-reports of sexual arousal in the presence of a same-race or other-race researcher. Also, Janssen et al. (2003) have shown that the sex of the researcher may affect the kinds of films chosen for sexual arousal studies, which in turn may influence participants' responses to erotica. Therefore, race or ethnicity of the researcher choosing the erotic stimuli is another factor that should be taken into account. Finally, our results point to the need to consider not only the race or ethnicity of the participants, but also the race and ethnicity of the actors/characters in erotic stimuli when selecting sexually explicit materials and the order in which the stimuli are shown. Black women reported more arousal to the Black video overall and White women reported equal arousal to both erotic videos; however, the order of presentation moderated sexual arousal.

One theory which may be useful in understanding the sexual arousal of women of different races or ethnicities is sexual involvement theory. Sexual involvement theory (Mosher, 1988) posits that for sexual arousal to occur, the actors and actions portrayed in the sexually explicit materials have to match the viewer's sexual scripts and preferences. For example, women may be more aroused by female-oriented erotica than male-oriented erotica because women have an easier time imagining themselves in the roles of the actors in female-oriented erotica, i.e., the female-oriented erotica is a better match with their sexual scripts than the male-oriented erotica (Pearson & Pollack, 1997). Similarly, Black and White women may develop different sexual scripts because of historical experiences, cultural standards, and in-group biases. These scripts may determine what stimuli are or are not sexually arousing and with whom women can or cannot have sexual relationships. Also, erotic stimuli such as films and writings may be more similar to fantasy sexual scripts that do not necessarily reflect the sexual script that guides a person's sexual behavior. Sexual fantasies are very common but they do not necessarily represent behavior that the person will act on (Leitenberg & Henning, 1995). The study of the sexual fantasies of Black and White women might elucidate whether those fantasies predict sexual arousal to materials portraying other-race actors or interracial relationships, and the likelihood of becoming sexually involved with someone of another race.

INTRODUCTION REFERENCES

Davis, G. L., and H. J. Cross. 1979. Sexual stereotyping of Black males interracial sex. *Archives of Sexual Behavior* 8: 169–79.

Exton, N., T. Truong, M. Exton, S. Wingenfeld, N. Leygraf, B. Saller, et al. 2006. Neuroendocrine response to film-induced sexual arousal in men and women. *Psychoneuroendrocrinology* 25: 187–99.

Youn, G. 2006. Subjective sexual arousal in response to erotica: Effects of gender, guided fantasy, erotic stimulus, and duration of exposure. *Archives of Sexual Behavior* 35: 87–97.

REFERENCES

Abramson, P. R., & Mosher, D. L. (1975). Development of a measure of negative attitudes toward masturbation. *Journal of Consulting and Clinical Psychology, 43,* 485–490.

Adams, H., Wright, L., & Lohr, B. (1996). Is homophobia associated with homosexual arousal? *Journal of Abnormal Psychology, 105,* 440–446.

Apt, C. & Hurlbert, D. F. (1992). The female sensation seeker and marital sexuality. *Journal of Sex and Marital Therapy, 18,* 315–324.

Baumeister, R. F., & Tice, D. M. (2001). *The social dimension of sex.* Boston: Allyn and Bacon.

Belcastro, P. A. (1985). Sexual behavior differences between Black and White students. *The Journal of Sex Research, 21,* 56–67.

Chivers, M. L., Rieger, G., Latty, E., & Bailey, J. M. (2004). A sex difference in the specificity of sexual arousal. *Psychological Science, 15,* 736–744.

Cowan, G., & Campbell, R. R. (1994). Racism and sexism in interracial pornography: A content analysis. *Psychology of Women Quarterly, 18,* 323–338.

Fiebert, M. S., Karamol, H., & Kasdan, M. (2000). Interracial dating: Attitudes and experience among American college students in California. *Psychological Reports, 87,* 1059–1064.

Gaither, G. A., & Sellbom, M. (2003). The sexual sensation seeking scale: Reliability and validity within a heterosexual college student sample. *Journal of Personality Assessment, 81,* 157–167.

Gerrard, M. (1982). Sex, sex guilt, and contraceptive use. *Journal of Personality & Social Psychology, 42,* 153–158.

Glascock, J. (2005). Degrading content and character sex: Accounting for men and women's differential reactions to pornography. *Communication Reports, 18,* 43–53.

Graham, C. A., Sanders, S. A., Milhausen, R. R., & McBride, K. R. (2004). Turning on and turning off: A focus group study of the factors that affect women's sexual arousal. *Archives of Sexual Behavior, 33,* 527–538.

Janssen, E., Carpenter, D., & Graham, C. A. (2003). Selecting films for sex research: Gender differences in erotic film preference. *Archives of Sexual Behavior, 32,* 243–251.

Knox, D., Zusman, M. E., Buffington, C., & Hemphill, G. (2000). Interracial dating attitudes among college students. *College Student Journal, 34,* 69–71.

Korgen, K. O., Mahon, J., Wang, G. (2003). Diversity on college campuses today: The growing need to foster campus environments capable of countering a possible "tipping effect". *College Student Journal, 37,* 16–26.

Kurtz, J. P., & Zuckerman, M. (1978). Race and sex differences on the sensation seeking scales. *Psychological Reports, 43,* 529–530.

Langlois, J. H., Kalakanis, L., Rubenstein, A. J., Larson, A., Hallam, M., & Smoot, M. (2000). Maxims or myths of beauty? A meta-analytic and theoretical review. *Psychological Bulletin, 126,* 390–423.

Laumann, E. O., Gagnon, J. H., Michael, R. T., & Michaels, S. (1994). *The social organization of sexuality: Sexual practices in the United States.* Chicago: University of Chicago Press.

Leitenberg, H. & Henning, K. (1995). Sexual fantasy. *Psychological Bulletin, 117,* 469–496.

Middleton, D. R. (2002). *Exotics and erotics: Human cultural and sexual diversity.* Prospect Heights, IL: Waveland Press.

Mosher, D. L. (1987). Revised Mosher Sex Guilt Inventory. In D. H. Davis, W. Yarber, & S. Davis (Eds.), *Sexuality-related measures: A compendium* (pp. 152–155). Lake Mills, IA: Graphic Publishing Co.

Mosher, D. L. (1988). Pornography defined: Sexual involvement theory, narrative context, and goodness-of-fit. *Journal of Psychology & Human Sexuality, 1,* 67–85.

Mosher, D. L., Barton-Henry, M., & Green, S. E. (1988). Subjective sexual arousal and involvement: Development of multiple indicators. *The Journal of Sex Research, 25,* 412–425.

Mosher, D. L., & McIan, P. (1994). College men and women respond to x-rated videos intended for male or female audiences: Gender and sexual scripts. *The Journal of Sex Research, 31,* 99–109.

Nagel, J. (2003). *Race, ethnicity, and sexuality: Intimate intersection frontiers.* New York: Oxford University Press.

Pearson, S. E., & Pollack, R. H. (1997). Female response to sexually explicit films. *Journal of Psychology & Human Sexuality, 9,* 73–88.

Rellini, A. H., McCall, K. M., Randall, P. K., & Meston, C. M. (2005). The relationship between women's subjective and physiological sexual arousal. *Psychophysiology, 42,* 116–124.

Rubin, Z. (1973). *Liking and loving: An invitation to social psychology.* Oxford, England: Holt, Rinehart, & Winston.

Stephens, D. P., & Phillips, L. D. (2003). Freaks, gold diggers, divas, and dykes: The sociohistorical development of adolescent African American women's sexual scripts. *Sexuality & Culture: An Interdisciplinary Quarterly, 7,* 3–49.

Todd, J., & McKinney, J. L. (1992). Attitudes toward interracial dating: Effects of age, sex, and race. *Journal of Multicultural Counseling and Development, 20,* 202–208.

U.S. Bureau of the Census (2004, September 15). *Table MS-3. Interracial married couples: 1980 to 2002.* Retrieved June 1, 2005, from http://www.census.gov/population/socdemo/hh-fam/tabMS-3.pdf.

White, G. L., Fishbein, S., & Rutsein, J. (1981). Passionate love and the misattribution of arousal. *Journal of Personality & Social Psychology, 41,* 56–62.

Wiederman, M. W. (1999). Volunteer bias in sexuality research using college student participants. *The Journal of Sex Research, 36,* 59–66.

Wiederman, M. W., Maynard, C., & Fretz, A. (1996). Ethnicity in 25 years of published sexuality research: 1971–1995. *The Journal of Sex Research, 33,* 339–342.

Williams, S. (1982). The effects of sensation seeking and misattribution of arousal on attraction toward similar or dissimilar strangers. *Journal of Research in Personality, 16,* 217–226.

Wyatt, G. E., & Dunn, K. M. (1991). Examining predictors of sex guilt in multiethnic samples of women. *Archives of Sexual Behavior, 20,* 471–485.

Yancey, G. (2002). Who interracially dates: An examination of the characteristics of those who have interracially dated. *Journal of Comparative Family Studies, 33,* 179–190.

Zuckerman, M., Kolin, E., Price, A., & Zoob, I. (1964). Development of a sensation seeking scale. *Journal of Consulting Psychology, 28,* 477–482.

PART IV

Sexuality and the Life Cycle: Middle and Later Adulthood

The woman of 60, flying to her winter home in Florida, conveyed a somewhat convoluted saga to her seatmate. Her latest boyfriend, a 70-year-old businessman, had recently acquired a mark of distinction from his peers when sued by a young female employee for sexual harassment. Although neither the woman nor the jury faulted her boyfriend, it troubled her mother, age 85, whose 91-year-old fifth husband had read about it in a professional business journal he had received in his office (Clendinen 2000). Such copy may seem to set the stage for an off-Broadway play, but this actually occurred, epitomizing "third-stage adulthood"—the fastest growing demographic category in America.

It was not until the second half of the twentieth century that changing demographics, resulting from the "graying of America," spawned the fertile field of geriatrics to care for America's fastest growing population, the elderly. In this process a face was finally placed on sexuality throughout a lengthening life span. Sex therapists and sexuality educators with a life-span perspective have responded to the need to expand their services to encompass new markets. Sexuality researchers have also expanded their parameters beyond the issues of the early adolescent and the young adult years, as reflected in the selections in this unit that showcase

sexuality in the middle and later years. Regardless of the market or issues, a firm understanding of life-span sexuality development can contribute to personal happiness or professional success. This knowledge is especially important for today's aspiring sexuality professionals who will work with myriad populations in search of individual and family stability.

In an offering new to this Part, Jay Teachman investigates whether or not premarital sex and/or cohabitation might be among the obstacles that threaten marital stability. Teachman uses nationally representative data from the 1995 National Survey of Family Growth to estimate the association between intimate premarital relationships, either premarital sex or premarital cohabitation, and subsequent marital dissolution among women. Surprisingly, the literature on the relationship between premarital intercourse and divorce is limited, while research showing a strong association between premarital cohabitation and divorce is fairly common. Teachman extends prior research by studying the joint effects of both types of intimate premarital relationships.

The *selection perspective* and the *experience perspective* are the two views used in research to explain the links between cohabitation and marital dissolution. The *selection perspective* assumes that cohabitors and non-cohabitors possess differing characteristics that affect marital outcomes (Dush, Cohen, and Amato 2003), while the *experience perspective* assumes that something about the process of cohabitation itself increases the likelihood of problems possibly leading to divorce. The offering included here is unique in that it combines a measure of both perspectives by considering the relationship histories pertaining to premarital sex as well as the experience of premarital cohabitation itself. Students will be intrinsically interested in the topic that addresses a life-style experienced by more than 5.1 million heterosexual couples in the United States today (Olson and Olson-Sigg 2007). This number represents a ten-fold increase since the 1970s, a time remembered by their parents as the era of open marriage, communes and group marriages. From all of the former alternate life-styles practices, cohabitation is the only one that still thrives today, an interesting topic for a class discussion.

Helping couples decode the language of their sexuality in "Passionate Marriage," David Schnarch addresses what he calls the vortex of the emotional struggle in marriage. He believes that in order to grow, each must hold on to self in the context of the other. This seasoned therapist is a founder of the Sexual Crucible Approach, which conceptually integrates individual, sexual, and marital therapies. The article included here is not just for those few who would be sex therapists. It is included because it illustrates that sexual-marital therapy is an excellent context for developing personal growth and relationships. This selection is a timely feature about the middle adult years, one of the foci of this unit. When marriages end through divorce at this juncture in life, they usually do so because of having been "neglected to death." As such malaise is addressed, nearly always, sexuality is raised as an issue. Those whose interest is piqued by this article are referred to Schnarch's (1991) breakthrough book, *Constructing the Sexual Crucible: An Integration of Sexual and Marital Therapy*. In presenting the reality of our struggles with sex, he engages in highly explicit discussion of

what goes on in bed. The time spent reading this selection will yield rich dividends.

Middle-aged individuals have never been much of a focus for sex researchers. While the prospect of developing treatments for erectile dysfunction has resulted in increasing interest in the physiological sexual functioning of middle-aged men, for the most part, women in mid-life have been ignored by researchers. This is evidenced by the fact that there is still not a clear understanding of how menopause really affects women's sexuality. In addition, the emotional aspects of middle-age sexuality have been largely neglected. The article by Carpenter, Nathanson, and Kim included here is a significant attempt to correct such imbalances.

In this intriguing analysis of data from the 1992 National Health and Social Life Survey (NHSLS), Carpenter et al. explore the role of physical and relational aspects of sexuality in predicting the physical and emotional sexual satisfaction of middle-aged women and men. These researchers question why the belief that men's sexual satisfaction is unrelated to relationship factors persists in the absence of empirical support for this view. Although most students may not be innately interested in reading about this age group, this article is one that should be assigned because it will almost certainly lead to interesting class discussions that challenge a number of stereotypes held by students regarding middle-aged sexuality. Topics to discuss include the importance of relationships in sexual satisfaction, the effect of menopause, and erectile dysfunction, among others.

The article by John Delamater and Sarah Moorman presents a secondary analysis of data collected for the American Association of Retired Persons (AARP). The sample is large and representative, though it may suffer from volunteer bias, which is an issue with any research that relies on volunteer participants. Nonetheless, it represents one of the best and most scientific approaches to understanding sexuality among aging adults. The study utilizes a biopsychosocial perspective which enables an understanding of the dynamics of sexuality from a biological, psychological, and social standpoint and facilitates the incorporation of various theories (Kruger 2007).

Like the Carpenter et al. chapter, this research also examines gender stereotypes. It explores which of two predictors of sexual activity, biological sex or relationship status, is the more important. In reporting the greater level of sexual activity by older men than women, the authors consider if such findings are a function of diminished desire or interest on the part of women or if they are due to the fact that older women are far more likely to be without a partner. Students will be challenged to account not only for the greater levels of sexual activity reported by men compared to women but to examine other unfounded stereotypical thinking. For example, the sparse research that does exist has noted the impact of aging on the sexuality of the baby-boomer generation, but not how the approaches to sexuality at mid-life displayed by this cohort differs from those suggested by cultural stereotypes.

The most valuable contribution of the Delamater and Moorman article may be in its presentation of the idea that sexual intimacy later in life is very much a changing reality that may assume many different faces. The finding that satisfying sexual relationships are as likely to occur in middle age and later life as in young adulthood may be a novel idea to many young readers who have a difficult time perceiving older adults, such as parent or grandparent figures, as sexual beings.

Prior to 1998, erectile dysfunction was either treated with psychotherapy or, if there was clearly a physiologically-based cause, with rather intrusive physical methods including injections and suppositories inserted directly into the penis as well as penile implants and pumps. A relatively recent development in sexology is the "medicalization" of sexual dysfunction. Now that there are medical treatments for erectile dysfunction, there has been a de-emphasis on the psychological aspects of this disorder. Further, the normal changes of age are now viewed as symptoms to be treated with medications such as Viagra. Barbara Marshall discusses this "new regime of compulsory tumescence" (p. 357) in a fascinating examination of the historical landscape of erectile dysfunction and the concept of male menopause. This focus on the need for strong, hard erections regardless of situation or age has its counterpart in the development of the concept of *female sexual dysfunction*, a medical treatment in search of a disorder (Tiefer 2006).

Marshall's article is a natural follow-up to the two previous chapters. Whereas the studies by Carpenter et al. as well as by Delamater and Moorman are empirically-based examinations of the reality of middle-aged and older adult sexual expression, the Marshall piece takes a more philosophical approach. Her focus is on the implications of a lifetime of sexuality. Accordingly, the fact that sexuality remains important throughout life even though sexual functioning does not stay the same, is a much-to-be celebrated gift of life.

REFERENCES

Buss, D. M. 1994. *Evolution of desire: Strategies of human mating.* New York: Basic Books.

Clendinen, D. 2000. Third-stage adulthood is fast-growing demographic. *New York Times,* 14 July, 15A.

Dush, C. M. K., C. L. Cohan, and P. R. Amato. 2003. The relationship between cohabitation and marital quality and stability: Change across cohorts. *Journal of Marriage and Family* 65: 539–49.

Kruger, D. J. 2007. The importance of multi-level theoretical integration in biopsychosocial research. *Psychological Topics* 16: 225–40.

Olson, D. H., and A. Olson-Sigg. 2007. *Overview of cohabitation research.* Minneapolis: Prepare/Enrich Life Innovations.

Schnarch, D. 1991. *Constructing the sexual crucible: An integration of sexual and marital therapy.* New York: Norton.

Smith, T. W. 1994. Attitudes toward sexual permissiveness: Trends, correlates, and behavioral connections. In *Sexuality across the life course* (pp. 63–97), ed. A. S. Ross. Chicago: University of Chicago Press.

Tiefer, L. 2006. Female sexual dysfunction: A case study of disease mongering and activist resistance. *PLoS Medicine* 3: 436–40.

CHAPTER 16

Premarital Sex, Premarital Cohabitation, and the Risk of Subsequent Marital Dissolution Among Women

Jay Teachman

Made in Heaven, Settled in Court *(Mitchelson 1979), the title of a book that addressed legal issues surrounding unmarried cohabitation reflected the American fascination with and ambivalence toward alternative lifestyles in the 1970s. The research on nontraditional family forms, which has increased dramatically since that time, mirrored a period of rapid social change. While the vast majority of Americans still marry, have children, live in single-family households, and prefer heterosexuality and permanent sexual exclusivity, increasingly, as the evidence indicates, other lifestyles have been embraced.*

Actually, it is a myth that even in the "good old days" there were no variations from the traditional nuclear family. But in earlier times, social and economic circumstances usually dictated alternative patterns, while today free choice is exercised in such matters. The fact is that the practice of cohabitation has been around since antiquity, existing in all types of cultures to varying degrees, even though both church and state tried to legally prohibit such behavior (Trost 1979). Even in the United States, alternative lifestyles are not new concepts. Judge Ben Lindsey proposed a trial, or "companionate," marriage as long ago as 1927 (Russell 1928). Later, during the 1960s, futurist Vance Packard (1968) urged a 2 year confirmation period for marriage partners, and anthropologist Margaret Mead (1966) proposed a "two-stage marriage," an "individual" and a "parental" marriage. That none of these earlier proposals gained widespread cultural acceptance is self-evident.*

Fairly consistent research findings concerning patterns of cohabitation today were confirmed in The Social Organization of Sexuality (Laumann, et al. 1994), the nation's most comprehensive, representative survey of sexual behavior in the general population to date. The study reported that those most likely to cohabit less frequently attended religious services, were from nonintact families, had sexual intercourse earlier, were less educated, and, for women only, had fathers with higher levels of education.

About one-half of cohabitations today are short-lived, ending within the year by either separation, marriage or death. The large proportion of cohabitations (40 percent) that end in marriage were the subject of the following investigation by Teachman, who studied the association between intimate premarital relationships and subsequent marital dissolution among women married up to 25 years. His research extends previous cohabitation research by considering the relationship histories pertaining to both premarital sex and premarital cohabitation, making it a "must read assignment" for most who are still trolling the waters for prospective marriage partners.

Unmarried heterosexual cohabitation has become very common in the United States. Among recent birth cohorts of young men and women, the majority will cohabit at some point in their lives (Smock, 2000). Bumpass and Lu (2000) estimate that nearly 60% of unions formed in the early 1990s began with cohabitation. At the same time that cohabitation has increased, so has the incidence of premarital intercourse. Among women born between 1950 and 1954, nearly one quarter experienced their first instance of sexual intercourse within marriage (Abma, Chandra, Mosher, Peterson, & Piccinino, 1997). For women born between 1965 and 1969, only about 10% had first sex within marriage. These trends clearly signify a continuing separation of marriage from the initiation of sexual intimacy and coresidential living.

Social scientists have asked what these trends mean for the nature and functioning of marriage. One of the most clearly defined correlates of cohabitation is an increased risk of marital dissolution (Bumpass, Martin, & Sweet, 1991; DeMaris & McDonald, 1993; Smock, 2000;

Teachman & Polonko, 1990). Marriages preceded by a spell of cohabitation are as much as 50% more likely to end in divorce at any marital duration than marriages not preceded by cohabitation. Although less well researched, there is also evidence to suggest that premarital intercourse is associated with an increased risk of marital disruption (Kahn & London, 1991). Using a nationally representative sample of women, I seek to extend research on the effects of intimate premarital relationships on marital stability in two ways. First, I consider the joint relationship between both premarital cohabitation and premarital intercourse and the risk of marital dissolution. Clearly, premarital sex and premarital cohabitation overlap, yet no prior research has considered their effects simultaneously. Second, I consider the effects of variations in histories of intimate, premarital relationships. In particular, I distinguish between premarital cohabitation and premarital intercourse that is limited to a woman's eventual husband from intimate relationships that occur with other men. I find that neither premarital intercourse nor premarital cohabitation, if limited to a woman's husband, is linked to the subsequent risk of marital disruption. However, intimate premarital relationships with other men are associated with a substantial increase in the likelihood of divorce.

PRIOR RESEARCH ON PREMARITAL RELATIONSHIPS AND THE RISK OF DIVORCE

Premarital Cohabitation

One of the most robust predictors of marital dissolution that has appeared in the literature is premarital cohabitation. Beginning with reports by Booth and Johnson (1988) and Bennett, Blanc, and Bloom (1988), virtually all studies of the relationship between premarital cohabitation and divorce have found a positive link. Early investigators expressed surprise at this result because it had sometimes been theorized that premarital cohabitation would act as a screening device, allowing couples to choose a mate with whom they could form a successful marriage. Two alternative explanations have been put forward to explain the consistently positive link between cohabitation and marital disruption.

The first thesis used to explain the higher risk of divorce experienced by marriages preceded by a spell of cohabitation is selectivity. A number of authors have argued that people who cohabit before marriage possess different characteristics compared with those who do not cohabit, and these characteristics are tied positively to the risk of divorce. The characteristics thought to be important in distinguishing cohabitors from noncohabitors include less commitment to marriage as a permanent institution, acceptance of divorce as an appropriate means to end a poor relationship, an emphasis on individualism, poor relationship skills, and so on. A number of studies have found evidence of selectivity, either through direct measurement of differences on important characteristics (DeMaris & MacDonald, 1993; Thomson & Colella, 1992; Thornton, Axinn, & Hill, 1992) or the use of statistical procedures that adjust for unmeasured heterogeneity distinguishing cohabitors from noncohabitors (Lillard, Brien, & Waite, 1995).

The second thesis linking premarital cohabitation to the risk of divorce focuses on the experience of cohabitation itself. That is, it is argued that there is a causal effect of having lived with someone outside of marriage that cannot otherwise be attributed to differences on other, preexisting characteristics that may be associated with the risk of marital disruption. The underlying notion in this thesis is that cohabitation allows individuals to learn about intimate living outside of marriage, provides information about alternatives to marriage, and acts to erode their belief in the permanence of marriage. Although less well researched than the selectivity argument, the thesis of a causal effect of cohabitation has also received empirical support (Axinn & Barber, 1997).

Premarital Intercourse

The literature on the relationship between premarital intercourse and divorce is limited. Kahn and London (1991) found a relatively strong positive relationship between the two. They suggested, as is the case for premarital cohabitation, that the relationship may be due to either selectivity on preexisting characteristics or altered perceptions of marriage and alternatives to marriage that occur as the result of engaging in premarital sex. Their statistical modeling strategy suggests that selectivity may be the more important mechanism to consider. Unfortunately, no study has attempted to directly measure differences in characteristics affecting the risk of divorce that might exist between women who do and women who do not engage in premarital intercourse, nor has their been any research indicating that experience with premarital sex alters attitudes toward and expectations about marriage.

EXTENDING PRIOR RESEARCH

Joint Effects of Premarital Intercourse and Premarital Cohabitation

Although the research findings are consistent, prior research can be extended in at least two ways. First, no study has simultaneously considered the relationship between both premarital cohabitation and premarital intercourse and marital dissolution. Clearly, the two are linked, and failure to consider both variables simultaneously may yield biased estimates of their effects on divorce. For example, it is reasonable to assume that women who cohabit prior to marriage are more likely to have engaged in premarital sex than women who do not cohabit before marriage. If premarital sex is the primary force driving an increased risk of marital dissolution and it is not measured, the effect of premarital cohabitation will be overstated. I take this possibility into account by including measures of both premarital intercourse and premarital cohabitation in my analysis. In particular, I can determine whether the effect of premarital sex depends on the occurrence of premarital cohabitation.

The Variable Meaning of Premarital Intercourse and Premarital Cohabitation

Another limitation of prior research is that, with few exceptions, diversity in histories of premarital relationships has not been considered. Most studies of the relationship between premarital cohabitation and divorce have used a simple variable indicating whether the respondent (usually the wife) cohabited before marriage. This measurement strategy ignores with whom the cohabitation occurred (the person the respondent married or someone else); if the question about cohabitation refers specifically to the person married, it ignores previous cohabitations. The importance of making such distinctions is illustrated by research conducted by DeMaris and MacDonald (1993) and Teachman and Polonko (1990), who found that premarital cohabitation limited to one's spouse does not increase the risk of marital instability (either marital dissolution or perceived risk of marital dissolution). Only respondents who had cohabited with someone in addition to their spouse were at a higher risk of marital instability.

The use of a simple measurement strategy may lead to biased estimates; for example, such a strategy may not measure the extent to which diversity in histories of premarital relationships is linked to either selectivity on variables affecting the risk of divorce or learned behaviors and attitudes related to the stability of marriage. For example, there is a growing literature suggesting that there may be two broadly different groups of cohabiting couples. One group consists of cohabiting couples who plan to marry and are using cohabitation as a newly evolved stage in the courtship process. The second group consists of very different couples who have no plans to marry and are using cohabitation as an alternative to marriage. The first group tends to resemble married couples on various dimensions of relationship quality, and the latter group appears to have lower quality relationships (Brown & Booth, 1996; Skinner, Bahr, Crane, & Call, 2002).

Even though fewer data are available, the same may be said for premarital intercourse. A significant majority of couples in today's marriage market engage in premarital intercourse, and for some couples it may simply be another stage in the courtship process. Indeed, data on premarital pregnancies indicate premarital sex with one's future spouse was not uncommon in the past (Teachman, 1985). Recent data from the 1995 National Survey of Family Growth indicate that premarital sex and marriage are linked for a nontrivial proportion of women (Abma et al., 1997). Among ever-married women who have had premarital sex, nearly 15% experienced first intercourse within 12 months of marriage and more than 25% had first sex with their husband. In addition, about 25% of all women who have had sex have had only one partner in their lifetime, most often their husband.

If premarital sex and, increasingly, premarital cohabitation have become a normal and accepted part of the courtship process in the contemporary United States, for at least some couples, one might expect little association between the risk of subsequent marital dissolution if it is limited to one's eventual marital partner. However, an intimate premarital relationship with someone other than one's marital partner may indicate increased risk to subsequent marital disruption. Multiple premarital sexual partners may indicate less commitment to the idea of a permanent relationship with one individual. Multiple sexual partners may also weaken the marital bond by heightening awareness of alternatives to one's marital partner as sources of sexual intimacy and fulfillment. Similar to the case for premarital sex, multiple coresidential unions prior to marriage may indicate a range of personal attitudes and beliefs that might undermine the stability of unions. In addition, a coresidential relationship that does not lead to marriage may provide firsthand experience with the process of ending a union, reducing transaction costs of future disruptions.

This line of reasoning leads me to expect that premarital cohabitation or sex that is limited to one's spouse will not be linked to the risk of subsequent marital dissolution. As part of the normal and expected courtship pattern, such behavior does not indicate reduced commitment to marriage and likely does not provide socializing experiences that might weaken the marital union. However, either premarital cohabitation or sex that occurs with someone other than one's spouse is expected to be related to an increased risk of marital dissolution. These individuals are either selected on characteristics that increase the risk of divorce or their experiences with disrupted unions lead to destabilizing influences on marriage.

Change across time in the effect of premarital cohabitation. At least one author has suggested that the meaning of cohabitation has changed over time. Schoen (1992) argues that early cohabitors were selective of people more willing to break social norms and less committed to marriage. However, as cohabitation has become more common, it has become less selective of people possessing characteristics related to marital stability. Given more accepting attitudes toward cohabitation in recent years, premarital cohabitation is also less likely to provide experiences that weaken subsequent marriages. The same argument can be applied to premarital sex. As an increasing proportion of people have experienced premarital sex, it is less likely to be a marker of characteristics or experiences that raise the risk of marital disruption.

This perspective suggests changes over time in the relationship between intimate premarital relationships and subsequent marital stability, although at least one study has failed to find a change in the association between premarital cohabitation and divorce over a wide range of marriage cohorts (Teachman, 2002). However, offsetting changes could have occurred according to type of cohabiting union. For example, it could be the case that premarital cohabitation

with one's spouse has become more acceptable (leading to a decreased risk of marital dissolution over time), whereas premarital cohabitation with multiple partners has become increasingly selective of people less committed to marriage (leading to an increased risk of marital dissolution over time). Even though available evidence is not sufficient to posit a firm expectation, there is enough justification to investigate whether the association between marital stability and premarital cohabitation and sex has varied across time.

In the following analysis, I estimate the effects of different histories of premarital cohabitation and sex on the risk of marital disruption, using a nationally representative sample of women. I control for a wide range of potentially confounding variables that have been identified in the literature. These confounding variables reflect variation in attitudes and values that are related to marital stability, as well as differences in ability to engage in the exchange of expressive and instrumental goods and services between husbands and wives that act to increase their interdependence (Becker, 1991; Teachman, 2002). The characteristics included are measures of race, religion, education, parental education, parental marital history, premarital births and conception, and spouse homogeneity with respect to race, religion, and age.

Method

Data

The data are taken from the 1995 round of the National Survey of Family Growth (NSFG). The NSFG is a national area probability survey, a cross-sectional sample of 10,847 civilian non-institutionalized women aged 15–45 residing in the United States (National Center for Health Statistics, 1998). The NSFG collected extensive life history data from women that detail their premarital relationships, as well as the dates at which each of their marriages began and ended.

For analysis, I select a subset of ever-married women whose first marriages were contracted between 1970 and 1995. The resulting sample size is 6,577 women.

Measures

Dependent variable. The dependent variable of interest is the rate at which first marriages are disrupted and is estimated using information on the duration of first marriages. Marriages are considered to be disrupted at either the date of divorce, or the date of separation, whichever came first.

Independent variables. The NSFG contains information about the beginning and ending dates for each nonmarital, cohabiting union experienced by women in the sample and whether these unions ended in disruption or marriage. From this information, I created two variables. The first variable is whether the woman ever cohabited prior to her first marriage. The second variable contains four categories (essentially dividing women who had ever cohabited prior to marriage into categories according to their histories of cohabitation): women who did not cohabit before first marriage, women who cohabited before their first marriage but only with their husband, women who cohabited before their first marriage with someone other than their husband, and women who cohabited two or more times before their first marriage, including with their husband and at least one other man.

The NSFG also contains information about the dates at which women initiated sex with each of their sexual partners, as well as information about their relationship to each of these partners (i.e., whether the sexual partner was a husband or cohabiting partner that she married, someone with whom she was cohabiting but did not marry, or someone else). From this information, I again created two variables. The first variable is whether the woman ever had sex prior to her first marriage. The second variable has three categories: women who did not have sex before first marriage, women who had premarital sex but only with their husbands, and women who had premarital sex with their husbands and at least one other man.

Control variables. A number of commonly used family background, life course, and socioeconomic variables pertaining to women are available in the NSFG, and I use them to limit the likelihood that any effects of premarital cohabitation and premarital sex are spurious.

The NSFG also contains data on husbands that can be used to create variables that have been linked to the risk of marital disruption (see Teachman, 2002).

Nearly 35% of the women in the sample reported that their first marriages had ended, with 34% ending within the first 10 years. Nearly 40% of women had cohabited prior to marriage, most (31%) with their eventual husband. As expected, a much larger percent of women had experienced premarital sex (about 82%). Contrary to the situation for premarital cohabitation, a majority of women had first sex with someone other than their husband (55%).

About 18% of women in the sample did not have premarital sex and did not cohabit prior to marriage. Nearly 19% of women had premarital sex with their husband only and did not cohabit, and another 8% of women had premarital sex with their husband only and cohabited with him. More women (25%) had premarital sex with their husband and another man but did not cohabit. Nearly as many women (about 23%) had premarital sex with their husband and another man and cohabited with their husband only. Fewer women (6%) had sex and cohabited with their husband and another man, and still fewer women had sex with their husband and another man and cohabited only with the other man.

Limitations. First, the data contain no information about relationship skills or attitudes, values, or beliefs that can be used to distinguish between groups of women defined according to their histories of premarital relationships. Although the NSFG contains information tapping attitudes toward marriage and family roles, this information is limited to 1995 and therefore may be as much a consequence of premarital sex, premarital cohabitation, marriage, and divorce as a determinant of these events. Second, there is no information pertaining to the premarital relationship histories of husbands (other than information ascertaining whether a husband was married before). Thus, the reported associations between marital disruption and premarital relationships are specific to the experiences of women.

Because the upper age limit in the NSFG is 45, resulting in the truncation of marriages begun prior to 1970, marriages of long duration are not observed. The longest marital duration considered in this analysis is 25 years.

Multivariate Results

Results for Model 1 indicate effects that are similar to those found in previous research (Bumpass et al., 1991; Teachman, 2002). In particular, the risk of divorce is greater for women who marry earlier, are Black, have a premarital birth or conception, have fewer siblings, have less educated mothers, and have experience with other than a two-parent family. In addition, women who marry men with less education, men who were married before, men of a different race or religion, men who are at least 2 years younger, or men who believe that religion is important to very important are at a higher risk of marital disruption.

Model 2 indicates that premarital cohabitation is associated with a 33% increase in the likelihood of marital disruption at each point in marriage. Model 3 indicates that women who had their first sexual encounter prior to first marriage are about 34% more likely to experience marital dissolution at each point in their marriages (and for each year that they delay sex, the risk of marital disruption is reduced by about 8%). These results closely replicate prior research by indicating that intimate premarital relationships, either premarital cohabitation or

premarital sex, are linked to an increased risk of marital dissolution.

The coefficients associated with premarital cohabitation in Model 1 are positive and statistically significant for two of the three situations compared with not having premaritally cohabited (the effect for having cohabited only with someone other than the woman's husband is not statistically significant but is based on a relatively small number of women). The effect for having cohabited twice is about 44% larger (a statistically significant difference) than the effect for having cohabited only with her husband. The effects for premarital sex in Model 2 indicate that it is only women whose first sex was with someone other than her husband who experience an increased risk of marital disruption (114%).

The results in Model 3, which includes the effects of both premarital cohabitation and premarital sex (compared with women who did not cohabit before marriage and did not engage in premarital sex), show that the risk of marital dissolution is higher when the woman cohabited twice (by about 28%) and when her first sex was with someone other than her husband (by about 109%). Combining premarital cohabitation and premarital sex in the same model reduces the effect of having cohabited solely with one's husband to nonsignificance. This pattern results because women who cohabited with their husband only are more likely than women who did not cohabit before marriage to have had first sex with someone other than their husband (73% vs. 41%). That is, for these women, it is not the fact that they cohabited before marriage that is important for marital dissolution; it is the fact that they had at least one other sexually intimate relationship prior to marrying.

To better understand the pattern of results, I estimated an additional model using a cross-tabulation of two variables used to measure premarital intimate relationships. The following categories resulted (women with no premarital sex or premarital cohabitation serve as the baseline): women who had premarital sex with their husband only but did not cohabit with him; women who had premarital sex with their husband only and cohabited with him, women whose first premarital sex was with another man but who never cohabited, women whose first premarital sex was with another man and who cohabited with her husband, women whose first premarital sex was with another man and cohabited with him as well as her husband, and a small number of women whose first premarital sex was with another man and who cohabited with him but not her husband.

It is clear that an intimate premarital relationship limited to a woman's husband does not affect the risk of marital disruption. However, having at least one other intimate relationship prior to marriage is linked to an increased risk of divorce (from 53% to 166%). There is a substantially higher risk of marital dissolution if the woman both had sex with another man and cohabited with him (166% vs. 53%–119% for other patterns of premarital relationships involving someone other than one's husband, a difference that is statistically significant). That is, there is an interaction between having multiple premarital sexual partners and cohabiting multiple times.

DISCUSSION

The results presented in this article replicate findings from previous research: Women who cohabit prior to marriage or who have premarital sex have an increased likelihood of marital disruption. Considering the joint effects of premarital cohabitation and premarital sex, as well as histories of premarital relationships, extends previous research. The most salient finding from this analysis is that women whose intimate premarital relationships are limited to their husbands—either premarital sex alone or premarital cohabitation—do not experience an increased risk of divorce. It is only women who have more than one intimate premarital relationship who have an elevated risk of marital disruption. This effect is strongest for women who have multiple premarital coresidental unions. These findings are consistent with the notion that premarital sex and cohabitation have become part of the normal courtship pattern in the United States. They do not indicate selectivity on characteristics linked to the risk of divorce and do not provide couples with experiences that lessen the stability of marriage.

To be sure, this research is limited by the lack of information pertaining to the relationship histories of men. Only information pertaining to the premarital relationships of women is available in the NSFG. Thus, the results cannot be extrapolated to the premarital relationships of men, and there is no immediate basis for expecting the effects of such relationships to be either similar to or different from those of women. The current results also cannot be used to ascertain the joint effects of the premarital relationships of both men and women (e.g., the likelihood of marital disruption if both partners had cohabited with someone else prior to marriage). Again, this remains an issue for subsequent research to address in full. These results are also limited to marriages formed prior to 1995 and marriages of relatively short duration. As changes in premarital sex and cohabitation continue to occur, it would prove useful to consider the effects of these variables on marital stability.

It remains the case, however, that women with more than one intimate relationship prior to marriage have an elevated risk of marital disruption. The risk of divorce is particularly great for women who cohabited with both their husbands and another man. Unfortunately, this study does not provide any information that allows us to better determine whether the effect of having multiple premarital relationships is based on differences on preexisting characteristics that are tied to the risk of divorce or whether having multiple relationships generates environments where relationship skills or attitudes and values about the permanency of marriage are somehow altered. It remains the task of subsequent research to consider these alternatives more fully. This limitation notwithstanding, the results presented here should shift attention away from research that focuses on the selection of individuals into cohabitation and premarital sex to a focus on the selection of individuals who do not marry the individuals with whom they first cohabit or initiate first sex. It may well be the case that, irrespective of the legal status of the relationship, the relevant distinction to make is between people who form multiple relationships and people who form a single, longer lasting relationship.

INTRODUCTION REFERENCES

Laumann, E. O., J. H. Gagnon, R. T. Michael, and S. Michaels. 1994. *The social organization of sexuality: Sexual practices in the United States.* Chicago: University of Chicago Press.

Mead, M. 1966. Marriage in two steps. *Redbook*, July 1966.

Michelson, M. M. 1979. *Made in heaven, settled in court.* New York: Warner.

Packard, V. 1968. *The sexual wilderness.* New York: Mckay.

Russell, B. 1928. *Marriage and morals.* New York: Liveright.

Trost, J. E. 1979. *Unmarried cohabitation.* Vasteras, Sweden: International Library.

REFERENCES

Abma, C., Mosher, W., Peterson, L., & Piccinino, L. (1997). Fertility, family planning, and women's health: New data from the 1995 National Survey of Family Growth. *Vital and Health Statistics, 23(19).* Washington DC: National Center for Health Statistics.

Axinn, W., & Barber, J. (1997). Living arrangements and family formation attitudes in early adulthood. *Journal of Marriage and the Family, 59,* 595–611.

Becker, G. (1991). *A treatise on the family.* Cambridge, MA: Harvard University Press.

Bennett, N., Blanc, A., & Bloom, D. (1988). Commitment and the modern union: Assessing the link between premarital cohabitation and subsequent marital instability. *American Sociological Review, 53,* 127–138.

Booth, A., & Johnson, D. (1988). Premarital cohabitation and marital success. *Journal of Family Issues, 9,* 255–272.

Brown, S., & Booth, A. (1996). Cohabitation versus marriage: A comparison of relationship quality. *Journal of Marriage and the Family, 58,* 668–678.

Bumpass, L., & Lu, H. (2000). Trends in cohabitation and implications for children's family contexts in the United States. *Population Studies, 54,* 29–41.

Bumpass, L., Martin, T., & Sweet, J. (1991). The impact of family background and early marital factors on marital disruption. *Journal of Family Issues, 12,* 22–42.

DeMaris, A., & MacDonald, W. (1993). Premarital cohabitation and marital instability: A test of the unconventionality hypothesis. *Journal of Marriage and the Family, 55,* 399–407.

Kahn, J., & London, K. (1991). Premarital sex and the risk of divorce. *Journal of Marriage and the Family, 53,* 845–855.

Lillard, L., Brien, M., & Waite, L. (1995). Premarital cohabitation and subsequent marital dissolution: A matter of self-selection? *Demography, 32,* 437–457.

National Center for Health Statistics. (1998). Sample design, sampling weights, imputation, and variance estimates in the 1995 National Survey of Family Growth. Washington DC: U.S. Government Printing Office.

Schoen, R. (1992). First unions and the stability of first marriages. *Journal of Marriage and the Family, 54,* 281–284.

Skinner, K., Bahr, S., Crane, D., & Call, V. (2002). Cohabitation, marriage, and remarriage. *Journal of Family Issues, 23,* 74–90.

Smock, P. (2000). Cohabitation in the United States: An appraisal of research themes, findings, and implications. *Annual Review of Sociology, 26,* 1–20.

Teachman, J. (1985). Historical and subgroup variations in the association between marriage and first childbirth. *Journal of Family History, 10,* 379–401.

Teachman, J. (2002). Stability across cohorts in divorce risk factors. *Demography, 39,* 331–351.

Teachman, J., & Polonko, K. (1990). Cohabitation and marital stability in the United States. *Social Forces, 69,* 207–220.

Thomson, E., & Colella, U. (1992). Cohabitation and marital stability: Quality or commitment? *Journal of Marriage and the Family, 54,* 259–267.

Thornton, A., Axinn, W, & Hill, D. (1992). Reciprocal effects of religiosity, cohabitation, and marriage. *American Journal of Sociology, 98,* 628–651. allison.

CHAPTER 17

Passionate Marriage

David M. Schnarch

Individuals for whom orgasm is the ultimate in sexual functioning may find David Schnarch's article simply boring. His counter-belief that sexual potential extends far beyond the physical point of release is skillfully woven into the case of Betty and Donald, an actual married couple with real-life issues. Challenging the common foci of many sex therapists, i.e., sexual technique, reversal of sexual symptoms, or the pursuit of intimacy for intimacy's sake, Schnarch proposes another theory. From his perspective, it is within what he calls the "sexual crucible" that unresolved individual and relationship problems surface to reveal themselves in common dysfunctional sexual styles.

One does not have to be an aspiring sex therapist to be enlightened and liberated by this important work. Of the many insights to be gained, two points are especially helpful for young persons just embarking on their personal odysseys. The first is the distinction between a person's genital prime, the peak years of physical reproductive maturity, and one's sexual prime, the human capacity for adult eroticism and emotional connection. The potential for sex to be even better in the sexual prime that occurs with age than in the genital prime of youth has to be an intriguing concept for all mortals because aging is seldom an option. The second point, concerning the author's thesis that

mutual completion of the sexual response cycle is not the same thing as intimacy, is well-supported. Although this assertion may be assumed to be self-evident, the number of failed marriages among Americans perhaps belies this assumption. This is a definitely not-to-be-missed offering.

———

Betty, a designer in a high-powered advertising firm, and Donald, a college professor bucking for tenure, had been married for 15 years. They spent the first 10 minutes in my office invoking the standard litany of our times as an explanation for their lousy sex life–they were both just too busy. Not that this focus precluded blaming each other for their difficulties. "Betty gets home from work so late that we barely see each other anymore, let alone have sex," said Donald resentfully. "We're collaborators in child raising and mortgage paying, but we're hardly lovers anymore. I've taken over a lot of the household chores, but she often doesn't get home until 9 p.m.—and most nights, she says she's just 'too tired' for sex." Betty sighed in exasperation. "Sometimes I think Donald wants me to leap from the front door to the bedroom and take care of him," she said. "But I'm being swallowed up by a sea of obligations—my boss, the kids, the house, the dog, Donald, everybody wants a big chunk of me. Right now, I feel there's nothing left of me for *me*, let alone for *him*. He just doesn't get it that I need more time for myself before I'm interested in sex." I asked them to be specific

From "Passionate Marriage" by D. Schnarch. 1997. *Family Therapy Networker*, September/October, pp. 42, 44–49. Copyright © 1997, *The Psychotherapy Networker*. Reprinted by permission.

about how the stress from their very demanding lives revealed itself in bed—exactly what happened, and in what order, when they had sex. Several moments of awkward silence and a number of false starts ensued before another, much more intimate, level of their marital landscape revealed itself.

Betty looked hard at Donald, then at me. "The fact of the matter is, he doesn't even know how to kiss me!" she said grimly.

"How would you know? It's been so long since you *let* me kiss you!" hissed Donald.

When I asked them to describe their foreplay, Betty looked embarrassed and Donald sounded frustrated. "During sex, she turns her face to the side and I end up kissing her cheek. She won't kiss me on the mouth. I think she just wants to get sex over with as fast as possible. Not that we have much sex." Betty shook her head in distaste. "He always just rams his tongue halfway down my throat—I feel like I can't breathe. Besides, why would I want to kiss him, when I can't even talk to him! We don't communicate at all."

Over the years, I've worked with many couples who complain bitterly that the other kisses—or touches, fondles, caresses, strokes—the "wrong" way. I used to take these complaints at face value, trying to help the couple solve their problems through various forms of marital bargaining and forbearance—listen empathetically, give a little to get a little, do something for me and I'll do something for you—teach them the finer points of sexual technique and send them home with detailed prescriptions (which they usually didn't follow) until I realized that their sexual dissatisfactions did not stem from ignorance, ineptitude or a "failure to communicate." On the contrary, "communicating" is exactly what Donald and Betty were already doing very well, only neither much liked the "message" the other was sending. The way this couple kissed each other, indeed their "vocabulary" of foreplay, constituted a very rich and purposeful dialogue, replete with symbolic meanings. Through this finely nuanced, but unmistakable language, both partners expressed their feelings about themselves and each other and negotiated what the entire sexual encounter would be like—the degree and quality of eroticism, connection and intimacy, or their virtual absence.

Donald and Betty had tried marital therapy before, but their therapist had taken the usual approach of dealing with each complaint individually—job demands, parenting responsibilities, housework division and sexual difficulties—as if they were all separate but equal situational problems. Typically, the clinician had tried to help Donald and Betty resolve their difficulties through a skill-building course on compromise, setting priorities, time management and "mirroring" each other for mutual validation, acceptance and, of course, better communication. The net result of all this work was that they felt even worse than before, even more incompetent, inadequate and neurotic, when sex didn't improve.

Knowing that Betty and Donald were most certainly communicating something via their gridlocked sexual styles, I asked them, "Even if you are not talking, what do you think you might actually be 'saying' to each other when you kiss?" After a minute, Donald said resentfully, "She's telling me I'm inadequate, that I'm not a good lover, I can't make her happy and she doesn't want me anyway." Betty defensively countered, "He's saying he wants me to do everything exactly his way and if I don't just cave in, he'll go ahead and do what he likes, whether I like it or not!" I asked her why she was willing to have intercourse at all if she didn't even want to kiss him. "Because he is such a sullen pain in the ass if I don't have sex," Betty replied without hesitation. "Besides, I like having orgasms."

Donald and Betty perfectly illustrated the almost universal, but widely unrecognized, reality that sex does not merely constitute a "part" of a relationship, but literally and metaphorically embodies the depth and quality of the couple's entire emotional connection. We think of foreplay as a way couples establish connection, but more often it's a means of establishing disconnection. Betty was a living rebuttal of the common gender stereotype that all women always want more foreplay; she cut it short so they could get sex done with as quickly as possible—and Donald understood. Donald returned the compliment by "telling" Betty he knew she didn't like him much, but he was going to get something out of her anyway—with or without her presence, so to speak.

Clearly, foreplay for this couple was not simply a mechanical technique for arousal, amenable to the engineering, skill-building approach still dictated by popular sex manuals. Nor were they likely to improve sex just by being more "open" with each other, "asking for what they wanted"—another popular remedy in self-help guides and among marital therapists—as if they weren't already "telling" each other what each did and did not want, and what each was or was not willing to give. Instead of trying to spackle over these normal and typical "dysfunctional" sexual patterns with a heavy coat of how-to lessons, I have learned that it makes much more sense to help the couple analyze their behavior, to look for the meaning of what they were already doing before they focused on changing the mechanics.

Rather than "work on their relationship" as if it were some sort of hobby or home-building project, Betty and Donald, like every other couple I have seen, needed to understand that what they did in bed was a remarkably salient and authentic expression of themselves and their feeling for each other. The nuances of their kissing style may have seemed trivial compared to the screaming fights they had about money or long days of injured silence, but in fact was an open window into their deepest human experience—who they were as people, what they really felt about each other, how much intimacy they were willing to risk with each other and how much growing up they still had to do.

As in any elaborate and nuanced language, the small details of sex carry a wealth of meaning, so while Donald and Betty were surprised that I focused on a "little thing" like kissing, rather than the main event—frequency of intercourse,

for example—they were startled to find how truly revealing it was, about their personal histories as well as their marriage. I told Betty I thought she had probably come from an intrusive and dominating family that never dealt openly or successfully with anxiety and conflict. "So now, you have a hard time using your mouth to tell Donald not to be so overbearing, rather than turning it away to keep him from getting inside it. You've become very good at taking evasive action to avoid being overwhelmed," I said. "You're right about my family," Betty said softly, "we kids didn't have any privacy or freedom in my family, and we were never allowed to complain openly about anything—just do what we were told, and keep our mouths shut."

On the other hand, I said, I imagined Donald had never felt worthwhile in his family's eyes. He had spent a lot of time trying to please his parents without knowing what he was supposed to do, but he got so little response that he never learned how to read other people's cues—he just forged blindly ahead, trying to force his way into people's good graces and prove himself without waiting to see how he was coming across. "Come back here and give me a chance to prove myself!" his behavior screamed. "Are you so used to being out of contact with the people you love that you can successfully ignore how out of sync you are with them?" I asked. To Donald's credit, he didn't dodge the question, though he seemed dazed by the speed with which we'd zoomed in on such a core issue.

Nevertheless, Donald and Betty discovered that their discomfort in describing, in exact detail, what was done by whom, when, how and where, was out-weighed by their fascination at what they were finding out about themselves—far more than was remotely possible from a seminar on sex skills. Betty, for example, had suggested that once kissing had stopped and intercourse had started, her sexual life was just fine—after all, she had orgasms and she "liked" them. But when I asked her to describe her experience of rear-entry intercourse—a common practice with this couple—she did not make it sound like a richly sensual, erotic or even particularly pleasant encounter. During the act, she positioned herself on elbows and knees, her torso held tense and rigidly parallel to the mattress while she protectively braced her body for a painful battering. Instead of moving into each thrust from Donald, she kept moving away from him, as if trying to escape. He, on the other hand, clasped her hips and kept trying to pull her to him, but never got a feeling of solid physical or emotional connection.

In spite of the fact that both were able to reach orgasm—widely considered the only significant measurement of successful sex—Betty and Donald's minute-by-minute description of what they did made it obvious that a lot more was happening than a technically proficient sex act. I told Betty I was glad she had told me these details, which all suggested that she thought it was pretty hopeless trying to work out conflicts with people she loved. "I suspect you've gotten used to swallowing your disappointment and sadness without telling anybody, and just getting along by yourself as best you can," I said. "It sounds very lonely." At that point, much to Donald's shock, Betty burst into tears. I said to Donald that he still seemed resigned to chase after people he loved to get them to love and accept him. "I guess you just don't believe they could possibly love you without being pressured into it. In fact, I think both of you use sex to confirm the negative beliefs you already have about yourselves."

For several seconds Donald looked at his lap, while Betty quietly cried in the next chair. "I suppose we must be pretty screwed up, huh?" Betty snuffled. "Nope," I said. "Much of what's going on between you is not only understandable, it's predictable, normal and even healthy—although it doesn't look or feel that way right now." They were describing the inevitable struggle involved in seeking individual growth and self-development within the context of marriage.

Betty said she used to enjoy sex until she became overinvolved with her job, but I suggested that the case was more likely the reverse—that the demands of her job gave her a needed emotional distance from Donald. Her conscious desire to "escape" from Donald stemmed from emotional fusion with him—she found herself invaded by his worries, his anxieties, his insecurities and his needs as if she had contracted a virus from him. "You may feel that you don't have enough inside you to satisfy his needs and still remain a separate, whole person yourself," I said. "Your work is a way of keeping some 'self' *for* yourself, to prevent being absorbed by him. That's the same reason you turn your head away when he tries to kiss you."

I suggested that Donald's problem was a complementary version of the same thing: in order to forestall the conviction that he had no worthwhile self at all, he felt he had to pressure Betty, or anybody he loved, to demonstrate they loved him—over and over. Donald, of course, did not see that he was as important to Betty as she was to him, but their mutual need for each other was really a function of two fragile and insecure selves shoring each other up.

Like most of us, neither Betty nor Donald was very mature when they married; neither had really learned the grown-up ability to soothe their own emotional anxieties or find their own internal equilibrium during the inevitable conflicts and contretemps of marriage. And, like most couples after a few years of marriage, they made up for their own insecurities by demanding that the other provide constant, unconditional acceptance, empathy, reciprocity and validation to help them each sustain a desired self-image. "I'm okay if, but only if, you think I'm okay," they said, in effect, to each other, and worked doubly hard both to please and be pleased, hide and adapt, shuffle and dance, smile and agree. The more time passes, the more frightened either partner is of letting the other know who he or she *really* is.

This joint back-patting compact works for a while to keep each partner feeling secure, but eventually the game becomes too exhausting to play. Gradually, partners becomes less inclined to please each other, more resentful of the cost of continually selling themselves out for ersatz peace and tranquillity, less willing to put out or give in. The ensuing "symptoms"—low sexual desire, sexual boredom, control battles, heavy silences—often take on the coloring of a deathly struggle for selfhood, fought on the implicit assumption that there is only room for one whole self in the marriage. "It's going to be my way or no way, my self or no self!" partners say in effect, in bed and out—leading to a kind of classic standoff.

Far from being signs of a deeply "pathological" marital breakdown, however, as Donald and Betty were convinced, this stalemate is a normal and inevitable process of growth built into every marriage, as well as a golden opportunity. Like grains of sand inexorably funneling toward the "narrows" of an hourglass, marriage predictably forces couples into a vortex of emotional struggle, where each dares to hold onto himself or herself in the context of each other, in order to grow up. At the narrowest, most constricting part of the funnel—where alienation, stagnation, infidelity, separation and divorce typically occur—couples can begin not only to find their individual selves, but in the process acquire a far greater capacity for love, passion and intimacy with each other than they ever thought possible.

At this excruciating point in a marriage, every couple has four options: each partner can try to control the other (Donald's initial ploy, which did not succeed), accommodate even more (Betty had done so to the limits of her tolerance), withdraw physically or emotionally (Betty's job helped her to do this) or learn to soothe his or her own anxiety and not get hijacked by the anxiety of the other. In other words, they could work on growing up, using their marriage as a kind of differentiation fitness center par excellence.

Differentiation is a lifelong process by which we become more uniquely ourselves by maintaining ourselves in relationship with those we love. It allows us to have our cake and eat it too, to experience fully our biologically based drives for both emotional connection and individual

self-direction. The more differentiated we are—the stronger our sense of self-definition and the better we can hold ourselves together during conflicts with our partners—the more intimacy we can tolerate with someone we love without fear of losing our sense of who we are as separate beings. This uniquely human balancing act is summed up in the striking paradox of our species, that we are famously willing both to die for others, and to die rather than be controlled by others.

Of all the many schools of hard experience life has to offer, perhaps none but marriage is so perfectly calibrated to help us differentiate—if we can steel ourselves to take advantage of its rigorous lessons, and not be prematurely defeated by what feels at first like abject failure. Furthermore, a couple's sexual struggle—what I call the sexual crucible—is the most powerful route both to individual maturity and the capacity for intimate relationship, because it evokes people's deepest vulnerabilities and fears, and also taps into their potential for profound love, passion, even spiritual transcendence.

In the typically constricted sexuality of the mid-marriage blues, Betty and Donald's sexual repertoire consisted of "leftovers"—whatever was left over after eliminating every practice that made one or the other nervous or uncomfortable. The less differentiated a couple, the less they can tolerate the anxiety of possibly "offending" one another, the more anxiety of possibly "offending" one another, the more anxiety they experience during sex and the more inhibited, rigid and inflexible their sexual style becomes: people have sex only up to the limits of their sexual and emotional development. Unsurprisingly, Donald and Betty's sexual routine had become as predictable, repetitious, unadventurous and boring as a weekly hamburger at McDonald's. This is why the standard advice to improve sex by negotiating and compromising is doomed to failure—most normally anxious couples have already long since negotiated and compromised themselves out of any excitement, variety or sexual passion, anyway.

And yet, it would have been pointless and counterproductive to march Donald and Betty through a variety of new sexual techniques. Using sex as a vehicle for personal and relational growth is not the same as just doing something new that raises anxieties. Rather, it depends on maintaining a high level of personal connection with someone known and loved during sex—allowing ourselves to really see and be seen by our partners, feel and be felt, know and be known by them. Most couples have spent years trying not to truly reveal themselves to each other in order to maintain the illusion of complete togetherness, thus effectively smothering any true emotional connection, with predictably disastrous effects on sex.

Donald and Betty were so obsessed with sexual behavior, so caught up in their anxieties about who was doing or failing to do what to whom in bed, that they were not really emotionally or even physically aware of each other when they touched. Like people "air kissing" on social occasions, they were going through the motions while keeping a kind of emotional *cordon sanitaire* between them. Their sex was more like the parallel play of young children than an adult interaction—except that they each watched the other's "play" with resentment and hurt feelings. Betty complained that Donald touched her too roughly—"He's crude and selfish!" she said, "and just uses me to please himself." Her complaint undercut Donald's sense of self, and he defensively accused her of being a demanding bitch, never satisfied and fundamentally unpleasable—thereby undermining her sense of self.

In order to help them each find a self and each other, I had to redirect their gaze away from their obsession with mutually disappointing sexual behavior, and encourage them to "follow the connection"—rediscover or establish some vital physical and emotional link as a first building block to greater intimacy. To consciously "follow the connection," however, requires the full presence and consent of both partners, each purposely slowing down and giving full attention to

the other, feeling and experiencing the other's reality.

The next session, Donald reported that he now understood why Betty felt he was too "rough"; he said the experience made him realize that he usually touched her with about as much care and sensitivity as if he was scouring a frying pan! But slowing down to really become conscious of what he was doing made him experience a sudden jolt of emotional connection with Betty. This awareness was an unnerving sensation for someone who had spent his life performing for other people (including his wife) rather than actually being *with* them.

Betty, too, was shaken by the jarring reality of their connection. She hadn't liked being touched roughly, but the concentration and attention in Donald's hands as he really felt and got to know her body was deeply disturbing; she found herself suddenly and unexpectedly sobbing with grief and deprivation for the warmth and love she'd missed as a child, and that she had both craved and feared in her marriage. Later that night, they had the best sex they had experienced in a very long time.

Buoyed by this first success, more hopeful about their future together, they both wanted to know how they could enhance this new and still tentative sense of connection. I suggested they try something called "hugging till relaxed," a powerful method for increasing intimacy that harnesses the language and dynamics of sex without requiring either nudity or sexual contact. Hugging, one of the most ordinary, least threatening gestures of affection and closeness, is also one of the most telling. When they hugged, Betty complained that Donald always leaned on her—making her stagger backward—while Donald accused Betty of pulling away from him, letting go "too soon," and leaving him "hugging air."

I suggested that Betty and Donald each stand firmly on their own two feet, loosely put their arms around each other, focus on their own individual experience and concentrate on quieting themselves down while in the embrace—neither clutching nor pulling away from or leaning on each other. Once both partners can learn to soothe themselves and maintain their individual equilibrium, shifting their own positions when necessary for comfort, they get a brief, physical experience of intimate connection without fusion, a sense of stability and security without overdependency.

While practicing hugging until relaxed with Donald, Betty found that as she learned to quiet her own anxiety, she could allow herself to be held longer by Donald without feeling claustrophobic. Just relaxing in the hug also made her realize that she normally carried chronic anxiety like a kind of body armor. As Betty calmed down and began to melt peacefully into the hug, not pulling away from fear that Donald would, literally, invade her space, he noticed his own impulse to break it off before she wanted to. When they each could settle down in the hug, they discovered that together they eventually would enter a space of great peace and tranquillity, deeply connected and in touch with each other but secure in their self.

Soon, they could experience some of the same kind of deep peace during sex, which not only eliminated much of the anxiety, resentment and disappointment they had felt before, but vastly increased the eroticism of the encounter. Now that they knew what they were looking for, they could tell when it was absent. Later, in my office, while Betty gently stroked his arm, Donald teared up as he told me about the new sense of quiet but electric connection he felt with her. "I just had no idea what we were missing; she seemed so precious to me that it almost hurt to touch her," he said, his voice thick with emotion.

This leap in personal development didn't simply occur through behavioral desensitization. Sometimes, Betty and Donald got more anxious as their unresolved issues surfaced in their physical embrace. At times, when Betty dared to shift to a more comfortable position, Donald felt she was squirming to avoid him. It was my job to help them see how this reflected the same emotional dynamics present in other aspects of their marriage. Betty was attempting to "hold onto herself" while remaining close to someone she loved, and likewise, Donald was refusing to chase after a loved one to get himself accepted. Insight alone didn't help much; a lot of self-soothing was required. Ultimately, they stopped taking each other's experience and reaction as a reflection on themselves and recognized that two separate realities existed even during their most profound physical union.

Building on their new stockpiles of courage earned in these experiments with each other, I suggested that Donald and Betty consider eyes-open sex, the thought of which leaves many couples aghast. Indeed, Donald's first response to the suggestion was that if he and Betty tried opening their eyes during sex, they wouldn't need birth control because the very thought made him so anxious he could feel his testicles retreating up into his windpipe! But eyes-open sex is a powerful way of revealing the chasm between sensation-focused sex and real intimacy. Most couples close their eyes in order to better tune out their partners so that they can concentrate on their physical feelings; it is a shocking revelation that to reach orgasm—supposedly the most intimate human act—most people cannot tolerate too much intimacy with their partners, so they block the emotional connection and concentrate on body parts.

Eyes-open sex is not simply a matter of two pairs of eyeballs staring at each other, but a way to intensify the mutual awareness and connection begun during foreplay; to really "see" and "be seen" is an extension of feeling and being felt when touching one another. But if allowing oneself to be known by touch is threatening, actually being seen can be positively terrifying. Bravely pursuing eyes-open sex in spite of these misgivings helps couples not only learn to tolerate more intimacy, it increases differentiation—it requires a degree of inner calm and independent selfhood to let somebody see what's inside your head without freaking out.

But the experience was also exhilarating. As Donald and Betty progressed from shy, little, peekaboo glimpses into each other's faces to long, warm gazes and soft smiles, each found their encounters more deeply moving. Betty slowly realized that whereas before she had wanted to escape from Donald, now she yearned to see all of him, and for him to see all of her. "I felt so vulnerable, as if he could see all my inadequacies, but the way he looked at me and smiled made all that unimportant." Donald gradually relinquished the self-image of a needy loser; he no longer needed to pursue Betty for reassurance and found, to his delight, that she wanted him—a breathtaking experience. "Her eyes are so big and deep, I feel I could dive into them," he said in wonder.

Both began to experience an increasing sense of self-acceptance and personal security. "We're having better sex now than we've ever had in our lives," Betty reported, "And I thought we were getting to be too old and far too married for exciting sex." Donald agreed. Betty and Donald, like society at large, were confusing genital prime—the peak years of physical reproductive maturity—with sexual prime—the specifically human capacity for adult eroticism and emotional connection. "Are you better in bed or worse now than you were as an adolescent?" I asked them. "Most people definitely get better as they get older, at least potentially. No 17-year-old boy is sufficiently mature to be capable of profound intimacy—he's too preoccupied with proving his manhood; and a young woman is too worried about being 'used' or too hung up about romance and reputation to really experience her own eroticism. Most 50-year-olds, on the other hand, have a much better developed sense of who they are, and more inner resources to bring to sex. You could say that cellulite and sexual potential are highly correlated."

As far as issues of gender equality are concerned, both men and women become more similar as they age and approach their sexual potential. Men are not as frightened of letting their partners take the lead in making love to them, and they develop far greater capacity and appreciation for emotional connection and tenderness than they had as young men. Women, on the other hand, become more comfortable with their own sexuality, more likely to enjoy sex for its own sake and less inclined to apologize for their eroticism or hide behind the ingenue's mask of modesty. As they age, women feel less obligated to protect their mate's sexual self-esteem at the cost of their own sexual pleasure.

Once a couple's sexual potential has been tapped, partners are no longer afraid to let their fantasies run free with each other. Donald, for example, let Betty know that he dreamed of her tying him up and "ravishing" him sexually—so one day, she bought four long, silk scarves and that night, wearing three-inch high heels and a little black lace, she trussed him to the bed and gave him what he asked for, astounding him and surprising herself with her own dramatic flair. Betty had always secretly cherished a fantasy of being a dangerous, sexually powerful femme fatale, but Donald's clingy neediness had dampened her enthusiasm for trying out the dream—also she had been afraid it would make him even more demanding. But now, knowing he was capable of being himself regardless of what she did or did not do, Betty felt much more comfortable expressing her own sense of erotic play.

The Sexual Crucible Approach encourages people to make use of the opportunity offered by marriage to become more married and better married, by becoming more grown-up and better at staking out their own selfhood. But the lessons learned by Betty and Donald, or any couple, extend far beyond sex. The same emotional development that makes for more mature and passionate sexuality also helps couples negotiate the other potential shoals of marriage—money issues, childrearing questions, career decisions—because differentiation is not confined to sex. In every trouble spot, each partner has the same four options: dominate, submit, withdraw or differentiate. Differentiation does not guarantee that spouses can always have things their own individual way and an unfailingly harmonious marriage besides. Marriage is full of hard, unpleasant choices, including the choice between safety, security and sexual boredom, on the one hand, and challenge, anxiety and sexual passion, on the other.

But spouses who have learned to stand on their own two feet within marriage are not as likely to force their own choices on the other or give in or give up entirely just to keep their anxiety in check and shore up their own frail sense of self. Learning to soothe ourselves in the middle of a fight with a spouse over, say, the choice of schools for our child or a decision to move, not only helps keep the discussion more rational, but makes us more capable of mutuality, of hearing our partner, of putting his or her agenda on a par with our own. The fight stops being, for example, a struggle between your personal needs and your spouse's personal needs, often regarded by each as my "good idea" and her/his "selfishness," but which is really often my fragile, undeveloped self versus his/her equally fragile, undeveloped self. Instead, we can begin to see that the struggle is inside each of us individually, between wanting what we want for ourselves personally, and wanting for our beloved partner what he or she wants for himself or herself. Becoming more

differentiated is possibly the most loving thing you can do in your lifetime—for those you love as well as yourself. Someone once said that if you're going to "give yourself" to your partner like a bouquet of flowers, you should at least first arrange the gift!

There is no way this process can be foreshortened into a technical quick-fix, no matter how infatuated our culture is with speed, efficiency and cost containment. Courage, commitment, a willingness to forgo obvious "solutions," tolerating the anxiety of living without a clear, prewritten script, as well as the patience to take the time to grow up are all necessary conditions, not only for a good marriage, but for a good life. At the same time, reducing all marital problems to the fallout from our miserable childhoods or to gender differences not only badly underestimates our own ability to develop far beyond the limitations of our circumstances, but misjudges the inherent power of emotionally committed relationships to bring us (drag us, actually, often kicking and screaming) more deeply and fully into our own being. Marriage is a magnificent system, not only for humanizing us, maturing us and teaching us how to love, but also perhaps for bringing us closer to what is divine in our natures.

CHAPTER 18

Physical Women, Emotional Men

Gender and Sexual Satisfaction in Midlife

Laura M. Carpenter
Constance A. Nathanson
Young J. Kim

Most college students don't like to think of their middle-aged parents as sexually active. Even in a time of relative sexual enlightenment, some may believe that sexual expression stops when one reaches a certain birthday or when one becomes a parent. A study done by Pocs and Godow (1977) found that students underestimated by a large degree the frequency with which their parents engaged in various sexual acts. The students who participated in that study are now likely the parents of college students themselves, and understand firsthand that even though bodies may change during adulthood, desire and passion remain. Generally, middle-aged people enjoy sex at least as much as they did when they were younger.

However, in the middle-aged years, bodily changes occur that potentially affect health and physical features in a way that can be an impediment to a fully satisfying sexual relationship. In

addition, many women who are middle-aged feel less attractive than in the previous years, which can have a negative impact on their sexual desire and enjoyment, frequency of intercourse, and their experience of orgasm (Koch et al. 2005).

In the following, there are some surprises to be found regarding the physical and emotional satisfaction of middle-aged men and women in sexual relationships. Before you read the chapter, take a minute to list the stereotypes that are generally held regarding age, men, women, and sex. Then, as you read, keep track of how many of the research findings appear to contradict those stereotypes. You might also want to think about the implication of the current human life span extending well past that of our ancestors as well as the role that sexuality plays in a long-term relationship when the time for procreation has passed.

From "Physical Women, Emotional Men: Gender and Sexual Satisfaction in Midlife" by L. M. Carpenter, C. A. Nathanson, and Y. J. Kim. 2009. *Archives of Sexual Behavior 38*: 87–107. Copyright © 2009, Springer. With kind permission from Springer Science + Business Media.

The runaway success of Viagra and other new pharmaceutical treatments for sexual dysfunction in men, and drug companies' eager quest to devise equivalent medications for women, have brought unprecedented public attention to sexuality in mid- and later life. Popular media accounts often ask whether these medical "fixes" truly deliver on their promise to enhance individuals' and couples' sexual satisfaction and whether heterosexual women always appreciate the drugs' effects on their partners (Croissant, 2006; Vares & Braun, 2006). In turn, these treatment-specific questions raise more general concerns about the relationships among age, gender, and sexual satisfaction, and about the relative importance of biological, social, cultural, and psychological factors in explaining variations in sexual life.

Until recently, scholars in sexuality and gender studies had all but neglected the sexual lives of middle-aged and older women and men, focusing instead on adolescents or adults of "childbearing" age. Conversely, experts on aging rarely asked questions about sex (Calasanti & Slevin, 2001). Much of the literature on aging and sexuality is narrowly concerned with factors, especially physiological factors, that affect sexual "function"—the ability to perform sexually—and with the more quantifiable aspects of sexuality, such as frequency of sexual activity. Yet, the importance of understanding the subjective dimensions of sexuality, like physical and emotional satisfaction, and the ways they are patterned by aging and gender, cannot be underestimated. What, for instance, can one make of the observation that men and women have sex less often as they get older without knowing whether this change brings them frustration or relief?

Better understanding of the dynamics of sexual satisfaction is particularly crucial. Sexual satisfaction has been shown to enhance individuals' well-being as well as the stability of marriages and other intimate relationships (Henderson-King & Veroff, 1994; Sprecher, 2002). Expanded knowledge of the factors that enhance and diminish sexual satisfaction can pave the way for more effective clinical and policy responses to sexual problems (Bancroft, 2002). More generally, understanding sexuality in later life is becoming increasingly imperative as the U.S. population ages, as individuals live longer, healthier lives, and as beliefs about the nature of aging and gender and the importance of sexuality for personal happiness are transformed (Calasanti & Slevin, 2001).

This article addresses critical gaps in the literature by exploring social, cultural, and physiological factors that contribute to age and gender differences in sexual satisfaction among sexually-active, middle-aged, heterosexual adults in the United States. Recent studies have indicated that sexual satisfaction begins to decline in late middle age, especially among women (AARP, 1999; Laumann, Gagnon, Michael, & Michaels, 1994). Yet, researchers have yet to establish fully the social dynamics responsible for these patterns. Many studies treat gender cursorily and few adequately distinguish between the effects of aging and generation. Our analysis of data from the 1992 National Health and Social Life Survey (NHSLS) examined how women's and men's satisfaction with their sexual relationships was influenced—possibly differentially—by aging, physical health, sexual functioning, partners' health and functioning, relationship factors, sexual practices and attitudes, and birth cohort.

AGE, GENDER, AND SEXUAL SATISFACTION

Measuring Sexual Satisfaction

Researchers have conceptualized sexual satisfaction and problems/dissatisfaction in diverse ways. Early studies often used the frequency of sexual intercourse or orgasms as proxies for sexual satisfaction (Henderson-King & Veroff, 1994). Recently, scholars have measured satisfaction more directly (e.g., through self reports). They have also begun to address affective as well as physical dimensions of satisfaction and to include relationship factors and (less often) cultural context alongside physiology and personality as possible determinants of sexual satisfaction (Christopher & Sprecher, 2000). Scholars disagree as to whether the physical and emotional dimensions of sexual satisfaction merit separate analyses. Many studies employ composite measures; however, some analyses find that the predictors of physical and emotional satisfaction differ (e.g., Waite & Joyner, 2001). Researchers also disagree about the relative utility of objective versus subjective measures. As Bancroft, Loftus, and Long (2003) demonstrated, objective measures of sexual problems (e.g., lubrication difficulty, painful intercourse) are not always accompanied by subjective reports of distress or dissatisfaction, and vice versa. This article focuses on middle-aged adults' subjective (i.e., self-reported) satisfaction with the emotional and physical dimensions of their primary sexual relationships.

Our conceptual framework posits gendered patterns of sexual satisfaction in midlife to be shaped by the interaction of factors at the levels of the individual, the relationship, and the broader culture (Bancroft et al., 2003). Key individual-level factors include personal sexual history and attitudes, as well as physical condition, including normal bodily aging, health status, and medical treatments. At the relationship level, the type, quality, and duration of the relationship, partner's health and availability, and patterns of sexual activity are central. The cultural level encompasses widely shared beliefs and expectations about sexuality. The dynamics of sexual satisfaction are influenced at all three levels by age, gender, and cohort/generation.

On balance, research indicates that older adults are less sexually satisfied than their younger counterparts and that women are less satisfied than men. Methodologically diverse studies have found lower levels of sexual satisfaction among older participants (Haavio-Mannila & Kontula, 1997; Laumann et al., 1994). However, the majority of middle-aged and older adults describe sex as feeling as good or better than when they were younger (Starr & Weiner, 1981) and men's sexual satisfaction levels appear to change little with age (Schiavi, 1996). Several large-scale studies have observed men to be more sexually satisfied than women (Laumann et al.,

1994; Waite & Joyner, 2001; but see AARP, 1999). Studies assessing the intersection of age and gender generally observe a more pronounced decline in sexual satisfaction among women, starting in late midlife (ages 50–60 or 65) or early old age (ages 60 or 65–75) (Edwards & Booth, 1994; Laumann et al., 1994); some even show increased enjoyment of sex among aging men (Wiley & Bortz, 1996). The American Association of Retired Persons (AARP) (1999) survey is an exception, finding that, although sexual satisfaction declined with age for both genders, within age groups, men were more dissatisfied than women.

Individual Influences on Satisfaction

Physical changes associated with normal aging may reduce sexual desire, physiological sexual response, and therefore satisfaction with the physical aspects of sex (Segraves & Segraves, 1995). These effects differ by gender. For men, the major changes are difficulties getting and sustaining erections and ejaculating, due to decreasing testosterone, muscle tone, and blood circulation with age (Marsiglio & Greer, 1994). For women, the major physiological changes include decreased vaginal lubrication and more painful intercourse (Huyck, 1994). However, sexual distress among women may be more closely associated with a lack of arousal or genital tingling than with difficulty lubricating (Bancroft et al., 2003). Women often experience physiological changes at menopause; yet, scholars disagree as to how adversely menopause affects women's sexuality. A longitudinal study of middle-aged Australian women found that, while sexual arousal, orgasm, and enjoyment declined for all women, regardless of menopause status, menopause was specifically linked to increased pain during intercourse and decreased sexual desire, frequency, and positive feelings for one's partner (Dennerstein, Dudley, & Burger, 2001). Yet, other studies indicate that many women experience few adverse changes in arousal and orgasm at menopause (Deeks & McCabe, 2001), and many find their sex lives enhanced by freedom from possible pregnancy (Barbre, 1998). Physical and mental health, smoking, and male partners' sensitivity to menopausal symptoms may have a greater impact on women's sexual functioning than menopause per se (Winterich, 2003).

Aging-related illnesses, such as high blood pressure and diabetes, and their treatments may also reduce sexual desire and physiological response, and thus sexual satisfaction (Segraves & Segraves, 1995). Poor mental health is associated with diminished sexual satisfaction (Bancroft et al., 2003); ironically, however, many antidepressants reduce sexual desire or change people's sexual lives in other dissatisfying ways. Physiological factors may also affect emotional satisfaction. Insofar as U.S. culture posits erections as virtually indispensable to masculine sexuality, anxiety about erectile dysfunction may affect older men's enjoyment of sex, even prompting some to avoid sexual encounters altogether (Loe, 2001).

Sexual attitudes represent another individual-level predictor of sexual satisfaction—one that is patterned by gender and generation (Laumann et al., 1994). People with permissive beliefs (e.g., approving of casual sex) report higher levels of satisfaction than their less-permissive counterparts (Haavio-Mannila & Kontula, 1997). Our analysis departed from previous studies by treating sexual attitudes not merely as the property of individuals, but as reflections of the degree to which particular women and men subscribe to mainstream sexual culture.

Most studies find little or no relationship between sexual satisfaction and race, ethnicity, socioeconomic status, and/ or religion (Christopher & Sprecher, 2000). One exception found more pleasure among Blacks than Whites and less satisfaction among women with higher income (Henderson- King & Veroff, 1994). Some studies have observed fewer sexual problems among the college educated, possibly reflecting an educational difference in choosing scale

options (Bancroft et al., 2003; Laumann et al., 1994).

Relational Influences on Satisfaction

Relationship-level factors also contribute to age and gender differences in sexual satisfaction. Overall, married people are more sexually satisfied than cohabiters and singles (Laumann et al., 1994), while committed daters are more satisfied than the sexually-active unattached (Pedersen & Blekesaune, 2003). Relationship type seems to affect emotional satisfaction more strongly than physical pleasure (Waite & Joyner, 2001), consistent with the commonsense assumption that people invest greater emotion in more committed relationships. Relationship quality appears to be reciprocally related to sexual satisfaction, with each enhancing the other (Sprecher, 2002). Monogamous relationships are more conducive to sexual pleasure than non-monogamous ones, perhaps because monogamy facilitates learning one's partner's sexual preferences; however, it could be that dissatisfied partners seek sex outside the relationship (Laumann et al., 1994).

Sexual satisfaction tends to decline as relationships (of all types) endure over time, likely because familiarity makes sex routine or even boring (Laumann et al., 1994; Pedersen & Blekesaune, 2003). The effects of duration account, in part, for the lower levels of satisfaction observed with increasing age. Using data from NHSLS, Liu (2003) found that longer relationships predicted lower sexual satisfaction among married 18–59-year-olds, but age did not.

Cultural stereotypes suggest that women's enjoyment of sex depends more on relational factors than does men's, but empirical evidence is mixed. The duration of heterosexual college students' relationships was better predicted by relationship satisfaction for women and by sexual satisfaction for men (Sprecher, 2002) and sexual satisfaction was more closely linked to the expectation of a lifelong relationship among women than men (Waite & Joyner,

2001). Yet, other studies have found that middle-aged and older men rated having a romantic relationship and a sensitive partner as more important to sexual satisfaction than did women (AARP, 1999) and that reciprocal love was a significant predictor of sexual satisfaction for men but not women (Haavio-Mannila & Kontula, 1997).

Sexual satisfaction also depends on one's partner's health and availability. Vaginal intercourse with a male partner who has difficulty sustaining an erection or ejaculating, or who ejaculates prematurely, or with a female partner who has trouble lubricating, may be physically uncomfortable and/or emotionally frustrating (Bancroft et al., 2003). Male partners' ill health or sexual dysfunction, and/or their insensitivity to menopausal women's lubrication difficulties, may also inhibit pleasure (Avis, 2000; Winterich, 2003). Having a partner who is unavailable for sexual activity—as when couples work different shifts—may also be dissatisfying (Keith & White, 1990). However, co-residing with children under 18 (which is correlated with relationship satisfaction and sexual frequency) does not appear to affect sexual satisfaction (Liu, 2003).

What couples do sexually represents another relational component of sexual satisfaction. Orgasm, the archetypal measure of physical pleasure, has been linked to higher levels of sexual satisfaction for both genders (Waite & Joyner, 2001). Women climax less regularly than men (Laumann et al., 1994); however, orgasms appear to be more important for men's sexual satisfaction (Nicolson & Burr, 2003). People who engage in sexual activity relatively frequently report higher levels of sexual satisfaction than those who have sex less often (Waite & Joyner, 2001); this may hold especially true among women (Pedersen & Blekesaune, 2003). It is not clear whether satisfying sex inspires more frequent encounters or frequent sex improves technique; however, sexual satisfaction declines more slowly than frequency over time (Christopher & Sprecher, 2000). People who employ diverse sexual techniques in their encounters report greater satisfaction than the less adventuresome (Haavio-Mannila & Kontula, 1997), at least in part because many women require manual or oral clitoral stimulation, instead of, or in addition to, vaginal intercourse to achieve orgasm.

Cultural Influences on Satisfaction

Cultural norms equating sexual desirability and expression with youth may make middle-aged and older people feel ashamed of their sexual desires, in turn inhibiting their enjoyment of sex (Levy, 1994), or may prompt them to accept as inevitable reductions in sexual satisfaction that result from factors other than normal aging (Schiavi, 1996). People who reject this "aging as decline" model for a newer perspective emphasizing "healthy aging" may, conversely, harbor unrealistic expectations about sexuality in mid- and later life, and may feel dissatisfied if their sexual lives are adversely affected by normal aging or illnesses (Schiavi, 1996). Women may feel the impact of ageist cultural beliefs about sexuality with particular force, given the greater cultural emphasis on appearance and youth for female desirability (Gibson, 1993). Men who endorse prevailing cultural beliefs about masculine sexuality, which emphasize strength, competence, and assertiveness (not to mention erection capacity), may have trouble enjoying sex when their bodies start changing with age (Loe, 2001). Yet, some adults reject these mainstream beliefs, responding to aging-related bodily changes in ways that help maintain sexual satisfaction, whether by adopting new sexual practices (e.g., emphasizing caressing rather than coitus) or revising their expectations (e.g., accepting less frequent orgasms) (Loe, 2001; Wiley & Bortz, 1996). Those who subscribe to the widespread belief that "real" sex entails penile-vaginal penetration and ejaculation may resist changing their practices and enjoy sex less (e.g., Winterich, 2003).

Cultural beliefs about sexuality, aging, and gender vary by generation (Riley, 1987). Social forces in the late 1960s and early 1970s, including the youth counterculture, effective contraceptives, Baby Boom, and rising divorce rates, helped to bring about a general liberalization of sexual mores and conduct, especially among people who were relatively young at the time (D'Emilio & Freedman, 1988). Longitudinal studies show that members of younger cohorts engage in more frequent sexual activity than members of older cohorts at the same ages (George & Weiler, 1981), although individual variations in sexual desire and conduct endure across the life course. Sexual satisfaction may be similarly patterned. Baby Boomers express greater approval of non-coital practices, such as oral sex, than do their parents, which may make them better prepared to adapt to aging-related physiological changes (Gagnon & Simon, 1987).

Cohort differences are especially pronounced among women, not least because second-wave feminism prompted many women to reject the sexual double standard (Luria & Meade, 1984). One survey found that objective sexual "problems" (e.g., difficulty lubricating) were more common in older women, but more distressing to younger women—likely a cohort effect (Bancroft et al., 2003). Feminism and the youth counterculture also worked to replace the view of "real" men as "sexual animals" to "competent lovers," possibly heightening performance anxiety for some men (especially Baby Boomers) (Marsiglio & Greer, 1994). The advent of medications like Viagra is also liable to have differential effects across generation (Loe, 2001).

In sum, although research on sexual satisfaction is burgeoning, much remains to be understood. Since most studies focus on young adults, examining sexual satisfaction among middle-aged and older people will help to reveal whether similar factors influence satisfaction at every stage of the life course.

Better distinguishing between the effects of aging and cohort will help to enhance our understanding of the ways aging and cultural change impact sexual life. Closer examination of women's and men's subjective experiences can shed new light on heretofore mixed findings about gender and sexual satisfaction. More also remains to be known about the extent to which the physical and emotional dimensions of sexual satisfaction diverge from one another. Finally, key methodological issues must be addressed. Samples that include only currently-married people are common, many studies exclude one gender or the other, and some fail to distinguish consistently between people with and without partners (Wiley & Bortz, 1996).

Hypotheses

Based on our review of the literature and our understanding of the dynamics of physical and emotional satisfaction, we developed seven hypotheses about gender, aging, and sexual satisfaction. At the individual level (holding age, race/ethnicity, and socioeconomic status constant):

(H1) People who were in poor health will report lower levels of pleasure, especially physical pleasure (H1a), than people who were in good health.

(H2) People who experienced sexual "problems" will report lower levels of pleasure, especially physical pleasure (H2a), than people who were "problem-free."

At the relationship level:

(H3) People who were married or cohabiting, in a relatively long-term relationship, and who knew their partner relatively well before having sex will report higher levels of satisfaction than people who were single, in relatively short-term relationships, and/or relatively unfamiliar with their partner before sex.

(H3a) These relationship factors will have greater bearing on emotional than physical satisfaction.

(H4) People whose partners were in poor health or who experienced sexual "problems" will report lower levels of pleasure, especially physical pleasure

(H4a), than people with healthy, problem-free partners.

(H5) People who had sex relatively frequently, achieved orgasm regularly, had relatively lengthy sexual encounters, and engaged in activities other than vaginal intercourse will report greater pleasure than people who had sex seldom, often did not orgasm, had brief encounters, and engaged only in vaginal sex.

(H5a) Sexual practices will affect physical pleasure especially and (H5b) will have a stronger impact on men than on women.

At the cultural level:

(H6) People with more traditional beliefs about sexual morality and gender differences in sexuality will report lower satisfaction than their less-traditional peers.

(H6a) Sexual attitudes should have a more pronounced effect for women, given the greater impact of post-1960s liberalization on women's sexuality.

(H7) The effects of sexual attitudes and of age will be mediated by generation (Baby Boom versus WWII).

METHOD

Participants

Data for this study come from the NHSLS, a unique data set containing a wealth of detailed information about sexual conduct and attitudes (Laumann et al., 1994). Fielded in 1992, the NHSLS conducted in-person interviews with 3,432 English-speaking adults, aged 18–59 years, randomly drawn from a national sample of U.S. households, using an area probability design and oversampling for African Americans and Hispanics. People in the military and/or residing in institutions were excluded. The response rate was almost 80%.

Of the NHSLS participants who self-identified as heterosexual, 1,240 were middle-aged, between 40 and 59, at the time of the survey. Our analysis focused on the 1,035 (83.4%) of these middle-aged participants who reported having a sexual partner in the previous year. They are broadly representative of the U.S. population in terms of gender, racial-ethnic background, education, household income, and religion. We would have liked to include gay, lesbian, and bisexual participants in our analyses; yet, only 14 NHSLS participants aged 40–59 self-identified as anything other than heterosexual.

The subsample of the NHSLS that we analyzed included people born as early as 1933 and as late as 1952. Following convention, we classified participants born between 1933 and 1945 as members of the Great Depression/World War II generation and those born from 1946 onward as Baby Boomers. The NHSLS must likewise be situated in historical context. It was conducted before the advent of Viagra and anti-retroviral therapies for HIV, and at a time when moral conservatives were gaining considerable influence over U.S. public policy.

Procedure and Measures

The major advantage of the NHSLS is the plethora of detailed information it included about almost every aspect of sexual behavior, beliefs, and fantasy. Crucial for our purposes, the questionnaire distinguished between the physical and emotional dimensions of sexual satisfaction. The NHSLS also employed an especially inclusive definition of "sexual activity," encompassing any voluntary "direct physical contact with the genitals...of someone else" where "sexual excitement or arousal occurred...even if intercourse or orgasm did not occur." This definition was well-suited for our research, since aging-related difficulties with erection and ejaculation may impair couples' ability to engage in vaginal intercourse but not other kinds of sex (see Calasanti & Slevin, 2001).

The dependent variables in our analyses were participants' reports of physical pleasure and emotional satisfaction within their primary sexual relationship in the 12 months before the survey. We determined individuals' satisfaction based their own responses to the questions: "How physically pleasurable did you find your relationship with (PARTNER) to be?" and "How emotionally satisfying did you find your relationship with (PARTNER) to be?" Physical pleasure and emotional satisfaction were closely correlated. We opted to analyze the two dimensions of satisfaction separately not only because they are imperfectly correlated, but also because we expected that they might be influenced by different factors.

Our analyses distinguished between people who were currently cohabiting (94% of whom were married) and people who were not (who may be single, separated, or divorced). Although some studies of sexual satisfaction find cohabiters to resemble singles more than the married, we grouped married and cohabiting people together. Participants were designated as having sexual "problems" if they experienced one or more of seven conditions in the year preceding the survey. This measure was not ideal, insofar as it disregarded whether a participant found a particular functional experience problematic or distressing; however, it was the best measure available. Since NHSLS did not include direct measures of partners' health or sexual problems, we used age as a proxy— comparing partners aged under 40, 40–59, and 60 and older— on the grounds that certain sexual difficulties, and many health conditions that impair sexual function, become more common with age. Regrettably, NHSLS did not ask participants to assess the quality of their relationships. We measured cultural factors broadly, through two attitudinal variables meant to capture sexual conservatism (beliefs about sex without love and sex before marriage), which has been linked to lower levels of satisfaction, and one intended to assess gender traditionalism. Believing that men need sex more than women do may reflect adherence to traditional understandings of masculine sexuality (men as active penetrators) and feminine sexual worth (emphasizing youth and beauty),

which may impede adjustment to aging-related sexual changes.

RESULTS

Women overall described their relationships as less satisfactory, physically and emotionally, than did men. The level of physical pleasure men received from their sexual relationships varied little by age. Women, however, reported significantly lower levels of physical pleasure at older ages, especially after age 56. The proportion of women describing their relationships as extremely emotionally satisfying likewise decreased with age, while the opposite was true for men (the pattern was statistically significant for women only).

To better understand these patterns, we used regression to predict the relative risk of a respondent finding his or her primary sexual relationship (1) extremely *physically* pleasurable or not-so-pleasurable, compared with very pleasurable, and (2) extremely *emotionally* satisfying or not-so-satisfying, compared with very satisfying. For both dimensions of satisfaction, we tested models including various combinations of six categories of independent variables, mapping to the individual, relationship, and cultural levels of sexual life.

Individual Level Factors

Our predictions about the effects of health status and sexual problems, especially on physical pleasure, received partial support. Men in fair or poor health reported significantly lower levels of physical pleasure than healthy men. This pattern appears to reflect the direct results of ill health and/or medical treatments, for having sexual problems in the past year also predicted lower levels of physical pleasure. These variables became statistically non-significant when sexual practices were added to the model, suggesting that health and sexual problems affected men's physical satisfaction chiefly through their influence on sexual frequency, duration, and orgasm.

Health status did not predict physical pleasure for women, but healthy women were more likely than unhealthy women to report both extremely emotionally satisfying and not-so-emotionally satisfying relationships. Women who experienced sexual problems were over twice as likely to describe their relationships as physically and emotionally not-so-pleasurable than problem-free women. Menopause status did not significantly predict either dimension of satisfaction. Our findings for men supported our hypotheses that health and sexual problems would primarily affect physical pleasure; however, these factors (especially health) had a greater impact on women's emotional than physical satisfaction.

Although age is an individual attribute, our hypotheses focused on the relationship of age to generation; we therefore discuss age alongside cultural-level factors. We did not develop hypotheses about the effects of race/ethnicity, education, and income, expecting that they would not affect satisfaction once other factors were accounted for. By and large, we were correct. However, women of color were about twice as likely as white women to express dissatisfaction with the physical aspects of their sexual relationships. Men who completed at least some college were significantly less likely to report extremely emotionally satisfying relationships than men with high school degrees.

Relationship Level Factors

Our hypotheses about relationship-related variables received support in two cases. First, men who were not cohabiting/married reported significantly lower levels of physical pleasure than cohabiting/married men, though this effect became non-significant when attitudes about sex without love were added to the model. Second, women who knew their partners more than a year before having sex were significantly less likely to report not-so-emotionally satisfying relationships than women who had known their partners more briefly. The latter finding

supported our prediction that relationship factors would have greater bearing on emotional than physical satisfaction, while the former suggested the converse. Relationship duration was not a significant predictor of physical or emotional satisfaction in any of the models we tested, for men or women.

Our prediction of less pleasure among people whose partners were in poor health or who experienced sexual problems was supported only for women, and only in the case of emotional satisfaction. Women with partners aged 60 or older were significantly less likely than women with younger partners to describe their relationships as extremely emotionally satisfying, controlling for relationship factors and sexual practices. This effect became non-significant when generation was taken into account.

We found considerable support for our hypothesis linking bodily aspects of sexual conduct to greater sexual satisfaction; yet, bodily practices seemed just as important for emotional as physical pleasure and appeared to be more central to women's pleasure than to men's. Women rated their sexual relationships more physically and emotionally pleasurable if their most-recent sexual encounter lasted a comparatively long time; less physically pleasurable if they had orgasms only sometimes (versus always); and less physically and emotionally pleasurable if they had sex relatively infrequently. Men whose most-recent sexual encounters lasted 16–29 min reported more physical pleasure than men whose encounters were shorter and men who had sex relatively rarely reported less emotional satisfaction than men who had sex more often.

Cultural Level Factors

We found some support for our hypothesis that levels of sexual satisfaction would be partly explained by agreement with the dominant sexual culture. As predicted, women who believed that men have greater sexual needs than women were less likely to report extremely physically satisfying relationships than their less-traditional counterparts. This relationship remained significant when generation was included in the model, indicating the influence of variations in belief among members of the same generation. Attitudes about gender and sexuality were not associated with women's emotional pleasure or with either dimension of satisfaction for men. These findings were consistent with our prediction that attitude effects would be more pronounced among women, given the greater impact of late-1960s social changes on women. Beliefs about premarital sex did not predict levels of sexual satisfaction in any of the models we tested.

Men who disapproved of sex without love were significantly more likely to rate their relationships as extremely physically and emotionally satisfying than men who approved, and women who disapproved of sex without love reported higher levels of emotional satisfaction. We had, however, predicted that sexual conservatism would be associated with lower levels of satisfaction. Beliefs about sex without love can be interpreted as indicating not only agreement with dominant cultural mores, but also the quality of a person's relationship with her/his sexual partner—at least to the extent that people who disapprove of loveless sex tend to be in love with their partners. This latter finding suggested a closer link between beliefs and satisfaction for men than women; although our finding about beliefs about gender differences in sexual needs suggested the converse.

Our hypothesis that generation would mediate the effects of sexual attitudes was not supported. Generation was not a significant predictor of physical or emotional satisfaction, for men or women, in any of the models we tested. However, generation did appear to mediate the effects of age. Age was not associated with men's physical or emotional satisfaction, except that older men were more likely to be extremely emotionally satisfied. In contrast, with each additional year of age, women were significantly less likely to describe their

relationship as extremely physically and/or emotionally satisfying in every model, except those including generation. Women were also less likely to report not-so-emotionally-satisfying relationships with advancing age. Although the proportion of emotionally-dissatisfied women varied little by age, the proportion of extremely-satisfied women decreased (i.e., women shifted from "extremely" to "very" happy). These age effects became non-significant for women and men when generation was added to the models.

DISCUSSION

Individual Level Factors

Poor health negatively affected men's physical pleasure, as hypothesized; however, health affected women's emotional rather than physical satisfaction. Sex differences in morbidity may help to explain this pattern. Many illnesses affect sexual functioning in men disproportionately and men suffer from them at earlier ages than do women (Schiavi, 1994). The women in our sample may simply have been too young for poor health to impair their physical sexual pleasure. Insofar as good *and* poor health were associated with lower levels of emotional satisfaction among women, it may be that healthy women have higher expectations for sex, and so are more easily dissatisfied, while less-healthy women experience emotional frustration due to the inability to have sex in favored ways. Similarly, our prediction that sexual problems would affect physical rather than emotional pleasure held true for men (in models excluding sexual practices), whereas women with sexual problems reported significantly lower levels of both physical and emotional pleasure. These patterns—which are broadly consistent with previous research (Marsiglio & Greer, 1994; Segraves & Segraves, 1995)—suggest that these two dimensions of sexual satisfaction may be more closely intertwined for women than for men. For men, health and sexual problems appeared to diminish sexual satisfaction insofar as they impacted sexual practices, whereas for women, the effects of sexual problems and health remained independent, persisting as variables measuring sexual practices were incorporated into the model.

Previous research can shed some light on our unanticipated findings about racial/ethnic background and education. Belonging to a racial/ethnic minority was associated with lower levels of physical satisfaction only for women, while higher education was associated with lower levels of emotional satisfaction only for men. These findings contrast with research showing greater enjoyment among Blacks than Whites (Henderson-King & Veroff, 1994) and fewer sexual problems among the college educated (Laumann et al., 1994), but are consistent with the claim that such differences may stem from cultural/educational differences in ways of talking about sex and using survey scale options (Bancroft et al., 2003). Perhaps physical sexual pleasure is more subject to systematic racial/ethnic differences in women's ways of talking about sex, while emotional satisfaction is more subject to educational differences in men's talk about sex. It could also be that some aspect of higher education raised men's expectations about the emotional aspects of sexual relationships, such that they found real life more disappointing than men whose expectations had not been raised thusly.

Relationship Level Factors

The relationship variables we tested were, by and large, poor predictors of sexual satisfaction. Although many studies have linked relationship duration to sexual satisfaction, we found no such association in any of the models we tested, among men or women. For women, the only relationship-related variables associated with satisfaction were cohabitation status (physical) and time-partner-known-before-sex (emotional). Cohabitation status did not predict women's physical satisfaction once sexual practices were introduced into the model, suggesting

that bodily practices (which may differ by cohabitation status) were more central to women's physical pleasure. For men, the only significant relationship variable was cohabitation status, which predicted greater physical pleasure until sexual attitudes were included in the model.

We suspect that disapproval of sex without love reflected an emotional dimension of participants' actual relationships rather than simply a cultural orientation toward sex. To the extent that beliefs about sex without love reflected the quality of participants' relationships, relationship quality appeared to be a better predictor of satisfaction for men than women. Disapproval of sex without love was associated with greater emotional pleasure for both genders, and with greater physical pleasure for men only. Causality should be interpreted with caution. Beliefs may shape behavior, such that people who disapproved of sex without love had sex only with beloved partners, and their love enhanced sexual satisfaction. Alternatively, men may have interpreted physically pleasurable sex as a sign of love, and then associated love with sex. People in satisfying sexual relationships may have declared that sex should be confined to loving couples because that was their own experience, whereas less-satisfied people may have distinguished love and sex because they had been separate in their own lives.

Our findings of greater emotional pleasure among women who knew their partners well before sex and among men and women who disapproved sex without love supported our prediction that relationship factors would have greater bearing on emotional than physical satisfaction, while the findings that men who cohabited and men who disapproved of sex without love experienced more physical pleasure suggested that relationship factors have more bearing on physical pleasure. In short, our research partially challenged and partially supported the commonsense assumption that emotional factors primarily affect emotional happiness. By a similar token, we found mixed evidence about gender differences. Some relationship-related factors affected women and men differently, while others acted in similar ways. These mixed findings are consistent with the literature, but somewhat unusual in a single study.

Partner's age, our proxy for partner's health and sexual function, significantly predicted emotional rather than physical enjoyment, but only for women, and only in models excluding generation. This suggested that older women's partners, almost all of them still-older men, may disproportionately lack skills related to the emotional aspects of sex, even when relationships are otherwise loving. Such skills may vary by generation, rather than age per se (Ehrenreich, Hess, & Jacobs, 1986). A study using direct measures of partner's health and sexual function would help to unravel this relationship further. Moreover, exceedingly few men had partners older than 59, the ages at which aging-related changes in health and sexual function become increasingly common among women.

For women, physical satisfaction and emotional pleasure were both associated with the frequency and duration of sexual encounters, and physical satisfaction was additionally linked with the regularity of orgasm. In contrast, for men, physical satisfaction was associated only with sexual duration and emotional pleasure only with sexual frequency. Broadly speaking, these findings were as we hypothesized; however, our predictions of greater effects on physical pleasure and among men were not supported. Indeed, bodily sexual practices appeared to be better predictors of physical and emotional satisfaction for women than relational factors, whereas for men, relational factors seemed to be better predictors of both types of satisfaction. This counterintuitive finding should prompt additional study. It is possible that previous studies have overstated gender differences; or, alternatively, that men and women's approaches to sex grow more similar over the life course.

Regarding specific sexual practices, although sexual encounters longer than 15 min predicted enhanced physical pleasure for both genders, women reported significantly more satisfaction if their encounters lasted 16–29 or 30+ min, whereas, for men, only 16–29 min encounters predicted greater satisfaction. Relatively lengthy sexual encounters may have contributed to greater physical pleasure for both sexes through the physiological mechanisms that promote arousal and climax; however, our research suggested that women's threshold for "long enough" sex was higher than men's, perhaps because women achieve arousal and orgasm more slowly. This stands in contrast to studies in which men offer significantly longer ideal intercourse times than women (Miller & Byers, 2004); but supports findings that men rate rapid ejaculation as more troubling than do their female partners (Byers & Grenier, 2003). Notably, regular orgasms were also a significant predictor of physical pleasure for women, suggesting that longer encounters were important in their own right. Longer encounters may have enhanced women's emotional sexual satisfaction by allowing for more romantic expression between partners or by indicating that one's partner was concerned with ensuring mutual pleasure, which knowledge might have heightened satisfying feelings of intimacy. (Conversely, people who were emotionally dissatisfied with their sexual partners may have avoided prolonged sexual encounters). Our analyses also indicated gendered thresholds for "regular enough" orgasms, consistent with previous research. For men, for whom orgasm during sex is understood as routine, regularity of orgasms was not predictive of sexual satisfaction; but for women, for whom orgasms during vaginal sex are less routine, climaxing only sometimes (versus always) reduced physical pleasure. Our failure to find a positive association between varied sexual practices and sexual enjoyment could have stemmed from our narrow measure of variety (limited to oral sex).

As noted, bodily practices evinced somewhat different relationships to physical and emotional pleasure, but not as we expected. For women, sexual frequency and duration were associated with both aspects of pleasure, but orgasm was linked only with physical satisfaction. This finding helps to illuminate a tension in the literature, whereby some studies find orgasm to be relatively unimportant to women's sexual pleasure (Nicolson & Burr, 2003) while others find just the opposite (Haavio-Mannila & Kontula, 1997). For men, physical satisfaction was associated only with sexual duration and emotional pleasure only with sexual frequency. These patterns make sense considering that sexual duration depends largely on physiological phenomena like erectile capacity, while the emotional quality of a couple's relationship would likely be linked to the frequency with which they have sex.

Cultural Level Factors

Our hypothesis that traditional sexual beliefs would predict lower levels of satisfaction received scant support. Women who agreed that men have greater sexual needs reported less physical pleasure than women who disagreed, but this relationship did not hold true for men or for emotional satisfaction for either gender. This pattern suggested that subscribing to traditional views of masculine sexuality, which may be more difficult to embody with advancing age, did not impair either aspect of men's sexual satisfaction; while holding traditional views of women's sexuality, which may imply a greater emphasis on youthful appearance, decreased women's physical but not emotional pleasure. (Alternatively, women who did not particularly enjoy sex may, accordingly, have felt they needed sex less than men do).

Our findings about beliefs about sex without love and premarital sex likewise tended to disconfirm our hypothesis. In contrast with studies linking permissive sexual attitudes with greater sexual satisfaction (Haavio-Mannila & Kontula, 1997), beliefs about premarital sex did not predict levels of sexual satisfaction in any of the models we tested. Moreover, approval of sex without love predicted less physical and emotional satisfaction among men and less emotional satisfaction among women. As noted, we suspect that these patterns reflected the impact

of relationship quality on sexual satisfaction, rather than the broader cultural processes our hypotheses was intended to tap.

Finally, our analyses supported the hypothesis that age effects on sexual satisfaction would be mediated by generation. Although previous research indicates that sexual satisfaction declines with advancing age, especially for women, few studies adequately distinguish between age and generation. As in other research, women in our study expressed less physical and emotional satisfaction with advancing years, whereas men reported greater emotional satisfaction at older ages. The age effects we found became non-significant when generation was added to the models, suggesting that these age patterns were largely due to differences between the Baby Boom and WWII cohorts. It therefore appears that is it not age per se, but generation that influenced women's and men's sexual satisfaction. However, the generation effect was not strong enough (or was too intertwined with other variables) for generation to be a significant predictor of satisfaction in its own right.

Notably, the effect of generation cannot be reduced to cohort differences in sexual attitudes, for these were independent predictors of sexual satisfaction. More complex forces appeared to be at work. For example, Baby Boomer women may have systematically described their sexual experiences using more dramatic terms than older women; perhaps they were socialized to express more enthusiasm about sex. It could also be that the pre-Boom generation had to a greater extent internalized the image of older women as sexually undesirable; thus, they may have perceived themselves as less sexy as they age, and gotten less emotional (or even physical) enjoyment from sex accordingly.

CONCLUSION

Taken together, our analyses highlight the nuanced ways in which gender, age, and generation shape the physical and emotional dimensions of sexual satisfaction. Overall, we found the factors contributing to sexual satisfaction to be more numerous and complex for women than for men. Contrary to popular assumptions, bodily sexual practices appeared to be better predictors of physical and emotional satisfaction for women than relational factors, whereas for men, relational factors seemed to be better predictors of both types of satisfaction. As anticipated, physical and emotional sexual satisfaction were influenced by somewhat different factors, but not always in the way commonsense assumptions would predict. Although women expressed less physical and emotional satisfaction with advancing years, while men reported greater emotional satisfaction at older ages, these age effects became non-significant when generation was added to the models, suggesting that generational differences between the Baby Boom and WWII cohorts underlay patterns by age.

At the outset of this article, we stressed the need to know more about the relative importance of biological, cultural, and psychological factors in explaining variations in sexual life. Our findings revealed how all three dimensions of human life, along with relational factors, worked together in complicated, sometimes unexpected ways, to shape sexual satisfaction. Our research also advanced knowledge about the subjective aspects of sexuality by linking levels of self-reported satisfaction to the more easily quantifiable factors on which so much sexuality research focuses. Sexual frequency, duration, and regularity of orgasm were (positively) associated with sexual satisfaction, as were objectively-measured sexual "problems" (negatively), in ways complicated by gender, generation, and age.

Our research can be usefully extended in several ways. By collecting longitudinal data on sexuality, scholars could more effectively disentangle the effects of aging from those of cohort and begin to assess questions of cause and effect. In-depth interviews and other qualitative methods could help to illuminate middle-aged

women and men's subjective understandings of sexual satisfaction and the means through which they attempt to enhance it. It would also be useful to examine the same issues among women and men aged 60 and older, especially as life expectancies continue to rise, and to chart the sexual lives of the Baby Boomers as they age. Future research could utilize additional, more direct measures of relationship quality and distinguish sexual problems that cause distress from those that do not.

A positive end in its own right, satisfying sexual activity is integral to mental health and associated with marital/ relationship stability (SIECUS, 2002). Sexual satisfaction is also seen as a hallmark of healthy/ successful aging, among those who subscribe to that paradigm. Our findings about gender and sexual satisfaction in midlife recommend optimism as well as concern. On the upside, contrary to popular stereotypes, the majority of sexually-active middle-aged heterosexual women and men are highly satisfied with the physical and emotional dimensions of their sexual relationships. On the downside, a sizeable minority of middle-aged heterosexual men and especially women describe their sexual lives as mediocre at best. Both genders would benefit from efforts to improve the overall health of older adults; to treat aging-related illnesses in ways that have fewer adverse effects on sexual life; and to counteract the ageist and sexist images that pervade American popular culture. Older women might also gain from initiatives aimed at enhancing the sexual techniques of their male partners.

Our counterintuitive findings about the importance of bodily practices for women's sexual satisfaction and the importance of relationships for men's provide particular food for thought. Why, for instance, does the cultural belief that men's sexual happiness is relatively independent from relational factors persist, when scholarly research regularly demonstrates otherwise? Our research also supports scholars (Calasanti & Slevin, 2001; Loe, 2001) who warn that Viagra alone cannot ensure men's sexual happiness, insofar as relationships play an important role in men's sexual satisfaction. For women, whose pleasure depends in large part on physical aspects of sex (contrary to widespread assumptions), medical sexual treatments should prove helpful, but not sufficient—for, as we have shown, the underpinnings of women's sexual satisfaction are complex. The relational nature of men's sexual satisfaction is cause for optimism for both genders—for men may well be eager to learn new ways of bringing their women partners physical pleasure.

INTRODUCTION REFERENCES

Pocs, O., and A. G. Godow. 1977. Can students view parents as sexual beings? *The Family Coordinator* 26: 31–6.

Koch, P. B., P. K. Mansfield, D. Thurau, and M. Carey. 2005. "Feeling frumpy": The relationship between body image and sexual response changes in midlife women. *The Journal of Sex Research* 42: 215–23.

REFERENCES

AARP. (1999). *AARP/modern maturity sexuality study.* Washington, DC: American Association for Retired Persons.

Avis, N. E., Stellato, R., Crawford, S., Johannes, C., & Longcope, C. (2000). Is there an association between menopause status and sexual functioning? *Menopause, 7,* 297–309.

Bancroft, J. (2002). The medicalization of female sexual dysfunction: The need for caution. *Archives of Sexual Behavior, 31,* 451–455.

Bancroft, J., Loftus, J., & Long, J. S. (2003). Distress about sex: A national survey of women in heterosexual relationships. *Archives of Sexual Behavior, 32,* 193–208.

Barbre, J. W. (1998). Meno-boomers and moral guardians: An exploration of the cultural construction of menopause. In R. Weitz (Ed.), *The politics of women's bodies: Sexuality, appearance, and behavior* (pp. 242–252). Oxford: Oxford University Press.

Brecher, E. M. (1983). *Love, sex, and aging: A Consumers Union report.* Boston: Little, Brown.

Byers, E. S., & Grenier, G. (2003). Premature or rapid ejaculation: Heterosexual couples' perceptions of men's ejaculatory behavior. *Archives of Sexual Behavior, 32,* 261–270.

Calasanti, T. M., & Slevin, K. F. (2001). *Gender, social inequalities, and aging.* Walnut Creek, CA: Altamira Press.

Christopher, F. S., & Sprecher, S. (2000). Sexuality in marriage, dating, and other relationships: A decade review. *Journal of Marriage and the Family, 62,* 999–1017.

Croissant, J. (2006). The new sexual technobody: Viagra in the hyperreal world. *Sexualities, 9,* 333–344.

Deeks, A. A., & McCabe, M. (2001). Sexual function and the menopausal woman: The importance of age and partner's sexual functioning. *Journal of Sex Research, 38,* 219–225.

D'Emilio, J., & Freedman, E. B. (1988). *Intimate matters: A history of sexuality in America.* New York: Harper & Row.

Dennerstein, L., Dudley, E., & Burger, H. (2001). Are changes in sexual functioning during midlife due to aging or menopause? *Fertility and Sterility, 76,* 456–460.

Edwards, J. N., & Booth, A. (1994). Sexuality, marriage, and well-being: The middle years. In A. S. Rossi (Ed.), *Sexuality across the life course* (pp. 233–259). Chicago: University of Chicago Press.

Ehrenreich, B., Hess, E., & Jacobs, G. (1986). *Re-making love: The feminization of sex.* New York: Doubleday.

Gagnon, J. H., & Simon, W. (1987). The sexual scripting of oral genital contacts. *Archives of Sexual Behavior, 16,* 1–25.

George, L. K., & Weiler, S. J. (1981). Sexuality in middle and late life: The effects of age, cohort, and gender. *Archives of General Psychiatry, 38,* 919–923.

Gibson, H. B. (1993). Emotional and sexual adjustment in later life. In S. Arber & M. Evandrou (Eds.), *Ageing, independence, and the life course* (pp. 104–118). London: Jessica Kingsley.

Haavio-Mannila, E., & Kontula, O. (1997). Correlates of increased sexual satisfaction. *Archives of Sexual Behavior, 26,* 399–419.

Henderson-King, D. H., & Veroff, J. (1994). Sexual satisfaction and marital well-being in the first years of marriage. *Journal of Social and Personal Relationships, 11,* 509–534.

Huyck, M. H. (1994). Marriage and close relationships of the marital kind. In R. Blieszner & V. H. Bedford (Eds.), *Aging and the family* (pp. 181–200). Westport, CT: Praeger.

Keith, B., & White, L. (1990). The effect of shift work on the quality and stability of marital relations. *Journal of Marriage and the Family, 52,* 453–463.

Laumann, E. O., Gagnon, J. H., Michael, R. T., & Michaels, S. (1994). *The social organization of sexuality: Sexual practices in the United States.* Chicago: University of Chicago Press.

Levy, J. A. (1994). Sex and sexuality in later life stages. In A. S. Rossi (Ed.), *Sexuality across the life course* (pp. 287–309). Chicago: University of Chicago Press.

Liu, C. (2003). Does quality of marital sex decline with duration? *Archives of Sexual Behavior, 32,* 55–60.

Loe, M. (2001). Fixing broken masculinity: Viagra as a technology for the production of gender and sexuality. *Sexuality and Culture, 5,* 97–125.

Luria, Z., & Meade, R. (1984). Sexuality and the middle-aged woman. In G. Baruch & J. Brooks-Gunn (Eds.), *Women in midlife* (pp. 371–397). New York: Plenum Press.

Marsiglio, W., & Greer, R. A. (1994). A gender analysis of older men's sexuality: Social, psychological, and biological dimensions. In J. E. H. Thompson & M. S. Kimmel (Eds.), *Older men's lives* (pp. 122–140). Thousand Oaks, CA: Sage.

Miller, S. A., & Byers, E. S. (2004). Actual and desired duration of foreplay and intercourse: Discordance and misperception within heterosexual couples. *Journal of Sex Research, 41,* 301–309.

Nicolson, P., & Burr, J. (2003). What is "normal" about women's (hetero)sexual desire and orgasm? A report of an in-depth interview study. *Social Science & Medicine, 57,* 1735–1745.

Pedersen, W., & Blekesaune, M. (2003). Sexual satisfaction in young adulthood: Cohabitation, committed dating or unattached life? *Acta Sociologica, 46,* 179–193.

Riley, M. W. (1987). On the significance of age in sociology. *American Sociological Review, 52,* 1–14.

Schiavi, R. C. (1994). Effect of chronic disease and medication on sexual functioning. In A. S. Rossi (Ed.), *Sexuality across the life course* (pp. 313–339). Chicago: University of Chicago Press.

Schiavi, R. C. (1996). Sexuality and male aging: From performance to satisfaction. *Sexual and Marital Therapy, 11,* 9–13.

Segraves, R. T., & Segraves, K. B. (1995). Human sexuality and aging. *Journal of Sex Education and Therapy, 21,* 88–102.

SIECUS. (2002). SIECUS position statement on "sexuality of the aging." *SIECUS Report: Sexuality and aging revisited, 30,* 2.

Sprecher, S. (2002). Sexual satisfaction in premarital relationships: Associations with satisfaction, love, commitment, and stability. *Journal of Sex Research, 39,* 190–197.

Starr, B. D., & Weiner, M. B. (1981). *The Starr–Weiner report on sex and sexuality in the mature years.* New York: McGraw-Hill.

Vares, T., & Braun, V. (2006). Speading the word, but what word is that? Viagra and male sexuality in popular culture. *Sexualities, 9,* 315–332.

Waite, L. J., & Joyner, K. (2001). Emotional and physical satisfaction with sex in married, cohabiting, dating sexual unions: Do men and women differ? In E. O. Laumann & R. T. Michael (Eds.), *Sex, love, and health in America: Private choices and public policies* (pp. 239–269). Chicago: University of Chicago Press.

Wiley, D., & Bortz, W. M. I. (1996). Sexuality and aging – usual and successful. *Journal of Gerontology, 51A,* M142–M146.

Winterich, J. A. (2003). Sex, menopause, and culture: Sexual orientation and the meaning of menopause for women's sex lives. *Gender & Society, 17,* 627–642.

CHAPTER 19

Sexual Behavior in Later Life

John DeLamater
Sarah M. Moorman

The sexuality of older adults is difficult to study for a variety of reasons. Older adults tend to be from a generation that has always been less comfortable discussing sexual matters than are their younger adult counterparts. There is also the idea, held by many, that sex is only for the young. This misconception might tend to make older research participants less willing to reveal anything about their sexual lives. In addition, many older adults, particularly women, find themselves without mates and thus unable to participate in partnered sex, which may be, for some, the only form of sexual expression to which they are willing to admit.

Nonetheless, as time goes on, researchers are gaining a better understanding of what changes over time are inevitable, and which ones are a function of generation and partner status. The following study by Delamater and Moorman uses a biopsychosocial perspective which enables an understanding of the dynamics of sexuality from a biological, psychological, and social standpoint.

This article helps combat the myth that sexual activity is not prevalent among the elderly. It confirms the reality that sexual needs do not change abruptly with age; that in fact, the potential for sexual expression continues until death. But it also raises related questions that may have surprising

answers. Is sexual vigor necessarily age-related? Does age have comparable effects on both men and women as physiological changes occur during the later years? What roles do touching, caressing, masturbation, and sexual intercourse play in the lives of later-age seniors?

Unfortunately, a lack of informed opinion about aging and sexuality is not limited to the public. Despite an explosion of knowledge about sexuality, most physicians receive little, if any, sexuality education in medical school, especially that which pertains to the elderly. Similarly, nursing-home staffs are only moderately knowledgeable about sexuality in older persons and are often, as a result, highly restrictive and judgmental in their attitudes and rules about elderly sexuality. What are the sources of such oppression of sexual fulfillment for the elderly? Certainly, lack of knowledge is one factor. But, the negative reaction of health professionals may also be a manifestation of their own fears of aging or perhaps lack of acceptance of their own sexuality. Which would you guess?

If social scientists from an alien planet wished to learn about Earthling behavior from reading our scientific research literature, they might well conclude that sexuality is not important to humans older than 50. Remarkably few scientific studies address sexual behavior in mid- and later life or the ways in which sexuality changes over the life course. In this article, we seek to narrow this gap in knowledge: We examine the biological and psychosocial factors associated with frequency of sexual behavior in adults aged 45 and older.

Cross-sectional surveys report that the frequency of sexual behavior declines in successively older age groups. This finding holds in nationally representative samples (Call, Sprecher, & Schwartz, 1995; National Council on Aging, 1998) as well as in large nonrandom samples (Matthias, Lubben, Atchison, & Schweitzer, 1997; Starr & Wiener, 1981), and samples from outside the United States (Kontula, 2002). The largest of these studies (Call et al., 1995) included 6,785 married persons aged 19 and older who were participants in the National Survey of Families and Households. Although 96% of married persons aged 19 to 24 had engaged in sexual intercourse at least once in the past month, as had 83% of those aged 50 to 54, only 27% of those aged 75 or older had. Noncelibate couples in this oldest age group had sex an average of 3 times per month.

Three explanations for these findings have been forwarded. First, age may be a proxy for duration of relationship. Monotony or habituation to sex with a long-term partner may lead to a decline in frequency of sexual behavior (Call et al., 1995). In a review of the literature, however, Burgess (2004) concludes that although duration has effects on frequency, the effects of age are strong and independent.

Second, the cross-sectional finding that older adults engage in sex less frequently than do younger adults may be the result of cohort, rather than age, effects. Reviewers of the literature have concluded that both factors are at work. Noting dramatic changes in attitudes about sexuality since World War II, as well as increases in healthy life expectancy, Burgess (2004) predicts that future cohorts of older adults will be more sexually active than are current cohorts. Edwards and Booth (1994) conclude that although members of later cohorts enjoy more sexual variety and frequency than

do members of earlier cohorts, sexual activity becomes less frequent with age for all cohorts.

Third, increasing age may represent increasing problems with physical health. A sizeable literature suggests that chronic illnesses (Marumo & Murai, 2001) or common medications (Trudel, Turgeon, & Piche, 2000) interfere with sexual function. Most sex research on older adults focuses on illness (Burgess, 2004).

A much smaller literature emphasizes psychosocial factors, such as self-image, religious values, psychological well-being, social connectedness, and relationship satisfaction (Marsiglio & Donnelly, 1991; Matthias et al., 1997). In this article we seek to unite the two emphases, using the biopsychosocial perspective, to contribute a much-needed theoretical basis to the literature on sexuality and aging (DeLamater & Hyde, 2004). In addition, most research is based on limited measures of sexual functioning; the data presented here include measures of sexual desire as well as partnered and unpartnered sexual behavior.

We argue for a broad biopsychosocial perspective on health, as presented by Lindau, Laumann, Levinson, and Waite (2003). This perspective is characterized by seven core principles: (a) Researchers should attend to health rather than illness but (b) retain the capacity to study health or illness as outcomes; (c) biological, psychological, and social domains contribute equally to health outcomes; (d) causality is bidirectional (i.e., biopsychosocial factors influence health outcomes and vice versa); (e) health depends not only on the individual but also on interactions with family and ties to other social networks; (f) life-course trajectories influence health; and (g) biopsychosocial influences can be helpful or harmful to health.

Hypothesis 1: Age will be negatively associated with frequency of sexual behavior, but the association will be greatly reduced following the addition of measures of biological and psychosocial influences.

BIOLOGICAL ASPECTS OF SEXUALITY

Although the biopsychosocial model emphasizes good health, prior research has focused on sexuality and poor health. This literature suggests that we cannot ignore the effects of illness and its treatment on sexual behavior. Moreover, because the effects of psychological and social variables on sexuality in later life have not been tested before, we can draw conclusions about their relative importance only through comparison with the effects of biological variables.

Aging and Chronic Illness

Most of the research on health in the aging population has measured incidence of illness. Chronic illnesses, such as cardiovascular disease, diabetes, arthritis, depression, benign prostate conditions, and cancers of the reproductive organs, are commonly associated with sexual problems in older people (Feldman, Goldstein, Hatzichristou, Krane, & McKinlay, 1994; Johannes et al., 2000; Stead, 2004). For instance, in a study of 120 women with diabetes and 180 age-matched healthy controls, women with diabetes were significantly more likely to report sexual dysfunction than were nondiabetic women (Enzlin et al., 2002). Diabetes was associated with pain during sex, decreased desire, and decreased arousal. Schiavi, Stimmel, Mandeli, and Rayfield (1993) found that diabetic men, in comparison with aged-matched healthy controls, showed large decrements in sexual activity and satisfaction. Furthermore, the diabetic men reported decreased penile sensitivity and a range of ejaculatory and orgasmic difficulties, which are well-established complications of diabetes (Veves, Webster, Chen, Payne, & Boulton, 1995).

Aging and Medication Use

Medications used to treat chronic illnesses also interfere with sexual functioning. Many medications prescribed today slow the autonomic nervous system, reducing responsiveness and sensitivity to stimulation. For instance, antiandrogen treatment for prostate cancer can reduce sexual drive and cause erectile dysfunction (Marumo & Murai, 2001). Medications may also interfere with capacity for sustained sexual thought or fantasy. Antihypertensive drugs represent the single largest medication group implicated in the development of sexual side effects, including difficulties in attaining orgasm for both women and men (Masters et al., 1994).

Hypothesis 2: In the biological domain, chronic illnesses and their medical treatment will be negatively associated with frequency of sexual activity. A participant's self-reported physical or emotional sexual limitations will also be negatively associated with sexual frequency.

Lindau, Laumann, Levinson, and Waite (2003) call attention to the role of social ties in determining healthy functioning, and many sexual behaviors require a partner. If a respondent's physical or emotional sexual limitations are negatively related to frequency of sexual behavior, any limitations of his or her partner can also be expected to have negative effects on the couple's sexual frequency. The greatest decrements in functioning would be expected when both respondent and partner are limited.

Hypothesis 3: Participant and partner sexual health limitations will have interactive effects on frequency of sexual behavior.

PSYCHOSOCIAL ASPECTS OF SEXUALITY

The meaning and significance of sexuality in individual lives—that is, *sexual attitudes*—are important determinants of reactions to sexual changes associated with aging (Schiavi, 1999). Many older persons do not believe that sexual expression is natural and healthy for elderly people (Trudel et al., 2000). Many older persons look to the "middle-aged" or the "young" as a reference group. Comparison to either reference group creates dissatisfaction with changing appearance and abilities, which in turn can lead to sexual dissatisfaction. A survey of older women found that those who endorsed statements such as "romantic involvement between older people looks foolish" reported significantly lower levels of sexual activity (Johnson, 1998).

Sexual desire is a prerequisite for enjoyable sexual activity (DeLamater & Sill, 2005). Desire is defined here as conscious thought about or interest in sexual activity. Desire is the psychological manifestation of an interaction between biological factors, cognitive factors, learned behavior, and past experience. An important premise of the biopsychosocial model is that characteristics of the person's social network influence sexual expression (Lindau et al., 2003). The presence or absence of a sexual partner is extremely important in understanding differing levels of sexual activity among aging women and men. Many older people consider sexual intimacy to be only or most appropriate in marriage; thus death and divorce leave many older Americans without a sexual partner. Single women are particularly disadvantaged because the sex ratio becomes increasingly imbalanced with age.

Many older people who are without a sexual partner for an extended amount of time drift into a state of sexual disinterest. Masters et al. (1994) suggest that women "turn off" their interest as a coping mechanism: Not wanting sex prevents frustration and depression. In Schiavi's (1999) study sexual interest and behavior in men decreased greatly when there was no sexual partner or the sexual partner was without sexual desire.

For those who do have a sexual partner, satisfaction with the relationship is an important influence on sexuality. Laumann, Gagnon, Michael, and Michaels (1994) measured how physically pleasurable and emotionally satisfying the relationship with one's partner was. These factors, in addition to duration of relationship (Burgess, 2004), may affect the frequency and quality of sexual activity.

> *Hypothesis 4*: In the psychosocial domain, negative attitudes toward sexual activity in later life and low sexual desire will be negatively associated with frequency of sexual activity. Having a healthy sexual partner and being satisfied with that relationship will be positively associated, and long relationships, negatively associated, with frequency of sexual activity.

METHODS

Participants

We analyzed secondary data provided to us by the American Association of Retired Persons (AARP). The AARP Modern Maturity Sexuality Survey was a mail survey completed by 1,384 women and men ages 45 and older. The survey was designed by the editorial staff of Modern Maturity and the AARP Research Group with the assistance of the New England Research Institute and NFO Research. A commercial data collection agency, NFO maintains a consumer panel of 565,000 individuals who are broadly representative of the population of the United States and who have agreed to participate in surveys. Surveys were mailed to all of the 1,709 individuals (not couples) who agreed to participate (77% of those contacted); 1,384 returned completed surveys (81% of those who were sent the survey, 62% of those contacted). These final data were weighted to reflect United States Census Bureau estimates for age and gender of the population over age 45, resulting in a sample of 745 women and 639 men.

Independent Variables

Age. Male participants ranged in age from 45 to 89 years old, female participants from 45 to 94.

Illnesses. All participants were asked to indicate if they had been diagnosed with any of eight chronic conditions. More than 10% of the men and of the women reported being diagnosed with diabetes, hypertension, arthritis, or depression. Other conditions (e.g., HIV/AIDS) were reported by fewer persons. Male participants were asked if they had ever been diagnosed with benign and/or malignant prostate problems, and female participants were asked if they had ever been diagnosed with gynecological (breast, cervical, and/or ovarian) cancer.

Treatment. Participants who had been diagnosed with an illness were asked to indicate whether or not they were receiving treatment for that illness.

Sexual restrictions. Participants were asked, "Do you have any physical or emotional limitations or illnesses which restrict your sexual activity?"

Attitudes toward sex. Attitudes toward sex were measured with a series of nine items. For both men and women, Factor 1 consisted of three items assessing respondents' attitudes about sex for the self. Items included, "I do not particularly enjoy sex," "I would be quite happy never having sex again," and "Sex is only for younger people." Again, for both men and women, Factor 2 included three items: "Sexual activity is important to my overall quality of life," "Sexual activity is a critical part of a good relationship," and "Sexual activity is a duty to one's spouse/partner." These items assess attitudes toward sex in relationships.

Sexual desire index. Level of sexual desire was measured by two questions: "How frequently do you feel sexual desire? This feeling includes wanting to have sexual experiences, planning to have sex, and feeling frustrated due to lack of sex," and "How frequently do you have sexual thoughts, fantasies, or erotic dreams?" Each question was answered using a 8-point scale (8 = more than once a day, 7 = once a day, 6 = 2 or 3 times per week, 5 = once a week, 4 = 2 or 3 times per month, 3 = once per month, 2 = less than once per month, 1 = not at all).

Characteristics of the sexual partner. Participants were asked if they currently had a sexual partner. Seventy-nine percent of the men and

60% of the women had partners. In more than 96% of the cases, the partner was a spouse. Less than 1% of participants reported a same-sex partner; these participants were excluded from analyses. If a participant had a partner, he or she responded to a series of questions that were not asked of participants without partners. Length of relationship could range from *less than 6 months; 6 to 11 months; 1 to 2 years; 3 to 5 years; 6 to 10 years; 11 to 20 years;* to *more than 20 years*). This item was highly skewed as 70% of participants were in partnerships of 20 years or more, and none reported a partnership shorter than 3 to 5 years. Therefore we dichotomized the variable into a measure of long relationships: 20 years or fewer, more than 20 years. Two items assessed facets of sexual satisfaction. The participant answered the questions, "In the past 6 months, how emotionally satisfying was your relationship with your partner?" and "In the past 6 months, how physically pleasurable was your relationship with your partner?" Finally, participants were asked whether the partner had any physical or emotional limitations that restricted the couple's sexual activity.

Dependent Variables

Five sexual behaviors (four partnered, one nonpartnered) were assessed. Participants were asked, "During the past 6 months, how often, on average, have you engaged in the following sexual activities?" The behaviors included kissing or hugging, sexual touching or caressing, oral sex, sexual intercourse, and masturbation. Response alternatives for all items were *not at all, less than once a month, once or twice a month, about once a week, more than once a week,* and *daily.*

Analytic Strategy

Analyses were run separately for men and women. The four partnered behaviors were restricted to the subset of participants (503 men and 446 women) who reported having sexual partners, because few participants reported having no regular partner but engaging in partnered behaviors. Note that limiting to participants with partners affects the age distribution of the sample, especially for women. The median age of partnered women is 55, whereas the median age of women without partners is 69. The median age of partnered men is 57, whereas the median age of men without partners is 66.

Modeling. Model 1 tests the effects of age alone, Model 2 tests the effects of age and biological variables, and Model 3, age and psychosocial variables. Model 4 tests the effects of all variables. Model 5 tests the effects of all variables plus the interaction term Respondent's Sexual Limitations x Partner's Sexual Limitations.

RESULTS

Hypothesis 1: Age negatively associated with frequency of sexual behavior, association reduced following the addition of measures of biological, psychological, and social influences.

Age was negatively associated with the frequency of all five sexual behaviors for both men and women. Age had the largest effect on frequency of oral sex for both men and women (Model 1). Second, following the addition of biological, psychological, and social variables (Model 4), the effect size of age was reduced for all five outcomes across gender.

Hypothesis 2: Chronic illnesses and their treatment negatively associated with frequency of sexual activity. Self-reported sexual limitations negatively associated with sexual frequency.

Although we predicted that illnesses and their treatments would be negatively associated with frequency of sexual activity, very few of the coefficients were significant (Model 2). Several significant effects were opposite to the hypothesis: Treatment for high blood pressure was associated with higher frequency of hugging and kissing for women, a diagnosis of depression was associated with higher frequency of intercourse for women, and male participants who reported

a sexual limitation masturbated more frequently than did male participants who were not limited.

Other effects supported our hypothesis. Among women, a diagnosis of high blood pressure was associated with lower frequency of hugging and kissing, and a report of sexual limitation was associated with lower frequency of both oral sex and intercourse. Among men, treatment for a benign prostate condition was associated with lower frequency of oral sex, a report of sexual limitation was associated with lower frequency of intercourse, and treatment for depression was associated with lower frequency of masturbation.

Hypothesis 3: The interactive effects of participant and partner sexual health limitations.

For women, the interaction of participant's sexual health limitations and partner's sexual health limitations was not significant for any outcome (Model 5). For men, the interaction term was significant for intercourse. This effect is opposite to the direction hypothesized: Couples with two limited partners have more frequent intercourse than do couples with one or no limited partners. The small number of individuals reporting that both they and their partners suffer limitations (37 women and 50 men) introduces power problems into our analyses; thus our findings should not be regarded as definitive.

Hypothesis 4: Negative attitudes toward sexual activity in later life and low sexual desire negatively associated with frequency of sexual activity. Having a healthy sexual partner and being satisfied with that relationship positively associated, long relationships negatively associated with frequency of sexual activity.

In the psychosocial domain (Model 3), positive attitudes toward sexuality for the self and for the relationship and high sexual desire were, in general, associated with more frequent sexual activity. For men, negative attitudes toward sex in relationships were associated with higher frequency of masturbation.

Satisfaction with a partner was associated with higher frequency of kissing and hugging and sexual touch in men and in women. Greater physical satisfaction with the relationship was associated with more frequent oral sex for women. Physical satisfaction with the partner was associated with higher frequencies of intercourse for men and for women, and women with healthy partners had more frequent intercourse than did women with sexually limited partners. Both men and women without partners engaged in more frequent masturbation than did men and women with partners. Men who were less physically satisfied with their partners masturbated more often than did men who were more physically satisfied with their partners. Women with sexually limited partners masturbated more frequently than did women with healthy partners. Men and women in shorter relationships engaged in more frequent oral sex than did men and women in long relationships.

DISCUSSION

In this study, we found that although age was negatively associated with frequency of partnered and nonpartnered sexual behavior, accounting for biological and psychosocial variables attenuated this effect, as predicted by the biopsychosocial model. Diagnosed illnesses and their associated treatments exerted surprisingly little influence on frequency of sexual behavior. Positive attitudes about and desire for sex and having a physically satisfying relationship were strongly associated with greater frequency of sexual behaviors in both men and women.

Cohort

Our findings support the conclusion of Edwards and Booth (1994) that members of younger cohorts engage in more varied forms of sex than do members of older cohorts. Out of all five behaviors, increasing age was most strongly associated with infrequent oral sex. Whereas only 44% of women and 38% of men ages 45

to 49 reported never having oral sex, more than 75% of men and women in all age groups over 65 reported never engaging in this behavior. But those over 65 did engage in intercourse, even though intercourse is more physically demanding than oral sex. Furthermore, independent of age, long relationships were significantly negatively associated only with oral sex, such that individuals in relationships shorter than 20 years engaged in more frequent oral sex than did individuals in relationships longer than 20 years. We speculate that younger cohorts view oral sex as a more acceptable and desirable part of the sexual repertoire than older cohorts do.

Age, Gender, and Partnership

In the majority of our analyses, adding biological, psychological, and social variables to the model did not eliminate the significant effect of age. For women, age likely represents biological variables not available for inclusion in the model. For instance, the hormonal changes associated with women's menopause often result in inadequate lubrication and vaginal atrophy, which may cause pain during intercourse (Dennerstein, Dudley, & Burger, 2001). What the remaining age effect represents is less obvious for men, but these may involve biological and psychosocial variables. Burgess (2004) notes that in a cultural context that equates men's sexual performance with penile performance, an aging man may believe himself to be an inadequate sexual partner when his penis no longer responds as it did when he was younger.

Few gender differences emerged. Intercourse was strongly and negatively associated with having or being a male partner who had restrictions, and men's restrictions were associated with more frequent masturbation among their partners. Indeed, the presence or absence of a partner was far more influential than gender, supporting the assertion that social network characteristics are relevant to understanding sexual expression. Men and women without partners masturbated more frequently than did persons with partners.

The frequency of all partnered behaviors was positively associated with physical satisfaction in the relationship.

Representativeness

Because participants knew the topic of the study before they agreed to respond, the representativeness of our data is an obvious concern. We can compare some of our behavioral data with the results of the National Health and Social Life Survey (NHSLS; Laumann et al., 1994). The NHSLS sample included persons aged 18 to 59 in 1992. We can compare the reported frequency of masturbation by persons 45 to 59 in the AARP data with those in the NHSLS data. We compared reports by persons 45 to 49, 50 to 54, and 55 to 59 separately for men and women. Both data sets include reports of at least weekly masturbation. The reports of men in the two samples are similar, with reports in all three age groups ranging from 31% to 38% (Laumann et al., 1994). The reports of women are also very similar, ranging from 1% to 9%. Turning to reports of intercourse, men in the three age groups in the AARP sample are more likely to report at least weekly intercourse (56%, 52%, and 57%) than men in the NHSLS (37%, 27%, and 18%; Laumann et al., 1994). Women in the AARP sample are also more likely to report at least weekly intercourse (55%, 50%, and 40%) than were women in the NHSLS (27%, 20%, and 7%). Thus the results are similar for masturbation, whereas AARP participants report more frequent partnered activity. Differences may be due to mode of data collection (the AARP data were collected via mailed survey; the NHSLS, via face-to-face interviews) and/or to cohort differences (Edwards & Booth, 1994).

A similar comparison can be made with the results the National Council on Aging (NCOA) survey (1998). Questionnaires were mailed to a representative sample and 1,292 completed surveys were returned. We can compare reports of sexual activity at least once a month in the past year for men and women ages 60 to 69 and 70 to 79. For men in the AARP sample,

71% and 64%, respectively, report sexual activity in the past year, compared with 71% and 57% (NCOA, 1998); for women in the AARP sample, the result is 47% and 26%, compared with 51% and 30%. These percentages are quite similar, the largest difference being 7%. These comparisons give us some confidence that the AARP data are representative of older Americans in the 1990s.

LIMITATIONS

Our study has several limitations of note. First, like all sex research, we must rely on self-reports of sexual behavior, although our results are consistent with those reported by others. Second, we rely on secondary data. Variables such as race/ethnicity, religious affiliation, and living arrangements may affect sexual expression, but this information is not available to us in these data. We have only a measure of depression diagnosis. Study participants without an official diagnosis could have been experiencing depressive symptoms that interfered with sexual functioning. We have many measures of illness but no measures of healthy biological functioning, and the biopsychosocial model posits that health is as influential as illness. Third, more than 99% of the members of the sample were in heterosexual relationships; too few persons reported same-gender partners to allow for analyses. Finally, this study is cross-sectional, and so we cannot determine causal direction. For instance, we may conclude that individuals in satisfying relationships have more sex, or we may conclude that individuals who have more sex are more satisfied with their relationships.

CONCLUSIONS

Our purpose was to test a biopsychosocial model of the influences on sexual expression of men and women over the age of 45. Individuals who are healthy and satisfied with their relationship remain sexually active into their 70s and

80s. The nature of sexual expression in later life reflects the interplay of body, mind, and social context.

REFERENCES

Burgess, E. O. (2004). Sexuality in midlife and later life couples. In J. Harvey, A. Wenzel, & S. Sprecher (Eds.), *The handbook of sexuality in close relationships* (pp. 437–454). Mahwah, NJ: Erlbaum.

Call, V., Sprecher, S., Schwartz, P. (1995). The incidence and frequency of marital sex in a national sample. *Journal of Marriage and the Family, 57*(3), 639–652.

DeLamater, J., & Hyde, J. (2004). Conceptual and theoretical issues in studying sexuality in close relationships. In J. Harvey, A. Wenzel, & S. Sprecher (Eds.), *The handbook of sexuality in close relationships* (pp. 7–30). Mahwah, NJ: Erlbaum.

DeLamater, J., & Sill, M. (2005). Sexual desire in later life. *Journal of Sex Research, 42*(2), 138–149.

Dennerstein, L., Dudley, E., & Burger, H. (2001). Are changes in sexual functioning during midlife due to aging or menopause? *Fertility and Sterility, 76*, 456–460.

Edwards, J. N., & Booth, A. (1994). Sexuality, marriage, and well-being: The middle years. In A. S. Rossi (Ed.), *Sexuality across the life course* (pp. 233–259). Chicago: University of Chicago Press.

Enzlin, P., Mathieu, C., Van Den Bruel, A., Bosteels, J., Vanderschueren, D., & Demyttenaere, K. (2002). Sexual dysfunction in women with Type I diabetes. *Diabetes Care, 25*(4), 672–677.

Feldman, H., Goldstein, I., Hatzichristou, D., Krane, R., & McKinlay, J. (1994). Impotence and its medical and psychosocial correlates: Results of the Massachusetts Male Aging Study. *The Journal of Urology, 151*(1), 54–61.

Johannes, C., Araujo, A., Feldman, H., Derby, C., Kleinman, K., & McKinlay, J. (2000). Incidence of erectile dysfunction in men 40 to 69 years old: Longitudinal results from the Massachusetts Male Aging Study. *The Journal of Urology, 163*(2), 460–463.

Johnson, B. K. (1998). A correlational framework for understanding sexuality in women age 50 and older. *Health Care International for Women, 19*, 553–564.

Kontula, O. (2002, November). *Human sexuality and aging: An empirical study.* presented at the annual meeting of the Society for the Scientific Study of Sexuality, Montreal, Canada.

Laumann, E. O., Gagnon, J. H., Michael, R. T., & Michaels, S. (1994). *The social organization of sexuality: Sexual practices in the United States.* Chicago: University of Chicago Press.

Lindau, S., Laumann, E. O., Levinson, W., & Waite, L. (2003). Synthesis of scientific disciplines in pursuit of health: The interactive biopsychsocial model. *Perspectives in Biology and Medicine, 46*(3), S74–S86.

Marsiglio, W., & Donnelly, D. (1991). Sexual relations in later life: A national study of married persons. *Journal of Gerontology: Social Sciences, 46*, S338–S344.

Marumo, K., & Murai, M. (2001). Aging and erectile dysfunction: The role of aging and concomitant chronic illness. *International Journal of Urology, 8*, S50–S57.

Masters, W., Johnson, V., & Kolodny, R. (1994). *Heterosexuality.* New York: Harper Collins.

Matthias, R. E., Lubben, J. E., Atchison, K. A., & Schweitzer, S. O. (1997). Sexual activity and satisfaction among very old adults: Results from a community-dwelling Medicare population survey. *The Gerontologist, 37*, 6–14.

National Council on Aging. (1998). *Healthy sexuality and vital aging: Executive summary.* Washington, DC: The National Council on Aging.

Schiavi, R. (1999). *Aging and male sexuality.* Cambridge: Cambridge University Press.

Schiavi, R., Stimmel, B., Mandeli, J., & Rayfield, E. (1993). Diabetes mellitus and male sexual function: A control study. *Diabetologia, 36*, 745–751.

Starr, B. D., & Weiner, M. B. (1981). *The Starr-Weiner report on sex and sexuality in the mature years.* Briarcliff Manor, NY: Stein & Day.

Stead, M. L. (2004). Sexual function after treatment for gynecological malignancy. *Current Opinion in Oncology, 16*, 492–495.

Trudel, G., Turgeon, L., & Piche, L. (2000). Marital and sexual aspects of old age. *Sexual & Relationship Therapy, 15*(4), 381–406.

Veves, A., Webster, L., Chen, T., Payne, S., & Boulton, A. (1995). Aetiopathogenesis and management of impotence in diabetic males: Four years experience from combined clinic. *Diabetic Medicine: A Journal of the British Diabetic Association, 12*(1), 77–82.

The New Virility

Viagra, Male Aging, and Sexual Function

Barbara L. Marshall

If you are a man, what do you expect your sexual functioning to be like as you age? If it doesn't meet your expectations, how much intervention are you willing to accept? If you have a male partner with erectile dysfunction (ED), to what extent would you want him to pursue a medically-based solution? Would you feel that your partner desires you less if he needs a medical solution to erectile dysfunction?

In the following article, Barbara Marshall provides an interesting overview of the change in views of aging male sexuality over the years, in part, due to the development of effective erectile dysfunction medications. While Viagra and related drugs reflect the current state of the art regarding treatment for ED, there might well be other treatments in the future. Viagra, while very effective for many, does have its share of side effects and can cause relationship complications.

One of the more interesting aspects of this reading is the discussion of the concept of "male menopause." Women, of course, go through the climacteric period resulting in menopause generally between the ages of 45–55. This change in reproductive function is hormonally-based, universal,

and inevitable. There have always been a few medical professionals who have suggested that there might be a comparable process in men due to a decline in testosterone levels, sometimes termed "andropause." You will need to read the article to learn what Marshall has to say about this idea.

Over the last century, a variety of expert discourses–including psychiatry, gerontology, sexology, endocrinology, and urology–have been central in the construction and reconstruction of sexual lifecourses. Traditionally, the assumption that sexual function and virility naturally decline with age grounded the efforts of the sexological sciences to help men manage and adjust to what was considered a finite bodily resource. However, late in the 20th century, as the sexual capacities of aging men were opened up to new biomedical treatments and consumerist lifestyle projects, what were previously considered to be "normal" changes in sexual capacities associated with bodily aging became pathologized as sexual dysfunctions. While not entirely responsible for this reconfigured understanding of the aging male, the success of the blockbuster drug Viagra (sildenafil citrate) in securing a particular understanding of sexuality and sexual function across the lifecourse cannot be underestimated. As a site of convergence between the "biomedicalization of aging" (Estes and Binney, 1989;

Gilleard and Higgs, 1998) and that of sexuality (Tiefer, 1996), the reconceptualization of what might have been considered normative experiences related to bodily aging as dysfunctions which demand correction means that masculine vitality itself has increasingly become framed as a biochemical problem in both medical and popular discourses. John Hoberman (2005: 71), in his history of testosterone, credits the "Viagra boom" with being the catalyst for reviving scientific interest in the sexual effects of testosterone on aging men which had for years been "suppressed by old taboos and the timidity of potential sponsors".

This article explores the contemporary bodily configuration, still in the making, of the virile, sexually-fit aging male. I analyze scientific and clinical texts on aging and sexuality, as well as health promotion and marketing initiatives directed at older men, to trace both the history and contemporary dimensions of the new culture of virility. The first part of the article reviews shifting scientific and cultural narratives of the sex/age problematic in men over the course of the 20th century. The varying significance accorded to changing sexual capacities is illustrated from early assertions of the natural waning of sexual powers with age to the more contemporary emphasis on continued sexual functionality as a marker of successful aging. The latter part of the article explores how the newly robust "men's health" industry has expanded the medicalization of masculinity in later life, particularly via the recuperation of the "male menopause" as "androgen deficiency in the aging male", and has framed emerging understandings of risk, health and surveillance in relation to sexual function.

REJUVENATION AND THE AGING MALE: FROM FRINGE TO MAINSTREAM

Historically, aging was viewed as a process of de-sexualization, and both medical and moral authorities in the late 19th and early 20th centuries extolled the virtues of the post-reproductive, post-sexual life. Popular author Sylvanus Stall (1901: 59), suggesting that it was nature's course to diminish sexual power in men once their peak reproductive fitness had passed, reminded his readers of the benefits of accepting and adjusting to sexual decline, promising that "the stress of passion will be past, the imagination will become more chastened, the heart more refined, the lines of intellectual and spiritual vision lengthened, the sphere of usefulness enlarged". The conviction that men's sexual powers naturally declined with age could lead only to a counsel of acceptance, and advice similar to Stall's was widely repeated in the early 20th-century literature. For example, Frederic Sturgis (1930: 312) advised that "Where old age is the cause of impotence, there is, alas! no remedy, except to submit as gracefully as possible to the decrees of fate, and by carefully husbanding the sexual resources to prolong the usefulness of the genital organs as far as possible".

Not all early 20th-century scientists embraced the counsel of graceful acceptance of decline. Some contended that the secret to masculine vitality–and the secret to forestalling its loss in the aging process—lay in the sex glands themselves. While there has certainly been a long-standing belief that masculine virility, valor and vigor are rooted in the testes, assumptions of the testicular basis of masculinity came to the fore in the organotherapy and rejuvenation experiments of the late 19th and early 20th centuries. Sengoopta (2001: 644) calls the 1920s the "decade of the testicle" as it was then that "physiological and clinical research on testicular functions came together in what, for a time, seemed to be a spectacularly successful synthesis". Austrian scientist Eugen Steinach, after a period of experimentation with testicular transplants, became famous for the "Steinach operation". This was essentially a vasectomy which supposedly let the body reabsorb testicular fluid instead of discharging it, hence reaping the benefits of its invigorating power (Sengoopta, 2003).

By the 1920s, other scientists around the world, such as Harry Benjamin and Peter Schmidt, had taken up Steinach's theories and were conducting their own trials with surgical rejuvenation (Schmidt, 1929).

Relatively few men actually underwent the procedures advocated by the rejuvenation enthusiasts, and what success those who did may have claimed is now suspected to be largely a placebo effect (Cussons et al., 2002). By the 1930s, surgical rejuvenation was largely discredited as a medical practice and was consigned to the fringes of quackery (Jaheil, 1992). But as commentators such as Susan Squier (1999) and John Hoberman (2005) have noted, the ideas of rejuvenation and life-extension retained both cultural and medical significance throughout the 20th century. In particular, the public imagination was captured by the idea that science could forestall, or even reverse, the effects of age on the body.

Sexual rejuvenation in aging men was a subject of some ambivalence, even for its promoters. While organotherapy and rejuvenation unequivocally linked masculine vitality and vigor to glandular secretions, interest in rejuvenation therapies was largely motivated by worries about declines in masculine productivity, not virility. To be sure, restoration of sexual function was part of the promise of rejuvenation, but this was treated as almost a side effect of the restoration of general masculine vigor. Steinach himself stressed the non-sexual benefits of rejuvenation, seeking to ward off not only the physical disorders of age (cancer, heart disease, hypertension) but also the "paralyzing fatigue, disinclination to work, failing memory, indifference and depression, all of which hinder or preclude progress and every kind of competition" (cited in Hirshbein, 2000: 285). In a spirited defense of rejuvenation science, Paul Kammerer (1924: 185) argued that: "If reawakened manhood, a by-product of rejuvenation, occasionally is criticized as an immoral disadvantage of rejuvenation as a whole, then the simultaneously reawakened love of, and ability to work, should be considered a sufficient compensation". Similarly,

in reviewing the literature on rejuvenation therapies, George Ridley Scott (1953: 9–10) suggested that "much of the hostility towards rejuvenation has been engendered through its association with sex" and countered almost apologetically that "there is no way of extending the physical and mental powers of the individual into advancing years without coincidentally keeping the sexual and endocrinal glands functioning".

This ambivalence towards sexual rejuvenation of aging men continued as hormone therapy moved into mainstream medical practice via testosterone treatment for the "male climacteric" in the 1930s and 1940s. While notions of a male climacteric as a parallel process to the female menopause had circulated in the medical literature since the early 19th century, it was not until August Werner's reintroduction of the concept to mainstream American medicine in 1939 that it had a clinical presence (Werner, 1939). Yet Werner, though arguing that the climacteric "is due primarily to a function of the sex glands" (1939: 1441), and asserting that, as a result, "man is subject to varying degrees of sexual function" (Werner, 1946: 194), did not view the restoration of sexual function as a central goal of testosterone therapy. In other words, even though sexual dysfunction might be a key *symptom* of the climacteric, it was not the main concern in *treating* it. Although potency might inadvertently be stimulated by testosterone therapy, Werner (1945: 710) insisted that it should not be given for this purpose, and in fact suggested that "it is perhaps better for older men if this phase of the reaction does not result". This emphasis on the non-sexual aspects of restoring masculine vitality is reiterated in a discussion of Werner's work by Charles Dunn, who reminded readers that

the male climacteric is an important syndrome because it occurs chiefly in men with important responsibilities, men who require sustained energy, physical and mental throughout the day to perform competently their assigned responsibilities . . . The true climacteric patient is more concerned with constitutional rehabilitation than he is with sexual stimulation. (Dunn, 1945: 710)

The specter of immorality still cast a shadow over sexual rejuvenation of aging men, reiterating the long-held assumption that old age should be a time of asexuality (Marshall and Katz, forthcoming). If acceptance of the male climacteric as a clinical disorder, and its treatment with hormone replacement therapy, was to be accepted in mainstream medical practice, then the emphasis had to be placed on the non-sexual aspects of treatment. Despite this, the concept never really caught on. Rather than as a medical disorder, the "male climacteric" was viewed as a period of psychological or emotional upheaval—a "midlife crisis" (Hepworth and Featherstone, 1998). Ironically—at least from the perspective of those such as Werner—it took the post-Viagra re-centering of sexual function and its restoration to revitalize the concept of male menopause as a medical disorder in the late 20th century.

POSITIVE AGING AND THE RE-SEXUALIZATION OF THE AGING MALE

Ambivalence towards the importance of sexual function in medical discourse around aging and masculinity illustrates the dilemma in which the emerging sciences of aging and sexuality found themselves in the early to mid-20th century. On the one hand, sexual science had enshrined sexual decline as an inevitable aspect of bodily aging. On the other hand, the new professional discourse of gerontology emphasized vitality, activity and independence, challenging previously negative stereotypes of later life (Katz, 1996). Discourses of "positive aging" in sexology and gerontology did find some common ground in the mid-20th century as shifting etiologies of sexual dysfunction resulted in their agreement that psychological, rather than organic, factors were central (Marshall and Katz, 2002).

Sexual decline was no longer characterized as a "natural" consequence of bodily aging for which graceful acceptance was the appropriate response. Aging men were increasingly told that it was their anxiety over their supposed loss of sexual function—their *fear* of loss of potency—that was causing their premature sexual decline. In addition, men were told that to cease having sex would itself hasten aging. Common wisdom by the middle of the 20th century was that continued sexual activity, and especially sexual intercourse, was a healthy and necessary component of successful aging.

In the 1980s new developments in urology effected a decisive change in understanding the sexual capacities of the aging body. Specifically, urological research reconceptualized the male erection as a vascular, physiological event after it was demonstrated that erections could be induced by chemical injection, severing the mechanism of erection from any sort of emotional arousal or tactile stimulation (Brindley, 1986; Virag, 1982). Impotence–which by the 1990s was referred to as "erectile dysfunction"—became a treatable, physiological disorder. The effect of this move was to see sexual decline as neither the inevitable by-product of bodily aging nor the result of psychological difficulties. Erectile dysfunction resulted from "modifiable, para-aging phenomena" (Feldman et al., 1994: 54). Reversing the old belief that psychological distress acted to produce physiological sexual dysfunction, it was now argued that, left untreated, physiological sexual dysfunction had serious emotional and psychological effects. As one of the many mass-market books on male sexual function to emerge in the wake of Viagra put it: "no malfunction of the human apparatus—not even cancer or heart disease–can be more painful to the male ego or catastrophic to the male psyche than sexual impotence" (Melchiode and Sloan, 1999: 17). These catastrophic effects, coupled with the reportedly epidemic rates of men suffering from erectile difficulties, and the expected increase in incidence given aging populations in western societies, transformed age-related sexual dysfunction into a serious public health problem demanding redress.

By the late 1990s, scientific and commercial interests converged in reconceptualizing sexual disorders as requiring biotechnical, rather than therapeutic, fixes, and sexual-function products were now added to the legitimate marketplace of products geared to aging consumers (Katz and Marshall, 2003). In contrast to the manner in which the restoration of sexual function was treated as an almost regrettable byproduct of rejuvenation in the first half of the 20th century, there was nothing coincidental or apologetic about the central place accorded to sexual function in the emerging arsenal of anti-aging products and related health promotion discourses.

The discourses of positive aging have contributed to the unmooring of sexual decline from the limits of the aging body, in part as a means of redressing negative, ageist stereotypes. One of the problems with the discourses of positive aging, however, has been the assumption that successful aging really means not aging. As Stephen Katz (2001/2002: 27) asserts, "the ideals of positive aging and anti-ageism have come to be used to promote a widespread anti-aging culture, one that translates their radical appeal into commercial capital". Against this landscape, the concatenation of masculinity, sexual functionality and successful aging stands out. While the negative association of aging and active sexuality is, of course, ageist, the reversal of this association will not necessarily be liberating if narrow sexist (and heterosexist) sexual stereotypes are reasserted in the process (Marshall and Katz, forthcoming). As a number of critical analyses have demonstrated, restoration of aging male sexuality via the rehabilitation of the erection with Viagra (and its successor drugs) has been premised on a narrow and limiting understanding of both "sex" and "masculinity" (Loe, 2001; Mamo and Fishman, 2001; Marshall, 2002). Masculinity, at least as it is portrayed in pharmaceutical advertising and "men's health" promotion

around erectile dysfunction, "remains anchored in the erect penis across the lifecourse" (Marshall and Katz, 2002: 63). Calasanti and King (2005: 16) summarize the impact of the new culture of virility on aging men: "Sexual functioning now serves as a vehicle for reconstructions of manhood as 'ageless' . . . To the extent that men can demonstrate their virility, they can still be men".

Aging women, of course, have long been subject to biomedical restoration of their "femininity" via hormone replacement therapy. Nelly Oudshoorn (1997) has suggested several reasons why, at least until recently, the problems of the aging male were not medicalized to the same degree as those of women. First, the success in defining female menopause as a treatable hormone deficiency gave a clear motive for the hormone replacement industry to target women. Gynecological clinics were able to facilitate both research on and treatments to their clientele, while parallel institutions were not available for men. Oudshoorn argues that men's more passive attitudes towards seeking treatment for health problems and the continued marginalization of men's health in the organizational structures of institutionalized medicine were key factors in undermedicalizing the male menopause, in comparison to women's. As she puts it, "health problems can only be classified as illness and be medicalized if there exists a cultural climate and a medical infrastructure that actively transforms health complaints into diseases" (Oudshoorn, 1997: 143). This "active transformation" is evident in the post-Viagra years, as both the cultural climate and medical infrastructure have absorbed the assumption of a biochemical basis for sexual dysfunction (Marshall, 2002). The clinical and market success of Viagra was pivotal in paving the way for the development of a lucrative men's health industry and for the construction of the aging male body as a site of biomedical intervention. An expanded range of institutional and discursive structures have not only accommodated, but nurtured, the medicalization of masculinity in mid- and late life. Professional associations, journals, conferences and clinics focusing on men's sexual health and aging have proliferated. The pharmaceutical industry has worked hard to legitimate and publicize the disorders for which they have a potential treatment by sponsoring and disseminating research favorable to their products. That there is profit to be made here cannot be denied: according to industry reports, the therapeutic areas of male sexual dysfunction and male menopause are expected to lead the way in expanding the already $17 billion dollar world market in pharmaceuticals for "men's health" (*Biotech Week*, 2003). By the late 20th century, the aging male body was understood as a series of functional subsystems amenable to constant monitoring and biotechnical intervention. While Viagra was seen as the solution to malfunction in one of these subsystems (vascular flow to the penis), the problems of the aging male were now increasingly opened up to diagnosis and treatment. By the turn of the 21st century, the concept of the male climacteric, menopause, or "andropause" as an organic disorder was poised to undergo a renaissance, but this time with the restoration of sexual virility at its center.

"IF YOU THINK YOU CAN VIAGRA YOUR WAY OUT OF THIS ONE, THINK AGAIN": THE RETURN OF TESTOSTERONE

According to the report of the Third International Conference on the Management of Erectile Dysfunction, held in 2003: "Although it is now possible for almost all men with ED to regain their erections, getting those men to use their erections regularly is more complicated" (Nehra et al., 2003: S3). With a reported 50–60 per cent of men discontinuing medical treatments for erectile dysfunction, attention has increasingly turned to the problem of waning sexual *desire*. As one newspaper feature put it: "If you think you can Viagra your

way out of this one, think again: It and similar drugs might help with the mechanics, but not with desire; testosterone is what fires the libido" (Werland, 2004: 9).

As discussed in an earlier section of the article, the concept of the "male climacteric" or "male menopause" as an organic disorder never really caught on in mainstream medicine. However, from the late 1990s to the present, the male menopause, now referred to as "andropause", or ADAM (androgen deficiency in the aging male), has circulated widely through both the clinical and popular health literatures. Here, the andropause is reconceptualized as an age-related physiological disorder treatable with testosterone therapy. Despite a mass of contradictory scientific evidence on the existence of the disorder and both the efficacy and safety of testosterone therapy, it is reiterated that "andropause is a fact, not a fiction" (Nicholls, 2003: 99), and "andropause is a testosterone deficiency that develops gradually over a number of years in all men aged 50 and older" (Anderson et al., 2002: M796). The ADAM questionnaire developed by a team at the University of St Louis and at Organon, one of the key manufacturers of pharmaceutical testosterone products, has been widely promoted as a clinical screening tool that identifies "a symptom complex associated with the age-related decline in testosterone that may be amenable to therapeutic intervention" (Morley et al., 2000: 1241).

The foregrounding of erectile dysfunction as a key symptom of andropause appears more related to the post-Viagra willingness of men to present with this disorder than it does to any evidence linking erectile dysfunction to low testosterone levels. Dunsmuir (1999: 138) confirms that "much of the lay public equates the male menopause with erectile failure", in spite of the fact that studies of men presenting at clinics with erectile dysfunction show that the incidence of low testosterone in this group is small (Johnson and Jarow, 1992; T'Sjoen et al., 2003). Indeed the Massachusetts Male Aging Study, which is cited so ubiquitously to establish the relationship between age and erectile function, found no significant correlations between the latter and testosterone levels (Feldman et al., 1994). Yet the ADAM questionnaire treats a positive response to the question about erectile dysfunction as immediately identifying the respondent as "at risk" for androgen deficiency (Morley et al., 2000).

Significantly, marketing the new virility has revived some very old configurations of masculinity. A doctor with a men's clinic recounts a typical success story of modern treatment modalities. Here, a 40-year-old man presented complaining of erectile dysfunction and low libido. After he "treated the erectile dysfunction and prescribed oral testosterone for the man's low libido" the patient returned after six weeks:

> He was vibrant. He had quit his job and gone into business for himself–something he said that he always wanted to do but never believed in himself enough to follow through . . . The man's marriage was wonderful and his sex life was great. He had a great sense of vitality and a positive attitude towards life. (Powell, 2000: D2)

Not only is treatment for erectile dysfunction (presumably with Viagra) coupled with treatment for diminished libido (testosterone), but sexual decline and its reversal are linked, just as in the early 20th-century rejuvenation movement, with the restoration of masculine productive power more generally. Not unlike the "feminine forever" message with which women were bombarded by proponents of hormone replacement therapy in the 1960s, the newly remedicalized menopause for men reasserts a chemical basis for masculinity itself. Decline in sexual function, sports performance, work success – these all become markers of the equation of aging with demasculinization, and all become treatable in a program of virility maintenance.

THE NEW VIRILITY: RISK FACTORS, SURVEILLANCE AND SEXUAL HEALTH

A number of commentators on health and medicine in contemporary western societies have argued that individuals are increasingly being enrolled into programs of self-surveillance and risk management. For example, Anthony Pryce, drawing on Deborah Lupton's (1999) analysis of "risk" in late modernity, has suggested that the medical gaze now reaches beyond the walls of the clinic:

> Surveillance is relocated through the individual citizen's reflexive observation of their 'self' for signs of contamination, disease or dysfunction within cultures increasingly constructed as morally, socially, environmentally and biologically dangerous or 'risky'. The recruitment and self-examination by the 'active patient' is central to governmentality and the construction of a new health citizenship. (Pryce, 2000: 104)

Similarly, Andrew Webster (2002) notes that new discourses of health and illness have created the "worried well" as a significant market. It is not difficult to see these trends as evident in the new discourses of men's sexual health. The widespread publicity given to the "epidemic" of sexual dysfunction, coupled with the close cultural association between sexual virility and masculinity, has fostered an environment of amplified risk for many men, promoting self-surveillance and monitoring. And no longer is sexual dysfunction just a concern for men in their old age, but anxiety over the prospect of sexual decline is fostered at increasingly younger ages. As Margaret Gullette (1998: 17) notes, "everyone has been getting older younger".

While the original disease model of erectile dysfunction focused on clearly discernable age-related physiological factors relating to impaired vascular function, the efficacy of Viagra in producing erections regardless of the etiology has expanded the parameters of the disease. The Viagra user is no longer just an older man who, due to a physiological problem, is unable to get or keep an erection most of the time, but is just as likely to be a younger man, with no identified organic disorder, who worries about his erections being less reliable than he thinks they should be. This is clearly reflected in the marketing campaigns for Viagra (and its successor drugs). Originally marketed to an older audience, erectile dysfunction drugs have been pitched to ever younger markets. One widely-used print advertisement for Viagra in the United States features a man, appearing to be in his early 40s, telling us that he knows "a lot of guys have occasional erection problems", but that he chose not to accept his by seeing his doctor and asking about Viagra.

The downloading of risk and anxiety about age-related changes in sexual capacities to younger and younger men is borne out by research on whom those prescriptions are going to. A study of prescription claims data in the US in the first five years of Viagra's availability found that younger men (aged 18 to 45) were the fastest growing group of users (Delate et al., 2004). Similarly, the renewed medicalization of the male menopause has meant medicalizing mid-life, rather than late-life, masculinity–according to two reports cited by the National Institute of Medicine, most testosterone prescriptions were given to men in the 45–65 age group, not to men over 65, where decreased levels of circulating testosterone are most evident (Liverman and Blazer, 2004: 25). The construction of ever-younger aging males as "active patients" occurs against an expanded horizon of risk, increasing responsibility of both the individual and the health professional to undertake virility surveillance, and an expansion of the very concept of "sexual health".

The transformation of erectile dysfunction and low libido into organic disorders originally linked them with other bodily disorders which act as risk factors–for example, diabetes, prostate cancer, obesity and hypogonadism. However,

age, as the most clearly articulated risk factor puts all men at risk. The specter of sexual dysfunction has also been taken up by various health promotion discourses in terms of lifestyle factors that may increase the risk of sexual dysfunction. These include both official campaigns, such as Health Canada's anti-smoking campaign ("Tobacco use can make you impotent"), and unofficial ones, as in "People for the Ethical Treatment of Animals" (PETA) promotion of vegetarianism ("Eating meat can cause impotence"). When the popular magazine *Men's Health* ran a feature educating men on how to assess their risk for developing erectile dysfunction (McDonald, 2000), the highest-risk case study was a 31 year old who currently has sex every day. While he doesn't have problems yet, we are told his "poor diet, sedentary lifestyle and family history will eventually catch up to him", and that if doesn't start to exercise and eat right, his "sex-life expectancy" has only about 10 years to run. The message here is not only one of constant vigilance, even where no immediate problems are apparent, but also one of equating the loss of erectile power with the end of life itself. Thus, the onus is on the individual to take responsibility for managing risk through new regimes of bodily discipline which must start long before the onset of "old age".

In addition to preventative lifestyle changes, men are exhorted to continually monitor and assess their sexual function, and to take remedial action where necessary.

Pfizer's "three steps to better erections" plan illustrates well the construction of the active patient in this respect. In brochures and on web sites, men are instructed to assess their erectile capacity (by filling out a short form of the International Index of Erectile Function), compare it to a standardized model (via their score on that quiz) and seek action by visiting their doctor and asking for a starter pack of Viagra. This process is replicated for those worried that they might be suffering from andropause–take a quiz, go to your doctor, actively ask about a treatment. Not only is the individual increasingly enrolled into regimes of self-surveillance, but physicians are also increasingly called upon to be more pro-active in diagnosing sexual dysfunctions in their patients. A number of articles in periodicals directed at front-line family physicians encourage "proactive sexual health interviews" (Nusbaum and Hamilton, 2002) and suggest that information about sexual function should be "actively solicited as part of the routine medical history" (Lightner, 2002). Also suggested is the use of questionnaires to identify symptom complexes–either physician administered or left in the physician's waiting room for the patient to self-administer (MacIndoe, 2003). It is no wonder that the pharmaceutical industry has invested so heavily in developing the myriad questionnaires, indices and scales aimed at diagnosing dysfunctions.

The concept of "sexual health", once focused on sexually transmitted disease and reproductive concerns (Giami, 2002) has now broadened out to a concern with maintenance and enhancement of sexual desire and performance. Sexual function has now come to dominate many uses of the concept of sexual health—for example, one of the newer indices on the block, the Male Sexual Health Questionnaire, deals only with erections, ejaculations and sexual satisfaction (Rosen et al., 2004). A brochure entitled "Men's Sexual Health", distributed in physicians' waiting rooms, has four pages on erectile dysfunction and its treatment, two pages on loss of sexual desire linked to androgen deficiency, and two pages on prevention of STDs. Thus three-quarters of the brochure conceptualizes "sexual health" as "sexual function". Given that health "has become a duty as much as a right of citizenship" (Porter, 2002: 201; Tiefer, 1997), seeing sexual health primarily in terms of meeting some standardized model of sexual function makes it a moral imperative. A critical aspect of being a responsible late modern citizen is to take charge of one's health—including one's sexual health–by adopting particular sorts of lifestyles, and by the consumption of appropriate forms of expertise and products.

CONCLUSIONS

The success of Viagra in securing a new regime of compulsory tumescence is an exemplary case of the manner in which bodies are reconstructed as sites for biomedical intervention and incorporated into consumerist "lifestyle" projects. A reinvigorated sense of masculinity as a life-long project is configured by the new biology of the body which has emerged in relation to pharmaceutical therapies geared towards functionality and performativity. The post-Viagra expansion of the "men's health" industry, which promotes a standardized model of sexual function as its raison d'etre, has an ever-expanding kit-bag of therapies for an ever-younger aging patient. Not only sexual function, but masculine vitality itself, is presumed to be at stake here, as anxieties over aging are crystallized in terms of biochemical demasculinization. Yet qualitative research with older men (and women), demonstrates that:

> there is no standard experience of a 'functional' erection, even less so a 'dysfunctional erection'; there appears to be no necessary relationship between a particular type of erection and a satisfying sexual relationship; and there is no definitive view of what constitutes 'normal' masculinity or 'being a man' in relation to erectile 'functionality'. (Potts et al., 2004: 498)

Perhaps the recognition that "manhood changes" (Calasanti and King, 2005: 5), rather than diminishes with age can be the starting point for challenging the post-Viagra culture of virility.

REFERENCES

Anderson, J. K., Faulkner, S., Cranor, C., Briley, J., Gevirtz, F. and Roberts, S. (2002) "Andropause: Knowledge and Perceptions among the General Public and Health Care Professionals", *Journal of Gerontology: Medical Science* 57A(12): M793–M796.

Biotech Week (2003) "Sexual Dysfunction and Andropause Lead Strong Growth in Men's Segment", *Biotech Week* (10 September): 289.

Brindley, G. S. (1986) "Pilot Experiments on the Actions of Drugs Injected into the Human Corpus Cavernosum Penis", *British Journal of Pharmacology* 87(3): 495–500.

Calasanti, T. and King, N. (2005) "Firming the Floppy Penis: Age, Class and Gender Relations in the Lives of Old Men", *Men and Masculinities* 8(1): 3–23.

Cussons, A., Bhagat, C. I., Fletcher, S. J. and Walsh, J. P. (2002) "Brown-Sequard Revisited: A Lesson from History on the Placebo Effect of Androgen Treatment", *Medical Journal of Australia* 177(2): 678–9.

Delate, T., Simmons, V. A. and Motheral, B. R. (2004) "Patterns of Use of Sildenafil among Commercially Insured Adults in the United States: 1998–2002", *International Journal of Impotence Research* 16: 313–18.

Dunn, C. (1945) "Discussion of August Werner's 'The Male Climacteric: Report of Fifty-Four Cases'", *Journal of the American Medical Association* 127: 710.

Dunsmuir, W. D. (1999) "Male Sexual Dysfunction: The Male Menopause", in R. S. Kirby, M. G. Kirby and R. N. Farah (eds) *Men's Health*, pp. 137–46. Oxford: Isis Medical Media.

Estes, C. and Binney, E. (1989) "The Biomedicalization of Aging", *The Gerontologist* 29: 587–96.

Feldman, H. A., Goldstein, I., Hatzichristou, D. G., Krane, R. J. and McKinlay, J. B. (1994) "Impotence and its Medical and Psychosocial Correlates: Results of the Massachusetts Male Aging Study", *Journal of Urology* 151: 54–61.

Giami, A. (2002) "Sexual Health: The Emergence, Development and Diversity of a Concept", *Annual Review of Sex Research* 13: 1–35.

Gilleard, C. and Higgs, P. (1998) "Ageing and the Limiting Conditions of the Body", *Sociological Research Online* 3(4), URL (accessed March 2006): http://www.socresonline.org.uk/3/4/4.html.

Gullette, M. M. (1998) "Midlife Discourses in the Twentieth Century United States: An Essay on the Sexuality, Ideology, and Politics of 'Middle-Ageism'", in R. Shweder (ed.) *Welcome to Middle Age! (and Other Cultural Fictions)*, pp. 3–44. Chicago, IL: University of Chicago Press.

Hepworth, M. and Featherstone, M. (1998) "The Male Menopause: Lay Accounts and the Cultural Reconstruction of Midlife", in S. Nettleton and J. Watson (eds) *The Body in Everyday Life*, pp. 276–301. London: Routledge.

Hirshbein, L. (2000) "The Glandular Solution: Sex, Masculinity and Aging in the 1920s", *Journal of the History of Sexuality* 93(3): 277–304.

Hoberman, J. (2005) *Testosterone Dreams: Rejuvenation, Aphrodisia, Doping.* Berkeley: University of California Press.

Jaheil, J. (1992) "Rejuvenation Research and the American Medical Association in the Early Twentieth Century: Paradigms in Conflict", unpublished PhD thesis, Department of History, Boston University.

Johnson, A. R. and Jarow, J. P. (1992) "Is Routine Endocrine Testing of Impotent Men Necessary?" *Journal of Urology* 147: 1542–3.

Kammerer, P. (1924) *Rejuvenation and the Prolongation of Human Efficiency.* London: Methuen.

Katz, S. (1996) *Disciplining Old Age: The Formation of Gerontological Knowledge.* Charlottesville: University Press of Virginia.

Katz, S. (2001/2002) "Growing Older without Aging? Positive Aging, Anti-Ageism, and Anti-Aging", *Generations* 25(4): 27–32.

Katz, S. and Marshall, B. L. (2003) "New Sex for Old: Lifestyle, Consumerism and the Ethics of Aging Well", *Journal of Aging Studies* 17(1): 3–16.

Lightner, D. (2002) "Female Sexual Dysfunction: A Concise Review for Clinicians", *Mayo Clinic Proceedings* 77(7), 698–702.

Liverman, C. T. and Blazer, D. G. (eds) (2004) *Testosterone and Aging: Clinical Research Directions.* Washington, DC: National Academies Press, Institute of Medicine.

Loe, M. (2001) "Fixing Broken Masculinity: Viagra as a Technology for the Production of Gender and Sexuality", *Sexuality and Culture* 5(3): 97–125.

Lupton, D. (1999) *Risk.* London: Routledge.

MacIndoe, J. H. (2003) "The Challenges of Testosterone Deficiency", *Postgraduate Medicine* 114(4): 51–62.

Mamo, L. and Fishman, J. (2001) "Potency in All the Right Places: Viagra as a Technology of the Gendered Body", *Body & Society* 7(4): 13–35.

Marshall, B. L. (2002) "'Hard Science': Gendered Constructions of Sexual Dysfunction in the 'Viagra Age'", *Sexualities* 5(2): 131–58.

Marshall, B. L. and Katz, S. (2002) "'Forever Functional': Sexual Fitness and the Aging Male Body", *Body & Society* 8(4): 43–70.

Marshall, B. L. and Katz, S. (forthcoming) "From Androgyny to Androgens: Re-Sexing the Aging Body", in T. Calasanti and K. Slevin (eds) *Age Matters.* New York: Routledge.

McDonald, K. (2000) "Who Will Be Impotent First?" *Men's Health* October: 70–2.

Melchiode, G. and Sloan, B. (1999) *Beyond Viagra: A Commonsense Guide to Building a Healthy Sexual Relationship for Both Men and Women*. New York: Owl Books, Henry Holt and Co.

Morley, J. E., Charlton, E., Patrick, P., Kaiser, F. E., Cadeau, P., McCready, D. and Perry, H. M. I. (2000) "Validation of a Screening Questionnaire for Androgen Deficiency in Aging Males", *Metabolism* 49(9): 1239–42.

Nehra, A., Steers, W. D., Althof, S. E., Andersson, K.-E., Burnett, A., Costabile, R. A., Goldstein, I., Kloner, R. A., Lue, T. F., Morales, A., Rosen, R. C., Shabsigh, R., Siroky, M. B. and King, L. (2003) "Third International Conference on the Management of Erectile Dysfunction: Linking Pathophysiology and Therapeutic Response", *Journal of Urology* 170: S3–S5.

Nicholls, E. H. (2003) "Andropause for Thought", *Endeavor* 27(3): 99.

Nusbaum, M. R. H. and Hamilton, C. D. (2002) "The Proactive Sexual Health History", *American Family Physician* 66(9): 1705–12.

Oudshoorn, N. (1997) "Menopause, Only for Women? The Social Construction of Menopause as an Exclusively Female Condition", *Journal of Psychosomatic Obstetrics and Gynecology* 18: 137–44.

Porter, D. (2002) "The Healthy Body", in R. Cooter, R. Pickstone and J. Pickstone (eds) *Medicine in the 20th Century*, pp. 201–16. Amsterdam: Harwood Academic Publishers.

Potts, A., Grace, V., Gavey, N. and Vares, T. (2004) " 'Viagra Stories': Challenging Erectile Dysfunction' ", *Social Science and Medicine* 59: 489–99.

Powell, B. (2000) "The Stuff of Manhood or Falsehood? Testosterone Gel Prods Debate over the Essence of Maleness", *Toronto Star* (25 August): D1.

Pryce, A. (2000) "Frequent Observation: Sexualities, Self-Surveillance, Confession and the Construction of the Active Patient", *Nursing Inquiry* 7: 103–11.

Rosen, R. C., Catania, J., Pollack, L., Althof, S. E., O'Leary, M. and Seftel, A. D. (2004) Male Sexual Health Questionnaire (MSHQ): Scale Development and Psychometric Validation', *Urology* 64(4): 777–82.

Schmidt, P. (1929) "Six Hundred Rejuvenation Operations: A Nine-Year Survey", in N. Haire (ed.) *Third Congress of the World League of Sexual Reform*, pp. 574–81. London: Kegan Paul, Trench, Trubner and Co.

Scott, G. R. (1953) *The Quest for Youth: A Study of All Available Methods of Rejuvenation and of Retaining Physical and Mental Vigour in Old Age*. London: Torchstream.

Sengoopta, C. (2001) "Transforming the Testicle: Science, Medicine and Masculinity, 1800–1951", *Medicina nei Secoli* 13(3): 637–55.

Sengoopta, C. (2003) " 'Dr. Steinach Coming to Make Old Young!' Sex Glands, Vasectomy and the Quest for Rejuvenation in the Roaring Twenties", *Endeavour* 27(3): 122–6.

Squier, S. (1999) "Incubabies and Rejuvenates: The Traffic between Technologies of Reproduction and Age-Extension", in K. Woodward (ed.) *Figuring Age: Women, Bodies, Generation*, pp. 88–111. Bloomington: Indiana University Press.

Stall, S. (1901) *What a Man of Forty-Five Ought to Know*. Philadelphia: VIR Publishing Co.

Sturgis, F. R. (1930) *Sexual Debility in Man* (2nd edn). Chicago, IL: Login Bros.

T'Sjoen, G., Feyen, E., De Kuyper, P., Comhaire, F. and Kaufman, J. F. (2003) "Self-Referred Patients in an Aging Male Clinic: Much More Than Androgen Deficiency Alone", *The Aging Male* 6(3): 157–65.

Tiefer, L. (1996) "The Medicalization of Sexuality: Conceptual, Normative and Professional Issues", *Annual Review of Sex Research* 7: 252–82.

Tiefer, L. (1997) "Medicine, Morality and the Public Management of Sexual Matters", in L. Segal (ed.) *New Sexual Agendas*, pp. 103–12. London: Macmillan.

Virag, R. (1982) "Intracavernous Injection of Papaverine for Erectile Failure", *The Lancet* 2: 938.

Webster, A. (2002) "Innovative Health Technologies and the Social: Redefining Health, Medicine and the Body", *Current Sociology* 50(3): 443–57.

Werland, R. (2004) "Manhood Checkup", *Chicago Tribune* (27 June): 9.

Werner, A. (1939) "The Male Climacteric", *Journal of the American Medical Association* 112: 1441–3.

Werner, A. (1945) "The Male Climacteric (Including Therapy with Testosterone Propionate): Fifty-Four Cases", *Journal of the American Medical Association* 127(12): 705–10.

Werner, A. (1946) "The Male Climacteric: Report of Two Hundred and Seventy-Three Cases", *Journal of the American Medical Association* 132 (September): 188–94.

PART V

Gender and Sexuality

"Sex Drugs for Women?" Several years ago, *Harper's Bazaar* posed this question in a lead article that focused attention on University of Chicago survey data which revealed sexual dysfunction to be a bigger problem for women than for men (Fishman 2000). At that time, the writer suggested it was possible that within 2 years, women would have their own tested version of Viagra. But, not so fast, warned Irwin Goldstein, a physician at Boston University School of Medicine. A leader in the science of female sexual response, it was Goldstein who, ironically, had authored a 1998 paper showing that Viagra—an angina drug that had the unwanted side effect of producing erections— was a safe and effective treatment for male erectile dysfunction. According to Goldstein, results for women are 20 years behind those of men mainly because female sexual dysfunction is underresearched and a poorly understood area of medicine (Fishman 2000). Apparently, he is correct. In the years since the Fishman publication, men now have three additional choices of "sex drugs" (*Levitra, Cialis,* and *Uprima*), but the score for women is still zero compared to men!

In Part V, gender, as it pertains to sexuality, is addressed from several perspectives. But, before students encounter various approaches to understanding this issue so vital to their sexual health and well-being, a challenge might be in order. They could be encouraged to search the offerings for any clues that might help explain a female-male imbalance such as that evidenced in the drug research.

Pavlov wrote to the academic youth of Soviet Russia in 1935 just before his death, "Do not become the archivists of facts. Try to penetrate to the secret of their occurrence..." (Elias 1979, p. 73). More than three-quarters of a century later, sexuality researchers must still resist the tendency to become "archivists of facts" in their efforts to correctly assess changes in sexual attitudes and behaviors. Jenna Mahay, Edward Laumann, and Stuart Michaels seem to have mastered this feat in their chapter, "Race, Gender, and Class in Sexual Scripts." Although many scholars have documented group differences in sexual behaviors and attitudes, this research team "penetrates the secret of their occurrence" by examining the broader sexual scripts in which specific acts are embedded and by determining how gender, race/ethnicity, and class intersect to shape those scripts.

Beginning with the premise that changes in sexual attitudes and behaviors can only be understood in relation to other elements in the fabric of our social structure, the authors explore what they labeled as master status variables: age, religion, marital status, and family composition. Readers will be intrigued with the differences in sexual attitudes and behavior that surfaced between race/ethnicity, gender, and class when these master statuses were controlled. Certainly, this compelling chapter will not be quickly read, but the lack of technical research jargon does make it student friendly.

To state that sexual desire is a popular pastime among young adults today may be a classic understatement, without any dissenters. But add the subject of gender to the mix of sexual desire and the screen immediately scrolls down to the category of "debate." Pepper Schwartz and Virginia Rutter manage a fascinating, readable combination of the two often disparate topics, addressing many of the fallacies and facts along the way. Their promise is alluring: Who we're attracted to and what we find sexually satisfying is not just a matter of the genital equipment we're born with. This chapter explains why.

Beginning with the thesis that gender is the most significant dimension of sexuality, Schwartz and Rutter take issue with the assumptions that sexuality is naturally gendered, being rooted in biology, and that women and men are different sexually. They aptly review three competing explanations of differences in sexual desire between women and men to substantiate their claims: the biological; the sociobiological and evolutionary psychological; and the social constructionist view. But the authors expand what could be just a well-done review of the three opposing perspectives about gender differences in sexual desire when they propose the use of an "integrative" view. Defining *integrationist* as "one who will raise questions about biology when social context is emphasized as cause and will raise questions about social contexts when biological causes are emphasized," they encourage students to reason for themselves (Schwartz

and Rutter, 1998, p. 36). This is a lengthy piece, but one that is guaranteed to pique the interest of even the most reluctant of readers.

"How refreshing it is to find a book that sees through 30 years of blather about sexual politics and calls a gene a gene; a reproductive strategy, a reproductive strategy; a survival mechanism, a survival mechanism" (Angier 2000, *Frontspiece*). Erica Jong's observation in the *New York Observer* was but one of numerous accolades praising Natalie Angier's book, *Woman: An Intimate Geography*, a *New York Times* prizewinning bestseller that has been translated into 21 languages. Pulitzer-Prize winning author Angier, science writer for the *New York Times*, challenges widely accepted Darwinian-based gender stereotypes in her award-winning book. She shows how cultural biases have influenced research in evolutionary psychology, leading to what she describes as dubious conclusions about female nature. In the chapter, "Venus in Furs: Estrogen and Desire," Angier admits that we do not understand how estrogen works on the brain to elicit desire. But, in her words, "there are enough indirect strands of evidence to knit a serviceable thinking cap with which to mull over estrogen's meaning" (Angier 2000, p. 214). Not only will students resonate to the message Angier sends, they will also appreciate the language with which she offers an optimistic, fresh vision of womanhood. Some may even be motivated to read more on this topic than required.

One of the conundrums posed by research findings on gender differences in sexual behavior is that traditionally, men have reported more sexual activity and more sexual partners than women. The word "partner" means "one of a pair." Therefore, for each man who has engaged in a sexual experience with a woman, there should be a woman who has engaged in a sexual experience with a man. Since the standard research sample has largely consisted of heterosexual college students, the extent of sexual activity and number of sexual partners for women and men should be equivalent. Researchers have tried to uncover an explanation for this apparent mismatch, proposing a variety of possible explanations (Wiederman 1997).

The research by Alexander and Fisher presented in the final selection is yet another attempt to account for the difference. Their study involved a classic social psychology methodology, the bogus pipeline, to try to determine if different social roles for men and women lead to differences in reports of sexual behavior in the typical sexuality study. After students read this chapter, it might be a good time to discuss some of the major theories of sex differences so that students may debate which best accounts for the findings: evolutionary psychology (Buss 2003), social-role theory (Eagly and Wood 1999), or the gender similarities hypothesis (Hyde 2005). Indeed, a discussion of these various theoretical approaches may shed new light on the previous readings as well.

REFERENCES

Angier, N. 2000. *Woman: An intimate geography.* New York: Anchor Books.

Buss, D. M. 2003. *The evolution of desire: Strategies of human mating.* New York: Basic Books.

Eagly, A. H., and W. Wood. 1999. The origins of sex differences in human behavior: Evolved dispositions versus social roles. *American Psychologist* 54: 408–23.

Elias, V. D. 1979. Interpreting data on sexual conduct and social change. In *The frontiers of science,* ed. V. L. Bullough 71–76. Buffalo, NY: Prometheus.

Fishman, S. 2000. Sex drugs for women? *Harper's Bazaar,* March, 388–92.

Hyde, J. S. 2005. The gender similarities hypothesis. *American Psychologist* 60: 581–92.

Schwartz, P., and V. Rutter. 1998. *The gender of sexuality.* Thousand Oaks, CA: Pine Forge.

Wiederman, M. W. 1997. The truth must be in here somewhere: Examining the gender discrepancy in self-reported lifetime number of sex partners. *Journal of Sex Research* 34: 375–86.

CHAPTER 21

Race, Gender, and Class in Sexual Scripts

Jenna Mahay
Edward O. Laumann
Stuart Michaels

What do your race/ethnicity, gender, and class have to do with your sexuality? How do your cultural scenarios differ from those of your best friends? Or, just how unique is your interpersonal script, *which translates abstract sexual scenarios into strategies appropriate to particular situations? Certainly your* interpsychic script, *your sexual dialogue with self that elicits and sustains sexual arousal, is unlike that of any other. Or is it? You as a sexuality student, and perhaps even your erudite professors will be interested in discovering answers to these rather personal questions in this chapter.*

Using the rich descriptive resources of the National Health and Social Life Survey (NHSLS), Mahay, Laumann, and Michaels weave the variables of race/ethnicity, gender, and class into a piece that avoids the limitations of previous studies. The use of master status variables, that is, age, religious affiliation, marital status, and family composition, in analyzing each category was a massive undertaking, but one that spelled

success for the authors, who broke new ground on old premises. As you read this chapter, challenge yourself to make two lists: one with findings that surprise you and one with reaffirmations of your long-held attitudes about race/ethnicity, gender, and class as related to sexuality. Regardless of which list is longer, the contents of both are guaranteed to challenge you with new unanswered questions and offer a fertile field for class discussion.

While sexuality is popularly described in highly individualistic terms, this chapter examines the ways in which sexual norms, practices, and preferences are shaped by race, gender, and class. Many scholars have already documented group differences in specific sexual behaviors, such as age at first sex, use of condoms, and number of partners. This chapter examines the broader sexual scripts in which these specific acts are embedded and how race, gender, and class intersect to shape those scripts.

A middle-aged, working-class African American man explains what he sees as racial differences in sexual scripts:

> When it comes to woman and man relationships, white people have a tendency to be too damn

From "Race, Gender, and Class in Sexual Scripts" by J. Mahay, E. O. Laumann, and S. Michaels. 2001. In *Sex, Love, and Health in America*, E. O. Laumann and R. T. Michael, eds., 197–238. Chicago: University of Chicago Press. Copyright © 2001, University of Chicago Press. Reprinted by permission.

intellectual. Now that is not one of the true prerequisites of making love. It's the emotion, the passion. You don't have time to ask a woman what kind of degree she has. You see what I'm saying? (quoted in Duneier 1992, 44)

A white woman describes how gender shapes the way she approaches sex with her partner:

It is sort of an issue that I don't initiate sex. I would always wait for him. And finally he said, "Look, I'm not going to initiate sex all the time," and I would give him the argument: "Oh, men say they want women to initiate sex, but really when it happens they're, like, 'I have a headache tonight, honey.'" So in my mind there was a reason not to initiate it because it threatened him. (quoted in Blumstein and Schwartz 1983, 212)

An African American woman discusses how class plays a part in who she believes is a suitable partner:

It is difficult to find a person that one is truly compatible with, and that's especially true for a highly educated woman whose expectations often differ from those of most women and are not always consistent with the eligible pool [similar status] of men, who seem to have some preference for "traditional" women. (quoted in Staples 1981, 83)

Race, gender, and class, however, do not operate independently in forming sexual scripts; they "intersect" (cf. Connell 1995; Nagel 1999). In the third quote presented above, for example, ideas of who is a suitable partner and of the difficulties the woman has in finding one have to do not only with class but with race and gender as well. Unfortunately, until recently, there has been an absence of data allowing simultaneous comparisons by race/ethnicity, gender, and class on the broad range of sexual attitudes, practices, and preferences that make up sexual scripts. This chapter uses the rich descriptive resources of the National Health and Social Life Survey (NHSLS) to overcome this limitation. We first develop a theoretical

perspective on the systematic variations in the sexual scripts adopted by persons with particular status attributes. We then analyze the similarities and differences in the sexual scripts of racial/ethnic groups and the gender and class variations within those groups.

THEORIZING VARIATIONS IN SEXUAL SCRIPTS

Sexual scripts operate at three levels: the cultural, the interpersonal, and the intrapsychic (Simon and Gagnon 1987b). *Cultural scenarios* are the societal norms and narratives that provide guidelines for sexual conduct, thereby broadly indicating appropriate partners and sex acts, where and when to perform those acts, and even what emotions and feelings are appropriate. Thus, actors engaged in sexual interactions create *interpersonal scripts* that translate abstract cultural scenarios into scripts appropriate to particular situations. Interpersonal scripts, then, are the strategies for carrying out an individual's own sexual wishes with regard to the actual or anticipated responses of another person. While interpersonal scripts can be seen as "sexual dialogues" with others, *intrapsychic scripts* are sexual dialogues with the self. The intrapsychic script is a person's sexual fantasies, the sequence of acts, postures, objects, and gestures that elicit and sustain sexual arousal (Simon and Gagnon 1987b). Intrapsychic scripts should be seen, not merely as expressions of an individual's biologically generated appetites or drives, but rather as inextricably linked to what that person has learned to mean or understand as *being sexual*.

In the United States, cultural scenarios frequently stipulate that people of races or ethnicities different from one's own are inappropriate for sexual partnerships. In addition, because sex partners are generally chosen from a circumscribed group of people who are met through mutual friends, at work, or in neighborhood activities, the high level or racial segregation in these areas of social life also results in choosing others from the same racial/ethnic group. Indeed, as was reported in *The Social Organization of Sexuality (SOS)*, 93 percent of those who were married in the last ten years chose marriage partners of the same race or ethnicity. Even among those who had a very short-term sexual relationship, 91 percent chose partners of the same race or ethnicity. In short, *SOS* (p. 255) reported that racial homophily was higher than all the other types of homophily, including age, education, and religious affiliation.

Because sexual partnering is so highly segregated racially, we would expect different sexual scripts to develop within these segregated subpopulations with their distinctive age, class, religious, and marital compositions. Sexual scripting creates and stages a drama wherein the roles take on meaning in relation to the enactment of related roles and the specific cast of actors (Simon and Gagnon 1987a). Thus, we would expect different dramas and roles to be staged when distinctive and segregated casts of actors perform them. Because sexual scripts are *socially* produced, individuals must call on shared meanings and expectations to produce them. Thus, we would expect an independent effect of race/ethnicity after controlling for age, religion, class, and marital status.

In addition to race, gender centrally organizes sexual scripting. Most sexual scripts involve gendered roles, where certain sexual practices take on meaning as either masculine or feminine in relation to the enactment of particular roles by the "appropriate" sex. Cultural scenarios, interpersonal scripts, and intrapsychic scripts all involve assumptions about gender differences in sexuality. For example, at the level of the cultural scenario, the social norm may be that boys are expected to have sex before marriage but that girls are not. At the level of the interpersonal script, it may be that men are generally more aggressive in initiating sexual encounters and that women are more passive sexually. At the intrapsychic level, men and women may find different sexual practices appealing or have different kinds of sexual fantasies. As sexual scripts vary between racial/ethnic groups, so will the gender roles and expectations regarding men's and women's sexual behavior.

Finally, many have speculated on the relation between race and class in sexual behavior, but the data limitations of previous studies have precluded an evaluation of their relative importance. This chapter examines the effects of race and class separately, to test whether racial/ethnic differences in sexual behavior can, in fact, be explained by class alone, after taking into account gender, marital status, age, religion, and family composition.

OTHER STUDIES OF RACE, GENDER, AND CLASS IN SEXUAL BEHAVIOR

Racial/Ethnic Differences in Sexual Behavior

Social scientists have long studied race and ethnicity in American society and its effect on attitudes and social life (cf. Jaynes and Williams 1989), but only limited attention has been paid to sexual practices. While some ethnographic studies of particular racial/ethnic communities have included information on their sexual attitudes and practices, this qualitative information does not readily lend itself to comparisons across groups. Quantitative studies, on the other hand, have made such comparisons but have been restricted only to adolescent sexual practices or a very limited range of adult sexual practices. One more comprehensive analysis (Weinberg and Williams 1988) identified interesting differences across racial and class groupings but was based on different samples drawn at different times and different geographic locations. What has been lacking are data from representative samples of the major racial/ethnic groups collected at the same time and covering a wide range of sexual behaviors.

It is clear from the literature that the sexual practices and attitudes of different racial/ethnic groups must be analyzed in relation to each other because sexual relations within racial/ethnic groups are often affected and defined by the race relations between groups (Spelman 1988, 106). For example, in his ethnography of middle-aged working-class African American men in Chicago, Duneier (1992) found his informants to be very aware of the stereotype of themselves as sexual-exploiters, an image they self-consciously tried to live down. But Bowser (1994) claims that the hypersexuality attributed to African Americans by whites has been incorporated into the self-identity of younger African Americans, motivating them to become experienced as soon as possible and to prove to themselves and their partners that they are sexually superior. In addition, the influence of race relations on specific sexual practices is shown by Sterk-Elifson's (1994) finding that many African Americans considered birth control, masturbation, and anal and oral sex evils that white people invented.

Only a very limited range of sexual experiences has been studied in existing quantitative work on racial/ethnic differences in sexual practices, however. Many studies focus on age at first intercourse, condom use, and teenage pregnancy and thus are concerned mainly with adolescent sexuality (see, e.g., Udry and Billy 1987; Duncan and Hoffman 1991; Furstenberg et al. 1987; Lauritsen 1994; Brewster 1994). There have been several national surveys of the sexual behavior of adolescents, such as John Kantner and Melvin Zelnik's 1971 and 1976 National Surveys of Young Women and the 1979 National Survey of Young Men and Women. Sonenstein has more recently conducted the 1988 and 1990 National Surveys of Adolescent Males.

While numerous studies have been conducted on specific sexual practices (e.g., sexual debut and condom use), we know much less about the prevalence and meanings given to such sexual practices as masturbation, oral sex, anal sex, and same-gender sexual activity. The General Social Survey (GSS) included only a limited number of questions about sexual behavior in its national surveys, and the 1990 National AIDS Behavioral Surveys asked detailed questions about vaginal and anal intercourse only of respondents who reported an HIV risk factor. Moreover, sexual behavior cannot be understood apart from the attitudes that give insight into the meaning of various sexual activities. The NHSLS provides a much more comprehensive and detailed picture of people's sexual activities, preferences, and attitudes than has previously been available.

Gender Differences in Sexual Practices

Most sexual practices are highly gendered, meaning that certain sexual practices, such as engaging in a high frequency of sex and having multiple sex partners, are identified as masculine, others, such as waiting until marriage to have sex, as feminine. Many studies of sexual behavior, however, study only one gender (see, e.g., Sterk-Elifson 1994; Gilmore, DeLamater, and Wagstaft 1996; Brewster 1994). This makes it very difficult to compare the experiences and sexual roles of men and women in relation to each other within and across racial and ethnic groups.

Several studies of gender differences in sexuality have been conducted within specific racial/ethnic and class groups. Anderson (1990) found that adolescent African American men and women living in the ghetto have sharply contrasting orientations toward sexuality. Anderson describes the "game" of men and the "dream" of women. Men see women as objects of a sexual game to be won as trophies for their own personal aggrandizement; sex is used as an important means of enhancing their social status among their male peers. Women dream of having a boyfriend, a financé, or a husband and the fairy-table prospect of living happily ever after with one's children in a nice house in a good neighborhood: the dream of a middle-class lifestyle and the nuclear family. The reality of inner-city African American men's poor employment prospects means that this dream is not likely to be realized (Anderson 1993).

Gender roles also have an important but different effect on sexual behavior among Latinos (see, e.g., Marín 1996). Women cannot be sexual if they want to be considered "good," resulting in the feelings of discomfort about sex commonly reported by Latino women. At the same time, men are expected to be passionate and to have a constant sexual desire that, once ignited, is beyond their control. For a Latino man, sexual conquest is a proof of masculinity. Because men generally have more status and power than women in Latino culture, women are at a disadvantage in dealing with coercion by men. The norms requiring virginity for women and encouraging men to seduce women create an ongoing tension between the sexes. In Mexican culture, men are allowed to have multiple sex partners, while women are required to be faithful. When a young women does engage in premarital intercourse, her sexuality is more accepted if it is seen as "bounded." For example, she was in love with her boyfriend and gave in to his sexual demands in a moment of passion (Horowitz 1983). Among mainly middle-class whites, Blumstein and Schwartz (1983) found that gender also affects what a person desires in a relationship and how he or she behaves in one. Men are expected to be more aggressive sexually and are thought to be more lustful than women, while women are supposed to be more passive.

While the literature has clearly documented significant gender differences in sexual scripts within racial/ethnic groups, studies typically treat only a single racial or ethnic group and fail directly to compare gender differences *across* racial and ethnic groups. Some authors have speculated that gender differences in sexual practices are smaller for African Americans than for whites. Bowser (1994) argues that African American gender differences in sexual practices are smaller because it is more acceptable for African American women to engage in casual sex. African American men assume that African

American women are, like the men themselves, having sex before marriage and having multiple sex partners. Sterk-Elifson (1994) found that many young African American women felt pressured to have sex because they feared that their partners would leave them if they did not.

Weinberg and Williams (1988) found male-female differences in sexual practices were substantially larger among African Americans than among whites. Compared to African American women, African men have first intercourse at a much younger age, have a higher frequency of premarital sexual activity, and have more sex partners. They suggest that this is because African American men are in a social milieu that is sexually permissive and in which sexual opportunities are relatively available, while white men are more constrained by their cultural environment. These conclusions were based on data collected only through 1970 and may not accurately represent women and men who came of age after the sexual revolution.

The Effect of Education on Sexual Practices

Studying racial/ethnic differences in sexual scripts is difficult because race and ethnicity are themselves highly correlated with educational attainment. Findings regarding the relative effect of education versus race on sexual practices have been contradictory. Numerous studies have shown that class has an effect on age at first intercourse (Kinsey, Pomeroy, and Martin 1948; Hollingshead 1949; Sterk-Elifson 1994). In an early sociological community study, Hollingshead (1949) found that class was a major factor in shaping white adolescents' sexual practices. Adolescents in the lower classes tended to begin having sexual intercourse at an earlier age than those in the working or middle classes. Most lower-class couples did not use contraception, and there was a high rate of pregnancy before marriage. In more recent analysis comparing two different studies, Weinberg and Williams (1980) found that class, as measured by education level, is important among males in predicting the onset of sexual activity and the incidence and frequency of such sexual behaviors as masturbation and oral sex during adolescence. For females, class was negatively related to early sexual activity and positively related to good feelings about first sexual experiences.

The increasing polarization of the African American population by socioeconomic class (Wilson 1978) suggests that class may have an even greater effect on African Americans' sexual behavior. Hogan and Kitagawa (1985) examined the linkages between social status, family structures, and neighborhood characteristics as they affected fertility patterns among adolescent African American women in 1979. They found that social class was a significant factor, inversely related to teenage pregnancy.

Anderson (1993) also argues that black ghetto sexual behaviors and values are a result of the "economic noose" in the ghetto—the structural conditions that allow girls to conclude that they have no future to derail by having a baby and boys to conclude that they will be unable to become economically self-reliant and support a family. The same strains are not experienced by middle-class blacks. In addition, middle-class youths have a much higher level of practical education about birth control and sexuality in general.

Other studies have shown that sexual relationships are still sharply organized around racial and ethnic categories. *SOS* found a higher degree of race than class homophily (as measured by education) in sexual partnerships. Weinberg and Williams (1988) concluded that cultural differences between races override differences in social class, finding that the effects of race were still prominent even after class was taken into account. Regardless of class status, African Americans were more likely to engage in premarital sex earlier and more frequently than whites. African American men had a greater number of partners, and African Americans in

general were more liberal and accepting of sex, pursued it more, and reported fewer problems with it. They found no support for Kinsey's hypothesis that these differences are explained by social class. Weinberg and Williams (1988) argued that their finding that social class is not a complete explanatory factor for racial differences in sexual behavior is due to a distinct subculture created by African Americans as a result of their specific historical and social circumstances, which have given particular meaning to sexuality for them. In addition, the continuing segregation of blacks and whites regardless of social class has sustained these cultural patterns.

Measuring Class

Furstenberg et al. (1987) conclude that African Americans have sex earlier than whites because of racial differences in attitudes and norms regarding sexual behavior and that this is particularly true for African Americans in highly segregated schools. They found that African Americans are more likely to expect parenthood before or at the same time as marriage and that they are more likely to report having peers who are sexually active. These studies lead one to expect that race will have a larger effect on sexual scripts than class, given that distinctive sexual scripts will develop in racially segregated populations.

One difficulty in comparing the effects of race/ethnicity and class is that, while *race* and *ethnicity* are reasonably well-defined, socially sanctioned categories, *class* is less easily defined and measured. Previous studies of sexuality that have focused simply on age at first sex, number of partners, and condom use have defined *class* as the potential for upward mobility and thus have used complex composite measures that take into account parents' education, occupation, family income, and labor force experience (cf. Hogan and Kitagawa 1985). However, the concept of class most pertinent to our analysis of broader sexual scripts is that of groups of individuals who share a "style of life," social positions that are characterized by value orientations, attitudes, behavior, and conventions. Thus, each dimension of lifestyle, including the sexual, expresses a similar logic. Education has often been thought to be a better measure of this conception of class than occupation or income since cultural capital has a greater influence on one's values and beliefs than does economic capital (Mayer 1997; DiMaggio 1994). Thus, although it is not a perfect measure, we use respondent's education as a simple measure of class and the potential for upward mobility and a factor that largely defines the pool of potential sex partners. We have broken education into three categories: no high school degree, high school degree, and more than high school degree (which includes vocational degree, some college, college degree, and advanced degrees). We grouped those with vocational degrees and some college with those who had a college or an advanced degree because, in general, they are more similar to the latter than to the high school graduates.

Racial/Ethnic Categories

There are definitional issues related to ethnicity that also require careful consideration. First, race and ethnicity are not mutually exclusive. Some respondents, primarily Hispanics, do not consider themselves white or black, selecting the category *other* on the question about race, and, when queried, specify their race as Hispanic. For this reason, in following what is the standard practice in reporting census data, we start by dividing the population into Hispanic and non-Hispanic, then break the later into racial categories: white, black, Asian/Pacific Islander, or Native American. However, the Hispanic group does not form a single homogeneous entity in terms of either race or national origin. It is therefore problematic to treat Hispanics as a single category when comparing them to blacks and whites. One solution is to break them into smaller, more homogeneous groupings. Since

Mexican Americans constitute the majority of Hispanics in the United States, we analyze them as a separate group. Unfortunately, no other Hispanic subgroups in our sample are large enough to analyze separately.

Second, the fact that Hispanics are very heterogeneous reminds us that whites also have many ethnic origins. According to the GSS (1988–94), no more than 20 percent of whites in the United States under sixty years of age came from any one country of origin. The most common white family origin is Germany (18 percent), followed by England (12 percent) and Ireland (11 percent). Smaller percentages report family origins in Italy (5 percent), Scotland (3 percent), and Poland (3 percent). Reflecting this diversity in countries of origin is the religious heterogeneity among whites. Whites reporting a religious affiliation in the NHSLS were evenly divided among Catholics, Mainline Protestants, and Fundamentalist Protestants.

UNDERSTANDING RACIAL/ETHNIC DIFFERENCES

Whites

The whites have, on the average, more school years completed when compared to the other three racial and ethnic groups. Only about 11 percent of the whites in our sample did not finish a high school degree, while over 60 percent had at least some college or vocational training. They were also somewhat older. About 40 percent of the whites were between forty and fifty-nine years of age. Whites were very heterogeneous in terms of religious affiliation, almost evenly divided among Catholicism, Mainline Protestantism, and evangelical and fundamentalist Protestantism, with about 12 percent reporting no religious affiliation. About 55 percent of the men and 59 percent of the women were married at the time of the survey. The white profile is generally older, married, and college educated, but religion is mixed.

African Americans

Compared to the whites in our sample, African Americans had a lower level of educational achievement. About 22 percent of the African Americans had not finished high school, twice the percentage of whites, and only about 40 percent had at least some college or vocational school. African Americans had an age composition similar to that of whites, with about 36 percent between forty and fifty-nine years of age. A much lower percentage of African Americans than whites were currently married. Only 39 percent of the men and 36 percent of the women were married at the time of the interview. The vast majority, 64 percent of the men and 75 percent of the women, were affiliated with more conservative Protestant denominations, such as the Baptist and Pentecostal Churches. The African American profile is thus typified by older, moderately educated, and unmarried conservative Protestants.

Mexican Americans

Of our four racial and ethnic groups, Mexican Americans had the lowest level of educational attainment. Almost 38 percent had not completed high school. Mexican Americans in our sample also tended to be much younger than representatives of the other groups. Almost 80 percent of the Mexican American women were between eighteen and forty, and 45 percent were between eighteen and twenty-nine. Almost 70 percent of Mexican American men were between eighteen and forty years of age, and 49 percent were between eighteen and twenty-nine. Despite their younger ages, however, the proportion married was similar to the proportion of whites married, with 50 percent of the men and 57 percent of the women married at the time of the interview. The vast majority of Mexican Americans in our sample were Catholic, 75 percent of the men and 67 percent of the women. Mexican Americans were concentrated in the Southwest. The Mexican American profile is one of young, less-educated, strongly Catholic married couples.

DATA AND METHODS

To study cultural scenarios, we analyze the responses to the NHSLS questions regarding sexual attitudes. These questions ask respondents whether they think that certain sexual practices are wrong, and the answers to these questions thus form a picture of the social guidelines and norms surrounding sexual behavior. Second, we examine interpersonal scripts by analyzing the responses to the NHSLS questions regarding the sexual practices in which the respondents have engaged, both in their lifetime and in their last sexual event. Third, to study intrapsychic scripts or individual fantasies and desires, we analyze the responses to the NHSLS questions regarding which sexual practices the respondent finds appealing.

DEFINITION OF VARIABLES

Master Statuses

Age is divided into four cohorts: eighteen to twenty-nine, thirty to thirty-nine, forty to forty-nine, and fifty to fifty-nine. The oldest cohort reached adolescence well before the sexual revolution; the youngest cohort came of age after the AIDS epidemic began (1981).

There are four categories of religious affiliation: no religious affiliation, Mainline Protestant, Evangelical Protestant, and Catholic. Mainline Protestant mainly includes such Protestant denominations as the Episcopalians, Lutherans, Presbyterians, and Methodists. Evangelical Protestant includes the Baptists and Pentecostals and other fundamentalist sectarian churches.

Respondent's marital status was treated differently for different dependent variables. When the dependent variable pertained to sexual activities performed over the lifetime, such as whether the respondent had ever experienced fellatio, marital status distinguished between the ever married and the never married. When the dependent variable referred to sexual activities in the past twelve months, marital status distinguished the currently married from the not currently married.

Family composition was determined from the question, "Were you living with both your own mother and father when you were 14?" (if no: "With whom were you living around that time?") Three categories were identified: (1) lived with both biological parents; (2) lived with a parent and a stepparent; and (3) lived with a single parent.

Measures of Cultural Scenarios

Aspects of sexual cultural scenarios were measured by the respondents' attitudes toward certain sexual practices. These attitudes concern the age at which the respondent believes sex is appropriate, the appropriate relationship to one's sex partner, the feelings one is supposed to have for one's sex partner, the sexual acts deemed appropriate in a sexual encounter, and the appropriate gender of a sex partner. *SOS* reported a cluster analysis of nine attitudes that identified three broad normative orientations toward sexuality: traditional, relational, and recreational.

Strongly disapproving attitudes toward premarital sex and teenage sex as well as agreement with the statement that religious beliefs shape the respondent's sexual behavior are used to indicate support for the traditional cultural scenario that regards reproduction as the sole purpose of sex, which should take place only within marriage. This orientation is rooted in religious convictions, with the Roman Catholic and more conservative Protestant churches being strong advocates of these ideas. Respondents were asked, "If a man and a woman have sex relations before marriage, do you think it is always wrong, wrong only sometimes, or not wrong at all?" and, "What if they are in their teens, say 14–16 years old?" Those who answered always wrong or almost always wrong to these questions were coded as having a traditional cultural scenario. In addition, respondents were asked to respond to the statement, "My religious beliefs have shaped and guided my sexual behavior." Those who responded strongly agree or agree were coded as having a traditional cultural scenario (*SOS*).

Relational orientation toward sexuality was identified by agreement with the statement, "I would not have sex with someone unless I was in love with them." Those who answered strongly agree or agree were coded as holding a cultural scenario in which sex should take place in an intimate, loving relationship (thus, a relational cultural scenario allows for premarital sex, but only within a loving relationship).

A recreational cultural scenario is one in which attitudes toward sexual practices do not relate directly either to procreation or to the intimacy of the relationship. This was measured by asking respondents whether they agreed with the statement, "Any kind of sexual activity between adults is okay as long as both persons freely agree to it." Again, those who answered strongly agree or agree were coded as holding a recreational attitude toward sexuality. This item was used because it was thought to measure a modern, pleasure-centered view of sex, where sex is considered a good in itself as long as it does not hurt anyone.

Finally, respondents' attitudes toward homosexuality are often quite distinct from any of their attitudes toward other sexual matters, and we thus analyze this issue separately. We distinguished between those who regarded homosexual activity as always or almost always wrong and those who said that it was wrong only sometimes or not wrong at all.

Measures of Interpersonal Scripts

We examined the respondent's actual sexual practices, including both adolescent and adult sexual experiences. Interpersonal scripts can be divided, like cultural scenarios, into three categories: traditional, relational, and recreational.

Two central aspects of interpersonal scripts are the age at the time of first sexual intercourse and the relationship to one's first sex partner. Respondents were asked, "How old were you the *first* time you had vaginal intercourse with a (…male/female)?". It was specified that the interviewer was asking only about the first intercourse after puberty, not about childhood sexual experiences before puberty. We coded those who had sex before age sixteen as having an early initiation into sexual activity and thus have a less traditional interpersonal script. Respondents were then asked, "What was your relationship to this person [i.e., the person with whom respondent had first vaginal intercourse]?". Those who were married to their first sex partner at the time they had their first sex can be seen as being traditional on this measure. Those who reported that they were in love with their first sex partner (but not necessarily married) were considered to be more relational in their sexual practices than people who reported that they were not in love with their first sex partner. People who reported their first sex as being with someone with whom they were not in love were considered more recreational in their sexual practices.

Another aspect of interpersonal scripts concerns the reasons people report for having decided to have sex for the first time. First, we asked whether this first sexual intercourse was "something you wanted to happen at the time?…something you went along with, but did not want to happen?…[or] something that you were forced to do against your will?". For those whose first sex was wanted, the interviewer continued: "What was the main reason you decided to go along with having sexual intercourse this first time?". The answers fell mainly into four categories: affection for partner, curious/ready for sex, physical pleasure, and wedding night. Those who reported their first sex because it was their wedding night were considered more traditional in their interpersonal scripts. Having first sex because of affection for one's partner indicated a relational script, while having it because of curiosity/readiness or for physical pleasure indicated a more recreational script. We also asked respondents how many sex

partners they had in the past twelve months. Those who reported having three or more partners in the last year were considered more recreational in their sexual practices.

Finally, we asked about the sexual acts occurring in sexual encounters. To determine whether respondents had ever had fellatio or cunnilingus, they were asked, "Have you ever performed oral sex on a [opposite sex: man/woman]?" and, "Has a [opposite sex: man/woman] ever performed oral sex on you?" Regarding heterosexual anal sex, we asked, "Have you ever had anal sex with a [opposite sex: man/woman]?". The sexual acts in which people engage are not readily associated with particular normative orientations, but they do seem to indicate conventional interpersonal scripts (never having experienced oral or anal sex) as opposed to elaborated interpersonal scripts (ever having experienced oral or anal sex).

Measures of Intrapsychic Scripts

The respondent's own sexual preferences will serve as measures of his or her intrapsychic scripts. Respondents were asked whether they found certain sex acts, such as vaginal intercourse, watching their partner undress, a partner performing oral sex on them, or performing oral sex on a partner, very appealing, somewhat appealing, not appealing, or not at all appealing. We simply dichotomized the responses into the categories appealing and not appealing. Those who found only vaginal intercourse appealing, a substantial majority of the NHSLS respondents, will be treated as being more conventional in their intrapsychic scripts, while those who find any other sexual act appealing will be regarded as having more elaborated intrapsychic scripts.

ANALYSES AND RESULTS

Race, Gender, and Class in Sexual Cultural Scenarios

Overall, the majority of both men and women in all the racial/ethnic groups considered do not believe that premarital sex is wrong but do believe that teenage sex (between the ages of fourteen and sixteen years) is wrong. The majority also agree that any sexual activity between two consenting adults is OK. Finally, the majority believe that homosexual activity is wrong. Even after controlling for the other master statuses, the attitudes of Mexican Americans and African American women are more traditional where sex is concerned, while whites are less traditional, and African American men are the least traditional of all.

More specifically, Mexican Americans are more than twice as likely as whites to regard premarital sex as wrong when we control for the other master statuses. Mexican American women are also three times more likely than white women to believe that teenage sex is wrong, and Mexican American men are more than twice as likely as white men to believe that religion shapes their sexual behavior. Thus, Mexican Americans are more likely than whites to embrace traditional sexual attitudes. Mexican American women are also over three times more likely than white women to report that homosexual activity is wrong.

In comparison to Mexican Americans, who hold mostly traditional attitudes, whites are more secular and less traditional. For example, whites are less likely than Mexican Americans to report that religion shapes their sexual behavior. Whites are also less likely than Mexican Americans to regard premarital sex as wrong. In addition, whites, and particularly white women, are much more liberal in their attitudes toward homosexual activity. While the vast majority of whites believe that teenage sex is wrong, white women are less likely than Mexican American women to believe this, particularly after taking into account the other master statuses.

The attitudes of African Americans are similar to those of whites on several issues, such as premarital sex and teenage sex. However, gender differences between African American men and women are so large that it is difficult to analyze them together. The attitudes of African American women are more traditional than those of whites in some respects, while those of African American men are not. For example, after controlling for other master-status characteristics, African American women are almost twice as likely as white women to say that their religion shapes their sexual behavior. They are also slightly more likely than white women to regard premarital sex as wrong, although this result is reduced to nonsignificance when other master statuses are taken into account. Although the attitudes of African American men are also very similar to those of white men where sex is concerned, African American men are significantly less likely than men of other racial/ethnic groups to say that they would have sex only if they were in love. African American men, in short, hold less relational attitudes than men and women of other racial/ethnic groups.

While the racial/ethnic differences are significant, gender plays the central role in shaping sexual attitudes. In fact, attitudes toward teenage sex, one's relationship to one's sex partner, and religious beliefs guiding sexual behavior differ more by gender than by race or ethnicity. More women than men in all racial/ethnic groups regard premarital and teenage sex as wrong and assert that their religious beliefs shape their sexual behavior and that they would not have sex unless they were in love. This may reflect the sexual double standard that places more restrictions on women's sexuality than on men's. The gender gap appears largest among African Americans. While 77 percent of African American women say that they would have sex only if they were in love, only 43 percent of African American men agree. And, while 69 percent of African American women say that their religious beliefs shape their sexual behavior, only 50 percent of African American men say this. The gender gap in attitudes toward premarital sex and teenage sex is also large for Mexican Americans. However, there are no significant gender differences in attitudes toward recreational sexual activity and homosexuality, with the exception of white men's and women's attitudes toward homosexuality.

What are the effects of class and other master-status variables on sexual attitudes? Education, age, religion, marital status, and family composition during adolescence do not diminish racial/ethnic differences in the attitudes toward premarital sex, teenage sex, religious influence on sexual behavior, and having sex only if in love. The one exception is that African American women do not differ from whites in regarding premarital sex as wrong once the other master statuses are taken into account.

In most cases, when we control for these other social factors, racial/ethnic differences are even stronger. For example, only after controlling for these other master statuses are Mexican American men more than twice as likely as white men to regard premarital sex as wrong and to say that their religious beliefs shape their sexual behavior. Differences for Mexican American and other Hispanic women (compared to white women) in the influence of religion on sexual behavior also approach significance once these other social factors are taken into account. Education, for example, has an effect on women's attitudes toward teenage sex; women with a college education are more likely to regard teenage sex as wrong. For men, education has an effect on men's reporting that their religious beliefs shape their sexual behavior. In the end, however, these attitudes are still largely organized around racial/ethnic lines, with variations according to age and religion.

Other sexual attitudes, however, appear to be more a function of class than of race/ethnicity. Attitudes about recreational sexual and homosexual activity are strongly affected by education. Controlling for education does diminish racial/ethnic differences in attitudes toward homosexual activity and other sexual practices between adults. Those with at least some college are significantly less likely to believe that homosexual activity is wrong. After controlling for education, age, religion, marital status, and family composition, there are no significant racial/ethnic differences among men in attitudes toward homosexuality. The difference in attitudes toward homosexuality between African American women and white women is diminished, although the difference between Mexican American women and white women is only slightly reduced, suggesting perhaps that there is a particular proscription against homosexuality in Mexican American culture.

Education also has a significant effect on whether the respondent believes that any sexual activity between two consenting adults is OK. Among both men and women, those with at least some college are about half as likely as those who did not finish high school to believe that any sexual activity between two consenting adults is OK. Controlling for these other variables, the difference between Mexican American women and white women is reduced to nonsignificance, but the difference between African American women and white women remains.

In conclusion, education has the strongest effect on attitudes toward recreational sexual practices and homosexuality, at times causing racial/ethnic differences to disappear. This suggests that these attitudes are more related to class and other social characteristics, such as age and religious affiliation, than racial/ethnic group affiliation. However, for other sexual attitudes, racial/ethnic differences largely remain, or become even stronger, after controlling for education and these other social characteristics. Thus, attitudes toward premarital and teenage sex, religious influence on sexual behavior, and having sex only if in love vary more by race and ethnicity than by class.

Race, Class, and Gender in Interpersonal Scripts

Now that we have a picture of the role of race, gender, and class in sexual cultural scenarios, how do these relate to interpersonal scripts or actual sexual practices? Recall that interpersonal scripts refer to the ways in which cultural scenarios are used and adapted to fit specific situations, representing the actor's response to the external world. We first briefly summarize the racial/ethnic similarities and differences in sexual practices and then examine the effects of class and other master statuses on these sexual practices.

Just as in the case of cultural scenarios, racial/ethnic groups share basic interpersonal scripts. For example, the majority of men and women in all racial/ethnic groups have had premarital sex. The majority of men and women also report that their first sex was something they wanted to do at the time. In terms of current sexual practices, the majority of people had fewer than three sex partners in the past year and had sex once a week or more in the past twelve months.

Despite these basic similarities among racial/ethnic groups, it is clear that significant differences also exist among the racial/ethnic groups in almost all aspects of interpersonal scripts examined here. For example, even after controlling for other master statuses, whites have sex later in adolescence but engage in more elaborated sexual practices, including oral and anal sex, as adults. Mexican Americans' adolescent sexual behavior is similar to that of whites, but the former are much less likely to engage in oral sex as adults. African Americans have had sex earlier, and have a much higher rate of premarital sex, but are still very conventional in terms of adult sexual practices, being much less likely to engage in oral and anal sex.

When we compare actual sexual practices to the cultural scenarios of the racial/ethnic groups, we find that these two levels of sexual scripts do not always coincide. For example, while Mexican Americans have more traditional attitudes than whites toward premarital sex and teenage sex, their sexual practices are little different from those of whites. And, while African American women hold more traditional sexual attitudes than white women, their actual sexual practices are less traditional. While African American men hold attitudes similar to those of men in other racial/ethnic groups regarding premarital

sex and teenage sex, they are much less traditional and relational in practice. These disjunctures between the cultural scenario and the interpersonal script suggest that the situational contexts of sexual encounters for racial/ethnic groups are different, leading to differences in the ways in which those cultural scenarios are used.

Adolescent Interpersonal Scripts

Whites are slightly more conventional than other racial/ethnic groups in terms of their early sexual experiences. While the vast majority of whites have had premarital sex, most did not have sex until after they were sixteen. About three-fourths of white women were in love with their first sex partner and reported wanting their first sex at the time. There is a significant gender difference, however, in that only 42 percent of white men reported being in love with their first sex partner. In addition, most white men report wanting their first sex out of curiosity/readiness, while most white women report wanting their first sex because of affection for their partner.

Despite the fact that Mexican Americans have more traditional attitudes than whites, there is no significant difference between the two groups in the proportion who have had teenage sex or premarital sex. Over 90 percent of the men and about 80 percent of Mexican American women had premarital sex, and about 30 percent of the men and 20 percent of the women had sex before they were sixteen. Mexican American women are twice as likely as white women, however, to report being in love with their first sex partner, after controlling for the other master statuses. The higher percentage of Mexican American women who report being in love with their first sex partner is consistent with the feminine ideal in the Mexican American community that makes premarital sex more acceptable for a women if it is done out of love for her boyfriend (Horowitz 1983). Despite the fact that a higher proportion of Mexican American women report being in love with their first sex partner, almost 30 percent of Mexican American women also report that their first sex was something they went along with but did not want. This, too, may reflect the Mexican American feminine ideal that requires submission to the sexual demands of a boyfriend, particularly when in love.

Although the attitudes of African Americans toward premarital sex and teenage sex are not significantly different from those of whites, African Americans do have higher rates of premarital and teenage sex and are less likely than whites to be in love with their first sex partner, even after controlling for the other master statuses. Almost 98 percent of African American men and 93 percent of African American women had premarital sex. African Americans also had a higher rate of teenage sex, with 51 percent of African American men and 24 percent of African American women having sex before they were sixteen. African American women are also the least likely to report that their first sex was wanted at the time even after controlling for other master statuses.

Differences in interpersonal scripts among racial/ethnic groups, despite similarities in cultural scenarios, may be the result of the different situational contexts in which the cultural scenario is used. For example, barriers to their economic success may help explain why African American men have sex before they are sixteen more often than do men in other racial/ethnic groups (despite shared attitudes about teenage sex). In a situation where economic opportunities are blocked, sex during early adolescence is likely to have meaning beyond the sexual, affirming identity as a socially competent, high-status person (Simon and Gagnon 1987b). As noted before, twice as many African American men as white men have no high school degree, an indicator of limited later socioeconomic success. However, even after controlling for education, African American men are still three times more likely than white men to have had sex before they were sixteen. In short, blocked opportunities, as measured by education at least, cannot account for all the effects of race on early sexual intercourse.

While having sex early may be a way for African American adolescent males to affirm their status, the literature does not offer the same explanation with regard to African American women. For some African American women, early sex may instead be something that they go along with because they have no future to derail (Anderson 1993). First, African American women are significantly more likely than white women to report that their first sex was something that they went along with but did not want to happen. This may be a result of the very different cultural scenarios with which African American men and women approach the sexual encounter. Education, (a measure of future opportunities) has a very strong effect on age at first sex for women at both the high school and the college level. For women, then, the racial/ethnic differences in the percentage having sex before age sixteen disappear when we control for education and the other master statuses.

Gender differences in the percentage actually having sex before age sixteen reflect the differences in attitudes toward teenage sex that are part of the cultural scenarios. A significantly lower percentage of women than men had premarital and teenage sex in most racial/ethnic groups. Women are also more likely than men to be in love with their first sex partner and to have sex because of affection for their partner. In all racial/ethnic groups, however, women are significantly less likely than men to report that their first sex was wanted.

Adult Interpersonal Scripts

We now turn to an examination of sexual practices occurring in the past twelve months. Compared to other racial/ethnic groups, whites have lower numbers of sex partners but much greater elaboration in sexual practices. The vast majority of whites (90 percent of the men and 96 percent of the women) have fewer than three sex partners in the past twelve months, and most whites have sex once a week or more. About three-fourths of whites have engaged in oral sex, with 30 percent of the men and 21 percent of the women having experienced fellatio in the last event and similar percentages having experienced cunnilingus.

Mexican Americans' number of partners in the last twelve months is very similar to that of whites. There is also no significant difference in the frequency of partnered sex. However, Mexican Americans are more conventional with regard to other sexual practices, being less than half as likely as whites to engage in oral sex, even after controlling for the other master statuses.

African American men and women are more likely than those in other racial/ethnic groups to have three or more partners in the last twelve months, although, for women, this difference disappears after controlling for other master statuses. Despite the fact that a higher proportion of African American men have three or more sex partners in the past twelve months, there is no significant racial/ethnic difference in the frequency of partnered sex. In terms of other sexual practices, African Americans are more conventional than whites, with African American women being less likely than white women to have ever performed fellatio and African American men and women both being less likely than whites ever to have experienced cunnilingus. African American women are also significantly less likely than white women to have had anal sex, although there is no racial difference among men.

Race, Class, and Gender in Intrapsychic Scripts

Let us now turn to racial/ethnic similarities and differences in individuals' sexual desires and fantasies, key elements of the intrapsychic sexual script. We find that the intrapsychic scripts of racial/ethnic groups generally coincide with their interpersonal scripts. For example, as with their interpersonal scripts, whites had more elaborated intrapsychic scripts than African Americans and Mexican Americans when one counted the number of sexual techniques, such

as oral or anal sex and manual stimulation, that respondents found very appealing. White men had the highest mean number of *very appealing* responses, 2.60. African American men had a significantly lower mean number of *very appealing* responses, 2.47, and Hispanic men had an even lower mean number, 2.38. Women in all the racial/ethnic groups had lower mean numbers of *very appealing* responses than men, but they also differed significantly between racial and ethnic groups. White women reported a mean of 1.68 techniques to be very appealing, which was close to Hispanic women's mean of 1.65. African American women, however, found a mean of only 1.48 techniques very appealing. In general, African Americans and Hispanics find fewer sexual techniques very appealing.

Vaginal intercourse enjoys almost universal appeal and constitutes a part of the vast majority of people's intrapsychic scripts in all the racial/ethnic groups. However, there are some racial/ethnic variations among women in the appeal of vaginal intercourse. Other Hispanic women are significantly less likely than women of the other racial/ethnic groups analyzed here to find vaginal intercourse very or somewhat appealing. However, there were no racial or gender differences in whether vaginal intercourse occurred in the last event. When we look at the percentage of people who both find vaginal intercourse appealing and actually had vaginal intercourse in the last event, we find that African American and Mexican American women who find vaginal intercourse appealing are more likely than white women or other Hispanic women to have had vaginal intercourse in the last event.

While vaginal intercourse is almost universally appealing, the appeal of oral sex varies greatly by race and ethnicity. While the vast majority of white men (82 percent) find fellatio appealing, a substantially lower proportion of African American men (55 percent) find it appealing. Mexican American and the other Hispanic men find fellatio appealing more often than African American men do but still less often than white men do. Similarly, while 55 percent of white women find fellatio appealing, only 25 percent of African American women do. It is apparent that there are also significant gender differences in the percentage finding fellatio appealing in all racial/ethnic groups. For example, among African Americans, more than twice as many men as women find fellatio appealing.

The appeal of cunnilingus also varied widely among racial/ethnic groups. A much higher percentage of white men (77 percent) than African American men (42 percent) reported that they found cunnilingus appealing. Likewise, a higher percentage of white women (65 percent) than African American women (40 percent) found cunnilingus appealing. Again, Mexican Americans and the other Hispanics are between African Americans and whites in the percentage finding cunnilingus appealing. However, unlike for fellatio, there is no significant gender difference in the proportion finding cunnilingus appealing, except among whites. There is also a significant difference between white men and white women in the percentage who both find cunnilingus appealing and reported that it occurred in the last sexual event: a higher percentage of white men than white women who find cunnilingus appealing reported that it occurred in the last event.

When we control for education and other master statuses, racial/ethnic differences in the proportion finding oral sex appealing remain. While education does have a significant effect on preferences for cunnilingus and fellatio, as it does for the actual practice of these acts, the racial/ethnic differences are not diminished.

Thus, while vaginal intercourse is part of the intrapsychic scripts of all four racial/ethnic groups, whites include fellatio and cunnilingus to a larger degree in their intrapsychic scripts, while Mexican Americans and other Hispanics include these sexual practices to a lesser extent. African Americans are the least likely to include fellatio and cunnilingus in their intrapsychic scripts.

SUMMARY: RACIAL/ETHNIC SIMILARITIES AND DIFFERENCES IN SEXUAL SCRIPTS

First, we found that racial and ethnic groups share many aspects of their sexual scripts. The majority of people in all racial/ethnic groups, for example, believe that teenage sex and same-gender sex are wrong and report that they would not have sex unless they were in love. In terms of sexual practices, most people have had premarital sex but waited until they were at least sixteen to have sexual intercourse, have fewer than three sex partners in the last twelve months, and have sex once a week or more. In intrapsychic scripts, vaginal intercourse is found to be almost universally appealing, but only smaller pluralities find most other sexual practices appealing.

However, even after controlling for other master status variables, there are still significant racial/ethnic variations in these aspects of sexual scripts and even larger differences in the practices of other sexual activities, such as oral sex. Because race and ethnicity are highly correlated with other master statuses, different sexual scripts develop within these sexually segregated racial/ethnic groups. These sexual scripts become the norm for those in racial/ethnic groups and are used even by members of those groups who differ on other master statuses. Thus, we get an independent effect for racial and ethnic group affiliation after controlling for the other master statuses. Below, we summarize the predominant sexual scripts for whites, African Americans, and Mexican Americans.

Secular Cultural Scenario, Relational-Elaborated Interpersonal Scripts

Regarding interpersonal scripts, whites can best be described as relational-elaborated. While the overwhelming majority of whites had premarital sex and thus cannot be considered traditional in that respect, they are more likely than African

Americans to say that they were in love with their first sex partner, indicating a more relational orientation. Whites are also much more likely than the other racial/ethnic groups to engage in elaborated sexual behavior, such as oral and anal sex. One hypothesis is that the more elaborated and less procreation-oriented sexual script of whites is due to a weakening of religious influence on sexual attitudes and practices. A lower proportion of whites than of the other racial/ethnic groups assert that their religious beliefs shape and guide their sexual behavior in every age cohort younger than fifty to fifty-nine, even after the other master statuses are taken into account. Evidence that religion is linked to less elaborated sexual practices is found in the fact that respondents who agree that their religious beliefs shape and guide their sexual behavior are less than half as likely to have ever engaged in fellatio or cunnilingus.

GENDERED CULTURAL SCENARIO, RECREATIONAL-CONVENTIONAL INTERPERSONAL SCRIPTS

Characterizing the cultural scenarios of African Americans as a whole is difficult because men and women embrace such different sexual scripts. African American women hold more traditional and relational attitudes toward premarital sex, homosexuality, teenage sex, the influence of religion on sexual behavior, and having sex only if in love than African American men. They are much less likely to describe their first sexual experience as wanted at the time than women in any other group.

Regarding interpersonal scripts, African Americans are typically recreational-conventional in orientation. They are more likely than the other groups to report that they were not in love with their first sex partner, that they had their first sex because of curiosity/readiness or physical pleasure, and that they had three or more partners in the past year. At the same time, they are much more conventional than whites in what they do in sexual encounters, being much less likely to engage in oral or anal sex.

One explanation for the more conventional features of African Americans' sexual scripts is the legacy of fundamentalist and evangelical Protestantism. About 64 percent of African American men and 75 percent of African American women are affiliated with conservative Protestant churches, and similar proportions were raised in such churches. This is over twice, and sometimes more than three times, the rate of affiliation for any of the other racial/ethnic groups. African Americans, particularly women, are especially likely to say that their religious beliefs shape and guide their sexual behavior. Support for the hypothesis that conventional sexual practices are the result of conservative religious affiliation is found in the fact that whites affiliated with fundamentalist and evangelical Protestant churches are also much less likely to have had experience with oral or anal sex. More research is surely needed to clarify how recreational scripts came to dominate the orientations of African American men.

Traditional Cultural Scenario, Relational-Conventional Interpersonal Scripts

Mexican Americans' cultural scenarios are traditional in orientation with respect to attitudes toward premarital sex, homosexuality, religious influences on sexual behavior (for men), and attitudes toward teenage sex (for men), and attitudes toward teenage sex (for women).

Regarding interpersonal scripts, Mexican Americans are relational-conventional. They cannot be considered traditional because the vast majority have engaged in premarital sex. They are, however, relational in their interpersonal scripts because Mexican American women are twice as likely as white women to report that they were in love with their first sex partner, after controlling for the other master statuses.

Mexican Americans are also less likely than African Americans to have had three or more partners in the last year. In terms of specific sex acts, Mexican Americans are more conventional than whites in that they are less likely to engage in fellatio or cunnilingus.

Mexican Americans' traditionalism in sexual scripts may be rooted in their Catholicism, which emphasizes procreational sexual practices within the context of marriage. Three-fourths of Mexican American men and two-thirds of Mexican American women are Catholic. Over 50 percent of Mexican American men and over 60 percent of Mexican American women report that their religious beliefs shape and guide their sexual behavior.

Although Mexican American women overwhelmingly reported being in love with their first sex partner, a fairly high percentage (30 percent) also reported that their first sex was something they went along with but did not want.

Elaboration of Sexual Script by Class, Age, Religious Affiliation, and Marital Status

Master statuses other than race and ethnicity also exert significant effects on sexual attitudes, preferences, and practices. The younger age cohorts are less traditional in their attitudes and more likely to have sex earlier, to have more sex partners, to have sex more frequently, and to engage in oral sex. The college educated are also significantly more likely to engage in cunnilingus and fellatio, to find those practices appealing, and to express more liberal views toward homosexuality. Those who are conservative Protestants are less likely to engage in or find oral sex appealing and more likely to regard teenage sex, premarital sex, and homosexual activity as wrong. Married people, compared to the never married, are more likely to regard premarital sex and teenage sex as wrong. They report fewer sex partners but have partnered sex more frequently.

CONCLUSION

While racial/ethnic groups share basic similarities in their sexual scripts, important differences remain even after one takes the effects of education, religion, age, and marital status into account. We hypothesize that the racial/ethnic segregation of sexual partnering results in sexual scripts that are particularized to each group. When a specific sexual script becomes the norm in a group, it may be used by other members of the group regardless of their other master statuses. Because the script is *socially* produced, individuals must call on shared meanings and expectations in order to enact them. Further research must be conducted if we are to understand how actual networks and social contexts of sexual partnering facilitate the development and transmission of sexual scripts.

The sexual scripts approach also revealed the complex patterns in which specific sexual practices are embedded. For example, while African Americans may be less traditional in their age at and the context of first intercourse, they are actually more traditional in their actual sexual practices in adulthood. We also found contradictions between the cultural scenarios and the interpersonal scripts of some groups. These disjunctures highlight the different contexts in which these generally shared cultural narratives are applied in actual situations. Along these lines, some have argued that the racial/ethnic differences in sexual behavior are really an effect of class locations. But we found that, although education does have a significant effect on many sexual behaviors, race/ethnicity retains an independent effect.

Finally, we found that, for many aspects of sexual scripts, gender differences are more substantial than racial/ethnic differences. And, where the gender differences in cultural scenarios were the greatest, so were the number of women who reported that their first sex was something that they went along with but did not want. Gender is thus an integral part of sexual scripts, with profound consequences for men's and women's sexual experiences.

REFERENCES

Anderson, E. 1990. *Streetwise: Race, class, and change in an urban community.* Chicago: University of Chicago Press.

Anderson, E. 1993. Sex codes and family life among poor inner-city youths. In *The ghetto underclass: Social science perspectives*, ed. W. J. Wilson. Newbury Park, Calif.: Sage.

Blumstein, P., and P. Schwartz. 1983. *American couples: Money, work, sex.* New York: Morrow.

Bowser, B. 1994. African-American male sexuality through the early life course. In *Sexuality across the life course*, ed. A Rossi. Chicago: University of Chicago Press.

Brewster, K. L. 1994. Race differences in sexual activity among adolescent women: The role of neighborhood characteristics. *American Sociological Review* 59 (June): 408–24.

Connell, R. W. 1995. *Masculinities: Knowledge, power and social change.* Berkley and Los Angeles: University of California Press.

DiMaggio, P. 1994. Social stratification, life-style, and social cognition. In *Social stratification: Class, race, and gender in sociological perspective*, ed. D. B. Grusky. Boulder, Colo.: Westview.

Duncan, G. J., and S. D. Hoffman. 1991. Teenage underclass behavior and subsequent poverty: Have the rules changed? In *The urban underclass*, ed. C. Jencks and P. Peterson. Washington, D.C.: Brookings.

Duneier, M. 1992. *Slim's table: Race, respectability, and masculinity.* Chicago: University of Chicago Press.

Furstenberg, F., P. Morgan, K. Moore, and J. Peterson. 1987. Race differences in the timeing of adolescent intercourse. *American Sociological Review* 52:511–18.

Gilmore, S., J. DeLamater, and D. Wagstaff. 1996. Sexual decision making by inner city black adolescent males: A focus group study. *Journal of Sex Research* 33, no. 4:363–71.

Hogan, D., and E. Kitagawa. 1985. The impact of social status, family structure, and neighborhood on the fertility of black adolescents. *American Journal of Sociology* 90, no. 4:825–55.

Hollingshead, A. B. 1949. *Elmtown's youth: The impact of social classes on adolescents.* New Brunswick, N.J.: Rutgers University Press.

Horowitz, M. J. 1983. *Honor and the American dream: Culture and identity in a Chicano community.* New Brunswick, N. J.: Rutgers University Press.

Jaynes, G. D., and Robert M. Williams, ed. 1989. *A common destiny: Blacks and American society.* Washington, D.C.: National Academy Press.

Kinsey, A. C., W. B. Pomeroy, and C. E. Martin. 1948. *Sexual behavior in the human male.* Philadelphia: W. B. Saunders.

Laumann, E. O., J. H. Gagnon, R. T. Michael, and S. Michaels. 1994. *The social organizations of sexuality: Sexual practices in the United States.* Chicago: University of Chicago Press.

Lauritsen, J. L. 1994. Explaining race and gender differences in adolescent sexual behavior. *Social Forces* 72, no. 3:859–84.

Marin, B. V. 1996. Cultural issues in HIV prevention for Latinos: Should we try to change gender roles? In *Understanding and preventing HIV risk behavior: Safer sex and drug use*, ed. S. Oskamp and S. C. Thompson. Thousand Oaks, Calif.: Sage.

Mayer, S. 1997. *What money can't buy: Family income and children's life chances.* Cambridge, Mass.: Harvard University Press.

Nagel, J. 1999. Ethnosexual frontiers: Constructing and crossing racial, ethnic, nationalist, and sexual boundaries. Paper presented at the annual meeting of the American Sociological Association, 9 August.

Simon, W., and J. H. Gagnon. 1987a. Sexual scripts: Permanence and change. *Archives of Sexual Behavior* 52:97–120.

Simon, W., and J. H. Gagnon. 1987b. A sexual scripts approach. In *Theories of human sexuality*, ed. W. T. O'Donohue. New York: Plenum.

Sonenstein, F. L., J. H. Pleck, and L. C. Ku. 1989. Sexual activity, condom use, and AIDS awareness among adolescent males. *Family Planning Perspectives* 21:152–158.

Staples, R. 1981. *The world of black singles: Changing patterns of male/female relations.* Westport, Conn.: Greenwood.

Sterk-Elifson, C. 1994. Sexuality among African-American women. In *Sexuality across the life course*, ed. A. S. Rossi. Chicago: University of Chicago Press.

Udry, J. R., and J. Billy. 1987. Initiation of coitus in early adolescence. *American Sociological Review* 52:841–55.

Weinberg, M., and C. Williams. 1980. Sexual embourgeoisement? Social class and sexual activity, 1938–1970. *American Sociological Review* 45:33–48.

Weinberg, M., and C. Williams. 1988. Black sexuality: A test of two theories. *Journal of Sex Research* 25, no. 2:197–218.

Wilson, W. J. 1978. *The declining significance of race.* Chicago: University of Chicago Press.

Zelnik, M., and J. F. Kantner. 1980. Sexual activity, contraceptive use, and pregnancy among metropolitanarea teenagers, 1971–1979. *Family Planning Perspectives* 12:230–37.

CHAPTER 22

Sexual Desire and Gender

Pepper Schwartz
Virginia E. Rutter

Fisher, Buss, and Schwartz are all names instantly recognized by colleagues in their respective disciplines of anthropology, psychology, and sociology. What do these different professionals have in common? All have written about the subject of sexual desire. Helen Fisher and David Buss are but two of the names of researchers you will encounter in the following chapter as Schwartz and Rutter carefully review the current knowledge about the intriguing subject of sexual desire and gender.

In anthropologist Helen Fisher's (2004) book, Why We Love: The Nature and Chemistry of Romantic Love, *she postulates that romantic love is a primary motivation system in the brain, a fundamental human mating drive. She accepts neuroscientist Don Pfaff's definition of a* drive *as a "neural state that energizes and directs behavior to acquire a particular biological need to survive or reproduce" (Fisher, 2004, 74). In her research, Fisher and colleagues worked with a team of scientists who scanned the brains of people who had just fallen "madly in love." The scans revealed that specific areas of the brains of "in love" subjects actually "light up" with increased blood flow. The research team concluded that romantic passion is hardwired into our brains by*

millions of years of evolution; it is not an emotion, but a drive as powerful as hunger, even if less predictable.

Buss's work, reported in The Evolution of Human Desire: Strategies of Human Mating (2003), *was based on the most massive study of human mating ever undertaken. It encompassed more than 10,000 people of all ages from thirty-seven (37) world-wide cultures. According to Buss, to understand the elusive subject of sexual desire, we must look into our evolutionary past. Presenting a unique theory of human mating behavior, he details what women want, what men want, and then explains why their desires differ radically.*

After reading this chapter from Schwartz and Rutter's book, The Gender of Sexuality, *you will be better able to claim your own territory in the land of sexual dissention. Ask yourself if you fit most neatly into the biological camp, the evolutionary psychological one, or the social-constructionist one. Or perhaps with Schwartz and Rutter, you will embrace the position of an integrationist, questioning biology when social contexts are emphasized as cause and questioning social contexts when biological causes are emphasized. Whatever your answers, when you have finished reading this next offering, your opinion will be better informed than before.*

The gender of the person you desire is a serious matter seemingly fundamental to the whole business of romance. And it isn't simply a matter of whether someone is male or female; how well the person fulfills a lover's expectations of masculinity or femininity is of great consequence, as two examples from the movies illustrate.

In the movie *The Truth About Cats & Dogs* (1996), Brian falls in love with Abby over the phone, and she with him. They find each other warm, clever, charming, and intriguing. But she, thinking herself too plain, asks her beautiful friend Noelle to impersonate her when the man and woman are scheduled to meet. Although the man becomes very confused about which woman he really desires, in the end the telephone lovers are united. The match depended on social matters far more than physical matters.

In the British drama *The Crying Game* (1994), Fergus, an Irish Republican Army underling, meets and falls in love with the lover (Dil) of Jody, a British soldier whom Fergus befriended prior to being ordered to execute him. The movie was about passionate love, war, betrayal, and, in the end, loyalty and commitment. Fergus seeks out Jody's girlfriend in London out of guilt and curiosity. But Fergus's guilt over Jody's death turns into love, and the pair become romantically and sexually involved. In the end, although Fergus is jailed for terrorist activities, Fergus and Dil have solidified their bond and are committed and, it seems, in love. The story of sexual conquest and love is familiar, but this particular story grabbed imaginations because of a single, crucial detail. Jody's girlfriend Dil, Fergus discovers, turns out to be (physically) a man. Although Fergus is horrified when he discovers his lover is biologically different from what he had expected, in the end their relationship survives.

These movies raise an interesting point about sexual desire. Although sex is experienced as one of the most basic and biological of activities, in human beings it is profoundly affected by things other than the body's urges. Who we're attracted to and what we find sexually satisfying is not just a matter of the genital equipment we're born with. This chapter explains why.

Before we delve into the whys and wherefores of sex, we need to come to an understanding about what sex is. This is not as easy a task as it may seem, because sex has a number of dimensions.

On one level, sex can be regarded as having both a biological and a social context. The biological refers to how people use their genital equipment to reproduce. In addition, as simple as it seems, bodies make the experience of sexual pleasure available—whether the pleasure involves other bodies or just one's own body and mind. It should be obvious, however, that people engage in sex even when they do not intend to reproduce. They have sex for fun, as a way to communicate their feelings to each other, as a way to satisfy their ego, and for any number of other reasons relating to the way they see themselves and interact with others.

Another dimension of sex involves both what we do and how we think about it. *Sexual behavior* refers to the sexual acts that people engage in. These acts involve not only petting and intercourse but also seduction and courtship. Sexual behavior also involves the things people do alone for pleasure and stimulation and the things they do with other people. *Sexual desire*, on the other hand, is the motivation to engage in sexual acts. It relates to what turns people on. A person's *sexuality* consists of both behavior and desire.

The most significant dimension of sexuality is *gender*. Gender relates both to the biological and social contexts of sexual behavior and desire. People tend to believe they know whether someone is a man or a woman not because we do a physical examination and determine that the person is biologically male or biologically female. Instead, we notice whether a person is masculine or feminine. Gender is a social characteristic of individuals in our society that is only sometimes consistent with biological sex. Thus, animals, like people, tend to be identified as male and female in accordance with the reproductive function, but only people are described by their gender, as a man or a woman.

When we say something is *gendered* we mean that social processes have determined what is appropriately masculine and feminine and that gender has thereby become integral to the definition of the phenomenon. For example, marriage is a gendered institution: The definition of marriage involves a masculine part (husband) and a feminine part (wife). Gendered phenomena, like marriage, tend to appear "naturally" so. But, as recent debates about same-sex marriage underscore, the role of gender in marriage is the product of social processes and beliefs about men, women, and marriage. In examining how gender influences sexuality, moreover, you will see that gender rarely operates alone: Class, culture, race, and individual differences also combine to influence sexuality. This chapter explores and takes issue with the assumptions that sexuality is naturally gendered and rooted in biology, that men and women are different sexually, and that this difference is consistent and universal across societies.

Sexuality is a complex bit of business. The study of sexuality presents methodological challenges. Sexual thoughts and behavior are typically private. Researchers must rely on what people say they want and do sexually, and these reports, as much as the desire and behavior itself, are influenced by what people believe they are supposed to feel and say. We will piece together this puzzle of acts, thoughts, and feelings with insights provided by survey research, physiological studies, ethnography, history, philosophy, and even art, cinema, and literature.

DESIRE: ATTRACTION AND AROUSAL

The most salient fact about sex is that nearly everybody is interested in it. Most people like to have sex, and they talk about it, hear about it, and think about it. But some people are obsessed with sex and willing to have sex with anyone or anything. Others are aroused only by particular conditions and hold exacting criteria. For example, some people will have sex only if they are positive that they are in love, that their partner loves them, and that the act is sanctified by marriage. Others view sex as not much different from eating a sandwich. They neither love nor hate the sandwich; they are merely hungry, and they want something to satisfy that hunger. What we are talking about here are differences in desire. As you have undoubtedly noticed, people differ in what they find attractive, and they are also physically aroused by different things.

Many people assume that differences in sexual desire have a lot to do with whether a person is female or male. In large representative surveys about sexual behavior, the men as a group inevitably report more frequent sex, with more partners, and in more diverse ways than the women as a group do. We will review that evidence. First, we should consider the approaches we might use to interpret it. Many observers argue that when it comes to sex, men and women have fundamentally different biological wiring. Others use the evidence to argue that culture has produced marked sexual differences among men and women. We believe, however, that it is hard to tease apart biological differences and social differences. As soon as a baby enters the world, it receives messages about gender and sexuality. In the United States, for example, disposable diapers come adorned in pink for girls and blue for boys. In case people aren't sure whether to treat the baby as masculine or feminine in its first years of life, the diaper signals them. The assumption is that girl babies really are different from boy babies and the difference ought to be displayed. This different treatment continues throughout life, and therefore a sex difference at birth becomes amplified into gender difference as people mature.

Gendered experiences have a great deal of influence on sexual desire. As a boy enters adolescence, he hears jokes about boys' uncontainable desire. Girls are told the same thing and told that their job is to resist. These gender messages have power not only over attitudes and behavior (such as whether a person grows up to prefer sex with a lover rather than a stranger) but also over physical and biological experience. For example, a girl may be discouraged from vigorous competitive activity, which will subsequently influence how she develops physically, how she feels about her body, and even how she relates to the adrenaline rush associated with physical competition. Hypothetically, a person who is accustomed to adrenaline responses experiences sexual attraction differently from one who is not.

What follows are three "competing" explanations of differences in sexual desire between men and women: a biological explanation, sociobiological and evolutionary psychological explanations, and an explanation that acknowledges the social construction of sexuality. We call these competing approaches because each tends to be presented as a complete explanation in itself, to the exclusion of other explanations. Our goal, however, is to provide a clearer picture of how "nature" and "nature" are intertwined in the production of sexualities.

THE BIOLOGY OF DESIRE: NATURE'S EXPLANATION

Biology is admittedly a critical factor in sexuality. Few human beings fall in love with fish or sexualize trees. Humans are designed to respond to other humans. And human activity is, to some extent, organized by the physical equipment humans are born with. Imagine if people had fins instead of arms or laid eggs instead of fertilizing them during intercourse. Romance would look quite different.

Although biology seems to be a constant (i.e., a component of sex that is fixed and unchanging), the social world tends to mold biology as much as biology shapes humans' sexuality. Each society has its own rules for sex. Therefore, how people experience their biology varies widely. In some societies, women act intensely aroused and active during sex; in others, they have no concept of orgasm. In fact, women in some settings, when told about orgasm, do not even believe it exists, as anthropologists discovered in some parts of Nepal. Clearly, culture—not biology—is at work, because we know that orgasm is physically possible, barring damage to or destruction of the sex organs. Even ejaculation is culturally dictated. In some countries, it is considered healthy to ejaculate early and often; in others, men are told to conserve semen and ejaculate as rarely as possible. The biological capacity may not be so different, but the way bodies behave during sex varies according to social beliefs.

Sometimes the dictates of culture are so rigid and powerful that the so-called laws of nature can be overridden. Infertility treatment provides an example: For couples who cannot produce children "naturally," a several billion dollar industry has provided technology that can, in a small proportion of cases, overcome this biological problem (Rutter 1996). Recently, in California, a child was born to a 63-year-old woman who had been implanted with fertilized eggs. The cultural emphasis on reproduction and parenthood, in this case, overrode the biological incapacity to produce children. Nevertheless, some researchers have focused on the biological foundations of sexual desire. They have examined the endocrine system and hormones, brain structure, and genetics. Others have observed the mechanisms of arousal. What all biological research on sex has in common is the proposition that many so-called sexual choices are not choices at all but are dictated by the body.

The Influence of Hormones

Biological explanations of sexual desire concentrate on the role of hormones. *Testosterone*, sometimes called the male sex hormone, appears to be the most important hormone for sexual function. Numerous research studies identify testosterone as an enabler for male sexual arousal (Bancroft 1978; Masters, Johnson, and Kolodny 1995). But we cannot predict a man's sexual tastes, desires, or behavior by measuring his testosterone. Although a low level of testosterone in men is sometimes associated with lower sexual desire, this is not predictably the case. Furthermore, testosterone level does not always influence sexual performance. Indeed, testosterone is being experimented with as a male contraceptive (Wu et al. 1996), thus demonstrating that desire and the biological goal of reproduction need not be linked to sexual desire.

Testosterone has also been implicated in nonsexual behaviors, such as aggression. Furthermore, male aggression sometimes crosses into male sexuality, generating sexual violence. But recent research on testosterone and aggression in men has turned the testosterone-aggression connection on its head: Low levels of testosterone have been associated with aggression, and higher levels have been associated with calmness, happiness, and friendliness (Angier 1995).

Testosterone is also found in women, although at levels as little as one-fifth those of men. This discrepancy in levels of testosterone has incorrectly been used as evidence for "natural" gender differences in sex drives. However, women's testosterone receptors are simply more sensitive than men's to smaller amounts of testosterone (Kolodny, Masters, and Johnson 1979).

Estrogen, which is associated with the menstrual cycle, is known as the female hormone. Like testosterone, however, estrogen is found in both women and men. Furthermore, estrogen may be the more influential hormone in human aggression. Researchers are currently investigating the association between adolescents' moodiness and their levels of estrogen (Angier 1995). Of course, many social factors—such as changes in parental behavior toward their teenagers—help explain moodiness among adolescents (Rutter 1995).

Some biological evidence indicates that a woman's sexual desire may be linked to the impact of hormones as levels change during her reproductive cycle. (No evidence shows men's sexual desire to be cyclical.) Some scientists believe that women's sexual arousal is linked

to the fertile portion of their cycle (Stanislaw and Rice 1988). They believe that sexual interest in women is best explained as the product of thousands of years of natural selection. Natural selection would favor for survival those women who are sexually aroused during ovulation (the time women are most likely to become pregnant). These women would be reproductively successful and therefore pass on to their children the propensity for arousal during ovulation. Neat though this theory is, it doesn't fit all the data. Other research (Bancroft et al. 1983) finds no evidence of increased sexual interest among women who are ovulating. Instead, the evidence suggests that women's sexual interest actually tends to peak well before ovulation. Still other evidence finds no variation in sexual desire or sexual activity in connection to the menstrual cycle (Meuwissen and Over 1992).

Testosterone and estrogen are not clearly linked to either men's desire or women's. Research shows a complicated relationship between hormones and sexuality. Hormonal fluctuations may not be the central cause of sexual behavior or any social acts; instead, social circumstances may be the cause of hormonal fluctuation.

The Mechanisms of Arousal

Biological explanations of gender differences in sexuality owe a great deal to the work of William Masters and Virginia Johnson, who studied the human sexual arousal system. Unlike other researchers, who had relied on self-reports, these pioneers actually hooked up their participants to machines that could provide information on physiological responses to sexual stimuli. They based their findings on laboratory observation of over 10,000 sexual episodes experienced by 382 women and 312 men (Masters and Johnson 1966). The research team photographed the inside of women's vaginas during arousal and observed circulatory and nipple response, and they observed the rise and fall of men's penises.

Notice that Masters and Johnson focused on bodies rather than the social and relationship contexts in which sex occurs. From the start, the research was limited to information about the mechanisms of sexuality. It's not hard to imagine that the responses of men and women hooked to machines and under observation might well be different from a loving couple's first (or 91st) sexual episode. In addition, the participants were far from "typical" or randomly selected. To the contrary, they were sexual extroverts such as prostitutes, who, as far as we can tell, were not really representative of the population.

Nevertheless, with this information Masters and Johnson created the new field of sex therapy, which sought to understand and modify the mechanisms of human sexual response or, as the case might be, nonresponse. The sexual therapies they developed were based on what they inferred from their data to be differences between male and female patterns of arousal.

One of Masters and Johnson's most important observations was a sexual difference between men and women in the timing of the excitement cycle. The key difference is that male sexual physiology has a quicker trigger. Comparing men's and women's sexual responses is like comparing sprinters (men) to long-distance runners (women). Men are excited sooner, have an orgasm sooner, relatively quickly lose their erection, and require a "refractory" period before sexual excitation and erection can begin again. This refractory period among young or exceptional men could be very brief. But for the majority of men, 20 minutes, an hour, or even a day might be necessary.

The female cycle is, in general, a slower and more sustained proposition. The increase of blood to the genital area that accompanies arousal takes longer and remains longer after orgasm. This slower buildup may in part account for the longer time it typically takes women to be ready for sexual intercourse. Additionally, the longer time women take to reach and stay in the plateau phase theoretically makes orgasm less automatic than it is for men. However, the fact that blood leaves the genital area slowly after orgasm means that many women require little or no refractory period if restimulated. Consequently, Masters and Johnson described women as potentially "multi-orgasmic." In other words, some women can have more than one orgasm in fairly short succession.

These physiological findings were the basis for a theory about female and male mating styles. Masters and Johnson considered men's more quickly triggered mechanisms to be at odds with the slower mechanisms of women. On the other hand, the ability of women to have more than one orgasm suggested that women might be the superior sexual athletes under certain conditions. Masters and Johnson's followers work within a model that addresses sexual problems by matching male and female sexual strategies more closely than they believe nature has done. In fact, it might be argued that Masters and Johnson's general approach to sexual counseling was to teach men to understand and cope with the slower female sexual response and to modify their own sexual response so that they do not reach orgasm before their partner is fully aroused.

SOCIOBIOLOGY AND EVOLUTIONARY PSYCHOLOGY

The past few decades of research on sexuality have produced a new school of human behavior—*sociobiology* and a related discipline, *evolutionary psychology*—that explains most gender differences as strategies of sexual reproduction. According to evolutionary psychologist David Buss (1995), "Evolutionary psychologists predict that the sexes will differ in precisely those domains in which women and men have faced different sorts of adaptive problems" (p. 164). By "those domains," Buss refers to reproduction, which is the only human function that depends on a biological difference between men and women.

The key assumption of sociobiological/ evolutionary theory is that humans have an innate, genetically triggered impulse to pass on their genetic material through successful reproduction: This impulse is called *reproductive fitness*. The human species, like other species that sociobiologists study, achieves immortality by having children who live to the age of reproductive maturity and produce children themselves. Sociobiologists and evolutionary psychologists seek to demonstrate that almost all male and female behavior, and especially sexuality, is influenced by this one simple but powerful proposition.

Sociobiologists start at the species level. Species are divided into *r* and *K reproductive categories*. Those with *r* strategies obtain immortality by mass production of eggs and sperm. The *r* species is best illustrated by fish. The female manufactures thousands of eggs, the male squirts millions of sperm over them, and that is the extent of parenting. According to this theory, the male and female fish need not pair up to nurture their offspring. Although thousands of fertilized fish eggs are consumed by predators, only a small proportion of the massive quantity of fertilized eggs must survive for the species to continue. In the *r* species, parents need not stay together for the sake of the kids.

In contrast, humans are a *K*-strategy species, which has a greater investment in each fertilized egg. Human females and most female mammals have very few eggs, especially compared to fish. Moreover, offspring take a long time to mature in the mother's womb and are quite helpless after they are born, with no independent survival ability. Human babies need years of supervision before they are independent. Thus, if a woman wants to pass on her genes (or at least the half her child will inherit from her), she must take good care of her dependent child. The baby is a scarce resource. Even if a woman is pregnant from sexual maturation until menopause, the number of children she can produce is quite limited. This limitation was particularly true thousands of years ago.

Before medical advances of the nineteenth and twentieth centuries, women were highly unlikely to live to the age of menopause. Complications from childbirth commonly caused women to die in their 20s or 30s. Where the food supply was scarce, women were less likely to be successful at conceiving, further reducing the possibility of generating offspring.

Sociobiologists and evolutionary psychologists say that men inseminate, women incubate. The human female's reproductive constraints (usually one child at a time, only so many children over a life cycle, and a helpless infant for a long period of time) shape most of women's sexual and emotional approaches to men and mating. According to their theory, women have good reason to be more selective than men about potential mates. They want to find a man who will stick around and continue to provide resources and protection to this child at least until the child has a good chance of survival. Furthermore, because a woman needs to create an incentive for a man to remain with her, females have developed more sophisticated sexual and emotional skills specifically geared toward creating male loyalty and commitment to their mutual offspring.

Sociobiologists and evolutionary psychologists say that differences in reproductive capacity and strategy also shape sexual desire. Buss asserts that reproductive strategies form most of the categories of desire: Older men generally pick younger women because they are more fertile; younger women seek older men who have more status, power, and resources (a cultural practice known as *hypergamy*) because such men can provide for their children. Furthermore, health and reproductive capacity make youth generally sexier, and even certain shapes of women's bodies (such as an "ideal" hip-to-waist ratio epitomized by an hourglass figure, which correlate with ability to readily reproduce), are widely preferred (Buss 1994)—despite varying standards of beauty across cultures. Likewise, men who have demonstrated their fertility by producing children are more sought after than men who have not (Buss 1994).

According to evolutionary psychologists, men's tastes for recreational sex, unambivalent lust, and a variety of partners are consistent with maximizing their production of children. Men's sexual interest is also more easily aroused because sex involves fewer costs to them than to women, and the ability for rapid ejaculation has a reproductive payoff. On the other hand, women's taste for relationship-based intimacy and greater investment in each sexual act is congruent with women's reproductive strategies.

In a field that tends to emphasize male's "natural" influence over reproductive strategies, evolutionary anthropologist Helen Fisher (1992) offers a feminist twist. Her study of hundreds of societies shows that divorce, or its informal equivalent, occurs most typically in the third or fourth year of a marriage and then peaks about every four years after that. Fisher hypothesizes that some of the breakups have to do with a woman's attempt to obtain the best genes and best survival chances for her offspring. In both agrarian and hunter-gatherer societies, Fisher explains, women breast-feed their child for three or four years—a practice that is economical and sometimes helps to prevent further pregnancy. At the end of this period, the woman is ready and able to have another child. She reenters the mating marketplace and assesses her options to see if she can improve on her previous mate. If she can get a better guy, she will leave the previous partner and team up with a new one. In Fisher's vision, unlike the traditional sociobiological view, different male and female reproductive strategies do not necessarily imply female sexual passivity and preference for lifelong monogamy.

Sociobiologists and evolutionary psychologists tell a fascinating story of how male and female reproductive differences might shape sexuality. To accept sociobiological arguments, one must accept the premise that most animal and human behavior is driven by the instinct to reproduce and improve the gene pool. Furthermore, a flaw of sociobiology as a theory is that it does not provide a unique account of sexual behavior with the potential to be tested empirically. Furthermore, other social science explanations for the same phenomena are supported by more immediate, close-range evidence.

THE SOCIAL ORIGINS OF DESIRE

Your own experience should indicate that biology and genetics alone do not shape human sexuality. From the moment you entered the world, cues from the environment were telling you which desires and behaviors were "normal" and which were not. The result is that people who grow up in different circumstances tend to have different sexualities. Who has not had their sexual behavior influenced by their parents' or guardians' explicit or implicit rules? You may break the rules or follow them, but you can't forget them. On a societal level, in Sweden, for example, premarital sex is accepted, and people are expected to be sexually knowledgeable and experienced. Swedes are likely to associate sex with pleasure in this "*sex positive*" society. In Ireland, however, Catholics are supposed to heed the Church's strict prohibitions against sex outside of marriage, birth control, and the expression of lust. In Ireland the experience of sexuality is different from the experience of sexuality in Sweden because the rules are different. Certainly, biology in Sweden is no different from biology in Ireland, nor is the physical capacity to experience pleasure different. But in Ireland, nonmarital sex is clandestine and shameful. Perhaps the taboo adds excitement to the experience. In Sweden, nonmarital sex is acceptable. In the absence of social constraint, it may even feel a bit mundane. These culturally specific sexual rules and experiences arise from different *norms*, the well-known, unwritten rules of society.

Another sign that social influences play a bigger role in shaping sexuality than does biology is the changing notions historically of male and female differences in desire. Throughout history, varied explanations of male and female desire have been popular. At times, woman was portrayed as the stormy temptress and man the reluctant participant, as in the *Bible* story of Adam and Eve. At other times, women were seen as pure in thought and deed while men were voracious sexual beasts, as the Victorians would have it.

These shifting ideas about gender are the social "clothing" for sexuality. The concept of gender typically relies on a dichotomy of male versus female sexual categories, just as the tradition of women wearing dresses and men wearing pants has in the past made the shape of men and women appear quite different. Consider high heels, an on-again off-again Western fashion. Shoes have no innate sexual function, but high heels have often been understood to be "sexy" for women, even though (or perhaps because) they render women less physically agile. So feminine are high heels understood to be that a man in high heels, in some sort of visual comedy gag, guarantees a laugh from the audience. Alternatively, high heels are a required emblem of femininity for cross-dressing men. Such distinctions are an important tool of society; they provide guidance to human beings about how to be a "culturally correct" male or female.

THE SOCIAL CONSTRUCTION OF SEXUALITY

Social constructionists believe that cues from the environment shape human beings from the moment they enter the world. The sexual customs, values, and expectations of a culture, passed on to the young through teaching and by example, exert a powerful influence. When Fletcher Christian sailed into Tahiti in Charles Nordhoff's 1932 account, *Mutiny on the Bounty*, he and his nineteenth-century English crew were surprised at how sexually available, playful, guilt-free, and amorous the Tahitian women

were. Free from the Judeo-Christian precepts and customs that inhibited English society, the women of Tahiti regarded their sexuality joyfully and without shame. The Englishmen were delighted and refused to leave the island. The women back in England had been socialized within their Victorian culture to be modest, scared of sex, protective of their reputation, and threatened by physical pleasure. The source of the difference was not physiological differences between Tahitian and English women; it was sexual *socialization* within their differing families and cultures.

If we look back at the Victorian, nineteenth-century England that Nordhoff refers to, we can identify *social structures* that influenced the norms of women's and men's sexuality. A burgeoning, new, urban middle class created separate spheres in the division of family labor. Instead of sharing home and farm or small business, the tasks of adults in families became specialized: Men went out to earn money, women stayed home to raise children and take care of the home. Although this division of labor was not the norm in all classes and ethnicities in England at the time, the image of middle-class femininity and masculinity became pervasive. The new division of labor increased women's economic dependence on men, which further curbed women's sexual license but not men's. When gender organizes one aspect of life—such as men's and women's positions in the economy—it also organizes other aspects of life, including sex.

In a heterogeneous and individualistic culture like North America, sexual socialization is complex. A society creates an "ideal" sexuality, but different families and subcultures have their own values. For example, even though contemporary society at large may now accept premarital sexuality, a given family may lay down the law: Sex before marriage is against the family's religion and an offense against God's teaching. A teenager who grows up in such a household may suppress feelings of sexual arousal or channel them into outlets that are more acceptable to the family. Or the teenager may react against her or his background, reject parental and community opinion, and search for what she or he perceives to be a more "authentic" self. Variables like birth order or observations of a sibling's social and sexual expression can also influence a person's development.

As important as family and social background are, so are individual differences in response to that background. In the abstract, people raised to celebrate their sexuality must surely have a different approach to enjoying their bodies than those who are taught that their bodies are a venal part of human nature. Yet whether or not a person is raised to be at ease with physicality does not always help predict adult sexual behavior. Sexual sybarites and libertines may have grown up in sexually repressive environments, as did pop culture icon and Catholic-raised Madonna. Sometimes individuals whose families promoted sex education and free personal expression are content with minimal sexual expression.

Even with the nearly infinite variety of sexuality that individual experience produces, social circumstances shape sexual patterns. For example, research shows that people who have had more premarital sexual intercourse are likely to have more extramarital intercourse, or sex with someone other than their spouse (Blumstein and Schwartz 1983). Perhaps early experience creates a desire for sexual variety and makes it harder for a person to be monogamous. On the other hand, higher levels of sexual desire may generate both the premarital and extramarital propensities. Or perhaps nonmonogamous, sexually active individuals are "rule breakers" and resist not only the traditional rules of sex but also other social norms they encounter. Sexual history is useful for predicting sexual future, but it does not provide a complete explanation.

To make explanations more useful, sociologists refer to societal-level explanations as the *macro* view and to individual-level explanations as the *micro* view. At the macrolevel, the questions pertain to the patterns among different groups. For example, we may note in our culture that some women wear skirts and all men do not. Why do women and men, generally speaking, differ in this way? *Social conflict theory*, which examines the way that groups gain and maintain power over resources and other groups, is often used to address macrolevel questions. One might ask: Whose interest does this custom serve, and how did it evolve? What does it constrain or encourage? If the custom changes, what social forces have promoted the change?

Symbolic interactionism supplements this macrolevel view by looking at the microlevel: How does a particular custom gain its meaning through social interaction? For example, what is really happening when a man opens a door for a woman? *Symbolic interactionism* proposes that social rules are learned and reinforced through everyday interaction in both small acts, such as a man's paying for a woman's dinner, and larger enactments of male and female roles, such as weddings, manners, movies, and television. Through such everyday social interaction, norms are confirmed or resisted. When an adult tells a little girl "good girls don't do this," or when boys make fun of her for wanting to be on the football team, or when she sees women joining a military school getting hazed and harassed, she is learning her society's rules of behavior.

When it comes to sexuality, all these social and behavioral theories hold that biological impulses are subservient to the influence of social systems. Consider high heels again. As anyone who has done so knows, wearing high heels has physical consequences, such as flexed calves while wearing them and aching feet at the end of an evening. But nothing in the physiology of women makes wearing high-heeled shoes necessary, and the propensity to wear high heels is not programmed into women's DNA. A sociobiologist might note that any additional ways a society can invent for women to be sexy accelerate reproductive success. A symbolic interactionist would counter that most rules of sexuality go way beyond what's needed for reproductive success. Society orchestrates male and female sexuality so that its values are served. A social conflict theorist would go a step further and note that the enactment of gendered fashion norms serves the political agenda of groups in power (in this case men) at the macrolevel.

An astounding example of gender-based social control of sexuality was the practice of binding the feet of upper-class women in China starting around the tenth century. Each foot was bound so tightly that the last two toes shriveled and fell off. What was left was so deformed that the woman could barely walk and had to be carried. The function was to allow upper-class men to control the mobility of their women. Bound feet, which were thus associated with status and wealth, became erotically charged. Unbound feet were seen as repugnant. By the eighteenth and nineteenth centuries, even poor women participated in this practice. This practice was so associated with sexual acceptability and marriageability that it was difficult to disrupt, even when nineteenth century missionaries from the West labeled the practice barbaric and unsafe. Only later, in the twentieth century, did foot binding become illegal (Greenhalgh 1977).

Social Control of Sexuality

So powerful are norms as they are transmitted through both social structures and everyday life that it is impossible to imagine the absence of norms that control sexuality. In fact, most images of "liberated" sexuality involve breaking a social norm—say, having sex in public rather than in private. The social norm is always the reference point. Because people are influenced from birth by the social and physical contexts of sexuality, their desires are shaped by those norms. For the past two centuries in North America, people have sought "true love" through personal choice in dating and mating (D'Emilio and Freedman 1988). Although this form of sexual liberation has generated a small increase in the number of mixed pairs—interracial, interethnic, interfaith pairs—the rule of *homogamy*, or marrying within one's class, religion, and ethnicity, still constitutes one of the robust social facts of romantic life. Freedom to choose the person one loves turns out not to be as free as one might suppose.

Despite the norm of true love currently accepted in our culture, personal choice and indiscriminate sexuality have often been construed across cultures and across history as socially disruptive. Disruptions to the social order include liaisons between poor and rich; between people of different races, ethnicities, or faiths; and between members of the same sex. Traditional norms of marriage and sexuality have maintained social order by keeping people in familiar and "appropriate" categories. Offenders have been punished by ostracism, curtailed civil rights, or in some societies, death. Conformists are rewarded with social approval and material advantages. Although it hardly seems possible today, mixed-race marriage was against the law in the United States until 1967. Committed same-sex couples continue to be denied legal marriages, income tax breaks, and health insurance benefits; heterosexual couples take these social benefits for granted.

Some social theorists observe that societies control sexuality through construction of a dichotomized or gendered (male-female) sexuality (Foucault 1978). Society's rules about pleasure seeking and procreating are enforced by norms about appropriate male and female behavior. For example, saying that masculinity is enhanced by sexual experimentation while femininity is demeaned by it gives men sexual privilege (and pleasure) and denies it to women.

Societies control sexuality in part because they have a pragmatic investment in it. Eighteenth-century economic theorist T. R. Malthus ([1798] 1929) highlighted the relationship between reproductive practices and economics in *The Principle of Population*. According to Malthus, excessive fertility would result in the exhaustion of food and other resources. His recommendation to curb the birth rate represents an intervention into the sexual behavior of individuals for the well-being of society. A more recent example is the one-child policy in modern China.

Alarmed by the predictions of famine and other disastrous consequences of rapid population growth, Mao Tse-tung and subsequent Chinese leaders instituted a program of enforced fertility control, which included monitoring women's menstrual cycles, requiring involuntary abortions, and delaying the legal age for marriage. To this state, sexual behavior isn't really an intimate, private act at all; it is a social and even economically significant activity. Such policies influence society at large, but they influence private experience as well. In China, raising the legal age for marriage resulted in a shift toward tolerance regarding premarital sex, a practice that became more common.

Society's interest in controlling sexuality is expressed in the debates regarding sex education. Debates about sex education in grade school and high school illustrate the importance to society of both the control of desire and its social construction. The debates raise the question, does formal learning about sex increase or deter early sexual experimentation? The point is, opponents and proponents of sex education all want to know how to control sexuality in young people. Those who favor sex education hold that children benefit from early, comprehensive information about sex, in the belief that people learn about sexuality from birth and are sexual at least from the time of puberty. Providing young people with an appropriate vocabulary and accurate information both discourages early sexual activity and encourages safe sexual practices for those teenagers who, according to the evidence, will not be deterred from sexual activity (Sexuality Information and Education Council of the United States [SIECUS] 1995). On the other hand, opponents of sex education are intensely committed to the belief that information about sex changes teenagers' reactions and values and leads to early, and what they believe are inappropriate, sexual behaviors (Whitehead 1994). Conservative groups hold that sex education, if it occurs at all, should emphasize abstinence as opposed to practical information.

These conflicting points of view about sex education are both concerned with managing adolescent sexual desire. Conservatives fear that education creates desire; liberals feel that information merely enables better decision making. So who is correct? In various studies, a majority of both conservative and liberal sex education programs have demonstrated little effect on behavior.

[But] the passionate debate about sex education is played out with high emotions. Political ideology, parental fears, and the election strategies of politicians all influence this mode of social control. In the final analysis, however, teaching about sex clearly does not have an intense impact on the pupil. In terms of trends within groups, however, it appears that sex education tends to delay sexual activity and makes teenage sex safer when it happens.

To summarize, social constructionists believe that a society influences sexual behavior through its norms. Some norms are explicit, such as laws against adult sexual activity with minors. Others are implicit, such as norms of fidelity and parental responsibility. In a stable, homogeneous society, it is relatively easy to understand such rules. But in a changing, complex society like the United States, the rules may be in flux or indistinct. Perhaps this ambiguity is what makes some issues of sexuality so controversial today.

AN INTEGRATIVE PERSPECTIVE ON GENDER AND SEXUALITY

Social constructionist explanations of contemporary sexual patterns are typically pitted against the biology of desire and the evolutionary understanding of biological adaptations. Some social constructionists believe there is no inflexible biological reality; everything we regard as either female or male sexuality is culturally imposed. In contrast, *essentialists*—those who take a biological, sociobiological, or evolutionary point of view—believe people's sexual desires and orientations are innate and hard-wired and that social impact is minimal. Gender differences follow from reproductive differences. Men inseminate, women incubate. People are born with sexual drives, attractions, and natures that simply play themselves out at the appropriate developmental age. Even if social constraints conspire to make men and women more similar to each other, people's essential nature is the same: Man is the hunter, warrior, and trailblazer, and woman is the gatherer, nurturer, and reproducer. In short, essentialists think the innate differences between women and men are the cause of gendered sexuality; social constructionists think the differences between men and women are the result of gendering sexuality through social processes.

Using either the social constructionist or essentialist approach to the exclusion of the other constrains understanding of sexuality. We believe the evidence shows that gender differences are more plausibly an outcome of social processes than the other way around. But a social constructionist view is most powerful when it takes the essentialist view into account. We describe this view of gender differences in sexual desire as *integrative*. Although people tend to think of sex as primarily a biological function—tab B goes into slot A—biology is only one part of the context of desire. Such sociological factors as family relationships and social structure also influence sex. A complex mix of anatomy, hormones, and the brain provides the basic outline for the range of acts and desires possible, but biology is neither where sexuality begins nor where it ends. Social and biological contexts link to define human sexual possibilities.

The integrative approach follows from a great deal that sexuality researchers have observed. A very personal matter that seems to be utterly physical—penile erection, or more specifically a man's inability to get an erection. How might an erection be socially constructed? It is more or less understood in the United States that a penis should be hard and ready when a man's sexual opportunity is available. And it is more or less understood that the failure to get or maintain an erection in a sexual situation has two meanings: The guy isn't "man enough," or the other person isn't attractive enough. But there are many other explanations, not the least of which has been poetically explained by Shakespeare (and scientifically documented):

> Lechery, sir, [alcohol] provokes and unprovokes: it provokes the desire, but it takes away the performance. Therefore much drink may be said to be an equivocator with lechery: it makes him, and it mars him; it sets him on, and it takes him off; it persuades him; and disheartens him; makes him stand to, and not stand to; in conclusion, equivocates him in a sleep, and, giving him the lie, leaves him. (*Macbeth*, Act II, Scene iii)

The Shakespearean speech refers to the way in which alcohol can undermine robust sexual desire by leaving the penis flaccid. The performance is not the intimate interaction of bodies in pursuit of pleasure; it is strictly focused on the penis, which ought to "stand to." The speech emphasizes the humiliation—the "mar"—for a man who fails to sustain an erection. Though the speech refers to the toll that alcohol takes on the circulatory system that assists penises in becoming erect, the discussion is about the social experience of a man failed by his penis.

Even in the absence of drinking, penises are not nearly so reliable as the mythology of masculinity and attraction would maintain. Erections appear to come and go with odd timing. For example, erections rise and fall on babies and young boys; men often wake up with erections. None of these instances has to do with machismo or sexual desire. Erections are not always evidence of romantic interest, though our culture tends to interpret them as such. But their absence or presence, which is a physical phenomenon, takes on great meaning thanks to Western culture's prevailing beliefs and norms.

Even biological research has supported the integrative perspective. A quarter century ago, one team of scientists found that homosexual men had lower testosterone levels than a matched group of heterosexual men (Kreuz, Rose, and Jennings 1972). The traditional interpretation at the time of the study was that homosexual men were less "masculine" than the comparison group and that their lower testosterone levels explained why they were gay. But a group of active military men were also measured and found to be low in testosterone. The researchers were loath to believe that an unusual number of military men were gay or that military men were below average hormonally, so they found an alternative explanation for low testosterone. The researchers speculated that stress, anxiety, and similar negative emotions had temporarily lowered hormone levels in both soldiers and homosexuals. The stressful social context—as either a gay man living in a straight world or as a military man being bossed around constantly—had shaped a biological response, the researchers concluded. Hormones were the cart, not the horse. Biology influences desire, but social context influences biology and gives meaning to bodily sensation.

What do these examples from research illustrate? Sexual desire—in fact, all sexuality—is influenced by the cultural, personal, and situational. But these examples also tell us that people can't escape the biological context of sex and sexuality—nor can they rely on it. Such an *integrative approach*—the intimate relationship between social context and biological experience—is central to understanding sexuality.

What are the implications of using an integrative approach to sexuality? First, an integrationist will raise questions about biology when social context is emphasized as cause, and will raise questions about social context when biological causes are emphasized. The point is, everything sexual and physical occurs and achieves meaning in a social context.

Sexual Identity and Orientation

Nowhere does the essentialist versus social constructionist argument grow more vehement than in the debate over *sexual identity* and *sexual orientation*. These terms are used to mean a variety of things. We use these terms to refer to how people tend to classify themselves sexually—either as *gay, lesbian, bisexual,* or *straight.* Sexual behavior and sexual desire may or may not be consistent with sexual identity. That is, people may identify themselves as heterosexual, but desire people of the same sex—or vice versa.

It is hard to argue with the observation that human desire is, after all, organized. Humans do not generally desire cows or horses. More to the point, humans are usually quite specific about which sex is desirable to them and even whether the object of their desire is short or tall, dark or light, hairy or sleek.

In the United States, people tend to be identified as either *homosexual* or *heterosexual*. Other cultures (and prior eras in the United States) have not distinguished between these two sexual orientations. However, our culture embraces the perspective that, whether gay or straight, one has an essential, inborn desire, and it cannot change. Many people seem convinced that homosexuality is an essence rather than a sexual act. For essentialists, it is crucial to establish the primacy of one kind of desire or another and to build a world around that identity. People tend to assume that the object of desire is a matter of the gender of the object. That is, they think even homosexual men desire someone who is feminine and that homosexual women desire someone who is masculine. In other words, even among gay men and lesbians, it is assumed that they will desire opposite-gendered people, even if they are of the same sex.

Historians have chronicled in Western culture the evolution of homosexuality from a behavior into an identity (e.g., D'Emilio and Freedman 1988). In the past, people might engage in same-gender sexuality, but only in the twentieth century has it become a well-defined (and diverse) lifestyle and self-definition. Nevertheless, other evidence shows that homosexual identity has existed for a long time. The distinguished historian John Boswell (1994) believes that homosexuals as a group and homosexuality as an identity have existed from the very earliest of recorded history. He used evidence of early Christian same-sex "marriage" to support his thesis. Social scientist Fred Whitman (1983) has looked at homosexuality across cultures and declared that the evidence of a social type, including men who use certain effeminate gestures and have diverse sexual tastes, goes far beyond any one culture. Geneticist Dean Hamer provides evidence that sexual attraction may be genetically programmed, suggesting that it has persisted over time and been passed down through generations.

On the other side of the debate is the idea that sexuality has always been invented and that sexual orientations are socially created. A gay man's or lesbian's sexual orientation has been created by a social context. Although this creation takes place in a society that prefers dichotomous, polarized categories, the social constructionist vision of sexuality at least poses the possibility that sexuality could involve a continuum of behavior that is matched by a continuum of fantasy, ability to love, and sense of self.

The jury is still out on the scientific origins of heterosexuality and homosexuality. One series of studies on the brain (LeVay 1993) identified some differences in the makeup of the brains of heterosexual and homosexual men. This research has been criticized because the brain samples for the homosexual population were taken from men who had died from AIDS, which may have systematically altered the brain structure of the men. Nevertheless, some researchers believe that sexual orientation is wired into the brain, perhaps even dictating the intensity and specificity of sexual tastes.

Genetics researcher Michael Bailey and colleagues looked at identical twins (who have identical genetic material) reared apart. The studies found a likelihood much greater than chance that if one male twin is homosexual, the other will also be homosexual (Bailey et al. 1993). Because the twins in the study did not share the same environment, this finding suggests that the twins' common genes made them similar in their sexual orientation. On the other hand, other recent genetic and twin studies have highlighted the fact that having a certain *genotype* (DNA coded for a particular characteristic, such as heart disease) does not always produce the corresponding *phenotype* (the physical expression of that characteristic, such as actually suffering from heart disease). Researchers speculate that environment and individual history influence the expression or suppression of genetic types (Wright 1995).

These are just a few of the studies that, in some people's opinions, support the idea that homosexuality is not a choice but a naturally occurring phenomenon in a predetermined proportion of births. By extension, they believe, much human sexual desire and behavior must be biologically determined. Of course, social constructionists would disagree. But if biology does not determine whether one is heterosexual or homosexual, is sexual orientation a choice? Not exactly. The notion that sexuality is a preference supposes a person goes to a sexuality bazaar and picks out what to be today. That is not the case either. Physical and social structures and individual biography join together to produce sexual desire and behavior in an individual that may vary over time. Because of powerful social norms regarding sexuality, people are more likely to sustain a single sexual orientation throughout adulthood. The overwhelming evidence supports the idea that biology is a player in the game of sexual orientation but is not the only player or even captain of the team.

The Continuum of Desire

Variation among people has been examined more than changes in sexual orientation within an individual. Alfred Kinsey (see Kinsey, Pomeroy, and Martin 1948), in his pioneering studies on human sexualities in the late 1940s and 1950s, introduced the Kinsey Heterosexual-Homosexual Rating Scale. A person was coded using a zero for "completely heterosexual," a six for "completely homosexual," or a number in between to represent a more ambiguous orientation. Kinsey measured his participants' reports of interest in or attraction to and explicit past experiences with both same-sex and other-sex people and figured out where his participants fit on the continuum. However, his measurements were more of an art than a science. One cannot weigh or calibrate sexuality so finely. But Kinsey did examine actual behavior, fantasy, intensity of feeling, and other important elements that contribute to a person's sexuality.

Although such a rating scale may be an imperfect way of providing individuals with some sort of sex score, Kinsey made the point that a dichotomous vision of sexual orientation is even more inadequate and inaccurate. The Kinsey scale still defines the polarities of sexuality as heterosexuality and homosexuality, and in that sense it is essentialist. However, it provides alternatives beyond "yes," "no," or "in denial."

Kinsey opened the door to thinking in terms of the diversity of sexualities. People may use dichotomous terms in everyday life, but the idea that many people have the capacity to relate sexually to both males and females (at a single point in their life or intermittently over a lifetime) is part of the legacy of Kinsey's sex research.

By using a sexual continuum that blurs the edges of heterosexuality and homosexuality, Kinsey advanced the idea of bisexuality. The mere existence of *bisexuality* (the common term for some history of attraction to or sex with both men and women) is troubling for essentialists, who see sexuality as fixed and linked to procreation. However, biologists can show that bisexuality exists in the animal kingdom. Evolutionary psychologists and anthropologists hypothesize that bisexuality could be useful for a group's bonding and thus have survival value (Fisher 1992). The explanation is that adults who are like aunts and uncles to children—and who are intimate with parents—provide additional support for maintaining a family. But committed essentialists do not usually buy the idea that "true" bisexuality exists. Instead, they

code men and women as "true" heterosexuals or homosexuals who have some modest taste in the other direction.

Given the evidence, it is possible to believe that the biological context tends to encourage an individual to acquire one sexual orientation or another but also to believe that society exerts greater influence than biology over behavior. Kinsey's data, as well as controversial data from a small gay and lesbian subsample from the National Health and Social Life Survey (NHSLS; Laumann, Michael, and Gagnon 1994), indicate that many more people report homosexual desire and behavior than those who claim homosexuality or bisexuality as their main sexual orientation or sexual identity. Essentialists might say people who admit to homosexual behavior but deny being homosexuals are kidding themselves. Social constructionists say people are always kidding themselves; in other words, people acquire the desires and behaviors that are available and appealing. These choices will be based on personal history as well as social norms and will emerge in idiosyncratic and diverse ways across the continuum of sexuality. They will also be based on the costs and benefits in a given social system. How many people might code their fantasies differently if it were prestigious to be bisexual? Surely people's impulse to code themselves dichotomously is in part influenced by the social and emotional costs of doing otherwise.

An interesting issue that puzzles essentialists is how different male homosexuality seems to be from female homosexuality. More men than women identify as homosexual, but more women claim homosexual desire and/or behavior than men in those categories. In Lever's (1994) *Advocate Survey*, as well, more men than women identify themselves as homosexual. Indeed, much of the sexual attraction and behavior between women is not labeled as sexual. Women hug and kiss each other with impunity, and not necessarily with specific sexual intent. They can have extended sex play in their youth, or even in adulthood, without being instantly labeled as homosexual, as men who engaged in similar behavior would be. Women are also more likely to report that a same-sex sexual episode had less to do with sexual attraction than with love.

Historically, the waters are even murkier. As Lillian Faderman illustrates in *Surpassing the Love of Men* (1981), eighteenth- and nineteenth-century women were allowed such license to love each other that they could declare truly passionate feelings for one another without labels and identities being bandied about. For example, Faderman (1981) quotes Rousseau's eighteenth-century novel *La Nouvelle Héloïse*, in which Julie writes to Clair: "The most important thing of my life has been to love you. From the very beginning my heart has been absorbed in yours" (p. 77). If these women expressed these sentiments today, observers would assume them to be homosexual. Are these the words simply of passionate friends? Essentialists would say these were lesbian lovers who did not have social permission to know who they really were. Historians and sociologists are divided as to whether these women experienced their love as sexual or romantic in the contemporary understanding of those feelings. It is difficult to label people's emotions for them after the fact and from a different historical and psychological vantage point. Just as beliefs and biases influence the way social science is conducted in the present, so such biases influence the views and interpretations of the past. We need to remember that sexual orientation, along with desire and other manifestations of sexuality, is socially constructed and culturally specific.

GENDER AS THE BASIS FOR SEXUAL IDENTITY

Sexual orientation, as nearly everyone in Western culture has come to understand the phrase, signifies the identity one has based on the gender of the sexual partners one tends to pair with—either at a particular time or over a lifetime.

In our culture, gender is the focus of sexual identity. Thus, the whole notion of sexual identity requires strict distinctions between male and female. The fact that the gender of sexual partners is of great social interest highlights yet again how gender organizes the definitions of sexuality.

Few can resist gendered distinctions. But a challenge comes from *transsexuals*, men and women who believe they were born in the wrong body. Although anatomically they are one sex, transsexuals experience themselves as the other sex, much the way we described Dil, in *The Crying Game* at the beginning of the chapter, who felt like a woman but was built like a man. Sometimes transsexuals "correct" their bodies with surgery or hormone treatments. And their sexual orientations are diverse. Some male-to-female transsexuals pair with men, some with women. The same is true for female-to-male transsexuals. One male-to-female person, speaking at a sexuality conference in the 1970s, declared, "Personally, I feel it is sexist to love on the basis of gender. You love the person, whatever their sex might be!"

CONCLUSION

There are, it seems, two arguments that help explain the way the genders express sexual desire. On the one hand are the images and statistics showing that men and women have distinct (albeit shifting) patterns of sexual expression, regardless of sexual orientation. On the other hand, the wide range of sexualities among men or among women also calls for an explanation. A continuum of passion, of desire, of sexual acts and feelings is a useful way to reconcile these phenomena. Furthermore, it helps to recognize that sexual phenomena are socially scripted but also highly individualized. Although sexual desire tends to be described in orderly and quantifiable terms, sexual desire is a chaotic playing field on which we, as sociologists, attempt to place some order to understand it better.

Biology or, more simply stated, bodies are the site for passionate experience, even if that experience is in the brain, in the absence of actual sensations in the skin or other sexual organs. In this sense, biology is a prominent context for sexuality. However, interpersonal, biographical, social, and political contexts influence sexuality and interact with biology in surprising ways. Thus, the continuum of sexuality we propose becomes even more diverse.

Diversity and change in behavior are at the center of social science. Sexuality is one of the most diverse, pervasive, and enigmatic of human experiences. Therefore, far from naming a single sexuality or a dichotomous sexuality, we may more accurately say that there are as many sexualities as there are people. Yet detecting patterns within the diversity can advance an understanding of gender, sex, and society and show how differences and similarities among groups of men and women came into being and are sustained through social practices. The categorical language of sexuality is difficult to avoid.

INTRODUCTION REFERENCES

Buss, D. M. 2003. *The evolution of desire: Strategies of mating*, Rev. ed. New York: Basic Books.

Fisher, H. 2004. *Why we love: The nature and chemistry of romantic love*. New York: Henry Holt.

REFERENCES

Angier, N. 1995. "Does Testosterone Equal Aggression? Maybe Not." *New York Times*, June 20, p. A1.

Bailey, J. M., R. C. Pillard, M. C. Neale, and Y. Agyei. 1993. "Heritable Factors Influence Sexual Orientation in Women." *Archives of General Psychiatry* 50:217–23.

Bancroft, J. 1978. "The Relationship between Hormones and Sexual Behavior in Humans." Pp. 493–519 in *Biological Determinants of Sexual Behavior*, edited by J. B. Hutchinson. New York: Wiley.

Bancroft, J., D. Sanders, D. Davidson, and P. Warner. 1983. "Mood, Sexuality, Hormones, and the Menstrual Cycle: III. Sexuality and the Role of Androgens." *Psychosomatic Medicine* 45:508–24.

Boswell, J. 1994. *Same-Sex Unions in Pre-Modern Europe*. New York: Villard.

Buss, D. 1994. *The Evolution of Desire: Strategies of Human Mating*. New York: Basic Books.

Buss, D. 1995. "Psychological Sex Differences: Origins through Sexual Selection. *American Psychologist* 50:164–68.

D'Emilio, J. D. and E. Freedman. 1988. *Intimate Matters: A History of Sexuality in America*. New York: Harper & Row.

Faderman, L. 1981. *Surpassing the Love of Men: Romantic Friendship and Love between Women from the Renaissance to the Present*. New York: William Morrow.

Fisher, H. (2004). *Why we love: The nature and chemistry of romantic love*. New York: Henry Holt.

Fisher, H. E. 1992. *Anatomy of Love: The Natural History of Monogamy, Adultery, and Divorce*. New York: Norton.

Foucalt, M. 1978. *A History of Sexuality: An Introduction*. New York: Pantheon.

Greenhalgh, S. 1977. "Hobbled Feet, Hobbled Lives: Women in Old China." *Frontiers* 2:7–21.

Kinsey, A. C., W. B. Pomeroy, and C. E. Martin. 1948. *Sexual Behavior in the Human Male*. Philadelphia: W. B. Saunders.

Kolodny, R. C., W. H. Masters, and V. E. Johnson. 1979. *Textbook of Sexual Medicine*. Boston: Little, Brown.

Kreuz. L. E., R. M. Rose, and J. R. Jennings. 1972. "Suppression of Plasma Testosterone Levels and Psychological Stress: A Longitudinal Study of Young Men in Officer Candidate School." *Archives of General Psychiatry* 26:479–82.

Laumann, E. O., R. T. Michael, and J. H. Gagnon. 1994. *The Social Organization of Sexuality: Sexual Practices in the United States*. Chicago: University of Chicago Press.

LeVay, S. 1993. *The Sexual Brain*. Cambridge: MIT Press.

Lever, J. 1994. "The 1994 Advocate Survey of Sexuality and Relationships: The Men." *The Advocate: The National Gay and Lesbian News Magazine*, August 22, pp. 22–30.

Malthus, T. R. [1798] 1929. *An Essay on the Principle of Population as It Affects the Future Improvement of Society*. New York and London: MacMillan.

Masters, W. H., V. E. Johnson. 1966. *Human Sexual Response*. Boston: Little, Brown.

Masters, W. H., V. E. Johnson, and R. C. Kolodny. 1995. *Human Sexuality*. 5th ed. New York: Harper Collins College.

Meuwissen, I. and R. Over. 1992. "Sexual Arousal across Phases of the Human Menstrual Cycle." *Archives of Sexual Behavior* 2:101–19.

Nordhoff, C. and J. N. Hall. 1932. *Mutiny on the Bounty.* Boston: Little, Brown.

Rutter, V. 1995. "Adolescence: Whose Hell Is It?" *Psychology Today*, January/February, pp. 54–66.

Rutter, V. 1996. "Who Stole Fertility?" *Psychology Today*, March/April, pp. 44–70.

Sexuality Information and Education Council of the United States. 1995. A Report on Adolescent Sexuality. New York: SIECUS.

Stanislaw, H. and F. J. Rice. 1988. "The Correlation between Sexual Desire and Menstrual Cycle Changes." *Archives of Sexual Behavior* 17:499–508.

Whitehead, B. D. 1994. "The Failure of Sex Education." *Atlantic Monthly*, October, pp. 55–80.

Whiteman, F. 1983. "Culturally Invariable Properties of Male Homosexualities: Tentative Conclusions from Cross-Cultural Research." *Archives of Sexual Behavior* 12:207–26.

Wright, L. 1995. "A Reporter at Large: Double Mystery. *New Yorker* 8/7:44–50.

Wu, F. C., T. M. Farley, A. Peregondon, and G. M. Waites. 1996. "Effects of Testosterone Enanthate in Normal Men: Experience from a Multicenter Contraceptive Efficacy Study." *Fertility and Sterility* 65:626–36.

CHAPTER 23

Venus in Furs

Estrogen and Desire

Natalie Angier

The biology of scorpions, disputes over the Human Genome Project, the ubiquitousness of philandering in the animal kingdom, and estrogen and desire: How could this wide array of scientific topics possibly be related? As you read this chapter from Natalie Angier's book, Woman: An Intimate Geography *(2000) you can sense why this science writer for the* New York Times *won a Pulitzer Prize in the category of "Beat Reporting" for a series of articles on such topics. And, you will understand why Angier's book has been so highly lauded. According to the* Washington Post, *"ultimately this grand tour of the female body provides a new vision of the role of women in the history of our species" (Angier, 2000, ii). Gloria Steinem quipped, "Think you know it all? Think again. [It] is nothing less than liberation biology. . . . Anyone living in or near a female body should read this book" (Angier, 2000, ii).*

But, before you read this tell-tale chapter about estrogen and sexual desire, ask yourself, what do I currently know about the relationship of estrogen to sexual behavior? To check this out, label the following statements as myths or facts:

There is a positive correlation between a woman's ovulatory cycle and

- *Frequency of sexual intercourse*
- *Frequency of orgasm*
- *Frequency of sexual fantasy*
- *Frequency of masturbation*
- *Physical arousability (genitals swell and lubricate)*
- *Sexual hunger*
- *A rise in hemlines*

You will find the answers to these less than academic-sounding questions in the pages of this chapter, along with a wealth of other scientific information couched in readable language. Whether you are of the female or male sex, some surprises may be in store for you as you mine this fertile field of sexuality information about estrogen and desire. And, without a doubt, this reading has the potential to invoke still other questions that might lead to a lively class debate among inquiring minds.

A female rat can't mate if she is not in estrus. I don't mean that she doesn't want to mate, or that she won't find a partner if she's not in heat and sending forth the appropriate spectrum of olfactory and auditory enticements. I mean that she is physically incapable of copulating. Unless she is in estrus, her ovaries do not secrete estrogen and progesterone, and without hormonal stimulation, the rat can't assume the mating position known as *lordosis*, in which she arches her back and flicks aside her tail. The lordosis posture changes the angle and aperture of the vagina, making it accessible to the male rat's penis once he has mounted her from behind. There is no rat's version of the *Kama Sutra*. An ovariectomized female won't assume lordosis, and hence she can't mate—unless, that is, she is given hormone shots to compensate for the loss of the natural ablutions of the ovarian follicle.

For the rats, as well as for many other female animals, mechanics and motivation are intertwined. Only when she is in heat is the female driven to seek a mate, and only when she is in heat can her body oblige her. Estrogen controls her sexual appetite and sexual physics alike.

A female primate can copulate whenever she pleases, whether she is ovulating or not. There is no connection between the mechanics of her reproductive tract and the status of her hormones. Estrogen does not control the nerves and muscles that would impel her to hoist her rear end in the air, angle her genitals just so, and whip her tail out of the way, if she has one. A female does not have to be capable of becoming pregnant in order to partake of sex. She can have sex every day, and if she's a bonobo, she will have sex more than once a day, or once an hour. A female primate has been unshackled from the tyranny of hormones. In an almost literal sense, the *key* to her door has been taken away from her ovaries and placed in her hands.

Yet she still cycles. Her blood bears estrogen from place to place, including to the portions of the brain where desire and emotion and libido dwell, in the limbic system, the hypothalamus, the amygdala. The female primate has been freed from the rigidity of hormonal control. Now she can take the sex steroid and apply it subtly, to integrate, modulate, and interpret a wealth of sensory and psychological cues. For rats, hormones are thumpish, unmistakable, the world in black and white; for primates, they act like a box of crayons, the sixty-four pack, with a color for every occasion and at least three names for

every color. Do you want it in pink, blush, or fuchsia?

"In primates, all the effects of hormones on sexual behavior have become focused on psychological mechanisms, not physical ones," Kim Wallen, of Emory University, says to me. "The decoupling of physical from psychological allows primates to use sex in different contexts, for economic reasons or political reasons. Or emotional reasons, or to keep from getting bored." As Wallen speaks, we watch a group of five rhesus monkeys at the Yerkes Primate Research Center chase two other rhesus monkeys around and around in their enclosure, all seven swearing back and forth at each other in rhesus-ese, as you can tell because the more they scream, the faster everybody runs. In a primate, Wallen continues, hormone pulses may not make the female bow down in lordosis, but they clearly influence her sexual motivation. He points at the group of rhesus monkeys. The seven samurai are still screaming and running. Several other monkeys look on with rapt anxiety, like bettors at a racetrack. One large, scruffy male ignores everything and picks his teeth. None is doing anything remotely sexual. Rhesus monkeys are Calvinists, Wallen says, prudish and autocratic in matters of sex. When a female rhesus is alone with a familiar male and no other monkeys are there to spy on her, she will mate with the male regardless of where she is in her breeding cycle. But a female under the constraints of the social group does not have the luxury of freewheeling carnality. If she sidles up to a male and begins engaging in a bit of heavy petting, other group members strive to intervene, raucously and snappishly. A female rhesus doesn't often bother defying convention. What does she look like, a bonobo?

Hormones change everything. They tint her judgement and sweep her from Kansas to Oz. When she is ovulating and her estrogen levels soar, her craving overcomes her political instincts and she will mate madly and profligately, all the while out snarling those who would dare to interfere.

We know that there's a macaque darting about in the genomic background and that we feel like monkeys and can act like them too. The moment a young girl enters adolescence, she begins dwelling on sex, consciously, unconsciously, in her dreams, alone in the bath— however or wherever it happens, it happens. Her desire is aroused. The changes of puberty are largely hormonal changes. The shifting of the chemical setting stirs desire. Intellectually, we accept the idea that sexuality is a hormonally inflected experience, but we still resent the connection. If hormones count, we worry that they count too much and that therefore we have no free will, and so we deny that they count, all the while knowing that they count, because we see it in our teenage children and we remember, please goddess, our teenage greed.

Rather than denying the obvious, we should try to appreciate the ways in which estrogen and other hormones affect behavior. Granted, our knowledge of neurobiology is primitive. We don't understand how estrogen or any other substance works on the brain to elicit desire, or feed a fantasy, or muffle an impulse. But there are enough indirect strands of evidence to knit a serviceable thinking cap with which to mull over estrogen's meaning.

If you don't reproduce during a particular cycle, it won't kill you. Humans are long-lived creatures who operate on the implicit assumption that they will have many opportunities to breed and can afford to override the whims and impulses of Eros for months, years, decades, and, oops, a lifetime if conditions of the moment are not quite optimal. Animals in whom reproductive drives are as relentless as thirst are short-lived species who may have only one or two breeding seasons in which to leave their Mendelian badge on the world. A corollary of longevity is a rich emotional life and a complex sexuality. We mistakenly equate emotionality with the primitive and rationality with the advanced, but in fact the more intelligent the animal, the deeper its passions. The greater the intelligence, the greater the demand on the emotions to expand their capacity and multiply their zippers and compartments.

We impugn emotions, but we are lucky to be so thick with them. They give us something to think about and decode. We are brilliant because of them, not in spite of them. Hormones are part of the suitcase, and they are part of the contents. They relay information about themselves, and they carry information about others. They do not make us do anything, but they may make the doing of something easier or more pleasurable when all else conspires in favor of it.

Estrogen, puckish estrogen, works through many intermediaries in the brain, many neuropeptides and neurotransmitters. It works through nerve growth factor, and it works through serotonin, a neuropeptide best known for its role in depression. It works through natural opiates and it works through oxytocin. It may be thought of as a conjoiner or a facilitator, or as leavening, like yeast or baking soda. Estrogen has no particular emotion in mind, yet it permits emoting. For years researchers have sought to link estrogen levels to women's sexual behavior. The assumption is logical. Estrogen concentrations rise steadily as the egg follicle grows each month; peaking with the moment of ovulation, when the egg is released into the fallopian tube. If the egg has a need, a desire to be fertilized, in theory it could make the need known to the brain through estrogen, and estrogen would then stimulate a neuropeptide to encourage a particular behavior—to wit, seeking a sexual partner like a thirsty pedestrian seeks a water fountain.

The difficulties of correlating estrogen to human sexual behavior are considerable. What sort of behavior are you looking at? What are the relevant data points? Frequency of intercourse? Frequency of orgasm? Frequency of masturbation or sexual fantasy? The sudden urge to buy *Cosmopolitan*? Here is what we know. There is no association between rate of intercourse and where a woman is in her ovulatory cycle. Women do not have sex more often during ovulation than they do at any other time of the month, unless they're consciously on the fertility quest. But the completion of a behavior tells you little about the subliminal provocations of that behavior. If you plot the incidence of intercourse among couples, you'll see an amazing statistical high point, and it's called the weekend—not because people necessarily feel sexy each Sunday, but because people have sex when it's convenient, when they're not exhausted by work, and when they have the whole day to toy with. A hormone may lead you to water, but it can't make you drink.

There is also no correlation between estrogen levels and physical arousability—the tendency of the genitals to swell and lubricate in response to an overt sexual stimulus, such as a lovemaking scene in a movie. Women have been shown to be fairly invariate in their display of physiological arousal, regardless of their cycle. But physiological arousal says little about meaningful sexual motivation or hunger, for some women will lubricate during rape, and Ellen Laan, of the University of Amsterdam, has shown that women's genitals congest robustly when they watch pornography that the women later describe as stupid, trite, and distinctly unerotic.

We get a somewhat better kinship between hormones and sexuality when we look at desire rather than at genital performance. Some studies have taken female initiation of sex as the marker of desire. The results have varied considerably, depending on the type of birth control used, but they list in the predicted direction. Women on oral contraceptives, which interfere with normal hormonal oscillations, are no more likely to come on to their partners at the middle of the cycle than they are at other times. When the birth control method is reliable but nonhormonal—a vasectomized husband, for example—women show a tendency to be the initiators of sex at the peak of ovulation more than they are during other times of the month, suggesting that the estrogen high is beckoning to them. Add in the complicating factor of a less trustworthy barrier, such as a diaphragm or condom, and the likelihood of midpeak propositioning subsides. No great enigma there: if you

don't want to get pregnant, you might not be eager to fool around when you think you're at your most fertile. In a study of lesbian couples, who have no fear of pregnancy, don't use birth control, and are free of supposedly confounding factors of male expectations and manipulations, psychologists found that women were about 25 percent more likely to initiate sex and had twice as many orgasms during the midpoint of their cycle than at other times of the month.

The strongest correlations between hormones and sexuality are seen when pure, disembodied desire is the object of scrutiny. In one large study, five hundred women were asked to take their basal temperatures every day for several months and to mark down the day of the month when they first noticed the stirrings of sexual desire. The pooled results show an extraordinary concordance between the onset of sexual hunger and the time that basal temperature readings suggest the women were at or nearing ovulation. Women may even express desire through unconscious body language. In a study of young women who spent a lot of time dancing in nightclubs, the scientists found that as the women approached the day of ovulation, their outfits became progressively skimpier, more flaunting of flesh: the hemlines rose with estrogen levels as if with a bull market. (Of course, it doesn't hurt that midcycle is also the best time to wear your tightest and most revealing clothing, as that is when you are free of premenstrual water retention and blemishes and any fear of leaking menstrual blood.)

A number of researchers lately have suggested that it is testosterone, not estrogen, that is the "true" hormone of libido, in men and women alike. They point out that the ovaries generate testosterone as well as estrogen and that androgen levels spike at midcycle just as estrogen levels do. How can we neglect testosterone when men have so much of it and men love sex so madly, don't they? Many textbooks on human sexuality declare flatly that testosterone is the source of all lust, and some women have added testosterone to their hormone replacement regimens in an effort to shore up their ebbing libido. But if testosterone is relevant to female lust, evidence suggests that it is as a handmaiden to estrogen rather than as Eros descended. As it happens, some proteins in the blood will cling to both testosterone and estrogen and in so clinging prevent the hormones from penetrating the barrier between blood and brain. Estrogen accelerates the production of these binding proteins, but the proteins have a slight preference for testosterone. Hence, as the levels of sex hormones and binding proteins climb with the menstrual cycle, the binding proteins seek out testosterone prejudicially, defusing it in the blood below before it can accomplish much of psychodynamic interest above. The testosterone proves useful indirectly, though: by occupying the binding proteins, it frees estrogen to reach the brain unimpeded. This power of distraction could explain why testosterone therapy works for some women with low libidos: it keeps the blood proteins busy and lets estrogen breaststroke straight to the brain.

But to view estrogen as the hormone of libido is to overstate it and underrate it. If estrogen is the messenger of the egg, we should expect the brain to pay attention, but not in any simple, linear fashion. Just as the mechanics of our genitals have been released from the hormonal chokehold, so have our motives and behaviors. We would not appreciate a hormonal signal that is a blind nymphomaniac, an egg groupie, telling us we're horny and must fornicate. We do not want to indulge an egg just because it is there. We live in the world, and we have constraints and desires of our own. What we might like, though, is a pair of well-appointed glasses, to read the fine print better. Estrogen's basic behavioral strategy is to hone the senses. It pinches us and says, Pay attention. A number of studies have suggested that a woman's vision and sense of smell are heightened at ovulation. So too do the senses shine at other times of high estrogenicity, such as right before menstruation, when your progesterone levels have dropped way down and left estrogen to act unopposed. During pregnancy,

you can smell a dirty cat box from two flights away, and you can see dim stars and the pores on every face you meet. It must be emphasized that we don't need estrogen to pay attention or to smell a thing, but there it is, coursing from blood to brain and lending the brain a mild buzz, just as it does the bones and heart and breast and little gray basket.

If estrogen is to help at all, it should help us best when our minds must be wonderfully concentrated. Ovulation is a time of danger and of possibility. Estrogen is like hunting magic, the hallucinogenic drug that Amazonian Indians extract from the skin of the poison-dart frog to lend them the sensorial strength of heroes. The more we are of the world, the greater are our chances of meeting others who suit us, but the more incumbent it is on us to notice and assess those around us. If there is such a thing as feminine intuition, it may lie in the occasional gift of a really sweet estrogen high, the great emulsifier, bringing together disparate observations. But estrogen is also at the behest of history and current affairs: If you are in a sour, reclusive mood to begin with, the hump of estrogen at ovulation, or its unopposed premenstrual energy, may make you feel more rather than less reclusive. Estrogen is a promoter, not an initiator. We can understand this by considering how estrogen contributes to breast cancer. The hormone is not, strictly speaking, a carcinogen. It does not crack or destabilize the genetic material of breast cells, in the way radioactivity or toxins such as benzene can. Yet if an abnormal cell exists, estrogen may stoke and stimulate it, abetting its growth until a minor aberration that might otherwise regress or be cleaned up by the immune system survives and expands to malignant dimensions.

The strength of estrogen lies in its being context-dependent. It does not make us do anything, but it may make us notice certain things we might otherwise neglect. Estrogen may enhance sensory perception, giving us a slight and fluctuating advantage overlaid on the background of the self. If we are good, we may have our moments of being very, very good, and if we are mediocre, well, we can blame it on our hormones. They are there to be used.

As a lubricant for learning, estrogen is of greatest benefit in young women, who are sorting themselves out and gathering cues and experiences. Young women may reap advantages from intuition for lack of anything better to draw on as they assess the motives and character of another. But we can become too enamored of our intuitive prowess, our insight into others, and believe too unshakably in the correctness of our snap judgments. The older we get, the softer the peaks and valleys of our estrogen cycles are, and the less we need them. Experience, after all, is a trustworthier friend than intuition. How many times do you have to encounter a man who reminds you of your cold, aloof, angry, hypercritical, and infinitely alluring father before you can recognize the phenotype in your sleep and know enough to keep your eyes and nose and hormones far, far away?

Each of us is a privately held chemistry lab, and we can play with ourselves if we want. You may find your ovarian cycle too boring to dwell on or you may try to explore its offerings, and you may be disappointed or you may not. It took me many years to realize that my orgasms were very strong at midcycle. I always knew that they were good right before menstruation, but I thought that had to do with mechanics, the congesting of the pelvis with premenstrual fluid, and I didn't attend to the other side of the equation, because I didn't believe in it. When I started to investigate the link between rising estradiol and the quality of climax, I found a wonderful connection. The midway orgasms are deep and resounding, accentuated, maybe by estrogen, maybe by decoy testosterone, maybe by autohypnosis. I could be experiencing a placebo aphrodisiac. It doesn't matter. As a chemist, I'm an amateur, and I can't do a controlled experiment with myself. Nevertheless, on matters that count I'm a quick study, and I've learned to find my way home to ecstasy whatever the moon, month, menses, may be doing.

We each of us have but one chemistry set and brain to explore, and the effects of estrogen will vary from head to head. Yet if there is a principle to be drawn from the general recognition that hormones can stimulate and emulsify the brain and sensitize it to experience and input, it is this: puberty counts. Under the influence of steroid hormones, the brain in early adolescence is a brain expanding, a Japanese flower dropped in water. It is also vulnerable to the deposition of dreck and pain, which can take a lifetime to dump back out again. The plasticity of the pubertal mind is grievously underestimated. We've obsessed over the brain of early childhood and the brain of the fetus, and though those brains matter deeply to the development of all-round intelligence, character, and skill, the adolescent brain counts in another way. As the brain stumbles toward maturity, and as it is buffeted by the output of the adrenal glands at age ten and of the gonads a year or two later, it seeks to define itself sexually and socially. The brain of a prepubertal girl is primed to absorb the definitions of womanness, of what counts and what doesn't, of what power is and how she can get it or how she will never get it. We've all heard about the crisis of self-confidence that supposedly strikes girls as they leave childhood and climb the Bunker Hill of junior high, but what has been less recognized is the correspondence between this period of frailty, this tendency for the personality to mutate beyond recognition, and the hormonal squall in the head. The pubertal brain is so aware of the world that it throbs, it aches, it wants to find the paths to calm it down and make sense of the world. It is an exposed brain, as tender as a molted crab, and it can be seared deeply. Who can forget adolescence? And who has ever recovered from it?

At the same time that hormones challenge the pubertal brain, they change the body. A girl's high estrogen content helps in the deposition of body fat on the breasts, hips, thighs, and buttocks, subcutaneously, everywhere. Because of estrogen and auxiliary hormones, women have more body fat than men. The body of the average woman is 27 percent fat, that of the average man 1.5 percent fat. The leanest elite female athletes may get their body fat down to 11 or 12 percent, but that is nearly double the percentage of body fat found on the elite male athlete, who is as spare as a pronghorn antelope. We can look at the deposition of body fat that comes with womanhood and say it's natural for girls to fatten up when they mature, but what natural means is subject to cultural definition, and our culture still hasn't figured out how to handle fat. On the one hand, we're getting fatter by the year, we westerners generally and North Americans particularly, and why should we expect otherwise? We are stapled to our desks; food is never far from our hands and mouths, and that food tends to be starchy and fatty and overrich; and we get exercise only if we exert willpower, not because sustained body movement is an integrated feature of work, social life, or travel. On the other hand, we are intolerant of fatness, we are repulsed by it, and we see it as a sign of weak character and sloth. Contradictory messages assail us from all sides: we must work all the time, the world is a competitive place, and technology requires that our work be sedentary, cerebral, but we must not get too fat, because fat is unhealthy and looks self-indulgent. So we must exercise and control our bodies, because our natural lives won't do it for us.

Girls, poor girls, are in the thick of our intolerance and vacillation. Girls put on body fat as they pass into adulthood. They put on fat more easily than boys do, thank you very much, Lady Estradiol. And then they are subject to the creed of total control, the idea that we can subdue and discipline our bodies if we work very very hard at it. The message of self-control is amplified by the pubescent brain, which is flailing about for the tools to control and soothe itself and to find what works, how to gather personal and sexual power. Dieting becomes a proxy for power, not simply because girls are exposed through the media to a smothering assemblage of slender, beautiful models, but because adolescent girls today are laying down a bit of fat in an era when

fat is creeping up everywhere and is everywhere despised. How is a girl to know that her first blush of fatness will ever stop, when we're tearing our hair out over how the national fat index keeps on rising and we must wrestle it to the ground right now?

There are other, obvious reasons that a girl's brain might decide that a fixation on appearance is the swiftest route to power. There are too many of these Beauty 'n' You, Beast magazines around, far more than when I was a prepubescent girl circa 1970. (There were too many of them back then.) Supermarkets now offer no-candy checkout aisles for parents who don't want their children screaming for Mars bars as they wait in line. Where are the no-women's-magazine aisles? Where are the aisles to escape from the fascism of the Face? Any sane and observant girl is bound to conclude that her looks matter and that she can control her face as she controls her body, through makeup and the proper skin care regimen and parsing her facial features and staying on guard and paying attention and thinking about it, really thinking about it. No wonder a girl loses confidence. If she is smart, she knows that it is foolish to obsess over her appearance. It is depressing and disappointing; for this she learned to read, speak passable Spanish, and do calculus? But if she is smart, she has observed the ubiquitous Face and knows of its staggering power and wants that power. A girl wants to learn the possible powers. By all indications, a controlled body and a beautiful face practically guarantee a powerful womanhood.

I'm not saying anything new here, but I argue that people should see adolescence as an opportunity, a fresh coat of paint on the clapboards of the brain. Girls learn from women: fake women, amalgamated women, real women. The Face is inescapable, but it can be raspberried, sabotaged, emotionally exfoliated. Repetition helps. Reassuring a girl that she is great and strong and gorgeous helps. The exhilarating, indoctrinating rah-rah spirit of the new girl-power movement helps. Girls helping each other helps, because girls take cues from other girls as well as from women. Ritual helps, and antiritual helps. We can denude totemic objects and reinfuse them with arbitrary mania. Girls can use lipstick to draw scarification patterns on each other's backs or faces, or a line of supernumerary nipples from armpit to pelvis. Build a hammock with brassieres and fill it with doughnuts and Diet Coke. Combine the covers of women's magazines with cutout parts from nature magazines to make human-animal chimerical masks: Ellephant MacPherson, Naomi Camel. Glue rubber insects and Monopoly hotels onto the top of a bathroom scale. Girls can imagine futures for each other, with outrageous careers and a string of extraordinary lovers, because it is easier to be generous to another than to yourself, but imagining greatness for a friend makes it thinkable for yourself. Sports help. Karate helps. Sticking by your girlfriends helps. Writing atonal songs with meaningless lyrics helps more than you might think. Learn to play the drums. The world needs more girl drummers. The world needs your wild, pounding, dreaming heart.

CHAPTER 24

Truth and Consequences

Using the Bogus Pipeline to Examine Sex Differences in Self-Reported Sexuality

Michele G. Alexander
Terri D. Fisher

When the following article was published, it received extensive media attention. Very quickly, headlines about the study became some version of "women lie about sex." Why were people so willing and eager to believe that women were "lying" when for some variables, the reports of men were also influenced by testing condition? And, were these women really lying, or was something else going on? The answer to these questions lies buried in the fact that we live in a society in which casual sex or sex with many different partners is considered less acceptable for women than for men. This double-standard is reflected in our language, with "stud" or "player" being terms that are typically used to describe a man who is believed to have had a large number of sexual partners, whereas "slut" or "ho" are the terms most likely applied to a woman who has had sex with many partners. Although "stud" and "player" are generally viewed as complimentary and desirable terms, "slut" and

"ho" hold quite negative connotations. Therefore, many women may be motivated to do what is necessary to avoid these epithets, including perhaps distorting their sexual histories when discussing them with friends or a new partner, or when responding to sexual surveys.

Researchers have always known that people may hesitate to be completely forthcoming about their sexual behavior. Alexander and Fisher set out to examine whether or not women and men are differentially affected by social norms, as reflected by their willingness (or lack thereof) to report certain behaviors. They made use of a fake lie detector test to encourage participants to be more honest in their reports about their sexual activity. The researchers wanted to learn if sex differences disappeared or diminished when participants believed that their honesty was being monitored by a lie detector.

After you complete this reading, think about its implications for our understanding of gender differences in sexual behavior. Which of the three conditions used in the study is most comparable to the manner in which survey-based sex research is usually undertaken? Do you think that researchers have a good understanding of the

From "Truth and Consequences: Using the Bogus Pipeline to Examine Sex Differences in Self-Reported Sexuality" by M. G. Alexander, and T. D. Fisher. 2003. *The Journal of Sex Research* 40: 27–35. Reprinted by permission of the publisher (Taylor & Francis, http://www.informaworld.com).

differences between women and men with regard to their sexual behavior? What are some ways to reduce the influence of social norms on reports of sexual activity? And lastly, consider whether you as a research subject would have answered the questions honestly.

—————————

Research on self-reported sexual attitudes and behavior consistently indicates that men are more inclined than women to engage in sexual behavior outside of committed relationships and are less discriminating with regard to quality and quantity of sexual partners (Baumeister, Catanese, & Vohs, 2001; Laumann, Gagnon, Michael, & Michaels, 1994). Men, compared with women, are more approving of casual sex and report more frequent and explicit sexual fantasies (Hyde & Oliver, 2000; Okami & Shackelford, 2001). Additionally, men report an earlier age of first intercourse, a greater number of sexual partners (Smith, 1992), and a higher incidence of intercourse and masturbation (Oliver & Hyde, 1993). Women, on the other hand, report more sexual caution than do men (Hyde & Oliver, 2000). Furthermore, sex stereotypes exist such that men are expected to be more sexually permissive than are women (Cohen & Shotland, 1996).

Several of these well-established sex differences in sexual behavior are somewhat bewildering. Researchers have questioned the statistical improbability of men having more heterosexual intercourse partners than women, as these numbers should be equivalent for the sexes (Pedersen, Miller, Putcha-Bhagavatula, & Yang, 2002; Wiederman, 1997). Similar paradoxes exist with regard to men reporting more frequent intercourse than women. Because a partner is required, it is impossible for men to engage in heterosexual intercourse more often than their female counterparts. Furthermore, males typically report an earlier age of first intercourse than do females (Oliver & Hyde. 1993). Although it is plausible that males have their first sexual experiences with older females, it seems

unlikely, given that adolescent females prefer older sexual partners (Elo, King, & Furstenberg, 1999). In light of these illogicalities, it is reasonable to speculate that some of the sex differences in self-reports of sexuality are not due to actual sex differences in behavior, but rather to differences in reporting as a function of differential normative expectations for men and women.

GENDER ROLES, NORMS, AND SEXUALITY

Gender roles and gender-typed expectations may have direct implications for men's and women's sexual attitudes and behavior. In general, men are expected to take agentic roles, being assertive, independent, and dominant, and women are expected to serve communal roles, being relationship oriented, selfless, and submissive (Cejka & Eagly. 1999; Glick. 1991). Such expectations encourage and foster role-consistent behavior by men and women both privately (Wood, Christensen, Hebl, & Rothgerber, 1997) and publicly (Eagly, Wood, & Diekman, 2000). If women are expected to be relationship oriented, they may also be expected to disapprove of and avoid sexual behaviors that are perceived as being threatening to relationships or self-serving, such as casual sex, masturbation, and use of hard-core or softcore erotica. In contrast, frequent and early recreational sex as well as autoerotic sexual behaviors are more socially approved of and encouraged for men than for women. These behaviors are considered more agentic and independent than sexual behavior associated with long-term commitment, and men can enhance their dominance and power by participating in a greater number of short-term rather than close, long-term relationships (Baumeister & Sommer, 1997; Gabriel & Gardner, 1999). Consistent with this gender role perspective of sexuality, the only large sex differences reported in Oliver and Hyde's (1993) meta-analysis of various sexual domains were for attitudes toward casual sex and reported incidence of masturbation.

The potential effects of these broad gender expectations on sexuality are currently evident in the sexual scripts that regulate men's and women's sexual behavior. In sexual encounters, men are expected to initiate and women are expected to react and comply (Shotland & Hunter, 1995). Some researchers have suggested that differences in sexual desire between men and women could be attributed to the social pressures that are placed on women to stifle their sexuality, as dictated by sexual scripts (Leiblum, 2002). Furthermore, many people still accept some version of the sexual double standard, in which men are afforded more sexual freedom than women, and women are expected to be more reluctant than men to acknowledge their desire for sex (Gentry, 1998). Women and men can anticipate different consequences when deviating from their prescribed behavior: Men are likely to find their sexual orientation or potency questioned, while women risk being labeled "sluts" or "whores." Indeed, societal judgments of sexually permissive women continue to be harsher than those of sexually permissive men in certain circumstances (Milhausen & Herold, 2001).

Given the connection between gender roles and sexuality, sex differences based on self-reports may partly reflect *false accommodation* to gender role norms, that is, self-presentation strategies used by men and women to appear consistent with gender role expectations and to avoid the negative consequences associated with deviating from these expectations. False accommodation might result in answers distorted in opposite directions for men and women such that men may be motivated to report approving of sexual behavior and to exaggerate the frequency and variability of their sexual encounters, whereas women may be motivated to understate theirs. These distorted self-presentations could occur intentionally through biased reporting or unintentionally through selective recall. Recent discussions of

the susceptible nature of self-reports of sexuality to social desirability responding (Meston, Heiman, Trapnell, & Paulhus, 1998) indicate that it is not clear how closely self-reports of sexuality resemble true attitudes and behavior. The differences reported in previous sex research could reflect actual sex differences, or they could merely be a result of self-presentation strategies on the parts of men and women. To the extent that sex differences in self-reported sexuality result from false accommodation to gender role norms, research contexts that encourage gender-typed self-presentation strategies, such as an *exposure threat* situation in which anonymity is not guaranteed, may yield larger self-reported sex differences than contexts in which such self-presentation strategies are discouraged, as with the *bogus pipeline method*.

BOGUS PIPELINE METHODOLOGY

The bogus pipeline procedure may be useful for identifying or controlling false accommodation to gender role norms on self-reports of sexual attitudes and behavior. With this procedure, participants are attached to a nonfunctioning polygraph and are led to believe that dishonest answers given during an interview or on a survey can be detected by the machine (Jones & Sigall, 1971). Their responses are typically compared with a control group not attached to the device; those in the bogus pipeline condition tend to report higher frequency of socially sensitive or socially undesirable behaviors (Tourangeau, Smith, & Rasinski, 1997). A meta-analysis of 31 studies using the bogus pipeline method indicated that the technique is an effective means of reducing biased responding and shifting self-reports toward veracity (Roese & Jamieson, 1993). Apparently the procedure eliminates positive self-presentation by evoking a motivational shift from self-enhancement to self-protection (Roese & Jamieson, 1993). If a self-enhancing presentation (e.g., conformity to gender role norms) is inconsistent with one's true attitudes and behavior (e.g., deviance from gender role norms), an individual who gives self-enhancing responses risks being detected as lying or as lacking self-awareness. The bogus pipeline method motivates individuals to eschew self-enhancement in favor of honest and accurate answers to avoid embarrassment (Sabini, Siepmann, & Stein, 2001).

THE PRESENT RESEARCH

We designed a laboratory experiment to assess the effects of false accommodation on sex differences in self-reported sexual behaviors and attitudes. To manipulate the likelihood of false accommodation, we had male and female college students complete a sexual attitudes and behavior questionnaire under three testing conditions. In the exposure threat condition, participants were led to believe that their responses might be seen by a peer (i.e.. a research assistant). We expected participants in this condition to be influenced by gender role norms, rendering sex differences. In the anonymous condition, in which participants were given strong assurances of anonymity, we expected the lack of identifiability to reduce the magnitude of sex differences by relaxing the pressure to adhere to gender role norms. Finally, in the bogus pipeline condition, we expected that participants would use an honesty self-presentation strategy, thus reducing false accommodation to gender role norms resulting in few if any sex differences. Altogether, we expected the magnitudes of sex differences in reports of erotophilia and erotophobia (i.e., positive and negative emotional orientation toward sexuality), sexual attitudes, and sexual experience to vary as a function of testing condition. We expected this pattern of responses especially on specific sexual behaviors for which gender role expectations diverge for men and women (e.g. number of sexual partners, age at first intercourse, masturbation, exposure to hardcore & softcore erotica).

A differential impact of testing context on men's and women's reported sexuality, evidenced by an interaction between participant sex and testing condition, would suggest that normative expectations for men and women play a role in reporting sexual activity. Such results would provide support for the idea that sex differences in reports of sexual behavior and attitudes are at least in part due to differences in social expectations.

METHOD

Participants

An initial sample of 248 male and female undergraduates participated. To keep the sample somewhat homogenous, we used only data from unmarried, heterosexual, 18- to 25-year-old participants. The 47 participants who did not fit this description were dropped, leaving a final sample of 201 participants.

Measures

Manipulation checks

To assess the effectiveness of the bogus pipeline procedure for reducing social desirability responding, we included a brief version of the Marlowe-Crowne Social Desirability Scale (Strahan & Gerbasi, 1972) at the end of the survey packet.

We also gave 50 participants who were attached to the polygraph three items asking how accurate they thought the machine was in measuring their true attitudes and behavior, how much influence they thought the machine had on their responses, and how much pressure they felt from the lie detector to answer questions honestly.

Sexual attitudes

The 21-item Sexual Opinion Survey (Fisher, Byrne. & White, 1983) was used to measure erotophobia-erotophilia. We measured sexual attitudes with the Attitudes Toward Sexuality Scale (Fisher & Hall, 1988).

Sexual experience and behavior

Sexual behavior was measured using the Cowart Pollack scale of sexual experience (Cowart-Steckler & Pollack, 1988), which assesses the breadth of men's and women's sexual experience. Because we were especially interested in examining responses to three items highly relevant to gender role norms (masturbation, exposure to softcore erotica, and exposure to hardcore erotica), we created a subscale using these three items.

We also asked participants to indicate the age at which they had first engaged in consensual sexual intercourse and the number of partners with whom they had engaged in sexual intercourse.

Procedure

Overview

The experimenter, a student research assistant, took them to a small, private testing room where they were tested individually. We examined participants' self-reported sexual attitudes and behavior in three testing conditions. Two testing conditions entailed connecting participants to a bogus pipeline apparatus at some point, either while completing the sex questionnaire (bogus pipeline condition) or while completing a filler task (anonymous condition). Participants in the bogus pipeline condition were attached to the pipeline apparatus while completing the sex questionnaires and were unattached during the filler task. Participants in the anonymous condition were attached to the apparatus during the filler task and unattached while completing the sex questionnaires. We attached participants to the bogus pipeline apparatus in both testing conditions to ensure that they were treated similarly in the two testing conditions, controlling for potential confounds produced by the invasive procedure of the bogus pipeline (i.e., contact or physical proximity with experimenter: see Ostrom, 1973). The third condition (exposure threat) did not involve the bogus pipeline or the filler task.

Participants were randomly assigned to one of the three testing conditions. For the bogus pipeline and anonymous conditions, participant sex, experimenter sex, and task order were counterbalanced using all possible combinations of these variables. For the exposure threat condition, participant sex and experimenter sex were counterbalanced. Upon finishing the experiment, participants who had been attached to the polygraph completed the manipulation check and were debriefed and questioned for suspicion. No participants reported being suspicious of the bogus recording device.

Bogus pipeline condition

The experimenter informed participants in this condition that they would be completing a questionnaire about their sexual attitudes and behaviors and would view and rate a brief videotape. They were told that during a portion of the experiment they would be connected to a physiological monitor similar to a polygraph or "lie detector" to maximize honesty in responding.

As the experimenter placed electrodes on participants' hands, forearms, and neck, he or she told participants that the polygraph could assess truthfulness by measuring vital signs such as heart rate and galvanic skin response. To "calibrate the machine to ensure that it worked correctly," and to enhance the believability of the bogus pipeline, the experimenter asked participants to respond "yes" to two questions, one of which evoked a false response and one of which evoked a true response. The experimenter showed everyone the same bogus printout, which clearly differentiated the false response from the truthful response. Reminding them that the machine was sensitive enough to detect dishonesty even in written responses, the experimenter urged participants to respond accurately, handed them the sex questionnaire, and exited the room, closing the door to provide privacy. When finished, participants placed their completed surveys in a locked box in the room.

Anonymous condition

Participants in the anonymous condition were attached to the polygraph during the filler task, but not while completing the sexuality questionnaires. They were told that their answers would be completely anonymous and they were left alone in the small room with the door fully closed. They placed their completed surveys in a locked box before exiting the room.

Exposure threat condition

In this condition, we did not use the polygraph. Participants were led to believe that the experimenter, a college student peer, might view their responses because they were instructed to directly hand the completed questionnaire to the experimenter when finished. They completed the questionnaires in the small room with the door open and the experimenter sitting just outside in full view as a reminder of the impending possibility of exposure. In actuality, when participants attempted to give their completed survey to the experimenter, they were instead told to place the questionnaire in the locked box in the testing room.

RESULTS

Manipulation Checks

Responses on the Marlowe-Crowne Social Desirability scale for all three conditions were compared with analysis of variance (ANOVA), which indicated a significant main effect for testing condition among the three groups. As predicted, social desirability scores were lowest in the bogus pipeline condition, intermediate in the anonymous condition, and highest in the exposure threat condition.

Sexual Attitudes and Behaviors

Sexual attitudes

For the Sexual Opinion Survey, the ANOVA yielded a significant main effect for participant sex with a moderate effect size with men reporting greater erotophilia than women. There was

also a main effect for testing condition, with participants in the bogus pipeline condition reporting more erotophilic attitudes than participants in the exposure threat condition.

Sexual experience and behavior

The ANOVA on the sexual experiences scale yielded no significant effects. Results on the composite score of gender-role-relevant sexual behaviors (i.e., masturbation, exposure to hardcore and softcore erotica) yielded a significant interaction between participant sex and testing condition. Planned comparisons revealed that although there were significant sex differences (with men scoring higher) in all three conditions, the differences were much larger in the exposure threat condition, than in the anonymous condition or the pipeline condition. An analysis further indicated no significant differences among the men as a function of testing condition. Among the women, however, those in the pipeline condition, and in the anonymous condition reported engaging in significantly more of these behaviors than did those in the exposure threat condition.

Number of sexual partners

The ANOVA on self-reports of the number of sexual partners yielded no significant effects, but the data did strongly favor the predicted pattern. That is, men reported more sexual partners than did women in the exposure threat condition (3.7 vs. 2.6), where gender expectations are most salient. The magnitude of the sex difference decreased in the anonymity condition (4.2 vs. 3.4), and the direction of the difference actually reversed in the bogus pipeline condition, with men reporting fewer partners than women (4.0 vs. 4.4).

Age of first intercourse

A two-way ANOVA on participants' reports of the age of their first intercourse indicated no main effects of sex of participant or testing condition, but did yield a significant interaction. Planned comparisons revealed no sex difference between reported age of first intercourse in the pipeline condition. In the anonymous condition however, women reported a significantly earlier age of first intercourse than did men, indicating a reversed pattern of typical self-report research. In the exposure threat condition, men reported an earlier age of first intercourse than did women, although the difference did not quite reach significance. The effect of testing condition was significant for the women, but not for the men.

DISCUSSION

Though not as clear as we had expected, the pattern of results generally supported the idea that men and women use gender-specific self-presentation strategies when reporting their sexual behaviors. Sex differences were greatest in the exposure threat condition, which encouraged gender role accommodation, and were smallest in the bogus pipeline condition, which discouraged stereotypical responses and encouraged honest responding instead. These findings suggest that some sex differences found by sex researchers may reflect false accommodation to gender role norms when reporting sexuality, particularly on the part of women. This pattern was more apparent for self-reports of sexual behaviors than of attitudes toward sexuality.

The results were clearest for autonomous sexual behaviors (i.e., masturbation, exposure to hardcore & softcore erotica), which are considered more appropriate for males than females. Typical sex differences, with more men than women reporting having engaged in these behaviors, were found in the exposure threat condition. These sex differences were smaller in the anonymous condition and even more diminished in the bogus pipeline condition. Participants' reports of the age of their first consensual intercourse also significantly differed by sex and testing condition, with almost no sex differences evident in the bogus pipeline condition and a typical sex difference with men

reporting a 6-month younger age than women in the exposure threat condition (although not quite significant). Surprisingly, women reported an earlier age than men in the anonymous condition.

Sex differences in self-reports of the number of sexual partners also showed the predicted trend, although it was not significant. The sex difference was greatest in the exposure threat condition, which encouraged gender role accommodation, and decreased in the anonymous condition. In the bogus pipeline condition, which encouraged honesty rather than social desirability, women actually reported more sexual partners than did men. This pattern should be interpreted cautiously because the overall interaction between participant sex and testing condition was not significant. Nonetheless, the trend is intriguing and may help explain why heterosexual males report a greater number of sexual partners than do heterosexual females (Wiederman, 1997).

Women's reports of sexual experiences fluctuated more than did men's as a function of testing condition. This is not altogether surprising, given the different expectations for the sexes regarding sexual behavior, with more constraints placed on women (Schwartz & Rutter, 1998). Gender expectations consistent with the sexual double standard may be responsible for heightening women's sensitivity to the degree of privacy or pressure to respond honestly more so than men's, especially in the exposure threat condition. Men have a history of enjoying and expressing sexual freedom, autonomy, and liberation, and therefore may be more comfortable than women expressing their sexuality on self-report measures. Because men do not face the same negative consequences for expressing their sexuality as do women, they may not experience the need to inhibit these responses to the same degree.

The lack of significant effects of testing condition on sex differences in erotophilia and sexual attitudes is interesting and requires further explanation. in light of some of the significant findings related to behavior. One plausible explanation is that reports of sexual attitudes and opinions are not as influenced by normative expectations for men and women as are reports of sexual behaviors. This would account for fluctuations found in self-reported behavior but not attitudes across testing conditions. A second possible explanation is that individuals, particularly women, experience more constraints placed on their sexual behaviors than on their sexual attitudes, which may pressure them to falsely accommodate to behavioral norms more so than to attitudinal norms for sexuality. Thus, sexual behaviors may be more susceptible to social desirability responding and self-presentation strategies than are sexual attitudes. If this is the case, findings on sex differences in self-reported sexual attitudes may indicate real differences between the sexes whereas the typical patterns found in self-reported sexual behavior may not accurately reflect true sex differences.

It is well known that response bias can weaken the credibility and validity of findings obtained with the traditional survey approach (Catania. Gibson, Marin, Coates, & Greenblatt, 1990). As the present study suggests, self-presentation strategies relevant to gender role norms also affect self-reports of sexual behavior. Much of the data reported on sexuality are collected in settings more similar to our exposure threat condition than either the bogus pipeline or the anonymous conditions. Thus, in sex research based on self-reports, sex differences may be exaggerated due to false accommodation to gender role norms. These differences may reflect respondents' ideas of what they are expected to report rather than their actual experience. Although it is not practical to use the bogus pipeline technique in all sex research, our results illustrate the need for researchers to do everything possible to minimize the likelihood that participants' responses are tainted by social expectations.

Future researchers interested in using the bogus pipeline method should be aware of a potential weakness in our procedure stemming from an attempt to control for confounds between the bogus pipeline and the anonymous conditions. Although participants in our anonymous condition were not attached to the bogus pipeline while completing the sex survey, they had been made aware of the experimenter's desire to obtain honest responses by being attached to the pipeline while completing the video filler task (although half of the time this occurred after the sex survey had been completed). The anonymous condition we designed was therefore unlike that used by most sex researchers.

Lately there has been heated debate regarding the origins of sex differences in sexual behavior and attitudes (Pratto & Hegarty, 2000; Wood & Eagly, 2002), with two distinct explanations prevalent in the psychological literature. Evolutionary psychologists attribute sex differences to the evolved dispositions of men and women, with differential patterns of sexual behavior developing over time due to their likelihood of maximizing reproductive success (Buss, 1998; Buss & Schmitt, 1993). In contrast, social role theorists (Eagly, 1987) suggest that sex differences in social behavior mirror gender roles and stereotypes, which originate from the differential distribution of men and women into social roles in domestic and paid labor. Thus, evolutionary theorists favor distal explanations whereas social role theorists favor proximal explanations. Although our study does not directly address the origins of sex differences in sexuality, it does suggest that reports of sex differences based on self-reports may reflect conformity to normative expectations for men and women rather than actual differences in behavior. When the impact of normative expectations for men and women was muted by pressure to be honest in the bogus pipeline condition, sex differences were minimized. When existing gender norms seemed most appropriate to use, as in the exposure threat condition, men's and women's reports corresponded to gender role norms for sexuality more closely, with men reporting more sexual experiences than women. Participants seemed to alter their self-presentations to meet the demands of the testing condition, which lends support to the social role perspective that sex differences in sexuality stem from gender-differentiated normative pressures that designate men as more sexual than women.

In closing, one reason that the results are not as strong as we had hoped is that the very sex differences that we sought to explain were not particularly robust. Main effects of participant sex were evident only on the 3-item composite measure of sexual experience and the erotophilia-erotophobia measure. No sex differences, for example, were found on the Attitudes Toward Sexuality Scale, a measure that has consistently yielded sex differences in the past (Fisher & Hall, 1988). This overall lack of sex difference findings may indicate a broader shift in gender role norms which has implications for men's and women's attitudes and behavior. Several recent sexuality surveys have found no sex differences in self-reported sexual behavior (Browning, Kessler, Hatfield, & Choo, 1999), incidence of casual sexual interactions (Paul. McManus, & Hayes, 2000), number of sexual partners in the past year (Brown & Sinclair, 1999), or desired number of lifetime sexual partners (Pedersen et al., 2002). The lack of sex differences in these studies and in our analysis may reflect currently shifting gender roles and their subsequent impact on normative expectations and expressions of sexual behavior.

References

Baumeister, R. F., Catanese, K. R., & Vohs, K. D. (2001), Is there a gender difference in strength of sex drive? Theoretical views, conceptual distinctions, and a review of relevant evidence. *Personality and Social Psychology Review, 5*, 242–273.

Baumeister, R. F., & Sommer, K. L. (1997). What do men want? Gender differences and the two spheres of belongingness: Comment on Cross and Madson. *Psychological Bulletin, 122*, 38–44.

Brown, N. R., & Sinclair, R. C. (1999). Estimating lifetime sexual partners: Men and women do it differently. *The Journal of Sex Research, 36*, 292–297.

Browning, J. R., Kessler. D., Hatfield, E., & Chop, P. (1999). Power, gender, and sexual behavior. *The Journal of Sex Research, 36*, 342–347.

Buss, D. M. (1998). Sexual strategies theory: Historical origins and current status. *The Journal of Sex Research, 35*, 19–31.

Buss, D. M., & Schmitt. D. P. (1993). Sexual strategies theory: An evolutionary perspective on human mating. *Psychological Review, 100*, 204–232.

Catania, J., Gibson. D. R., Marin, B., Coates. T. J., & Greenblatt, R. M. (1990). Response bias in assessing sexual behaviors relevant to HIV transmission. *Evaluation and Program Planning, 13*, 19–29.

Cejka, M. A., & Eagly, A. H. (1999). Gender-stereotypic images of occupations correspond to sex segregation of employment. *Personality and Social Psychology Bulletin, 25*, 413–423.

Cohen. L. L., & Shotland, R. (1996). Timing of first sexual intercourse in a relationship: Expectations, experiences, and perceptions of others. *The Journal of Sex Research, 33*, 291–299.

Cowart-Steckler, D., & Pollack, R. H. (1988). The Cowart-Pollack Scale of Sexual Experience. In C. M. Davis, W. L. Yarber, & S. L. Davis (Eds.). *Sexuality related measures: A compendium* (pp. 91–92). Lake Mills, IA: Graphic Publishing.

Eagly, A. H. (1987). *Sex differences in social behavior: A social role interpretation.* Hillside, N J: Erlbaum.

Eagly, A. H., Wood, W., & Diekman, A. (2000). Social role theory of sex differences and similarities: A current appraisal. In T. Eckes & H. M. Trautner (Eds.), *The developmental social psychology of gender* (pp. 123–174). Hillsdale, NJ: Erlbaum.

Elo, I. T., King, R. B., & Furstenberg. F. F. (1999). Adolescent females: Their sexual partners and the fathers of their children. *Journal of Marriage & Family, 61.* 74–84.

Fisher, T. D., & Hall. R. G. (1988). A scale for the comparison of sexual attitudes of adolescents and their parents. *The Journal of Sex Research, 24.* 90–100.

Fisher, W. A., Byrne, D., & White, L. A. (1983). Emotional barriers to contraception. In D. Byrne & W. A. Fisher (Eds.), *Adolescents, sex, and contraception* (pp. 207–239). Hillsdale, NJ: Erlbaum.

Gabriel, A., & Gardner, W. L. (1999). Are there "his" and "hers" types of interdependence? The implications of gender differences in collective versus relational interdependence for affect, behavior and cognition. *Journal of Personality and Social Psychology, 77,* 642–655.

Gentry, M. (1998). The sexual double standard: The influence of number of relationships and level of sexual activity on judgments of women and men. *Psychology of Women Quarterly, 22,* 505–511.

Glick, P. (1991). Trait-based and sex-based discrimination in occupational prestige, occupational salary, and hiring. *Sex Roles, 25,* 351–378.

Hyde, J. S., & Oliver, M. B. (2000). Gender difference in sexuality: Results from a meta-analysis. In C. B. Tavris & J. W. White (Eds.). Sexuality, society, and feminism (pp. 57–77). Washington, DC: American Psychological Association.

Jones, E. E., & Sigall, H. (1971). The bogus pipeline: A new paradigm for measuring affect and attitude. *Psychological Bulletin. 76,* 349–364.

Laumann, E. O., Gagnon, J. H., Michael, R. T., & Michaels, S. (1994). The social organization of sexuality: *Sexual practices in the United States.* Chicago: University of Chicago Press.

Leiblum, S. R. (2002). Reconsidering gender differences in sexual desire: An update. *Sexual and Relationship Therapy, 17,* 57–68.

Meston, C. M., Heiman. J. R., Trapnell. P. D., & Paulhus, D. L. (1998). Socially desirable responding and sexuality self-reports. *The Journal of Sex Research, 35,* 148–157.

Milhausen, R. R., & Herold, E. S. (2001). Reconceptualizing the sexual double standard. *Journal of Psychology and Human Sexuality, 13,* 63–83.

Okami, P., & Shackelford. T. K. 12001). Human sex differences in sexual psychology and behavior. *Annual Review of Sex Research, 12,* 186–241.

Oliver, M. B., & Hyde, J. S. (1993). Gender differences in sexuality: A meta-analysis. *Psychological Bulletin, 114,* 29–51.

Ostrom, T. M. (1973). The bogus pipeline: A new ignis fatuus? *Psychological Bulletin, 79,* 252–259.

Paul, E. L., McManus. B., & Hayes. A. (2000). "Hookups": Characteristics and correlates of college students' spontaneous and anonymous sexual experiences. *The Journal of Sex Research, 37,* 76–88.

Pedersen, W. C., Miller, L. C., Putcha-Bhagavatula, A., & Yang. Y. (2002). Evolved sex differences in the number of partners desired? The long and short of it. *Psychological Science, 13,* 157–161.

Pratto, F., & Hegarty, P. (2000). The political psychology of reproductive strategies. *Psychological Science, 11,* 57–62.

Roese, N. J., & Jamieson. D. W. (1993). Twenty years of bogus pipeline research: A critical review and meta-analysis. *Psychological Bulletin, 114,* 363–375.

Sahini, J., Siepmann. M., & Stein, J. (2001). The really fundamental attribution error in social psychological research. *Psychological Inquiry, 12,* 1–15.

Schwartz., P., & Rutter, V. (1998). *The gender of sexuality.* Thousand Oaks, CA: Pine Forge Press.

Shotland, R. L., & Hunter, B. A. (1995). Women's "token resistant" and compliant sexual behaviors are related to uncertain sexual intentions and rape. *Personality and Social Psychology Bulletin, 21,* 226–236.

Smith, T. (1992). Discrepancies between men and women in reporting number of sexual partners: A summary from four countries. *Social Biology, 39,* 203–211.

Strahan., R., & Gerbasi. K. C. (1972). Short, homogeneous versions of the Marlowe Crowne Social Desirability Scale. *Journal of Clinical Psychology, 28,* 191–193.

Tourangeau, R., Smith. T. W., & Rasinski, K. A. (1997). Motivation to report sensitive behaviors on surveys: Evidence from a bogus pipeline experiment. *Journal of Applied Social Psychology, 27,* 209–222.

Wiederman. M. W. (1997). The truth must be in here somewhere: Examining the gender discrepancy in self-reported lifetime number of sex partners. *The Journal of Sex Research, 34,* 375–386.

Wood, W., Christensen, P. N., Hebl, M. R., & Rothgerber, H. (1997). Conformity to sex-typed norms, affect, and the self-concept. *Journal of Personality and Social Psychology, 73,* 523–535.

Wood, W., & Eagly, A. H. (2002). A cross-cultural analysis of the behavior of women and men: Implications for the origins of sex differences. *Psychological Bulletin, 128,* 599–727.

PART VI

Relationships and Sexuality

Sexuality and relationships are integrally connected. Though not every romantic relationship is a sexual relationship, relationship satisfaction and sexual satisfaction are closely linked, and appear to strongly influence one another (Byers 2005). Problems in one domain are often linked to problems in the other domain. Thus, it is heartening that researchers have begun to pay attention to sexuality in close relationships, even though it is methodologically more difficult to study than sexual behavior as an individual process.

A natural opening for Part VI is the Decade Review by Scott Christopher and Susan Sprecher which highlights research advances made in the study of sexuality in close relationships. The authors critically review the major empirical data, beginning with a discussion of theoretical and methodological issues. Other than the increase in the numbers of scholars who employed an evolutionary perspective, they found that the theoretical advancements in sexuality research were somewhat limited in the last decade of the twentieth century. Questioning this atheoretical stance, Christopher and Sprecher (1998) note at least six theories applicable to sexuality that were featured in a special

issue of *The Journal of Sex Research*, which was devoted to theory.

A number of topics are covered in this review: sexual activity and satisfaction in marriages and committed gay and lesbian relationships, premarital sexual involvement, sexual assault, sexual coercion, and extramarital sex. The concluding recommendations for the study of sexuality in the next decade are noteworthy, particularly because both authors are well-known for their prolific sexuality research and publications. This chapter, as a fitting framework for the readings that follow, is a must read for both the serious and the not-so-serious consumer of the sexuality literature.

Many relationships do not stand the test of time. Some relationships end because of incompatibility; others end because of infidelity. There are many modern obstacles to monogamy. Life in large cities, with its anonymity, lends itself to extramarital relationships far more than does life in small-town America. Media messages, with their glossy images of playmates, offer alluring alternatives to monogamous devotion. In the world of work, women and men are often thrown into close contact with attractive colleagues, leading to potential sexual interest. But economic inequality may be the largest obstacle to lasting monogamy and a major player in extramarital sexual involvement. According to evolutionary psychologists, women seek the protection, resources, and genes of successful men, and men seek success to attract women, especially younger ones (Buss 2003). Helen Fisher, the renowned anthropologist who is the author of the second chapter in this section, shares this evolutionary view of human love and sex. She has characterized the human mating pattern as serial monogamy with covert infidelity. Fisher was widely quoted in the media when she first advanced her theory that the natural life span of a human relationship is about four years, because she feels that is how long it takes to raise a child to semi-independence (Fisher 1992).

Fisher has enhanced her anthropological approach with neuroscience research. In Chapter 26, she discusses the biochemical basis of sexual desire and romance, highlighting the specific neurotransmitters which play a role in three components of interpersonal attraction: lust, romantic attraction, and attachment. She argues that these three phenomena are triggered by different neurochemicals.

Students are likely to have a mixed response to Fisher's presentation. She intersperses her presentation of biochemistry with poetry and linguistic studies, making fascinating reading, but perhaps frustrating prose for both the more scientific as well as the more literary-leaning students. Happily, these diverse reactions could lead to an intense and informed discussion of the world of science and of letters, and how the two may inform one another.

A hot-button issue in the United States, at present, is the question of gay marriage. Individuals with a same-sex orientation would like the opportunity to make a legal and public spiritual commitment to their partners that is considered the same as marriage between a man and a woman. Many people would like to see the right to marry afforded everyone, regardless of sexual orientation, while others are opposed to the idea for religious, moral, or philosophical reasons.

Attitudes toward gay marriage seem to be more accepting among young people, so it is likely just a matter of time until this right to legal marriage is afforded to all, regardless of sexual orientation.

Even without legally married status, many lesbians and gay men are in committed relationships. Based on various surveys, the reported percentages of lesbian women who are in committed romantic relationships range from 45 percent to 80 percent compared to 40 percent to 60 percent for gay men (Kurdek 1995). More recent and precise data are unavailable in the research literature at this time.

The big news about same-sex relationships is that, with a few exceptions, they are very much like mixed-sex relationships. The chapter by Peplau and Fingerhut reviews what is known about same-sex relationships, focusing on the formation and quality of the relationship, sexuality, division of labor, conflict, and relationship stability. Students may be surprised to learn that many of the widely-held stereotypes about same-sex relationships are not true. This article will be a revelation to many heterosexual students who think of homosexuality only in terms of sexual behavior.

Just as infants have different types of emotional bonds (or lack thereof) to their parents, adults have different styles of emotional connections to their romantic partners. This is a major tenet of attachment theory, reinforcing the idea that our early love relationships within our family set the tone for our subsequent partnerships. Attachment theory has become quite common in relationship research. What is unusual about the Butzer and Campbell study presented in this Part is their application of attachment theory to the understanding of sexuality among married couples. Butzer and Campbell have expanded our understanding of how sexual relationships are impacted by the nature of our emotional relationships. Specifically, they have examined how adult attachment style moderates the correlation between relationship satisfaction and sexual satisfaction. Students should be intrigued to learn how attachment style can influence the role that sexuality plays within a relationship, since relationships for many are a lifetime affair.

References

Buss, D. M. 2003. *The evolution of desire: Strategies of human mating*. New York: Basic Books.

Byers, E. S. 2005. Relationship satisfaction and sexual satisfaction: A longitudinal study of individuals in long-term relationships. *Journal of Sex Research* 42: 113–18.

Fisher, H. E. 1992. *Anatomy of love: The natural history of monogamy, adultery, and divorce*. New York: W. W. Norton and Company.

Kurdek, L. A. 1995. Lesbian and gay couples. In *Lesbian, gay, and bisexual identities over the lifespan*, eds. A. R. D'Augelli and C. J. Patterson, 243–61. New York: Oxford University Press.

CHAPTER 25

Sexuality in Marriage, Dating, and Other Relationships

A Decade Review

F. Scott Christopher
Susan Sprecher

Before reading this chapter, consider first the good news and then the bad! That relationship variables such as attraction, satisfaction, intimacy, equity, love, communication, and stability are receiving increasing emphasis in the science of interpersonal relationships is certainly good news. Because scholars in the field are examining the relationship of sexuality to these phenomena, you as a university student can anticipate scholarly answers to some of the more pressing issues of your time. The bad news, however, reflects the general lack of government funding for research on intimate relationships, especially sexually intimate relationships. This circumstance means that most investigations are limited to smaller convenience samples, that is, university students, family planning clinics, and the readership of popular magazines.

Given this scenario, how would you, as a consumer of sexuality research, assess the major effects of such sample limitations? Other than sample limitations, what other negative effects may derive from using convenience samples? From your perspective, what should be the role of government in funding research? As a voter, how could your opinion be expressed? After reading the reviews of the impressive array of sexuality research that was done in the previous decade, what would you, as a sexuality researcher, be most interested in pursuing? Such questions posed here may seem irrelevant to you now as a student. But, as lifetime consumers of scientific discoveries, we all have a part to play in the enactment of reason.

From "Sexuality in Marriage, Dating, and Other Relationships: A Decade Review" by F. S. Christopher, and S. Sprecher. 2001. In *Understanding Families into the New Millennium: A Decade in Review*, ed., R. M. Milardo, 218–236. Minneapolis: National Council on Family Relations. Copyright © 2001 by the National Council on Family Relations, 3989 Central Avenue NE, Suite 550, Minneapolis, MN 55421. Reprinted by permission.

Sexuality is woven into the fabric of many close relationships. It is sanctioned in marriage; it is often explored in dating; and it is an intricate part of other committed romantic relationships. The past decade saw a marked increase in scholarly interest in sexuality within a relational context. This increased interest posed a challenge for us as we developed the foci of this review. In deciding what areas of research to review, we considered the interests of family scientists balanced with the sexual phenomena explored by scholars from a variety of disciplines, including but not limited to family studies, sociology, psychology, communication, public health, and women's studies. More specifically, the purpose of our review was to identify, summarize, and critique theoretical, methodological, and empirical breakthroughs in sexuality research from the 1990s as they relate to marriage and other relationships that occur prior to or outside of marriage.

We open by identifying major theoretical and methodological advancements in sexuality research of the 1990s that have relevance to marriage, dating, and committed relationships. In the second section, we review the empirical literature from the 1990s on sexuality in marriage and other committed relationships. In the third section, we review the past decade's literature on sexuality in dating (premarital) relationships. Although most of our review concentrates on sexuality's positive aspects, sexuality also has a "dark side" involving sexual coercion and assault. Hence, our review of the literatures on marital and dating sexuality includes findings on this aspect of sexuality. We end the review with recommendations for research on sexuality for the coming decade.

Because of page limits, we could not review all topics relevant to sexuality. For example, we did not include a review of adolescent sexuality, contraceptive use, or teenage pregnancy (for reviews see Gullotta, Adams, & Montemayor, 1993; Moore, Miller, Glei, & Morrison, 1995). Furthermore, although the 1990s saw an increase in research on risk behaviors and individual and family outcomes related to AIDS, these topics are also beyond the scope of this review (see Kelly, 1995, for a review). Moreover, the topics we were able to cover were limited primarily to research conducted in North America, although advances were also made in sexuality research in other countries and cross-culturally.

ADVANCEMENTS IN THE 1990S

We wish to identify several advancements in sexuality research in the 1990s that have relevance to family science. These can be aggregated broadly into two areas: (1) advancements in conceptualization and theory involving sexuality-related phenomena and (2) advancements in methodology.

The 1990s witnessed an increased focus on sexuality within a relational context, which broadened the concepts, topics, and theories linked to sexuality (e.g., McKinney & Sprecher, 1991). The science of interpersonal relationships is one of the most rapidly growing areas in behavioral sciences (Berscheid & Reis, 1998), and it is now chronicled in two multidisciplinary journals (*Journal of Social and Personal Relationships* and *Personal Relationships*) that have published several articles on sexuality. Scholars from the close relationships field have examined how sexuality is related to such relationship phenomena as attraction, satisfaction, intimacy, equity, love, communication, and stability. Reflecting the general lack of government funding for research on intimate relationships, most of these investigations are based on smaller convenience samples (Gierveld, 1995). However, because the issues examined by relationship scholars have not, in general, also been examined in the larger, national studies, we highlight some of their findings in this review because of their insights and heuristic promise.

Overall, theoretical advancements in sexuality research were somewhat limited during this past decade. However, there was an increase in the number of scholars who employed an evolutionary perspective, either as an explanation for their findings or to test *a priori* hypotheses derived from this perspective. Evolutionary approaches focus on distal causes of sexual behavior and argue that current patterns of sexual behavior, including gender differences in these behaviors, exist because they have been associated with reproductive success in our ancestral past. According to this perspective, current gender differences in a variety of sexual behaviors can be traced to the smaller investment that men, relative to women, need to make in order to create offspring, balanced against women's more limited access to resources needed to ensure their offsprings' survival. In particular, evolutionary perspectives were used to explain gender differences in extramarital behavior, jealousy reactions to extradyadic affairs, sexual conflict in marriage, and choice of sexual influence tactics in dating. Despite the increase in evolutionary-based research, more of the research on sexuality in the 1990s was atheoretical than theoretical (see discussion by Weis, 1998). There is little reason for this to continue. Near the end of the decade, *The Journal of Sex Research* devoted a special issue to theory, which included reviews and critiques of social constructionism (DeLamater & Hyde, 1998), sexual strategy theory (Buss, 1998), social exchange (Sprecher, 1998); symbolic interactionism (Longmore, 1998), social learning theory (Hogben & Byrne, 1998), and systems theory (Jurich & Myers-Bowman, 1998) as they apply to sexuality. This collected work provides a solid reference for informing sexual research in the coming decade.

A number of methodological advances were worthy of recognition. First, there was an increased availability of large-scale national studies that included sexuality data. Knowledge of patterns of sexual behavior was increased significantly with the publication of data from the National Health and Social Life Survey (NHSLS; Laumann, Gagnon, Michael, & Michaels, 1994; Michael, Gagnon, Laumann, & Kolata, 1994). For this study, a probability sample of 3,432 Americans, aged 18 to 59, was interviewed, and respondents completed a brief questionnaire with more sensitive questions about sexuality. Approximately 54 percent of the sample were married, and another 7 percent were in cohabiting relationships. Several other ongoing and first-time large-scale probability studies provided data about adult or adolescent sexuality in the 1990s (e.g., General Social Survey—GSS, The National Survey of Men—NSM, The National Study of Adolescent Health—Add Health). In general, it became more legitimate to ask about sexual behaviors and attitudes in national studies because information on sexual patterns was relevant to the AIDS crisis. More government and private funding was placed into this type of research.

Another methodological advancement was the maturation of several longitudinal studies conducted with married or committed couples. Researchers who began longitudinal studies in the 1980s continued to follow the couples over several years and multiple waves, which allowed them to examine, when sexuality data were available, how sexual phenomena change over time, and how the sexual health of the relationship at one time might be related to a future outcome of the relationship. Two longitudinal studies in particular have included measures of sexuality over time: The Early Years of Marriage Project, based on a sample of Black and White married couples in the Detroit area (e.g., Oggins, Leber, & Veroff, 1993); and the Marital Instability over the Life-course Project, which was based on a national sample of married individuals obtained through random digit dialing (e.g., Edwards & Booth, 1994).

A final methodological advancement we want to note is an increase in the sophistication and accessibility of information on particular methods and measurement. For example, a recent issue of *The Journal of Sex Research* was devoted to methodological advances (Catania, 1999a). Several of the works will likely prove valuable to family scientists into the next decade. Gribble, Miller, Rogers, and Turner (1999) reviewed the advantages of incorporating new technologies into survey work, including computer-assisted personal and telephone interviewing. These are technologies that, when compared to traditional survey and interview methods, appear to increase respondents' reports of engaging in sensitive sexual practices. Morrison, Leigh, and Gillmore (1999) provided a useful comparison of three different methods of daily data collection: individual-initiated phone calls, investigator-initiated phone calls, and self-administered questionnaires. Wiederman (1999) identified volunteer biases among college students who typically participate in sexuality research. Catania (1999b) provided a thoughtful analysis of the origins of reporting biases in interviews. Finally, Binik, Mah, and Kiesler (1999) examined ethical issues connected with conducting research using the Internet, a practice that will likely increase in the coming decade. In addition, several methodological issues were discussed in an edited volume sponsored by the Kinsey Institute (Bancroft, 1997). Furthermore, Davis, Yarber, Bauserman, Schreer, and Davis (1998) published a handbook of over 200 sexuality measures, including information on their reliability and validity. The advances in methodology, coupled with an increased accessibility of measures of sexuality-related variables, will likely increase the volume of research conducted on sexuality in the next decade.

In addition to advances in conceptualizations, theory, and methods, scholars' empirical investigations revealed new insights into the sexuality of adults in relationships. We begin our review of these findings by examining sexuality in marriage and other committed romantic relationships.

SEX IN (AND OUTSIDE OF) MARRIAGE AND OTHER COMMITTED RELATIONSHIPS

The most socially approved context for sexual activity is the marital relationship. Because sex and marriage are legally and morally linked, marital sex is generally not viewed as a social problem or as a phenomenon likely to lead to negative outcomes. As a result, marital sex has not been the central focus of much research in the past decade. This scarcity of research on marital sex has also been noted in previous decades (Greenblat, 1983). Nonetheless, several studies were conducted in the 1990s that included data on sexuality in marriage or other committed relationships, as described below.

Descriptive Information about Sexual Activity

One issue that received research attention, before and during the 1990s, is the frequency of couples' sexual activity. Scientific interest in frequency of marital sex is based in part on its association with both fertility and quality of marriage. Although data collected on this topic prior to 1990 were based on nonprobability samples (e.g., Blumstein & Schwartz, 1983; Kinsey, Pomeroy, & Martin, 1948; Kinsey, Pomeroy, Martin, & Gebhard, 1953), this past decade yielded data on sexual frequency from national probability samples.

Because the national samples included respondents from across the life-span, how sexual frequency is associated with marital duration or age, two passage-of-time variables that are highly confounded, was examined. The National Survey of Families and Households (NSFH), based on interviews conducted in 1987–1988 (Wave 1) with a randomly selected sample of over 13,000 Americans, included a question on frequency of sexual intercourse in the self-administered questionnaire completed by the respondents. Call, Sprecher, and Schwartz (1995) reported that the NSFH Wave 1 married respondents had an overall mean frequency of sex of 6.3 times per month. Couples under the age of 24 had a mean frequency of 11.7, but the frequency declined with each subsequent age group. For example, in the 75 and older age group, the mean frequency was slightly less than once per month. Call, Sprecher, and Schwartz (1996) reported a similar negative association of sexual frequency with age at Wave 2 (1992–1994) of the NSFH. With slightly different foci and subsamples from the NSFH Wave 1 data, Rao and DeMaris (1995), Marsiglio and Donnelly (1991), and Donnelly (1993) published similar findings about marital sexual frequency. The decline in sexual frequency seems to be due to both psychological and biological factors associated with the aging process. Any decreases due to habituation resulting from being with the same partner seem to occur early in the marriage (Call et al., 1995). A habituation perspective can also explain the finding from NSFH (Call et al., 1996) that a remarriage was associated with an increase in marital sex, controlling for other factors including age.

Measures of sexual frequency were included in the National Health and Social Life Survey [NHSLS] (Laumann et al., 1994; Michael et al., 1994), the large-scale national study referred to earlier. The researchers provided data on the sample members' frequency of sexual activity in various ways, but, for our interests, reported a mean frequency of sexual activity per month of 6.9 for married men and 6.5 for married women. The cohabitors had a higher level of sexual activity (which was also found in the NSFH data; e.g., Call et al., 1995; Rao & DeMaris, 1995), whereas the single individuals had the lowest level of sexual activity. Laumann and colleagues (1994) also reported the ubiquitous decrease in sexual frequency with age, although the data were presented for the entire sample, married and unmarried.

The General Social Survey (GSS), an interview study on a variety of attitudes and experiences conducted biennially by the National Opinion Research Center with probability samples of Americans, also contains data on sexual frequency. As reported in Smith (1994b, based on 1993 GSS data), married respondents engaged in sexual intercourse an average of 67 times per year, or slightly over once a week. The frequency rates were highest among the young and those married less than 3 years.

Only a few longitudinal studies were conducted in the 1990s that included information on sexual frequency, but their findings confirm a decrease in sexual frequency with marital duration. In a longitudinal study of newly married couples selected randomly from central Pennsylvania, Huston and Vangelisti (1991) found that a decrease in sexual activity and

interest began in the first 2 years of marriage. Preliminary analyses based on both waves of the NSFH data (Call et al., 1996) indicated that the younger couples in the original sample experienced a decrease in sexual frequency between Waves 1 and 2. In a four-wave longitudinal study conducted with 570 pregnant women and their husbands or partners, Hyde, DeLamater, Plant, and Byrd (1996) found that the respondents reported having sex 4–5 times per month during pregnancy, had almost no sex in the first month post-partum, said they resumed sexual intercourse approximately 7 weeks postpartum, and had a sexual frequency rate at 4 and 12 months postpartum that was similar to the rate during pregnancy (4–5 times per month). More long-term longitudinal studies are needed to examine the pattern of sexual activity with the passage of time and with other family transitions, including the launching of children and retirement.

The rates of marital sexual activity found in the national probability samples of the 1990s appear to be similar to, and in some cases slightly lower than, those reported in nonprobability samples conducted in previous decades. The major advancement in the 1990s on this topic was the examination of a wide range of possible predictors of sexual frequency through multivariate analyses. Passage of time (i.e., age, duration of marriage) was found to have the strongest (negative) association with frequency of marital sex, although marital satisfaction also had a unique and strong (positive) association with sexual frequency (e.g., Call et al., 1995; Smith, 1994b). Social and background characteristics, such as race, social status, and religion, were generally unrelated to marital sexual frequency, with the exception of a few modest associations, such as a Catholic background being associated with a lower frequency (Call et al., 1995). The multivariate results conducted in the 1990s on predictors of sexual frequency indicated only a modest amount of variance in marital sexual frequency explained, despite a notable number of predictor variables (e.g., 20 percent was explained in Call et al., [1995], using the NSFH data and 18 predictors), suggesting that future research needs to broaden the type of predictors considered.

There was very little discussion in the 1990s of measurement issues associated with sexual frequency. The sexual frequency question varied slightly in format across the studies described above. For example, the question in the NSFH referred to "sexual intercourse" and was open-ended, whereas the NHSLS asked about "sex" and elicited closed-ended responses. Responses might vary in systematic ways as a function of the format of the item, although we suspect not by much. The NHHLS study further explored what couples do when they have sex and found that almost all of the married men and women (95 percent) had vaginal intercourse in their last sex act. Although a majority of the respondents had engaged in oral sex in their lifetime, less than one-fourth of the married respondents reported having oral sex during their last sex act. Anal sex was even less common, 1–2 percent reported having had it during their last episode, although 9.7 percent of married men and 7.3 percent of married women reported engaging in anal sex during the past year. Oral and anal sex were more common among the more highly educated and the White respondents.

A continued focus on documenting frequency of marital sex and its predictors might not be as fruitful as examining other issues about sexual frequency, including how married respondents believe their frequency compares to that of other couples and to what they desire or expect, and the implications of these comparisons. In addition, we suggest that the focus of research move from how often couples have sex overall (e.g., each week on average) to the degree of variation, week to week, both in frequency of sexual activity and in the specific behaviors engaged in and the length of time sex lasts. This intracouple variation (over time) is likely to be linked in complex ways to relationship phenomena, including balance of power, conflict, and communication. We encourage research on this issue, possibly through daily diaries kept by

married individuals, a method used infrequently in the 1990s.

Sexual Satisfaction

Married individuals' assessments of the quality of their sexual relationship also received research attention in the 1990s. Consistent with findings from previous decades (e.g., Blumstein & Schwartz, 1983), married couples were generally sexually satisfied. For example, Laumann and colleagues (1994), in the NHSLS, found that 88 percent of the married individuals in the sample were either extremely or very physically pleased in their relationship. When asked about the specific feelings they experienced after having sex, a majority of the participants reported positive feelings (i.e., felt "loved," "thrilled and excited") and only a small minority reported any negative feelings (e.g., "anxious and worried"). Married respondents, particularly if they were monogamous, reported the highest level of sexual satisfaction; cohabiting and single (i.e., dating) respondents had slightly lower levels of sexual satisfaction. Greeley (1991) also found high sexual satisfaction among his married respondents, obtained from the 1988 and 1989 GSS and from telephone interviews conducted by the Gallup Organization using a national probability sample of married couples. High levels of marital sexual satisfaction were reported in several other studies as well (e.g., Edwards & Booth, 1994; Lawrance & Byers, 1995; Oggins et al., 1993). Couples who become sexually dissatisfied, however, might be less likely to be in these studies because of their greater risk of having divorced early in marriage.

Less consistent information is available on how sexual satisfaction might change with marital duration or age, although the accumulating evidence suggests that it does not decline as rapidly or as dramatically as does frequency of sex. For example, Laumann and colleagues (1994) reported that most of their respondents, regardless of age, were happy with their partnered sex. Although physical pleasure was found to be lower for women over the age of 40 than for women under 40, their analyses were based on all respondents, married and unmarried. Men did not experience the same drop in physical pleasure with age, which, as explained by the authors, might be due to divorced and widowed men's greater likelihood of obtaining new and younger sex partners, relative to their female counterparts. Edwards and. Booth (1994), in their national sample of married individuals, found no differences in sexual happiness as a function of age, although wives in their late middle years (48–60) were more likely than younger wives to say that loss of interest in sex was a problem in their relationship (nonetheless, only a small minority had this view). Men and women tended to agree that it was the wife who was more likely to lose interest. Their longitudinal analyses revealed a significant decrease in happiness with sex and a significant increase in loss of interest in sex in the sample over 9 years of marriage. Greeley (1991), in a cross-sectional analysis based on a national sample of married couples, also found a decline in sexual satisfaction with age (and therefore marital duration).

Not surprisingly, sexual satisfaction is associated with sexual frequency. Couples who have the most frequent sex are the most sexually satisfied (Greeley, 1991; Laumann et al., 1994). This past decade, however, did not yield any findings of import about this association. For example, no significant knowledge was gained about how the quantity and quality of sexual activity influence each other over time (is one more likely to lead to the other?), the specific processes that might mediate the association, and the degree to which the strength of the association differs based on other characteristics of the couple such as their ages and relationship duration. That sexual frequency appears to decline more rapidly than sexual satisfaction with age (and marital duration) suggests that the association between the quantity and quality of sex might change with the passage of time. These are issues that need more investigation in the next decade.

In the previous section, we reported that social and demographic characteristics are generally unrelated to frequency of sex. Research conducted in the 1990s indicated that social and demographic variables also are generally unrelated to the degree of sexual satisfaction (e.g., Davidson, Darling, & Norton, 1995; Henderson-King & Veroff, 1994; Laumann et al., 1994). An exception is that at Wave 1 of the Early Years of Marriage Project, Black spouses reported more sexual enjoyment than White spouses, controlling for other demographic variables, including income (Henderson-King & Veroff, 1994; Oggins et al., 1993). These researchers also found that higher household income was associated with less sexual satisfaction for women and speculated that higher family income is associated with one or both partners working longer hours or having more work stress, which might be detrimental to women's sexual satisfaction. However, with a national sample, Greeley (1991) reported that after controlling for age there was no association between the wife working and sexual satisfaction in marriage. Another work variable, working different shifts, was found to be associated with sexual problems or sexual dissatisfaction in a national sample of married individuals (White & Keith, 1990).

Investigations designed to identify predictors of sexual satisfaction have been generally atheoretical and focused on personality attributes (as noted by Lawrance & Byers, 1995); these studies are beyond the scope of this review. More relevant to this review, however, are investigations that have focused on how sexual satisfaction might be predicted by behavior and affect in sexual and nonsexual aspects of the relationship. Lawrance and Byers (1995) developed a model of sexual satisfaction that focuses on the interpersonal context and is based on exchange theory. Their Interpersonal Exchange Model of Sexual Satisfaction states that sexual satisfaction is affected by rewards, costs, comparison level, comparison level for alternatives, and equality within the sexual area of the relationship, as well as by relationship satisfaction. Evidence for components of this model was found in a study of married and cohabiting men and women (Lawrance & Byers, 1995), a study of daters (Byers, Demmons, & Lawrance, 1998), and a study of Chinese married men and women (Renaud, Byers, & Pan, 1997). Sexual satisfaction also has been found to be associated with other aspects, of the interpersonal environment, including quality of sexual communication (Cupach & Comstock, 1990), sexual self-disclosure as mediated by relationship satisfaction (Byers & Demmons, 1999), and equity (Henderson-King & Veroff, 1994).

Investigations in the 1990s that focused on predictors of sexual satisfaction most often were based on smaller, geographically limited samples, although their strength was the frequent use of either multi-item scales with known reliability and validity, multidimensional measures, or both (e.g., Lawrance & Byers, 1995; Oggins et al., 1993), in contrast to the use of single-item global measures of sexual satisfaction typical of national studies. Ideally, research in the future will combine good sampling techniques with sophisticated measures of sexual satisfaction. In addition, more theoretically driven research is needed to identify how factors associated with the individual, the relationship, and "the environment" might interact to affect sexual satisfaction.

In the next section, we discuss how sexual satisfaction, as well as level of sexual activity, are related to overall relationship satisfaction and other relationship outcome variables.

The Association Between Sexual Dimensions of the Relationship and Relationship Quality

In our discussion of findings from the 1990s on sexual frequency, we noted that sexual frequency was found to be associated positively with general relationship satisfaction in married couples (e.g., Call et al., 1995; Smith, 1994b). What appears to be a more important predictor of marital satisfaction, however, is sexual satisfaction or other feelings about sex (Greeley,

1991). Several studies conducted in the past decade have demonstrated that sexual satisfaction is associated with higher marital satisfaction (Cupach & Comstock, 1990; Edwards & Booth, 1994; Haavio-Mannila & Kontula, 1997; Henderson-King & Veroff, 1994; Kurdek, 1991). The quality and quantity of sex also appear to be associated with feelings of love for one's spouse or partner, especially a passionate or erotic type of love (e.g., Marston, Hecht, Manke, McDaniel, & Reeder, 1998; Sprecher & Regan, 1998). Sexual intimacy, however, has been found to be a weaker predictor of love or of general relationship quality than have other forms of intimacy, including degree of affection expressed (Huston & Vangelisti, 1991) and supportive communication (Sprecher, Metts, Burleson, Hatfield, & Thompson, 1995).

In the examination of how a sexuality variable (e.g., sexual satisfaction) is associated with a general relationship construct (e.g., relationship satisfaction), caution must be exercised so that the two variables do not overlap in measurement content (e.g., Fincham & Bradbury, 1987). For example, several marital satisfaction scales (e.g., Roach, Frazier, & Bowden, 1981; Spanier, 1976) include an item or two about sexual activity. Measures of other relationship dimensions, including intimacy, love, interdependence, maintenance strategies, and exchange, have also included elements referring to sexuality (for a discussion, see Sprecher & McKinney, 1993). One solution has been to delete from the scale measuring the general relationship construct any items that refer to sexuality (e.g., Kurdek, 1991).

On a broader conceptual level, researchers must determine whether the sexuality variable is the independent or dependent variable. One's theoretical framework guides the determination of the specific causal connections between partners' feelings about the sexual relationship and the overall evaluation of the relationship. In most research, the focus has been on a sexuality variable as the predictor and on a general relationship quality measure as the variable to be explained, often within a multivariate framework (e.g., Edwards & Booth, 1994). However, the reverse causal direction is proposed in some models, such as the interpersonal Exchange Model of Sexual Satisfaction described earlier (e.g., Lawrance & Byers, 1995). Furthermore, Henderson-King and Veroff (1994), among others, have speculated that marital well-being and sexual feelings are reciprocal and that both causal directions operate over time. More multiple-wave, longitudinal investigations are needed to adequately address the possible reciprocal relation between these variables over time.

Research in the 1990s also examined whether sexual satisfaction predicts marital stability versus dissolution. Oggins et al. (1993), using data from the Early Years of Marriage Project, reported that sexual dissatisfaction at Year 1 predicted marital dissolution by Year 4 of marriage. Based on later analyses, however, Veroff, Douvan, and Hatchett (1995) found that sexual (dis)satisfaction measured in the 3rd year of marriage was not a significant predictor of later relationship dissolution. In their longitudinal study of married individuals, Edwards and Booth (1994) found that a decline in sexual satisfaction over time was associated with the increased likelihood of divorce. Furthermore, in a national study of married individuals (White & Keith, 1990), a measure of sexual problems or dissatisfaction at Time 1 was associated positively with the likelihood of divorce by Time 2, controlling for general marital happiness and other variables. Thus, these limited findings suggest that sexual satisfaction contributes to marital stability. To our knowledge, however, no research has examined the effects of frequency of sexual activity on the likelihood that marriages dissolve over time.

In the next section, we discuss extramarital sex, which has also been found to be associated with negative outcomes for the relationship.

Extramarital Sex

Although sex in marriage is the most socially approved form of sexual outlet, sex by married persons with someone other than their spouse is one of the most stigmatized. The GSS has included an attitudinal question on extramarital sexuality, and, consistently through the years, 70–80 percent of Americans express complete disapproval of a married person having sex with someone other than his or her spouse, and most others express at least some disapproval (e.g., Smith, 1994a). The NHSLS (Laumann et al., 1994) included a similar attitudinal question and found that 77 percent of participants said extramarital sex was always wrong. Considerable research has been done to examine predictors of attitudes about extramarital sex, although most of this research was conducted in the decades prior to 1990 (for reviews, see Glass & Wright, 1992; Sponaugle, 1989). Among the variables that have been found to be associated with permissive attitudes toward extramarital sex are: premarital sexual permissiveness, high education, low religiosity, and being male.

Research conducted in the past decade on the incidence of extramarital sex has yielded rates lower than those reported in earlier studies based on nonprobability samples (for a review of the earlier research, see Thompson, 1983). In the NHSLS study (Laumann et al., 1994), approximately 25 percent of married men and 15 percent of married women reported having engaged in extramarital sex at least once. Less than 4 percent of married respondents reported having engaged in sex with someone other than their spouse in the prior year. Similar low rates have been found in other national studies, including the GSS (e.g., Smith, 1994b; Wiederman, 1997), the 1991 National Survey of Men (Billy, Tanfer, Grady, & Klepinger, 1993), the 1991 National Survey of Women (Forste & Tanfer, 1996), and a national sample based on the National AIDS Behavioral Study (Choi, Catania, & Dolcini, 1994). Nonetheless, these percentages translate into a significant number of Americans who have experienced sex with someone other than their spouse at least once. Furthermore, individuals who divorce are less represented in married samples but perhaps more likely to have experienced sex with someone other than their spouse.

Cohabitors have a higher rate of non-monogamy than do married couples (Forste & Tanfer, 1996). In addition, a higher lifetime incidence of extramarital sex is found among men, Blacks, remarried individuals, those in the lowest and highest education categories, those in urban areas, and those low in religiosity (e.g., Laumann et al., 1994; Wiederman, 1997).

Perhaps because of the relatively low incidence of extramarital sex, few studies in the past decade have focused on its association with marital satisfaction. There are two major issues that can be examined, however, about this association: First, does marital dissatisfaction lead to extramarital sex? Second, what are the effects of a partner's infidelity on one's marital satisfaction?

The limited research from the 1990s on the first issue suggests that marital dissatisfaction might play only a small role in married individuals' decision to engage in extramarital sex. For example, Greeley (1991) reported that marital dissatisfaction has only an indirect influence on the likelihood of extramarital sex, mediated by such factors as premarital sexual permissiveness and a lower value placed on fidelity. However, several studies prior to 1990 (reviewed in Bringle & Buunk, 1991, and in Edwards & Booth, 1994) did show an association between extramarital sex and marital dissatisfaction, especially for women. Opportunity and having a reference group that supports nonmonogamy also seem to be important factors leading to the behavior.

Concerning the second issue, research suggests that spouses become upset with a partner's infidelity. Not all spouses find out about a partner's infidelity, but those who do tend to have negative reactions (e.g., Bringle & Buunk, 1991) or say they would if it were to happen (Shackelford & Buss, 1997). Gender differences in negative reactions to partner's real, or hypothetical infidelity have been a focus of several studies conducted in the 1990s. This research suggests that men become more upset by the sexual aspect of a partner's infidelity, whereas women become more upset by the emotional aspect. These gender difference are explained most frequently from an evolutionary perspective (e.g., Buunk, Angleitner, Oubaid, & Buss, 1996). In the aggregate, however, it appears that marital satisfaction is rarely affected by the threat of extramarital sex. For example, in their national study of married individuals, Edwards and Booth (1994) reported that only about 5 percent of the sample reported that extramarital sex caused a problem in their marriage. However, those who perceived it as a problem were more likely to be dissatisfied in their marriage.

Although laypersons and family scholars alike might not agree on the extent to which extramarital sex is a social problem, most can agree that forced sex in marriage or other committed relationships is indeed a problem and a dark side to human sexuality. We discuss sexual assault and coercion in marriage next.

Husbands' Sexual Assault and Coercion of Wives

In spite of important foundational studies in the 1980s (e.g. Finkelhor & Yllo, 1985; Russell, 1982), husbands' sexual assault and coercion of their wives remains one of the most understudied areas of marriage and sexuality. Perhaps this reflects society's struggle with accepting that sexual assault in marriage actually occurs. The American Law Institute's Model Penal Code recommends exempting spouses from sexual assault laws (Poser & Silbaugh, 1996). Four states follow this recommendation by exempting spouses from sexual assault statutes if a married couple co-resides. In addition, many states' statutes allow spouses partial exemptions from their sexual assault laws when a spouse is mentally incapacitated or disabled or, in one state, no penetration occurs.

Knowledge about the exact prevalence of marital sexual assault and coercion remains elusive. Laumann et al. (1994), in their national survey, asked women whether they had been "forced to do something sexual they did not want to" (p. 334). Twenty-two percent of the women had been sexually forced by a man and in 9 percent of these cases the women referred to a spouse. Extrapolating from these percentages suggests a rate of 2 percent for married women, although the wording of this item is at best a rough indicator of sexual assault, a problem readily acknowledged by the investigators. The 2 percent rate is notably lower than the marital rape rates of 10 percent (Finkelhor & Yllo, 1985) and 14 percent (Russell, 1982) found in earlier investigations that used area-probability samples and more exact measures.

Knowledge about the marital dynamics associated with sexual coercion and assault in marriage remained equally elusive. Using the first wave of NSFH data, DeMaris (1997) found that the monthly sexual frequency of couples with violent husbands was 2.5 times higher than that for couples with nonviolent husbands, when controlling for other factors. Based on previous findings of an overlap between husbands' physical and sexual abuse of their wives, DeMaris hypothesized that violent husbands sexually coerced their wives into this higher frequency of sexual activity. Unfortunately, the data set contained no direct measures of sexual coercion, although indirect measures provided some support for his hypothesis. Additional work with Swinford (DeMaris & Swinford, 1996) using the National Family Violence Survey also provided partial support for the hypothesis. DeMaris and Swinford's analyses revealed that husbands' previous attempted or completed rapes of their spouses significantly predicted wives' fear of being hit. Hence, husbands' sexual and physical violence co-occur in some marriages. DeMaris (1997) provides insights into these wives' mental states; couples' coital frequency was positively related to wives' depression if husbands were violent, or, in instances where both spouses were violent, if wives but not husbands suffered physical injuries.

The lack of empirical and theoretical attention to sexual assault and coercion in marriage in the 1990s is striking. Work in the 1980s that combined qualitative and quantitative methods painted compelling and vivid pictures of patriarchal terrorism (see Johnson, 1995, for a definition) and of the long-term effects of these women's experiences (e.g., Finkelhor & Yllo, 1985; Russell, 1982). The role of social, familial, couple, and individual factors in sexual coercion and assault in marriage is unclear at this time. Moreover, investigations have centered primarily on wives and have excluded husbands' reports. We echo the call of others in noting the great need for scholarly attention to this area.

Research also documents that forced sex occurs in other committed relationships, including gay and lesbian relationships (e.g., Waldner-Haugrud & Gratch, 1997). The more positive aspects of sex in gay and lesbian relationships, however, will be discussed next.

Sex in Gay and Lesbian Committed Relationships

Although considerable research was done in the past decade on the sexual behavior of homosexuals, particularly gay men, the focus of most of this research was on risky versus safe-sex behavior (e.g., Barrett, Bolan, & Douglas, 1998). Very little research focused on sexuality in committed, long-term homosexual relationships. Furthermore, the national probability studies conducted on sexuality (e.g., Laumann et al.'s [1994] NHSLS) did not include enough homosexual participants to systematically analyze their results separately. Thus, the Blumstein and Schwartz (1983) study from the 1980s continues to be the most extensive study on the sexuality of gay and lesbian couples to date.

The research that did include gay and lesbian samples and a focus on sex in a relational context (e.g., Deenen, Gijs, & van Naerssen,

1994; Kurdek, 1991; Lever, 1995) suggests that sexuality in committed lesbian and gay relationships is similar to sexuality in heterosexual married couples. For example, Kurdek (1991) found no differences in sexual satisfaction across four types of couples: gay, lesbian, heterosexual cohabiting, and heterosexual married. He also found that in all four couple types, sexual satisfaction was associated with general relationship satisfaction. Lesbian couples might have sex slightly less often than women in heterosexual marriages (Lever, 1995), and gay couples might have sex slightly more often than other couples, at least early in the relationship. However, sexual frequency declines with relationship duration in lesbian and gay relationships, just as it does among heterosexual married couples. One characteristic that continues to distinguish gay male couples from both heterosexual married couples and lesbian couples is their higher rates and acceptance of nonmonogamy (Kurdek, 1991).

The reliance on volunteer samples, including magazine surveys (e.g., Lever, 1995), for data on sexuality in committed gay and lesbian couples is problematic because sexuality in couples open about their sexual orientation might differ from those who are less public. National probability samples have oversampled for other groups in society with small populations (e.g., Blacks, Hispanics, certain religious groups) and then allowed for a weight adjustment based on probability of selection when the data are analyzed in the aggregate; future national studies could also oversample homosexual couples. In addition, studies of married couples should not automatically exclude committed gay and lesbian couples simply because they do not have a legal tie. Realistically, however, it can be expected that most of the research on sex in gay and lesbian relationships will continue to rely on nonprobability samples. We encourage such research because it is through the accumulation of such findings that we can build a knowledge base about the role of sexuality in committed gay and lesbian relationships.

SEXUALITY IN DATING RELATIONSHIPS

General Trends in Sexual Behavior and Attitudes in Dating

Then-current and representative studies in the 1990s attested to a striking shift in coital incidence of adolescents during this decade. Four cross-sectional, national probability samples of high school students from the Youth Risk Behavior Survey, collected between 1991 and 1997, showed an 11 percent increase in the incidence of virgin adolescents (Centers for Disease Control and Prevention, 1998). Change was not uniform; male but not female youths, and White and Black but not Hispanic youths contributed to this increase. This represents a significant reversal from the higher incidence of nonvirginity among adolescents during the 1970s and 1980s.

Such decreases in coital experiences were not evident for the single adult population. Analysis of the National Survey of Men ages 20–39 indicated that 88 percent of never-married men were coitally experienced (Billy et al., 1993). When investigators asked about the previous 1.5 years, most of these men had a single coital partner, but 18.3 percent had four or more partners. Laumann and colleagues (1994) reported similar findings. When they queried never-married men ages 18–29 about the previous 12 months, they found that 40.7 percent had one partner, 30.5 percent had two to four partners, and 14.2 percent had five or more.

Comparable findings were reported for women. Tanfer and Cubbins' (1992) use of the National Survey of Unwed Women (NSUW) ages 20–29 showed that 80.75 percent were nonvirgins. Seidman, Mosher, and Aral's (1992) examination of the 1988–1996 GSS data indicated that 7.9 percent of never-married women ages 15–44 had two or more partners over a 3-month period. Using a 12-month period, Laumann and colleagues (1994) reported that 56.6 percent of never-married women ages 18–29 had one partner, 24.2 percent had two to four partners, and 6.2 percent had five or more. Taken together, these findings from multiple sources suggest that young, single, adult men and women continue to be sexually active. Possibly this is an outgrowth of the delay in marriage that characterizes this age cohort (U.S. Bureau of the Census, 1988), combined with the overall acceptance of engaging in sex before marriage (Smith, 1994a).

In light of this coital activity, some scholars have investigated predictors of having multiple intercourse partners. Bogaert and Fisher's (1995) smaller scale study suggests age, hypermasculinity, sensation seeking, and testosterone levels are associated positively with men's experiences of high numbers of coital partners. Youthful coital experiences and low levels of religiosity predicted number of partners for Black and White women, and living in a major city was an additional and positive predictor for Whites (Seidman et al., 1992).

Other scholars have examined predictors of coital frequency among unmarried young adults. Analysis of the 1983 NSUW data demonstrated that single Black and White women engaged in coitus more frequently if they experienced early onset of coitus, were in a relationship, and were protected from pregnancy (Tanfer & Cubbins, 1992). Living independently, not being religious, and being in the early stages of dating additionally predicted coital frequency for White women. Comparable analyses were unavailable for single men and represent a well-defined gap in our knowledge.

As in much research from previous decades, a general correspondence continued to be found between the coital activity of singles and societal attitudes about sex before marriage (Roche & Ramsbey, 1993; Smith, 1994b). Using data from the 1972–1991 GSS, Smith (1994b) notes fewer respondents have rated sexual relations before marriage as always wrong, and more have rated them as not wrong at all, in recent as compared to earlier years. Smith interpreted these changes as a shift towards being morally neutral about engaging in coitus prior to marriage. Nonetheless, Smith demonstrated that societal approval of premarital sexual relationships has generally remained stable since 1982. Since 1982, roughly 38 percent of respondents have rated sex before marriage as not wrong at all, with an approximate 23 percent seeing it as only sometimes wrong. Smith found that predictors of such sexual permissiveness paralleled pre-1990s findings. Multivariate tests revealed that greater acceptance corresponded most strongly with low religiosity, with not having teens in the household, and with being young, politically liberal, Black, male, single (Smith, 1994b). Roche and Ramsbey's (1993) more limited study does show, however, that young adults' sexual permissiveness for dating varies with the commitment level of those involved; higher levels of dating commitment coincide with greater approval for engaging in sexual intercourse. Sprecher and Hatfield (1996) found similar results.

Although these findings collectively demonstrate that most never-married young adults accepted premarital coitus and were sexually active, they concurrently demonstrate that some young adults remain virgins. There are at least four groups of reasons, derived from factor analysis, for this choice (Sprecher & Regan, 1996): (1) not experiencing enough love, (2) feeling fearful (of AIDS, STDs, pregnancy), (3) holding beliefs supportive of virginity, and (4) feeling inadequate or insecure. Women rate the first three of these as more important than men do; the reverse holds for the final group of reasons.

Empirically scrutinizing the general trends in singles' coital behavior and sexual attitudes highlighted in this section continues to be important in light of these variables' association with the increased incidence of STDs such as chlamydia and AIDS among single heterosexuals. Aside from this compelling need, however, this research additionally points to ethnic differences that are not well understood. Researchers typically investigate ethnicity either by making comparisons across ethnic groups or by calculating separate models for each ethnic group. Although these practices increase our knowledge about the similarities among ethnic groups and uniqueness within them, scholars have yet to grapple with the larger question of why ethnic subcultures approach sexuality before marriage uniquely. Measuring ethnicity by using categorical variables fails to capture the richness and complexity that is inherent in ethnicity as a variable. The time is ripe for scholars to take a more comprehensive, possibly qualitative look at the relationship between ethnicity and sexuality, rather than simply to continue documenting commonalties and differences.

Besides ethnic influences, investigations in the last decade revealed that relationship and sexual experiences are often interrelated. We review the findings in this area in the next section.

Sexuality and Dating Relationship Experiences

The 1990s witnessed scholars' increased recognition that sexual and relational experiences covary in myriad ways. This recognition translated into different empirical foci. Issues of sexual influence and consent, including initiating sexual involvement, sexual resistance, and complying with a partner's sexual wishes, constituted one empirical focus. For instance, Greer and Buss (1994) identified sexual initiation tactics that men and women perceived were effective and were commonly used. There was considerable overlap in the tactics men and women used and had used on them, including the tactics of implying commitment, increasing attention, and displaying status cues. Men initiated sexual activity more frequently than women, although no gender difference appeared to exist in how frequently men and women considered initiating sex (O'Sullivan & Byers, 1992). There were more frequent sexual initiations in steady as compared to less committed dating relationships, and these initiations involved both indirect verbal messages and nonverbal behaviors for both men and women.

Some investigations of sexual compliance focused on singles who consent to unwanted sexual acts without sexual coercion or aggression. Women most often comply unwillingly with partners' sexual wishes as a form of relationship maintenance (O'Sullivan & Gaines, 1998). In later dating stages, compliant women did not want to disappoint their partners or risk damaging the relationship. Men resist their partners' sexual initiations at times. In fact, examinations of women's attempts to influence reluctant male partners found these to be common experiences, especially in steady dating relationships (O'Sullivan & Byers, 1993). In such instances, men more than women offered the inappropriateness of the relationship as the reason for their reluctance, whereas women more than men identified problems with the time or place.

Scholars have additionally focused on token resistance, as when individuals say "no" but mean "yes" to intercourse. Sprecher, Hatfield, Cortese, Potapova, and Levitskaya (1994) sampled college students in the United States, Russia, and Japan and found that the U.S. samples had the lowest incidence of token resistance among nonvirgins. Gender comparisons that included virgins and nonvirgins revealed that more men than women engaged in token resistance; comparisons within nonvirgins only revealed no gender differences. O'Sullivan and Allgeier (1994) asked singles why they used token resistance, and found that the most frequently offered reasons reflected emotional, relational, and practical concerns. Only a small minority of individuals offered control or game-playing reasons for their actions. Token resistance might also be a sign of ambiguity in coital decision making. Shotland and Hunter (1995) revealed that the use of token resistance was more prevalent among women who had previously engaged in coitus with their partners and might have involved women changing their coital intentions from "no" to "yes" over the course of a date. Such ambivalence about engaging in coitus is often associated with more general concerns about the relationship (O'Sullivan & Gaines, 1998).

This collection of studies demonstrates that issues of influence and sexual consent are complex. Although the use of force by a dyad partner is a clear index of sexual aggression, it is not always clear whether the lack of forceful influence by one dating partner corresponds with the other partner's willing consent to engage in sexual activity. Given that initiations and consent usually involve nonverbal signals, opportunities for miscommunication that can affect the relationship exist. Hence, it is important to continue this line of research into the next decade. Operationalizing variables of influence and consent, however, must be done carefully. For instance, Muehlenhard and Rogers' (1998) recent work demonstrates the need to provide respondents with multiple memory cues, such as asking about incidents with current and past partners, when measuring token resistance. Similarly, O'Sullivan and Allgeier's (1998) careful conceptualization and operationalization of sexual consent demonstrates the importance of differentiating undesired from nonconsensual sexual involvement.

Another research focus during the 1990s centered on motivations, and beliefs about motivations, for sexual expression for singles. Hill and Preston's (1996) examination of motivations for engaging in coitus revealed that feeling nurturing towards one's partner, emotionally valuing one's partner, and experiencing pleasure all predicted individuals' engagement in vaginal, oral, and anal intercourse. Emotionally valuing a partner, however, motivated women more than men to engage in coitus. Women's sexual motivations might be important for predicting sexual involvement for dating couples. Cohen and Shotland (1996) found the concordance between individuals' sexual expectations and actual experiences holds more strongly for women than for men. Thus women's desire to pair emotional and sexual experiences played a more direct role in couples' sexual interactions. Research has consistently shown such a gender difference across pre-1990s studies, so it is not surprising that Oliver and Hyde's (1993) meta-analysis found women less accepting of casual sex than men.

Findings that women link their relationship experiences with their sexual expression resonates with young adults' belief that single women's sexual desire is keyed by professing love and that women's sexuality is strongly related to their relationship experiences (Regan, 1997; Regan & Berscheid, 1995). Women's sexuality, however, might actually be more complicated than this. In a series of studies, Cyranowski and Andersen (1998; Andersen & Cyranowski, 1994) showed that young women's sexual schemas, or self views, include not only estimations of how romantic and passionate they are—clear indicants of relational experiences—but also self judgments about how sexually open and direct or how embarrassed and sexually conservative they are.

Additional work points to a range of relationship properties that are related to different facets of couples' sexuality. Regan and Berscheid (1999) combined previous conceptualizations of love with empirical evidence to argue that sexual desire is a component of romantic love and that sexual desire is popularly perceived to be part of the experience of being in love. Long, Cate, Fehsenfeld, and Williams (1996) found sexual conflict related negatively to sexual and relationship satisfaction and positively to dyadic conflict and feelings of obligation to engage in intercourse. Byers and colleagues (1998) found dating individuals' sexual satisfaction strongly related to their relationship satisfaction, as was perceived equality of sexual costs and comparisons of sexual rewards to such costs. Lally and Maddock (1994) proposed that the meaning couples assign to their sexual involvement (i.e., affection, communication, recreation or play) is important. They showed that engaged couples were more apt to develop a joint meaning when those couples cohabited, had attained higher education levels, had the same religious affiliation, and agreed on family planning options.

Although the above investigations focused on relationship experiences that either preceded or were concurrent with sexual involvement, other investigations during this decade explored the effects of sexual involvement on short- and long-term relationship outcomes. For instance, Cate, Long, Angera, and Draper (1993) examined the impact of first coitus in a dating relationship on later relational development. Relationships improved for men and women when relationship quality played a role in coital decision making and when they were sexually satisfied. Being sexually permissive was an additional predictor of improved relationship quality for men. Other investigators looked beyond dating to consider outcomes of sexuality in family and marriage. Using data on women from the 1982 National Survey of Family Growth (NSFG), Miller and Heaton (1991) examined the relationship between age at first coitus and the later timing of marriage and childbirth. They showed that after controlling for other factors, early onset of coitus among adolescents corresponded with earlier age at forming a family and with an increased probability that the family would begin with childbirth—as opposed to marriage. Finally, Kahn and London (1991) queried whether engaging in premarital sexual intercourse would put women at risk for divorce. Using White respondents from the 1988 NSFG data, and controlling for other factors, they revealed that women who were virgins at marriage were less likely to be separated or divorced than nonvirgins 10 years into marriage. This difference disappeared when potential differences between virgins and nonvirgins were taken into account (mother's education, strictness of rules, and religiosity at age 14). Kahn and London speculated that women who are virgins at marriage might find divorce less acceptable than would women who are nonvirgins, although this hypothesis could not be directly tested with the data.

These findings extend the previous body of research in this area (see Sprecher & McKinney, 1993, for a review) by illustrating different ways in which sexuality is intertwined with relational experiences for singles and ways in which premarital sexual experiences potentially influence marital and familial experiences. For instance, these studies reveal that singles' relationship satisfaction is associated with a number of sexually related variables. There is a need, however, to develop theory-based models for how sexual cognitions, evaluations, and interactions are intertwined with the relationship dynamics for dating individuals. Byers and colleagues (1998) take important steps in this direction with their use of social-exchange theory, but more comprehensive models are needed.

Sexual Coercion and Aggression in Dating

Scholarly interest in sexual coercion and aggression in dating flourished during the 1990s. The corpus of work developed to the point where a number of general reviews and critiques were written (i.e. Koss & Cleveland, 1997; Marx, Van We, & Gross, 1996), and midlevel theoretical models were proposed (Byers, 1996; Malamuth, 1998; Thornhill & Thornhill, 1992). Space limitations prevent us from reviewing all advances in this area. Instead, we highlight new research directions generally not included in previous reviews.

The first of these areas reflects early experiences with and influences on sexual coercion. Evidence continued to accumulate that some adolescents fall victim to sexual coercion (Erickson & Rapkin, 1991; Jordan, Price, Telljohann, & Chesney, 1998). Sexually coerced teens were more sexually active, had poorer peer relationships, and had more same-sex friends who also were sexually active than those who had not suffered coercion (Vicary, Klingaman, & Harkness, 1995). Those who experienced unwanted coitus also were older, experienced less parental monitoring and more parental sexual abuse, and conformed more to peers (Small & Kerns, 1993). A number of investigations pointed to the role that early developmental influences play in later acts of sexual coercion. These include experiences of family violence (Dean & Malamuth, 1997), early history of behavior problems (Lalumiere & Quinsey, 1996), and delinquency (Calhoun, Bernat, Clum, & Frame, 1997).

A second new area of research further illuminated the role that dating experiences play in men's sexual coercion. Sexually coercive men, when compared to noncoercive men, were more apt to endorse a Ludic love style—a style characterized by a noncommittal, manipulative, game-playing approach to love (Kalichman at al., 1993). They experienced conflict and ambivalence with their coerced partners; experiences that directly predicted their acts of sexual coercion (Christopher, Madura, & Weaver, 1998; Christopher, Owens, & Stecker, 1993a). Such men might also lack skills for communicating well in a relationship. Based on responses to videotapes in which women respond in a variety of ways to a man's sexual advances, Malmuth and Brown (1994) suggest that sexually coercive men use cognitive schemas that discount the truthfulness of women's rejection messages. Hence, sexually coercive men might have a propensity to inaccurately decode women's sexual rejections.

Research evidence also reveals that sexually coercive men are different from noncoercive men in their approach to relationships and sexuality. They date more frequently (Byers & Eno, 1991), begin sexual activity at an early age (Malamuth et al., 1995), and have high numbers of sexual partners (Christopher et al., 1993a, 1993b; Lalumiere, Chalmers, Quinsey, & Seto, 1996), especially in uncommitted dating relationships (Lalumeire & Quinsey, 1996). They also prefer novel and casual sexual encounters (Lalumeire et al., 1996). Koss and Cleveland (1997), in reviewing such findings, speculate that sexually coercive men take a predatory approach to their sexual interactions with women.

Finally, a limited number of investigators in the 1990s focused on female-initiated sexual coercion. Studies comparing single women's and single men's coercion experiences reveal that fewer women are sexually coercive; and when women are coercive, they use less forceful techniques (Christopher et al., 1998). Moreover, when men are victims of coercion, they experience less and shorter term emotional upset as a consequence of their experiences, than women

(O'Sullivan, Byers, & Finkelman, 1998). These results must be interpreted carefully, because few men in these studies experienced violent sexual aggression. Comparing men who experienced no coercion to those who experienced pressure or violence reveals that men who experienced violent sexual coercion were angrier and more depressed than men in the other two groups (Zweig, Barber, & Eccles, 1997). Examination of the sexual outcomes of coercive acts showed that men's experiences with being coerced most often do not advance beyond kissing or fondling whereas women's experiences most often result in intercourse (Waldner-Haugrud & Magruder, 1995).

Attempts to identify correlates of female-initiated sexual coercion revealed that women who use coercion see themselves as more open, and rate themselves higher in self-esteem and in relationship satisfaction, than female victims of coercion (Busby & Compton, 1997). They also feel hostile towards men, possess a brooding anger, have a history of being sexually coercive, and experience relational conflict with and ambivalence about their coerced partners (Christopher et al., 1993b; Christopher et al., 1998).

Of the new research directions we have highlighted, two are particularly noteworthy. First, the corpus of our knowledge about sexual coercion and aggression in dating relationships is largely limited to what occurs among college students. Sampling from early- and middle-adolescent populations represents an important first step in breaking out of this limitation. The next decade should see an expansion of investigations into the more general single adult population. Second, research to date has focused primarily on individual-level predictors of sexual aggression. We are encouraged that investigators have tested models that additionally included relational (e.g., conflict) and social (e.g., peer association) variables (Christopher et al., 1998). Such integrated approaches will likely continue to prove useful in advancing our understanding of this phenomenon.

FUTURE DIRECTIONS

Throughout this review, we have suggested possible areas for research in the coming decade. In closing, we want to highlight three directions that hold heuristic promise and represent important next steps in the study of sexuality.

We identified new and noteworthy findings about marital sexuality in this review. More is known about sexuality in marriage at this time than has ever been true in the past. Yet we still have only a limited view of how sexuality is integrated into the normal flow of married life—how it influences and is influenced by other marital phenomena. Thus there exist several viable research questions for the coming decade. Does sexuality play a role in maintaining marital relationships? Does it contribute to couples' commitment or to family cohesion? How is sexuality related to dyadic conflict? How do married couples communicate about their sexuality, and does this communication play a role in relationship functioning? Addressing these and similar questions will provide a better understanding of sexual expression in its most socially approved context.

This review additionally attests that research that includes close relationship and sexuality constructs provides useful insights into sexual phenomena. Sexual interaction takes place in a dyadic context, so it should not be surprising that relational and sexual variables co-vary. To date, however, this developing literature suffers limitations common to many fields, including small samples that disproportionately represent college students, cross-sectional designs, and a high number of atheoretical investigations. Nonetheless, the findings generated from these empirical efforts are intriguing and should be investigated further, albeit with better designed investigations. We encourage sexuality researchers in the coming decade to include relational constructs in their investigations while simultaneously addressing current shortcomings.

Finally, the 1990s saw theoretical and methodological advances in the study of sexuality. Although the advances in theory were moderate, important foundational and exemplary work now exists (Weis, 1998). Methodological advances were more robust and included insights into survey design and the increased use of national data sets. We end our review with the perennial but necessary comment of other reviewers of social science advances. We encourage sexuality researchers to build from these advances. We encourage the increased use of theory, probability sampling, and longitudinal designs. Incorporating these advances into new research in the coming decade will allow researchers to test causal models that more accurately reflect complex influences on sexual expression and will thereby extend our understanding of sexuality in close relationships.

REFERENCES

Andersen, B. L., & Cryanowski, J. M. (1994). Women's sexual self-schema. *Journal of Personality and Social Psychology, 67,* 1079–1100.

Bancroft, J. (Ed.) (1997). *Researching sexual behavior: Methodological issues.* Bloomington, IN: Indiana University Press.

Barrett, D. C., Bolan, G., & Douglas, J. M., Jr. (1998). Redefining gay male anal intercourse behaviors: Implications for HIV prevention and research. *The Journal of Sex Research, 35,* 381–389.

Berscheid, E., & Reiss, H. T. (1998). Attraction and close relationships. In D. R. Gilbert, S. T. Fisk, & G. Lindzey (Eds.), *The handbook of social psychology* (Vol. 2, 4th ed., pp. 196–281). New York: McGrawHill.

Billy, J. O. G., Tanfer, K., Grady, W. R., & Klepinger, D. H. (1993). The sexual behavior of men in the United States. *Family Planning Perspectives, 25*; 52–60.

Binik, Y. M., Mah, K., & Kiesler, S. (1999). Ethical issues in conducting sex research on the internet. *The Journal of Sex Research, 26,* 82–90.

Blumstein, P., & Schwartz, P. (1983). *American couples.* New York: William Morrow.

Bogaert, A. F., & Fisher, W. A. (1995). Predictors of university men's number of sexual partners. *The Journal of Sex Research, 32,* 119–130.

Bringle, R. G., & Buunk, B. E. (1991). Extradyadic relationships and sexual jealousy. In K. McKinney &

S. Sprecher (Eds.), *Sexuality in close relationships* (pp. 135–153). Hillsdale, NJ: Erlbaum.

Busby, D. M., & Compton, S. V. (1997). Patterns of sexual coercion in adult heterosexual relationships: An exploration of male victimization. *Family Process, 36,* 81–94.

Buss, D. M. (1998). Sexual strategies theory: Historical origins and current status. *The Journal of Sex Research, 35,* 19–31.

Buss, D. M., Larsen, R., Westen, D., & Semmelroth, J. (1992). Sex differences in jealousy: Evolution, physicology, and psychology. *Psychological Science, 3,* 251–255.

Buunk, B., Angleitner, A., Oubaid, V., & Buss, D. (1996). Sex differences in jealousy in evolutionary and cultural perspectives: Tests from the Netherlands, Germany, and the United States. *Psychological Science, 7,* 359–363.

Byers, E. S. (1996). How well does the traditional sexual script explain sexual coercion? Review of a program of research. *Journal of Psychology & Human Sexuality, 8,* 7–25.

Byers, E. S., & Demmons, S. (1999). Sexual satisfaction and sexual self-disclosure within dating relationships. *The Journal of Sex Research, 36,* 180–189.

Byers, E. S., Demmons, S., & Lawrance, K. (1998). Sexual satisfaction within dating relationships: A test of the interpersonal exchange model of sexual satisfaction. *Journal of Social and Personal Relationships, 15,* 257–267.

Byers, E. S., & Eno, R. J. (1991). Predicting men's sexual coercion and aggression from attitudes, dating history, and sexual response. *Journal of Psychology and Human Sexuality, 4,* 55–70.

Calhoun, K. S., Bernat, J. A., Clum, G. A., & Frame, C. L. (1997). Sexual coercion and attraction to sexual aggression in a community sample of young men. *Journal of Interpersonal Violence, 12,* 392–406.

Call, V., Sprecher, S., & Schwartz, P. (1995). The incidence and frequency of marital sex in a national sample. *Journal of Marriage and the Family, 57,* 639–650.

———. (1996, November). Changes over time in the incidence and frequency of marital sex: Longitudinal data from a U.S. National Sample. Paper presented at the National Council on Family Relations. Portland, OR.

Catania, J. A. (1999a). A comment on advancing the frontiers of sexological methods. *The Journal of Sex Research, 36,* 1–2.

———. (1999b). A framework for conceptualizing reporting bias and its antecendents in interviews assessing human sexuality. *The Journal of Sex Research, 36,* 25–38.

Cate, R. M., Long, E., Angera, J. J., & Draper, K. K. (1993). Sexual intercourse and relationship development. *Family Relations, 42,* 158–164.

Centers for Disease Control and Prevention. (1998, September 18). Trends in sexual risk behaviors among high school students—United States, 1991–1997. *Morbidity and Mortality Weekly Report [Online] 47,* 749–751. Available: http://www.cdc.gov/epo/mmwr/preview/mmwrhtml/00054814.htm.

Choi, K., Catania, J. A., & Dolcini, M. M. (1994). Extramarital sex and HIV risk behavior among US adults: Results from the national AIDS behavioral survey. *American Journal of Public Health, 84,* 2003–2007.

Christopher, F. S., Madura, M., & Weaver, L. (1998). Premarital sexual aggressors: A multivariate analysis of social, relational, and individual variables. *Journal of Marriage and the Family, 60,* 56–69.

Christopher, F. S., Owens, L. A., & Stecker, H. L. (1993a). Exploring the dark side of courtship: A test model of male premarital sexual aggressiveness. *Journal of Marriage and the Family, 55,* 469–479.

Cohen, L. L., & Shotland, R. L. (1996). Timing of first sexual intercourse in a relationship: Expectations, experiences, and perceptions of others. *The Journal of Sex Research, 33,* 291–299.

Cupach, W. R., & Comstock, J. (1990). Satisfaction with sexual communication in marriage. Links to sexual satisfaction and dyadic adjustment. *Journal of Social and Personal Relationships, 7,* 179–186.

Cyranowski, J. M., & Andersen, B. L. (1998). Schemas, sexuality, and romantic attachment. *Journal of Personality and Social Psychology, 74,* 1364–1379.

Davidson, J. K., Sr., Darling, C. A., & Norton, L. (1995). Religiosity and the sexuality of women: Sexual behavior and sexual satisfaction revisited. *The Journal of Sex Research, 32,* 235–243.

Davis, C. M., Yarber, W. L., Bauserman, R., Schreer, G., & Davis, S. L. (Eds.) (1998). *Handbook of sexuality-related measures.* Thousand Oaks, CA: Sage.

Dean, K. E., & Malamuth, N. M. (1997). Characteristics of men who aggress sexually and of men who imagine aggressing: Risk and moderating variables. *Journal of Personality and Social Psychology, 72,* 449–455.

Deenen, A. A., Gijs, L., & van Naerssen, A. X. (1994). Intimacy and sexuality in gay male couples. *Archives of Sexual Behavior, 23,* 421–431.

DeLamater, J. D., & Hyde, J. S. (1998). Essential versus social constructionism in the study of human sexuality. *The Journal of Sex Research, 35,* 10–18.

DeMaris, A. (1997). Elevated sexual activity in violent marriages: Hypersexuality or sexual extortion? *The Journal of Sex Research, 34,* 361–373.

DeMaris, A., & Swinford, S. (1996). Female victims of spousal violence: Factors influencing their level of fearfulness. *Family Relations, 45,* 98–106.

Donnelly, D. A. (1993). Sexually inactive marriages. *The Journal of Sex Research, 30,* 171–179.

Edwards, J. N., & Booth, A. (1994). Sexuality, marriage, and well-being: The middle years. In A. S. Rossi (Ed.), *Sexuality across the life course* (pp. 233–259). Chicago: University of Chicago Press.

Erickson, P. I., & Rapkin, A. (1991). Unwanted sexual experiences among middle and high school youth. *Journal of Adolescent Health, 12,* 319–325.

Fincham, E. D., & Bradbury, T. N. (1987). The assessment of marital quality: A reevaluation. *Journal of Marriage and the Family, 49,* 797–809.

Finkelhor, D., & Yllo, K. (1985). *License to rape: Sexual abuse of wives.* New York: Holt, Rinehard & Winston.

Forste, R., & Tanfer, K. (1996). Sexual exclusivity among dating, cohabiting, and married women. *Journal of Marriage and the Family, 58,* 33–47.

Gierveld, J. J. (1995). Research into relationship designs: Personal relationships under the microscope. *Journal of Social and Personal Relationships, 12,* 583–588.

Glass, S. P., & Wright, T. L. (1992). Justifications for extramarital relationships: The association between attitudes, behaviors, and gender. *The Journal of Sex Research, 29,* 361–387.

Greeley, A. M. (1991). *Faithful attraction: Discovering intimacy, love, and fidelity in American marriage.* New York: Doherty.

Greenblat, C. S. (1983). The salience of sexuality in the early years of marriage. *Journal of Marriage and the Family, 45,* 289–299.

Greer, A. E., & Buss, D. M. (1994). Tactics for promoting sexual encounters. *The Journal of Sex Research, 31,* 185–201.

Gribble, J. N., Miller, H. G., Rogers, S. M., & Turner, C. F. (1999). Interview mode and measurement of sexual behaviors: Methodological issues. *The Journal of Sex Research, 36,* 16–24.

Gullotta, T. P., Adams, G. R., & Montemayor, R. (Eds.) (1993). *Adolescent sexuality.* Newbury Park, CA: Sage.

Haavio-Mannila, E., & Kontula, O. (1997). Correlates of increased sexual satisfaction. *Archives of Sexual Behavior, 26,* 399–419.

Henderson-King, D. H., & Veroff, J. (1994). Sexual satisfaction and marital well-being in the first years of marriages. *Journal of Social and Personal Relationships, 11,* 509–534.

Hill, C. A., & Preston, L. K. (1996). Individual differences in the experience of sexual motivation: Theory and measurement of dispositional sexual motives. *The Journal of Sex Research, 33,* 27–45.

Hogben, M., & Byrne, D. (1998): Using social learning theory to explain individual differences in human sexuality. *The Journal of Sex Research, 35,* 58–71.

Huston, T. L., & Vangelisti, A. L. (1991). Socioemotional behavior and satisfaction in marital relationships: A longitudinal study. *Journal of Personality and Social Psychology, 61,* 721–733.

Hyde, J. S., DeLamater, J. D., Plant, E. A., & Byrd, J. M. (1996). Sexuality during pregnancy and the year postpartum. *The Journal of Sex Research, 33,* 143–151.

Johnson, M. P. (1995). Patriarchal terrorism and common couple violence: Two forms of violence against women. *Journal of Marriage and the Family, 57,* 283–294.

Jordan, T. R., Price, J. H., Telljohann, S. K., & Chesney, B. K. (1998). Junior high school students' perceptions regarding nonconsensual sexual behavior. *Journal of School Health, 68,* 289–300.

Jurich, J. A., & Myers-Bowman, K. S. (1998). Systems theory and its application to research on human sexuality. *The Journal of Sex Research, 35,* 72–87.

Kahn, J. R., & London, K. A. (1991). Premarital sex and the risk of divorce. *Journal of Marriage and the Family, 53,* 845–855.

Kalichman, S. C., Sarwer, D. B., Johnson, J. R., Ali, S. A., Early, J., & Tuten, J. T. (1993). Sexually coercive behavior and love styles: A replication and extension. *Journal of Psychology & Human Sexuality, 6,* 93–106.

Kelly, J. A. (1995). Advances in HIV/AIDS education and prevention. *Family Relations, 44,* 345–353.

Kinsey, A. C., Pomeroy, W. B., & Martin, C. E. (1948). *Sexual behavior in the human male.* Philadelphia: Saunders.

Kinsey, A. C., Pomeroy, W. B., Martin, C. E., & Gebhard, P. H. (1953). *Sexual behavior in the human female.* Philadelphia: Saunders.

Koss, M. P., & Cleveland, H. H. (1997). Stepping on toes: Social roots of date rape lead to intractability and politicization. In M. D. Schwartz (Ed.), *Researching sexual violence against women: Methodological and personal perspectives* (pp. 4–21). Thousand Oaks, CA: Sage.

Kurdek, L. A. (1991). Sexuality in homosexual and heterosexual couples. In K. McKinney & S. Sprecher

(Eds.), *Sexuality in close relationships* (pp. 177–191). Hillsdale, NJ: Erlbaum.

Lally, C. E, & Maddock, J. W. (1994). Sexual meaning systems of engaged couples. *Family Relations, 43,* 53–60.

Lalumiere, M. L., Chalmers, L. J., Quinsey, V. L., & Seto, M. C. (1996). A test of the mate deprivation hypothesis of sexual coercion. *Ethology and Sociobiology, 17,* 299–318.

Lalumiere, M. L., & Quinsey, V. L. (1996). Sexual deviance, antisociality, mating effort, and the use of sexually coercive behaviors. *Personality and Individual Differences, 21,* 34–48.

Laumann, E. O., Gagnon, J. H., Michael, R. T., & Michaels, S. (1994). *The social organization of sexuality: Sexual practices in the United States.* Chicago: University of Chicago Press.

Lawrance, K., & Byers, E. S. (1995). Sexual satisfaction in long-term heterosexual relationships: The interpersonal exchange model of sexual satisfaction. *Personal Relationships, 2,* 267–285.

Lever, J. (1995, August 22). Lesbian sex survey. *The Advocate,* 21–30.

Long, E. C. J., Cate, R. M., Fehsenfeld, D. A., & Williams, K. M. (1996). A longitudinal assessment of a measure of premarital sexual conflict. *Family Relations, 45,* 302–308.

Longmore, M. A. (1998). Symbolic interactionism and the study of sexuality. *The Journal of Sex Research, 35,* 44–57.

Malamuth, N. M. (1998). The confluence model as an organizing framework for research on sexually aggressive men: Risk moderators, imagined aggression, and pornography consumption. In R. G. Geen & E. Donnerstein (Eds.), *Human aggression: Theories, research, and implications for social policy* (pp. 227–245). San Diego, CA: Academic Press.

Malamuth, N. M., & Brown, L. M. (1994). Sexually aggressive men's perceptions of women's communications: Testing three explanations. *Journal of Personality and Social Psychology, 67,* 699–712.

Malamuth, N. M., Lintz, D., Heavey, C. L., Barnes, G., & Acker, M. (1995). Using the confluence model of sexual aggression to predict men's conflict with women: A 10-year follow-up study. *Journal of Personality and Social Psychology, 69,* 353–369.

Marsiglio, W., & Donnelly, D. (1991). Sexual intercourse in later life: A national study of married persons. *Journal of Gerontology, 46,* 338–344.

Marston, P. J., Hecht, M. L., Manke, M. L., McDaniel, S., & Reeder, H. (1998). The subjective experience of intimacy, passion, and commitment in heterosexual loving relationships. *Personal Relationships, 5,* 15–30.

Marx, B. P., Van Wie, V., & Gross, A. M. (1996). Date rape risk factors: A review and methodological critique of the literature. *Aggression and Violent Behavior, 1,* 27–45.

McKinney, K., & Sprecher, S. (Eds.). (1991). *Sexuality in close relationships.* Hillsdale, NJ: Erlbaum.

Michael, R. T., Gagnon, J. H., Laumann, E. O., & Kolata, G. (1994). *Sex in America: A definitive survey.* Boston: Little, Brown.

Miller, B. C., & Heaton, T. B. (1991). Age at first sexual intercourse and the timing of marriage and childbirth. *Journal of Marriage and the Family, 53,* 719–732.

Moore, K. A., Miller, B. C., Glei, D., & Morrison, D. R. (1995). Adolescent sex, contraception, and childbearing: A review of recent research. Washington, DC: *Child Trends.*

Morrison, D. M., Leigh, B. C., & Gillmore, M. R. (1999). Daily data collection: A comparison of three methods. *The Journal of Sex Research, 36,* 76–81.

Muehlenhard, C. L., & Rodgers, C. S. (1998). Token resistance to sex. *Psychology of Women Quarterly, 22,* 443–463.

Oggins, J., Leber, D., & Veroff, J. (1993). Race and gender differences in black and white newlyweds' perceptions of sexual and marital relationships. *The Journal of Sex Research, 30,* 152–160.

Oliver, M. B., & Hyde, J. S. (1993). Gender differences in sexuality: A meta-analysis. *Psychological Bulletin, 114,* 29–51.

O'Sullivan, L. F., & Allgeier, E. R. (1994). Disassembling a stereotype: Gender differences in the use of token resistance. *Journal of Applied Social Psychology, 24,* 1035–1055.

———. (1998). Feigning sexual desire: Consenting to unwanted sexual activity in heterosexual dating relationships. *The Journal of Sex Research, 35,* 234–243.

O'Sullivan, L. F., & Byers, E. S. (1992). College students' incorporation of initiator and restrictor roles in sexual dating interactions. *The Journal of Sex Research, 29,* 435–446.

———. (1993). Eroding stereotypes: College women's attempts to influence reluctant male sexual partners. *The Journal of Sex Research, 30,* 270–282.

O'Sullivan, L. F., Byers, E. S., & Finkelman, L. (1998). A comparison of male and female college students' experiences of sexual coercion. *Psychology of Women Quarterly, 22,* 177–195.

O'Sullivan L. F., & Gaines, M. E. (1998). Decision-making in college students' heterosexual dating relationships: Ambivalence about engaging in sexual activity *Journal of Social and Personal Relationships, 15,* 347–363.

Posner, R. A., & Silbaugh, K. B. (1996). *A guide to America's sex laws.* Chicago: University of Chicago Press.

Rao, K. V., & DeMaris, A. (1995). Coital frequency among married and cohabiting couples in the U.S. *Journal of Biosocial Science, 27,* 135–150.

Regan, P. C. (1997). The impact of male sexual request style on perceptions of sexual interactions: The mediational role of beliefs about female sexual desire. *Basic and Applied Social Psychology, 19,* 519–532.

Regan, P. C., & Berscheid, E. (1995). Gender differences in beliefs about the causes of male and female sexual desire. *Personal Relationships, 2,* 345–358.

Regan, P. C., & Berscheid, E. (1999). *Lust: What we know about human sexual desire.* Thousand Oaks, CA: Sage.

Renaud, C., Byers, E. S., & Pan, S. (1997). Sexual and relationship satisfaction in mainland China. *The Journal of Sex Research, 34,* 1–12.

Roach, A. J., Frazier, L. P., & Bowden, S. R. (1981). The marital satisfaction scale. *Journal of Marriage and the Family, 40,* 537–546.

Roche, J. P., & Ramsbey, T. W. (1993). Premarital sexuality: A five-year follow-up study of attitudes and behavior by dating stage. *Adolescence, 28,* 67–80.

Russell, D. E. H. (1982). *Rape in marriage.* Bloomington, IN: Indiana University Press.

Seidman, S. N., Mosher, W. D., & Aral, S. O. (1992). Women with multiple sexual partners: United States, 1988. *American Journal of Public Health, 82,* 1388–1394.

Shackelford, T. K., & Buss, D. M. (1997). Anticipation of marital dissolution as a consequence of spousal infidelity. *Journal of Social and Personal Relationships, 14,* 793–808.

Shotland, R. L., & Hunter, B. A. (1995). Women's "token resistant" and compliant sexual behaviors are related to uncertain sexual intentions and rape. *Personality and Social Psychology Bulletin, 21,* 226–236.

Small, S. A., & Kerns, D. (1993). Unwanted sexual activity among peers during early and middle adolescence: Incidence and risk factors. *Journal of Marriage and the Family, 55,* 941–952.

Smith, T. W. (1994a). Attitudes toward sexual permissiveness: Trends, correlates, and behavioral connections. In Rossi, A. S. (Ed.), *Sexuality across the life course* (pp. 63–97). Chicago: University of Chicago Press.

Smith, T. W. (1994b). *The demography of sexual behavior.* Menlo Park, CA: Kaiser Family Foundation.

Spanier, G. B. (1976). Measuring dyadic adjustment. *Journal of Marriage and the Family, 38,* 15–28.

Sponaugle, G. C. (1989). Attitudes toward extramarital relations. In K. McKinney & S. Sprecher (Eds.), *Human sexuality: The societal and interpersonal context* (pp. 187–209). Norwood, NJ: Ablex.

Sprecher, S. (1998). Social exchange theories and sexuality. *The Journal of Sex Research, 35,* 32–43.

Sprecher, S., & Hatfield, E. (1996). Premarital sexual standards among U.S. college students: Comparison with Russian and Japanese students. *Archives of Sexual Behavior, 25,* 261–288.

Sprecher, S., Hatfield, E., Cortese, A., Potapova, E., & Levitskaya, A. (1994). Token resistance to sexual intercourse and consent to unwanted sexual intercourse: College students' dating experiences in three countries. *The Journal of Sex Research, 31,* 125–132.

Sprecher, S., & McKinney, K. (1993). *Sexuality.* Newbury Park, CA: Sage.

Sprecher, S., Metts, S., Burleson, B., Hatfield, E., & Thompson, A. (1995). Domains of expressive interaction in intimate relationships: Associations with satisfaction and commitment. *Family Relations, 44,* 203–210.

Sprecher, S., & Regan, P. C. (1996). College virgins: How men and women perceive their sexual status. *The Journal of Sex Research, 33,* 3–15.

———. (1998). Passionate and companionate love in courting and young married couples. *Sociological Inquiry, 68,* 163–185.

Tanfer, K., & Cubbins, L. A. (1992). Coital frequency among single women: Normative constraints and situational opportunities. *The Journal of Sex Research, 29,* 221–250.

Thompson, A. (1983). Extramarital sex: A review of the research literature. *The Journal of Sex Research, 19,* 1–22.

Thornhill, R., & Thornhill, N. W. (1992). The evolutionary psychology of men's coercive sexuality. *Behavioral and Brain Sciences, 15,* 363–421.

U.S. Bureau of the Census. (1988). Households, families, marital status, and living arrangements: March, 1988 [Advance Report] (Current Population Reports, Series P-20, No. 432). Washington, DC: Government Printing Office.

Veroff, J., Douvan, E., & Hatchett, S. J. (1995). *Marital instability: A social and behavioral study of the early years.* Westport, CT: Praeger.

Vicary, J. R., Klingaman, L. R., & Harkness, W. L. (1995). Risk factors associated with date rape and sexual assault of adolescent girls. *Journal of Adolescence, 18,* 289–306.

Waldner-Haugrud, L. K., & Gratch, L. V. (1997). Sexual coercion in gay/lesbian relationships: Descriptives and gender differences. *Violence and Victims, 12,* 87–98.

Waldner-Haugrud, L. K., & Magruder, B. (1995). Male and female sexual victimization in dating relationships: Gender differences in coercion techniques and outcomes. *Violence and Victims, 10,* 203–215.

Weis, D. L. (1998). The use of theory in sexuality research. *The Journal of Sex Research, 35,* 1–9.

White, L., & Keith, B. (1990). The effect of shift work on the quality and stability of marital relations. *Journal of Marriage and the Family, 52,* 453–462.

Wiederman, M. W. (1997). Extramarital sex: Prevalence and correlates in a national survey. *The Journal of Sex Research, 34,* 167–174.

———. (1999). Volunteer bias in sexuality research using college student participants. *The Journal of Sex Research, 36,* 59–66.

Zweig, J. M., Barber, B. L., & Eccles, J. S. (1997). Sexual coercion and well-being in young adulthood. *Journal of Interpersonal Violence, 12,* 291–308.

Web of Love

Lust, Romance, and Attachment

Helen Fisher

When we "click" with someone and feel an instant attraction, we sometimes refer to it as "chemistry." According to Helen Fisher, that is exactly what is responsible for the feelings of excitement and arousal that occur when we are physically attracted to someone. But, chemistry also leads to the intense feelings of romance that we have early in a relationship and to the warm glow that we feel about a long-term partner. There is a different mix of neurotransmitters that results in each set of feelings.

Other theorists have attributed instant attraction to various other factors such as pheromones, which are chemical messages sent between people. We know that pheromones function as attractants in the world of many animals. Do they play a role in human attraction as well? And, what about the various signals that indicate potential mates have good genes to pass along? Research has indicated that we are drawn to people who are more symmetrical (which indicates fitness) and whose bodies have a different chemical makeup from our own (which indicates that they are likely not our relatives).

As you read this chapter, you may want to talk with your classmates about the research findings

that Fisher's theory explains and those it doesn't explain. You won't be able to keep from thinking about personal experiences you may have had that fit (or don't fit) her ideas. Do you agree with Fisher that lust, attraction, and love all boil down to one's body chemistry? Or, is there anything else that could play a role in to whom and how you have been attracted and attached? Do you, as a human being, have any control over all of this?

There are unlikely to be final answers to these and any other questions that for so long have been debated by sages of many disciplines. Just make sure that the next time you meet "that certain someone," you aren't so busy analyzing the chemistry of the experience that the magic of the moment is missed!

From *Why We Love: The Nature and Chemistry of Romantic Love* (Chapter 4) by H. Fisher. 2004. New York: Henry Holt and Company. Copyright 2004 by Helen Fisher. Reprinted by arrangement with Henry Holt and Company, LLC.

Love is a harmony, as Shakespeare wrote, sometimes even a cacophony of sensations. Exuberance, tenderness, compassion, possessiveness, rapture, adoration, longing, despair: romance is a kaleidoscopic pattern of shifting needs and feelings all tethered to a celestial being on whose slightest word or smile one dangles, spinning with hope and joy and craving. Complexity, thy name is love.

Yet with time and circumstance, nature has built a few major chords within this symphony. Romantic love is deeply entwined with two other mating drives: lust—the craving for sexual gratification; and attachment—the feelings of calm, security, and union with a long-term partner.

Each of these basic mating drives travels along different pathways in the brain. Each produces different behaviors, hopes, and dreams. And each is associated with different neurochemicals. Lust is associated primarily with the hormone testosterone in both men and women. Romantic love is linked with the natural stimulant dopamine and perhaps norepinephrine and serotonin. And feelings of male-female attachment are produced primarily by the hormones oxytocin and vasopressin.

Moreover, each brain system evolved to direct a different aspect of reproduction. Lust evolved to motivate individuals to seek sexual union with almost *any* semi-appropriate partner. Romantic love emerged to drive men and women to focus their mating attention on a preferred individual, thereby conserving invaluable courtship time and energy. And the brain circuitry for male-female attachment developed to enable our ancestors to live with this mate at least long enough to rear a single child through infancy together.[1]

All three of these brain networks—lust, romantic attraction, and attachment—are multipurpose systems. In addition to its reproductive purpose, the sex drive serves to make and keep friends, provide pleasure and adventure, tone muscles, and relax the mind. Romantic love can stimulate you to sustain a loving partnership or drive you to fall in love with a new person and initiate divorce. And feelings of attachment enable us to express genuine affection for children, family, and friends, as well as a beloved.

Nature is conservative. When she has a good design, she sticks with it, expanding its uses to suit many situations. But the primary purpose of these interlocking drives is to motivate us to seek an array of sexual partners, choose one to dote upon, then remain emotionally engaged with "him" or "her" at least long enough to rear a child together—the basics of the mating game.

ON LUST

Lust is a primordial human feeling. It is unpredictable, too. The craving for sexual fulfillment can pop up in your mind as you are driving in your car, watching a movie on TV, reading in the office, or daydreaming on the beach. And this urge is very different from the feeling of romantic love. In fact, few people in Western societies confuse the elation of romance with the longing for sexual release.[2]

People in far different cultures also easily distinguish between these feelings.[3] On the Polynesian island of Mangaia, "real love" is called *inangaro kino*, a state of romantic passion quite distinct from one's sexual desires. In their native language, the Taita of Kenya call lust *ashiki* while they refer to love as *pendo*. And in Caruaru, a town in northeast Brazil, locals say, "*Amor* is when you feel a desire to always be with her, you breathe her, eat her, drink her, you are always thinking of her, you don't manage to live without her." *Paixao*, on the other hand, is "horniness" and *tesao* is "a very strong sexual attraction for a person."

These people are correct to regard these feelings as distinct. Scientists have recently established that lust and romantic love are associated with different constellations of brain regions.[4] In one study researchers scanned the brains of a group of young heterosexual men using the fMRI brain scanner. The men were shown three types of videos: some were erotic, some relaxing, some related to sports.[5] Each volunteer wore a custom-built pneumatic pressure cuff around his penis to record firmness. The pattern of brain activity was quite different from the one we found among the love-sick subjects in our brain scanning project.

Lust and romantic love are not the same.

And just as people everywhere have concocted love potions to spur romance, they have tried all sorts of potions to trigger lust—what an Italian proverb calls "the oldest lion of them all."

THE HORMONE OF DESIRE

Everywhere humankind has used what they hoped was an aphrodisiac to trigger lust. When the tomato first crossed the Atlantic from the Americas, the Europeans thought this juicy red fruit would spark the sexual appetite; they called it the "love apple." Shark's fins, bird's nest soup, powdered rhinoceros horn, curry, chutney, mandrake root, chocolate, hyena eyes, caviar, clams, oysters, lobsters, dove brains, goose tongues, apples, bananas, cherries, dates, figs, peaches, pomegranates, asparagus, garlic, beer, perspiration: scents and tastes and ointments of dazzling variety have been employed to charm reluctant partners into bed.

The Elizabethans served free prunes in brothels because they were convinced this spurred lust. In past centuries Arabs tried to lure hesitant women into sampling a bit of camel hump to pique their sexual desire. Pliny wrote that hippopotamus snouts would do the trick. The Aztecs saw sexual magic in goat and rabbit parts because these animals were fast breeders. Sea slugs caught the fancy of the Chinese, largely because these strange animals enlarge when touched. And Europeans historically pulverized a certain type of beetle found in southern Europe to incite sexual desire; they called it Spanish fly.

Eating increases blood pressure and the pulse rate, raises body temperature, and sometimes makes us sweat, physiological changes that also occur with sex. Perhaps this is why men and women have long associated different foods with sexual excitement. But nature has made only one true substance to stimulate sexual desire in men and women—testosterone, and to a lesser degree, its kin, the other male sex hormones.

This is well established. Men and women who have higher circulating levels of testosterone tend to engage in more sexual activity.[6] Male

athletes who inject testosterone to elevate their strength and stamina have more sexual thoughts, more morning erections, more sexual encounters, and more orgasms. And women who take testosterone in middle age boost their sexual desire. The male libido peaks in the early twenties, when levels of testosterone are highest. And many women feel more sexual desire around ovulation, when levels of testosterone increase.[7]

As elevated levels of testosterone stimulate the sex drive, declining levels dampen it. Both sexes have fewer sexual fantasies, masturbate less regularly, and engage in less intercourse as they age.[8] Poor health, unhappiness, overwork, lack of opportunity, laziness, and boredom undoubtedly contribute to this waning lust. But with age, levels of testosterone decline, often depressing sex desire.

Some two-thirds of middle-aged women do not experience any decline in libido, however.[9] This, too, may be due to testosterone. As the estrogens decline with menopause, levels of testosterone and the other androgens become unmasked: these potent hormones can finally express themselves more fully. Indeed, they do. In one study of middle-aged women, almost 40 percent complained that they were not having enough sex.[10]

When it comes to sexual desire, people vary, in part because levels of testosterone are inherited.[11] Levels also fluctuate according to the day, the week, the year, and the life cycle. Moreover, the balance of testosterone, estrogen, and other bodily ingredients, as well as social circumstances and a host of other factors, all play a role in when, where, and how often we feel lust.[12] Nevertheless, testosterone is central to this appetite. And this primordial chemical can swamp the thinking brain.

Men and women are often sexually stimulated by different things, however. Men like to look. They are sexually turned on by visual stimuli. Even when men fantasize, they conjure up vivid images of body parts and copulation.[13] This lascivious peering probably boosts levels of testosterone. When male monkeys see a sexually available female or watch a companion copulate with a female, their levels of testosterone soar.[14] So the men who go to strip bars or look at "girlie" magazines are probably boosting levels of testosterone and triggering lust.

Women are generally more turned on by romantic words, images, and themes in films and stories. Women's sexual fantasies also include more affection, commitment, and sex with familiar partners.[13] And women like to yield. About 70 percent of American men and women fantasize while making love.[15] But as conquest is at the core of most men's mental plots, active surrender is prevalent in women's sexual reveries.[16]

These tastes for conquest and surrender have nothing to do with rape. Less than half of 1 percent of men enjoy forcing a woman into coitus; and less than half of 1 percent of women want to be coerced into copulation.[16] Still, American women are twice as likely as men to actively fantasize about being "done to" as opposed to "doing."[13]

Danger, novelty, particular smells and sounds, love letters, candy, endearing conversations, sexy clothes, swaying music, elegant dinners: many cues can trigger the sex drive. How do feelings of romantic love affect this primordial brain circuit, lust?

ROMANCE TRIGGERS LUST

Surely you have noticed that when you fall in love, your ardor stimulates the sex drive. Novelists, dramatists, poets, and songwriters all rhapsodize about this urge to kiss, cuddle, and make love to someone you adore.

Why do we feel lust when we fall in love?

Because dopamine, the liquor of romance, can stimulate the release of testosterone, the hormone of sexual desire.[17]

This relationship between elevated levels of dopamine and sexual arousal, frequency of intercourse, and positive sexual function is common in animals.[18] When dopamine is injected into a male rat's bloodstream, for example, it stimulates copulatory behaviors.[19] Moreover, when a male laboratory rat is placed in an adjacent cage where he can see or smell an estrous female, he becomes sexually excited; with this, levels of dopamine also rise.[20] And when the barrier is removed and he is allowed to copulate, levels of dopamine rise even higher.[20]

Dopamine can also stimulate lust in humans.[21] When men and women who are depressed take drugs that elevate levels of dopamine in the brain, their sex drive regularly improves.[22]

A friend of mine in her thirties told me a remarkable story regarding this. She had been mildly depressed for several years, so recently she began to take one of the newer antidepressants (one without negative sexual side effects) that elevates levels of dopamine in the brain. A month after starting this drug she not only thought more about sex, but she had also begun to have multiple orgasms with her boyfriend. I suspect her sudden change in sexual desire and sexual function occurred because the pill she was taking daily to enhance dopamine triggered the release of testosterone as well.

This positive relationship between dopamine and testosterone may also explain why people feel so sexy when they go on vacation, try some new trick in the bedroom, or make love to a new partner. Novel experiences drive up levels of dopamine in the brain—hence they can also trigger the brain chemistry of lust.

Norepinephrine, another stimulant that probably plays a role in romantic love, also stimulates the sex drive. Addicts who take amphetamines, known as "uppers" or "speed," say their sex drive can be constant. This lustiness probably stems from the same biological equation: amphetamines largely boost norepinephrine (as well as dopamine). And norepinephrine can stimulate the production of testosterone.[23]

Once again some caveats: the dosage of all these chemicals, as well as the timing of their release in the brain, makes a difference. None of these interactions are direct or simple.

But generally speaking, dopamine and norepinephrine spark sexual desire,[24] most likely by elevating levels of testosterone. No wonder new lovers stay up all night caressing. The chemistry of romance ignites the most powerful urge of nature: the drive to copulate.

This chemical connection between romantic love and lust makes evolutionary sense. After all, if romantic love evolved to stimulate mating with a "special" other, it *should* trigger the drive to have sex with this beloved, too.

DOES LUST TRIGGER ROMANCE?

But is the reverse true? Can lust stimulate amour? Can you climb in bed with "just a friend" or even a stranger, then suddenly fall in love with him or her?

Ovid, a man who had many love affairs, believed that a strong sexual attraction could often provoke a person to fall in love.[25] But lust does not always trigger romantic ardor, as many people know. Most sexually liberated contemporary adults have had sex with someone they were not in love with. Many have even copulated with this "friend" regularly. But, alas, they never felt the exhilaration of romantic passion for this bed partner. Lust does not necessarily lead to the passion and obsession of romantic love.

In fact, there is a great deal of data to the contrary. Athletes who inject synthetic androgens to build muscles don't fall in love as they take their drugs. When middle-aged men and women inject testosterone or apply testosterone cream to various body parts to stimulate their sex drive, their sexual thoughts and fantasies increase.[26] But they don't fall in love either. The brain circuitry of lust does not necessarily ignite the furnace of romance.

This is not to say that lust never triggers romantic love. It can. A middle-aged friend of mine is a good example. She had been having sex with "just a friend" for almost three years. These were sporadic events, she told me; she and her friend had sex no more than two or three times annually. Then one summer evening, about five minutes after coupling with him, she fell profoundly in love with him. At that moment the obsessive thinking, the pining, and the rapture started. In the weeks and months that followed, she told me, she lay awake at night and thought of him constantly, waited by the phone to hear his voice, dressed attractively to win him, and fantasized about a life together. Fortunately he loved her, too.

"*Naso pasyo, maya basyo.*" Women in rural western Nepal use this off-color saying to express the same phenomenon. It means, "The penis entered and love arrived."

I think biology contributes to this spontaneous love for a sex partner. Sexual activity can increase brain levels of dopamine and norepinephrine in male rats.[27] Even without sexual activity, increasing levels of testosterone can elevate levels of dopamine[28] and norepinephrine[29] as well as suppress levels of serotonin.[30] In short, the hormone of sexual desire can trigger the release of the brain's elixirs for romantic passion. As my friend cuddled and copulated with "just a friend," I think she triggered her brain circuit for romance and fell in love.

That "ol' black magic" is a fickle force. The chemistry of romantic love can trigger the chemistry of sexual desire and the fuel of sexual desire can trigger the fuel of romance. This is why it is dangerous to copulate with someone with whom you don't wish to become involved. Although you intend to have casual sex, you might just fall in love.

Romantic passion also has a special relationship with feelings of attachment.

ON ATTACHMENT

Love changes over time. It becomes deeper, calmer. No longer do couples talk all day or dance till dawn. The mad passion, the ecstasy, the longing, the obsessive thinking, the heightened energy: all dissolve. But if you are fortunate, this magic transforms itself into new feelings of security, comfort, calm, and union with your partner. Psychologist Elaine Hatfield calls this feeling "companionate love," a feeling of happy togetherness with someone whose life has become deeply entwined with yours.[31] I call this complex feeling "attachment."

And just as men and women intuitively distinguish between the feelings of romantic love and those of lust, people just as easily distinguish between feelings of romance and attachment.

Nisa, a !Kung Bushman woman of the Kalahari Desert of Botswana, explained this feeling of man-woman attachment succinctly to anthropologist Marjorie Shostak. "When two people are first together," Nisa said, "their hearts are on fire and their passion is very great. After a while, the fire cools and that's how it stays. They continue to love each other, but it's in a different way—warm and dependable."[32]

The Taita of Kenya would agree. They say that love comes in two forms, an irresistible longing, a "kind of sickness," and a deep enduring affection for another. Brazilians have a poetic proverb that distinguishes between these two feelings, saying, "Love is born in a glance and matures in a smile." And for the Koreans, "*sarang*" is a word close to the Western concept of romantic love, while "*chong*" is more like feelings of long-term attachment. But perhaps Abigail Adams, the wife of America's second president, said it best, writing to John in 1793, "Years subdue the ardor of passion, but in lieu thereof friendship and affection deep-rooted subsists, which defies the ravages of time, and whilst the vital flame exists."[33]

THE CHEMISTRY OF ATTACHMENT

Scientists began to examine this brain system, attachment, decades ago when British psychiatrist John Bowlby proposed that humans have evolved an innate attachment system consisting of specific behaviors and physiological responses.[34] Only recently, however, have researchers begun to understand which brain chemicals produce this feeling of fusion with a long-term mate. Most now believe that vasopressin and oxytocin, closely related hormones made largely in the hypothalamus and the gonads, produce many of the behaviors associated with attachment.

But to grasp how these hormones generate the sensation of union with a sweetheart, I must introduce you to prairie voles. These brown-gray, mouselike rodents form pair-bonds to rear their young; some 90 percent mate for life with a single partner. A few years ago neuroscientists Sue Carter, Tom Insel, and others pinpointed the cause of this attachment in males. As the male prairie vole ejaculates, levels of vasopressin increase in the brain, triggering his spousal and parenting zeal.[35]

Is vasopressin nature's cocktail for male attachment?

To investigate this hypothesis, scientists then injected vasopressin into the brains of *virgin* male prairie voles raised in the lab. These males immediately began to defend the space around them from other males, an aspect of pair formation in prairie voles. And when each was introduced to a female, he became instantaneously possessive of her.[36] Moreover, when these same scientists blocked the production of vasopressin in the brain, male prairie voles acted like cads instead—copulating with a female, then abandoning her for another mating opportunity.

Nature has given male mammals a chemical to feel the paternal instinct: vasopressin.

OXYTOCIN: ANOTHER COCKTAIL FOR DEVOTION?

Few poets write about the durable feeling of attachment, perhaps because this drive rarely compels one to compose passionate verse in the dead of night. Yet the feeling of attachment must be a common sensation among all birds and mammals, because it is associated not only with vasopressin but also with oxytocin—a related hormone that is ubiquitous in nature.[37]

Like vasopressin, oxytocin is made in the hypothalamus, as well as in the ovaries and testes. Unlike vasopressin, oxytocin is released in all female mammals (including women) during the birthing process.[38] It initiates contractions of the uterus and stimulates the mammary glands to produce milk. But scientists have now established that oxytocin also stimulates bonding between a mother and her infant.

More important, many now believe that oxytocin is also involved in the feelings of adult male-female attachment.[39]

You have undoubtedly felt the power of these two "satisfaction hormones," as vasopressin and oxytocin are sometimes called. We secrete them at two poignant moments during sexual intercourse: during stimulation of the genitals and/or nipples[40] and during orgasm. At orgasm, levels of vasopressin dramatically increase in men and levels of oxytocin rise in women.[39] These "cuddle chemicals" undoubtedly contribute to that sense of fusion, closeness, and attachment you can feel after sweet sex with a beloved.

How does the chemistry of attachment affect feelings of lust and romantic love?

DOES LUST DAMPEN ATTACHMENT?

The chemical components of attachment have complex effects on both the sex drive and feelings of romantic passion.

In short, the chemistry of attachment can trigger lust and the chemistry of lust can trigger expressions of attachment.

But all these hormones can also have negative effects on one another. Increasing levels of testosterone can sometimes drive down levels of vasopressin (and oxytocin) and elevated levels of vasopressin can *decrease* levels of testosterone.[41] This inverse relationship between lust and attachment is "dose-dependent"; it varies depending on the quantities, timing, and interactions among several hormones.[42] But high levels of testosterone can reduce

attachment. And there is a great deal of evidence that this happens to people regularly—sometimes with disastrous effects.

Men with high baseline levels of testosterone marry less frequently, have more adulterous affairs, commit more spousal abuse, and divorce more often. As a man's marriage becomes less stable, his levels of testosterone rise. With divorce, his testosterone levels rise even more. And single men tend to have higher levels of testosterone than married men.[43]

The reverse can also happen: as a man becomes more and more attached to his family, levels of testosterone can decline. In fact, at the birth of a child, expectant fathers experience a significant decline in levels of testosterone.[44] Even when a man holds a baby, levels of testosterone decrease.

This negative relationship between testosterone and attachment is also seen in other creatures. Male cardinals and blue jays flit from one female to the next; they never stick around to parent their young. These profligate fathers have high levels of testosterone. Males of species that form monogamous pair-bonds and remain with this mate to father infants, however, have much lower levels of testosterone during the parenting phase of the breeding season.[45] And when scientists surgically pumped testosterone into monogamous male sparrows, these faithful fathers abandoned their nests, their young, and their "wives" to court other females.[46]

As I have said, the interactions between these chemical systems for lust and attachment are complex and variable. But there is data to suggest that as people grow like "two lovely berries moulded on one stem," the chemistry of attachment can dampen lust. This is probably why men and women in long stable marriages tend to spend less time in their bedroom making love.

But what about romance? How does dopamine, the fuel of romantic love, affect levels of vasopressin and oxytocin, the brain's intoxicants for attachment? Do deep feelings of union and attachment enhance or stifle romantic passion?

ROMANCE AND ATTACHMENT?

Nature isn't tidy. She likes options. And there is no definite relationship between the neurotransmitters of romance and the hormones of attachment. As should be said of all these chemical interactions: it depends.

Under some circumstances, dopamine and norepinephrine can stimulate the release of oxytocin and vasopressin[47]—and contribute to one's growing feelings of attachment. But increasing levels of oxytocin (found in both men and women) can also interfere with dopamine and norepinephrine pathways in the brain, decreasing the impact of these excitatory substances.[48] Hence the chemistry of attachment can quell the chemistry of romance.

There is a great deal of anecdotal evidence for this negative chemical relationship between attachment and romantic love. People around the world say the exhilaration of romance wanes as their marriage or partnership becomes increasingly stable, comfortable, and secure. Some even go to psychiatrists or marriage counselors to try to renew romantic passion in their relationship. Some seek romance outside their marriage instead. Some divorce. And many settle into a long-term partnership devoid of romantic bliss.

I have mixed feelings about this fate nature has decreed. First, many of us would die of sexual exhaustion if romantic love flourished endlessly in a relationship. We wouldn't get to work on time or concentrate on anything except "him" or "her." Moreover, as romantic love matures, it often expands into hundreds of complex and fulfilling feelings of attachment that produce an enormously intricate, interesting, and emotionally rewarding union with another living soul.

Romantic love did not evolve to help us maintain a stable, enduring partnership. It evolved for different purposes: to drive ancestral men and women to prefer, choose, and pursue specific mating partners, then start the mating process and remain sexually faithful to "him" or "her" long enough to conceive a child. After the child is born, however, parents need a new set of chemicals and brain networks to rear their infant as a team—the chemistry of attachment. As a result, feelings of attachment often dampen the ecstasy of romance, replacing it with a deep sense of union with a mate.

THE TRELLIS OF LOVE

In spite of this evolutionary trajectory of loving, in which romantic passion gradually transforms into feelings of deep attachment, these three brain circuits—lust, romantic love, and attachment—can ignite in any combination.

In the traditional Western course of events, you meet a man or woman. You talk and laugh and begin to "date." Rapidly or gradually you fall in love. As the camaraderie escalates to bliss, your sex drive surges into higher action. Then after months or years of joyous times together, your raging romantic passion and raw sexual hunger begin to wane, replaced by what Theodor Reik called that warm "afterglow,"[49] attachment. In this scenario, romantic love has triggered lust; then with time, these raw feelings of passion and desire have settled into a sinew of emotional union and commitment—attachment.

Lust, romance, and attachment can visit you in other sequences, however. You may begin a liaison with someone for whom you feel only sexual desire. For a few months you have sex irregularly. Then one day you begin to feel possessive. Soon you fall in love with "him" or "her." And over time you become deeply emotionally entwined. In this case, lust has preceded romance, which then led to attachment.

Then there are couples who actually begin their relationship with feelings of attachment. They quickly achieve emotional union in the college dorm, at the office, or in their social circle. They become fast friends. With time, this attachment metamorphoses into romantic passion—which finally triggers lust.

Alas, many of us also have periods in our lives when these three mating drives—lust, romantic love, and attachment—do not focus on the same person. It seems to be the destiny of humankind that we are *neurologically* able to love more than one person at a time. You can feel profound attachment for a long-term spouse, *while* you feel romantic passion for someone in the office or your social circle, *while* you feel the sex drive as you read a book, watch a movie, or do something else unrelated to either partner. You can even swing from one feeling to another.

Lust, romantic love, and deep attachment can visit you in such different and unexpected combinations that many people have come to believe the mixture of sensations that draws you to another is mysterious, elusive. But once you begin to envisage lust, romantic love, and attachment as three specific mating drives, each producing many gradations of feeling that endlessly combine and recombine in countless different ways, love takes on tangibility.

THE MAD SYMPHONY OF ROMANCE

Romantic love certainly has subtle variations, as well as intricate and varied relationships with its kindred reproductive drives, lust, and attachment. Love is a symphony of feelings with many notes and chords.

To make matters even more complex, the brain network for romantic love melds with many more brain systems with circuits for other basic drives, as well as with many emotions, memories, and thoughts. All these ingredients add fantastic depth, nuance, and spice to our feelings of romance.

Certainly our emotions contribute to romantic passion. Human emotions lie along a continuum, from those that are so basic that they are almost impossible to hide (such as disgust) to those like envy that we can more easily conceal.

Certainly the drive to love commandeers all basic emotions at one time or another. As you feel an irresistible urge to phone "him" or "her," you can become engulfed with fear that your lover has gone out with a rival, then overwhelmed with joy as he or she answers the phone and says, "I love you," then pummeled by surprise and disappointment as this celestial being breaks the dinner date you had planned together. Romantic love is also linked to a host of more complex feelings. Respect, admiration, loyalty, gratitude, sympathy, apprehension, bashfulness, nostalgia, remorse, even the sense of fairness. We tack on dozens of these complex emotions while we are in the throes of romantic love.

Calm, tension, contentment, anxiety, mild pain, mild pleasure, and other general bodily states also contribute to feelings of romantic love. As neurologist Antonio Damasio puts it, these "background emotions" provide the landscape of the body, the persistent mood that accompanies us as stronger emotions and motivations ebb and surge.[40] Only occasionally do these background states gush into your conscious mind. But these steady undercurrents of anxiety, pain, and pleasure certainly color our feelings for a beloved.

Most compelling, this trellis of emotions and motivations is hierarchically ordered in the brain. Fear can overcome joy, for example. Jealousy can stifle tenderness. The juxtapositions are manifold. But in this pecking order of basic and complex emotions, background feelings and powerful drives, romantic love holds a special place: close to the zenith, the pinnacle, the top. Romantic love can dominate the drive to eat and sleep. It can stifle fear, anger, or disgust. It can override one's sense of duty to family and friends. It can even triumph over the will to live.

Like a chord on a piano, the feeling of romantic passion harmonizes with myriad other feelings, drives, and thoughts to create different melodies in different keys. Moreover, each of us is wired somewhat differently. Some are predisposed to happiness; others to calm, anxiety, fear, or anger; some are insatiably curious; others wonderfully amusing. Scientists say that about 50 percent of our temperament is inherited; the rest is molded by our upbringing and environment. But we all share this wondrous—and devilish—thing called romantic love.

References

1. Fisher, H. 1999. *The First Sex: The Natural Talents of Women and How They Are Changing the World.* New York: Random House.

2. Hatfield, E., & R. Rapson. 1996. *Love and Sex: Cross-Cultural Perspectives.* Needham Heights, Mass.: Allyn and Bacon.

3. Jankowiak, W. 1995. Introduction. In *Romantic Passion: A Universal Experience?*, ed. W. Jankowiak. New York: Columbia University Press.

4. Karama, S., A. R. Lecours, J. M. Leroux, P. Bourgouin, G. Beaudoin, S. Joubert, and M. Beauregard. 2002. Areas of brain activation in males and females during viewing of erotic film excerpts. *Human Brain Mapping* 16(1):1–13.

5. Arnow, B. A., J. E. Desmond, L. L. Banner, G. H. Glover, A. Solomon, M. L. Polan, T. F. Lue, S. W. Atlas. 2002. Brain activation and sexual arousal in healthy, heterosexual males. *Brain* 125 (pt 5):1014–23.

6. Sherwin, B. B. 1994. Sex hormones and psychological functiong in post-menopausal women. *Experimental Gerontology* 29(3/4):423–30.

7. Van Goozen, S., V. M. Wiegant, E. Endert, F. A. Helmond, and N. E. Van de Poll. 1997. Psychoendocrinological assessment of the menstrual cycle: The relationship between hormones, sexuality, and mood. *Archives of Sexual Behavior* 26(4):359–82.

8. Edwards, J. N., and A. Booth. 1994. Sexuality, Marriage, and Well-Being: The Middle Years. In *Sexuality across the Life Course*, ed. A. S. Rossi. Chicago: University of Chicago Press.

9. Hållström, T., and S. Samuelsson. 1990. Changes in women's sexual desire in middle life: the longitudinal study of women in Gothenburg. *Archives of Sexual Behavior* 19(3):259–68.

10. Tavris, C., and S. Sadd. 1977. *The Redbook Report on Female Sexuality.* New York: Delacorte.

11. Meikle, A., J. Stringham, D. Bishop, and D. West. 1988. Quantitating genetic and nongenetic factors influencing androgen production and clearance rates in men. *Journal of Clinical Endocrinology Metabolism* 67: 104–9.

12. Nyborg, H. 1994. *Hormones, Sex and Society.* Westport, Conn.: Praeger.

13. Ellis, B. J., and D. Symons. 1990. Sex differences in sexual fantasy: An evolutionary psychological approach. *Journal of Sex Research* 27: 527–55.

14. Blum, D. 1997. *Sex on the Brain. The Biological Differences between Men and Women.* New York: Viking.

15. Reinisch, J. M, and R. Beasley. 1990. *The Kinsey Institute New Report on Sex.* New York: St. Martin's Press.

16. Laumann, E. O., J. H. Gagnon, R. T. Michael, and S. Michaels. 1994. *The Social Organization of Sexuality: Sexual Practices in the United States.* Chicago: University of Chicago Press.

17. Hull, E. M., J. Du, D. S. Lorrain, and L. Matuszewich. 1997. Testosterone, preoptic dopamine, and copulation in male rats. *Brain Research Bulletin* 44(4):327–33.

18. Liu, Y.-C., B. D. Sachs, and J. D. Salamone. 1998. Sexual behavior in male rats after radiofrequency or dopamine-depleting lesions in nucleus accumbens. *Pharmacology Biochemistry and Behavior* 60(1):585–92.

19. Ferrari, F., and D. Giuliani. 1995. Sexual attraction and copulation in male rats: Effects of the dopamine agonist SND 919. *Pharmacology, Biochemistry, and Behavior* 50(1):29–34.

20. Hull, E. M., J. Du, D. S. Lorrain, and L. Matuszewich. 1995. Extracellular dopamine in the medial preoptic area: Implications for sexual motivation and hormonal control of copulation. *Journal of Neuroscience* 15(11):7465–71.

21. Clayton, A. H., E. D. McGarvey, J. Warnock, et al. 2000. Bupropion as an antidote to SSRI-induced sexual dysfunction. Poster presented at the New Clinical Drug Evaluation Unit Program (NCDEU), Boca Raton, Fla.

22. Coleman, C. C., L. A. Cunningham, V. J. Foster, S. R. Batey, R. M. J. Donahue, T. L. Houser, and J. A. Ascher, 1999. Sexual dysfunction associated with the treatment of depression: a placebo-controlled comparison of bupropion sustained release and sertraline treatment. *Annals of Clinical Psychiatry* 11(4):205–15.

23. Mayerhofer, A., R. W. Steger, G. Gow, and A. Bartke. 1992. Catecholamines stimulate testicular testosterone release of the immature golden hamster via interaction with alpha- and beta-adrenergic receptors. *Acta Endocrinologia* 127(6):526–30.

24. Fabre-Nys, C. 1998. Steroid control of monoamines in relation to sexual behavior. *Reviews of Reproduction* 3(1):31–41.

25. Hopkins, A. 1994. *The Book of Courtly Love: The Passionate Code of the Troubadours.* San Franciso: HarperSanFranciso.

26. Sherwin, B. B., and M. M. Gelfand. 1987. The role of androgen in the maintenance of sexual functiong in oophorectomized women. *Psychosomatic Medicine* 49:397.

27. Yang, S. P., K. Y. F. Pau, D. L. Hess, and H. G. Spies. 1996. Sexual dimorphism in secretion of hypothalamic gonadotropin-releasing hormone and norepinephrine after coitus in rabbits. *Endocrinology* 137(7):2683–93.

28. Hull, E. M., D. S. Lorrain, J. Du, L. Matuszewich, L. A. Lumley, S. K. Putnam, and J. Moses. 1999. Hormone-neurotransmitter interactions in the control of sexual behavior. *Behavioural Brain Research* 105(1):105–16.

29. Jones, T. J., G. Dunphy, A. Milsted, and D. Ely. 1998. Testosterone effects on renal norepinephrine content and release in rats with different Y chromosomes. *Hypertension* 32(5): 880–885.

30. Netter, P., J. Hennig, B. Meier, and S. Rohrmann. 1998. Testosterone as an indicator of altered 5-HT responsivity in aggressive subjects. *European Psychiatry* 13(4):181s.

31. Hatfield, E. 1988. Passionate and companionate love. In *The Psychology of Love*, ed. R. J. Sternberg and M. L. Barnes. New Haven: Yale University Press.

32. Shostak, M. 1981. *Nisa: The Life and Words of a !Kung Woman*. Cambridge, Mass.: Harvard University Press.

33. McCullough, D. 2001. *John Adams*. New York: Simon and Schuster.

34. Bowlby, J. 1980. *Attachment and Loss: Loss* (vol. 3). New York: Basic Books.

35. Pitkow, L. J., C. A. Sharer, X. Ren, T. R. Insel, E. F. Terwilliger, and L. J. Young. 2001. Facilitation of affiliation and pair-bond formation by vasopressin receptor gene transfer into the ventral forebrain of a monogamous vole. *Journal of Neuroscience* 21(18): 7392–96.

36. Wang, Z. Z., C. F. Ferris, and G. J. De Vries. 1994. The role of septal vasopressin innervation in paternal behavior in prairie voles (*Microtus ochrogaster*). *Proceedings of the National Academy of Sciences (USA)* 91:400–404.

37. Carter, C. S., A. C. DeVries, and L. L. Getz. 1995. Physiological substrates of mammalian monogamy: the prairie vole model. *Neuroscience and Biobehavioral Reviews* 19(2):303–14.

38. Pederson, C. A., J. D. Caldwell, G. F. Jirikowsk, and T. R. Insel, eds. 1992. *Oxytocin in Maternal, Sexual and Social Behaviors*. New York: New York Academy of Sciences.

39. Young, L. J., Z. Wang, and T. R. Insel. 1998. Neuroendocrine bases of monogamy. *Trends in Neurosciences* 21(2):71–75.

40. Damasio, A. R. 1994. *Descartes' Error: Emotion, Reason, and the Human Brain*. New York: G. P. Putnam's Sons.

41. Thomas, A., N. B. Kim, and J. A. Amico. 1996. Differential regulation of oxytocin and vasopressin messenger ribonucleic acid levels by gonadal steroids in postpartum rats. *Brain Research* 738(1):48–52.

42. Delville, Y., and C. F. Ferris. 1995. Sexual differences in vasopressin receptor binding within the ventrolateral hypothalamus in golden hamsters. *Brain Research* 68(1):91–96.

43. Booth, A., and J. M. Dabbs. 1993. Testosterone and men's marriages. *Social Forces* 72(2):463–77.

44. Berg, S. J., and K. E. Wynne-Edwards. 2001. Changes in testosterone, cortisol, and estradiol levels in men becoming fathers. *Mayo Clinic Proceedings* 76(6):582–92.

45. De Ridder, E., R. Pinxten, and M. Eens. 2000. Experimental evidence of a testosterone-induced shift from paternal to mating behavior in a facultatively polygynous songbird. *Behavioral Ecology and Sociobiology* 49(1):24–30.

46. Wingfield, J. C. 1994. Hormone-behavior interactions and mating systems in male and female birds. In *The Differences Between the Sexes*, ed. R. V. Short and E. Balaban. New York: Cambridge University Press.

47. Galfi, M., T. Janaky, R. Toth, G. Prohaszka, A. Juhasz, C. Varga, and F. A. Laszlo. 2001. Effects of dopamine and dopamine-active compounds on oxytocin and vasopressin production in rat neurohypophyseal tissue cultures. *Regulatory Peptides* 98(1–2):49–54.

48. Van de Kar, L. D., A. D. Levy, Q. Li, and M. S. Brownfield. 1998. A comparison of the oxytocin and vasopressin responses to the 5-HT$_{1A}$ agonist and potential anxiolytic drug alnespirone (S-20499). *Pharmacology, Biochemistry, and Behavior* 60(3):677–83.

49. Reik, T. 1964. *The Need to Be Loved*. New York: Bantam.

CHAPTER 27

The Close Relationships of Lesbians and Gay Men

Letitia Anne Peplau
Adam W. Fingerhut

While much research on sexuality within relationships has focused on mixed-sex couples, such research on same-sex couples has been sparse. That is changing, reflecting not only theoretical interest but sheer numerical expediency. The number of same-sex couples increased by almost 30 percent between the 2000 Census and the 2005 American Community Survey, with the largest increase occurring in the Midwest (Gates 2006). Same-sex couples reside in every Congressional district of the United States, for an estimated total of nearly 777,000.

Regardless of whether same-sex couples are legally allowed to marry or not, they will still continue to form partnerships and families. As you will learn in this chapter, there are very few differences between same-sex and mixed sex couples. However, one of the greatest differences is that mixed-sex couples do not face the discrimination and lack of social support that is common for same-sex couples. Such prejudice is an extra burden to be borne by lesbian and gay partnerships.

From "The Close Relationships of Lesbians and Gay Men" by L. A. Peplau and A. W. Fingerhut. 2007. Annual *Review of Psychology* 58: 405–424. Copyright © 2007 by Annual Reviews (www.annualreviews.org). Reprinted with permission from the *Annual Review of Psychology*.

Before reading this chapter, think about the role that gender plays in mixed-sex relationships. What do you think happens when scripts are not assigned as a function of who is male and who is female? Review the gender differences that have been found in sexual behavior, and develop some hypotheses about what you would expect when two women or two men are in a relationship together. After finishing the article, you will know how many of your hypotheses were correct.

In the past half century, the close relationships of lesbians and gay men have moved from the shadows of society as a "love that dares not speak its name" to center stage in a national and international debate about same-sex marriage. The increasing visibility of same-sex couples has challenged researchers to provide scientific information that can illuminate the relationship experiences of lesbians and gay men. Research findings can also inform legal and policy questions that have been raised by ongoing efforts to achieve equal rights for same-sex couples.

This review focuses on the experiences of same-sex couples in the United States. We begin with up-to-date estimates about the number of same-sex couples. Next, we review the research literature on same-sex couples and identify major empirical findings. When possible, we compare the experiences of same-sex couples to those of heterosexual couples in order to indicate areas of commonality and of difference. It is noteworthy that research on same-sex couples began slowly in the 1970s, grew in the 1980s, and then diminished as researchers shifted their attention to the impact of the AIDS epidemic on the gay community. Much of the research we review was conducted 10 or 20 years ago.

In the past few years, however, research on same-sex couples has been revitalized and has shifted to a new set of topics. We highlight three recent research directions: the legalization of same-sex relationships through civil unions and same-sex marriage, the experiences of same-sex couples raising children, and the impact of societal prejudice and discrimination on same-sex partners. We conclude with general comments about the role of empirical research in four areas: debunking negative stereotypes about same-sex couples, testing the generalizability of theories about close relationships, informing our understanding of gender and close relationships, and providing a scientific basis for public policy.

COUNTING SAME-SEX COUPLES

Although same-sex couples have a clear and growing presence in American society, several factors make it difficult to provide an accurate estimate of the number of lesbians and gay men who are currently in a same-sex relationship. First, some lesbians and gay men are reluctant to reveal their sexual identity or the nature of their romantic attachments. Second, lacking the equivalent of legal heterosexual marriage and divorce, we have no public records of how many lesbians and gay men are currently in a serious relationship or have experienced the loss of a serious relationship through breakup or the death of a partner. Third, researchers have used differing and noncomparable questions to assess the relationship status of lesbians and gay

men, asking, for instance, if an individual is in a romantic/sexual relationship, has a steady partner, has been together with a partner for six months or more, or currently lives with a romantic partner.

Nonetheless, available evidence suggests that many gay men and lesbians are in couple relationships. Recently, the U.S. Census and other national surveys added the category "unmarried partner" to their household roster, making it possible to estimate the number of gay and lesbian adults who live together with a same-sex partner. According to the 2000 Census, there were approximately 600,000 same-sex couples living together in the United States, with roughly equal numbers of men and women (Gates & Ost 2004). Approximately 16% of same-sex couples included at least one Hispanic partner, and 14% included at least one black partner. One estimate is that about 28% of gay men and 44% of lesbians are currently living with a same-sex partner (Black et al. 2000). Although same-sex couples are more common in urban areas, they are located in all parts of the United States.

BASIC FINDINGS ABOUT SAME-SEX COUPLES

In the sections that follow, we review major findings from research on same-sex couples and offer suggestions about areas in need of further investigation. Prior to turning to these findings, it is useful to comment briefly on the sources of data that have been used in research on same-sex couples. Most studies have been conducted in the United States with individuals who self-identify as gay or lesbian, for instance by volunteering to participate in a study about gay and lesbian couples. Like many studies of heterosexual couples, studies of same-sex couples have typically recruited younger, well-educated, middle-class, white volunteers. Many studies have relied on questionnaires and have obtained reports from only one partner in a couple.

In addition to many small-scale studies, there have been a few major research programs focusing on same-sex couples. For example, in a project known as the American Couples Study, Blumstein & Schwartz (1983) obtained responses to lengthy questionnaires from both partners in 957 gay male, 772 lesbian, 653 heterosexual cohabiting, and 3656 heterosexual married couples. A subset of participants also completed an 18-month follow-up questionnaire. More recently, Kurdek conducted two longitudinal studies involving repeated assessments of both partners in same-sex couples and married heterosexual couples (Kurdek 1994a, 2004a). Our review encompasses both small-scale studies and larger programs of research.

Relationship Formation

Several studies have compared the qualities that lesbians, gay men, and heterosexuals seek in romantic partners (Peplau & Spalding 2000). Regardless of sexual orientation, most individuals value affection, dependability, shared interests, and similarity of religious beliefs. Men, regardless of sexual orientation, are more likely to emphasize a partner's physical attractiveness; women, regardless of sexual orientation, give greater emphasis to personality characteristics. Like their heterosexual counterparts, lesbians and gay men report that they often meet potential dates through friends, at work, at a bar, or at a social event (Bryant & Demian 1994). Urban areas with visible gay and lesbian communities provide expanded opportunities to meet potential partners. In addition, the Internet has rapidly become a way for gay men and lesbians to meet each other. There is some evidence that lesbians and gay men, like their heterosexual counterparts, rely on fairly conventional scripts when they go on dates with a new partner (Klinkenberg & Rose 1994).

For lesbians and gay men, the boundaries between friendship and romantic or sexual relationships may be particularly complex (Diamond & Dube 2002). Rose et al. (1993), for example, found that many lesbian romantic relationships began as a friendship, then developed into a love relationship, and later became sexual. Some women reported difficulties with this pattern of relationship development, such as problems in knowing if a relationship was shifting from friendship to romance and in gauging the friend's possible sexual interest. In addition, lesbians and gay men may be especially likely to remain friends with former sexual partners (Solomon et al. 2004). In a recent study (Harkless & Fowers 2005), lesbians and gay men were more likely than were heterosexuals to agree, "When a relationship is ending, one of my biggest fears is that I will lose the friendship" or that it is important "to remain friends with someone with whom I've had a serious relationship." Lesbians and gay men were also more likely than were heterosexuals to report continued phone calls and social contacts with ex-partners. The factors that encourage same-sex ex-partners to remain friends are not well understood but may include the small size of some gay and lesbian social networks, the norms of particular gay and lesbian communities, and the benefits that can accrue from transforming ties with ex-lovers into friendship (Nardi 1999, Weinstock 2004).

The Division of Household Labor and Power

Traditional heterosexual marriage is organized around two basic principles: a division of labor based on gender and a norm of greater male power and decision-making authority. Researchers have investigated how same-sex couples, who lack biological sex as a basis for assigning tasks and status, organize their lives together.

Turning first to the division of labor, it is important to emphasize that most gay men and lesbians are in dual-earner relationships, so neither partner is the exclusive breadwinner and each partner has some measure of economic independence. When it comes to housework, same-sex couples are likely to divide chores fairly equitably. Kurdek (1993) compared the division of housework (e.g., cleaning, cooking, and shopping) in cohabiting same-sex couples and married heterosexual couples, none of whom had children. In heterosexual couples, wives typically did most of the housework. In contrast, lesbian and gay couples divided the household tasks more equally (Kurdek 2006). Lesbian partners tended to share tasks; gay male partners were more likely to have each partner specialize in certain tasks. In a review of research on this topic, Kurdek (2005, p. 252) concluded that "although members of gay and lesbian couples do not divide household labor in a perfectly equal manner, they are more likely than members of heterosexual couples to negotiate a balance between achieving a fair distribution of household labor and accommodating the different interests, skills, and work schedules of particular partners."

Questionnaire studies may not capture the nuanced complexities of domestic work for cohabiting couples. An in-depth study of dual-earner heterosexual families (Hochschild & Machung 1989) showed that although most wives did the bulk of housework, many couples found ways to characterize their allocation of housework as balanced. Similarly, based on in-depth interviews and home observations, Carrington (1999) suggested that same-sex couples' reports of equal sharing of household activities may reflect their ideals but often mask substantial observable differences between partners' actual contributions. He found that equal sharing of domestic activities was far from universal: It was most common among affluent couples who relied on paid help, and when both partners had less demanding jobs with more flexible schedules.

When researchers assess power in close relationships, they typically try to characterize the overall pattern of dominance to determine whether one partner is more influential than the other is. The lesbians and gay men who participate in psychological research tend to be advocates of power equality in their relationships. In an early study, 92% of gay men and 97% of lesbians defined the ideal balance of power as one in which both partners were "exactly equal" (Peplau & Cochran 1980). In a more recent study, partners in gay and lesbian couples rated power equality as important in an ideal relationship, although lesbians scored significantly higher on the value of equality than did gay men (Kurdek 1995a). This strong endorsement of power sharing may reflect, in some measure, the tendency for researchers to recruit participants who are well educated and generally liberal in their attitudes.

Not all couples who strive for power equality achieve this ideal. Reports of the actual balance of power vary from study to study. When Peplau & Cochran (1980) asked lesbians and gay men "who has more say" in your relationship, only 38% of gay men and 59% of lesbians characterized their current relationship as "exactly equal." Equal power was reported by 59% of the lesbians studied by Reilly & Lynch (1990) and by 60% of the gay men studied by Harry & DeVall (1978).

Social exchange theory predicts that greater power accrues to the partner who has relatively greater personal resources, such as education, money, or social standing. Studies of gay men have supported this hypothesis. Harry found that gay men who were older and wealthier than their partner was tended to have more power (Harry 1984). Blumstein & Schwartz (1983, p. 59) concluded that "in gay male couples, income is an extremely important force in determining which partner will be dominant." For lesbians, research results are less clear-cut, with some studies finding that income is significantly related to power (Caldwell & Peplau 1984, Reilly & Lynch 1990) and others not (Blumstein & Schwartz 1983). Dunne (1997, p. 180) concluded that "lesbian women are comfortable neither with dominating nor with being dominated in their partnerships." Further research on the balance of power is needed to clarify these inconsistent results and to broaden our knowledge about correlates of power imbalances.

Love and Satisfaction

Stereotypes depict gay and lesbian relationships as unhappy and dysfunctional, especially in comparison with heterosexual relationships (Crawford & Solliday 1996, Testa et al. 1987). In fact, empirical research finds striking similarities in the reports of love and satisfaction among contemporary lesbian, gay, and heterosexual couples. Peplau & Cochran (1980) found no significant differences in scores on standardized Love and Liking scales among matched samples of lesbians, gay men, and heterosexuals who were all currently in a romantic/sexual relationship. In a longitudinal study of married heterosexual and cohabiting homosexual couples, Kurdek (1998) found similar results. Controlling for age, education, income, and years cohabiting, the couples did not differ in relationship satisfaction at initial testing. Over the five years of his study, all types of couples tended to decrease in relationship satisfaction, but no differences were found among gay, lesbian, or heterosexual couples in the rate of change in satisfaction. A survey of African American lesbians and gay men in committed relationships (Peplau et al., 1997) also found high levels of relationship satisfaction and closeness. Further, the partner's race was unrelated to relationship satisfaction: Interracial couples were no more or less satisfied, on average, than same-race couples.

Researchers have begun to identify factors that enhance or detract from satisfaction in same-sex relationships. Like their heterosexual counterparts, gay and lesbian couples generally benefit when partners are similar in background, attitudes, and values (Kurdek & Schmitt 1987). Additionally, consistent with social exchange theory, happiness tends to be high when partners perceive many rewards and few costs from their relationship (Beals et al. 2002). A study of lesbian relationships found support for another exchange theory prediction, that satisfaction is higher when partners are equally involved in or committed to a relationship (Peplau et al. 1982). For lesbian couples, greater satisfaction has also been linked to perceptions of greater equity or fairness in the relationship (Schreurs & Buunk 1996). Finally, several studies of lesbians and gay men have found that satisfaction is higher when partners believe they are relatively equal in power and decision-making (Peplau & Spalding 2000).

Sexuality

Sexuality has been a popular topic of investigation in studies of gay and lesbian couples. A comprehensive review of this literature is provided by Peplau et al. (2004). Research on the frequency of sex in relationships has identified several consistent patterns. Among same-sex and heterosexual couples, there is wide variability in sexual frequency and a general decline in frequency as relationships continue over time. In the early stages of a relationship, gay male couples have sex more often than do other couples. Further, research consistently finds that lesbian couples report having sex less often than either heterosexual or gay male couples.

Considerable attention has been given to the low frequency of sex reported by lesbians, in part because this pattern may reflect broader issues about female sexuality (Peplau & Garnets 2000). One suggestion is that gender socialization leads women to repress and ignore sexual feelings, and this effect is magnified in a relationship with two female partners. Another view is that women have difficulty taking the lead to initiate sexual activities with a partner, resulting in low levels of sexual activity. A third possibility is that men are generally more interested in sex than are women, leading to higher levels of sexual activity in couples that include a male partner. A fourth possibility is that traditional conceptions of sexuality, which equate "sex" with penile penetration, may not adequately capture lesbian women's sexual experiences. Finally, there may be methodological problems with the ways researchers have asked questions about women's sexuality (Rothblum 2000).

In addition to studying sexual frequency, researchers have also investigated sexual satisfaction in gay and lesbian couples. High levels of sexual satisfaction have been reported in studies of students and young adults (Peplau & Cochran 1981, Peplau et al. 1978), predominantly white adult samples (Blumstein & Schwartz 1983, Kurdek 1991), and samples of African American lesbians and gay men (Peplau et al. 1997). Not surprisingly, sexual satisfaction and sexual frequency are linked. Sexual satisfaction is also associated with global measures of relationship satisfaction in gay and lesbian as well as heterosexual couples (Bryant & Demian 1994).

Research has documented differences between gay, lesbian, and heterosexual couples concerning the issue of sexual exclusiveness versus openness. First, there are differences in attitudes about monogamy (Bailey et al. 1994). In the American Couples Study, only 36% of gay men indicated that it was important to be sexually monogamous, compared with 71% of lesbians, 84% of heterosexual wives, and 75% of husbands. Second, there are major differences in reports of actual behavior (Bryant & Demian 1994). In the American Couples Study, only a minority of lesbians (28%), wives (21%), and husbands (26%) reported having engaged in extradyadic sex, compared with 82% of gay men. Third, among those individuals who had engaged in extradyadic sex, gay men reported having a greater number of sex partners. Finally, Kurdek (1991) found that sexual fidelity was positively related to relationship satisfaction for lesbian and heterosexual couples, but not for gay male couples. This may reflect the norms of the gay male community and the fact that some male couples have agreements that extradyadic sex is acceptable (Hickson et al. 1992).

We know little about possible changes in sexual attitudes and behavior that may have occurred among lesbians and gay men in recent years, both in response to the AIDS epidemic and the greater attention being given to same-sex marriage. Rutter & Schwartz (1996) suggested that from the 1970s to the 1990s gay men's attitudes shifted toward greater endorsement of monogamy but their actual sexual behavior did not undergo a corresponding change.

CONFLICT AND PARTNER VIOLENCE

Few couples avoid occasional disagreements and conflicts. Lesbian, gay male, and heterosexual couples report a similar frequency of arguments and tend to disagree about similar topics, with finances, affection, sex, criticism, and household tasks heading the list (Kurdek 2005, 2006; Metz et al. 1994). How well do lesbians and gay men solve problems that arise in their relationships? Available research indicates that their problem-solving skills are at least as good as are those of heterosexual couples. In a study of homosexual and heterosexual couples, Kurdek (1998) found no differences in the frequency of using positive problem-solving styles such as negotiating or compromising. Nor were differences found in the use of poor strategies, such as launching personal attacks or refusing to talk to the partner. A study that observed couples discussing relationship conflicts in a laboratory setting found that gay and lesbian partners used somewhat more positive communication styles than did heterosexual couples (Gottman et al. 2003). Finally, as with heterosexual couples, happy lesbian and gay male couples are more likely than are unhappy couples to use constructive problem-solving approaches (Kurdek 2004).

Recently, researchers have begun to document the existence and nature of violence in same-sex relationships (Potoczniak et al. 2003). It is impossible to estimate accurately the frequency of same-sex domestic violence, not only because of underreporting to the police but also because research studies have been based on small, unrepresentative samples. Interviews with abused gay and lesbian individuals (Renzetti & Miley 1996) have documented a cycle of escalating abuse in some same-sex couples. This pattern, in which one partner uses violence and threats of violence to intimidate and control the other, bears many similarities to violence in heterosexual couples that Johnson (2006) has characterized as "intimate terrorism." We know less about other types of violence in same-sex relationships, including violent resistance to abuse by a partner and situational violence that occurs when a verbal conflict turns physical. We also lack information about the correlates of domestic violence among same-sex couples. In male-female couples, traditional attitudes about gender roles, differences in physical size and strength, and differences in financial resources can all contribute to patterns of abuse. How do these factors affect same-sex couples? In addition, are there other factors unique to lesbians and gay men that contribute to violence, including experiences of discrimination or the stress of belonging to a sexual minority group (Balsam & Szymanski 2005)?

COMMITMENT AND RELATIONSHIP STABILITY

Three general factors contribute to partners' psychological commitment to each other and to the longevity of their relationship; all three appear to be relevant to same-sex couples (Peplau & Spalding 2000). Of obvious importance are positive attraction forces, such as love and satisfaction, that make partners want to stay together. A second factor is the availability of alternatives to the current relationship, most often a more desirable partner. Partners who perceive few alternatives are less likely to leave a relationship. Finally, barriers that make it difficult for a person to leave a relationship also matter (Kurdek, 2000). Barriers include investments that increase the psychological, emotional, or financial costs of ending a relationship, as well as moral or religious feelings of obligation or duty to one's partner. A model including all three predictors of commitment was tested by Beals et al. (2002) using data on lesbian couples from the American

Couples Study. Their analyses found that relationship satisfaction, the quality of alternatives, and investments each predicted psychological commitment, which in turn predicted relationship stability.

There is evidence that married heterosexual couples perceive more barriers than do gay, lesbian, or cohabiting heterosexual couples (Kurdek 1998). A relative lack of barriers may make it less likely that lesbians and gay men will be trapped in miserable and deteriorating relationships. On the other hand, weaker barriers may also allow partners to end relationships that might have improved if given more time and effort. In a longitudinal study, Kurdek (1998) found that barriers to leaving the relationship were a significant predictor of relationship stability over a five-year period. Today, as lesbians and gay men gain greater legal recognition for their relationships, the barriers to ending same-sex relationships may become more similar to those of heterosexuals. The impact of such trends on the stability of same-sex relationships is an important topic for future investigations.

Given the weaker barriers to ending same-sex relationships, we might anticipate that there would be fewer long-term relationships among lesbians and gay men compared with heterosexuals. Unfortunately, we currently know little about the longevity of same-sex relationships. No information comparable to divorce statistics for heterosexual marriages is available. Several studies have documented the existence of very-long lasting gay and lesbian relationships (Johnson 1990, McWhirter & Mattison 1984). Longitudinal studies provide further clues about relationship stability. In a five-year prospective study, Kurdek (1998) reported a breakup rate of 7% for married heterosexual couples, 14% for cohabiting gay male couples, and 16% for cohabiting lesbian couples. Controlling for demographic variables, cohabiting gay and lesbian couples were significantly more likely than were married heterosexuals to break up (see also Kurdek 2004).

RECENT RESEARCH DIRECTIONS

The twenty-first century has seen renewed interest in research on same-sex couples, spurred by the increasing visibility of lesbians and gay men and by public policy debates about same-sex marriage and gay adoption. A shift has also occurred from viewing same-sex couples through the lens of abnormality and dysfunction toward viewing lesbians and gay men as members of a sexual minority group dealing with social stigma and discrimination.

Legalizing Same-Sex Relationships: Marriage, Civil Unions, and Domestic Partnerships

For heterosexual couples, marriage represents both a public sign of commitment and a legal status affecting many aspects of life. The General Accounting Office (2004) has estimated that marriage affects 1138 federal rights, including taxes, Social Security, and veterans' benefits. Not surprisingly, lesbians and gay men have actively sought to make legal recognition of their relationships a reality. In a national survey (Kaiser Family Foundation 2001), 74% of lesbians and gay men said that if they could legally marry someone of the same sex, they would like to do so someday. In recent decades, advances have been made in achieving formal recognition for same-sex relationships. Within gay and lesbian communities, same-sex couples are holding commitment ceremonies to celebrate their relationships, and some religious groups now perform same-sex wedding ceremonies. Additionally, increasing numbers of employers provide domestic partner benefits to same-sex partners. Despite this progress, the substantial social and legal benefits and protections accorded to legally married couples by state and federal laws are still beyond the reach of most same-sex partners in the United States.

Efforts to legalize same-sex relationships have met with considerable opposition. Reflecting public sentiment, President Clinton signed the Defense of Marriage Act in 1996, clarifying that for the federal government, marriage is defined as "a legal union of one man and one woman as husband and wife" and that spouse should be defined only as "a person of the opposite sex who is a husband or a wife." A majority of state governments have also taken steps to restrict marriage to heterosexual couples (Human Rights Campaign 2006). Recent national poll data indicate that a 53% majority of Americans oppose allowing gay men and lesbians to marry legally, with only 36% in favor of same-sex marriage and 11% uncertain (The Pew Forum on Religion and Public Life 2005). For many Americans, opposition to same-sex marriage is strongly correlated with the belief that homosexuality is immoral (Lewis 2006). Despite opposition to same-sex marriage, an increasing percentage of Americans endorses extending legal rights and protections to lesbians and gay men. In national surveys (Kaiser Family Foundation 2001), more than two-thirds of Americans support providing inheritance rights, health insurance, and social security benefits to same-sex domestic partners. For the first time in 2005, a 53% majority of those polled favored permitting lesbians and gay men to enter into civil unions that would give them many of the same rights as married couples (The Pew Forum on Religion and Public Life 2005). Public attitudes and governmental policies differ from state to state. Currently, only Massachusetts offers legal marriage to same-sex couples, and six other states recognize some form of same-sex civil union.

In addition to information about heterosexuals' attitudes toward same-sex marriage, researchers have also gathered information about the attitudes of gay men and lesbians. Lannutti (2005) used an open-ended Web-based survey to examine the attitudes of 288 lesbians and gay men toward same-sex marriage. Her findings revealed complex and nuanced views. Virtually all participants emphasized fairness and equal rights: Legal marriage would be a sign that lesbians and gay men had achieved first-class citizenship. Many positive aspects of same-sex marriage were noted. Marriage would help couples feel closer and strengthen their relationships, in part by creating structural barriers to relationship dissolution. Respondents also suggested that marriage would reduce the stress that same-sex couples experience, by increasing legal rights and benefits, reducing societal prejudice, and diminishing internalized homophobia among lesbians and gay men. At the same time, respondents expressed concerns that the availability of legal unions might put pressure on individuals to get married "for the wrong reasons" or might create status hierarchies within the gay/lesbian community that could stigmatize those who choose not to marry. Another concern was that legalizing same-sex marriage might lead to assimilation into mainstream heterosexual norms and values that would change and harm unique features of the gay/lesbian community.

Currently, we have very little information about American couples who seek civil unions or same-sex marriage. Solomon, Rothblum and colleagues (Solomon et al. 2004, Todosijevic et al. 2005) studied the first cohort of couples to obtain civil unions in Vermont. For comparison purposes, the researchers asked gay and lesbian respondents to nominate a married heterosexual sibling and the sibling's spouse as well as a gay or lesbian couple from their friendship circle who were not in a civil union. Results from this research replicated many findings from previous studies concerning sexuality, conflict, and the division of housework and childcare among same-sex couples. Few differences were found among same-sex couples based on their civil union status.

As time goes by, researchers will be able to investigate the impact of civil unions and same-sex marriage on gay and lesbian couples more thoroughly. An important goal will be to identify factors that distinguish same-sex couples who seek legal recognition from those who do not, including their motives and the extent to which couples emphasize the symbolic and psychological meaning of legal recognition or the financial and legal benefits that

recognition may confer. A further question concerns the impact of legal recognition itself on the nature and longevity of same-sex relationships. Will legalization increase the stability of same-sex relationships? Data from Norway and Sweden, where registered same-sex partnerships have been available since the 1990s, indicate that the rate of dissolution within five years of entering a legal union is higher among same-sex partnerships than among heterosexual marriages, with lesbian couples having the highest rates of dissolution (Andersson et al. 2006). Unfortunately, the Scandinavian data do not permit comparisons with the longevity of same-sex couples who did not seek legal recognition. Many other questions remain unanswered (Patterson 2004a). For example, do the social and economic benefits of legal recognition affect relationship functioning and satisfaction? Does legal recognition change the way in which couples or their family and friends think about their relationship? Does legalization lead to better physical and mental health for gay and lesbian people (Herdt & Kertzner 2006, King & Bartlett 2006)? Finally, does the form of legal recognition—marriage, civil union, domestic partnership—make a difference?

Same-Sex Couples with Children

Based on data from the 2000 U.S. Census (Gates & Ost 2004), it has been estimated that among adults aged 22–55, 34% of lesbian couples who live together and 22% of gay male couples who live together are raising children. Consequently, approximately 250,000 children under the age of 18 are being raised by same-sex couples. Although the experiences of these children are beyond the scope of our review, it is important to note that research has documented that they are comparable to children of heterosexual parents on measures of psychological well-being, self-esteem, cognitive abilities, and peer relations (Fulcher et al. 2006, Tasker 2005).

Gay- and lesbian-headed families are created in a variety of ways (Patterson 1995a). Some lesbians and gay men, perhaps the majority at present, had children in a previous heterosexual relationship. Growing numbers of lesbians and gay men are choosing to have children within the context of a same-sex relationship. In a national poll, 49% of gay men and lesbians who were not parents said they would like to have or adopt children of their own (Kaiser Family Foundation 2001). Given the obstacles to parenthood faced by self-identified gay men and lesbians, there is a high likelihood that their children are strongly desired and planned.

Several paths to parenthood are available to same-sex couples, each affecting the biological relatedness of the child to the parents. Some couples adopt, in which case neither parent is biologically related to the child. Some gay male couples turn to surrogacy, so that the partner who provides the sperm is biologically related to the child. Some lesbian couples use donor insemination, so that the lesbian who carries the child is biologically related to the child. Other lesbian couples use in vitro fertilization so that one woman contributes the egg and the other woman is the birth mother. There are also differences in the legal relations between parents and children. Some states permit two same-sex partners to be the legal parents of a child, whereas many others do not. In states that do not allow second-parent adoption by a same-sex partner, only one partner in the couple is a legal parent. It is likely that the family experiences of lesbians and gay men differ, depending on how they become parents and the nature of their biological and legal relationship to their children.

Although census data provide basic information about same-sex couples with children, small-scale studies provide richer details about the experiences of these couples. Several studies have investigated relationship satisfaction among lesbian couples with children (Patterson 1995a). There is some evidence that relationship satisfaction may decline shortly after the birth of a child, as is generally true for heterosexual couples. A recent longitudinal study followed lesbian couples from one month before the birth of

a child to three months after the birth (Goldberg & Sayer 2006). All couples used donor insemination. For both the biological and nonbiological mother, love for the partner typically declined and conflict increased with the transition to parenthood. Patterns of change were affected by the women's neuroticism, expectations about social support from family, and features of the partners' interaction. Other studies have compared lesbian parenting couples with other couples. In an illustrative study, Flaks et al. (1995) compared 15 lesbian couples to 15 heterosexual couples, all with children between the ages of three and nine who were conceived through donor insemination. No significant differences were found between the lesbian and heterosexual couples on the Dyadic Adjustment Scale, a standard measure of relationship quality.

Does the egalitarian division of household labor typically found among gay and lesbian couples without children hold for those with children? Although limited, available research indicates that parenthood does not change the general pattern of shared household responsibilities for same-sex couples (Parks 1998). This is particularly true for the allocation of household chores and decision-making (Patterson et al. 2004). The division of childcare responsibilities, on the other hand, is less clear-cut.

Research consistently demonstrates that lesbian couples with children endorse an egalitarian division of childcare as their ideal (Chan et al. 1998, Patterson et al. 2004). This is in contrast to heterosexual couples, who tend to endorse a nonegalitarian division, with the wife ideally doing more childcare than the husband does. Research on the actual division of childcare among lesbian mothers is less consistent. Some studies have reported that lesbian partners share equally in childcare (Hand 1991, Patterson et al. 2004), but others have reported that lesbian couples adopt a less-than-egalitarian division of childcare (Ciano-Boyce & Shelley-Sireci 2002, Patterson 1995b). The reasons for these differences are not understood. They may result from the use of relatively small samples. It seems likely, however, that other factors are also at play. In particular, the biological and legal relationship of each parent to the children may make a difference. It may be, for example, that biological mothers tend to be more involved in childcare than are nonbiological mothers. Research systematically examining these issues is needed.

Currently, research on same-sex couples with children is quite limited. Research on gay fathers is rare (Patterson 2004b). Studies of ethnic minority families and low-income families are also needed. Further, it would be useful for researchers to go beyond studying relationship satisfaction and the division of labor to address a broader set of issues in the lives of same-sex couples raising children and to go beyond description toward specifying underlying mechanisms affecting couples' functioning. Longitudinal approaches to studying same-sex couples as they transition into parenthood may prove especially useful.

Societal Stigma: Stress and Social Support

The stigma of homosexuality affects lesbians, gay men, and their relationships in many ways. Personal experiences of rejection and discrimination are common. In a national survey (Kaiser Family Foundation 2001), 74% of lesbians and gay men reported experiencing discrimination based on sexual orientation, with 23% reporting that discrimination occurred "a lot." Additionally, 34% reported that their family or a family member had refused to accept them because of their sexual orientation. Discrimination often comes in the form of minor daily hassles, such as derogatory remarks or poor service. Swim (2004) utilized daily experience accounts to assess gay and lesbian people's experience with these everyday hassles. Over a one-week period, participants reported experiencing an average of two hassles related to their sexual orientation. Two-thirds of these hassles were verbal, including jokes, comments based on stereotypes, hostile or threatening comments, and comments expressing general dislike of gay

men and lesbians. In an experimental study, Jones (1996) demonstrated that same-sex couples requesting a hotel room with a shared bed were denied a room significantly more often than were other-sex couples making an identical request. Lewis et al. (2001) identified several types of gay-related stressors that are specific to lesbians and gay men. One type concerned family reactions and included rejection, lack of support, or ignoring the person's sexual orientation. Other gay-related stressors involved the need to hide one's sexual orientation, fear of being exposed as homosexual, violence and harassment, lack of societal acceptance, and discrimination.

Gay and lesbian couples are also vulnerable to hate crimes based on their sexual orientation. In 2002, a lesbian couple and their infant son barely escaped with their lives when arsonists set their home on fire, only days after the women had sued the University of Montana for failing to provide domestic partner benefits. In 1999, two brothers claiming to be carrying out God's will brutally murdered long-term gay partners Gary Matson, 50, and Winfield Mowder, 40, while they slept in their home. In a national survey, 32% of lesbian and gay respondents reported having been the target of physical violence against them or their property because of their sexual orientation (Kaiser Family Foundation 2001).

Researchers have consistently shown that lesbians and gay men who experience greater levels of discrimination are at greater risk for poor psychological adjustment and stress-related psychological disorders (Mays & Cochran 2001; Meyer 2003). Indeed, researchers are now testing the applicability of models of minority stress, first developed with regard to ethnic minorities, to the experiences of lesbian and gay individuals (Meyer 2003). Unfortunately, we currently have little information about how social stigma and discrimination affect same-sex couples. Research with heterosexual married couples has clearly demonstrated that high levels of stress from sources outside a relationship (e.g., financial difficulties, lack of social support) are associated with lower marital satisfaction and declines in satisfaction over time (Karney & Bradbury 2005). Further, during times of high stress, married couples report experiencing more marital problems.

It is reasonable to assume that discrimination based on sexual orientation places strains on gay and lesbian couples (Otis et al. 2006). A study of same-sex couples in civil unions (Todosijevic et al. 2005) found a significant association between reports of more gay-specific stressors and lower relationship satisfaction for lesbian couples but not for gay male couples. The effects of gay-related stress on couple functioning may be direct, for example, through limited access to important resources such as jobs and housing, or rejection of the couple or their children by family, neighbors, or peers at work or school. Discrimination may also affect couples indirectly, by diminishing the self-esteem or mental health of the partners or their ability to function effectively in a relationship. Research to determine the ways in which discrimination affects same-sex couples is needed.

Equally important will be studies of the resilience of same-sex couples in the face of prejudice and discrimination. Central to understanding how couples cope with discrimination will be analyses of social support. Research consistently shows that, compared with heterosexuals, lesbians and gay men perceive less social support from their family of origin (Elizur & Mintzer 2003; Kurdek 2006). Of course, these average differences can be misleading. Some gay men and lesbians have strong and supportive family ties that are undoubtedly a valuable source of aid and comfort in times of need. At the other extreme, some lesbians and gay men have negative relations with their families, ranging from grudging acceptance to outright rejection of them and/or their partner. There is evidence that greater social support from relatives is associated not only with greater personal well-being but also with greater relationship satisfaction in same-sex couples (Kurdek 1995b). In addition, there may be distinctive

types of social support that are of special relevance to lesbians and gay men. Preliminary evidence that support for a woman's lesbian identity may be particularly important to psychological wellbeing comes from a two-week-long daily experience study of lesbians (Beals & Peplau 2005).

A further consistent finding is that lesbians and gay men may compensate for lower levels of family support by establishing closer ties with friends. Some lesbians and gay men create "families of choice," that is, a network of friends who provide love and support, celebrate holidays and rituals, share leisure activities, and offer assistance in time of need (Carrington 1999). Oswald (2002) referred to the creation of these families as "choosing kin" and noted commonalities between these flexible family networks and the fictive kinship patterns seen in African American and Latino communities. Studies of the impact of supportive friends on the well-being of same-sex couples would be valuable (Elizur & Mintzer 2003).

Social relations can be a mixed blessing (Rook 1998). On the one hand, supportive relationships are a source of aid and comfort in times of stress. On the other hand, social relations can be powerful sources of conflict, hostility, and disappointment that create stress. Further research on sources of stress and support for same-sex couples is needed, along with explicit analyses of how models of minority stress may apply to same-sex couples.

In this section, we have reviewed three relatively new topics of research about same-sex couples: legal recognition of same-sex relationships, same-sex partners as parents, and the impact of gay-related stress on gay and lesbian couples. An important direction for future research will be to use better and more varied research methodologies. The recent availability of information about same-sex couples gathered from large, representative samples including the U.S. Census and other major surveys has been a major advance. Survey research can fruitfully be augmented with daily experience methods, longitudinal assessments, behavioral observations in controlled settings, and experimental designs. In-depth interviews, participant observations, and ethnographies can provide rich descriptions of the daily lives of same-sex couples within a specific cultural, historical, and social context. Studies specifically focusing on couples from diverse ethnic and social class backgrounds would fill an important gap in existing knowledge.

Concluding Comments

The growing body of research on same-sex couples has contributed to our understanding of close relationships in several important ways. One contribution has been to challenge the accuracy of negative social stereotypes about gay and lesbian relationships and to provide more reliable information (Peplau 1991). For decades, the media have depicted homosexuals as unhappy individuals who are unsuccessful in developing stable romantic ties and so end up frustrated and lonely. Both the women lovers in Radclyffe Hall's popular 1928 novel, *The Well of Loneliness* (Hall 1928), and the male lovers in the award-winning film, *Brokeback Mountain*, reflected this theme. Contrary to these media images, research has documented that many contemporary lesbians and gay men establish enduring intimate relationships. Research has also debunked a second stereotype, that gay and lesbian relationships are dysfunctional or inferior in quality to those of heterosexuals. Instead, studies have shown that on standardized measures of love, satisfaction, and relationship adjustment, same-sex and heterosexual couples are remarkably similar. This is not to say that all same-sex relationships are happy and problem-free, but rather that gay and lesbian couples are not necessarily more prone to relationship difficulties than are heterosexuals. A third stereotype, that same-sex relationships universally mimic heterosexual marriages by creating "husband" and "wife" roles, has also

been discredited. Historical and anthropological accounts have documented that masculine-feminine distinctions have sometimes been important in structuring same-sex relations, and this may continue to be true among some Americans today (Murray 2000, Peplau 2001). However, most contemporary gay and lesbian couples in the United States share homemaking tasks and financial provider responsibilities, rather than dividing them such that one partner is the "husband" and the other partner is the "wife" (Kurdek 2005).

A second contribution of research on gay and lesbian relationships has been to test the generalizability of relationship concepts and theories that were based, implicitly or explicitly, on heterosexual couples. We reviewed research showing the applicability of social exchange models of commitment and stability to same-sex couples. Although same-sex couples may differ from heterosexual couples in their mean level of exchange variables, such as barriers to dissolution, the hypothesized associations among key constructs have been strongly supported. This research provides evidence for the general usefulness of exchange models. It also suggests that researchers studying gay and lesbian relationships can build on the existing theoretical literature about close relationships, rather than having to start anew. We agree with Kurdek (2005, p. 253), who observed that "despite external differences in how gay, lesbian and heterosexual couples are constituted, the relationships of gay and lesbian partners appear to work in much the same way as the relationships of heterosexual partners." A promising new direction is provided by studies applying ideas from adult attachment theory to same-sex couples (Elizur & Mintzer 2003, Kurdek 2002).

A third contribution of research on same-sex relationships has been to provide a new way to investigate how gender affects close relationships. For example, by comparing how women behave with male versus female partners, we can begin to disentangle the effects on social interaction of an individual's own sex and the sex of their partner. This comparative research strategy is obviously not identical to an experiment, but can nonetheless be informative. Research on social influence in close relationships is illustrative. Studies of heterosexuals have shown that men and women tend to use somewhat different tactics when trying to influence an intimate partner, but could not clarify if these differences were due to the sex of the influence agent, the sex of the target, or some other factor such as relative power in the relationship. Studies including gay, lesbian, and heterosexual couples (Falbo & Peplau 1980, Howard et al. 1986) have demonstrated that regardless of gender or sexual orientation, partners with relatively less power in a relationship tend to use "weak strategies" such as withdrawal or supplication. In contrast, partners with relatively more power tend to use "strong strategies" including bargaining or bullying.

A fourth contribution of empirical research on same-sex relationships has been to provide a scientific basis for policy and legal decisions. Activities of the American Psychological Association (APA) are illustrative. In July 2004, the APA Council of Representatives issued a resolution on sexual orientation and marriage. It stated, "APA believes that it is unfair and discriminatory to deny same-sex couples legal access to civil marriage and to all its attendant benefits, rights and privileges." The resolution explicitly referred to research on same-sex couples and concluded that research provides no evidence to justify discrimination against same-sex couples. The APA has also submitted research-based legal briefs *amicus curiae* for court cases challenging state marriage laws in Nebraska, New Jersey, New York, Oregon, and Washington (Herek 2006).

As this review suggests, research on same-sex couples has been reinvigorated by the continuing public debate about same-sex marriage, by the availability of improved research methods, and by general theoretical advances in the field of close relationships.

INTRODUCTION REFERENCE

Gates, G. G. 2006, October, *Same-sex couples and the gay, lesbian, bisexual population: New estimates from the American Community Survey.* Los Angeles: The Williams Institute on Sexual Orientation Law and Public Policy, UCLA School of Law. http://www.law.ucla.edu/williamsinstitute/publications/SameSexCouplesandGLBpopACS.pdf.

LITERATURE CITED

Am. Psychol. Assoc. 2004. Resolution on sexual orientation and marriage. http://www. apa.org/pi/lgbc/policy/marriage.pdf.

Andersson GT, Noack T, Seierstad A, Weedon-Fekjaer H. 2006. The demographics of same-sex marriages in Norway and Sweden. *Demography* 43:79–98.

Bailey JM, Gaulin S, Agyei Y, Gladue BA. 1994. Effects of gender and sexual orientation on evolutionarily relevant aspects of human mating psychology. *J. Personal. Soc. Psychol.* 66:1081–93.

Balsam KF, Szymanski DM. 2005. Relationship quality and domestic violence in women's same-sex relationships: the role of minority stress. *Psychol. Women Q.* 29:258–69.

Beals KP, Impett EA, Peplau LA. 2002. Lesbians in love: why some relationships endure and others end. *J. Lesbian Stud.* 6:53–63.

Beals KP, Peplau LA. 2005. Identity support, identity devaluation, and well-being among lesbians. *Psychol. Women Q.* 29:140–48.

Black D, Gates G, Sanders S, Taylor L. 2000. Demographics of the gay and lesbian population in the United States. *Demography* 37:139–54.

Blumstein P, Schwartz P. 1983. *American Couples.* New York: Morrow. 656 pp.

Bryant AS, Demian. 1994. Relationship characteristics of American gay and lesbian couples: findings from a national survey. In *Social Services for Gay and Lesbian Couples,* ed. LA Kurdek, pp. 101–17. New York: Haworth.

Caldwell MA, Peplau LA. 1984. The balance of power in lesbian relationships. *Sex Roles* 10:587–600.

Carrington C. 1999. *No Place Like Home: Relationships and Family Life Among Lesbians and Gay Men.* Chicago: Univ. Chicago Press. 273 pp.

Chan RW, Brooks RC, Raboy B, Patterson CJ. 1998. Division of labor among lesbian and heterosexual parents: associations with children's adjustment. *J. Fam. Psychol.* 12:402–19.

Ciano-Boyce C, Shelley-Sireci L. 2002. Who is mommy tonight? Lesbian parenting issues. *J. Homosex.* 43:1–13.

Crawford I, Solliday E. 1996. The attitudes of undergraduate college students toward gay parenting. *J. Homosex.* 30:63–77.

Diamond LM, Dube EM. 2002. Friendship and attachment among heterosexual and sexual-minority youths. *J. Youth Adolesc.* 31:155–66.

Dunne GA. 1997. *Lesbian Lifestyles: Women's Work and the Politics of Sexuality.* Toronto: Univ. Toronto Press. 258 pp.

Elizur Y, Mintzer A. 2003. Gay males intimate relationship quality: the roles of attachment security, gay identity, social support, and income. *Pers. Relat.* 10:411–36.

Falbo T, Peplau LA. 1980. Power strategies in intimate relationships. *J. Personal. Soc. Psychol.* 38:618–28.

Flaks DK, Ficher I, Masterpasqua F, Joseph G.1995. Lesbians choosing motherhood: a comparative study of lesbian and heterosexual parents and their children. *Dev. Psychol.* 31:105–14.

Fulcher M, Sutfin EL, Chan RW, Scheib JE, Patterson CJ. 2006. Lesbian mothers and their children. In *Sexual Orientation and Mental Health: Examining Identity and Development in Lesbian, Gay, and Bisexual People*, ed. AM Omoto, HS Kurtzman, pp. 281–99. Washington, DC: Am. Psychol. Assoc.

Gates G, Ost J. 2004. *The Gay and Lesbian Atlas.*Washington, DC: Urban Inst. Press. 232 pp.

Gen. Account. Off. 2004. Defense of Marriage Act: update to prior report. Document GAO-04–353R. Washington, DC: GAO.

Goldberg AE, Sayer A. 2006. Lesbian couples' relationship quality across the transition to parenthood. *J. Marriage Fam.* 68:87–100.

Gottman JM, Levenson RW, Swanson C, Swanson K, Tyson R, Yoshimoto D. 2003. Observing gay, lesbian and heterosexual couples' relationships: mathematical modeling of conflict interaction. *J. Homosex.* 45:65–91.

Hall R. 192 8. *The Well of Loneliness.* New York: Bard Avon. 506 pp.

Hand SI. 1991. *The lesbian parenting couple.* PhD thesis. San Francisco: Prof. School Psychol.

Harkless LE, Fowers BJ. 2005. Similarities and differences in relational boundaries among heterosexuals, gay men, and lesbians. *Psychol. Women Q.* 29:167–76.

Harry J. 1984. *Gay Couples.* New York: Praeger. 151 pp.

Harry J, DeVall WB. 1978. The *Social Organization of Gay Males.* New York: Praeger. 223 pp.

Herdt G, Kertzner R. 2006. I do, but I can't: the impact of marriage denial on the mental health and sexual citizenship of lesbians and gay men in the United States. *J. Sex. Res. Soc. Policy* 3(1):33–49, online ISSN 1553–6610.

Herek GM. 2006. Legal recognition of same-sex relationships in the United States: a social science perspective. *Am. Psychol.* 61:In press.

Hickson FC, Davies PM, Hunt AJ, Weatherburn P, McManus TJ, Coxon AP. 1992. Maintenance of open gay relationships: some strategies for protection against HIV. *AIDS Care* 4:409–19.

Hochschild A, Machung A. 1989. *The Second Shift: Working Parents and the Revolution at Home.* New York: Viking.

Howard JA, Blumstein P, Schwartz P. 1986. Sex, power, and influence tactics in intimate relationships. *J. Personal. Soc. Psychol.* 51:102–9.

Human Rights Campaign. 2006. *Statewide marriage laws.* http://www.hrc.org/Template.cfm? Section= Center&CONTENTID= 2822.5 &TEMPLATE=/Con tentManage ment/ContentDisplay.cfm.

Johnson MP. 2006. Violence and abuse in personal relationships: conflict, terror, and resistance in intimate partnerships. In *The Cambridge Handbook of Personal Relationships*, ed. A Vangelisti, D Perlman, pp. 557–78. New York: Cambridge Univ. Press.

Johnson S. 1990. *Staying Power: Long-Term Lesbian Couples.* Tallahassee, FL: Naiad Press. 333 pp.

Jones DA. 1996. Discrimination against same-sex couples in hotel reservation policies. *J. Homosex.* 31:153–59.

Kaiser Family Found. 2001. *Inside-Out: A Report on the Experiences of Lesbians, Gays and Bisexuals in America and the Public's View on Issues and Policies Related to Sexual Orientation*, Menlo Park, CA.

Karney BR, Bradbury TN. 2005. Contextual influences on marriage: implications for policy and intervention. *Curr. Dir. Psychol. Sci.* 14:171–74.

King M, Bartlett A. 2006. What same-sex civil partnerships may mean for health. J. Epidemiol. *Community Health* 60:188–91.

Klinkenberg D, Rose S. 1994. Dating scripts of gay men and lesbians. *J. Homosex.* 26:23–35.

Kurdek LA. 1991. Correlates of relationship satisfaction in cohabiting gay and lesbian couples. *J. Personal. Soc. Psychol.* 61:910–22.

Kurdek LA. 1993. The allocation of household labor in gay, lesbian, and heterosexual married couples. *J. Soc. Issues* 49(3):127–39.

Kurdek LA. 1994a. The nature and correlates of relationship quality in gay, lesbian, and heterosexual cohabiting couples. In *Lesbian and Gay Psychology: Volume 1*, ed. B Greene, GM Herek, pp. 113–55. Thousand Oaks, CA: Sage.

Kurdek LA. 1995a. Developmental changes in relationship quality in gay and lesbian cohabiting couples. *Dev. Psychol.* 31:86–94.

Kurdek LA. 1995b. Lesbian and gay couples. In *Lesbian, Gay, and Bisexual Identities over the Lifespan*, ed. AR D'Augelli, CJ Patterson, pp. 243–61. New York: Oxford.

Kurdek LA. 1998. Relationship outcomes and their predictors: longitudinal evidence from heterosexual married, gay cohabiting, and lesbian cohabiting couples. *J. Marr. Fam.* 60:553–68.

Kurdek LA. 2000. Attractions and constraints as determinants of relationship commitment: longitudinal evidence from gay, lesbian, and heterosexual couples. *Pers. Relat.* 7:245–62.

Kurdek LA. 2002. On being insecure about the assessment of attachment styles. *J. Soc. Personal. Relat.* 19:811–34.

Kurdek LA. 2004. Are gay and lesbian cohabiting couples really different from heterosexual married couples? *J. Marr. Fam.* 66:880–900.

Kurdek LA. 2005. What do we know about gay and lesbian couples? *Curr. Dir. Psychol. Sci.* 14:251–54.

Kurdek LA. 2006. Differences between partners from heterosexual, gay, and lesbian cohabiting couples. *J. Marr. Fam.* 68:509–28.

Kurdek LA, Schmitt JP. 1987. Partner homogamy in married, heterosexual cohabitating, gay, and lesbian couples. *J. Sex Res.* 23(2):212–32.

Lannutti PJ. 2005. For better or worse: exploring the meanings of same-sex marriage within the lesbian, gay, bisexual and transgendered community. *J. Soc. Personal. Relat.* 22:5–18.

Lewis GB. 2006. Thinking about gay marriage: putting the moral condemnation back into morality policy. Presented at Williams Inst. 5th Annu. Update Sex. Orientation Law Public Policy, Univ. Calif., Los Angeles.

Lewis RJ, Derlega VJ, Berndt A, Morris LM, Rose S. 2001. An empirical analysis of stressors for gay men and lesbians. *J. Homosex.* 42(1):63–88.

Mays VM, Cochran SD. 2001. Mental health correlates of perceived discrimination among lesbian, gay, and bisexual adults in the United States. *Am. J. Public Health* 91:1869–76.

McWhirter DP, Mattison AM. 1984. *The Male Couple: How Relationships Develop*. Englewood Cliffs, NJ: Prentice-Hall. 341 pp.

Metz ME, Rosser BRS, Strapko N. 1994. Differences in conflict-resolution styles among heterosexual, gay, and lesbian couples. *J. Sex Res.* 31:1–16.

Meyer IH. 2003. Prejudice, social stress, and mental health in lesbian, gay, and bisexual populations: conceptual issues and research evidence. *Psychol. Bull.* 129:674–97.

Murray SO. 2000. *Homosexualities*. Chicago: Univ. Chicago Press. 507 pp.

Nardi PM. 1999. *Gay Men's Friendships*. Chicago: Univ. Chicago Press. 253 pp.

Oswald RF. 2002. Resilience within the family networks of lesbians and gay men: intentionality and redefinition. *J. Marr. Fam.* 64:374–83.

Otis MD, Rostosky SS, Riggle EDB, Hamrin R. 2006. Stress and relationship quality in same-sex couples. *J. Soc. Personal. Relat.* 23:81–99.

Parks CA. 1998. Lesbian parenthood: a review of the literature. *Am. J. Orthopsychiatry* 68:3 76–89.

Patterson CJ. 1995a. Lesbian mothers, gay fathers, and their children. In *Lesbian, Gay, and Bisexual Identities over the Lifespan: Psychological Perspectives*, ed. AR D'Augelli, CJ Patterson, pp. 262–90. New York: Oxford Univ. Press.

Patterson CJ. 1995b. Families of the baby boom: parents' division of labor and children's adjustment. *Dev. Psychol.* 31:115–23.

Patterson CJ. 2004a. What difference does a civil union make? Changing public policies and the experiences of same-sex couples: comment on Solomon, Rothblum, and Balsam 2004. *J. Fam. Psychol.* 18:287–89.

Patterson CJ. 2004b. *Gay fathers. In The Role of the Father in Child Development*, ed. ME Lamb, pp. 397–416. New York: Wiley. 4th ed.

Patterson CJ, Sutfin EL, Fulcher M. 2004. Division of labor among lesbian and heterosexual parenting couples: correlates of specialized versus shared patterns. *J. Adult Dev.* 11:179–89.

Peplau LA. 1991. Lesbian and gay relationships. In *Homosexuality: Research Findings for Public Policy*, ed. JC Gonsiorek, JD Weinrich, pp. 177–96. Newbury Park, CA: Sage.

Peplau LA. 2001. Rethinking women's sexual orientation: an interdisciplinary, relationship-focused approach. *Pers. Relat.* 8:1–19.

Peplau LA, Cochran SD. 1980. *Sex differences in values concerning love relationships*. Presented at Annu. Meet. Am. Psychol. Assoc., Montreal.

Peplau LA, Cochran SD. 1981. Value orientations in the intimate relationships of gay men. *J. Homosex.* 6:1–19.

Peplau LA, Cochran SD, Mays VM. 1997. A national survey of the intimate relationships of African American lesbians and gay men: a look at commitment, satisfaction, sexual behavior, and HIV disease. In *Ethnic and Cultural Diversity among Lesbians and Gay Men*, ed. B Greene, pp. 11–38. Thousand Oaks, CA: Sage.

Peplau LA, Cochran SD, Rook K, Padesky C. 1978. Women in love: attachment and autonomy in lesbian relationships. *J. Soc. Issues* 34(3):7–27.

Peplau LA, Fingerhut AW, Beals KP. 2004. Sexuality in the relationships of lesbians and gay men. In *Handbook of Sexuality in Close Relationships*, ed. J Harvey, A Wenzel, S Sprecher, pp. 350–69. Mahwah, NJ: Erlbaum.

Peplau LA, Garnets LD, eds. 2000. Women's sexualities: new perspectives on sexual orientation and gender. *J. Soc. Issues* 56(2):181–364.

Peplau LA, Padesky C, Hamilton M. 1982. Satisfaction in lesbian relationships. *J. Homosex.* 8:23–35.

Peplau LA, Spalding LR. 2000. The close relationships of lesbians, gay men and bisexuals. In *Close Relationships: A Sourcebook*, ed. C Hendrick, SS Hendrick, pp. 111–24. Thousand Oaks, CA: Sage.

Potoczniak MJ, Mourot JE, Crosbie-Burnett M, Potoczniak DJ. 2003. Legal and psychological perspectives on same-sex domestic violence: a multisystemic approach. J. *Fam. Psychol.* 17:252–59.

Reilly ME, Lynch JM. 1990. Power-sharing in lesbian partnerships. *J. Homosex.* 19:1–30 Renzetti CM, Miley CH. 1996. *Violence in Gay and Lesbian Domestic Partnerships.* New York: Haworth. 121 pp.

Rook KS. 1998. Investigating the positive and negative sides of personal relationships: through a lens darkly? In *The Dark Side of Close Relationships*, ed. BH Spitzberg, WR Cupach, pp. 369–93. Mahwah, NJ: Erlbaum.

Rose S, Zand D, Cini M. 1993. Lesbian courtship scripts. In *Boston Marriages: Romantic but Asexual Relationships Among Contemporary Lesbians*, ed. ED Rothblum, KA Brehony, pp. 70–85. Amherst: Univ. Mass. Press.

Rothblum ED. 2000. Sexual orientation and sex in women's lives: conceptual and methodological issues. *J. Soc. Issues* 56(2):193–204.

Rutter V, Schwartz P. 1996. Same-sex couples: courtship, commitment, context. In *The Diversity of Human Relationships*, ed. AE Auhagen, M von Salisch. pp. 197–223. New York: Cambridge Univ. Press.

Schreurs KMG, Buunk BP. 1996. Closeness, autonomy, equity and relationship satisfaction in lesbian couples. *Psychol. Women Q.* 20:577–92.

Solomon SE, Rothblum ED, Balsam KF. 2004. Pioneers in partnership: lesbian and gay male couples in civil unions compared with those not in civil unions and heterosexual married siblings. *J. Fam. Psychol.* 18:275–86.

Swim JK. 2004. *Day to day experiences with heterosexism: heterosexist hassles as daily stressors.* Work. Pap., Dept. Psychol., Penn. State Univ.

Tasker F. 2005. Lesbian mothers, gay fathers, and their children: a review. *J. Dev. Behav. Pediatr.* 26(3):224–40.

Testa RJ, Kinder BN, Ironson G. 1987. Heterosexual bias in the perception of loving relationships of gay males and lesbians. *J. Sex Res.* 23:163–72.

The Pew Forum on Religion and Public Life. 2005. *Abortion and rights of terror suspects top court issues; strong support for stem cell research.* http://pewforum.org/docs/index.php?Doc ID=91.

Todosijevic J, Rothblum ED, Solomon SE. 2005. Relationship satisfaction, affectivity, and gay-specific stressors in same-sex couples joined in civil unions. *Psychol. Women Q.* 29:158–66.

Weinstock JS. 2004. Lesbian FLEX-ibility: friend and/or family connections among lesbian ex-lovers. *J. Lesbian Stud.* 8(3/4):193–238.

CHAPTER 28

Adult Attachment, Sexual Satisfaction, and Relationship Satisfaction

A Study of Married Couples

Bethany Butzer
Lorne Campbell

When in a relationship, do you worry a lot about being rejected by your partner? If so, you may be high in the relationship trait known as anxiety. *Are you a bit remote, and unwilling to get too close to the other person? If this characterizes you, it is possible that you may be high in the relationship trait called* avoidance. *According to research by attachment theorists, the nature of your romantic relationships is related to the quality of the relationship that you had with your parents when you were very young. Sometimes emotional incompatibility within a couple may be due to the two partners having different templates for what relationships should be like or the role that partners should play.*

In the following article, Bethany Butzer and Lorne Campbell present research indicating that the general approach that one takes to relationships, called attachment *style, is very much related not only to relationship satisfaction, but also to sexual satisfaction, and to the correlation between*

the two. Thus, sexual problems within a couple could be due to incompatibility in attachment styles.

The Butzer and Campbell study is a fascinating look at the different roles that sex can play in a relationship as a function of one's sense of emotional security or insecurity. It is remarkable that the emotional climate within one's family of origin can have such far-reaching effects in adulthood. After reading this chapter, you might spend some time recalling the relationships and interactions you observed while growing up in your own family of orientation. You should then have a better understanding of the complex role that emotional baggage can play in a couple's sexual encounters. You might also develop some additional insight and empathy for a partner whose attachment style is different than your own.

Sexuality is an integral part of most romantic relationships, with society emphasizing marriage as the main dyadic relationship within which sex occurs (Sprecher, Christopher, & Cate, 2006). One theoretical perspective that is particularly applicable to research on sexuality is attachment theory, as this theory focuses on the processes involved in the development of close affectional bonds with others (Feeney & Noller, 2004). Using a large community sample of married couples, the present research tests specific hypotheses regarding sexual and marital satisfaction from an attachment perspective.

ADULT ATTACHMENT THEORY

Bowlby (1969, 1980) posited that early interactions with significant others instill expectations and beliefs that subsequently shape social perceptions and behavior regarding what relationships and relationship partners should be like during adulthood. Two relatively orthogonal dimensions define individual differences in adult attachment (Brennan, Clark, & Shaver, 1998). The first dimension, labeled avoidance, reflects the degree to which individuals feel comfortable with closeness and emotional intimacy in relationships. People who score higher on avoidance tend to be less invested in their relationship and strive to remain psychologically and emotionally independent of their partners (Hazan & Shaver, 1994). The second dimension termed anxiety, taps the degree to which individuals worry and ruminate about being rejected or abandoned by their partners. Prototypically secure people tend to score lower on both attachment dimensions.

Mikulincer and Shaver (2007) introduced a model that specifies the activation and operation of the adult attachment system. According to this model, the primary strategy of the attachment system involves seeking proximity to attachment figures during times of need. A secure attachment style tends to develop when attachment figures are available and responsive to an individual's needs. In this case, the individual experiences a sense of felt security, which encourages the formation of close affectional bonds with others. On the other hand, if attachment figures are consistently unavailable or unresponsive, this indicates that the primary strategy of proximity seeking is unsuccessful, which results in the use of secondary attachment strategies

to deal with the resulting sense of insecurity. These secondary strategies involve hyperactivation or deactivation of the attachment system. The main goal of hyperactivating strategies is to get an unresponsive attachment figure to pay attention to the individual and provide care and support, a strategy that is most typical of individuals who score highly on attachment anxiety. Thus, anxiously attached individuals make strong attempts to maintain proximity to attachment figures and monitor their relationship partners closely for signs of deficient or waning physical or emotional proximity (Simpson, Ickes, & Grich, 1999).

Deactivating strategies, on the other hand, involve the inhibition of proximity seeking in response to an unavailable attachment figure, which is most typical of individuals who score highly on attachment avoidance. Thus, avoidantly attached individuals seek to maintain independence and self-reliance, while also denying needs or emotional states that might activate the attachment system (Mikulincer & Shaver, 2007). As such, highly avoidant people often do not allow themselves to become close to their romantic partners (Campbell, Simpson, Kashy & Rholes, 2001) or turn to their partners for support in times of distress (Simpson, Rholes, & Neligan, 1992).

ADULT ATTACHMENT AND SEXUALITY

Adult romantic relationships involve the integration of three behavioral systems, namely, attachment, caregiving, and sexual mating (Shaver, Hazan, & Bradshaw, 1988). The least studied of the three behavioral systems is the sexual mating system, but attempts to link adult attachment styles with sexuality have resulted in a number of intriguing empirical findings (Birnbaum, 2007; Davis et al., 2006). Researchers, however, have conducted little work on the links between adult attachment and sexual satisfaction specifically, with most prior work focusing on beliefs about sex and types of sexual behaviors in undergraduate students.

Due to their successful use of the primary attachment strategy of proximity seeking during times of need, prior research suggests that securely attached individuals should have more positive sexual experiences and more positive sexual satisfaction in their relationships (Mikulincer & Shaver, 2007). Indeed, securely attached individuals tend to be comfortable with their sexuality, are open to sexual exploration, and enjoy a variety of sexual activities (Feeney & Noller, 2004). Securely attached individuals are also more likely to have sex with intimate relationship partners and are more likely to have sex that is mutually initiated (Brennan & Shaver, 1995; Feeney, Noller, & Patty, 1993). Finally, securely attached individuals are less likely to have casual or promiscuous sexual partners, one-night stands, or sex outside of their primary relationships (Bogaert & Sadava, 2002; Feeney & Noller, 2004).

The sexual relationships of anxiously attached individuals, however, tend to be organized around the hyperactivation of their attachment system, which causes them to be chronically dependent on others for approval and to be concerned about abandonment and rejection (Mikulincer & Shaver, 2007). For example, research shows that anxiously attached individuals report having sex to reduce insecurity and establish intense closeness, while also having low self-efficacy for sexual negotiation, fears that requests for sexual discussions will alienate partners, negative beliefs about condoms, lower levels of orgasmic responsivity, and higher levels of erotophobia (Birnbaum, 2007; Feeney, Kelly, Gallois, Peterson, & Terry, 1999; Feeney & Noller, 2004; Schachner & Shaver, 2004; Tracy, Shaver, Albino, & Cooper, 2003). In men, greater anxiety relates to more restrictive sexual behavior (Gentzler & Kerns, 2004) and a lower likelihood of using sex to cope with negative emotions or to bolster self-esteem (Cooper et al., 2006). In women, however, greater anxiety relates to a higher likelihood of having ever had sex, higher rates of infidelity, a younger age at first intercourse, and having sex to bolster self-esteem (Bogaert & Sadava, 2002; Cooper, Shaver, & Collins, 1998; Cooper et al., 2006). Thus, although attachment anxiety tends to relate to a desire to foster closeness in both males and females, the adverse effects of attachment anxiety on sexuality seem to be more pronounced for females.

In line with their goal of deactivating attachment concerns, avoidant individuals should find close sexual relationships uncomfortable and unrewarding due to their general discomfort with intimacy and a desire to avoid closeness (Mikulincer & Shaver, 2007). Overall, avoidant individuals attempt to deactivate their attachment system in two main ways with regards to sexual behavior. First, avoidant individuals can try to distance themselves from most sexual activities by, for example, having sex at a later age, engaging in fewer non-coital sexual behaviors, having greater concern about sexually transmitted diseases, and having stronger beliefs in the benefits of condoms (Bogaert & Sadava, 2002; Feeney, Peterson, Gallois, & Terry, 2000; Gentzler & Kerns, 2004). Second, avoidant individuals can engage in sexual relations only in contexts where intimacy is unlikely. For example, avoidant individuals have less restrictive attitudes towards sex, have sex to impress their peer group (as opposed to having romantic goals for sex), and have higher numbers of casual, uncommitted sex partners (Cooper et al., 1998; Gentzler & Kerns, 2004; Schachner & Shaver, 2004). This pattern of effects is very similar for both men and women, although they tend to be more pronounced in men (Cooper et al., 2006).

LINKS BETWEEN SEXUAL AND MARITAL SATISFACTION

Research shows that higher levels of sexual satisfaction are related to greater relationship quality and stability (Sprecher & Cate, 2004), with factor-analytic studies showing that sexuality is a core component of the prototype of relationship quality (Hassebrauck & Fehr, 2002). Birnbaum, Reis, Mikulincer, Gillath, and Orpaz (2006) note, however, that clinical evidence exists suggesting that some couples can be satisfied with their relationships in general but unsatisfied with their sexual relationship, and vice versa (Edwards & Booth, 1994). The link between sexual and marital satisfaction can therefore be stronger for some people than for others. For example, research shows that the use of sex to foster intense closeness and calm fears of rejection and abandonment in more anxiously attached individuals (Tracy et al., 2003) results in relatively strong links between day-to-day sexual experiences and subsequent relationship interactions; however, avoidant individuals do not show this association (Birnbaum et al., 2006). These results suggest that anxious individuals tend to use sexual experiences as a barometer of their relationship quality, whereas avoidant individuals do not.

LIMITATIONS OF PREVIOUS RESEARCH

Although investigators have made progress in the examination of adult attachment and sexuality in recent years, this research is limited in two important ways. First, researchers have conducted most of the previous work in this area on individuals, with very few studies focusing on sexuality and sexual satisfaction in dyads. While Birnbaum and colleagues (2006) examined the links between adult attachment, the daily experience of sexual intercourse, and relationship interactions (e.g., relationship enhancing vs. damaging behaviors) in a sample of cohabitating couples, this research did not examine how attachment might relate to individuals' overall satisfaction with their sexual relationship. Thus, the present study is unique in that it focuses on how individuals in long-term marital relationships feel about their sexual relationship as a whole, as opposed to focusing on feelings

and behaviors regarding a particular sexual episode.

Second, investigators have conducted most of the work in this area on samples of adolescents and undergraduate students, who, in most cases, have not yet had a chance to become involved in long-term, committed relationships, and generally have less sexual experience. In this sense, it is difficult to generalize these findings to more committed marital relationships.

HYPOTHESES

Attachment anxiety. Based on previous research showing that anxious individuals tend to defer to their partner's sexual needs, are distracted by relational concerns during sex, fear rejection and abandonment, and experience anxiety regarding sexual experiences (Birnbaum, 2007; Brennan et al., 1998; Davis et al., 2006), we hypothesized that more anxiously attached individuals would report lower levels of satisfaction with their sexual relationship. The possible links between one partner's anxious attachment and the other partner's sexual satisfaction, however, are unclear. For example, individuals with anxiously attached partners might be very satisfied with their sexual relationship since their partners may often sacrifice their own sexual needs for those of their partner (Davis et al., 2006). On the other hand, they may also begin to see sex as another way for their partner to display the clingy and dependent behavior that is characteristic of anxiously attached individuals (Campbell, Simpson, Boldry & Kashy, 2005). Thus, we made no specific hypotheses regarding the link between partner anxiety and sexual satisfaction.

In addition, consistent with prior research (Birnbaum et al., 2006), we expected that anxiety would moderate the link between sexual satisfaction and marital satisfaction. Specifically, we expected that individuals who were low in anxiety, as well as individuals with less anxious partners, would show similar levels of marital satisfaction regardless of their level of sexual satisfaction. On the other hand, we predicted that individuals who were high in anxiety, as well as individuals with more anxious partners, would report higher levels of marital satisfaction when they were also high in sexual satisfaction.

Attachment avoidance. Based on previous research suggesting that avoidant individuals experience aversive feelings and intrusive thoughts with regards to sex, prefer to distance themselves from intimate sexual activities, and experience lower levels of sexual intimacy and pleasure-related sexual feelings (Birnbaum, 2007; Birnbaum et al., 2006; Brennan et al., 1998; Cooper et al., 2006), we expected that avoidantly attached individuals would report lower levels of satisfaction with their sexual relationship. In addition, we expected that individuals with more avoidantly attached partners would show lower levels of satisfaction with their sexual relationship due to their partners' discomfort with closeness and intimacy, as well as their partners' tendency to focus on their own sexual needs (Birnbaum et al., 2006).

Finally, based on research suggesting that attachment avoidance inhibits the links between positive and negative sexual experiences and subsequent relationship behaviors (Birnbaum et al., 2006), we did not expect actor or partner avoidance to moderate the link between sexual satisfaction and marital satisfaction.

METHOD

Participants

Our sample consisted of 116 heterosexual married couples from London, Ontario, Canada who responded to advertisements in various local newspapers to participate in a Married Couples Survey. The average length of marriage was 10.02 years and ranged from 2 months to 53 years. The average age of participants was 38.56 years for men and 36.7 years for women. The majority of couples were Caucasian. Sixty percent of the married couples reported that they had children.

Procedure

Married couples attended a 2-hr laboratory session to separately and privately complete a booklet of questionnaires. The questionnaires asked about their perceptions of their attachment style, sexual satisfaction, and marital satisfaction. We informed participants that their responses would remain confidential and would not be shared with their partners.

Materials

Attachment style

Participants completed the Experiences in Close Relationships Questionnaire–Revised (ECR–R; Fraley, Waller, & Brennan, 2000). The ECR–R is a self-report questionnaire containing 18 items measuring avoidance and 18 items measuring anxiety. Examples of avoidance items include "I find it difficult to allow myself to depend on romantic partners" and "I get uncomfortable when a romantic partner wants to be very close." Examples of anxiety items include "I often worry that my partner doesn't really love me" and "I rarely worry about my partner leaving me". Participants rated each item on a 7-point scale, ranging from 1 (*strongly disagree*) to 7 (*strongly agree*).

Sexual satisfaction

We measured satisfaction with the sexual relationship using two scales. Fournier, Olson, and Druckman (1983) created the 10-item Enriching and Nurturing Relationship Issues, Communication, and Happiness (ENRICH) Sexual Relationship subscale to serve as an assessment tool for both personal and relationship issues for couples. Samples of items include: "Sometimes I am concerned that my spouse's interest in sex is not the same as mine" and "Our sexual relationship is satisfying and fulfilling to me." Participants responded to each item on a 7-point scale, ranging from 1 (*strongly disagree*) to 7 (*strongly agree*). We also measured satisfaction with the sexual relationship using the Index of Sexual Satisfaction (ISS; Hudson, Harrison, &

Crosscup, 1981). The ISS is a 25-item scale including items such as "I feel that my sex life is lacking in quality" and "My spouse does not satisfy me sexually." Participants responded to each item on a scale ranging from 1 (*none of the time*) to 7 (*all of the time*). Preliminary analyses revealed that the ISS and the Sexual Relationship subscale of the ENRICH were highly correlated. Thus, we aggregated the items for both scales to compute one composite score of sexual satisfaction.

Marital satisfaction

We used Hendrick's (1988) 7-item Relationship Assessment Scale to measure spouses' overall satisfaction with their marriage. Participants responded to items such as "In general, how satisfied are you with your relationship?" and "To what extent has your relationship met your original expectations?" on a 7-point scale (1 = *not at all/poor*, 7 = *a great deal/extremely good*).

RESULTS

The Actor–Partner Interdependence Model (APIM; Kenny, Kashy & Cook, 2006) guided the data analytic approach we adopted for testing our hypotheses. According to the APIM, when individuals are involved in an interdependent relationship, their outcomes depend not only on their own characteristics and inputs (called actor effects) but also on their partner's characteristics and inputs (called partner effects).

The means for anxiety and avoidance are similar to those found in previous studies using the ECR–R (Sibley, Fischer, & Liu, 2005). The only significant differences that emerged between husbands and wives on the study variables were for the avoidant attachment scores, with husbands reporting greater avoidance than wives. The correlations for both husbands and wives show that more anxious and avoidant individuals reported lower levels of marital satisfaction and sexual satisfaction. In addition, the correlations between marital satisfaction and

sexual satisfaction were positive and significant, indicating that if one partner was satisfied with their marriage in general and satisfied with their sexual relationship, the other one was also. Moreover, consistent with prior research, partners who were more sexually satisfied in their marriage were also more satisfied in general with their marriage.

Individuals who scored higher on the avoidance dimension also tended to report being more anxiously attached. Prior research using the Experiences in Close Relationships Questionnaire–Revised has also found positive correlations between the two attachment dimensions within individuals (Sibley et al., 2005).

In the first analysis, we estimated the actor and partner effects of the attachment orientations on reported sexual satisfaction. Sexual satisfaction served as the dependent variable in this analysis.

Consistent with predictions, a significant actor effect emerged for the anxious attachment dimension showing that more anxiously attached individuals reported lower levels of sexual satisfaction, controlling for their own level of attachment avoidance and their partner's scores on both attachment dimensions. Similarly, an actor effect for avoidant attachment emerged, showing that more avoidantly attached individuals also reported lower levels of sexual satisfaction, controlling for their own level of attachment anxiety and their partner's scores on both attachment dimensions. Also as predicted, a significant partner effect emerged for attachment avoidance, suggesting that people reported lower levels of sexual satisfaction when they had more avoidant partners, controlling for their partner's level of attachment anxiety and their own scores on both attachment dimensions. A partner effect for anxious attachment, however, did not emerge.

In the next analyses, we tested for the potential moderating effect of anxious attachment on the link between sexual satisfaction and marital satisfaction. Marital satisfaction served as the dependent variable in these analyses.

A significant main effect of gender emerged, suggesting that women reported lower levels of marital satisfaction than men when controlling for the main effects of both attachment dimensions and sexual satisfaction. In addition, a significant actor effect of sexual satisfaction emerged, suggesting that individuals who were more satisfied with their sexual relationship were also more satisfied with their marriage in general. Significant actor and partner effects also emerged for attachment anxiety. Specifically, individuals who reported higher levels of anxiety, as well as individuals with more anxious partners, reported lower overall levels of marital satisfaction. A significant actor effect also emerged for attachment avoidance, showing that individuals with higher levels of avoidance reported lower levels of marital satisfaction.

Some significant interactions emerged, however, that qualified these main effects. First, significant interactions between the actor and partner effects of attachment anxiety and the actor effect of sexual satisfaction emerged. The link between sexual satisfaction and marital satisfaction was fairly strong for more anxiously attached individuals, but was much weaker for individuals who were less anxiously attached. Similarly, sexual and marital satisfaction were significantly associated for individuals that had more anxiously attached partners, but were not significantly associated for individuals that had less anxiously attached partners.

An unexpected interaction between partner avoidance and actor sexual satisfaction also emerged. The link between sexual and marital satisfaction was fairly strong for individuals that had less avoidantly attached partners, but this link was only marginally significant for individuals that had more avoidantly attached partners.

DISCUSSION

Despite a number of advances that investigators have made in their work on adult attachment and sexuality, this work is limited in two important ways. First, researchers in this area tend to focus on individuals, despite the obviously dyadic nature of sexual experiences between couples. Second, researchers in this area tend to focus on adolescents and undergraduates, most of whom have probably not yet had a chance to become involved in long-term, committed sexual relationships. The present study addressed both of these limitations, and the results supported the hypotheses generated from attachment theory. Importantly, the present study conceptually replicates the findings of Birnbaum and colleagues (2006) in a different sample using more global measures of sexual and martial quality and also extends prior research by demonstrating the difficulty people may have in developing sexual intimacy and closeness with more avoidantly attached partners.

ADULT ATTACHMENT AND SEXUAL SATISFACTION

As predicted, higher levels of anxiety and avoidance were related to lower levels of sexual satisfaction at the individual level. In particular, more avoidant individuals reported lower levels of sexual satisfaction in their marriage, controlling for their own level of attachment anxiety and their partner's scores on both attachment dimensions. Thus, it appears to be the case that the discomfort that avoidant individuals feel about being close and intimate with others extends to their sexual relationship with their spouses. These findings are consistent with avoidant individuals' orientation toward deactivating their attachment system (Mikulincer & Shaver, 2007), and with the suggestion that avoidant individuals should find sexual relationships with their partners uncomfortable and unrewarding (Shaver & Hazan, 1988). In addition, these findings support previous research showing that avoidant individuals have aversive feelings about sex and tend to be uncomfortable with intimacy and closeness (Birnbaum et al.,

2006; Feeney & Noller, 2004). Thus, the present results suggest that avoidant individuals may be particularly uneasy regarding sexual encounters with their spouses and experience a less rewarding sexual relationship in their marriage.

In line with anxiously attached individuals' use of hyperactivating strategies (Mikulincer & Shaver, 2007), the present study provided support for the idea that anxious individuals should have difficulty experiencing sexual satisfaction and enjoyment, perhaps because they are often preoccupied with abandonment and tend to defer to their partner's sexual needs (Davis et al., 2006). Specifically, more anxious individuals displayed lower levels of sexual satisfaction in their marriage, controlling for their own level of attachment avoidance and their partner's scores on both attachment dimensions. Thus, the concerns about rejection and abandonment that anxious spouses commonly feel may influence their sexual satisfaction in a detrimental way. Indeed, Birnbaum (2007) found that attachment anxiety was positively correlated with intrusive thoughts during sex. Thus, it could perhaps be the case that, due to their chronic focus on potential cues of rejection, anxious individuals have difficulty enjoying sexual encounters, as they are often preoccupied with other matters.

A novel finding that emerged in the present research was that individuals with more avoidant partners reported being less sexually satisfied in their marriage, even after controlling for the individual's own level of avoidance. In other words, this partner effect suggests that having a spouse who is emotionally distant and uncomfortable with expressions of closeness relates to lower feelings of satisfaction with one's sexual relationship. This finding supports some of the theoretical assumptions of attachment theory as related to sexuality (Shaver & Hazan, 1988), and extends previous research by highlighting the importance of the dyadic relationship on sexual satisfaction.

We did not find a partner effect, however, for attachment anxiety. In other words, individuals with more anxious spouses did not report

being less satisfied with their sexual relationship. It could perhaps be the case that being married to an anxiously attached individual does not result in lowered sexual satisfaction for some people due to the desire of anxious individuals to foster intense closeness through sex (Schachner & Shaver, 2004). In addition, due to their chronic concerns about abandonment and their sensitivity to signs of waning physical or emotional proximity (Simpson et al., 1999), anxiously attached individuals might be more likely to defer to their partners' sexual needs (Davis et al., 2006). Thus, the partners of anxiously attached individuals may experience adequate levels of sexual satisfaction due to their sexual needs being met. This hypothesis is speculative, and future research will need to further explore the possible links between the anxious attachment of one partner and the sexual satisfaction of the other partner.

LINKS BETWEEN SEXUAL AND MARITAL SATISFACTION

The current study also provided support for previous research examining the moderating role of attachment anxiety on the relationship between daily sexual experiences and subsequent relationship interactions (Birnbaum et al., 2006). In particular, anxious individuals, and individuals with anxious partners, showed higher levels of marital satisfaction when they were also high in sexual satisfaction. On the other hand, individuals who were low in anxiety showed a weaker association between their sexual and marital satisfaction, while individuals with less anxious partners showed similar levels of marital satisfaction regardless of their level of sexual satisfaction. These results are consistent with previous research suggesting that, due to their sensitivity to cues that may connote support or rejection (Campbell et al., 2005), anxious individuals may use their sexual experiences as indicators of their overall relationship quality, and as a way to foster closeness to their partners (Birnbaum et al.,

2006; Tracy et al., 2003). Thus, anxious individuals appear to receive an extra "boost" in marital satisfaction when they experience positive and satisfying sexual encounters with their spouses, which may help to satisfy anxious individuals' needs for intimacy and closeness. This finding also suggests, however, that anxious individuals might have difficulty differentiating between aspects of their sexual experiences and their relationships as a whole, which could potentially result in relational instability if their sexual experiences are negative or unsatisfying (Birnbaum et al., 2006).

With regards to avoidance, the current findings support previous research suggesting that sexual satisfaction and relationship satisfaction are not strongly linked for avoidant individuals. Specifically, individuals in the current study who were high in avoidance reported lower levels of marital satisfaction, regardless of their levels of sexual satisfaction. This finding supports previous research suggesting that avoidant individuals tend to engage in sex for self-enhancing reasons that are extraneous to their relationships (Cooper et al., 2006). As Birnbaum and colleagues (2006) suggest, avoidant individuals may find such a pattern beneficial in the sense that distressing or unsatisfying sexual experiences with their partners may not negatively affect their overall relationship satisfaction. This pattern also suggests, however, that avoidant individuals do not experience the potentially beneficial enhancements to relationship satisfaction that can occur in the context of a positive or satisfying sexual relationship.

Unlike the results of Birnbaum and colleagues (2006), we found an unexpected interaction between actor sexual satisfaction and partner avoidance. This finding may be consistent with prior research focusing on links between avoidant attachment and relationship well-being. For instance, avoidantly attached individuals do not tend to develop a high degree of closeness or dependence with their romantic partners (Campbell et al., 2001), and people tend to be less satisfied overall with their more avoidant partners (Feeney, 1999). It may therefore be the case that when people find themselves less sexually satisfied with a less avoidant partner (i.e., someone who is comfortable with closeness and intimacy), it is particularly disheartening

CAVEATS AND CONCLUSIONS

The results of this study should be interpreted with some caveats in mind. First of all, the participants from this study self-selected to participate by responding to newspaper ads. Thus, it might be the case that these participants are more satisfied in general with their relationship, and perhaps also more satisfied with their sexual relationship, than married couples in the general population. In addition, we recruited participants from a fairly urban Canadian city, meaning that couples from more rural communities, or even from other countries, might display a different pattern of results. Second, the data from this study are correlational and cross-sectional. Thus, we cannot ascertain any cause and effect relationships between attachment style and sexual satisfaction based on the present research. The present study suggests that higher levels of anxiety and avoidance are related to lower levels of sexual satisfaction; however, we have not uncovered why this might be the case. For example, it is possible, as Davis and colleagues (2006) suggest, that inhibited communication of sexual needs mediates the relationship between attachment and sexual satisfaction. In addition, the aversive thoughts and feelings about sex that anxious and avoidant individuals experience could also potentially mediate the link between attachment and sexual satisfaction (Birnbaum et al., 2006).

Another potential limitation of the present research is that it focused specifically on sexual satisfaction in marriage and not on sexual behaviors or experiences. Future studies could benefit from the use of a larger number of measures of sexual satisfaction, in addition to measuring actual sexual behaviors in marital relationships.

Despite these limitations, the present study makes a number of important and unique contributions to our understanding of the relationship between adult attachment and sexual satisfaction. First of all, the present study addresses a number of limitations of previous research in this area by focusing on a relatively large community sample involving both members of married couples. Second, the present study reveals the importance of attachment style in relation to overall levels of sexual and relationship satisfaction in marriage. Our findings suggest that adult attachment might be an important factor to consider in the context of therapy for couples who are experiencing sexual issues in their marriage.

REFERENCES

Birnbaum, G. E. (2007). Attachment orientations, sexual functioning, and relationship satisfaction in a community sample of women. *Journal of Social and Personal Relationships, 24,* 21–35.

Birnbaum, G. E., Reis, H. T., Mikulincer, M., Gillath, O., & Orpaz, A. (2006). When sex is more than just sex: Attachment orientations, sexual experience, and relationship quality. *Journal of Personality and Social Psychology, 91,* 929–943.

Bogaert, A. F., & Sadava, S. (2002). Adult attachment and sexual behavior. *Personal Relationships, 9,* 191–204.

Bowlby, J. (1969). *Attachment and loss: Vol. 1. Attachment.* New York: Basic Books.

Bowlby, J. (1980). *Attachment and loss.* New York: Basic Books.

Brennan, K. A., Clark, C. L., & Shaver, P. R. (1998). Self-report measurement of adult attachment: An integrative overview. In J. A. Simpson & W. S. Rholes (Eds.), *Attachment theory and close relationships* (pp. 46–76). New York: Guilford Press.

Brennan, K. A., & Shaver, P. R. (1995). Dimensions of adult attachment, affect regulation, and romantic relationship functioning. *Personality and Social Psychology Bulletin, 21,* 267–283.

Campbell, L., Simpson, J. A., Boldry, J., & Kashy, D. A. (2005). Perceptions of conflict and support in romantic relationships: The role of attachment anxiety. *Journal of Personality and Social Psychology, 88,* 510–531.

Campbell, L., Simpson, J. A., Kashy, D. A., & Rholes, W. S. (2001). Attachment orientations, dependence, and behavior in a stressful situation: An application of the Actor-Partner Interdependence Model. *Journal of Social and Personal Relationships, 18,* 821–843.

Cooper, M. L., Pioli, M., Levitt, A., Talley, A. E., Micheas, L., & Collins, N. L. (2006). Attachment styles, sex motives, and sexual behavior: Evidence for gender-specific expressions of attachment dynamics. In M. Mikulincer & G. S. Goodman (Eds.), *Dynamics of romantic love: Attachment, caregiving, and sex* (pp. 243–274). New York: Guilford.

Cooper, M. L., Shaver, P. R., & Collins, N. L. (1998). Attachment styles, emotion regulation, and adjustment in adolescence. *Journal of Personality and Social Psychology, 74,* 1380–1397.

Davis, D., Shaver, P. R., Widaman, K. F., Vernon, M. L., Follette, W. C., & Beitz, K. (2006). "I can't get no satisfaction": Insecure attachment, inhibited sexual communication, and sexual dissatisfaction. *Personal Relationships, 13,* 465–483.

Edwards, J. N., & Booth, A. (1994). Sexuality, marriage, and well-being: The middle years. In A. S. Rossi (Ed.), *Sexuality across the life course* (pp. 233–259). Chicago: University of Chicago Press.

Feeney, J. A. (1999). Adult romantic attachment and couple relationships. In J. Cassidy & P. R. Shaver (Eds.), *Handbook of attachment: Theory, research, and clinical applications* (pp. 355–377). New York: Guilford Press.

Feeney, J. A., Kelly, L., Gallois, C., Peterson, C., & Terry, D. J. (1999). Attachment style, assertive communication, and safer-sex behavior. *Journal of Applied Social Psychology, 29,* 1964–1983.

Feeney, J. A., & Noller, P. (2004). Attachment and sexuality in close relationships. In J. H. Harvey, A. Wenzel, & S. Sprecher (Eds.), *The handbook of sexuality in close relationships* (pp. 183–201). Mahwah, NJ: Erlbaum Associates.

Feeney, J. A., Noller, P., & Patty, J. (1993). Adolescents' interactions with the opposite sex: Influence of attachment style and gender. *Journal of Adolescence, 16,* 169–186.

Feeney, J. A., Peterson, C., Gallois, C., & Terry, D. J. (2000). Attachment style as a predictor of sexual attitudes and behavior in late adolescence. *Psychology and Health, 14,* 1105–1122.

Fournier, D. G., Olson, D. H., & Druckman, J. M. (1983). Assessing marital and premarital relationships: The PREPARE/ENRICH inventories. In E. E. Filsinger

(Ed.), *Marriage and family assessment* (pp. 229–250). Newbury Park, CA: Sage.

Fraley, R. C., Waller, N. G., & Brennan, K. A. (2000). An item response theory analysis of self-report measures of adult attachment. *Journal of Personality and Social Psychology, 78,* 350–365.

Gentzler, A. L., & Kerns, K. A. (2004). Associations between insecure attachment and sexual experiences. *Personal Relationships, 11,* 249–265.

Hassebrauck, M., & Fehr, B. (2002). Dimensions of relationship quality. *Personal Relationships, 9,* 253–270.

Hazan, C., & Shaver, P. R. (1994). Attachment as an organizational framework for research on close relationships. *Psychological Inquiry, 5,* 1–22.

Hendrick, S. S. (1988). A generic measure of relationship satisfaction. *Journal of Marriage and the Family, 50,* 93–98.

Hudson, W. W., Harrison, D. F., & Crosscup, P. C. (1981). A short-form scale to measure sexual discord in dyadic relationships. *Journal of Sex Research, 17,* 157–174.

Kenny, D. A., Kashy, D. A., & Cook, W. L. (2006). *Dyadic data analysis.* New York: Guilford Press.

Mikulincer, M., & Shaver, P. R. (2007). *Attachment in adulthood: Structure, dynamics, and change.* New York: Guilford Press.

Schachner, D. A., & Shaver, P. R. (2004). Attachment dimensions and sexual motives. *Personal Relationships, 11,* 179–195.

Shaver, P. R., & Hazan, C. (1988). A biased overview of the study of love. *Journal of Social and Personal Relationships, 5,* 473–501.

Shaver, P. R., Hazan, C., & Bradshaw, D. (1988). Love as attachment: The integration of three behavioral systems. In R. J. Sternberg & M. Barnes (Eds.), *The psychology of love* (pp. 68–99). New Haven, CT: Yale University Press.

Sibley, C. G., Fischer, R., & Liu, J. H. (2005). Reliability and validity of the Revised Experiences in Close Relationships (ECR-R) self-report measure of adult romantic attachment. *Personality and Social Psychology Bulletin, 31,* 1524–1536.

Simpson, J. A., Ickes, W., & Grich, J. (1999). When accuracy hurts: Reactions of anxious-ambivalent dating partners to a relationship-threatening situation. *Journal of Personality and Social Psychology, 76,* 754–769.

Simpson, J. A., Rholes, W. S., & Neligan, J. S. (1992). Support seeking and support giving within couples in an anxiety-provoking situation: The role of attachment styles. *Journal of Personality and Social Psychology, 62,* 434–446.

Sprecher, S., & Cate, R. (2004). Sexual satisfaction and sexual expression as predictors of relationship satisfaction and stability. In J. H. Harvey, A. Wenzel, & S. Sprecher (Eds.), *The handbook of sexuality in close relationships* (pp. 235–256). Mahwah, NJ: Erlbaum.

Sprecher, S., Christopher, F. S., & Cate, R. (2006). Sexuality in close relationships. In A. Vangelisti, & D. Perlman (Eds.), *The Cambridge handbook of personal relationships* (pp. 463–482). New York: Cambridge University Press.

Tracy, J. L., Shaver, P. R., Albino, A. W., & Cooper, M. L. (2003). Attachment styles and adolescent sexuality. In P. Florsheim (Ed.), *Adolescent romantic relations and sexual behavior: Theory, research, and practical implications* (pp. 137–159). Mahwah, NJ: Erlbaum.

PART VII

Sexual Orientation

The word *homosexuality* was coined in 1869 when Hungarian Karoly Benkert first used the term; but it was British sexologist Havelock Ellis who introduced its English usage in the 1880s (Weeks 1981). Thereafter, the medical model of homosexuality as a form of mental disease was prevalent until the mid-1950s, when University of California psychologist Evelyn Hooker's pioneer study of matched samples of heterosexuals and homosexuals found that there were no significant differences in psychological functioning between the groups. However, it was not until 20 years later in 1974, after a number of other studies found similar results, that the American Psychiatric Association removed "self-accepting homosexuality" from its list of mental disorders (Troiden 1988).

The two basic perspectives of homosexuality in both popular and scientific thought are essentialism and social constructionism (Stein 1992). The popular, widespread view of essentialism relates homosexuality to biological or psychological factors. Ascribing a genetic causal model, this perspective is embraced by many scholars and researchers as well. Conversely, social constructionists question the universality of such categories as homosexuality and heterosexuality,

proposing instead that concepts of sexual orientation and practices have changed over time and that they vary across societies. Persons who subscribe to either of these positions can be pro-gay or anti-gay in their beliefs. Although social constructionism was mainly developed by pro-gay intellectuals who denied the innateness of homosexuality, in a twist of fate, some of their arguments of denial have been embraced by the right-wing anti-gays who use this position to support the view that homosexuality is a choice, and therefore, a sin (Laumann et al. 1994).

A difference in perspectives concerning the orientation of homosexuality is at the heart of many issues. The Parents and Friends of Lesbians and Gays (PFLAG) support organization is firmly behind any research that implicates biology as the source of homosexuality, possibly because it assuages any guilt for responsibility that they might feel. Conversely, many lesbians and gays have a growing skepticism about the search for the cause(s) of homosexuality, believing such a search implies that homosexuality is deviant and, therefore, needs to be cured. Hooker stated: "Why do we want to know the cause? If we understood...and accept it as a given, then we come closer to the kinds of attitudes that will make it possible for homosexuals to live a decent life in society" (Gelman, et al. 1992, p. 46).

One wonders if tolerance and acceptance of gays and lesbians would increase if we, without any reservations, could conclude that homosexuality is genetically linked. Or, if we discovered a homosexual gene, would pregnant women obtain an abortion if the fetus were lesbian or gay? Would these women echo the sentiments of the mother of an adult gay man, who in a *Newsweek* feature said, "Had I known that I was to have a gay child, I would probably not want to have a gay child" (Gelman et al. 1992, p. 50). Hard questions without easy answers are on the horizon for twenty-first century pilgrims. The articles on sexual orientation in Part VII enable readers to assess just how far society has progressed in its attitudes about homosexuality and, perhaps, the distance they themselves have traveled in their own journey.

Richard Pillard and Michael Bailey's technical, well-written review of the behavioral genetics research on sexual orientation includes studies of twins, the hypothalamus, and evolutionary trends. To determine if homosexuality runs in families, the authors examine sibling, twin, and adoption concordance rates that are compatible with the hypothesis that genes account for at least one-half of any variable in sexual orientation. Supporting the essentialist perspective of the authors, research findings are presented about gender atypicality as a forerunner of adult homosexuality, an unresolved topic that has been in the research literature for over a century. In raising the issue of a reproductive disadvantage of a homosexual orientation, this psychiatrist and psychologist team of Pillard and Bailey offers an evolutionary slant different from the William Byne selection that follows.

After considering the heritable component of sexual orientation, a number of important questions surface. For example, why do lesbians and gays have fewer children than heterosexuals? Why are women more often bisexual than men? Is the fact that gay men tend to be born

later into the family a significant factor to be explored in studying sexual orientation? Why are more gays found in urban than in rural areas? Is it because of more tolerance or anonymity there, or are other factors operating? And, finally, does homosexuality run in families? This selection is guaranteed to raise more questions than answers about an important and timely topic.

Byne is well-qualified to counter the argument that human sexual orientation has a heritable component. As a neuroanatomist and psychiatrist at Mt. Sinai School of Medicine, he studies correlations between brain structure and behavior in health and disease. He does not deny that all mental phenomena have a biological substructure, but he questions the precise contribution that certain biological factors may have in the development of sexual orientation. Although somewhat technical, the selection clearly and succinctly reviews several widely-acclaimed studies suggesting a biological basis for sexual orientation and draws surprising conclusions. Addressing what he believes to be incomplete or misleading findings, Byne makes a cogent case for controlled, carefully designed longitudinal studies. To properly debate the issue of the origin(s) of homosexuality, students will need the insights gained from this article as well as the previous one by Pillard and Bailey.

In the United States, it is estimated that at least 27 percent of same-sex couples are raising children under the age of eighteen (Gates and Ost 2004). More precise numbers are difficult to discern for various reasons—some obvious, others obscure. Obviously, many homosexual parents choose to remain anonymous because of discrimination, which can lead to loss of employment, loss of child custody, ostracism, or anti-gay and lesbian violence. Others may be ambivalent about their homosexuality, making it impossible for researchers to accurately assess the number of lesbian and gay parents. For example, when James McGreevey, the former governor of New Jersey, announced that he was gay in 2004, did his heterosexual family suddenly become a gay family? And, how might we best categorize families of bisexuals or transsexual/transgendered persons? Readers who wish to expand their knowledge beyond Susan Golombok and Fiona Tasker's rigorously designed study on these topics are referred to an article by therapists Ariel and McPherson (2000), who address a number of such issues in their work with lesbian and gay parents and children.

Of the hot topics pertaining to homosexual parenting, psychological stability is perhaps most debated. Do lesbian or gay parents differ from heterosexual parents in their ability to nurture children? Some people apparently believe so. A Florida court in 1996 removed a child from her biological mother, who was a lesbian, and awarded custody to the child's father, who had been convicted of murdering his first wife. Moreover, the mother mysteriously died when the case was being appealed (*Ward v. Ward*, No. 95–4184, 1996 Fla. App. LEXIX 9130 [Fla. Dis. Ct. App. Aug. 30, 1996]). Golombok and Tasker contrast biological and psychological theories as they address the subject of parental influence on the sexual orientation of children. An excellent, easy-to-follow review of various explanations of the causes of sexual orientation precedes the presentation of research in this British study.

The term, "queer theory," was first used in 1990 by Teresa de Lauretis, Professor of the History of Consciousness at the University of California, Santa Cruz, as a substitute term for the concept of "gay and lesbian studies." It very quickly caught on, and today, scholars in a variety of disciplines have "queered" the theories with which they work. According to David Halperin, a prominent queer theorist,

> This has resulted in a paradoxical situation: as queer theory becomes more widely diffused throughout the disciplines, it becomes harder to figure out what's so very queer about it, while lesbian and gay studies, which by contrast would seem to pertain only to lesbians and gay men, looks increasingly backward, identitarian, and outdated. (Halperin 2003, p. 342)

Elisa Abes and David Kasch, in their study, apply queer theory to the area of student development in the form of the life story of one prototypical student, KT. Thus, this reading introduces students to another approach that can be taken to the understanding of human sexuality: a case-study, viewed from a particular theoretical lens. Students who have gone through or are currently going through the coming-out process will likely identify at least a bit with KT. Students who are firm in their heterosexual identity will gain some empathy and insight with the plight of the sexual minority student. All students will develop a better understanding of the framework of queer theory.

Although much time and effort has been spent in an effort to understand the nature of sexual orientation, researchers are nowhere close to a definitive answer to the question of why most people find the other sex attractive, some people find the same sex attractive, and still others find both sexes attractive. The concept of bisexuality appears to be the most puzzling of all to those seeking a greater understanding of sexual orientation.

Roy Baumeister (2000) was among the first to argue that female sexuality is more fluid than male sexuality. This means, in part, that sexual expression tends to vary more significantly over the lifetime of a woman than a man. Sexual orientation seems to be a more static trait for men than for women. For women, a higher sex drive is related to greater sexual attraction to both sexes, whereas for men, a higher sex drive is related to more attraction to one sex or the other, but not both (Lippa 2006).

In the chapter by Lisa Diamond, changes in women's self-identified sexual orientation over a 10-year period of young adulthood are explored in an attempt to better understand the nature of bisexuality. Diamond examines the research evidence with regard to three different explanatory hypotheses regarding bisexuality, finding support for two of them. This longitudinal study is invaluable in expanding our conceptualization of what bisexuality is and shows how difficult it is to categorize the sexual orientation of many women.

Much sexuality research has focused on samples of participants who are largely heterosexual. Some research has examined those with a homosexual or bisexual orientation. But, what about those people who do not experience sexual desire for either sex? Asexuality, the focus of the Prause and Graham study, is a vastly understudied topic.

In 1980, Michael Storms tested his new conceptualization of sexual orientation in which heterosexual eroticism and homosexual eroticism were viewed as two independent dimensions, accommodating those who experienced attraction to both sexes as well as those who experienced attraction to neither sex. Since that time, however, there has been very little research on the concept of asexuality. The Internet, however, has enabled asexual individuals to form online communities, leading to greater visibility and perhaps allowing researchers to more easily reach individuals who self-identify as asexual.

The Prause and Graham study is a combination of qualitative and quantitative research, though the edited version presented in this volume focuses on the latter approach. The qualitative component of the study consisted of interviews with four self-identified asexual individuals. The information gleaned from these interviews led to the specific hypotheses tested in the quantitative portion of the study. Students will likely be eager to discuss the concept of asexuality. Some of them might self-identify as asexual, and others might have friends who they believe may fit the category. Indeed, asexuality is likely the answer to questions that some

students may have been asking. It may be a neglected piece to the puzzle of human sexual behavior.

REFERENCES

Ariel, J., and D. W. McPherson. 2000. Therapy with lesbian and gay parents and their children. *Journal of Marital and Family Therapy* 26: 421–32.

Baumeister, R. F. 2000. Gender differences in erotic plasticity: The female sex drive as socially flexible and responsive. *Psychological Bulletin* 126: 247–74.

Gates, G., and J. Ost. 2004. *The gay and lesbian atlas.* Washington, DC: Urban Institute Press.

Gelman, D., D. Foote, D. Barrett, and M. Talbot. 1992. "Born or Bred?" *Newsweek*, 24 February, 46–50, 52–53.

Halperin, D. M. 2003. The normalization of queer theory. *Journal of Homosexuality* 45: 339–43.

Laumann, E. O., J. H. Gagnon, R. T. Michael, and S. Michaels. 1994. *The social organization of sexuality: Sexual practices in the United States.* Chicago: University of Chicago Press.

Lippa, R. A. 2006. Is high sex drive associated with increased sexual attraction to both sexes? It depends on whether you are male or female. *Psychological Science* 17: 46–52.

Stein, E., ed. 1992. *Forms of desire: Sexual orientation and the social constructionist controversy.* New York: Routledge.

Storms, M. D. 1980. Theories of sexual orientation. *Journal of Personality and Social Psychology* 38: 783–92.

Troiden, R. R. 1988. *Gay and lesbian identity: A sociological analysis.* Dix Hills, NY: General Hall.

Weeks, J. 1981. Discourse, desire, and deviance: Some problems in a history of homosexuality. In *The making of the modern homosexual*, ed. K. Plummer, 76–111. London: Hutchinson.

CHAPTER 29

Human Sexual Orientation Has a Heritable Component

Richard C. Pillard
J. Michael Bailey

Before reading this article and the companion piece that follows, "Why we cannot conclude that sexual orientation is primarily a biological phenomenon," readers are referred to the fourth chapter of the Reiss and Reiss book, Solving America's Sexual Crises *for an excellent overview of homosexuality. These authors give an interesting, factual accounting of the homosexual revolution that began in 1969 at the Stonewall Inn, a popular gay bar in Greenwich Village in New York City. The subsequent birth of the Gay Liberation Front is detailed with amazing accuracy. Another excellent resource for understanding homosexuality is the beginning article in Part I by Bullough detailing the history of Kinsey's work on the topic of homosexuality from a different vantage point. Now, in this overview of behavioral genetics research on homosexual and heterosexual orientation, Pillard, a psychiatrist, and Bailey, a psychologist, team up to explore the heritability component of human sexual orientation. Against a backdrop of data about female and male sexual orientation, they impose recent research findings suggesting that*

sexual orientation is, at least in part, genetically based. Whether confirming or confounding for the reader, their research is an important contribution to understanding this still debatable topic.

A powerful generalization about human sexual desire is that members of the two sexes are attracted to each other but attracted by different qualities. Traditionally, men seek youth and beauty in a woman (although the standard of beauty may vary with time and place), whereas women seek in a man good health, high status, and evidence of willingness to provide for children (Symons 1979). These generalizations are intuitively compatible with evolutionary theory. The healthy, the young (women), and the rich (men) are more likely to produce viable offspring and raise them to maturity than the sick, the old, and the poor. (One example of fecundity enhanced by wealth and status: the late King Sombhuza of Swaziland was reported to have over 600 children).

For a given individual the selection of a mate may be an inexact marker of sexual attraction because in many societies the individual has limited mate choice and sometimes no choice at all. Community expectations and the social and political ambitions of the family often override

From "Human Sexual Orientation Has a Heritable Component" by R. C. Pillard, and J. M. Bailey. 1998. *Human Biology: The International Journal of Population Biology and Genetics 70*: 347–365. Copyright © 1998 Wayne State University Press, with the permission of Wayne State University Press.

individual desires. Also, atypical sexual desires result in censure and therefore may be effectively concealed. Nevertheless, heterosexual attraction, broadly speaking, must be the paradigmatic adaptation. Men and women attracted to one another sufficiently to copulate, pair bond, and raise children to self-sufficiency are a precondition for hominid evolution (Symons 1979).

The development and mechanisms of human sexual attraction have only recently become objects of study. Visual animals that we are, visual cues are doubtless important triggers of sexual response. Olfactory cues may also play a role in sexual attraction, although the nature of the cues and their relative strength remain in controversy (Kohl 1995). (It is interesting to note that blind persons report that they can be sexually attracted by a particular tone of voice.) Whatever cues attract men and women to each other, it is hard to escape the conclusion that they are more or less wired in, the product of an evolutionary history parallel to that of sexual reproduction itself.

Homosexuality, the sexual desire for a person of the same sex, is an interesting challenge to an evolutionary account of sexual attraction, one reason that psychosocial theories have been dominant. Homosexuality is not the only trait that poses the problem of the apparent selection of a reproductively disadvantageous trait. Schizophrenia is ubiquitous in humankind, too frequent to be the result of occasional mutations, and it is genetically influenced and results in decreased fecundity. What can one make of traits that seem so evidently to defeat the biological imperative of optimizing reproductive success?

Here, we present some background data about male and female sexual orientation and follow with some recent research that in our opinion suggests that sexual orientation has a genetic component. Finally, we comment on some possible explanations for the paradox presented by the persistence of a trait that appears inimical to reproductive success.

PHENOTYPE

Sexual orientation refers to an individual's erotic desire for a member of his or her own sex (homosexuality), the opposite sex (heterosexuality), or both sexes (bisexuality). Recognition of one's orientation generally comes during adolescence, although some individuals are aware of sex-specific attractions in childhood. A homosexual orientation may be concealed for practical reasons, but by adulthood it is almost always a conscious and more or less permanent personality trait. Psychological constructs such as "unconscious" or "latent" homosexuality have use for some clinicians but have dropped out of the research literature.

The ascertainment of an individual's sexual orientation for research purposes is generally done by a questionnaire or a sexual history interview, ideally conducted by a clinician with experience in sex history interviewing. Alfred Kinsey and his colleagues pioneered sex history interviewing with volunteer subjects, and a detailed account of the technique and content of the interviews upon which their survey research was based has been published (Kinsey et al. 1948). The information collected in a sexual history interview may include data about sexual feelings and behavior during the life epochs: childhood, adolescence, adulthood, and old age. Other information is obtained as the research protocol dictates, for example, the timing of developmental milestones (puberty, first sexual experience, marriage, menopause, etc.), the presence of sexual dysfunctions, safer sex practices, and sexual traumas.

As with any psychometric assessment, it is important to ensure the validity and reliability of the measures, and considerable work has been done on this issue (Bogaert 1996; Catania et al. 1995). Some researchers use physiological measures, such as penile plethysmography (Miner et al. 1995) or a vaginal probe, to evaluate sexual responsiveness to stimuli, usually presented by slides responsiveness to stimuli, usually presented by slides or videos. In this way responses to different erotic situations can be compared. These techniques, besides being somewhat invasive, require expensive instrumentation and their validity has not been fully established. Questionnaire and interview responses can be valid and reliable indicators of sexual behavior; as one example, respondents' accounts of their sexual activity can predict the occurrence of sexually transmitted diseases. The studies cited make use of interviews and questionnaires to ascertain the sexual orientation of research subjects. Despite sources of error, such as volunteer bias, pressure to give socially desirable responses, differences in interviewer technique and questionnaire items, these data give as clear and consistent a picture of the frequency and direction of sexual feeling and behavior as can be obtained from interview data on almost any other topic of interest to behavioral science.

FREQUENCY OF HOMOSEXUAL ORIENTATION

Some commentators in the early sexology literature believed that homosexuality was increasing because of the corrupting influences of city life (von Krafft-Ebing 1901). What they probably observed was the urbanization of nineteenth-century Europe bringing to the cities gays and lesbians who recognized that the opportunities for discreet liaisons were maximized there. More recently, Laumann et al. (1994) found that the percentage of gay men in large U.S. cities is much higher than that in rural areas. Some of this differential is the result of the migration of gays from country to city, but Laumann also found that gay men were disproportionately born in urban areas. This could result from environmental exposure, a reporting artifact (urban gays might be more candid about their orientation), or a genetic effect such that people with "gay genes" are more likely to be city dwellers.

Surveys of sexual orientation began with the Kinsey reports of 1948 and 1953 (Kinsey et al. 1948, 1953). With respect to sexual orientation,

the Kinsey team estimated the *relative* amounts of heterosexual and homosexual behavior, placing each subject on a 7-point scale from 0 (completely heterosexual) to 6 (completely homosexual) with intermediate points to describe mixtures of the two. Kinsey's data led to the much-cited estimate that 1 in 10 men are "more or less exclusively homosexual." Kinsey's colleague, Gebhard (1972), recognized the overrepresentation of subsamples with unusually high rates of homosexuality. By adjusting the sample weightings, Gebhard concluded that only 3–4 percent of men and 1–2 percent of women in the United States are exclusively homosexual or virtually so.

The Kinsey group also found that the frequency of more or less exclusive homosexuality was about the same in older subjects as in younger subjects. More recent surveys, although on a smaller scale, give estimates close to those from the Kinsey survey (as adjusted by Gebhard) a half-century ago (Seidman and Rieder 1994; Laumann et al. 1994). Thus, despite differences in definition, methodology, and time frame, these surveys taken together suggest that the frequency of gay and lesbian behavior in the United States has remained stable over several generations in spite of the revolutionary changes in the social status of homosexuality. Although comparable data from other countries would be useful, few are available. Some recent surveys report a frequency of homosexual behavior in the 1–2 percent range (Sell et al. 1995).

Bisexuality occupies a controversial place in the literature (Fox 1996). Kinsey suggested that bisexuality was both common and normal. His graphic presentations using a cumulative frequency distribution make it difficult for the reader to recognize that he found more respondents toward the extreme homosexual end of the spectrum (5 and 6 on the Kinsey scale) than in the intermediate range. Diamond (1993) concluded from his own survey that "exclusive or predominantly exclusive homosexual activities are more common than bisexual activities" (p. 291). In our experience this bimodality is more evident among men, whereas bisexuality is relatively more common in women.

Bisexuality is also more frequently endorsed among the young. Adult subjects are usually unequivocally able to say which sex they prefer in a partner, that is, which sex most strongly engages their fantasies and desires. On the other hand, people engage in sexual relations with the nonpreferred sex for any number of reasons, and therefore frequency counts of behavior alone, particularly if sampled over a stretch of time, often result in a pattern that appears more bisexual than would be the case if desire alone prompted behavior. By the time they reach their mid-twenties, most men and most women give a clear and unambiguous answer when asked, Would you rather have sex with a woman or a man?

GENDER ATYPICALITY

Gay men and to a lesser extent lesbian women are often labeled as gender atypical. The term "gender atypical" is chosen to avoid prejudging whether the behaviors at issue are typically those of the other sex or simply not typical of the assigned sex. For men atypicality is evidenced in childhood by association with girl playmates, preference for girls' toys and games, and avoidance of boyish rough-and-tumble play. In adulthood gay men often have preference for female-typical activities and vocations. Lesbian women recollect tomboy behavior in childhood and preference for boys' games and companionship. As adults, lesbians tend to adopt male-typical social and vocational roles more often than do heterosexual women.

Gender atypicality as a forerunner of adult homosexuality has been noted in the sexology literature for more than 100 years (Ulrichs 1994). It is a robust phenomenon confirmed in both prospective and retrospective studies (Bailey, Miller et al. 1993; Bailey and Zucker 1995; Bailey, Nothnagel et al. 1995; Green 1987; Phillips and Over 1995). Whitam found that gender

atypicality is a culturally invariable childhood trait for gay men (Whitam 1983) and women (Whitam and Mathy 1991) in such diverse cultures as Brazil, Peru, Guatemala, and the Philippines.

Of course there are many possible kinds of gender atypicality and many ways that a child or adult can feel and behave atypically. Nevertheless, comparing the gender behavior of gays and heterosexuals makes clear that this trait is not simply a matter of feeling lonely, isolated, different, or depressed. The feelings and behaviors are often strikingly and specifically those of the other sex (Pillard 1991).

Gender typical and atypical behaviors emerge in children at similar ages, around 2 to 4 years. Observes of gender-atypical children at play are struck by the pervasive and tenacious nature of this trait. Moreover, some gender-atypical children even look different. Zucker and his colleagues gave photographs of prepubertal gender-typical and gender-atypical boys (Zucker et al. 1993) and girls (Fridell et al. 1996) to raters blind to the child's behavior status. Raters described gender-atypical boys as "cuter," "prettier," and "more attractive" than the gender-typical boys and described the converse for the atypical girls. Apparently, in addition to their behavior, something in the physiognomy of these children marks them already in childhood as gender atypical. What we know about the natural history of this trait suggests that a larger than expected percentage will become gay and lesbian adults. A theory of the development of sexual orientation must take account of the robust and frequently replicated data on the coincidence of atypical behavior in early childhood followed by same-sex attraction in adolescence and adulthood [for an alternative view, see Bem (1996)].

With the onset of adolescence same-sex or opposite-sex attractions become prominent in the gay or lesbian adult-to-be, but some measure of gender atypicality usually remains. Standard personality tests often include so-called masculinity-femininity (M-F) scales purporting to reflect the degree to which an individual matches the "maleness" or "femaleness" typical of his or her sex. Most such items are transparent: "I think I would like the work of a nurse" or "I like to read *Popular Mechanics* magazine" obviously will have different endorsement rates for the two sexes. What is surprising is how large the differences are, how consistent they are across cultures, and how little they have changed over time despite the profound changes in available gender appropriate activities and role models (Gough et al. 1968). The endorsement of female-typical pursuits and interests by gay men found by Terman and Miles (1936) on their M-F scale can be replicated today, again despite profound changes in the roles and social status of women and of gays.

Are gays and lesbians also atypical in other domains in which the sexes differ, such as patterns of cognitive abilities, brain lateralization, or incidence of physical and mental illness? These questions have not been well studied, and results are uneven (Bogaert and Blanchard 1996; Hall and Kimura 1995; Reite et al. 1995). Furthermore, there are at least some traits on which gender atypicality seems to be minimal or absent; for example, gay men tend not to show a female-typical interest in child care (Stringer and Grygier 1976).

The research just cited naturally led investigators seeking neuroanatomical correlates of sexual orientation to look at the hypothalamus, because it subserves reproductive functions, and at nuclei within the hypothalamus known to be gender dimorphic. Two articles reported differences between gay and heterosexual men in the size of hypothalamic nuclei. LeVay (1991) found that gay men have a smaller anterior hypothalamic nucleus, which is also smaller in women than in men. However, Swaab and Hoffman (1990) found that gay men have a larger suprachiasmatic nucleus, although it is *not* gender dimorphic. It thus appears that homosexual attraction and gender atypicality are more complex than simply a skewed mix of typically masculine and feminine qualities.

BIRTH ORDER

Blanchard and Bogaert (1996) have recently reported that gay men tend to be born later in the sibship, and this trend is accounted for by the presence of older brothers but not older sisters. A psychosocial explanation for this observation certainly seems plausible. Perhaps having an older brother stimulates homosexual attraction, perhaps the family's reaction to a younger brother is such as to bend him in a homosexual direction. There are also purely biological possibilities; for example, placental cells invade the uterine endometrium, and it is now known that protein fragments from these cells may remain in the maternal system for many years. Their effect (if any) is unknown, but their existence raises the possibility of an influence on later gestations (Blanchard and Bogaert 1996).

FAMILIAL AGGREGATION OF MALE AND FEMALE SEXUAL ORIENTATION

Characteristics of interest to the behavioral geneticist generally run in families; familial aggregation suggests but does not prove a genetic contribution to the trait. Sexologists a half-century ago observed that sexual orientation may be familial (Hirschfeld 1936), but systematic research on the issue is relatively recent. Pillard and Weinrich (1986) used newspaper and radio advertisements to recruit subjects for studies of "personality, sexual behavior, and mental abilities." Some ads were placed in papers with a mostly gay readership to enrich the participation of the minority orientation and were written to be candid yet to conceal the specific hypotheses of the study. Volunteers were interviewed and given psychological tests; then permission was requested to recruit their sibs. A large number of sibs were enrolled and (to avoid bias) interviewed.

Pillard and Weinrich's (1986) primary finding was that nonheterosexual males (2–6 on the Kinsey scale) had an excess of nonheterosexual brothers (22 percent), whereas heterosexual males (0 or 1 on the Kinsey scale) had only 4 percent nonheterosexual brothers, close to the population average. We use the term "nonheterosexual" to highlight another finding: The few males who were bisexual (2–4 on the Kinsey scale) had as many gay brothers as did males who were exclusively gay. Individuals who had "more than occasional" gay contacts, even if most of their contacts were heterosexual, shared the tendency toward familial aggregation as strongly as did the exclusive homosexuals. An additional finding was that probands [brothers] were able to accurately report their sibs' orientation so long as they made the assessment with a high degree of confidence.

To summarize, we note that nonheterosexual males have from 2 to 5 times as many nonheterosexual brothers as do heterosexual males. The heterosexual males, in turn, have rates of nonheterosexuality among their brothers that are about equal to the population frequency, based on other large survey studies. Nonheterosexual women also appear to have more nonheterosexual sisters than do heterosexual women, although the familiality estimates for women vary more widely.

There is a trend for nonheterosexual men to have more nonheterosexual sisters [however, this was not found by Pillard and Weinrich (1986)], whereas nonheterosexual women tend to have more nonheterosexual brothers. However, the estimates varied considerably, leaving open the important issue of cofamiliality of male and female homosexuality.

Family trees with the systematically ascertained sexual orientation of parents, children, and other relatives of gay and lesbian probands are rarely published. Pillard et al. (1982) noted that, when males reported other gay or lesbian relatives, they usually came from the maternal side of the family, an observation also made by Hamer et al. (1993). This pattern suggests that some male homosexuality may be X-chromosome linked, an issue more fully discussed by Pattatucci (1998).

FEMALE AND MALE TWINS AND ADOPTEES

The traditional method used by behavioral geneticists to disentangle genetic and environmental components of trait variance is the comparison of concordance between monozygotic (MZ) twins, dizygotic (DZ) twins, and adopted siblings (i.e., biologically unrelated individuals) reared together. If the influence of genes is paramount, MZ twins will be frequently concordant, whereas DZ twins will have the same concordance as nontwin siblings (in the absence of a congenital factor). Adopted siblings, sharing the family's environment but not their genes, will share the trait no more often than an average sample of the population.

Several twin studies of sexual orientation have been conducted recently. Bailey and Pillard (1991) and Bailey, Pillard et al. (1993) recruited two kinds of gay males: those with twins and those with adopted brothers or sisters. Males were interviewed concerning the sexual orientation of their co-twin or adopted sib, who was contacted where possible. Males were generally accurate in assessing their sibling's sexual orientation. In the male sample 56 MZ twins were ascertained, 52 percent of whom were concordant for a nonheterosexual orientation, 54 DZ twins were ascertained, 22 percent of whom were concordant [the same as for nontwin brothers according to Pillard and Weinrich (1986)], and 57 adopted male sibs were ascertained, 11 percent of whom were concordant with the gay male sib.

The female study yielded concordance rates of 48 percent for MZ twins, 16 percent for DZ twins, and 6 percent for adopted sisters. Heritability estimates for women were likewise substantial. However, more recent data obtained by Bailey et al. (1996) on twins from an Australian twin registry showed little difference in concordance rates between female MZ and DZ twins and thus gave essentially zero heritability for females. This result may be due to the different manner in which the twins were recruited.

Neither age of first recognition of gay or lesbian feelings, extreme Kinsey scale score, nor extent of childhood gender atypicality related to genetic liability for a homosexual orientation. However, both male and female *concordant* MZ twin pairs were also highly similar in their gender atypicality scores, suggesting a genetic basis for this trait. Whitam et al. (1993) reported somewhat higher concordance rates for both MZ and DZ twins. They also reported three sets of triplets. One set consisted of an MZ male pair, concordant for homosexuality, and a heterosexual sister. A second set of three sisters consisted of an MZ pair, both lesbian, and a DZ heterosexual sister. The third set consisted of three MZ brothers, all gay.

The few available examples of MZ twins *raised apart* (Eckert et al. 1986; Whitam et al. 1993) show a degree of concordance, at least for males, similar to the cited observations of MZ twins raised together. Concordance in several male MZ pairs reared apart extended to an interesting variety of personality traits as well.

The conclusion that sexual orientation has a heritable component depends on a set of assumptions, which we now examine. The primary assumption is that volunteer bias does not distort the outcome. Probands [subjects] for the twin studies were obtained through advertisements in gay-oriented publications. It may be that persons who read these publications and who volunteer for a study are systematically different from the larger population of gay twins or siblings. This possibility can be tested by comparing volunteer data with those from a captive sample, such as from a clinic, or with subjects randomly drawn from a census tract or phone book.

There may also be a systematic concordant-dependent bias; that is, twins or sibs who share a trait may be more (or less) likely to volunteer than those who are discordant. The cited heritability analyses examined the effects of concordance-dependent bias and found that heritability estimates remained substantial over a wide range of assumptions about that kind of bias. Moreover, we found that the concordance rate of DZ twins was similar to the rate of nontwin siblings in other studies of men (Pillard and Weinrich 1986) and women (Bailey and Benishay 1993). We doubt that concordance estimates from the sibling studies were seriously biased because the hypothesis of those studies was concealed from subjects.

The possibility of *asymmetric* concordance-dependent bias could more seriously affect the heritability estimates. This could happen if, for example, concordant MZ twins were relatively more likely to volunteer than concordant DZ twins or adopted siblings. This possibility cannot be completely ruled out; however, the degree of volunteer asymmetry would have to be large to result in a true zero difference in concordance rates between MZ and DZ pairs.

Heritability calculations assume that MZ twins, DZ twins, and adopted siblings share environments that are not systematically different—in this case, not different on variables salient to sexual orientation. At first thought, it must seem that MZ twins are so alike that their family and friends could not help but treat them almost as one individual. Perhaps so, but studies suggest that a violation of the equal-environments assumption does not seem to have much effect. Twins whose parents make a deliberate effort to differentiate them (different clothing, names, schools, etc.) turn out to be as similar on a variety of personality traits as twins treated alike. Furthermore, MZ twins mistakenly thought by their family to be DZ twins are as similar as if they were correctly labeled (Plomin et al. 1990). However, it may be that we simply do not know the relevant environmental precursors of sexual orientation and so cannot judge the extent to which siblings share them.

Twin concordance estimates are affected by the way twins are selected. Hundreds of pairs may have to be screened to obtain a stable estimate of concordance for an infrequent trait. It is much easier just to advertise for twin probands [subjects] expressing the trait of interest. This proband-wise concordance will always produce an overestimate of true concordance simply because there are more concordant individuals eligible to respond. Probandwise concordance is the probability that a homosexual twin will have a homosexual co-twin.

For clarity of exposition the discussion to this point has tacitly assumed a simple causal model for sexual orientation, an assumption that is almost certainly incorrect. It seems likely, for example, that the orientation of women and men may be differently determined. As already noted, women and men experience sexual attraction in different ways; women are more often bisexual than men, there seems to be less familiality between than within the sexes, and the X-chromosome linkage site reported for men has not been replicated for women (Hu et al. 1995). Extrapolating from what is known about the genetics of other traits, one can see that there may be dozens or even hundreds of alleles [a series of two or more different genes that occupy the same location on a specific chromosome] relevant to sexual orientation. Some alleles may be quite rare, and some may interact with the environment in complex and unexpected ways. The physical and functional identification of genes for sexual orientation is still a distant goal.

EVOLUTIONARY SIGNIFICANCE

Many human traits are thought to have a genetic component because they run in families and because twin and adoptee concordance rates are compatible with the known principles of genetic transmission. Such traits include the shyness-extroversion axis, certain cognitive abilities, aggressiveness, manic-depressive illness, Tourette's syndrome, specific language disorders, self-esteem, some mental disorders, and some social attitudes (Plomin et al. 1994). A few of

these traits (e.g., spatial ability) are thought to have animal analogs. However, for none of the named traits has a specific gene (or genes) been found. The pathway from gene to behavior is unknown. Environmental sources of variance, substantial in our studies, may include the biological environment, for example, prenatal hormone exposure, the psychosocial environment, or some combination of the two. The interplay between genetic predisposition and environmental releasers or suppressers of a trait is presumably complicated, and at present, nothing is known with respect to sexual orientation.

The special problems posed by the evolution of traits that reduce fecundity have interested biologists since Darwin. If an individual possesses a gene that reduces his or her reproductive ability even slightly, that trait will be negatively selected, although it may reappear in other kindreds by means of a new mutation. But, as noted by Moran (1972), the frequency of homosexual orientation is too great by orders of magnitude to make plausible that it is replenished by random mutations.

The selective disadvantage of homosexuality must be very large in modern society. Bell et al. (1981) found that homosexuals have only one-fifth as many children as heterosexuals. Lesbians and gay men without children are a common feature of the urban milieu and give rise to the further paradox that social tolerance toward gays is the very condition that should promote the negative selection of "gay genes" (Hamer and Copeland 1994). In societies remote from Western influence, lesbians and gay men may more often marry and have children, but some probably adopt nonreproductive roles as celibates, priests, and so forth. In these societies the reproductive loss would be diminished but still present. If a genetic predisposition for a homosexual orientation exists, what advantage could it confer to pay the cost of lost reproduction to the individual?

Three sorts of answers are usually given to this question. One proposes a reproductive advantage to the heterozygote. Fisher (1922) pointed out that for a condition that is reproductively deleterious in the homozygote, there must be a selective advantage for the heterozygote. This issue has been developed by Weinrich and others (Weinrich 1987; MacIntyre and Estep 1993). The hypothetical advantage to the heterozygote need not have anything to do with sexual attraction. It could involve genes with other attributes: conferring resistance to an endemic disease, promoting a larger sibship or coding for personality traits or patterns of cognitive abilities that, for example, help their possessor to hunt the leopard or harvest the yams. It seems likely that the selecting environment "sees" other associated traits, and sexual desire or behaviors carried along as an exaptation.

A second possibility to account for the persistence of "gay genes" is that they prompt their possessor to undertake acts of altruism toward kin such that kin survival more than offsets the reproductive loss (in genetic terms) to the altruist. (Altruism is defined as an act that benefits another at a cost to the altruist.) Examples of kin altruism are reported for animal species and clearly are evolved behaviors (Packer et al. 1991). There is some evidence, both anecdotal and systematic, that gay persons behave more altruistically (Salais and Fischer 1995), but whether this is the behavior that maintains the genotype is of course anyone's guess.

A third possibility for persistence comes from the finding of a putative linkage site on the X chromosome (Hu et al. 1995). A gene conferring reproductive advantage to females (e.g., by making them more beautiful, more desirable as mates) could persist, although it is detrimental to males. Women have two X chromosomes, whereas men have only one, so a fairly small genetic advantage to a female could offset the cost to the male. We reiterate that the three mechanisms are simply speculations, arguments on the general question of the persistence of a phenotype that reduces fecundity. There is no evidence that any one of these mechanisms operates to maintain "gay genes" in a balanced polymorphism in human populations.

A limitation of the family and twin studies is that they can give no clue about where the "gay genes" are or what they do. Specific gene finding techniques are needed to address this issue. Should such genes be found, one question that begs for an answer is the transcultural nature of homosexuality. Herdt (1994) and others have described "third gender" members in various societies—shamans, priests, berdaches, celibates, etc. Some of these individuals are described as having cross-gender attributes and homosexual behaviors possibly analogous to gay and lesbian behavior in Western societies. One hypothesis is that there is a "gay genotype" of ancient origin, now widely dispersed in human societies, the phenotypic expression of which takes the many forms of third genderness described by social scientists.

Research on the presumed selective advantage of a gay genotype will be difficult to implement, first, because the environment that selected it, presumably over generations of prehistoric time, may be different from the one in which it now exists. Second, the selective advantage need be very small, only a percentage point or two, to balance the lost fertility of the individual gay or bisexual family member. These small effects are often buried in noise. Despite these formidable challenges to research on the genetics of sexual orientation, we believe that this topic has much to contribute to a more complete understanding of human nature.

REFERENCES

Bailey, J. M., and D. Benishay. 1993. Familial aggregation of female sexual orientation. *Am. J. Psychiatr.* 150: 272–277.

Bailey, J. M., and R. C. Pillard. 1991. A genetic study of male sexual orientation. *Arch. Gen. Psychiatr.* 48: 1089–1096.

Bailey, J. M., and K. J. Zucker. 1995. Childhood sex-typed behavior and sexual orientation: A conceptual analysis and quantitative review. *Devel. Psychol.* 31: 43–55.

Bailey, J. M., M. P. Dunne, and N. G. Martin. 1996. Distribution correlates and determinants of sexual orientation in a national twin sample. Unpublished.

Bailey, J. M., J. Miller, and L. Willerman. 1993. Maternally rated childhood gender nonconformity in homosexuals and heterosexuals. *Arch. Sex. Behav.* 22: 461–469.

Bailey, J. M., J. Nothnagel, and M. Wolfe. 1995. Retrospectively measured individual differences in childhood sex-typed behavior among gay men: Correspondence between self and maternal reports. *Arch. Sex. Behav.* 24: 613–622.

Bailey, J. M., R. C. Pillard, M. C. Neale et al. 1993. Heritable factors influence sexual orientation in women. *Arch. Gen. Psychiatr.* 50: 217–223.

Bell, A. P., M. S. Weinberg, and S. K. Hammersmith. 1981. *Sexual Preference: Its Development in Men and Women.* Bloomington, IN: Indiana University Press.

Bem, D. J. 1996. Exotic becomes erotic: A developmental theory of sexual orientation. *Psychol. Rev.* 103: 320–335.

Blanchard, R., and A. F. Bogaert. 1996. Homosexuality in men and number of older brothers. *Am. J. Psychiatr.* 153: 27–31.

Bogaert, A. F. 1996. Volunteer bias in human sexuality research: Evidence for both sexuality and personality differences in males. *Arch. Sex. Behav.* 25: 125–140.

Bogaert, A. F., and R. Blanchard. 1996. Handedness in homosexual and heterosexual men in the Kinsey interview data. *Arch. Sex. Behav.* 25: 373–378.

Catania, J. A., D. Binson, A. van der Straten et al. 1995. Methodological research on sexual behavior in the AIDS era. In *Annual Review of Sex Research: An Integrative and Interdisciplinary Review*, R. C. Rosen, ed. Mount Vernon, IA: Society for the Scientific Study of Sexuality, 77–125.

Diamond, M. 1993. Homosexuality and bisexuality in different populations. *Arch. Sex. Behav.* 32: 291–310.

Eckert, E. D., T. J. Bouchard, J. Bohlen et al. 1986. Homosexuality in monozygotic twins reared apart. *Br. J. Psychiatr.* 148: 421–425.

Fisher, R. A. 1922. On the dominance ratio. *Proc. R. Soc. Edinburgh* 42: 321–341.

Fox, R. C. 1996. Bisexuality: An examination of theory and research. In *Textbook of Homosexuality and Mental Health*, R. P. Cabaj and T. S. Stein, eds. Washington, DC: American Psychiatric Press, 147–172.

Fridell, S. R., K. J. Zucker, S. J. Bradley et al. 1996. Physical attractiveness of girls with gender identity disorder. *Arch. Sex. Behav.* 25: 17–31.

Gebhard, P. 1972. Incidence of overt homosexuality in the United States and Western Europe. In *National Institute of Mental Health Task Force on Homosexuality: Final Report and Background Papers*, J. Livingood, ed. DHEW Publication (HMS) 72–9116. Washington, DC: US Department of Health, Education, and Welfare, 22–29.

Gough, H. G., K. Chun, and Y. E. Chung. 1968. Validation of the CPI femininity scale in Korea. *Psychol. Rep.* 22: 155–160.

Green, R. 1987. *The "Sissy Boy Syndrome" and the Development of Homosexuality.* New Haven, CT: Yale University Press.

Hall, J. A. Y., and D. Kimura. 1995. Sexual orientation and performance on sexually dimorphic motor tasks. *Arch. Sex. Behav.* 24: 395–407.

Hamer, D., S. Hu, V. L. Magnuson et al. 1993. A linkage between DNA markers on the X chromosome and male sexual orientation. *Science* 261: 321–327.

Hamer, D., and P. Copeland. 1994. *The Science of Desire: The Search for the Gay Gene and the Biology of Behavior.* New York: Simon and Schuster.

Herdt, G., ed. 1994. *Third Sex, Third Gender: Beyond Sexual Dimorphism in Culture and History.* New York: Zone Books.

Hirschfeld, M. 1936. Homosexuality. In *Encyclopaedia Sexualis: A Comprehensive Encyclopedia/Dictionary of the Sexual Sciences*, V. Robinson, ed. New York: Dingwall-Rock, 321–334.

Hu, S., A. Pattatucci, C. Patterson et al. 1995. Linkage between sexual orientation and chromosome Xq28 in males but not in females. *Natur. Genet.* 11: 248–256.

Kinsey, A. C., W. B. Pomeroy, and C. E. Martin. 1948. *Sexual Behavior in the Human Male.* Philadelphia, PA: W.B. Saunders.

Kinsey, A. C., W. B. Pomeroy, C. E. Martin et al. 1953. *Sexual Behavior in the Human Female.* Philadelphia, PA: W. B. Saunders.

Kohl, J. V. 1995. *The Scent of Eros: Mysteries of Odor in Human Sexuality.* New York: Continuum Publishing.

Laumann, E., J. Gagnon, R. Michael et al. 1994. *The Social Organization of Sexuality: Sexual Practices in the United States.* Chicago, IL: University of Chicago Press.

LeVay, S. 1991. A difference in hypothalamic structure between heterosexual and homosexual men. *Science,* 255: 1034–1037.

MacIntyre, F., and K. W. Estep. 1993. Sperm competition and the persistence of genes for male homosexuality. *Biosystems* 31: 223–233.

Miner, M. H., M. A. West, and D. M. Day. 1995. Sexual preference for child and aggressive stimuli: Comparison of rapists and child molesters using auditory and visual stimuli. *Behav. Res. Ther.* 33: 545–551.

Moran, P. A. P. 1972. Familial effects in schizophrenia and homosexuality. *Aust. N.Z.J. Psychiatr.* 6: 116–119.

Packer, C., D. A. Gilbert, and A. E. Pusey. 1991. A molecular genetic analysis of kinship and cooperation in African lions. *Nature* 351: 562–564.

Pattatucci, A. M. L. 1998. Molecular investigations into complex behavior: Lessons from sexual orientation studies. *Hum. Biol.* 70(2): 367–386.

Phillips, G., and R. Over. 1995. Differences between heterosexual, bisexual, and lesbian women in recalled childhood experiences. *Arch. Sex. Behav.* 24: 1–20.

Pillard, R. C. 1991. Masculinity and femininity in homosexuality: "Inversion" revisited. In *Homosexuality: Research Implications for Public Policy*, J. Gonsiorek and J. D. Weinrich, eds. Newbury Park, CA: Sage Publications, 32–43.

Pillard, R. C., and J. D. Weinrich. 1986. Evidence of familial nature of male homosexuality. *Arch. Gen. Psychiatr.* 43: 808–812.

Pillard, R. C., J. I. Poumadere, and R. A. Carretta. 1982. A family study of sexual orientation. *Arch. Sex. Behav.* 11: 511–520.

Plomin, R., J. C. DeFries, and G. E. McClearn. 1990. *Behavioral Genetics: A Primer*. New York: W. H. Freeman.

Plomin, R., M. J. Owen, and P. McGuffin. 1994. The genetic basis of complex human behaviors. *Science* 264: 1733–1739.

Reiss, I. L., and H. M. Reiss. 1997. *Solving America's sexual crises*. Amherst, NY: Prometheus.

Reite, M., J. Sheeder, D. Richardson et al. 1995. Cerebral laterality in homosexual males: Preliminary communication using magnetoencephalography. *Arch. Sex. Behav.* 24: 585–593.

Rogers, S., and C. Turner. 1991. Male-male sexual contact in the USA: Findings from five sample surveys, 1970–1990. *J. Sex Res.* 28: 491–519.

Salais, D., and R. B. Fischer. 1995. Sexual preference and altruism. *J. Homosex.* 28: 185–196.

Seidman, S. N., and R. O. Rieder. 1994. A review of sexual behavior in the United States. *Am. J. Psychiatr.* 151: 330–341.

Sell, R. L., J. A. Wells, and D. Wypij. 1995. The prevalence of homosexual behavior and attraction in the United States, the United Kingdom, and France: Results of national population-based samples. *Arch. Sex. Behav.* 24: 235–248.

Stringer, P., and T. Grygier. 1976. Male homosexuality, psychiatric patient status, and psychological masculinity and femininity. *Arch. Sex. Behav.* 5: 15–27.

Swaab, D. F., and M. A. Hoffman. 1990. An enlarged suprachiasmatic nucleus in homosexual men. *Brain Res.* 537: 141–148.

Symons, D. 1979. *The Evolution of Human Sexuality*. New York: Oxford University Press.

Terman, L. A., and C. Miles. 1936. *Sex and Personality: Studies in Masculinity and Femininity*. New York: McGraw-Hill.

Ulrichs, K. H. 1994. *The Riddle of "Man-Manly" Love: The Pioneering Work on Male Homosexuality*, M. A. Lombardi-Nash, trans. Buffalo, NY: Prometheus Books.

von Krafft-Ebing, R. 1901. *Psychopathia Sexualis*, 3d ed., translation of 10th German ed. Chicago, IL: W. T. Keener.

Weinrich, J. D. 1987. *Sexual Landscapes*. New York: Scribner's.

Whitam, F. L. 1983. Culturally invariable properties of male homosexuality: Tentative conclusions from cross-cultural research. *Arch. Sex. Behav.* 22: 207–226.

Whitam, F. L., and R. M. Mathy. 1991. Childhood cross-gender behavior of homosexual females in Brazil, Peru, the Philippines, and the United States. *Arch. Sex. Behav.* 20: 151–170.

Whitam, F. L., M. Diamond, and J. Martin. 1993. Homosexual orientation in twins: A report of 61 pairs and three triplet sets. *Arch. Sex. Behav.* 22: 187–206.

Zucker, K., J. Wild, S. Bradley et al. 1993. Physical attractiveness of boys with gender identity disorder. *Arch. Sex. Behav.* 22: 23–36.

CHAPTER 30

Why We Cannot Conclude That Sexual Orientation Is Primarily a Biological Phenomenon

William M. Byne

After reading the previous article, claiming that human sexual orientation has a heritable component, readers will be challenged to broaden their conclusions by the Byne selection, which presents counterarguments to a number of scientific studies. For example, are the often quoted LeVay research findings focused more clearly by evidence that the medication used to treat AIDS causes change in the size of the hypothalamus gland? And what conclusions can be drawn from the information that the hormone profiles of gays and lesbians are reportedly indistinguishable from those of heterosexuals? These and other intriguing facts raise issues without answers. But the author, a medical researcher of brain structures and behavior, asks far more penetrating questions. Does biology simply provide a slate of neural circuitry upon which sexual orientation is inscribed by experience? Or do biological factors influence sexual orientation only indirectly by affecting personality variables that influence the environment in social relationships which in turn shape sexual orientation? Students, like more learned scholars, will be unable to answer the questions decisively after finishing this offering, but they will be farther along the path of scientific thought about this matter.

From "Why We Cannot Conclude That Sexual Orientation Is Primarily a Biological Phenomenon" by W. M. Byne. 1997. *Journal of Homosexuality 34*: 73–80. Copyright 1997 by Haworth Press Inc. – Journals. Reproduced with permission of Haworth Press Inc. – Journals in the format Textbook via Copyright Clearance Center.

I would like to challenge [the following statement]: "Sexual orientation is primarily a biological phenomenon," from three different perspectives. First, we have to ask whether sexual orientation is a unitary phenomenon that can be accounted for by a single explanation. If, as seems more likely, there are multiple pathways to the same endpoint of relative sexual attraction to men or to women, then biology might play a greater or lesser role for different individuals depending on the idiosyncrasies of their individual developmental pathways. [To say that]: "Sexual orientation is primarily a biological phenomenon," fails to anticipate the need for analysis at such a level of complexity.

Second, what do we mean when we assert that sexual orientation is "primarily biological"? All psychological phenomena are primarily biological in the sense that they cannot exist in the absence of the biological activity of a living brain. "Primarily biological" must mean something else—perhaps, that biological factors are more important than psychosocial or experiential factors. But the processes integral to experience, namely perception, internalization, association, and assimilation, are themselves inextricably enmeshed with biology. How, then, can biological and experiential factors be teased apart, and what are the units of measurement that would allow them to be individually quantified and weighed against one another in order to determine which is more important? I believe that it would be more productive to explore the pathways through which biological and experiential factors might interact, than to argue about the primacy of one set of factors over the other.

The final perspective from which I wish to challenge the debate statement is to address the weakness of the biological database itself. Much of the commonly offered biological evidence has yet to be replicated or has to be discounted because it has failed replication (Byne, 1995, 1996; Byne & Parsons, 1993; Fausto-Sterling, 1992). Even the replicable data are often uninterpretable because of confounded experimental designs (Byne, 1995; Fausto-Sterling, 1992). Beyond these difficulties the research to date has produced purely correlational data. Correlations, no matter how robust, cannot demonstrate that sexual orientation is primarily biological in the absence of adequately controlled longitudinal studies that delineate the intermediate causal mechanisms (Byne, 1996).

Much of the research is premised on assumptions of questionable validity. Most biological research that addresses sexual orientation seeks to demonstrate that the brains of homosexuals are in some ways like those of the other sex (Byne & Parsons, 1993). The rationale behind this research is as follows: First, sexual orientation is assumed to be a unitary brain function that is sexually dimorphic. By sexually dimorphic, I mean that it takes two forms and differs between heterosexual men and heterosexual women. Researchers then seek to define two archetypes for the human brain: One of these

they suggest would be shared by gay men and heterosexual women and would drive sexual attraction to men, while the other would be shared by heterosexual men and lesbians and would drive sexual attraction to women. Even a cursory review of human sexuality in historical and cross-cultural perspective suggests that these assumptions are culture bound and inadequate (Boswell, 1980; Ford & Beach, 1951).

Without questioning the validity of these assumptions, some researchers propose that the differentiation of these two archetypes is accomplished prenatally in response to sex differences in exposure to particular hormones (Allen & Gorski, 1992; Gladue et al., 1984; LeVay, 1991). This prenatal hormonal hypothesis draws upon animal research showing that a sexually receptive female mating posture called lordosis can be elicited from male rodents that were deprived of androgens during a critical period of brain development. Conversely, females that were experimentally treated with androgens during that same period fail to show lordosis in adulthood, but will show increased levels of male-typical mounting behavior (Goy & McEwen, 1980).

There are major problems in extrapolating from these findings to sexual orientation in humans. First, in the paradigm of the neuroendocrine laboratory, the male rat that shows lordosis [bending backward] when mounted by another male is considered the homosexual. But it is important to note that lordosis is little more than a reflex, and that the male that displays lordosis when mounted by another male will also display the posture if its back is stroked by a researcher. We cannot infer much about the sexual motivation of the male that exhibits this posture. Ironically, however, the animal that does display sexual motivation—the male that mounts another male—escapes scientific scrutiny and labeling as does the female that displays lordosis when mounted by another female. Some researchers have begun to acknowledge the problem of equating behaviors in rodents with sexual orientation, and have begun to employ a variety of strategies to actually assess partner preference in animals (Paredes & Baum, 1995).

But even these studies may have no relevance to human sexual orientation. This is because in order for the genetic male to behave as a female, with respect to either partner preference or lordosis behavior, he must be exposed to extreme hormonal abnormalities that are unlikely to occur outside the neuroendocrine laboratory. Not only must he be castrated as a neonate, depriving him of androgens, but in order to activate the display of female-typical behaviors and preferences, he must also be injected with estrogens in adulthood (Paredes & Baum, 1995).

It is difficult to see how this situation has any bearing on human sexual orientation when healthy gay men and lesbians have hormonal profiles that are indistinguishable from those of their heterosexual counterparts. Nor do the vast majority of homosexuals exhibit physical stigmata indicative of sexually atypical prenatal hormone levels (Meyer-Bahlburg, 1984).

However, if it proves to be replicable, Simon LeVay's report (1991) concerning the third interstitial nucleus of the anterior hypothalamus could be considered as evidence that some homosexual men experienced low androgen levels prenatally. Specifically, LeVay reported that the third nucleus is smaller in women and gay men than in presumed heterosexual men. The third nucleus in humans closely resembles a structure which, in rats, is much larger in males than in females. In rats, the size of this structure which is known as the sexually dimorphic nucleus of the preoptic area is primarily determined by perinatal hormones (Gorski et al., 1978).

LeVay's report that the size of the third nucleus varies with sexual orientation has been faulted for a number of technical reasons, such as small sample size, inadequate assessment of sexual orientation, and the reliance on the brains of gay subjects with AIDS. The small sample size really isn't a problem. In fact, statistical power analysis suggests that differences as large as those he reported could be detected with even smaller sample sizes. Also, by adding to uncontrolled variance, poor sexual histories would decrease rather than increase the probabitial of detecting statistically significant differences.

Unfortunately, there has been little discussion of the hormonal abnormalities associated with AIDS and the possible impact of such abnormalities on LeVay's findings. HIV-related hormonal abnormalities need to be taken into account because in some species the size of sexually dimorphic hypothalamic nuclei varies with the amount of testosterone in the adult animal's bloodstream (Commins & Yahr, 1984). Whether or not the nucleus is present is related to prenatal hormonal status. However, if an adult male is castrated, the size of his nucleus will decrease by half. This shrinkage can be prevented by the administration of testosterone, suggesting that testosterone is necessary to maintain the size of the nucleus in the mature animal (Commins & Yahr, 1984).

These findings are potentially highly relevant to LeVay's report because the testes fail in HIV infection and testosterone levels decline. Furthermore, some drugs used commonly to treat the opportunistic infections of AIDS also decrease testosterone levels and the side effects of other medications may elevate estrogen levels (Croxson et al., 1989). Thus, it is entirely possible that the effects on the size of the third nucleus that LeVay attributed to sexual orientation were actually due to some hormonal abnormality resulting from AIDS or its treatment. His inclusion of a few heterosexual men who died with AIDS did not adequately control for this possibility.

In interpreting his study, LeVat (1991) has suggested that the third interstitial nucleus is involved in the "generation of male-typical sexual behavior." But this suggestion is made on the basis of an imprecise reading of the literature. While he is technically correct when he writes that lesions in the region of the rat's sexually dimorphic nucleus disrupt male sexual behavior, the effective lesion site lies above, not within, that nucleus (Arendash & Gorski, 1983).

Furthermore, Gary Arendash and Roger Gorski at UCLA have shown that the sexually dimorphic nucleus can be destroyed on both sides of the brain without any effect on mounting behavior (Arendash & Gorski, 1983).

LeVay and Hamer (1994) conclude that similarly placed lesions in male rhesus monkeys cause them to become "completely sexually indifferent to females." But what the paper they cite actually shows is quite different. While dorsally placed medial preoptic lesions did decrease mounting, they by no means eliminated it (Slimp et al., 1978). Moreover, the males in this study pressed a lever for access to females more frequently following the lesions than before. So contrary to LeVay's interpretation, one cannot conclude that the lesioned males were sexually indifferent to females.

In another highly publicized neuroanatomical study, Laura Allen and Roger Gorski reported that the anterior commissure is larger in women and homosexual men than in presumed heterosexual men (Allen & Gorski, 1992). The major problem for this study is that the only other group to study the anterior commissure for sexual dimorphism found a sex difference but in the opposite direction (Demeter et al., 1988).

To summarize so far, then, the neuroendocrinological and neuroanatomical evidence does not allow one to resolve that sexual orientation is primarily biological, and as I will now show, the same can be said about the genetic evidence.

Until only two years ago, the evidence that heritable factors influence sexual orientation consisted only of reports that homosexuality tends to run in families and that identical twins are more likely to share the same sexual orientation than are fraternal twins (Byne & Parsons, 1993). Such studies are not helpful in distinguishing between biological and environmental influences because related individuals share environmental variables as well as genes. Adoption studies are necessary to avoid this confound.

One of the recent heritability studies did include an adoption component, and this suggested a significant environmental contribution to the development of sexual orientation (Bailey & Pillard, 1991). This study included not only identical and fraternal twins, but also the unrelated adopted brothers of the gay probands [subjects]. If there were no environmental effect on sexual orientation, then the rate of homosexuality among the adopted brothers should be equal to the base rate of homosexuality in the population, which recent studies place at somewhere between 2 and 5 percent (Hamer et al., 1993). The fact that the observed concordance rate was 11 percent—that is 2 to 5 times higher than expected—suggests a major environmental contribution—especially when we consider that the rate of homosexuality in the non-twin biological brothers was only 9 percent in the study of Bailey and Pillard (1991), and 13.5 percent in a study by Dean Hamer et al. (1993). If the concordance rate for homosexuality among non-twin brothers is the same whether or not the brothers are biologically related, the concordance cannot be explained genetically.

Of all the recent biological studies, the genetic linkage study by Dean Hamer's group (Hamer et al., 1993) is the most complex conceptually, and the most likely to be misinterpreted, especially by those unfamiliar with the rationale of linkage studies. While this study did suggest that homosexuality may be linked to the X-chromosome in at least one cohort of men, the study did not uncover any particular genetic sequence associated with homosexuality as is commonly believed.

The verdict is still out as to whether or not Hamer's study can be independently replicated. Recent work done by George Ebers's group in London, Ontario, raises doubt. This group is convinced that sexual orientation is genetically determined and is currently screening approximately 10 markers a day distributed across the human genome. While they are confident that they will eventually establish a genetic linkage for homosexuality, they are equally confident that it will not be to the X-chromosome. To date, their family studies based on over 200 gay probands have failed to show any evidence of X linkage (Ebers, personal communication).

In closing, we are a long way from understanding the factors that contribute to sexual orientation. Even if the size of certain brain structures does turn out to be correlated with sexual orientation, current understanding of the brain is inadequate to explain how such quantitative differences could produce qualitative differences in a psychological phenomenon as complex as sexual orientation. Similarly, confirmation of genetic linkage would make clear neither precisely what is inherited nor how the heritable factor influences sexual orientation. For instance, would the heritable factor influence the organization of hypothetical neural circuits that mediate sexual orientation? Or would it act more indirectly, perhaps influencing temperamental variants that in turn influence how one interacts with the environment in constructing the social relationships and experiences from which sexual orientation emerges (Byne, 1996)? The existing biological data are equally compatible with both scenarios, and certainly do not allow us to resolve that sexual orientation is primarily biological.

As research into the biology of sexual orientation proceeds, we should ask why we as a society are so emotionally invested in its outcome. Will it—or should it—make any difference in the way we perceive ourselves and others or in the way we live our lives and allow others to live theirs? Perhaps the answers to the most salient questions in this debate reside not in the biology of human brains, but within the cultures those brains have created.

References

Allen, L. S., & Gorski, R. A. (1992). Sexual orientation and the size of the anterior commissure in the human brain. *Proceedings of the National Academy of Sciences, USA, 89,* 7199–7202.

Arendash, G. W., & Gorski, R. A. (1983). Effects of discrete lesions of the sexually dimorphic nucleus of the preoptic area or other medial preoptic regions on the sexual behavior of male rats. *Brain Research Bulletin, 10,* 147–154.

Bailey, J. M., & Pillard, R. C. (1991). A genetic study of male sexual orientation. *Archives of General Psychiatry, 48,* 1089–1096.

Boswell, J. (1980). *Social tolerance, Christianity, and homosexuality.* Chicago, IL: University of Chicago Press.

Byne, W. (1995). Science and belief: Psychobiological research on sexual orientation. *Journal of Homosexuality 28,* 303–344.

Byne, W. (1996). Biology and homosexuality: Implications of neuroendocrinological and neuroanatomical studies. In R. P. Cabaj & T. S. Stein (Eds.) *Textbook of homosexuality and mental health* (pp. 129–146). Washington, DC: American Psychiatric.

Byne, W., & Parsons, B. (1993). Sexual orientation: The biological theories reappraised. *Archives of General Psychiatry, 50,* 228–239.

Commins, D., & Yahr, P. (1984). Adult testosterone levels influence the morphology of a sexually dimorphic area in the Mongolian gerbil brain. *Journal of Comparative Neurology, 224,* 132–140.

Croxson, T. S., Chapman, W. E., Miller, L. K., Levit, C. D., Senie, R., & Zumoff, B. (1989). Changes in the hypothalamic-pituitary-gonadal axis in human immunodeficiency virus-infected men. *Journal of Clinical Endocrinology and Metabolism, 89,* 317–321.

Demeter, S., Ringo, J. L., & Doty, R. W. (1988). Morphometric analysis of the human corpus callosum and anterior commissure. *Human Neurobiol, 6,* 219–226.

Fausto-Sterling, A. (1992). *Myths of gender: Biological theories about women and men.* New York: Basic Books.

Ford, C. S., & Beach, F. A. (1951). *Patterns of sexual behavior.* New York: Harper and Bros.

Gladue, B. A., Green, R., & Hellman, R. E. (1984). Neuroendocrine response to estrogen and sexual orientation. *Science, 225,* 1496–1499.

Gorski, R. A., Gordon, J. H., Shryne, J. E., & Southam, A. M. (1978). Evidence for a morphological sex difference in the medical preoptic area of the rat brain. *Brain Research, 148,* 333–346.

Goy, R. W., & McEwen, B. S. (1980). *Sexual differentiation of the brain.* Cambridge, MA: MIT Press.

Hamer, D. H., Hu, S., Magnuson, V. L., Hu, N., & Pattatucci, A. M. L. (1993). A linkage between DNA markers on the X chromosome and male sexual orientation. *Science, 261*, 321–327.

LeVay, S. (1991). A difference in hypothalamic structure between heterosexual and homosexual men. *Science, 253*, 1034–1037.

LeVay, S., & Hamer, D. (1994). Evidence for a biological influence in male homosexuality. *Scientific American, 270*, 44–49.

Meyer-Bahlburg, H. F. L. (1984). Psychoendocrine research on sexual orientation: Current status and future options. *Progress in Brain Research, 71*, 375–397.

Paredes, R. G., & Baum, M. J. (1995). Altered sexual partner preference in male ferrets given excitotoxic lesions of the preoptic area/anterior hypothalamus. *Journal of Neuroscience, 15*, 6619–6630.

Slimp, J. C., Hart, B. L., & Goy, R. W. (1978). Heterosexual, autosexual, and social behavior of adult male rhesus monkeys with medial preoptic anterior hypothalamic lesions. *Brain Res, 142*, 105–122.

CHAPTER 31

Do Parents Influence the Sexual Orientation of Their Children?

Susan E. Golombok
Fiona L. Tasker

A subject of major interest to many students is whether having a homosexual parent will predispose a person to a lesbian or gay identity. Golombok and Tasker investigate family environment as a causative factor in sexual orientation, identifying several factors that may influence whether children grow up to be heterosexual or homosexual. With one exception, they go a step beyond other investigations of adult daughters of lesbian mothers which have focused on children rather than on adults and have failed to address sexual orientation.

In addition, use of a comparison group of heterosexual parents definitely differentiates this research design from other such studies. But most important is its prospective nature, an approach that allows data about the sexual orientation of young adults reared by lesbian mothers to be examined. Thus, we receive a rare glimpse into the process through which childhood family characteristics and experiences may influence sexual orientation during the transition to adult life. Readers are cautioned, however, to interpret the

data with care because respondent attrition in the follow-up stage of the study substantially reduced the sample size. This ambitious piece of research, which challenges readers with far from staid conclusions or "pat" answers, may inspire or incite, yet it definitely will inform.

Opinion varies among biological and psychological theorists regarding the extent to which it is possible for parents to influence the sexual orientation of their children. From a purely biological perspective, parents should make little difference. In contrast, psychoanalytic theorists believe that relationships with parents in childhood are central to the development of sexual orientation in adult life. Research on adults raised in lesbian families provides an opportunity to test theoretical assumptions about the role of parents in their children's sexual orientation; if parents are influential in whether their children grow up to be heterosexual, lesbian, or gay, then it might be expected that lesbian parents would be more likely than heterosexual parents to have lesbian daughters and gay sons. With the exception of Gottman's (1990) investigation of adult daughters of lesbian mothers in which actual sexual behavior was not reported, research on lesbian families has focused on

From "Do Parents Influence the Sexual Orientation of Their Children?: Findings from a Longitudinal Study of Lesbian Families" by S. Golombok, and F. Tasker. 1996. *Developmental Psychology 32*: 3–11. Copyright © 1996 by the American Psychological Association. Adapted with permission.

children rather than adults, and sexual orientation has not been assessed (Golombok, Spencer, & Rutter, 1983; Green, Mandel, Hotvedt, Gray, & Smith, 1986; Patterson, 1992).

From the existing literature, it seems that no single factor determines whether a person will identify as heterosexual or homosexual. The current view is that there are a variety of influences, from the prenatal period onward, which may shape development in one direction or the other. Studies of gay men with twin brothers (Bailey & Pillard, 1991) and lesbian women with twin sisters (Bailey, Pillard, Neale, & Agyei, 1993) have found that a significantly greater proportion of monozygotic than dizygotic co-twins were gay or lesbian. The greater concordance between identical than nonidentical twin pairs indicates a genetic link to homosexuality, although this does not mean that a homosexual (or heterosexual) orientation is dependent on a specific genetic pattern. The identification of a genetic marker for male homosexuality has recently been reported by Hamer, Hu, Magnuson, Hu, and Pattatucci (1993). Of 40 pairs of brothers, both of whom were homosexual, 33 pairs were found to have a marker in a small region of the X chromosome, suggesting that there may be a specific gene, yet to be located, which is linked to male homosexuality. However, the presence of this gene, if it exists, would not necessarily determine a homosexual orientation, and not all homosexual men would necessarily possess the gene (the marker was not found in 7 pairs of brothers). Instead, it may be one of many factors that influence development along a homosexual rather than a heterosexual course.

Gonadal hormone levels may constitute another such factor. Although no consistent differences in gonadal hormone levels between heterosexual and homosexual adults have been identified (Meyer-Bahlburg, 1984), there is evidence to suggest that the prenatal hormonal environment may play some part in the development of sexual orientation. Studies of women with congenital adrenal hyperplasia (CAH), a genetically transmitted disorder in which malfunctioning adrenal glands produce high levels of androgens from the prenatal period onward, have found that these women were more likely to consider themselves to be bisexual or lesbian than were women who do not have the disorder, suggesting that raised levels of androgens prenatally may be associated with a lesbian sexual orientation (Dittman, Kappes, & Kappes, 1992; Money, Schwartz, & Lewis, 1984). In addition, a significantly greater proportion of women exposed in utero to the synthetic estrogen diethylstilbestrol (DES), an androgen derivative, reported bisexual or lesbian responsiveness compared with both unexposed women from the same clinic and their unexposed sisters (Ehrhardt et al., 1985). It is important to note, however, that most of the women with CAH, and most of the women prenatally exposed to DES, were heterosexual despite their atypical endocrine history.

On the basis of this research, together with animal research which has demonstrated that gonadal hormones influence the development of sex-typed behavior and sex differences in brain morphology (Goy & McEwen, 1980), it has been proposed that prenatal gonadal hormones may act on the human brain to facilitate development as heterosexual or homosexual (Hines & Green, 1990; Money, 1988). However, the mechanisms involved in the link between prenatal gonadal hormones, sex differences in brain morphology, and sexual orientation have not been established (Byne & Parsons, 1993). Although an anatomical difference in the hypothalamus of homosexual and heterosexual men has recently been identified (LeVay, 1991), the reason for this difference, and how it may influence sexual orientation, remains unknown.

A number of investigations point to a relationship between nonconventional gender role behavior in childhood and adult homosexuality. In retrospective studies, differences in childhood gender role behavior have been found between homosexual and heterosexual men (Bell, Weinberg, & Hammersmith, 1981; Whitam, 1977) and between lesbian and heterosexual women (Bell et al., 1981; Whitam & Mathy, 1991), with homosexual men and lesbian women consistently reporting greater involvement in cross-gender activities. Prospective studies of boys with gender identity disorder (American Psychiatric Association, 1994)—children who express a strong desire to be the other sex and characteristically engage in cross-gender behavior including a marked preference for friends of the other sex—have shown that more than two thirds of the children develop a bisexual or homosexual orientation in adulthood (Green, 1987). Nevertheless, the identification of a link between cross-gender behavior in childhood and homosexuality in adulthood does not mean that all or even most adults who identify as homosexual were nonconventional in their gender role behavior as children. A substantial proportion of gay and lesbian adults who participated in the retrospective studies reported no or few cross-gender behaviors in childhood, and the prospective studies examined gay men who had been referred in childhood to a clinic because of marked cross-gender behavior and thus were not representative of the general population of adult homosexual men. Investigations of parental influences on childhood gender nonconformity have failed to identify a clear and consistent association between the two, either for boys (Roberts, Green, Williams, & Goodman, 1987) or for girls (Green, Williams, & Goodman, 1982). However, to the extent that sexual orientation results from complex interactions between the individual and the social environment, studies that have demonstrated a link between boyhood cross-gender behavior and adult homosexuality suggest that feminine boys, and possibly masculine girls, in lesbian families may be more likely than their counterparts in heterosexual families to develop a sexual orientation toward partners of the same sex.

From the perspective of classical social learning theory, the two processes that are important for children's gender development are differential reinforcement and the modeling of same-sex individuals, particularly same-sex parents (Bandura, 1977; Lytton & Romney, 1991; Mischel, 1966). Although social learning theorists have focused on the development of gender role behavior rather than on sexual orientation, insofar as sexual orientation results from social learning, the processes of reinforcement and modeling would also apply. From this viewpoint, it could be expected that different patterns of reinforcement may be operating in lesbian than in heterosexual families, such that young people in lesbian families would be less likely to be discouraged from embarking upon lesbian or gay relationships. With respect to modeling, contemporary social learning theorists now believe that it is the modeling of gender stereotypes, rather than same-sex parents, that promotes gender development (Bandura, 1986; Perry & Bussey, 1979). Thus, girls would no longer be expected to adopt a lesbian identity simply by observing and imitating their lesbian mother. But by virtue of their nontraditional family, the sons and daughters of lesbian mothers may hold less rigid stereotypes about what constitutes acceptable male and female sexual behavior than their peers in heterosexual families, and they may be more open to involvement in lesbian or gay relationships themselves. Thus, from a social learning theory perspective, children's sexual orientation may be influenced by attitudes toward sexuality in the family in which they are raised.

In examining the cognitive mechanisms involved in gender development, cognitive developmental theorists, like social learning theorists, have focused on the acquisition of sex-typed behavior rather than on sexual orientation (Kohlberg, 1966; Martin, 1993). Cognitive developmental explanations of gender development emphasize that children actively construct for themselves, from the gendered world around them, what it means to be male or female, and they adopt behaviors and characteristics that they perceive as being consistent with their own sex. Again, gender stereotypes, rather than parents, are viewed as being the primary source of gender-related information. To the extent that cognitive processes are contributing to the adoption of a heterosexual or homosexual orientation, it would seem that young people seek out information that is in line with their emerging sexual orientation, and they come to value and identify with those characteristics that are consistent with their view of themselves as heterosexual, lesbian, or gay. Cognitive developmental theorists would place less emphasis on the role of parental attitudes than on prevailing attitudes in the wider social environment. Thus, the social context of the family, within a wider community that is either accepting or rejecting of homosexuality, would be considered to facilitate or inhibit respectively young people's exploration of relationships with partners of the same sex as themselves.

Social constructionist theories start from the premise that sexual feelings are not essential qualities that the individual is born with or that are socialized by childhood experiences (Kitzinger, 1987; Simon & Gagnon, 1987). What these approaches have in common is an emphasis on the individual's active role, guided by his or her culture, in structuring reality and creating sexual meanings for particular acts. Sexual identity is considered to be constructed throughout the life course; the individual first becomes aware of cultural scenarios for sexual encounters and then develops internal fantasies associated with sexual arousal and interpersonal scripts for orchestrating specific sexual acts (Gagnon, 1990). Identification with significant others is believed to be important for enabling an individual either to neutralize a homosexual potential or to construct a homosexual identity. For example, heterosexual parents may respond negatively to what they perceive as children's same-gender sexual activity (Gagnon, 1977). Plummer (1975) suggested that awareness of others who identify as homosexual validates feelings of same-gender attraction that might otherwise go unnoticed or be denied. From a social constructionist perspective, therefore, children raised in lesbian families would be expected to be more likely than children in heterosexual families to adopt a lesbian or gay identity themselves as a result of their exposure to lesbian lifestyles, and often to gay lifestyles as well.

Although psychoanalytically oriented theorists hold the view that homosexuality arises from disturbed relationships with parents (Freud, 1920/1955, 1933; Socarides, 1978), empirical studies of the influence of parent-child relationships on the development of a gay or lesbian identity have produced inconclusive results. In a study of psychoanalysts' reports of the family relationships of their male homosexual patients, the fathers of gay men were described as hostile or distant and the mothers as close—binding, intimate, and dominant (Bieber et al., 1962). With a nonpatient sample, Evans (1969) also showed a similar pattern of a close mother and a detached father. However, Bene (1965) found no evidence that homosexual men who were not in therapy were more likely to have been overprotected by, overindulged by, or strongly attached to their mother than heterosexual men, and in a well-controlled large-scale study by Siegelman (1974), no differences were identified in parental background between homosexual and heterosexual men who were low on neuroticism. Studies of the parents of lesbian women have similarly failed to produce consistent findings, although some investigations have reported mothers of lesbian women to be dominant and fathers to be inferior or weak (Bell et al., 1981; Newcombe, 1985).

Although existing research has failed to produce empirical evidence to demonstrate that parents' behavior influences the development of their children's sexual orientation, all of the studies to date have investigated heterosexual families. In addition, these studies have focused on the quality of parent-child relationships rather than on other aspects of the family environment. By investigating the sexual partner preferences of young adults who have grown up in a lesbian family, we hoped to examine the impact on sexual orientation of being raised by a lesbian mother, and thus to address the question of what influence, if any, parents may have in their children's development as heterosexual, lesbian, or gay. As data in this study were first collected from the families when the children were school age, this prospective investigation not only provides data on the sexual orientation of young adults raised by lesbian mothers, but it also allows an examination of the processes through which childhood family characteristics and experiences may influence the development of sexual orientation during the transition to adult life.

THE CURRENT STUDY

Method

Sample

Twenty-seven lesbian mothers and their 39 children and a control group of 27 heterosexual single mothers and their 39 children first participated in the study when the average age of the children was 9.5 years (Golombok et al., 1983). The two types of family were alike in that the children were being raised by women in the absence of a father in the household, but they differed with respect to the sexual orientation of the mother. The criteria for inclusion were that the lesbian mothers regarded themselves as predominantly or wholly lesbian in their sexual orientation and that their current or most recent sexual relationship was with a woman. The single-parent group was defined in terms of mothers whose most recent sexual relationship had been heterosexual but who did not have a male partner living with them at the time of the original study. The two groups were matched for the age and social class of the mothers, and all of the children had been conceived within a heterosexual relationship.

In 1992–1993, the children, who were 23.5 years old on average, were seen again. For ethical reasons, it was necessary to locate the mothers in the first instance to request permission to recontact their children. Fifty-one of the 54 mothers who participated in the original study were traced. The follow-up sample comprised 25 young adults raised in lesbian families (8 men and 17 women) and 21 young adults raised in heterosexual families (12 men and 9 women).

An examination of the demographic characteristics of the young people who participated at follow-up showed no statistically significant differences between those from lesbian and those from heterosexual single-parent homes with respect to age, gender, ethnicity, and educational qualifications. There were seven pairs of siblings in the lesbian group and five pairs of siblings in the heterosexual group. By the time of the follow-up study, all but one of the original group of heterosexual single mothers were reported by their children to have had at least one heterosexual relationship, and in most cases (18 out of 20), the new male partner had cohabited with the mother while the children were living at home. Likewise, all but one of the children in lesbian families reported that their mother had had at least one lesbian relationship, and in 22 out of 24 cases, their mother's female partner had resided with them. Thus, the large majority of children in both groups had lived in a stepfamily during their adolescent years.

Measures

Data on the young adults' sexual orientation were gathered in the follow-up study by using a semistructured interview with a standardized coding scheme that had been developed specifically for the present investigation (Tasker & Golombok, in press). Each man and woman was interviewed either at home or at the university by a female interviewer (Fiona Tasker). The psychosexual history section of the interview commenced with questions on experience of prepubertal sexual play with same-gender and opposite-gender children and about interest in other children's bodies and physical development during puberty. The men and women were then asked to recall their first crush and subsequent crushes from the beginning of puberty through to their first sexual relationship in order to establish the extent of same-gender and opposite-gender attraction. To further assess the presence or absence of same gender attraction, we asked the participants whether they had ever thought that they might be physically attracted to a friend of the same gender, and whether they had ever had sexual fantasies about someone of the same gender. A chronological sexual relationship history was then given by each interviewee detailing their age when the relationship began, the gender of their partner, the level of sexual contact, and the duration of the relationship. In addition, information was obtained regarding their current sexual identity as heterosexual, bisexual, lesbian, or gay.

Five variables relating to sexual orientation were derived from the interview material: (a) The presence of *same-gender attraction* was established from data on sexual object choice in crushes, fantasies, and sexual relationships from puberty onward. (b) *Consideration of lesbian or gay relationships* was rated according to whether participants had ever previously thought that they might experience same-gender attraction or relationships, or whether they thought it possible that they might do so in the future. (c) *Same-gender sexual relationships* ranged from a single encounter involving only kissing to cohabitation lasting over 1 year. (d) For the variable *sexual identity*, men and women were categorized according to whether they identified as bisexual, lesbian, or gay and expressed a commitment to a bisexual, lesbian, or gay identity in the future. (e) A composite rating of *same-gender sexual interest* was made for each participant.

Family Characteristics
Using an adaptation of a standardized interview previously designed to assess family functioning (Quinton, Rutter, & Rowlands, 1976), we obtained data on characteristics of the lesbian family environment that may be hypothesized to influence the development of children's sexual orientation from the lesbian mothers in the initial study when the children were school age. The variables derived from the initial study were the following: (a) number of years the child had been raised in a heterosexual home, (b) the

mother's warmth to the child, (c) the child's contact with his or her father, (d) the child's gender role behavior, (e) quality of the child's peer relationships, (f) quality of the mother's relationship with her current female partner, (g) the mother's relationship history, (h) the mother's openness in showing physical affection, (i) the mother's contentment with her sexual identity, (j) the mother's political involvement, (k) the mother's preference for the child's sexual orientation, and (l) the mother's attitude toward men. Comparable data from the initial study are not available for the young people raised in heterosexual families as it would not have been meaningful to ask the heterosexual mothers questions about lesbian relationships when they had not experienced any (e.g., about physical affection shown toward their female partner in front of the child).

Results

Sexual Orientation: Comparison Between Young Adults Raised in Lesbian and Heterosexual Families
There was no significant difference between adults raised in lesbian families and their peers from single-mother heterosexual households in the proportion who reported sexual attraction to someone of the same gender.

Distinct from the experience of same-gender attraction is consideration of having a lesbian or gay relationship. Significantly more of the young adults from lesbian family backgrounds stated that they had previously considered, or thought it a future possibility, that they might experience same-gender attraction or have a same-gender sexual relationship or both. Fourteen children of lesbian mothers reported this to be the case compared with 3 children of heterosexual mothers. Daughters of lesbian mothers were significantly more likely to consider that they might experience same-gender attraction or have a lesbian relationship than daughters of heterosexual mothers. There was no significant difference between sons from the two family types for this variable.

With respect to actual involvement in same-gender sexual relationships, there was a significant difference between groups such that young adults raised by lesbian mothers were more likely to have had a sexual relationship with someone of the same gender than young adults raised by heterosexual mothers. None of the children from heterosexual families had experienced a lesbian or gay relationship. In contrast, 6 children from lesbian families had become involved in one or more sexual relationships with a partner of the same gender. It was also found that all of the men and women from lesbian (as well as from heterosexual) backgrounds had experienced at least one opposite-gender sexual relationship.

In terms of sexual identity, the large majority of young adults with lesbian mothers identified as heterosexual. Only 2 young women from lesbian families identified as lesbian compared with none from heterosexual families. This group difference did not reach statistical significance.

Childhood Family Characteristics and Adult Sexual Orientation

To examine prospectively the processes that may result in the children of lesbian mothers being more likely to engage in same-gender relationships than those raised by heterosexual mothers, we correlated variables from the initial study relating to family characteristics with the overall rating of same-gender sexual interest for the group of young adults raised by lesbian mothers. Young adults whose mothers had reported greater openness in showing physical affection to their female partner when their children were school age and young adults whose mothers had reported a greater number of lesbian relationships when their children were school age were more likely to report same-gender sexual interest. No significant associations were found between same-gender sexual interest in adulthood and the number of years the child had been raised in a heterosexual household, the mother's warmth to the child, the child's contact with the father, the child's gender role behavior, the quality of the child's peer relationships, the quality

of the mother's relationship with her female partner, the mother's contentment with her sexual identity, the mother's political involvement, or the mother's attitude toward men. Similarly, data obtained from the heterosexual mothers in the initial study on the mother's warmth to the child, the child's contact with the father, the child's gender role behavior, and the quality of the child's peer relationships showed no significant association between these variables and the overall rating of the young adults' same-gender sexual interest.

Discussion

The sample studied in the present investigation is unique in that it constitutes the first group of young people raised in lesbian families to be followed from childhood to adulthood. As information about childhood family environment was collected before the participants began to engage in sexual relationships, the findings relating to the characteristics of the lesbian and heterosexual families in which these young people grew up are not confounded by knowledge of their sexual orientation in adult life.

Although no significant difference was found between the proportions of young adults from lesbian and heterosexual families who reported feelings of attraction toward someone of the same gender, those who had grown up in a lesbian family were more likely to consider the possibility of having lesbian or gay relationships, and to actually do so. However, the commonly held assumption that children brought up by lesbian mothers will themselves grow up to be lesbian or gay is not supported by the findings of the study; the majority of children who grew up in lesbian families identified as heterosexual in adulthood, and there was no statistically significant difference between young adults from lesbian and heterosexual family backgrounds with respect to sexual orientation.

It is important to remember that this research was conducted with volunteer samples of lesbian and heterosexual families, thus the generalizability of the findings is reduced. It is not possible to recruit a representative sample of lesbian mothers given that many do not publicly declare their sexual identity. However, both the lesbian and heterosexual groups reflected a diversity of families nationwide, from different socioeconomic backgrounds, and with different political or apolitical perspectives. Although our interviewees may have been reluctant to admit to same-gender sexual preferences, if underreporting took place, it seems reasonable to assume that this would have been more prevalent among men and women from heterosexual homes, as young adults from lesbian families appeared to be more comfortable in discussing lesbian and gay issues in general. Because of limitations of sample size, data have been presented for more than one child per family, which could have inflated significance. However, the 2 daughters who identified as lesbian were from different families, and of the 6 young adults from lesbian families who reported a same-gender relationship, only 2 belonged to the same family, suggesting that the findings cannot be explained in this way. To definitively address the questions raised in this article, one would require a large-scale epidemiological study following children of lesbian and heterosexual parents from childhood to adulthood with respect to their family characteristics and sexual identity development.

The greater proportion of young adults from lesbian families than from heterosexual families who reported consideration of, and involvement in, same-gender sexual relationships suggests an association between childhood family environment and these aspects of sexual development. Moreover, the association found in lesbian families between the degree of openness and acceptance of lesbian and gay relationships and young adults' same-gender sexual interest indicates that family attitudes toward sexual orientation, that is, as accepting or rejecting of gay and lesbian lifestyles, constitute one of the many influences that may shape development in either a heterosexual or a homosexual direction. It seem that growing up in an accepting atmosphere

enables individuals who are attracted to same-sex partners to pursue these relationships. This may facilitate the development of a lesbian or gay sexual orientation for some individuals. But, interestingly, the opportunity to explore same-sex relationships may, for others, confirm their heterosexual identity. In the present sample, 4 of the 6 young adults who had experienced same-gender sexual relationships identified as heterosexual in early adulthood. Although the findings suggest that daughters of lesbian mothers are more open to same-sex relationships than are sons, in the initial investigation, there was a higher ratio of sons to daughters in the lesbian group and a higher ratio of daughters to sons in the heterosexual group, which remained at the follow-up. Thus a higher proportion of women than men who reported consideration of, and involvement in, same-sex relationships may reflect this sampling bias.

It is important to point out that the mothers and children who participated in the research were genetically related to each other, and thus it is not possible to disentangle the influence of genetic and social aspects of the parent-child relationship, that is, the influence of parental genetic material as opposed to parental behavior. It cannot be ruled out that the outcomes for these young people would have been the same had they been raised by parents who were genetically unrelated to them (e.g., adoptive parents). However, the results suggest that the group difference in same-gender sexual interest is a consequence of the children's experiences with lesbian and heterosexual mothers while growing up, particularly in view of the finding that the childhood family environments of young adults from lesbian families who reported same-gender sexual interest were characterized by an openness and acceptance of a lesbian lifestyle. It should be noted that the young adults raised in lesbian households were no more likely than those from heterosexual households to experience mental health problems, and both groups obtained scores on standardized measures of emotional well-being that did not differ significantly from those of general population samples (Tasker & Golombok, in press).

Although not inconsistent with biological theories that propose that sexual orientation results from interactions between prenatal factors and postnatal experience (Money, 1988), the findings of this investigation are also compatible with social-cognitive and social constructionist explanations of the psychological mechanisms involved in gender development. What these latter theories have in common is the view that sexual orientation is influenced, to some extent at least, by social norms. From this perspective, if children grow up in an atmosphere of positive attitudes toward homosexuality, they would be expected to be more open to involvement in gay or lesbian relationships themselves. Different aspects of sexual orientation may be influenced to a greater or lesser degree by experiential factors such that sexual experimentation with same-gender partners may be more dependent on a conducive family environment than the development of a lesbian or gay identity. It is worth noting that none of the sons or daughters of lesbian mothers in the present investigation showed marked childhood cross-gender behavior of the type associated with a later lesbian or gay identity. In addition, no difference in childhood role behavior was found between young adults who reported same-gender sexual interest and those who did not.

Whereas there is no evidence from the present investigation to suggest that parents have a determining influence on the sexual orientation of their children, the findings do indicate that by creating a climate of acceptance or rejection of homosexuality within the family, parents may have some impact or their children's sexual experimentation as heterosexual, lesbian, or gay.

Growing attention has been paid in recent years to the social context of families and to the processes through which social environments affect family relationships. It is important to remember that the young adults in this study were born at a time when there was less social acceptance of lesbian women and gay men. As Gagnon (1990) pointed out, young

people are now better informed about lesbian and gay lifestyles and know about lesbian and gay possibilities at an earlier age. How the changing social climate may influence exploration of same-gender relationships remains open to speculation. It is conceivable, however, that children born at the present time to heterosexual parents who are accepting of lesbian and gay relationships will be just as open to same-sex exploration in adulthood as their counterparts from lesbian families are today.

REFERENCES

American Psychiatric Association. (1994). *Diagnostic and statistical manual of mental disorders* (4th ed.). Washington, DC: Author.

Bailey, J. M., & Pillard, R. C. (1991). A genetic study of male sexual orientation. *Archives of General Psychiatry, 48,* 1089–1096.

Bailey, J. M., Pillard, R. C., Neale, M. C., & Agyei, Y. (1993). Heritable factors influence sexual orientation in women. *Archives of General Psychiatry, 50,* 217–223.

Bandura, A. (1977). *Social learning theory.* Englewood Cliffs, NJ: Prentice Hall.

Bandura, A. (1986). *Social foundations of thought and action: A social cognitive theory.* Englewood Cliffs, NJ: Prentice Hall.

Bell, A. P., Weinberg, M. S., & Hammersmith, S. K. (1981). *Sexual preference: Its development in men and women.* Bloomington: Indiana University Press.

Bene, E. (1965). On the genesis of male homosexuality: An attempt at clarifying the role of the parents. *British Journal of Psychiatry, 111,* 803–813.

Bieber, I., Dain, H., Dince, P., Drellick, M., Grand, H., Gondlack, R., Kremer, R., Rifkin, A., Wilber, C., & Bieber, T. (1962). *Homosexuality: A psychoanalytic study.* New York: Basic Books.

Byne, W., & Parsons, B. (1993). Human sexual orientation: The biologic theories reappraised. *Archives of General Psychiatry, 50,* 228–239.

Dittman, R. W., Kappes, M. E., & Kappes, M. H. (1992). Sexual behavior in adolescent and adult females with congenital adrenal hyperplasia. *Psychoneuroendocrinology, 17,* 1–18.

Ehrhardt, A. A., Meyer-Bahlburg, H. F. L., Rosen, L., Feldman, L., Verdiano, N., Zimmerman, I., & McEwen, B. (1985). Sexual orientation after prenatal exposure to exogenous estrogen. *Archives of Sexual Behavior, 14,* 57–77.

Evans, R. (1969). Childhood parental relationships of homosexual men. *Journal of Consulting and Clinical Psychology, 33,* 129–135.

Freud, S. (1933). *Psychology of women: New introductory lectures on psychoanalysis.* London: Hogarth Press.

Freud, S. (1955). Beyond the pleasure principle. In J. Strachey (Ed.), *The standard edition of the complete works of Sigmund Freud* (Vol. 18, pp. 3–68). London: Hogarth Press. (Original work published 1920.)

Gagnon, J. H. (1977). *Human sexuality.* Glenview, IL: Scott Foresman.

Gagnon, J. H. (1990). Gender preference in erotic relations: The Kinsey scale and sexual scripts. In D. P. McWhirter, S. A. Sanders, & J. M. Reinisch (Eds.), *Homosexuality/heterosexuality: Concepts of sexual orientation* (pp. 177–207). Oxford, England: Oxford University Press.

Golombok, S., Spencer, A., & Rutter, M. (1983). Children in lesbian and single-parent households: Psychosexual and psychiatric appraisal. *Journal of Child Psychological Psychiatry, 24,* 551–572.

Gottman, J. S. (1990). Children of gay and lesbian parents. In F. W. Bozett & M. B. Sussman (Eds.), *Homosexuality and family relations* (pp. 177–196). New York: Harrington Park.

Goy, R. W., & McEwen, B. S. (1980). *Sexual differentiation in the brain.* Cambridge, MA: MIT Press.

Green, R. (1987). *The "sissy boy syndrome" and the development of homosexuality.* New Haven, CT: Yale University Press.

Green, R., Mandel, J., Hotvedt, M., Gray, J., & Smith, L. (1986). Lesbian mothers and their children: A comparison with solo parent heterosexual mothers and their children. *Archives of Sexual Behavior, 15,* 167–184.

Green, R., Williams, K., & Goodman, M. (1982). Ninety-nine "tomboys" and "non-tomboys": Behavioral contrasts and demographic similarities. *Archives of Sexual Behavior, 11,* 247–266.

Hamer, D., Hu, S., Magnuson, V., Hu, N., & Pattatucci, A. (1993). A linkage between DNA markers on the X-chromosome and male sexual orientation. *Science, 261,* 321–327.

Hines, M., & Green, R. (1990). Human hormonal and neural correlates of sex-typed behaviors. *Review of Psychiatry, 10,* 536–555.

Kitzinger, C. (1987). *The social construction of lesbianism.* London: Sage.

Kohlberg, L. (1966). A cognitive-developmental analysis of children's sex-role concepts and attitudes. In E. E. Maccoby (Ed.), *The development of sex differences* (pp. 82–173). Stanford, CA: Stanford University Press.

LeVay, S. (1991). A difference in hypothalamic structure between heterosexual and homosexual men. *Science, 253,* 1034–1037.

Lytton, H., & Romney, D. M. (1991). Parents' differential socialization of boys and girls: A meta-analysis. *Psychological Bulletin, 109,* 267–296.

Martin, C. L. (1993). New directions for assessing children's gender knowledge. *Developmental Review, 13,* 184–204.

Meyer-Bahlburg, H. F. L. (1984). Psychoendocrine research on sexual orientation: Current status and future options. *Progress in Brain Research, 61,* 375–398.

Mischel, W. (1966). A social learning view of sex differences in behavior. In E. E. Maccoby (Ed.), *The development of sex differences* (pp. 56–81). Stanford, CA: Stanford University Press.

Money, J. (1988). *Gay, straight or in-between: The sexology of erotic orientation.* New York: Oxford University Press.

Money, J., Schwartz, M., & Lewis, V. (1984). Adult heterosexual status and fetal hormonal masculinization and demasculinization: 46, XX congenital virilizing adrenal hyperplasia and 46, XY androgen-insensitivity syndrome compared. *Psychoneuroendocrinology, 9,* 405–414.

Newcombe, M. (1985). The role of perceived relative parent personality in the development of heterosexuals, homosexuals, and transvestites. *Archives of Sexual Behavior, 14,* 147–164.

Patterson, C. (1992). Children of lesbian and gay parents. *Child Development, 63,* 1025–1042.

Perry, D. G., & Bussey, K. (1979). The social learning theory of sex difference: Imitation is alive and well. *Journal of Personality and Social Psychology, 37,* 1699–1712.

Plummer, K. (1975). *Sexual stigma: An interactionist account.* London: Routledge & Kegan Paul.

Quinton, D., Rutter, M., & Rowlands, O. (1976). An evaluation of an interview assessment of marriage. *Psychological Medicine, 6,* 577–586.

Roberts, C. W., Green, R., Williams, K., & Goodman, M. (1987). Boyhood gender identity development: A statistical contract of two family groups. *Developmental Psychology, 23,* 544–557.

Siegelman, M. (1974). Parental background of male homosexuals and heterosexuals. *Archives of Sexual Behavior, 6,* 89–96.

Simon, W., & Gagnon, J. H. (1987). A sexual scripts approach. In J. H. Geer & W. T. O'Donahue (Eds.),

Theories of human sexuality (pp. 363–383). London: Plenum Press.

Socarides, C. W. (1978). *Homosexuality*. New York: Jason Aronson.

Tasker, F., & Golombok, S. (in press). *Growing up in a lesbian family*. New York: Guilford Press.

Whitam, F. (1977). Childhood indicators of male homosexuality. *Archives of Sexual Behavior, 6,* 89–96.

Whitam, F., & Mathy, R. (1991). Childhood cross-gender behavior of homosexual females in Brazil, Peru, the Philippines and the United States. *Archives of Sexual Behavior, 20,* 151–170.

Using Queer Theory to Explore Lesbian College Students' Multiple Dimensions of Identity

Elisa S. Abes
David Kasch

We live in a heteronormative world. That is, people are presumed to be heterosexual, unless and until they redefine themselves as something other than strictly heterosexual. Should that occur, regardless of whether one ultimately identifies as homosexual, bisexual, asexual, or something else, it is necessary to go through a process of redefinition.

In the following reading by Abes and Kasch, the coming-out and self-identification of a lesbian student, referred to as KT, is examined through the lens of queer theory, a newer perspective in sexuality and gender studies that seeks to combat heteronormativity. The authors contrast two theoretical frameworks to tell KT's identity story: Constructivist-Developmental Theory and Queer Theory. Each theory attempts to illuminate the relationships among KT's sexual-orientation identity and other dimensions of her life, including variables such as religion, gender, and social class.

To fully understand the chapter, you will need to learn the language of queer theory, a task that may be more comfortable for literary types than for social scientists. But, the fact that much of the chapter is based on first-person accounts makes the task less laborious. Nonetheless, after perusing the authors' simple explanations of the concepts, you will be able to see how an individual's experience can be expanded and transformed through a theoretical interpretation.

By describing the developmental trajectory of KT, Abes and Kasch challenge educators and personnel in student-affairs departments or divisions to reconsider how they see and interact with all students who are in the process of identity development, regardless of their sexual orientation. If you personally have had to come to grips with a sexual minority status, you will enjoy applying queer theory to your own life experiences. If you have not had to make such a transformation in your identity, you can still use queer theory to think about the meaning of labeling yourself as heterosexual

*and wonder at the ways your life is somewhat more
privileged as a result.*

Student development theory literature must include more attention to the ways in which social power structures, such as racism, classism, and heterosexism, mediate student development. In the context of heterosexism, Talburt (2004) and Renn and Bilodeau (2005) argued that gay, lesbian, and bisexual identity development theories that do not account for heterosexism reify heterosexual privilege. This research explores the relationship between heterosexism and student development theory by using queer theory to study the nature of lesbian college students' intersections of sexual orientation identity with other identity dimensions, such as religion, social class, and gender. What new insights about college students' negotiation of multiple identities are gained through the use of queer theory? What new insights into student development theory might queer theory uncover? To explore these questions, we focus on two tellings of the identity story of KT, one of the participants in a longitudinal study of lesbian college students' perceptions of their multiple dimensions of identity (Abes & Jones, 2004). Elisa [Eds: Abes] tells a story of KT's perceptions of her multiple identities using constructivist-developmental theory as the theoretical framework (Baxter Magolda, 2001; Kegan, 1994). Dave [Eds: Kasch] then applies a queer theoretical framework to KT's developmental story and retells her narrative through this perspective. Together, we hope to offer new understandings of how lesbian students' negotiate their multiple identities and how educators can support students in these identity negotiations.

LITERATURE REVIEW

We review the two theoretical frameworks that we use to tell and then retell a narrative about the relationships among KT's sexual orientation identity and other dimensions of her identity:

constructivist-developmental theory and queer theory.

Constructivist-Developmental Theory

Constructivist-developmental theorists suggest that people develop through a relatively linear trajectory of increasingly complex meaning-making structures, which are sets of assumptions that determine how an individual perceives and organizes life experiences (Kegan, 1994). Building on Kegan's constructivist developmental theory of self-evolution, Baxter Magolda (2001) described a framework for understanding young adult development. Specifically, Baxter Magolda described a process whereby young adults move from external to internal ways of making meaning of knowledge (cognitive domain), relationships with others (interpersonal domain), and who they are as individuals (intrapersonal domain).

Cognitive development theory describes how people perceive the nature of knowledge. Complex cognitive capacity enables a person to internally generate knowledge and beliefs rather than uncritically accepting knowledge claims from external authorities (Perry, 1970). Interpersonal development describes how people construct relationships. Mature relationships are characterized by mutuality (Jordan, 1997). Mutuality involves respect for both self and others' identities and the integration of multiple perspectives and needs. Intrapersonal development describes how people construct their identities. Complex identity construction requires the ability to reflect on and choose enduring values and beliefs that allow a person to internally develop a sense of self rather than relying on external influences to define identity (Baxter Magolda, 2001). These three domains are integrated; development in one domain typically fosters development in another. Complex meaning making in all three domains is necessary for a person to reach self-authorship, which is the internal capacity to construct one's beliefs, sense of self, and relationships with others (Baxter Magolda; Kegan, 1994).

Kegan also described postmodern development beyond self-authorship, the fifth order of consciousness, in which individuals demonstrate an ability through relationships to recognize their incompleteness and simultaneously author multiple forms of self-authorship. Kegan suggested that achieving the fifth order is rare and the earliest an individual does so is typically in his or her forties.

Writing about the first phase of the longitudinal study that provides the data for this analysis, Abes and Jones (2004) explored the relationship between constructivist-developmental theory and lesbian college students' perceptions of their sexual orientation identity and its relationships with other identity dimensions. They found that how context influenced participants' perceptions of their identity was related to the complexity of their meaning-making capacity. Participants with complex meaning-making capacity were able, more so than those with less developed capacity, to filter contextual influences, such as family background, peer culture, and social norms, and determine how context influenced their identity. Also based on the results of the first phase of that study, Abes, Jones, and McEwen (2007) focused in more depth on the role of meaning-making capacity in students' understanding of the salience of and relationships among their multiple identities. They found that meaning-making capacity mediated participants' perceptions of relationships among multiple identities and the ease with which sexual orientation was integrated or peacefully co-existed with other dimensions.

Queer Theory

Unlike constructivist-developmental theory, which explains development toward complex ways of understanding identity, queer theory critically analyzes the meaning of identity, focusing on intersections of identities and resisting oppressive social constructions of sexual orientation and gender. Queer theory is built from the poststructural theories of Foucault (1976/1978), Derrida (1967/1978), and Lyotard (1984). Sullivan (2003) stated: "poststructural theorists such as Foucault argue that there are no objective and universal truths, but that particular forms of knowledge, and the ways of being that they engender, become 'naturalised,' in culturally and historically specific ways" (p. 39). Queer theorists apply these ideas to gender and sexuality to suggest they are socially constructed (Butler, 1990). Genders and sexualities reflect the time and place in which they exist and the individuals who enact them. The expression of gender and sexuality is unstable, changing as the individual affects society and as society affects the individual. To narrow our focus within queer theory, we isolated three concepts that resonated with the development of multiple identities: heteronormativity, performativity, and liminality.

Heteronormativity is the use of heterosexuality as the norm for understanding gender and sexuality (Warner, 1991). Queer theory offers a threefold critique of this dominant social construction of gender and sexuality. First, heteronormativity creates a binary between identification as heterosexual and nonheterosexual in which nonheterosexuality is abnormal and measured in its difference from heterosexuality. This binary suggests that individuals separate into two distinct groups with identifiable differences. Second, heteronormativity consolidates nonheterosexuality into one essentialized group (Muñoz, 1999). The use of the label *LGBTQ* to represent students who identify as lesbian, gay, bisexual, transgender, or queer as one group is an example of consolidating nonheterosexual identities. Essentializing this diverse group of students reinforces the binary. Third, by privileging heterosexuality, society does not acknowledge gender and sexual orientation as reflections of social power structures (Foucault, 1976/1978). Heterosexuality's hegemony creates the perception (or lack thereof) that heterosexuality defines what is natural or acceptable (Britzman, 1997). Queer theory provides a framework for resisting heteronormativity.

The second concept that informs this analysis, performativity, uses heteronormativity as a point of tension. Performativity describes how individuals create genders and sexual identities through everyday behaviors or performatives (Butler, 1990). As performatives, actions do not represent identity; instead, actions create identity (Butler). As such, an individual's gender and sexuality do not exist before she or he performs them; they are not predetermined by physiological sex or attraction to a specific gender. Instead, the individual learns how to perform gender and sexual identity and socially constructs them into being through her or his behavior. Because individuals enact genders and sexualities that do not exist prior to their enactment, performatives provide the potential for resisting dominant social constructions of gender and sexuality. This process depends on creating an identity through repeating actions; however, an individual never repeats actions precisely the same. Thus, identity is always changing.

The third concept supporting this analysis is the idea of liminality, a transitional period of indeterminacy (van Gennep, 1909/1960). Liminality represents a state of flux between two distinct and stable stages of being. This idea is critical to understanding how heteronormativity and performativity play out in students' lives. For example, heteronormativity creates a binary of two fixed sexualities: heterosexuality and nonheterosexuality. Liminality is a resistance strategy in which elements of heterosexuality and nonheterosexuality are incorporated into one identity that rejects normalized definitions of either heterosexuality or nonheterosexuality. Liminality, as resistance, is a state of becoming (Grosz, 2004). It facilitates flexible genders and sexualities and reflects how an individual may perform a seemingly contradictory performative in ever-changing ways. As such, liminality provides a framework for understanding the complex ways in which an individual performs sexuality in resistance to and as part of heteronormativity. The "becoming" quality of liminality emphasizes the unstable meaning of gender and sexuality (Halberstam, 2005), reflecting queer theory's resistance to stable identities.

A key connection among these three ideas is the use of resistance as a primary force behind queer theory. Foucault (1976/1978) noted, "where there is power, there is resistance . . . and this resistance is never in a position of exteriority in relation to power" (p. 95). Queer theory creates complex intersections of identities through multiple strategies of resistance.

STUDY DESIGN

The data upon which the two tellings of KT's identity story are based came from the first two phases of Elisa's [Eds: Abes] longitudinal study of lesbian identity development (Abes & Jones, 2004). That study was guided by a constructivist theoretical perspective (Denzin & Lincoln, 2000) and a narrative inquiry methodology (Lieblich, Tuval-Mashiach, & Zilber, 1998). There were 10 participants, identified through purposeful sampling (Patton, 1990) in the first phase, and 8 in the second, all of whom were ages 18–25 over the span of the two study phases. These women, who identified as lesbian or queer, attended the same large public research university in the Midwest at the time of the first phase of the study. Data were collected through open-ended interviews that lasted between 1 and 3 hours. Interview questions elicited stories about how participants experienced their multiple identity dimensions. Examples of questions included: "Tell me what it means to you to be a lesbian," or "Tell me about a time that you were aware of your gender."

For this project, we chose to feature one participant, KT. By focusing on only one participant, we are able to richly analyze her identity stories. Focusing on only one participant is also a way to honor the unique story of one student typically considered on the margins, thus subverting the essentializing to which lesbian students are often subjected, which is one of the aims of queer theory (Muñoz, 1999). We chose to feature KT for several reasons. We identified a participant whose experiences might resonate with other lesbian or queer students. KT was not actively involved in queer student organizations, but instead, explored her identity through her family, work, and social life. She did not take courses that provided her the language to analyze her identity from an academic perspective; instead, she explored her identity and developed her own language through her lived experiences. KT earnestly, even if sometimes without realizing she was doing so, tried to integrate her multiple identity dimensions. She wanted an integrated identity so she could be honest with herself and others and reach her personal and professional goals. Although KT was initially tentative about participating in this study, explaining she had not thought about these issues, she deeply considered each question and thoughtfully articulated each response. Clearly, she had done more prior identity work than she realized. We now believe queer theory provides insights into why KT was unknowingly working so hard to understand her identity: she was living within the ambiguous liminality of her multiple identities.

For data analysis, we reanalyzed the data collected in both study phases. To create the constructivist-developmental narrative, we analyzed KT's interview transcripts. We first reviewed each line of the transcript, focusing on KT's words, and then grouped these words into concepts representing the same phenomena. We grouped these concepts into more abstract categories. We then considered these abstract categories in relationship to cognitive, interpersonal, and intrapersonal development.

To create the queer narrative, we reanalyzed KT's interview transcripts using queer theory. For purposes of this paper, we introduce queer theory as a new theoretical perspective only for data analysis to "queer" the constructivist narratives. To conduct the queer analysis, we reread KT's transcripts to understand how the queer notions of heteronormativity, performativity, and liminality were present in KT's stories.

Peer debriefing and member checking ensured trustworthiness (Patton, 1990). As part of peer debriefing, we conducted individual analyses of the data and then discussed our interpretations. For member checking, KT read both the constructivist and queer narratives. She commented that she readily saw herself in the constructivist narrative and was interested in the use of the three domains of development to explain her experiences. Not surprisingly, she found the queer theory analysis harder to get her head around, but the more she thought about it, the more she could see it as an intriguing way to describe her experiences.

KT's Constructivist-Developmental Narrative

Thoughtful and mature, KT is a goal-oriented person, proud of her educational and professional accomplishments. She received her undergraduate degree in physical education at age 22 during the first phase of the study, and then completed a master's degree in physical education in the time between the two phases. During the second phase, KT was in her first year as a physical education teacher. A White woman raised as a devout Catholic, KT realized she was a lesbian near the end of high school. Her mother conveyed immense disapproval, telling KT that as a lesbian she could no longer practice Catholicism, be professionally successful, or be feminine, each of which was important to KT. In the face of this critique, KT was proud of her decision to come out as a lesbian, a decision from which she has derived significant strength.

At the time of the first study phase, 4 years after that initial conversation, KT had not again discussed her sexual orientation with her parents, an avoidance which distressed her because she believed they deserved to know the truth. As KT was tentatively coming out to friends about her sexual orientation, everything she knew about what it meant to be a lesbian was based on negative stereotypes she heard from other people, especially her mother. During college, it became important to KT to be her own person as a lesbian rather than a stereotype. Before she could consider that possibility, however, she had to figure out whether or not the stereotypes were true, especially those related to the relationship between her sexual orientation and her religion, social class, and gender.

The first study phase was marked by KT experiencing dissonance between her mother's perspectives and the new perspectives she was exploring. This dissonance spurred cognitive, interpersonal, and intrapersonal development. Although KT was encouraged by glimmers of possible perspectives different from those of her mother, she was not ready to develop her own perspective on what it meant to be lesbian and how that related to her religion, gender, and social class. Over the next 18 months, KT experienced much development. Continuing to investigate multiple perspectives on what it meant to be a lesbian, KT was tentatively developing her own perspectives and starting to understand that her multiple identities were not mutually exclusive.

Sexual Orientation and Religion

KT was raised as a Catholic and had a deep faith in God; reconciling her religion and sexual orientation was among KT's most significant challenges. During the first study phase, KT reflected on a time when she believed others' perspectives that identifying as a lesbian precluded her from being religious. She explained: "My mother told me I can't be a lesbian [and Catholic]. I still want to be in touch with God. I want to go to church.... I felt that because of my mother I couldn't do that." KT sought out reading material to help her understand that her mother's interpretation of the Bible is not the only correct one. She cast her desire for religion as a future goal though still uncertain whether or not she could adopt a perspective different from what others taught her. Cognitively, she experienced some dissonance as she learned about multiple

perspectives, but was not yet prepared to adopt her own perspective.

KT's interpersonal development also interacted with her understanding of the relationship between her sexual orientation and religious identities. Because of her friends' attitudes toward religion, KT described herself as a "religious closet case": "None of my friends go to church. Knowing that I want to go to church, I really keep that a secret because everything that they say about religion is bad. I'm in the closet about religion." Although KT tentatively believed she could be religious and a lesbian (demonstrating her intrapersonal development), she had not yet developed agency in her relationships with her friends and thus hid her religious beliefs.

During the second study phase, and a result of continuing to seek out multiple perspectives, KT developed in how she understood her identity as a lesbian for whom religion is important. She more confidently believed there were multiple ways to be lesbian and religious, and started creating her own perspectives on this relationship. She explained:

> I know I can have God in my life and be gay and be everything I want to be. I can still put God first. I don't have to be in the church to pray.... I consider myself Catholic... but I go to a church where I'm welcome because of who I am.

For KT, a new supportive relationship mediated her intrapersonal and interpersonal development because her girlfriend respected her religious beliefs. This support allowed KT to reflect on prior relationships and see how she had allowed others to define her identity. KT explained that if her current girlfriend did not support her faith, "I would have issues with that.... it would be an issue with me right now if I just didn't see any kind of religious beliefs in [my girlfriend]." KT demonstrated development in all three domains. She was coming to understand multiple perspectives on the relationship between religion and sexual orientation (cognitive development); gaining a stronger sense of how she wanted to reconcile these two aspects of her identity (intrapersonal development); and hoping to maintain her religious beliefs in a relationship (interpersonal development).

Sexual Orientation and Social Class

KT also sought out concrete examples to help her learn that the stereotype that lesbians typically inhabit a lower social class was not necessarily true. Again, she was exposing herself to and seeing validity in multiple perspectives (cognitive development). Based on comments from her mother and exposure only to lesbians who were college students, KT believed for many years that identifying as a lesbian and as an upper-class professional were mutually exclusive. Through a relationship at the time of the first study phase with a "professional" woman, KT attended parties at nice homes owned by lesbians. Seeing these professional women allowed KT to consider, albeit tentatively, the possibility that identifying as a lesbian might not preclude her from achieving her professional and financial goals (intrapersonal development).

During the second phase, KT was more confident that her sexual orientation need not dictate her social class. KT attributed her new perspective that "you can be gay and successful" to her growing confidence that resulted from graduating from college and becoming a successful teacher. By accomplishing her educational goals, which her mother told her she could not do as a lesbian, KT gained the confidence to accept perspectives different from what her mother taught her and to believe in her own thinking (interpersonal development). KT's evolution in how she perceived the relationship between her sexual orientation and social class demonstrates development in all three domains as she is integrating into her sense of self (intrapersonal) her own perspectives on the relationship between her sexual orientation and social class (cognitive), rather than defining these possibilities through her mother (interpersonal).

Sexual Orientation and Gender

One of KT's obstacles in her journey toward reconciling her social class ambitions with her sexual orientation was her assumption that other people perceived lesbians to be masculine women. It was important to KT to always be professional in all aspects of her life, and she associated being professional with being feminine. From her perspective, especially during the first study phase, "masculine women" were not perceived as professional women. Even though she considered herself "a feminine woman who can be a little butch sometimes," KT assumed many people would think that because she was a lesbian she was also masculine and therefore unprofessional, which would hurt her career. This perception, again based on what others told her, was especially troubling as a physical education teacher because of the stereotypes about lesbians associated with this position. KT spoke to the pressure she felt teaching: "You almost have to be perfect in the schools as a teacher. So I don't want to be portrayed as a lesbian because I don't know where they stand, and I'm scared to death I'm going to get fired." However, by meeting other lesbians she considered to be professional and feminine, in particular one of her professors, she was coming to realize, again tentatively, the possibility of being perceived by others as feminine. Although KT still held onto gender stereotypes, she was starting to juggle multiple perspectives and entertain new possibilities for her identity.

KT did not give as much thought to her gender at the time of the second phase of the study. Still, she related gender and social class. When asked to describe her gender, KT, who was confident wearing short hair and stylish, athletic clothes, responded by saying "professional." Although she continued to equate professional with feminine, she was starting to define her own meaning of feminine rather than defining it through stereotypes. She explained: "When I am professional I try to be feminine. But feminine to me is more on the plain side. Just, you know, clean, nice clothes, sophisticated if you have to dress up, feminine in that way." Although she worried about being fired from teaching if others knew she was gay, she grew more comfortable portraying her gender in a way that makes her comfortable and in which she feels professional, rather than according to other people's standards. As with religion and social class, KT was not only entertaining the possibility of multiple perspectives, but was starting to develop her own perspectives (cognitive development) and defining her own identity (intrapersonal development), rather than losing herself in others' perceptions of her (interpersonal development).

At the end of the first phase, KT explained that she wanted her sexual orientation, gender, and social class to "come together" so she could be the person she aspires to be. Between the two study phases, KT's development toward self-authorship contributed to her multiple identities in fact coming closer together. Closer to self-authorship than before, KT reflected at the end of the second study phase that by gaining the ability to define her identities for herself and in less conflict with one another, she was "allowing [her] true self to evolve."

Queering KT's Constructivist-Developmental Narrative

Retelling KT's story from a queer theory perspective recasts it to reflect KT's resistance to stereotypes, as well as queer resistance to the linearity and heteronormativity of constructivist student development theory. KT's queer narrative is complex. Her life forms a text of resistance to heteronormative social constructions that exclude or oppress her sense of self (e.g., her mother's statements about how lesbians cannot be Catholics). It is a story of her enacting an identity performative in which she fluctuates between heteronormative constructions of self and constructions of self that resist heteronormativity. Initially, these fluctuations may appear to be a type of identity negotiation between heteronormative and nonheteronormative, but

KT's struggle is different from a simple negotiation. Instead, as detailed in the following narrative, KT is redefining the meaning of heteronormative and nonheteronormative identities. Prior to identifying as a lesbian, KT identified as a Catholic from a working class family and as a woman who conducts herself in a professional manner. Once identifying as a lesbian, the meaning of these prior identities became problematic for KT and caused her to question her sense of self. She formed her earlier identities based on a heteronormative understanding of the world (e.g., Catholics are straight, hard work can change a person's class status, and professional women must be feminine) and struggled to understand her conflicting experiences of these identities. KT's new primary identity as a lesbian created resistance to the stereotypes of lesbians her mother promoted because KT continued to engage each of these identities and be a lesbian, which her mother suggested was not possible. Still, she feared some of her own resistance, explaining:

> I was like one foot in the closet and one foot out of the closet. . . . I would tell certain people that I trusted. And I would not tell other people that I didn't trust because I felt that they would use it against me.

Heteronormativity, performativity, and liminality provide a framework for understanding how KT queered religion, gender, and social class.

Queering Catholicism

KT understood Catholicism to be exclusive of lesbians and to be a lesbian meant that she could no longer be a Catholic. This understanding was problematic because KT's faith was a pillar of how she understood herself. Her faith in God offered KT a cohesive sense of self, a sense of self built on the idea of only heterosexual partnerships. When KT first identified as a lesbian, she necessary excluded herself from the opportunity to have a relationship with God under this framework. This pushed KT into a liminal state, where she knew she believed in God but could not live her faith as she knew it. Instead she needed to create a new performative that resisted the idea of faith and God only supporting heterosexual relationships.

The constructivist narrative discussed KT's process of seeking support for a new understanding of religion that included her as a lesbian. KT sought out people, churches, and readings that resisted her mother's messages about the church's limited acceptance of lesbians and the gay community's limited acceptance of organized religion. These actions demonstrated KT's new performative of religion. Through this dual resistance she enacted the performative of "religious closet case." KT struggled to find acceptance in either community because she wanted to be part of both communities. KT explained:

> There were bad moments in my life, and it
> was when I didn't have religion, I didn't believe
> in it. When I think about it, I need it. So, I
> feel that's very important to who I am as a
> lesbian.

This quote reflects KT's complex construction of religion and sexuality: she believes in God as a lesbian. Her understanding of God depends on her understanding of her sexuality and her understanding of her sexuality depends on her understanding of God; the two identities are interwoven. This interwoven quality emphasizes an important queer feature of KT's new understanding of faith—her performative of faith changes as her understanding of her sexuality changes and vice versa. This conflation of religion and sexuality creates a unique identity in which KT is constantly redefining what it means to be a lesbian and what it means to be Catholic. She is performing a strategy of liminality in which these identities share the same identity material. Her faith in God is intelligible to her only as a lesbian because, for KT, the two are based on the same threads of identity.

Queering Social Class with Gender

One of the most complex identity constructions that KT describes is that of her gender. In the first study phase, KT defined gender as "professional." When pushed further about what professional means to her, KT connected hard work and social class. Professionalism, then, was the performative reflection of her work ethic based on a feminine gender: "I think gender and social class kind of go together for me because I always want to be portrayed as a woman and professional and lesbian." Gender for KT, then, is part of social class and sexual orientation. Through a physical performative, KT linked representations of woman, professional, and lesbian into one complex expression of identity. In doing so, KT is resisting the stereotypes that lesbians are masculine and masculine women are not professionally successful.

KT's understanding of sexuality and professionalism is another example of infused identities. No longer financially dependent on her family because of her post-college salary, KT explained: "I pay everything. I even pay a loan that my mom took out for me. . . . so, I'm taking more ownership of my sexuality now." For KT, professionalism and sexuality help to define her sense of self. Being a professional (gender/social class) and having income (social class) allow KT to "own," or create the meaning of, her sexuality. KT's sense of professionalism and gender influences how she understands the relationship between sexual orientation and social class and vice versa. The two groups are mutually influencing.

The meaning of KT's gender and sexuality are not pre-existent. KT brings them into being through the process of enacting them described in the idea of performatives. What is significant about this gender/social class performative is that it resists multiple constructions of heteronormative and nonheteronormative genders and sexualities at the same time. By defining her gender through social class, KT has subverted conventional understandings of gender.

KT noted, "I guess when I am looked at as a lesbian, I want to know that my job is something that I'm very happy with, I have a good living, I can make it on my own or with a partner." To KT, being a lesbian is now more than just a sexual orientation; it has an impact on work, happiness, and relationships. In subtle ways, KT's performative of social class and gender is defining work, happiness, and relationships through and with her sexuality.

Queering Identity Intersections

KT transformed the meaning of social class by combining social class with gender to create "professionalism." This performative of professionalism also depends on KT's construction of what it means to be a lesbian because this construction informs how she understands her gender. Given this relationship, KT's social class/gender is also a reflection of her Catholicism because her religion is important to who she is as a lesbian. As a result, the intersection of social class and gender in professionalism is also an intersection of religion and sexuality. Through professionalism, KT is enacting a time and place, unique reality of identity, specific to her. By enacting an identity that combines all of these identity dimensions, she is performing an infused identity.

From one perspective, KT's infused identity appears to be a negotiation of identities (a balancing of lesbian and Catholic lesbian and professional) rather than inter-connected identities; however, it is not that simple. This "negotiation of identities" perspective considers all of these identities as distinct but connected. KT's infusement, on the other hand, makes these elements of identity inseparable in her sense of self. KT's infusing of identities is a departure from simple intersections of identities. It reflects something more like "intrasections," where identities do not simply connect with each other, but rather they share the same identity material. In other words, each of these threads of identity (Catholic, professional, lesbian) are all the same identity. KT's infused identity is not evidence of progressively complex development, a constructivist-development theory suggests; it is a performative of inseparable identities.

KT's creation of infused, intrasected identities is a complex example of her resistance to heteronormativity through the performative of a liminal identity. For example, in her developmental narrative, KT's understanding of heteronormativity is inseparable from her understanding of her mother. To resist her mother's stereotypes of lesbians is to resist heteronormativity. KT created intrasections of identity that incorporate, build from, and refuse definitions of identities from her mother. KT used the definitions of lesbian, Catholicism and professionalism she learned from her mother and changed them to create her own unique identity that reflected KT's enactment of Catholicism and professionalism as a lesbian. KT redefined the meaning of each of these labels into one coherent intrasected identity by creating a singular identity that neither confirmed her mother's definitions nor created counter definitions.

Queering the Relationship Between KT and her External Environment

So far, this queer narrative has resisted the traditional structuralist framework of a binary between KT and society in which KT has the ability to affect society, society has the ability to affect KT, or the two influence each other. This structuralist binary is common in constructivist-developmental narratives (internal/external sources of authority). From a queer (poststructuralist) perspective, this binary is an artificial construction imposed upon KT and society. The binary does not exist until a third party chooses to locate KT and society as distinct and opposing entities. In using this KT/society binary, the subtle complexities of KT's performative, or the intrasections of KT's multiple dimensions of identity, are obscured, and a false sense of stability to the meaning of identities is created. Using a constructivist lens, KT's construction of identity initially appears to be a negotiation between heteronormative and non-heteronormative. It denies KT's queer development and the insight queer theory has into KT's on-going resistance to definitions of identity that obscure her "evolving" sense of "true self."

KT's queer narrative demonstrates the on-going performative of one woman creating an intrasected identity that resists engagement in traditional binaries. Using a queer perspective, both KT and the social constructions of identity become liminal, unstable, and constantly in states of becoming. These "becomings" resist binary frameworks in which the individual is abnormal in relation to her heterosexual environment. From the perspective of queer theory, KT's story is one of resistance to heteronormativity. By identifying as a lesbian, KT unknowingly began a process of resisting the heteronormativity of her mother and society. As KT's identification as a lesbian intensified, and her perception of the intersections between other identity dimensions and being a lesbian increased, her resistance to heteronormativity also intensified. KT also became increasingly aware of her resistance to heteronormativity and used that sense of awareness to develop her personal sense of agency. Rather than a story of developmental arrival, KT's queer narrative is a story of continued resistance and an ever-changing network of complex intrasections within dimensions of identity.

DISCUSSION

Implications for Student Development Theory

Queer-Authorship: Identity Construction as Social Change. From a constructivist-developmental perspective, KT is developing an increased capacity to construct the meaning of and relationships among her multiple identities through internally defined perceptions rather than defining herself through external expectations. From

a queer perspective, KT was reconstructing external authority by resisting heteronormativity and destabilizing structures it created. KT was enacting an identity that redefined her own identity *perceptions* in relationship to external influences (i.e., developing toward self-authorship), as she simultaneously redefined the *meaning* of those same external influences (i.e., deconstructing and reconstructing power structures). KT's performatives were creating a sexual orientation identity that no longer precluded her religious, social class, and gender identities because she changed the meaning of religious, social class, and gender identities to include her lesbian identity.

A queer theoretical perspective on development thus illuminates that for students who do not identify as heterosexual, identity development as part of the journey toward self-authorship requires resisting power structures that define one as abnormal. Whereas self-authorship focuses on how students construct internal frameworks to navigate external influences, queer resistance focuses on how students deconstruct and reconstruct external influences. Rather than challenging heteronormativity, self-authorship describes the developmental capacities students need to make meaning of their lives within a heteronormative society. When students necessarily deconstruct the heteronormative framework in order to reconstruct their identities, they offer a resistance that is development toward a form of self-authorship as social change, a type of development we call "queer-authorship."

Queer-authorship is the necessary deconstruction of heteronormativity that enables lesbian students to change the dominant social order in order to redefine the meaning of their multiple identities and the contexts in which their lives are situated. Queer-authorship suggests that self-authorship alone is an incomplete theoretical framework to describe the experiences of lesbian college students. It suggests that the developmental process looks different for lesbian college students, an observation suggesting that the nature of the developmental process might also be reexamined for other dimensions of identity, such as social class, race, and ethnicity.

To understand the social change aspect of queer-authorship, it helps to distinguish queer-authorship from the findings of other literature that explores how dissonance associated with marginalized identities fosters development toward self-authorship. Pizzolato (2003) described how high-risk college students who encountered challenges to their abilities developed self-authoring ways of knowing earlier than many participants in Baxter Magolda's (2001) longitudinal study. She found that students' encounters with provocative experiences, such as choosing to attend college despite a lack of community or family support, often prompted the disequilibrium needed to construct their own self-perceptions. Using a similar framework, it could be argued that the external influence of heteronormativity fostered complex development in KT, allowing her to develop toward self-authorship. Although likely true, this describes only part of KT's story. it describes only how KT positively defined herself in relationship to heteronormativity, accommodating this power structure rather than changing it. The queer view shifts the gaze from how KT is changing her self-perceptions within a heterosexist society, to how KT is changing the heterosexist society and thus her identity. Using a constructivist perspective, Pizzolato focused on the individual's development in response to marginalization, not how her participants changed the meaning of high risk, race, and class; however, her work suggests that a similar process may be taking place for high-risk students.

Further, it is insufficient to argue only that marginalization is an external factor that fosters development toward self-authorship because the theoretical framework of self-authorship does not wholly describe KT's development. Indeed, our research began with our mutual sense that student development theory was missing part of the developmental story of lesbian students.

We encountered this concern when initially analyzing KT's interview transcripts using a constructivist-developmental framework. Our analysis resulted in thinking that heterosexism was contributing to KT's complex cognitive capacity but stalling her interpersonal development given her tendencies to define herself though her mother, peers, and girlfriends. It felt wrong to describe KT's experiences as stalled interpersonal development, even though at first glance the way she defined herself in relationship to others was reminiscent of Kegan's (1994) third order or Baxter Magolda's (2001) early crossroads. It was evident that KT was trying to push back against dominant social structures, engaging in sophisticated interpersonal pursuits, and slowly defining herself in relation to others who tried to define her identity for her. Stepping outside of the self-authorship framework allowed us to incorporate KT's efforts at deconstructing heteronormativity into her development. Doing so led us to understand her development as more complex than what the language of self-authorship allows.

Queer-Authorship as Fluid, Nonlinear Development. The queer-authorship of KT serves as an example of how she must first form a resistance to heteronormative structures in her life before she exhibits development typically understood as self-authorship. Although we critique the heteronormativity of development toward self-authorship, Kegan's (1994) fifth order of consciousness, which he describes as a postmodern view of the world, explains some aspects of queer-authorship. He described the fifth order as:

> [Moving] form or system from subject to object, and brings into being a new "trans-system" or "cross-form" way of organizing reality. . . . the good working of the self and its recognition by the other begins with a refusal to see oneself or the other as a single system or form. The relationship is a context for sharing and an interacting in which both are helped to experience their "multipleness," in which the

many forms or systems that *each self is* are helped to emerge. (p. 313)

In the fifth order, people recognize that the relationship itself creates the individual elements rather than the individual elements creating the relationship. Differences among individuals are necessary for the relationship, and through the relationship, people recognize these differences within themselves. As described in KT's queer narrative, KT and the contexts in which she lives are a mutually influencing relationship; they are part of a "trans-system," with each bringing out "multipleness" of the other. As a social change agent, KT is changing the meaning of the context that influences the meaning of her multiple identities, while that changing context changes the meaning of her identity. The relationship between the two create multiple and changing meanings.

KT is exhibiting aspects of the fifth order at the same time that she has not yet reached the fourth order, or self-authorship. The concept of queer-authorship therefore suggests that the linear developmental trajectory associated with Kegan's (1994) orders, and upon which the concept of self-authorship is based, is insufficient to describe the experiences of all students. Rather than a linear developmental trajectory, queer-authorship suggests that people simultaneously exhibit qualities from multiple orders. This argument differs from the constructivist-developmental perspective that people don't always exhibit their most complex ways of making meaning. Although linear trajectories allow students to enact elements of previous stages of development, there remains a general notion that once a student achieves self-authorship she or he will be able to maintain or return to that higher level of development. This assumption suggests that student development is finite and measurable and that changes in students' expression of their identity reflect development along a trajectory. Using the notions of liminality and performativity, queer theorists argue that identities are always in flux and development

does not accommodate "arriving" at a stage of development (Halberstam, 2005; Sedgwick, 1990). Sullivan (2003) offered a similar observation about identity multiplicity:

> One's being in the world is always marked, molded, formed, and transformed in and through encounters with others and with a world. . . . Identity is never simply a question of self-authorship. . . . Identity categories are . . . continuously fracturing, multiplying, and metamorphosing. Identity, one could argue, is already always haunted by the other, by that which is not "I." (p. 149)

We recognize that according to Kegan (1994) most people do not reach the fifth order, and doing so is extremely unlikely for a traditional-aged college student. We are not suggesting that KT arrived at the fifth order. Instead, we are suggesting that this linear trajectory does not describe KT's development because her queer resistance causes her to interact with society in a manner similar to the fifth order, even though she might not have reached the fourth order. KT's development is more fluid than the process described by Kegan (1994) and Baxter Magolda (2001). Our argument is consistent with Talburt's (2006) proposed "queering of our ideas of development" in which "development does not occur in a straight line, so to speak," but is about "multiple practices, complex relations, and dynamic positionings across contexts" (p. 90).

Kegan (1994) acknowledged that his theory would not survive a deconstructive postmodern critique because it, like most theories, is not universally applicable. Citing Burbules and Rice (1991), Kegan distinguished between what he calls deconstructive and reconstructive postmodernism. Unlike deconstructive postmodernism, reconstructive postmodernism uses the products of deconstruction to create better theory that is constantly reforming. He argues that subject–object theory supports the reconstructive postmodern perspective because it avoids ideological absolutism, and meaning-making complexity allows for supporting others' positions on their own terms. Nonetheless, KT's queer narrative demonstrates that development toward self-authorship does not encompass the resistance and social change necessary for queer-authorship, thus resulting in an incomplete understanding of how lesbian college students experience their multiple identities.

The Fusion of Multiple Identities: Rethinking the Model of Multiple Dimensions of Identity. Queer theory also challenges the portrayal of multiple identities offered in the Model of Multiple Dimensions of Identity (Jones & McEwen, 2000), a conceptual depiction of students' perceptions of their identity. The model portrays how students' perceptions of the saliency of each of their multiple identity dimensions, portrayed as dots on ellipses surrounding a core sense of self, changes depending on contextual influences. Recently reconceptualized, the model includes meaning-making capacity, explained through constructivist-developmental theory, as a filter between contextual factors and students' perceptions of their multiple identities (Abes et al., 2007). Through the model's depiction of identity, Jones and McEwen remind educators the importance of "seeing students as they see themselves" (p. 412). In part a result of meaning-making capacity, students often see themselves as a combination of distinct and sometimes conflicting dimensions of identity (Abes et al.).

Queer theory, however, starts from the perspective that multiple identity dimensions are always fused (Fuss, 1989) intrasections rather than intersections. Although students might perform certain aspects of their identities more prominently than others at different times, depending on context, identities cannot be separated. By starting from this fused perspective, queer theory prompts an exploration as to why when lesbian students "see themselves," they often see identity dimensions as distinct. Starting from the perspective that students' identities

are fused prompts a focus on how heteronormativity contributes to students' perceptions of identity dimensions as distinct. Connecting queer theory with the model draws attention to social power structures with which students must contend in developing their multiple identities.

Further, when queer theory informs the model, the result portrays students as changing, through resistance, the meaning of the contextual factors that shape their identity. Thus, the interaction between context and identity dimensions is mutually influencing, which is not portrayed in the current model. Still further, viewing the model through a queer lens, the identity "dots" surrounding the core no longer could be portrayed as distinct, currently a possibility in the model, but merge together and change in meaning, depending on the meaning of each of the other changing identities. Because KT and society are simultaneously changing and mutually influencing, not only are KT's self-perceptions changing, but so too are the meaning of each of her multiple identities, each of which is in constant motion. This queer perspective opens up new possibilities for depicting the relationship between students' multiple identities and contextual influences. The queer perspective also challenges the heteronormative meaning-making filter recently incorporated into the reconceptualized model that filters external influences depending on development toward self-authorship (Abes et al., 2007).

The fusion of identities brings to light one of the limitations of this study. By choosing to focus on only the four identities most salient to KT, sexuality, religion, social class, and gender, we do not address how the meaning of each of those identities depends on the meaning of other social identities less salient to her, in particular her identity as a White woman. Not addressing KT's whiteness could contribute to one of the critiques of queer theory, namely that it has been blind when it comes to race (Sullivan, 2003).

Implications of Queer Theory for Student Affairs Practice

By describing how lesbian college students resist heteronormativity to construct their identities, this research raises the question as to how educators can support students' resistance, helping them identify and deconstruct heteronormative obstacles within and between identities. At the same time, it challenges educators to identify and deconstruct these same obstacles.

One of the challenges in KT's queer narrative is a call to re-examine how educators see and interact with students. Educators act as viewers and interpreters of students' life experiences. Aspects of T's queer narrative are about the viewer, not the viewed. It is the viewer's perception of KT's identities that constructs distinctions and unities among KT's dimensions of identity. The identity dimensions themselves do not change, but the viewer's perception of the relationships among the dimensions changes. One of the implications for practice, then, is the need to reconsider how educators frame students. Do educators align students along a trajectory and measure their development through a process of stages, or do educators move outside of linear models to consider the influence that students are having on their environment to reshape their contexts? KT's developmental and queer narratives are examples of how one student met situations in which she was on the subordinate side of power and what she did to resist larger heteronormative structures. KT's experiences can help sensitize educators to issues that students may face and offer insight into how educators can challenge their own understanding of student development theory and the heteronormative assumptions upon which it is built.

Perhaps one of the subtlest implications of queer theory for work with students is the commentary on power in the relationship between students and educators. How student affairs educators see students' development reflects how they position themselves in relation to the students. This is not a simple matter of trying to do no harm, but moving beyond that to carefully consider how they establish, maintain, and share power in relationships with students. One measure of how student affairs professionals build power relationships with students can be seen in how students cooperate or offer resistance to those relationships. This is a call to check and challenge the ways in which cultural power is expressed with students. As KT's narratives reflect, how "normal" is constructed can create tremendous obstacles and difficulties for students. Abes (in press) demonstrated the transformations that occurred for one college student in how she thought about relationships among her sexuality, ethnicity, and gender when educators intentionally challenged heteronormativity and the meaning of normal through classes and co-curricular experiences. One approach to helping students deconstruct heteronormativity is supporting and perceiving student organizations and experiences as sites of resistance rather than only means to help students (Renn & Bilodeau, 2005; Talburt, 2004). For instance, allowing students increased levels of freedom to define the purpose and mission of student groups, challenging school policy structures that expect students to all behave in similar ways (clothing, social attitudes, interests, and co-curriculars), and assuming that the pedagogical relationship between student and advisor moves from advisor down to student.

Where student affairs professionals have to exert caution is in making sure that the support offered to students does not create resistance groups that are reflections of the professionals' power rather than that of the students. This is not to say that students are always victims of power relationships. Talburt (2006) offered the challenge to move beyond the use of queer theory to reify a victimology of queer students; we take that challenge seriously. KT's queer narrative offers an alternative view of victimization. It offers a hopeful relationship in which educators help students define themselves in positive terms of what they value, rather than as survivors or victims of power structures they cannot control. It is a fundamental shift from being an onlooker with students to being an ally with students on their terms. When educators view students from a distance, imposing their own perspectives on how students are negotiating their multiple identities, they are too far removed to develop the caring relationships that nurture students. This reflects an "educator knows best" mentality in which students are passive receptors of knowledge or development. It is only where educators share a closer space with students, allowing students invested control of the relationship, that the real transformative work of helping students resist and influence heteronormativity occurs. Consistent with Noddings' (1984) ethic of care, in which care is demonstrated through "feeling with" (p. 30) another by receiving another into oneself rather than projecting oneself onto the other, it is important that educators work *with* students to identify and deconstruct the social constructions of their multiple identities rather than imposing their own power and perceptions onto the students.

CONCLUSION

By exploring the intersection of queer theory and constructivist-developmental theory, we are responding to calls within student development literature for attention to the relationship between power structures and student development. Just as gay, lesbian, and bisexual identity development theories that do not account for heterosexism reify heterosexual privilege (Renn & Bilodeau, 2005; Talburt, 2004), KT's queer narrative shows that student development theory does not yet adequately account for how heteronormativity contributes to lesbian students' negotiation of their multiple identities. Constructivist-developmental theory suggests that students are less developmentally complex if they are unable to overcome the heteronormativity that defines and separates their multiple identities. We do not intend to undermine the constructivist approach to development, which provides a rich understanding of the development of college students, but only to challenge its normative assumptions so that educators can more effectively work with the intrasections of students' identities.

REFERENCES

Abes, E. S. (in press). Applying queer theory in practice with college students: Transformation of a researcher's and participant's perspectives on identity. *Journal of Gay and Lesbian Issues in Education*.

Abes, E. S., & Jones, S. R. (2004). Meaning-making capacity and the dynamics of lesbian college students' multiple dimensions of identity. *Journal of College Student Development, 45*, 612–632.

Abes, E. S., Jones, S. R., & McEwen, M. K. (2007). Reconceptualizing the Model of Multiple Dimensions of Identity: The role of meaning-making capacity in the construction of multiple identities. *Journal of College Student Development, 48*, 1–22.

Baxter Magolda, M. B. (2001). *Making their own way: Narratives for transforming higher education to promote self-development* (1st ed.). Sterling, VA: Stylus.

Britzman, D. P. (1997). What is this thing called love?: New discourses for understanding gay and lesbian youth. In S. de Castell & M. Bryson (Eds.), *Radical in(ter)ventions: Identity, politics, and difference/s on educational praxis* (pp. 183–207). Albany: State University of New York Press.

Burbules, N. C., & Rice, S. (1991), Dialogue across differences: Continuing the conversation. *Harvard Educational Review, 61*, 393–416.

Butler, J. (1990). *Gender trouble: Feminism and the subversion of identity*. New York: Routledge.

Delgado, R., & Stefancic, J. (2001). *Critical race theory: An introduction*. New York: New York University Press.

Denzin, N. K., & Lincoln, Y. S. (2000). The discipline and practice of qualitative research. In N. K. Denzin & Y. S. Lincoln (Eds.), *Handbook of qualitative research* (2nd ed., pp. 1–28). Thousand Oaks, CA: Sage.

Derrida, J. (1978). *Writing and difference*. (A. Bass, Trans.). Chicago: The University of Chicago Press. (Original work published in 1967).

Foucault, M. (1978). *The history of sexuality: Volume 1, an introduction*. (R. Hurley, Trans.). New York: Vantage Books. (Original work published 1976)

Fuss, D. (1989). *Essentially speaking: Feminism, nature, and difference.* New York: Routledge.

Grosz, E. A. (2004). *The nick of time: Politics, evolution, and the untimely.* Durham, NC: Duke University Press.

Halberstam, J. (2005). *In a queer time and place: Transgender bodies and subcultural lives.* New York: New York University Press.

Jones, S. R., & McEwen, M. K. (2000). A conceptual model of multiple dimensions of identity. *Journal of College Student Development, 41,* 405–414.

Jordan, J. V. (Ed.). (1997). *Women's growth in diversity: More writings from the stone center.* New York: Guilford.

Kegan, R. (1994). *In over our heads: The mental demands of modern life.* Cambridge, MA: Harvard University Press.

Lieblich, A., Tuval-Mashiach, R., & Zilber, T. (1998). *Narrative research: Readings, analysis, interpretation.* Thousand Oaks, CA: Sage.

Lyotard, J-F. (1984). *The postmodern condition: A report on knowledge (theory and history of literature, volume 10).* Manchester, United Kingdom: Manchester University Press.

Mufioz, J. E. (1999). *Disidentifications: Queers of color and the performance of politics.* Minneapolis: University of Minnesota Press.

Noddings, N. (1984). *Caring: A feminine approach to ethics and moral education.* Berkeley, CA: University of California Press.

Patton, M. (1990). *Qualitative evaluation and research methods* (2nd ed.). Newbury Park, CA: Sage.

Perry, W. (1970). *Forms of intellectual and ethical development in the college years: A scheme.* Troy, MO: Holt, Rinehart, & Winston.

Pizzolato, J. E. (2003). Developing self-authorship: Exploring the experiences of high-risk college students. *Journal of College Student Development, 44,* 797–812.

Renn, K. A., & Bilodeau, B. (2005). Queer student leaders: An exploratory case study of identity development and LGBT student involvement at a midwestern research university. *Journal of Gay & Lesbian Issues in Education, 2*(4), 49–71.

Sedgwick, E. K. (1990). *Epistemology of the closet.* Berkeley: University of California Press.

Sullivan, N. (2003). *A critical introduction to queer theory.* New York: New York University Press.

Talburt, S. (2004). Constructions of LGBT youth: Opening up subject positions. *Theory into Practice, 43*(2), 116–121.

Talburt, S. (2006). Queer research and queer youth. *Journal of Gay & Lesbian Issues in Education, 3*(2/3), 87–93.

van Gennep, A. (1960). *The rites of passage* (M. B. Vizedom & G. L. Caffe, Trans.). Chicago: University of Chicago Press. (Original work published 1909).

Warner, M. (1991). Introduction: Fear of a queer planet. *Social Text, 29,* 3–17.

CHAPTER 33

Female Bisexuality from Adolescence to Adulthood

Results from a 10-Year Longitudinal Study

Lisa M. Diamond

Lisa Diamond, the author of the article that appears in this chapter, opens her 2008 book on sexuality and love in women with the following paragraph that nicely depicts the concept of sexual fluidity:

> *In 1997, the actress Anne Heche began a widely publicized romantic relationship with the openly lesbian comedian Ellen DeGeneres after having had no prior same-sex attractions or relationships. The relationship with DeGeneres ended after two years, and Heche went on to marry a man. The actress Cynthia Nixon of the HBO series* Sex and the City *developed a serious relationship with a woman in 2004 after ending a fifteen-year relationship with a man. Julie Cypher left a heterosexual marriage for the musician Melissa Etheridge in 1988. After twelve years together, the pair separated and Cypher—like Heche—has returned to heterosexual relationships.*
>
> *(Diamond 2008, 1)*

From "Female Bisexuality from Adolescence to Adulthood: Results from a 10-Year Longitudinal Study" by L. M. Diamond. 2008. *Developmental Psychology* 44: 5–14. Copyright © 2008 by the American Psychological Association. Adapted with permission.

Diamond questions, "What's going on? Are these women confused? Were they just going through a phase before, or are they in one now?" Searching for answers, the author explores the belief that female sexuality is more flexible and less specific with regard to the target of arousal. She interprets this to mean that more women are truly bisexual in their orientation than are men. Indeed, when exposed to erotic stimuli, the arousal response of men depends on their sexual orientation, while the arousal response of women does not (Chivers, Rieger, Latty, & Bailey, 2004). Also, women show comparable signs of physiological arousal regardless of the nature of the erotic stimulus. Indeed, women are even aroused by viewing erotic videos featuring bonobos (a type of chimpanzee), whereas men are not (Chivers & Bailey, 2005). This does not mean that all women are bisexual; it simply means that female arousal patterns are less categorizable.

This chapter reports on Diamond's 10-year longitudinal study that has examined the changes in self-identified sexual orientation in nearly 80 lesbian, bisexual, or unlabeled women over a 10-year period. After reading this article, you will likely have a rather different understanding of the concept of bisexuality than you did before.

Although basic research on sexual orientation has made significant strides over the past 20 years, one area that remains woefully under-investigated is bisexuality. Simply defining bisexuality remains problematic. Most researchers and laypeople view bisexuality as a pattern of erotic responsiveness to both sexes (Rust, 2002), yet even this broad conceptualization leaves many questions unanswered: Does any fleeting instance of same-sex attraction or fantasy "count," or must bisexuals experience regular, strong, and sustained attractions to both sexes? What about individuals who claim that although they do not currently experience attractions to both sexes, they have the potential to do so? For example, in their random, representative study of American adults, Laumann, Gagnon, Michael, and Michaels (1994) reported that a greater number of women found same-sex contact "appealing" than indicated being attracted to women. Are they bisexual?

Neither researchers nor gay/lesbian/bisexual individuals agree on the answers to such questions. As a result, many studies of same-sex sexuality have specifically excluded bisexually identified individuals over the years for the sake of conceptual and methodological clarity (Rust, 2000b).

This is somewhat ironic, given that studies using representative samples increasingly indicate that bisexual patterns of sexual attraction and behavior are more common than previously thought, and they are actually more common than exclusive same-sex sexuality among women (Kirk, Bailey, Dunne, & Martin, 2000; Mosher, Chandra, & Jones, 2005). Sexual-minority youth, too, appear increasingly likely to adopt bisexual and "unlabeled" identities rather than lesbian/gay identities, not only as a description of their attractions but also as an overarching philosophy embracing noncategorical, nongender-based models of sexuality (Savin-Williams, 2005). Yet, despite these changes in the cultural visibility and legitimacy of bisexuality (Diamond, 2005a; Firestein, 2007; Weinberg, Williams, & Pryor, 1994), many basic questions

about its nature and development remain unanswered. In particular, scientists and laypeople continue to debate whether bisexuality is (a) a temporary stage of denial, transition, or experimentation; (b) a "third type" of sexual orientation, characterized by fixed patterns of attraction to both sexes; or (c) a strong form of all individuals' capacity for sexual fluidity. Although these are not the only models of bisexuality that have been suggested over the years (Rust, 2000a), they remain among the most influential and widely held.

No prior research has systematically compared the evidence for these models, largely because such a comparison requires long-term longitudinal data on stability and change in women's attractions, behaviors, and identities. Such information is now available. In the present study, I use 10-year longitudinal data collected from 79 sexual-minority (i.e., nonheterosexual) women to examine the degree of empirical support for each of the aforementioned models of bisexuality. The findings advance not only researchers' specific understanding of bisexuality but also researchers' general understanding of female sexual development over the life course.

BISEXUALITY AND THE QUESTION OF CHANGE

Longitudinal data are indispensable for comparing the three aforementioned models of bisexuality because each entails a different perspective on *change over time* in sexual attractions, behaviors, and identities. The question of change has long garnered interest and controversy in research on sexual orientation, given that traditional, essentialist models of sexual orientation make no allowances for longitudinal change. According to an essentialist perspective, individuals are thought to be endowed with fixed, early developing sexual predispositions that manifest themselves in consistent patterns of same-sex or other-sex desire over the life course (DeCecco & Elia, 1993).

Bisexual attractions pose a quandary for this model because such attractions necessarily create the potential for change over time: alternating between same-sex and other-sex partners, for example, or altering one's self-described sexual identity according to the gender of one's current partner (Weinberg et al., 1994). Yet, the three aforementioned models of bisexuality predict different patterns of change, in different domains. For example, if bisexuality is simply a third "type" of sexual orientation, along with heterosexuality and homosexuality (Firestein, 1996; Snyder, Weinrich, & Pillard, 1994), then women's attractions themselves should remain relatively stable, even if her behavior and identity fluctuate as a result of situational or social factors.

Yet, stability should not be observed if bisexuality is a temporary stage. If most bisexuals are, in fact, either (a) gay-lesbian individuals who have not yet fully accepted their same-sex sexuality or (b) heterosexual individuals temporarily experimenting with or confused about same-sex relationships (Blumstein & Schwartz, 1977; Kitzinger, 1995), then as time goes on, bisexuals should eventually revert to exclusive patterns of behavior and attraction (either toward the same sex or the other sex), accompanied by adoption of heterosexual or lesbian labels.

Perhaps the broadest and most flexible conceptualization of bisexuality views it as a strong manifestation of all individuals' capacities for relatively malleable, situation-dependent, socially constructed sexual desires (Baumeister, 2000; Blumstein & Schwartz, 1990; Rust, 1993). Critiques of the rigid categorization of individuals as "gay/lesbian," "heterosexual," and "bisexual" have a long history. Kinsey, of course, famously argued that "The world is not to be divided into sheep and goats" (Kinsey, Pomeroy, & Martin, 1948, p. 639) and that same-sex and other-sex desires varied along a continuous dimension. More recently, this point of view has been articulated by researchers emphasizing the flexible, socially constructed nature of human sexuality (Blumstein & Schwartz, 1990;

Kitzinger & Wilkinson, 1995; Rust, 1993). As Paul (1985) succinctly summarized, "There is far more variability and fluidity in many people's sexual patterns than theoretical notions tend to allow, suggesting that researchers have imparted an artificial consistency to an inchoate sexual universe" (p. 21).

This may be particularly true with respect to women, given increasing evidence that women's desires are even more situation dependent and less "category specific" than those of men (Baumeister, Catanese, & Vohs, 2001; Chivers, Rieger, Latty, & Bailey, 2005; Lippa, 2006). Hence, variable patterns of same-sex and other-sex desire and behavior may emerge in any woman over time, and might simply be more pronounced among the subset of women who identify as bisexual. According to this view, the distinction between lesbianism and bisexuality is a matter of degree rather than kind, and women's adoption of a bisexual versus lesbian identity may have more to do with her self-concept, ideology, and intimate relationships than with her sexual "essence" (Golden, 1996; Rust, 1993).

PREVIOUS LONGITUDINAL RESEARCH

Is there any evidence that bisexual women's attractions, behaviors, and identities are, in fact, less stable over time than those of lesbians? Up until now, the only longitudinal studies of same-sex sexuality have been relatively short term (Dickson, Paul, & Herbison, 2003; Pattatucci & Hamer, 1995; Rosario, Schrimshaw, Hunter, & Braun, 2006; Weinberg & Williams, 1988), and therefore it is difficult to discern the overall prevalence and magnitude of change in different domains among bisexual versus lesbian women. For example, Pattatucci and Hamer (1995) collected 18-month follow-up data from 175 lesbian, bisexual, and heterosexual women recruited from lesbian/gay/bisexual organizations. The authors averaged respondents' Kinsey ratings (i.e., ratings on a 0 to 6 scale, with 0 representing *exclusive heterosexuality* and 6 representing *exclusive same-sex sexuality*) of sexual attraction, fantasy, behavior, and self-identification, thereby precluding comparisons between changes in different dimensions. The authors found fairly little change over the 18-month assessment period: Approximately 80% of their sample maintained the same rating, and those who changed ratings typically only did so by one point.

Stokes and his colleagues (Stokes et al., 1997) followed 216 bisexual men (recruited from gay/lesbian/bisexual community resources) over a 1-year period. They found that about one third changed Kinsey ratings in a more homosexual direction, and 17% changed in a more heterosexual direction. Longer follow-ups were conducted by Dickson et al. (2003), who sampled a cohort of approximately 1,000 New Zealanders born in the early 1970s. Over the 5-year assessment period, they found that nearly 30% of the men who reported ever having experienced same-sex attractions underwent a shift in their attractions between age 21 and 26, and two thirds of these changes were toward the same sex. Among women, about 45% of the women who had ever experienced a same-sex attraction reported a change in their attractions, and over 80% of these changes were toward the same sex.

Weinberg and colleagues (1994) also assessed change over a 5-year interval, but their sample was fairly small (N = 55) and self-selected, comprising individuals who were active participants in San Francisco's newly emergent bisexual community in the early 1980s. They found that approximately two thirds of their respondents reported changes in their self-reported ratio of same-sex to other-sex attractions over the 5-year period, and 85% reported changes in their ratio of same-sex to other-sex sexual behavior. A little over half of these changes were toward the same sex, and about 60% were 1-Kinsey point in magnitude. Rosario and colleagues (2006) examined changes in self-identification among 156 urban youths, nearly 80% of whom were ethnic minorities (in contrast to the other studies,

which sampled mainly White individuals). Over a 1 year period, about half the youths who had been bisexually identified at baseline transitioned to lesbian/gay labels, whereas only 7% of the lesbian/gay youths transitioned to bisexual labels.

Yet, each of these studies has shortcomings that make it difficult to interpret the findings, such as (a) short follow-up intervals, which may not be long enough for the full range of potential variability to become apparent; (b) the lack of direct comparisons between changes experienced by bisexual and lesbian women; (c) failure to differentiate between—or directly compare—changes in attractions versus behavior versus identity; (d) failure to include individuals who experience same-sex attractions but do not identify as gay/lesbian/bisexual, many of whom reported experiencing bisexual attractions; and (e) failure to assess other developmental and social factors that might influence longitudinal patterns of attraction, behavior, and identity. The present study aimed to correct these shortcomings and to provide a more comprehensive portrait of long-term stability and change in bisexual and lesbian women's attractions, behaviors, and identities.

THE PRESENT STUDY

Nearly 80 young sexual-minority women, identified as lesbian, bisexual, or unlabeled, have been assessed five times over a 10-year period, beginning in late adolescence and following through to early adulthood. The unlabeled women merit discussion. The scant research available on such individuals suggests that they typically experience attractions to both sexes (Diamond, 1998; Savin-Williams, 2005) but decline to label their sexuality either because they are still engaged in the process of sexual questioning or because they find the existing range of sexual identity categories, and the process of categorization altogether, to be limiting and restrictive. Hence, long-standing questions about the "true nature" of bisexual individuals' sexuality apply equally as well to unlabeled individuals. Accordingly, the hypotheses below refer to bisexual/unlabeled women as a single category. All data analyses, however, treat them as separate groups in order to permit investigation of the similarities and differences between them.

At each assessment, respondents provided detailed information on their sexual identities, attractions, behaviors, and their social and familial relationships. Using these data, I examine the evidence for the following conceptualizations of bisexuality:

1. *Bisexuality as a transitional stage*: This model suggests that most women who initially identified as bisexual or unlabeled will switch to heterosexual or lesbian identities over time and will report corresponding changes in their sexual attractions and behavior. As a result of these transitions, the number of women claiming bisexual or unlabeled identities should progressively decline as women grow older.

2. *Bisexuality as a third type of sexual orientation*: This model suggests that women with attractions to both sexes have a sexual orientation that is fundamentally distinct from—but just as stable as—lesbianism. Hence, contrary to the "transitional stage" model, women who claim bisexual/unlabeled identities should be more likely to *maintain* these identities than to switch to lesbian or heterosexual labels, and their degree of *attraction* to women versus men should remain stable over time (although their behavior might change as a function of opportunity, specific relationships, etc.).

3. *Bisexuality as a heightened capacity for fluidity*: This model suggests that some degree of fluidity in sexuality is a general feature of female sexuality, which may simply be stronger among bisexual women. Accordingly, there should be

overlap and change in the attractions, behaviors, and identities of bisexual/unlabeled and lesbian women, although more so in the former group. Additionally, because the passage of time should increase women's awareness of their own capacity for fluidity (as they encounter relationships and situations that facilitate variation in their sexuality), transitions to bisexual or unlabeled identities should be more likely over the long term than transitions away from such identities.

METHOD

Participants

Participants were 79 nonheterosexual women between the ages of 18–25 years who were initially interviewed as part of a longitudinal study of sexual identity development among young women (Diamond, 1998, 2000, 2003a, 2005b). Four follow-up interviews were conducted over the phone, each approximately 2 years apart. Initial sampling took place across a wide range of settings, including lesbian, gay, and bisexual community events (i.e., picnics, parades, social events) and youth groups in two moderately sized cities and a number of smaller urban and rural communities in central New York state (35% of sample); classes on gender and sexuality issues taught at a large private university in central New York (36%); and lesbian, gay, and bisexual student groups at a large private university, a large public university, and a small, private, women's college in central New York (29%).

This sampling strategy has known limitations: For example, organized community groups and activities tend to underrepresent sexual-minority individuals who do not openly identify as lesbian, gay, or bisexual. Although this is less of a problem when recruiting from college courses on gender and sexuality, such courses typically overrepresent White, highly educated, upper-middle-class women. In all, 85% of respondents were White, 5% African American, 9% Latina, and 1% Asian American.

At the beginning of each interview, each woman was asked, "How do you currently label your sexual identity to yourself, even if it's different from what you might tell other people? If you don't apply a label to your sexual identity, please say so." Lesbian- and bisexual-identified women were categorized according to their chosen identity labels. Women who declined to attach a label to their sexuality were classified as *unlabeled*. At the first assessment, the mean and median age of the participants was 19; at the fifth assessment, the mean and median age of the participants was 29. There were no significant age differences across settings or sexual identity categories.

Procedures

T1 assessments were scripted, face-to-face interviews conducted with each woman in 1995 by the primary investigator, approximately 90% of which lasted between 1–1.5 hr. When possible, interviews were conducted in a university office. When this was not feasible, interviews were conducted at a location of the participant's choosing, usually her home. Because of the sensitivity of the subject matter, interviews were not tape-recorded. Detailed notes were taken during the interview by the primary investigator and transcribed immediately afterward. The primary investigator reinterviewed participants in 1997 (Time 2 [T2]), 2000 (Time 3 [T3]), 2003 (Time 4 [T4]), and 2005 (Time 5 [T5]).

The final T5 sample size was 79, comprising 89% of the original respondents. During the consent procedure for each interview, women were informed that they would be asked about their prior and current sexual attractions, behaviors, and identification. The confidentiality of the interview was stressed, and each participant was instructed of her right to refrain from answering any of the interview questions or to terminate the interview at any time. None of the participants did so. At the close of each interview, women were given the opportunity to revise their answers to any of the questions or to add additional remarks.

As described in the first report on this sample (Diamond, 1998), T1 interviews assessed the timing and context of women's initial process of sexual questioning. This information is relevant to the present analyses because of long-standing stereotypes that women whose sexual questioning is triggered by environmental factors are less "authentically" gay, and therefore more likely to revert to heterosexuality over time, than women whose questioning is triggered by same-sex attractions (Diamond, 2006a). The factors that triggered women's questioning were coded into the following categories: (a) *Exposure to facilitative environment*, which included meeting, hearing about, or otherwise learning about lesbian/gay/bisexual people; discovering that a friend had same-sex attractions; discussing issues related to sexual orientation with friends; dating a bisexual man; or becoming the object of another woman's sexual interest; (b) *Same-sex attractions*, which included awareness of sexual desires for one or more women, unusual closeness to one or more women, fascination with women's bodies or women's beauty, intentional sexual contact with another woman, distinct disinterest in men, or a strong emotional attraction to a specific woman.

To assess the general distribution of their same-sex attractions, women were asked at each interview to report the percentage of their total attractions that were directed toward the same sex on a day-to-day basis; separate estimates were provided for sexual versus emotional attractions. This yields an estimate of the relative frequency of same-sex versus other-sex attractions, regardless of the intensity of these attractions or the total number of sexual attractions experienced on a day-to-day basis. To assess sexual behavior, participants were asked to report the total number of men and women with whom they *engaged in sexual contact* (defined as any sexually motivated intimate contact) between T1 and T2, T2 and T3, T3 and T4, and T4 and T5.

This information was translated into percentages so that 100% represents exclusive same-sex behavior, and 0% represents exclusive other-sex behavior.

RESULTS

Change in Identity

In all, 32% of women changed identities from T1 to T2, 25% from T2 to T3, 30% from T3 to T4, and 28% from T4 to T5 (these percentages were not significantly different). By the 10-year point, 67% of participants had changed their identities at least once since T1, and 36% had changed identities more than once. There was no association between identity change and SES when growing up, educational attainment, or the context of a woman's first questioning. Women who changed identities were, however, less likely to have had divorced parents, less likely to have come from middle- or upper-class backgrounds, and less likely to report antigay stigmatization/harassment/fear of violence. They were also no younger when they enrolled in the study than women with stable identities.

As noted earlier the transitional stage model of bisexuality would suggest that over the course of the study, most bisexual and unlabeled women will eventually switch to either heterosexual or lesbian identities. Bisexual and unlabeled women were, in fact, more likely to change their identity labels than were lesbian women over the 10 years of the study. In all, 73% of T1 bisexuals and 83% of T1 unlabeled women subsequently changed their identities, compared with 48% of T1 lesbians. Yet, the nature of these changes was not consistent with the transitional stage model. In particular, bisexual and unlabeled women were more likely to switch between bisexual and unlabeled identities than to settle on lesbian or heterosexual labels.

Of the T1 bisexuals, 92% identified as either bisexual or unlabeled 10 years later; only 1 claimed a lesbian label at T5, and 1 claimed a heterosexual label. Of the T1 unlabeled women,

61% identified as bisexual or unlabeled 10 years later; 5 women claimed a lesbian label at T5, and 5 claimed a heterosexual label. Notably, the total percentage of respondents who switched to a heterosexual identity from a bisexual or unlabeled identity during the study was larger—17%—but over half these women switched back to a bisexual or unlabeled identity by T5. Women who switched to lesbian labels did not show significant increases in their same-sex attractions over time, and those who switched to heterosexual labels did not show significant decreases. Rather, at T5, they showed largely the same pattern of same-sex and other-sex attractions that they reported at the beginning of the study.

These findings are therefore more consistent with the model of bisexuality as a stable identity than a transitional stage. Further evidence for the "stable identity" model is provided by the fact that the total percentage of respondents identifying as bisexual or unlabeled did not decline over the five waves of the study, as would be expected if women were progressively transitioning out of these labels.

The "bisexuality as heightened fluidity" perspective suggests that most women possess the capacity to experience sexual desires for both sexes, under the right circumstances. Hence, as time goes on, progressively more women should have the opportunity to become aware of this capacity and may adopt bisexual/unlabeled identities as a result. Consistent with this view, there were a greater number of transitions to (or between) bisexual and unlabeled identities than to either lesbian or heterosexual identities over the 10 years of the study. In all, two thirds of identity changes involved adopting either a bisexual or unlabeled identity, whereas about half as many (37%) involved adopting a lesbian or heterosexual identity. In fact, by the 10-year point, fully 80% of the sample had claimed a bisexual or unlabeled identity at some point (whereas 56% of the sample claimed a lesbian label at some point).

Because some models of sexual fluidity (Diamond, 2003b; Peplau, Spalding, Conley, &

Veniegas, 1999) emphasize the importance of relational contexts in prompting transitions in desire and identity, additional analyses were conducted to examine women's patterns of sexual involvement with men and women immediately prior to their identity changes. These analyses revealed that each of the bisexual/unlabeled women who switched to a heterosexual identity at some point during the study, and two thirds of the lesbians who switched to a bisexual/ unlabeled identity, had sexual contact with at least one man during the 2 years prior to the identity change. Thirty percent of the T1 lesbians ended up developing full-blown romantic relationships with men, and all of these women switched to unlabeled or bisexual identities. Of the women who adopted lesbian identities, 94% had sexual contact with at least one woman during the 2 years prior to the identity change.

Hence, women appeared to be adopting labels consistent with their relationship patterns. Notably, however, women's definitions of lesbianism appeared to permit more flexibility in behavior than their definitions of heterosexuality. In all, 76% of the women who switched to lesbian labels pursued sexual contact with both men and women during the 2 years prior to the identity change, compared with 30% of women who switched to heterosexual labels. This provides further support for the notion that female sexuality is relatively fluid and that the distinction between lesbian and bisexual women is not a rigid one. For example, of the women who identified as lesbian at T5, 15% reporting having sexual contact with a man within the previous 2 years. In contrast, none of the women who had settled on a heterosexual label by T5 reported having sexual contact with a woman within the previous 2 years.

Change in Attractions

To test for group differences in changes in attractions, analysis of variance (ANOVA) was conducted. The results revealed significant between-subjects effects of sexual identity on overall level of attraction, with the lesbian group showing consistently higher percentages of same-sex attractions than the bisexual and unlabeled groups. There was also a significant within-subject effect of time, and a trend-level interaction between sexual identity and time. Although there was a significant linear decline in same-sex attractions from T1 to T5 among the lesbians, this was not the case for the bisexual or unlabeled women. The change in attractions among the lesbian group is consistent with the "bisexuality as heightened fluidity" model, which predicts that most women possess some capacity for non-exclusive attractions, which should become progressively more evident as time goes by. Notably, however, when this analysis was repeated only among the bisexual/unlabeled women, it was found that those who eventually adopted lesbian identities did not show progressively increasing same-sex attractions over time, and those who eventually adopted heterosexual identities did not show progressive decreases. Thus, contrary to the transitional stage model, both groups of women continued to report bisexual patterns of attraction in T5, despite having given up bisexual/ unlabeled identities.

The "bisexuality as heightened fluidity" model suggests that bisexual and unlabeled women should undergo more overall fluctuation in their attractions over time. As expected, follow-up contrasts revealed that lesbian women had significantly smaller absolute changes in their attractions from assessment to assessment than did the bisexual women. The unlabeled women were intermediate between these groups and were not significantly different from either.

To determine whether factors other than sexual identity related to change over time, a series of additional models was computed. There were no associations between change in same-sex attractions and parental divorce, family SES, educational attainment, family disapproval of one's sexuality, experience with antigay stigma/harassment, or the context of first questioning.

Change in Sexual Behavior

To test for changes over time, ANOVA was computed. The results revealed significant effects of sexual identity, with the lesbian group reporting greater overall percentages of sexual contact with women versus men than the bisexual and unlabeled women, and the unlabeled women having greater percentages of same-sex versus other-sex contact than the bisexual women. A follow-up contrast detected a significant linear decline in the ratio of same-sex to other-sex contact across the sample as a whole. This is consistent with the "bisexuality as heightened fluidity" model, as it suggests that with the passage of time, women are increasingly likely to pursue sexual behavior with both sexes rather than with only one sex.

To determine whether factors other than sexual identity related to change over time, a series of additional models was computed. There were no effects associated with parental divorce, family SES, educational attainment, family disapproval, or experience with stigma/harassment. There was, however, a significant association between the context of a woman's first questioning and the degree of decline in same-sex behavior. Follow-up tests found a significant decline among women whose first attractions were prompted by exposure to a facilitative environment, but not among women whose first questioning was prompted by same-sex attractions. This is consistent with the notion that exposure to facilitative environments may temporarily heighten opportunities for same-sex contact among women who otherwise might not have pursued such opportunities.

There was a consistent decline in same-sex sexual behavior among all women from 1995–2005 that was not matched by a parallel decline in attractions (except among the T1 lesbians). In both time periods, same-sex attractions are fairly evenly distributed across the total

possible range, showing the overall prevalence of bisexual patterns of attraction. As for behavior, in 1995, it is also fairly evenly distributed across the possible range, with most women pursuing sexual contact with both men and women. Yet by 2005, a bimodal distribution has emerged, with most women pursuing either exclusively same-sex behavior or predominantly other-sex behavior. This is largely attributable to the fact that by 2005, most women were involved in long-term (i.e., over 1 year in length) monogamous relationships, and hence were pursuing all of their sexual contact with a single partner. Of the 31 women who reported that 100% of their sexual contact was pursued with women, 70% were currently involved in long-term same-sex relationships, and an additional 16% were involved in same-sex relationships lasting less than 1 year. Of the 27 women reporting exclusively other-sex sexual contact, all but 1 was involved in a long-term relationship with a man.

Interestingly, the fact that so many bisexual and unlabeled women ended up in long-term relationships contradicts the widespread stereotype that bisexual women are unable or uninterested in long-term monogamy (ostensibly because a relationship with one sex would not satisfy their desire for the other sex). To the contrary, T1 bisexuals were actually more likely than lesbian and unlabeled women to be involved, by 2005, in relationships lasting *at least 5 years*. In all, 63% of bisexual women were involved in such relationships, compared with 35% of lesbians and 30% of unlabeled women.

DISCUSSION

This research provides the first empirical examination of competing assumptions about the nature of bisexuality, both as a sexual identity label and as a pattern of nonexclusive sexual attraction and behavior. The findings demonstrate considerable fluidity in bisexual, unlabeled, and lesbian women's attractions, behaviors, and identities and contribute to researchers' understanding of the complexity of sexual-minority development over the life span.

Bisexuality as a Transitional Stage

The notion that bisexuality is a transitional stage that women adopt "on the way" to lesbian identification, or is an experimental phase among heterosexual women, is not consistent with the results of this study. Although women who entered the study with bisexual or unlabeled identities were significantly more likely to subsequently change their identities than were lesbian women (an effect that was large by conventional standards), most of these changes were between bisexual and unlabeled identities, and there was no evidence for large-scale shifts toward either lesbianism or heterosexuality. By the 10-year point, only 1 of the T1 bisexuals and 5 of the T1 unlabeled women had settled on a lesbian label; the same number settled on a heterosexual label. Furthermore, these women showed no evidence of progressive changes in their ratio of same-sex to other-sex attractions over the 10 years of the study. They were (and remain) sexually attracted to both men and women, but they label these attractions differently now than before.

Additional evidence against the transitional stage model comes from the fact that the overall number of women adopting bisexual or unlabeled identities did not decline over the course of the study. If bisexuality were a temporary stage, then one would expect fewer and fewer women to maintain these identities as they moved into adulthood. Yet, to the contrary, the percentage of women claiming a bisexual or unlabeled identity hovered between 50% and 60% at each wave of the study. Even more interesting, by the end of the study, 80% of women had adopted a bisexual or unlabeled identity at some point in time. These results do not rule out the possibility that some women adopt *bisexual* as a transitional label, but this pattern appears exceptional rather than normative.

This, of course, raises questions about the status of the unlabeled category, which proved (surprisingly) to be the most frequently adopted identity in the entire study. The present results suggest that women may adopt this label for different reasons at different times. Most women who adopted the unlabeled identity at T1 relinquished it before T2, suggesting that it initially served as a marker of ongoing sexual questioning. Yet, at every subsequent assessment, more women adopted an unlabeled identity than relinquished it. This suggests that *unlabeled* serves a unique function in the present sexual taxonomy, in some cases representing a state of "being attracted to the person, not the gender" (Diamond, 2006b); in other cases, representing an openness to future change in erotic experience (Diamond, 2005c); and in still other cases, representing patterns of "almost-but-not-quite-exclusive" same-sex attractions that women may consider inconsistent with both lesbian and bisexual labels. Hence, although individuals with unlabeled identities have been historically underrepresented in research on sexual orientation, these findings indicate that researchers must begin to systematically analyze these individuals' distinct social-developmental trajectories in order to build accurate models of sexual identity development over the life course.

Bisexuality as a Distinct Orientation and/or a Capacity for Fluidity

The present results provide evidence for both the "third orientation" and "heightened fluidity" models of bisexuality. The "third orientation" model would suggest that bisexual women's patterns of sexual attraction are stable over time, and notably distinct from those of lesbian women. Evidence for this view is provided by the fact that T1 bisexual and unlabeled women reported consistently lower percentages of same-sex attractions than did the lesbian women, and their average percentage of same-sex (relative to other-sex) attractions did not change over time. Nonetheless, bisexual and unlabeled women showed larger *absolute* fluctuations in their attractions from assessment to assessment than did the lesbian women. In other words, bisexual women's attractions varied over time, but these variations centered around a relatively stable set point. One potential interpretation, then, is that both the "third orientation" and "heightened fluidity" models of bisexuality are correct; that is, bisexuality may best be interpreted as a stable pattern of attraction to both sexes in which the *specific balance* of same-sex to other-sex desires necessarily varies according to interpersonal and situational factors. This is consistent with the observations of Weinberg et al. (1994), who noted that bisexual attractions entail a "lack of closure" that engenders fluctuations in attraction and behavior as individuals progress through different environments and relationships. This view is echoed in Peplau and colleagues' intimate careers model of female sexual orientation (Peplau et al., 1999), which suggests that contextual changes over the life course (such as intimate relationships) can redirect women's sexual-developmental pathways at any point.

The fact that such changes were observed in both lesbian and bisexual/unlabeled women supports the notion of generalized sexual fluidity. In fact, T1 lesbians reported progressively more "bisexual" patterns of attraction and behavior as the study progressed, which explains why transitions to bisexual/unlabeled identities were more common than transitions away from such labels. By T5, 60% of T1 lesbians had had sexual contact with a man, and 30% had been romantically involved with a man. Many of these women resolved the resulting contradiction between their lesbian identity and their other-sex attractions/behavior by switching to unlabeled or bisexual identities.

Such "post-coming-out" identity changes challenge the longstanding assumption that sexual identity questioning is permanently resolved as soon as the individual replaces his or her initial heterosexual identity with a gay/lesbian/bisexual identity. For many women,

this may be only the first of several such transitions: Two thirds of women changed their identity label after T1, and approximately half these women did so more than once. Hence, identity *change* is more common than identity *stability*, directly contrary to conventional wisdom. Furthermore, these changes do not appear attributable to social or developmental factors such as psychological immaturity, instability, or fear of stigmatization. If this were so, then one might expect a greater likelihood of identity change among younger women, women with a history of family disruption, and women who have experienced antigay stigmatization. But this was not the case.

Instead, women's identity changes reflected their own shifting experiences: All of the women who switched to a heterosexual identity reported having had sexual contact with men in the 2 years immediately prior to the change, and this was also the case for two thirds of the lesbians who switched to bisexual/unlabeled identities. Similarly, 90% of the women who switched to a lesbian label from an unlabeled or bisexual identity reported sexual involvement with women in the 2 years prior to the change. This suggests that when selecting an appropriate identity label, or subsequently altering this label, women seek to maximize fit with their prevailing pattern of attraction and behavior.

Yet, one of the interesting findings of the present study concerned the progressively increasing *discrepancy* between women's ratios of same-sex to other-sex attraction and their ratio of same-sex to other-sex behavior as they grew older. At the beginning of the study, when women were in their teens and early 20s, they tended to be involved in multiple successive relationships, and their ratio of same-sex to other-sex sexual contact tended to parallel their attractions. Yet 10 years later, most women had settled down into committed monogamous relationships. As a result, regardless of whether their relative percentage of same-sex to other-sex attractions tended to be 25%, 50%, or 75%, their sexual *behavior* was often 100% same-sex or 100% other-sex. It is interesting that this finding provides a notable counterpoint to the popular stereotype that bisexual women are incapable of committing to a single partner. Not only did bisexual women tend to pursue exclusive, monogamous relationships over time, but they were more likely to do so than either unlabeled or lesbian women.

CONCLUSION

The findings of this research suggest that there are, in fact, appreciable boundaries between the long-term developmental trajectories of lesbian, bisexual, and unlabeled women, but these boundaries are relatively fluid. Hence, the present study supports the notion of bisexuality as a third type of sexual orientation and also supports the notion of bisexuality as a capacity for context-specific flexibility in erotic response. In contrast, the findings are inconsistent with the long-debated notion of bisexuality as a transitional stage or "phase." Of course, this study is limited by its reliance on a small, exclusively female, disproportionately White and middle-class sample, and future research on larger and more diverse samples of sexual-minority women and men is important for determining the generalizability of the findings. Nonetheless, the results have important social and scientific implications.

INTRODUCTION REFERENCES

Chivers, M. L., and J. M. Bailey. 2005. A sex difference in features that elicit genital response. *Biological Psychology* 70: 115–20.

Chivers, M. L., G. Rieger, E. Latty, and J. M. Bailey. 2004. A sex difference in the specificity of sexual arousal. *Psychological Science* 15: 736–44.

Diamond, L. N. 2008. *Sexual fluidity: Understanding women's love and desire.* Cambridge, MA: Harvard University Press.

REFERENCES

Baumeister, R. F. (2000). Gender differences in erotic plasticity: The female sex drive as socially flexible and responsive. *Psychological Bulletin*, 126, 247–374.

Baumeister, R. F., Catanese, K. R., and Vohs, K. D. (2001). Is there a gender difference in strength of sex drive? Theoretical views, conceptual distinctions, and a review of relevent evidence. *Personality and Social Psychology Review*, 5, 242–273.

Blumstein, P., & Schwartz, P. (1977). Bisexuality: Some social psychological issues. *Journal of Social Issues*, 33, 30–45.

Blumstein, P., & Schwartz, P. (1990). Intimate relationships and the creation of sexuality. In D. P. McWhirter, S. A. Sanders, & J. M. Reinisch (Eds.), *Homosexuality/heterosexuality: Concepts of sexual orientation* (pp. 307–320). New York: Oxford University Press.

Chivers, M. L., Rieger, G., Latty, E., & Bailey, J. M. (2005). A sex difference in the specificity of sexual arousal. *Psychological Science*, 15, 736–744.

DeCecco, J. P., & Elia, J. P. (1993). A critique and synthesis of biological essentialism and social constructionist views of sexuality and gender. In J. P. DeCecco & J. P. Elia (Eds.), *If you seduce a straight person, can you make them gay? Issues in biological essentialism versus social constructionism in gay and lesbian identities* (pp. 1–26). New York: Harrington Park Press.

Diamond, L. M. (1998). Development of sexual orientation among adolescent and young adult women. *Developmental Psychology*, 34, 1085–1095.

Diamond, L. M. (2000). Sexual identity, attractions, and behavior among young sexual-minority women over a 2-year period. *Developmental Psychology*, 36, 241–250.

Diamond, L. M. (2003a). Was it a phase? Young women's relinquishment of lesbian/bisexual identities over a 5-year period. *Journal of Personality and Social Psychology*, 84, 352–364.

Diamond, L. M. (2003b). What does sexual orientation orient? A biobehavioral model distinguishing romantic love and sexual desire. *Psychological Review*, 110, 173–192.

Diamond, L. M. (2005a). "I'm straight, but I kissed a girl": The trouble with American media representations of female-female sexuality. *Feminism and Psychology*, 15, 104–110.

Diamond, L. M. (2005b). A new view of lesbian subtypes: Stable versus fluid identity trajectories over an 8-year period. *Psychology of Women Quarterly*, 29, 119–128.

Diamond, L. M. (2005c). What we got wrong about sexual identity development: Unexpected findings from a longitudinal study of young women. In A. Omoto & H. Kurtzman (Eds.), *Sexual orientation and mental health: Examining identity and development in lesbian, gay, and bisexual people* (pp. 73–94). Washington, DC: American Psychological Association.

Diamond, L. M. (2006a). The evolution of plasticity in female-female desire. *Journal of Psychology and Human Sexuality*, 18, 245–274.

Diamond, L. M. (2006b). How do I love thee? Implications of attachment theory for understanding same-sex love and desire. In M. Mikulincer & G. Goodman (Eds.), *Dynamics of romantic love: Attachment, caregiving, and sex* (pp. 275–292). New York: Guilford Press.

Dickson, N., Paul, C., & Herbison, P. (2003). Same-sex attraction in a birth cohort: Prevalence and persistence in early adulthood. *Social Science & Medicine*, 56, 1607–1615.

Firestein, B. A. (Ed.). (1996). *Bisexuality: The psychology and politics of an invisible minority*. Thousand Oaks, CA: Sage.

Firestein, B. A. (Ed.). (2007). *Becoming visible: Counseling bisexuals across the lifespan*. New York: Columbia University Press.

Golden, C. (1987). Diversity and variability in women's sexual identities. In Boston Lesbian Psychologies Collective (Ed.), *Lesbian psychologies: Explorations and challenges* (pp. 19–34). Urbana: University of Illinois Press.

Golden, C. (1996). What's in a name? Sexual self-identification among women. In R. C. Savin-Williams & K. M. Cohen (Eds.), *The lives of lesbians, gays, and bisexuals: Children to adults* (pp. 229–249). Fort Worth, TX: Harcourt Brace.

Kinsey, A. C., Pomeroy, W. B., & Martin, C. E. (1948). *Sexual behavior in the human male*. Philadelphia: W. B. Saunders.

Kirk, K. M., Bailey, J. M., Dunne, M. P., & Martin, N. G. (2000). Measurement models for sexual orientation in a community twin sample. *Behavior Genetics*, 30, 345–356.

Kitzinger, C. (1995). Social constructionism: Implications for lesbian and gay psychology. In A. R. D'Augelli & C. Patterson (Eds.), *Lesbian, gay, and bisexual identities over the lifespan* (pp. 136–161). New York: Oxford University Press.

Kitzinger, C., & Wilkinson, S. (1995). Transitions from heterosexuality to lesbianism: The discursive production of lesbian identities. *Developmental Psychology*, 31, 95–104.

Laumann, E. O., Gagnon, J. H., Michael, R. T., & Michaels, F. (1994). *The social organization of sexuality: Sexual practices in the United States*. Chicago: University of Chicago Press.

Lippa, R. A. (2006). Is high sex drive associated with increased sexual attraction to both sexes? It depends on whether you are male or female. *Psychological Science*, 17: 46–52.

Mosher, W. D., Chandra, A., & Jones, J. (2005). *Sexual behavior and selected health measures: Men and women 15–44 years of age, United States, 2002* (Advance data from vital and health statistics, No. 362). Hyattsville, MD: National Center for Health Statistics.

Pattatucci, A. M. L., & Hamer, D. H. (1995). Development and familiality of sexual orientation in females. *Behavior Genetics*, 25, 407–420.

Paul, J. P. (1985). Bisexuality: Reassessing our paradigms of sexuality. In F. Klein & T. Wolf (Eds.), *Two lives to lead: Bisexuality in men and women* (pp. 21–34). New York: Harrington Park Press.

Peplau, L. A., Spalding, L. R., Conley, T. D., & Veniegas, R. C. (1999). The development of sexual orientation in women. *Annual Review of Sex Research*, 10, 70–99.

Rosario, M., Schrimshaw, E. W., Hunter, J., & Braun, L. (2006). Sexual identity development among lesbian, gay, and bisexual youths: Consistency and change over time. *Journal of Sex Research*, 43, 46–58.

Rust, P. C. R. (1993). Coming out in the age of social constructionism: Sexual identity formation among lesbians and bisexual women. *Gender and Society*, 7, 50–77.

Rust, P. C. R. (2000a). Alternatives to binary sexuality: Modeling bisexuality. In P. C. R. Rust (Ed.), *Bisexuality in the United States* (pp. 33–54). New York: Columbia University Press.

Rust, P. C. R. (2000b). Criticisms of the scholarly literature on sexuality for its neglect of bisexuality. In P. C. R. Rust (Ed.), *Bisexuality in the United States: A reader and guide to the literature* (pp. 5–10). New York: Columbia University Press.

Rust, P. C. R. (2002). Bisexuality: The state of the union. *Annual Review of Sex Research*, 13, 180–240.

Savin-Williams, R. C. (2005). *The new gay teenager*. Cambridge, MA: Harvard University Press.

Shively, M. G., & DeCecco, J. P. (1977). Components of sexual identity. *Journal of Homosexuality*, 3, 41–48.

Snyder, P. J., Weinrich, J. D., & Pillard, R. C. (1994). Personality and lipid level differences associated with homosexual and bisexual identity in men. *Archives of Sexual Behavior*, 23, 433–451.

Stokes, J. P., Damon, W., & McKirnan, D. J. (1997). Predictors of movement toward homosexuality: A longitudinal study of bisexual men. *Journal of Sex Research*, 34, 304–312.

Weinberg, M. S., & Williams, C. J. (1988). Black sexuality: A test of two theories. *Journal of Sex Research*, 25, 197–218.

Weinberg, M. S., Williams, C. J., & Pryor, D. W. (1994). *Dual attraction: Understanding bisexuality*. New York: Oxford University Press.

CHAPTER 34

Asexuality

Classification and Characterization

Nicole Prause
Cynthia A. Graham

We live in a world that assumes that everyone experiences sexual desire. Referring to sexual desire, award-winning science writer Natalie Angier proclaimed, "It is a near-universal experience, the invisible clause on one's birth certificate stipulating that one will, upon reaching maturity, feel the urge to engage in activities often associated with the issuance of more birth certificates" (Angier 2007, para. 2). But, is this really a universal experience? About 1 percent of adults who have never experienced sexual desire and are not particularly distressed by that fact would say, "No."

In recent years, asexuals have begun to be more public about their lack of desire. The Asexuality Visibility and Education Network maintains a website that provides support and information about asexuality (www.asexuality.org). Asexuality is considered by some to be every bit as much a sexual orientation as heterosexuality, bisexuality, or homosexuality.

How would it feel to be part of such a small, silent minority, defined by what they don't feel?

Those around you would often be thinking about, talking about, joking about sex, and you wouldn't understand what the big fuss was all about. How could you tell your family and friends that your body doesn't react to erotic stimuli in the same way that their bodies react? How would you negotiate a romantic relationship with someone else who was interested in sex?

In the research reported in this chapter, one of very few studies of asexuality, Prause and Graham built on an initial small-scale, qualitative study of asexual individuals which helped them to develop hypotheses about variables that might be significantly different in asexual individuals than in others. Before you read this enlightening article, think about what hypotheses you would choose to test. After reading this chapter, if you still have questions about asexuality, you might think about ways to design the next study.

From "Asexuality: Classification and Characterization" by N. Prause and C. A. Graham. 2007. *Archives of Sexual Behavior* 36: 341–356. Copyright © 2007, Springer. With kind permission from Springer Science + Business Media.

INTRODUCTION

While researchers often assess sexual desire as one continuous dimension, individuals with very high or very low sexual desire typically are thought to be qualitatively distinct from others with "normal" sexual desire in clinical settings (cf. Haslam, 1995). The third edition of the *Diagnostic and Statistical Manual of Mental Disorders* (American Psychiatric Association, 1980) was the first to include psychosexual and, specifically, Inhibited Sexual Desire, disorders. Subsequently renamed "hypoactive sexual desire disorder" in the *DSM-IV-TR* (American Psychiatric Association, 2000), it is defined as a deficiency or absence of sexual fantasies and desire for sexual activity, which causes marked distress or interpersonal difficulty. The classification of sexual disorders in the *DSM* has recently come under criticism (Bancroft, Graham, & McCord, 2001; Tiefer, 2001), although sexual desire is still thought to play a fundamental role in the experience of sexuality (Brezsnyak & Whisman, 2004). The *DSM* acknowledges the problematic lack of normative age- or gender-related data on frequency or degree of sexual desire to delineate "deficient" sexual desire, and some have suggested cutoffs for defining normal levels of sexual desire (Riley & Riley, 2000). A group whose members identify as "asexual" has been appearing increasingly on the Internet (e.g., Jay, 2003), which brings a different perspective to what it might mean to have very low sexual desire. Asexuality raises questions concerning the role of "personal distress" in defining sexual desire problems. In this study, we attempt to better characterize the way that the label "asexual" is used and investigate what distinguishes those who identify as asexual from those who do not.

Implicit in the debate about what constitutes a "normal" level of sexual desire is an assumption that *some* level of sexual desire is normative. A person with no sexual desire seeking guidance from a clinician may be diagnosed with hypoactive sexual desire disorder or sexual aversion disorder, or may be referred for medical evaluation. Indeed, a decrease in sexual desire can signal psychological or physiological disorders (e.g., depression, hypothyroidism), but is low or absent sexual desire necessarily associated with pathology? "Pathologizing" has been defined as assigning a diagnosis on the basis of cognitions

or behaviors in the absence of substantive evidence that the cognitions or behaviors are maladaptive (Rubin, 2000). Currently, evidence does not suggest that cognitions and behaviors associated with asexuality necessarily signal a problem. All subsequent use of the term "asexual" in this article refers to those who identify as asexual.

One definition of "asexual" is lacking interest in or desire for sex (Editors of the American Heritage Dictionaries, 2000). Some have suggested that human asexuals are individuals who "do not experience sexual attraction" (Jay, 2003), who have never felt sexual attraction to "anyone at all" (Bogaert, 2004), or who have no "sexual interest" (Carlat, Camargo, & Herzog, 1997). In one study, participants were said to be asexual if they did not prefer either homosexual or heterosexual activities on a Sexual Activities and Preferences Scale (Nurius, 1983). Green (2000) described asexual transsexuals as having "a dearth of sexual attractions *or* behaviors" (p. 791, emphasis added). Women in lesbian relationships that may have had romantic components, but no sexual behaviors, have also been described as asexual (Rothblum & Brehony, 1993). It is unclear whether these characteristics are thought to be lifelong, or if they may be acquired.

Despite this lack of clarity, some researchers tend to characterize asexuality as negative. For example, they renounce the "asexuality" of older persons (Deacon, Minichiello, & Plummer, 1995), young lesbians (Zevy, 1999), and individuals with physical disabilities (Milligan & Neufeldt, 2001) or severe mental illness (Carmen & Brady, 1990). In summary, researchers have used the term "asexual" to refer to individuals with low or absent sexual desire or attractions, low or absent sexual behaviors, exclusively romantic non-sexual partnerships, or a combination of both absent sexual desires and behaviors, and they often consider the label pejorative.

Very little research has addressed asexuality. Recently, Bogaert (2004) used preexisting data from the U.K. National Survey of Sexual Attitudes and Lifestyles (Johnson, Wadsworth,

Wellings, & Field, 1994) to suggest that approximately 1% of their adult sample was asexual. Asexuals were defined as those who endorsed the statement: "I have never felt sexually attracted to anyone at all." The study compared the asexual group with the remaining "sexual" participants: those participants who reported that they had felt attracted to males, females, or both. Of the 15 variables investigated, many differentiated asexuals from non-asexuals. The variables predicting asexual classification included gender (more females than males), older age, marital status (more likely to be single), higher religiosity, short stature, low education, low socioeconomic status, poor health, later onset of sexual activity, later onset of menarche, fewer sexual partners, and less frequent sexual activity with a current partner. Analyses were also performed for each gender separately. Asexuality in women was predicted by age, socioeconomic status, education, race/ethnicity, height, menarche age, and religiosity. Asexuality in men was predicted by socioeconomic status, education, height, and religiosity.

This study had three primary limitations. First, only a single item defined individuals as asexual or sexual. The reliability of the item is unknown, its discriminant validity has not been established, and only limited evidence of convergent validity was provided. Second, by using preexisting data, constructs previously identified as potential features of asexual identity were not assessed. For example, sexual arousability was not available to assess. Additionally, the question used to identify asexuals assessed the direction of attraction, but there was no measure of the amount of sexual desire or attraction. Given the many authors who have defined asexuality in terms of a lack of sexual desire, this oversight neglects a potentially central aspect of asexual identity. Lastly, although Bogaert (2004) examined sexual behavior frequency as possible predictors of asexuality, there were no questions on solitary sexual activities, including masturbation. It was acknowledged that the study was primarily exploratory, required replication, and

that future work should investigate those who self-identify as asexual.

The current research was designed to better characterize individuals who self-identify as asexual and to provide exploratory data for future hypothesis-driven research. A convenience sample of 1,146 individuals ($N = 41$ self-identified asexuals) completed online questionnaires assessing their sexual history, sexual excitation and inhibition, sexual desire, sexual arousability, perceived advantages and disadvantages of asexuality, and their understanding of the term "asexual." The survey included several standardized questionnaires, but also an open-ended, essay-response questionnaire, which was subsequently evaluated by content analysis. The qualitative and quantitative data for asexuals and non-asexuals were compared to test our predictions concerning which variables were most predictive of asexual status.

First, it was hypothesized that individuals who identify as asexual have a specific lack of sexual desire, although they may not necessarily lack sexual motivation. Sexual motivation has been described as incentive motivation (Agmo, 1999) or desire for sexual behaviors that is driven by external cues, such as the desire to satisfy a romantic partner (Basson, 2001). Sexual desire, in this study, is conceptualized as the cognitive (or "felt") component of sexual arousal (Everaerd & Both, 2001). Asexuals may be willing to engage in sexually *motivated* behaviors to achieve nonsexual goals without experiencing sexual *desire*. Consequently, it was predicted that asexuals would report markedly lower sexual desire than non-asexuals, although they may or may not differ in their amount of behavioral sexual experience. Sexual desire was assessed by the Sexual Desire Inventory (Spector et al., 1996). Amount of sexual behavior was indexed by the number of lifetime sexual partners and frequency of masturbation. Second, asexuals were predicted to be less inclined to experience sexual arousal due to a higher threshold to sexual arousal than non-asexuals. Sexual arousability has been defined as an individual's characteristic rate of approach to orgasm as a result of sexual stimulation (Whalen, 1966). If asexuals have a higher threshold to experience sexual arousal, their scores on scales assessing sexual arousability and related constructs should be significantly lower than non-asexual individuals. Sexual arousability was assessed by the Sexual Arousability Inventory (Hoon, Hoon, & Wincze, 1976) and the SIS/SES [Sexual Inhibition and Sexual Excitation Scales] (Janssen et al., 2002).

Third, the interviews did not suggest that the participants were particularly concerned about their sexual functioning or about potential negative consequences of engaging in sexual activity, so we predicted that asexuals would not score higher on the two inhibition scales of the SIS/SES (Janssen et al., 2002) compared with non-asexuals. Specifically, SIS-1 includes fears such as losing sexual arousal too easily, worries about the sexual partner being satisfied, and concerns about performing well sexually. SIS-2 includes fears related to being caught having sex, experiencing negative consequences such as sexually transmitted infections, causing a partner pain, and having an appropriate partner (e.g., not too young).

Finally, the exploratory, qualitative portion of the survey included open-ended questions about the participant's definition of asexuality and the advantages and drawbacks of asexuality. These responses were first quantified using content analysis and then asexuals' and non-asexuals' responses were compared.

Method

Participants

Participants were recruited through convenience sampling from undergraduate psychology courses at a large university and by online advertisements (e.g., asexuality.org, kinseyinstitute.org). The introductory web page for the study did not mention asexuality, but informed potential volunteers that they would be asked about their "sexual feelings (or lack of feelings), sexual experience, and general personality."

Initially, 1,538 responses were obtained. Participants were excluded from analyses who did not complete all of the standardized questionnaires ($N = 357$), resubmitted identical or nearly identical responses ($N = 25$), or provided responses that clearly indicated that they were not responding seriously ($N = 5$). The final 1,146 participants ($N = 511$ women, 635 men) were between the ages of 18 and 59. Those recruited through the psychology courses ($N = 732$) tended to be younger than those recruited through the Internet.

Measures

Participants completed five questionnaires online presented in the same order. Online surveys have been shown to elicit greater reporting of behaviors that are socially undesirable (e.g., Ross, Tikkanen, & Mansson, 2000) and are a preferred method for reaching small populations efficiently (Birnbaum, 2004).

Sexual History Questionnaire (SHQ). Developed at The Kinsey Institute for Research in Sex, Gender, and Reproduction, the SHQ first collects general demographic and sexual information. Demographic questions included gender (male, female, other), age, education, and relationship status, and sexual information questions included number of lifetime sexual partners, number of lifetime sexual intercourse partners, masturbation frequency, worry about sexual problems, and orgasm consistency (% times reached orgasm when masturbating, % times reached orgasm when engaged in sexual activity with a partner). One question concerning attraction was similar to that used in the Bogaert (2004) study. It was worded slightly differently and asked "Would you describe the type of person you find most sexually attractive as:" and offered the response options "Only male," "Mostly male, but sometimes female," "Could be equally male or female," "Mainly female, but sometimes male," "Only female" or "None of the above."

The questions concerning the number of partners with whom they had experienced any sexual behaviors in their lifetime, and the frequency with which they masturbated, were used as indicators of "Sexual Experience." The "Lifetime sexual partners" measure was chosen to minimize the possibility that differences in attitudes toward sexual intercourse, as opposed to non-intercourse sexual behaviors, might underlie between-group differences. "Masturbation frequency" was selected to include sexual behaviors less subject to potential partner availability confounds.

The SHQ also provided a text box for participants to type in their sexual orientation. The purpose of allowing participants to write in their sexual orientation was to compare it with their subsequent response to a multiple-choice question about sexual orientation. The question was "Which of these commonly used terms would you use to describe yourself?" followed by the response options: Heterosexual/Straight; Homosexual/Gay; Bisexual; Asexual

Sexual Arousability Inventory. The SAI purports to measure "arousability." Participants indicated on a 7-point scale how arousing each of a list of 14 activities was to them (Hoon et al., 1976). The SAI can be completed by men or women, regardless of whether they currently have a sexual partner (Hoon & Chambless, 1998). Higher scores indicate that a person reports experiencing more sexual arousal to the list of potential sexual experiences.

Sexual orientation questionnaire. The final questionnaire was created for this study by the authors and included two multiple-choice questions, one multiple-selection question, and seven questions requiring write-in responses about sexual orientation development, feelings, and perceptions of asexuality. Responses to the three write-in questions relevant to definitions and perceptions of asexual identity were content analyzed. The questions were (1) "What kind of sexual or other experiences do you expect a person to have had if they call themselves asexual?" (2) "What drawbacks do you see for being asexual, if any?," and (3) "What benefits do you see for being asexual, if any?" One multiple-choice item was the follow-up question for the previous question that requested participants write in their sexual orientation. Allowing participants to self-identify their sexual orientation excludes other potentially important aspects of sexual identity (Sell, 1997) and does not account for label change over time (Diamond, 2005). However, since research supports the notion that self-identification indices typically covary strongly (Weinrich et al., 1993) and a main focus of this study was to begin to examine what self-identification as "asexual" means, self-identification of sexual orientation was used as the primary grouping variable.

Data Analyses

Between-groups (asexual vs. non-asexual) comparisons were made, although the nature of the samples precludes the possibility of drawing strong inferences since participants may differ systematically from a more representative sample from the population. Regarding gender and age, the only significant demographic difference between the groups was age, so between group comparisons were controlled for age, when possible, and corrected comparisons are reported if age changed the significance of the relationship.

Variables were conceptualized as indicators of either sexual desire level (Dyadic Sexual Desire, Solitary Sexual Desire), sexual arousability level (Sexual Arousability Inventory, Sexual Excitation Scale), sexual behaviors (Number of lifetime sexual partners, Masturbation frequency), or sexual inhibition (SIS-1, SIS-2). A substantial minority of participants had very low Solitary Sexual Desire scores. Solitary Sexual Desire was analyzed as a 4-category variable reflecting groups who have desire for sexual activity that occurs (1) rarely or never, (2) one to a few times per month, (3) one to a few times per week, or (4) once daily or more.

Qualitative content analyses were completed using methods outlined for textual analysis by Carpenter (2002) with the coding system criteria from Neuendorf (2002). Initially three coders (the first author and two trained research assistants) independently developed coding trees for each question in the Sexual Orientation Questionnaire by reviewing 20 non-overlapping, randomly selected participant's essays. The raters collaboratively integrated their coding trees for each question and drafted a codebook. Raters then randomly selected and independently coded 30 additional, non-overlapping cases. Following an open discussion of this revised codebook, adjustments were made to the coding trees. Finally, 201 participants were selected. These included all of those asexuals who provided at least one write in response ($N = 32$) and a randomly selected sample of non-asexuals ($N = 169$) who provided at least one write in response.

Results

Questionnaire Analyses

Demographic characteristics
There were no significant differences in the proportion of individuals who identified as asexual based on gender (women, men, or "other"). Asexuals were significantly older than non-asexual individuals. Also, asexuals and non-asexuals were predominantly single, and asexuals were more likely to have completed college.

Sexual orientation
The first opportunity for participants to provide their sexual orientation occurred in the SHQ and their responses were coded as: Heterosexual, Homosexual, Bisexual, Asexual, Mixed, Unsure/Don't Know, None ("N/A"), or as Miscellaneous (e.g., "eyes"). The second opportunity to provide their sexual orientation occurred in the multiple-choice question in the SOQ. Of the 40 participants who identified as "Asexual" in the multiple choice question, 22 (53.7%) had written

in their sexual orientation as "Asexual" earlier in the questionnaires.

In the current study, participants were asked a question concerning their sexual attraction. The predictive utility of this attraction question in classifying self-identified asexuals in this sample was evaluated. Only 17 of 41 (41.5%) self-identified asexuals in our sample reported that they were not attracted to men or women. Of the participants who reported no attraction to men or women ($N = 19$), 17 (89.5%) identified as asexual.

Sexual feelings and sexual behaviors
The Sexual Desire indicators (Dyadic sexual desire and Solitary sexual desire), a Sexual Arousability indicator (Sexual Arousability Inventory), and a Sexual Inhibition indicator (SIS-2) were significant predictors of asexual orientation.

A Sexual Desire indicator (Dyadic sexual desire) and Sexual Arousability indicator (Sexual Arousability Inventory) were the best predictors of asexual versus non-asexual identity. These were followed closely by the other Sexual Arousability indicator, the SES Scale. SIS-2 was less predictive of asexual status.

Concerns about sexual desire
Asexuals reported being no more worried about their level of sexual than non-asexuals. Furthermore, asexuals were not more likely than non-asexuals to want to speak with a health professional about their sexual desire level (56.1% of asexuals vs. 66.5% non-asexuals).

Content Analyses

Definition of asexuality
The five most common themes in participants' responses to what experiences they expected an asexual to have had included (1) a psychological problem, (2) a very negative sexual experience, (3) no/low sexual desire, (4) no/little sexual experience, and, (5) no differences from the experiences of non-asexuals. Of these, the most

common expectation reported was that asexuals would have low/no level of sexual desire. Non-asexuals were significantly more likely than asexuals to expect that asexuals would experience low/no sexual desire. In contrast, the expectation that asexuals would have low/no sexual experience was more often cited by asexuals than non-asexuals, although this difference was not statistically significant.

Of those participants who subsequently self-identified as asexual in a multiple-choice question, approximately half had also spontaneously written "asexual" as their sexual orientation in the earlier "write-in" question.

Advantages of asexuality

The four benefits of asexuality most commonly mentioned were (1) avoiding the common problems of intimate relationships, (2) decreasing risks to physical health or unwanted pregnancy, (3) experiencing less social pressure to find suitable partners, and (4) having more free time. A greater proportion of asexuals cited each benefit compared with non-asexuals. In particular, asexuals were much more likely to report "Lower health risks" and "Benefits of free time" as advantages of being asexual, as compared to non-asexuals.

Drawbacks of asexuality

The four drawbacks of asexuality stated most often were (1) problems establishing nonsexual, dyadic intimate relationships, (2) needing to find out what problem is causing the asexuality, (3) a negative public perception of asexuality, and (4) missing the positive aspects of sex. For all but one of the drawbacks mentioned, a greater proportion of asexuals cited each drawback as compared to non-asexuals. Asexuals were much more likely to report a drawback of asexuality as needing to find out what problem was causing the asexuality. Non-asexuals, however, were more likely to mention missing the positive aspects of sex as a drawback of asexuality.

DISCUSSION

This exploratory study attempted to better characterize individuals who identify as asexual and to provide exploratory data for future research. Asexuals were most clearly distinguished from non-asexuals by their lower/absent scores on the Dyadic Sexual Desire subscale, lower scores on the Solitary Sexual Desire subscale, and lower scores on the Sexual Arousability Inventory. Other variables that differentiated the groups less consistently included lower scores on SES (propensity to become excited sexually) and SIS-2 (inhibition due to threat of performance consequences). Also, asexuals did not express any greater interest in talking to a health professional about their low sexual desire, despite greater concern about their level of sexual desire. Finally, in the qualitative analyses, both the asexual and non-asexual groups cited no/low sexual desire and no/low sexual experiences most frequently as the two primary defining features of asexuality.

The fact that neither Sexual Inhibition scale was a strong predictor suggests that self-identified asexuals were not particularly sexually fearful, but that they had a lower excitatory drive. The lower excitatory drive was exemplified by their lower scores on the Dyadic Sexual Desire, Sexual Excitation, and Sexual Arousability Inventory questionnaires. This pattern of findings suggests several conclusions. First, asexuals were not well-described as motivated by avoidance, as relevant in social phobias and sexual aversion difficulties. Second, the results support the idea that excitation and inhibition can be conceptualized as relatively independent factors affecting sexual arousal (Bancroft, 1999). Finally, when assessing an individual's sexual desire level, it is possible that sexual excitation may be more relevant than sexual inhibition.

Self-identified asexuals exhibited similar SIS-1 scores and lower SIS-2 scores compared to non-asexuals. SIS-1 reflects concerns about sexual performance (e.g., erectile problems) while SIS-2 reflects concerns about performance consequences (e.g., contracting sexually transmitted infections, being caught having sex, etc.). The qualitative data support this concern, as asexuals were more likely to mention "avoiding disease" as a benefit of their asexual status. Both asexuals and non-asexuals may face common baseline difficulties in establishing intimate sexual relationships, hence not differing in their SIS-1 scores, but self-identified asexuals may feel that their low desire confers a lesser risk of subsequent sexual consequences. For instance, high sexual arousal may potentiate sexual risk taking (Strong, Bancroft, Carnes, Davis, & Kennedy, 2005). This may occur directly, through limiting attention paid to safety cues (Steele & Josephs, 1990), or indirectly through the reduced use, for instance, of alcohol to promote feelings of sexual arousal by self-identified asexuals (Brown, Goldman, Inn, & Anderson, 1980). In other words, asexuals may have lower SIS-2 scores because they feel less vulnerable about being carried away by feelings of sexual arousal into practicing unsafe sex since they do not experience strong sexual excitation or desire.

These data did not replicate several demographic and sexual experience predictors of asexual status reported by Bogaert (2004). First, we did not find a gender or relationship status difference between sexuals and asexuals. Given the younger age of our non-asexual sample, it is possible that they had less time available to have experienced a longer-term relationship. It is noteworthy that Bogaert reported that 44% of the empirically-defined asexuals in his sample were currently in or had been in long-term (cohabiting or married) relationships. Also, it is surprising that no gender differences emerged in this study given that women tend to report less sexual desire than men report on average (Beck, 1995). Second, these data indicated that a higher percentage of asexuals had completed at least a college degree as compared to non-asexuals, and this was not accounted for by the group age difference. The Bogaert study found the opposite. Third, there was no significant difference in the lifetime number of sexual partners reported by asexuals and non-asexuals, whereas in the Bogaert (2004) study asexuals reported fewer sexual partners. Finally, these data suggest that the item used in the Bogaert (2004) study to identify asexuals likely failed to identify many individuals who would have chosen to self-identify as asexual given the opportunity. Whatever the explanation for the divergent findings, it is clear that further research is needed on the correlates of asexuality.

This study utilized a multi-method approach combining qualitative and quantitative data. Collecting qualitative or quantitative data consistently represent some tradeoff in objectivity for phenomenological detail, and research that collects both qualitative and quantitative data has been recommended to maximize the objectivity and interpretability of data (Hyde, 2001). In our case, the qualitative data were helpful in understanding several differences found in the quantitative data. For instance, both groups of participants reported that asexuals would differ most from non-asexuals by their no/low sexual desire and their no/low sexual experience, but the quantitative data suggested that asexuals actually differed most in their sexual desire and sexual arousability levels, and not the amount of their sexual experience. It is possible that the concept of "arousability" was not identified as a theme in the qualitative data because it is simply not a term in common use by the lay public. Non-asexuals might believe that asexuals would not be sufficiently aroused to want to engage, or be able to engage, in sexual behaviors.

A second example of how the use of multi-method data collection is helpful is in understanding why asexuals were no more worried about their level of sexual desire and no more likely to want to speak to a health professional about their level of sexual desire than non-asexuals. This could simply reflect differences in conservatism in not wanting to discuss "inappropriate" personal sexual health with health professionals (e.g., sexuality concerns around pregnancy; Alteneder & Hartzell, 1997). Asexuals' written responses provided another possible explanation. While asexuals were significantly more likely to respond that being asexual meant that there was something wrong with the asexual person or that they had more relationship problems, they were also more likely to respond that there was a negative public perception of asexuals as compared to non-asexuals. Specifically, asexuals also frequently explained that what was wrong with asexuality was something outside of their control (e.g., "something wrong genetically," "hormone problem"). As discussed earlier, there is an expectation that a person should experience sexual desire, or they may be characterized as having "Hypoactive Sexual Desire Disorder" or "Sexual Aversion Disorder." Asexuals may feel pressure to conform to this expectation, but frame the abnormality as a problem with the social expectations (or their physical health), which is out of their control (Rubin, 2000). This has implications both for asexuals who may seek treatment and for understanding disorders of sexual desire.

The level of concern of asexuals was particularly relevant with regard to implications for diagnostic classification (Cole, 1993). As mentioned previously, personal distress is one of the criteria for diagnosing hypoactive sexual desire in the DSM-IV-TR (American Psychiatric Association, 2000). If personal distress is primarily due to conflicts with social expectations or worry that a physical problem exists, then a psychiatric diagnosis implying abnormality may exacerbate concerns in an asexual individual. While behavior that is statistically abnormal may be problematic without a person's full recognition of when they are behaving abnormally, as in schizophrenia, it remains to be determined to what extent asexuality is problematic in the absence of individual, personal distress.

This study had limitations. First, the sample was not randomly selected. In particular, the non-asexual sample was comprised mainly of younger students and the asexual sample was comprised primarily of individuals from the Internet, including asexuality sites. This difference could have caused the lack of

difference in relationship status between asexuals and non-asexuals. Non-asexuals were younger and perhaps less likely to be partnered as a result of insufficient time to locate a suitable partner rather than as a result of their non-asexual identity. Second, the on-line format introduced limitations. Despite the considerable advantages of online questionnaires, including increasing evidence that samples are not as select as was once feared (Birnbaum, 2004), online studies also have disadvantages; for example, they may be completed in undesirable circumstances (e.g., with a partner observing), and the anonymity may encourage deceptive responses. However, steps were taken to minimize the likelihood of these problems. For example, to encourage participants to complete the survey in private, the highly personal nature of the study was mentioned in introductory web pages. The effects of obvious deception and/or incomplete responses were reduced by thorough data cleaning. The advantages of the online format in reaching this likely small population and encouraging the reporting of socially undesirable sexual behaviors were judged to outweigh these disadvantages. Finally, the measures of sexual behavior (lifetime sexual partners and masturbation frequency) are subject to influences that may confound their interpretation (e.g., availability of sexual partners, abusive sexual experiences, etc.).

This study suggests a way of conceptualizing asexuality that leads to clear, testable hypotheses for future research. First, asexual self-identification was best predicted by low excitatory processes, but not necessarily high inhibitory processes. It may be that behavioral activation, as characterized by Gray (1987), is generally low among asexuals, or that depressogenic types are prevalent amongst self-identified asexuals. However, correlations between scales measuring general behavioral inhibition and activation and sexual excitation and inhibition have been low (Graham, Sanders, & Milhausen, 2006). Animal evidence also argues against this possibility. Sexually low-performing rams with low sexual incentive motivation appear strongly motivated in other domains, such as aggression in feeding (e.g., Alexander, Stellflug, Rose, Fitzgerald, & Moss, 1999).

Second, asexuals cited both more benefits and drawbacks of asexuality than non-asexuals. This simply may reflect a more complex consideration of the identity over time. However, it also may be that individuals who identify as asexuals face challenges unrecognized by others and may counteract those challenges by perceiving additional benefits. Third, asexuals appear to have similar levels of sexual behaviors to non-asexuals. Investigating emotionally intimate partner variables separately from sexuality variables could elucidate this finding. For example, asexuals may be engaging in unwanted, but consensual sex for the purpose of maintaining an intimate relationship with a sexual partner (O'Sullivan & Allgeier, 1998). The reason for the lack of difference is unclear and, given the nature of the sample, warrants replication.

Finally, after a better understanding of the asexual construct is developed, it may be useful to test the physiological and psychophysiological correlates of asexuality. These include, but are not limited to, responses to sexual stimuli, neurological evidence of affective experience (Cuthbert, Schupp, Bradley, Birnbaumer, & Lang, 2000), hormone abnormalities, or generalized, non-sexual motivated behaviors (Bindra, 1959). Indeed, a number of physical factors can affect feelings of sexual desire including menstrual phase (Hedricks, 1994), physical fatigue due to recent childbirth (Hyde, DeLamater, & Hewitt, 1998), or illness (Meuleman & van Lankveld, 2005), and central dopamanergic dysregulation in women (Bechara, Bertolino, Casabe, & Fredotovich, 2004) and men (Montorsi et al., 2003).

One direction that seems particularly promising is conceptualizing asexual development as a form of kindling. Kindling can be defined as sensitization to a previously sub-threshold stimulus. Non-copulating rats appear not to differ from copulating rats in baseline testosterone (Alexander et al., 1999). The present study data support the idea that human asexuals may have a higher excitatory threshold for sexual arousal. Future research concerning physical factors might focus on exploring generalized, cognitive "kindling" differences in those who do and do not identify as asexual. Although physiological mechanisms appear unlikely to completely explain asexuality, evidence of some biological basis for asexuality also may offer asexual individuals legitimacy, a conceptual framework for their feelings, and reduce the extent to which others blame them for assuming the identity (Irvine, 1993).

To our knowledge, this was the first study to investigate the defining features of individuals who self-identify as asexual. As such, it raises a number of empirical and theoretical questions about asexuality as well as about "normal" sexual functioning. Given these new questions and the paucity of research concerning asexuality, future research should continue to explore this population.

INTRODUCTION REFERENCE

Angier, N. 2007. Birds do it. Bees do it. People seek the keys to it. The *New York Times*, 10 April. Http://www.nytimes.com/2007/04/10/science/10desi.html (accessed December 24, 2008).

REFERENCES

Agmo, A. (1999). Sexual motivation–an inquiry into events determining the occurrence of sexual behavior. *Behavioural Brain Research*, 105, 129–150.

Alexander, B. M., Stellflug, J. N., Rose, J. D., Fitzgerald, J. A., & Moss, G. E. (1999). Behavior and endocrine changes in high-performing, low-performing, and male-oriented domestic rams following exposure to rams and ewes in estrus when copulation is precluded. *Journal of Animal Science, 77*, 1869–1874.

Alteneder, R. R., & Hartzell, D. (1997). Addressing couples' sexuality concerns during the childbearing period: Use of the PLISSIT model. *Journal of Obstetric, Gynecologic, & Neonatal Nursing, 26*, 651–658.

American Psychiatric Association. (1980). *Diagnostic and statistical manual of mental disorders* (3rd ed.). Washington, DC: Author.

American Psychiatric Association. (2000). *Diagnostic and statistical manual of mental disorders* (4th ed., text rev.). Washington, DC: Author.

Bancroft, J. (1999). Central inhibition of sexual response in the male: A theoretical perspective. *Neuroscience & Biobehavioral Reviews, 23*, 763–784.

Bancroft, J., Graham, C. A., & McCord, C. (2001). Conceptualizing women's sexual problems. *Journal of Sex & Marital Therapy, 27*, 95–103.

Basson, R. (2001). Using a different model for female sexual response to address women's problematic low sexual desire. *Journal of Sex & Marital Therapy, 27*, 395–403.

Bechara, A., Bertolino, M. V., Casabe, A., & Fredotovich, N. (2004). A double-randomized placebo control study comparing the objective and subjective changes in female sexual response using sublingual apomorphine. *Journal of Sexual Medicine, 1*, 209–214.

Beck, J. G. (1995). Hypoactive sexual desire disorder: An overview. *Journal of Consulting and Clinical Psychology, 63*, 919–927.

Bindra, D. (1959). Motivation: A systematic reinterpretation. New York: Ronald Press.

Birnbaum, M. H. (2004). Human research and data collection via the internet. *Annual Review of Psychology, 55*, 803–832.

Bogaert, A. F. (2004). Asexuality: Prevalence and associated factors in a national probability sample. *Journal of Sex Research, 41*, 279–287.

Brezsnyak, M., & Whisman, M. A. (2004). Sexual desire and relationship functioning: The effects of marital satisfaction and power. *Journal of Sex & Marital Therapy, 30*, 199–217.

Brown, S. A., Goldman, M. S., Inn, A., & Anderson, L. R. (1980). Expectations of reinforcement from alcohol: Their domain and relation to drinking patterns. Journal of *Consulting and Clinical Psychology, 48*, 419–426.

Carlat, D. J., Camargo, C. A., & Herzog, D. B. (1997). Eating disorders in males: A report on 135 patients. *American Journal of Psychiatry, 154*, 1127–1132.

Carmen, E., & Brady, S. M. (1990). AIDS risk and prevention for the chronic mentally ill. *Hospital and Community Psychiatry, 41*, 652–657.

Carpenter, L. M. (2002). Analyzing textual material. In M. W. Wiederman & B. E. Whitley (Eds.), *Handbook for conducting research on human sexuality* (pp. 327–343). Mahwah, NJ: Lawrence Erlbaum Associates.

Cole, E. (1993). Is sex a natural function?: Implications for sex therapy. In E. Rothblum & K. Brehony (Eds.), *Boston marriages: Romantic but asexual relationships among contemporary lesbians* (pp. 188–193). Amherst: University of Massachusetts Press.

Cuthbert, B. N., Schupp, H. T., Bradley, M. M., Birbaumer, N., & Lang, P. J. (2000). Brain potentials in affective picture processing: Covariation with autonomic arousal and affective report. *Biological Psychology, 52*, 95–111.

Deacon, S., Minichiello, V., & Plummer, D. (1995). Sexuality and older people: Revisiting the assumptions. *Educational Gerontology, 21*, 497–514.

Diamond, L. M. (2005). A new view of lesbian subtypes: Stable versus fluid identity trajectories over an 8-year period. *Psychology of Women Quarterly, 29*(2), 119–128.

Editors of the American Heritage Dictionaries. (2000). *The American heritage dictionary of the English language* (4th ed.). Boston: Houghton Mifflin Company.

Everaerd, W., & Both, S. (2001). Ideal female sexual function. *Journal of Sex & Marital Therapy, 27*, 137–139.

Graham, C. A, Sanders, S. A., & Milhausen, R. (2006). The Sexual Excitation and Sexual Inhibition Inventory for Women: Psychometric properties. *Archives of Sexual Behavior, 35*, 397–410.

Gray, J. A. (1987). Perspectives on anxiety and impulsivity: A commentary. *Journal of Research in Personality, 21*, 493–509.

Green, R. (2000). Birth order and ratio of brothers to sisters in transsexuals. P*sychological Medicine, 30*, 789–795.

Haslam, N. (1995). The discreteness of emotion concepts: Categorical structure in the affective circumplex. *Personality & Social Psychology Bulletin, 21*, 1012–1019.

Hedricks, C. A. (1994). Female sexual activity across the human menstrual cycle. *Annual Review of Sex Research, 5*, 122–172.

Hoon, E. F., & Chambless, D. (1998). Sexual Arousability Inventory (SAI) and Sexual Arousability Inventory-Expanded (SAI-E). In C. M. Davis, W. L. Yarber, R. Bauserman, G. Schreer & S. L. Davis (Eds.), *Handbook of sexuality-related measures* (pp. 71–74). Thousand Oaks, CA: Sage Publications.

Hoon, E. F., Hoon, P. W., & Wincze, J. P. (1976). An inventory for the measurement of female sexual arousability: The SAI. *Archives of Sexual Behavior, 5*, 291–300.

Hyde, J. S. (2001). The next decade of sexual science: Synergy from advances in related sciences. *Journal of Sex Research, 38*, 97–101.

Hyde, J. S., DeLamater, J. D., & Hewitt, E. C. (1998). Sexuality and the dual-earner couple: Multiple roles and sexual functioning. *Journal of Family Psychology, 12,* 354–368.

Irvine, J. M. (1993). Regulated passions: The invention of inhibited sexual desire and sex addiction. *Social Text, 37,* 203–226.

Janssen, E., Vorst, H., Finn, P., & Bancroft, J. (2002). The Sexual Inhibition (SIS) and Sexual Excitation (SES) Scales: I. Measuring sexual inhibition and excitation proneness in men. *Journal of Sex Research, 39,* 114–126.

Jay, D. (2003). Asexual visibility and education network. 2003, from http://www.asexuality.org/ info.htm.

Johnson, A., Wadsworth, J., Wellings, K., & Field, J. (1994). *Sexual attitudes and lifestyles.* Oxford: Blackwell Scientific Publications.

Meuleman, E. J. H., & van Lankveld, J. J. D. M. (2005). Hypoactive sexual desire disorder: An underestimated condition in men. *British Journal of Urology International, 95,* 291–296.

Milligan, M. S., & Neufeldt, A. H. (2001). The myth of asexuality: A survey of social and empirical evidence. *Sexuality & Disability, 19,* 91–109.

Montorsi, F., Perani, D., Anchisi, D., Salonia, A., Scifo, P., Rigiroli, P., et al. (2003). Apomorphine-induced brain modulation during sexual stimulation: A new look at central phenomena related to erectile dysfunction. *International Journal of Impotence Research, 15,* 203.

Neuendorf, K. A. (2002). *The content analysis guidebook.* London: Sage Publications.

Nurius, P. S. (1983). Mental health implications of sexual orientation. *Journal of Sex Research, 19,* 119–136.

O'Sullivan, L. F., & Allgeier, E. R. (1998). Feigning sexual desire: Consenting to unwanted sexual activity in heterosexual dating relationships. *Journal of Sex Research, 35,* 234–243.

Riley, A., & Riley, E. (2000). Controlled studies on women presenting with sexual drive disorder: I. Endocrine status. *Journal of Sex & Marital Therapy, 26,* 269–283.

Ross, M. W., Tikkanen, R., & Mansson, S. A. (2000). Differences between internet samples and conventional samples of men who have sex with men: Implications for research and HIV interventions. *Social Science and Medicine, 51,* 749–758.

Rothblum, E. D., & Brehony, K. A. (1993). *Boston marriages: Romantic but asexual relationships among contemporary lesbians.* Amherst: University of Massachusetts Press.

Rubin, J. (2000). William James and the pathologizing of human experience. *Journal of Humanistic Psychology, 40,* 176–226.

Sell, R. L. (1997). Defining and measuring sexual orientation: A review. *Archives of Sexual Behavior, 26,* 643–658.

Spector, I., Carey, M., & Steinberg, L. (1996). The Sexual Desire Inventory: Development, factor structure, and evidence of reliability. *Journal of Sex & Marital Therapy, 22,* 175–190.

Steele, C. M., & Josephs, R. A. (1990). Alcohol myopia: Its prized and dangerous effects. *American Psychologist, 45,* 921–933.

Strong, D. A., Bancroft, J., Carnes, L. A., Davis, L. A., & Kennedy, J. (2005). The impact of sexual arousal on sexual risk-taking: A qualitative study. *Journal of Sex Research, 42,* 185–191.

Tiefer, L. (2001). The "consensus" conference on female sexual dysfunction: Conflicts of interest and hidden agendas. *Journal of Sex & Marital Therapy, 27,* 227–236.

Weinrich, J. D., Snyder, P. J., Pillard, R. C., Grant, I., Jacobson, D. L., Robinson, S. R., et al. (1993). A factor analysis of the Klein Sexual Orientation Grid in two disparate samples. *Archives of Sexual Behavior, 22,* 157.

Whalen, R. (1966). Sexual motivation. *Psychological Review, 73,* 151–163.

Zevy, L. (1999). Sexing the tomboy. In M. Rottnek (Ed.), *Sissies and tomboys: Gender nonconformity and homosexual childhood* (pp. 180–195). New York: New York University Press.

PART VIII

Sexual Health

The vast majority of adults have engaged in sexual behavior that could potentially result in conception or sexually transmitted diseases, or both. We know this fact because only 2.8 percent of adults report never having had sex with a partner, and of those who have, 97 percent have had vaginal intercourse (Laumann et al. 1994). But, when connecting the dots in the game of "sex and consequences," a number of outcomes are possible, some of which are by choice and others by chance. Those variables subject to control are fertility and sexual practices. Disconnecting these dots at any point can separate the act of safer sex from the consequence of chance.

Sexual communication is very much related to sexual risk taking and sexual health, and its roots are in the family. Parents who have open and honest discussions with their children about sex set the tone for open and honest discussion with others about sex. Although parent-child sexual communication is not the panacea that many would like it to be, it certainly is related to adolescent sexual attitudes. Adolescents who have higher levels of sexual communication with their parents have sexual attitudes that are more highly correlated with those of their parents than do other adolescents (Fisher 1988). And, teenagers with close relationships

with their parents, regardless of whether or not they have talked about sex, are less likely to engage in risky sexual behavior.

Parent-child communication is explored in the article by Janna Kim and Monique Ward that examines an understudied population, Asian-American adolescents. This is an interesting group to study because Asians, in general, tend to be less permissive regarding sexuality than many other cultures. In such an environment, parent-child sexual communication likely plays more of an influential role in the socialization of sexual norms, yet little research exists to prove this assumption. Using both quantitative and qualitative methodology, Ward and Kim explore the messages from the Asian-American parents, searching for variables that help determine which messages are conveyed, and how often. Lack of a shared vocabulary was perhaps the most strikingly unique variable affecting communication for this population, while gender differences in type and amount were perhaps the most typical of the similar patterns found among other racial/ethnic groups. The results suggest that, as in other populations, implicit and nonverbal communication is used to impart sexual values.

Although the likelihood of contracting any STI is affected by behavioral risk factors, knowledge about STIs is not always associated with a reduction in risk-taking behavior. Large numbers of informed college students continue to report nonuse of condoms as well as sexual intercourse with persons just met, and sexual intercourse while under the influence of alcohol (Davidson et al. 2008). Research continues to indicate that sexual activity that is anonymous, casual, with multiple partners, or with high-risk partners substantially increases the likelihood of contracting an STI, but that condom use greatly reduces this likelihood (Hingson et al. 2003). Why then do so many sexually active persons fail to use condoms? Perhaps it is because consistent condom use is a complex issue, affected by psychological, interpersonal, and cultural factors.

In the second reading of this section, Abbey, Parkhill, Buck, and Saenz examine the predictors of condom use when sober and when intoxicated, in an attempt to better understand the complex relationship between alcohol use and condom use. In the past, research results concerning the link between alcohol consumption and sexual behavior have been mixed, depending on the characteristics of the individuals, their sex partners, and the situation. The findings offered by these researchers will highlight the importance of targeting beliefs about the disinhibiting effects of alcohol in STI and HIV prevention. Those students who are most aware of research methodology will likely raise methodological issues regarding the retrospective reports used as dependent variables in this study. Such questions can lead to a fruitful discussion regarding the ethical and practical limitations of research on certain topics.

Most sexuality research has focused on mainstream White, college-educated samples, with those studies that have examined sexuality within a specific U. S. subculture focusing on African-Americans, Asian-Americans, or Latinos. The culture-specific needs of Native Americans are often neglected because they are a minority among minorities. Compared to other racial/ethnic groups, Native Americans have received little attention in the

sexuality-research literature. Such an omission may be because they have had low reported rates of HIV/AIDS infection compared to other groups (McNaghten et al. 2005). Nevertheless, they exhibit a higher number of risk factors, for example, high rates of substance use and low rates of condom use, which put them at greater likelihood of contracting sexually transmitted infections in general and HIV/AIDs in particular than many other minority groups. It is, therefore, important to understand which variables are related to higher or lower levels of sexual risk-taking among this group.

The research by Marsiglia, Nieri, and Stiffman, like the study by Kim and Ward earlier in this section, examines the protective role of communication with parents about sexuality, among other family and cultural variables. Parent-child communication may be of even greater significance for this population because of the daily bicultural world of home and community in which the young Native American lives. In such an environment, resulting cultural conflicts may raise identity and sense-of-belonging questions that could impact the sexual experiences of youth who are still in the process of individuation. Students may enjoy the exercise of comparing and contrasting the methodology used and conclusions drawn by these two studies: one of Asian-Americans and one of Native Americans, both highlighting young persons who are very different in some ways and very similar in others.

More than 15 million Americans become infected with sexually transmitted diseases annually. Of these, the human papilloma virus (HPV), evidenced in genital warts, represents one-third of the cases. An estimated 20 million persons in the United States have HPV (Dailard 2003). Such numbers place our nation near the top of the HPV charts of the developed countries of the world. Like the genital herpes virus, HPV is a "gift" that keeps on giving, and as a result, over 6.2 million new cases of genital warts require treatment annually (CDC Fact Sheet, 2007). Not only can subsequent partners be affected, but HPV can also be transmitted to a baby during vaginal delivery if the warts are on the cervix or in the vagina.

In the new book, *Damaged Goods*, Adina Nack explores, for the first time, the qualitative experiences of women diagnosed with sexually transmitted infections [or sexually transmitted diseases (STD), the term still preferred by the Centers for Disease Control and Prevention and used by Nack]. Nack, a sexual-health educator and chronic STI sufferer herself, held in-depth interviews with women who are STI patients to learn how the disease modified the women's self-images and views of their sexual selves. The chapter included in this reader provides fascinating background and an overview of the book. The reader with a genuine interest in this topic will likely want to read the book in its entirety.

As suggested by several of the readings in this Part, the role that sex plays in our lives, our preferred means of sexual expression, and the degree to which we experience sexual guilt and pleasure are all influenced by our culture. Culture is also related to depression, a very common psychological disorder. It is not surprising, then, that culture plays a role in the interaction between sex and depression. As a disorder, depression is a disorder that is more than twice as common in women than in men. This imbalance has inspired two separate summit meetings sponsored by the American Psychological Association to explore the origins of this sex difference. The skewed female/male ratio appears to be due to a variety of causes, including genetic factors, sex hormones, life stress and trauma, and interpersonal relationships and cognitive style (Mazure, Keita, and Blehar 2002).

When it comes to sexual functioning, depressed individuals are victims of a "double-whammy." Not only is depression strongly related to lowered libido, the very antidepressant medications that may be used to treat this debilitating disorder have a number of sexual side-effects. Thus, when it comes to sexual functioning, the cure can be as bad as the disorder it was designed to treat.

In the final reading of this section, Dobkin, Leiblum, Rosen, Menza, and Marin discuss ways in which the link between depression and sexual dysfunction may differ as a function of culture, paying particular attention to African-American, Asian-American, and Hispanic women. Their article is a good illustration of the importance of cultural roots in our functions and dysfunctions, and the need for researchers and therapists to take culture into account when developing theories and treatments.

REFERENCES

Centers for Disease Control and Prevention Fact Sheet. December, 2007. *Genital HPV*. Retrieved November 17, 2008, from http://www.cdc.gov/STD/HPV/hpv-fact-sheet.pdf.

Dailard, C. 2003. HPV in the United States and developing nations: A problem of public health or politics? *The Guttmacher Report* 6(3): 1–5.

Davidson, J. K., Sr., N. B. Moore, J. R. Earle, and R. Davis. 2008. Sexual attitudes and behavior at four universities: Do region, race, and/or religion matter? *Adolescence* 43(170): 189–217.

Fisher, T. D. 1988. The relationship between parent-child communication about sex and the sexual behavior and attitudes of college students as a function of proximity to parents. *The Journal of Sex Research* 24: 305–11.

Hingson, R., T. Heeren, M. R. Winter, and H. Wechsler. 2003. Early age at first drunkenness as a factor in college students' unplanned and unprotected sex attributable to drinking. *Pediatrics* 111: 34–41.

Laumann, E. O., J. H. Gagnon, R. T. Michael, and S. Michaels. 1994. *The social organization of sexuality: Sexual practices in the United States*. Chicago: University of Chicago Press.

Mazure, C. M., G. P. Keita, and M. C. Blehar. 2002. *Summit on women and depression: Proceedings and recommendations*. Washington DC: American Psychological Association. Retrieved December 21, 2008, from http://www.apa.org/pi/wpo/women&depression.pdf.

McNaghten, A. D., J. J. Neal, J. Li, and P. L. Fleming. 2005. Epidemiologic profile of HIV and AIDS among American Indians/Alaska Natives in the USA through 2000. *Ethnic Health* 10: 57–71.

CHAPTER 35

Silence Speaks Volumes

Parental Sexual Communication Among Asian American Emerging Adults

Janna L. Kim
L. Monique Ward

What do parents talk about when communicating about sex with their children? Generally, mothers, and less frequently fathers, stick to biological and reproductive facts, with only some parents venturing into information about how to minimize sexual risks. Fewer still seem brave enough to discuss sexual feelings and ways to maximize the pleasures of sexuality with their adolescent offspring. Nonetheless, in the process of discussing or not discussing sex, parental values are often conveyed that adolescents tend to adopt (Fisher 2004).

How much have you discussed the various aspects of sexuality with your parents? If asked, could you accurately recall the topics that you have discussed, and the messages that they have conveyed to you? At the time, do you remember feeling that much more was being conveyed than the actual facts that they were verbalizing? Do you recall how much of the message seemed to have been communicated through body language? You may wish to recall these earlier memories of communication about sexuality in your own family as you read the following chapter by Janna Kim and Monique Ward, who explore parent-child communication about sexuality among Asian-American families. This topic, though commonly studied in other populations, has rarely been examined among Asian-Americans. As the authors lift the veil on this generally private aspect of parent-child relationships from a culture that may not be like your own, compare or contrast this to your family.

The real question, then, is whether or not parent-child sexual communication among Asian-Americans is similar, in either quality or quantity, to that of other ethnic/racial families, and to what degree enculturation and language difficulties may have an impact on family discussions about sex. This study takes a unique approach to examining parent-child communication about aspects of sexuality, and contributes greatly to our understanding of this complex process.

Although research has shed considerable light on how parents educate about sexual roles and relationships, much of our knowledge is derived from studies of White, European American families (for a review, see DiIorio, Pluhar, & Belcher, 2003). In one line of inquiry, researchers examine the amount or incidence of sexual communication occurring between parents and children. These studies show that although parents often report *wanting* to be the primary sexuality educators of their children (Alexander & Jorgensen, 1983), in reality, they tend to be reluctant and infrequent transmitters of sexual information (Hutchinson & Cooney, 1998). Parents' rates of communication depend, in part, on the sexual topic in question (Hepburn, 1983), a finding that has prompted many researchers to abandon global measures of communication (e.g., "Have your parents talked to you about sex?") in favor of scales that make distinctions between different sexual topics. It is unfortunate that small but persistent differences in the wording of such scales make it difficult to draw broad conclusions across these studies. However, DiIorio et al. (2003) estimated that the percentage of adolescents and young adults who reported having ever discussed sexual topics with at least one parent ranged from 37% to 93% for menstruation, 11% to 70% for birth control, 12% to 84% for sexually transmitted diseases (STDs), 31% to 80% for sexual intercourse, and 66% to 80% for pregnancy.

Knowing whether or not sexual communication takes place is most informative if the substance of that communication is identifiable. Therefore, a second line of inquiry, typically qualitative, concentrates on the content or tone of the sexual messages that parents provide. Research reveals that much of this communication is indirect and subtle (Hepburn, 1983), with parents conveying messages about sexual morality more often than they provide children with explicit sexual information or facts (King & Lorusso, 1997). Parents' messages tend to be negative or cautionary in tone (e.g., Ward & Wyatt, 1994) and often emphasize the potential for adverse sexual outcomes (O'Sullivan, Meyer-Bahlburg, & Watkins, 2001).

Despite these broad trends in the literature, research suggests that parental sexual communication is rarely uniform but is instead shaped by salient characteristics of the family environment. Gender differences are pervasive. Studies find that mothers are more likely to impart sexual knowledge to their children than are fathers (DiIorio, Kelley, & Hockenberry-Eaton, 1999; Miller, Kotchick, Dorsey, Forehand, & Ham, 1998) and that daughters are the more likely recipients of this communication than are sons (Fisher, 1993). In addition, the content of parents' messages often conveys a sexual double standard. Whereas messages to sons sometimes promote sexual exploration and pleasure (Downie & Coates, 1999), messages to daughters are overwhelmingly restrictive in tone, stressing the negative consequences of sexual activity (Downie & Coates, 1999).

Differences have also emerged based on race or ethnicity (Hutchinson & Cooney, 1998). In their study comparing Black and White young women, Hutchinson and Cooney (1998) found that at least two thirds of Black participants, but less than half of White participants, had discussed birth control, postponing sex, and sexual protection with their mothers. This finding is consistent with earlier studies in which Black mothers were found to discuss sexuality with their daughters earlier than White mothers and were more likely to initiate conversations about "sensitive" sex-related topics (Fox & Inazu, 1980). Latino mothers, in contrast, have been shown to communicate less frequently than White mothers (Davis & Harris, 1982) and to use more power-assertive techniques to dominate discussions about sex with children (Lefkowitz, Romo, Corona, Au, & Sigman, 2000).

Parental Sexual Communication among Asian Americans

Whereas research on parental sexual communication is relatively extensive on White families and is increasingly focusing on Blacks and Latinos, research on Asian Americans is nascent at best. The lack of attention to Asian Americans is not surprising, given that this group is frequently identified as being at low-risk for STDs and unwanted teenage pregnancies. Indeed, in the relatively few sexuality-related studies that do consider Asian American adolescents (for a review, see Okazaki, 2002), these youth have been found to initiate sexual activity at later ages (Upchurch, Levy-Storms, Sucoff, & Aneshensel, 1998), to report fewer sexual partners (Grunbaum, Lowy, Kann, & Pateman, 2000), and to prefer more restrictive sexual timetables (East, 1998) than teens in other ethnic groups. Although such cross-cultural comparisons of sexual outcomes are informative, they add little to our understanding of the sexual socialization processes occurring within this unique sociocultural context. As a result, even the most basic questions about parental sexual communication among Asian Americans have not yet been answered.

Currently, Asian Americans make up the third largest and most rapidly growing ethnic minority group in the United States. However, to our knowledge, only three studies have provided initial insight into sexual communication in Asian American families. Abramson, Moriuchi, Waite, and Perry (1983) found that second- and third-generation Japanese American parents were less likely than White parents to persist in talking about sexual topics with their children in the face of discomfort. More than a decade later, Harman and Johnson (1995) conducted a multiethnic study of college students' sex education experiences, reporting that the 14 Asian American participants in their study understood what sexual intercourse was at an older age than non-Asian participants and that only one Asian American identified parents as a primary source of sex education. Finally, in the most in-depth study to date, Chung et al. (2004) conducted a series of focus group interviews with first- and second-generation Filipino American adolescents, parents, and grandparents. Although most participants identified school as teenagers' primary sex education source, they were dissatisfied with the education that schools provided. Parents were also critical of mainstream American parents'

open, friend-like communication with children, arguing that these ideals contributed to children's loss of respect for elders.

Despite their initial contributions, previous studies are marked by a number of limitations, including the use of samples that are too small to perform statistical tests (Harman & Johnson, 1995) or the inclusion of only a single ethnic subgroup (Chung et al., 2004). A related shortcoming is that they fail to examine within-group variation. Asian Americans represent a large and heterogeneous group, and dramatic differences in parental sexual communication may emerge with respect to a number of basic and culturally relevant demographic factors, including parents' education level, religiosity, ethnicity, immigration history, English proficiency, and acculturation to the dominant U.S. culture. Finally, a major shortcoming of past studies is their omission of gender as a key variable, given its central role in past sexual socialization research, in particular. Like many other cultures steeped in patriarchal ideology, traditional Asian cultures uphold different norms and expectations for the sexual conduct of women and men. Specifically, female virginity is valued more highly, and thus regulated more closely, than male virginity (Lam, Shi, Ho, Stewart, & Fan, 2002), suggesting that Asian American daughters might receive more prohibitory messages about sex from their parents than might Asian American sons.

This Study

Given the small amount of research in this area, the purpose of our study was to build a descriptive base of the amount and content of parental sexual communication recalled by Asian American youth. We approached this topic from a cultural psychological framework (Shweder et al., 1998), viewing culture as a process that could shape the nature and tone of sexual communication in Asian American families rather than as an index on which ethnic group differences may (or may not) emerge.

Placing Asian Americans at the center of our study helped us theorize about how characteristics of traditional Asian cultures (i.e., shared belief systems, norms, values, traditions) could shape parental sexual communication in Asian American families. Specifically, they led us to expect reports of sexual reticence from parents and gender-specific communication that would be especially negative for women. In traditional Asian cultures, there is a cultural taboo that relegates displays of sexual expression to private spheres and deems sexuality an inappropriate topic to be discussed with others (Okazaki, 2002). Therefore, with respect to the amount of communication recalled, we expected Asian American participants to report that their parents offered minimal communication about sex.

Yet, whereas some characteristics of Asian cultures may encourage sexual reticence, these tendencies are likely to be offset by parents' need to clearly convey their sexual values and expectations to their children and especially to their daughters. Indeed, although dominant sexual attitudes in Asian cultures stem from different cultural philosophies (e.g., Confucianism, Hindu beliefs), they are similar in their stigmatization of sexuality and their strong condemnation of nonmarital sexual activity (Okazaki, 2002). The onset of puberty is frequently marked by parents' stricter rules about dress, comportment, and activities, in particular among daughters, whose sexual conduct is a symbol of their families' honor (Inman, Ladany, Constantine, & Morano, 2001). Thus, with respect to the types of sexual messages that parents provided, we expected women and men to report receiving higher levels of sexually prohibitive messages than sexually permissive messages and for daughters to recall receiving more sexual information and more sexually prohibitory messages from parents than sons.

A cultural psychological framework drew our attention to the potential for within-group variation among Asian Americans with respect to basic and culturally relevant demographic factors, such as parents' education level, religiosity, ethnic subgroup, generation status, parents' acculturation to mainstream American norms, and the presence of language discrepancies in the home. Past studies exploring demographic predictors of parental sexual communication have produced a rather mixed body of findings.

As a result, our analyses of within-group variation were largely exploratory in nature. However, based on our review of the literature, we offered three specific hypotheses. First, we expected participants who perceived their parents to be more highly acculturated to mainstream American norms and values to recall receiving more communication about sexual topics overall, fewer messages about sex as a taboo topic, and more messages conveying their acceptance of premarital sex. Second, we expected more religious participants to recall receiving more sexually prohibitive messages than less religious participants. Third, because research suggests that an intergenerational discrepancy in language use (i.e., a child is predominantly English-speaking and the parent is predominantly non-English-speaking) is associated with less frequent parent-child discussions, greater discomfort and miscommunication, and greater difficulties in expressing complex ideas or emotions (Tseng & Fuligni, 2000), we expected participants reporting a language barrier in the home to recall receiving less sexual communication from parents than those without such barriers.

Finally, a cultural psychological framework underscored the importance of using culturally appropriate measures that were sensitive to the ways in which Asian immigrant parents may communicate their sexual values and beliefs. Therefore, in the quantitative component of our study, we asked, "How much 'information' (i.e., facts, attitudes, or values) was *communicated to you* by your mother and father?" and in the qualitative component, we allowed participants to write at length about parents' sexual messages without forced response choices. In doing so, we anticipated that the most prominent and memorable of parents' sexual messages would emerge, perhaps shedding light on culture-specific messages that would not be detected by existing quantitative measures.

METHOD

Participants

Participants were 165 Asian American college students who were recruited from an introductory psychology subject pool at a large, Midwestern university. Students were not aware of the purpose of the study prior to arriving at the session, and their participation partially fulfilled a course requirement. The sample was made up of 74 women (45.1%) and 91 men, ranging in age from 17 to 25 years ($M = 19.41$ years). Among these participants, 97 were of East Asian ancestry (e.g., China, Japan, Korea), 55 were of South Asian ancestry (e.g., India, Pakistan), 7 were of Pacific Island ancestry (e.g., The Philippines), 4 were of Southeast Asian ancestry (e.g., Vietnam, Laos), and 3 were multiracial or multiethnic. With regard to their immigration status, 58 participants (35.2%) identified themselves as first-generation, or born abroad; 102 (61.8%) as second-generation, or born in the United States to immigrant parents; and 5 (3.0%) as third-generation or higher.

Participants' level of religiosity during their formative years was assessed by three questions: (a) "How religious were you?" (*not at all* to *very*); (b) "How often did you attend religious services?" (*never* to *very regularly, more than once a week*); and (c) "How often did you pray?" (*never* to *very regularly, at least once a day*). Individual responses were coded on a 5-point scale and summed to produce scores that could range from 0 to 12. The mean level of religiosity in this sample was 6.69; however, the modal level was 10, and more than 40% of the sample scored a 9 or higher, suggesting that a substantial proportion of the sample was highly religious. Participants came from highly educated families. Indeed, more than 70% of mothers and close to 90% of fathers had earned an undergraduate college or more advanced degree.

Intergenerational language discrepancy

Participants identified whether they used English or an Asian language when speaking with their mothers and their fathers and whether their mothers and fathers used English or an Asian language when speaking to them. A variable was then created that reflected whether or not participants experienced an intergenerational language discrepancy at home.

Perceived parental acculturation

A series of four questions asked participants to rate each parent's level of acculturation. The questions read, "How 'traditional' (i.e, Asian or non-Western) is your mother/father in her/his attitudes and behavior?" and "How 'mainstream American' (i.e., Western) is your mother/father in her/his attitudes and behavior?" Participants responded on a 5-point scale (0 = *not at all*, 4 = *extremely*). Parents' levels of "Asianness" were coded, such that higher scores represented parents' perceived acculturation to mainstream American values.

Sexual Communication Measures

Amount of sexual communication

We used an adapted measure from Fisher (1993) to assess the incidence and amount of sexual communication provided by mothers and fathers. On a 4-point scale (0 = *none*, 1 = *a little*, 2 = *some*, 3 = *a lot*), participants indicated how much information (i.e., values, norms) each parent provided about the following 10 specific sexual topics: menstruation, dating norms and expectations, necking and petting, fertilization/conception, sexual intercourse, pregnancy, birth control, STDs, abortion, and homosexuality.

Types of parental sexual messages

Surveys included two means of assessing the content of parents' sexual communication. First, an open-ended item asked participants to spontaneously recall the types of sexual messages parents provided during their formative years. In total, participants generated 385 statements that were subjected to qualitative analysis.

Second, to compare more directly the content of parental messages across participants, we used an adapted version of The Childhood and Adolescent Sexual Messages scale (Caruthers & Ward, 2002), a cued-recall measure that assesses how often parents, peers, and the media convey several specific sexual themes. Participants were asked to indicate how frequently parents conveyed each message on a 4-point scale ranging from 0 (*never*) to 3 (*a lot*). To adapt the scale for use with an exclusively Asian-American sample, six items were added to capture messages about sex being a taboo, private, and shameful activity.

Three resulting subscales reflected conservative or prohibitory attitudes toward sexuality, whereas one subscale reflected a permissive sexual attitude. The seven-item Abstinence Until Marriage subscale stressed the importance of remaining abstinent until marriage (e.g., "Sex belongs in married relationships only"). The six-item Sex Is Relational subscale described sexual intercourse as an intimate activity that takes place in the context of a loving and committed relationship (e.g., "Sex should be a deep and beautiful expression of love between two people"). The five-item Sex Is a Taboo Topic subscale described sex as a private topic that should not be discussed with others (e.g., "Sex is a private matter and should not be discussed in public"; "It is not appropriate to hug and kiss your partner in front of members of your family"). The six-item Acceptance of Premarital Sex subscale conveyed notions that premarital sexual intercourse is a normal, positive, and frequently nonrelational activity among adults (e.g., "Having sex should be viewed as a normal part of dating relationships"). The fifth subscale conveyed a sexual double standard and could therefore be interpreted as sexually prohibitive for women and sexually permissive for men. This 12-item Gendered Sexual Roles subscale

described men as sex-driven initiators of intercourse and women as passive sexual limit-setters (e.g., "It is up to women to limit the sexual advances of men and to keep men from going 'too far' "). A mean score was computed for each subscale with higher scores signifying greater parental communication about that theme.

RESULTS

Amount of Parental Communication about Sexuality

The topic that participants were most likely to report receiving information about was menstruation among girls and their mothers, and dating norms and expectations for both sexes. Whereas fathers' rates of communication were strikingly low across the remaining topics for both daughters and sons (never surpassing 34%), mothers' rates exhibited more variability. For all topics, the rates of parental communication reported by Asian American students are markedly lower than those recalled by Black, White, and Latino students.

Next, we assessed the amount of parents' communication about these topics. Participants reported receiving minimal information about most sexual topics. In general, dating norms and pregnancy ranked among the two most frequently discussed topics, whereas necking and petting emerged as the least frequently discussed topic by parents. Again, communication was perceived to be especially limited from fathers. Indeed, with the exception of their communication about dating norms, the mean amount of communication recalled from fathers by both daughters and sons never exceeded the 0.50 mark, a quantitative assessment that corresponds with a response between "none" and "a little." Mothers were perceived to be similarly uncommunicative about most sexual topics by sons, but less so by daughters, who, on average, reported receiving at least "a little" information about menstruation, fertilization, dating norms and expectations, and pregnancy.

Did mothers and fathers differ significantly in the amount of communication they reportedly provided to children? Among daughters, the amount of communication recalled from mothers significantly exceeded that of fathers for every single sexual topic. Among sons, however, mothers were only perceived to be significantly more communicative than fathers for three topics: menstruation, pregnancy, and homosexuality.

Daughters reported receiving significantly more sexual communication from parents than did sons. There was no sexual topic assessed for which men reported receiving more communication than women. Indeed, compared with sons, daughters received significantly more sexual information from parents, overall, and for half of the 10 individual sexual topics (i.e., menstruation, dating norms and expectations, fertilization, pregnancy, and birth control).

Cued Recall of Parent-Provided Sexual Messages

What types of sexual messages did participants recall receiving from parents during their formative years? We had predicted that both sons and daughters would recall receiving more sexually prohibitive messages than sexually permissive messages from parents. Consistent with expectations, women recalled receiving more prohibitive messages [Abstinence Until Marriage; Sex Is Relational; Sex Is a Taboo Topic; and Gendered Sexual Roles, which are restrictive for women] than the permissive message conveying an Acceptance of Premarital Sex. Similarly, men recalled receiving more prohibitive messages about Abstinence Until Marriage; Sex is Relational; and Sex Is a Taboo Topic, than permissive messages conveying an Acceptance of Premarital Sex and Gendered Sexual Roles, respectively.

We next examined whether Asian American women reported receiving more sexually prohibitive messages from their parents than did their male counterparts. Women did indeed recall receiving more prohibitive messages about abstinence until marriage, sex as relational, sex as a taboo topic, and gendered sexual roles than did men. Parents were perceived to be equally unlikely to convey to sons and daughters their acceptance of premarital sex.

Qualitative Analyses of Parental Sexual Messages

Our next set of analyses explored the types of sexual messages that participants *independently* recalled receiving from parents in response to an open-ended query.

The most common theme overall, appearing in 24% of men's statements and 12% of women's, described sexual and romantic relationships as a taboo topic, one that either never naturally came up in conversations in the home or was actively avoided by both parents and children. As one Indian American man stated plainly, "This was not talked about in my family," and an Indian American woman clarified, "Growing up, the word *sex* was never mentioned." In their written responses, many participants expressed difficulty in remembering any parent-provided messages about romantic or sexual topics at all. Typical responses to this question included, "Nothing I can remember," "They pretty much never said anything to me about it at all," and "I can't remember anything they ever told me." However, some participants suggested that although explicit communication about sex was silenced, parents made their sexual values clear via nonverbal or indirect means. Indeed, several participants stated that "it was just understood" that they were not supposed to date or engage in sexual behavior. As one Korean American woman elaborated, "They never talked to me about sex; it was just understood that it was bad and I wasn't supposed to do it." Consistent with earlier quantitative results, significantly more men than women recalled receiving no verbal or direct communication from parents.

The second most common theme, emerging in 17% and 13%, respectively, of women's and men's recollections, dealt with parents' disapproval of dating. In contrast to the previous one, this theme was mentioned equally by women and men. According to some participants, parents strongly discouraged their children from dating, portraying romantic partners as distractions from important life goals, such as getting into college or working toward a successful career. According to one Korean American woman, her parents told her, "Studying and schoolwork is more important than dating a guy," and one Chinese American man stated simply, "Sex can wait—career first." Some parents were perceived as prioritizing their children's academic achievement over and above their social lives. Women were told, "There's no need to date when you are still young," "Boys will mess you up and make you distracted," and "Concentrate on your studies." Similarly, men were advised to "wait until after college to start dating," "put school first; worry about relationships later," and that "dating will hurt grades/classwork." Some parents set rules that prohibited dating, and these rules were based on chronological age (e.g., "Dating was not allowed until I was 25"), academic accomplishments (e.g., "Don't date until you're done with grad school"), or other major life transitions (e.g., "Don't date 'til you are ready to get married," "Romance is for marriage, and *not before*"). Taken together, these messages suggest that a portion of Asian parents did not view dating as a normative component of adolescent development, which stands in contrast to expectations conveyed by the dominant U.S. culture through avenues such as peers or the media.

The third most common theme described sexual activity as existing only within the confines of marriage. Messages in this category were strikingly similar across gender, ethnicity, and generation status. Participants were told to "wait until marriage for sex," that there should be "nothing physical before marriage," and that "you can't have sex until you're married."

The fourth most common theme dealt with parents' advice concerning the norms and features of romantic relationships. Messages to both sexes were comparable in content, with many focusing on the importance of men being respectful toward women. Messages recalled by women, such as "Boys should treat me well and with respect," and "Find someone with good manners and confidence," complemented those recalled by men (e.g., "Men should always be polite to ladies"; "You should treat her right—nice and respectful"). Parents were also seen as providing descriptions of the qualities of a suitable partner (to women, "Choose to date someone kind, relatively good-looking," and to men, "You should get girls who are attractive," and "You should find someone smart, pretty"). Nine participants, both male and female, reported that their parents specified the desired ethnicity of their future dating or marriage partners. One Chinese American woman recalled her parents saying, "Get an Asian. It's easier to communicate." Similarly, a Vietnamese American man recalled hearing, "Just grow up and marry a Vietnamese girl."

The next two themes, which appeared in at least 5% of men's and women's recollections, focused on protecting oneself, either physically or emotionally. First, some participants recalled receiving cautionary statements from parents that warned them about the negative physical consequences of sexual activity. In many cases, these warnings were vague; participants were told to "be careful," to "be responsible," and "not to make mistakes." However, a few women recalled more specific messages from parents about rape and physical victimization. For example, one Chinese American woman wrote that her parents told her, "Be careful at parties—always keep your drink with you—guys will take advantage of you," and one Taiwanese American woman was warned, "The people that rape you are your friends." Messages to men more often involved information about STDs and contraception, implying that many parents either knew or assumed that their sons were already sexually active. For example, a Taiwanese American man wrote that he was informed about "basically any disease-related precautions I could take."

Similarly, one Chinese American man said that his father told him, "When you have sex, use a condom," and another Taiwanese American man specified, "Mostly they just wanted to make sure I didn't get any STDs or any girls pregnant before I was married." Second, some parents validated participants' ability to make their own dating and sexual decisions but also warned them about the perils of bad choices. Notably, the underlying message was often sexually prohibitive. For example, one Korean American woman wrote, "I think they had faith in me, that I'm the type of person that would stay away from such things," and one Chinese American man reported that his parents said pointedly, "I know you know what is right and wrong." Messages recalled by women suggested that parents were also preoccupied with their daughters' potential to be taken advantage of by men. Parents reportedly warned them to "never be in a relationship that makes me uncomfortable," "never to feel pressured by anyone when it comes to sex," and to "never be controlled; always be the one in control in relationships." Significantly more women than men reported receiving such messages.

Three additional themes appeared in at least 5% of either men's or women's recollections. They included vague warnings to sons and daughters not to have sex (e.g., "Don't do it"; "No fooling around!"; "Sex will ruin your life!"), information that was educational in nature ("How babies are born"; "My mom basically explained the idea of sex to me when I was younger"), and gender-related norms (e.g., "If you give in too easily, your partner will not respect you"; "When doctors would ask if I was sexually active, my dad would say, 'No, she's a good girl'"). Notably, significantly more women than men reported receiving gendered messages, and these messages often conveyed sexual stereotypes about men (e.g., "Boys have bad intentions"; "Guys will lie to get what they want, but then not care for you"; "You can't trust guys").

The remaining six themes were recalled by fewer than 5% of male and female participants.

They included negative threats about the consequences of pregnancy (e.g., "If you get pregnant I will kick you out!"), messages that linked sexuality to religious values (e.g., "Sex is a sin"; "You should not let [your relationships] distract you with your personal relationship with God"), and messages that affirmed sexual activity (e.g., "Sex is intimate and something to be shared with someone important"; "Sex is a natural thing").

Within-Group Variation in Parental Sexual Communication

Our final set of analyses examined parental sexual communication based on the following five dimensions of family background—parents' education level, ethnicity, religiosity, parents' acculturation to American norms, and the presence of a language discrepancy in the home—and two sets of dependent variables—parents' overall amount of sexual communication and their communication of messages about abstinence until marriage, sex as relational, sex as a taboo topic, their acceptance of premarital sex, and gendered sexual roles. Because all of our hypothesized associations were expected to appear in the same direction for men and women, this set of analyses combined male and female participants' responses. First, we conducted exploratory analyses examining the role of parental education and ethnic subgroup. Parents with more formal schooling were perceived as providing higher overall amounts of sexual communication to their children, but no differences in the types of messages provided. A series of tests compared the two largest ethnic subgroups in the sample, East Asian Americans (e.g., Chinese, Korean) and South Asian Americans (e.g., Indian). No differences emerged in the amount of communication received, but South Asian American participants reported receiving significantly more messages about abstinence until marriage and about sex being a taboo topic than did East Asian American participants.

Our analyses next turned to the three specific hypotheses we offered based on our review of the literature. First, we had predicted that participants with highly acculturated parents would recall receiving more sexual communication overall, fewer messages about sex as a taboo topic, and more messages conveying an acceptance of premarital sex than would participants with less acculturated parents. Parents' acculturation level was unrelated to the overall amount of information they were perceived as providing or the frequency with which they transmitted messages about sex being a taboo topic. However, more acculturated parents were perceived as providing more messages conveying their acceptance of premarital sex. Second, we had predicted that participants from more religious families would recall receiving more sexually prohibitive messages and fewer sexually permissive messages. Results indicated that more religious participants did indeed report receiving more messages about abstinence until marriage and sex as a taboo topic, and fewer messages conveying an acceptance of premarital sex. However, there were no associations between religiosity and messages about gendered sexual roles or about sex being relational.

Finally, we had predicted that participants who encountered a language discrepancy in the home would receive lower amounts of sexual communication overall from both mothers and fathers. Participants with a language discrepancy in the home received less information from their mothers than those without such a discrepancy. No differences were apparent in fathers' mean amount of communication.

Discussion

Although significant advances have been made in documenting parental sexual communication, Asian Americans are consistently overlooked in this literature. Our study addressed this omission by providing data on the amount and types of parental sexual communication in Asian American families, according to retrospective reports by Asian American college students. Whereas quantitative analyses of survey data allowed us to test hypotheses and evaluate within-group variation, qualitative analyses provided greater depth and clarity to participants' sexual socialization experiences. Several noteworthy findings emerged.

Our first set of hypotheses addressed the amount of communication that participants reported receiving from parents during their formative years. Initially, quantitative results depicted Asian American homes as shrouded in silence about sexuality. Indeed, participants reported receiving minimal information about a variety of sexual topics ranging from biological processes (e.g., menstruation, fertilization) to potential sexual outcomes (e.g., pregnancy, abortion). In fact, among sons, the modal level of information they reported receiving from both mothers and fathers was "none" for *every* sexual topic assessed. This pattern also held among daughters, with the exception of mothers' communication about menstruation, pregnancy, and dating norms and expectations. Furthermore, investigations of rates reported by teens in other ethnic groups suggest that Asian American youth may receive considerably less sexual communication from their parents, by comparison.

Why do Asian Americans recall receiving such little communication about sexuality from their parents? Although we could not test this assumption directly, it seems likely that a cultural taboo about sex and/or expectations for hierarchical familial relationships deter open and explicit communication about this sensitive topic. If parents do not initiate these discussions because of the taboo, as was suggested by many of the open-ended responses, then their children may feel that it is not their place to ask such questions. At the same time, a lack of shared vocabulary or difficulty in expressing complex ideas may also create obstacles to intergenerational knowledge or values transmission in some immigrant families. We found that participants who spoke to parents in English but were spoken to in an Asian language recalled significantly less sexual communication from mothers than participants who encountered just one language in the home, whether that language was solely English or solely of Asian origin. Although we did not find a significant relation between language use and fathers' communication, this finding could be attributed to a lack of variability or a floor effect in fathers' communication amounts.

Similar to previous studies, we found that parents were not uniformly silent about sexuality. Gender differences were quite striking, with results suggesting that male family members were less engaged in the sexual socialization process. Sons recalled receiving less sexual information than did daughters, and fathers were perceived as providing substantially less information than mothers about almost all sexual topics. Mothers spoke to daughters most frequently about topics that were related to anatomy and biological reproduction, like menstruation and fertilization, or about topics that were less overtly sexual, such as dating norms and expectations. However, it is noteworthy that a substantial proportion of Asian American women reported that their mothers gave them "a lot" of information about pregnancy. This set of findings stimulates several interesting questions for further research. For example, at what age and in what context do parents deliver sexual information to daughters? Do mothers provide extensive information about pregnancy to daughters due to concerns about family honor, daughters' academic success, or other reasons? In the absence of parental communication about sexuality, to which sources do Asian American boys and young men turn to learn about sex?

Our second set of analyses addressed the types of sexual messages parents provided. Despite initial reports of sexual reticence, most participants could remember receiving a number of specific sexual messages. Furthermore, in response to an open-ended question, participants generated 385 messages, only 20% of which indicated that no verbal or direct communication was provided from parents. These findings are not incompatible but suggest that parents who do not directly provide their children with sexual facts use indirect ways to make their sexual

values clear and that their children are generally sensitive to these cues. In this study, parents who informed their sons and daughters that "romance is for marriage" or that "dating can wait until college" conveyed clear expectations about their children's sexual conduct without ever explicitly referring to sexual intercourse. Future researchers using Asian American samples are advised to pay special attention to the implicit ways that Asian American parents make their sexual values known, perhaps by creating separate scales of parents' nonverbal and indirect sexual communication.

Although all participants reported receiving more sexually prohibitive messages than sexually permissive messages, daughters reported receiving more prohibitive messages from parents than did sons. Yet, despite this evidence of a sexual double standard, the themes identified in qualitative analyses were only sometimes gender-specific. For example, women and men were equally likely to recall receiving messages from parents that discouraged dating or promoted sexual abstinence until marriage. Notably, messages about romance being a serious threat to academic achievement were slightly more prevalent than messages about sexual morality. This finding may be an artifact of the sample's composition; most participants came from highly educated families and all were attending a prestigious university, suggesting that they may hold academic achievement in higher regard than may the general Asian American population. Qualitative analyses also indicated that whereas sons were sometimes educated about STDs and safer sex practices, daughters were usually advised to avoid social situations and/or men altogether. Indeed, many parents were concerned that their daughters would be physically or emotionally victimized by men and warned them to guard themselves against this risk. Future studies should examine how Asian American girls and young women contend with conflicting cultural expectations about dating and sexuality.

One of our key objectives for this study was to examine how background characteristics of participants' families influence the amount and types of sexual messages that Asian Americans recalled. Consistent with expectations, we found that the content of parents' messages was more consistently correlated with demographic factors than parents' sheer communication amounts. For example, compared with East Asian Americans, South Asian Americans reported receiving more sexual messages that encouraged abstinence until marriage and regarded sex as a taboo topic but similar amounts of sexual information overall. Participants from more religious backgrounds reported receiving more messages about the inappropriateness of premarital sex and about sex as a taboo topic and fewer messages conveying an acceptance of premarital sex. More acculturated parents were perceived as providing more messages accepting premarital sex, but not more sexual information overall or more messages about sex being a taboo topic. The latter results could be attributed, in part, to the limitations of the four-item acculturation measure developed for this study. Although the process of acculturation may lead to parents' more lax attitudes toward sexual activity, it is also possible that parents are perceived to be more acculturated by their children *because* they provide more permissive messages about sex, or that a third, unmeasured variable explained these relationships. We chose to assess five culturally relevant demographic factors in this study: parents' education level, religiosity, ethnicity, parents' acculturation level, and language use. Future studies may benefit from considering a more comprehensive set of moderators and testing these associations longitudinally.

We recognize other limitations of this study. First, we acknowledge that the select nature of our sample may have constrained our ability to find more within-group variation and also limited the generalizability of our findings. Participants in this study came from highly educated families, attended a prestigious university in the Midwest, and were predominantly East Asian or South Asian in origin. Future studies should

aim to recruit larger and more diverse Asian American samples with respect to age, socioeconomic status, ethnicity, and immigration history. Parental sexual communication may be quite different among Asian American families living in more impoverished or ethnically diverse communities. Second, because our measures of parental sexual communication were based on retrospective reports by Asian American college students, it is fair to ask whether participants accurately recalled the amount and type of sexual communication their parents had provided during childhood and adolescence. However, like previous researchers using this widely used technique (e.g., Hutchinson & Cooney, 1998), we argue that it is children's perceptions of past communication that are important, as it is these perceptions that will be called to mind during their subsequent sexual encounters. Finally, parents represent just one of many sources of adolescents' sexual socialization. In addition to examining peers and the media, we advise future researchers to explore other sources with culture-specific considerations in mind. Given Asian Americans' heavier reliance on extended family networks, future studies should examine how nonparental family members, such as grandparents, siblings, aunts, and cousins, contribute to the sexual socialization process.

INTRODUCTION REFERENCE

Fisher, T. D. 2004. Family foundations of sexuality. In *The handbook of sexuality in close relationships*, eds., J. Harvey, A. Wenzel, & S. Sprecher, 385–409. Mahwah, NJ: Lawrence Erlbaum.

REFERENCES

Abramson, P. R., Moriuchi, K. D., Waite, M. S., & Perry, L. B. (1983). Parental attitudes about sexual education: Cross-cultural differences and covariate controls. *Archives of Sexual Behavior, 12*, 381–397.

Alexander, S. J., & Jorgensen, S. R. (1983). Sex education for early adolescents: A study of parents and students. *Journal of Early Adolescence, 3*, 315–325.

Baldwin, J. D., Whiteley, S., & Baldwin, J. L. (1992). The effect of ethnic group on sexual activities related to contraception and STDs. *Journal of Sex Research, 29,* 189–205.

Caruthers, A. S., & Ward, L. M. (2002, April). *Mixed messages: The divergent nature of sexual communication received from parents, peers, and the media.* Paper presented at the Society for Research on Adolescence, New Orleans, LA.

Chung, P. J., Borneo, H., Kilpatrick, S. D., Lopez, D. M., Travis, R., Jr., Lui, C., Khandwala, S., & Schuster, M. A. (2005). Parent-adolescent communication about sex in Filipino American families: A demonstration of community-based participatory research. *Ambulatory Pediatrics, 5,* 50–55.

Davis, S. M., & Harris, M. B. (1982). Sexual knowledge, sexual interests, and sources of sexual information of rural and urban adolescents from three cultures. *Adolescence, 17,* 471–492.

Dilorio, C., Kelley, M., & Hockenberry-Eaton, M. (1999). Communication about sexual issues: Mothers, fathers, and friends. *Journal of Adolescent Health, 24,* 181–189.

Dilorio, C., Pluhar, E., & Belcher, L. (2003). Parent-child communication about sexuality: A review of the literature from 1980–2002. *Journal of HIV/AIDS Prevention and Education for Adolescents and Children, 5,* 7–32.

Downie, J., & Coates, R. (1999). The impact of gender on parent-child sexuality communication: Has anything changed? *Sexual and Marital Therapy, 14,* 109–121.

East, P. L. (1998). Racial and ethnic differences in girls' sexual, marital, and birth expectations. *Journal of Marriage and the Family, 60,* 150–162.

Fisher, T. D. (1993). A comparison of various measures of family sexual communication: Psychometric properties, validity, and behavioral correlates. *Journal of Sex Research, 30,* 229–238.

Fox, G. L., & Inazu, J. K. (1980). Mother-daughter communication about sex. *Family Relations, 29,* 347–362.

Grunbaum, J. A., Lowy, R., Kann, L., & Pateman, B. (2000). Prevalence of health risk Behaviors among Asian American/Pacific Islander high school students. *Journal of Adolescent Health, 27,* 322–330.

Harman, M. J., & Johnson, J. A. (1995). Cross-cultural sex education: Aspects of age, source, and sex equity. *TCA Journal, 23,* 1–11.

Hepburn, E. H. (1983). A three-level model of parent-daughter communication about sexual topics. *Adolescence, 18,* 523–534.

Hutchinson, M. K., & Cooney, T. M. (1998). Patterns of parent-teen sexual risk communication: Implications for intervention. *Family Relations, 47,* 185–194.

Inman, A. G., Ladany, N., Constantine, M. G., & Morano, C. K. (2001). Development and preliminary validation of the Cultural Values Conflict Scale for South Asian Women. *Journal of Counseling Psychology, 48,* 17–27.

King, B. M., & Lorusso, J. (1997). Discussions in the home about sex: Different recollections by parents and children. *Journal of Sex and Marital Therapy, 23,* 52–60.

Lam, T. H., Shi, H. J., Ho, L. M., Stewart, S. M., & Fan, S. (2002). Timing of pubertal maturation and heterosexual behavior among Hong Kong Chinese adolescents. *Archives of Sexual Behavior, 31,* 359–366.

Lefkowitz, E. S., Romo, L. F., Corona, R., Au, T. K., & Sigman, M. (2000). How Latino American and European American adolescents discuss conflicts, sexuality, and AIDS with their mothers. *Developmental Psychology, 36,* 315–325.

Miller, K. S., Kotchick, B. A., Dorsey, S., Forehand, R., & Ham, A. Y. (1998). Family communication about sex: What are parents saying and are their adolescents listening? *Family Planning Perspectives, 30,* 218–235.

Okazaki, S. (2002). Influences of culture on Asian American sexuality. *Journal of Sex Research, 39,* 34–41.

O'Sullivan, L. F., Meyer-Bahlburg, H. F., & Watkins, B. (2001). Mother-daughter communication about sex among urban African American and Latino families. *Journal of Adolescent Research, 16,* 269–292.

Thornburg, H. D. (1981). The amount of sex information learning during early adolescence. *Journal of Early Adolescence, 1,* 171–183.

Tseng, V., & Fuligni, A. J. (2000). Parent-adolescent language use and relationships among immigrant families with East Asian, Filipino, and Latin American backgrounds. *Journal of Marriage and the Family, 62,* 465–476.

Upchurch, D. M., Levy-Storms, L., Sucoff, C., & Aneshensel, C. S. (1998). Gender and ethnic difference in the timing of first sexual intercourse. *Family Planning Perspectives, 30,* 121–127.

Ward, L. M. (1995). Talking about sex: Common themes about sexuality in the prime-time television programs children and adolescents view most. *Journal of Youth and Adolescence, 24,* 595–615.

Ward, L. M., & Wyatt, G. E. (1994). The effects of childhood sexual message on African-American and White women's adolescent sexual behavior. *Psychology of Women Quarterly, 18,* 183–201.

CHAPTER 36

Condom Use with a Casual Partner
What Distinguishes College Students' Use When Intoxicated?

Antonia Abbey
Michele R. Parkhill
Philip O. Buck
Christopher Saenz

The first year of college is a time that most students are enjoying the freedom of living apart from parents for the first time, a freedom that presents both positive and negative benefits. In the absence of restrictions, college students are subject to various social influences that may lead to alcohol consumption. First-year male college students who were binge drinkers in high school will drink more in college if they have a roommate who was also a binge drinker in high school (Duncan et al. 2005).

College students are also known to sometimes engage in ill-advised or risky sexual acts. To what degree is high-risk sexual behavior linked to the use of alcohol? There is a considerable amount of research that has examined this relationship, with findings that are more complex than previously perceived. Researchers have found that the role that excessive alcohol use plays in safer sex practices depends on variables such as attitudes toward sexuality and condom use, as well as one's perception of the impact of alcohol (Cooper 2006).

If you were interested in studying the effect of alcohol on condom use, how would you go about doing so? As you likely already know, to demonstrate a cause-effect relationship, you would have to do an experiment. Could you design an ethical and safe experiment to examine the impact of drinking on use of condoms? You might decide that the best you could do would be a correlational study to look at the relationship between the two variables without drawing conclusions as to cause and effect. But, even a correlational approach may not prove to be all that simple to implement.

In the study to follow by Abbey et al. (2007), the researchers asked college students to retrospectively report on their condom use, both when sober and when intoxicated. Before reading the

From "Condom Use with a Casual Partner: What Distinguishes College Students' Use When Intoxicated?" by A. Abbey, M. R. Parkhill, P. O, Buck, and C. Saenz. 2007. *Psychology of Addictive Behaviors* 21: 76–83. Copyright © 2007 by the American Psychological Association. Adapted with permission.

surprising results of the study, think about the variables that you believe would be most likely to predict willingness to use condoms when intoxicated. Then, read this chapter to find out if you were right.

———

Approximately 19 million STD infections are diagnosed annually in the United States, and almost half occur among individuals between the ages of 15 and 24 (Weinstock, Berman, & Cates, 2004). At least half of all new HIV infections in the United States are estimated to occur among people under the age of 25, with African Americans disproportionately affected (Centers for Disease Control and Prevention, 2004). Rates of heterosexual transmission have been increasing, particularly among young women.

Nationally representative surveys of college students suggest that many engage in high-risk sexual behaviors. Approximately 80% of college students have engaged in sexual intercourse, yet only about one third report that they regularly use condoms (Wechsler et al., 2000). About one quarter of college students report having had six or more lifetime sexual partners (Douglas et al., 1997), and 6% report having had more than one partner in the past 30 days (Wechsler et al., 2000). Self-reported lifetime rates of STD infections range from 12% to 25% among sexually experienced students (Cooper, 2002), with rates of human papilloma virus and chlamydia during the past school year of approximately 1.5% (American College Health Association, 2005). Hightow et al. (2005) observed that most college students do not feel personally at risk for contracting HIV and AIDS and engage in many high-risk behaviors that allow STDs to spread rapidly.

Sexual risk taking and heavy drinking frequently co-occur (Perkins, 2002). For example, 16% of a national sample of college students reported that they had had sex without a condom when intoxicated during the past school year (American College Health Association, 2005). The co-occurrence of drinking and unprotected sex does not demonstrate a causal relationship or elucidate what types of individual and situational factors contribute to intoxicated sexual risk-taking behavior. The study presented in this paper examines the cross-sectional predictors of heterosexual college students' frequency of condom use when intoxicated, after controlling for their frequency of condom use when sober.

MIXED EVIDENCE REGARDING THE RELATIONSHIP BETWEEN INTOXICATION AND RISKY SEXUAL BEHAVIOR

Acute alcohol consumption impairs higher-order cognitive processing and activates relevant expectancies (Curtin & Fairchild, 2003; Fillmore & Blackburn, 2002). Thus, sexual encounters that take place when individuals are intoxicated are expected to involve more high-risk sexual behavior because of drinkers' diminished decision-making capacities, coupled with their beliefs that intoxication reduces their sexual inhibitions. Despite the large body of theory and research that supports this hypothesis, delineating alcohol's role in risky sexual behavior has been more challenging than originally anticipated (Cooper, 2002; Weinhardt & Carey, 2000). Personality traits, such as impulsivity and sensation seeking, may lead to both heavy drinking and willingness to engage in unprotected sex (Justus, Finn, & Steinmetz, 2000). This concern has led many researchers to focus on studies in which participants are asked to report on multiple sexual events. If the same individuals are more likely to engage in unprotected sex when intoxicated compared to when sober, then the relationship between alcohol and condom use cannot be attributed to personality or other stable individual differences.

Although some multiple-event studies have supported the hypothesis that alcohol consumption increases the likelihood of engaging in risky sexual behavior, here, too, the findings are mixed

(Graves & Hines, 1997; Morrison et al., 2003). Some authors have found stronger results when the outcome measure was number of casual sexual partners than when it was frequency of condom use (Cooper, 2002). For example, in a national study of young adults, Graves and Hines (1997) found that alcohol consumption was more common in sexual events that involved partners known for a short period of time; however, results regarding the relationship between alcohol consumption and condom use were inconsistent. Corbin and Fromme (2002) asked college students to report on their first and most recent sexual experiences with their current partners. Among those participants who had strong sex-related alcohol expectancies, condom use was negatively related to alcohol consumption during first sexual experiences with the current partner. This pattern did not continue for most recent intercourse with current partner, suggesting that alcohol is most likely to contribute to risky sexual behavior early in a sexual relationship.

The interrelationships between partner type, intoxication, and condom use make it difficult to disentangle alcohol's role in unprotected sex. Cooper and Orcutt (2000) interviewed more than 1,000 sexually active young adults. Participants reported that they were more likely to use condoms and to drink alcohol with casual partners than with serious partners. Alcohol consumption was unrelated to condom use when partner type was not controlled. In contrast, when analyses were conducted separately for casual and serious partners, alcohol and condom use were negatively related for both types of partners. The authors suggest that when partner type is not controlled for in data analyses, it may mask the relationship between alcohol consumption and condom use.

Gender differences in the relationship between intoxication and condom use have also been hypothesized. Men consume alcohol more frequently and in larger quantities than do women (O'Malley & Johnston, 2002). Cooper and Orcutt (1997) hypothesized that the situations in which sexual decisions create the most conflict differ for men and women; thus, the situations in which intoxication leads to greater sexual risk taking should also differ. They posited that having sex on a first date would be unappealing for most young women but would create conflict for most young men as they tried to balance their sexual desire and social prohibitions. In support of this theoretical reasoning, they found that young men's drinking on a first date was a significant predictor of engaging in intercourse; however, young women's drinking on a first date was unrelated to the likelihood of engaging in intercourse.

THE ROLE OF SELF-EFFICACY AND OUTCOME EXPECTANCIES IN CONDOM USE

Although alcohol researchers focus on alcohol's role in risky sexual behavior, many theories of health behavior have been applied to sexual risk taking and STD and HIV prevention (Albarracin et al., 2005). Bandura (1997) has successfully applied social-cognitive theory to explain college students' condom-use behaviors. This theory emphasizes the critical role of self-efficacy in determining whether people initiate safer sexual behaviors and persist despite challenges. A number of studies have supported the hypothesis that individuals who feel more self-efficacious about condom use are more likely to use condoms (Baele, Dusseldorp, & Maes, 2001; Dilorio, Dudley, Soet, Watkins, & Maibach, 2000). For example, Wulfert and Wan (1993) found that confidence about one's ability to use condoms was a strong predictor of the frequency of condom use for both women and men. Because condom use is inherently interpersonal, some researchers have emphasized the importance of feeling confident about partners' acceptance of condoms and the ability to be assertive about expressing the desire to use a condom (Zamboni, Crawford, & Williams, 2000).

Outcome expectancies are another important component of the social-cognitive model. Bandura (1997) argued that outcome expectancies are important to consider when the quality of performance does not fully determine the types of outcomes that will be experienced. Thus, people who expect to experience negative outcomes, such as reduced physical pleasure or partner disapproval, should be less likely to use condoms; whereas people who expect to experience positive outcomes should be more likely to use condoms (Dilorio et al., 2000). In support of this hypothesis, data from 1,380 students from six different colleges indicated that the stronger students' expectations that condom use would be associated with positive outcomes, the more frequently they used condoms (Dilorio et al., 2000).

OVERVIEW OF STUDY AND HYPOTHESES

To examine the effects of alcohol consumption on condom use, two parallel sets of regression analyses were compared. In the first set, participants' frequency of condom use with a new or casual partner when sober was predicted with measures representing the domains of demographics (gender, age), personality (sensation seeking, assertiveness), alcohol (expectancies, consumption), and social-cognitive theory (self-efficacy, outcome expectancies). In the second set of regressions, we used the same independent variables to predict the same individuals' frequency of condom use when intoxicated, adding condom use when sober as a predictor. Because condom use when sober was controlled for, the predictors of condom use when intoxicated explain variance that is unique to condom use while intoxicated. Therefore, individual differences can be ruled out as a plausible alternative explanation for any divergence in the predictors of condom use while sober compared with condom use while intoxicated. Personality, alcohol, and

social-cognitive variables were selected because they reflect different theories regarding condom use and alcohol's role in sexual risk taking. There are many reasons that college students engage in unprotected sex, and different individuals can be motivated to use condoms by different constellations of factors (Albarracin et al., 2005).

Although the primary focus was on condom use when intoxicated, it needs to be considered in the context of individuals' condom use when sober. We anticipated that condom use when sober and condom use when intoxicated would be strongly positively correlated and that they would share many of the same predictors. We focused on condom use with casual partners because most U.S. adults and college students report low levels of condom use with regular partners (Anderson, Wilson, Doll, Jones, & Barker, 1999). Age and gender are included because past research suggests that men and younger individuals are more likely to report using condoms than are women and older individuals (Sheeran et al., 1999). Based on past research, we hypothesized that individuals high in sensation seeking would be less likely to use condoms with casual partners when sober and that individuals high in social assertiveness would be more likely to do so (Justus et al., 2000; Zamboni et al., 2000). We also hypothesized that self-efficacy regarding negotiating condom use with one's partner and positive outcome expectancies regarding condom use would be associated with increased frequency of condom use when sober (Dilorio et al., 2000).

We expected that when we controlled for condom use when sober, only alcohol-related variables would remain significant predictors of condom use when intoxicated. Based on past research and theory, alcohol expectancies about sexual risk taking and self-efficacy regarding condom use when intoxicated were expected to be significant predictors of frequency of condom use with casual partners when intoxicated (Abbey, Saenz, & Buck, 2005). A measure of usual alcohol consumption was included, although our expectation was that it would not be significant when drinking within the sexual situation was already taken into account. Women express more concern than men do about the consequences of unprotected sex and have less positive attitudes about casual sexual relations (Oliver & Hyde, 1993). Intoxication may cause women to be less focused on these concerns and feel more comfortable about unprotected sex with a casual partner. Thus, we explored the possibility that gender might interact with personality characteristics and attitudes, such that women who are high in sensation seeking or who strongly believe that alcohol makes them take sexual risks would be least likely to use condoms when intoxicated.

METHOD

Participants

College students from a large urban university participated in this study (195 women and 103 men). Participants' ages ranged from 21–35, with an average age of 24 years.

Procedures

Participants were recruited from lists provided by the registrar's office and flyers posted on campus. Participants were required to be of the legal drinking age, to be social drinkers, and to date people of the opposite sex so that they could relate to the stimulus materials. Individuals who met the study's criteria were mailed an information sheet describing the study, a self-administered questionnaire, and two prestamped envelopes. Seventy percent of eligible individuals returned the questionnaire. Because of this paper's focus on condom use, participants who had never had sexual intercourse and students who did not answer all of the condom questions were not included in data analyses, leaving a sample of 298 individuals.

Measures

Social desirability

Ballard's (1992) 13-item short version of the Marlowe–Crowne Social Desirability Scale was used to measure and control for social-desirability response bias. Sample items include, "No matter who I'm talking to, I'm always a good listener," and "I'm willing to admit it when I make a mistake." Participants responded either *true* or *false*.

Sensation seeking

Eysenck and Eysenck's (1977) 11-item sensation-seeking measure was used. Sample questions include, "Do you enjoy taking risks?" and "Would you do almost anything for a dare?" Responses were made on 5-point scales, with options ranging from *not at all* to *very much*.

Social assertiveness

A 12-item subset of Rathus's (1973) Assertiveness Schedule was used to measure social assertiveness. Sample items include, "I am open and frank about my feelings," and "I enjoy starting conversations with new acquaintances and strangers." Responses were made on 6-point scales with options ranging from *not at all like me* to *exactly like me*.

Alcohol expectancies

Two of Dermen and Cooper's (1994) alcohol-expectancy subscales were used to assess alcohol expectancies relevant to sexual risk taking. They were combined into a single measure. A sample sexual risk item is, "After a few drinks of alcohol, I am less likely to take precautions before having sex," and a sample disinhibition item is, "After a few drinks of alcohol, I become uninhibited." Responses were made on 5-point scales, with options ranging from *not at all* to *very much*.

Alcohol consumption

Participants were asked to think back over the past 12 months and indicate how many days they consumed beer, wine, wine coolers, or liquor in a typical month. They were then asked how many drinks they usually consumed per day on the days they drank alcohol. These two questions were multiplied to create a quantity by frequency measure of total monthly alcohol consumption (Cahalan, Cisin, & Crossley, 1969). Quantity by frequency measures of alcohol consumption are strongly correlated with measures based on daily diaries (Midanik & Greenfield, 2003).

Outcome expectancies associated with condom use

The pleasure subscale from the UCLA Multidimensional Condom Attitudes Scale (Helweg-Larsen & Collins, 1994) was used to assess positive expectancies regarding condom use. This 5-item subscale assesses expectations that condom use will be associated with pleasurable outcomes. Sample items include, "The use of condoms can make sex more stimulating," and "Condoms are a lot of fun." Responses were made on 7-point scales, with options ranging from *strongly disagree* to *strongly agree*.

Condom use self-efficacy

Several subscales were included from the Condom Use Self-Efficacy Scale (Brien et al., 1994). The 5-item partner and 3-item assertiveness subscales were combined to assess self-efficacy regarding negotiating condom use with partners. Sample items include, "I feel confident in my ability to discuss condom usage with any partner I might have," and "If I were unsure of my partner's feelings about using condoms, I would not suggest using one." The 3-item self-efficacy regarding condom use when intoxicated subscale was also used. A sample item is, "I feel confident in my ability to discuss condom usage with any partner even after I have been drinking." Responses were made on 5-point scales, with options ranging from *strongly disagree* to *strongly agree*.

Sexual experiences

Participants were asked several questions regarding their past consensual sexual behavior. They were asked how many consensual sexual intercourse partners they had in their lifetime, the number of partners they had sexual intercourse with on only one occasion, their number of oral sexual partners, and their number of anal sexual partners.

Condom use

In separate questions, participants were asked how often they used a condom when they had sexual intercourse when sober with a new or casual partner of the opposite sex and when drinking alcohol with a new or casual partner of the opposite sex. Responses were made on 7-point scales with options ranging from *never* to *always*. Participants reported on their lifetime pattern of use. A measure of overall condom use that did not specify partner type or alcohol use was correlated with condom use with a casual partner when sober and with condom use with a casual partner when intoxicated.

Experiments that have compared diary reports with retrospections of up to a year find that retrospective recall of condom use is very accurate (Graham, Catania, Brand, Duong, & Canchola, 2003).

RESULTS

Descriptive Information

There was no significant difference in men's and women's number of sexual intercourse partners. Compared with women, men reported having significantly more partners with whom they had sex on only one occasion, more anal sex partners, and more oral sex partners.

Bivariate Analyses

Social desirability was not significantly correlated with frequency of condom use when sober or intoxicated. Surprisingly, gender and sensation seeking were unrelated to condom use when sober or intoxicated. All of the other predictor variables were significantly correlated with both condom-use measures except alcohol consumption (which was only significantly correlated with frequency of condom use when intoxicated). This is not surprising, given the strong correlation between the two condom-use measures.

Multiple Regression Analyses

The first multiple regression analysis examined how often participants had sex without a condom when sober with a new or casual partner (Cohen, Cohen, West, & Aiken, 2003). The first step included control and demographic variables: social desirability, age, and gender. The second step included personality measures: sensation seeking and social assertiveness. The third step included alcohol measures: alcohol expectancies about sexual risk taking and alcohol consumption. The final step included variables from social-cognitive theory: self-efficacy regarding communication with partner about condoms, self-efficacy regarding condom use when intoxicated, and positive outcome expectancies regarding condom use.

None of the demographic or control variables were significant predictors of condom use when sober. On the second step, social assertiveness was positively related to frequency of condom use when sober. On the third step, alcohol expectancies about sexual risk taking were significantly negatively related to frequency of condom use when sober. On the fourth step, self-efficacy regarding condom use when intoxicated and positive outcome expectancies regarding condom use were both significant predictors of frequency of condom use when sober.

The same predictor variables were used to predict condom use when intoxicated, with one exception. Condom use when sober was added to the first step; thus, variables added on later steps are explaining the variance in condom use when intoxicated that is not explained by condom use when sober. As anticipated, condom use when sober was a strong predictor of condom use when intoxicated. On the second step,

neither of the personality variables had significant effects after controlling for condom use when sober. On the third step, alcohol expectancies regarding sexual risk taking remained a significant predictor. On the fourth step, self-efficacy regarding condom use when intoxicated remained a significant predictor. In a fifth step, interactions between gender and each of the personality, alcohol, and social-cognitive variables were examined. None of the interactions were significant.

DISCUSSION

The findings from this study replicate and extend past research. As hypothesized, frequency of condom use with casual partners was associated with social assertiveness, alcohol expectancies regarding sexual risk taking, self-efficacy, and positive outcome expectancies regarding condom use. Also as hypothesized, alcohol expectancies regarding sexual risk taking and self-efficacy regarding condom use when intoxicated were associated with frequency of condom use both when intoxicated and when sober. Beliefs about alcohol influenced condom use when intoxicated, even after controlling for condom use when sober, social desirability, age, gender, personality traits, and general alcohol consumption.

Some of our hypotheses were not supported. Despite the gender difference in number of one night stands and number of anal and oral sexual partners, gender was not significantly related to frequency of condom use when sober or intoxicated. Age was also not a significant predictor of condom use. Although younger adults and men are more likely to report using condoms, the magnitude of these relationships is typically low (Sheeran et al., 1999), and this sample had a constricted age range. Surprisingly, sensation seeking was not significantly related to condom use when sober or when intoxicated. There may be unique characteristics of individuals who are sensation seekers in the sexual domain. In contrast, the expectancy measure specifically focused on individuals' beliefs about alcohol; yet it was strongly related to condom use when sober and when intoxicated. This is partially due to the strong relationship between people's condom use when intoxicated and when sober. It also is likely that alcohol expectancies about sexual disinhibition share variance with general risk-taking measures; thus, this measure may have tapped into general individual differences in sexual risk taking. Future research is needed to examine the relationship between alcohol expectancies and general personality traits. Additionally, although self-efficacy regarding condom-use negotiation with partners was significantly correlated with condom use, it was not a significant multivariate predictor of condom use. The strong correlation between self-efficacy regarding partner negotiation and self-efficacy when intoxicated suggests that there is a core aspect of self-efficacy that is invariant across situations.

As Cooper (2002) noted, "the relationship between alcohol use and risky sexual behavior appears to be both complex and highly circumscribed" (p. 115), varying with characteristics of the individual drinker and the sexual situation. This study focused on individuals' frequency of condom use, rather than condom use on specific occasions. This measurement approach has the advantage of representing a broad range of sexual experiences; however, it raises concerns about accuracy of recall.

Implications

Intoxication does appear to affect risky sexual behavior, but only for some drinkers and only under some circumstances. There is a need for more sophisticated theories that include potential moderators to identify which individual drinkers are most likely to engage in risky sexual behavior when intoxicated. It is important to recognize that the strongest predictor of condom use when intoxicated

is condom use when sober. This suggests that even when interventionists are concerned about condom use when intoxicated, prevention strategies that encourage general condom use may be most effective from a public health perspective.

Furthermore, this study's findings indicate that college students are less likely to use condoms if they strongly believe that alcohol makes them sexually disinhibited and if they feel less confident that they can successfully use a condom when drinking. These findings highlight the need for prevention programs that challenge these beliefs and provide students with skill-building exercises that increase their confidence about their ability to use condoms under all types of circumstances, including intoxication. Prevention programs should also encourage students to question whether they should be having sex if they feel temporarily unable to correctly use a condom due to intoxication, exhaustion, anxiety, or any other reason.

INTRODUCTION REFERENCES

Cooper, M. L. 2006. Does drinking promote risky sexual behavior? A complex answer to a simple question. *Current Directions* 15: 19–23.

Duncan, G. J., J. Boisjoly, M. Kremer, D. M. Levy and J. Eccles. 2005. Peer effects in drug use and sex among college students. *Journal of Abnormal Child Psychology* 33: 375–85.

REFERENCES

Abbey, A., C. Saenz, and P. O. Buck. 2005. The cumulative effects of acute alcohol consumption, individual differences, and situational perceptions on sexual decision making. *Journal of Studies on Alcohol* 66: 82–90.

Albarracin, D., J. C. Gillette, A. N. Earl, L. R. Glasman, M. R. Durantini, and M-H. Ho. 2005. A test of major assumptions about behavior change: A comprehensive look at the effects of passive and active HIV-prevention interventions since the beginning of the epidemic. *Psychological Bulletin* 131: 856–897.

American College Health Association. (2005). The American College Health Association National College Health Assessment (ACHANCHA) Spring 2003 reference group report. *Journal of American College Health, 53,* 199–210.

Anderson, J. E., Wilson, R., Doll, L., Jones, T. S., & Barker, P. (1999). Condom use and HIV risk behaviors among U.S. adults: Data from a national survey. *Family Planning Perspectives, 31,* 24–28.

Baele, J., Dusseldorp, E., & Maes, S. (2001). Condom use self-efficacy: Effect on intended and actual condom use in adolescents. *Journal of Adolescent Health, 28,* 421–431.

Ballard, R. (1992). Short forms of the Marlowe-Crowne Social Desirability Scale. *Psychological Reports, 71,* 1155–1160.

Bandura, A. (1997). *Self-efficacy: The exercise of control.* New York: Freeman.

Brien, T. M., Thombs, D. L., Mahoney, C. A., & Wallnau, L. (1994). Dimensions of self-efficacy among three distinct groups of condom users. *Journal of American College Health, 42,* 167–174.

Cahalan, D., Cisin, I., & Crossley, H. (1969). *American drinking practices.* New Brunswick, NJ: Rutgers Center for Alcohol Studies.

Centers for Disease Control and Prevention. (2004). *HIV/AIDS surveillance report, 2003* (Vol. 15). Atlanta, GA: US Department of Health and Human Services.

Cohen, J., Cohen, P., West, S. G., & Aiken, L. S. (2003). *Applied multiple regression/correlation analysis for the behavioral sciences* (3rd ed.). Mahwah, NJ: Erlbaum.

Cooper, M. L. (2002). Alcohol use and risky sexual behavior among college students and youth: Evaluating the evidence. *Journal of Studies on Alcohol,* (Suppl. 14), 101–117.

Cooper, M. L., & Orcutt, H. K. (1997). Drinking and sexual experience on first dates among adolescents. *Journal of Abnormal Psychology, 106,* 191–202.

Cooper, M. L., & Orcutt, H. K. (2000). Alcohol use, condom use and partner type among heterosexual adolescents and young adults. *Journal of Studies on Alcohol, 61,* 413–419.

Corbin, W. R., & Fromme, K. (2002). Alcohol use and serial monogamy as risks for sexually transmitted diseases in young adults. *Health Psychology, 21,* 229–236.

Curtin, J. J., & Fairchild, B. A. (2003). Alcohol and cognitive control: Implications for regulation of behavior during response conflict. *Journal of Abnormal Psychology, 112,* 424–436.

Dermen, K. H., & Cooper, M. L. (2000). Inhibition conflict and alcohol expectancy as moderators of alcohol's relationship to condom use. *Experimental and Clinical Psychopharmacology, 8,* 198–206.

Dilorio, C., Dudley, W. N., Soet, J., Watkins, J., & Maibach, E. (2000). A social cognitive-based model for condom use among college students. *Nursing Research, 49,* 208–214.

Douglas, K. A., Collins, J. L., Warren, C., Kahn, L., Gold, R., Clayton, S., et al. (1997). Results from the 1995 National College Health Risk Behavior Study. *Journal of American College Health, 46,* 55–66.

Eysenck, S. B., & Eysenck, H. J. (1977). The place of impulsiveness in a dimensional system of personality description. *British Journal of Social and Clinical Psychology, 16,* 57–68.

Fillmore, M. T., & Blackburn, J. (2002). Compensating for alcohol induced impairment: Alcohol expectancies and behavioral disinhibition. *Journal of Studies on Alcohol, 63,* 237–246.

Graham, C. A., Catania, J. A., Brand, R., Duong, T., & Canchola, J. A. (2003). Recalling sexual behavior: A methodological analysis of memory recall bias via interview using the diary as the gold standard. *The Journal of Sex Research, 40,* 325–332.

Graves, K. L., & Hines, A. M. (1997). Ethnic differences in the association between alcohol and risky sexual behavior with a new partner: An event-based analysis. *AIDS Education and Prevention, 9,* 219–237.

Halpern-Felsher, B. L., Millstein, S. G., & Ellen, J. M. (1996). Relationship of alcohol use and risky sexual behavior: A review and analysis of findings. *Journal of Adolescent Health, 19,* 331–336.

Helweg-Larsen, M., & Collins, B. E. (1994). The UCLA multidimensional condom attitudes scale: Documenting the complex determinants of condom use in college students. *Health Psychology, 13,* 224–237.

Hightow, L. B., MacDonald, P. D. M., Pilcher, C. D., Kaplan, A. H., Foust, E., Nguyen, T. Q., & Leone, P. A. (2005). The unexpected movement of the HIV epidemic in the Southeastern United States. *Journal of Acquired Immune Deficiency Syndrome, 38,* 531–537.

Justus, A. N., Finn, P. R., & Steinmetz, J. E. (2000). The influence of traits of disinhibition on the association between alcohol use and risky sexual behavior. *Alcoholism: Clinical and Experimental Research, 24,* 1028–1035.

Midanik, L. T., & Greenfield, T. K. (2003). Telephone versus in-person interviews for alcohol use: Results of the 2000 National Alcohol Survey. *Drug and Alcohol Dependence, 72,* 209–214.

Morrison, D. M., Gilmore, M. R., Hoppe, M. J., Gaylord, J., Leigh, B. C., & Rainey, D. (2003). Adolescent drinking and sex: Findings from a daily diary study. *Perspectives on Sexual and Reproductive Health, 35,* 162–168.

Oliver, M. B., & Hyde, J. S. (1993). Gender differences in sexuality: A meta-analysis. *Psychological Bulletin, 114,* 29–51.

O'Malley, P. M., & Johnston, L. D. (2002). Epidemiology of alcohol and other drug use among American college students. *Journal of Studies on Alcohol,* (Suppl. 14), 23–39.

Perkins, H. W. (2002). Surveying the damage: A review of research on consequences of alcohol misuse in college populations. *Journal of Studies on Alcohol,* (Suppl. 14), 91–100.

Rathus, S. A. (1973). A 30-item schedule for assessing assertive behavior. *Behavior Therapy, 4,* 398–406.

Sheeran, P., Abraham, C., & Orbell, S. (1999). Psychosocial correlates of heterosexual condom use: A meta-analysis. *Psychological Bulletin, 125,* 90–132.

Wechsler, H., Lee, J. E., Kuo, M., Seibring, M., Nelson, T. F., & Lee, H. (2000). Trends in college binge drinking during a period of increased prevention efforts: Findings from 4 Harvard School of Public Health College Alcohol Study surveys: 1993–2001. *Journal of American College Health, 50,* 203–217.

Weinhardt, L. S., & Carey, M. P. (2000). Does alcohol lead to sexual risk behavior? Findings from event-level research. *Annual Review of Sex Research, 11,* 125–157.

Weinstock, H., Berman, B., & Cates, W., Jr. (2004). Sexually transmitted diseases among American youth: Incidence and prevalence estimates, 2000. *Perspectives on Sexual and Reproductive Health, 36,* 6–10.

Wulfert, E., & Wan, C. K. (1993). Condom use: A self-efficacy model. *Health Psychology, 12,* 346–353.

Zamboni, B. D., Crawford, I., & Williams, P. G. (2000). Examining communication and assertiveness as predictors of condom use: Implications for HIV prevention. *AIDS Education and Prevention, 12,* 492–504.

CHAPTER 37

HIV/AIDS Protective Factors Among Urban American Indian Youths

Flavio F. Marsiglia
Tanya Nieri
Arlene Rubin Stiffman

Although Native Americans at present do not have a disproportionate number of HIV/AIDS cases, they have an increasing STI rate relative to all other subgroups in the United States. This appears to be due to a combination of behavioral, attitudinal, cultural, and geographic factors (Ramirez et al. 2002). Family discussions about health-threatening issues are thought to be key variables in promoting HIV/AIDS knowledge among children and teens. This may be especially true for those from Native American families, who know less about this disease than their non-Native American counterparts. Therefore, higher levels of family communication skills about HIV/AIDS would possibly be useful in reducing sexual risk-taking among this population.

However, to say that family communication is subject to many trials and tribulations is an understatement. Even in the best of circumstances, teenagers and their parents often seem at cross purposes in their exchange of information. Add to this dilemma a conundrum: For both teens and their parents, sexual behavior seems quite natural and inviting, while sexual discussions seem unnatural and foreboding. Satirically, although sexual information and family communication skills are sorely needed by this population because of their increasing rates of STIs, comprehensive sexuality is unlikely to be taught in their schools, and classes in communication skills occur even more rarely. What do such omissions reveal about our society concerning the welfare of this population?

In the following study, Marsiglia, Nieri, and Stiffman explore the role of various individual, cultural, and family factors, including family HIV/AIDS communication in reducing high-risk sexual behaviors among Native American youth. As you read the chapter, you will learn that the solution to this public health problem is not always as simple as it might seem.

While there is a growing body of research on HIV/AIDS in the general population, less is known about the protective and risk factors associated with HIV/AIDS infection among American Indian youth. Relative to other racial/ethnic groups, American Indians have received minimal attention because they have had low reported rates of infection since the early days of the epidemic.[2,10,27,36] Yet, over two decades into the epidemic, reported rates of infection among American Indians have begun to increase, especially among youth, who make up a large portion of the American Indian population.[2,4] The change in rates raises questions about this group's vulnerability to HIV/AIDS and marks a need to better understand the factors that may lead to or prevent behaviors associated with disease contraction in this group. Toward that end, this study uses a sample of sexually active, urban American Indian youth and explores the influence of family and individual factors on behaviors associated with HIV/AIDS risk: having multiple recent sexual partners, substance use during sex, and unprotected sex.

American Indian youth and HIV/AIDS

According to the Centers for Disease Control (CDC),[5] there were 1,506 American Indians living with AIDS at the end of 2004, less than 1% of the total U.S. AIDS cases. At that same time, there were 11.1 American Indians with HIV/AIDS per 100,000 population, based on the CDC's 33-state surveillance estimates.[5] The accuracy of these official numbers has been questioned by people who believe that actual rates may be higher.[4,30] Poor record keeping by the Indian Health Service (IHS), poor and under-reporting of disease, racial/ethnic misclassification of American Indians, and low levels of HIV testing among American Indians may explain the suspected underestimates.[4,11,27,30]

Some researchers have described HIV as the new smallpox, an epidemic that could decimate entire American Indian communities in a way reminiscent of the epidemics caused by early European colonization.[2,3] The fact that many American Indian communities present risk factors commonly associated with HIV infection contributes to the concern. For example, American Indians report high rates of substance

use, especially alcohol use,[2,7,8,12] and high rates of sexually transmitted diseases.[8] Furthermore, American Indians face high rates of poverty and low rates of educational achievement, which may constitute barriers to prevention and access to health services.[3,7] On the other hand, the community's past low levels of infection necessitate further research to identify possible protective factors. Once these protective factors are identified and better understood, they can be integrated into effective and culturally grounded prevention programs.

The urban context

Despite their identified high HIV-risk behaviors, American Indians are sometimes thought to be better protected from HIV/AIDS than other groups because many live on tribal lands in rural, isolated areas. Residence on tribal lands may provide risk-reducing social support and cultural connectedness due to proximity to family and other tribe members and traditional events.[17] Urban areas, in contrast, have been associated with greater HIV/AIDS risk because residents are exposed to more infected people, behavior norms associated with greater HIV/AIDS risk, and other problems, such as homelessness, which may ultimately increase the risk of infection.[26] In fact, the majority of American Indian HIV cases are in urban areas.[11] However, it is important to recognize that urban areas may also be protective in some respects. For example, American Indians residing in urban areas may benefit from greater access to HIV/AIDS knowledge and education than people living on reservations have.[2]

For American Indian youth, living in an urban area involves navigating through two worlds and a mix of risk and protective factors. As adolescents, they are already experiencing multi-faceted changes in their lives.[31] Their daily bicultural experience of home and community may produce cultural conflicts and raise questions about identity and sense of belonging.[22] American Indian identity may take on greater salience as the youths interact with students and teachers of other racial/ethnic backgrounds. They may come to be viewed narrowly as Indian, and negative interactions may lead to poorer self-appraisal.[18]

Sexual behavior and HIV/AIDS

Sexual activity continues to be the main mode of HIV transmission for adolescents in general,[9,10] and American Indian youth are no exception.[10] Among sexually active youth the number of sexual partners, substance use during sex, and non-use of condoms have been associated with HIV/AIDS infection. Although national data on sexually active youths' number of recent sexual partners are not available, evidence suggests that the number of partners may increase HIV risk when no protective measures are taken.[9] Unfortunately, American Indian youth, like youth from other racial/ethnic backgrounds, are inconsistent and infrequent users of protection.[10,13] Nationally, 42% of youth of all racial/ethnic backgrounds report no condom use during the last sexual intercourse.[14] Relative to their non-Native peers, American Indian youth are about half as likely to use contraceptives.[15]

Studies in the general adolescent population show that condom use is less likely when youth are under the influence of substances.[9] According to a national survey of adolescents aged 15 to 24, 11% report having used alcohol or drugs during the most recent sexual intercourse.[14] Studies among American Indian adults have linked substance use to less condom use, especially by females.[4,8] Few studies have explored this link among youth.

Some research has explored the family's role in encouraging healthy sexual behavior, although few studies thus far have explored this association among American Indian youth. Existing research suggests that parental monitoring, positive family relations, and parent-child discussions about sex can protect against risky sexual behavior among American Indian youth.[1,7,16,19]

Other research has documented the relationship between family relations and substance use.[20,21] Family members have been found to have both positive and negative effects on American Indian youths. Family members' substance use can motivate youths to avoid using alcohol and other drugs because they witness closely its negative consequences or it can foster substance use because the youths are invited to use alongside their family members.[20] Supervision by family members may give youths a sense that they are protected and cared for, thereby decreasing their interest in substance use.[20] Closeness to and low conflict with family members has also been associated with less substance use.[21]

Cultural factors also are key variables in prevention for American Indians.[6,10,37] The belief is that developing cultural pride will strengthen youth's perceptions of their own value, thereby motivating them to engage in healthy behaviors.[3] Although some research demonstrates the success of culturally grounded programs for American Indian adults,[37] little research on American Indian youth has tested this association in relation to HIV/AIDS risk. One study found that American Indian adolescents' cultural connectedness and Native religious involvement had no effect on sexual behaviors.[19] In contrast, another study found that youth in more culturally traditional families became sexually active at later ages and had higher rates of condom use,[2] suggesting an important prevention role for the family's culture.

A contextual approach to American Indian youth sexual behavior

The standard knowledge-attitudes-behavior (KAB) approaches to explaining risky sexual behavior (e.g., the theory of reasoned action,[23] the theory of self efficacy,[24] and the health belief model[25]) focus on the individual. The models generally posit that people with greater knowledge of HIV transmission and modes of prevention and greater self efficacy will be less likely to engage in risky sexual behavior and more likely to engage in risk reduction behavior. Thus, the research has explored such individual variables as the extent to which individuals have correct knowledge of HIV and sexuality, perceive themselves to be personally vulnerable to HIV infection, are willing to use condoms or negotiate safe sex, and have confidence in their ability to protect themselves from HIV.[2] Although this approach has helped to generate needed information on existing HIV knowledge and attitudes, it has been less effective in explaining adolescents' actual sexual behavior. Knowledge and attitudes do not consistently predict behavior.[2,26,28] Walters and Simoni, for example, found in their study of adult urban American Indians that trauma was a better predictor of HIV risk behavior than social cognitive variables.[26]

The inconsistent findings have been explained, in part, in terms of a failure to account for context. A person's ability to translate knowledge and norms into healthy behavior may be encouraged or constrained by the context in which he or she lives.[28,32,33] This limitation of the KAB approach, among others, has prompted some researchers to call for less individual, more contextual approaches, and for more strength- or resiliency-based rather than risk-based approaches to understanding and preventing HIV/AIDS among youth.[35] In addition, some researchers have stressed the importance of taking into account community-level experiences, such as communities' historical oppression as a group, and cultural contexts when examining American Indians' health behaviors.[6,29,30,34,37,38]

Given the limitations of standard approaches and the importance of context for American Indians, we advance a contextual model for examining the relationship between American Indian youth and HIV/AIDS protective and risk behaviors. Calling upon Bogenschneider's[39] Ecological Risk/Protective Theory, we explore family factors that form part of the social context that may influence sexual behavior.

Bogenschneider's theory explains youth outcomes in terms of adolescents' personal attributes and the dynamic environments in which youth live. It accounts for protective factors that may offset risks in adolescents' lives. From this perspective, we hypothesize that urban American Indian adolescents' family context may include supports and stressors that influence sexual behavior and, consequently, exposure to HIV/AIDS.

We propose to examine individual factors and contextual family factors, specifically family relations, family communication about HIV/AIDS, and family cultural involvement among urban American Indian youth. The study is guided by the hypothesis that family relations, family communication, and family cultural involvement are associated with the presence or absence of selected sexual risk behaviors among sexually active, urban American Indian youth.

Methods

This article reports the findings of a secondary data analysis using data from the first wave of the urban American Indian Multisector Help Inquiry (AIM-HI), which examined the service use of a representative sample of 200 American Indian youths living in a large metropolitan area of a Southwestern state in the U.S. Youth aged 12–19 years were randomly selected from complete tribal enrollment and school district records. One child per household was enrolled and interviewed in 2001.

Interviewers administered a brief interview exploring behavior and functioning; the interview was structured, using material from the Youth Self Report,[40] the child version of the Columbia Impairment Scale,[41] and substance use questions from the Youth Risk Behavior survey.[42] Of the youth who completed the brief interview, half were randomly sampled to complete a long interview. An additional 50 youth, who were not randomly selected but were identified as being in great need of services, based on the brief interview, were added to the sample. Additional details on the study are summarized by Stiffman, Striley, Brown, Limb, and Ostmann.[43]

Sample

The sub-sample consisted of the 89 urban youth who reported that they had ever had sex and were not married. The sub-sample was older, with a mean age of 16.2 years, whereas unselected youth from the original sample had a mean age of 15.3 years. The sub-sample reported greater family and personal involvement in American Indian cultural activities than the sample as a whole.

Demographics

Respondents' ages ranged from 14–20 years with an average of 16.5 years. Almost the entire sample (87%) reported that they had ever been taught in school about HIV/AIDS infection.

Measures

We analyzed three outcomes: having more than one sexual partner in the last three months, alcohol or drug use during last sexual intercourse and sexual intercourse without a condom during last encounter.

Family relations were measured by an index with five items.[44] The respondent indicated the frequency with which: the family gets on their nerves, they really enjoy their family, they can really depend on their family, their family argues too much, and they feel like a stranger in their family.

Family communication about HIV/AIDS was measured by a single item indicating whether the youth ever talked about HIV/AIDS infection with his/her parents or other adults in his/her family.

Individual and family involvement in American Indian culture was measured using questions from Oetting and Beauvais' Orthogonal Cultural Identity Scale.[45] Family cultural involvement was measured by a single item assessing the degree of family involvement in American Indian traditions. Individual cultural involvement was measured by a set of items assessing the respondent's involvement in American Indian traditions, including memorials/feasts, powwows/dances, giveaways, healing ceremonies, sweats, religious events, naming ceremonies, talking circles, spiritual running, and other traditional activities, and private American Indian spiritual activities.

Substance use was captured by a dichotomous variable distinguishing users from non-users. It was a composite of several measures capturing lifetime experience with alcohol, tobacco, and other drugs.

Results

Analyses of the outcome variables revealed that 11% of the youth reported having more than one sex partner in the last three months. Sixteen percent reported using alcohol or drugs during last sexual intercourse, five percentage points higher than national figures. Finally, 32% reported not using a condom during last sexual intercourse, 10 percentage points lower than national figures. Although the pattern is that boys were more likely to have had more recent sex partners and use substances at last intercourse and girls were more likely to have had sex without a condom, these differences were not statistically significant.

Additional analyses revealed high levels of family support in the sample. On average youths reported that they had positive family relations for "a good part of" the last six months. Sixty percent reported that they had ever talked about HIV/AIDS with parents or other adults in their family. On average, the youth reported that their families had some involvement in American Indian traditions. Personal involvement was somewhat lower. On average, the adolescents reported only a little personal involvement in American Indian cultural traditions. The vast majority reported recreational substance use experience.

A pattern of protection appeared for two of the three outcomes. Fewer youth in families that talk about HIV/AIDS reported substance use or no condom use at last intercourse, relative to youth in families that do not discuss HIV/AIDS. However, more youth in these families reported sex with multiple recent partners.

These results indicate that family HIV/AIDS communication, but not positive family relations or family involvement in American Indian cultural traditions, are related to HIV/AIDS risk behavior. In particular, family communication about HIV/AIDS has a positive effect on the likelihood of having had more than one sex partner in the last three months and a negative effect on the likelihood of having used substances at last intercourse. Relative to youth without family communication about HIV/AIDS, youth who discuss HIV/AIDS with their parents or other adult family members had greater odds of having multiple recent sex partners and lower odds of using substances at last intercourse. Family HIV/AIDS communication was not related to the likelihood of having unprotected sex.

At the individual level, only substance use was significant. A powerful predictor, it was associated with a much greater likelihood of having multiple recent sex partners and using substances at last intercourse. However, it was not associated with condom non-use. Individual American Indian cultural involvement, age, sex, and socioeconomic status, measured by financial assistance, had no effect on the three outcomes.

Discussion

This study examined the prevalence of three sexual risk behaviors among sexually active American Indian youth, providing needed information on an understudied group by exploring the relationship between individual and contextual family factors and HIV/AIDS risk. The findings provide a snapshot of the risk status of a selected group of sexually active American Indian youth residing in a large metropolitan area of the Southwest U.S. The finding of lower than national average rates of unprotected sex is reassuring, but it runs counter to previous research[15] and warrants further investigation. It may reflect resources and supports unique to these urban American Indian youth. In particular, it may reflect greater access to condoms and HIV/AIDS information due to urban residence or some other factor. The vast majority of the sample (98%) reported receiving HIV education in school. This programming may be accompanied by a condom distribution plan, thereby facilitating condom use in this particular sample. If so, this finding would suggest that greater access to HIV/AIDS prevention resources fosters lower risk among urban American Indian youth, though further study is required to confirm this possibility.

The finding of higher than national rates of substance use during sex lends credence to some concerns voiced by researchers about the under-reported risk for HIV/AIDS in this population.[3,4] It is important to remember that the original sample included an additional group of youth identified as having a greater need for services. This fact limits any comparisons with national rates. The high rates of lifetime substance use in this sample and among American Indian youth in general, however, contribute to the salience of this risk behavior in this population.

Of the family factors assessed here, only family communication about HIV/AIDS was a significant factor. Positive family relations had no effect. The measure may be too general to explain a youth's sexual risk behavior. It may be that sex-specific family attitudes and norms, such as those reflected in conversations about sex or HIV/AIDS, are more salient predictors in this group of already sexually active youth. Furthermore, the finding of no effect does not necessarily mean that families are not protective or have no influence on American Indian youth's sexual behaviors. It may mean that good relations alone will not foster healthy sexual activity. Targeted family intervention, such as family communication about HIV/AIDS, may be required to have an impact on HIV/AIDS risk.

It appears that family communication has an impact, but that impact can be positive or negative, possibly depending on the content of the conversations. The finding of their impact, coupled with the finding of generally positive family relations in the sample, suggests that the family may be a resource for prevention. The seriousness of HIV/AIDS as a topic of conversation may make family HIV/AIDS communication a more salient factor than general family relations. Some families may speak only rarely about sex such that when they do, the experience resonates loudly for the youth, influencing their subsequent behavior.

Due to the cross-sectional nature of the data, causal ordering is unclear, and detailed information about the content and tone of the family HIV/AIDS conversations is unknown. It may be that family members initiate conversations about HIV/AIDS when they realize or suspect that the youth is having sex. Alternatively, it may be that these conversations portray sex as a normal, healthy human activity, thus fostering sexual activity and reducing the need to rely on substance use to get through the experience. Family conversations may, however, fail to distinguish the circumstances under which sexual activity can threaten health, such as unprotected sex with multiple partners. Further exploration of the content of family exchanges about HIV/AIDS, with more comprehensive measures, may yield information important for possible prevention interventions.

Family involvement in American Indian culture had neither a protective nor a risk effect on the outcomes. Individual involvement also had no effect. There were low levels of both types of involvement in the sample as a whole, perhaps due to the urban composition of the sample and the consequent bicultural perspective of the respondents. In addition, because the cultural involvement variable assessed only American Indian culture, it may have failed to distinguish between youth with high and low involvement in mainstream culture, thus suppressing a possible protective effect of Native orientation as well as a risk effect of mainstream orientation. It is worth noting that the one other study of American Indian youth sexual practices that was identified also found no relationship between cultural involvement and safer sexual practices.[19]

Youth with lifetime substance use experience were more likely to report having multiple sex partners and using substances at last intercourse, and the effects were very strong. The finding is consistent with prior research linking substance use and sexual risk behavior.[4,8,9,14] It suggests that lifetime substance use is a robust predictor of sexual risk behavior and that HIV/AIDS prevention programs must address substance use as a separate but related behavior.

No family or individual variable predicted condom non-use. Prior research has found substance use to be a consistent predictor of condom non-use.[9] The surprising absence of an effect here may be due to the failure to include more proximal variables, such as partner or sexual encounter characteristics, which have been found to be related to condom use.[28,32,33]

Conclusion

This study provides important descriptive information on the HIV/AIDS risk and protective factors associated with sexually active American Indian youth, an understudied group. It also identified important contextual family factors that are related to HIV/AIDS risk and protection. Future researchers must continue to examine contextual factors, using longitudinal data, to develop greater understanding of the influences on American Indian adolescents' sexual behaviors and their implications for HIV/AIDS prevention. In particular, there is a need to explore the conditions under which family HIV/AIDS communication is associated with risk and protection and whether topic-specific family communication can be employed to protect against other outcomes.

Future research could also explore the role of family factors, comparing sexually active youth with non-sexually active youth, since there is some evidence that family factors may differ for the two groups.[16]

INTRODUCTION REFERENCE

Ramirez, J. R., W. D. Crano, R. Quist, M. Burgoon, E. M. Alvaro, and J. Grandpre. 2002. Effects of fatalism and family communication on HIV/AIDS awareness variations in Native American and Anglo parents and children. *AIDS Education and Prevention* 14: 29–40.

REFERENCES

1. Fingerson L. Do mothers' opinions matter in teens' sexual activity? J Fam Issues. 2005 Oct;26(7):947–74.
2. Mitchell CM, Kaufman CE; the Pathways of Choice and Healthy Ways Project Team. Structure of HIV knowledge, attitudes, and behaviors among American Indian young adults. AIDS Educ Prev. 2002 Oct;14(5):401–18.
3. Vernon IS. Killing us quietly: Native Americans and HIV/AIDS. Lincoln: University of Nebraska Press, 2001.
4. Vernon I, Jumper-Thurman, P. The changing face of HIV/AIDS among native populations. J Psychoactice Drugs. 2005 Sep;37(3):247–55.
5. Centers Centers for Disease Control and Prevention. HIV/AIDS Surveillance Report, 2004. Vol. 16. Atlanta, GA: US Department of Health and Human Services, Centers for Disease Control and Prevention, 2005. Available at http://www.cdc.gov/hiv/stats/ hasrlink.htm.
6. Scott KD, Gilliam A, Braxton K. Culturally competent HIV prevention strategies for women of color in the United States. Health Care Women Int. 2005 Jan;26(1): 17–45.
7. Ramirez JR, Crano WD, Quist R, et al. Effects of fatalism and family communication on HIV/AIDS awareness variations in Native American and Anglo parents and children. AIDS Educ Prev. 2002 Feb;14(1):29–40.
8. Saylors K, Jim N, Plasencia AV, et al. Faces of HIV/AIDS and substance abuse in Native American communities. J Psychoactive Drugs. 2005 Sep;37(3):241–5.
9. Shrier LA, Emans SJ, Woods ER, et al. The association of sexual risk behaviors and problem drug behaviors in high school students. J Adolesc Health. 1996 May; 20(5):377–83.
10. Aguilera S, Plasencia AV. Culturally appropriate HIV/AIDS and substance abuse prevention programs for urban native youth. J Psychoactive Drugs. 2005 Sep;37(3): 299–304.
11. Foley K, Duran B, Morris P, et al. Using motivational interviewing to promote HIV testing at an American Indian substance use treatment facility. J Psychoactive Drugs. 2005 Sep;37(3): 321–9.
12. Spear S, Longshore D, McCaffrey D, et al. Prevalence of substance use among white and American Indian young adolescents in a Northern Plains state. J Psychoactive Drugs. 2005 Mar;37(1):1–6.
13. Shafer M, Boyer CB. Psychosocial and behavioral factors associated with the risk of sexually transmitted diseases, including human immunodeficiency virus infection, among urban high school students. J Pediatr. 1991 Nov; 119(5): 826–33.
14. Sexuality Information and Education Council of the United States. The truth about adolescent sexuality. SIECUS Fact Sheet. Washington, DC: Sexuality Information and Education Council of the United States, 2003.
15. Edwards S. Among Native American teenagers, sex without contraceptives is common. Fam Plann Perspect. 1992 Jul–Aug; 24(4):189–91.
16. Oman RF, Vesely SF, Aspy, CB. Youth assets and sexual risk behavior: the importance of assets for youth residing in one-parent households. Perspect Sex Reprod Health. 2005 Mar;37(1):25–31.
17. Sullivan C. Pathways to infection: AIDS vulnerability among the Navajo. AIDS Educ Prev. 1991 Fall;3(3):241–57.
18. Beiser M, Sack W, Manson SM, et al. Mental health and the academic performance of first nations and majority-culture children. Am J Orthopsychiatry. 1998 Jul; 68(3):455–67.
19. Chewning B, Douglas J, Kokotailo PK, et al. Protective factors associated with American Indian adolescents' safer sexual patterns. Matern Child Health J. 2001 Dec; 5(4):273–80.
20. Hurdle D, Okamoto SK, Miles BW. Family influences on alcohol and drug use by American Indian youth: implications for prevention. J Family Social Work 2003; 7(1):53–68.

21. East PL, Khoo ST. Longitudinal pathways linking family factors and sibling relationship qualities to adolescent substance use and sexual risk behaviors. J Fam Psychol. 2005 Dec;19(4):571–80.

22. Machamer AM, Gruber E. Secondary school, family, and educational risk: comparing American Indian adolescents and their peers. J Educ Res. 1998;91(6):357–369.

23. Fishbein M. AIDS and behavior change: an analysis based on the theory of reasoned action. Interamerican J Psychology. 1990;24:37–56.

24. Bandura A. Social cognitive theory and exercise of control of HIV infection. In: DiClemente RJ, Peterson JL, eds. Preventing AIDS: theories and methods of behavioral interventions. New York: Plenum Press, 1994; 25–59.

25. Janz NK, Becker MH. The Health Belief Model: a decade later. Health Educ Q. 1984 Spring; 11(1):1–47.

26. Walters KL, Simoni JM, Harris C. Patterns and predictors of HIV risk among urban American Indians. Am Ind Alsk Native Ment Health Res. 2000;9(2):1–21.

27. Greabell L, Cordes P, Klein SJ. HIV/AIDS and Native Americans: the health departments' response. J Psychoactive Drugs. 2005 Sep;37(3):267–72.

28. Crosby RA, DiClemente RJ, Wingood GM, et al. Identification of strategies for promoting condom use: a prospective analysis of high-risk African American female teens. Prev Sci. 2003 Dec;4(4):263–70.

29. Saylors K, Daliparthy N. Native women, violence, substance abuse and HIV risk. J Psychoactive Drugs. 2005 Sep;37(3):273–80.

30. Hamill S, Dickey M. Cultural competence: what is needed in working with Native Americans with HIV/AIDS? J Assoc Nurses in AIDS Care. 2005 Jul–Aug;16(4):64–9.

31. Sweeney MM, Zionts P. The "second skin": perceptions of disturbed and nondisturbed early adolescents on clothing, self-concept, and body image. Adolescence. 1989 Summer;2(94):411–20.

32. Vernon IS. Violence, HIV/AIDS, and Native American women in the twenty-first century. American Indian Culture and Research J 2002;26(2):115–33.

33. Browne DC, Clubb PA, Aubrecht AM, et al. Minority health risk behaviors: an introduction to research on sexually transmitted diseases, violence, pregnancy prevention, and substance use. Matern Child Health J. 2001 Dec;5(4):215–24.

34. Speier T. Special Projects of National Significance and the Alaska Tribal Health System: an overview of the development of a best practice model for HIV/AIDS care and treatment in Alaska. J Psychoactive Drugs. 2005 Sep;37(3):305–12.

35. DiClemente RJ, Wingood GM, Crosby RA. A contextual perspective for understanding and preventing STD/HIV among adolescents. In: Romer D, ed. Reducing adolescent risk: toward an integrated approach. Thousand Oaks, CA: Sage Publications, 2003; 366–73.

36. McNaghten AD, Neal JJ, Li J, et al. Epidemiologic profile of HIV and AIDS among American Indians/Alaska Natives in the USA through 2000. Ethn Health. 2005 Feb; 10(1):57–71.

37. Nebelkopf E, Penagos M. Holistic Native network: integrated HIV/AIDS, substance abuse, and mental health services for Native Americans in San Francisco. J Psychoactive Drugs. 2005 Sep;37(3):257–64.

38. Walters KL, Simoni JM, Evans-Campbell T. Substance use among American Indians and Alaska natives: incorporating culture in an "indigenist" stress-coping paradigm. Public Health Rep. 2002;117 Suppl 1:S104–17.

39. Bogenschneider K. An ecological risk/protective theory for building prevention programs, policies, and community capacity to support youth. Fam Relat. 1996 Apr; 45(2):127–38.

40. Achenbach TM. Manual for the youth self-report and 1991 profile. Burlington, VT: University of Vermont Department of Psychiatry, 1991.

41. Bird HR, Shaffer D, Fisher P, et al. The Columbia Impairment Scale (CIS): Pilot findings on a measure of global impairment for children and adolescents. Int J Methods Psychiatr Res. 1993;3(3):167–76.

42. Kann L, Warren CW, Harris WA. Youth risk behavior surveillance—United States, 1995. MMWR CDC Surveill Summ. 1996 Sep 27;45(4):1–84.

43. Stiffman AR, Striley C, Brown E, et al. American Indian youth: who Southwestern urban and reservation youth turn to for help with mental health or addictions. J Child Fam Stud. 2003 Sep;12(3):319–33.

44. Hudson WW, Acklin JD, Bartosh JC. Assessing discord in family relationships. Social Work Research and Abstracts. 1980;16(3):21–29.

45. Oetting ER, Beauvais F. Orthogonal cultural identification theory: the cultural identification of minority adolescents. Int J Addict. 1990–1991;25(5A–6A):655–85.

CHAPTER 38

Damaged Goods

Mixing Morality with Medicine

Adina Nack

Human papillomavirus (HPV), believed to be the most common STI in the United States, has been identified as the major cause of cervical cancer, and to have a strong association with cancer of the vulva, vagina, anus, and penis. Commonly called genital warts, the virus primarily affects persons ages 15–40. These highly contagious warts are transmitted through direct bodily contact during vaginal, oral, or anal intercourse as well as through nongenital contact. The problem is magnified because many infected male sex partners have no visible signs of these warts, which may be only inside the urethra. Additionally, a partner may be a carrier of the virus, which has not as yet produced warts. Therefore, the most common form of transmission is by a person who is asymptomatic. Adding to the bad news, no accurate screening test is currently available for this STI.

Such a bleak outlook raises several questions for the sexually active college student. How would you feel if you suddenly found out that you had contracted this or some other sexually transmitted infection from somebody with whom you were sexually intimate? Would it matter if it were a casual partner or someone with whom you had a long-term relationship? What if the infection was passed along to you as the result of infidelity? Would you feel differently if you had been using condoms than if you had not taken precautions? What if it was an infection for which there is no cure?

There are several sexually transmitted diseases that, once contracted, can not be cured. Contracting a disease such as HPV, genital herpes, or HIV/AIDS is therefore life-altering. HPV is related to cancer, genital herpes can increase the likelihood of contracting HIV and HIV/AIDS is often a terminal illness. In addition to the physical risks and discomfort of such an infection, there is also a psychological impact. The emotional effect of having a sexually transmitted disease is somewhat different for women than for men, in part because of the sexual double standard: It is still more acceptable for men to be sexually adventurous than for women. As Adina Nack points out in the following reading, the stigma of contracting a sexually transmitted disease is therefore stronger for women. This piece, the first chapter of her book, Damaged Goods?: Women Living with Incurable Sexually Transmitted Diseases, lays out her methodology and hints at her conclusions. After reading this tantalizing first chapter, you want to read the entire book.

I never thought it would happen to me. . . .

A 20-year-old undergraduate receives a phone call from her ex-boyfriend. He nervously informs her that he has just been diagnosed with genital warts and is in the process of having them "frozen off" with liquid nitrogen. He explains that he called her because there was a chance that he might have had *this* when they had last *been together*. He adds that he is not sure she is at risk because he had not noticed symptoms until recently. She quickly thanks him for calling, hangs up the phone, and sits in stunned silence.

She thinks to herself: *How could this have happened to me? I'm not a slut: I've only had sex with three guys and always used condoms. I talked with both my ex-boyfriends and current boyfriend before we ever had sex—they told me about their sexual histories and sexual health. These guys had all tested negative for HIV so they were "safe"—healthy and trustworthy—right? My high school sex education focused on HIV/AIDS, so I've only been worried about fluids being transmitted. Is it possible to get a disease even when you're using condoms?*

A series of scary questions runs through her mind. *Do I have warts, too? How could I? My last annual gynecological exam was less than six months ago, and my Pap smear results were normal. Wouldn't my doctor have noticed if had warts? Could I have warts that are so tiny I've never noticed them? Have I already infected my current boyfriend?*

With no answers to any of these questions, one horrific image appears in her mind with unsettling clarity: inspired by the one film about sexually transmitted diseases (STDs) that was shown in her high school health class, she envisions her vulva sprouting cauliflower-like growths, more and more fleshy warts, ultimately covering her genitals inside and out. This image brings her to tears. As she begins to cry, she wonders: *Will any guy ever want me? Will I ever get married or be able to have a healthy baby?*

MORE THAN JUST AN INFECTION: GENDERED MORALITY AND SEXUAL DISEASES

The preceding snapshot gives one example of how it feels to find out that you have a STD. Many infected individuals feel "dirty," disgusted by the bumps and sores that require medical attention and mar body parts, which are supposed to be the most private, sensual, and erotic. These negative feelings are compounded by the social acceptability of blaming infected individuals for their illnesses. Often the blame comes with judgments, such as *irresponsible, naïve, or stupid*. Others will likely view this illness as a sign of immorality and label the infected person a promiscuous *slut*, having low character and bad values. This kind of disease will likely be experienced not only as a health crisis but also as an identity crisis. It is easy to understand why many Americans with STDs are left wondering if they are, in fact, *damaged goods*—their bodies and reputations so spoiled that they may never again feel healthy, whole, and valuable.

Every year, versions of this scenario become reality for many of the over 15 million Americans who contract a STD. Chronic STDs are a significant part of this epidemic in the sexually-active population: U.S. rates of genital human papillomavirus infections (HPV—the virus that causes anogenital warts and cervical lesions) are as high as 75 percent (ASHA 2006a), and genital herpes infections (HSV) are estimated at more than 20 percent (ASFIA 2006b). Since 2000, HPV infection has ranked as the most common STD infecting American youth (Weinstock et al. 2004). Medical experts believe that these rates will continue to rise, in part because genital HSV and HPV infections are often asymptomatic and frequently transmitted by individuals who do not know that they are infected. If present, symptoms may be mild, mistaken for other conditions, or seem to be "cured" during long periods of latency. The failure to recognize symptoms of these infections translates into a serious public health problem because both of these viruses are contagious, even in the absence of noticeable symptoms.

A recent study pointed out that, "[w]hile these diseases are of epidemic proportion, we actually see surprising little about them in the media, and we talk about them even less" (Cline 2006:353). In an era of public health campaigns and mandated education targeting HIV/ AIDS, the use of latex condoms is more and more the behavioral norm for "safer" sex. However, both HPV and HSV are transmitted by skin-to-skin contact. So, even when a latex condom is used consistently and correctly, it will provide a barrier for only a portion of the genital skin that will likely come in contact with a partner's skin during sexual intercourse. In addition to the promotion of using latex condoms as the standard for "safer sex," HIV-testing has also been successfully promoted as a sexual responsibility norm. Currently, more than 50 percent of adults have only been tested for HIV and not for any other STDs (ASHA 2006c). Given our medical norm of annual gynecological exams for women, but no comparable exam for men, a significant portion of the sexually-active population is not regularly screened for any STDs.

When individuals do seek sexual health exams, less than one-third of US physicians consistently screen these patients for the full range of sexually transmitted diseases, leaving many patients unaware of their infection status with regard to either HPV or HSV (ASHA 2006c). Some sexual health educators believe that, because these two diseases are understood as nonfatal, there has been less funding for research, education, and prevention efforts. However, genital herpes and HPV infections can have devastating effects if transferred from mother to fetus, and medical researchers have linked certain strains of HPV to cervical and anal cancers.

Odds are, you have not heard of the "HPV vaccine." On the other hand, if you live in the U.S., then you have probably seen or heard one of many ads promoting a "cervical cancer" vaccine sold by Merck as GARDASIL. Originally, this vaccine was called what it actually is: a vaccine to protect against several strains of sexually transmitted human papillomavirus (HPV). When the press began to cover the trials of this HPV vaccine, several conservative organizations protested. The Family Research Council (FRC), for example, was initially concerned that the HPV vaccine equated to a "license" for young people to have premarital sex. Strong objections from such socially-conservative organizations, in addition to focus groups conducted by the CDC, may have informed Merck's marketing campaign of GARDASIL, in which all advertisements, marketing, and health education materials aim to sell this to the American public as a vaccine that protects against cervical cancer. Parry (2007) notes that this is not an easy plan or necessarily a solution to the problem of longstanding negative stigma against STDs: "Promoting an anti-cancer vaccine and, at the same time, making it clear that HPV is a sexually transmitted infection will require deft handling in the wording of policy, education and publicity materials" (90). Many health organizations, including the American Cancer Society, expressed concerns that acceptance of the drug would be influenced by whether the American public perceives the vaccine to be one aimed at reducing the risk of cervical cancer, or as a vaccine designed to prevent a sexually transmitted virus.

So, is there really a "cervical cancer" vaccine? In short, the answer is "No." Merck's vaccine, trademarked as GARDASIL, protects against four HPV types, which together are associated with 70 percent of cervical cancers, but these cancers are relatively rare. The American Cancer Society estimated that, in 2006, approximately 9,710 women were diagnosed with invasive cervical cancer and another 3,700 died from it (2007). In June 2006, the Food and Drug Administration (FDA) licensed GARDASIL, a prophylactic vaccine, that prevents over 95 percent of HPV infections, caused by four types of virus: Together, these are estimated to be responsible for about 70 percent of cervical cancers and 90 percent of genital warts (Temte 2007). This vaccine is not an effective treatment for existing HPV infections (genital warts, cervical cancers or precancerous lesions). It has been tested and approved for use on girls and women from 9 to 26 years of age. Given the expense, limitations, and controversies surrounding this new approach to the prevention of HPV, the ultimate impact of this vaccine remains to be seen. As this new vaccine protects against only four strains of HPV, girls and women who receive the vaccine will need to continue routine gynecological exams and practice safer sexual behaviors, as these individuals will be vulnerable to infection with the dozen or so other strains of this virus. As for the ongoing work on developing an HSV (herpes) vaccine, medical researchers are not sure whether a safe and effective one will be developed. Those who study pediatric infectious diseases have noted that, "Once an efficacious herpes vaccine is available, its effectiveness will depend ultimately on vaccine acceptance by professional organizations, healthcare professionals, and parents" (Rupp et al. 2005, 31).

The development and widespread use of any STD vaccines will not necessarily result in a world that is kinder and gentler to those who become infected. In fact, there is reason to believe that STD-related stigma may negatively affect the public's response to the new vaccine that is being marketed as a "cervical cancer" vaccine. A recent behavioral health article on HPV and cervical cancer emphasized the need for research that explores how the nature of this virus being sexually-transmitted affects the experiences of those who test positive. These findings could help us to better understand how individuals will make decisions about cervical cancer screening (Waller et al. 2004).

The cost of diagnosing and treating all sexually transmitted diseases in the U.S. is about $8 billion per year. HPV and HSV account for a sizeable portion of these costs (ASHA 2006c): HPV infections alone add up to health care expenses of over $2 billion per year (CDC 2006). It is difficult, however, to put a price tag on the variety of personal costs to infected individuals. Individuals experience social and psychological costs of these infections differently, depending upon their sex, socioeconomic status, ethnicity, age, religious upbringing, and other factors. Sex differences are the most obvious: HPV and HSV present more negative consequences for women, in terms of both reproductive health and self-concept. A woman's reproductive health can be greatly compromised by a cervical HPV infection that necessitates the removal of significant amounts of her cervix, the bottom portion of the uterus, which must be thick enough and strong enough to bear the weight of a growing fetus. Should she be able to carry the baby to term, there is the additional risk that, genital infections of both HPV and HSV can pass from mothers to babies during vaginal deliveries.

Although the CDC reports that few women suffer serious reproductive consequences of HPV and HSV infections, the typical infected American woman is likely to experience one of these incurable STDs as a severe stress on her sense of wellbeing. This negative shift can occur even at the receipt of a diagnostic result, which merely indicates the possibility of HPV infection: Zimet (2006, 23) documented "the emotional suffering associated with abnormal Papanicolaou (Pap) test results." In a U.S. society, which supports a double-standard of sexual behavior and, consequently, a sexist magnification of the negative impact of STDs for women, a clinically minor problem (like an abnormal Pap result) can quickly become a cause for major concern.

Most Americans subscribe to a gender ideology in which girls and women are morally and socially demeaned by non-marital sexual encounters, whereas these same behaviors serve to elevate the social statuses of boys and men (Eyre, Davis, and Peacock 2001). Sexual health researchers find that the traits which U.S. society associates with contracting STDs—"indiscriminate promiscuity, pollution, and uncleanness" (Lawless, Kippax, and Crawford 1996, 1371)—are incongruous with cultural definitions of feminine "goodness." In this climate, a woman with a lifelong STD tends to become fearful about how others will view her.

CHRONIC STDS AS TURNING POINTS IN WOMEN'S LIVES

To understand how women view themselves with chronic STDs, I use the theoretical lens of *symbolic interactionism* in which, "Identities are meanings attributed to self, by others and by self. They are developed in interaction as others respond to particular presentations of self" (Kelly 1992, 395). An *interactionist* would say that how we see ourselves and how others see us are interdependent concepts because we construct personal identities through social interactions. Contracting an incurable sexually transmitted disease creates a "turning-point moment" (Strauss 1959) for most American women, in that the illness initiates an "identity dilemma." As Charmaz (1994) found, "Identity dilemmas result from losing valued attributes, physical functions, social roles, and personal pursuits through illness and their corresponding valued identities" (269). In many social contexts and social roles, a person's sexual health status may have little, if any, impact on how they view themselves or how others view them, but STDs present a particular threat to an individual's *sexual self*.

Damaged Goods draws on women's firsthand experiences to explore how social constructions of female sexual morality merge with stereotypes about STDs to threaten women's sexual selves: Individuals' views of themselves as sexual beings that exist in relation to their general views of themselves. My conceptualization of a *sexual self* draws on components of Dowd's (1996) theory of a *secret self*: Privacy allows individuals to have a secret self, which may be a sphere of behavior that is engaged in behind closed doors, out-of-view, and which the actor would prefer to keep

separate from the "public sphere" (249). In this sense, the term "sexual self" signifies a typically private self, shaped by emotions, cognitions, and memories of sexual experiences.

I conceive of the sexual self as encompassing individuals' self-evaluations of their own sexual desirability and how they think of their own imagined and experienced erotic sensuality. Other researchers have posited similar operational definitions of the term *sexual self* (Breakwell and Millward 1997; Cranson and Caron 1998; Sandstrom 1996) to refer to something fundamentally different from a gender identity or a sexual identity. I agree with Breakwell and Millward that, "the structure of the sexual self-concept is significantly influenced by dominant social representations of gender differences and relationships" (1997, 29).

While a few other researchers and theorists have referred to the sexual self-concept, this term's definition has not been agreed on. I posit the components of a sexual self to include the level of sexual experimentation, emotional memories of sexual pleasure (or lack thereof), perception of one's body as desirable or undesirable, and perception of one's sexual body parts as healthy or unhealthy. Research has yet to explore why the sexual self is uniquely susceptible to damage. Applying Goffman's (1963) concept of a "spoiled identity," I propose that STDs, in addition to other traumatic experiences, may create, add to, or maintain a *spoiled sexual self*, resulting in both intrapersonal and interpersonal costs: these traumas include molestation, rape, homophobia, self-loathing brought on by social constructions of attractiveness, and other sexually-related medical conditions (infertility, breast cancer, and impotency). Social interactions that communicate that some physical bodies are less attractive, particular sexual preferences are unacceptable, or certain levels of sexual experience are immoral, can also transmit messages that damage sexual selves. *Damaged Goods* expands on the work of medical sociologists (Charmaz 1994; Sandstrom 1996; Swanson and Chenitz 1993) by examining how these women are transformed during each stage in their illness experiences. At each of the six stages, particular factors create, maintain, challenge, and reshape how they see themselves as sexual beings.

THE ROOTS OF STD STIGMA

Ancient Greeks used the descriptive term "stigmata" to refer to visible marks which signified the bearer as one who was tainted and deserved to be ostracized. Manzo (2004) clarified Goffman's (1963) conceptualization of stigma by looking for the qualities that made social scientists likely to label a condition as "stigmatizing." He determined that STDs fit the criteria of being stigmatizing because of contagiousness and culpability. Manzo highlights a key point of Goffman's earlier work, "that stigma attaches not only to persons but to specific social contexts" (Manzo 2004, 414). Stigma is not simply a discrediting attribute; rather, each stigma is the product of a process of social interactions within a cultural context.

Centuries before the first case of HIV/AIDS, the social stigma and health ramifications of other sexually transmitted diseases scarred the lives of many around the world. The experiences of U.S. women and men today must be seen in historical context. Sexual health services in the U.S. became strongly influenced by moral objectives when, in the late 1800s, male physicians "professionalized" midwifery. The growing preference and respect for scientifically educated male professionals in the field of women's health allowed for sexist moral agendas to shape American medical philosophy and public health services related to STDs. Public opinion and public health campaigns have often targeted sexually active, working-class and minority women as the "vectors and vessels" of sexual disease (Davidson 1994; Luker 1998; Mahood 1990). Scholars have elaborated on the class dynamics of these campaigns. Ehrenreich and English (1973) found that

Victorian-era upper-class women received an abundance of medical care, whereas lower-class women received almost no general health care services. However, the lower-classes, and lower-class women in particular, have been viewed as the transmitters of disease to the wealthier classes.

During the social hygiene movement of the Progressive Era (1890–1913), physicians and women moral reformers combined forces to explicitly shape the moral boundaries of sexual behavior, under the justification of public good/health. However active the women reformers may have been, these boundaries were decidedly sexist. The doctrine of "physical necessity" was deemed to justify, and often excuse, men's forays into promiscuity. As early as 1910, Dock pointed out the bias in how the (then popular) *theory of innate depravity* was applied to "fallen women" and not to their male counterparts, whose sexual escapades were equally, if not more, shameful than those of the women.

Historical documents reveal that, during this period of the early 20th century, physicians had constructed a spectrum of culpability, positing "innocent patients" at one end—those children and married women who had been infected via an adulterous husband—and infected married men and "problem girls" at the other end (Davidson 1994). Not only had these "problem girls" contracted diseases willfully, but they were also the "major vectors of disease" by virtue of their promiscuity and low morals.

This view of women regained momentum in the 1980s when early AIDS research studies viewed women "not as victims of the disease but as risk factors to others," and the public regarded HIV infections in women as "simply the natural consequence of the way they choose to live, the 'wages of sin' "—(Nechas and Foley 1994, 98; 101). A recent overview of findings from qualitative studies of HIV-positive women asserts that women's experiences of HIV-related stigma were intensified because they were female: They had been socialized to believe in gender norms and values that meant that their social relations and moral identity were threatened by others' awareness of their infection status (Sandelowski, Lambe and Barroso 2005). Beyond HIV, studies have examined the gendered nature of American attitudes toward other STDs, looking at the interplay between negative social constructions of STDs and culturally defined gender roles in differentially shaping patients' experiences of diagnoses, symptoms, and treatment (Meyer-Weitz et al. 1998). Eng and Butler (1997) have argued that sexual mores *explicitly* shaped public health policy and are reflected in past and present societal attitudes toward sexual health. Society's focus on assigning moral culpability to illness encouraged policy makers to ignore the social and environmental factors that contributed to disease and reinforced the tendency to reject, ridicule or simply ignore those who suffer from an illness.

A few researchers have charted social histories of the moralization of STDs (Brandt 1987; Davidson 1994; Luker 1998) and illuminated issues of social power and subordination. Others have examined the ways in which public perceptions of health policy and practice have reflected social acceptance of the sexual subordination of women (Lock and Kaufert 1998; Lorber 1993). The social history of sexually transmitted diseases in the United States reflects a tradition of not only assigning moral responsibility to those infected with STDs, but also of differentially assigning moral stigma on the basis of gender, race, and class (Brandt 1987; Luker 1998).

Social stereotypes of sexual immorality and disease are specific to sex, gender, ethnicity, and socioeconomic status. Researchers have found that biased norms of sexual morality have influenced a wide range of sexual health programs: "Current campaigns against STDs which are aimed at women are infused with the same moral judgments found in earlier campaigns" (Leonardo and Chrisler 1992, 1). In addition to inaccurately targeting populations for outreach, biased health research has increased the likelihood that the more complex issues faced by individuals with STDs will

not he addressed. Lock (2000) explained how the targeting of certain populations on the basis of ascribed traits, such as sex and ethnicity, sets the stage for medically ineffective and socially destructive health policies and programs. She cautioned that it becomes easy to overlook true inequalities, like poverty, when we are comfortable blaming individuals' biological traits, such as ethnicity and sex, for their designation as "high-risk" groups for particular diseases.

Thus we need to examine women's experiences of STD diagnostic and treatment interactions within a larger social context of how female sexuality and sexual morality have been constructed in the United States. In line with Mechanic's (1989) conceptualization of illness experiences as "shaped by socio-cultural and social-psychological factors," my research explores women's experiences of chronic STDs within medico-moral interactions that are shaped by race, class, and gender norms of sexual health and behavior.

SEX, GENDER AND STD STIGMA

Feminist scholars have highlighted the resilience and salience of gender: "despite the impact of feminism and deconstruction, gender has not been abolished, but continues to be reinscribed in our identities, desires, and thought" (Thomson and Holland 1997:2). While it is true that gender norms may be influenced by norms of race/ethnicity, sexuality, age, etc., a woman negotiates her sense of self and identity by referring to and measuring herself against the gender norms that have been constructed as most important in her life experiences. Hughes (1945) conceptualized a "master status" as a social identity that is dominant and influences the way in which individuals are viewed. As long as being a woman is one's master status in common contexts (intimate relationships, the gynecologist's office, and motherhood), then one is expected to meet stereotypical expectations of femininity, including sexual behavior norms and sexual morality norms.

Looking back at the late 19th and early 20th centuries, the meaning of "femininity" created categories for women on either side of the sexual morality dichotomy: "God's police" posed in opposition to "damned whores" (Summers 1975). Historically, these labels gave one group of women a sense of duty to keep a critical eye on their *sinful* sisters and to dole out stigmatizing labels when necessary. Current debates about surveillance and sexual health question the value of public health professionals labeling certain groups as "at-risk" (O'Byrne and Holmes 2005). This type of labeling has been linked to promoting sexism, racism, and homophobia, both inside and outside the U.S. Researchers on AIDS in Africa found significant gender differences with regard to stigma: "Popular ideas about STDs suggest little stigma is attached to male infection. Having an STD is almost regarded as a rite of passage into manhood, proof of sexual activity: 'A bull is not a bull without his scars'" (Bassett and Mhloyi 1991, 143). These researchers found that African women experienced greater degrees of stigmatization and ostracism as a result of a HIV infection. Other researchers, looking at the gendered implications of non-HIV sexual transmitted diseases, confirmed that, "women feel particularly shamed and isolated as a result of the infection" (Pitts et al. 1995, 1303). A recent study of adolescents' views of sex found one ideology dominant among young women and young men: "the gender ideology linked with the 'double standard' in which males are morally elevated by multiple sexual encounters, while females are morally demeaned" (Eyre, Davis and Peacock 2001, 13).

Across cultures, sexually transmitted diseases have been connected to promiscuity. The traits our society has traditionally associated with contracting an STD—promiscuity, irresponsibility, uncleanness, immorality, and even naïveté— were incongruous with cultural definitions of being a "good" girl/woman. In this way, the context of gender is especially important for understanding both the social construction of sexual disease in the United States and why contracting a STD, especially an incurable one, can be a severely stigmatizing illness experience for women.

Goffman (1963) discussed stigma as contextual phenomena: "Not all undesirable traits are at issue, but only those which are incongruous with our stereotype of what a given type of individual should be" (3). From a symbolic interactionist perspective, individuals intersubjectively create meanings about STD infection during interactions. Interactions between medical practitioners and lay people have been found to be the conduits through which STD stigma are reinforced (Brandt 1987). Social constructionist, labeling and conflict theories enhance our understanding of how people come to understand different illnesses: individuals and social control agents (medical practitioners), "construct particular acts as deviance and individuals as deviants" via processes that entail the creation of and sharing of meanings (Best 2006). *Damaged Goods* illuminates important facets of stigma in the "moral careers" (Goffman 1959) of female STD patients.

Social prejudices have been found to intensify against individuals, such as those infected with STDs, who were believed to have caused their own stigmatization (Goffman 1963). Tewksbury and McGaughey (1997) applied this concept to the development of HIV-related stigma. They contended that the physiological and social qualities of this disease make it likely for persons living with HIV to experience the three faces of stigma as put forth by Goffman (1963, 4): "Abominations of the body . . . blemishes of individual character . . . tribal stigma." Given the global devastation resulting from HIV/AIDS, the majority of contemporary scholarship on chronic illness, moral identity, and the self has focused on this disease. However, *Damaged Goods* is the first book to focus exclusively on the social-psychological impact of two other incurable STDs. While the physiological impacts of these viral infections differ greatly from HIV,

I argue that genital herpes and HPV infections similarly challenge women's perceptions of themselves with regard to health, morality, and social status.

MEDICAL SOCIOLOGICAL STUDIES OF SEXUAL HEALTH

American sexual health policies and attitudes have always been shaped, in part, by prevailing medical beliefs and practices. In the 1970s, American cultural views of health shifted from a focus on germ theory—that certain microorganisms cause disease—to an emphasis on individual responsibility for behaviors that might cause disease. Epidemiological studies from that period show that behavioral choices, such as smoking and exercise, influence ill health. "No longer would disease be viewed as a random event; it would now be viewed as a failure of individual control, a lack of self-discipline, an intrinsic moral failing" (Brandt 1997, 64). The ways in which both medical and lay people speak about particular diagnoses have often denoted blame and individual responsibility to the sick. When we feel comfortable blaming the sick for their own illnesses—if their own "bad" choices caused their health problems—then the rest of us who are making "good" choices can all feel less at-risk.

Along with scholars who have documented the popularity of blaming individuals for their own poor health, researchers have also examined the role of medical practitioners in the social construction of health and illness. Medical practitioners, in addition to controlling health information and services, also have the capacity to serve as social control agents, in that they have implicit authority to assign moral statuses to different illnesses. Early work on hospital staff documented the prevalence of "moral evaluations" of patients (Roth 1972). Foucault (1978) argued that social control in the field of medicine had become more professionalized and oriented to the surveillance of deviant behavior. Social responses to STDs illustrate how medico-moral discourses have served to construct and regulate sexuality (Foucault 1978, Mort 1987, Davenport-Hines 1991, Davidson 1994).

Pryce (1998) pointed to a critical gap—the "missing" sociology of sexual disease—and asserted that this application of sociology should focus on the social construction of the body as central in the medical and social understandings of STDs. Sociological research on sexual morality and health has primarily addressed HIV/AIDS (Fernando 1993; Matthews 1988; Nechas and Foley 1994; Plumridge and Chetwynd 1998; Ray 1989). The overwhelming focus of social scientific studies of STDs, other than HIV, has been on evaluating the effectiveness of education/prevention strategies, environmental determinants, and understanding risk assessment and risk-taking behaviors (Beadnell et al. 2006; Rogers 1999; Shrier et al. 1999; Thomas et al. 1999).

Most research on morality in the socio-medical politics of STDs has addressed the issue from a national level. Few studies examine micro-level interactions in sexual health services, especially from patients' perspectives. Such studies can illuminate issues that occur at the interface between medical practitioners and patients. As such, qualitative studies have not fully examined affected individuals' "illness behaviors," which Mechanic (1982) defines as "the manner[s] in which persons monitor their bodies, define and interpret their symptoms, take remedial actions, and utilize the health-care system" (1). A more recent study focused on how the stigma of sexually transmitted diseases may affect one particular illness behavior—that of seeking treatment for STD infections. Lichtenstein (2003) found that African-Americans' willingness to access sexual health treatment at public health facilities was directly and indirectly impacted by STD-related stigma: specifically, religious ideation, privacy fears, racial attitudes, and the fear of being "scarlet lettered" proved to impact individuals' willingness to seek medical treatment.

The practitioner-patient interactions that comprise STD diagnoses differ from other chronic illness in that there are explicit and implicit threats of negative health *and* negative moral consequences. A study on media coverage of herpes in the early 1980s found that the stories stressed "a psychological and social deadliness"—evidence that the detrimental effects of herpes diagnoses extended beyond the physical (Signorielli 1993, 60). Medical research determined "the most common and usually the most devastating problem of having genital herpes is its psychological impact" (Bettoli 1982, 925). However, most studies of individuals infected with herpes have neglected to address the identity impacts of the physical, moral, and social consequences of receiving a diagnosis (Reiser 1986; Rosenthal et al. 1995; Swanson and Chenitz 1993). Two articles (Melville et al. 2003; Breitkopf 2004) confirmed the presence and ramifications of stigma experienced by individuals living with genital herpes. The later concluded that the stigma experienced by those living with herpes will lessen as we see more media portrayals of these individuals as normal and the infection as treatable. Commercials for *Valtrex*, a popular antiviral medication, have portrayed infected individuals as active (riding mountain bikes) and happily involved in intimate relationships (embracing a significant other while professing their understanding that even correct and consistent use of this medication does not guarantee protection for an uninfected partner).

With regard to HPV, most studies of affected individuals focus on risk evaluation/risk-taking behavior (Ford and Moscicki 1995). One clinical study (Keller et al. 1995) advised practitioners to be aware of the psychosocial aspects of HPV diagnoses, but did not examine why these negative implications exist or how they might affect patients in different ways. While this study noted the "potentially traumatic nature of HPV infection" (Keller et al. 1995, 356), my study is the first to fully analyze the social-psychological impacts of having HPV. HPV-related stigma may create

feelings of embarrassment and fear of rejection, which could lead to infected individuals choosing not to disclose their HPV-positive status to sexual partners (Keller et al. 2000). This dangerous public health consequence of STD stigma emphasizes the urgency for a more complete understanding of how being diagnosed with a chronic sexually transmitted disease may affect the self-concepts and decision-making processes of infected individuals.

For the past two decades, interactionist medical sociologists have studied first-hand accounts of illness experiences. Analyses of chronic illness, in particular, have led to the creations of theories about the social and psychological consequences for those affected. Scholars have examined the challenges posed by chronic illness to self and identity (e.g. Charmaz 1994; Frank 1991; Sandstrom 1996). Medical sociologists have specifically explored the impact of stigma by focusing on how chronically ill individuals manage both identity dilemmas and interpersonal relationships (Conrad and Schneider 1980; Tewksbury and McGaughey 1997; Weitz 1991).

Interactionist studies of chronic illness have begun to explore sexual-self concepts. Sandstrom (1996) sought to fill an important gap in the literature on the self in chronic illness by exploring how HIV/AIDS, "affects the sexuality and sexual identity work of diagnosed individuals" by examining men's "sexual self-images" (242). Other research on HIV/AIDS has looked at how the diagnosis serves to redefine not only affected individuals' health statuses, but also their sexual statuses (Sandstrom 1990; Weitz 1991). These scholars have documented redefinitions of self and status; however, none of these researchers have addressed infections, like genital herpes and genital HPV, which are lifelong but manageable.

Genital HPV and herpes infections, as sexually stigmatizing chronic illnesses, pose specific challenges to infected women's selves and identities. Pioneers in researching the connection between self-conception and sexual health, Swanson and Chenitz (1993) used qualitative methods to examine the relationship between herpes infections and a "valued" self, which began analysis at the point of diagnosis. While these researchers theorized a three-stage model of regaining a valued sense of self after herpes diagnoses, their findings indicate a more complex process that begins well before the point of contracting an STD and is shaped by social dynamics of gender, race, class, sexuality, etc. In *Damaged Goods*, I detail six stages of how chronic STDs transform women's sexual selves and include stages prior to diagnosis.

ON METHODOLOGY: RESEARCHING AN INVISIBLE POPULATION

Motivated by personal experience, I entered this research setting as a "complete member" (Adler and Adler 1987). At age 20, I was diagnosed with a cervical HPV infection. In fact, the prose "snapshot" that began this chapter is actually the beginning of my own story. Self-education helped me to manage the initial stress of diagnosis and treatment. Then, volunteer involvement with sexual health education and outreach became the foundation for my research and provided me with insights and legitimacy to connect with others facing STD diagnoses.

As a professional sexual health educator in the late 1990s, I began to question how individuals infected with chronic STDs managed the intrapersonal and interpersonal challenges. To more fully understand the social and psychological impact of chronic STDs on women, I aimed to uncover how these women created, maintained, and transformed the meanings of their STD illness experiences. My goal was to collect data that could provide an empirical foundation from which to test the prevailing medical, sociological, and lay assumptions about women living with chronic STDs.

Women with STDs are a hidden population, their identities protected by medical confidentiality. Aware of the negative social attitudes toward infected women, most keep their sexual health statuses a secret. In this sense, their stigmatized condition is *discreditable* (Goffman 1963), and the women can *pass* as sexually healthy in most social contexts. With this norm of secrecy, women with non-HIV STDs are also a fragmented population, unlikely to engage in support groups or identity politics for fear of outing themselves.

Having conducted a survey study that found women strongly preferred maintaining the confidentiality of their sexual health statuses, I determined that one-on-one interviews were the best method of data collection. As this topic is sensitive and laden with sociocultural "baggage," talking with these women individually created an intimate research space in which I had the best chance for high construct validity. In this manner, I was able to develop what Blumer (1973, 798) described as, "a close, flexible and reflective examination" of contemporary social facts about women with STDs. The data I collected can be conceptualized both as *sexual stories* (Plummer 1995) and as *illness narratives* (Frank 1993), in that each woman spoke about intimate, sexual, and sensual aspects of her life; while she also described her encounters with the medical profession as a patient being treated for one or more STDs.

As with many studies of individuals living with HIV/AIDS (Cranson and Caron 1998; Grove, Kelly, and Liu 1997; Sandstrom 1996), I employed a mixture of convenience and snowball sampling (Biernacki and Waldork 1981) because of the research topic's sensitive nature. In keeping with the principles of grounded theory, I sampled for theory construction, rather than for representativeness (Charmaz 1995). In all, I interviewed forty-three women who had been diagnosed with genital herpes and/or HPV infections for this study. My final sample size resulted from ethical restrictions on subject recruitment. Given doctor-patient confidentiality, there was no way for me to obtain a list of the women who met the sampling criteria and then engage in any form of random or purposive sampling. In sum, due to the sensitive topic, medical policies, and research ethics, I was limited in my ability to create a more diverse sample.

The women who participated in my study ranged in age from 19 to 56 years old at the time of their interviews. In terms of ethnicity, thirty-eight identified as European American (including Jewish, Greek, and Persian ethnicities), three as Latinas, one as African-American, and one as Native-American. Socioeconomically, they ranged from upper-class to working class, with the majority identifying as lower-middle, middle, or upper-middle class. The participants represented a variety of religious upbringings and current practices: Buddhists, Jews, Muslims, Pagans, and Christians (Catholics, Protestants, and Southern Baptists). Catholics were the largest group, but fourteen women had been raised with no religion, and nineteen reported being currently nonreligious. With regard to sexual identity, the majority (37) identified as heterosexual, five identified as bisexual, and one identified as a lesbian.

In-depth, semi-structured interviews allowed me the flexibility in the data gathering process to uncover what having a chronic STD meant to this sample of women. Constant comparative analysis (Glaser and Strauss 1967; Glaser 1978) provided the guidelines by which I was able to ferret out the shared meanings of STD stereotypes, symptoms, diagnoses, and treatments from the subjective point of view of those living with these infections and accompanying social stigma. Utilizing a symbolic interactionist approach to guide my data collection and analysis, I tested emerging hypotheses about the empirical realities of women with STDs, via a thorough and continuous examination of their world (Blamer 1969).

While their identities are protected by pseudonyms in this work, the details of their stories are exactly as they told them to me. No story is identical to another, but many shared similar motivations for participation in this research: (1) To help others by giving voice to the real struggles of millions of women who live with these infections, and (2) To personally benefit from managing their STD stigma, via cathartic disclosure, relief from the burden of secrecy (Adler and Adler 2006). My goal, in sharing their stories, via sociological analysis, is to frame their individual struggles within a larger, social context and highlight opportunities for improvement in sexual health education and medical services for women and their sexual partners.

SIX STAGES OF SEXUAL SELF-TRANSFORMATION

Damaged Goods draws on in-depth interviews with women who have been diagnosed with genital HSV and/or HPV infections. Highlighting the voices of these women, I write about the transformations of their *sexual selves*—how they see themselves as sexual beings—and how they understood and made choices about sexual health issues. I document the physical, moral, and social consequences of living with these diseases, by analyzing their experiences within a six-stage framework. I use symbolic interactionist, social psychological, and feminist theories to explore the ways in which these women's sexual-selves are transformed throughout their STD illness experiences.

The women I interviewed came from a variety of backgrounds, but common threads emerged, as illustrated by their quotes and anecdotes, that conveyed the interplay between socio-demographic factors, cultural constructions of health, gender, and sexual morality, and structural norms of the American medical system.

I created a model that illuminates stages in the "moral careers" (Goffman 1959) of STD patients and documents the event series that ultimately shape changes in patients' sexual selves and social relationships. This theoretical model represents "ideal types" in the sense that not all women went through each stage in the same manner. In stage one, *Sexual Invincibility*, early portions of women's socio-sexual histories create and maintain beliefs in a myth of STD immunity. In stage two, *STD Anxiety*, women's experiences of initial symptoms or practitioners' suggestions of possible infection replace feelings of invincibility with anxiety. In stage three, *Immoral Patient*, they experience practitioners' deliveries of STD diagnoses as imparting health, moral, and social stigma. In stage four, *Damaged Goods*, women employ individual stigma management strategies within interpersonal relationships. In stage five, *Sexual Healing*, they face the interpersonal, physical, emotional, and financial challenges of treatments. Finally in stage six, *Reintegration*, many women reconcile the meanings of their illness experiences by integrating risk awareness and desire for intimacy within revised sexual selves.

Damaged Goods expands discussions of moral identity and sexuality in chronic illness by examining genital herpes and HPV from social-psychological and interactionist perspectives. Highlighting the role of social power, it focuses on how their illness experiences serve to create "turning-point moments" (Strauss 1959).

References

Adler, Patricia A. and Peter Adler. 1987. *Membership Roles in Field Research*. Newbury Park, CA: Sage.

Adler, Patricia A. and Peter Adler. 2006. *Constructions of Deviance: Social Power, Context, and Interaction (Fifth Edition)*. Belmont, CA: Thomson Wadsworth.

American Social Health Association Server. 2006a. "Quick Facts about HPV." *National HPV and Cervical Cancer Resource Center*: www.ashastd.org/hpv/hpvre/facti.html.

American Social Health Association Server. 2006b. "Quick Facts about Herpes." *National Herpes Resource Center*: www.ashastd.org/herpes/hrc/info1.html.

American Social Health Association Server. 2006c. "Fact Sheet on HPV." *National HPV Cervical Cancer Resource Center*: http://www.ashastd.org/pds/HPS_factsheet.pdf.

Bassett Mary. T. and M. Mhloyi. 1991. "Women and AIDS in Zimbabwe: The making of an epidemic." *International Journal of Health Services*, 21, 1:143–56.

Beadnell, Blair, Baker, Sharon A., Morrison, Diane M., Huang, Bu, Stielstra, Sorrel, and Susan Stoner. 2006. "Change Trajectories in Women's STD/HIV Risk Behaviors Following Intervention." *Preventive Science*, 7:321–331.

Best, Joel. 2006. "Deviance: The Constructionist Stance." In Patricia A. Adler and Peter Adler (eds.) *Constructions of Deviance: Social Power, Context, and Interactions*, pp. 92–95. Belmont, CA: Thomson/Wadsworth.

Bettoli, E.J. 1982. "Herpes: facts and fallacies." *American Journal of Nursing*: 924–29.

Biernacki, Patrick, and Dan Waldorf. 1981. "Snowball Sampling." *Sociological Research Methods*, 10:141–63.

Blumer, Herbert, 1973. "A Note on Symbolic Interactionism." *American Sociological Review*, 38, 6:797–98.

Brandt, Allan M. 1987. *No magic bullet: A social history of venereal disease in the United States since 1880*. New York: Oxford University Press.

_____. 1997. "Behavior, Disease, and Health in the Twentieth Century United States: The Moral Valence of Individual Risk." In A. Brandt and Paul Rozin (eds.) *Morality and Health*, pp. 53–77. New York: Routledge.

Breakwell, Glynis M. and Lynne J. Millward. 1997. "Sexual self-concept and sexual risk-taking." *Journal of Adolescence*, 20:29–41.

Breitkopf, Carmen Radecki. 2004. "The Theoretical Basis of Stigma as Applied to Genital Herpes. *HERPES*, 11, 1:4–7.

Centers for Disease Control and Prevention (CDC), Division of Sexually Transmitted Disease Prevention. 2006. "HPV Vaccine: Questions and Answers." August 2006: accessed online May 31, 2007. http://www.cdc.gov/std/hpv/STDFact-HPV-vaccine. html.

Charmaz, Kathy. 1994. "Identity Dilemmas in Chronically Ill Men." *Sociological Quarterly*, 35:269–88.

_____. 1995. "Learning Grounded Theory". In Jonathon Smith, Rom Harré, and Luk Van Langenhove (eds.) *Rethinking Methods in Psychology*, pp. 27–49. London: Sage Publications.

Cline, J. Steven. 2006. "Sexually Transmitted Diseases: Will this Problem Ever Go Away?" *North Carolina Medical Journal*. 67, 5:353–58.

Conrad, Peter, and Joseph W. Schneider. 1980. *Deviance and Medicalization: From Badness to Sickness*. St. Louis, MO: The C.V. Mosby Company.

Cranson, Denis A. and Sandra L. Caron. 1998. "An Investigation of the Effects of HIV on the Sex Lives of Infected Individuals." *AIDS Education and Prevention*, 10, 6:506–22.

Davenport-Hines, R. 1991. *Sex, Death and Punishment: Attitudes to Sex and Sexuality in Britain since the Renaissance.* London: W. Heinemann/Reed Books.

Davidson, Roger. 1994. "Venereal Disease, Sexual Morality, and Public Health in Interwar Scotland." *Journal of the History of Sexuality,* 5, 2:267–94.

Dock, Lavinia. 1910. *Hygiene and Morality: A Manual for Nurses and Others, Giving an Outline of the Medical, Social and Legal Aspects of the Venereal Diseases.* New York: G.P. Putnam's Sons.

Dowd, James J. 1996. "An Act Made Perfect in Habit: The Self in the Post-modern Age." *Current Perspectives in Social Theory,* 16:237–63.

Ehrenreich, Barbara and Deirdre English. 1973. *Complaints and Disorders: The sexual politics of sickness.* Old Westbury, NY: Feminist Press.

Eng, Thomas and William Butler. 1997. *The Hidden Epidemic: Confronting Sexually Transmitted Diseases.* Washington, DC: National Academy Press.

Eyre, S.L., Davis, E. W., & Peacock, B. 2001. "Moral Argumentation in Adolescents' Commentaries About Sex." *Culture, Health, and Sexuality,* 3, 1:1–17.

Fernando, M. Daniel. 1993. *AIDS and Intravenous Drug Use: the Influence of Morality, Politics, Social Science, and Race in the Making of a Tragedy.* London: Praeger.

Ford, Carol A. and Anna-Barbara Moscicki. 1995. "Control of Sexually Transmitted Diseases in Adolescents: The Clinician's Role." *Advances in Pediatric Infectious Diseases,* 10:263–305.

Foucault, Michael. 1978. *The History of Sexuality,* volume 1. New York: Pantheon.

Frank, Arthur W. 1991. *At the Will of the Body.* Boston, MA: Houghton Mifflin Company.

———. 1993. "The Rhetoric of Self-change: Illness Experience as Narrative," *The Sociological Quarterly* 34, 1:39–52.

Glaser, Barney G. 1978. *Theoretical sensitivity.* Mill Valley, CA: Sociological Press.

Glaser, Barney G., and Anselm L. Strauss. 1967. *The Discovery of Grounded Theory: Strategies for Qualitative Research,* Chicago: Aldine.

Goffman, Erving. 1959. "The Moral Career of the Mental Patient." *Psychiatry,* 22, 2: 23–42.

———. 1963. *Stigma: Notes on the Management of Spoiled Identity.* Englewood Cliffs, NJ: Prentice Hall.

Grove, Kathleen A., Donald P. Kelly, and Judith Liu. 1997. "But Nice Girls Don't Get It: Women, Symbolic Capital, and the Social Construction of AIDS." *Journal of Contemporary Ethnography,* 26, 3: 317–37.

Hughes, Everett. 1945. "Dilemmas and Contradictions of Status." *American Journal of Sociology,* March: 353–59.

Keller, Mary L., Mims, L. Fern, and Judith J. Egan. 1995. "Genital Human Papillomavirus Infection: Common but Not Trivial." *Health Care for Women International,* 16:351–64.

Keller, Mary L., von Sadovszky, V., Pankratz, B., and J. Hermsen. 2000. "Self-disclosure of HPV infection to sexual partners." *Western Journal of Nursing Research,* 22:285–96.

Kelly, Michael. 1992. "Self, identity and radical surgery." *Sociology of Health & Illness,* 14, 3:390–415.

Lawless, Sonia, Susan Kippax, and June Crawford. 1996. "Dirty, Diseased and Undeserving: the Positioning of HIV Positive Women." *Social Science and Medicine,* 43, 9:1371–77.

Leonardo, Cecilia and Joan C. Chrisler. 1992. "Women and Sexually Transmitted Diseases." *Women & Health,* 18, 4:1–15.

Lichtenstein, Bronwen. 2003. "Stigma as a barrier to treatment of sexually transmitted infections in the American deep south: issues of race, gender and poverty." *Social Science & Medicine,* 57:2435–2445.

Lock, Margaret and P. Kaufert. 1998. *Pragmatic Women and Body Politics.* Cambridge: Cambridge University Press.

Lock, Margaret. 2000. "Accounting for Disease and Distress: Morals of the Normal and Abnormal." In Albrecht, Fitzpatrick, and Scrimshaw (eds.) *Handbook of Social Studies in Health and Medicine,* pp. 259–76. London: Sage Publications.

Lorber, Judith. 1993. "Believing is Seeing: Biology as Ideology." *Gender and Society,* 7, 4:568–81.

Luker, Kristin. 1998. "Sex, Social Hygiene, and the State: The Double-Edged Sword of Social Reform." *Theory and Society,* 27, 5:601–34.

Mahood, Linda. 1990. "The Magdalene's Friend: Prostitution and Social Control in Glasgow, 1869–90." *Women's Studies International Forum,* 13, 1/2:49–61.

Manzo, John F. 2004. "On the Sociology and Social Organization of Stigma: Some Ethnomethodological Insights." *Human Studies,* 27:401–16.

Matthews, Eric. 1988. "AIDS and Sexual Morality." *Bioethics,* 2, 2:118–28.

Mechanic, David (ed.). 1982. *Symptoms, Illness Behavior, and Help-Seeking.* New York: Prodist.

———. 1989. *Painful Choices: Research and Essays on Health Care.* New Brunswick, NJ: Transaction Publishers.

Melville, J., Sniffen, S., Crosby, R., Salazar, L., Whittington, W., Dithmer-Schreck, D., DiClemente, R., and

A. Wald. 2003. "Psychosocial impact of serological diagnosis of herpes simplex virus type 2: a qualitative assessment." *Sexually Transmitted Infections*, 79:280–85.

Meyer-Weitz, A., Reddy, P., Weijts, W., van den Borne, B., and G. Kok. 1998. "The socio-cultural contexts of sexually transmitted diseases in South Africa: implications for health education programmes." *AIDS Care*, 10, 1:539–55.

Mort, F. 1987. *Dangerous Sexualities: Medico-Moral Politics in England since 1830*. London: Routledge & Kegan Paul.

Nechas, Eileen and Denise Foley. 1994. *Unequal Treatment: What You Don't Know About How Women Are Mistreated by the Medical Community*. New York: Simon & Schuster.

O'Bryne, Patrick and Dave Holmes. 2005. "Re-Evaluating Current Public Health Policy: Alternative Public Health Nursing Approaches to Sexually Transmitted Infection Testing for Teens and Males who Have Sex with Males." *Public Health Nursing* 22, 6:523–28.

Parry, J. 2007. Vaccinating against cervical cancer. *Bulletin of the World Health Organization*, 85, 89–90.

Pitts, Marian, Margaret Bowman and John McMaster. 1995. "Reactions to Repeated STD Infections: Psychosocial Aspects and Gender Issues in Zimbabwe." *Social Science and Medicine*, 40, 9:1299–1304.

Plummer, Ken. 1995. *Telling Sexual Stories: Power, change, and social worlds*. London: Routledge.

Plumridge, E.W., and S.J. Chetwynd. 1998. "The Moral Universe of Injecting Drug Users in the Era of AIDS: Sharing Injecting Equipment and the Protection of Moral Standing." *AIDS Care,* 10: 6:723–33.

Pyrce, Anthony. 1998. "Theorizing the Pox: A Missing Sociology of VD." Presented to the *International Sociological Association*.

Ray, Laurence J. 1989. "AIDS as a Moral Metaphor. An Analysis of the Politics of the Third Epidemic." *Archives Europeennes de Sociologie*, 30, 2:243–73.

Reiser, Christa. 1986. "Herpes: A Physical and Moral Dilemma." *College Student Journal*, 20, 3:260–269.

Rogers, Susan Matthews. 1999. "Sexual Behavior and Risk of Sexually Transmitted Diseases: Do Community Characteristics Moderate the Relationship between Individual Behaviors and STD Risk?" *Dissertation Abstracts International*, A: *The Humanities and Social Sciences*, 60, 4, Oct, 1341-A.

Roth, Julius A. 1972. "Some Contingencies of the Moral Evaluation and Control of Clientele: The Case of Hospital Emergency Staff." *American Journal of Sociology*, 77, 5:839–56.

Rosenthal, Susan L., Frank M. Biro, Sheila S. Cohen, Paul A. Succop, and Lawrence R. Stanberry. 1995. "Strategies for Coping with Sexually Transmitted Diseases by Adolescent Females." *Adolescence*, 30, 119:655–66.

Rupp, R., Rosenthal, S., and L. Stanberry. 2005. "Pediatrics and herpes simplex virus vaccines." *Seminars in Pediatric Infectious Diseases*, 16, 1:31–37.

Sandelowski, Margarete, Lambe, Camille, and Julie Barroso. 2004. "Stigma in HIV-Positive Women." *Journal of Nursing Scholarship*, 36, 2:122–128.

Sandstrom, Kent L. 1990. "Confronting Deadly Disease: The Drama of Identity Construction among Gay Men with AIDS." *Journal of Contemporary Ethnography*, 19, 3:271–94.

_____. 1996. "Redefining Sex and Intimacy: The Sexual Self-Images, Outlooks, and Relationships of Gay Men Living with HIV/AIDS." *Symbolic Interaction* 19:241–62.

Shrier, Lydia, A., Elizabeth Goodman, and S. Jean Emans. 1999. "Partner Condom Use among Adolescent Girls with Sexually Transmitted Diseases." *Journal of Adolescent Health*, 1999, 24, 5:357–61.

Signorielli, Nancy. 1993. *Mass Media Images and the Impact on Health: A Sourcebook*. Wesport, CT: Greenwood Press.

Strauss, Anselm L. 1959. *Mirrors and Masks*. Mill Valley, CA: Sociology Press.

Swanson, Janice M., and W. Carole Chenitz. 1993. "Regaining a Valued Self: The Process of Adaptation to Living with Genital Herpes." *Qualitative Health Research*, 3, 3:270–97.

Summers, Ann. 1975. *Damned Whores and God's Police: the Colonization of Women in Australia*. Melbourne, Australia: Penguin Books.

Temte, Jonathan L. 2007. "HPV Vaccine: A Cornerstone of Female Health." *American Family Physician*, 75, 1:28–30.

Tewksbury, Richard, and Deanna McGaughey. 1997. "Stigmatization of Persons with HIV Disease: Perceptions, Management and Consequences of AIDS." *Sociological Spectrum*, 17:49–70.

Thomas, James C., Michele Clark, Jadis Robinson, Martha Monnett, Peter H. Kilmarx, and Thomas A. Peterman. 1999. "The Social Ecology of Syphilis." *Social Science & Medicine*, 48, 8:1081–94.

Thomson, Rachel and Holland, Janet. 1994. "Young Women and Safer (Hetero) Sex: Context, Constraints and Strategies", in Sue Wilkinson and Celia Kitzinger (eds.) *Women and Health: Feminist Perspectives*, pp. 13–32. London: Taylor & Francis.

Waller, Jo, McCaffery, Kirsten, Forrest, Sue, and Jane Wardle, 2004. "Human Papillomavirus and Cervical Cancer: Issues for Biobehavioral and Psychosocial Research." *Annals of Behavior Medicine*, 27, 1:68–79.

Weinstock, H., Berman, S., and W. Cates, Jr. 2004. "Sexually Transmitted Diseases among American Youth:

Incidence and Prevalence Estimates, 2000." *Perspectives on Sexual and Reproductive Health*, 36, 1:6–10.

Weitz, Rose. 1991. *Life with AIDS*. New Brunswick. NJ: Rutgers University Press.

Zimet GD. 2006. "Understanding and overcoming barriers to human Papillomavirus vaccine acceptance." *Current Opinion in Obstetric Gynecology*. 18:1:S23–28.

CHAPTER 39

Depression and Sexual Functioning in Minority Women

Current Status and Future Directions

Roseanne D. Dobkin

Sandra R. Leiblum

Raymond C. Rosen

Matthew Menza

Humberto Marin

Depression is a common psychological disorder than can affect many aspects of life, including sexuality. Depressed individuals tend to have lower levels of sexual desire. If they turn to anti-depressant medication as treatment, these formerly depressed patients may start to feel much better, but they may well experience some sort of sexual dysfunction due to the medication. However, many people report that the relief from the antidepressants is worth whatever sexual price they have to pay. This complex sexological Catch-22 has been primarily studied in those from the mainstream United States culture.

From "Depression and Sexual Functioning in Minority Women: Current Status and Future Directions" by R. D. Dobkin, S. R. Leiblum, R. C. Rosen, M. Menza, and H. Marin. 2006. *Journal of Sex & Marital Therapy 32*: 23–36. Reprinted by permission of the publisher (Taylor & Francis, http://www.informaworld.com).

Research has indicated that African-Americans, Asian-Americans, and Hispanics differ significantly from each other and from European-Americans with regard to sexual behavior and attitudes. These differences are then reflected in terms of the impact of various contextual variables on sexual behavior. Not only are there direct effects of culture, there are sometimes interactions as well. The following article by Dobkin, Leiblum, Rosen, Menza, and Marin examines the various ways in which the links between depression and sexuality may differ as a function of culture.

This is clearly an issue of interest to therapists and clients, but what about the typical student who does not have to deal with issues of depression? Whether you know it or not, you have friends or relatives who are depressed, or who are on antidepressant medication. In addition, it is estimated that 16% of people will eventually experience depression (Strine et al., 2008). Many of those people are unaware of the impact that depression or treatment for depression has on their sexual functioning. After reading this article, you will be in a better position to understand some of the complex psychological, medical, and cultural dynamics related to depression and sexuality that you or your loved ones may experience at some point in your lives.

Sexual dysfunction and depression often co-occur; both have a negative impact on relationship satisfaction and quality of life (Heiman, 2002; Laumann, Paik, & Rosen, 1999). There is a greater prevalence of both depression (Altshuler, 2002) and sexual difficulties (Heiman, 2002) in women, and unfortunately, many of the medications used to treat depression further compromise sexual desire, arousal, and orgasm. In fact, lower rates of medication adherence may occur as a result of unwanted sexual side effects (Rosenberg, Bleiberg, Koscis, & Gross, 2003; Zajecka, 2000). These issues may be particularly salient for specific groups of minority women (e.g., African-American, Hispanic, Asian-American), yet this area of research has been relatively unexamined.

OVERVIEW

Although there is a considerable body of research on both depression and sexuality, there has been little empirical investigation focusing on the prevalence of sexual problems in depressed African-American, Hispanic, or Asian-American women. It is known, for example, that women are 2 to 3 times more likely than men to experience a depressive episode, with lifetime prevalence rates estimated to be as high as 21% (Altshuler, 2002). However, it is not known to what extent ethnicity and culture affects these rates. It is also recognized that minority status frequently is associated with impoverished living conditions and reduced access to healthcare, which pose additional risk factors for both depression and sexual dysfunction.

In fact, despite the increasing numbers of non-Caucasians in the United States, the overwhelming majority of research into both depression and sexuality has been conducted predominantly with European-American (White) samples (Cain et al., 2003; Miranda et al., 2003). Less than 1% of the depressed patients included in the American Psychological Association's treatment guidelines for depression were classified as African-American and none were Hispanic (U.S. Department of Health and Human Services, 2001). Moreover, two major peer-reviewed sexual research articles surveying all published papers between 1971 and 1995 found that ethnicity was assessed in only 26.4% of the studies and analyzed as a variable 7.3% of the time (Wiederman, Maynard, & Fretz, 1996).

In general, African-Americans were more than twice as likely to be included as Hispanics or Asian-Americans. Although there is greater awareness of ethnicity as an independent variable in recent publications, the majority of studies continue to report data on European-American (White) samples. Thus, the assessment and treatment of sexual dysfunction in depressed African-American, Hispanic, and Asian-American women (three growing subgroups of minority females) is an area that warrants attention.

PREVALENCE OF FEMALE SEXUAL DYSFUNCTION

Female sexual dysfunction is prevalent, with estimates ranging from 25% to 63% in community samples (Heiman, 2002). Differences in prevalence rates can be attributed to discrepancies in sampling and varying definitions of sexual distress (dysfunction, problems, difficulty, reaction to life stress). However, even when conservative definitions (problem + distress) are used (e.g., Bancroft, Loftus, & Long, 2003), prevalence rates still typically exceed 25%.

For example, the National Health and Social Life Survey (Laumann et al., 1999) assessed 1,749 women between the ages of 18 and 59. In this sample, approximately one-third of women reported low sexual interest, whereas one-fourth noted orgasm difficulties. An additional 20% had problems with lubrication, and 20% stated that sexual activity was not enjoyable. In a review of population-based studies, Simons and Carey (2001) echoed the above findings, noting that approximately 5–40% of women sampled experienced impaired orgasm or hypoactive sexual desire, whereas 6–21% of women endorsed arousal problems. Anxiety during sexual activity (38.1%), lack of enjoyment (16.3%) and orgasm (15.4%) and arousal (13.6%) difficulties also were found in a study of healthy women in an out-patient gynecological clinic (Rosen, Taylor, Leiblum, & Bachman, 1993).

Potential reasons for the discrepancy in reporting rates include differences in definitions of sexual problems or dysfunction, use of different questionnaires or survey instruments from one study to another, variations in the age or ethnic composition of the samples, and other sources of variability between studies (Rosen & Laumann, 2003). Overall, these studies show that sexual problems frequently are reported by women and that lack of interest or desire is consistently among the most common problems noted.

Although little data exists regarding prevalence rates of sexual dysfunction among specific groups of minority women, limited information suggests that sexual concerns are common for women from all ethnic backgrounds. Specifically, Laumann et al. (1999) found that African-American women reported a higher incidence of hypoactive sexual desire and less sexual pain compared with Caucasian women, whereas Hispanic women reported the fewest sexual complaints (which may indicate a reluctance to acknowledge sexual concerns rather than the absence of difficulties). Asian-American women were not represented in this sample.

The Study of Women Across the Nation (SWAN) was the first large multisite longitudinal study to explore sexual functioning, attitudes, and practices among 3,262 community based ethnically diverse mid-life women as they transitioned through menopause (Cain et al., 2003). In this sample, socioeconomic status and demographic characteristics were controlled for in all analyses. Results from the baseline cohort indicated that Chinese and Japanese women reported lower levels of sexual desire than Caucasian, Hispanic, and African-American women. Caucasian women reported fewer problems with sexual arousal and less sexual pain than women in all other ethnic groups. African-American women reported engaging in sexual activity more frequently than Caucasian women, who reported more activity than Japanese women. Of interest, no ethnic differences were observed in emotional satisfaction or physical pleasure derived from sexual encounters. With the exception of pain during intercourse, all results were independent of menopausal status.

Moreover, Kameya (2001) noted that the incidence of female sexual desire disorders is considerably lower in Japan than in other countries because Japanese women do not typically view low sexual desire as a problem and thus are not distressed about it. Additional prevalence data regarding ethnicity and sexual functioning is needed before meaningful comparisons can be made both between and within various ethnic groups.

Factors such as age, education, socioeconomic status, and emotional distress have been linked to reports of impaired sexual functioning. Higher education and increasing age have been associated with fewer sexual problems and high levels of stress, negative emotions and economic and social declines have been linked with increasing rates of sexual dysfunction for women (Laumann et al., 1999). For example, women experiencing financial difficulties were more likely to report impaired sexual desire and arousal, as well as less emotional and physical satisfaction from sex, than more financially secure women. Lower-income women also were considered to be at the greatest risk for all types of sexual difficulties (Cain et al., 2003). These risk factors may be highly prevalent in minority populations.

THE ASSOCIATION BETWEEN DEPRESSION AND SEXUAL FUNCTION

Depression has been predicted to become the second most debilitating condition worldwide by 2020 (Murray & Lopez, 1997), with similar prevalence rates (2–18%) reported for those of Caucasian, Hispanic, and African-American descent (U.S. Department of Health and Human Services, 2001; Vega et al., 1998). Sexual dysfunction is a common correlate of major depression (Baldwin, 2001), and the antidepressants commonly used to treat depression often further impair sexual function (Clayton et al., 2002). For example, individuals with major depression frequently suffer from low sexual desire, which may be exacerbated by antidepressant treatment. Although the direction of the relationship between depression and sexual dysfunction often is unclear, improvement in one of these areas often is associated with improvement in the other.

General Background

Women with mood disorders have significantly lower levels of sexual functioning than individuals without a psychiatric history (Clayton, McGarvey, Clavet, & Piazza, 1997). Low sexual desire is commonly associated with depression and has been reported in approximately 50–70% of depressed patients (Casper et al., 1985). A lifetime history of major depression has been found at double the rate in individuals presenting with primary hypoactive sexual desire compared with those without disturbance in sexual functioning, whereas women with a history of major depression have reported that their initial depressive episode and impaired libido developed concurrently (Schreiner-Engel & Schiaivi, 1986).

Frequency of and interest in sexual activity tends to decline with more severe depression, whereas orgasm and arousal difficulties also are common in depressed women (Kennedy, Dickens, Eisfeld, & Bagby, 1999). For example, Hawton, Gath, and Day (1994) found that depressed women described sexual activity as less enjoyable, more unpleasant, and less satisfying than nondepressed women. In another study of depressed women, Kennedy et al. (1999) found that 50% of women reported low sexual desire and decreased arousal, 40% noted lubrication difficulties, approximately 35% experienced a decreased interest in sexually explicit material, fantasy, and masturbation, and 15% experienced orgasm delays.

Frohlich and Meston (2002) confirmed the above results in a depressed college sample. Forty-seven depressed college women reported significant decreases in arousal, orgasm, satisfaction, and pleasure as well as increased pain during intercourse (due to lack of lubrication) compared with nondepressed female students. The depressed students also noted increased frequency of masturbation, which the authors attribute to greater rumination about sex, the desire to engage in a self-soothing behavior, or the inability to achieve orgasm with a partner.

Finally, in the Zurich cohort study (Angst, 1998), the prevalence of sexual dysfunction in individuals with both treated (63%) and untreated depression (45%) was significantly higher than that of controls (26%). Yet, the prevalence of sexual dysfunction in specific groups of depressed minority women, such as African-American, Hispanic, or Asian-American women, is unexplored.

SEXUAL FUNCTIONING IN DEPRESSED MINORITY WOMEN

Little is known about sexual functioning in specific groups of depressed minority women

(African-American, Hispanic, Asian-American). Yet, antidepressant medications (e.g., Selective Serotonin Reuptake Inhibitors (SSRIs), Selective Norepinephrine Reuptake Inhibitors (SNRIs), tricyclics, bupropion) often are first-line treatment for depression. Because women have a higher prevalence of both depressive and anxiety disorders, which may be chronic conditions, there is a greater likelihood that they will be prescribed antidepressants and use them for longer periods of time than men in order to facilitate remission and prevent relapse (Hensley & Nurnberg, 2002). Several studies have noted a link between antidepressant initiation and sexual dysfunction, with prevalence rates as high as 73% (Rosen, Lane, & Menza, 1999 and Montgomery, Baldwin, & Riley, 2002), and more severe sexual side effects in women (Hensley & Nurnberg, 2002).

However, the near-overwhelming majority of participants in both survey studies and clinical trials involving depression and sexual dysfunction have been European-American (White). In fact, in the literature examining the impact of antidepressant use on sexual functioning or treatment of sexual concerns in a depressed population, ethnicity has rarely been analyzed as a separate variable. Thus, there is a paucity of information about the prevalence and treatment of sexual dysfunction in African-American, Hispanic, or Asian-American women receiving antidepressant therapy and about ways to potentially minimize sexual difficulties in these populations. Yet, some literature suggests that the treatment with and the side-effects of antidepressants may be particularly salient for certain groups of minority women.

Cultural Influences on Antidepressant Treatment

Limited research conveys that ethnicity and culture may influence response to antidepressant treatment. First, in two independent studies, Hispanic patients were found to be less likely to report concerns about their antidepressant medications or to complain about the side effects of the antidepressants to their physicians, compared with their non-Hispanic peers (Sleath, Rubin, & Wurst, 2003). Yet, Marcos and Cancro (1982) found that Hispanic patients experienced more antidepressant side effects compared with other groups.

Second, Sleath, Rubin, and Huston (2003) noted that primary care doctors prescribing psychotropics gave significantly less information about antidepressant medication with their Hispanic patients, compared with their non-Hispanic counterparts, and that these patients also were less adherent to their medication regimen. Third, high rates of somatization are observed within the Hispanic population (U.S. Department of Health and Human Services, 2001). Because somatizers are very sensitive to physical discomfort, they may be especially disturbed by medication side effects (Meserman, Horowitz, & Bein, 1995).

Fourth, both African-American and Hispanic patients tend to be less likely to find antidepressant medications acceptable and often hold more negative beliefs about their effectiveness (Cooper et al., 2003). Fifth, African Americans have demonstrated higher rates of pretermination and shorter duration of treatment (Sue, Fujino, Hu, Takeuchi, & Zane, 1991). For example, in a treatment trial comparing the effectiveness of interpersonal psychotherapy and medication management (Brown, Schulberg, Sacco, Perel, & Houck, 1999), significantly fewer African-American patients completed the continuation phase (71% versus 35%) and complied with the medication regimen (48% versus 69%) compared with Caucasian participants. Noncompliance was associated with premature termination and African-American patients also were less tolerant of medication side effects. Last, ethnicity has been found to predict the type and dosage of antidepressant medication received (Melfi, Croghan, Hanna, & Robinson, 2000), which may impact side-effect profile.

Cultural Influences on Sexuality

Cultural norms and values may influence the manner in which different subgroups of minority women experience sexuality and react to sexual dysfunction and sexual side effects. Conceptions of sexuality may differ across cultures because cultural norms may dictate what is considered proper and sexually appealing (Leiblum, Wiegel, & Brickle, 2003). Moreover, terms such as sexual desire and arousal may carry different connotations in different cultures (Cain et al., 2003). However, the sociocultural factors that shape sexual desire and dysfunction have received limited attention in the literature (Leiblum et al., 2003). Cultural differences in sexual attitudes and practices are further discussed below.

EXPERIMENTAL STUDIES

In SWAN, described earlier, sexuality and sexual functioning appeared to be extremely important for African-American women, compared with women from other ethnic backgrounds (Cain et al., 2003). African-American women also reported a higher incidence of frequent sexual intercourse compared with other groups. In contrast, the Hispanic women in SWAN were the least likely of the ethnic groups represented to indicate that they engaged in sex for pleasure and the most likely to report that the desire to get pregnant was the main motivator for sexual activity. They also were very likely to engage in sexual relations in order to please their partner, rather than for self-fulfillment.

The Asian-American sociocultural context has historically deemphasized the sexual needs of women. In the SWAN sample, Japanese and Chinese women were more likely to report sex as unimportant, compared with other women in the sample. In addition, Japanese women were the most likely to engage in sex to please their partners. Similarly, in a large cross-sectional study, Meston, Trapnell, and Gorzalka (1996) found that Asian undergraduates were

significantly more conservative regarding sexual behavior than non-Asian students. Asian students were less likely to participate in oral sex, masturbation, and petting, with significantly fewer Asian females participating in intercourse compared with their non-Asian peers. Asian undergraduates typically were older during their first sexual encounter, were less likely to fantasize about having sex in unusual positions, and endorsed a lower frequency of intercourse. Non-Asian students also reported a higher lifetime number of sexual partners and one-night stands and were more likely to fantasize about a person other than their significant other. In a second study, Meston et al. (1998) stated that Asian students were less sexually informed and demonstrated less accurate sexual knowledge compared with peers of other ethnic backgrounds. Finally, a separate multisite cross-sectional study (Leiblum et al., 2003) also found Asian students to possess more conservative sexual attitudes, compared with their Caucasian counterparts. However, the overall sample possessed fairly liberal beliefs, suggesting an impact of acculturation on individuals from diverse backgrounds.

CLINICAL OBSERVATIONS

Additional themes regarding cultural influences on sexuality have been discussed in the context of case and observational studies. Villarruel (1998) interviewed Puerto-Rican and Mexican-American adolescents and their mothers to further elucidate cultural influences on sexuality in these populations of women. Culturally prescribed gender roles, gender differences in dating rules, and the importance of virginity were identified as factors clearly linked to sexual desire and behavior. Concerns about rape and abuse by strangers and acquaintances, because sex often occurred in a violent context in these women's neighborhoods, also tempered enthusiasm for sexual behavior. Church and family structure also were found to be strong predictors of sexual behavior among Mexican-American adolescents (DuRant, Pendergrast, & Seymore, 1990).

Although motivators for and conceptualizations of sexual activity may vary within the Hispanic community, some preliminary empirical evidence suggests that Hispanic women, compared with other ethnic groups, are at a greater risk for depression when aspects of their sexual capabilities are altered (Adams, DeJesus, Trujillo, & Cole, 1997). Santos-Ortiz and Vazquez (1989) also reported that Hispanic women often felt inadequate when they were unable to become aroused for sexual activity. However, they did not simply want to be viewed as machines when they felt unable to perform sexually (Fontes, 2001).

Moreover, Stephens, and Phillips (2003) commented on factors associated with sexuality in the African-American community. With female African-American adolescents at significantly greater risk for unplanned pregnancy, HIV/AIDS, sexually transmitted diseases, early age of first sexual experience, multiple and older sexual partners, and violent first sexual encounters than their Caucasian and Hispanic-American peers, these factors have impacted the women's sexual attitudes and behaviors. Power also has been linked with sexuality in the African-American community. Thus, as stated above, culture plays a significant role in defining a woman's sexuality and needs to be considered when addressing sexual dysfunction.

CONCLUSIONS

In sum, women report higher rates of depressive disorders than men and often experience more severe sexual side effects of antidepressant medication—a first line treatment. Because the overwhelming majority of participants in both clinical trials and survey studies investigating depression and sexual functioning have been European-American (White), little is known about the sexual functioning of depressed African-American, Hispanic, or Asian-American women. Sexual dysfunction has been shown to have a deleterious effect on quality of life, relationship satisfaction, and treatment outcome. Because culture may influence women's response to both antidepressant treatment and sexual dysfunction, further research with a specific emphasis on gender and culture is needed to elucidate the prevalence, impact, and treatment of sexual dysfunction in specific subgroups of depressed minority women.

Although the differences between European-American, African-American, Hispanic, and Asian-American women have been highlighted in this article, it also is important to mention that noteworthy variability may exist within these subgroups of women. For example, women from India may espouse different attitudes about sex compared with other Asian-American women, whereas Puerto Rican and Mexican-American women may hold divergent conceptions of sexuality. Thus, it is important that future research investigate similarities and differences that exist both between and within various cultures.

It is critical to be sensitive to the specific cultural messages that women from different ethnic groups hold about sexual functioning and associated interventions. Further research will help delineate appropriate clinical recommendations, enabling physicians to provide a high level of culturally sensitive and effective clinical care. Overall, this heightened level of sensitivity coupled with culture specific research has the potential to maximize mental health, relationship satisfaction, quality of life, and treatment adherence in diverse groups of women presenting with both depression and sexual dysfunction.

INTRODUCTION REFERENCE

Strine, T. W., A. H. Mokdad, L. S. Balluz, O. Gonzalez, R. Crider, J. T. Berry, et al. 2008. Depression and anxiety in the United States: Findings from the 2006

Behavioral Risk Factor Surveillance System. *Psychiatric Services* 59: 1383–90.

REFERENCES

Adams, J., DeJesus, Y., Trujillo, M., & Cole, F. (1997). Assessing sexual dimensions in Hispanic women. Development of an instrument. *Cancer Nursing, 20,* 251–259.

Altshuler, L. L. (2002). The use of SSRIs in depressive disorders specific to women. *Journal of Clinical Psychiatry, 63*(7), 3–7.

Angst, J. (1998). Sexual problems in healthy and depressed persons. International Clinical *Psychopharmacology, 13*(Suppl. 6), S1–4.

Baldwin, D. S. (2001). Depression and sexual function. *British Medical Bulletin, 57,* 81–99.

Bancroft, J., Loftus, J., & Long, J. S. (2003). Distress about sex: A national survey of women in heterosexual relationships. *Archives of Sexual Behavior, 32,* 193–208.

Brown, C., Schulberg, D. S., Perel, J. M., & Houck, P. R. (1999). Effectiveness of treatments for major depression in primary medical care practice: A post hoc analysis of outcomes for African American and white patients. *Journal of Affective Disorders, 53,* 185–192.

Cain, V. S., Johannes, C. B., Avis, N. E., Mohr, B., Schocken, M., Skurnick, J., & Ory, M. (2003). Sexual functioning and practices in a multi-ethnic study of midlife women: Baseline results from SWAN. *The Journal of Sex Research, 40,* 266–276.

Casper, R. C., Redmond, Jr., D. E., Katz, M. M., Scaffer, C. B., Davis, J. M., & Koslow, S. H. (1985). Somatic symptoms in primary affective disorder: Presence and relationship to the classification of depression. *Archives of General Psychiatry, 42,* 1098–1104.

Clayton, A. H., McGarvey, E. L., Clavet, G. J., & Piazza, L. (1997). Comparison of sexual functioning in clinical and nonclinical populations using the changes in sexual functioning questionnaire (CSFQ). *Psychopharmacology Bulletin, 33,* 747–753.

Clayton, A. H., Pradko, J. F., Croft, H. A., Montano, B., Leadbetter, R. A., Bolden-Watson, C., Bass, K. I., Donahue, R. M. S., Jamerson, B. D., & Metz, A. (2002). Prevalence of sexual dysfunction among newer antidepressants. *Journal of Clinical Psychiatry, 63,* 357–366.

Cooper, L. A., Gonzales, J. J., Gallo, J. J., Rost, K. M., Meredith, L. S., Rubenstein, L. V., Wang, N. Y., & Forn, D. E. (2003). The acceptability of treatment for depression among African-American, Hispanic, and white primary care patients. *Medical Care, 41,* 479–489.

DuRant, R. H., Pendergrast, R., & Seymore, C. (1990). Sexual behavior among Hispanic female adolescents in the United States. *Pediatrics, 85,* 1051–1058.

Fontes, L. A. (2001). The new view and Latina sexualities: Pero no soy una m´aquina! *Women & Therapy, 24,* 33–37.

Frohlich, P., & Meston, C. (2002). Sexual functioning and self-reported depressive symptoms among college women. *The Journal of Sex Research, 39,* 321–325.

Hawton, K., Gath, D., & Day, A. (1994). Sexual function in a community sample of middle-aged women with partners: Effects of age, marital, socioeconomic, psychiatric, gynecological, and menopausal factors. *Archives of Sexual Behavior, 23,* 375–395.

Heiman, J. R. (2002). Sexual dysfunction: Overview of prevalence, etiological factors, and treatments. *The Journal of Sex Research, 39,* 73–78.

Hensley, P. L., & Nurnberg, H. G. (2002). SSRI sexual dysfunction: A female perspective. *Journal of Sex & Marital Therapy, 28,* 143–153.

Kameya, Y. (2001). How Japanese culture affects the sexual functions of normal females. *Journal of Sex & Marital Therapy, 27,* 151–152.

Kennedy, S. H., Dickens, S. E., Eisfeld, B. S., & Bagby, R. M. (1999). Sexual dysfunction before antidepressant therapy in major depression. *Journal of Affective Disorders, 56,* 201–208.

Laumann, E. O., Paik, A., & Rosen, R. C. (1999). Sexual dysfunction in the United States: Prevalence and predictors. *The Journal of the American Medical Association, 281,* 537–544.

Leiblum, S., Wiegel, M., & Brickle, F. (2003). Sexual attitudes of U.S. and Canadian medical students: The role of ethnicity, gender, religion and acculturation. *Sexual and Relationship Therapy, 18,* 473–491.

Marcos, L. R., & Cancro, R. (1982). Pharmacotherapy of Hispanic depressed patients: Clinical observations. *American Journal of Psychotherapy, 36,* 505–512.

Melfi, C. A., Croghan, T. W., Hanna, M. P., & Robinson, R. L. (2000). Racial variation in antidepressant treatment in a Medicaid population. *Journal of Clinical Psychiatry, 61,* 16–21.

Meresman, J. F., Horowitz, L. M., & Bein, E. (1995). Treatment assignment, dropout, and outcome of depressed patients who somaticize. *Psychotherapy Research, 5,* 245–257.

Meston, C. M., Trapnell, P. D., & Gorzalka, B. B. (1996). Ethnic and gender differences in sexual behavior between Asian and non-Asian university students. *Archives of Sexual Behavior, 25,* 33–72.

Meston, C. M., Trapnell, P. D., & Gorzalka, B. B. (1998). Ethnic, gender and length-of-residency influences on sexual knowledge and attitudes. *The Journal of Sex Research, 35,* 176–188.

Miranda, J., Chung, J. Y., Green, B. L., Krupnick, J., Siddique, J., Bevick, D. A., & Belin, T. (2003). Treating depression in predominantly low income young minority women: A randomized controlled trial. *Journal of the American Medical Association, 290,* 57–65.

Montgomery, S. A., Baldwin, D. S., & Riley, A. (2002). Antidepressant medications: A review of the evidence for drug-induced sexual dysfunction. *Journal of Affective Disorders, 69,* 119–140.

Murray, C. J. L., & Lopez, A. D. (1997). Alternative projections of mortality and disability by cause 1990–2020: Global burden of disease study. *Lancet, 349,* 1498–1504.

Population by Race and Hispanic or Latino Origin for the United States: 1990 and 2000 (2001, March 12). United States Census 2000. (Retrieved June 3, 2004.) http://www.census.gov/population/www/cen2000/phc-t.html.

Rosen, R. C., Lane, R. M., & Menza, M. (1999). Effects of SSRI's on sexual function: A critical review. *Journal of Clinical Psychopharmacology, 19,* 67–85.

Rosen, R. C., & Laumann, E. O. (2003). The prevalence of sexual problems in women: How valid are comparisons across studies?; Commentary on Bancroft, Loftus, and Long's (2003) "Distress about sex: A national survey of women in heterosexual relationships." *Archives of Sexual Behavior, 32,* 209–211.

Rosen, R. C., Taylor, J. F., Leiblum, S. R., & Bachmann, G. A. (1993). Prevalence of sexual dysfunction in women: Results of a survey study of 329 women in outpatient gynecological clinic. *Journal of Sex & Marital Therapy, 19,* 171–188.

Rosenberg, K. P., Bleiberg, K. L., Koscis, J., & Gross, C. (2003). A survey of sexual side effects among severely mentally ill patients taking psychotropic medications: Impact on compliance. *Journal of Sex & Marital Therapy, 29,* 289–296.

Santos-Ortiz, M. C., & Vazquez, M. M. (1989). An exploratory study of the expression of female sexuality: The experience of two groups of Puerto Rican women from different social backgrounds. In C. T. Garcia Coll & M. L. Matteir (Eds.), *The psy-*chosocial development of Puerto Rican women. (pp. 141–165). New York: Praeger.

Schreiner-Engel, P., & Schiavi, R. C. (1986). Lifetime psychopathology in individuals with low sexual desire. *Journal of Nervous & Mental Disease, 174,* 646–651.

Simons, J. S., & Carey, M. P. (2001). Prevalence of sexual dysfunctions: Results from a decade of research. *Archives of Sexual Behavior, 30,* 177–219.

Sleath, B., Rubin, R. H., & Huston, S. A. (2003). Hispanic ethnicity, physician-patient communication and antidepressant adherence. *Comprehensive Psychiatry, 44,* 198–204.

Sleath, B., Rubin, R. H., & Wurst, K. (2003). The influence of Hispanic ethnicity on patients' expression of complaints about and problems with adherence to antidepressant therapy. *Clinical Therapeutics, 25,* 1739–1749.

Stephens, D. P., & Phillips, L. D. (2003). Freaks, gold diggers, divas, and dykes: The sociohistorical development of adolescent African American women's sexual scripts. *Sexuality & Culture, 7,* 3–49.

Sue, S., Fujino, D. C., Hu, L., Takeuchi, D. T., & Zane, N. W. S. (1991). Community mental health services for ethnic minority groups: A test of the cultural responsiveness hypothesis. *Journal of Consulting and Clinical Psychology, 59,* 533–540.

U.S. Department of Health and Human Services. (2001). *Mental Health: Culture, Race, and Ethnicity—A Supplement to Mental Health: A Report of the Surgeon General.* http://www.ncbi.nlm.nih.gov/books/bv.fcgi?rid=hstat5.chapter.971 (Retrieved May 4, 2004.)

Vega, W. A., Kolody, B., Aguilar-Gaxiola, S., Alderte, E., Catalano, R., & Caraveo-Anduaga, J. (1998). Lifetime prevalence of DSM-II-R psychiatric disorders among urban and rural Mexican Americans in California. *Archives of General Psychiatry, 55,* 771–778.

Villarruel, A. M. (1998). Cultural influences on the sexual attitudes, beliefs, and norms of young Latina adolescents. *Journal of the Society of Pediatric Nurses, 3*(2), 69–79.

Wiederman, M. W., Maynard, C., & Fretz, A. (1996). Ethnicity in 25 years of published sexuality research: 1971–1995. *The Journal of Sex Research, 33,* 339–342.

Zajecka, J. M. (2000). Clinical issues in long-term treatment with antidepressants. *Journal of Clinical Psychiatry, 61*(2), 20–25.

PART IX

Sexual Victimization and Compulsion

As illustrated by the topics in Part IX, sexual victimization and compulsion can run the gamut, ranging from child sexual abuse to cybersex. The one variable inherent in all victimization is power and its misuse. Even though all sexual relationships include an element of power, when this power is shared, partners are empowered and relationships strengthened. But, coercive sexuality is characterized by a clash of personal power (Carroll and Wolpe 1996). Whether evidenced in child sexual abuse, sexual aggression, sexual harassment, or cyber sex, an unequal power structure inevitably results in harm.

All adults in our society are called upon to play a role in stemming the tide of sexual victimization. When underage children or adolescents are victims of sexual abuse, laws mandate that any person with knowledge of the incident must play the role of reporter. Once the abuse becomes known and verified by the authorities, professionals become involved. The role of medical and mental-health professionals is assessment and, eventually, the role of the therapist is to address healing (Faller 1995). Legal roles may also play a part in the sexual victimization picture as evidenced by various state laws and institutional policies pertaining to sexual aggression and sexual harassment in occupational, educational, medical, and therapeutic settings. But the laws and roles involved in the protection against sexual victimization are not always clear-cut or embraced by everyone. As readers will see, some people question whether or not the government should have any role at all when the setting is in the bedroom.

A number of models of sexual abuse have been advanced, but a comprehensive theory of sexual aggression has yet to be proposed. Such a theoretical vacuum exists in spite of the fact that almost one-half of Americans are affected by this serious social problem as either victims or perpetrators (Laumann, Gagnon, Michael & Michaels, 1994). Viewing sexual aggression only as a societal problem ignores the horrendous personal emotional pain experienced by millions. But, neither is it a purely personal problem. Sexual aggression should be considered a broad mix of both social processes and interpersonal relationships.

Any theoretical model for child sexual abuse must take into account possible immediate causes of sexual abuse, such as the psychology of the abuser and interpersonal relationships as well as possible contextual factors such as social variables and values that make children more or less likely to be victimized (Glaser & Frosh, 1988). Sexual victimization of the young arises from two sources: outside factors, including child and adolescent sex rings, pornography, adolescent runaways, and juvenile prostitution, and inside factors, including incest, a family affair. The Young, Harford, Kinder, and Savell article examines the aftereffects of sexual victimization in a college student sample, with some predictable and some surprising findings.

Researchers Zöe Peterson and Charlene Muehlenhard have long been interested in the concept of "unacknowledged rape," which is when an encounter fits the definition of rape but is not identified as such by the victim. In a 2004 study, they examined the role played by "rape myths" and "stereotypic rape scripts" in women's sexual experiences and found that when a woman's nonconsensual sexual encounters did not fit her script for a rape, she was less likely to define it as a rape (Peterson & Muehlenhard, 2004). Many students still accept many rape myths and tend to envision rape as involving the proverbial stranger jumping out of the bushes. It is these distorted stereotypes about rape that lead to many victims of rape not fully acknowledging what has occurred.

In the study contained in this Part, Peterson and Muehlenhard examined the role of consent and "wantedness" in sexual interactions as well as the role of these variables in identifying a situation as rape. Students will likely be eager to talk about many of the concepts and contradictions contained in the chapter. This selection will lead students into what may be uncharted waters in search of answers to dilemmas that can occur when sexual scripts collide with reality.

In previous chapters, students have read about gender differences related to sexuality on a number of dimensions: desire, sexual dysfunction, and drug research to name only a few. The research by Cindy Struckman-Johnson, David Struckman-Johnson, and Peter Anderson investigates gender differences in a subject long

considered to be uniquely a feminine experience: sexual coercion. Based on the assumption that language is power, the chapter challenges students to clarify the term "sexual coercion" and its various uses. Struckman-Johnson and colleagues define sexual coercion for their purposes as the act of using pressure, alcohol, drugs, or force to have sexual contact with someone against her or his will. The fact that the sample studied in this research consists of university women and men makes the research believable, if not a *déjà vu* experience, for students.

But, upon finishing this selection, students may find themselves with more questions than answers and in considerable disagreement with their classmates. What constitutes verbal pressure? What constitutes force? Does sexual coercion include threats of physical force as well as physical force? And, just how intoxicated does the person have to be for absence of consent to exist? Does the alcohol or drug need to be given by the perpetrator? What if both persons are intoxicated? Clearly, most readers will be interested in what this research offers to clarify such cloudy issues. And, those who are motivated to expand their thinking beyond these obvious questions will find at least some other recent research on the topic.

One of the more interesting studies in this area investigated the subject of gender and coercive sexual behavior within the framework of "social rules." Researchers posed two questions: (1) Are there social rules regarding sexual behavior that indicate when sex may be desired, expected, or obligatory? (2) Do some rules legitimize a man's initiation of sex with a woman, regardless of the woman's desires or intentions (Anderson, Taylor-Simpson, & Herrmann, 2004)? Using the "Rules About Sex" questionnaire, which was developed to study these questions, gender differences were discovered in the use of rules that would indicate when sex may be desired. Girls and women endorsed fewer rules than did boys and men, and university students endorsed fewer rules than did middle-school children. An association between boys' and men's self-reported sexually-coercive behavior and beliefs about who should initiate sex was also found. Students who explore relationships between these findings and those in the Struckman-Johnson et al. study will exercise their critical thinking skills and, perhaps, even those of their professor.

The United States makes use of many immigrant workers, documented as well as undocumented. Unfortunately, some employers use these workers not only for their labor, but for sexual gratification as well. In 1997, Diana Vellos addressed the sexual harassment faced by Latina domestic workers, concluding that it is due to a mix of sexism, classism, racism, and nationalism, with undocumented workers being particularly vulnerable (Vellos, 1997). These women feel isolated, lonely, and ultimately, helpless to do anything to address their situation for fear of job loss and deportation. Nine years later, Gloria González-López addressed the same problem in Latino male workers, resulting in the article presented in this Part. The researcher presents the results of detailed interviews she held with 20 male Mexican immigrants, most of whom reported experiences with sexual harassment, generally on the part of other men, and coercion to engage in same-sex sexual activity.

The González-López study will be an eye-opener for students. It paints a bleak picture of the lives of many immigrants, and provides vivid details about the role that sex plays in the lives of these men as they navigate tricky employment and survival dynamics. It also depicts the fluidity of heterosexuality for many men. Perhaps more so than most other chapters, this piece clearly presents sex as a commodity. It will expand the thinking of students as to what constitutes sexual harassment and who the victims of such harassment may be.

Handwritten love letters carried by Pony Express, telephone conversations between lovers on different continents, and online chats in cyberspace. What are the differences? Years of technological advances in communication. The September-October 2002 issue of the *Family Therapy Magazine* was devoted to the subject "relationships in cyberspace" (Occhetti, 2003). It featured several articles illustrating that human communication in its many forms is vital to the fabric of all societies. The Jennifer Schneider chapter, highlighting cybersex addiction and its effects on the family, is an important feature in Part IX on sexual victimization and compulsion. The survey, which was completed by women and men who had experienced serious adverse consequences of their partner's cybersex involvement, offers a wealth of information on a relatively new and controversial subject.

One of the more significant facts revealed by the survey was that almost one-third of the respondents indicated that the cybersex activities of their spouse were a continuation of preexisting compulsive sexual behaviors. This finding raises interesting questions about cause and effect: Does Internet use cause or is it the result of an addiction? Also, what is normal Internet usage? And, what about terminology? Is such behavior an addiction or is it sexual compulsivity?

Eli Coleman (1992), Director of the Human Sexuality Program at the University of Minnesota Medical School, has argued that sexual activity, if inadequately controlled, is an obsessive-compulsive disorder (OCD). Thus, he believes that the syndrome should be called *sexual compulsivity* rather than *sexual addiction*. Coleman points to the fact that, unlike OCD, the syndrome of sexual addiction has never been included in the standard diagnostic classification system used in the United States—*The Diagnostic and Statistical Manual of Mental Disorders* (American Psychiatric Association, 1994). Gold (2001) has stated, "The lack of a clear, widely agreed upon definition of sexual addiction itself has created considerable confusion about the concept and its practical application" (p. 347). Not surprisingly, the Internet itself has spawned a proliferation of websites with personal and professional opinions about this puzzle. Students surfing the Internet will discover new terms emerging, such as Pathological Internet Use (PID) and Internet Addiction Disorder (IAD) (Occhetti, 2003). Most authorities, however, believe the jury is still out on the subject of what inadequately controlled sexual behavior on the Internet should be called. There appears to be an ever widening circle of choices: IAD, PID, OCD, or CA (cybersex addiction).

Although answers about causal relationships between online behavior and its effects are lacking, research does confirm that online usage is a problem when it interferes with a person's normal life and relationships (Kraut et al., 1998). All of which begs the question: "If a rose by any other name is a rose," is a problem by any other name a problem? The scenarios in this offering will, without question, infuse a dose of reality into the minds of students, most of whom have spent an entire lifetime in a cyberspace world. We can all hope that, as a jury, they will reach reasoned opinions on this subject.

REFERENCES

American Psychiatric Association. 1994. *Diagnostic and statistical manual of mental disorders, Fourth edition.* Washington, DC: Author.

Anderson, V. N., D. Taylor-Simpson, and D. J. Hermann. 2004. Gender, age, and rape-supportive rules. *Sex Roles 50:* 77–90.

Carroll, J. L., and P. R. Wolpe. 1996. *Sexuality and gender in society.* New York: HarperCollins.

Coleman, E. 1992. Is your patient suffering from compulsive sexual behavior? *Psychiatric Annuals 22:* 320–25.

Faller, K. C. 1995. Assessment and treatment in child sexual abuse. In *Handbook of child and adolescent sexual problems,* ed. G. A. Rekers, 209–31. New York: Lexington.

Glaser, D., and S. Frosh. 1988. *Child sexual abuse.* Chicago: Dorsey.

Gold, S. N. 2001. Sexual addiction. In *Encyclopedia of clinical and deviant behavior, vol. 3, Sexual deviance,* vol. eds. N. Davis and G. Geis, 347–50. Philadelphia: Taylor & Francis.

Kraut, P., M. Patterson, V. Lundamark, S. Kiesler, T. Mukophadhyay, and W. Scherlis. 1998. Internet paradox: A social technology that reduces social involvement and psychological well-being? *American Psychologist 53:* 1017–31.

Laumann, E. O., J. H. Gagnon, R. T. Michael, and S. Michaels. 1994. *The social organization of sexuality: Sexual practices in the United States.* Chicago: University of Chicago Press.

Occhetti, D. R. 2003. E-communication: Pros and cons. *Family Therapy Magazine,* September–October 16, 28–31.

Peterson, Z. D., and C. L. Muehlenhard. 2004. Was it rape? The function of women's rape myth acceptance and definitions of sex in labeling their own experiences. *Sex Roles 51:* 129–44.

CHAPTER 40

The Relationship Between Childhood Sexual Abuse and Adult Mental Health Among Undergraduates

M. Scott Young
Kelli-Lee Harford
Bill Kinder
Jodi K. Savell

In 1990, David Finkelhor and colleagues published a study which is regarded as the "gold standard" concerning child sexual abuse (CSA) in the United States. Based on a national probability sample, this study revealed that 27 percent of women and 16 percent of men reported having been a victim of CSA (Finkelhor, Hotaling, Lewis, & Smth, 1990). These figures, that were shocking to many, indicated that CSA was a much larger problem than had been commonly believed. Finkelhor et al. found that the strongest predictor of victimization was an unhappy family life, which means that those who are most likely to be targets of CSA already have the deck of life stacked against them.

Eight years after the Finkelhor et al. study, history was made again when a meta-analytic study

was published in Psychological Bulletin, *a top peer-reviewed journal published by the American Psychological Association. Rind, Tromovitch, and Bauserman (1998) presented an analysis of 59 studies of the effect of CSA in college student samples. After controlling for the effect of family environment, the authors concluded that the data did not support the notion that CSA is inevitably harmful, though they were careful to add that "lack of harmfulness does not imply lack of wrongfulness." (p. 47). An uproar resulted, fueled by conservative talk radio personality, "Dr. Laura" Schlessinger, which eventually led to a condemnation of the research by the United States Congress. Somehow, an objective, scientific study had been twisted and misinterpreted as an endorsement of adult-child sexual contact. In the words of Thomas Oellerich (2000), "The Rind et al. study of the impact of CSA among college students is politically incorrect but scientifically correct" (p. 79).*

It is not disputed that girls are more likely to have been the victims of CSA than boys (Gorey & Leslie, 1997), and therefore, much of the literature on CSA has concentrated on female subjects.

In this chapter, the research by Scott Young, Kelli-Lee Harford, Bill Kinder, and Jodi Savell focuses on the potential long-term impact of CSA in both male and female college students. Would you expect the effect to be stronger on one sex or the other, or do you think the impact would be similar? After reading this chapter, you will learn if you are correct. You will also see that the findings of this study differ from those of the Rind et al. (1998) meta-analysis, and you may want to spend some time thinking and talking about why that might be.

A large body of research has documented the harmful effects of childhood sexual abuse (CSA) on adult mental health among females, but less work has examined this issue among males. For example, Browne and Finkelhor's (1986) seminal review on the effects of CSA only described the effects of sexual abuse on females. The authors contended that there were not sufficient studies on male victims of sexual abuse from which to draw conclusions about this population. The literature on male victims of CSA has grown more recently, but research on gender differences related to the prevalence and sequelae of CSA is still in its infancy.

PREVALENCE OF CSA

In 1984, the Second National Incidence and Prevalence Study of Child Abuse and Neglect was mandated by Congress. This study demonstrated that girls were significantly more likely to be victims of sexual abuse than boys. The incidence rate of sexual abuse among girls was found to be 3.28 per 1,000, whereas for boys it was 1.00 per 1,000 (Cappelleri, Eckenrode, & Powers, 1993). Putnam (2003) reported that studies using community samples typically find that the prevalence of CSA is between 12% and 35% for females and between 4% and 9% for males. International data indicate that prevalence rates around the world are comparable to those in the United States. Finkelhor (1994)

conducted a review of studies from 19 countries and found that the rates of CSA in women were between 7% and 36% and in men were between 3% and 29%.

Commenting on the range of prevalence rates, Putnam (2003) suggested that they "vary widely as a function of the selection and response rate, the definition used, and the method by which the history is obtained" (p. 270). After adjusting for factors such as sample-related variation, response rates, and differences in definition, Gorey and Leslie (1997) found the prevalence rates of CSA to be 16.8% for women and 7.9% for men.

Definitions of CSA that have been used in the research literature differ primarily along four dimensions: (a) whether physical contact is a necessary condition, (b) the specific age difference, if any, that is required between the victim and perpetrator, (c) the age at which the victim is no longer considered to be a child, and (d) the relationship between the victim and perpetrator. The varying definitions of CSA and their fairly wide range of prevalence rates underscore the need to assess CSA in a consistent, standardized fashion so that results can be compared across isolated studies. In response, Bartoi and Kinder (1998) developed the Early Sexual Experiences survey (ESE), a standardized measure of CSA. Slightly higher rates of CSA have been retrospectively reported among adult female undergraduates in studies using the ESE. For instance, Bartoi and Kinder (1998) found that 40% of undergraduate females reported a history of CSA, and Bartoi, Kinder, and Tomianovic (2000) later found a similar rate in another undergraduate female sample.

Some researchers have speculated that true prevalence rates of CSA may be higher because many individuals fail to report abusive incidents for various reasons (Dimock, 1988; Finkelhor, 1994). This may be especially significant for cases involving male victims of CSA (King & Woollett, 1997; Lab, Feigenbaum, & De Silva, 2000), possibly contributing to the lower rates documented among males.

PSYCHOLOGICAL CONSEQUENCES OF CSA

A large body of research has shown that adult victims of CSA exhibit greater levels of mental health problems relative to individuals who were not sexually abused as children. Internalizing effects such as depression, anxiety, posttraumatic stress disorder (PTSD), fear, distress, guilt, and shame have been reported in individuals who have been sexually abused (Johnson & Kenkel, 1991; Kendall-Tackett, Williams, & Finkelhor, 1993; Saywitz, Mannarino, Berliner, & Cohen, 2000). Some externalizing behaviors that have been identified by researchers as possibly stemming from CSA include aggression, over-sexualized behavior, eating disorders, substance abuse, self-injurious behaviors, and somatic complaints (Browne & Finkelhor, 1986; Inderbitzen-Pisaruk, Shawchuck, & Hoier, 1992; Monahan & Forgash, 2000; Saywitz et al., 2000; Saywitz, Mannarino, Smith, & Smith, 1999).

Browne and Finkelhor (1986) suggested that one of the most common effects of CSA among females is depressive symptomatology, including suicidal ideation and attempts. Many studies have documented that both male and female victims of CSA report higher levels of depression than their same-sex counterparts without a history of CSA, including studies with clinical samples of crisis center inpatients (Briere, Evans, Runtz, & Wall 1988) and psychiatric inpatients (Sansonnet-Hayden, Haley, Marriage, & Fine, 1987; Stiffman, 1989). In their review article, Dhaliwal et al. (1996) noted that CSA history is associated with elevated levels of depression for both males and females, and that most investigations have failed to find differences in the rates of depression among male and female survivors of CSA. Aside from depression, this same general pattern of findings has been found with regard to suicidal ideation and attempts (Garnefski & Diekstra, 1997; Martin, Bergen, Richardson, Roeger, & Allison, 2004) and distress levels (Marx & Sloan, 2003).

Though most studies have found that history of CSA is detrimental to both male and female adult mental health, there are some exceptions. Some studies have found that females with CSA histories experienced significantly more negative mental health consequences than their male Counterparts. Rind, Tromovitch, and Bauserman's (1998) meta-analysis of studies using undergraduate samples concluded that females with CSA histories suffered from more adjustment problems than males with a history of CSA. Banyard, Williams, and Siegel (2004) concluded that history of CSA was associated with higher levels of sexual concerns among females, but not among males.

Few studies have found that history of CSA is more detrimental to adult mental health among males than females. Using Symptom Checklist 90-Revised (SCL-90-R) with a clinical sample, Gold, Lucenko, Elhai, Swingle, and Sellers (1999) found that males with a history of CSA exhibited significantly more interpersonal sensitivity, depression, anxiety, and phobic anxiety than women with a history of CSA.

Some studies have found that males and females may differ with regard to the specific types of mental health problems they experience as a result of being sexually abused as a child. This pattern of findings might be expected given that females are more likely to develop internalizing disorders in response to distress, with males being more likely to develop externalizing problems. In their study of a community sample of CSA survivors, MacMillan et al. (2001) found that female survivors were more likely to report internalizing disorders like anxiety and major depressive, whereas male survivors were more likely to report externalizing behaviors like alcohol or drug abuse/dependence and antisocial behaviors.

Though most studies suggest that history of CSA is damaging to adult mental health among both males and females, several factors contribute to the inconsistent findings. These include differences between studies in the definitions of CSA, different domains of mental health that were assessed, different measures of the same mental health domain, and different samples.

Even though the body of research on males who have been sexually abused is growing, information on males is still sparse in comparison to the available literature on females. Few CSA studies have included both male and female participants, and even fewer have used standardized measures to assess the prevalence and sequelae of CSA. Studies meeting these expectations have typically included only a small number of male participants with a history of CSA, or they have been based on clinical samples. Clinical samples are biased to include participants most adversely affected by CSA. Because undergraduates can be considered a highly functioning nonclinical sample, these samples are biased to include participants least affected by CSA. It is important to examine the relationship between CSA and adult mental health among both clinical and nonclinical samples. In an effort to improve on some of the methodological shortcomings of and discrepancies between previous studies, the current investigation adds to the literature by using standardized measures of CSA and mental health to examine the relationship between gender, CSA history, and adult mental health in a mixed gender undergraduate sample. Based on previous studies, it was hypothesized that history of CSA would be related to higher rates of depression and overall distress. It was further hypothesized that this would not vary across genders.

METHOD

Participants

Participants ($N = 406$) ranged in age from 18 to 30, averaging 20.23. The sample was predominantly Caucasian (54.5%), though African Americans (20.8%), Hispanics (13.9%), Asians (3.7%), and other ethnicities (7.2%) were also represented.

Materials

ESE

The ESE (Bartoi & Kinder, 1998) is an 11-item measure developed to assess participants' history of CSA. Items ask whether respondents experienced various types of sexual encounters before the age of 16, including: participation in oral, vaginal, or anal intercourse with someone at least 5 years older; participation in genital manipulation with someone at least 5 years older; being touched in a way that made them feel violated; or being coerced into unwanted sexual activity. Participants were considered to have a history of CSA if they endorsed one or more of the ESE items.

Brief Symptom Inventory (BSI)

The BSI (Derogatis, 1993) was designed to assess common psychological symptoms. Each item represents a problem, with respondents indicating the extent to which each item has distressed them over the past week. The measure assesses the following nine primary symptom dimensions: depression, interpersonal sensitivity, anxiety, phobic anxiety, paranoid ideation, somatization, obsessive-compulsive, hostility, and psychoticism. The BSI also provides a global severity index to indicate overall mental health functioning.

Because the sample included both males and females, it was necessary to analyze gender-specific normative T-scores rather than raw scores because males and females have different normal levels of mental health symptomatology. Participants were classified as to the presence or absence of psychological distress according to criteria outlined in the BSI manual (Derogatis, 1993).

Procedure

Participants were recruited through undergraduate psychology and human sexuality courses. The data were collected in groups ranging in size from 5 to 12. To ensure privacy of responses, participants were asked not to sit next to one another.

RESULTS

Prevalence of CSA

Overall, 155 participants (38.2%) reported a history of CSA as indicated by endorsement of one or more items from the ESE survey. The types of abusive experiences most commonly reported included genital manipulation with someone at least 5 years older and being touched in a manner that made participants feel violated. A significantly greater proportion of females (41.6%) than males (30.7%) reported a history of CSA. Rates of CSA also varied significantly by ethnicity. The highest rates were reported among Hispanics (51.8%), followed by "other" ethnicities (44.8%), African Americans (44.0%), Caucasians (31.8%), and Asians (26.7%).

RELATIONSHIP BETWEEN GENDER, CSA, AND ADULT MENTAL HEALTH

Main effects of gender were observed on only the somatization scale, indicating that females reported significantly greater levels of somatization compared to males. Main effects of CSA history were observed on hostility, paranoid ideation, psychoticism, and the global severity index; participants reporting a history of CSA endorsed significantly greater levels of hostility, paranoid ideation, psychoticism, and global mental health symptomatology as compared to participants not reporting a history of CSA. There were no significant interactions between CSA and gender.

A similar proportion of males (55.9%) and females (64.2%) were classified as being psychologically distressed, though a significantly greater proportion of participants reporting a history of CSA were classified as being psychologically distressed (72.9% vs. 54.6%).

Similar analyses performed separately for males and females indicated that this pattern of results was consistent across genders.

A similar proportion of males (29.9%) and females (28.0%) were classified as being severely distressed, though participants reporting a history of CSA were more likely to be classified as being severely distressed (24.3% vs. 35.5%). CSA status was significantly related to severe distress in females (34.5% vs. 23.3%) but not in males (38.5% vs. 26.1%). The gender-specific effect sizes were identical across genders, suggesting that the gender discrepancy in statistically significant findings was a function of the different sample sizes rather than being because of true gender differences.

DISCUSSION

This study found that experiences of CSA were commonly reported among a nonclinical sample of male and female undergraduates. Nearly a third of males reported a history of CSA, with more than 40% of females reporting such a history. These rates are higher than those found in previous investigations using different definitions of CSA (Cappelleri et al., 1993; Putnam, 2003), but they are consistent with rates obtained among women using the same measure applied in this study (Bartoi et al., 2000). The types of abusive incidents most commonly reported included genital manipulation with someone at least 5 years older and being touched in a manner that made participants feel violated. Incidents involving force or anal intercourse were less frequently reported, and few participants (3.6%) reported receiving psychological treatment in which sexual abuse issues were covered.

Compared to participants not reporting a history of CSA, this study found that participants reporting such a history experienced significantly higher average levels of recent mental health symptomatology as measured by the

BSI global severity index. Aside from this global mental health difference, more specific analyses of each BSI primary dimension scale average score indicated that participants with a history of CSA reported increased levels of hostility, paranoid ideation, and psychoticism compared to participants with no history of CSA. A significantly greater proportion of participants with a history of CSA was classified as being distressed (72.9% vs. 54.6%) or severely distressed (35.4% vs. 23.3%), and this pattern of results was consistent across males and females. These findings underscore the clinical significance of the statistical differences found between participants varying in CSA status and provide further support for the lack of gender differences in this undergraduate sample.

Though history of CSA was associated with higher levels of adult mental health symptomatology, this study failed to find that gender moderated the effects of CSA on adult mental health. These findings regarding the significant effects of CSA and the lack of significance of the gender by CSA interaction are consistent with previous studies examining this issue among clinical (Briere et al., 1988) and nonclinical (Marx & Sloan, 2003) mixed-gender samples. Though these studies found that participants reporting a history of CSA have elevated levels of adult mental health symptomatology, the effects were not found to differ by gender.

There are several practical implications of these findings. More than 40% of females and more than 30% of males reported experiencing sexually abusive incidents during childhood. These rates are likely much higher than those thought by the general public. Because public awareness of a problem is often a first step toward dedicating appropriate resources and attention necessary to help solve it, the public should be made aware of how commonly male and female children are sexually abused. Additionally, as indicated by Dhaliwal et al. (1996), there is also a need for more professionals to educate themselves on the issue of CSA of males. These professionals include school personnel, clergy, and child protective workers, as well as persons working in the fields of law enforcement, mental health, or medicine. Practical treatment implications follow from the findings that history of CSA was associated with higher levels of hostility, paranoid ideation, and psychoticism. For instance, anger management techniques may be well suited for survivors of CSA reporting high levels of hostility. Also, because persons high on psychoticism or paranoid ideation are often socially isolated, CSA survivors high on these dimensions may benefit from social skills training.

Limitations of the study include the likelihood that important variables were not measured. It is possible that the effects of CSA on adult mental health may be related to characteristics of the abuse not measured in this study, including the relationship to the perpetrator (Bauserman & Rind, 1997), gender of perpetrator (Coxell & King, 1996), age of onset (Murphy et al., 1988; Russell, 1986), and duration of abuse (Briere & Runtz, 1988; Wind & Silvern, 1992). Though significant relationships between CSA and adult mental health were revealed in this study, their small to medium (Cohen, 1988) effect sizes suggest that other unexamined factors are influential.

This study found that rates of CSA varied significantly by ethnicity, with the highest rates reported by Hispanics, "other" ethnicities, and African Americans. Future research in this area should examine ways in which cultural factors may influence the expression of the effects of CSA. Loeb et al. (2002) suggested that different ethnic groups may differ in the set of circumstances surrounding the abuse, in the way that the abuse is processed, and in the effects of the abuse. For example, Wyatt (1990) reported that African American women were more likely than Caucasian women to avoid men resembling the perpetrator. This line of research is still in its infancy, and more studies are needed to examine whether the effects of sexual abuse are different for males and females in different cultures.

INTRODUCTION REFERENCES

Finkelhor, D. Hotaling, G., Lewis, I. A., & Smith, C. 1990. Sexual abuse in a national survey of adult men and women: Prevalence, characteristics, and risk factors. *Child Abuse & Neglect 14*: 19–28.

Gorey, K., & Leslie, D. 1997. Prevalence of child sexual abuse: Integrative review adjustment for potential response and measurement biases. *Child Abuse & Neglect 21*: 391–398.

Oellerich, T. D. 2000. Rind, Tromovitch, and Bauserman: Politically incorrect—scientifically correct. *Sexuality and Culture 4*: 67–81.

Rind, B., Tromovitch, P., & Bauserman, R. 1998. A meta-analytic examination of assumed properties of child sexual abuse using college samples. *Psychological Bulletin 124*: 22–53.

REFERENCES

Banyard, V. L., Williams, L. M., & Siegel, J. A. (2004). Childhood sexual abuse: A gender perspective on context and consequences. *Child Maltreatment, 9*(3), 223–238.

Bartoi, M., & Kinder, B. (1998). Effects of child and adult sexual abuse on adult sexuality. *Journal of Sex and Marital Therapy, 24*, 75–90.

Bartoi, M., Kinder, B., & Tomianovic, D. (2000). Interaction effects of emotional status and sexual abuse on adult sexuality. *Journal of Sex and Marital Therapy, 26*, 1–23.

Bauserman, R., & Rind, B. (1997). Psychological correlates of male child and adolescent sexual experiences with adults: A review of the nonclinical literature. *Archives of Sexual Behavior, 26*(2), 105–141.

Briere, J., Evans, D., Runtz, M., & Wall, T. (1988). Symptomatology in men who were abused as children: A comparison study. *American Journal of Orthopsychiatry, 58*, 457–461.

Briere, J, & Runtz, M. (1988). Symptomatology associated with childhood sexual victimization in a nonclinical adult sample. *Child Abuse & Neglect, 12*, 51–59.

Browne, A., & Finkelhor, D. (1986). Impact of child sexual abuse: A review of the research. *Psychological Bulletin, 99*(1), 66–77.

Cappelleri, J. C., Eckenrode, J., & Powers, J. L. (1993). The epidemiology of child abuse: Findings from the second national incidence and prevalence study of child abuse and neglect. *American Journal of Public Health, 83*, 1622–1624.

Cohen, J. (1988) *Statistical power analysis for the behavioral sciences* (2nd ed.). Hillsdale, NJ: Lawrence Erlbaum Associates.

Coxell, A., & King, M. (1996). Male victims of rape and sexual abuse. *Sexual and Marital Therapy, 11*(3), 297–308.

Derogatis, L. R. (1993). *Brief Symptom Inventory: Administration, scoring, and procedures manual* (4th ed.). Minneapolis, MN: NCS Pearson Assessments, Inc.

Dhaliwal, G. K., Guazas, L., Antonowicz, D. H., & Ross, R. R. (1996). Adult male survivors of childhood sexual abuse: Prevalence, sexual abuse characteristics, and long term effects. *Clinical Psychology Review, 16*(7), 619–639.

Dimock, P. T. (1988). Adult males sexually abused as children: Characteristics and implications for treatment. *Journal of Interpersonal Violence, 3*(2), 203–221.

Elliott, D. M., & Briere, J. (1992). The sexually abused boys: Problems in manhood. *Medical Aspects of Human Sexuality, 26*, 68–71.

Finkelhor, D. (1994). The international epidemiology of child sexual abuse. *Child Abuse & Neglect, 18*(5), 409–417.

Garnefski, N., & Diekstra, R. F. W. (1997). Child sexual abuse and emotional and behavioral problems in adolescence: Gender differences. *Journal of the American Academy of Child & Adolescent Psychiatry, 36*(3), 323–329.

Gold, S. N., Lucenko, B. A., Elhai, J. D., Swingle, J. M., & Sellers, A. H. (1999). A comparison of psychological/psychiatric symptomatology of women and men sexually abused as children. *Child Abuse & Neglect, 23*(7), 683–692.

Gorey, K., & Leslie, D. (1997). Prevalence of child sexual abuse: Integrative review adjustment for potential response and measurement biases. *Child Abuse & Neglect, 21*, 391–398.

Inderbitzen-Pisaruk, H., Shawchuck, C., & Hoier, T. (1992). Behavioral characteristics of child victims of sexual abuse. *Journal of Clinical Child Psychology, 21*, 14–19.

Johnson, B. K., & Kenkel, M. B. (1991). Stress, coping, and adjustment in female adolescent incest victims. *Child Abuse & Neglect, 15*, 293–305.

Kendall-Tackett, K., Williams, L., & Finkelhor, D. (1993). Impact of sexual abuse on children: A review and synthesis of recent empirical studies. *Psychological Bulletin, 113*, 164–180.

King, M., & Woollett, E. (1997). Sexually assaulted males: 115 men consulting a counseling service. *Archives of Sexual Behavior, 26*(6), 579–588.

Lab, D. D., Feigenbaum, J. D., De Silva, P. (2000). Mental health professionals' attitudes and practices towards male childhood sexual abuse. *Child Abuse & Neglect*, 24(3), 391–409.

Loeb, T. B., Williams, J. K., Carmona, J. V., Rivkin, I.,Wyatt, G. E., Chin, D., et al. (2002). Child sexual abuse: Associations with the sexual functioning of adolescents and adults. In G. M. Wingood & R. J. DiClemente (Eds.), *Handbook of women's sexual and reproductive health: Issues in women's health* (pp. 307–345). New York: Kluwer Academic/Plenum.

MacMillan, H. L., Fleming, J. E., Streiner, D. L., Lin, E., Boyle, M. H., Jamieson, E., et al. (2001). Childhood abuse and lifetime psychopathology in a community sample. *American Journal of Psychiatry*, 158, 1878–1883.

Martin, G., Bergen, H. A., Richardson, A. S., Roeger, L., & Allison, S. (2004). Sexual abuse and suicidality: Gender differences in a large community sample of adolescents. *Child Abuse & Neglect*, 28, 491–503.

Marx, B., & Sloan, D. (2003). The effects of trauma history, gender, and race on alcohol use and post-traumatic stress symptoms in a college sample. *Addictive Behaviors*, 28, 1631–1647.

Monahan, K., & Forgash, C. (2000). Enhancing the health care experiences of adult female survivors of childhood sexual abuse. *Women & Health*, 30(4), 27–41.

Murphy, S., Kilpatrick, D., Amick-McMullan, A., Veronen, L., Paduhovich, J., Best, C., et al. (1988). Current psychological functioning of childhood sexual abuse survivors: A community study. *Journal of Interpersonal Violence*, 3(1), 55–79.

Putnam, F. W. (2003). Ten-year research update review: Child sexual abuse. *Journal of the American Academy of Child and Adolescent Psychiatry*, 42, 269–278.

Rind, B., Tromovitch, P., & Bauserman, R. (1998). A meta-analytic examination of assumed properties of child sexual abuse using college samples. *Psychological Bulletin*, 124, 22–53.

Russell, D. (1986). *The secret trauma: Incest in the lives of girls and women.* New York: Basic Books.

Sansonnet-Hayden, H., Haley, G., Marriage, C., & Fine, S. (1987). Sexual abuse and psychopathology in hospitalized adolescents. *Journal of the American Academy of Child and Adolescent Psychiatry*, 26, 753–757.

Saywitz, K. J., Mannarino, A. P., Berliner, L., & Cohen, J. A. (2000). Treatment for sexually abused children and adolescents. *American Psychologist*, 55, 1040–1049.

Saywitz, K., Mannarino, A., Smith, M., & Smith, M. (1999). A stimulus control intervention in the gynecological exam with sexual abuse survivors. *Women & Health*, 30, 39–51.

Stiffman, A. (1989). Physical and sexual abuse in runaway youth. *Child Abuse & Neglect*, 13, 417–426.

Wind, T. W., & Silvern, L. (1992). Type and extent of child abuse as predictors of adult functioning. *Journal of Family Violence*, 7, 261–281.

Wyatt, G. E. (1990). The aftermath of child sexual abuse of African American and White American women: The victim's experience. *Journal of Family Violence*, 15, 61–81.

CHAPTER 41

Conceptualizing the "Wantedness" of Women's Consensual and Nonconsensual Sexual Experiences

Implications for How Women Label Their Experiences with Rape

Zöe D. Peterson
Charlene L. Muehlenhard

What does it mean to want sex? What does it mean to consent to sex? Is it possible that nonconsensual sex could still be wanted? If it is wanted, then is nonconsensual sex still rape? This intriguing study is unusual in the annals of sexuality research because of its use of first-person narrative responses guaranteed to evoke thoughtful reader reactions.

Using clever methodology, Zöe Peterson and Charlene Muehlenhard have explored the concepts of "wantedness" of sex and consent for sex in an effort to determine whether or not these are independent dimensions. Their research findings suggest that rape is a more complex issue than many believe.

From "Conceptualizing the 'Wantedness' of Women's Consensual and Nonconsensual Sexual Experiences: Implications for How Women Label Their Experiences with Rape" by Z. D. Peterson, and C. L. Muehlenhard. 2007. *Journal of Sex Research* 44: 72–88. Reprinted by permission of the publisher (Taylor & Francis, http://www.informaworld.com).

In December, 2008, the United States Government released a report of crime statistics in which the number of reported rapes had increased by 25 percent over the past 2 years (Human Rights Watch, 2008). While such a statistic may initially sound quite alarming, it is possible that the jump in reported sexual assaults is due to a change in the methodology used for collecting such statistics from victims. Now, instead of talking to a computer, those who have been victimized are able to talk to real people who can assist them in defining the nature of the assault. It is possible that such victims are now better able to assess the nuances of a sexual encounter in which wanting sex and agreeing to sex were independent issues.

Students will probably ask themselves several questions after reading this selection. How does one determine if sex is wanted or not? How does one make clear the consent or refusal to have sex? What are the implications of consenting to sex that is not wanted? The answers to these and other related questions are surely significant to the sexual well-being of students, putting this article at the top of their must-read list.

Many people, including the public and researchers, treat sex as either wanted or unwanted, with wanted sex being consensual and unwanted sex being nonconsensual. Real life, however, is often more complicated. For example, one woman, recalling her thoughts immediately before experiencing nonconsensual sex, wrote,

> I was thinking, "I really shouldn't be doing this," but on the other hand, almost like the devil on one shoulder and the angel on the other, I was saying, "he is so cute and I really like him and he will probably think I was just leading him on if I don't do it." (Peterson & Muehlenhard, 2000)

She expressed reasons for wanting to have sex and reasons for not wanting to have sex. Furthermore, although she expressed reasons for wanting to have sex, her questionnaire responses made it clear that she had not consented.

Can sex be wanted *and* unwanted? Can sex be *wanted but nonconsensual*? These questions have important scientific, clinical, legal, and interpersonal implications.

In this article, we describe what we view as the prevailing dominant model used to conceptualize sexual wanting. We then present a new model of sexual wanting and use it to explore women's feelings about consensual sex and rape.

THE DOMINANT MODEL OF SEXUAL WANTING

In the dominant model of sexual wanting, sex is conceptualized as either wanted or unwanted, reflecting a unidimensional, dichotomous model. Wanted sex is treated as consensual, and unwanted sex is treated as nonconsensual,

reflecting a model that conflates wanting and consenting (Muehlenhard & Peterson, 2005). Researchers do not explicitly delineate this model, and, if asked, they might view it as problematic. Nevertheless, much research seems consistent with this model.

Examples Reflecting a Unidimensional, Dichotomous Conceptualization of Wantedness

The dominant model, which is often apparent in research on sexuality, is unidimensional and dichotomous. The dominant model is implicit when sex is conceptualized unproblematically as either wanted or unwanted, when questionnaires refer to "wanted" sex or "unwanted" sex and ask respondents to recall incidents that fit one or the other and when questionnaires do not allow participants to express their ambivalence.

In a study investigating token resistance to sex, Muehlenhard and Hollabaugh (1988) asked women if they had been in the following situation: "You were with *a guy who wanted to engage in sexual intercourse and you wanted to also*, but for some reason you indicated that *you didn't want to . . .*" (p. 874). By referring to "wanted" sex and not allowing for ambivalence, this question conformed to the dominant model in which sex is assumed to be wanted or unwanted but not both. Similar questions have been used in other studies (Muehlenhard & Rodgers, 1998; Sprecher, Hatfield, Cortese, Potapova, & Levitskaya, 1994).

Research on sexual assertiveness also reflects the wanted—unwanted dichotomy. Morokoff et al.'s (1997) Sexual Assertiveness Scale was designed to measure several aspects of women's sexual assertiveness, including "initiation of *wanted sexual experience*" and "refusal of *unwanted sexual experience*" (p. 791). The measure includes items such as, "I begin sex with my partner *if I want to*" and "I refuse to let my partner touch my breasts *if I don't want that*, even if my partner insists" (p. 804). These items and the underlying concepts seem to be based on an implicit unidimensional, dichotomous model of wanting.

Examples Reflecting the Conflation of Wanting and Consenting

The dominant model also equates wanting sex with consenting to sex. This model is reflected when respondents are asked about "unwanted" sex, but their responses are treated as incidents of nonconsensual sex, thus making unwanted consensual sex conceptually impossible. This model is also reflected when, to qualify as having experienced nonconsensual sex, respondents must report sex that was not only nonconsensual but also unwanted, thus making wanted nonconsensual sex conceptually impossible.

Muehlenhard and Linton (1987, p. 188) defined rape as sexual intercourse when the woman "did not want to" and made that clear to her partner, but he did it anyway. In a nationwide survey of college students, Koss, Gidycz, and Wisniewski (1987) defined rape as sexual intercourse or other sexual penetration "*when you didn't want to* because a man gave you alcohol or drugs" or "*when you didn't want to* because a man threatened or used some degree of physical force" (p. 167). Similar definitions have been used in other studies (Shapiro & Schwarz, 1997; Testa & Dermen, 1999). These definitions imply that sex must be unambiguously unwanted to qualify as rape. Consistent with the dominant model, sex is treated as unwanted or wanted, and wantedness and consent are treated as equivalent.

PROBLEMS WITH THE DOMINANT MODEL

Problems With the Wanted—Unwanted Dichotomy

Although the dominant model treats sex as either wanted or unwanted, many people report ambivalence about sex. In O'Sullivan and Gaines's (1998) study of sexual decision making in college students, for example, over 80%

of the participants reported a situation in which they felt ambivalent about engaging in a sexual activity. Muehlenhard and Rodgers (1998) collected narrative data that captured participants' ambivalence. One woman wrote, "although my body wanted him my mind knew better" (p. 449). Another wrote, "I wanted to sleep with him, but I didn't know how he viewed the relationship" (p. 450). Similarly, Tolman and Szalacha (1999) found that many adolescent girls reported simultaneously experiencing reasons for wanting sex (feelings of pleasure) and for not wanting it (feelings of vulnerability).

Problems With Conflating Wanting and Consenting

Although the dominant model equates wanting and consenting, we argue that it is useful to conceptualize wanting and consenting as distinct concepts. In our conceptualization, to *want* something is to desire it, to wish for it, to feel inclined toward it, or to regard it or aspects of it as positively valenced; in contrast, to *consent* is to be willing or to agree to do something. Wanting may influence individuals' decisions about whether to consent, but wanting and consenting need not correspond. Individuals can agree or be willing to do things that do not correspond with their wishes or their inclinations (someone may not want to go to work on Monday morning yet still may be willing to go). Conversely, individuals can want or wish for something but decide not to consent to it (someone may want to go out drinking with friends but decide to stay home and study).

Evidence that Consensual Sex Can Be Unwanted

Many people report having consented to unwanted sex (O'Sullivan and Allgeier, 1998; Reneau & Muehlenhard, 2005). For example, O'Sullivan and Allgeier (1998) found that 50% of women and 26% of men in committed dating relationships reported consenting to unwanted sex during a 2-week period. The most commonly cited reasons were satisfying a partner's needs, promoting intimacy, and avoiding relationship tension. Other studies have identified reasons such as avoiding hurting a partner's feelings, feeling obligated because of something a partner did for them, and enhancing their sexual experience or image (Reneau & Muehlenhard, 2005).

Evidence that Nonconsensual Sex Can Be Wanted

In the dominant model, sex that is both nonconsensual and wanted is conceptually impossible. However, when wanting and consenting are conceptualized as distinct, wanted nonconsensual sex is possible. An individual might want to engage in a sexual activity, meaning that the individual desires or wishes for the activity or regards aspects of the activity as positively valenced but might nevertheless decide not to and thus be unwilling to engage in the activity. Little research has systematically tested the idea that nonconsensual sex can be wanted. However, when Satterfield and Muehlenhard (1996) asked college women and men about an experience with nonconsensual, unwanted sex, many of them described nonconsensual sex that was both wanted and unwanted. Their reasons for wanting the sexual experience included feeling sexually aroused, wanting to enhance the relationship, and wanting to enhance their image.

Unacknowledged Rape as a Possible Consequence of the Wanting-Consenting Conflation

It is possible that equating wantedness and consent contributes to unacknowledged rape. In Koss, Dinero, Seibel, and Cox's (1988) nationwide study of rape, 73% of the rape victims were *unacknowledged rape victims*—that is, they reported an experience meeting the researchers' operational definition of rape but did not label their experience as "rape." In subsequent studies, 73% (Layman, Gidycz, & Lynn, 1996), 62%

(Peterson & Muehlenhard, 2004), 58% (Kahn, Jackson, Kully, Badger, & Halvorsen, 2003), and 47% (Fisher, Daigle, Cullen, & Turner, 2003) of rape victims were unacknowledged rape victims.

Why might women refrain from labeling their experiences as rape? One explanation involves the conflation of wanting and consenting inherent in the dominant model. In some cases of rape, especially in cases of acquaintance rape, nonconsensual sex may be unwanted in some ways and wanted in others. Rape victims who accept the narrow definition of rape promoted by the dominant model and who had reasons for wanting to have sex may believe that their experience does not qualify as rape. They may believe that wanted but nonconsensual sex is either impossible or possible but not rape. A model of wanting that distinguishes between wanting and consenting would allow for a broader definition of rape and, therefore, would allow victims of nonconsensual sex to label their experience as rape regardless of whether the experience was wanted, unwanted, or both.

THE CURRENT STUDY

The current study addressed three primary objectives. Objective 1 was the further development of a new model of sexual wanting. Elaborating on a model suggested in other studies (Muehlenhard, Peterson, MacPherson, & Blair, 2002; Muehlenhard & Rodgers, 1998), we used a model that included the following components: (a) multiple gradations of wanting rather than a dichotomy; (b) multiple dimensions, acknowledging that sex can be wanted in some ways and unwanted in other ways; (c) an act–consequences distinction, acknowledging that wanting or not wanting a sexual act differs from wanting or not wanting its consequences; and (d) a wanting–consenting distinction, acknowledging that wanting or not wanting sex differs from consenting or not consenting to sex.

Objective 2 involved applying this new model to women's experiences with consensual and nonconsensual sex. Women who had experienced consensual sexual intercourse and women who had experienced rape completed a questionnaire developed to measure components of the new model. We explored global wantedness ratings and reasons for wanting and not wanting the intercourse.

Objective 3 involved the use of the new model to understand how women who had been raped labeled their experiences. We used the new model to assess whether ambivalence regarding wanting was related to rape victims' status as acknowledged or unacknowledged rape victims.

Conducting this study required that we choose a definition of rape. We chose to use a relatively narrow definition of rape, including only penile–vaginal intercourse (although some legal definitions include *digital penetration*, *oral sex*, etc.) and including only sex that was clearly nonconsensual because of force or fear of force or because the victims was too intoxicated to consent or to resist (Muehlenhard, Powch, Phelps, & Giusti, 1992; Posner & Silbaugh, 1996). We chose a narrow definition for two reasons: (1) If our definition had been broader than legal definitions, we might have inappropriately labeled some participants as *unacknowledged rape victims* in cases in which their experience fit our definition but did not fit the legal definition in their state. In exploring why some women did not label their nonconsensual sexual experience as *rape*, we wanted to avoid making psychological interpretations when the actual explanation was that they knew the law. (2) We hoped that by including only clear cases of rape, any results showing that some rape victims reported reasons for wanting to have sex would be more compelling. Our decision about whether to include a participant in the rape group did not mean that her experience was or was not rape in any absolute sense.

METHOD

Participants

The measures for our study were completed by 339 undergraduate women taking introductory psychology at the University of Kansas. Their mean age was 19, and most were in their 1st year of college. The ethnic composition of the sample was as follows: European American (81.4%), Hispanic American (6.2%), Asian American (3.8%), African American (2.9%), biracial or multiracial (2.1%), international student (0.9%), and other 0.9%). Almost all ($n = 323$; 95.3%) identified their sexual orientation as heterosexual. From this group, we identified a sample of women who had been raped (the "rape group") and a sample of women who had experienced consensual sexual intercourse (the "consensual sex group").

Identifying Members of the Rape Group

We used a 4-step procedure to identify group members. Step 1 involved the use of mass testing to identify individuals likely to meet the criteria for this group. On the screening measure for this study, the women were asked if they had experienced either of two situations. Question 1 asked about a situation in which (a) "you were 14 or older," (b) "you had penile—vaginal intercourse when you did not consent or agree to," and (c) "this experience occurred because you were incapable of giving consent or resisting due to intoxication." Question 2 asked about a situation in which (a) "you were 14 or older," (b) "you had penile—vaginal intercourse when you did not consent or agree to," and (c) "this experience occurred because the other person used physical force or some how made you afraid to say no." The screening measure did not use the word *rape*; however, anyone having been in one of these situations had been raped as defined by our research definition and by the laws of this state (*Kansas State Annals*, 1995, 21-3501). Of the 1,862 women who completed the screening measure, 61.0% reported having had penile—vaginal intercourse either willingly or unwillingly, and 6.9% reported having experienced nonconsensual sex.

In Step 2, all 128 women who had reported nonconsensual sex were contacted and invited to participate in the study. In addition, because we wanted to protect the women's privacy, and because of the possibility that some women who had been raped did not construe it as nonconsensual, we also invited an equal number of women who had indicated that they had not experienced nonconsensual sex obtained through intoxication, force, or fear.

Step 3 involved eliciting respondents' narrative descriptions of their experiences. The Sexual Experiences Questionnaire (SEQ) included Questions 1 and 2 from the screening questionnaire. Respondents who checked *yes* to Questions 1 or 2 were asked to describe their most recent experience with nonconsensual intercourse. Respondents who checked *no* were asked if they had had an experience "similar to" those described in these questions.

In Step 4, for all participants who reported nonconsensual sexual intercourse ($n = 78$) or a similar experience ($n = 66$), the two coinvestigators coded participants' narrative descriptions to determine whether the experiences fit the definition of rape used in this study. Our goal was to identify "false positives" and "false negatives." We relied on participants' narratives rather than relying solely on whether they had checked *yes* or *no* to Questions 1 and 2. We coded narratives as meeting our definition of rape if they clearly met the following criteria:

1. The participant was 14 years of age or older at the time of the incident.
2. The incident involved completed penile—vaginal intercourse.
3. The participant had not consented.
4. Either the other person had used physical force or had made the participant afraid to say no for fear of force (the force criterion) or the participant had been unable to

consent or resist because of the effect of alcohol or drugs, which would have been reasonably apparent to the other person (the intoxication criterion).

Of the 78 participants who had checked yes to the questions about experiencing nonconsensual sexual intercourse obtained through intoxication or force (*yes* to Questions 1 or 2), 89.7% were judged to qualify as rape victims on the basis of the definition used in this study. Of the 66 who had reported a "similar" experience (*no* to Questions 1 and 2 but had described a similar experience), 10.6% were judged to qualify as rape victims. Thus, the rape group consisted of 77 women who answered our measures on the basis of an experience with rape as defined in this study.

Identifying Members of the Consensual Sex Group

Potential members of the consensual sex group were recruited through the Psychology Department's Web-based sign-up system, which allowed introductory psychology students—the same population from which we drew the rape group—to sign up for a day and time to complete the questionnaires. This Web site specified that only women were eligible to participate but did not mention the topic of the study. Those participants who, on the SEQ, reported engaging in consensual sexual intercourse were included in the consensual sex group. This group included 87 women who answered our measures on the basis of their most recent experience with consensual sexual intercourse.

Measures

The SEQ

Narrative descriptions of participants' experiences. The first part of the SEQ differed for the rape and consensual sex groups. Participants who were recruited through mass testing (potential members of the rape group) were presented again with Questions 1 and 2 from the mass testing questionnaire that asked about nonconsensual sexual intercourse. Those who had had such an experience were asked to describe it. Those who had not had such an experience were asked to describe a similar situation, if applicable. Those who had not experienced nonconsensual intercourse or a similar situation were asked to describe a fictional situation; data from these participants were not used in the analyses.

Participants who were recruited through the Web-based system (potential members of the consensual sex group) were asked to describe their most recent experience with consensual intercourse, if applicable. Those who had not had consensual intercourse were asked to describe an experience with nonconsensual intercourse or something similar, if applicable. Those who had never had intercourse were asked to describe a fictional situation; data from these participants were not used in the analyses.

All participants were instructed to answer the rest of the questionnaire on the basis of the sexual experience they described.

The labels participants applied to their experiences. On the next section of the SEQ, participants were asked how they labeled the consensual or nonconsensual sexual experience. First they wrote open-ended responses. Then they were given a list of 25 possible labels and asked to check any label applicable to their experience. Possible labels included "rape," as well as options such as "a good sexual experience," "a bad sexual experience," "an exciting sexual experience," "a mistake on my part," and "a mistake on the other person's part." Among participants who reported an experience that fit our definition of rape, those who checked the label "rape" were considered acknowledged rape victims; those who did not check "rape" were considered unacknowledged rape victims.

Questions regarding consent. The SEQ then asked participants about their feelings and expressions of consent during the experience. *Consent* can be conceptualized both as a state

of mind (an internal feeling of willingness) and as a behavior (a verbal or physical expression of willingness; Hickman & Muehlenhard, 1999). In order to address both forms of consent, participants were asked to rate on a 7-point scale their agreement with the following statements: "I felt that I consented or agreed to this experience," "I communicated to the other person that I consented or agreed to this experience," and "I communicated to the other person that I did not consent or agree to this experience." Participants also were asked to describe in a narrative format how they communicated their consent or nonconsent.

Wanting Questionnaire

Finally, we assessed participants' reasons, if any, for wanting and not wanting the sexual experience, first via open-ended questions and next via the Wanting Questionnaire, the objective questionnaire based on our new model of wanting (Muehlenhard et al., 2002). The Wanting Questionnaire presented a list of possible reasons for wanting or not wanting the sexual act itself, the consequences of engaging in the sexual act, and the consequences of not engaging in the sexual act. Reflecting themes from previous research (Muehlenhard & Cook, 1988; Satterfield & Muehlenhard, 1996), questionnaire items described reasons for wanting or not wanting sex that related to sexual arousal, values, situational characteristics, social status, fear of pregnancy and STDs, and relationship concerns. Respondents indicated whether each item was true for them using a 7-point scale ranging from −3 (*a strong reason for not wanting to have sex*), to 0 (*not a reason for wanting or not wanting to have sex*), to 3 (*a strong reason for wanting to have sex*). Participants also made three global ratings of wantedness. The global wantedness items were as follows: "Overall, how much did you want or not want to engage in the SEXUAL INTERCOURSE ITSELF (not considering the consequences)?," "Overall, how much did you want or not want the POSSIBLE CONSEQUENCES OF ENGAGING in the sexual intercourse?," and "Overall, how much did you want or not want to engage in sexual intercourse in this situation (taking into account the intercourse itself, the possible consequences of engaging in the intercourse, and the possible consequences of not engaging in the intercourse)?" These three items were also rated on a scale ranging from -3 (*strongly unwanted*) to 3 (*strongly wanted*).

Procedure

All participants completed the measures in groups of 25 or fewer under the supervision of female research assistants. To protect participants' privacy, they were seated in alternate seats, they completed the measures anonymously (except for those who volunteered to be interviewed), and they placed their completed questionnaires in manila envelopes so that everyone turned in identical blank manila envelopes.

Interviews

Individual follow-up interviews were conducted with a subsample of participants who expressed interest on the interview-request form in their questionnaire packet. Women who described a real sexual experience on the SEQ and who expressed interest in being interviewed were contacted and invited to participate. Interviews were completed with 6 women from the rape group, 1 woman from the consensual sex group, and 1 woman who wrote about an experience that was "similar to" nonconsensual sex but that did not meet our definition of rape.

RESULTS

Objective 1: Development of a Multidimensional Model of Sexual Wanting

The first objective of this study was the further development of a multidimensional

model of sexual wanting. Toward this end, we explored the factor structure of the Wanting Questionnaire.

Exploratory Factor Analyses

The exploratory factor analysis included data from 213 participants who had completed the questionnaire according to the directions and who had described a real experience with sexual intercourse (consensual sex, nonconsensual sex, or something "similar" to nonconsensual sex). For the factor analysis of reasons for wanting sex, 60 items with a positive mean were included in the factor analysis. On the basis of the interpretability of the factors, 13 factors were retained. For the factor analysis of the reasons for not wanting sex, 43 items with a negative mean rating were included in the factor analysis; 12 factors were retained.

Objective 2: Comparisons of the Rape and Consensual Sex Groups

The second objective of this study was to apply the new model to women's experiences with consensual and nonconsensual sex.

Global Ratings of Wantedness

A one-way multivariate analysis of variance (MANOVA) was conducted to explore the relationship between consenting and wanting. The independent variable was membership in the rape or consensual sex group. The dependent variables were the three global ratings of wantedness. Significant differences were found between the rape and the consensual sex groups on the dependent measures. Compared with the rape group, the consensual sex group reported higher levels of wantedness for the sexual act, the consequences, and the intercourse overall. On the average, the consensual sex group rated the sexual act itself and the intercourse overall as wanted, whereas the rape group rated both as unwanted. Both groups rated the consequences as unwanted.

Although there were between-group differences, there were also notable within-group variations. Some members of the rape group rated the act itself, the consequences, and the intercourse overall as wanted. Conversely, some members of the consensual sex group rated the act itself, the consequences, and the intercourse overall as unwanted.

Reasons for Wanting and Not Wanting Sexual Intercourse

Compared with the rape group, the consensual sex group rated their experience with intercourse as more wanted because they were in the mood, they hoped to strengthen their relationship with the other person, they and the other person were not intoxicated, and they and the other person were not virgins. Compared with the consensual sex group, the rape group rated the intercourse as more wanted because they expected negative consequences if they refused and because they feared physical harm if they refused.

Compared with the consensual sex group, the rape group rated sex as more unwanted because they were not in the mood, they expected negative consequences from sex, they lacked confidence in their ability to perform, they disliked the other person, and they feared negative social consequences.

Objective 3: Comparisons of Acknowledged and Unacknowledged Rape Victims

The third objective of this study was to assess whether ambivalence about wanting sex was related to rape victims' status as acknowledged or unacknowledged rape victims. Among women in the rape group, those who checked the label *rape* as applying to their experience were considered acknowledged rape victims; those who did not were considered unacknowledged rape victims. On the basis of this criterion, 45.5% were acknowledged victims, and 54.5% were unacknowledged victims. There were no

significant group differences in whether nonconsensual sex had been obtained through force or intoxication or in the nature of the participants' prior relationship with the perpetrator (whether he was an acquaintance, friend, boyfriend, etc.).

Global Ratings of Wantedness

There were significant differences between the acknowledged and the unacknowledged groups. Acknowledged rape victims reported wanting the sexual intercourse itself less than unacknowledged rape victims. Rape acknowledgment was not significantly related to wantedness of the consequences.

Reasons for Wanting and Not Wanting Sexual Intercourse

For the analysis with the Reasons for Wanting Sex subscales, there were significant differences between the acknowledged and unacknowledged groups. Of the follow-up analyses, one reached statistical significance. Compared with acknowledged rape victims, unacknowledged rape victims reported wanting sex more because they were in the mood.

Secondary Analyses: Consent

Consent Ratings of the Rape and Consensual Sex Groups

Participants had rated on a 7-point scale the extent to which they had felt like they were consenting, had expressed their consent, and had expressed their nonconsent. Compared with the rape group, the consensual sex group had higher consent ratings and lower nonconsent ratings. Group differences were less clear-cut than might be expected, however. For example, for the item, "I felt that I consented or agreed to this experience," the modal response was 1 (*not at all true*) for the rape group (given by 54% of the group) and 7 (*very much true*) for the consensual-sex group (given by 88% of this group). However, responses of the rape group ranged from 1 to 7, and responses of the consensual sex group ranged from 4 to 7.

Consent as Related to Rape Acknowledgment

Compared with unacknowledged rape victims, acknowledged rape victims reported that the intercourse had felt less consensual and that they had expressed less consent to the other person.

DISCUSSION

Support for the New Model of Sexual Wanting

Wanting as a Continuous and Multidimensional Concept

Findings from the current study, in combination with findings from previous studies (Muehlenhard et al., 2002), provide support for conceptualizing sexual wanting as continuous and multidimensional. The continuous nature of wanting was demonstrated by the fact that for global ratings of wantedness, participants used the entire scale, not just the endpoints. The analysis of the Wanting Questionnaire produced multiple interpretable factors, supporting the multidimensional nature of sexual wanting.

Additionally, in response to open-ended questions, many participants described reasons for both wanting and not wanting sex. For example, a participant in the rape group described her reasons for wanting the intercourse ("I was sexually aroused from the previous making out/petting, I was highly attracted to my boyfriend, and I was under the influence") and for not wanting it ("We hadn't been dating long, I was really tired, I didn't feel good, I wasn't ready physically or emotionally").

Wanting the Act as Distinct from Wanting the Consequences

Results also supported distinguishing between wanting a sexual act and wanting its consequences. On average, women in the consensual sex group reported strongly wanting the intercourse itself but not wanting the consequences.

In their qualitative responses, both the rape and consensual sex groups often described reasons for wanting the intercourse but not wanting its consequences. A woman in the rape group wrote that she wanted the sexual act ("I was horny or just didn't know where to place all my hormonal energy") but did not want the consequences ("I didn't want to put my family to shame. I didn't want to reuine [sic] my relationship with God"). A woman in the consensual sex group described her reasons for wanting the sexual act ("I liked him, I was drunk, and it felt good") but not the consequences ("I wasn't ready and didn't want to get pregnant, I didn't love him").

Wanting as Distinct from Consenting

Not surprisingly, wanting sex and consenting to sex were closely related; on average, nonconsensual sex was less wanted than was consensual sex. However, the results demonstrated that individuals sometimes consent to unwanted sex and sometimes do not consent to wanted sex. When rating the wantedness of the sexual act, the consequences, and the intercourse overall, both the rape and consensual sex groups used almost the entire 7-point scale from −3 (*strongly unwanted*) to 3 (*strongly wanted*). About one fifth (19%) of the women in the rape group rated the sexual act as wanted to some degree, and half of the women in the consensual sex group rated the consequences of sex as unwanted to some degree. Even on the measure of overall wantedness, 5% of the rape group rated the intercourse as wanted, and 6% of the consensual sex group rated the intercourse as unwanted.

One participant in the rape group rated the intercourse as *strongly wanted* overall. She described an experience with an abusive boyfriend who often intentionally got her drunk to the point of almost passing out. He would then have sex with her despite her protests. Although clearly nonconsensual, the sex was not entirely unwanted. She wrote about her reasons for wanting to have sex, saying, "I loved him and wanted him to be happy.... I was horny too until he got controlling and his whole personality changed." Although she did not consent, she wrote that she "innerly wanted sex." The fact that the intercourse was wanted overall did not mean that the rape was not upsetting, however; she described it as an "emotionally painful" experience.

Conversely, 1 participant in the consensual-sex group described the intercourse as consensual and enjoyable, but she nevertheless rated it as *strongly unwanted* overall. She wrote,

> My sexual experiences are very few. I lost my virginity a little while ago. The last time I had sex I was still exploring.... I enjoy it, but I do get spasms of guilt feelings for doing it before marriage.

The distinction between wanting and consenting was also apparent on the subscales. On two Reasons for Wanting Sex subscales, the rape group scored higher than the consensual sex group. Although the women in the rape group did not consent, many of them reported reasons for wanting to have sex, such as fear of hurting the other person's feelings or angering the other person by refusing or fear of being physically harmed if they refused. On one hand, when women report wanting sex because of a fear of retaliation if they refuse sex (e.g., fear that the other person would physically harm them, fear that the other person would accuse them of being a "tease," etc.), it seems problematic to think of these fears as a reason for wanting sex in the same way that being aroused or wanting to strengthen the relationship is a reason for wanting sex. On the other hand, some women in this study did rate these as reasons that they wanted to have sex. This again highlights the importance of distinguishing between wanting and consenting; clearly "wanting" sex to avoid harm is different than freely consenting to sex.

Applications of the New Model
The new model could be useful in research on ways in which sex is wanted and unwanted in happy versus unhappy relationships and in

research on whether feelings about wanting or not wanting sex relate to sexual dysfunction. This model also has applications for unacknowledged rape.

Wantedness as a Predictor of Rape Acknowledgment
Although legal definitions of rape vary from state to state, generally such definitions are based on use of force or lack of consent (Posner & Silbaugh, 1996) not on whether the sexual act is wanted or unwanted. Nevertheless, the current study provides evidence that many women used levels of wanting in their decision about whether their experience qualified as rape. Compared with acknowledged rape victims, unacknowledged rape victims rated the sexual act itself as more wanted and reported wanting the intercourse more because they were in the mood (because they were aroused, expected sex to be pleasurable, or were attracted to the other person).

The qualitative data provided further support for this idea. In response to open-ended questions, several unacknowledged rape victims mentioned wanting the sexual act. One described wanting sex because of "curiosity [sic] b/c I was a virgin." Another, who was drunk to the point of unconsciousness during the intercourse, wrote, "...when I get drunk I am usually horney [sic] so I probably wanted it as bad as him."

Implications of the Relationship Between Wantedness and Rape Acknowledgment
The distinction between wanting sex and consenting to sex could have important implications for rape victims, clinicians, victim advocates, and juries. When rape is conceptualized as unwanted sex, any evidence that the victim wanted to have sex (flirtatious behavior prior to the rape, sexual arousal during the rape) can be interpreted to mean that the incident was not really rape. As a result, rape victims may

experience blame or guilt for having "asked for it," even though they did not consent to it.

A woman who does not consider her experience rape is unlikely to report it to the police or to seek support in dealing with her distress. There is some evidence that unacknowledged victims may have more difficulty recovering from their rape than do acknowledged victims. Research suggests that, compared with acknowledged rape victims, unacknowledged victims tend to experience more emotional problems that interfere with their work, feel less happy, feel less supported, and consume more alcohol following their rape (Botta & Pingree, 1997). If acknowledging rape facilitates adjustment, rape victims may benefit from educational or therapeutic interventions that emphasize the distinction between wanting sex and consenting to sex and that emphasize nonconsent rather than a lack of wantedness as the defining feature of rape.

Other Findings

Although not the primary purpose of the current study, participants' qualitative responses and the results of the secondary quantitative analyses offered insights into the definitional ambiguity of rape, the complexity of consent, and possible consequences of acknowledging versus not acknowledging rape for individual women.

Definitional Ambiguity of Rape

Research on rape often involves providing participants with an operational definition of rape; those who report an experience that meets this operational definition are considered rape victims. This approach is based on the assumption that participants and researchers are interpreting the questions the same way. In the current study, we coded participants' narrative descriptions of their experiences, and we found evidence of both false positive and false negative reports of rape on the basis of our research definition. This finding highlights the difficulties in deciding which incidents should count as rape.

Coding participants' narratives as rape or as not rape was often difficult, especially for incidents that did not involve force and thus would qualify as rape only under the intoxication criterion. The legal definition of rape in Kansas, which guided our research definition, includes cases of intercourse in which "the victim is incapable of giving consent . . . because of the effect of any alcoholic liquor, narcotic, drug or other substance, which condition was known by the offender or was reasonably apparent to the offender" (*Kansas State Annals*, 1995, 21-3502). It is unclear how intoxicated a woman must be in order to be "incapable of giving consent" and in order for the condition to be "reasonably apparent to the offender."

It seemed clear that an experience would meet the legal definition of rape if the woman was unconscious or barely coherent, or if the intercourse occurred despite her expression of nonconsent. However, not all experiences in which the woman was intoxicated seemed coercive or nonconsensual. For example, we excluded one woman from our rape group although she reported having been drunk and high on marijuana. She wrote, "The guy was hot and drunk sex is the best," and she described enthusiastically participating in the intercourse.

Particularly confusing were cases in which the woman reported "blacking out"—that is, being unable to recall portions of the situation due to intoxication. In these cases, participants recalled only fragments, if any, of the sexual encounter. If the woman was intoxicated enough to forget the intercourse, then it might seem reasonable to assume that she was too intoxicated to give consent.

Cases in which the woman gave in to intercourse as a result of fear were also sometimes difficult to classify. The legal definition of rape in Kansas includes intercourse in which "the victim is overcome by force or fear" (*Kansas State Annals*, 1995, 21-3502). It is unclear what type of fear should count. We decided to count fear of physical harm but not fear of social repercussions or relationship conflict.

The Ambiguity of Consent

On average, acknowledged rape victims in the current study rated the sexual act as less consensual than unacknowledged rape victims. However, it was evident that consent and nonconsent, like wanting and not wanting, are not clear-cut or easily defined. Many participants in the current study seemed to view consent as continuous rather than dichotomous.

In addition, many participants expressed idiosyncratic ideas about what constitutes having consented. Some regarded passivity as consent ("I guess you could say I 'consented' by not saying yes and just letting it happen". This response was consistent with past findings that the modal way that college women and men reported expressing their consent for sexual intercourse was to do nothing (Hickman & Muehlenhard, 1999).

Some participants regarded being in a particular situation as having consented. One unacknowledged rape victim rated her sexual experience as somewhat consensual, despite having said "no" and pushed the other person away. In an interview, she explained that she believed that she demonstrated consent by putting herself in a sexually risky situation:

> Well, the fact that I was there and wasn't telling my friend to take me home or telling one of the guys there that was sober to take me home, you know.... Kind of by not making a big deal out of, like being alone in there with him.... You know, by staying and by not saying anything about the awkward situation of being alone in there with a guy that I just met like twice before, that was kind of like consenting to it.

Effects of Acknowledging or Not Acknowledging Rape on Individual Women

There is evidence that acknowledging rape is beneficial for psychological recovery from rape (Botta & Pingree, 1997). Consistent with this point, in the current study, when asked how she would feel differently if she thought her experience was a rape, an unacknowledged rape victim stated, "I wouldn't blame myself as much if it was rape because I had control and I let it happen so I do get angry with myself for letting it happen."

Although labeling an act as rape may decrease self-blame and aid in recovery for some women, it may have negative consequences for others. Lamb (1999) suggested that many women do not want to think of themselves as "victims" because the term "revives the original feeling of helplessness and vulnerability" (pp. 125–126). Because our culture emphasizes individual responsibility, she wrote that it is reasonable that individuals would want to emphasize their own "resiliency, agency, and strength" (p. 126) by rejecting the victim label. Along these lines, one rape victim in the current study checked the label *rape* as applying to her experience but expressed reservations about using the label:

> I never say rape—I'm not really sure why. I tell people my 1st experience was not by my choice, it was forced.... I think that it makes me less upset to say. It seems less abrasive. Also, I think I worry a lot about how other people will think of me or react if I say rape.

Several unacknowledged rape victims suggested that they had considered calling their experience rape and had rejected that label for a variety of reasons. For example, one woman described the problems that labeling her experience as rape could have caused:

> It's really weird because ... I went back to my house the next morning, and one of the first things I felt was, "I really want to take a shower," but then I thought, "Ohh, but you're not supposed to do that ... in case you feel it matters or anything," and then I was like, "No, that would just be weird." I don't think I could do that to my parents and to him and to everybody else and to come out and say I was raped.... I mean, among other things, it would just be word against word. I just didn't see any pretty way of handling it, really, I mean for anybody, because my parents don't know I drink, so that would be bad. I'm definitely not proud of my conduct.... I've heard

that through trials everything comes out, and you know, they look for every reason they can to make it look like you said yes or whatever. It's almost easier to think of it as an accident.

She also suggested that she avoided labeling her experience as rape because it would have made her feel uncomfortable to think of the other person as a rapist.

> *Participant*: I guess the weird thing about considering it rape would be I would have to consider him the person who did it and that's really weird.
>
> *Researcher*: Is it hard to think of him as a rapist?
>
> *Participant*: Yeah.
>
> *Researcher*: Why is that hard?
>
> *Participant*: He's a normal horny college guy, a next-door neighbor, funny, um, well, not that intelligent [laughs]. Um, he just seems like a lot of guys I've met. Maybe not someone I'd want to date, but someone I'd want to hang out with. And if he can do that, if he's a rapist, or even a potential, then that makes me start going, "What about that guy, and what about that guy, and what about that guy?"

Another unacknowledged rape victim conveyed similar themes:

> I think I would be a lot more upset about it [if it had been rape]. I think it would have affected me for longer than it did. Because the next morning I was like, "I can't believe that happened," but I wasn't like, "Oh my gosh, I got raped, and now I need to do something about it." I was like, "Wow that was a big mistake and that won't happen again."

Labeling her experience "a big mistake" allowed her to feel less traumatized and more in control. For her, avoiding the term "rape" may have been empowering.

Thus, this study suggested two sets of reasons for why women might not label their nonconsensual sexual intercourse as rape. One set of

reasons relates to how they conceptualize sexual wanting: If they regard wanting sex as consenting to sex, and if they had reasons for wanting sex, then they might conclude that their experience does not qualify as rape or that they are not entitled to call their experience *rape*. The other set of reasons relates to the perceived consequences applying the term *rape* to their own experience: Labeling an incident as rape might make them feel obligated to act, such as by reporting the incident to the police. It might lead to negative interpersonal or practical consequences. It might increase their feeling of vulnerability. It might make the experience more traumatizing. In some cases, then, rejecting the label *rape* might be a constructive and empowering choice.

A FINAL POINT

At first glance, it might seem inappropriate or harmful to claim that some rape victims actually wanted to have sex. After all, "She wanted it" is a rape myth used to blame rape victims or to dismiss claims of rape (Lonsway & Fitzgerald, 1995). We argue that, to the contrary, this concept can actually be helpful to rape victims.

Most people would probably agree that it is possible to want to have sex but to decide not to consent. If the other person proceeds despite the lack of consent, it is rape, regardless of how strongly the sex was wanted. Contemporary thinking about rape has expanded to include circumstances that, in the past, would have disqualified the incidents from counting as rape. Currently, many people are willing to say that if the victim did not consent, it is rape, even if the victim flirted with the perpetrator, even if the victim had been drinking, or even if the victim experienced sexual arousal or orgasm during the incident. It seems constructive to expand current thinking about rape to say that if the victim did not consent, it is rape, even if the victim wanted to have sex. Rape is about the absence of consent, not the absence of desire—an idea that could be liberating to many rape victims.

INTRODUCTION REFERENCE

Human Rights Watch. 2008, December 18. U. S.: Soaring rates of rape and violence against women. Http://www.hrw.org/en/news/2008/12/18/us-soaring-rates-rape-and-violence-against-women (accessed December 25, 2008).

REFERENCES

Botta, R. A., & Pingree, S. (1997). Interpersonal communication and rape: Women acknowledge their assaults. *Journal of Health Communication*, 2, 197–212.

Fisher, B. S., Daigle, L. E., Cullen, F. T., & Turner, M. G. (2003). Acknowledging sexual victimization as rape: Results from a national-level study. *Justice Quarterly*, 20, 535–570.

Hickman, S. E., & Muehlenhard, C. L. (1999). "By the semi-mystical appearance of a condom": How young women and men communicate sexual consent in heterosexual situations. *Journal of Sex Research*, 36, 258–272.

Kahn, A. S., Jackson, J., Kully, C., Badger, K., & Halvorsen, J. (2003). Calling it rape: Differences in experiences of women who do and do not label their sexual assault as rape. *Psychology of Women Quarterly*, 27, 233–242.

Kansas State Annals. §§ 21–3501–3502 (1995 & Supp. 1999).

Koss, M. P., Dinero, T. E., Seibel, C. A., & Cox, S. L. (1988). Stranger and acquaintance rape: Are there differences in the victim's experience? *Psychology of Women Quarterly*, 12, 1–24.

Koss, M. P., Gidycz, C. A., & Wisniewski, N. (1987). The scope of rape: Incidence and prevalence of sexual aggression and victimization in a national sample of higher education students. *Journal of Consulting and Clinical Psychology*, 55, 162–170.

Lamb, S. (1999). Constructing the victim: Popular images and lasting labels. In S. Lamb (Ed.), *New versions of victims: Feminists struggle with the concept* (pp. 108–138). New York: New York University Press.

Layman, M. J., Gidycz, C. A., & Lynn, S. J. (1996). Unacknowledged versus acknowledged rape victims: Situational factors and posttraumatic stress. *Journal of Abnormal Psychology*, 105, 124–131.

Lonsway, K. A., & Fitzgerald, L. F. (1995). Attitudinal antecedents of rape myth acceptance: A theoretical and empirical reexamination. *Journal of Personality and Social Psychology*, 68, 704–711.

Morokoff, P. J., Quina, K., Harlow, L. L., Whitmire, L., Grimely, D. M., Gibson, P. R., & Burkholder, G. J. (1997). Sexual Assertiveness Scale (SAS) for women: Development and validation. *Journal of Personality and Social Psychology*, 73, 790–804.

Muehlenhard, C. L., & Cook, S. W. (1988). Men's self-reports of unwanted sexual activity. *Journal of Sex Research*, 24, 58–72.

Muehlenhard, C. L., & Hollabaugh L. C. (1988). Do women sometimes say no when they mean yes? The prevalence and correlates of women's token resistance to sex. *Journal of Personality and Social Psychology*, 54, 872–879.

Muehlenhard, C. L., & Linton, M. A. (1987). Date rape and sexual aggression in dating situations: Incidence and risk factors. *Journal of Counseling Psychology*, 34, 186–196.

Muehlenhard, C. L., & Peterson, Z. D. (2005). Wanting and not wanting sex: The missing discourse of ambivalence. *Feminism and Psychology*, 15, 15–20.

Muehlenhard, C. L., Peterson, Z. D., MacPherson, L. A., & Blair, R. L. (2002, June). *First experiences with sexual intercourse: Wanted, unwanted, or both? Application of a multidimensional model*. Paper presented at the Midcontinent and Eastern Region Joint Conference of the Society for the Scientific Study of Sexuality, Big Rapids, Ml.

Muehlenhard, C. L., Powch, I. G., Phelps, J. L., & Giusti, L. M. (1992). Definitions of rape: Scientific and political implications. *Journal of Social Issues*, 48, 23–44.

Muehlenhard, C. L., & Rodgers, C. S. (1998). Token resistance to sex: New perspectives on an old stereotype. *Psychology of Women Quarterly*, 22, 443–463.

O'Sullivan, L. F., & Allgeier, E. R. (1998). Feigning sexual desire: Consenting to unwanted sexual activity in heterosexual dating relationships. *Journal of Sex Research*, 35, 234–243.

O'Sullivan, L. F., & Gaines, M. E. (1998). Decision-making in college students' heterosexual dating relationships: Ambivalence about engaging in sexual activity. *Journal of Social and Personal Relationships*, 15, 347–363.

Peterson, Z. D., & Muehlenhard, C. L. (2000). *Rape myth acceptance and situational characteristics as predictors of rape acknowledgment*. [Unpublished raw data].

Peterson, Z. D., & Muehlenhard, C. L. (2004). Was it rape? The function of women's rape myth acceptance and definitions of sex in labeling their own experiences. *Sex Roles*, 51, 129–144.

Posner, R. A., & Silbaugh, K. B. (1996). *A guide to America's sex laws*. Chicago: University of Chicago Press.

Reneau, S. E., & Muehlenhard, C. L. (2007). *Unwanted consensual sexual activity in heterosexual dating relationships*. Manuscript submitted for publication.

Satterfield, A. T., & Muehlenhard, C. L. (1996, November). *The role of gender in the meaning of sexual coercion: Women's and men's reactions to their own experiences*. Paper presented at the Annual Meeting of the Society for the Scientific Study of Sexuality, Houston, TX.

Shapiro, B. L., & Schwarz, J. C. (1997). Date rape: Its relationship to trauma symptoms and sexual self-esteem. *Journal of Interpersonal Violence, 12*, 407–419.

Sprecher, S., Hatfield, E., Cortese, A, Potapova, E., & Levitskaya, A. (1994). Token resistance to sexual intercourse and consent to unwanted sexual intercourse: College students' dating experiences in three countries. *Journal of Sex Research, 31*, 125–132.

Testa, M., & Dermen, K. H. (1999). The differential correlates of sexual coercion and rape. *Journal of Interpersonal Violence, 14*, 548–561.

Tolman, D. L., & Szalacha, L. A. (1999). Dimensions of desire: Bridging qualitative and quantitative methods in a study of female adolescent sexuality. *Psychology of Women Quarterly, 23*, 7–39.

Tactics of Sexual Coercion
When Men and Women Won't Take No for an Answer

Cindy J. Struckman-Johnson
David L. Struckman-Johnson
Peter B. Anderson

Some of you reading this chapter about tactics of sexual coercion may find yourself in the "been there done that" category. Perhaps you could even add your own scenarios to the firsthand accounts of the respondents' experiences with post-refusal sexual persistence: persistent attempts to have sexual contact with someone who has already refused, using pressure, alcohol or drugs, or force. But, things are changing in this respect.

Rape is but one result of coercive sexual behavior but it is a category in which a change of views seems almost as mercurial as the nightly news. In fact, new laws defining rape today are light years ahead of the public's perceptions of rape when your parents and grandparents were on university campuses or were already young adults in the world of work. As recently as the 1970s, rape was viewed as a sexual act in which a man had responded to a woman's sexual provocations. In 1971, MacDonald wrote, "[A] woman who accepts a ride home from a stranger, picks up a hitchhiker, sunbathes alone,

or works in a garden in a two-piece bathing suit which exposes rather than conceals her anatomy invites rape" (1971, 311).

Then there were the years of terminological confusion. During the decade of the 1970s, feminist writers began to question the way that rape was commonly conceptualized. Brownmiller (1975) and Griffin (1971) began to depict rape as violence. Griffin characterized it as an act of aggression in which the victim is denied her "self-determination." Further, she emphasized that the fear of rape also limits women's freedom.

More recently, in the word game of terminology, more questions have been posed: Should the term "rape" be replaced with "sexual assault" in order to emphasize the violent nature of the act? Do we more correctly refer to "rape survivor" than to "rape victim," a less empowering word? Muehlenhard and Highby (1997) in their prolific writing on the subject concluded in the late 1990s that there was no clear consensus on these questions in law, popular media, research literature, or feminist writing.

But once again, the "order of the day" seems to be change, with troubling questions on the horizon about rape and consent. In January 2003, the California Supreme Court ruled that a man can

From "Tactics of Sexual Coercion: When Men and Women Won't Take No for an Answer" by C. Struckman-Johnson, D. Struckman-Johnson, and P. B. Anderson. 2003. *The Journal of Sex Research* 40: 76–86. Reprinted by permission of the publisher (Taylor & Francis, http://www.informaworld.com).

be convicted of rape if a woman first consents, but later asks him to stop the sexual activity (Chiang 2003). In July 2003, a rape law was enacted in the State of Illinois that further clarified the issue of consent by emphasizing that people can change their mind while having sex. Simply stated, if a person in Illinois says "no," the act of sex becomes rape (McKinney 2003). In an Op-Ed column of the Boston Globe, *Cathy Young (2003) characterized the broad scope of such actions as "hailed by some as a sign of progress and denounced by others as a sign of an anti-male witch-hunt" (p. A15). Young concluded that although there are many unresolved and troubling questions about force, consent, and credibility in rape cases, the principle is sound: forced sex is always rape. You may be amazed or amused at some of the archaic concepts of sexual assault and other forms of sexual coercion that have occurred over the years. As you somehow try to fit together the pieces of the puzzle, however, we hope your conscience will comprehend the seriousness of any kind of forced sexual activity.*

Following this reading about sexual coercion, what changes on your campus could you suggest as prevention strategies for destructive sexual behaviors? Do any of them pertain to personal attitudes that need to be strengthened or modified? Could sharing these ideas with others in your social groups lead to broad social change about an important topic? Remember, when scrolling down the screen under the subject of sexual coercion, with a click of the mouse, anyone can instantly move from the virtual category of "problem" to "solution." By speaking up and adding your voice to the din about sexual coercion, however, you will move from the everyday category of "problem" to "solution." Your movement will not be as instantaneous as it would be online, but it will be more real and more life changing.

The Prevalence of Sexual Coercion

Sexually coercive behavior, defined in this paper as the act of using pressure, alcohol or drugs, or force to have sexual contact with someone against his or her will, has been studied among young adult populations for decades. From 1950 through the 1980s, the research focused on female victims and male perpetrators. One of the most influential studies was by Koss, Gidycz, and Wisniewski (1987), who found that 15 percent of the women in a national sample of over 6,000 college students had experienced rape. About 4 percent of the men indicated that they had perpetrated rape. In this survey, like many others conducted during this time period, only women were asked about being victims, and only men were asked about being perpetrators of coercive sexual behavior (Allgeier, 2002; Struckman-Johnson & Anderson, 1998).

In the late 1980s, a small number of investigators began to ask men as well as women about their experiences as victims of sexual coercion. Struckman-Johnson (1988) documented that 16 percent of men and 22 percent of women surveyed at a university reported being forced to have sexual intercourse while on a date. In the 1990s and early 2000s, at least a dozen more studies that included both male and female sexual victims appeared in the literature. For example, Lottes (1991) discovered that 24 percent of the men and 35 percent of the women in a classroom sample of college students reported that they had been coerced into sexual intercourse.

Tactics of Sexual Coercion

The present [chapter] is about gender differences in the tactics that are used in sexual coercion. In our review of the literature, we learned that men and women have been the victims of and have used a wide variety of coercive strategies for sexual contact. Most of the research has focused on the tactics men used to gain sexual access to women. Notably, Koss and her colleagues initiated a large body of research using the Sexual Experiences Survey (SES; Koss et al., 1987), which assessed a list of coercive tactics that men use to have sexual contact with women. For example, Koss et al. (1987) found that college women reported engaging in unwanted sexual intercourse because men had used verbal coercion (reported by 25 percent of the women), had threatened or used force (9 percent), had given the women alcohol or drugs (8 percent), and had misused authority (2 percent).

Anderson and Aymami (1993) measured college women's use of tactics for initiating sexual contact with men. One of the most commonly reported tactics was attempting to arouse the partner (cited by 79 percent of women). However, about *half* of the women reported initiating sex with a drunken man, 15 percent reported getting a man drunk or stoned, and 6 percent reported using physical force.

A few studies have explored male victims' perspectives on sexually coercive tactics used by female perpetrators. Struckman-Johnson and Struckman-Johnson (1998) found that 43 percent of college men had been subjected to at least one coercive sexual act with a woman since the age of 16. The most frequently cited tactics were verbal coercion (reported by 75 percent of male victims), being encouraged to get drunk (40 percent), and threats that the woman would withdraw her love (19 percent). Only 8 percent of male victims said that they were physically restrained by a woman. Surveying college men, Fiebert and Tucci (1998) documented that 70 percent reported being subjected to some form of sexual coercion perpetrated by a woman in the past 5 years. Most of the coercive activities fell into categories labeled mild (e.g., 17 percent to 39 percent experienced unwanted sexual touching and kissing) and moderate (e.g., 24 percent had unwanted sex with an insistent woman). Severe coercion involving a woman's threats or physical force was reported by only 1 percent to 3 percent of men.

Numerous studies have compared the coercive tactics experienced by male and female victims. In a classic work, Muehlenhard and Cook (1988) examined gender differences in reasons why college men and women engaged in unwanted sexual activity. The authors used factor analysis to create 13 categories of reasons for engaging in unwanted sexual activity, some of which reflected coercive tactics by the partner (e.g., verbal coercion by the partner) and some of which did not (e.g., peer pressure from the respondents' friends). Overall, they found that more women than men reported engaging in unwanted sexual activity because of the partner's verbal coercion (reported by 34 percent of the women and 27 percent of the men) and physical coercion (reported by 31 percent of the women and 24 percent of the men). None of the reasons for engaging in unwanted sexual activity were reported by more men than women.

Waldner-Haugrud and Magruder (1995) surveyed college students about unwanted sexual behavior in a dating context. According to self reports, more women than men were subjected to tactics of detainment, persistent touching, lies, and being held down. More men than women reported being victimized by the tactics of blackmail and use of a weapon. Larimer, Lydum, Anderson, and Turner (1999) used a gender-neutral version of the SES to assess sexual coercion among college students in Greek organizations. Similar percentages of men and women reported having unwanted sexual intercourse because they were pressured by continual arguments and were given alcohol and drugs. However, for attempts at sexual intercourse, more women than men reported being given alcohol and drugs (17 percent vs. 9 percent) and being subjected to physical force (5 percent vs. 1 percent).

Finally, we found two studies that analyzed differences in tactics used by male and female perpetrators of sexual coercion. Hogben and Waterman (2000) measured the extent to which college men and women used a variety of tactics to engage in sex with someone against his or her will. They found that more men than women reported having engaged in the behaviors of touching above clothing, removal of clothing, and verbal attempts to obtain intercourse. However, men and women did not differ significantly in their reported use of violence or threats of violence. Zurbriggen (2000) found that similar percentages of men and women reported that they used tactics of complaining of sexual frustration, threatening to end a relationship, and getting a little drunk and forcing someone to have sex. However, more men than women said that they gave the silent treatment (40 percent vs. 16 percent, respectively), got someone purposefully drunk for sex (32 percent vs. 18 percent), or threatened that their feelings of affection would change (25 percent vs. 11 percent).

The preponderance of studies revealed that greater percentages of women than men had been subjected to the full range of tactics of sexual coercion from verbal pressure to physical force. The most commonly experienced tactics of sexual coercion, regardless of gender, appeared to be techniques of sexual arousal (e.g., persistent kissing and touching) and verbal pressure such as continual arguments. The least commonly experienced tactics were those involving physical force and harm. There is consistent evidence that more women than men were deceived for purposes of sexual access (e.g., Waldner-Haugrud & Magruder, 1996). There are contrasting findings for the tactic of taking advantage of intoxicated persons. Although at least one study indicates that more women than men were subjected to this tactic (Lottes & Weinberg, 1996), some studies found no gender difference (e.g., Lane & Gwartney-Gibbs, 1985). A majority of studies indicated that more women than men were subjected to tactics involving physical force, yet several studies found few differences or numbers of reports too small to analyze (e.g., Hogben & Waterman, 2000).

THE PRESENT STUDY

We designed the present research to study gender differences in the experience and use of tactics of sexual coercion using methods that would remedy many of these complications. Our first objective was to study tactics that could clearly be defined as sexually coercive, asking both women and men about both experiencing and using these tactics. We chose to study a behavior that we termed "post-refusal sexual persistence," defined as the act of pursuing sexual contact with a person after he or she has refused an initial advance. In our thinking, all acts of post-refusal sexual persistence are sexually coercive in that the receiver has already indicated that he or she does not consent to the action. While acts such as removing a receiver's clothing or making repeated requests would be considered noncoercive in an initial sexual advance, the same behaviors can be defined as coercive if the person continues to do them after the receiver has said no.

A second objective was to organize tactics that have been identified in past research into categories that reflect increasing levels of sexual exploitation. Based on our past research and a review of the literature, we proposed four levels of tactics.

Level 1 includes nonverbal sexual arousal tactics, such as persistent touching and kissing and clothing removal, that are intended to change the receiver's mind about saying no to sex. Because these tactics are normative acts of sexual seduction in consensual situations and do not involve verbal pressure or duplicity, use of drugs, or physical force, we considered them to be the least exploitative of sexually persistent acts.

Level 2 consists of tactics of emotional manipulation and lies. This category includes tactics that are typically termed verbal or psychological pressure, such as repeated requests, questions about a person's sexuality, threats of breaking up the relationship, deception, and blackmail. These tactics are exploitative in that they are intended to wear down the receiver's resistance, to take unfair advantage of the receiver's needs and desires for a relationship, and to deceive and trick the receiver into having sexual contact.

Level 3 includes tactics related to alcohol and drug intoxication, such as taking advantage of someone who is already drunk or purposely getting someone intoxicated to obtain sexual contact. We regard these tactics as a higher level of exploitation than manipulation or lies because the receivers may be too inebriated to consider requests, to give knowledgeable consent, to detect deception, or to physically escape the situation.

Level 4, tactics of physical force and harm, is the highest level of exploitation because the receiver is forced to engage in behaviors against her or his will. Injury and harm may occur. Depending upon the sexual outcome, behaviors in Levels 3 and 4 meet the legal definition of rape in many states.

A final objective of our study was to gain understanding of the dynamics of post-refusal sexual persistence by examining participants' descriptions of recent experiences. We used structured and open-ended questions to assess relationships between receivers and perpetrators, how the tactics were employed, and how participants were affected by the incidents.

Method

We distributed the survey to 656 college students: 213 men and 247 women from a Midwestern university and 62 men and 134 women from a Southern university. The average age was 21 years for men and 20 years for women. The survey was administered anonymously to students in general psychology, social psychology, sex roles, and human sexuality classes. This procedure prevents a problem in sexual coercion research in which men in classroom administrations tend to leave a large number of items blank (Senn, Verberg, Desmarais, & Wood, 2000). Over 95 percent of questionnaires were returned. A majority of the participants (82 percent) indicated on the questionnaire that they were Caucasian.

Measures

The post-refusal sexual persistence item read "Since the age of 16, how many times has a male [female; always the opposite sex from the participant] used any of the tactics on the list below to have sexual contact (genital touching, oral sex, or intercourse) with you after you have

indicated 'no' to his [her] sexual advance?" Participants were further instructed to write in the space next to each tactic the number of times, to the best of their memory, that a male or female had used a tactic against them. Participants were then asked to answer questions about the most recent incident of sexual persistence they had experienced (if any). [They] were asked: "In your own words, please explain how this happened. What exactly did the male or female do when he or she tried to have sexual contact with you?" We then asked participants multiple-choice questions about their relationship with the perpetrator and what sexual activity took place. Participants rated the extent to which the incident affected them and their relationship with the perpetrator and wrote descriptions of these effects. We asked participants the same questions about their own use of post refusal sexual persistence tactics since age 16 and in the most recent incident.

Results

Receivers of Post-refusal Sexual Persistence
Chi-square tests determined that the distributions of sexual persistence experiences for receivers did not differ between the two university samples, so the two samples were combined. The results revealed that 58 percent of the male sample and 78 percent of the female sample had been subjected to at least one tactic of sexual persistence.

Most frequently reported tactics across genders. The tactics category reported most frequently was sexual arousal, with 65 percent of all participants being subjected to at least one experience. Within this category, persistent kissing and touching was the most cited tactic. Emotional manipulation and deception was the next most frequently reported category, with 60 percent of participants being subjected to at least one experience. Within this category, participants cited the specific tactics of repeated requests and telling lies most often. Intoxication was the third most frequently reported category, with 38 percent of all participants being subjected to at least one tactic. More participants reported being taken advantage of while already intoxicated than being purposely intoxicated. The category with the lowest frequency of reports was physical force and harm, with 28 percent of participants being subjected to at least one tactic. The most frequently reported acts were having the retreat route blocked, being physically restrained, and being harmed. Less than 2 percent of participants reported that weapons were used against them.

Gender differences in receivers' experiences of tactics. Results revealed that more women than men reported being subjected to at least one sexual arousal tactic. Within this category, more women than men cited persistent kissing and touching. A greater percentage of women than men reported being subjected to at least one tactic of emotional manipulation or lies. Within this category, more women than men reported repeated requests and being told lies.

More women than men reported experiencing at least one intoxication tactic. This difference held for cases in which the participant was already intoxicated and for cases in which the perpetrator purposefully intoxicated the participant. There was no significant difference between the percentages of women and men who reported being subjected to at least one tactic of physical force and harm. However, within this category, a greater percentage of women than men reported being subjected to physical restraint and being threatened with harm.

Perpetrators of Post-refusal Sexual Persistence

Most frequently reported tactics across genders. As reported, 43 percent of men and 26 percent of women reported having perpetrated at least one tactic of sexual persistence. Although there were fewer perpetrators than receivers, the two groups showed similar patterns for the most frequently occurring tactics. For perpetration of sexual persistence, the most frequently reported

category was sexual arousal. Within the category, kissing and touching was the most used tactic. The second most frequently reported category was emotional manipulation and lies. Within this category, 20 percent reported using repeated requests, and 8 percent reported using lies. Only 8 percent of participants said that they had used at least one intoxication tactic, with 8 percent taking advantage of an intoxicated person and 3 percent using purposeful intoxication. Only 3 percent of participants reported using a tactic in the physical force and harm category.

Gender differences in use of tactics. More men than women reported using at least one tactic in the sexual arousal category (40 percent vs. 26 percent, respectively). Within this category, more men than women reported persistent kissing and touching and removing the receivers' clothing. More men than women also reported using at least one tactic of emotional manipulation and lies. Within this category, more men than women reported using repeated requests and lying.

For the category of intoxication, more men than women reported using at least one tactic. The difference held for taking advantage of an intoxicated person and for purposely getting someone intoxicated. There was no significant difference in the percentage of men and women who reported the use of at least one force tactic.

Variables Related to Most Recent Incidents

There were no gender differences for the relationship variable among the receivers or among the perpetrators. Half of the receivers reported being with an acquaintance, friend, or new date, and 38 percent reported being with a boyfriend, girlfriend, steady date, or fiancé. A majority of perpetrators reported being with a steady partner, and 30 percent reported being with acquaintances or new partners. Fewer than 5 percent of all incidents occurred with strangers. There were no gender differences for sexual outcome of the most recent incident among the receivers or among the perpetrators. The most recent incident resulted in sexual intercourse for 48 percent of receivers and 55 percent of perpetrators.

Written Descriptions

Free response descriptions of most recent incidents were provided by 375 receivers (131 men and 244 women) and 174 perpetrators (95 men and 79 women). We sorted the descriptions according to the most exploitative tactics that were used in an incident. Our intent was not to conduct a systematic content analysis of the descriptions, but to record the variety of ways the tactics were carried out.

The tactics are illustrated with verbatim descriptions of incidents collected in the questionnaires. Spelling and grammar errors are left intact. We also summarize descriptions of the context and effects of the incidents.

Level 1: Sexual arousal. The incident usually began when the perpetrator either asked for sex or began touching and kissing the receiver. When the receiver expressed his or her refusal, the perpetrator usually responded first with persistent touching and kissing and removal of clothing. Leg, back, and genital massages were frequently mentioned in descriptions.

A woman wrote about what happened with a boyfriend. The outcome was sexual touching.

> We left a party & went to park. He was on top of me kissing me & stuff & trying to take all of my clothes off. He kept putting my hands down his pants & I kept pulling away. I made up some excuse for us to leave.

A man wrote about the following experience with a female acquaintance. Only sexual touching occurred. He reported that the incident hurt their friendship.

> We were at her parents house getting intoxicated. She went to "go take a shower," but came out of the bathroom with only a robe on. She removed it and was naked and tried to grope me.

Another man described what happened with a female friend. The outcome was sexual intercourse. He reported that the incident ruined their friendship.

> She asked me to bring her to the bank to get some money which was close to my house. Then she asked if I wanted something to eat I said yes, so we went to my apartment where she tried to kiss me. I told her to quit. She then grabbed my genitals and I quickly removed her hand. She then took off her clothes and said take me. I laughed at her. She asked why didn't I want her. I replied because I have a girlfriend. Then she kept pushing the issue until I gave in.

The perpetrator's perspective was given by a woman who said that she had persuaded reluctant men on many occasions. In this instance, the man was an acquaintance, and the outcome was sexual intercourse. She said that the incident had no bad effects on her.

> I told him how sexy he was & that he turned me on. And asked for sex. He refused. I retreated for a while but then continued to ask & say erotic things to him (putting ideas in his head) and every chance I could I would touch his genitals or buttox (sic).

Level 2: Emotional manipulation and lies. The most common form of emotional manipulation experienced by men and women was repeated requests. About twice as many men as women made repeated requests. One reason, we speculate, is that men are more practiced at verbalizing their desire in their role as sexual initiators. Perhaps women are not as comfortable as men with making direct sexual requests. Men and women often used repeated requests in conjunction with sexual arousal techniques.

According to descriptions, perpetrators often used deception when the tactics of sexual arousal and repeated requests failed to overcome the receivers' refusal. About twice as many women as men reported being lied to, and about five times as many men as women reported lying. Giving truth to an old stereotype (Zilbergeld, 1978), the lies told by men were usually false claims of love or affection. Another lie told by older men was that they were the same age as the college women. Presumably, this made the men seem more trustworthy. Men broke promises about not inserting their penises and told tales of "blue balls" and other peculiarities about their sexual anatomy and functioning.

A woman described being deceived by a male acquaintance. The outcome was sexual intercourse. She reported that the incident had no negative effects.

> He kissed and touched me in private places. He performed oral sex on me. He was begging and trying to trick me by saying it was his finger. It was his penis though. Afterwards, I threw him off of me.

Some women reported being manipulated emotionally by men who told them that they were "abnormal" to refuse because "everybody is doing it." Women were warned that their relationships with the men would end if they did not have sex. A few women were told that sex is what good friends do for each other or that sex with a new person is the best way to get over a breakup. Women were complimented by men, were told that they were the right kind of girl or the man's fantasy, or were told that they would be respected in the morning.

In the following description, a male perpetrator explained his manipulation tactic with a female acquaintance. The outcome was sexual touching.

> I first got her in my bed & started to kiss her, but after awhile she didn't want to so I stopped & then I told her exactly what she wanted to hear. (she asked me what I look for 'in a girl'). Then we started to kiss & she stopped my [first] attempt at her breast, & after I tried again she let me & after 3 attempts she let me in her pants.

He wrote that the woman hated him afterwards. He regretted his action and subsequently stopped trying when a woman said no.

Another man wrote about a lie that he did not mean to tell to a female acquaintance. The outcome was sexual intercourse.

> It was like this: She, before engaging in sex, asked me if it wasn't just a one-night stand. I told her no, it wasn't. At the time I thought I meant it but in the morning I didn't feel that way. Maybe the liquor?

The man said that they never spoke again. He added that he no longer started a relationship that he did not intend to finish.

Men were deceived by women who claimed to be in love with them or to care about them. Men's emotions were manipulated by women who complimented them, questioned their masculinity or heterosexuality, offered them sex as a perk of friendship, and asked them why they (the women) were not good enough or pretty enough or loved enough for sex.

In the excerpt below, a woman explained how she manipulated her boyfriend. The outcome was sexual intercourse.

> We were alone together and he didn't want to have sex cause he wanted it to be special. I felt rejected, telling him 'what it's not special enough that it's just you & me.' I started crying and basicly [sic] guilted him into having sex w/me.

The woman reported that their relationship was hurt. She said that much later she came to regret that she had hurt someone.

Several men were blackmailed by women. In the following case, a man had sexual intercourse with an ex-girlfriend:

> We had gone out for the previous two years and recently broken up. I had a new girlfriend of about four months, but cheated on her with my ex once before. My ex came over and tried to make out or have sex with me. I refused and she told me she would tell my girlfriend about last time if I didn't have sex with her. I gave in.

The man added that his ex-girlfriend told his current girlfriend about the incident and he never spoke to either one again.

Some men encountered threats of suicide and self-harm when they turned down women. One man wrote about his ex-girlfriend. The outcome was sexual touching. He said that the incident hurt their relationship.

> Entered my apt. to discuss recent break up, began to get real 'handsy.' Stated that if I didn't stop the pain by having sex with her she would find a way to 'end it all.' I could only assume she meant herself.

Level 3: Exploitation of the intoxicated.

Of the respondents, 30 percent of the men and 42 percent of the women reported being sexually exploited when they were already intoxicated. According to written descriptions, receivers were often lured to an isolated area, such as a bedroom at a party house or outside away from the crowd. In numerous instances, the perpetrators simply waited for the receivers to pass out in a convenient bedroom. As documented, 19 percent of participants reported that they were purposefully intoxicated, with the percentage of female receivers being double that of male receivers. According to descriptions, perpetrators accomplished this by buying drink after drink for receivers, engaging the receivers in drinking games, and rarely, drugging drinks.

Some exploited women were so drunk that they had little memory of what happened, as in the following case. The woman was with an acquaintance, and the outcome was sexual intercourse. She said that the incident had a very negative effect on her sex life.

> I was very intoxicated and I don't remember the details. He was just very pressuring; he kept trying to talk me into it and messing around until I didn't have the ability to resist anymore.

Another woman wrote about being purposely drugged by an acquaintance. The outcome was sexual intercourse. She reported that the incident had a very negative effect on her dating and sex life.

> He gave me a drink that had drugs in it. I passed out and awoke while he was on top of me having sex.

A common scenario for male receivers was being led to a bed or being joined in bed by a female perpetrator who tried to arouse him by removing his clothing or initiating oral sex. Sometimes, the woman got on top of an aroused man and inserted his penis. In some cases, inebriated men became so aroused that they became a willing participant in the sex. In the following case, a man described how an acquaintance took advantage of his intoxicated state. The outcome was sexual intercourse. He said that the incident had a negative effect on him.

> Alcohol was involved. She undressed me, tried to arouse me by touching my genitals, oral sex, and trying to force me inside of her.

Several men wrote that they were taken advantage of by women who were sometimes undesirable to them and who wanted to start a relationship with them. One female perpetrator reflected this motive in her description of sexually touching a drunken man:

> I liked this guy and I thought the only way we'd ever hook up is if we got drunk and fooled around.

The woman wrote that no relationship developed as a consequence. She added that she came to realize that a relationship should be based on more than just a drunken one night stand.

One man reported that he was purposefully intoxicated by a female acquaintance. He said that the incident did not have a negative effect on him.

> We were drunk and she kept buying me drinks. Later she grabbed my crotch & asked if it turned me on. Then unzipped my pants & proceeded with oral sex.

Another man described how a female stranger used multiple strategies, including purposeful intoxication, to have sex with him. Sexual intercourse was the outcome.

> At a party, she came up and began talking to me. I was already drinking some at the time. While playing cards, she talked me into finishing several of her drinks and beers. She said there was another party, and convinced me to go. I was too drunk to drive so she drove us. The 'party' seemed to lack other people. After about 1/2 hour of kissing/making out, I was tired and wanted to go home. She said no and told me she wanted to have sex. I said no, but she continued to kiss me and try to talk me into it. When she produced a condom, I gave in.

The man wrote that he was a virgin at the time and that he felt somewhat used afterwards.

Level 4: Physical force and harm. Similar percentages of men and women reported that someone tried to block their retreat, a minor form of physical force. According to participants' descriptions, the most common acts were when perpetrators stood in front of doors, locked doors, or locked car doors. About twice as many women as men reported being physically restrained, a more serious act.

In the following case, the woman was with an acquaintance whom she had turned down for sex when she was sober. She said that she ended the friendship after it happened.

> I was at a party and I was drunk but still knew what I was doing. He asked me to go for a walk with him. I told him I would go but we were just going to walk down the street and back. He made sure my glass was full before we left. He talked me into jumping on a trampoline & he then pushed me down and pulled my pants down & forced his penis into me. Then told me that if I told anyone they won't believe me.

Another woman wrote how an acquaintance physically forced her into sexual intercourse. She said that she avoided him afterwards.

> We were all drinking (I was with my older sister). This guy offered to bring me to go get cigarettes. Already being drunk I said yes. Trusting this guy. Well we never made it to the store. He brought me to the lake. That's when he brought himself on me. He was to strong. I couldn't get him off.

In the following case, a woman described how she was harmed by a stranger. The outcome was sexual intercourse.

> Forced himself on me after a few drinks in a bar. When I tried to leave in my car (intoxicated) he climbed in and agressively [sic] attacked me sexually leaving numerous bruises on my backside. He kept slapping me on my ass, hurting me repeatedly.

The woman wrote that the man tried unsuccessfully to contact her again for a date. She added that she quit drinking.

The male perpetrators' descriptions of force tactics were sparse. Not many men reported using a force tactic, and those who did often left out descriptions, wrote about their regrets rather than about the incident, or cited memory loss due to intoxication. In the following example, the man was with a female acquaintance.

> This girl and I occasionaly got together and had intercourse. Once when I was very drunk, she said we had anal intercourse when she wasn't willing. I don't remember this part of the night no matter how hard I try. Fortunatly [sic] I don't drink at all these days.

The man reported that their relationship was hurt. He added that the incident caused him to become more sensitive and passive when having sex with women.

Women were unlikely to use high levels of physical force with male receivers. Instead, they occasionally tried to grab and hold on to men, push them down on beds and sit or lay on them, and tie them up. Here is a description from a man who was physically restrained by a woman he had previously dated. He said that the incident had no effects on their limited relationship.

We had 'made out' the weekend before, but I didn't want to continue any further because I was already dating a different girl. She got drunk and so did I, she wanted to 'hook up again.' But I thought it was a bad idea. She pinned me down at one point (it was kind of thrilling) but I left.

In several instances, women bit, pinched, slapped, and hit male receivers. In some cases, a woman's harmful act appeared to be a means of persuasion; in others it seemed to be a way of "punishing" a man for refusing her.

I already had a girlfriend and she tried to have sex with me. I told her no and she kept kissing me and touching me. She kept asking and trying to make me have sex with her.

Female perpetrator descriptions of using force tactics were rare. In this example, the woman was with a male acquaintance. The outcome was sexual touching.

I locked the room door that we were in. I kissed and touched him. I removed his shirt and unzipped his pants. He asked me to stop. I didn't. Then, I sat on top of him. He had had two beers but wasn't drunk.

She wrote that the man refused to speak to her or get near her again after it happened.

DISCUSSION

A major finding of our study is that a form of sexual coercion that we call post-refusal sexual persistence is a fairly common experience among our college student sample. Nearly 70 percent of the participants had been subjected to at least one tactic of post-refusal sexual persistence since the age of 16. One-third of our participants said that they had used a tactic. We found that the most frequently reported tactics were sexual arousal and emotional manipulation and lies: categories that we consider to be less exploitative than intoxication and physical force. However, well over a third of our participants had

been sexually exploited while intoxicated, and over one-fourth of our participants had been subjected to a tactic of physical force.

Our study is consistent with past research that has shown that women are more likely than men to report being sexually coerced (e.g., Byers & O'Sullivan, 1998). More women than men were subjected to at least one tactic of sexual arousal, emotional manipulation and lies, and exploitation due to intoxication. Although there was no difference in the percentage of men and women who had been subjected to at least one tactic categorized as physical force, a greater percentage of women than men had been subjected to the specific tactics of physical restraint and threats of harm.

Our study is also consistent with past research (e.g., Struckman-Johnson & Anderson, 1998) in finding that substantial percentages of men were subjected to the sexually persistent behavior of female perpetrators. Our study found that women generally used gentler or less exploitative tactics than men did when confronted with a sexual refusal. That is, women more than men appeared to restrict their behavior to tactics of sexual arousal and repeated requests. Still, moderate percentages of women reportedly engaged in deception, taking advantage of intoxicated men, and blocking men's retreat. However, reports of women engaging in serious acts of physical restraint or causing serious harm were uncommon.

In some respects, we found more similarities than differences in the ways that men and women were subjected to sexual persistence. Statistical tests revealed significant gender differences for only 7 of the 19 tactics. For example, approximately equal percentages of men and women were subjected to the tactics of having their clothes removed by a perpetrator, being threatened with a breakup, having their sexuality questioned, having their retreat blocked, and being physically harmed.

Our results are consistent with past research that indicates a strong relationship between drinking and sexual coercion (e.g., Larimer et al., 1999; Tewsbury & Mustaine, 2001). Nearly 40 percent of the participants in our study fell victim to sexual exploitation due to intoxication. We surmise that this tactic is used because it can be so easily accomplished by both men and women. Perpetrators do not have to worry about their attractiveness to the target, what to say, or how to prevent the target from leaving. One idea for future research would be to explore the motives of individuals who use specific tactics such as intoxication to gain sexual access to others.

Our research underscored the problems that result from sexually coercive behavior. We found that many of our victims of post-refusal sexual persistence reported long lasting negative effects from the incidents. In particular, we were struck by the number of respondents who reported in their written descriptions that romantic relationships and friendships were ruined by an incident of post-refusal sexual persistence.

One limitation of our research is that participants were asked to report incidents that had happened since the age of 16. It is possible that their recollections of postrefusal sexual persistence were influenced by the passage of time. In addition, some participants' memories of specific incidents may have been influenced by alcohol consumed at the time of the incident.

Another limitation is that our four categories of sexual exploitation may not be hierarchical as we propose. For example, one could argue that our *Level 1 tactic of sexually persistent touching* is equally or more exploitative than verbal coercion. This question could be investigated in future research by having respondents rate the perceived exploitation value of different tactics of sexual coercion.

Our study raises an interesting question about the disparity between the relatively large number of participants who reported being receivers of sexual persistence and the much smaller number who reported being perpetrators. To reiterate a question asked by many researchers in this area (e.g., Anderson & Sorensen, 1999; Lottes,

1991), who is committing the sexual persistence reported by our receivers? It could be that a small number of perpetrators are committing acts with numerous partners or that receivers are socializing with a population not included in our survey. It is also possible that participants did not report perpetration due to social undesirability of the acts. Our research method may have contributed to this effect: Respondents who were first asked to report having a tactic used against them may have been reluctant to then report that they had used such tactics.

Another explanation is that participants did not perceive their behaviors as tactics of sexual persistence. Many of our participant perpetrators qualified their behaviors as playful or beneficial, indicating that the behaviors were intended to improve their relationships. Numerous female perpetrators and some male perpetrators wrote that their partners changed their minds and were pleased to have sex. After reading so many receivers' complaints, we wonder if some of our perpetrators were unaware of the negative effects of their behavior. These speculations and others that may explain the receiver-perpetrator gap are ripe for future research.

INTRODUCTION REFERENCES

Brownmiller, S. 1975. *Against our will: Men, women, and rape.* New York: Simon and Schuster.

Chiang, H. 2003, January 7. "Court says sex after rescinded consent is rape/state justices hear case of 2 teens." *San Francisco Chronicle,* A17.

Griffin, S. 1971. "Rape: The All-American crime." *Ramparts* 10: 26–35.

MacDonald, J. M. 1971. *Rape offenders and their victims.* Springfield, IL: Thomas.

McKinney, D. 2003, July 29. "Clarifications of rape law signed by governor." *Chicago Sun-Times,* 6.

Muehlenhard, C., and Highby, B. J. 1997. "Sexual assault and rape." In *The International Encyclopedia of Sexuality,* Vol. 3, ed. R. T. Francoeur, 1546–1555. New York: Continuum.

Young, C. C. 2003, January, 20. "Troubling questions about rape and consent." *Boston Globe,* A15.

REFERENCES

Allgeier, E. R. (2002). Interpreting research results. In M. W. Wiederman & B. E. Whitley, Jr. (Eds.), *Handbook for conducting research on human sexuality* (pp. 371–392). Mahwah, NJ: Lawrence Erlbaum.

Anderson, P. B., & Aymami, R. (1993). Reports of female initiation of sexual contact: Male and female differences. *Archives of Sexual Behavior, 22,* 335–343.

Anderson, P. B., & Sorensen, W. (1999). Male and female differences in reports of women's heterosexual initiation and aggression. *Archives of Sexual Behavior, 28,* 243–253.

Byers, E. S., & O'Sullivan, L. F. (1998). Similar but different: Men's and women's experiences of sexual coercion. In P. B. Anderson and C. Struckman-Johnson (Eds.), *Sexually aggressive women: Current perspectives and controversies* (pp. 144–168). New York: Guilford.

Fiebert, M. S., & Tucci, L. M. (1998). Sexual coercion: Men victimized by women. *Journal of Men's Studies, 6,* 127–133.

Hogben, M., & Waterman, C. K. (2000). Patterns of conflict resolution within relationships and coercive sexual behavior of men and women. *Sex Roles, 43,* 341–357.

Koss, M. P., Gidycz, C. A., & Wisniewski, N. (1987). The scope of rape: Incidence and prevalence of sexual aggression and victimization in a national sample of higher education students. *Journal of Consulting and Clinical Psychology, 55,* 162–170.

Lane, K., & Gwartney-Gibbs, P. (1985). Violence in the context of dating and sex. *Journal of Family Issues, 6,* 45–59.

Larimer, M. E., Lydum, A. R., Anderson, B. K., & Turner, A. P. (1999). Male and female recipients of unwanted sexual contact in a college sample: Prevalence rates, alcohol use, and depression symptoms. *Sex Roles, 40,* 295–308.

Lottes, I. I. (1991). The relationship between non-traditional gender roles and sexual coercion. *Journal of Psychology and Human Sexuality, 4,* 89–109.

Lottes, I. I., & Weinberg, M. (1996). Sexual coercion among university students: A comparison of the United States and Sweden. *The Journal of Sex Research, 34,* 67–76.

Muehlenhard, C. L., & Cook, S. (1988). Men's self-reports of unwanted sexual activity. *The Journal of Sex Research, 24,* 58–72.

Senn, C. Y., Verberg, N., Desmarais, S., & Wood, E. (2000). Sampling the reluctant participant: A random-sample response-rate study of men and sexual coercion. *Journal of Applied Psychology, 30,* 96–105.

Struckman-Johnson, C. J. (1988). Forced sex on dates: It happens to men, too. *The Journal of Sex Research, 24,* 234–240.

Struckman-Johnson, C., & Anderson, P. B. (1998). "Men do and women don't": Differences in researching sexually aggressive women. In P. B. Anderson and C. J. Struckman-Johnson (Eds.), *Sexually aggressive women: Current perspectives and controversies* (pp. 9–18). New York: Guiford.

Struckman-Johnson, C. J., & Struckman-Johnson, D. L. (1998). The dynamics and impact of sexual coercion of men by women. In P. B. Anderson and C. J. Struckman-Johnson (Eds.), *Sexually aggressive women: Current perspectives and controversies* (pp. 121–169). New York: Guiford.

Tewsbury, R., & Mustaine, E. E. (2001). Lifestyle factors associated with sexual assault of men: A routine activity theory analysis. *Journal of Men's Studies, 9,* 153–182.

Waldner-Haugrud, L. K., & Magruder, B. (1995). Male and female sexual victimization in dating relationships: Gender differences in coercion techniques and outcomes. *Violence and Victims, 10,* 203–215.

Zurbriggen, E. L. (2000). Social motives and cognitive power-sex associations: Predictors of aggressive sexual behavior. *Journal of Personality and Social Psychology, 78,* 1–23.

CHAPTER 43

Heterosexual Fronteras

Immigrant Mexicanos, Sexual Vulnerabilities, and Survival

Gloria González-López

The U.S. Equal Employment Opportunity Commission defines sexual harassment as:

> *Unwelcome sexual advances, requests for sexual favors, and other verbal or physical conduct of a sexual nature constitutes sexual harassment when submission to or rejection of this conduct explicitly or implicitly affects an individual's employment, unreasonably interferes with an individual's work performance or creates an intimidating, hostile or offensive work environment. (U.S. Equal Employment Opportunity Commission, 2002)*

Sexual harassment is illegal, and there are steps that may be taken in order to rectify such a situation. But, imagine being an undocumented immigrant to the United States. You know very few people, and of those, you don't know who you can trust. You may not yet speak English very well. You have a job that you can't afford to leave, or a living situation that you are unable to change. In order to keep the job or the apartment, you are asked to provide sexual favors to your employer, or your landlord, or your roommate. This is clearly sexual harassment, but not the sort that can be reported.

While sex with a loving and desired partner can be the most wonderful of experiences, undesired sex is one of the worst experiences of a lifetime. And for the male Mexican immigrants that you will meet in this chapter, unwanted sex or pressure to have unwanted same-sex sexual activity is a commonplace experience.

Gloria González-López has used an ethnographic approach to gain a better understanding of the lives of Latino immigrants. She has uncovered the distressing reality that sex, for these men, is often a commodity that is traded, albeit unwillingly, in order to survive. This fascinating, but disturbing article is one that you will not forget.

From "Heterosexual Fronteras: Immigrant Mexicanos, Sexual Vulnerabilities, and Survival" by G. González-López. 2006. *Sexuality Research and Social Policy 3*: 67–81. Copyright © 2006 by the National Sexuality Research Center. Reprinted by permission of the University of California Press.

Some of my employers call me many times to offer me a job late at night. . . . They tell me it's easy, that I am going to enjoy it, and that they are going to pay me a lot for not doing much. They are offering money to have sexual relations. And they are young, older, of all ages. Seventy percent are White men. (Eugenio)

Eugenio is a single man in his early 40s who said he felt offended whenever he received this type of invitation. Unlike some other men on the margins of society, he had never had sexual relations with strangers in order to get a meal or a place to sleep. Eugenio left Mexico City to immigrate to the United States and had lived in Los Angeles for more than 10 years. He had a place to live but it had never been easy or predictable for him on the north side of the border. He had lived in extreme poverty and at one point was even homeless, sleeping on the busy streets of the megacity. Despite the hardships, he had not given up hope. He got up every day when it was still dark wondering about what kind of job he would get so he could survive *al día*—one day at a time. Before the sun rose, he joined thousands of other undocumented men from Latin America who were looking for informal jobs as *jornaleros*, or day laborers.

Every day in Los Angeles County thousands of men like Eugenio look for work as day laborers (Valenzuela, 2003). At busy street corners in cities (and more recently at centers sponsored by immigrants' rights organizations), immigrant men establish informal groups as they decipher the work of underpaid labor and wait for a transaction. These men offer their skills in carpentry, construction, plumbing, landscaping, roofing, and painting for menial wages that often barely cover their expenses for the day. In addition to being vulnerable to economic exploitation, these men are at risk for sexual harassment by other men.

According to the U.S. Equal Employment Opportunity Commission (EEOC), "Sexual harassment is a form of sex discrimination that violates Title VII of the Civil Rights Act of 1964" (2002, ¶ 1). The EEOC also indicates that "unwelcome sexual advances, requests for sexual favors, and other verbal or physical conduct of a sexual nature constitutes sexual harassment when submission to or rejection of this conduct explicitly or implicitly affects an individual's employment, unreasonably interferes with an individual's work performance or creates an intimidating, hostile or offensive work environment" (¶ 2). Sexual harassment can include a wide variety of attitudes and behaviors, from subtle and nuanced, to rape (Giuffre & Williams, 2002).

WHY SEXUAL VULNERABILITY, HETEROSEXUAL MEXICANOS, AND INEQUALITY?

Sexuality research that examines the sex lives of self-identified heterosexual Mexican immigrant men from a perspective of gender relations and socioeconomic and racial inequality is practically invisible. Why? First, since the 1970s, sexuality research on Mexican men has focused primarily on the experiences of gay and bisexual men. Gender and sexuality research with Mexican and Mexican immigrant populations has just begun to look at heterosexual love and sex experiences (Carrillo, 2002; González-López, 2005; Hirsch, 2003). For instance, sexuality research that has studied *down* on sex has analyzed the experiences of groups (mainly gay men and lesbians) that have been historically oppressed and marginalized within the structure of power and control in society. Studying *up* on sex, or examining the sexual experiences of those who represent sexual privilege (i.e., heterosexuals) within that same social structure, has been rare. Scholars such as Michael Messner (1996), Chrys Ingraham (2005), and Lynne Segal (1994) have advocated for critical examinations of heterosexuality in the power structure. Thus, studying up on the sex lives of heterosexual Mexican immigrant men allows us to uncover the reasons why not all heterosexual individuals or groups are privileged. The men who are the subjects of this study simultaneously experienced diverse forms of inequality in the United States as the result of their race/ethnicity, citizenship and language, intra-male hierarchical interactions, and socioeconomic marginality, among other expressions of inequality associated with migration contexts and globalized economies.

Second, sexuality research on Mexican men who live in the United States has taken place largely within the behavioral sciences, public health, and epidemiology. A special concern about the HIV/AIDS epidemic has also resulted in extensive studies of Latino populations. Publications (Diaz, 1998; Marín, Gómez, & Hearst, 1993; Organista, Organista, Bola, García de Alba, & Castillo Morán, 2000) have traditionally examined Latino men and sexuality from the perspectives of acculturation and assimilation, and the theoretical categories that have dominated this extensive body of literature have included familism, machismo, and Catholicism, all of which have been associated with a so-called Latino culture.

Third, the extensive literature on the sociology of immigration has analyzed labor markets, economics, and political activism and more recently has paid attention to family relations, religion, and gender. Research on day laborers from Latin America (Malpica, 2002; Valenzuela, 2003) has provided insightful and groundbreaking studies on their living conditions, their marginality, and the social injustices they encounter. While these publications have examined conditions of inequality and exploitation, they have ignored immigrants' sex lives. In short, Mexican immigrants have traditionally been desexualized in research about them (González-López, 2005). Until recently, sexuality research that has been done with this population has focused on the sex lives of gay Mexican immigrants (Cantú, 1999), young couples' redefinitions of marital quality and sexuality across borders and between generations (Hirsch, 2003), and the sociology of immigration and heterosexual immigrants (González-López, 2005).

Fourth, research on sexual harassment and work has made important contributions toward an understanding of gender, power relations, and sexism at the workplace and has examined ethnicity/race, sexual orientation, and citizenship dynamics (Welsh, Carr, MacQuarrie, & Huntley, 2006), including the experiences of Latina immigrant women—who are also vulnerable to sexual harassment while deciphering underpaid work at the bottom of the power structure (Cortina, 2004;). Interestingly, research on male-on-male sexual harassment is relatively recent (Giuffre & Williams, 2002; Smith & Kimmel, 2005), and there are no major research studies or statistics on either sexual harassment of or commercial sex with day laborers.

This article reports on ethnographic data collected from in-depth individual interviews with 20 Mexican immigrant adult men and establishes a bridge between gender/sexuality and immigration studies in order to explain the ways in which self-identified heterosexual Mexican men working on the margins of society have experienced two contrasting categories of same-sex sexual activity. While both will be shown to expose the unstable nature of heterosexuality for some men, each of them is caused by and prompts different forms of sexual vulnerability. The first category consists of same-sex interactions between an immigrant man and his employer (frequently a White gay man) and involves structural power inequality between them. In this situation, the immigrant man is not only economically exploited but also sexually objectified from a location that places him at the bottom of a social structure made from a complex web of interdependent factors including, but not limited to, class, ethnicity/race, sexuality, language, and legal/citizenship status (González-López, 2005). The immigrant men in such situations are exposed to sexualized negotiations that may include sexual harassment, commercial sex (either voluntary or coercive), and other forms of sexual violence. In these sexualized transactions, the men are not only surviving; they are also responding to prescriptions for masculinity that enforce their presumed responsibilities as fathers, sons, and brothers to their financially dependent families back home (see LeVine, 1993).

The second category of sexual interactions involves self-identified heterosexual Mexican immigrant men engaging in same-sex activities with other immigrant men. These activities involve less significant power differentials;

coercion between partners rarely occurs; and the interactions result more frequently from immigrants' own agency. However, these activities are often prompted by migration-related conditions such as crowded housing, alcohol and drug use, and other socioeconomic forces affecting the personal and sex lives of these men. Both of these categories of same-sex sexual activities can be explained, at least in part, by two central dynamics: a political economy characterized by both globalization and sexual exploitation and a notion that can be described as the borders of heterosexuality.

A Political Economy of Globalization and Sexual Exploitation

These men's experiences of sexual objectification and exploitation are in response to two interconnected processes taking place at both local and global levels. Class, ethnicity, language barriers, socioeconomic segregation, citizenship status, occupational incorporation, and the objectification of Latino men within White gay communities as "exotic, dark, and passionate" (Díaz, 1998, p. 125) have combined locally to make day laborers vulnerable to exploitation by other men who occupy higher racial and economic levels within the intra-male hierarchy of power and control. My study demonstrates that some White middle- and upper-middle-class gay men may engage in these complex dynamics. Such potential sexual harassment on the part of a gay employer should be viewed as the result of power differentials and not of sexual orientation or sexuality per se.

Globalization, sexual tourism, and new forms of capitalism are interlocking processes prompting these sexualized processes (Altman, 2001). On the one hand, poor heterosexual men of color who migrate north or who go from less developed to more industrialized nations are often relegated to the margins of society and, thus, become vulnerable to commercial sex as an avenue for survival. On the other hand, White (gay) men who go south from developed to developing or underdeveloped nations

for purposes of commercial sex and tourism do not operate in a socioeconomic vacuum:

> Their sexual taste for 'Others' reflects not so much a wish to engage in a specific sexual practice as desire for an extraordinarily high degree of control over the management of self and others as sexual, racialized, and engendered beings. (O'Connell Davidson & Sanchez Taylor, 2004, p. 454)

Thus, in the microcosmos of the global city of Los Angeles (Sassen-Koob, 1984), both social images overlap: Some White gay men in Los Angeles look for the exotic Other (those who come from the South) to sexually objectify them and to financially exploit their highly needed and underpaid day labor within contexts of perverse racial, socioeconomic, and language inequalities (see O'Connell Davidson & Sanchez Taylor).

The Borders of Heterosexuality

Heterosexuality is a paradoxical social construction (Ingraham, 2005). It is both normative—that is, heterosexuality is the hegemonic norm that promotes idealized and socially expected values and practices of sexual desire, behavior, and identity and represents sexual supremacy and social privilege—and simultaneously is neither firm nor stable. From this perspective, heterosexuality can be seen to be fragile and susceptible to changing socioeconomic contexts and conditions.

The interviews with the self-identified heterosexual Mexican immigrant men in my study demonstrated how the changing socioeconomic situations and other circumstances involved in their migration experiences revealed the paradoxical nature of heterosexuality, especially its vulnerable side. Thus, like gender (Hondagneu-Sotelo, 1992) and sexuality in general (González-López, 2005), heterosexuality is fluid and unstable and can be remade through migration. Migration-related conditions selectively shaped the sexual desires, behaviors, and identities of these self-identified heterosexual immigrant men. Crowded housing, alcohol and drug use, poverty, a stressful lifestyle, and peer pressure, among other factors prompted by social inequality and injustice, pushed some of these men to engage in same-sex experiences with other immigrants (González-López, 2005). And as they incorporated into and became part of the socioeconomic landscape of the United States, additional forces promoting inequality may have further blurred their former notions of heterosexuality. Men who sent remittance to families left behind may have felt forced to accept the sexualized advances of a male employer or compelled to engage in commercial sex for economic reasons. At the same time, when their heterosexuality was perceived to be vulnerable, these men may have felt the need to protect and reinforce it. Through such a process, these Mexican men exercised agency by defending their sense of manhood as traditionally associated with heterosexual masculinity, especially when the sexual advances made by potential employers compromised their sense of personal dignity and respect.

The testimonies of the immigrant Mexican men in my study should not be viewed as stories of the powerful versus the powerless. Even though forces associated with power may oppress some poor immigrant men, the men in my study were not simply passive victims who automatically accepted perceived expressions of sexual harassment in the workplace. Indeed, a clear sense of sexual agency was expressed in their same-sex experiences with other immigrant men. Similarly, an immigrant possesses some degree of sexual agency through his capacity for subjective negotiation in challenging or resisting such sexual propositions. At the same time, the men's sexual agency was shaped by their linguistic skills, citizenship status, and financial need, as well as by other factors including but not limited to personal histories of child sex abuse. Some of these Mexican workers also used homophobia symbolically as a way to resist sexual advances from their employers, because their homosexuality

was what made some of their employers vulnerable. In the case of their same-sex sexual encounters with their peers, sexual activities happened under conditions of marginality but also as part of voluntary exchanges of friendship and camaraderie.

METHOD

This article presents data obtained from in-depth individual interviews with 20 Mexican immigrant men. These interviews were part of a larger study I conducted with 40 women and 20 men who were born and raised in Mexico and who immigrated to Los Angeles as adults (González-López, 2005). All of the men had experienced poverty during migration and settlement. They migrated from either Jalisco or Mexico City at the age of 20 years or older, and they had all lived in the Los Angeles area for at least 5 years. All of them identified themselves as heterosexual.

I used a snowball sampling technique to recruit the 20 informants. In order to identify them, I visited and contacted professionals at four community-based agencies and three elementary schools in Los Angeles. In addition, I attended meetings at the Consulate of Mexico in Los Angeles and established contacts with representatives of hometown associations, community organizations, and employment centers for day laborers. After contacting some of these representatives, I scheduled and attended meetings at these sites where I introduced myself as a sociologist and as a couple and family therapist who conducted sexuality research with Mexican immigrant populations. Some of them qualified for the study and voluntarily accepted to be interviewed. I personally conducted all of the interviews in Spanish and in a private space primarily in agencies, schools, employment centers, or homes.

Study participants were between the ages of 25 and 45 years at the time of their interviews; their average age was 38. Half of the sample consisted of 10 men born and raised in the state of Jalisco, Mexico; the other half had been born and raised in Mexico City. As the birthplace of tequila, mariachi music, and traditional charro cultures, Jalisco has played an essential role in the creation of Mexican masculinist identities. All participants had lived permanently in the United States for between 5 and 20 years.

Participants worked in a wide variety of occupations. They included construction and maintenance workers, truck drivers, equipment operators, supervisors, and technicians. Five of the informants were day laborers at the time of our interviews.

For this article, I examined these men's responses to the themes related to what they had identified as dangerous and high-risk employment opportunities for Mexican men after immigrating to the United States.

RESULTS

Political Economy of Globalization and Sexual Exploitation

While not all informants had been exposed personally to sexual harassment at their jobs, the vast majority had been told stories about such harassment by relatives, friends, or acquaintances. Many of them recalled stories involving work, money, and sex with White employers.

Alfredo explained how after trying unsuccessfully to get a job in Los Angeles, he had left for northern California to explore the job market there. During a short stay in San Francisco, he learned about a place he identified as *El Cachadero* (from "to catch," to get a job), which was often visited by affluent gay men. He explained the experience he had after being hired by a man at this site who drove him to his house in a sparkling Corvette:

We arrived at his home and he asked me to mow the lawn. So, I asked, "What else do you want me to do?" "Clean the windows." I agreed. So everything was fine. But when I was cleaning the windows, he was inside his house already wearing this bikini. So, I said to myself, if this guy is gay, he is giving me that kind of a signal. . . . This guy wants something else. Later on he told me that he wanted me to fix something in the bathroom. . . . I tell him, "I have to fix this and that," and the guy is right there, standing in front of me wearing this bikini. "Isn't it hot? Why don't you make yourself more comfortable?" he said. And I replied, "You know what? I am going to feel more comfortable if you pay me and I am going to leave right away because this place requires a lot of work, and I don't even know if you are going to pay me to begin with." He said, "How much do you charge?" "$350," I replied. Then, he said, "Yes, I pay you. Do you want to drink a soda?" Then I told him, "I know what you want from me." "No," he says. "But look, you need to understand." [He pleaded]. So I said, "No, not with me."

Just as Eugenio explained in the introduction to this article, Alfredo claimed he never accepted these attractive offers, even in times of extreme poverty. Marcos, Nicolás, and Ernesto told similar stories involving work, money, and invitations for sex with their employers. They also reported witnessing other immigrant men practicing commercial sex out of financial need. "That is very common," said Ernesto, who went on to explain:

That is why I did not like to look for work by standing at the corner, never. I was not going to stand there. Someone could kidnap me and nobody would ever hear from me again. I know you find a lot of racist people over here who may hurt you.

Ernesto once shared an apartment with 10 immigrant men from Mexico, Guatemala, and El Salvador, and he reported that they had talked about their job-hunting experiences. He said, "One of my roommates was picked up by this homosexual man," and added:

He told me that when he arrived at the house and started to clean, the other man put this pornographic movie in the VCR and started to touch him. And he used to tell me that this man paid him very well.

I asked Ernesto if he knew whether his friend had engaged in that type of activity with his employer voluntarily. "He accepted out of need, he was financially needy," he said. "He had to send a check to Guatemala, so what else was he supposed to do?"

The experiences of Eugenio, Alfredo, and Ernesto illustrate day laborers' exposure not only to sexual harassment and coercion but also to temptation into sexualized encounters for money. Research with other immigrants, though not only day laborers, has found that commercial sex is still an avenue for survival for those who are unemployed or financially needy, as described by Bronfman and López Moreno (1996) in their article about their findings with immigrants living in northern California.

How did these immigrants react in situations of sexual harassment? Some resisted. In certain instances, expressions of discrimination were used to respond to the sexual harassment. For example, Alfredo made fun of his employer, using effeminate mannerisms and making homophobic gestures, and as indicated by their comments, Alfredo and Ernesto had sufficient linguistic skills to challenge the sexual invitations to them. Their use of humor and sexualized jokes demonstrated the resilience of some of the men. In addition, giving up job opportunities before they could become sexual threats represented the expressions of dignity and respect that I consistently identified in these men's narratives concerning sexual harassment. For instance, with teary eyes, Eugenio told me that he was *un hombre pobre pero decente*—a poor but decent man—who would never compromise his values of decency and dignity, not even while surviving extreme poverty. Many other informants expressed a similar sentiment during our interviews. The men used humor in order to maintain a sense of dignity as they deciphered potentially abusive encounters and

grappled with their multifaceted feelings, emotions, and subjective interpretations.

The Borders of Heterosexuality

All informants reported having personally experienced and/or witnessed a wide expression of same-sex sexualized exchanges in all-male settings. These exchanges included teasing, harassing, joking and bragging about sex, talking with sexual innuendos, touching, seducing, and having voluntary or coercive sex. They reported that these experiences had taken place before migrating and at times had been prompted by factors related to social inequality and marginality. In Los Angeles, such exchanges were triggered in part by crowded housing, drug and alcohol use, poverty, and peer pressure, as well as social isolation and emotional loneliness.

I met Mauricio (26 years old, from Mexico City, a construction worker, cohabiting, and the father of two young girls) at a center for day laborers. He told me that he had been involved in same-sex sexual practices, something he had kept private from his circle of close friends but had been public about with casual acquaintances and roommates. He described the intense mixed feelings he had regarding his experiences of peer pressure and alcohol and drug use as he embarked on voluntary and involuntary sexual contact with other immigrant men. I asked him about the number of occasions he had received oral sex from other men in Los Angeles. He said:

> About twenty times or more. Yes, and with different men because they would arrive at our apartment and when you get drunk or drugged, and I did not know, by the time they told, they had already got me undressed, but I was not aware of it when they did it. I did not like it.

Mauricio reported that some of his self-identified heterosexual migrant friends had also participated in similar exchanges. He explained, however, that his "friends had homosexual friends, but they had them only so they could give them oral sex, not to have sexual relations." With regard to himself, he said, "I have had oral sex with homosexuals, when I had just arrived to this country. But not relationships in which they penetrate." I asked him, "Do you identify yourself as homosexual?" Assertively, he replied, "No."

Sexuality research with Mexican men has examined this pattern extensively. Self-identified heterosexual men who have sex with men do not identify themselves as "homosexual" when they play the active role during anal penetration (Alonso & Koreck, 1993; Carrier, 1985; Szasz, 1998) or when they receive oral sex (Bronfman & López Moreno, 1996). In addition, for these self-identified heterosexual men who play the insertive role, penetration may be an expression of honor, power, and masculinity (Prieur, 1998). The assumption that men can split the sexual from the emotional (Rubin, 1983) may facilitate these men's sexual involvement with other men. Even though penetrating another man does not compromise a man's sense of masculinity, being penetrated by the other man may. I asked Mauricio if he liked men or if he felt sexually attracted to them. He reacted emphatically:

No, no! And that is what I think about. And I ask myself, "Why?" In other words, when I am drunk, I do it. But then, after I do it, I do not like myself. But then I say, "What if later on I begin to feel attracted to men?"

Mauricio began to engage in same-sex behaviors before migrating. As an adolescent he was seduced by a friend he identified as homosexual. Mauricio had agreed to have sex with him on three or four occasions as an obligation; he had helped Mauricio get a job and offered him a room in which to live. Mauricio explained that there was one common denominator between his pre- and post-migration sexual experiences: On either side of the border, being under the influence of drugs or alcohol always prompted sexual activity with other men.

Other day laborers also mentioned the combined effect of drug and alcohol use, peer pressure, and isolation on some men's sexual behavior. Alfredo (36 years old, a construction worker, cohabiting, and a father of a 13 year-old girl) and Alejandro (37 years old, a small-business owner, married, and the father of a girl and a boy) were from Mexico City and said at the times of their interviews that they were sober. Ernesto (43 years old, from Guadalajara, a technician, married, and the father of a girl and a boy) described himself as "shy with women" and "shocked" by what he saw while living with other immigrant men right after he migrated. This trio of men gave their views on what they had observed within their groups of Latino friends. Sounding defensive, Alfredo explained what he had observed at a bar:

When they drink, it's like homosexuality takes over, because they say "I like you, I love you," that kind of words. It's OK for them to say to a person, "I am fond of you, I love you, I like you as a friend," within what's normal. But when they get drunk, they get closer and they want to hold you and that makes you think. . . . [They have told me] "I even feel like giving you a kiss." [And I say] "Hey! Get away from here!"

With a similarly guarded attitude, Alejandro made sure I understood he did not hang out with immigrants who had same-sex desire, though he knew some. He said:

Men do it out of loneliness. A friend of mine, well, he is not my friend like that, right? He told me that he used drugs and also alcohol and then he started to have an inclination toward men. So it was loneliness. He found out that he was alone and perhaps his friends pushed him to do other kinds of sex acts.

Ernesto stated, "I saw it, and nobody is going to tell me about [men having sex with other men] because I actually saw it!" Then he elaborated:

My bed was right there, and the table and the big chair were over there [pointing with his hands].

So, yes, I saw when they would drink and I saw when more than one of my friends would screw this man, you know, a friend they had . . . but they did it when they were already drunk and everything.

Ernesto explained that this man, his roommates' friend, approached him; however, he never accepted his invitations to engage in sex. Like Mauricio, he also explained that his roommates would penetrate and receive oral sex from their friend, a man he described as "very masculine with the people outside, but when he talked to us, he then would loosen up, you know, he would be more queer." Defensively, he explained, "I respect people who are homosexual, I hug them and play with them, and chat, you know, but when they want more than that, I get away."

In addition to activities done under the influence of alcohol and drug use, similar behaviors emerged from emotional isolation, socioeconomic segregation, and crowded housing. Raúl (34 years old, from Mexico City, a technician, divorced, and a father of a baby girl) and Alfredo explained:

> I lived with these buddies, and they were about 15 men living in one apartment. They lived like sardines inside the apartment. Suddenly *el albur* [sexual wordplay] made them start touching each other on their buttocks because they did not have anyone to socialize or even go out with. (Raúl) I lived with these five men in an apartment who were also immigrants, and every week they rented pornographic movies. And I did not like to join them, because you see that movie with a group, and then what? In 15 minutes your sexuality changes, you end up doing things you shouldn't. That is when some men reveal their homosexuality.

These men's voices resonated with research in Mexico that looked at a variety of sexual exchanges taking place in all-male settings among working-class men, including having collective sex, touching each other, and joking and bragging about sex in different contexts such as their neighborhood streets, soccer fields, and work crews (Szasz, 1998). These testimonies also expanded on extensive research looking at the connection between alcohol use and eroticism between men. De la Vega (1990) examined how some self-identified heterosexual Latino men who lived in the United States engaged in sex acts with other men when they were under the influence of alcohol and other substances. In reporting on a group of immigrant men living in rural California, Bronfman and López Moreno (1996) explained that sex took place among these men because being "under the influence of alcohol did not count. . . . Alcohol consumption constituted another effective mechanism to protect masculinity and reinforced the separation of roles" (p. 59). Research by Brandes (2002) with a group of working-class men in Alcoholics Anonymous in Mexico who were in primary loving relationships with women found that "homosexual wishes and encounters are part of their dark alcoholic past" (p. 127). Interestingly, these findings seemed to indicate that becoming heterosexual is part of an alcoholic man's recovery, as heterosexuality becomes the ideal of sobriety.

A Professional Opinion

Daniel Malpica has spent long hours doing research with jornaleros. I asked him, "Why do you think these White men approach these day laborers?" He replied, "I think there is a White gay–Latino man thing going on. Latino jornaleros are sort of seen as exotic, sort of macho type, so I think that is one of the reasons why they are objectified." "Another reason?" He said:

> I also think that they are easy targets because, you know, in the eyes of a lot of people you can screw a lot of these men. They are sort of disposable; they are always there. Everyone can sort of abuse them, with regard to labor, sex, everything. They are undocumented, and that is a big factor because in the eyes of the people who are sexually harassing these young men, they actually think

they can get away with it. That is what I think; that is my reading of it.

Malpica's words suggested a process of dehumanization of these Mexican immigrant men. The sexual objectification of jornaleros by opportunistic people can also be understood as a reflection of additional and more complex dynamics. I argue that the fact that an employer has the economic power to buy the cheap labor of a poor man may give the employer a sense of sexualized entitlement over the poorer man. That is, an employer may have embraced the idea that he has the right and power to do whatever he pleases to his employee. And the fact that the jornalero has agreed to work at his employer's home or business can make him even more vulnerable to sexual harassment by the employer.

I also asked Daniel Malpica, "Why do you think some of these day laborers accepted the sexual invitations?" Recalling what Ernesto had expressed, Malpica responded, "I would actually think it is because they are so desperate; a lot of them are in such an urgent need to actually earn money that actually they go ahead and do this."

Both Daniel Malpica and the vast majority of my informants reported a deep awareness of the extreme economic plight and marginality surrounding the everyday life of jornaleros. All of my informants seemed to agree that *un hombre de verdad* (a real man) should not tolerate being sexually harassed, should not engage in sexual activities with an employer, and should not practice prostitution as a way to survive. For them, however, un hombre de verdad was also financially responsible for the welfare of the family he left behind, which left them with a struggle to understand the tension between their sense of manhood and their need to survive.

DISCUSSION

Heterosexual men are the protagonists of privilege and power in patriarchal societies such as Mexico. However, migration and socioeconomic incorporation within North American societies complicate such a clear-cut dynamic. The results from this study demonstrated that self-identified heterosexual Mexican men who were poor and who had immigrated to and assimilated into the marginalized communities of Los Angeles were exposed to segregation, socioeconomic exploitation, and racism. Their underprivileged socioeconomic location made their sex lives vulnerable. An examination of this social inequality revealed the paradoxical nature of heterosexuality as the social norm. Those who left a wife and children behind never anticipated what their sexual destiny would be in the United States. First, for those who looked for work as day laborers, sexual harassment by a potential employer became a potential threat, which they need to negotiate with limited language skills while simultaneously encountering the effects of racism and socioeconomic marginality. Second, the immigrant men who reported engaging in same-sex activities with other immigrants did so in part as a consequence of migration-related factors related to socioeconomic inequality and marginality, including but not limited to crowded housing, alcohol and drug use, poverty, peer pressure, and loneliness.

Race, ethnicity, class, citizenship status, and other factors appeared to contribute in nuanced and complex ways to the promotion of sexual exploitation of the men in this study, who lived at the margins of society in the United States and at times in their own countries of origin. While White gay men may also represent expressions of subordinate masculinities vis-à-vis White middle-class heterosexual men (Connell, 1995), their relationship to disadvantaged immigrant men complicates this picture. When they interacted with the poor Mexicanos described in this study, the gay men who hired them appeared to exercise their privileges based on class, ethnicity/race, citizenship, and language. The working-class men in these stories were at the bottom of the social structure yet still felt the pressure to fulfill social prescriptions of masculinity; these men, especially those who left wives and children behind, were expected to be good providers for their families in Mexico who depended on their remittances (LeVine, 1993).

The protagonists of these sexualized interactions were not alone in their adventures. They experienced these processes within a larger international system and were part of a globalized political economy of sexuality (Hennessy, 2000). The Mexican immigrant men's experiences united them with other Latin American men who have similarly been exposed to multiple forms of inequality within larger hierarchical systems and structures of power and control. Late capitalism has given birth to racist and classist expressions of both sexuality and commodification, as some White gay employers and some Latin American male immigrant day laborers attempt to get their respective erotic and survival needs satisfied. These interactions may be seen to resemble the negotiations between White men from developed nations who visit Cuba for sexual tourism. Some Cuban *pingueros* (young male sex workers) who engage in commercial sex with foreign men have been shown to do so only to earn money for personal and family survival (Hodge, 2001). Thus, poor men of color who interact with White middle-class gay men, whether in Havana or in Los Angeles, are vulnerable to new capitalist market relations that serve to globalize and commodify their bodies.

In such race and class clashes, White gay men are not the only ones responsible for these dynamics. Poor dark men from rural areas migrating to Mexico City have been exposed to very similar dynamics. For example, Gutmann (1996) examined Patricio Villalva's research on the experiences of hundreds of *prostitutos*—adolescent, indigenous men who did not identify themselves as homosexual or bisexual and were sometimes married and had children—who were often hired by lighter-skinned men from Mexico City who took advantage of these poor men's vulnerability after they arrived in the big city.

Under conditions of great structural inequality, some immigrant males may feel that they have no option but to engage in sexual activities that have been prompted by conditions of coercion and constrained choice. As I thought about the situation of the particular group of men in my study, I was challenged by the difficulty of theorizing the fine boundaries between sexual coercion and sex work, especially in relation to the challenges these immigrant men may have experienced when identifying and labeling themselves as having been sexually harassed (Welsh et al., 2006) and while living in conditions of marginal survival and undocumented status. Few of my informants reported that they had themselves been sexually solicited during a day laborer job, and none of my informants revealed their actual involvement in sex work activities with their employers. Embarrassment, shame, concern, and fear of deportation might have been some of the reasons why such accounts were not revealed. Also, they might have felt more comfortable sharing stories that had taken place voluntarily under less coercive circumstances.

The "White gay man–Latino man" sexualized interaction described by Malpica while relevant is clearly not the exclusive social force underlying the relationships between men described in this article. Future research is needed in order to explain additional processes contributing to these dynamics, including examinations of other forms of sexual and racial harassment and coercion by nongay men, non-White men, and women who also hire these immigrants.

The question arises as well if some of these informants and their acquaintances and friends might have been gay or bisexual men who did not know their identity until after they had migrated. I believe that sexuality is a complex, fluid, and sophisticated process that goes beyond the categories of sexual orientation labeled as homosexual, bisexual, and heterosexual. For those who migrate between countries (and between different socioeconomic contexts), sexuality can be shaped by different economic, political, and ethnic/racial factors as well as by modes of settlement and incorporation. For instance, for men like Mauricio who had been involved in long-term romantic relationships with women, sexual desire for men was not reported as part of their sexual repertoire of feelings and emotions. Even though Mauricio may have found pleasure while receiving oral sex from men, he reported that for him sex with other men had always been prompted by conditions that had to do with inequality and marginality, such as crowded housing, the effects of drugs or alcohol, or a sense of moral responsibility for someone who had helped him while he struggled with poverty. Thus, while men like Mauricio may embrace heterosexuality as their sexual identity and as the main organizer of their romantic choices, their actual sexual behaviors may also be affected by the changing social contexts that they experience.

Interestingly, Mauricio and other informants blushed or became defensive and anxious when I carefully asked if they had ever felt sexual attraction toward men. And when I asked them why a man would actually have sex with another man, they associated negative factors (i.e., alcohol, drugs, crowded housing, isolation, and pornographic movies) with such behaviors. While these factors may explain in part why these sexualized interactions took place and often negatively impact the sexual health of this population (González-López, 2005), my informants less frequently described same-sex desire and sexual pleasure as part of these exchanges. Their feelings of homophobia might have not allowed them to directly express their authentic erotic desire when we discussed these specific issues. Thus, further research is needed to explore how and why same-sex desire and pleasure may inform the behaviors of nongay-identified migrant jornaleros who have sex with men before and after migration.

In sum, these men's experiences exposed heterosexuality's complex fluidity and potential fragility. Heterosexuality can thus be viewed as a paradox, socially powerful and vulnerable at the same time. The voices of these men also served to support the argument that heterosexuality—as an institution and as the hegemonic sexual

norm—has to be consistently reproduced and reinforced in order to preserve its dominance. Their voices may also be seen to extend the findings from other critical studies that have examined heterosexuality with the purpose of "revealing and demystifying the mechanisms of power, identifying their internal contradictions and cleavages, so as to inform movements for change" (Messner, 1996).

FINAL REFLECTIONS

The voices of immigrant men presented in this article show how macro and micro conditions of immigration sometimes push at the fronteras of heterosexuality. On the one hand, these men have been exposed to structural coercion and commercial sex within oppressive racialized and sexualized intra-male hierarchies and larger and globalized socioeconomic forces, and on the other, they have reported engaging in same-sex experiences within migration contexts and through their own agency. In the first case, I have described a larger structural power inequality that has influenced the sex lives of these immigrant Mexicanos. In the second case, no one had significant power over anyone else. I have argued that these two patterns of sexual behavior are not part of the same phenomenon—one does not necessarily lead to the other—and that they belong to different categories of same-sex sexual activity. Each one of these processes is complex, however, and requires further research.

Sexuality research with U.S. Latino populations has traditionally used and abused paradigms that focus on a so-called Latino culture based on concepts such as machismo, marianismo, religiosity, familism, and acculturation. I argue that it is time to go beyond such simplistic culture-based paradigms in order to identify and critically examine other social forces affecting and shaping the sex lives of these populations. The objective of my research with Mexican populations is to challenge stereotypical representations of Latina women and Latino men in sexuality research. In addition, I am interested in addressing why in-depth sociological examinations are overdue. These sociological examinations are crucial for a better understanding of the sex lives of the poor immigrant men who may become sexually disempowered while surviving in an increasingly complex and exploitative capitalist society.

INTRODUCTION REFERENCE

U.S. Equal Employment Opportunity Commission. 2002, June 27. *Facts about sexual harassment.* Http://www. eeoc.gov/facts/fs-sex.html (accessed December 26, 2008).

REFERENCES

Alonso, A. M., & Koreck, M. T. (1993). Silences: "Hispanics," AIDS, and sexual practices. In H. Abelove, M. A. Barale, & D. M. Halperin, (Eds.), *The lesbian and gay studies reader* (pp. 110–126). New York: Routledge.

Altman, D. (2001). *Global sex.* Chicago: University of Chicago Press.

Brandes, S. (2002). *Staying sober in Mexico City.* Austin: University of Texas Press.

Bronfman, M., & López Moreno, S. (1996). Perspectives on HIV/AIDS prevention among immigrants on the U.S.-Mexico border. In S. I. Mishra, R. F. Conner, & J. R. Magaña (Eds.), *AIDS crossing borders* (pp. 49–76). Boulder: Westview Press.

Cantú, L. (1999). *Border crossings: Mexican men and the sexuality of migration.* Dissertation manuscript, University of California, Irvine.

Carrier, J. M. (1985). Mexican male bisexuality. In F. Klein & T. J. Wolf (Eds.), *Bisexualities: Theory and research* (pp. 75–85). New York: Haworth Press.

Carrillo, H. (2002). *The night is young: Sexuality in Mexico in the time of AIDS.* Chicago: University of Chicago Press.

Connell, R. W. (1995). *Masculinities.* Berkeley: University of California Press.

Cortina, L. M. (2004). Hispanic perspectives on sexual harassment and social support. *Personality and Social Psychology Bulletin, 30*(5), 570–584.

de la Vega, E. (1990). Considerations for reaching the Latino population with sexuality and HIV/AIDS information and education. *SIECUS Report, 18*(3), 1–8.

Díaz, R. M. (1998). *Latino gay men and HIV: Culture, sexuality, and risk behavior.* New York: Routledge.

Giuffre, P. A., & Williams, C. L. (2002). Boundary lines: Labeling sexual harassment in restaurants. In C. L. Williams & A. Stein (Eds.), *Sexuality and gender* (pp. 427–447). Oxford, England: Blackwell.

González-López, G. (2005). *Erotic journeys: Mexican immigrants and their sex lives.* Berkeley, CA: University of California Press.

Gutmann, M. C. (1996). *The meanings of macho: Being a man in Mexico City.* Berkeley: University of California Press.

Hennessy, R. (2000). *Profit and pleasure: Sexual identities in late capitalism.* New York: Routledge.

Hirsch, J. S. (2003). *A courtship after marriage: Sexuality and love in Mexican transnational families.* Berkeley: University of California Press.

Hodge, G. D. (2001). Colonization of the Cuban body: The growth of male sex work in Havana. *Report on Gender, NACLA Report on the Americas, 34*(5), 20–28.

Hondagneu-Sotelo, P. (1992). Overcoming patriarchal constraints: The reconstruction of gender relations among Mexican immigrant women and men. *Gender & Society, 6*(3), 393–415.

Ingraham, C. (2005). *Thinking straight: The promise, the power, and the paradox of heterosexuality.* New York: Routledge.

LeVine, S. (1993). *Dolor y alegría: Women and social change in urban Mexico.* Madison: University of Wisconsin Press.

Malpica, D. M. (2002). Making a living in the streets of Los Angeles: An ethnographic study of day laborers. *Migraciones Internacionales, 1*(3), 24–148.

Marín, B. V., Gómez, C. A., & Hearst, N. (1993). Multiple heterosexual partners and condom use among Hispanics and non-Hispanic Whites. *Family Planning Perspectives, 25,* 170–174.

Messner, M. A. (1996). Studying up on sex. *Sociology of Sport Journal, 13*(3), 221–237.

O'Connell Davidson, J., & Sanchez Taylor, J. (2004). Fantasy islands: Exploring the demands for sex tourism. In M. S. Kimmel & M. A. Messner (Eds.), *Men's lives* (6th ed., pp. 454–466). Boston: Allyn and Bacon.

Organista, K. C., Organista, P. B., Bola, J. R., García de Alba, J. E., & Castillo Morán, M. A. (2000). Predictors of condom use in Mexican migrant laborers. *American Journal of Community Psychology, 28*(2), 245–265.

Prieur, A. (1998). *Mema's house, Mexico City: On transvestites, queens, and machos.* Chicago: University of Chicago Press.

Rubin, L. B. (1983). *Intimate strangers: Men & women together.* New York: Harper & Row Publishers.

Sassen-Koob, S. (1984). The new labor demand in global cities. In M. P. Smith (Ed.), *Cities in transformation: Class, capital and the state* (pp. 139–171). Beverly Hills: Sage.

Segal, L. (1994). *Straight sex: Rethinking the politics of pleasure.* Berkeley: University of California Press.

Smith, T., & Kimmel, M. (2005). The hidden discourse of masculinity in gender discrimination law. *Signs: Journal of Women in Culture and Society,* 30(3), 1827–1849.

Szasz, I. (1998). Masculine identity and meanings of sexuality: A review of research in Mexico. *Reproductive Health Matters,* 6(12), 97–104.

U.S. Equal Employment Opportunity Commission (EEOC). (2002). Retrieved August 24, 2006, from http://www.eeoc.gov/facts/fs-sex.html.

Valenzuela, A., Jr. (2003). Day labor work. *Annual Review of Sociology,* 29(1), 307–333.

Welsh, S., Carr, J., MacQuarrie, B., & Huntley, A. (2006). "I'm not thinking of it as sexual harassment": Understanding harassment across race and citizenship. *Gender and Society,* 20(1), 87–107.

Effects of Cybersex Addiction on the Family

Results of a Survey

Jennifer P. Schneider

What are anonymous, convenient, and readily available to potential partners, making them a major conduit for unhappiness in many marriages? Cybersex and Internet affairs (Schnarch & Morehouse 2002). Relatively "new kids on the block," interpersonal relationships in cyberspace were unheard of before the past decade. In fact, few persons other than professionals in research laboratories and universities had even used the Internet. By 2008 there were an estimated 135 million Internet users, with the numbers expected to continue to grow (Nielson Online, 2008). Jennifer Schneider used e-mail to survey persons identified by therapists as dealing with cybersex problems in the family, illustrating the dramatic difference a decade can make, even in research methods.

The most frequently searched topic on the Internet today is a three-letter word, spelled "sex" (Freeman-Longo & Blanchard 1998). And, the statistics are daunting. In a survey by MSNBC, over nine million users were found to visit adult entertainment websites, and of these, 23 percent of the women and 50 percent of the men surfed for visual erotica (Cooper, McLoughlin, & Campbell 2000). The use of cybersex on the Internet occupies, on average, 11 hours per week for the compulsive user (Cooper, Putnam, Planchon, & Boies 1999). But, herein may lie another problem of terminological confusion. Of 7,000 persons surveyed by MSNBC, over 60 percent did not consider cybersex with another person to be marital infidelity (Cooper et al., 2000). It was considered instead to be more like pornography and less like a real relationship.

David Schnarch and Ruth Morehouse (2002), Co-Directors of the Marriage and Family Health Center in Evergreen, Colorado, have helped to clarify the confusion by defining three related concepts from their perspectives as therapists:

- Cybersex involves the use of computerized text, images, or sound files for sexual stimulation;
- Cyber infidelity occurs when a partner in a committed relationship uses a computer to violate agreements of sexual exclusivity; and
- Internet affairs involve the use of interactive computer chat rooms to create exchanges to sexually arouse self or others as well as creating shared sexual excitement, often

From "Effects of Cybersex Addiction on the Family: Results of a Survey" by J. P. Schneider. 2000. *Sexual Addiction & Compulsivity* 7: 31–58. Reprinted by permission of the publisher (Taylor & Francis, http://www.informaworld.com).

culminating in simultaneous masturbation (p. 15).

Giving cybersex addiction a psychological spin, Schnarch and Morehouse contend that many people are so afraid of rejection, or so inexperienced at initiating novel sexual experiences, that they prefer to express their sexuality in the obscurity of the Internet. The therapists believe there are predictable, progressive steps in the development of Internet affairs:

- *Conducting nonsexually explicit flirting;*
- *Using sexual innuendos and explicit repartee;*
- *Scheduling sex-laced chats;*
- *Discussing sexual preferences and fantasies;*
- *Engaging in simultaneous masturbation online; and*
- *Planning face-to-face meetings for physical contact (Schnarch & Morehouse 2002, p. 15).*

Even though it is far too early to predict the extent of cybersex addiction or its effects on the family of the twenty-first century, this reading will at least acquaint you with the concept and the inherent conundrums surrounding the issue. After reading Schneider's work, you will be better able to agree or disagree with the definitions and opinions of Schnarch and Morehouse concerning cybersex. Regardless of varying opinions about terminology, researchers (including sociologists, psychologists, and family therapists), are currently involved in gathering data about destructive sexual behaviors, many of which are related to the Internet. Soon, we should know more about the warning signs of compulsive sexual behavior on the Internet, which would enable earlier intervention. Eventually, we will get to the "how" and the "why" factors. When we understand more about the cause and not just the effect, what then? Then parents, schools, churches, media, and all of the social institutions that influence a child's healthy sexuality will share in the responsibility to ensure its development.

———————

It felt like there was another woman or a "something" there that was competing for his attention. I felt like he was choosing between me and "it," and "it" usually won. I felt that I should have been first in his heart, but "it" was. I guess that I was a co-addict, as I considered sex and love as the same, and when he was choosing the computer, he was rejecting me. When I was home nights, and he would finally come to bed, then say he was too tired, I would try to interest him, and when I was unsuccessful, I would go into the living room and cry for hours.

He said that the computer was only a small part of the sex addiction, that pornography and meeting other people was a greater part, but the computer was an object that I could see, and, I guess, hate. When he was away from home, he could make up excuses for what he was doing, but when he was sitting in front of the computer and conversing for hours, there was no doubt what he was doing.

The kids knew what was going on, to an extent. My son says there is no way that he can trust his dad, but my son also has been visiting porn sites, until we found out and talked to him about it.

I resented the computer for years, until I finally accepted the fact that it was the user, not the machine that was causing the problem.
—*41-year-old woman, married 23 years*

I knew my husband was masturbating all the time, but I thought it was my fault. When I found the computer disk going back five years, everything made sense. I had been in denial about how much I knew, and how much my life was out of control. I feel very used and violated because of this behavior, and I have lost my trust.

My husband would blame me when I would catch him masturbating at the computer. He would not do any chores when I was out; when I returned, he would throw the blinds and turn off the light really fast. He would keep looking at his pants to see if I could tell he had an erection. He would run out of the bedroom like he was just changing. He would call me and say he was coming right home at 4:00, and not show up until 7:00. He would say he was working really hard and not to give him a hard time.

I knew he would be masturbating if I left the house. I never said no to sex unless he was wasted drunk, I was not feeling well, or I was working. I believed that if I had sex more often, or if I were better at sex, he would not masturbate as much. I surveyed my friends to see if they'd caught their husbands masturbating, to see how often they thought it was normal to masturbate, to see what kind of sex they had with their husbands and how often.

I thought I was not good enough because I did not look like the girls in the pictures. I thought that if I dressed and looked good it would keep him interested. I would give up competing with his masturbating and not want to have sex with him. I would not walk into the room at night because I did not want to walk in on him.

If the kids and I were coming home from somewhere and his car was there, I would run into the house first and be loud so the kids would not walk in on him. I found semen on my office chair and pubic hair on my mouse. I would get dressed fast so I would not have to have sex with him. I stopped making dinner because I would not know when he would be coming home. I would have to mentally prepare myself for sex. I tried to talk with him about masturbation and how often he wanted to have sex. I was in denial about how unhappy I was.

My husband does not believe he has an addiction. He doesn't think it's a big deal because he says he was never with anyone else. He thinks all he needs is a more loving wife.

—*38-year-old woman, married 15 years, divorcing*

When I know that my husband has masturbated to cyberporn, I don't want him to touch me. I feel like I am leftovers, not first-run as I should be. My self-esteem is damaged beyond belief. To be honest, our sex life is pretty incredible—we are not prudes by any means. I just don't understand. How can it be soooo good for both of us but still not enough for him?

—*31-year-old woman, married one year*

The growth of the Internet has been phenomenal. Before 1993 the Internet was used by only a few persons in laboratories and universities. [Today, an] increasing number of people are drawn into using Internet access to obtain sexual satisfaction. Most of these people are "recreational users," analogous to recreational drinkers or gamblers, but a significant proportion have preexisting sexual compulsions and addictions that are now finding a new outlet. For others, with no such history, cybersex is the first expression of an addictive sexual disorder, one that lends itself to rapid progression, similar to the effect of crack cocaine on the previously occasional cocaine user.

In contrast to pornographic bookstores and theaters, involvement with prostitutes, exhibitionism and voyeurism on the street, purchase of pornographic magazines, and anonymous sex in hotels and parks, the Internet has several characteristics which make it the ideal medium for sexual involvement (Cooper, Putnam, Planchon, & Boies, 1999). It is widely accessible, inexpensive, legal, available in the privacy of one's own home, anonymous, and does not put the user at direct risk of contracting a sexually transmitted disease. It is also ideal for hiding the activities from the spouse or significant other (SO), because it does not leave obvious evidence of the sexual encounter. It takes some computer savvy on the part of the spouse to retrace the user's online adventures.

METHODS

To learn more about the effects of cybersex on the SO and family of the user, I employed the same qualitative research method used in previous studies of the effect of sex addiction on couples (Schneider, Corley, & Irons, 1998). The only difference was that the research was done entirely via e-mail, as I assumed that the target population would have access to a computer. A cover letter was sent to approximately 20 therapists who treat sex addicts, and they were asked to forward the letter to any persons they knew who were dealing with cybersex involvement in the family. The letter explained the nature of the research and invited the client to e-mail me to obtain a brief survey.

The survey asked questions both about the adverse effects of cybersex use on the partners and about their efforts at resolution of the problems, either individually or as a couple. When reading the overwhelmingly pained, discouraged, and negative comments of the SOs, it is helpful to know that many of the same writers later describe recovery from their codependency and their pain, whether or not they are still in the relationship. In a number of cases, the cybersex user is taking major positive steps toward recovery from the addiction, and the couple relationship has changed significantly for the better.

This survey of partners of cybersex users did not attempt to formally diagnose sex addiction in the (mostly) men described by the respondents, and by its nature represents only the perspective of the respondents. Any addictive disorder comprises loss of control (i.e., compulsive behavior), continuation despite adverse consequences, and obsession or preoccupation with the activity. It is likely that the vast majority of the cybersex users fulfill these criteria and indeed have an addictive sexual disorder. However, this study was not designed to ascertain this. Therefore, use of the term "cybersex addict" in this article is informal and should not be construed as a definitive medical diagnosis.

RESULTS

Demographics

Responses were obtained from 94 persons whose spouse or partner was heavily involved in cybersex activities. The 94 SOs comprised 91 women and 3 men. One woman and 2 men reported being in a homosexual relationship. The 94 cybersex addicts were 92 men and 2 women. The mean age of the 94 respondents was 38.0 years, with a range of 24–57 [years]. They had been in the relationship for a mean of 12.6 years and a range of 0.5–39 years. In response to the question, "Are you still in the relationship?" 78.7 percent replied yes, 9.6 percent no, and 11.7 percent were separated. That is, 21.5 percent were living apart. Several partners who were still living with the spouse stated that the marriage was essentially over and that they were planning to divorce.

The cybersex involvement had been a problem for the partners for a mean of 2.4 years and a range of 1 month to 8.5 years. Several, however, commented that although they had learned about the behavior very recently, they now recognized that it had been going on for a long time and was probably responsible for problems in the relationship whose nature they had not understood before.

What Partners Told About the Cybersex Addicts

Sexual Activities

When asked about the addict's sexual activities, all responses included viewing and/or downloading pornography along with masturbation. Other behaviors were reading and writing sexually explicit letters and stories, e-mailing to set up personal meetings with someone, placing ads to meet sexual partners, visiting sexually oriented chat rooms, and engaging in interactive online affairs with same- or opposite-sex people, which included real-time viewing of each other's bodies using electronic cameras connected to the computer. Related activities included phone sex with people met online, and online affairs that progressed to real affairs. Several SOs knew that the addict was participating in unacceptable or illegal online activities such as sadomasochism and domination/bondage, bestiality, viewing child pornography and pornographic pictures of teenagers, and having sex with underage persons. One man reportedly signed on as a teenage girl and solicited lesbian sex, and another man posed as a teenage boy in teen chat rooms.

Live or Offline Sexual Activities
One might hypothesize that offline or live sexual encounters would be more problematic for a relationship than virtual encounters. Compared with the 57 people who had reportedly not had offline affairs, the 28 who did have live affairs were on the average older and had been in the relationship longer.

Online Sex Is a Continuation of a Preexisting Addictive Sexual Disorder
In 30.9 percent [of the reports], the cybersex activities were said to be a continuation of other compulsive sexual behaviors. Because some SOs may not have known about other behaviors, or may not have thought to mention them, this figure is likely to be an underestimate. Behaviors included phone sex, voyeurism, seeing prostitutes, and going to massage parlors. Most common was heavy involvement with pornography (magazines, videos, movies, etc.), often since the teen years.

Progression, Including Live Sex with Others
A well-known characteristic of addictions is tolerance, which is the need to do more and more to get the same results. This may involve an increase in the quantity of the drug or behavior, or an escalation in the type of activity. For sex addicts, this may mean more hours on the Internet, a larger number of partners, or more bizarre or riskier activities, or going from virtual to actual sexual encounters.

> Cybersex really accelerated the addiction on his part. It went from just magazines and movies to spending hours on end on the computer looking at images to hours on end chatting with anyone who would 'talk.' It took only 3 months to go from simple e-mail to all this, and he said it would have only been a matter of time before he

did start to meet women in person had I not found the disk. [30-year-old woman who found a porn disk in the drive]

Their partner's cybersex activities [17.6 percent] had indeed progressed to live encounters with other people. In some cases these were people they met online in chat rooms, via e-mail, etc. In other cases, the computer sexual activity triggered other addictive behaviors which involved other people. For example, a gay man wrote that his partner's bathhouse activities with other people had increased. Women wrote that their husbands had begun new activities such as a sexual massage parlor, visits with prostitutes, the first real affair, or an additional affair.

Denial, Minimization, and Blame
Some SOs wrote that their spouses were now attending 12-step meetings for sex addicts and/or going to counseling. Many others, however, explained that their spouses did not believe they had a problem or, even if they did recognize this, were not motivated to do anything about it. Several SOs had separated, divorced, or were planning to leave because of their spouse's refusal to recognize the problem, go to counseling, or seek other help.

Effect of Addict's Cybersex Involvement on Partners

On the Partner's Emotions
Most SOs described some combination of devastation, hurt, betrayal, loss of self-esteem, mistrust, suspicion, fear, and a lack of intimacy in their relationship. Other responses were extreme anger or rage, feeling sexually inadequate or feeling unattractive and even ugly, doubt one's judgment and even sanity, severe depression, and, in two cases, hospitalization for suicidality.

> This behavior has left me feeling alone, isolated, rejected, and 'less than.' Masturbation hangs a sign on the door that says 'You are not needed, I can take care of myself thank you very much.' I have threatened, manipulated, tried to control,

cried, gave him the cold shoulder, yelled, tried to be understanding, and even tried to ignore it. Denial and codependence are my character defects. [55-year-old woman, married 36 years]

Trust was a major casualty of the secrecy of cybersex addiction. Many SOs felt that this was at least as harmful to the relationship as the sexual activities themselves. Partners reported losing all trust in their mate and in anything he/she told them. Many reported that despite the addict's promises, "behavior has continued, but he has learned to be much more secretive about it." A common theme was, "The lies he told me concerning his whereabouts, while he looked me straight in the eye, have hurt worse than his having sex with them."

Three women reported having engaged in extramarital affairs or encounters, either to shore up their own self-esteem or else to get revenge on their spouses.

Effect on the Sexual Relationship

A 34-year-old woman who had learned of her husband's cybersex involvement only weeks earlier, described the effects on the couple's sexual relationship:

> I realize now that many of the things he most liked and requested when we made love were recreations of downloaded images. He is unable to be intimate, he objectifies me, he objectifies women and girls on the streets, he fantasizes when we're together. I feel humiliated, used, and betrayed, as well as lied to and misled. It's almost impossible for me to let him touch me without feeling really yucky and/or crying. I tried to continue being sexual with him initially (and in fact, being 'more' sexual, trying to fix it by being sexier, better than the porn girls), and I couldn't do it. We have now been consensually abstinent for 3 weeks.

This description contains various themes that were brought up recurrently by survey respondents: a feeling of being objectified, comparing herself with the cybersex women, initial attempt to increase the quantity and/or variety of sexual activities, and a decreased desire to have sexual relations with the addict. This woman did not experience the most common complaint: Loss of interest by the addict in having sex with the partner.

Two-thirds of respondents (68.1 percent) described sexual problems in the couple relationship that were generally related to the cybersex addict's sexual activities. In some cases these problems had resulted in decreased interest by the cybersex user in relational sex. In others it was the SO who had lost interest, and in some cases both partners had a decreased interest. In only 31.9 percent [of] coupleships were both partners still interested in sex with each other.

When asked about the effect of cybersex on their sexual relationship, fully half (52.1 percent) said that their husbands were not interested, or hardly interested in sex with them. Note that 65.3 percent of those who had decreased sexual interest stated that they now have less sex than they want. The remaining 18.1 percent reported that they too had shut down sexually, so that the lack of sexual activity at the same time of reporting was mutual in 17 couples.

In summary, 34 percent of the SOs complained that they were feeling deprived of relational sex, and another 16 percent of SOs reported that it was only the cybersex user who was unhappy with the lack of relational sex. Twice as many SOs as cybersex users wanted more sex with their relational partner than they were getting.

The SOs who were not interested in sex with the cybersex addict attributed their loss of interest primarily to their negative reaction to the Internet user's sexual activities with cybersex, phone sex, live encounters, etc. In total, half of the cybersex addicts and one third of the partners were no longer interested in marital sexual relations. This was reportedly not a problem for the addicts, who had substituted cybersex for sex with SO, but was definitely a problem for the partners, who felt angry, hurt, rejected, and often sexually unfulfilled.

Respondents who reported that the cyber-sex addict had been sexually compulsive (paper pornography, phone sex, etc.) even before the Internet came on the scene often stated that the couple's sexual relationship had been infrequent in those days as well. Some added that the problems in the sexual relationship had intensified since the cybersex activities began.

Cybersex Addict Alone Has Lost Interest in Couple Sex

[Although] 34 percent reported that they still wanted a sexual relationship, the cybersex addict had withdrawn his sexual (and general) attention from the partner and family and devoted his (or her) time and energy instead to computer sex. Recurrent themes here follow:

- The partner felt hurt, angry, sexually rejected, inadequate, and unable to compete with cyber images and sexy online women (or men) who were willing to do anything.
- The addict made excuses to avoid sex with the partner (not in the mood, too tired, has already climaxed and doesn't want sex, the children might hear).
- During relational sex, the addict appeared distant, emotionally detached, and interested only in his/her own pleasure.
- The partner ended up doing most or all of the initiating, either to get her/ his own needs met, or else in an attempt to get the addict to decrease the online activities.
- The addict blamed the partner for their sexual problems.
- The addict wanted the partner to participate in sexual activities which she/he found objectionable.

Since my husband was living in a fantasy world of Internet porn, I was the only one who initiated sex. I thought if I didn't we would never have sex and this would cause him to go elsewhere. He would respond but always seemed to be in another world during sex. When confronted with why he was not interested in sex, he said that "it was not as important to him as it is to other men." [28-year-old woman, married 8 years]

Partner Alone Has Lost Interest in Couple Sex

In 15 cases, the cybersex addict maintained his/her desire for sex with the SO, but the partner was less interested. In some cases the partner refused to have sex; in others, the partner didn't want to but continued out of fear of driving the addict further into online activities. Major themes reported follow:

- The partner's initial response in some cases was to increase the sexual activities in order to "win back" the addict. This early response was only temporary.
- The partner felt repelled and disgusted by the addict's online or real sexual activities and no longer wanted to have relationship sex. The partner could no longer tolerate the addict's detachment and lack of emotional connection during sex.
- The partner's anger over the addict's denial of the problem interfered with her/his sexual interest.
- In reply to pressure or requests by the addict to dress in certain ways or perform new sexual acts, the partner felt angry, repelled, used, objectified, or like a prostitute.
- Partner fears sex with the addict because the partner fears catching a disease from the addict, or has already caught one.

At first we had sex more than ever as I desperately tried to prove myself, then sex with her made me sick. I get strong pictures of what she did and lusted after, and I get repelled and feel bad. I used to see sex as a very intimate loving thing. We always had a lot of sex and I thought we were intimate. Now that I found out my wife was not on the same page, I can't be intimate or vulnerable–sex is now more recreational or just out of need. [44-year- old man, married 26 years]

Both Partners Have Lost Interest in Couple Sex

In 18.1 percent, loss of interest by both partners put a virtual end to sexual relations between them. Typical dynamics were a man who was more interested in sex with the computer than with the wife, and a woman who felt rejected, angry, and unable to compete—i.e., a combination of the individual themes.

Comparison With Online Sexual Partners

The knowledge that the addict's head is full of cybersex images inevitably produces in the SO a comparison between the spouse and the fantasy woman in terms of appearance, desirability, and repertory of sexual behaviors. Both addicts and partners were reported to make such comparisons. The SO feels she/he is competing with the computer images and people. ("If only I were perfect like his porn, then he would want the real thing and love me.") The result is often confusion—on the one hand, desire to emulate and better the cyberwoman (or man), on the other [hand] revulsion at the lack of intimacy and mechanical nature of the sex. Survey respondents reported vacillating between these two polarities.

> He's never been physically unfaithful, but he has had experiences with others. I feel cheated. I never know who or what he is thinking of when we are intimate. How can I compete with hundreds of anonymous others who are now in our bed, in his head? By chatting sex, he and others made up fantasies and pretended. How can reality ever satisfy him now? When he says something sexual to me in bed, I wonder if he has said it to others, or if it is even his original thought. Now our bed is crowded with countless faceless strangers, where once we were intimate. With all this deception, how do I know he has quit, or isn't moving into other behaviors?
> [34-year old woman, married 14 years to a minister]

Partner Increases Sexual Activities to Combat the Problem

Some partners attempted a sexual solution to the cybersex addiction problem, typically either increasing the frequency of sexual activities with the addict, or else joining with the addict in his preferred activities:

> My husband is a minister who was stationed overseas for a year. We chatted daily, but never sexually. Then I learned about his cybersex activities, and felt cheated. Why wouldn't he ask me to have cybersex? I wasn't comfortable with this, but I thought I could 'rescue' him. So we began a cybeysex relationship. But much to my horror, he never quit with all the anonymous partners. So he lumped me together with all the online whores. When he returned, he continued his cybersex even though we were reunited.
> [34year-old woman, still in a long-term marriage]

What's the Big Deal About Online Sex?

This is the most common question that is asked by persons who focus on the absence of skin-to-skin contact during cybersex activities, and cannot understand why marriages actually break up over this issue. This question elicited the most emotional and eloquent responses of the survey.

Concern about escalation. Tolerance—the need to do more to get the same results—is a common feature of addictive disorders. Online viewing, which begins as harmless recreation, can become an all-consuming activity and can also lead to real sexual encounters, either with sexual partners met online or escalation of the sex addiction in general. Even when the sex involves only the computer, there is often escalation of conflict in the relationship.

> I might say to those who say, 'it's only cyber[sex]' that it's so easy to go on to more from there! I never thought the cyber addiction would be so hard to control, and I nearly went on to meet individual men myself. If I had, I think I would be dead right now because I was becoming so

lackadaisical in personal protection issues. [51-year-old woman who is herself recovering from sex addiction and is married to a sex addict]

It's still cheating/a mental affair/adultery. Thirty respondents explained why they consider online sex activities the same as adultery. The most important reasons are:

1. Having interactive sex with another person is adultery, whether or not they have skin-to-skin contact.
2. Cybersex results in lying, hiding one's activities, and covering up, and the lies are often the most painful part of the affair.
3. The spouse feels betrayed, devalued, deceived, "less than," abandoned—same as with a real affair.
4. Cybersex takes away from the sexual relationship of the couple.
5. A real-life person cannot compete with fantasy. The cybersex addict loses interest in his spouse because he has "ideal" relationships where there is no hassle.
6. Cybersex takes the addict away from his partner—in terms of time and emotions. It results in emotional detachment from the marriage.

Effect on self-esteem. The reason some respondents gave for why cybersex is so destructive is the adverse effect on their self-esteem.

> True, you don't have the risk of the diseases, but it is still an emotional thing. It's hard to think that the sex addict wants to do it without the actual touch–how can it be better for them? Especially since they have to do all the work themselves! It really hurts your self-esteem, and most of us don't have a very good self-esteem as it is. [37-year-old woman, married 17 years]

I can't compete with fantasy/can't measure up. Cybersex taps into partners' deepest insecurities about their ability to measure up. The need to compete with interactive sex online pressures them into unwanted sexual activities. "Sex with

the fantasy leaves practically nothing left to be desired when compared with the all-too human and flawed spouse," explained one woman.

On the Internet it is possible to find groups of people who are interested in all kinds of unusual or even deviant sexual practices. Interacting with these people desensitizes the user to these activities and "normalizes" them. Some cybersex users eventually come to blame their partners for being unwilling to engage in these behaviors.

It has adversely affected our relationship. Some SOs focused not on the adultery aspect of cybersex, but rather on the overall effect on the couple relationship:

> Not everyone who looks at pornography is an addict, some are merely curious. But when the addict never admits to viewing pornography, when he lies about his use of pornography to the marriage counselor he's agreed to go to because he wants to save his marriage, that's when it becomes a problem. I tell them I knew something was wrong in our intimate relationship and I always wondered who he was making love to, because it never was me. [39-year-old woman, divorced after an 8-year marriage]

Partners Who Have Experienced Both
Several partners who had dealt with both cyber affairs and live affairs said they hurt the same.

> They should try it for themselves one time, and see how it feels to be less important to their partner than a picture on a computer screen! They should see what it feels like to lie in bed and know their partner is on the computer and what he is doing with it. It's not going to do much for the self-esteem. My husband has actually cheated on me and it FEELS NO DIFFERENT. The online 'safe' cheating has just as dirty, filthy a feel to it as does the 'real-life' cheating. [38-year-old woman, married 18 years]

Effects on the Children

The most commonly reported adverse consequence was that one or both parents were unavailable to spend time or pay attention to the children. Respondents complained of the addict's unavailability to the children, and failure to fulfill family responsibilities: "One afternoon he was so caught up in the computer that he failed to meet my daughter coming off the school bus. I told my husband that the only way the kids recognize him is by the back of his head." The other parent may also be unavailable because of preoccupation with the addict. SOs who got divorced or were separated mentioned that their children had lost their two-parent home.

Even if children did not see the online sexual images, they observed arguments and stress in the home; this was the second most commonly mentioned adverse effect. Two women wrote of the children witnessing episodes of domestic violence. Thirty percent of those with children believed that their young children, and adult children who were out of the home, were not significantly affected by the family problems related to online sex addiction.

Other adverse effects were related to viewing pornography (and occasionally masturbation) and to exposure to the cybersex addict's objectification of women. Some SOs reported that their children had found pornography that had been left on the computer, had walked in when the cyberaddict was chatting in a chat room, had overheard the addict having phone sex, or had observed the addict having interactive sex online. As a result, one woman wrote, "One daughter became promiscuous, the other wants me to leave him. My son now thinks that hurting women is normal." Other consequences were that the children became "horrified, ashamed, and embarrassed," got angry at the father and/or lost respect for him. Teenage children began viewing online pornography themselves. Others began selling it: "My son found old porn movies I was told had been disposed of, and he and a friend copied them and were selling them at school. My 14-year-old baby had a porn ring going!"

Several mothers were worried because their husbands surfed the Internet while supposedly watching younger children, who got to view the pornography and sometimes the masturbation.

> My daughter caught him masturbating once and told me about it. I felt sick. I am scared that someday, when she gets to the age of the women that he likes to look at, that he will hurt her. I am confused about how to talk to my children about love, sex, and masturbation. [27-year-old woman, married 3 years and still in the relationship]

When Both Partners Are Cybersex Users

There are many legitimate dating services on the Internet which have facilitated single people meeting each other. The risks and advantages of meeting in this way have been discussed before (Cooper & Sportolari, 1997). However, when two people meet online specifically for sex, then later attempt to convert the relationship to a more traditional one, there are predictable risks. A 46-year-old woman met a man online in a sexually oriented chat room. They participated in cybersex for many months, then finally met in person.

> I met him online five years ago. I thought he was "faithful" to our online relationship. I found out a few months ago that he has been nonmonogamous from almost the very first time we met in person. He was into porn extensively, and into meeting 'swingers.' I assumed he was honest with me, but I found out otherwise. We had an amazing, exciting, and satisfying sexual relationship until he disclosed to me a few months ago. Then it turned sour.... I met him on online, and now I know... it is no different than meeting someone in 3D. People are people, and sickness and addictions are everywhere.

She reports that currently she is experiencing major depression, related to the sense of betrayal and the ending of the relationship.

Both men and women, many of them sexually compulsive, engage in online sexual activities. Not surprisingly, a sexually addicted couple can get drawn into cybersex activities. One of the survey respondents wrote that she and her husband had both been actively involved in cybersex activities with other people. Her marriage is in trouble because she is now sexually sober but her spouse is still acting out on the computer. If one member of such a couple bottoms out and seeks recovery before the other, the relationship will become destabilized.

Discussion

In planning this survey, I was very concerned with issues of anonymity and privacy. It was surprising to me, therefore, that only 3 of the 94 respondents returned the survey by regular mail, thereby remaining completely anonymous. In some cases their willingness to e-mail me was situational—several commented in their survey that they were familiar with my writings. I would hypothesize that the comfort of other respondents with e-mail reflected the ease of use of the computer and sense of anonymity of the internet culture.

One-third of respondents volunteered the information that their partner's online sexual activities had been preceded by years of other compulsive sexual behaviors. As stated earlier, the actual numbers are likely to be significantly higher. Cooper, Delmonico, and Burg (2000) reported that 4.6 percent of a large sample of cybersex participants were sexually compulsive, as determined by their scores on a sexual compulsivity scale. The present sample, in contrast to Cooper's cohort, was selected specifically because the cybersex use had caused significant problems for the partner. It is likely that the majority of the remaining cybersex users in the present study belonged to the "at-risk" group, those with prior vulnerability to compulsive Internet involvement.

Divorce and separation were two other consequences of cybersex addiction which were common in this survey. We may speculate that more couples get divorced over cybersex addiction than over excessive time spent on the Internet in general. Also, it is probable that workers who use company time to access the Internet are more likely to get fired if the content of their Internet activity was sexual than if it was not.

The Stages of Prerecovery of the Cybersex Coaddict

In this study, SOs were aware of the cybersex addict's online activities for time periods ranging from eight years to just a month or two. It is possible to infer from the survey responses the time course of responses by the partner to the cyberaddict's ongoing involvement with online sex.

Stage 1: Ignorance/Denial

The partner recognizes there is a problem in the relationship but is unaware of the contribution of cybersex to the problem. ("I knew something was wrong the first two years of our marriage, but I could not identify it.") The SO believes the addict's denials, explanations, and promises. She tends to ignore and explain away her own concerns, and may blame herself for the sexual problems. When cybersex addiction is present, a frequent problem is lack of interest by the addict in marital sex; in response the SO may try to enhance her own attractiveness to the addict. Self-esteem is likely to suffer, but the partner is unlikely to seek help at this point.

Late in this stage, suspicions may increase and "detective behaviors" begin. However, snooping or detective behaviors are accentuated at a later stage.

Stage 2: Shock/Discovery of the Cybersex Activities

At some point the partner learns of the cybersex addict's activities. In some cases this occurs accidentally, either because the partner comes upon the addict in the midst of the activities, or because the SO turns on the computer and discovers a cache of pornographic pictures. In other cases, the discovery is the result of deliberate investigations by the SO. No matter how the discovery occurs, the result is that the partner's ignorance and denial are over.

Discovery often leads to strong emotions of shock, betrayal, anger, pain, hopelessness, confusion, and shame. Because the pull of the computer is so strong and its availability in the home and at work is so great, there is a great tendency for the addict to return to cybersex activities even after discovery by the spouse, no matter how sincere the initial intention to quit. The result is that many respondents described a cycle of discoveries, promises made and broken, and additional discoveries and promises.

Feelings of shame, self-blame, and embarrassment often accompany the early days of dealing with a partner's cybersex addiction. These feelings may prevent the SO from talking with others and appealing for help, and the resultant isolation worsens the situation. Covering up for the addict is part of this stage.

> We have only told our therapists about this problem. It's so hard to go to family events and everyone thinks we're doing great. I don't want to tell them because I don't want this to be all that they think of when they think of my husband. And we don't feel like we can trust any of our friends with our 'secret.' So we're dealing with this alone and that hurts. [25-year-old woman, married 2 years, just recently discovered the cybersex addiction]

Stage 3: Problem-Solving Attempts

The partner is now energized to take action to resolve the problem, which is perceived as the cybersex behaviors. At this stage the classic sexual coaddictive behaviors peak–snooping, bargaining, controlling access to the computer, giving ultimatums, asking for full disclosure after every episode, obtaining information for the addict on sex addiction and addiction recovery, and (early in this stage) increasing the frequency and repertory of sexual activities with the addict in hopes of decreasing his desire for cybersex.

The breaking point became his willingness to lie to me to cover his activities and his shame. We both knew this would not work and I especially would spiral downhill when I would find out he had broken his promises. At some point I had asked that if he acted out that he tell me right away so that we could work with it. My preference of course was that he come to me when he felt like acting out, but that didn't happen. I could deal with the addiction if it were out in the open, because we would both begin to gain insights into the why's of this complicated issue. [38-year-old woman, married 8 year]

This type of agreement rarely works for long. It provides a measure of comfort for the wife to know what is going on and gives her the illusion of control. But the result establishes a parent-child dynamic between the couple, engenders resentment in the addict, and typically ends up in continued lying.

A sexual solution to the sexual problem seems to make sense in this stage. SOs may agree to sexual practices with which they are not comfortable, have sex even when tired, and think about improving their appearance by undergoing breast enhancement surgery or liposuction. For the cybersex user, none of these methods are likely to diminish the lure of the Internet.

The partner believes that additional information will enhance her or his ability to manage the situation. This leads to "snooping" or "detective" behaviors. Co-addicts who are computer savvy learn how to trace the addict's activities, and in some cases may even try to entice him by logging on into the same chat rooms themselves.

When the cybersex activities come to light, the couple tries to come to some agreement to try to limit the addict's use of the computer. This may consist simply of promises not to use it, or to restrict usage to legitimate needs. Often, the SO, with the addict's agreement or at least knowledge, assumes control of the access. In addition, the SO or the couple may purchase filtering software (e.g., Net Nanny) which prevents access to sexually-oriented sites. None of these "negative" methods tend to be successful for long if they are not accompanied by "positive" recovery-oriented activities.

The above three stages—ignorance/denial, shock/discovery of the cybersex, and problem solving attempts—are specific applications of the phases of prerecovery of sexual co-addicts described by Milrad (1999). She found that the prerecovery stage, lasting approximately 4–8 years, was divided into two phases—a denial phase, when partners recognize there is a problem but remain in denial about its cause, and a more active phase, when they come out of denial about the addict's problem and seek active solutions, but remain in denial as to their own issues.

The findings of this survey support Milrad's phases. As she observed in her study, the end of the prerecovery phase and the beginning of recovery is an awareness by sexual co-addicts that they are in crisis and need help. In the present study, SOs entered the crisis stage when they realized that their problem-solving efforts were unsuccessful and when the costs of remaining in the status quo became intolerable— depressive symptoms, isolation, loss of libido, a "dead" marriage, their own dysfunctional behaviors in some cases (affairs, excessive drinking, violence), and awareness of the effects on the children of the family dysfunction. This is the stage when the SO seeks help for herself/himself rather than in order to fix the addict, and learns that she/he did not cause the problem and cannot solve it. Once the SO is in therapy and getting help, the chances increase that the marriage or relationship will end unless the cybersex addict too becomes committed to recovery.

Limitations of This Study
The chief limitation of this study is that it includes only a self-selected population of people who have experienced significant adverse consequences as a result of their partner's cybersex addiction. It can provide no information about (a) the nature of the consequences, if any, to families of recreational or occasional cybersex users or (b) the prevalence among all cybersex users of significant consequences to the family. A random sample of partners of all cybersex users would be needed to provide such information.

INTRODUCTION REFERENCES

Cooper, A., Putnam, D. A., Planchon, L. A., & Boles, S. C. 1999. Online sexual compulsivity: Getting tangled in the net. *Sexual Addiction & Compulsivity* 6: 79–104.

Cooper, A., McLoughlin, I. P., & Campbell, K. M. 2000. Sexuality in cyberspace: Updates for the 21st century. *CyberPsychology & Behavior 3*: 521–536.

Freeman-Longo, I. B., & Blanchard, G. 1998. *Sexual abuse in America: Epidemic of the 21st century*. Brandon, VT: Safer Society Press.

Nielsen Online. 2008, August 12. *Nielsen Online Reports Topline U.S. data for July*. New York: Author.

Schnarch, D., & Morehouse, R. 2002. September– October. Online sex: Dyadic crises, and pitfalls for MFTs. *Family Therapy Magazine*, 14–19.

REFERENCES

Cooper, A., Delmonico, D. L., & Burg, R. (2000). Cybersex users, abusers, and compulsives: New findings and implications. *Sexual Addiction & Compulsivity, 7*, 5–29.

Cooper, A., Putnam, D. A., Planchon, L. A., & Boies, S. C. (1999). Online sexual compulsivity: Getting tangled in the Net. *Sexual Addiction & Compulsivity, 6*, 79–104.

Milrad, R., (1999). Coaddictive recovery: Early recovery issues for spouses of sex addicts. *Sexual Addiction & Compulsivity, 6*, 125–136.

Schneider, J. P., Corley, M. D., & Irons, R. R., (1998). Surviving disclosure of infidelity: Results of an international survey of 164 recovering sex addicts and partners. *Sexual Addiction & Compulsivity, 5*, 189–218.

PART X

Sexuality and Public Policy

With changes in technology making pornography "easier to order into the home than pizza" and court decisions that offer broad legal protection to vendors, selling sex has become a $10 billion industry in the United States (Egan, 2000). Meanwhile, the "crazy aunt in the attic" phenomenon has been spawned: "everyone knows she is there, but no one is talking about her!" It seems that legal issues about sexuality and money have become silent partners. American Telephone and Telegraph, Time Warner, Marriott International, and the Hilton Corporation are all corporations with a big financial stake in the adult-video film market, but all remain low-key about pornography profits. With market players of such magnitude, it is logical to question the relationship of economic factors to laws that have been or could be affected, especially those pertaining to sexual behavior and sexual exploitation. Part X flushes out significant sociological questions related to legal, economic, and educational issues surrounding sexuality and public policy.

Legal issues are critically related to the sexual health of Americans and inextricably bound to public policy. To understand how legal issues influence sexuality, one must be somewhat knowledgeable about legislative and legal processes. Basically, the levels of jurisdiction throughout the country begin locally, progressing from city, to county, to state, and, finally, to federal government, each with its own legal code. Additionally, even the military has a legal code of its own. All laws are subject to the provisions of the Constitution of the United States and, likewise, laws governing sexuality at any level cannot be inconsistent with the next highest level of governance.

In any storyline, one first identifies the principal players. Frank Rich does a masterful job of this assignment in his *New York Times Magazine* article, "Naked Capitalists" in which both nakedness and capitalism are exposed. He flushes out the characters who are conducting an annual $10 to $14 billion business in the United States called the "Adult Industry" or the "Porn Business." Rich characterizes the business as "a mirror image of Hollywood," contending that the arrival of home video revolutionized pornography as much as sound had revolutionized Hollywood. And, his facts are staggering: Considering even the low-end $10 billion estimate, pornography is a bigger business than professional football, basketball, and baseball combined. More money is spent for pornography than regular movie tickets or than all of the performing arts together.

The byword for access to pornography today appears to be "no effort, no fear." In writing about pornography and sexual deviance, Bryant and Zillman (2001) contend that the benefits of living in the information age, with ready access to large quantities of information and communication options, can prove to be a proverbial two-edged sword: Not all access to mediated messages is beneficial or desirable. The negative social and psychological effects that appear to stem from repeatedly using hard-core pornography are cited as an example of the "dark side" of ready access to modern mediated communication.

College students likely represent a microcosm of varying opinions in the pornography debates: For example, free speech versus censorship issues have created some unlikely allies. Antipornography feminist scholars find themselves allied with Christian evangelical leaders in antipornography debates, and law professors specializing in First Amendment issues are themselves defending the rights of publishers of the most graphically explicit materials in anticensorship litigation (Carroll, 2005).

But, the issue of pornography nowhere has been more divisive than among feminists themselves. Antipornography feminist leaders Catherine MacKinnon and Andrea Dworkin contend that pornography is less about sex than power over women. They claim that it reinforces male dominance and increases sexual and physical abuse against women (LeVay & Valente, 2003). Anticensorship feminists, such as Camille Paglia (1994) and Nadine Strossen (1995), argue that censorship of sexual materials will be used to suppress feminist writings about erotica, endangering women's rights and freedom of expression. Extensive arguments on both sides of the censorship issue are so compelling that readers are often left with feeling that the answer to the question "Are you for or against censorship of pornography?" is "yes."

Putting a face on the women and men who are in this multibillion-dollar business, Rich reveals how they feel about their work, why they got into the adult industry, and interesting trivia, such as whether they themselves watch pornography. Understanding their motives, missions, and misgivings will provide students with a better knowledge base from which to formulate their own opinions about pornography and the women and men who promote it. Historian Vern L. Bullough advanced a convincing argument that society itself plays a key role in promoting the sex industry. In writing from a historical perspective about prostitution, a largely illegal (except in Nevada) form of deviant sexual behavior, he proposed that the prostitute herself is the traditional woman in a specialized occupation. Bullough argued that as women become more assertive, the prostitute herself will change. He observed "to label a woman sick for what all women have been acculturated to do is ahistorical" (Bullough, 1979, p. 93).

Readers will find this offering different from most of those on pornography. It is neither a moral brief nor a passionate defense of pornography. Although Rich does not sift through the large body of research on the topic, he does inform students about many of the pertinent facts surrounding the Adult Film Industry. And, all of this is accomplished through the eyes of women and men who are leaders in the industry. As their human interest stories unfold, stereotypes are guaranteed to be dispelled.

The chapter, "Desire, Demand, and the Commerce of Sex" is an important addition to the Sexuality and Public Policy unit. In her award-winning book, *Temporarily Yours: Intimacy, Authenticity, and the Commerce of Sex*, Sociologist Elizabeth Bernstein uses an ethnographic lens to examine the meaning and context of sex work in contemporary culture. For this impressive study, Bernstein held intensive interviews with clients of sex workers, reviewed various print and electronic media, and explored the commercial sex markets of several cities in the State of California and in Western Europe.

Based on the compilation of such data, the book provides detailed descriptions and theoretical interpretations of commercial sex. This engaging, provocative piece will captivate readers from the beginning.

While the scholarly literature on prostitution has typically viewed sexual commerce through the narrow lens of the female prostitute, this exposé renders male sexual clients visible, enabling a change of focus that permits evolving parameters of commercial sex to be formulated. Accordingly, Bernstein postulates that in today's post-industrial cities, street prostitution has become increasingly replaced by a "brave new world of commercially available intimate encounters that are subjectively normalized for sex workers and clients alike" (Bernstein, 2007, p. 7). With such services less likely to be viewed as a deviant form of sexual pleasure, both sex workers and their clients are less stigmatized than in the past. This significant work reveals, however, that the normalization of this activity appears to coexist with a greater tendency on the part of government to enforce the laws surrounding sex work and to attempt to "redirect" the behavior of clients.

By focusing the lens of research on this timely topic, *Temporarily Yours*, as does most high quality research, raises more questions than answers for readers. Nevertheless, the interface of the personal and the social so deftly described in this offering definitely makes it a must-read for students committed to exploring the intersection of sexuality and public policy.

Searching for the operative word in the chapter concerning risk, identity, and love in the age of AIDS, students will discover that the word is community. From Judith Levine's controversial book, *Harmful to Minors: The Perils of Protecting Children From Sex*, this exposé about sexuality education and HIV prevention programs among youth clearly features the concept of *community as process*. However, this emotionally-charged phrase represents more than the usual meanings ascribed to the word *community*: "consensus, socialization, and solidarity." Levine's concept of

community is more analogous to "community-feeling", or *gemeinschaft*, a word Alfred Adler (1924) used to describe a sense of relationship between the individual and the community. Adler contended that out of community-feelings "... are developed tenderness, love of neighbor, friendship and love, and the desire for power unfolding itself in a veiled manner and seeking secretly to push its way along the path of group consciousness" (Hinsie & Campbell, 1970, p. 139). Therapists have long emphasized the value of such a sense of community by including socio-environmental and interpersonal influences in their treatment protocols. Theoretically, at least, patients who identify with a social group will modify their social attitudes and behavior because of a growing awareness of their roles in relationships with others (Wilmer, 1958).

Reading about Levine's field work in the Minneapolis and St. Paul, Minnesota area to study the issue of AIDS, students will encounter what is described as "an imperiled, yet flourishing community of gay, lesbian, bisexual, and homeless youth [who] are the recipients of some extraordinary adult care and attention" (Levine, 2000, p. 202). Could such success be expressly because of community feeling? Perhaps. It will be hard for students to read this chapter without putting a face on their own sense of community. They will at least find this broad sense of community in the two principles that Levine believes to be essential in successful programs that target prevention of AIDS: (1) to recognize the urgency of the problem and the pressing needs of the people targeted, and (2) to respect social norms, identities, values, and desires of clients as expressed in the relationships between individuals and within communities. Readers of this offering may learn the simple lessons of meeting people where they are and of respecting their choices—both valuable lessons for community programs and for life.

Virginity pledges became popular in the 1990s as an attempt to encourage adolescents to remain virgins until they married. Studies examining the effectiveness of such public affirmations are problematic due to the tendency of adolescents to later deny having pledged to remain a virgin after becoming sexually active (Rosenbaum, 2006). However, the chapter by Felicia Mebane, Eileen Yam, and Barbara Rimer presents the findings of a very different sort of study that ultimately might provide students with another critical thinking tool for their kit. Rather than a survey, an experiment, or a case-study, these authors undertook a content analysis of newspapers, examining the conceptual frames used in media coverage of virginity pledges, with interesting, albeit unsurprising, conclusions.

In reading this article, it will be confirmed: Americans are newshounds! According to the Pew Research Center, in 2004, 59 percent of American adults regularly watched local television news and 33 percent regularly watched nightly network news while 42 percent read a daily newspaper, and 29 percent accessed online news sites at least three times per week (The Pew Center for the People and the Press, 2004). It is clear that American lives are influenced by mass media messages daily, but what may not be so obvious is the factor that makes a discernable difference. It is not just the dissemination of news that matters, it is how the messages are framed as well as how balanced or not balanced the reporting of facts occurs.

Could it then be true? Could the one-liners coined in the 1960s by the famous father and leading prophet of the electronic age, Marshall McLuhan, apply today? "News, far more than art, is artifact." If so, "The medium is the message," as also suggested by this technological pioneer of long ago (Kappelman, 2001). The savvy student today is likely to have much to say about the design and the conclusion of this study. Your class might well be enthusiastic about approaching another sexuality-related topic in this same manner.

The Terrance Olson chapter on sexuality education is an updated one for this edition of *Speaking of Sexuality.* The author was assigned a difficult task when he was asked to review the research literature about sexuality education and attempt a rational analysis of the realities reflected in the current situation, within philosophical and practical parameters. Because this work is not an exercise in technical writing but, instead, one that often finds itself embedded in the midst of deepest values, it would be a challenge for any scholar undertaking such a project to maintain a professional detachment, permitting a value-free approach to the process. This chapter is one person's Olympian effort to do just that. Yet, as we read, it is important to remember, "anything approaching impersonality of experimental science will only succeed in purifying the subject out of its actual existence in the world of human affairs" (Kovel, 1976, p. xiii).

Although sexuality education is moored in ideology, it is expressed in real practice. This author conducts an inquiry into the inner assumptions that guide the practice of sexuality education, grounds his findings with philosophy, and, best of all, does not pretend that "the observer stands separate from the observed" (Kovel, 1976, p. xiii). Well-equipped to do this project, Olson has been engaged in the field of family science for a number of years, developing and evaluating sexuality education programs as well as training teachers throughout the United States and abroad.

But, sexuality education is an ideological debate. As in all ideological warfare, when like-minded people band together, they are probably not going to hear both sides of the story. In remarks about the two major political parties, the Republicans and the Democrats, Robert Baron, a social psychologist at the University of Iowa, offered this commentary, "The discussion will be twisted and biased, emphasizing those things that support the dominant form and disparaging or questioning the credibility of things that contradict" (Bishop, 2004, p. Al). Our hope is that the English poet Robert Blake (1757–1827) was correct in his assertion: "Without contraries [there] is no progression" (Kovel, 1976, p. xiii). If this admonition is true, we seem to be making significant progress in the field of sexuality education today, with our numerous "contraries" much in evidence. This chapter must be read to see that Olson does accomplish his assignment without undue polemics. That he gives ample space to the actual contradictions in the political and moral landscapes is hopeful.

After reading the chapters in Part X, readers will be more aware of the effect of social problems pertaining to sexuality in this new millennium and certain that they cannot be adequately solved with archaic public polices. Pouring "new wine into old wineskins" will not work. But, neither can workable solutions be secured without some form of wineskins. Whether these are called norms, mores, or values, a judicious mix of old and new is required: As always, change must be balanced with continuity.

REFERENCES

Adler, A. 1924. *The practice and theory of individual psychology*. Translated by P. Radin London: Humanities Press.

Bishop, B. 2004, 8 April. The growing cost of political uniformity. *Austin American-Statesman, pp. Al, A6.*

Bryant, J., and D. Zillman. 2001. Pornography, Models of effects of sexual deviancy. In *Encyclopedia of criminal and sexual deviance, vol. 3., Sexual deviance,* vol. eds. N. Davis and G. Geis, 241–244. Philadelphia, PA: Taylor & Francis.

Bullough, V. L. 1979. Prostitution, psychiatry, and history. In *The frontiers of sex research,* ed. V. L. Bullough, 87–96. Buffalo, NY: Prometheus.

Carroll, J. L. 2005. *Sexuality now: Embracing diversity.* Belmont, CA: Wadsworth.

Egan, T. 2000. U.S. corporations finding sex sells. *Austin American-Statesman,* 23 October Al, A8.

Hinsie, L. E., and R. E. Campbell. 1970. Community. In *Psychiatric dictionary,* 4th Ed., eds. L. E. Hinsie and R. E. Campbell. New York: Oxford University Press.

Kappelman, T. 2001. *Marshall McLuhan: The medium is the message.* Richardson, TX: Probe Ministries.

Kovel, J. 1976. *A complete guide to therapy from psychoanalysis to behavioral modification.* New York: Pantheon.

LeVay, S., and S. M. Valente. 2003. *Human sexuality.* Sunderland, MA: Sinauer Associates.

Levine, J. 2002. *Harmful to minors: The perils of protecting minors from sex.* Minneapolis: University of Minnesota Press.

Paglia, C. 1994. *Vamps and tramps.* New York: Vintage.

Rosenbaum, J. E. 2006. Reborn a virgin: Adolescent's retracting of virginity pledges and sexual histories. *American Journal of Public Health* 96: 1098–1103

Strossen, N. 1995. *Defending pornography: Free speech, sex, and the fight for women's rights.* New York: Scribner.

The Pew Research Center for the People and the Press. 2004. *News audiences increasingly politicalized: Online news audience larger, more diverse.* 8 June http://people-press.org/reports/display.php3? PageID=833.

Vellos, D. 1997. Immigrant Latina domestic workers and sexual harassment, *American University Journal of Gender and the Law* 5: 407–32.

Wilmer, H. A. 1958. Toward a definition of community. *Journal of Psychiatry* 114: 824–33.

CHAPTER 45

Naked Capitalists

Frank Rich

In 1993, college student Marc Andreessen created the Mosaic Web Browser, the first tool that allowed ordinary people to easily explore the Internet. He then developed Netscape, a commercial version of Mosaic, and quickly became a "wealthy wunderkind" when two years later the company went public. Eventually, when he lost the browser war to Microsoft Corporation, Netscape became part of Time-Warner, Inc's AOL (Geewax, 2004).

So, what is the relevance of this story? As you read Frank Rich's exposé, "Naked Capitalists," you may be reminded of the childhood fable of "Pandora's Box." If you remember, once Pandora's box was opened and the contents scattered, they could never be contained again. In the Netscape story, you may recognize Andreessen as a modern-day Pandora who opened the door to the sex industry as it is known today. The privacy provided by the technology that spawned the Internet, as well as cable television and VCRs, brought pornography to people who would never go to adult theaters or bookstores. This phenomenon, perhaps more than any other one factor, is responsible for the explosion of what is euphemistically called the "Adult Industry."

In this chapter, adapted from an article in the New York Times Magazine, you will find familiar concepts, but the context within which they are presented may be surprising. Rich has written about the astonishing relationship between pornography and capitalism with such verve that you seldom notice that the reading is an assignment. You may wonder, what are the names of Fortune 500 Corporations, such as Marriott, AT & T, and AOL Time Warner doing in such a selection? If you stay tuned for the facts as they unfold, you may discover what most adults in the United States do not currently know. But, as you read, you may need to first lay aside your stereotypes, lest they be destroyed in the process. Then, prepare to be both entertained and informed by the author as he artfully uses the human interest approach to explore the business of adult entertainment.

Even though Rich focuses on the amazing partnership between our dollars and senses, his chapter may raise basic questions about pornography itself. Some readers may align themselves with those who wonder why pornography is allowed at all, but others may be more comfortable in the company of those who wonder, "What's the big deal? Why do some people even question its existence?" Do not expect all of your questions about pornography to be answered here. In spite of two Presidential commissioned reports on pornography, one in 1970 and the other, sixteen years later, in 1986, there still are many debatable issues about this explosive topic.

At the time the first investigation began, the greatest concern in the legal area was the interpretation of the word obscene (Neff, 2001a). This struggle was apparent in a statement by Supreme Court Justice Potter Stewart concerning obscenity: "I shall not further attempt to define [obscenity], and perhaps I couldn't ever succeed in intelligibly doing so. But, I know it when I see it" (Jacobellis v. Ohio 1964). Previously, in 1957, the U.S. Supreme Court in Roth v. United States had upheld laws against obscenity and found that obscene materials were not entitled to the protections accorded to "speech" in the First Amendment of the U.S. Constitution. However, during the first Commission's investigation, the Court, using Stanley v. Georgia (1969), modified the Roth decision and ruled that individuals have the right to read or view obscene materials in the privacy of their homes (Neff, 2001a). Later, a legal ruling on the definition of obscenity occurred when in Miller v. California (1973), the U.S. Supreme Court imposed three new criteria that must be met for materials to be considered obscene:

- The average person, applying contemporary community standards, would find that the work, taken as a whole, appeals to the prurient interest.
- The work depicts/describes, in a patently offensive way, sexual conduct specifically defined by applicable state law.
- The work, taken as a whole, lacks serious literary, artistic, political, or scientific value. (Miller v. California 413 U.S. 15, 1973)

Both Presidential Commissions raised awareness levels about pornography and their findings resulted in much spirited public and professional debate. The 1970 Commission Report recommended that all legislation prohibiting the sale, exhibition, or distribution of sexual materials to consenting adults be repealed, but that legislation should prohibit such materials to children (Neff, 2001a). A Minority Report was written with opposite conclusions by six dissenters, stating that pornography should be prohibited for adults.

Although President Lyndon B. Johnson had commissioned the 1970 Commission Report, it was completed after President Richard B. Nixon took office. President Nixon characterized the Report as "morally bankrupt," and the U.S. Senate voted 60 to 5 to reject and censure the Commission Report, as did other groups, such as the National Conference of Catholic Bishops (Neff, 2001a).

The 1986 Report, prepared by the Meese Commission, reflected many of the same issues as did the 1970 Commission Report, except for the addition of child pornography. But, the results were dramatically different (Neff, 2001b). Among the 92 recommendations of the Meese Report were conclusions such as these items:

- A linkage exists between the pornography industry and organized crime;
- A causal relationship exists between exposure to pornography and aggression toward women; and
- A need exists for criminal laws on pornography and obscenity (Neff, 2001b).

The second Report received as much criticism as did the first one, but with a significant difference: while conservatives had criticized the 1970 Report for being too liberal, the liberals criticized the 1986 Report for being too conservative (Neff, 2001b). The two female members of the Commission refused to sign the 1986 Report on the grounds that it was biased and did not consider all available facts. Neff concluded her excellent analysis of the Meese Commission Report by offering these observations:

> While sexually explicit materials wake strong sentiments and emotions in most people, there is no consensus on how society should respond to those beliefs. Expecting a small group of political appointees to make policy on such issues seems to only sharpen the divisions and conflicts that arise over such emotionally charged issues (Neff 2001b, p. 247).

Even if you were not already aware of the historical information about the two Presidential

Commission Reports on pornography, as sexuality students, you probably do know more about the issues surrounding pornography than you do about the business side of the equation illuminated by Rich. As he reframes and interrelates the subjects of pornography and economics, you will be sometimes amazed, sometimes amused, but at all times informed.

In late January 1998, during the same week that America first heard the ribald tale of the President and the intern, *Variety* tucked [in] a business story that caused no stir whatsoever. Under a Hollywood dateline, the show-biz trade paper reported that the adult-video business "saw record revenues last year" of some $4.2 billion in rentals and sales. It soon became clear to me that these bicoastal stories, one from the nation's political capital and the other from its entertainment capital, were in some essential way the same story.

In the weeks that followed, Washington commentators repeatedly predicted that the public would be scandalized by the nonmissionary-position sex acts performed illicitly in the White House. But just as repeatedly, voters kept telling pollsters that they weren't blushing as brightly as, say, Cokie Roberts. The *Variety* story, I realized, may have in part explained why. An unseemly large percentage of Americans was routinely seeking out stories resembling that of the President and the intern—and raunchier ones—as daily entertainment fare.

The $4 billion that Americans spend on video pornography is larger than the annual revenue accrued by either the N.F.L., the N.B.A. or Major League Baseball. But that's literally not the half of it: the porn business is estimated to total between $10 billion and $14 billion annually in the United States when you toss in porn networks and pay-per-view movies on cable and satellite, Internet Web sites, in-room hotel movies, phone sex, sex toys and that archaic medium of my own occasionally misspent youth, magazines. Take even the low-end $10 billion estimate (from a

1998 study by Forrester Research in Cambridge, Mass.), and pornography is a bigger business than professional football, basketball and baseball put together. People pay more money for pornography in America in a year than they do on movie tickets, more than they do on all the performing arts combined. As one of the porn people I met in the industry's epicenter, the San Fernando Valley, put it, "We realized that when there are 700 million porn rentals a year, it can't just be a million perverts renting 700 videos each."

Yet in a culture where every movie gross and Nielsen rating is assessed ad infinitum in the media, the enormous branch of show business euphemistically called "adult" is covered as a backwater, not as the major industry it is. Often what coverage there is fixates disproportionately on Internet porn, which may well be the only Web business that keeps expanding after the dot-com collapse but still accounts for barely a fifth of American porn consumption. Occasionally a tony author—David Foster Wallace, George Plimpton and Martin Amis, most recently—will go slumming at a porn awards ceremony or visit a porn set to score easy laughs and even easier moral points. During sweeps weeks, local news broadcasts "investigate" adult businesses, mainly so they can display hard bodies in the guise of hard news. And of course, there is no shortage of academic literature and First Amendment debate about pornography, much of it snarled in the ideological divisions among feminists, from the antiporn absolutism of Catherine MacKinnon and Andrea Dworkin to the pro-porn revisionism of Sallie Tisdale and Susie Bright.

I'm a lifelong show-biz junkie, and what sparked my interest in the business was what I strumbled upon in *Variety*—its sheer hugeness. Size matters in the cultural marketplace. If the machinations of the mainstream TV, movie and music industries offer snapshots of the American character, doesn't this closeted entertainment behemoth tell us something as well? At $10 billion, porn is no longer a sideshow to the mainstream like, say, the $600 million Broadway theater industry—it *is* the mainstream.

And so I went to the San Fernando Valley, a.k.a. Silicone Valley, on the other side of the Hollywood Hills, to talk with the suits of the adult business. I did not see any porn scenes being shot. I did not talk to any antiporn crusaders or their civil-libertarian adversaries. I did not go to construct a moral brief. I wanted to find out how some of the top players conduct their business and how they viewed the Americans who gorge on their products.

Among other things, I learned that the adult industry is in many ways a mirror image of Hollywood. Porn movies come not only in all sexual flavors but also in all genres, from period costume dramas to sci-fi to comedy. Adult [film industry] has a fabled frontier past about which its veterans wax sentimental—the "Boogie Nights" 70s, when porn was still shot only on film and seen in adult movie theaters. (The arrival of home video revolutionized porn much as sound did Hollywood.) Adult also has its own *Variety (Adult Video News)*, its own starmaking machinery (the "girls" at Vivid and Wicked are promoted like bygone MGM contract players), its own prima donnas and cinéastes. It has (often silent) business partners in high places: two of the country's more prominent porn purveyors, Marriott (through in-room X-rated movies) and General Motors (though its ownership of the satellite giant DirecTV), were also major sponsors of the Bush-Cheney Inaugural. Porn even has its own Matt Drudge—a not-always-accurate Web industry gossip named Luke Ford, who shares his prototype's political conservatism and salacious obsessiveness yet is also, go figure, a rigorously devout convert to Judaism.

I didn't find any porn titans in gold chains, but I did meet Samantha Lewis, former real-estate saleswoman and current vice president of Digital Playground, whose best-selling "Virtual Sex" DVDs are, she says, "the Rolexes and Mercedeses of this business." I talked with Bill Asher, the head of Vivid, who is an alumnus of Dartmouth and U.S.C. (for his M.B.A.). I listened to the story of John Stagliano, who was once a U.C.L.A. economics major with plans "to teach at the college level" but who instead followed his particular erotic obsession and became Buttman, the creator of hugely popular improvisational *cinema-vérité* porn videos that have been nicknamed "gonzo" in honor of the free-wheeling literary spirit of Hunter S. Thompson. A political libertarian, [he] was for a while a big-time contributor to the Cato Institute.

If the people who make and sell pornography are this "normal"—and varied—might not the audience be, too? It can't be merely the uneducated and unemployed who shell out the $10 billion. Porn moguls describe a market as diverse as America. There's a college-age crowd that favors tattooed and pierced porn performers; there's an older, suburban audience that goes for "sweeter, nicer, cuter girls," as Bill Asher of Vivid Pictures puts it. There is geriatric porn and there's a popular video called "Fatter, Balder, Uglier." Oral sex sells particularly well in the Northeast, ethnic and interracial videos sell in cities (especially in the South), and the Sun Belt likes to see outdoor sex set by beaches and pools.

Yet such demographics are anecdotally not scientifically obtained. So few Americans fess up when asked if they are watching adult product, says Asher, "that you'd think there is no business." But in truth, there's no business like porn business. Porn is the one show that no one watches but that, miraculously, never closes.

"Porn doesn't have a demographic—it goes across all demographics," says Paul Fishbein, the compact and intense man who founded *Adult Video News.*

There were 11,000 adult titles last year versus 400 releases in Hollywood. There are so many outlets that even if you spend just $15,000 and two days—and put in some plot and good-looking people and decent sex—you can get satellite and cable sales. There are so many companies, and they rarely go out of business. You have to be really stupid or greedy to fail.

He points me toward the larger producers whose videos top *AVNs* charts and have the widest TV distribution. There are many successful companies, but some of them cater to niche markets (like gay men) that as of yet haven't cracked the national mass market of TV, where pay-per-view pornographic movies, though priced two or three times higher and not promoted, often outsell the Hollywood hits competing head to head. In a business with no barrier to entry—anyone with a video camera can be a director or star—there are also countless bottom feeders selling nasty loops on used tape. Whatever the quality or origin of a product, it can at the very least be exhibited on one of the 70,000 adult pay Web sites, about a quarter of which are owned by a few privately held companies that slice and dice the same content under different brands.

Fishbein has a staff of 62 to track it all. He seems smart, sensible and mercurial—in other words, just like any other successful editor. And like almost everyone else I met in porn, he says he fell into it by accident. While a journalism student at Temple University in his hometown, Philadelphia, he managed a video store and found that customers kept asking him how to differentiate one adult tape from another. It was the early 80s, and the VCR was starting to conquer America, its popularity in large part driven by the easier and more anonymous access it offered to porn. Prior to home video, pornography had a far smaller audience, limited mainly to men willing to venture into the muck of a Pussycat Cinema—the "raincoaters," as the trade refers to that dying breed of paleo-consumer. The VCR took porn into America's bedrooms and living rooms—and, by happenstance, did so at the same time that the spread of AIDS began to give sexual adventurers a reason to stay home. There is no safer sex than porn.

As adult titles on tape proliferated, Fishbein started a newsletter to rate them. Other video-store owners, uncertain about which porn films to stock, took a look. Now, some 18 years later, Fishbein runs an empire that includes 10 Web sites and spinoff journals like *AVN Online*. He also stages trade shows and presents the *AVN* Awards in Vegas in January. An issue of *AVN* can run in excess of 350 slick pages, much of it advertising, in which a daunting number of reviews (some 400 a month) jostle for space with sober reportage like "For Adult, Ashcroft Signals Circle the Wagons Time." Fishbein has a soft spot for porn veterans like Al Goldstein, the 65-year-old paterfamilias of *Screw* magazine who writes a column for Fishbein's main Web site, *AVN.com*, in which Goldstein sometimes rails against the new corporate generation of pornographers who have no memory of the daring and sacrifice of their elders. "Al Goldstein took 19 arrests for this business," Fishbein says reverently.

Though he embodies the corporatization of porn, Fishbein exudes a certain swagger:

> I'm here by accident, and now that I'm here, I'm proud of what I do, he says. My mother sits at my awards table each year when girls accept awards for oral sex. Sex sells and it drives the media, and it always has. Billboards, movies, ads, commercials. It's what we're thinking about at all times of the day. We're told it's bad, and it manifests itself as political debates.

Fishbein assures me that he has no "naked girls running through the office," and alas, he is right—though a staff member does wander in with a photo to ask, "Was that the naked sushi party?" But there's a pleasant buzz and bustle about the place—one I associate with journalism. "This could be a magazine about pens and pencils," Fishbein says.

The browsers on the two computers behind his desk are kept on *CNN.com* and *AVN.com*, which is modeled on CNN's as a (porn) news portal. The décor of his large, meticulous office is mostly movie memorabilia. A film buff as well as a news junkie, Fishbein is a particular fan of the high-end comedies of Woody Allen, Albert Brooks and Preston Sturges, and he could be a highly articulate, slightly neurotic leading man out of one of them. He speaks glowingly of having just taken his 12-year-old stepdaughter to "Yi Yi." Does he watch the movies that *AVN* reviews? He flinches. "I haven't watched an adult movie without fast-forwarding since I saw one in a theater at 18. I watch them for business reasons. My wife and I don't watch them for entertainment. It is hard for me to look at it as more than product."

Many of the top porn producers are within blocks of Fishbein's office in the utterly anonymous town of Chatsworth—an unhurried, nondescript sprawl of faded strip malls, housing developments and low-slung (and usually unmarked) business complexes that look more like suburban orthodontic offices than porn factories. Everyone in the business seems to know one another. "There's a certain camaraderie among those who are on the fringe of society, a similarity to outlaws," Fishbein says. Yet he seems like anything but an outlaw; he was about to fly off to the Super Bowl and then a skiing vacation. I ask if organized crime is a factor in today's porn world. "When I got here, I heard there were mob companies," he answers. "But I've never even been approached by a criminal element. I've never been threatened or bribed. So if it ever existed, it's part of the history of the business." He almost sounds disappointed.

Russell Hampshire, who owns one of the biggest companies, VCA Pictures, did do time in jail—nine months in 1988 for shipping obscene videotapes across state lines to federal agents in Alabama. [He], who runs VCA with his wife of 10 years, Betty, has an Oscar Madison look—Hawaiian shirts, gym shorts and a baseball cap. I wouldn't want to get on his bad side. He's big and leathery and sounds like Lee Marvin as written by Damon Runyon. Asked why the sign outside says "Tray Tech" instead of VCA, he says he wants to stay "as innoculous as possible."

He has been in the business since 1978 and waxes nostalgic for the early video days, when you could transfer a prevideo Marilyn Chambers classic to cassette and sell it wholesale for up to a hundred bucks. Now his top movies wholesale for $18 or $19, sometimes lower. "There used

to be only 10 to 12 titles to choose from in a video store," he says. "Now there are thousands of titles." A typical release may sell only 2,000 units or less—7,500 would be a modest hit—but thanks to TV and international sales, Hampshire says he makes money "on every title." Though the total income from a hit is pocket money by Hollywood standards, Hollywood should only have such profit margins. An adult film that brings in $250,000 may cost only $50,000 to make—five times the original investment. Production locations are often rented homes, shooting schedules run less than a week, and most projects are not shot on the costly medium of film. There are no unions or residuals. Marketing costs are tiny since quote ads run in *AVN* and skin magazines, not in national publications or on TV. Most economically of all, porn movies don't carry the huge expense of theatrical distribution: video killed off adult movie theaters far more effectively than it did regular movie theaters.

Still, Hampshire resents the lower overhead of porn's newcomers: "I have 80 employees. I have a 100 percent medical plan for everyone's family—dental and vision care too. Some of my guys have been working here 17 or 18 years. And I'm up against amateurs with $800 Handicams." He also grouses about the new administration in Washington, as many in the industry do, fearing there could be a replay of the war on porn during the Reagan years, when Attorney General Edwin Meese called for restrictions on live sex shows and the dissemination of pornographic materials. "I like the rest of Bush's cabinet—just not Ashcroft," Hampshire says.

With the company's in-house press rep, a former preschool teacher named Mischa Allen, in tow, Hampshire takes me on a tour of VCA's 40,000-square-foot operation, proudly showing off the state-of-the-art video-editing bays, the room containing 3,000 video-duplication decks (churning out 400,000 tapes a month) and the prop room in which I spot a neon sign for "Bada Boom" from the set of the recent "Sopornos 2." The mechanized assembly line on which the tapes are boxed and shrink-wrapped is as efficient as that for bottling Coke.

But more than anything, VCA resembles the corporate headquarters of a sports franchise. Only on close inspection do I realize that a towering glass case full of what look like trophies in the reception area in fact contains awards such as the 1996 Best Group Sex Scene, bestowed upon the "Staircase Orgy" from "New Wave Hookers 4." Hampshire, an avid golfer and bowler, has lined VCA's corridors with his collection of autographed sports jerseys, the latest from Tiger Woods. On one wall are plaques of appreciation from the Hampshires' philanthropic beneficiaries, including a local school to which they donate video equipment and free yearbook printing.

Hampshire's own office is spacious, outfitted with leather furniture, but—characteristically for the business—looks like a bunker. Above his desk is a console of TV screens tuned into the feeds from security cameras. Incongruously, this inner sanctum's walls are festooned with another variety of pompously framed "collectibles"—autographed letters and photographs from Anwar Sadat, Menachem Begin, Jimmy Carter and Richard Nixon. Hampshire says they're all copies, but he points to a melted-looking clock and says, "I've got Salvador Dalis all over the place—*authentic* Salvador Dalis." He also shows off a vintage group photo of Murder, Inc.

He almost never goes to a set, where the hurry-up-and-wait pace makes it as "boring as Hollywood." He ticks off his duties: "Dealing with distributors and OSHA rules and regulations. I have to write reviews of all my department heads and decide raises."

As I leave his office I notice still another framed artifact: a Bronze Star for "exceptionally valorous action on 12/8/67" while serving as a Company C rifleman in combat in Vietnam. The citation says that Hampshire "continually exposed himself to hostile fire" while saving the lives of his fellow soldiers. It's the only thing that seems to embarrass him. "I buried it for so long," he says. "When I first came out here, I was ashamed to say anything because people might say I'm a bad person."

Almost every adult company is pursuing innovative media, preparing for Internet broadband and interactive hotel-room TV. At Wicked Pictures' newly revamped Web site, for instance, a visitor can cross-index a particular porn star with a sexual activity, then watch (and pay for) just those scenes that match. Digital Playground's "Virtual Sex" DVDs resemble video games in how they allow the user to control and inject himself into the "action."

As in nonadult video, DVD is cutting into videocassette sales—even more so in adult, perhaps, because DVDs have the added virtue of being more easily camouflaged on a shelf than cassettes. Hampshire is particularly proud of VCA's DVD technology. With his vast catalog, he is following the model of Hollywood studios by rereleasing classics—"The Devil in Miss Jones 2," "The Opening of Misty Beethoven"—in "Collectors Editions," replete with aural commentaries from original stars like Jamie Gillis. As with Hollywood's DVD rereleases, they are pitched at nostalgic consumers in the "boomer-retro" market. "These aren't 'adult'—they're pop culture now," says Mischa Allen.

But VCA aims far higher than merely recycling golden oldies. In a windowless VCA office, I meet Wit Maverick, the head of its DVD production unit. He is 37, and with his blue Oxford shirt, goatee and glasses, he could be a professor somewhere—perhaps at Cal Arts, where he got a masters in film directing. He ended up at VCA, he says, because it was "the best opportunity to push the envelope of technology."

Maverick knocks mainstream studios for providing only a linear cinematic experience on their DVD's. "There's a great hubris in Hollywood," he says. "They think the way the director made the film is the only way the story can be told. We have a lot more humility. If a viewer wants something different, we give it to him." As an example he cites "Being With Juli Ashton," VCA's take on "Being John Malkovich." The viewer, Maverick says, "can go inside the head of the person having sex with Juli Ashton, male or female. He can choose which character to follow. He can re-edit the movie. Would James Cameron let anyone do that with 'Titanic'? I feel like filmmakers 100 years ago," Maverick continues. "It's a great technology, but we still don't know what to do with it. A hundred years from now I want grad students to read what I've done on DVD the way I read about D.W Griffith."

Wit Maverick collaborates on his DVDs at VCA with Veronica Hart, 44, one of the business's most prominent female executives and, before that, a leading porn star of the late 70s and early 80s. Universally known as Janie—her real name is Jane Hamilton—she is typical of the mostly likable people I met in the porn world. She combines hard-headed show-biz savvy and humor with an utter lack of pretension and even some actual candor—a combination unheard of on the other side of the hills.

"The difference between us and Hollywood," she elaborates, "is money and ego. We deal with thousands of dollars, not millions. In mainstream, people are more cutthroat and pumped up about themselves. We're just like regular people—it has to do with exposing yourself. If you show something this intimate, there isn't a lot you can hide behind. You're a little more down to earth. We're not curing cancer. We're providing entertainment."

Hart studied theater at the University of Nevada in her hometown, Las Vegas. After acting leads in plays by Pinter and García Lorca—as far east as Kennedy Center's annual college theater festival—she passed through the music business in England and worked as a secretary at *Psychology Today* magazine in New York before ending up in movies like "Wanda Whips Wall Street." While we are talking in her office she looks up Veronica Hart's 100-plus performing credits on the Internet, including some non-hard-core B movies with faded mainstream actors like Farley Granger and Linda Blair. "In this one I played a stripper," she says while scrolling down the list. "*That* was a real stretch."

She pulls back from the computer screen and sums up her career: "I was lucky enough to be a performer in the golden age of porn cinema. I'm no raving beauty, and I don't have the best body in the world, but I look approachable. And I've always really enjoyed sex." More recently, she played a cameo as a judge in "Boogie Nights," but she disputes that movie's historical accuracy about porn's prevideo age. "We never shot in L.A. back then, only in New York and San Francisco," she says. Indeed, adult exactly mimicked movie-industry history—beginning in New York, then moving west.

In 1982, at the top of her career, Hart fell in love and left the business. "AIDS had just started up, and I lost every gay person I knew," she says, listing close friends who worked on the production side of the straight-porn business. She had two sons and helped support her family in part by stripping. Though not intending to re-enter porn, eventually she did, as a producer and director.

Hart has been in adult longer than anyone I met and has done "everything" in it, she jokes, "including windows." She warns me that any blanket statement about the business is meaningless because it's so big that every conceivable type of person can be found in it:

You'll find someone who's into it to provide spiritual uplift and educational self-help. . . . And if you want to find rotten, vicious, misogynistic bastards—you'll find them. You'll find everyone who fits the stereotype and everyone who goes against the stereotype. In the loop and disposable-porno section of our business, you'll find the carnival freak-show mentality. There has to be a geek show somewhere in our society. What ticks me off is that all of adult is classified according to the lowest that's out there. We've always been legal. Child molestation has never been in mainstream adult. We've always policed ourselves. There's no coerced sex. But there are little pipsqueaks who get their disgusting little videos out there. There's a trend in misogynistic porn, and it's upsetting. I've been in the business for more than 20 years, and I helped make it possible for these guys to make these kinds of movies. I don't believe that's what America wants to see.

As for her own movies, Hart, like many of her peers, is preoccupied with the industry's biggest growth market—women and couples. The female audience was thought to be nearly nil when consuming pornography required a visit to a theater, an adult book store or the curtained adult section of a video store. But now hardcore is available at chains like Tower (though not Blockbuster), through elaborate Web sites like *Adultdvdempire* that parallel Amazon and by clicking a pay-per-view movie on a TV menu (where the bill won't specify that an adult title was chosen).

The Valley's conventional wisdom has it that women prefer more romance, foreplay and story, as well as strong female characters who, says Bill Asher of Vivid, "are not only in charge of the sex but the rest of the plot." Hart isn't sure. "Just because women like romance doesn't mean we want soft sex," she says. "We want hot and dirty sex just like anybody else. For instance, many women love the fantasy of being taken—but how do you portray it without sending a message to some guys to abduct?"

Hart, who thought of herself as a sexual pioneer when she was a porn performer, finds that there is no shortage of women who want to appear in adult now. She never has to search for new talent; willing performers call her "from all over the country." The men? "They're props."

Today's porn stars can be as temperamental as their Hollywood counterparts, or more so. "I assume Sarah Jessica Parker and Kim Cattrall show up on the set on time," said Paul Fishbein rather tartly when I asked about Jenna Jameson, the industry's reigning It girl of recent years. Though he was trying to give her a free vacation as thanks for her work as host of the recent *AVN* awards, Jameson wasn't returning his calls. "In adult, they don't show up and don't care,"

Fishbein says. "Lots of girls in this business—and guys, too—are dysfunctional. The girls get here at 18 and aren't mature. They do it because they're rebels or exhibitionists or need money. They think they're making real movies and get really upset when they don't win awards or get good reviews."

Some porn directors have similar pretensions. They can receive grandiose billing—"A Brad Armstrong Motion Picture"—and are sometimes grudgingly indulged with a "big budget" project ($250,000 tops) made on film, even though sex scenes are far harder to shoot on film (with its trickier lighting and shot setups) than on video—and even though adult films are almost never projected on screens. "We have our own Brad Pitts wanting to make 'Seven Days in Tibet,'" said one executive. Performers are paid at fairly standardized rates—by the day or sex scene, as much as $1,000 per day for women, as little as $200 for men. The contract girls at Vivid and Wicked sign for $100,000 and up a year, in exchange for which they might make nine movies, with two sex scenes each, over that time, along with any number of brand-boosting promotional appearances at consumer conventions and video stores. The top stars double or triple that figure by running their own subscription Web sites, marketing autographs and most lucratively, dancing in the nation's large circuit of strip clubs at fees that can top $10,000 a week.

But porn stars have an even shorter shelf life than Hollywood's female stars and fare worse in love. Though HIV and drug testing, as well as condom use, are rigorous at the top adult companies, one producer asks rhetorically, "Who wants to date a woman who's had sex with 60 people in two months?"

Since I've rarely found actors to be the most insightful observers of the movie business, I wasn't eager to sample the wisdom of porn stars. But I did seek out Sydnee Steele, a newly signed Wicked contract girl who is by many accounts a rarity in the business—she's happily married. Her husband is Michael Raven, a top adult director. They met in Dallas in the early

90s, when she was a jewelry saleswoman in a shopping mall and he was a car salesman who sold her a mariner blue Miata. Eventually they drifted into the local swingers' scene. (One porn worker would later tell me, "Texas, Florida and Arizona are where all the swingers and strippers come from, though no one knows why.")

"The industry looks up to our relationship," Raven says when I meet the couple, now married nine years, at Sin City, another production company in Chatsworth. Avid porn fans in Texas, they migrated to the Valley to turn their avocation into a livelihood. Like many of the directors and male performers in the business, Raven is a somewhat lumpy everyman, heading toward baldness and sporting a meticulous goatee. A Kandinsky poster decorates the Sin City office. "I've gotten jealous on occasion," Raven allows. "I'm not jealous of her because of sex in movies; I'm jealous when her work takes her away from me. I get lonely if she's gone two weeks on the road."

"Sometimes I'm too tired for my husband," Steele says. "We love what we do, but it's hard work—lots of 12-hour days." By now, I've watched some of what she does and find it hard to square the rapacious star of "Hell on Heels" with the woman before me, who is softer-spoken, prettier and considerably less animated than her screen persona. Maybe she can act.

The daughter of a college professor, Steele comes from what she calls a " 'Leave It To Beaver' nuclear family," Raven from a religious one. "I've leaned toward the right in my politics," he says, "but I'm bothered by the Republicans' association with the religious right. I know from my experience of religious people that those who protest and scream the loudest usually have the biggest collection of adult under their bed." He wishes they'd protest violent entertainment instead: "In video games, you're supposed to destroy, maim and dismember an opponent. But if one person is giving pleasure to another in adult, that's evil. Sex on TV is more destructive than hard core. You can depict a rape on TV—we don't touch that subject."

Like his wife, Raven is increasingly recognized by strangers—largely because "Behind the Scenes" documentaries about his movies appear on DVDs and on cable erotic networks, much like *Backstory* features on American Movie Classics. But Raven no longer stays in contact with his own family. And Steele's parents, she says, "don't totally know what I'm doing and don't ask. We don't lie, but they've never really been told."

Bryn Pryor is the Director and a writer of "The Money Shot." He's an *AVN* staff member who arrived in the Valley after nine years in the theater, much of it children's theater, in Arizona. "Everyone at *AVN* writes under a pseudonym. We have people here who don't want anyone to know their real name." Variations on this theme were visible everywhere I went in the Valley. Receptionists at porn companies tend to answer the phone generically: "Production Company" or "Corporate Office."

Typifying this ambivalence is Steve Orenstein the owner of Wicked Pictures. He made his accidental entrance into the porn business through his mother—who got him a part-time job when she worked as a bookkeeper at an adult-book distributor and he was 18. But he does not seem eager to reveal his calling to his 9-year-old stepdaughter.

"Being in the business you walk that line all the time—do you say what you do or not?" he says. Orenstein has revealed his true profession to only a handful of people whom he and his wife have met on the PTA circuit. "I'm comfortable with what I do," he says, "but I don't want parents of our child's friends saying their kids can't play with her because of it." His stepdaughter has noticed the Wicked logo on his shirt. "She knows I make something only adults can see."

The Orensteins have spoken to a therapist about the inevitable day of reckoning with their child. "The counselors say don't tell her yet," he says, "don't overexplain." But surely she'll guess by adolescence? Orenstein, a slight, nervous man with a reputation as a worrier, merely shrugs. For the moment, he's more concerned about protecting the child from prime-time television, citing a recent episode of the sitcom "The King of Queens" on CBS. He recalls: "The guy's rolling off his wife, and my 9-year-old asks, 'What do they mean by that?' Should I be letting her watch it?"

Russell Hampshire's gambit is to tell strangers he's in "the video-duplication business." Allen Gold, a VCA executive with daughters ages 1 and 3, says he's "in the DVD business." Paul Fishbein doesn't bring either *AVN* or adult product[s] into his house. Michael Raven and Sydnee Steele have decided for now not to have children.

I ask Veronica Hart, whose two teenage sons are at magnet schools for the highly gifted, what they have made of her career. "It's horrible for them," she says.

> I'm their loving mommy, and nobody likes to think of their parents having sex and being famous for it. I'm not ashamed of what I do. I take responsibility for who I am. I chose. From the time they were kids, my stripping gear was washed and hanging in the bathtub. At the same time I apologize to my kids for how the choices in my life have affected them. They're well adjusted and can joke with me about it: 'I know I'm going to spend the rest of my life on the couch.'

No wonder the porn industry has its finger on the pulse of American tastes. Not only do its players have a lifestyle more middle class than that of their Beverly Hills counterparts, but in their desire to keep their porn careers camouflaged in a plain brown wrapper, they connect directly with their audience's shame and guilt. Still, the next generation of porn consumers and producers alike may break with that puritan mind-set. The teenagers who grew up with cable and the VCR "come to the table already saturated with sex," says Bryn Pryor. "They've never known a time without Calvin Klein ads and MTV. By the time they see porn, they've already seen so many naked people they're pre-jaded."

This may explain why Americans are clamoring for ever more explicit fare. In mainstream TV, sex is no longer sequestered on late-night public access shows like "Robin Byrd." At HBO, Sheila Nevins, the highly regarded executive in charge of its nonfiction programming, has been stunned by the success of sexual documentaries like "Real Sex," now in its 11th year, and "Taxicab Confessions." Focus groups complain to HBO that another hit series, "G-String Divas," doesn't go far enough. "They know what really happens in a strip club," Nevins says, and find HBO's version "too R-rated." Though HBO, known for its heavy promotions of "The Sopranos" and "Sex and the City," spends nothing to advertise its sex series, they always are among the network's most watched. "I can do all the shows I want about poverty in the Mississippi Delta," Nevins says, "but this is what hard-working Americans want to see. At first we were embarrassed by the sex shows, and producers didn't want their names on them. Now we have Academy Award producers, and their names can't be big enough."

At Playboy, Jim English, the head of its TV division, and his boss, Christie Hefner, have felt the heat. Its Playboy and Spice channels have been squeezed from both sides in the cable-satellite marketplace. The softer, if X-rated, cuts of hard-core movies that it runs are no longer much more explicit than regular cable programming at HBO, Showtime ("Queer as Folk") and MTV ("Spring Break"). Meanwhile, erotic networks like Hot and Ecstasy, which run XX films, are cannibalizing Playboy's audience from the other end of the erotic spectrum. The result: Playboy plans to start "Spice Platinum Live," which edges toward XXX. (I'll leave the codified yet minute clinical distinctions separating X, XX and XXX to your imagination.)

Even in an economic downturn, everything's coming up porn. Newly unemployed dot-com techies who can't find jobs in Silicon Valley are heading to Silicone Valley, where the work force is expanding, not contracting. "Vivid overall has doubled, tripled revenues and profits in the past couple of years," says Bill Asher. While he says there's no such thing as a

Hollywood-style "home run" in porn—unless another celebrity like Pamela Anderson turns up in a sex video, intentionally or not—he sees potentially "a tenfold jump" in profits as distribution increases through broadband and video-on-demand. "There are opportunities here that Paramount will never have in terms of growth," Asher says. "Our product travels well internationally and is evergreen. Five-year-old product is still interesting to someone; it's not yesterday's news like a five-year-old Hollywood blockbuster. Our costs are relatively fixed. As there's more distribution, 90 cents of a dollar hits the bottom line." The absence of adult retail stores in conservative pockets of the country is no longer a barrier. "You can get a dish relatively anywhere," Asher says, "and get whatever you want."

When Vivid took over and expanded the Hot Network in 1999, Asher says, "there was no outcry: We got thank-you letters and sales boomed. We put up two more channels in months. Cable companies were begging for them. It doesn't take a genius to do this. Literally the customers say, I like what you've got—give me some more of it." Entertainment-industry executives not directly involved in the adult business confirm its sunny future. Satellite and cable companies have found that the more explicit the offerings, the more the market grows. *AVN* reports that TV porn may actually be increasing video-store sales and rentals rather than cannibalizing them—by introducing new customers to the product. Though some cable companies say they don't want adult, only one of the country's eight major cable providers, Adelphia, forbids it. The others are too addicted to the cash flow to say no. The organized uproar that recently persuaded a teetering Yahoo to drop its adult Web store—but not its gateways into other adult sites—is the exception, not the rule.

And despite a rumor that one porn mogul keeps a Cessna waiting at Van Nuys airport to escape to Brazil if there's a government crackdown, the odds of that look slim. Too many Fortune 500 corporations with Washington clout, from AT & T to AOL Time Warner, make too much money on porn—whether through phone sex, chat rooms or adult video. At the local level, the Supreme Court's 1973 "community standard" for obscenity may be a non sequitur now that there's a XX national standard disseminated everwhere by satellite and the Web. A busted local video retailer in a conservative community can plead that his product is consistent with what the neighbors are watching on pay-per-view—as one such owner successfully did in Utah last fall.

Should John Ashcroft's Justice Department go after porn, smart betting has him pursuing shadowy purveyors of extreme porn on the Internet (though it's not clear that the actionable stuff originates in the United States) and child pornography, all of which is condemned by the professional adult industry. "No one in this business will complain if Ashcroft goes for the kid angle," Fishbein says.

Jim English of Playboy suggests that one way to meet the typical American porn audience en masse is to accompany him to a live broadcast of a hit Playboy show called "Night Calls 411." Fittingly, "Night Calls" is televised from a studio in Hollywood, right by the old Gower Gulch, where low-budget studios long ago churned out early features in bulk much as the adult business does now.

Two underclad hostesses, Crystal Knight and Flower, intersperse wisecracks and sex tips with viewers' phone calls. Though only a few callers get on the air, as many as 100,000 try to get through, with still more deluging the show with "Miss Lonelyhearts" e-mail. It's not "Larry King Live," but in some ways it could be an adult version of the "Today" show, whose fans cross the country with the hope of being in view as the camera pans Rockefeller Center. The "Night Calls" devotees go further: many of them are engaging in sex when they call. "Having sex is not enough of a turn-on in America—you have to be on TV too," jokes English. The callers often ask that the hosts talk them through to what *The*

Starr Report called completion, and the women oblige—hoping for slam-bam speed so they can move on to the next caller. I'm struck by how much the male and female callers alike mimic porn performers, with their clichéd sex talk and over-the-top orgasmic shrieks. The adult audience apes its entertainers as slavishly as teenagers do rock idols.

By now, I've become intimately familiar with the conventions of adult entertainment, having asked those I met in the business to steer me to their best products. I've watched Wicked's "Double Feature," a multiple winner of *AVN* awards, among them "Best Comedy," and found it full of erudite cinematic references, including a campy spoof of Ed Wood films. I've seen Vivid's new "Artemesia," a costume drama set in sixteenth-century Italy and given *AVN's* highest rating; it is laced with high-flown ruminations on the meaning of art, somewhat compromised by the tattoos on the performers. From Video Team, a company specializing in interracial porn, there is a thriller called "Westside" with a social conscience reminiscent of "West Side Story" soundtrack that features music by Aaron Copland and a take on the drug wars that wouldn't be out of place in "Traffic."

It's no wonder, though, that Stagliano's gonzo, in which the performers just get it on, has such a following. All the plot and costuming and set decoration and arty cinematography—why bother? The acting—who needs it? (In "Flashpoint," Jenna Jameson, cast as a female firefighter, sounds the same when sobbing over a colleague's death as she does in coital ecstasy.) The films are tedious, and I'm as tempted to fast-forward through the sex scenes as the nonsex scenes. No matter what the period or setting, no matter what the genre, every video comes to the same dead halt as the performers drop whatever characters they're supposed to be assuming and repeat the same sex acts, in almost exactly the same way, at the same intervals, in every film. At a certain point, the Kabuki-like ritualization of these sequences becomes unintentionally farcical, like the musical numbers in a 30s Hollywood musical or the stylized acrobatics in a martial-arts film. Farcical, but not exactly funny. All the artful *mise-en-scene* in the world cannot, for me anyway, make merchandised sex entertaining or erotic.

I tell Bryn Pryor of *AVN* and "The Money Shot" my reaction. He's a professional porn critic. Is this the best that adult has to offer? "The top of the heap in porn is the bottom in mainstream," he says.

> The sad fact is that while consumers are more aware than they've ever been, nobody cares if it's a good movie, and we all know that. They care if it's hot in whatever subjective way it's hot to them. Most porn directors don't even watch the sex; they just direct the dialogue. They tell the camera people they want three positions and then go off and eat.

He continues: "Porn is not a creative medium. Everyone in the porn industry says he's on the way to something else, like waiters and bartenders, but it may be that most of us belong here. If we were really good, we'd be doing something else." Pryor envisions a day when adult and Hollywood will converge, but in a sense that's already the case. If much of porn ranges from silly to degrading, what's the alternative offered on the other side of the hills? The viewer who isn't watching a mediocre porn product is watching what? "Temptation Island"? WWF?

Moralists like to see in pornography a decline in our standards, but in truth it's an all-too-ringing affirmation of them. Porn is no more or less imaginative than much of the junk in the entertainment mainstream—though unlike much of that junk, it does have an undeniable practical use. In that regard, anyway, there may be no other product in the entire cultural marketplace that is more explicitly American.

INTRODUCTION REFERENCES

Geewax, M. 2004, March 29. Extolling the virtues of hiring overseas. *Austin American-Statesman*, 1E.

Jacobellis v. Ohio, 378 U.S. 184 (1964).

Miller v. California, 413, U.S. 15 (1973).

Neff, J. L. (2001a). Pornography—First Presidential Commissions report. In *Encyclopedia of criminal and deviant behavior*, vol. 3, Sexual deviance, vol. eds., N. Davis and G. Geis, 238–240. Philadelphia, PA: Taylor & Francis.

Neff, J. L. (2001b). Pornography—Second Presidential Commissions report. In *Encyclopedia of criminal and deviant behavior*, vol. 3, Sexual deviance, vol. eds., N. Davis and G. Geis, 245–247. Philadelphia, PA: Taylor & Francis.

Stanley v. Georgia, 394 U. S. 557 (1969).

CHAPTER 46

Temporarily Yours

Desire, Demand, and the Commerce of Sex

Elizabeth Bernstein

As one of the more enticing chapters in Part X, "Sexuality and Public Policy," the following "read" provides a different take on what has traditionally been referred to as the world's oldest profession, prostitution. Regardless of how authorities frame prostitution, they agree that today it has become a stratified, specialized profession, with prostitutes for "every social class, every special occasion and every conceivable location" (Simon, 2001, p. 264). Over time, the definition of prostitution has expanded to include teen prostitutes, male adults with female clients, bisexual prostitution, prostitution by telephone, and internet sexual services (Flowers, 1998). In the apparent economic hierarchy that exists, call girls and corporate prostitutes, typically young and beautiful aspiring models or actresses, rank above middle-class and working-class prostitutes while street-walkers and sexual slaves are relegated to the lower rungs of the ladder (Simon, 2001).

Recent media attention, including sources such as Forbes *magazine and* Newsweek, *has focused on the economic aspect of prostitution. Online news blogs portray prostitution as the recession-proof career, suggesting that it is based on the one commodity that never loses its value (Noer, 2006). But, according to recent financial data, sex for money may be recession resistant, not recession proof. In Nevada, the only state with legalized prostitution in some rural counties in the form of licensed brothels, all is not well. Recently, revenue for the 25 brothels in the Nevada Brothel Owners' Association is down as much as 45 percent (Ramirez, 2008).*

Economists Lena Edlund and Evelyn Korn (2002) raised professional angst when they proposed a controversial theory of prostitution in the academic publication, Journal of Political Economy. *Their theory proposed that "wives and whores" were economic goods that could be substituted, one for another. But, within these new approaches, old questions remain: Who buys? Who sells? For how much? Who is being arrested? Symbolically reflecting Western civilization's double standard of sexual norms, prostitution may be the only crime in which two persons engage in an act of mutual consent but traditionally, only one, the prostitute, is likely to be arrested (Flowers, 1998).*

The following chapter from Elizabeth Bernstein's award-winning book, Temporarily Yours: Intimacy, Authenticity, and the Commerce of Sex, *explores the topic from yet another perspective.*

Shedding new light on an old subject, the author researches the changing landscape of commercial sex and the intimate intersection of politics, economics, and desire. Suggesting that there is a sizeable shift occurring in the world of commercialized sex, Bernstein describes the shape of the emerging paradigm, one that binds the relational with the recreational. This exposé of the motivations of the customers of sex workers yields findings that may challenge some of your long-held paradigms regarding commercialized sexuality. As you read, consider the following questions: Why would a man prefer to purchase sexual services as opposed to trying to form an ongoing intimate relationship? Why would a client lose interest in a sexual encounter if the sex worker didn't charge for the act? Aside from the obvious financial benefits, what might be some of the motivations of sex workers who engage in this line of work? And, finally, why would there be such increasing demand for "the girlfriend experience"?

After reading this chapter, you will be better able to discern if these questions are merely conundrums, that is, problems with no solutions, or, whether such queries represent puzzles with real life solutions buried in research, such as that offered in the Bernstein study. Regardless of individual answers, a lively class discussion is likely.

———

Suddenly, the car takes off. We're moving again, but I'm not quite sure whom we're following. Apparently, a woman has gotten into the car ahead of us with a date. We proceed at full speed about a block or two, over train tracks, to a deserted stretch of territory with few cars or people. The area is in fact completely barren except for a few abandoned warehouses. Despite the gleaming California sunshine, the atmosphere is tense.

Everything happens in a flash. In mere minutes, it's all over, we slam the brakes on, and two of the officers hop out. They motion for me to join them.

The other members of the Street Crimes unit have already arrived on the scene. They have stopped a blue Chevrolet truck and handcuffed the driver, a large but trembling man who is trying

to be obsequious in spite of being terrified. Two of the officers have their guns pointed toward him. In addition to the arresting officer, the sergeant and another policeman also surround the suspect. Meanwhile, the female officers beckon the passenger, Carla, from her seat and begin to talk to her. They are trying to get her side of the story so that they can use it as evidence. Carla is high on drugs and rather weary but still lucid. She is apparently one of the numerous street prostitutes whom the officers know by name, since she has been arrested repeatedly during the ten or so years that she has been working. But today she is not the main focus of their attention.

I hover in the background, absorbing the drama of the surrounded man, the drawn guns, the momentary displays of power and fear. My heart pounding, I try to listen, feeling vaguely guilty about being a part of this. The arresting officer delivers a rapid-clip, tough-guy, made-for-TV monologue:

> I want you to tell me what happened. . . . Remember, we've spoken to her so we know. . . . What were you thinking? . . . Did you use a condom? . . . No? So you came in her mouth? . . . Did you even look at her? Did you see that disgusting shit she has on her hands? Now it's all over your wee-wee. . . . Do you have a wife or girlfriend? Now you're going to go home and give whatever you just got to her. Every man's thought of it, but you don't need to take chances. Next time you're feeling horny, why don't you just buy some porn and jack off?

Before releasing their detainee, the officers issue him a written citation and a court date.

Much later that same evening, I arrive at a famed "erotic theater" with a friend, tired but intrigued. The theater has a reputation for being one of the most upscale of the seventeen legal sex clubs in the area, where striptease, lap dances, and, in recent years, hand jobs and blow jobs are widely if unofficially available for purchase. We wade through the small crowd of Asian businessmen standing outside and make our way to the entrance. A middle-aged man with glasses politely takes our money ($45 each) with no perceptible surprise that we should choose to come here—even though we are clearly the evening's only female customers. A basket of condoms sits prominently by the door.

Again in straightforward fashion, an employee proceeds to give us a tour and to describe the various shows. The rooms have names like the "VIP Club" and the "Luxury Lounge." The premises are dimly lit but clean, orderly, and rather spare. The floors are bare yet spotless. We head over to the main stage in the back room, where a young tanned and toned woman in a sparkly thong bikini is doing a dance to the accompaniment of strobe lights and disco. She twists and turns, gyrates and thrusts, opens and closes her legs. Her featured partner is a long, silver pole that protrudes upright from the floor. As the male customers watch the show, I watch them. They crane their necks to get a better view of the dancer. All of the seats are filled, and it's standing room only. "Imagine coming home to that," gushes a forty-something, white man in a dark business suit and red tie to one of his colleagues. The performance concludes with the dancer making her way into the audience and sidling up to individual men, who caress the surface of her body and push $20 bills under her garter.

Many of the customers are extremely young: under twenty-five, perhaps under twenty, white, baseball-capped and sporting casual attire. These contingents have clearly come in groups. The thirty- and forty-something, suited white businessmen seem to comprise another category, and also cluster together in groups of three or four. Then there are the loners—again, typically under fifty years of age, predominantly white, with a sprinkling of blacks and Latinos. All are able-bodied, of average looks and builds. By mere appearances, they certainly belie the stereotype that the sex industry is geared toward older men who can't find partners.

In a room called "Copenhagen Live," a central stage is encircled by a sunken ring of little cubicles, each partitioned off from the performance area by fine, black mesh curtains. This design allows the heads and bodies of the customers to protrude through to the stage, and for the women to protrude back through to the booths in the other direction. A surrounding wall of mirrors above the cubicles means that each customer can see every other customer, as well as the performers. Two young, beautiful women come out, both with gleaming, waist-length hair and very high heels, naked but for black-and-white midriff corsets which leave their breasts and genitals exposed. They perform a highly choreographed and stylized sex act together, kissing and licking. Then, despite an earlier staff person's admonishment that body parts must remain within the booths, the women come over individually to each booth to ask if anyone would like a "show." Both of them soon descend into the dark cubicles where they are grasped by eager hands, momentarily disappearing from our line of vision.

Field Notes, San Francisco Bay Area, May 1999

Feminists and other scholars have debated theoretically what is "really" purchased in the prostitution transaction. Is it a relationship of domination? Is it love, an addiction, pleasure? Can sex be a service like any other? Only recently have they begun to tackle this question empirically. This chapter draws on field observations of and interviews with male clients of commercial sex workers as well as the state agents who are entrusted with regulating them in order to probe the meanings ascribed by different types of consumers to commercial sexual exchange, and to situate such exchanges within the broader context of postindustrial transformations of sexuality and culture.

I begin with the two paradoxical ethnographic images above. The first describes the new and growing phenomenon of the arrest of clients of female street prostitutes, an unprecedented strategy of direct state intervention in public expressions of heterosexual male desire. In the late 1990s, for the first time ever, U.S. cities such as San Francisco and New York began to boast arrest rates of male clients which approached those of female prostitutes, reversing a historical pattern that feminists had long criticized.[1] The second takes us to a local strip club, where (technically illegal) commercial sex acts are consumed as relatively unproblematic instances of sexual entitlement and male bonding.

In Western Europe and the United States, recent state efforts to problematize men's demand for sexual services—rising client arrests and reeducation via diversion programs such as "John School"; vehicle impoundment; stricter domestic and international laws on the patronage of illegal migrant or underage prostitutes and the possession of child pornography—have occurred in the face of an increasingly unbridled ethic of sexual consumption. During the last thirty years, demand for commercially available sexual services has not only soared but become ever more specialized, diversifying along technological, spatial, and social lines. These contradictory social developments reveal a tension between sex-as-recreation and the normative push for a return to sex-as-romance, a cultural counterpart of which can be found in the simultaneous emergence of Viagra and twelve-step languages of masculine sexual addiction. "Sex" as cultural imperative and technical quest, now freed from the bounds of domesticity and romance, and the rendering of nonrelationally bound erotic behavior as a pathological "addiction" are products of the same place and time.[2] The goal of this chapter is to unravel this paradox.

Some have attributed recent attempts to reform male sexuality to the gains of second-wave feminism, and even described a shift in social stigma from the seller to the buyer of sexual services.[3] Yet the influence of larger, structural factors has been neglected in most discussions. In fact, state interventions in (a typically lower-class tier of) male heterosexual practices, and the regendering of sexual stigma in certain masculine middle-class fractions can both be linked to some of the broader transformations that have produced the burgeoning demand for sexual services in the first place. In the industrializing nineteenth and early twentieth centuries, the "wrong" in prostitution was seen to reside in the prostitute herself, and, in the classical writings of social science, prostitution as a social institution was portrayed as the supreme metaphor for the exploitation of wage labor. With the transition from a production-based to a consumption-based economy, the focus of moral critique and political reform is gradually being displaced: the prostitute is increasingly normalized as either a "victim" or "sex worker," while attention and social sanction—at municipal, national, and transnational levels—are directed away from labor practices and toward consumer behavior.

In what follows, I first sketch a brief genealogy of the academic and political discourses surrounding male sexual desire and consumer demand that have developed over the past century. I next take the reader to a variety of settings in which commercial sexual consumption takes place, in order to explore the meanings and motivations that contemporary clients ascribe to their own activities. In the final section, I contrast these framings with recent attempts by state agencies to reshape demand in the wake of a booming and diversifying sexual marketplace. My discussion throughout is based on fifteen in-depth interviews with male sexual consumers, a review of local newspapers and other print and electronic media, and ethnographic fieldwork in commercial sexual markets collected in five cities.

EXPLAINING COMMERCIAL SEXUAL DEMAND

Like that of social policy, the scholarly literature on prostitution has typically viewed the varied phenomena of sexual commerce through a narrow focus on the etiology, treatment, and social symbolism of the female prostitute. Although the moral reformers in the late nineteenth-century United States sought to problematize male sexuality, their campaign to replace the prevailing double standard of sexual behavior with a single female standard that would be officially encoded into state policy met with little success.[4] After the Progressive Era, far less social or scholarly attention was paid to prostitution, as sociology and psychology both reinscribed the double standard and rendered prostitution not only unproblematic for the male clientele but structurally integral to the institution of marriage. In the 1970s and the 1980s, both the sociology of deviance and feminist theory saw the prostitute (but not the client) as a symbolically laden precipitate of larger social currents. Although some second-wave feminists critiqued the lack of attention to male clients, as well as the sexual double standard that underpinned it, empirical literature with a sustained focus on male sexual clients has been slow to emerge.[5]

Over the course of the last two decades, a small but growing number of ethnographic and interview-based studies of client behavior have been undertaken by a new generation of social researchers. Meanwhile, building on Kinsey's earlier—if methodologically flawed—work, as well as heeding feminist calls to render male sexual clients visible, quantitative researchers have begun to correlate proclivity for client behavior with other sociodemographic patterns. Analyzing data from the 1993 University of Chicago National Health and Social Life Survey, researchers Elliot Sullivan and William Simon found factors such as age cohort, military experience, education, and racial/ethnic background to be statistically significant predictors of commercial sexual purchase. In terms of racial patterns, for example, Sullivan and Simon found that, among men with no military experience, African American and Hispanic men were twice as likely as white men to have visited a prostitute.[6]

Commercial sexual proclivity has furthermore been shown by recent sociological researchers to vary systematically with a variety of attitudinal dispositions, including "socio-emotional problems," as measured by reported feelings of emotional and physical dissatisfaction, feeling unwanted and sexually unsatisfied, and, most interestingly, by "not hav[ing] sex as an expression of love."[6] It has also been correlated with a "commodified" view of sexuality, as measured by number of sexual partners, use of pornography, and the belief that one needs to have sex immediately when aroused.[7]

Finally, client behavior has increasingly been featured as a key component of broader qualitative studies on commercial sexual exchange. A primary agenda of this work has, again, been to subject the heretofore invisible male sex buyer to a sociological and political gaze. Drawing on field data and interviews, qualitative researchers have generated typologies of clients and consumer motivations. Whereas sociological research on female prostitutes has typically been driven by questions of etiology (How did she get that way? Why would a woman do that?), this research highlights differences between men, but typically takes men's status as purchasers for granted. The primary motivations identified by these authors include clients' desire for sexual variation, sexual access to partners with preferred ages, racialized bodies, and specific physiques, the appeal of an "emotion-free" and clandestine sexual encounter, loneliness, marital problems, the quest for power and control, the desire to be dominated or for other "exotic" sex acts, and the thrill of violating taboos. While provocative and insightful, one deficit that characterizes the majority of this work is the failure to explain client motives with historical specificity, or to link clients' motives to social and economic institutions that might themselves structure the relations of gender dominance that are implied by the explanatory categories listed above. In general, typologies are presented as if they were distinct attributes of a transhistorical and unwavering masculinity.

Two notable exceptions to this tendency are the diversely situated anthropological and sociological accounts of client behavior by

Anne Allison and Monica Prasad. In Allison's *Nightwork*, an ethnography of a Tokyo "hostess club" where beautiful young women serve businessmen drinks and light their cigarettes, keep the banter flirtatious, and make their bodies available for groping, all at corporate expense, Allison draws on Frankfurt school theory in order to argue that "the convergence of play and work and player and worker, supposed and presupposed by the institution of company-paid entertainment, is a feature of any society progressing through the late stages of capitalism."[8] According to Allison, Japanese businessmen's nightly participation in the mizu shobai, or erotic nightlife, as well as their emotional distance from their wives and families, epitomizes this historical trend.

Meanwhile, in an article that draws on telephone interviews with male sexual customers and which engages economic sociologists' classic distinction between market and premarket societies, Prasad argues that the prostitution exchange contains within it a form of morality that is specific to mass-market societies. Her interviews reveal that

> customers conduct the prostitution exchange in ways that are not very different from how most market exchanges are conducted today: information about prostitution is not restricted to an elite but is widely available; social settings frame the interpretation of this information; the criminalization of prostitution does not particularly hinder the exchange; and whether the exchange continues is often dictated by how well the business was conducted. In short, according to these respondents, in late-capitalist America sex is exchanged almost like any other commodity.[9]

Noting that her interviewees "praise 'market exchange' of sex for lacking the ambiguity, status-dependence, and potential hypocrisy that they see in the 'gift exchange' of sex characteristic of romantic relationships," Prasad goes on to remark that in the "fervently free-market 1980s and 1990s, romantic love might sometimes be

subordinated to, and judged unfavorably with, the more neutral, more cleanly exchangeable pleasures of eroticism."[9]

Unlike many treatments of sexual clients, the contributions of Allison and Prasad situate sexual consumption within the context of an expanded and normalized field of commercial sexual transactions. Their analyses begin to reveal a shift from a relational to a recreational model of sexual behavior, a reconfiguration of erotic life in which the pursuit of sexual intimacy is not hindered but facilitated by its location in the marketplace.

THE SUBJECTIVE CONTOURS OF MARKET INTIMACY

I'm by myself a lot, used to it, but sometimes I crave physical contact. I'd rather get it from someone I don't know because someone I do will want more. You get lonely. There's this girl right now I'm seeing. I like the attention. But that's it, in a nutshell. I find [prostitution] exciting, kind of fun. It's amazing that it's there. More people would participate if it weren't illegal. A lot of frustration in both sexes could be eliminated.

DON, 47, house painter

I feel guilty every time I cheat on my wife. I'm not a psychopath. I try to hide it as much as possible. I had a nonprofessional affair once. It was nice, and intimate, and I didn't have to pay! But I felt more guilty about that, messing with someone else's life, even though she knew I was married. You don't ever have to worry about that when you pay for it. I'm conservative by nature, but I believe in freedom of choice. If a woman wants to do it, more power to her! She's providing a service. I'm not exploiting her. Exploitation would be finding some hot 25-year-old who doesn't know any better and taking her to lunches, then to bed.

STEVE, 35, insurance manager

I started seeing escorts during a time when I didn't have many venues to meet women. I felt isolated. My friends had moved away, and I was lacking motivation. It's more real and human than jacking off alone. My first preference was to pick up women for casual sex. Since that wasn't happening, I got into the habit. It was so easy.

DAN, 36, research analyst

Theorists of gender have sometimes regarded the recent growth of the commercial sex industry as a reactionary reassertion of male dominance in response to the gains of second-wave feminism, or as compensation for men's economic disempowerment in the postindustrial public sphere. In such scenarios, the role of commercial sex is to provide the male client with a fantasy world of sexual subservience and consumer abundance that corrects for the real power deficits that he experiences in his daily life. While not disputing such accounts, I would like to suggest that men's quest for market-mediated sexual intimacy is guided by an additional set of historical transformations.

"Compensatory" arguments regarding men's persistent desire for commercial sexual encounters rest on the implicit premise that prostitution as an institution caters to needs that would preferably and more fulfillingly be satisfied within an intimate relationship in the private sphere of the home. Yet for many sexual clients, the market is experienced as enhancing and facilitating desired forms of nondomestic sexual activity. This is true whether what the client desires is a genuine but emotionally bounded intimate encounter, the experience of being pampered and "serviced," participation in a wide variety of brief sexual liaisons, or an erotic interlude that is "more real and human" than would be satisfying oneself alone. The by now platitudinous insight that sexuality has been "commodified"—and by implication, diminished—like everything else in late capitalism does not do justice to the myriad ways in which the spheres of public and private, intimacy and commerce, have interpenetrated one another and been mutually transformed, making the postindustrial consumer marketplace a prime arena for securing varieties of

interpersonal connection that circumvent this duality.

For many clients, one of the chief virtues of commercial sexual exchange is the clear and bounded nature of the encounter. In prior historical epochs, this "bounded" quality may have provided men with an unproblematic and readily available sexual outlet to supplement the existence of a pure and asexual wife in the domestic sphere. What is unique to contemporary client narratives is certain men's explicitly stated preference for this type of bounded intimate engagement over other relational forms. For at least some clients, paid sex is neither a sad substitute for something that one would ideally choose to obtain in a noncommodified romantic relationship, nor the inevitable outcome of a traditionalist Madonna/Whore double standard. Don, a forty-seven-year-old, never-married man from Santa Rosa, California, described the virtues of the paid sexual encounter this way:

> I really like women a lot, but they're always trying to force a relationship on me. I'm a nice guy, and I feel this crushing thing happen. Right now, I know a woman, she's pretty, nice, but if I make love to her, she'll want a relationship. But I'm really used to living by myself. I go and come when I want, clean when I want. I love women, enjoy them, they feel comfortable around me. I've always had a lot of women friends. I flirt and talk to them, but I don't usually take the next step, because it leads to trouble!

Much is lost if we try to subsume Don's statements under pop-psychologizing diagnoses such as "fear of intimacy," or even a more covertly moralistic social-psychological descriptor like "techniques of neutralization."[10] In Don's preference for a life constructed around living alone, intimacy through close friendships, and paid for, safely contained sexual encounters, we also see evidence of a disembedding of the (male) individual from the sex-romance nexus of the privatized nuclear family. This is a concrete example of the profound reorganization of personal life

608 SEXUALITY AND PUBLIC POLICY

that diverse social analysts have noticed occurring during the last thirty or so years.

An additional advantage of market-mediated sexual encounters was articulated by Steve, a married, thirty-five-year-old insurance manager from a middle-class California suburb. Frustrated that sexual relations with his wife had been relatively infrequent since the birth of their child, Steve had decided to look for sex elsewhere. Although elements of Steve's story invoke the sexual double standard of eras past, the reasoning that he displayed during our interview also revealed a decidedly new twist. For Steve, the market-mediated sexual encounter is morally and emotionally preferable to the "nonprofessional affair" because of the clarifying effect of payment. Though he characterized himself as "conservative by nature," Steve had incorporated a fair amount of sex-worker rights rhetoric into his own discourse, describing the sexual agency of his paid "service providers" with tangible awe. Having grappled with feminist critiques of male sexual indulgence as "exploitative," he concluded that true exploitation resided in the emotional dishonesty of the premarket paradigm of seduction, rather than in the clean cash-for-sex market transactions that he participated in.

In my interviews with clients, many men were insistent that their patronage of the commercial sexual economy did not in any way result from problems or deficits in their primary sexual relationships. Rick, a sixty-one-year-old data processor from San Francisco, emphasized that his sexual relationship with his wife was just fine, and likened his desire to pay different women for sex to other, less socially problematic consumer experiences ("There's a Vietnamese restaurant...that I love, but I don't want to eat there every day"). Rick's statement may be seen as a variant of the classic argument that prostitution is an expression of the male "natural appetite"—a perspective which, like Steve's above, is of course premised on a notion of the sexual double standard. As Carole Pateman has pointed out, in such arguments, "The

comparison is invariably made between prostitution and the provision of food."[11] Significantly, however, Rick's explicit justification for patronizing prostitutes is less one of essential, biological drives than it is one of simple and entitled consumer choice. Rick's stated preference for variety presumes an underlying model of sexuality in which sexual expression bears no necessary connection to a domestic-sphere relationship, and in which a diversity of sexual partners and experiences is not merely substitutive but desirable in its own right.

Interviewees like Rick challenge a common second-wave feminist presupposition that prostitution exists simply to satisfy sexual demands which nonprofessional women find distasteful or are too inhibited to perform. Though sexual dissatisfaction within marriage may have at least partly characterized the motivations of a prior era of male sexual clients, in the contemporary sexual marketplace paid sex is often not seen as compensation for something lacking in men's primary domestic relationships. Rather, commercial sex provides access to multiple attractive partners that—in the wake of the historical shift from the family-based "good provider role" to the unfettered, consumeristic "playboy philosophy"—many male sexual clients feel that they are *entitled* to.[12] This philosophy is also made apparent in the upscaling of commercial sex venues that has occurred in U.S. cities since the 1980s, what the anthropologist Katherine Frank has described as the "intensified focus on the creation of 'atmosphere' and luxury."[13] Over the last two decades, "gentleman's clubs" and commercial sexual services with names like "Platinum Crown Escorts," "Prestige Escorts," "The Gold Club," and "VIP Massage" have proliferated to cater to clients' fantasies of consumptive class mobility. Within the terms of this new cultural logic of male dominance, clients conjure the sexual marketplace as the great social equalizer, where consumer capitalism democratizes access to a caliber of goods and services that in earlier eras would have been the exclusive province of a restricted elite.

BOUNDED AUTHENTICITY AND THE "GFE"

Here is another man's account of his commercial sexual activity, this time from an Internet chat room for patrons of strip clubs:

> I finally got to spend some quality time in the city by the Bay, compliments of my employer, who decided that I needed to attend a conference there last week. So, armed with a vast array of knowledge regarding the local spots, I embarked on a week of fun and frolicking. Unfortunately, I ended up spending too much time with conference goers so I only made three trips to clubs. I had an absolutely incredible time at both places.... At the first club, I adjourned to the Patpong Room with Jenny, who asked me what I was interested in. I said that a couple of nude lap dances were on the agenda and I inquired as to her price: $60 each. Okay, no problem. I forked over the cash. After the two long dances she offered me a blow job for another $120.
> I said that would be heavenly and handed her the money.... It was an absolutely fabulous experience. I spent $30 on cover charges, $10 on tips, $240 with Jenny, and $300 with another girl named Tanya for a total of $580. Not bad for just over two hours of illicit fun. I'm used to paying that for decent outcall so this was a nice change of pace.

Like many of the interviewees described above, this man is unself-conscious about constructing his experience as a form of light and unproblematic commercial consumption ("two hours of illicit fun," "a nice change of pace"). For clients such as this (who may describe themselves as "hobbyists" or "enthusiasts" in Internet chat rooms), prostitution is primarily a pampering diversion financed by and casually sandwiched in between a week's worth of requisite, and presumably less pleasurable, professional activities.

Yet the paid sexual encounter may also represent to clients something more than just an ephemeral consumer indulgence. In their 1982 article, Harold Holzman and Sharon Pines argued that it was the fantasy of a mutually desired, special, or even romantic sexual encounter that clients were purchasing in the prostitution transaction—something notably distinct both from a purely mechanical sex act and from an unbounded, private-sphere romantic entanglement. They observed that the clients in their study emphasized the warmth and friendliness of the sex worker as characteristics that were at least as important to them as the particulars of physical appearance. Katherine Frank has also noted the ways in which patrons of strip clubs frequently pursue signs of a female dancer's "sincerity" before choosing to interact with her (many comment that they specifically avoid dancers "who [are] doing this just to make money").[13] The clients that I interviewed were similarly likely to express variants of the statement that "If her treatment is cold or perfunctory, I'm not interested." And in Web-based client guides to commercial sexual services such as "The World Sex Guide," reviewers are consistently critical of sex workers who are "clockwatchers," "too rushed and pushy," who "don't want to hug and kiss," or who "ask for a tip mid-sex act."

One of the most sought after features in the prostitution encounter has thus become the "girlfriend experience," or GFE. Ads for escorts in print media and online now routinely feature this in their advertisements, and there are entire Web pages where people who specialize in this service can advertise.

Here is a description of what a GFE session might consist of, an account that was posted to an Internet chat forum by one sexual client:

> A typical non-GFE session with an escort includes one or more of the basic acts required for the customer to reach a climax at least one time, and little else. A GFE type session, on the other hand, might proceed much more like a non-paid encounter between two lovers. This may include a lengthy period of foreplay in which

the customer and the escort touch, rub, fondle, massage, and perhaps even kiss passionately. A GFE session might also include activities where the customer works as hard to stimulate the escort as she works to stimulate him. Finally, a GFE session usually has a period of cuddling and closeness at the end of the session, rather than each partner jumping up and hurrying out as soon as the customer is finished.

Earlier, we saw how San Francisco's white middle-class sex workers often strived to obtain a sense of emotional authenticity in their work, tailoring this experience into a purchasable (and desirable) commodity for their clients. The first tier of paid "intimacy providers" to offer their clients the GFE were indeed white, native-born sex workers in possession of sufficient cultural and bodily capital to fulfill their clients' fantasies of sex with a social equal. More recently, however, in client chat rooms and on Internet bulletin boards, men have begun to note that "foreign" women are also highly skilled practitioners of the service. One client observed that "Asian, Latin, and Eastern European women . . . are in my experiences the most intimate and open to this type of physical intimacy." As the GFE expands from a local, elite specialty service to a broadly advertised, mass-market sexual commodity (even constituting a standard feature of the "menus" of sexual services available in brothels worldwide), the initially broad and ill-defined spectrum of activities offered under this banner has metamorphosed into simple shorthand for modern prostitution's conventionally denied mouth-to-mouth kiss. The most "natural" of intimate gestures, now offered back to the client in denaturalized and explicitly commodified form, the kiss has become a highly prized emblem of intimacy and authenticity.

As with other forms of service work, successful commercial sexual transactions are ones in which the market basis of the exchange serves a crucial delimiting function that can also be temporarily subordinated to the client's fantasy of authentic interpersonal connection, as the following chat room description of an encounter in a commercial sex club illustrates:

> At the club, I had a memorable experience with a light-skinned black girl named Luscious. . . . We adjoined to the backstage area for one full-service session during the course of my visit. This time I brought my condoms. We began with the usual touchy feely. . . . I could feel she was just soaking, an indication her moans were not faked. Several minutes later I shot my load and used the conveniently located Kleenex dispenser to wash up. The most unusual aspect of this encounter is that Luscious didn't ask for money up front which is a first for a place of this type. I tipped her $60.

Even when the encounter lasts only minutes, from the client's perspective it may represent a meaningful and authentic form of interpersonal exchange. Clients such as the one quoted above are indeed seeking a real and reciprocal erotic connection, but a precisely delimited one. For these men, what is (at least ideally) being purchased is a sexual connection that is premised on bounded authenticity. As with the above client's invocation of the physical tangibility of Luscious's desire, other clients boasted of their ability to give sex workers authentic sexual pleasure, insisted that the sex workers they patronized liked them enough to offer them freebies or to invite them home for dinner, and proudly proclaimed that they had at times even dated or befriended the sex workers they were seeing.

Clients' repeated claims of authentic interpersonal connection are particularly striking to consider in light of the fact the vast majority of sex workers (even those who were themselves pursuing a meaningful experience in their work) imposed very clear emotional boundaries between their customers and their nonprofessional lovers. Amanda, one of the few San Francisco sex workers that I spoke with who admitted to occasionally looking for lovers among her client pool, said that she had given up the practice of offering her preferred clients "bargain rates" or unpaid sexual arrangements because it inevitably met with dire results:

> They pretend to be flattered, but they never come back! If you offer them anything but sex for money they flee. There was one client I had who was so sexy, a professional dancer and tai chi practitioner, and really fun to fuck. Since good sex is a rare thing, I told him I'd see him for $20 (my normal rate is $250). Another guy, he was so sexy, I told him "come for free." Both of them freaked out and never returned. The men want an emotional connection, but they don't want any obligations. They don't believe they can have no-strings-attached sex, which is why they pay. They'd rather pay than get it for free.

Christopher, a male sex-worker who had also once tried to redefine his relationship with a client, recounted something similar: "I called a trick once because I wanted to have sex with him again. . . . We agreed in advance that it was just going to be sex for sex's sake, not for pay, and that was the last time I ever heard from him!" Critics of commercialized sex may misconstrue clients' desire for bounded authenticity if their implicit point of reference is the modernist paradigm of romantic love, premised on monogamous domesticity and intertwined life trajectories. Thus, Carole Pateman asks why (if not for the sake of pure domination) would "15–25 per cent of the customers of the Birmingham prostitutes demand what is known in the trade as 'hand relief,'" something which could presumably be self-administered.[11] Yet, as one client insisted, after explaining to me that he studied and worked all the time and consequently didn't have much opportunity to even meet women, let alone to pursue a romantic relationship, "It's more real and human than jacking off alone." This client reveals an underlying sexual paradigm which blends the "relational" with the "recreational"—a mode of eroticism that is compatible with the rhythms of his individually oriented daily life and, increasingly, with those of other men with similar white, middle-class sociodemographic profiles.

CONSUMPTION, COMPULSIVITY, AND SHAME

This is not to suggest that all of the clients that I spoke with regarded their patterns of sexual consumption with nonchalance and ease. Gary, an unpartnered forty-seven-year-old contractor from a small Bay Area city, was one of several clients I encountered who were too ashamed of their behaviors to even meet me for a face-to-face interview. Currently in therapy to deal with his compulsive behaviors around sexuality in general (and commercial sex in particular), throughout our telephone conversation Gary's emotional state oscillated between shameful frenzy and depressive desperation. In fact, he told me that he had answered my ad in the first place because he was feeling compulsive and out of control, and thought that by calling me (instead of a sex worker) he would be doing something to help himself: "reaching out," not "acting out."

Here is an excerpt from Gary's account of shopping for commercial sex:

> If I thought about it logically, I wouldn't do it. There are triggers. I work hard, long hours, live alone, and am comfortable enough. A lot of times I'll be home on a Friday night, I'll pick up the newspaper, look at the ads, get enticed, and then I'm gone. It's so easy. . . .
>
> But, you know, it's a tremendous financial drain. I've spent enough money in the massage parlors over the last twenty-seven years to buy myself a house. Some people snort houses, I do this. . . . You start to feel you can't get this unless you pay for it. That's the personal blow from this that you take that you keep to yourself. Plus there's the loss of money. It's like guilt, too, and shame. But you block that out when you're doing it, even if you feel it soon after. You feel like you're letting yourself down by not pursuing a relationship in more conventional ways. You're cheating yourself. As time goes on, you feel more and more distant from being able to have a normal relationship. Plus having such a secret

aspect to your life, you feel dishonest with your world. People don't really know you. Although it's strange, I also know people who brag about it and are very open. . . .

Likening his subjective experience of buying sex to snorting drugs. Gary is clearly describing an "addictive," or at least compulsive, experience of his commercial sexual activity. This framing is in stark contrast to the deliberate, carefully considered redemptions of market intimacy and bounded authenticity described above, as well as to the open and bragging behavior that Gary has witnessed in some of his associates. Gary's guilt and shame around the purchase of sex congeal around the vast sums of money he has spent and the orienting of the self away from "normal relationships" and toward this easy yet esteem-damaging alternative. In various of my interviews with sexual clients—even ones in which the interviewees had first praised the benefits of market-mediated sexual exchange— similar themes of compulsivity, guilt, and shame emerged.

Several men described feeling "out of control" and "powerless" before making the purchase, driven and desperate while in active pursuit, and ashamed, secretive, fearful, or disappointed following the event. The extracts below convey some of these men's subjective experiences of the prostitution encounter. All are quotes from men who had spent the earlier part of their interviews extolling the virtues of commercial sex:

Nobody knows I do this. Nobody knows. Something comes over me. I could be driving along, and if I get a sexual thought, I need to take care of it. It could be going to a sexual arcade, or hiring someone. It's completely compulsive! I don't think about it in the morning. If I have a few hundred dollars, I want to see someone in twenty minutes.

STEVE, 35

Sometimes, I'll be prowling the streets at night until 3:00 or 4:00 a.m., and come in to work after only four hours of sleep. I know that it's

compulsive. One time, I was in Cape Cod on vacation, and I thought, "I have to get back to San Francisco, because there are no hookers here." The most uncomfortable part is definitely the compulsivity, the feeling like you don't have any power. And unfortunately, I'm one of those guys who feel let down afterwards. Afterwards, I worry: Did I get a disease? Are there pimps? How do I get home? Was my car broken in to? What will she use the money for? And I always want to spend more time. I think of all the negatives, that it was too rushed and disconnected. What I really want is some connection. . . .

RICK, 61

How might we explain why some of the very same men who in one moment celebrate the safe parameters of market intimacy in the next breath describe their engagement with that intimacy as so very compulsive and psychically problematic? With Foucault-inspired critics such as Janice Irvine and Helen Keane, we could problematize the post-1970s discourses of addiction, whereby individuals' unfulfilled desires and consumptive excesses are interpreted as symptoms of underlying pathology. Through their internalization of these discourses, individuals themselves come to participate in the regulatory regimes of the psychotherapy industry and the state.[14] Alternatively, we might interpret these men's accounts of subjective suffering as both symbolic and material in origin—as an effect not only of Foucauldian biopower but of tangible, embodied conflicts with the mores of late-capitalist consumer culture. Thus Anthony Giddens suggests that the normalization of nonrelationally bound sexuality, on the one hand, and the emergence of so much psychic stress around sexuality (in the form of compulsions and addictions), on the other hand, necessarily emerge in tandem. In this view, the more that sexual and other cultural practices are disembedded from their traditional ritual supports, the more the solitary self must subsume these behaviors under the banner of individual "lifestyle choices," and, for many, the subjective burdens prove to be overwhelming.

Further insight into these men's accounts of the occasionally "addictive" quality of sexual purchase can also be gleaned from the works of diverse theorists of postmodern life, who argue that it is precisely the flexibility, transience, and flux of postmodernity that create simultaneous subjective longings for stability and permanence. These longings are evident in the postmodern surge of disparate forms of nostalgias and fundamentalisms—from the moral critique of consumerism to the ideology of family values to the quest for true love. In the case of commercial sex, this reactivity can serve to explain clients' accounts of their desires for both bounded and unbounded authenticity, for commodified erotic exchange and the proverbial "free love." Clients' self-conflicting desires bespeak the very moment of social flux which has produced both normalized and "compulsive" engagements with commercial sexual activity. The act of sexual purchase thus serves as a temporary salve to clients' contradictory desires for both transience and stability, for fungible intimacy as well as durable connection. Meanwhile, culturally prominent discourses of "sex addiction" not only recast these conflicts in individualized terms but seek quite literally to capitalize on them, to rechannel clients' disparate needs and longings into more socially desirable directions.

THE STATE AND THE REDIRECTION OF DESIRE

It's 9 a.m. on a Saturday morning. In one of the only occupied rooms of the San Francisco Hall of Justice, I am seated in the back row of "John School," the city's pretrial diversion program for men who have been arrested for soliciting prostitutes. The city is proud of its program, which boasts a recidivism rate of less than 1 percent of first-time arrestees, who, for a mere $500, can have their records cleared. Approximately fifty or sixty men are in the room this morning, of diverse class and ethnic backgrounds.

*More striking still is that there is nearly an equal number of media representatives in the room. By the end of the first hour, I have been introduced to journalists from TV20, the **London Times**, and **Self Magazine**. "There are representatives from different media organizations here each month," announces Evelyn, the program's feisty director, to the men. "I never do this class without media coverage."*

Yet according to the johns I chat with during the coffee breaks, very few are passively absorbing the information that is presented to them, and they are far from being persuaded of the error of their ways. The men say that John School is even worse than Traffic School—an all-day ordeal in a stuffy room with a whole procession of equally stuffy speakers. "This is bullshit." "I was trapped." "It's so hypocritical." "It should be legalized" "They act like it's something special, but all men do it. . . . Men and women just think differently. Men will fuck sheep, boys, anything. They are dogs."

The first presentation is led by an assistant district attorney and is entitled "Prostitution Law and Street Facts." Although John School is officially available to all men arrested for soliciting a prostitute, the structure of the program demonstrates that those who do get arrested comprise only a small and special subgroup of clients. This program is clearly geared for heterosexual men who shop the streets. During his presentation, the DA, trying to get the group to engage, asks: "How many of you were picked up in the Tenderloin? How many of you were picked up in the Mission?" He does not ask how many were picked up at the local erotic theater, or with an escort, or while cruising for a sex worker online, or even on Polk Street (where male and transgender street prostitutes work).

The DA's objective is to scare the men out of their established patterns of behavior by gruesomely cataloging the potential legal repercussions of what they are doing—what it's like to get booked, to be herded into the paddy wagon, to spend the night in jail, or to be forced to take an HIV test—all likely consequences of a second arrest. He shows the class a brief video reviewing the laws. I am at first confused by the last image in the sequence: the captionless depiction of a man hunched over a computer screen. The DA's final words to the men are even more remarkable: "Next time you're thinking of going out on the street, do like this guy. Go on the Internet if you have to—but stay away from minors!"

The final presentation before the lunch break features a former street prostitute and ex-heroin addict who now runs a program to help prostitute women transform their lives and get off the streets. Seated beside her is a panel of three other formerly homeless and drug-addicted streetwalkers. Now clean and sober, well-scrubbed, well-fed, and conservatively attired, their appearances are not much different from other thirty- to forty-year-old professional women. Only their scathing and effusively expressed anger betrays a difference.

For the men, this is no doubt the most riveting panel of the day—at last, their attention seems focused; they sit tense and upright in their chairs. From their facial expressions and inclining postures, some even seem to be vaguely aroused. The rhetorical tactic employed by the women is a combination of shock therapy and a firm reassertion of the primacy of marital domesticity. "Most of the women I have worked with started turning tricks as children or teens," says one woman in a harsh, accusatory voice. "I learned a long time ago that it's not pedophiles involved in that, but the men that sit here in this room." Through teary eyes and clenched teeth, another panelist tells the men her own story of early sexual abuse, addiction, and rape. Her narrative, gripping and theatrical, ends with the following admonition:

Once, I remember being crusty and dope sick, wearing yellow shorts, and walking around with blood caked on my thighs for two days. No one asked me what was wrong. I felt like a fallen woman that God, society, and my family would never forgive.... We're not out there because we like to suck dick, and you're not out there because you like us. You're the cause of our suffering, and you can become statistics yourselves. Try and realize, if you have to go back out—these women were hurt! A lot of you men are husbands, fathers,

and grandfathers. What did you tell your significant others today? Hopefully, someday soon you'll learn how to have healthy relationships—with your wives.

In the afternoon, there are three additional presentations: one featuring representatives from organized neighborhood and merchant groups, another with a sergeant from the vice squad on the dynamics of pimping, and the final presentation by a therapist on "Sexual Compulsivity and Intimacy Issues." The neighborhood groups are represented by two men and a woman, white residents and small shopkeepers from the Tenderloin district. Together with the vice cop, they paint the johns as aggressors against family, community, and—rather ironically—business. The harms that the johns are held responsible for are both symbolic and material. "Do you have sex in front of your children?" they ask. "Little boys in my neighborhood blow up condoms like balloons! You hear about victimless crimes, but our whole neighborhood is a victim! Fifteen-year-old girls turn tricks and twenty minutes later deliver babies. Millions of dollars pass through these girls, but at the end of the day they have nothing. All the way through this business, there are victims."

The final session, led by a licensed marriage and family counselor, relies on a twelve-step sexual addiction model of client behavior. The counselor is a white, middle-class, casually dressed man in his late thirties, an exemplar of northern California therapeutic culture and soft-spoken masculinity. He begins his presentation with a definition: "Sex addicts have trouble thinking of sex and love together, in the same relationship. They say, 'I love my wife, but I have sex with a prostitute.' The challenge is to do them together, to learn how to nurture relationship."

After distributing a "Sexual Addiction Screening Test" to the members of the class (with questions such as "Do you often find yourself preoccupied with sexual thoughts?" and "Has your sexual activity interfered with your family life?"), the therapist tries to enlist the class in a discussion about why men visit prostitutes. "Stress," *volunteers one man. "Curiosity," says another. "Anger? Loneliness?" offers the therapist, and some of the men agree. Finally, one john rouses himself out of boredom to protest. "Come on already! It should just be legalized! Guys need a place to get relief." A police officer from the Street Crimes unit who is seated to my left leans over to me and whispers in my ear: "I agree. Anyway, I bet most of these men will now just go indoors, where they don't have to worry about any of this."*

Field Notes, San Francisco, May 1999

Feminists have bemoaned—but also taken for granted—the sexual double standard in the treatment of prostitution by the criminal justice system. In 1993, the scholar and prostitutes' rights activist Gail Pheterson persuasively argued that

> Of course, the customer is also party to prostitution transactions and in countries where sex commerce is illegal, he is equally guilty of a crime. But such laws are not equally applied to customer and prostitute. . . . Nowhere is equal punishment enforced, however, partly because law officials are either customers themselves or they identify with customers.[5]

Pheterson and other critics would never have predicted that, by the mid-1990s, municipal and national governments might actually intervene to challenge and reconfigure patterns of male heterosexual consumption, and even mobilize feminist arguments in the service of such interventions. Nor did they foresee that, despite a shared gender and sexual identification with customers, male authorities might be beholden to other social forces and political agendas that could lead them to curtail the prerogatives of heterosexual interest. And they did not anticipate how programs such as "John School" and the expanding and diversifying market in commercial sexual services might represent what only seem to be paradoxical facets of interconnected social trends.

Since the mid-1990s, "John Schools," "First Offender Programs," and "Client Reeducation Projects" have sprung up in American cities as diverse as San Francisco and Fresno, California; Brooklyn and Buffalo, New York; Portland, Oregon; Las Vegas, Nevada; Kansas City, Kansas; Norfolk, Virginia; and Nashville, Tennessee, as well as in Toronto and Edmonton in Canada and Leeds in the United Kingdom. Numerous other cities throughout the United States and Western Europe have also considered implementing similar programs. After decriminalizing prostitution in the late 1960s, in 1998 Sweden became the first national government to unilaterally criminalize the purchase of sexual services by male customers. In the United States, although the first sporadic and fleeting gestures toward the arrest of male clients date back to the 1970s, contemporary client reeducation programs must be seen as part of a new strategy of state intervention in male sexual behavior.

In both Oklahoma City and Kansas City, for example, city officials have begun to broadcast on cable television the photos and names of male clients arrested by police for prostitution-related offences.[15] In Huntington Woods, Michigan, the police released the names of 16,000 alleged prostitution customers on CD-ROM.[16] Police in various municipalities have also arranged for the names and faces of arrested clients to appear on city billboards and Web sites and in local newspapers.[17] Perhaps the most provocative recent example of john "outing" is "Webjohn," an online database organized by "concerned community members," featuring johns caught on video picking up or communicating with a known prostitute. The site's Mission Statement notably posits johns, not prostitutes, as vectors of disease, and declares two official aims: "to deny johns their anonymity" and "to offer any residential or business community in North America a cost-free and lawsuit-free mechanism to suppress street-level prostitution in the area." Taken together with a revision of legal codes to facilitate client arrests and to stiffen criminal penalties, "public outings" in the mass media, vehicle impoundment, revocation of driver's licenses, as well as fiercer prohibitions against the patronage of child prostitutes and the possession of child pornography, the new spate of social policies and cultural interventions constitutes an unprecedented attempt to regulate male heterosexual behavior.

"John Schools" are the outcome of an alliance between feminist antiprostitution activists, organized groups of predominantly lower middle-class community residents and shopkeepers, and politicians and big businesses with interests in gentrifying neighborhoods such as San Francisco's Tenderloin and Mission districts. These are neighborhoods which are home to the city's principal streetwalking strolls and the most socially marginal sectors of the commercial sex trade, yet which also stand close to the business district and to highly valuable real estate. Although the three groups indicated have disparate ideological and material agendas, as part of their agenda to eliminate street prostitution as a whole, they have joined forces to target the male patrons of prostitution's most public domain. In contrast to the moral wars of a century ago, contemporary campaigns against prostitution are chiefly concerned with cleaning up the gritty underbelly of an industry that is in practice left alone so long as it remains behind closed doors.[15]

In this way, the district attorney's advice to the attendees of "John School" to turn on their computers can be rendered decipherable as an important step toward cleaner streets and gentrified neighborhoods. Thus, in 1994, when the San Francisco Board of Supervisors assembled a task force to investigate revisions to the city's prostitution policy, the primary and explicitly stated impetus was community and merchants' objections to disruptions on their streets.[18] Although police representatives and municipal politicians continue to frame their street-focused enforcement strategy as being in accordance with the preponderance of citizens' complaints, the effect of their policies is clearly to divert sex workers

and customers into indoor and online commercial sex markets.

The new social policies targeting male sexual conduct and commercial consumption are not, however, absent of moral focus or content. The various strands of the ideological agenda behind programs such as "John School," like the interest groups behind it, are multiple but interweaving. Many contemporary feminist activists, like their feminist forerunners, are keen on challenging the male half of the sexual double standard. Given the emergence of the sexually consumeristic "playboy" ideal in the 1960s, the deregulation and normalization of pornography in the 1970s, and other predominantly male benefits of the sexual revolution, the reassertion of sexual domesticity and marital fidelity may be experienced as particularly crucial. Responding to a similar constellation of concerns, the Tenderloin's middle-class residents and small-scale merchants can be seen as participating in both a material and a symbolic crusade against the incursion of market forces into a longed-for, protected sphere of family, neighborhood, and community.

CONCLUSION

The two historically unique and contradictory tendencies that I have documented here, namely burgeoning consumption and increased state intervention, should be understood within a broad array of economic and cultural transformations that have unfolded over the last thirty-five years and crystallized even more dramatically during the last decade. The pursuit of bounded authenticity that is encapsulated in men's demand for sexual commerce has been fostered by the shift from a relational to a recreational model of sexual intimacy, by the symbiotic relationship between the information economy and commercial sexual consumption, by the ways in which tourism and business travel facilitate the insertion of men into the commercial sexual marketplace, and, more generally, by the myriad mergings and inversions of public and private life that are characteristic of our era.

At the same time, the corresponding phenomena of postindustrial poverty and the gentrification of the inner city have led to an overlapping of ambitions between municipal politicians, developers, and feminist antiprostitution activists, who are jointly interested in "cleaning up" the male desires that contribute to the sullying of urban streets. "John Schools," as well as other measures that penalize a subgroup of the male clients of commercial sex workers, have emerged out of the confluence of these disparate political agendas. The recent crackdowns on johns and the normalization of other forms of commercial sex thus go hand in hand because, in addition to struggles over sex and gender, both the state policing of the street-level sex trade and the normalization of the sex business reveal a shared set of underlying economic and cultural interests: the excision of class and racial Others from gentrifying inner cities, the facilitation of the postindustrial service sector, and the creation of clean and shiny urban spaces in which middle-class men can safely indulge in recreational commercial sexual consumption.

INTRODUCTION REFERENCES

Edlund, L., and E. Korn. 2002. A theory of prostitution. *Journal of Political Economy* 110: 181–214.

Flowers, R. B. 1998. *The prostitution of women and girls.* Jefferson, NC: McFarland.

Noer, M. 2006, February 14. The economics of prostitution. Http://www.*forbes*.com/2006/02/11economics-prostitution-marriage (accessed October 10, 2008).

Ramirez, J. 2008, June 16. Feeling the pinch: Nevada's brothels hit hard times. Http://www.*newsweek*.com/id/141848/output/print (accessed October 6, 2008).

Simon, D. R. (2001). Prostitution-female. In *Encyclopedia of criminology and deviant behavior, vol. 3, Sexual deviance* (pp. 264–66), eds. C. D. Bryant (Editor-in-Chief), N. Davis and G. Geis (Vol. Eds.). Philadelphia: Taylor & Francis.

REFERENCES

1. Lefler, Julie. 1999. "Shining the Spotlight on Johns: Moving toward Equal Treatment of Male Customers and Female Prostitutes." *Hastings Women's Law Journal* 10 (1): 11–37.

2. Irvine, Janice M. 1993. "Regulated Passions: The Invention of Inhibited Sexual Desire and Sex Addiction." *Social Text* 37: 203–27.

3. Kulick, Don. 2005. "Four Hundred Thousand Swedish Perverts." *GLQ* 11 (2): 205–35.

4. Luker, Kristen. 1998. "Sex, Social Hygiene, and the State: The Double-Edged Sword of Social Reform." *Theory and Society* 27: 601–34.

5. Pheterson, Gail. 1993. "The Whore Stigma: Female Dishonor and Male Unworthiness." *Social Text* 37: 39–65.

6. Sullivan, Elroy, and William Simon. 1998. "The Client: A Social, Psychological, and Behavioral Look at the Unseen Patron of Prostitution," in *Prostitution: On Whores, Hustlers, and Johns*, ed. James Elias et al. Amherst, NY: Prometheus Books, pp. 134–55.

7. Monto, Martin. 2000. "Why Men Seek Out Prostitutes," in *Sex for Sale: Prostitution, Pornography, and the Sex Industry*, ed. Ron Weitzer. New York: Routledge, pp. 67–85.

8. Allison, Anne. 1994. *Nightwork: Sexuality, Pleasure, and Corporate Masculinity in a Tokyo Hostess Club.* Chicago: University of Chicago Press.

9. Prasad, Monica, 1999. "The Morality of Market Exchange: Love, Money, and Contractual Justice." *Sociological Perspectives* 42 (2): 181–215.

10. Sykes, Gresham M., and David Matza. 1957. "Techniques of Neutralization: A Theory of Delinquency." *American Sociological Review* 22: 664–70.

11. Pateman, Carole. 1988. *The Sexual Contract.* Stanford: Stanford University Press.

12. Ehrenreich, Barbara. 1983. *The Hearts of Men: American Dreams and the Flight from Commitment.* New York: Doubleday.

13. Frank, Katherine. *G-Strings and Sympathy: Strip Club Regulars and Male Desire.* Durham: Duke University Press.

14. Keane, Helen. 2002. *What's Wrong with Addiction?* New York: New York University Press.

15. Weitzer, Ron. 2000. "The Politics of Prostitution in American," in *Sex for Sale: Prostitution, Pornography, and the Sex Industry*, ed. Ron Weitzer. New York: Routledge, pp. 159–81.

16. "Names of Alleged U.S. Prostitute Clients Released." 1999. Reuters Online, Jan. 13, http://www.infonautics.com (last access March 3, 2000).

17. Conroy, John. 2006. "The Electronic Pillory." *Chicago Reader*, April 7, sec. 1.

18. San Francisco Task Force on Prostitution. 1996. *Final Report*. Submitted to the Board of Supervisors of the City and County of San Francisco, California. Available online at http://www.bayswan.org/1TF.html (last accessed May 17, 2006).

CHAPTER 47

Community

Risk, Identity, and Love in the Age of AIDS

Judith Levine

The type of "love" in the age of AIDS highlighted in this offering may surprise you. In her controversial book, Harmful to Minors: The Perils of Protecting Children from Sex, *Judith Levine provides prescriptions for how adults might do better in guiding children toward "loving well," meaning safely, pleasurably, and with respect for others and themselves. But, the love featured in this chapter is about* agape *love, a Greek word meaning "selfless love."*

Levine is a journalist of national renown whose lively writing about sex, gender, and families has spanned two decades. She is well-qualified to report on the success of the sexuality education and HIV prevention programs she investigated in the Minneapolis and St. Paul areas. Do not expect academic "program evaluations," however, from this hands-on "beat-reporter." She uses interviews with young people and their parents, stories drawn from today's headlines, as well as visits to classrooms and clinics to inform her writing. And, in the process she will inform your opinion. Chronicling the lives of the gay, lesbian, bisexual, and homeless youth in the Twin Cities, she poignantly portrays a community of caring adults who embody the essence of agape love in their programs and practice.

Levine's chapter promises to challenge your critical thinking. On the one hand, it may raise anxieties, on the other, it may provoke questions about conflicting views. In either case, you will be among friends—that large group of people who admit that they do not yet have all the answers about sex or about agape love.

"But what about AIDS?" The question arises immediately, almost every time I hazard the opinion that sex is not harmful to minors. Often it is not a question at all but a kind of preemptive statement: as long as there is AIDS, there cannot be adolescent sex. In 1981, when only gay men and their friends knew about the incipient epidemic, "chastity education" was a laughingstock. But as soon as HIV hit the cover of *Newsweek*, not far behind was the remarkable popular consensus that no-sex was the best thing to teach and the best thing for teens to practice. Just when mass public education about transmission, condoms, and nonpenetrative forms of sex was most crucial, AIDS became the rationale for not talking about sex. "The right wing's demand to 'teach' abstinence created the next generation's paradox," wrote Cindy Patton in

From "Community: Risk, Identity, and Love in the Age of AIDS" by J. Levine. 2002. In *Harmful to Minors: The Perils of Protecting Children from Sex*, by J. Levine, 199–217. Minneapolis: University of Minnesota Press. Copyright 2002 by Judith Levine. Reprinted with permission of the author and the University of Minnesota Press.

her searing *Fatal Advice: How Safe-Sex Education Went Wrong.* "[E]quating 'no sex' and safe sex suggests that no sex is safe."[1]

That paradox did not yield mass abstention. Sex continued more or less unabated, but instead of safely, many youths did it ignorant of the difference between those acts that abetted HIV transmission, those that were relatively safer, and those that virtually precluded transmission. And exactly as the militant AIDS activist group ACT UP warned, silence has equaled death. By the mid-1990s, a young person was being infected with HIV every hour of every day.[2] And while AIDS deaths dropped in the general U.S. population,[3] the disease became the leading cause of mortality for people ages twenty-five to forty-four, many of whom had likely contracted the virus in their teens.[4]

If abstinence is not the key, what is? Public-health experts have long observed that the populations hit hardest by AIDS overlap in predictable ways with those otherwise afflicted by poor health, education, or housing—and a poor standing in America's social hierarchies. Infection rates have fallen dramatically among adult men who have sex with men, especially white, middle-class, out gay men.[5] Nevertheless, it was estimated in the 1990s that 20 to 30 percent of gay youths would be infected by their thirtieth birthday.[6] Of all HIV-infected American youths in 1998, 63 percent were black.[7] And a survey of young, gay men of color conducted in six major cities by the National Centers for Disease Control from 1998 to 2000 revealed an even more astonishing figure: almost a third of gay black men in their twenties are HIV positive.[8]

People in extremis, as usual, are at more extreme risk. Runaway teens show infection rates as high as 10 percent.[9] Half of New York City's people with HIV in the 1990s were intravenous drug users,[10] many of whom were young and marginally housed or employed.

These patterns are even more baldly visible globally. For instance, as the disease has ravaged Africa and steadily crept over South Asia, the United Nations reports that the near-total sexual, social, and economic abjection of women in those regions is translating into catastrophic rates of HIV infection and AIDS deaths among them.[11] The 1997 International AIDS Conference had predicted such dire developments. "Social norms and structural factors" exert a major impact on the spread and containment of the epidemic, the conferees concluded, advising policymakers to start paying more attention to such factors.[12]

Risk, in other words, is like sex itself: it is made up of acts that are given meaning and relative gravity by social context. Without basic changes in the most encompassing of those contexts (those "structural factors" such as economic, racial, and gender inequality), the AIDS plague will not end. Stagnant social structures are the reason the relatively wealthy, middle-class, urban, gay white male populations of the United States were able to stem the spread of the disease relatively quickly in the 1980s and why today many seropositive men in those communities are living longer, healthier lives with the help of expensive drugs and medical care. It's also why the same thing has not happened among poor people of color, women, and drug addicts in America and Eastern Europe. In Africa, countries already decimated by war and famine now watch their populations stagger while international lawyers adjudicate their "rights" to buy cheaper generic versions of exorbitantly expensive AIDS drugs patented in the global North.

The good news is that social norms even within these stubborn structures can change—if people feel it's in their interest to change and if what they're changing to isn't vastly more onerous than what they are used to doing. The failure of abstinence education may prove less about the intransigence of young people's mores (these can turn on an advertiser-flipped coin) than about the plain fact that sex is more appealing than abstinence. Abstaining promises a definite negative (you don't have sex, and you don't get pregnant or sick) in place of a positive linked only to a possible negative (you do have sex, and you may not get pregnant or sick).

The norm of safe sex has taken hold most firmly where it has represented not a wholesale reversal of already established norms but rather a variation on those norms. Some early gay AIDS activists such as Larry Kramer and Michelangelo Signorelli have since repented of their earlier sexual libertarianism and indicted the "promiscuity" of gay men for their own demise. But other activist-intellectuals such as Douglas Crimp and Jeffrey Weeks argue far more persuasively that the inventive public sexual culture that defined the liberationist gay community also provided the motherlode of techniques from which safe sex was mined and the sexual frankness and intimate networks that got the word out. Similarly, AIDS-prevention workers in distressed communities have adopted the strategy of "harm reduction": they don't try to make drug addicts stop using before getting help, for instance (though they offer treatment when possible). Instead, they promote needle sterilization and clean-needle exchange programs so that intravenous users won't share dirty needles, one of the main transmitters of HIV.

Successful AIDS prevention, then, must be based on at least two principles: It must recognize the urgency of the problem of HIV and the exigencies, both personal and structural, of the people it is targeting. And it must respect their social norms: their identities, values, and desires, expressed in the relationships between individuals and within communities.

To witness sexuality education and HIV prevention where these principles are taken intelligently, creatively, and passionately to heart, I traveled in the spring of 1998 to Minneapolis and St. Paul, Minnesota, where the imperiled yet flourishing communities of gay, lesbian, bisexual, and homeless youths are the recipients of some extraordinary adult care and attention.[13]

As communities go, the Twin Cities are hardly the worst place to be young, gay, homeless, or at risk of dropping out, having a baby, getting HIV, or otherwise losing your way. A slow-moving, leafy metropolis of manageable size, with a history of progressive politics and philanthropy, a well-funded network of social service agencies, a university that has done groundbreaking work on sexuality and AIDS, and a cottage industry of "recovery" facilities, the Twin Cities are also blessed with a committed cadre of gay and lesbian public-health and youth workers. These people are determined to make growing up gay happier and safer for this generation than it was for theirs.

Not everything is perfect in the Twin Cities, of course. There aren't enough beds for homeless kids, for instance. As elsewhere, some of the neediest clients slip through the cracks: by definition runaways and street kids are fliers by night. The majority of youth and AIDS professionals in the Twin Cities are male, white, educated, healthy, and handsome, whereas many of their clients meet few of the above descriptions. State policymakers don't always appear to be on the same page as the workers on the ground. For instance, during the snack break of a student-taught HIV-prevention class run by a drop-in agency for homeless youth called Project Offstreets, the young staffer told me her program was about to lose its funding. Why? Because youth AIDS cases were diminishing in the Twin Cities. "Well duh-uh," commented the frustrated worker. "Maybe prevention is working."

If AIDS prevention is working, why is it? How are the strategies developed over twenty years by progressive grassroots gay and lesbian organizers and public-health educators being applied? What lessons can we take from the Twin Cities about sex and safe-sex education as part of young people's lives?

MEET PEOPLE WHERE THEY ARE: IDENTITY AND EXIGENCY

Out-of-the-closet gay youths have one thing going for them. Whereas abstinence-only sex education gives straight kids the message that sex is not a seminal part of adolescence, when a kid announces his identity in sexual terms, the people around him have no choice but to deal with him as a sexual person. That's both a blessing and a curse.

Coming out can give a kid a secure affiliation, a way to fit into the scheme of things. But the evil twin of affiliation is conformity, and the rigidly homophobic monoculture of the average high school hallway dictates that "queers" be punished—that they be reminded continually that they don't fit anywhere in the scheme. Some states, with Minnesota in the lead, have instituted legal antiharassment policies and student-faculty gay-straight alliances throughout the public schools. Nevertheless, facing ostracism and violence, gay students drop out at high rates.

Family life can be awful for a homosexual child, too. Youth who come out meet with parental grief, confusion, denial, or rage so hot that, for everyone involved, the prospect of the child eating from dumpsters and sleeping under bridges may be preferable to coexisting under the same roof. "My brother says to my mom, 'You have a faggot-ass son,'" said Stephen Graham, a twenty-year-old African American gay activist, recalling his early teens. He was speaking at a sexuality-education conference for teachers run by the young denizens of District 202, Minneapolis's drop-in center run "by and for gay, lesbian, bi, and transgendered youth." "My mom just said to me, 'I can't agree with it. I can't love you.'" Stephen's pastor also branded him a sinner and banished him from the church. The boy ended up in state institutions, in squats, and crashing at friends' places throughout much of his adolescence.

Family hostility, in fact, is a leading cause of homelessness among gay youth. Of 150 youngsters surveyed in 1997 at District 202, 40 percent said they had been homeless at some time.[14] In cities nationwide, 25 to 40 percent of homeless youth identify themselves as gay or lesbian.[15] And what they do when they leave home isn't always the safest things. "Parents' abandonment or overt rejection of homosexual adolescents is partially responsible for the dramatic rise of teen male prostitution in the United States,"

wrote adolescent public-health doctors Martha Sturdevant and Gary Remafedi in a review of the special health needs of homosexual youth.[16] If you're fourteen and can't get a worker's permit or even a driver's license, sex is one of the few services you've got to offer on the labor market. "This may be the most politically unsavvy thing I can say," averred Paul Thoemke, Offstreets' gay lesbian bisexual transsexual (GLBT) case manager. "But I sometimes think the greatest risk for these kids is their families."

It is hardly surprising that among gay and lesbian youth drug and alcohol use is high,[17] and while getting high does not cause people to take risks, people tend to do a number of dangerous and self-destructive things at the same time.[18] Despair plus disinhibition can equal death, as the disproportionate number of gay and lesbian kids in the suicide statistics suggests.[19]

A gay identity can present other, less obvious troubles in growing up and shaping a self. A straight kid's straightness does not box his identity in; he is straight, yes, but mostly he's seen as African American or Filipino or Jewish, a jock or a gangsta or a nerd. But a gay kid is defined by what he is not: he is not straight. That makes it hard even for a securely gay or lesbian teen to express his or her individuality. "Coming out gives kids the freedom to express and explore their sexuality," said Ed Kegle, a youth worker at District 202. "But it's also limiting, because that's the only way other people see you, as 'that little fag' or 'that little dyke.'" A sixteen-year-old lesbian activist summed up the dilemma: "I love being queer," she told me, running a hand through her cherry-red crew cut. "But sometimes I just wanna be Jenny, not Queer Jenny."

Many kids may feel that a gay identity describes them no more accurately than the names they inherited from the communities that expelled them. In one study of seventh- to twelfth-graders in Mineapolis, more than 10 percent said they were unsure of their sexual orientation.[20] "I meet a lot more kids who say they're bi, or just 'sexual,' not homo or hetero," said Rob Yaeger, the high-wattage risk-reduction educator for the community-based Minnesota AIDS Project and member of the Safer Sex Sluts. Courie Parker, a District 202 youth who identifies herself as bisexual, described her orientation this way: "There are the consonants and the vowels—a, e, i, o, u, and sometimes y. That's me: *sometimes y*.'"

The dangers of coming out and teens' disinclination to join one sexual "team" or another can flummox those who are trying to deliver culturally specific or community-based safe-sex education to them. This is especially true when the adults, like those in Minneapolis, come from strongly gay-identified politics, social circles, and even career paths. One way everyone seems to have dealt with this fluidity of identity is to classify it as an "identity," too. In the lengthening train of labels attached to "queer" youth, GLBTQ, the Q stands not for "queer" but for "questioning." In a sense, it's a description that could fit almost every teenager.

Of course, sexuality is not the only way that people identify themselves. Even if their parents may sometimes regard them as foundlings, queer youngsters are not born in some independent offshore Queer Nation and imported to Boston's Italian American South Side or Utah's Mormon Salt Lake City. Nor do all kids reject their religious or ethnic communities of origin, even when some people in those communities reject them. The best safe-sex education takes into account the complex interplay of identities and loyalties in any given person or group.

In the African American community of north Minneapolis, a group of young women and men calling themselves the Check Yo'self Crew got started producing one poster with the slogans "Check yo'self before you wreck yo'self," "Educate your mind, protect your body," and "No parachute, no jump" emblazoned over a photo of a bunch of hip-looking black kids. After their poster won an award, they got grants to put up six billboards of the same image and message, and then they hunkered down in the neighborhood, channeling gangs' energy into HIV peer education and establishing a free condom source on every block. A similar project was later undertaken in a Latino community in town.

Some of the smartest and most moving culturally specific HIV/AIDS youth work in the Twin Cities is masterminded by the Minnesota American Indian Task Force. Its Director is Sharon Day, a forty-six-year-old Ojibwa Indian, out lesbian, mother of two, and custodial grandmother of one. "We need to understand what has allowed us native people to survive since time began," Day told me in a voice as soft and tough as chamois. Her theater work began with that and related questions. "If the birth rate is an indication of the frequency of the sex act," she reasoned, Native Americans' high birth rate "shows we haven't gotten so depressed that we've lost that ability to be sexual. Why is that?" Western psychological models don't explain it. Even if parents are alcoholic or otherwise "dysfunctional," Native American children like herself have survived intact by gleaning intimacy and security from the extended family and the wider community. In directing the task force's youth theater troupe, which travels to community centers, schools, and reservations statewide, doing AIDS-awareness plays, Day said "We are trying to recapture those traditions and expressions that have kept our people emotionally and sexually healthy."

My Grandmother's Love, written by Day in collaboration with the young actors, is one part family soap opera, one part Native American vision quest, one part safe-sex agit-prop political propaganda skit. It opens with four boys beating one large drum and chanting the traditional men's songs in their high children's voices. Then it moves to short reminiscences about grandmothers, whose photos are projected onto a large screen. "She's a good cook, her hair is all black, no gray," one boy says. "She's a basic grandma." The main story concerns a gay college boy (played by an androgynous fourteen-year-old girl) who returns home to tell his family he is HIV positive. "You little faggot!" the father explodes, pounding his fist on the kitchen table.

Scared and depressed, the young man withdraws. But he is sustained, and finally restored, by his grandmother's unconditional love and a dream-vision of running to safety. In the final scene, the group chants his vision—"I have been to the brink, to the rim of the canyon. I've looked over the edge. It's not so scary to me anymore"— and asks the audience to pray for the ill. Family, spirituality, community, said Day: "This is what has enabled native people to survive, gay or straight."

By the same token, Day knows that as much as sex education must focus on specific cultural beliefs and practices, it must also be catholic enough to accommodate young people who fall victim to those same beliefs and practices. Stephen Graham, the gay boy rejected by his pastor, for instance, was lucky to find another African American church whose dogma and liturgy resembled his old congregation's, with the major difference that this one embraced him, sexuality and all. Other gay youth have felt driven more radically from their faith communities by antagonism toward homosexuality, so they've had to find other sources to satisfy their spiritual needs. In the 1997 District 202 survey, almost every respondent filled in the blank under religious affiliation. But the largest single group called themselves Pagan.

DON'T BOX PEOPLE IN: THE "RISK-GROUP" FALLACY

Identities are multiple. Their facets sometimes harmonize; at other times they are dissonant. In AIDS prevention, the challenge is to find people where they affiliate and speak to their sense of belonging for the purpose of instilling and reinforcing safe-sex values and habits. But the construction of categories can also be perilous. Indeed, the error (some say the fatal error) of AIDS prevention over the past two decades has been its strategy of labeling groups of people, not as potentially powerful allies in fighting the

disease, but as collections of mutually antagonistic virus-carrying harm-spreaders, or "risk groups."

The first decade of public-health AIDS education told us there were two kinds of people in the world of AIDS. The "high-risk groups" included gay men, Haitian immigrants, and intravenous drug users and their sex partners and babies. These people used to be called AIDS victims but were actually thought of as AIDS victimizers. In the "low- or no-risk groups" were suburban teens, heterosexuals, white Yuppies—as Patton put it, the people who qualified as bona fide "citizens." Prevention for the "low-risk" folks meant avoiding the poisonous populations, first, by steering clear of people who looked suspicious and, second, by practicing "partner selection": interrogating potential partners for their possible inclusion or interaction with "high-risk" persons and rejecting those who might be "unsafe" lovers.[21] Teens did not have to perform this discretionary process. They were instructed to say no to everyone.

The concept of the risk group helped neither presumptive group. The people supposedly inside it were either stigmatized (and neglected by policymakers) for their allegedly self-destructive lifestyles or ignored. Some of those relegated to this status used it as a powerful political motivator—ACT UP emerged from gay men's rage at being excluded as legitimate recipients of health care resources. For others, however, being branded "at risk" only induced fatalism. The idea that one is likely to die simply by virtue of being a certain kind of person does not concentrate the mind wonderfully on life-saving strategies. And for already hurt people, this new denigration only compounded hopelessness. "Individuals who have been at high risk," like kids who have been abused, lived on the streets, or turned tricks, "are likely to see themselves as at risk of getting HIV," said Gary Remafedi, Director of the University of Minnesota's Youth & AIDS Project. "Or they'll say, 'I'm gay. It's inevitable I'm gonna die. So what?'" According to Jeffrey Escoffier, a New York public educator, sociologist, and AIDS activist, research shows that gay men who learn that all gay-associated sex, including fellatio, is equally fatal come to believe they are doomed, so they engage in more of the riskiest behaviors. In one San Francisco survey of seventeen- to nineteen-year-old men who have sex with men, 28 percent had recently had unprotected anal sex, the behavior carrying the highest risk for HIV transmission;[22] in a six-city study of young gay men of color, almost half had done so in the preceding six months.[23]

For people both "inside" and "outside," however, the risk-group theory had a profound flaw: *there is no such thing as a discrete social-sexual population.* No group is an island; all risk is shared, potentially, with a limitless universe of partners. While in America most people travel in social ruts, apart from other races and classes, not even the most insular, cautious people always stay in those ruts. Drug users don't congregate only in crack houses; they also frequent trendy nightclubs. And a man who has unprotected sex with a seropositive teenage hustler in a downtown city park may have sex the next day with a guy he knows from a neighborhood bar, and that guy will have sex with his middle-class suburban wife the next.

One way to circumvent the hazards of the risk-group assumption, while being realistic about the fact that it's been drummed into everybody's head, is to use it to get people's attention, then redirect their thinking. Rather than choosing or rejecting certain people or "kinds" of people, specific *behaviors* can be rejected. As a pamphlet displayed with a couple dozen others on District 202's wall put it: "Being young and gay does NOT have to mean being at risk for HIV & AIDS.... But being unsafe does."

Taking a kernel of wisdom from the "risk-group" concept—that individuals within certain social or sexual groups may more commonly engage in behaviors that can transmit HIV—and tempering it with the understanding of the fluidity of communities and individual diversity within them, AIDS-prevention professionals

have lately conceived the notion of "target populations." These comprise not people who are "by nature" risk-prone but those who live in situations of high risk, say, in a neighborhood or social circle a large number of whose members are seropositive. Most important, educators identify these populations by sexual behavior: not by how they dress, where they drink, or what they call themselves, but by what acts they do. MSM, for example, is HIV/AIDS shorthand for "men who have sex with men, a category that takes in both the Puerto Rican husband and father who lives in upper Manhattan but occasionally goes to a bar in the Bronx and has sex with a man and the teenage Anglo who dies his hair green and marches in the Castro Street Gay Pride parade in a goatee and tutu."

In Minneapolis, I watched numerous AIDS-ed workers in various settings, from off-the-cuff conversations in a scruffy city park to the makeshift stage in a Native American cultural center, from a peer-run class in a high school for returning dropouts to sex-and AIDS-ed sessions at District 202. In all of these, instructors started with the acts they believed their students might engage in, making these broadest determinations by the group's sexual or age identity or perhaps its religious or ethnic affiliation. But they assumed nothing about the specifics of any individual's predilections. A lesbian group at District 202 discussed the use of a square of latex called a dental dam that can be laid over a partner's vagina before performing cunnilingus. At the Center's conference for teachers, a quick safe-sex rap by the twenty-year-old peer educator Toyin Adebanjo reminded the audience not to forget such youth-specific contaminated-blood risks as body piercing and tattooing. At the same time, the woman addressing the young lesbians talked about contraceptive and safe-sex precautions for penile-vaginal intercourse. And a youth worker addressing fifteen-year-olds did not neglect information on the HIV transmission risks of breast feeding.

Gary Remafedi, who educates young gay men, described the balance of the main message, identity, and personal taste this way: "One message is, 'Always use condoms while you're fucking.' But that assumes that every gay man fucks. So the other message is, 'Fucking is not a fundamental part of being a gay man. Not everyone likes it. And everyone can enjoy safe sex behavior that is not intercourse.'"

RESPECT PEOPLE'S CHOICES AS RATIONAL

A fair number of the youngsters who find their way to Offstreets, District 202, or Remafedi's program at the university either regularly or occasionally turn to prostitution to get by. In the risk-benefit calculus of life on the street, sex is both a plus and a minus.[24] "Survival sex"—sex in trade for a bed, a shower, or a pair of shoes— may also offer some personal rewards, such as adult companionship and affirmation. And like other adult-minor sex, it is not always an interaction of utter abjection on the young person's side. "A lot of the youth don't see survival sex as prostitution," said Ludfi Noor, the easy-going Director of Offstreets' HIV education. Added Gonne (pronounced "Honnah") Asser, a young outreach worker, "This youth was talking the other day, saying, 'I was going to clubs and getting lucky. Older people wanted to have sex with me.'" Of the here-to-day-gone-tomorrow relationships between youngsters and adults, she added, "It can be a relationship that lasts a week, but to the kid, it's still a relationship."

Of course, prostitution without even that rudimentary relationship poses its own risks. Working girls (and boys) have long adopted their own health and safety practices, notably condom use. Among homeless youth, it appears that when the trick is a stranger, condom use is also the rule.[25] No educator should underestimate a young person's ability to make informed decisions about sex. To make informed decisions, though, people need information, and

some AIDS experts argue that what they need is the kind of detailed information about risk that is available throughout most of Europe but that U.S. Health Departments are reluctant to give out. Rather than listing acts as either safe or unsafe, period, so-called relative-risk data disseminated in Paris or Berlin tell you that such-and-such behavior has led to HIV transmission in a particular number of known cases in this or that country, or that findings about this other behavior are still inconclusive. Armed with such data, people can make choices about their sex lives in the same way they craft the rest of their lives: by weighing desires and rewards against dangers and unwanted consequences.

That said, there are a lot of reasons not to put on a rubber if you're a young person selling or bartering sex. Sex without a condom demands a higher price than sex with one, so taking a higher risk per trick in order to turn fewer tricks overall may feel like a reasonable business decision. (Other considerations go into the equation, too: receiving fellatio, a fairly common act of male prostitution, is of extremely low risk to the receptor. For a young woman in heterosexual sex, the opposite is true: as the giver of oral sex and the receiver of vaginal intercourse, she takes practically all the risk of HIV and other STD transmission.)[26]

A homeless kid turning a trick may not protect himself or herself for some subtler and sadder reasons as well. Such youngsters typically have been the victims of inordinate violence; "more than half have been physically abused, more than one-third, sexually abused, more than one-third beaten by an intimate partner during the last year," said a report of Minneapolis's gay, lesbian, bisexual, and transgender homeless youth conducted by the Wilder Research Center in 1996.[27] About once a week, said Paul Thoemke, a girl comes into Offstreets and says she's been raped. For people who have been treated with routine cruelty, particularly by their "loved" ones, self-care can be a foreign concept. "A lot of women and girls don't see sex as a source of pleasure or their bodies as something they have control over," noted Beth Zemsky, a lesbian AIDS educator who works on gay and lesbian student issues at the University of Minnesota. Ine Vanwesenbeeck, in a study of sexual power and powerlessness among Dutch prostitutes and other young women, found that those who capitulated to johns' demands that they forgo a condom were more often younger, drug users, and immigrants and "had experienced more victimization, both in childhood and in adult life, both on and off the job." Once they'd become known as "risk takers," they were "most often visited by recalcitrant condom users."[28]

AIDS prevention for the street kids of the Twin Cities, then, means more than pressing a bundle of condoms into a hustler's tight jeans pocket. "So many of the youth I work with have been treated in such a disrespectful way, they can't respect themselves," said Youth & AIDS Project caseworker Jerry Terrell. "A third of the people I see are suicidal, a fifth are actively using chemicals, and then for the homeless youth, there's no tomorrow; everything is today. The main thing is helping them to imagine that there is a future and beginning to get a toehold in whatever that might be. HIV is at the end of a long line of other issues."

Those issues are both emotional and material. When the Wilder researchers queried homeless youth on what would really make a difference in their lives, their sights usually focused somewhere between hand and mouth. Several suggested access to a free washing machine. "I can wear dirty clothes, pants, shirts, and stuff," said one girl. "As long as I can have clean underwear, I'm okay." Under such circumstances, safe sex can be a rather abstract and distant notion. "Safety means finding a bed tonight," explained Amber Hollibaugh, former Head of the Lesbian AIDS Project at GMHC in New York. "Putting on a condom is not exactly the Number One priority."[29]

Still, risk taking should not be considered a symptom of pathology, as it so often is among teachers, adolescent psychologists, and

public-health professionals. Instead, said Jeffrey Escoffier: "People are also doing a rational assessment of their environments. They tally the odds." On the street, kids know their lives are by definition unsafe, that they can't eliminate all risk. So the task is to figure out the route of greatest reward—financial, practical, emotional—with the least endangerment along the way. It is the job of prevention workers to understand that calculus, too, and help young people incrementally refigure the emotional and material factors so that they can make more self-protective decisions in their sexual behavior and stick to them. In "sex education" with his young hustlers, Jerry Terrell told me, "most of what I do is not about sexuality."

RETHINK ALL ASSUMPTIONS: PLEASURE, LOVE, AND TRUST

Street kids are not another species. Even for them, sex is not all work, exploitation, or pain. "Sex is nice, it's intimate, it's fun, it doesn't cost anything," Project Offstreets' Thoemke said, in answer to my question about the role of pleasure in his clients' lives. "These kids, not having close relationships with their families, or if they were abused, sex was a really awful thing. To find sex as a pleasure, that's so great." He grumbled at the relentless Lutheran-ness of the bureaucrats who check up on his agency. "They come in, and they're appalled that we have condoms available at our front door or the kids are watching cartoons or smoking cigarettes." Homeless kids carry all the responsibilities of adult independence, he reasoned. Why not get a few of the perquisites? He paused. "But sex is the easiest thing in the world. It's love that's hard to find."

The personality structures and circumstances of disenfranchised youths vex the already difficult search for love. On one hand, as abused or rejected children, they are desperate to love, to plunge into trusting. On the other, as abused or rejected children-turned-street rats, they are trained in mistrust, and touchy, sometimes paranoid. They want stability and monogamy, yet they are also hot to try out their sexuality, sometimes with many partners (these last two contradictory desires are often split by gender, with girls and women rushing to the altar, so to speak, and boys and men reveling in sexual novelty, variety, and quantity). On balance, though, homeless boys and girls want what everyone wants, Thoemke insists: love *and* sex, plus a measure of security—"a permanent partner and not to worry about how the bills will get paid."

Love? A permanent partner? Regular bill paying? These wishes would bring sunshine to the hearts of the bureaucrats at Offstreets' door or to the abstinence-until-marriage campaigners, who claim that a committed relationship is the best and only prophylactic against AIDS. But the fact is, love is no fortress against sexual risk. One of the biggest paradoxes of HIV prevention is that love—not just careless love, but also love that is desperately coveted and conscientiously nurtured—may compound the dangers of sex. Contrary to the propaganda that advertises the perils of the backroom or the bathhouse, *people, both gay and straight, are more likely to have unsafe sex inside a committed, loving relationship than in casual encounters.*[30] Trust, conceived in the way we currently conceive it, can be "a risky practice."[31]

"One of the most striking and consistent findings of behavioral research on gay men is that high-risk sex is more frequently reported with someone described as a 'regular partner or lover,'" wrote the British medical sociologist Graham Hart. In a study of 677 men, Hart and his colleagues found that "unprotected intercourse...was a way of expressing the love and commitment to a shared life that the men felt."[32] Sarah Phillips's survey of heterosexual adolescents' condom use came to similar conclusions: "[B]oth young men and women who claimed to be in love with their partners were significantly more likely to agree to sexual intercourse without a condom than were those who reported that they were not in love."[33] The certainty that the other person is perfectly monogamous is

viewed, by people of all classes, as an automatic right conferred in loving that person. "Once I'm married, that's it," declared Keisha, a seventeen year-old Minneapolis peer educator, ramming a firm fist into her hip and raising an instructing finger to face height. "If he brings me home AIDS, then I have a right to kill him." If the implicit agreement of Keisha's marriage is that her husband knows he'll be "killed" if he admits to having been unfaithful—and therefore feels he can't tell her—then he may end up killing her too, only more slowly.

Although many definitions of trust cross gender lines, those that do not tend to put women at a disadvantage. "There was a strong shared understanding that 'steady' relationships are based on trust," wrote the psychologist Carla Willig, paraphrasing the conclusions of some researchers who interviewed inner-city young women. "At the same time [the women] identified a tendency to define a relationship as 'steady' in order to justify sex. Since discontinuation of condom use can signify increasing commitment to a relationship, condom use within 'steady' relationships is difficult to maintain." Among a group of Canadian college students, "for women [the implicit compact between committed lovers] meant trusting that one's partner would disclose relevant information, and for men it meant trusting that one's partner had nothing to disclose. As a result, women found it very difficult to request condom use from partners whom they knew well, but ironically, 'they were most able to protect themselves from all three dangers—pregnancy, disease, and emotional hurt—in casual encounters.'"[34] The prejudice that respectable girls are nonsexual (except with the current partner), moreover, makes safe sex additionally difficult for young women. Planned HIV prevention can give a girl a bad reputation, sex educator Rob Yaeger said. "Girls say, 'If I pull out a condom, he'll think I'm a slut.'" Because women are far more likely to contract HIV from a male partner than vice versa, and young women's vaginal linings are more fragile than mature women's and therefore additionally infection-prone, these gendered assumptions endanger young women disproportionately.

For many people, simply bringing up the subject of protection is so threatening to trust that trust requires absolute censorship. Some of the people Willig interviewed went so far as to say that requiring long-term couples to start talking about or, worse, using condoms would mean an irreparable rent in the social fabric. "I mean there's got to be some sort of element of trust somewhere," said a young man named John, "unless life as we know it ain't gonna happen."[35]

True love is monogamous, trust depends on monogamy and monogamy on trust, and trust is the cornerstone of love: unfortunately, from the point of view of the sexually transmitted virus, this formulation is heavy with potential dangers. First, although statistics vary widely depending on the surveyor, the way the questions are asked, and the sexuality of the subjects, at least a significant number of married and committed couples stray at least once, at least a third of teens do,[36] and even youths who are monogamous are only serially so.[37] Meanwhile, fewer than 60 percent of sexually active adolescent boys who use only condoms say they use them every time.[38]

Yet many of these people predicate their relationship on unerring fidelity. That sets up an untenable dilemma: the confession of a lapse fatally threatens the relationship, but keeping a secret fatally threatens both the person and his or her beloved. Carla Willig's informant John accepted that maintaining a societal and personal contract of trusting silence might mean the sacrifice of a few "innocent victims" whose partners committed crimes of omission.[39] Is the symbolic and moral risk of abandoning loving trust "as we know it" really greater than the risk of rampaging HIV infection? Federally funded abstinence-only education says yes, by teaching, contrary to evidence, that the only safe sex is within a "traditional" committed (read unquestionably monogamous) heterosexual marriage.

Fortunately, some independent AIDS educators are going wholeheartedly in the other direction. "I tell them, *love is not the answer*," said Rob Yaeger. "Love will not protect you. The virus doesn't care if you're in love, if you're married. It doesn't care what your favorite song is." And it doesn't care what your favorite song says love is, either. Given the urgent historical circumstances, a policy of confession and forgiveness when a partner strays from intended monogamy might be *more* loving than censorship enforced by the expectation of rage and rejection. But such ways of relating require less dependency, less jealousy, less unwavering confidence in the other person's ability and willingness to take care of you, and at the same time, more personal maturity, flexibility, independence, and self-esteem, and more altruism from both partners.

Aside from altruism, these emotions are different from the ones we are used to associating with love. Nevertheless, it is these qualities and values, not the blind faith of "true" love and, the hound dog's acuity for "risky" partners, that we need to be nurturing in kids.

CULTIVATE THE BEST VALUES: CREATE BRAVE NEW COMMUNITIES

Plenty of the teens who flow through the agencies where I hung out in Minneapolis and St. Paul are notoriously tough cases. It's hard to get them back to the clinic for a follow-up visit, much less to a GED class or job-training program. District 202 youth volunteer Courie Parker, who has been homeless herself, explained why homeless kids drift further and further from "normalizing," adult-overseen institutions such as school and work. "You can't plug in an alarm clock under a bridge," she said simply.

But exclusion from the mainstream can also engender tight affiliation, and as history has shown for blacks, women, gays, and the disabled, collective survival is the first step toward the creation of a resistant community identity. Homeless youth form scruffy mutual-aid societies, tight little tribes that scavenge food or locate shelter for each other, often moving about with a brace of equally disenfranchised dogs. To the Offstreets kids, group cohesiveness is everything, said Thoemke. "They always want to say 'we.' If we could harness that good energy, we'd have a powerful community."

During the early years of gay liberation, despised communities harnessed the energy of the hatred directed at them and transformed it into pride—for instance, appropriating as flags of distinction the derogatory terms *dyke, faggot,* and *queer.* When the AIDS epidemic hit them, gay men and women turned that energy toward aggressive political confrontation that, for all its outward rage, was fueled by love, both fraternal and erotic. "The AIDS crisis, in all its frightening impact, bearing the burden of fear of disease and death in the wake of pleasure and desire, seems to many to embody the downside of the transformation of sexuality in recent years, a warning of the dangers of things 'going too far,'" wrote the British social critic Jeffrey Weeks. "Yet in many of the responses to it we can see something else: a quickening of humanity, the engagement of solidarity, and the broadening of the meanings of love, love in the face of death."[40]

Self-love and self-esteem are necessary to practicing safe sex. But this history speaks of love that goes beyond the self and even beyond the beloved. This is *communal* love, a kind of modern agape, based in shared pride of identity and collective self-defense and practiced within circles of personal friendship and desire. *Love and loyalty, the same feelings that can discourage safe sex, can also motivate it.* People care about their communities even when their communities are hostile to them, and they put on a condom with that caring in mind. "When people are asked why they practice safe sex," said Jeffrey Escoffier, "one of the main reasons they give is altruism." He cited a study of gay Latino men, done by the Rafael Diaz Center for AIDS Prevention Studies in San Francisco. "The most common response was, 'There are people who count on me.'" Escoffier noted that the people who depend on

those men were not necessarily part of any gay community but rather family members, friends, and neighbors in their Latino communities of origin. What this study and others uncovered, he said, was "a high level of integration even into a community that they feel ambivalent about. A lot of [HIV] prevention aims at self-interest," he concluded. "That's a mistake."

America has made many grievous mistakes in trying to protect its children from the dangers of sex. Underlying these errors is fear. Some is "good" fear, that they will be sickened or traumatized, will lose their direction, their ambition, their sense of self. But much is fear of eros, to which we attribute anarchic, obliterating power—the power to destroy individuals and civilization itself.

Yet eros is not a wild animal prowling outside the civilizing meanings we assign it, beyond the moralities with which we govern it. We create eros for ourselves and for our children; it is we who teach our young the meanings and moralities of sex. In the age of AIDS, we must invent new iterations of the best old values, creating new expressions of love, trust, loyalty, and mutual protection. Inspired and sheltered by the values of caring, young people can discover their sexual power without dominating or diminishing others; they can find romance without surrendering self-protection. They can arrive at the divine oblivion of sex consciously, with responsibility, forethought, and consent.

While laboring to vanquish AIDS and the conditions that abet it, we must remember what we were taught by the gay and lesbian heroes of one of modern sexuality's most terrible epochs. The infinite gifts of the erotic can empower people and unite communities. The embrace of pleasure can be the greatest defense against peril.

References

1. Cindy Patton, *Fatal Advice: How Safe-Sex Education Went Wrong.* (Durham, NC: Duke University Press, 1996), 34.

2. Bill Alexander, "Adolescent HIV Rates Soar; Government Piddles," *Youth Today* (March/April 1997): 29.

3. Lawrence K. Altman, "AIDS Deaths Drop 48% in New York," *New York Times*, February 3, 1998, A1.

4. Philip J. Hilts, "AIDS Deaths Continue to Rise in 25–44 Age Group, U.S. Says," *New York Times*, January 16, 1996, A22.

5. Centers for Disease Control, Atlanta, Ga., March 1996.

6. Interview with Gary Remafedi, Director of the University of Minnesota/Minneapolis Youth & AIDS Project, 1998.

7. "Rate of AIDS Has Slowed," *New York Times*, April 25, 1998, A9.

8. Lawrence K. Altman, "Study in 6 Cities Finds HIV in 30% of Young Black Gays," *New York Times*, February 6, 2001.

9. Cherrie B. Boyer and Susan M. Kegeles, "AIDS Risk and Prevention among Adolescents," *Social Science Medicine* 33, no. 1 (1991): 11–23.

10. New York City Health Department, phone interview, April 1999.

11. Barbara Crossette, "In India and Africa, Women's Low Status Worsens Their Risk of AIDS," *New York Times*, February 26, 2001 [sic].

12. B. R. Simon Rossner, "New Directions in HIV Prevention," *SIECUS Report 26* (December 1997/January 1998): 6.

13. The following remarks from people in the Twin Cities came from interviews that I conducted during my visit there in 1998.

14. *District 202 Youth Survey* (Minneapolis, 1997).

15. *District 202 Youth Survey*.

16. Marsha S. Sturdevant and Gary Remafedi, "Special Health Needs of Homosexual Youth," in *Adolescent Medicine: State of the Art Reviews* (Philedelphia: Hanley and Belfus, 1992), 364.

17. R. Stall and J. Wiley, "A Comparison of Alcohol and Drug Use Patterns of Homosexual and Heterosexual Men: The San Francisco Men's Health Study," *Drug and Alcohol Dependence* 22 (1988): 63–73.

18. Marina McNamara, "Adolescent Behavior II. Socio-Psychological Factors," *Advocates for Youth Fact Sheet*, Washington, D.C., September 1997 [sic].

19. Alan Bell and Martin Weinberg, *Homosexualities* (New York: Simon and Schuster, 1978).

20. Gary Remadefi, Michael Resnick, Robert Blum, and Linda Harris, "Demography of Sexual Orientation in Adolescents," *Pediatrics* 89, no. 4 (April 1992).

21. Patton, *Fatal Advice*.

22. U.S. Conference of Mayors, "Safer Sex Relapse: A Contemporary Challenge," *AIDS Information Exchange* 11, no. 4 (1994): 1–8.

23. Altman, "Study in 6 Cities."

24. D. Boyer, "Male Prostitution and Homosexual Identity," *Journal of Homosexuality* 9(1984): 105.

25. S.L. Bailey et al., "Substance Use and Risky Sexual Behavior Among Homeless and Runaway Youth," *Journal of Adolescent Health* 23 (December 1998): 378–388.

26. Amy Bracken, "STDs Discriminate," *Youth Today* (March 2001): 7–8.

27. *Minnesota's Youth Without Homes* (St. Paul: Wilder Research Center, 1997), 5.

28. Ine Vanwesenbeeck, "The Context of Women's Power(lessness) in Heterosexual Interactions," in *New Sexual Agendas*, ed. Lynne Segal (New York: New York University Press, 1997), 173.

29. Author interview, New York, 1999.

30. E. Matinka-Tyndale, "Sexual Scripts and AIDS Prevention: Variations in Adherence to Safer Sex Guidelines in Heterosexual Adolescents," *Journal of Sex Research* 28 (1991): 45–66.

31. Carla Willig, "Trust as a Risky Practice," in *New Sexual Agendas*, ed. Segal, 125–135.

32. Graham Hart, "'Yes, but Does It Work?' Impediments to Rigorous Evaluations of Gay Men's Health Promotion," in *New Sexual Agendas*, ed. Segal, 119.

33. Sarah R. Phillips, "Turning Research into Policy: A Survey on Adolescent Condom Use," *SIECUS Report* (October/November 1995): 10.

34. Willig, "Trust as a Risky Practice," 126.

35. Willig, "Trust as a Risky Practice," 130.

36. Pepper Schwartz and Philip Blumstein, *American Couples: Money, Work, Sex* (New York: Pocket Books, 1983).

37. Susan L. Rosenthal et al., "Heterosexual Romantic Relationships and Sexual Behaviors of Young Adolescent Girls," *Journal of Adolescent Health* 21 (1997): 238–243.

38. Freya L. Sonenstein and Joseph H. Pleck et al., "Change in Sexual Behavior and Contraception among Adolescent Males: 1998 and 1995," *Urban Institue Report*, Washington, D.C., 1996 [sic].

39. Willig, "Trust as a Risky Practice," 130.

40. Jeffrey Weeks, *Invented Moralities: Sexual Values in an Age of Uncertainty* (New York: Columbia University Press, 1995), 42.

CHAPTER 48

Sex Education and the News

Lessons from How Journalists Framed Virginity Pledges

Felicia E. Mebane
Eileen A. Yam
Barbara K. Rimer

Our view of the world is strongly influenced by various media (television, films, newspapers, books, the Internet, etc.). News stories provide an interpretation of various events and phenomena and often impact the way we think about an issue. If you enter the term "virginity pledge" into an Internet search engine, you will encounter thousands of news stories discussing the concept, the effectiveness, and the pervasiveness of these public affirmations to refrain from sexual intercourse until marriage. Felicia Mebane, Eileen Yam, and Barbara Rimer undertook the huge task of analyzing news stories on virginity pledges over a 14-year period in order to determine what approaches or "frames" were used in the stories.

According to Gamson, Croteau, Hoynes, and Sasson (1992),

> *Participants in symbolic contests read their success or failure by how well their preferred meanings and interpretation are doing in various media arenas. . . . Essentially, sponsors of different frames monitor media discourse to see how well it tells the story they want told, and they measure their success or failure accordingly. (p. 385)*

With regard to virginity pledges, there are clearly at least two different "sponsors": Those for whom the pledges appear to be the solution to the perceived problem of adolescent sexual activity and those who worry that the pledges will be ineffective, leaving teens more vulnerable to unprotected sexual activity than if they had not pledged to remain a virgin. But wait: if each position is viewed as a solution by some and a problem by others, how are the facts weighed? The answer is usually with great difficulty.

After learning what Mebane et al. discovered about the news media's framing of virginity pledges and the impact that it may have on public perception, you will probably never look at news coverage quite the same way. To test this theory, read the following paragraph.

"Hold the press!" shouts the Editor of the Daily News *as still another story reporting virginity*

From "Sex Education and the News: Lessons from How Journalists Framed Virginity Pledges" by F. E. Mebane E. A. Yam, and B. K. Rimer. 2006. *Journal of Health Communication* 11: 583–606. Reprinted by permission of the publisher (Taylor & Francis, http://www.informaworld.com).

pledge outcomes moves across the wire services. The newspaper headline reads, "New findings challenge the belief of true believers in virginity pledges." The reporter opines, "Rosenbaum (2009) concludes that virginity pledgers are as likely to have premarital sexual intercourse as nonpledgers, and less likely to use condoms or other contraception if they do have intercourse before marriage." And, his column concludes, "We can anticipate that supporters of the Virginity Movement will cast aspersions upon the latest study, as they have with others, claiming methodological flaws."

While the research is real in the above paragraph, the wire service news account is bogus. It is used here to illustrate the message being conveyed in this chapter, that the different frames (i.e., approaches) used in reporting an incident influence our thinking about the subject. Re-read the bogus news story, and then answer these questions. Would you judge the writer of the above piece to be a supporter or opponent of virginity pledges? Which sentence justifies your answer? At what point did you begin to understand the writer's preferred meanings and interpretations? Do you think the sponsor of these "frames" measures the story as successful? By sharing your opinions with your classmates, a spirited discussion should follow concerning the merits and demerits of media coverage.

———

The negative consequences of the sexual behaviors of American youth remain a serious health concern in the United States. Teenage birth rates in the United States are higher than those of other Western industrialized nations, and out-of-wedlock births account for 7 of 10 births to American women under age 20 (Ozer, Brindis, Millstein, Knopf, & Irwin, 1998). Teenage parents are less likely to complete school and more likely to end up on welfare than nonchildbearing teens. The children of teenage parents tend to have less supportive home environments, more behavioral problems, and poorer health (Kirby, 2001).

One of the most heated, ongoing reproductive health debates is how to prevent unwanted teen pregnancies and the resulting negative consequences. While most people may agree on the goal of reducing the number of unplanned pregnancies among teens, researchers, religious leaders, youth advocates, educators, and parents often differ sharply about what strategies and policies should be used to achieve this common goal. The contention surrounding sex education is a case in point. Sex education curricula may include a comprehensive range of approaches to prevent pregnancy (abstinence as well as contraception) or focus on one message only (abstinence as the only option outside of marriage). Supporters of comprehensive sexuality education contend that teaching about contraceptives and condom use delays the onset of sexual intercourse and reduces high-risk behaviors that contribute to teen pregnancies (Landry, Kaeser, & Richards, 1999). Proponents of the abstinence-only approach argue that teaching about contraception sends a contradictory message, in essence promoting sexual activity under the auspices of an educational curriculum that claims to encourage abstinence (Howell, 2001).

Another factor that complicates sex education choices is the various levels at which these strategies are being considered. On a personal level, individual families and religious congregations, for example, are directly affected by teen pregnancies, and they often promote preventive programs motivated by personal experiences and values. In the public arena, policymakers, parents, public health experts, and others concerned about the sexual and moral health of today's adolescents grapple with how to most cost effectively use government resources to address the problem. Throughout the country, local school boards have held hearings to address the adoption of comprehensive sex education curricula. In 2003, the federal government allocated $117 million to support abstinence-only education programs, an increase of about 1000% over the past 22 years (The National Campaign to Prevent Teen Pregnancy, 2003); and school systems are deciding whether to allow school nurses to refer students to clinics that provide contraception. Although teen pregnancy currently is not the top issue that Americans want governments to address, it is clearly a public health and policy issue with which governments, families, and individuals at all levels are grappling.

The decision of what to teach youth about sex as part of school curricula is made more complex by a lack of consensus in the scientific community about the efficacy of various public health programs designed to change teens' sexual behaviors and reduce teen pregnancies. For example, while abstinence advocates tout research studies showing the positive impact of abstinence-only programs, detractors point to the methodological weaknesses of these studies. Increasingly, this type of evidence-based disagreement is addressed via a credible evidence review conducted using well-accepted procedures by an appropriate team. Unfortunately, on the topic of sex education, there is no guidance in this regard. We did not find reviews conducted by the U.S. Preventive Services Task Force (2005) or the Centers for Disease Control and Prevention's *Guide to Community Preventive Services* (2005) that definitively determine the impact of abstinence-only programs. Thus, although research is underway to investigate the effectiveness of different sex education programs, taken as a whole, the currently available data are inconclusive. In other words, some studies show a positive effect for virginity pledges or abstinence programs and some data do not.

In the vacuum left by a lack of scientific consensus on how to most effectively affect teens' sexual behavior, policymakers make sex education policy decisions in the context of public discussions and debates that consider a range of factors and perspectives. Because the problem of teen pregnancies involves highly charged topics, such as sex, teens, morals, and religion, it attracts the attention of a wide range of groups that have a stake in how the problem is addressed. These debates often pit public health experts or health care professionals against religious groups, with both sides disseminating information to promote their preferred approaches. Thus, the outcome of these sex education policy debates depends, in part, on how successful stakeholders are in promoting their respective perspectives and arguments (scientific evidence or religious principles) for consideration by the public and policymakers.

This study is motivated by the conviction that government policies on sex education should be informed, at least in part, by scientific evidence. While we recognize that multifaceted debates involving teens, sex, and pregnancy often must take into account several potentially conflicting considerations, including religious and political, we argue that all discussions of sex education alternatives should include at least a reference to the related research on their likely public health impacts. Even noting a lack of consensus on the impact of such programs would allow policymakers and the public to incorporate the best available scientific evidence among the other equally important values and principles that form the basis of public policies.

One approach to determine whether discussions about topics related to teens' sexual behaviors are being informed by scientific evidence is to examine the messages disseminated by a key source of information for policymakers and the public: news organizations. News outlets are an important source of policy information because they reach large audiences, and news messages can influence how the general public and other political actors view policies on issues such as sex education.

Although news consumption has fallen over the past decade, millions of American adults regularly attend to the news (The Pew Research Center for the People and the Press, 2004). In 2004, 59% of adults regularly watched local television news; about one-third regularly watched nightly network news. Forty-two percent of adults read a newspaper on the day prior to the survey, and 29% accessed news on-line at least three times a week.

More specifically, millions of Americans use mass media for health, medical, and health policy news. In 1997, 40% of Americans relied on television as their primary source of medical and health news. Similarly, 72% of Americans said they relied on television for nutrition information (American Dietetic Association, 2002).

In addition, each year the Kaiser Family Foundation (KFF) conducts several surveys in which they ask respondents from the general public how closely they have been following news stories on health and non-health-related topics tracked by the KFF. In 2003, the KFF's summary of these Health News Interest Index polls showed that public health and health policy stories were of interest to the general public. According to their surveys conducted between 1996 and 2002, adults followed *very closely* 20%, 17% and 14% of public health, disease/medical stories, and health policy stories, respectively. By comparison, adults followed *very closely* 34% of top non-health news stories (Brodie, Hamel, Altman, Blendon, & Benson, 2003). In sum, news messages on public health topics are conveyed to millions of Americans each day through a variety of media, and millions of Americans pay attention to them.

Once public health messages are disseminated, how they are presented or "framed" influences what attributes of these issues are readily available when the public is asked for their opinions. The highlighted attributes then are used to help the public decide what issues governments should address and how (Andsager & Powers, 1999; Iyengar, 1991; Rogers Dearing, & Chang, 1991). Numerous studies have demonstrated connections between news frames and support for public policy solutions (Huebner, Fan, & Finnegan, 1997; Menashe & Siegel, 1998; Ryan, 1991; Wallack et al., 1993). In the final link to policy outcomes, news influences public opinion polls about the public's priorities, and these opinions become part of the input policymakers use to adopt policy positions. In sum, by presenting particular interpretations of problems and policies, news frames can form the basis for public policy decisions (Wallack, Dorfman, Jernigan, & Themba, 1993).

For example, "a majority of the public supports the rights of persons with AIDS when the issue is framed [in a survey question] to accentuate civil liberties considerations—and supports as well mandatory testing when the issue is framed to accentuate public health considerations" (Sniderman, Brody, & Tetlock, 1991, p. 52). This kind of shift in support based on a change in the framing of an issue can dramatically shift policy outcomes. In a similar example, the Jacobson and colleagues (1993) study of antismoking legislation in six states shows that legislative outcomes favored antismoking advocates when public health issues dominated debates, and that statewide antismoking legislation stalled when debates shifted to personal freedoms. In conclusion, to maximize the likelihood that public policies will be based on scientific evidence about which sex education strategies should reduce teen pregnancies, we must be sure that news reports include public health frames on the evidence.

In addition to demonstrating how issue frames can affect policy outcomes, several of the studies discussed here also identify a lack of balance in news reporting of frames related to public health issues. For example, Menashe and Siegel (1998) found that tobacco industry frames dominated public health frames in *The New York Times* and *Washington Post* coverage from 1985 to 1996. Similarly, Lima and Siegel (1999) showed that discussions of the tobacco settlement in 1997–1998 tended to exclude discussions of the public health policy aspects of the agreement, focusing instead on the generation of new revenue. Given the wide range of frames likely to be promoted by stakeholders interested in policies aimed at youth and sex, these results suggest that news coverage of sex education policies also may lack a balance of public health or scientific frames. In addition, the growing range of immediate and often targeted and tailored news sources available via the Internet and print media have increased the complexity of messages to which the public is exposed daily. As a result, media scholars and public health advocates agree that it is important to assess and understand the representation of public health issues disseminated via news organizations.

As a case study to consider the balance of scientific versus nonscientific information in policy debates about strategies to reduce unwanted teen pregnancies, this analysis focuses on how newspaper reports "framed" discussions of two very different news events related to "virginity pledges." These pledges are the focus because they have been presented as viable options for affecting teens' sexual behavior. Policymakers have specifically cited virginity pledges in policy discussions considering how to influence teens' sexual behaviors in venues ranging from school board meetings to hearings in the U.S. Congress. In a 2001 hearing on teenage pregnancy before the House Subcommittee on Human Resources that included discussion of the reauthorization of the 1996 welfare reform legislation's substantial funding provision for abstinence-until-marriage education programs, virginity pledges were cited three times. For example, Dr. Joe McIlhaney of the Medical Institute for Sexual Health proclaimed,

> [The Add Health study] . . . showed that kids who took pledges of abstinence, that those pledges were the biggest influence in the lives of those children who were delaying the onset of sexual activity. . . . The pledges were at first ridiculed by the scientific community. No more. (Teenage Pregnancy Prevention, 2001)

In that same hearing, Assistant Secretary for Planning and Evaluation Bobby P. Jindal of the U.S. Department of Health and Human Services stated,

> Specific findings . . . show that virginity pledges have been successful, in many instances, in convincing teens to delay their first sexual intercourse. . . . However, it also shows that if teens do become sexually active, they are less likely to protect themselves. (Teenage Pregnancy Prevention, 2001)

The initial virginity pledge news events analyzed in this study compose the phenomenon of the virginity pledge campaigns themselves. The so-called pledge "movement" has served as an activist element in the broader abstinence-until-marriage movement, which recently has grown in popularity. Pledges and organizations that promote them, like the Southern Baptist True Love Waits (TLW) virginity pledge program, have attracted a notable level of news attention. Another news event that prompted news coverage about virginity pledges is the publication of the Add Health study described below, which examined the impact pledges had on teens' sexual behavior. Our analysis focuses on newspaper coverage of both news events over a 14-year period.

The purpose of this study is to examine what frames are used to provide context for newspaper stories related to virginity pledges. We assessed both pledge campaigns and a scientific study, because stories about these two news events likely will yield very different frames that could inform public policy debates. Virginity pledge campaigns generally are sponsored by religious organizations that promote abstinence based on moral values or ideological principles. Stories about virginity pledge campaigns are likely to use frames that reflect this motivation and other positive aspects of the pledge phenomenon. By contrast, news coverage of scientific studies likely will focus on the research findings and the implications for teens' sex behaviors.

The following main premises of this study concern the connections between scientific evidence and public discussions about sex education in news coverage:

(1) News reports on events related to sex education programs should include some mention of the most current conclusions about their public health impacts.

(2) News coverage of scientific evidence should include some mention of the programs or debates that the study results might inform.

By including scientific context in news coverage on religion-based virginity pledge programs and by incorporating reference to the sex education debate as a context for news reports on scientific studies, policymakers and the public following news coverage of virginity pledges will be more likely to incorporate science into sex education policy decisions and to support evidence-based policies that may help reduce teen pregnancies. We predict that a large majority of the pledge program stories will not include frames related to the public health impact of virginity pledges. Conversely, a large majority of the scientific stories will not include frames related to the broader policy implications of the study findings on the health impact of such pledge programs.

BACKGROUND

True Love Waits

The TLW program is a prominent virginity pledge program created by the Southern Baptist Convention Sunday School Board in April 1993. Both young people who have never had sex as well as those who have been sexually active in the past are encouraged to take the pledge and to commit to sexual purity from that day until their wedding day. The TLW pledge reads: "Believing in True Love Waits, I make a commitment to God, myself, my family, my friends, my future mate, and my future children to be sexually abstinent from this day until the day I enter into a biblical marriage relationship" (LifeWay, 2002).

The TLW movement, which began with 59 pledgers in Nashville, Tennessee, eventually expanded to include hundreds of churches, schools, and college chapters throughout the country. In July 1994, at a mass rally in Washington, DC, pledgers displayed more than 200,000 pledge cards on the National Mall, and in February 1996, a similar display took place at the Georgia Dome in Atlanta. TLW leaders reported that more than one million adolescents have taken the virginity pledge since the program's inception (LifeWay, 2002). Although TLW was neither the first nor the only program to use chastity vows to encourage sexual abstinence, it was unprecedented in its scale and reach, with a growth rate described by observers as "phenomenal" (Bearman & Bruckner, 2001).

In the 1990s, the TLW program was not the only event related to virginity pledges that could have informed people's views of sex education programs aimed at teens. Public health experts also conducted and published studies on the impact of virginity pledges on teen sexual behavior.

Add Health Study

Researchers who developed the National Longitudinal Study of Adolescent Health (Add Health), a representative, longitudinal, cohort survey of teenagers nationwide, were particularly interested in studying the sexual behavior of American youth. From 1994 to 1996, responding to recent news coverage of virginity pledges, researchers added a survey question to assess whether respondents had ever taken a public or written pledge to remain a virgin until marriage. In 1997, researchers analyzed Add Health interview data from 12,118 seventh through twelfth graders and concluded that those who had taken a virginity pledge were 75% less likely to report having ever had sexual intercourse (Resnick et al., 1997). More comprehensive findings on the effectiveness of virginity pledges were released to the public in the January 2001 issue of the *American Journal of Sociology*. The findings were mixed, offering ammunition for either abstinence-only or comprehensive sex education proponents, depending on which findings were emphasized. Several major findings are relevant here (Bearman and Bruckner, 2001; National

Institute of Child Health and Human Development, 2001):

- Pledgers began sexual activity on average 18 months later than nonpledgers.
- Pledging had little effect among older teens (18 and older).
- The vow was effective only in environments where fewer than 30% of a school's students were pledgers, thus allowing pledgers to form identities unique from the majority of other students.
- Among those teens who eventually did have intercourse, pledgers were less likely to use contraception than nonpledgers.

News Frames

For this analysis, we viewed journalists as processors of information who produce "interpretive packages" of issues that can influence and reflect a topic's "issue culture" (D'Angelo, 2002). While news reports often go beyond simply reporting "who, what, when, where, why, and how," they do not have the space or resources to capture every fact and perspective on a topic. Reporters and editors routinely make choices about what information to include and what to exclude, often using a "frame" or "central organizing idea or story line" to tie information together or to provide emphasis (Gamson & Modigliani, 1987). Although different audiences may interpret and process news frames differently based on their individual experiences, for this study we viewed news frames as independent variables that can influence an audience's perception of a range of perspectives and opinions about public health issues. Since the salience of a given frame varies based on the interaction of the text and the audience, a frame's presence in a news report does not guarantee its influence on the audience. However, its inclusion or exclusion may influence readers' understanding of issues (D'Angelo, 2002). Researchers have used this framework for considering news messages in analyses of news coverage of issues such as breast cancer and

gun policy (Andsager & Powers, 1999; Woodruff, 2000).

The relevance of news frames to public policy formation lies in their importance in defining and suggesting solutions to social problems. Whether intentionally or not, journalists' decisions to report "some aspects of a perceived reality and make them more salient in a communicating text... [can] promote a particular problem definition, causal interpretation, moral evaluation, and/or treatment recommendation for the item described" (Entman, 1993, p. 52). The merits or weaknesses of various policy arguments often are secondary to the relative success of proponents and opponents in having their issue frame included in news coverage (Wallack et al., 1993). Even when a policy suggestion is not explicitly stated, policy options or preferences can be implied in the news text by the selective presentation of various positive or negative aspects of an issue or proposed solution (Pan & Kosicki, 1993). Analyses of news frames can reveal which aspects of a discussion or debate are being emphasized and which are being ignored or downplayed.

In addition to its content, the physical placement of a frame also provides a clear signal about the importance and salience of the information. The headline and lead or first paragraph of a story are the most powerful suggestive cues regarding the central message of the text (Pan & Kosicki, 1993). The writer of a news headline is charged with the challenging task of relating the content of a news article in just a few words and in a manner that is intriguing enough to attract headline-scanning readers, some of whom may not go on to read the article. Consequently, headlines often are remembered when the text of the article is not.

Finally, in addition to the packages of ideas journalists generate to present stories, they also rely on sources to provide frames. The impact of the frames provided by news sources depends on both the message and attributes of the source. Generally, news audiences are more likely to accept or take cues from information attributed to credible sources (Mondak, 1990). An audience members' assessment of source credibility and the impact of that assessment may vary depending on his background, experiences, views about the source's motives, the content of the message, motivations, etc. (Perloff, 1993; Pornpitakpan, 2004; Slater & Rouner, 1997). An analysis of the sources attributed in the news coverage highlights the connection between source credibility and the impact of news frames.

Research Questions

This analysis focuses on two separate news events: (1) virginity pledge programs taking place in the United States between 1987 and 2001, and (2) the 2001 publication of Add Health study findings regarding the effectiveness of virginity pledges. This combination of news events permits comparison between news coverage of an event promoted by a religious group for social and moral reasons and the news coverage of the publication of research results on the public health impact of these pledges. The contrasting nature of the two news events and their sponsors invites journalists to use different frames, though the health topic is the same.

Our aim is to understand how newspaper outlets presented various perspectives about the prevalence and effectiveness of virginity pledge programs that could have influenced the public's and policymakers' understanding of and support for abstinence-only sex education programs. Specifically, we are interested in whether stories that focus on pledge programs provide scientific evidence frames as context and whether stories on scientific studies also mention broader policy discussions or debates. The results of this study address the following questions:

- How extensive was newspaper coverage of virginity pledges between 1987 and 2001?
- How did newspaper coverage frame virginity pledge programs?
- How did frames in newspaper reports about virginity pledge programs differ

from the frames in news reports covering the Add Health study?
- How did messages presented in headlines of articles reporting on the Add Health study differ from those presented in the text of these newspaper articles?
- What sources provided frames for the newspaper articles of the virginity pledge program and the Add Health study?

METHODS

Currently, there is no standardized approach to conduct framing analyses. Our methods were derived from generally accepted guidelines for text analysis and similar studies of public health issues (Neuendorf, 2002).

We selected news articles on virginity pledges using the LexisNexis news database to search U.S. newspapers and wire services in each of the four regions of the country (Midwest, Southeast, Northeast, and West). The database consisted of 329 U.S. newspapers and newswire services. Search terms were keywords "abstinence or virginity or chastity" within five words of "pledge or vow or promise" between January 1, 1987, and December 31, 2001. Although virginity pledge programs received international news media attention, we focused only on American news coverage.

After applying exclusion criteria, 142 newspaper articles remained. The distribution of the articles was as follows: 130 general articles on virginity pledges (TLW became a focus of this analysis because it was the virginity pledge program that earned the most news coverage at the time) and 12 articles on the Add Health study findings on pledge effectiveness.

Using an adapted version of a news analysis tool for developing frames (Winett, 1997), the second author read the full text of each article and recorded the catch phrases, images, or arguments invoked by reporters and spokespersons discussing virginity pledges or the Add Health results. The authors then categorized these presentation techniques and tools into categories representing frames or overarching ideas related to virginity pledges. Each frame is connected to representative metaphors, images, and principles.

We then coded each article for whether it included any of the five frames determined to be the primary ways of discussing pledges in the articles. In addition to tracking these frames in article texts, for each of the 12 articles that reported on the Add Health study, we analyzed the messages contained in the article headlines.

After the frames for each article were established, the lead author coded to whom the frame was attributed. A frame was considered "Unattributed" when it was not explicitly linked to a source in quotes or with phrases such as "says Pastor Smith" or "according to sex educators." The "Miscellaneous" category groups all sources linked to a particular frame only once.

Finally, the second author served as primary coder for the frames, coding the entire sample.

RESULTS

A large majority (68%) of the 142 reports specifically mentioned the TLW program. The amount of coverage over time varied with the occurrence of related newsworthy events. In 1994, for instance, virginity pledges were showcased at two major events: a Washington, DC, virginity pledge rally on the National Mall and the annual Southern Baptist meeting. Accordingly, in 1994, there was a marked increase in news coverage of virginity pledge campaigns. The passage of welfare reform legislation in 1996, which included an abstinence-until-marriage education provision allowing states to apply for federal funds to pay for such programs, corresponded with a second spike in news coverage of virginity pledges. The final blip in news coverage took place in 2001, during which the Add Health survey's virginity pledge results were published.

Based on an initial reading of virginity pledge news reports, five organizing ideas were both central to the coverage and representative of various ways of thinking about virginity pledges. One of the frames is labeled "abstinence is 'in'". This moniker captures the idea that taking a virginity pledge is a new way for teens to be "cool" or "popular." Catch phrases such as "new sexual revolution" and "new era of chastity" were used to describe the popularity of virginity pledges. In addition, some stories combined the image of teen role models with their public choice to remain virgins, thus characterizing virginity pledges as popular because of their association with "hip" public figures. As an example of how the frame was presented, a youth pastor described virginity this way in a January 14, 1994, report in *The Virginian-Pilot* (Copley, 1994, p. 1): "There are kids who, a year ago, would have been ashamed to admit they're virgins.... It's cool now." The article explained that "Part of virginity's coolness comes from high-profile entertainers and athletes, such as alternative musician Juliana Hatfield and Phoenix Suns power forward A.C. Green, who are open about their decisions to wait." By placing virginity pledges in a popular light, this frame creates a positive, almost trendy aura around the use of moral values as the basis for teens' decisions about having sex. It also appeals to teens' desire to be accepted and well regarded by their peers and to emulate the behavior of famous role models.

The "social movement" frame takes the level of acceptance of virginity pledges among teens a step further. It presents the idea that the virginity pledge movement is not an isolated, individual phenomenon, but one on par with the sexual revolution of the late 1960s. The implication is that virginity pledges are significantly changing society. A July 26, 1994, *Washington Times* article (Wetzstein, 1994, p. A1) described it this way: "A quarter century after Woodstock, a new youth rebellion is afoot. The anthem of this new generation: True love waits." Both the "social movement" and "abstinence is in" frames suggest that programs based on moral or religious principles of abstinence until marriage can change teens' sexual behaviors. With respect to public policy, these frames imply that virginity pledges can be a viable alternative for sex education, because peer pressure and the desire to be part of something meaningful and large in scope will encourage teens to take the pledges and to keep them. Thus, the movement can reduce the rate of teen pregnancies.

The "faulty education" frame criticizes comprehensive sex education programs, arguing that moral values and principles should be the focus of sex education instead of discussion of contraception or condoms. In an August 13, 1994, article, *The Press-Enterprise* (Moore, 1994, p. B01) attributed the following statements about the health curriculum in a local school district to a school board trustee and middle school teacher:

> Park said the books impart a message that says, "If you decide to have sex, then as long as you are responsible, you can feel good about yourself." She said it is wrong to give young people a "smorgasbord" of choices.

The prevailing image for this frame is of teachers explaining how and why to use condoms and other aspects of sex experience and implicitly promoting sex. In other words, comprehensive sex education is not viable because it instructs teens on how to have sex and, therefore, encourages them to do so. This frame appeals to the principle of the importance of properly protecting and educating teens and also implies that religious principles should be a guide. The policy implication is that comprehensive sex education programs should not be the primary public policy for affecting teens' sexual behaviors.

The "lack of trust in teens" concepts focus on the idea that adults do not trust teens not to have sex, and that adults have been sending the message that they do not expect teens to be able to control their sexual impulses. In news coverage, pledgers spoke of how, on the contrary, youth are indeed capable of keeping abstinence vows, and that adults are misguided in thinking that such pledges inevitably would be broken. In a June 15, 1994, article in the *St. Petersburg Times* (Billitteri, 1994, p. 1A), one teen commented,

"A lot of adults think we're sexually active and we're a bunch of animals who can't control ourselves." The images that arise from this frame are of lax, resigned parents and wild teens. In this presentation, teens are attracted to pledges in direct response to adults' view about them. In this news report this same teen said, "I wanted to make a stand and let them know we can—that we're not all doing it" (Billitteri, 1994, p. 1A). This frame sets the stage for support for virginity pledge programs, with youth themselves demonstrating that they can prove adults wrong by remaining abstinent until marriage.

The "faulty pledge" frame exudes skepticism about the effectiveness of pledges in affecting teens' behaviors. This frame uses scientific evidence and arguments based on the difficulty of getting teens to change other risky behaviors, like smoking, to argue that expecting teens to adhere to virginity pledges may be harmful or unrealistic. As a state public health official put it in a July 15, 1997, article in the *Charleston Daily Mail* ("Abstinence-only program attacked," 1997, p. 5A), "Vows of abstinence break more often than condoms do. (An abstinence-only program) does not give them the skills to conduct responsible sexual behavior." The implication is that scientific evidence and experience should inform public policy. As a university professor and advocate of comprehensive sex education put it in a February 8, 1996, article (Longino, 1996, p. 01D), "*the True Love Waits* approach can be positive for some people." He added, however,

> You cannot build your policy on what you want children to do; you have to build it also on what they are doing. And a very high percentage of teenagers in the United States are having sex. There have to be sources of information other than parents out there.

"Faulty pledges" appeals to the principle of putting public health practices and principles at the forefront of efforts to educate and protect youth and affect teens' behaviors. With regard to public policy, this frame implies that comprehensive sex education is the most effective way to reduce teen pregnancies and, more generally, that practical experience and scientific evidence should inform public policy.

In sum, these frames show a range of arguments, images, and policies presented in news coverage of virginity pledges. Each one could prime the audience to consider particular perspectives and opinions in their evaluation of virginity pledges and, by extension, in their assessment of the validity of abstinence-only sex education as a strategy to reduce teen pregnancy. Next, as a measure of the overall messages the news coverage presented on virginity pledges, we describe what proportion of the news coverage displayed each of these frames.

Among the 130 newspaper articles focusing on virginity pledge events and not on the Add Health study, about one half (52%) contained the "social movement" frame, and nearly one quarter included the "abstinence is in" ideas. The next most frequent frame, "lack of trust in teens," was included in almost one third of these reports (32%). Nearly one quarter of the news reports (22%) were skeptical of the effectiveness of virginity pledges ("faulty pledges") and only one tenth (12%) were critical of comprehensive sex education ("faulty education").

In contrast, among the 12 articles that reported on the Add Health findings related to the effectiveness of virginity pledges, 8 contained the frame "social movement," and a large majority (10 articles) was skeptical of or offered caveats about the effectiveness of such pledges ("faulty pledges"). None of the other 3 analyzed frames were present in the Add Health articles.

Despite the lack of an explicit endorsement of virginity pledge programs in the body of the articles, almost all the news articles about the Add Health study had headlines that only mentioned the effectiveness of virginity pledges in delaying sex. Caveats to these claims often were buried in the text after the content already had been framed by highly suggestive headlines such as "Virginity pledge helps teens wait" and "Virginity pledges by teenagers can be highly effective, federal study finds." The headlines overwhelmingly conveyed the perspective that virginity pledges are effective. A large majority of the frames coded in newspaper articles on the pledges (69%) were unattributed or provided by journalists. In addition, the most used source varied by frame. Journalists provided 94% of the "social movement" frames that were recorded compared with only 15% of the "lack of trust in teens" frame. Teens and church officials were most likely to account for the "Lack of trust in teens" frames, with 34% and 22%, respectively. The "faulty pledges" frame was most often unattributed (25%) or provided by professionals who teach in schools or develop school curricula (18%). Researchers accounted for only 11% of the "faulty pledges" frame. "Abstinence is 'in'" was provided most often by the journalist (68%) or church officials (13%). Finally, the "faulty education" frame was most often provided by a mix of several sources that were mentioned only once (41%). For this frame, the miscellaneous category contained 7 sources and was followed in attributions by youth or representatives of religious youth groups (a combined 30%) and supporters of abstinence-only education programs. When the reports focused on the Add Health study, 83% of the two frames mentioned, "social movement" and "faulty pledges," were attributed to the study authors.

DISCUSSION

This study was motivated by what we argue should be key aspects of communications in the policymaking process. First, public policy decisions should be informed by scientific evidence to ensure that they promote public health. Second, for policies to be informed, the science must reach policymakers and the general public. Third, researchers should collaborate with professionals skilled in dissemination to ensure that important information reaches policymakers and the public. Finally, journalists also have an important role in disseminating scientific and policy information to policymakers and the public. This article focuses on journalists and public health experts' roles in the flow of sex education policy messages.

Journalists have several goals for reporting on sex education, including to attract audiences' attention. They achieve this goal by reporting on the objective aspects of events and studies related to topics such as virginity pledges or sex education. They also selectively choose how to frame or present stories in a way that highlights the ideological conflict, human interest element, or any other aspect of stories that make them newsworthy. Many journalists also have "service journalism" as a secondary goal, providing the public with news it can use to make policy decisions or to take social action. In news coverage of debates about sex education policy, responsible service journalism entails some mention of the available scientific evidence. Similarly, in reports about events related to teens' sexual behaviors, journalists would do their audience a service if they connected events to broader public debates. This study begins to consider how well journalists were providing information the public could use in reporting on virginity pledges by answering the following questions: When journalists had a choice about how to discuss virginity pledges, how often did they mention the public impact of the program? Similarly, when evidence was reported, was it linked to policy debates to facilitate usage when making those choices? Finally, who provided those frames?

Our study of how newspaper journalists reported on TLW virginity pledge campaigns and the Add Health study confirms that these topics were newsworthy; newspaper coverage of the virginity pledges increased throughout the mid-1990s, providing increasing opportunities for these news frames to affect audiences' views. We also found that when reporting on virginity pledges outside the context of scientific studies, reporters excluded from a majority of the articles the possibility that pledges may not effectively change most teens' behaviors. In contrast, at least half the articles on pledge campaigns framed the pledges as a social movement,

implying a significant impact on teens' behaviors. These results suggest that news coverage of TLW may have contributed to what proponents describe as a new culture of chastity. Thus, audiences reading these stories may have been more likely to support abstinence-only education.

Analysis of news reports on the 2001 Add Health study reveals a markedly different breakdown in the distribution of the analyzed frames in the text of articles. Only those frames pertaining to the scale of the virginity pledge movement and skepticism and caveats about the effectiveness of pledging were present in these articles. In sum, newspaper journalists' coverage of the Add Health results centered on the scientific evidence without providing the additional policy-related frames that had been presented in the other news coverage of virginity pledges. One possible explanation for this more narrow range of frames used to describe the Add Health findings is that the Add Health researchers presented only a couple of frames when interviewed. Alternatively, researchers, public officials, or other sources may have presented a range of frames that then were narrowed by journalists. In either case, most newspaper reporters covering the Add Health findings missed an opportunity to provide a broader context for readers to consider the results or link them to specific policy options.

With respect to the messages in the headlines of articles on pledge programs, newspaper reports sent the public contradictory information during the period in which our analysis was conducted. Even when the less promising data on virginity pledge effectiveness was included in article texts, the messages presented first and with the most emphasis were positive proclamations in the headlines. Thus, readers would have received different messages about virginity pledges depending on how much attention was paid to the text of the article.

The likely impact of the headline frames is striking. Readers glancing at newspapers at a newsstand or skimming headlines over breakfast could have been left with the impression that abstinence vows are a new solution to problems of unwanted teenage pregnancies. A likely conclusion would be that virginity pledge programs should be included as part of sex education programs, because they are effective for all teens. This result is not surprising in that headlines are limited in space, and there is little room for explanations of caveat-riddled research findings. Furthermore, headlines are intended to attract attention with titillating "teasers" about what follows. One solution is to find ways to tease and leave room for some uncertainty, distinctions, or nuances. To attract audiences to read further, uncertainty could be presented as a puzzle or controversy. For example, the headline could add a question mark ("Virginity pledges help teens wait?") or emphasize nuances in other ways ("Virginity pledges by teenagers *can* be highly effective, federal study finds.").

The analysis of the sources mirrors the lack of balance shown in the distribution of frames. A large majority of the general stories containing two of the frames not connected with research effects, "social movement" and "abstinence is 'in,' " were presented as the journalists' own view or synthesis of features of the story. By contrast, the third frame that was not based on science, "lack of trust in teens" was presented most often as the view of youth who were interviewed because they had or planned to take a virginity pledge or church officials promoting the pledges. The fact that the founder of the TLW virginity pledge campaign was quoted as presenting this frame suggests that it may have been even more salient for youth taking the pledges because it was reinforced with messages from the campaign. The two frames that could have been linked to a scientific context or researchers were "faulty pledges" and "faulty education." During this period, the "faulty education" frame was not based on research, but on the promotion of using religious values as a basis for sex education. The "faulty pledges" frames were supported with a sizable proportion of public health researchers and educator as the sources.

This lack of balance in frame sources could be addressed by providing reporters with a list of sources with varying views on virginity pledges and sex education in advance of an event, educating journalists on the issues surrounding sex education and teens' sexual behavior so that the frames they put around the quotes and facts are more balanced, or by training expert sources to alert journalists to the variety of perspectives surrounding this debate.

Nevertheless, given the comparatively small number of articles that included any arguments in opposition to virginity pledges, it was apparent that stories about virginity pledge programs tended to favor supportive messages and generally were not balanced with public health arguments, evidence-based skepticism, or public policy implications.

CONCLUSION

In battles over the public's support for evidence-based sex education policies, public health practitioners and researchers often overlook the power of news organizations to shape attitudes, beliefs, and policies. When advocacy campaigns and scientific studies create public, teachable moments about sex education strategies such as virginity pledges, experts should provide reporters and news outlets, especially wire services, with information guided by an awareness of the lack of balance in the frames and sources that have been employed in previous news reports on this topic. Whether the news reports focus on comprehensive sex education or abstinence-only programs, providing additional, contextual information about the controversies or varying viewpoints on sex education could add to the newsworthiness of the event or study, thereby providing an incentive for journalists to more consistently convey a wider range of information on this topic. With a concerted effort to collaborate with journalists by providing context along with their perspectives, media-savvy public health experts might gain more opportunities to influence public perceptions of potential solutions to societal problems such as teenage pregnancy.

By focusing on the balance of frames and their sources, experts should advocate that journalists understand the range of debates surrounding sex education and recognize that abstinence-only advocates tend to use religious principles while public health experts tend to rely on science. By including a public health frame in virginity pledge stories that focus on religion-oriented pledge events, science is more likely to inform the audiences' views about sex education and the resulting policy implications. Additionally, public health experts interviewed for stories about studies such as Add Health should clearly link their results to policy options in order to help the audience connect the dots between research findings and policy choices.

Finally, options for accessing news via mass media are more varied than ever in our history. Consumers are bombarded with information from many sources, and they can be proactive information-seekers who control their information exposure. Moreover, the Internet has given consumers the ability to produce and widely disseminate health information. Even in this complex and rich information environment, news organizations remain a powerful force behind the dissemination of health information in U.S. society. It is still important that researchers examine the content and impact of news coverage on our collective knowledge, attitudes, and behaviors and provide a balance of information needed for journalists, policy-makers, and the public to make informed decisions.

INTRODUCTION REFERENCES

Gamson, W. A., D. Croteau, W. Hownes, and T. Sasson. 1992. Media images and the social construction of reality. *Annual Review of Sociology* 18: 373–93.

Rosenbaum, J. E. 2009. Patient teenagers? A comparison of the sexual behavior of virginity pledgers and matched nonpledgers. *Pediatrics* 123: 110–20.

REFERENCES

Abstinence-only program attacked. (July 15, 1997). *Charleston Daily Mail*. 5A.

American Dietetic Association. (2002). *Nutrition and you: Trends 2002*. Retrieved June 1, 2004, from http://www.eatright.org.

Andsager, J. L. & Powers, A. (1999). Social or economic concerns: How news and women's magazines framed breast cancer in the 1990s. *Journalism & Mass Communication Quarterly, 76*(3), 531–550.

Bearman, P. S. & Bruckner, H. (2001). Promising the future: Virginity pledges and first intercourse. *American Journal of Sociology, 106*(4), 859–912.

Billitteri, T. J. (1994, June 15). Sex is a 4-letter word: Wait. *St. Petersburg Times*, p. 1A.

Brodie, M., Hamel, E., Altman, D., Blendon, R., & Benson, J. (2003). Health news and the American public: 1996–2002. *Journal of Health Politics, Policy & Law, 28*(5), 297.

Centers for Disease Control and Prevention. (2005). *Guide to community preventive services*. Retrieved May 16, 2005, from http://www.thecommunityguide.org/.

Copley, R. (1994, January 14). Saying no to sex; More young people are taking pride in committing themselves to remaining virgins until they are married. *The Virginian-Pilot*, p. 1.

D'Angelo, P. (2002). News framing as a multiparadigmatic research program: A response to Entman. *Journal of Communication, 52*(4), 870–888.

Entman, R. M. (1993). Framing: Toward clarification of a fractured paradigm. *Journal of Communication, 43*(4), 51–58.

Gamson, W. A. & Modigliani, A. (1987). The changing culture of affirmative action. In: R. G. Braungart & M. M. Braungart (Eds.), *Research in political sociology* (pp. 137–177). Greenwich: JAI Press.

Howell, M. (2001). The future of sexuality education: Science or politics? *Transitions, 1*, 12–13.

Huebner, J., Fan, D. P., & Finnegan, J. (1997). Death of a thousand cuts—The impact of media coverage on public opinion about Clinton's health security act. *J Health Communication, 2*(4), 253–270.

Iyengar, S. (1991). *Is anyone responsible? How television news frames political issues*. Chicago: University of Chicago Press.

Jacobson, P. D., Wasserman, J., & Raube, K. (1993). The politics of antismoking legislation: Lessons from six states. *Journal of Health Politics, Policy, and Law, 18*, 787–819.

Kirby, D. (2001). *Emerging answers: Research findings on programs to reduce teen pregnancy (summary)*. Washington, DC: The National Campaign to Prevent Teen Pregnancy.

Landry, D. J., Kaeser, L., & Richards, C. L. (1999). Abstinence promotion and the provision of information about contraception in public school district sexuality education policies. *Family Planning Perspectives, 31*(6), 280–286.

LifeWay. (2002). *True Love Waits: Leader FAQs*. Retrieved December 20, 2002, from http://www.lifeway.com/tlw/ldr_faq_home.asp.

Lima, J. & Siegel, M. (1999). The tobacco settlement: An analysis of newspaper coverage of a national policy debate, 1997–98. *Tobacco Control, 8*, 247–253.

Longino, M. (1996, February 8). Abstinence: Saying yes is saying no. *The Atlanta Journal and Constitution*, p. 01D.

Menashe, C. L. & Siegel, M. (1998). The power of a frame: An analysis of newspaper coverage of tobacco issues—United States, 1985–1996. *J Health Commun, 3*, 307–325.

Mondak, J. J. (1990). Perceived legitimacy of supreme court decisions: Three functions of source credibility. *Political Behavior, 12*(4), 363–384.

Moore, S. (1994, August 13). Vote on sex education in Hemet set tuesday. *The Press-Enterprise*, p. B01.

The National Campaign to Prevent Teen Pregnancy. (2003). *Summary of teen pregnancy related funding*. Retrieved May 3, 2003, from http://www.teenpregnancy.org/press/pdf/AppropriationsFY2004.pdf.

National Institute of Child Health and Human Development. (2001). *Virginity pledge helps teens delay sexual activity*. Bethesda: National Institutes of Health.

Neuendorf, K. A. (2002). *The content analysis guidebook*. Thousand Oaks, CA: Sage Publications.

Ozer, E. M., Brindis, C. D., Millstein, S. G., Knopf, D. K., & Irwin, C. E., Jr. (1998). *America's adolescents: Are they healthy?* San Francisco: University of California, San Francisco, National Adolescent Health Information Center.

Pan, Z. & Kosicki, G. M. (1993). Framing analysis: An approach to news discourse. *Political Communication, 10*, 55–75.

Perloff, R. (1993). *The dynamics of persuasion*. Hillsdale, NJ: Erlbaum.

The Pew Research Center for the People and the Press. (2004). *News audiences increasingly politicized: Online news audience larger, more diverse*. Retrieved June 20, 2004, from http://people-press.org/reports/display.php3?PageID = 833.

Pornpitakpan, C. (2004). The persuasiveness of source credibility. A critical review of five decades' evidence. *Journal of Applied Social Psychology, 34*(2), 243–281.

Resnick, M. D., Bearman, P. S., Blum, R. W., Bauman, K. E., Harris, K. M., Jones, J., et al. (1997). Protecting adolescents from harm: Findings from the national longitudinal study on adolescent health. *JAMA, 278*(10), 823–831.

Rogers, E., Dearing, J., & Chang, S. (1991). AIDS in the 1980s: The agenda-setting process for a public issue. *Journalism Monographs, 126*, 1–47.

Ryan, C. (1991). *Prime time activism: Media strategies for grassroots organizing*. Boston: South End Press.

Slater, M. & Rouner, D. (1997). How message evaluation and source attributes may influence credibility assessment and belief change. *Journalism and Mass Communication Quarterly, 73*(4), 974–991.

Sniderman, P., Brody, R., & Tetlock, P. E. (1991). *Reasoning and choice: Explorations in political psychology*. Cambridge: Cambridge University Press.

Teenage Pregnancy Prevention: Hearing before the Subcommittee on Human Resources of the House Committee on Ways and Means, 107th Cong., 1st Sessn. (2001, November 15). Retrieved 12 August 2005, http://waysandmeans.house.gov/legacy/humres/107cong/11-15-01/107-8final.htm.

U.S. Preventive Task Force. (2005). Retrieved May 16, 2005, from http://www.ahcpr.gov/clinic/uspstfix.htm.

Wallack, L., Dorfman, L., Jernigan, D., & Themba, M. (1993). *Media advocacy and public health: Power for prevention*. Newbury Park, CA: Sage Publications.

Wetzstein, C. (1994, July 26). With groups' help, teens take pride in virginity; Many vow abstinence until marriage. *The Washington Times*, p. A1.

Winett, L. (1997). Advocate's guide to developing framing memos. In S. Iyengar & R. Reeves (Eds.), *Do the media govern? Politicians, voters, and reporters in America*. Thousand Oaks, CA: Sage Publications.

Woodruff, K. (2000). *Issue 8: The debate on gun policies in U.S. and Midwest newspapers*. Berkeley, CA: Berkeley Media Studies Group.

CHAPTER 49

Finding a Match

How Contexts Inform Comprehensive and Abstinence-Based Sex Education Programs

Terrance D. Olson

In 2007, the primary approach in 35 percent of America's schools was "abstinence only" sex education, with an additional 50 percent of schools teaching "abstinence plus" in which various methods of contraception were discussed. Only the remaining 15 percent refused federal dollars in order to teach a more comprehensive sex education curriculum that included discussion of types of sex, contraception, masturbation, homosexuality, and abortion (Regnerus, 2007). Although abstinence-only programs are a priority of the federal government, they are not supported by either a majority of the public or the scientific community (Bleakley, Hennessy, & Fishbein, 2006). And, even among the one-third of parents who say schools should teach abstinence until marriage, a substantial number also want schools to arm their children with information about obtaining and using condoms, contraception, and abortion, in case they do become sexually active (Schemo, 2000). Is it any wonder that educators in the trenches often characterize our culture as sexually schizophrenic?

This great American ambivalence is illustrated in the different approaches to sexuality education at the beginning of the AIDS epidemic by the usually considered "conservative" Britons and the "liberal" Americans. The British inaugurated the nationwide "Don't Die of Ignorance" campaign after England had diagnosed only a few cases of AIDS. In the United States it took six years and thousands of cases of AIDS before the President even uttered the word in public. One professional offered this analysis:

> . . . [W]hile the British aim earnestly to protect their young from ignorance, we misguided Americans have [enlisted ignorance] in the fight! While the British motto might well be 'Just Say Know,' we offer, in place of the power of knowledge, 'Just Say No.' And who are the 'we'? We are the same adult community who can be seen saying 'yes' all day long in those endless television images, contradicting ourselves in the eyes of our young with every change of channels. (Roffman 1992, 7)

Straight talk is urged by experts in the field of sexuality education as an antidote to such adult "double speak." Roffman continues,

> Taking our cue from the sensible British, we might say: We love you and want you to be safe. The best

From "Finding a Match: How Contexts Informs Comprehensive and Abstinence-Based Sex Education Programs" by Terrance D. Olson. 2008. Unpublished manuscript, Brigham Young University.

way to do that is to abstain [from] any potentially risky behavior. Next best is to protect yourself and others as best you can. Here's how.... (1992, 7)

The Terrance Olson chapter about sexuality education will neither spell out nor recommend specific programs and practices. It will offer a philosophical perspective with which you can reframe this perennially controversial topic yourself.

SETTING THE STAGE

The discourse regarding what is appropriate or defensible sex education typically is carried out on a level that misses the mark regarding how to solve the problems that sex education itself addresses. Solutions to problems generally originate in ideas of either what the problems are or where the problems come from. If the debate over sex education were to be predicated on two contextual preconditions, the purposes of various sex education approaches could more likely be accomplished. The first of these preconditions involves being transparent regarding the philosophies of sexuality and of education that undergird research and practice. The second precondition requires that educational efforts be tailored specifically to social-relational contexts that research reveals to be related to the creation of the problems and to the solutions. The purpose of this chapter is to provide starting points for achieving a philosophical and practical match between such contexts and programs.

The *New England Journal of Medicine* published this observation about a sex education approach in the military:

A recent release from the Office of the Surgeon General reports a remarkable drop in the incidence of venereal disease [in the military].

... For the Army as a whole, the decrease amounted to 40 percent; for soldiers stationed in the United States, it was more than 50 percent.

This is an encouraging note in view of the trend toward increased rate in the civilian population as recently reported. The Surgeon General credits this accomplishment to a new approach on the part of the Army, based on "an intelligent appeal to the higher moral sense of the individual," with "moral, spiritual, psychological, as well as objective factors." In this program the reasons for good conduct are stressed through group and individual education and conferences.... This approach has supplanted prior concepts, which emphasized the aspects of prevention, with the implication that the soldier was not remiss so long as his illicit relations did not result in infection. Training films ... have been replaced by new films reflecting the current trend, dramatizing "The rewards of good conduct as well as the effect of social diseases on an individual's future health and happiness." (U. S. Army, 1948, p. 784).

At some point in the above paragraph it may have become obvious that this is an historical commentary, over 60 years old. The tip off might have been how the program was described approvingly, and by the use of judgmental terms such as "illicit" relations. But more to the point, the quote reveals that over two generations ago, at least two philosophical approaches to the consequences of sexual relations among the unmarried were being implemented—at least by the U.S. Army. This observation by the Surgeon General of the United States is just one pinpoint in the ongoing public debate regarding what the societal, public response to various sexual activities in the population—especially the adolescent population—ought to be. As soon as the debate centers on what kind of intervention—or what kind of education—should be initiated and delivered as a prevention for, or solution to, the consequences of nonmarital sexual activity, the issue becomes a matter of moral philosophy as well as social science and/or public policy. In short, there is no philosophy-free intervention program. Whether the decision is to deliver a "comprehensive" sex education program (commonly understood to include the biology of human reproduction as well as contraceptive information and abstinence options), or an abstinence-based program (including the biology of human reproduction and the preeminence of abstinence as a solution), some philosophy guides the delivery decisions.

Back (1983) suggested this reality when he noted that, in efforts to decrease adolescent pregnancy rates, scientists logically could focus on the two dimensions that generate the rates in the first place: the level of sexual activity among the adolescent population, and the level of contraception use in the same population. But Back indicated that up to the mid-1980s, this was not what had happened: "... we are struck by the preponderance of research and application on the second factor—the use of contraceptives, to the virtual exclusion of the first, the increase of teenage, nonmarital intercourse" (p. 2).

Over twenty years later, the debate has altered somewhat, with research now addressing both factors. Each group of researchers seem committed to solving the problem, but both groups espouse a distinct philosophy concerning the kind of sex education that would make "a meaningful difference"—referring to a description by Williams and Gantt (2002), that the moral "... is that which makes a meaningful difference to a human person in a given human context" (p. 11). The conclusions drawn regarding the value and pragmatic benefits of the content and delivery of various programs are conflicting. Deciding how to respond to those conflicting views (including what behaviors to target) is not a simple issue for those committed to intervention. To understand the conflicting starting points of intervention could be to grant that empirical work in social science is also guided by some philosophy of science (Slife & Williams, 1995).

It is assumed that any time social scientists create intervention programs, the motivation of the clinicians and practitioners so engaged are similar: to improve the quality of the human condition. Of course, if the issue is the quality of human experience, then judgments have to be made regarding what constitutes quality

living. Interventionists (such as therapists and family life or health educators) are inescapably addressing and drawing conclusions about what is moral or what is ethical, as evidenced by purposes that promote certain outcomes deemed to be of quality, over outcomes deemed to be less beneficial or even destructive. For example, one educator's solution to the problem of adolescent pregnancy (consistent, effective contraceptive use or abortion) ignores what another educator sees as a problem: sexual involvement by unmarried legal minors. These disagreements are typically addressed by those championing each position, citing research that buttresses the pragmatic benefits of their position.

Such debates are actually moral arguments, and illustrate how the moral or ethical domain is inherent in the study of human experience, and does not appear just when intervention is the issue. Counselors and educators—and perhaps especially sex educators, given the sensitive and central nature of their task, purpose, and topics—are seeking to make a meaningful difference in the lives of those exposed to sex education. It is assumed that the meaningful difference is in the quality of lives lived by those who are so educated, and thus are being issued an ethical call by any curriculum to live in the ways that will create the outcomes that would be in their best interests.

In recent years, social scientists have become more explicit about the reality and value of the moral domain concerning the kinds of interventions that are most valuable (see Doherty, 1995; Coles, 1988). In moral philosophy, many models of normative ethics-identifying principles that invoke that which is good or right have been presented over the years. Boyce and Jenson's (1978) integrated model is still a valid summary of conceptual possibilities. At least the questions about normative ethics have remained the same: In deciding what is "good" or quality human experience, do I take an instrumentalist view (Nothing is intrinsically good; all things are means, there are no ends.) or an intrinsic view (There are intrinsically good things; there are goods that are good in and of themselves.)? The latter view is a bit more complicated, because then a variety of intrinsic goods can be proposed: pleasure; something other than pleasure; pleasure plus something(s) other than pleasure—all are possibilities. In addition, once a concept of the good has been identified, the means to promoting that good must be decided. The possibilities involve taking only consequences into account (teleological positions), or taking only the nature of the action itself into account, or taking the nature of the act itself and the consequences into account (deontological positions) (Boyce & Jensen, 1978). These philosophical models of what is good usually invoke (although implicitly) some ontology of human being—some assumptions about what it means to be human and what humans are capable of.

It may be that interventionists do not see themselves as engaged in a philosophical enterprise that invokes some ethical stance, but it is likely that even if they have not been explicit about their views of what is good or what will bring to pass the good, or of what it is about human beings that makes it possible for them to choose the good, they are offering a moral possibility to their audiences—or, at the least, a possibility they believe is ethical. This is because interventions to foster the quality of human lives inescapably require making judgments about what constitutes quality living. Otherwise, why bother trying to educate or intervene in the first place? The only way intervention efforts could be considered not to be moral activity is if they were intended not to make any meaningful difference, which itself would make intervention efforts nonsensical.

Sexuality education is a controversial topic, not because science is in conflict with the values of nonscientist consumers of the sex education product—although sometimes the debates are characterized that way—but because of conflicting philosophies of what is good and ethical about how human sexuality is expressed. Neither scientists nor consumers can avoid taking some philosophical stance on this issue. And

while it is important to be fair and straightforward in interpreting research results, such interpretations are admittedly based on data that themselves were collected according to some philosophy or value position by those who constructed the research efforts. In summary, the reality of disagreement regarding quality, regarding the ethical and the moral, and regarding how to achieve or produce quality outcomes in the lives of adolescents, is what generates the debate central to all sex education efforts.

If we are to deliver sex education as a means of promoting the quality of life, we must decide what kind of knowledge is most appropriate, what practices we wish to promote, what contexts of conduct are most beneficial, and what practices are to be discouraged. For example, if we are to engage in prevention, exactly what are we to prevent, and why? Adolescent pregnancy prevention is deemed a worthwhile and realistic goal of sex education (SIECUS, 1996; Planned Parenthood, 1994; Kirby, 2007; Richard, 1990). But two "brands" or categories of sex education seem to describe most intervention efforts. Comprehensive Sex Education is described as providing accurate information, exploring sexual attitudes and values, developing interpersonal skills, and exercising responsibility regarding sexual relationships (SIECUS, 2003). Abstinence education is described as promoting appreciation for and practice of sexual abstinence until marriage through distribution of age-appropriate, factual, and medically accurate materials (Abstinence Clearinghouse, 2003). These approaches, in addition to offering knowledge about the biology and physiology of human sexuality, address the two factors contributing to adolescent pregnancy as noted by Back (1983): the level of use of contraception among participating teens, and the number of unmarried teens who participate in sexual intercourse at all.

The most widespread prevention efforts seem to be of the Comprehensive type (the SIECUS and Planned Parenthood Web sites offer lists of Comprehensive curricula), although a greater variety of abstinence-based programs now seem to be available (Abstinence Clearinghouse, 2003; Richard, 1990). Although both types of intervention are now generating empirical research, the types of studies and the meanings of the results continue to generate debate. Before numerous evaluation efforts were being reported extensively in the literature, Back (1983) attributed the disparity in types of prevention efforts not to how realistic a given approach may or may not be (to convince teens either to use condoms or to abstain altogether), but to ideology among social scientists who have already decided where the prevention line is to be drawn. A greater array of research results are now available, but the debate as to what best creates a meaningful difference is as intense as ever (see Rector, 2002; Kirby, 2007; Klein et al., 2005; SIECUS, 2008; Weed et al., 2008 for bibliographies of recent research).

For example, evidence that abstinence education is worthwhile includes a reduction in the onset of sexual activity, movement toward more abstinent attitudes toward sexual involvement, and a decrease in quality-of-life risk factors (i.e., inconsistent condom use) (Rector, 2002; Institute for Research & Evaluation, 2007; Weed, et al., 2008). For comprehensive sex educators, such abstinence efforts that warn of STIs through sexual involvement are frequently labeled guilt, shame, and fear-based (SIECUS, 2003). This is just one example of how prevention efforts based on one of the two philosophies are viewed askance by proponents of the other philosophy. Setting the stage for a mature dialogue about the consequences of risk taking, some professional journal articles often do reflect how it is possible to consider the possibility of multiple solutions, and to acknowledge that a key component that undermines the philosophy and practices of any program is the immature and irresponsible behavior of adolescents themselves. That is, some adolescents, in spite of their knowledge, and in spite of their skills, make self-destructive choices.

Systematic evaluations seem more frequent on the greater number of Comprehensive programs than on the fewer Abstinence-based programs. But neither category of curricula evaluations, irrespective of statistically significant differences in Random Clinical Trials (RCTs), suggests pragmatically stunning results. Both kinds of evaluations frequently show influence with only a modest percentage of the group receiving the treatment. It seems if that fact were acknowledged, each group could expend efforts to either target curricula for more specific audiences or to figure out how to focus on factors already shown to insulate youth from the earlier onset of sexual activity (such as familial, attitudinal, and cultural contexts). That is, if any given program is most effective with groups with certain demographic or attitudinal backgrounds, why not seek ways to enhance the influence of those backgrounds, and simultaneously undermine the pervasiveness of those contexts that correlate with risk-taking behaviors? Diverse intervention efforts, using different methods and content, have demonstrated marginal but worthwhile successes, and perhaps all educators should be grateful for the percent of adolescents who escape the potentially destructive consequences of high-risk behaviors and attitudes.

So to review, sexuality education begins in philosophy, not in curricula or research efforts. The latter two activities are expressions of philosophical starting points.

The Sex Information and Education Council of the United States (SIECUS) takes the position that early sexual involvement by teenagers is undesirable. The Council articulates guidelines and values that reveal a specific philosophy of human sexuality and of prevention:

1. Sexuality is a natural and healthy part of living.
2. All persons are sexual.
3. Sexuality includes physical, ethical, social, spiritual, psychological, and emotional dimensions.
4. Every person has dignity and self worth.
5. Young people should view themselves as unique and worthwhile individuals

within the context of their cultural heritage.

6. Individuals express their sexuality in varied ways.

7. Parents should be the primary sexuality educators of their children.

8. Families provide children's first education about sexuality.

9. Families share their values about sexuality with their children.

10. In a pluralistic society, people should respect and accept the diversity of values and beliefs about sexuality that exist in a community.

11. Sexual relationships should never be coercive or exploitative.

12. All children should be loved and cared for.

13. All sexual decisions have effects or consequences.

14. All persons have the right and the obligation to make responsible sexual choices.

15. Individuals, families, and society benefit when children are able to discuss sexuality with their parents and/or other trusted adults.

16. Young people develop their values about sexuality as part of becoming adults.

17. Young people explore their sexuality as a natural process of achieving sexual maturity.

18. Premature involvement in sexual behaviors poses risks.

19. Abstaining from sexual intercourse is the most effective method of preventing pregnancy and STDs/HIV.

20. Young people who are involved in sexual relationships need access to information about health care services. (SIECUS, 2003).

The starting point of the SIECUS philosophy is to see individuals as sexual beings who are to express their sexuality in responsible, knowledgeable ways. Sexuality education is preferably begun by responsible parents who are open and involved in providing sexual knowledge. This parental involvement is to include the transmission of parental values and beliefs regarding human sexuality. Embedded also in this philosophy of Comprehensive Sex Education are threads of relativism (all sexual values are to be respected and accepted—Point 10), and of individualism (young people develop their values about sexuality and explore sexuality as a natural process of becoming adults (Points 16–17). In addition, these guidelines suggest that all people are valuable and should attend to their cultural heritage (Point 5), and that parent-child discussions of sexual values and behavior are beneficial.

The Abstinence Clearinghouse also identifies guidelines for sex education, and includes the idea that sexuality is restricted to marriage in the definition of what is responsible, knowledgeable sexual expression. Thus, this view of sex education is that it "... promote the appreciation for and practice of sexual abstinence (purity) through the distribution of age-appropriate, factual and medically accurate materials." (Abstinence Clearinghouse, 2003). They support a variety of curricula that promote, in various ways, the abstinence-until-marriage message.

At the general level of analysis, these two organizations already reveal a difference in the philosophy that guides their sex education efforts. For SIECUS, the fundamental issue is that humans are sexual beings and should express their sexuality responsibly in a wide variety of possible practices and contexts. For the Abstinence Clearinghouse, humans are sexual beings whose responsible sexual practices are to be reserved for marriage. Both organizations affirm the destructiveness of manipulative, coercive sexual involvement, and both thus take a moral stand on sexual conduct generally based on a consideration of consequences. However, Abstinence Clearinghouse and most abstinence curricula extend a moral stance to include the context of the sexual involvement, and not just the conduct. This difference in approaches is grounded in differing philosophies of human being and of human sexuality and precedes any empirical work on these two distinct approaches to sexuality education. Comprehensive Sex Education (as presented by SIECUS and others) is extensive in addressing values, beliefs, practices, consequences, and sexual expression as a natural feature of being human. Abstinence curricula typically emphasize humans, at the least, as potentially capable managers of sexual feelings, and emphasize knowledge, consequences, beliefs and values—and the context of marriage as the appropriate domain of practice.

With the exception of acknowledging that sexual practices be mutual (noncoercive and nonexploitive), the ethical component of Comprehensive Sex Education seems to focus on guidelines regarding whether sexual practices manage to avoid destructive consequences. These consequences are most often thought of as physical (avoiding pregnancy, STIs, HIV, etc), but theoretically include social-emotional outcomes as well. The values and beliefs attending sexual participation are also seemingly seen as individualistic, with even the possibility of being unique. In this view, sexual practices are portable across a myriad of contexts, as long as the practices are mutual, freely chosen, and nondestructive. When only practices and behaviors are the targeted focus of sex education, the philosophy seems to lean toward defining, presenting, and promoting certain behaviors and practices, without prime attention to the contexts in which those practices might be carried out. Thus such curricula could be categorized as behavioral rather than contextual. In fact, they are philosophically "acontextual," with minimal attention paid to the relationship contexts where sexual activity takes place.

It might be argued that Comprehensive Sex Education acknowledges the context and primacy of parents in being the prime sex educators of their children. But given that the Comprehensive guidelines also indicate such relativistic values as "Individuals express their sexuality in varied ways," (SIECUS, 2003, Point 6) and "In a pluralistic society, people should respect and accept the diversity of values and beliefs about sexuality that exist in a community," (SIECUS, 2003, Point 10) the potential for conflict is great between what parents teach is *acceptable* sexual behavior and what the Comprehensive curricula teaches as merely *individual choice*. For example, for parents or students to "respect" sexual practices or contexts that some parents find morally reprehensible is unlikely, let alone to expect them to teach their children to "accept" them. Moreover, the practical degree of parental involvement in Comprehensive Sex Education may not be very extensive, as critiques by some abstinence educators suggest (Focus on the Family, 2001, p. 8). An alternative description of Point 10 that more parents might respond to positively would be a statement such as: "In a pluralistic society, some sexual practices might be promoted, some might be protected, and some might be prohibited. Individually, we have the right and obligation to declare our stance on such matters, and to view with compassionate tolerance those who disagree." Such a statement acknowledges that a philosophy of relativism need not be a feature of either approach to sex education, and that it is possible to acknowledge and support parental moral boundaries without justifying destructive attitudes towards those who differ—either in their moral arguments or in their sexual practices.

Abstinence education seems to be more attentive to contextual realities, with the ethical guideline being that sexual participation is only legitimate in a context of marriage. The exclusion of other sexual options for adolescents is no different from the context approved for adults. Both mutual consent and marriage are the essential contexts within which sexual activity is to take place. This stance places sexual activity in a relational context—a person-centered context—thus relegating a focus on sexual practices to secondary status. This disagreement between the two approaches is not grounded in conflicting empirical results, but in the incompatibility of conflicting moral philosophies. Abstinence educators are standing on ground that restricts adolescents, many of whom are, of course, also legal minors, from nonmarital sexual access. They are drawing the ethical boundary more restrictively than the limits drawn by the philosophy that underlies Comprehensive Sex Education, where mutual consent and nondestructive consequences are the prime moral boundaries.

In fact, at a more fundamental level, the differing philosophies of sex education illustrate different views of what attitudes and behaviors in a society are legitimate—or at least preferred. Abstinence educators see a society where both society and individuals benefit most when sexuality is expressed in marriage and not considered a matter of mere individual, noncoercive preference. Despite these differences, both philosophies of sex education do acknowledge abstinence as the best way to avoid a host of destructive consequences. But abstinence educators opt to teach that philosophy as preferred, while comprehensive sex educators see the marriage requirement as only one of many options, and seem to suggest a moral equivalency regarding almost any noncoercive sexual involvement. This view also informs how a society should address sexuality. The sexually-participating adolescent and adult population have every (moral) right—if not need—to sexually express themselves, on the assumption, of course, that coercion or manipulation is not a feature of the activity.

Observers of sexuality education may sometimes see Abstinence Education as teaching the way they believe society ought to be, while Comprehensive Education is teaching the way society actually is. Of course, since society consists of individuals who believe and can behave according to either philosophy we have discussed, abstinence education is, in fact, an expression of the beliefs and behaviors of one constituency in society, and comprehensive education is an expression of another. Again, the debate of what ought to be in sex education is as diverse as debates of what society should be like, and for good reason. Admittedly, the two distinct

philosophies described here are ideal types and in the sexuality-education arena, many curricula would claim to be a hybrid version of the two philosophies. Whether a coherent philosophical case for the hybrid idea could be presented is questionable, since, once a curriculum decides to offer counsel in favor of abstinence *and* to offer counsel recommending certain boundaries for acontextual sexual practices, the hybrid is now, by definition, merely Comprehensive Sex Education. Perhaps the recent statement from the American Academy of Pediatrics (Klein et al., 2005) affirming a hybrid approach, is looking at behavioral research results, but not attending to the contextual variables that those promoting comprehensive approaches admit help produce positive outcomes.

It could be, however, that if sex education were delivered according to the values, beliefs, and even behaviors of the audience, the content delivered could lose its hybrid nature, and be unique from either comprehensive or abstinence approaches. When the characteristics of an audience are assessed in advance, the content could be configured to benefit that specific group within certain moral boundaries—that is, within the concept of what content will make a meaningful difference. But U.S. approaches to sex education generally assume that the audience fits the already constructed curriculum. This seems not to be a problem if the issue is merely providing knowledge about practices and behaviors, but it is pedagogically and practically a big problem because the audience will receive those practices according to a pre-existing philosophy, and into many different relational contexts. The beliefs and behaviors of any given audience do not engage acontextually—devoid of specific contexts of action. Tailoring curricula to audiences is to acknowledge relevant and defensible contexts of sexual activity and the philosophies which justify behaviors and produce beneficial or destructive consequences.

In summary, the differences in the philosophies of sexuality that deem what kind of sex education is appropriate are not resolved in the research arena. The specific outcomes identified, the methods of measurement, and the interpretations of results do not dissolve the philosophical debate. Various programs, from a variety of philosophies, have achieved statistically significant results in the intended direction of the intervention curricula, but also have produced failures to change behavior significantly.

EMPIRICAL STUDIES

A few studies and results are illustrative of the division in the research community and especially among those intervening to make a meaningful difference. Two types of studies can be examined: those that provide background data on relevant factors describing the adolescent population, and direct intervention studies designed to make a meaningful difference.

An early survey study by Hanson, Myers, and Ginsburg (1987) of 10,000 never-married females, completed during their sophomore year of high school, and coupled with three years of follow-up surveys, found the following factors *not* related to the likelihood of a Black or White student having an out-of-wedlock birth as a teenager: 1) having had a school sex education course; 2) birth control knowledge. In other words, those two factors simply did not make a difference in the likelihood of a student in later years having an out-of-wedlock birth. The factors related to reducing the likelihood of an out-of-wedlock birth are, as reported by the authors, as follows:

> When adolescents and their parents endorse the values and accompanying behaviors that stress responsibility, the adolescents' chances of experiencing an out-of-wedlock childbirth are reduced. We found that girls who hold high educational expectations and have parents who are concerned about their activities (e.g., parents who monitor their child's homework and whereabouts) are less likely to bear a child out-of-wedlock than are girls with similar

> backgrounds, but who hold low expectations and have parents that express little concern. . . .
> [O]ur findings suggest that teenagers who are well behaved in school, indicating a strong sense of self-discipline and responsibility, are less likely to have a child as a teenager. For [W]hites, the likelihood of having a child is also reduced if teenagers attribute their successes to their own initiative and have parents who hold high educational expectations for their child. For [B]lacks, but not [W]hites, the chances of giving birth to a child are substantially increased for unmarried teenagers who [report they] *would* consider having a child out-of-wedlock. . . .
> For both [W]hites and [B]lacks, going steady increases the chances of having a child outside of marriage more than any other characteristic considered in the study (Hanson et al., 1987, pp. 250–251).

First of all, it is evident that the significant factors here are related to personal beliefs and values, and the contexts, relationships, families, and communities where such commitments were nurtured (or not). Parental concern, expectations, and monitoring contribute to self-discipline and responsibility. Although the relationship of sex education or contraceptive knowledge was not part of this study, the authors report an attitudinal connection: ". . . taking a sex education course and having greater knowledge of birth control increase the chances that a [B]lack teenager will consider giving birth while unmarried. Birth control knowledge but not sex education, increases these chances for [W]hites." (p. 251). Behaviorally, moreover, and for those most at risk, the knowledge was not a factor in changing their behavior. Notably, no data regarding participation rates in intercourse, or pregnancy rates, or abortion rates, were reported. Thus, it is not possible to draw conclusions regarding those factors that may or may not contribute to other problems of adolescent sexual involvement (including the contracting of STIs, for example, or of differential abortion rates in the categories analyzed). This is a common feature, both of background and intervention studies. The big picture of understanding statistically significant results is obscured by the telescopic focus on a few outcomes. Nevertheless, such studies give family life educators starting points of understanding the issues, even though definitive conclusions regarding the overall problem must be held in abeyance.

Perhaps knowledge and skills are incorporated into a culture when they are compatible with it, but ignored when counter to it. Generically speaking, sex education may not address the subcultures, either of the students most or least at risk for adolescent pregnancy. A significant feature of adolescent subcultures, however, is the relationship they have with their parents, and both Comprehensive Sex Education and Abstinence Education articulate values that include—at the theoretical level anyway—parental values and involvement. However, intervention efforts often fall short, for whatever reasons, of following through on their declared philosophy regarding parents. Even the conclusions of Hanson et al. (1987) in this background study seem misaligned with their results. Having just noted that beliefs, values, parental relationships, etc., are the significant antecedent conditions for lower rates of adolescent childbirth, more salient even than sex education or birth control knowledge, the authors recommend—more knowledge. In fairness, the authors call for school programs to include values and attitudes along with the technical knowledge, granting that parental values and influence are crucial to reducing rates of out-of-wedlock pregnancies. They do not go so far as to suggest that the schools should actually teach a philosophy consistent with the very values (usually fostered through parental involvement) which seem to be most helpful to adolescents.

Another early study, funded by the Ford Foundation, is the evaluation of a systematic and longitudinal treatment program for an extremely high-risk population with respect to adolescent pregnancy. The treatment group was adolescent women 17 or younger who were

pregnant or had already borne a child out of wedlock. The purpose of the program was to help the women avoid a repeat pregnancy and redirect them to "a path of economic self-sufficiency" (Polit & Kahn, 1985). This was a truly comprehensive program targeting economic self-sufficiency in the young women, and thus an array of counseling services (counseling, employment training, networking with service providers) were made available.

Four cities with groups of teens receiving the treatment program were matched for social and economic characteristics with four other cities also geographically similar. For 12 months, the treatment group was nurtured with an array of services, including employment training, contraceptive instruction, etc. At the end of one year, the repeat pregnancy rate of the targeted group was 14 percent as compared to 22 percent for the comparison group. This difference of 8 percent was statistically significant. In the following year, neither group received treatment. At the end of 24 months, the repeat pregnancy rate of the treatment group had increased to match that of the comparison group (45 percent and 49 percent), so that by the final interviews, no statistical difference in pregnancy rates was evident.

This study is strong in its thoroughness of research evaluation, although the reporting includes some odd omissions of information very relevant if the concern was with the meaning or context of repeat pregnancies. For example, almost three times as many of the comparison teens were married as were the project teens (3.3 percent vs. 8.9 percent), although their percentage of the total sample was small. Economically disadvantaged or not, a repeat pregnancy, or contraception, or employment and or school status might have a different meaning for a married teenager than an unmarried one. Yet, the conceptual significance of the study is the discouraging fact that, in spite of the skill training and available service providers, etc., and after an investment of one year in helping young women preserve their economic futures, and after a second year where the extensive nurturing of the experimental group was suspended, the group so targeted did as well (or poorly) as the groups who received no services. One plausible explanation would require examining the community connections. This high-risk group may be more in need of a nurturing community than of more knowledge and skill. After all, after one year of active nurturance of the experimental group, there was a statistical and practical reduction of their repeat pregnancy rate. But after two years, their repeat pregnancy rate rose to virtually match that of the comparison group.

Commendably, Polit (1989) revisited the sample in a five-year follow-up study. At this point, the statistically significant results included favorable improvements for the Redirection group in contrast to the Comparison group. The Redirection women reported a higher percentage of having held jobs, of working a greater number of hours per week, of receiving a smaller percentage of Aid to Families with Dependent Children help, fewer mean number of abortions (.3 vs .5), and a greater number of live births. No differences in aspects of contraceptive use were noted between the groups. Moreover, the most significant differences between the groups were in the social-emotional realm regarding their own children, with the Redirection mothers and their children "outperforming" those in the Comparison group on a variety of scales. In spite of not achieving differences in educational attainment between the two groups, these results suggest that Project Redirection did make a difference.

Again, potentially relevant contextual differences in the groups were not examined statistically. For example, the number of women in the five-year follow-up who were married was 24 percent, and "about one-third of the women were living with a male partner at the time of the most recent interview" (p. 166). Such contextual factors might be informative regarding such issues as contraceptive use, the context of repeat pregnancies, mean number of live births, accessibility to the workplace, etc. But no distinction is made regarding whether there

was a statistical difference between the groups in percent married, even though such a factor might help account for the differing abortion rates, and especially the better child well-being scores of the Redirection group. Is marriage a nonfactor, a positive factor, or a deleterious factor in the scores of the children on developmental measures? Nevertheless, as was the case with the Hanson et al. (1987) study, which ignored sexual activity factors and focused on a single outcome—out-of-wedlock pregnancies—Polit (1989) was looking primarily at economic and social well-being factors at follow-up. In addition, this study was cast, not as one concerned with the sexual involvement of the teens, but as an attempt to help them gain access to a better economic future through education. The common neglect by the two studies is the context of single, married, or live-in boyfriend factor and its impact on the well-being of the children. These three relational contexts of the two groups providing data might shed light on why the Redirection group had better scores. When the issue is how best to intervene, the more we know about contextual factors, the better we can focus any given intervention.

In a thorough review article of family factors associated with reducing risk of adolescent pregnancy, Miller, Benson and Galbraith (2001) note several variables that public schools might be able to build upon if the desire is to reduce the risk of pregnancy among its targeted school population. As paraphrased, the authors note:

1. Parent/child connectedness, defined as support, closeness and warmth, is related to lower adolescent pregnancy risk, and "is greatest for this effect through delaying and reducing adolescent sexual intercourse" (p. 24).
2. Parental supervision and monitoring generally are related to lower adolescent pregnancy risk.
3. Parental attitudes and values that disapprove of either sexual intercourse or unprotected intercourse and pregnancy

are related to lower adolescent pregnancy risk.

4. Although the direct effects of parent/child communication are noted as inconclusive, parent/child communication, linked with parental values and closeness of the parent/child relationship, "have important interactive effects on adolescent pregnancy risk through reducing sexual intercourse and/or increasing contraceptive use" (p. 25).

These variables are highlighted because they are the kind of contextual factors that both comprehensive and abstinence educators can support, but which do not seem to appear extensively in the content or recommended practices of curricula.

When sexuality educators, of whatever philosophy, take into account variables that contribute to reduced risk, such as family variables, and include discussions of family issues in the classroom, they are, at the least, addressing that portion of the audience whose family variables are relevant to prevention. While much of sex education addresses the "most at risk" portion of a student audience, it may be wise, relevant, and possible to structure components of a course that acknowledge the heterogeneous reality of any given class and deliver content designed to strengthen those students who already are less at risk, either because of their own beliefs and behavior, or because they are products of family variables that statistically reduce risk. Regarding contextual factors, parental influence ranks first or second, including influence regarding adolescents' sexual values, beliefs, and behavior (Miller, Benson, & Galbraith, 2001). But contextual factors are rarely a feature of sex education curricula.

IN SEARCH OF MEANING

Perhaps the realities of intervention in human affairs are so complex that it is simultaneously laudable and yet naïve to create sex education

programs when they cannot possibly deliver the dramatic results their creators, and society itself, might hope for. As Sarah Brown notes in the Foreword to a summary of pregnancy prevention efforts as compiled by the National Campaign to Prevent Teen Pregnancy (National Campaign, 2001):

> Although we believe that having accurate, research-based information can only help communities make good decisions about preventing teen pregnancy, the National Campaign recognizes that communities choose to develop particular prevention programs for many reasons other than research—including, for example, compatibility with religious traditions, available resources, community standards, and the personal values and beliefs of the leaders in charge. In this context, it is crucial for such leaders to understand that community-based programs are only part of the solution to the teen pregnancy challenge and that no single effort can be expected to solve this problem by itself. Teen pregnancy is, after all, a very complex problem, influenced by many factors, including individual biology, parents and family, peers, schools and other social institutions, religion and faith communities, the media, and the list goes on. In an ideal world, we would mount efforts to engage the help of all these forces, particularly popular culture, schools, faith communities, parents and other adults. But we are a long way from doing so. . . . The simple point is that no single approach can solve this problem alone, whether it be a national media campaign, a new move in faith communities to address this problem, or a well-designed community program. Advocates of any single approach . . . should therefore be modest in both their promises and their expectations (2001, p. iii).

This is a sobering assessment indeed. While it serves as a caution to those who continue to search for the best intervention content and methods, it highlights the possibility that however empirically worthy or philosophically defensible pregnancy prevention efforts prove to be, they are not available society-wide and are unlikely to be met with a unanimous supportive response anyway. The National Campaign (2001) reports research on programs from diverse philosophies and yet found rigorous evaluation to be lacking. Summarizing results from the many programs designed to reduce adolescent pregnancy or sexual activity is difficult, not only because of the diversity of methods and programs and audiences, but because the ever-expanding body of work makes definitive conclusions about where we are like pinpointing a moving ship at sea.

Nevertheless, Kirby's (2001) work, while acknowledging we have a long way to go in intervention efforts, is representative of the issues, the outcomes and the possibilities. He offers ten common characteristic actions of effective Sex and HIV Education Programs:

1. Focus on reducing sexual behaviors that lead to unintended pregnancy or HIV/ST[I]s. Use theoretical approaches that have been demonstrated to influence other health-related behavior and identify specific sexual antecedents to be targeted.
2. Deliver and consistently reinforce clear messages about abstaining from sexual activity and/or using condoms or contraception.
3. Provide basic, accurate information about the risks of teen sexual activity and ways to avoid intercourse or use methods of protection against pregnancy and ST[I]s.
4. Include activities that address social pressures that influence sexual behaviors.
5. Provide examples of and practice with communication, negotiation, and refusal skills.
6. Employ teaching methods that involve participants and personalizing information.
7. *Incorporate behavioral goals, teaching methods, and materials appropriate to the age, sexual experience, and culture of students.* [Emphasis ours]
8. Provide sufficient class time for curriculum.
9. Select teachers or peer leaders committed to the program and then provide adequate training. (Kirby, 2001, p. 10)

MATCH-MAKING: PHILOSOPHY AND RESEARCH-INFORMED PRACTICES

As long as sincere people are going to continue prevention efforts through sexuality-education curricula, the direction of their efforts should be re-examined. As difficult as it may seem, figuring out ways to highlight contextual factors and the kinds of beliefs and values that contribute to behavior change would improve the efforts. Sexuality education that focuses only on behaviors and skills is delivering information in a contextual vacuum. It is a bit like teaching an airplane mechanic how to use a special tool without paying attention to under what conditions the tool is to be used.

Moreover, research efforts on the effects of sexuality education are always limited relative to the total number of effects that could be measured. A truly comprehensive evaluation of sexuality education would have to take into account all relevant effects: sexual activity, contraceptive use, adolescent pregnancy, STI transmission (which ones, how frequently, how severe, etc.), social-emotional impacts, economic well-being, parenting practices, and so on. Of course, the standard limitations of research activity (time, money, access to appropriate samples, limited possibilities of proper experimental designs) seem to suggest that incremental improvement in prevention efforts may be insufficient to make a significant reduction in the problem without some kind of upheaval in other culture-wide factors.

In other words, the larger culture also is a factor in whether a meaningful difference is likely to occur in the adolescent population. Family background factors, cultural patterns of belief and behavior, media philosophies and images relevant to sexual issues, peer-group boundaries, individual responses to calls for responsible behavior—these are contexts in which all prevention efforts operate, and include major influences that a mere curriculum can hardly control.

Perhaps all school, agency, or government-based sex education is a compromise grounded in the idea that if parents are not going to do this, somebody has to. Sex education becomes a backup or replacement for parental neglect or inadequacy. The goal is to help children and adolescents protect themselves from self-destruction due to irresponsible or risky sexual involvement. But as previously noted, a neglected factor in choosing both the content and delivery of sex education is to examine the nature of the audience receiving the program. It may not be wise to assume that the audience for sex education efforts is a homogeneous group of adolescents with similar at-risk backgrounds and contextual factors.

Public sex education, perhaps of necessity, is delivered as if the receiving audience were homogeneous. That is, everyone is assumed to be equally at risk; the same knowledge, facts, and philosophy are assumed to be relevant to all. This need not be so. Comprehensive sexuality education could move toward more bold affirmations of abstinence being the best way to avoid a myriad of problems (National Campaign, 2001), but would need to do so while simultaneously acknowledging the philosophical realities that underlie such a viewpoint. Similarly, the philosophy guiding the notion of responsible sexual participation outside of marriage would also need to be articulated.

Sex education programs need to be evaluated both empirically and philosophically. Philosophical evaluation of the assumptions about human behaviors and beliefs relevant to targeted behaviors, practices and values needs to be made. A curriculum that rests on relativism—one feature of which might be that all noncoercive sexual relationships are of relatively equal quality—is philosophically different from curricula that are nonrelativistic and promote a specific relationship context. The difference is not between one approach that is devoid of philosophy and another that is philosophical. Every intervention is guided by some philosophy, articulated or not. Sex education programs are not usually examined for their philosophical underpinnings, but it may be that if they were, a program's philosophy—as well as the beliefs and values of the targeted audiences—could contribute to the program's effectiveness. At the very least, it would allow the possibility of matching the values and beliefs of audiences to curriculum content.

CITIZENSHIP AND SEXUALITY

One unique starting point of considering how philosophy of behavior might affect that behavior is to consider the idea of sexual behavior as a matter of citizenship. This would legitimize a call from both the abstinence and comprehensive sexuality educators that a quality community needs to attend to the sexual nature of human experience and foster those attitudes and behaviors that are nondestructive of human well-being. Sexuality is a matter of concern for the community. That is one reason why sexual practices and contexts are regulated by government. Community may be essential to understanding the solutions to social problems, including sexual problems.

Community is neither public nor private. It is an expression of a shared commitment or willingness to be connected. As Berry (1992) summarizes, "Community life is by definition a life of cooperation and responsibility. Private life and public life, without the disciplines of community interest, necessarily gravitate toward competition and exploitation" (p. 120).

Without citizenship or community, human action becomes a series of competing individualistic events regulated by some external entity like the government or the school system. Families become weak when they no longer nourish common interests across generations, and communities become weak for the same reasons. The possibility of making sex education a subset of citizenship education is symbolic of building community, where humans attend to one another's interests, affirming that the preferred context of human experience in a society or culture is more than just a group of individuals who are occupying the same place at the same time.

Currently in the United States, schools are too often seen as public arenas, rather than as communities. When sexuality is seen as a community issue, sexual involvement by unmarried legal minors would then be discussed as an act in which the community has an interest, and not as private behavior solely based on free choice. When the notion of community is excluded from prevention efforts, no conversations about citizenship, responsibility, morality, or acting in behalf of the next generation are appropriate, however practically or conceptually or relationally relevant they may be. In such circumstances, all that is left is for the public school to try to solve the problem by conveying knowledge or technical skill. In fact, the current few but recurring positive results of sexuality education obtained for some students from a variety of programs may best be understood according to the culture or sense of community the students already hold. If students already have a sense of community—of acting in behalf of the other person (socially, emotionally, spiritually, educationally, ethically, sexually), then Abstinence-based programs are more likely to succeed, and an ethical context could be just as central to Comprehensive approaches. If students have already lost a sense of community, they may defend their privacy without understanding its relationship to community. Behavioral approaches that minimize contextual factors seem not to have an impact in the aggregate. For example, while some programs report an increase in contraceptive use among the audiences for their programs, or a slight decrease

in premarital pregnancies—it is not quite sufficient to offset the frequent increase in sexual activity (See Franklin, et al., 1997; Weed et al., 2008, for reviews of a variety of programs). It seems we have everything to gain and little to lose by attending to malleable contextual factors that include beliefs and values as well as behaviors.

Perhaps if the idea of community is granted a place in the discussion of how to prevent or solve problems, debates about private behavior and public responsibility change in meaning. For example, the very fact that we debate whether sex education can, should, or will prevent problems such as adolescent pregnancy, sexually transmitted infections, AIDS, low birth-weight babies, etc., suggests we have abandoned the prior question of whether sexual involvement by unmarried legal minors is an act of good citizenship. When a culture thinks that a citizenship problem can be solved by providing various brands of knowledge or skill, it affirms that the culture has a built-in blindness to the source of the problem. Somehow we have adopted the notion that anything we do in the public arena to prevent the problems associated with teen sexual activity must see the sexual dimension of life as extracted from its contexts, cultures, families, and social-emotional-spiritual connections. Thus, sexual behavior is viewed as an activity not amenable to calls for responsible citizenship. Responsible citizenship, of course, is deeper and broader than responsible behavior. The latter is a matter of individual choice, while the former is a matter of contributing to the quality of life in a community. Sexual activity is a matter of citizenship because the consequences of sexual activity affect the community. Sexual involvement portends consequences far beyond the private acts of individuals.

Public schools could cast sex education efforts in an unabashed context of citizenship and community obligation, where that education would nurture the idea that even in (or especially in) the sexual domain, we must act as good citizens, in each others' best interests, and in ways that do not threaten community. Both approaches to sex education call for responsible decision making. The debate is over where we draw the line of responsible action. Granting community interests a stake in the outcomes is an additional invitation to adolescents to become citizens who foster the quality of their own futures as well as that of the communities they live in and help create.

RECOMMENDATIONS

Whether or not the philosophies of sexuality education become explicit in the next generation of educational efforts, the profession has given much attention to the task of evaluating sexuality education programs during the past three decades. These empirical evaluations suggest directions future interventions might take, and also reveal limitations in the way we go about evaluating outcomes. Some alterations in our assessment and evaluation activities would strengthen the outcomes and enhance family life educators' attempts to make meaningful differences.

1. Being more explicit about the philosophy guiding program choices will help consumers understand the risks and benefits of sexuality education.
2. Taking into account the developmental level of the recipients (moral, social, intellectual) could result in more developmentally appropriate curricula.
3. Including more parental dimensions in content and delivery contexts could act as an insulator against many risk-taking sexual behaviors of adolescents.
4. Acknowledging audience heterogenity in values, beliefs, practices, cultural patterns, and family circumstances, as well as the different responses to content, could temper the way concepts are delivered.
5. Examining the specific contexts of changes and outcomes could lead to

refinement of both content and delivery of sex education.
6. Addressing the ethical domain—especially regarding what it means to seek each other's best interests and to make a meaningful difference—would alter the content delivered.
7. Considering the possibility that the ideal curricula have not yet been created would spawn surprising approaches that might include new starting points altogether.
8. Admitting that a school curriculum may not be the major influence on sexual decision making of adolescents could lead to addressing destructive influences in the broader culture, beginning a dialogue and inviting everyone to consider new possibilities.

INTRODUCTION REFERENCES

Bleakley, A., M. Hennessey, and M. Fishbein. 2006. Public opinion on sex education in US schools. *Archives of Pediatrics and Adolescent Medicine* 160: 1151–1156.

Regnerus, M. D. 2007. *Forbidden fruit: Sex & religion in the lives of American teenagers.* New York: Oxford University Press.

Roffman, D. M. 1992. Common sense and nonsense about sex education. *Family Life Matters* 2: 7.

Schemo, D. J. 2000. Survey finds parents favor more detailed sex education. *New York Times*, 4 October, pp. 1A, 23A.

REFERENCES

Abstinence Clearinghouse (2003). Mission. http://www.abstinence.net/about/history.php.

Army, U. S. (1947, May 27). Army venereal disease rate drops as a result of new program. *The New England Journal of Medicine, 238,* 784.

Back, K. (1983). Teenage pregnancy: Science and ideology in applied social psychology. In R. F. Kidd & M. J. Saks (Eds.), *Advances in applied social psychology* (pp. 1–17). Hillsdale, NJ: Lawrence Erlbaum Associates.

Berry, W. (1992). *Sex, economy, freedom and community.* New York: Pantheon Books.

Boyce, W. D. & Jensen, L. C. (1978). *Moral reasoning: A psychological-philosophical integration.* Lincoln, NE: University of Nebraska Press.

Coles, R. (1988). *Harvard diary: Reflections on the sacred and the secular.* New York: Crossroad.

Doherty, W. J. (1995). Soul searching: *Why psychotherapy must promote moral responsibility.* New York, NY: Basic Books.

Franklin, D., Grant, D., Corcoran, J., Miller, P., & Bultman, L. (1997). Effectiveness of prevention programs for adolescent pregnancy: A meta-analysis. *Journal of Marriage and the Family, 59,* 551–567.

Focus on the Family (2001). *Take twelve: The truth about abstinence education.* Colorado Springs: Author.

Hanson, S. L., Myers, D. E., & Ginsburg, A. L. (1987). The role of responsibility and knowledge in reducing teenage out-of-wedlock childbearing. *Journal of Marriage and the Family, 49,* 241–256.

Institute for Research & Evaluation. (2007, June). *Abstinence or comprehensive sex education?* Salt Lake City, UT: Author.

Kirby, D. (2001). *Emerging answers: Research findings on programs to reduce teen pregnancy (Summary).* Washington, DC: National Campaign to Prevent Teen Pregnancy.

Kirby, D. (2007). *Emerging answers 2007: Research findings on programs to reduce teen pregnancy and sexually transmitted diseases (Summary).* Washington, DC: National Campaign to Prevent Teen Pregnancy.

Klein, J. D. & The Committee on Adolescence (2005). Adolescent pregnancy: Current trends and issues. *Pediatrics, 116,* 281–286.

Miller, B. C., Benson, B., & Galbraith, K. A. (2001). Family relationships and adolescent pregnancy risk: A research synthesis. *Developmental Review, 21,* 1–38.

National Campaign to Prevent Teen Pregnancy (2001). *Halfway there: A prescription for continued progress in preventing teen pregnancy.* Washington, D C: Author.

Planned Parenthood Federation of America (1994). *Mission statement and policy statement on sexuality education.* http://www.plannedparenthood.org/about/thisispp/mission.html#13Sexuality.

Polit, D. F., & Kahn, J. R. (1985). Project redirection: Evaluation of a comprehensive program for disadvantaged teenage mothers. *Family Planning Perspectives, 17,* 150–155.

Polit, D. F. (1989). Effects of a comprehensive program for teenage parents: Five years after Project Redirection. *Family Planning Perspectives, 21,* 164–169, 187.

Rector, R. (2002, April 5). The effectiveness of abstinence education programs in reducing sexual activity among youth. *The Heritage Foundation Backgrounder #1533.* Washington, DC: The Heritage Foundation.

Richard, D. (1990). *Has sex education failed our teenagers? A research report.* Colorado Springs, CO: Focus on the Family Publishing.

SIECUS (1996). *Guidelines for comprehensive sexuality education.* New York: SIECUS.

SIECUS (2003) *Sexuality education: Values inherent in the guidelines.* http://www.siecus.org/school/sex_ed/guidelines/guide0003.html.

SIECUS (2008, January). *Marginally successful results of abstinence-only program erased by dangerous errors in curriculum.* http://siecus.org/index.cfm?fuseaction=Future.show.

Slife, B. D., & Williams, R. N. (1995). *What's behind the research? Discovering hidden assumptions in the behavioral sciences.* Thousand Oaks, CA: Sage.

Weed, S. E., Ericksen, I. H., Lewis, A., Grant, G. E., & Wibberly, K. H. (2008). An abstinence program's impact on cognitive mediators and sexual initiation. *American Journal of Health Behavior, 32,* 60–73.

Williams, R. N., & Gantt, E. E. (2002). Pursuing psychology as the science of the ethical: Contributions of the work of Emmanuel Levinas. In E. E. Gantt & R. N. Williams (Eds): *Psychology for the other: Levinas, ethics and the practice of psychology* (pp. 1–31). Pittsburgh, PA: Duquesne University Press.

LaVergne, TN USA
19 July 2010
189967LV00004B/2/P